INVESTMENTS

EIGHTH CANADIAN EDITION

ZVI BODIE
BOSTON UNIVERSITY

ALEX KANE
UNIVERSITY OF CALIFORNIA, SAN DIEGO

ALAN J. MARCUS
BOSTON COLLEGE

STYLIANOS PERRAKIS
JOHN MOLSON SCHOOL OF BUSINESS,
CONCORDIA UNIVERSITY

PETER J. RYAN
MANSI CORP

LORNE N. SWITZER
JOHN MOLSON SCHOOL OF BUSINESS,
CONCORDIA UNIVERSITY
CONTRIBUTING AUTHOR

McGraw-Hill Ryerson

McGraw-Hill
Ryerson

Investments
Eighth Canadian edition

Copyright © 2015, 2011, 2008, 2005, 2003, 2000, 1997, 1993 by McGraw-Hill Ryerson Limited. All rights reserved. No part of this publication may be reproduced or transmitted in any form or by any means, or stored in a data base or retrieval system, without the prior written permission of McGraw-Hill Ryerson Limited, or in the case of photocopying or other reprographic copying, a licence from The Canadian Copyright Licensing Agency (Access Copyright). For an Access Copyright licence, visit www.accesscopyright.ca or call toll free to 1-800-893-5777.

Statistics Canada information is used with the permission of Statistics Canada. Users are forbidden to copy this material and/or redisseminate the data, in an original or modified form, for commercial purposes, without the expressed permission of Statistics Canada. Information on the availability of the wide range of data from Statistics Canada can be obtained from Statistics Canada's Regional Offices, its World Wide Web site at http://www.statcan.gc.ca, and its toll-free access number 1-800-263-1136.

The Internet addresses listed in the text were accurate at the time of publication. The inclusion of a website does not indicate an endorsement by the authors or McGraw-Hill Ryerson, and McGraw-Hill Ryerson does not guarantee the accuracy of information presented at these sites.

ISBN-13: 978-0-07-133887-5
ISBN-10: 0-07-133887-X

3 4 5 6 7 8 9 10 MQ 1 9 8 7 6

Printed and bound in Canada.

Care has been taken to trace ownership of copyright material contained in this text; however, the publisher will welcome any information that enables it to rectify any reference or credit for subsequent editions.

Director of Product Management: Rhondda McNabb
Senior Product Manager: Kimberley Veevers
Marketing Manager: Jeremy Guimond
Product Developer: Kamilah Reid-Burrell
Photo/Permissions Research: Indu Arora
Senior Product Team Associate: Marina Seguin
Supervising Editor: Joanne Limebeer
Copy Editor: Rodney Rawlings
Production Coordinator: Michelle Saddler
Manufacturing Production Coordinator: Lena Keating
Cover Design: Mark Cruxton
Cover Images: bear and bull: Corbis, RF; stock market: lovegull/Getty Images (RF)
Interior Design: Mark Cruxton
Page Layout: Aptara®, Inc.
Printer: Marquis

Library and Archives Canada Cataloguing in Publication

Bodie, Zvi, author
    Investments / Zvi Bodie, Boston University, Alex Kane, University of California, San Diego, Alan J. Marcus, Boston College, Stylianos Perrakis, John Molson School of Business, Concordia University, Peter J. Ryan, Mansi Corp, Lorne Switzer, John Molson School of Business, Concordia University. —Eighth Canadian edition.

Revision of: Investments / Zvi Bodie . . . [et al.]. — 7th Canadian ed.—
[Whitby, Ont.] : McGraw-Hill Ryerson, c2011.
Includes bibliographical references and indexes.
ISBN 978-0-07-133887-5 (bound)

    1. Investments—Textbooks. 2. Portfolio management—Textbooks.
I. Kane, Alex, author II. Marcus, Alan J., author III. Perrakis, Stylianos, 1938-, author IV. Ryan, Peter J., author V. Switzer, Lorne, 1954-, author VI. Title.

HG4521.I548 2014   332.6   C2014-902210-7

Zvi Bodie
BOSTON UNIVERSITY

Zvi Bodie is professor of finance and economics and the first Norman and Adele Barron Professor in Management at the School of Management at Boston University. He holds a Ph.D. from the Massachusetts Institute of Technology and has served on the finance faculty at the Harvard Business School and MIT's Sloan School of Management. Professor Bodie has published widely on pension finance and investment strategy in leading professional journals. His books include *Foundations of Pension Finance, Pensions in the U.S. Economy, Issues in Pension Economics*, and *Financial Aspects of the U.S. Pension System.* His textbook *Finance* is coauthored by Nobel Prize–winning economist Robert C. Merton. Professor Bodie is a member of the Pension Research Council of the Wharton School, University of Pennsylvania. His latest book is *Worry-Free Investing: A Safe Approach to Achieving Your Lifetime Financial Goals.*

Alex Kane
UNIVERSITY OF CALIFORNIA, SAN DIEGO

Alex Kane is professor of finance and economics at the Graduate School of International Relations and Pacific Studies at the University of California, San Diego. He has been visiting professor at the Faculty of Economics, University of Tokyo; at Graduate School of Business, Harvard; and at Kennedy School of Government, Harvard; and has been research associate at the National Bureau of Economic Research. An author of many articles in finance and management journals, Professor Kane's research is mainly in corporate finance, portfolio management, and capital markets, most recently in the measurement of market volatility and pricing of options.

Alan J. Marcus
BOSTON COLLEGE

Alan Marcus is professor of finance in the Wallace E. Carroll School of Management at Boston College. He received his Ph.D. in economics from MIT. Professor Marcus has been a visiting professor at the Athens Laboratory of Business Administration and at MIT's Sloan School of Management and has served as a research associate at the National Bureau of Economic Research. Professor Marcus has published widely in the fields of capital markets and portfolio management. His consulting work has ranged from new product development to provision of expert testimony in utility rate proceedings. He also spent two years at the Federal Home Loan Mortgage Corporation (Freddie Mac), where he developed models of mortgage pricing and credit risk. He currently serves on the Research Foundation Advisory Board of the CFA Institute.

Stylianos Perrakis
JOHN MOLSON SCHOOL OF BUSINESS
CONCORDIA UNIVERSITY

Stylianos Perrakis is the RBC Distinguished Professor of Financial Derivatives at the John Molson School of Business of Concordia University. He is the author of many articles published in leading academic and professional journals in economics and finance, especially in the areas of industrial organization, corporate finance, and option pricing. Professor Perrakis has served as a consultant to many private and governmental organizations, including the Institute of Canadian Bankers and the World Bank. He is also the author of *Canadian Industrial Organization* and has taught as a visiting professor in universities in Switzerland, France, Greece, and the United States. He is Fellow of the Royal Society of Canada and is currently serving as an elected member of the Board of Directors of the University of Macedonia in Greece.

Peter J. Ryan
MANSI CORP.

Peter Ryan is principal of Mansi Corp., which engages in financial advising. Professor Ryan's research interests include both contingent claims in general and the incentive effects of financial claims in corporate structures. His articles on the subject of options and financial instruments have been published in a number of international journals in finance and management science. He has been involved in developing the course material for the Canadian Securities Institute. Professor Ryan also serves as an expert witness on the execution of responsibilities by financial advisors.

Lorne N. Switzer (special contributor for Eighth Edition)
JOHN MOLSON SCHOOL OF BUSINESS
CONCORDIA UNIVERSITY

Lorne N. Switzer is a Professor of Finance and the Van Berkom Endowed Chair in Small Cap Equities at the John Molson School of Business (JMSB) at Concordia University. He has published several academic articles in leading finance and economics journals and serves on the editorial boards of *European Financial Management*, *La Revue du FINANCIER*, *International Journal of Business*, and *International Journal of Economic Issues*. He has done consulting work for many business firms and government organizations including the Bourse de Montréal, Caisse de Dépot et Placement du Québec, AMI Partners, Inc., Bank Credit Analysts Research Group, the C. D. Howe Institute, Keugler Kandestin LLC, Schlesinger, Newman, and Goldman, the Government of Canada, and Gouvernement du Québec. He is a graduate of the Wharton School, and obtained his Ph.D. from the University of Pennsylvania in 1982.

CONTENTS IN BRIEF

CONTENTS

PART THREE

EQUILIBRIUM IN CAPITAL MARKETS

CHAPTER 7
The Capital Asset Pricing Model 232

CHAPTER 8
Index Models and the
Arbitrage Pricing Theory 263

CHAPTER 9
Market Efficiency 313

PART SIX .

DERIVATIVE ASSETS

CHAPTER 18
Options and Other Derivatives Markets: Introduction   658

CHAPTER 19
Option Valuation   701

CHAPTER 20
Futures, Forwards, and Swap Markets   751

PART SEVEN

ACTIVE PORTFOLIO MANAGEMENT

CHAPTER 21
Active Management and Performance Measurement   804

CHAPTER 22
Portfolio Management Techniques   855

The first Canadian edition of this text was written more than two decades ago. The intervening years have been a period of rapid and profound change in the investments industry, and included as well a financial crisis of historic magnitude that hit the U.S. financial markets. The vast expansion in financial markets during the intervening period was due in part to an abundance of newly designed securities, in part to the creation of new trading strategies that would have been impossible without concurrent advances in computer technology, and in part to rapid advances in the theory of investments that have come out of the academic community.

Yet the financial crisis was also rooted in these developments. Many of the innovations in securities design facilitated high leverage and increased reliance on risk transfer strategies of dubious efficiency. These, coupled with relaxation of regulatory controls and reduced transparency, masked the increased exposure to risk of key financial institutions. Although these regulatory failures were not present in Canada, and for this reason the financial crisis was not felt as acutely in the Canadian markets, the new edition of our text reflects these world events.

This Eighth Canadian Edition of *Investments* is intended primarily as a textbook for courses in investment analysis. Our guiding principle has been to present the material in a framework that is organized by a central core of consistent fundamental principles. We make every attempt to strip away unnecessary mathematical and technical detail, and we have concentrated on providing the intuition that may guide students and practitioners as they confront new ideas and challenges in their professional lives.

This text will introduce you to major issues currently of concern to all investors. It can give you the skills to conduct a sophisticated assessment of current issues and debates covered by both the popular media and more specialized finance journals. Whether you plan to become an investment professional or simply a sophisticated individual investor, you will find these skills essential.

Our primary goal is to present material of practical value, but all five of us are active researchers in the science of financial economics and find virtually all of the material in this book to be of great intellectual interest. Fortunately, we think, there is no contradiction in the field of investments between the pursuit of truth and the pursuit of money. Quite the opposite. The capital asset pricing model, the arbitrage pricing model, the efficient market hypothesis, the option-pricing model, and the other centrepieces of modern financial research are as much intellectually satisfying as subjects of scientific inquiry as they are of immense practical importance for the sophisticated investor.

In our effort to link theory to practice, we have also attempted to make our approach consistent with that of the CFA Institute. In addition to fostering research in finance, the CFA and the ICFA administer an education and certification program to candidates seeking the title of chartered financial analyst (CFA). The CFA curriculum represents the consensus of a committee of distinguished scholars and practitioners regarding the core of knowledge required by the investment professional.

Many features of this text are designed to be consistent with and relevant to the CFA curriculum, with end-of-chapter questions from past CFA exams. Chapter 3 includes excerpts from the "Code of Ethics and Standards of Professional Conduct" of the CFA Institute; Chapter 24 presents the CFA Institute's framework for systematically relating investor preferences and constraints to ultimate investment policy.

In this Eighth Edition, we have extended our systematic collection of Excel spreadsheets that give students tools to explore concepts more deeply than previously possible. The spreadsheets are available on Connect, and provide a taste of the sophisticated analytic tools available to professional investors.

UNDERLYING PHILOSOPHY

Of necessity, our text has evolved along with the financial markets. In this edition, we address many of the changes in the investment environment.

At the same time, a few basic *principles* remain important. We believe that attention to these can simplify the study of otherwise difficult material, and that they should organize and motivate all study. These principles are crucial to understanding the securities already traded in financial markets and in understanding new securities that will be introduced in the future. For this reason, we have made this book thematic, meaning we never offer rules of thumb without reference to the central tenets of the modern approach to finance.

The theme unifying this book is that *security markets are nearly efficient*, meaning most securities are usually priced appropriately given their risk and return attributes. Free lunches are rarely found in markets as competitive as the financial markets. This simple observation is remarkably powerful in its implications for the design of investment strategies; as a result, our discussions of strategy are always guided by the implications of the efficient market hypothesis. While the degree of market efficiency is, and always will be, a matter of debate (in fact, we devote an entire chapter to the behavioural challenge to the efficient market hypothesis), we hope our discussions throughout the book convey a good dose of healthy criticism concerning much conventional wisdom.

Distinctive Features

Investments is designed to emphasize several important aspects of making investment decisions:

1. The central principle is the existence of near-informational-efficiency of well-developed security markets such as ours, and the general awareness that competitive markets do not offer arbitrage opportunities or free lunches to participants.

2. A second theme is the risk–return tradeoff. This too is a no-free-lunch notion, holding that in competitive security markets, higher expected returns come only at a price: the need to bear greater investment risk. However, this notion leaves several questions unanswered. How should one measure the risk of an asset? What should be the quantitative tradeoff between risk (properly measured) and expected return? The approach we present to these issues is known as *modern portfolio theory (MPT)*. This approach focuses on the techniques and implications of *efficient diversification*, and we devote considerable attention to the effect of diversification on portfolio risk and the implications of efficient diversification for the proper measurement of risk and the risk–return relationship.

3. This text puts greater emphasis on asset allocation than most of its competitors. We prefer this emphasis for two important reasons. First, it corresponds to the procedure most people actually follow. Typically, you start with all of your money in a bank account, only then considering how much to invest in something riskier that might offer a higher expected return. The logical step at this point is to consider other risky asset classes, such as stocks, bonds, or real estate. This is an asset allocation decision. Second, most of the time, in determining overall investment performance, the asset allocation choice is far more important than the set of security selection decisions. Asset allocation is the primary determinant of the risk–return profile of the investment portfolio, and so it deserves primary attention in a study of investment policy.

4. This text has a broader and deeper treatment of derivative securities than most investments texts. Markets for derivatives, including options, futures, and more complex instruments, have become both crucial and integral to the financial universe. Your only choice is to become conversant in these markets—whether you are to be a finance professional or simply a sophisticated individual investor.

NEW IN THE EIGHTH CANADIAN EDITION

The following is a guide to significant changes in the eighth Canadian edition. This is not an exhaustive outline but an overview of the important additions and changes in coverage from the previous edition. Aside from the frequent amplification and deletion of various topics, specific changes of note include:

Chapter 3 provides an update of the evolution of trading platforms and changing ownership structures of the Canadian securities markets.

Chapter 4 has been updated with considerable attention to evidence on tail risk and extreme stock returns.

Chapter 7 now includes a streamlined presentation of the traditional CAPM and a more thorough discussion of its assumptions, extensions, and tests.

Chapter 8 has expanded the discussion of the differences between the index model and the full Markowitz model.

Chapter 9 on market efficiency provides additional coverage of the debate between active and passive management and the small-cap anomaly.

Chapter 10 gives an amplified description of the use of price charts to describe, and perhaps predict, the trends in the price movement, by illustrating the use of moving averages and Bollinger bands in the charts.

Chapter 11 has expanded the coverage of tests of multifactor models of risk and return and the implications of these tests for extra-market hedging demands.

Chapter 12 includes new material on credit default swaps.

Chapter 15 responds to requests for more macroeconomic analysis; this is a completely new chapter on the subject, split off from the former Chapter 15 and greatly expanded. The new Chapter 16 consists largely of the remainder of the old chapter, with the expected updating of material and minor rephrasing. All the following chapters have been renumbered accordingly.

Chapter 16 has new material on ratios and fair value accounting in addition to use of up-to-date financial statements.

Chapter 19 (formerly 18) includes additional material on risk-neutral valuation methods and their implementation in the binomial model, and the implications of the option pricing model for tail risk and financial instability.

Chapter 23 has a greatly revised discussion of the issues surrounding international diversification in its discussion of the risk, return, benefits, and potential from diversifying portfolios to include international assets.

In addition, a great many new problems have been introduced to many chapters.

ORGANIZATION AND CONTENT

This Canadian edition is both an adaptation of the U.S. text for a Canadian audience and an extension of the material to incorporate several topics of specific Canadian interest. The adaptation has changed the presentation and examples of the basic material with respect to currency, the macroeconomic environment, tax rates and legislation, and other legal and institutional features of the Canadian economy. Substantial information about the U.S. institutions is included, as much of the investment activity by Canadian investors takes place in U.S. markets, implying that Canadian investment professionals cannot afford to ignore the situation south of their country's border. Not only does the U.S. market set the standards for most of the financial innovation and research in Canada, but it also paces many of the economic developments that underlie the performance of the Canadian financial system. Nevertheless, several Canadian financial aspects are unique and deserve more extended coverage in their theoretical and empirical aspects.

Part 1: Introduction

The first three chapters are introductory and contain important institutional material focusing on the financial environment. We discuss the major players in the financial markets, provide an overview of the types of securities traded in those markets, and explain how and where securities are traded.

The material presented in Part 1 should make it possible for instructors to assign term projects early in the course. These projects might require students to analyze in detail a particular group of securities. Many instructors like to involve their students in some sort of investment game, and the material in these chapters will facilitate this process.

Parts 2 & 3: Portfolio Theory & Equilibrium in Capital Markets

Parts 2 and 3 contain the core of modern portfolio theory. Chapter 4 reviews the historical returns to various classes of Canadian instruments and presents statistical techniques used in their analysis. It also compares the performance of the basic Canadian market portfolio with that of several U.S. portfolios. Chapter 5 discusses risk and risk aversion and then presents the capital allocation decision. Chapter 6 goes on from capital allocation to portfolio selection and the development of the capital market line. The next two chapters treat the development of the CAPM and its extensions and alternatives, such as the arbitrage pricing theory. Chapter 9 discusses the reasoning behind the idea that random price movements indicate a well-functioning or efficient market. Chapter 10 discusses behavioural finance and technical analysis. Chapter 11 reviews empirical evidence on security returns, including tests of the CAPM and other studies in the context of market efficiency.

Part 4: Fixed-Income Securities

Part 4 is the first of three parts on security valuation. This Part treats fixed-income securities—bond pricing (Chapter 12), term structure relationships (Chapter 13), and interest-rate risk management (Chapter 14). The next two Parts deal with equity securities and derivative securities. For a course emphasizing security analysis and excluding portfolio theory, one may proceed directly from Part 1 to Part 4 with no loss in continuity.

Part 5: Equities

The three chapters of this Part are devoted to the popular forms of security analysis—economywide and firm-specific fundamental and statement analysis. Macroeconomic analysis concerns national and industry economic concept. Fundamental analysis treats refinements of the dividend discount model, while statement analysis presents the traditional accounting approach to assessing value.

Part 6: Derivative Assets

Chapters 18 and 19 describe options, beginning with a description of the instruments, their payoffs, and the markets in which they trade, and then continuing to the details of models for valuation. Chapter 20 presents similar material for futures, forward contracts, and swaps. Together these chapters describe how risk management can be achieved.

Part 7: Active Portfolio Management

This Part presents active management as an alternative to passive acceptance of efficient markets. It describes how to measure the performance of individuals and institutions who attempt to time markets or select portfolios, and how they can practise the techniques such as selective indexing, or inclusion of active portfolio components. We also discuss in depth mutual funds and other investment companies, which have become increasingly important means of investing for individual investors. Finally, this Part addresses international investing as an added component of portfolios.

ACKNOWLEDGMENTS

We, the Canadian authors, would first like to express our gratitude to Professors Bodie, Kane, and Marcus for their continued improvement to what has been an outstanding text. Also, we appreciate their agreement to join in our production of a Canadian edition.

For granting permission to include many of their examination questions in the text, we are grateful to the Institute of Chartered Financial Analysts. We are grateful also to Qianyin Shan and Easton Sheahan-Lee for their invaluable help in preparing the ancillary material for this edition. Our thanks also go to BMO Nesbitt Burns for providing us with material on their beta estimates.

Many of the tables and graphs have been compiled from information provided through the cooperation of Statistics Canada. Readers wishing to obtain further information may contact Statistics Canada's Regional Offices, its Web site at **www.statcan.gc.ca**, and its toll-free access number 1-800-263-1136. Much credit is due also to the development and production team at McGraw-Hill Ryerson: our special thanks go to Kim Veevers, Senior Product Manager; Kamilah Reid-Burrell, Product Developer; Joanne Limebeer, Supervising Editor; Rodney Rawlings, Copy Editor and Proofreader; Indu Arora, Permissions Editor; and the rest of the development team.

Stylianos Perrakis
Peter J. Ryan
Lorne Switzer

WALKTHROUGH

PEDAGOGY

This book contains features designed to make it easy for the student to understand, absorb, and apply the concepts and techniques presented.

Current Event Boxes

Short articles from business periodicals are included in boxes throughout the text. The articles are chosen for relevance, clarity of presentation, and consistency.

Excel Spreadsheets

The Eighth Edition includes boxes featuring Excel® spreadsheet applications. A sample spreadsheet is presented in the text with an interactive version and related questions available on the Connect® site.

Concept Checks

A unique feature of this book is the inclusion of Concept Checks in the body of the text. These self-test questions and problems enable the student to determine whether they have understood the preceding material.

Summary and End-of-Chapter Problems

At the end of each chapter, a detailed Summary outlines the most important concepts presented. The Problems that follow the Summary (after the Key Terms and Selected Readings sections) progress from simple to challenging. Many of them are taken from CFA exams and represent the kinds of questions professionals in the field deem relevant; these are indicated by an icon next to the problem number.

Internet Exercises: E-Investments

These exercises provide students with a structured set of steps to finding financial data on the Internet. Easy-to-follow instructions and questions are presented so students can utilize what they've learned in class in today's Web-driven world.

connect McGraw-Hill Connect® is a Web-based assignment and assessment platform that gives students the means to better connect with their coursework, with their instructors, and with the important concepts that they will need to know for success now and in the future.

With Connect, instructors can access all the instructor support materials: the Instructor Outline, developed by William Lim of York University; the Instructor Solutions Manual; the Test Bank; PowerPoint slides; Excel templates; and the Image Bank. They can also deliver assignments, quizzes, and tests online; edit existing questions and author entirely new problems; track individual student performance—by question, by assignment, or in relation to the class overall—with detailed grade reports; and integrate grade reports easily with Learning Management Systems.

By choosing Connect, instructors are providing their students with a powerful tool for improving academic performance and truly mastering course material. Connect allows students to practise important skills at their own pace and on their own schedule. Importantly, students' assessment results and instructors' feedback are all saved online—so students can continually review their progress and plot their course to success.

Connect was developed for the eighth Canadian edition by William Lim of York University. It provides 24/7 online access to an eBook—an online edition of the text—to aid them in successfully completing their work, wherever and whenever they choose.

LEARNSMART No two students are alike. Why should their learning paths be? LearnSmart uses revolutionary adaptive technology to build a learning experience unique to each student's individual needs. It starts by identifying the topics a student knows and does not know. As the student progresses, LearnSmart adapts and adjusts the content according to his or her individual strengths, weaknesses, and confidence, ensuring that every minute spent studying with LearnSmart is the most efficient and productive study time possible.

SMARTBOOK As the first and only adaptive reading experience, SmartBook is changing the way students read and learn. SmartBook creates a personalized reading experience by highlighting the most important concepts a student needs to learn at that moment in time. As a student engages with SmartBook, the reading experience continuously adapts by highlighting content according to what he or she knows and doesn't know. This ensures the student's focus on the content needed to close specific knowledge gaps, while it simultaneously promotes long-term learning.

Superior Learning Solutions and Support

The McGraw-Hill Ryerson team is ready to help you assess and integrate any of our products, technology, and services into your course for optimal teaching and learning performance. Whether it's helping your students improve their grades, or putting your entire course online, the McGraw-Hill Ryerson team is here to help you do it. Contact your Learning Solutions Consultant today to learn how to maximize all of McGraw-Hill Ryerson's resources!

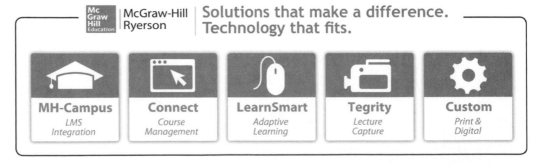

For more information on the latest technology and Learning Solutions offered by McGraw-Hill Ryerson and its partners, please visit us online: **www.mheducation.ca/he/solutions**.

INVESTMENTS

EIGHTH CANADIAN EDITION

CHAPTER

The Investment Environment

The world of investing looks much like a jungle to the uninitiated—a dangerous and exotic place, and definitely unfamiliar territory. Competent and intelligent professionals from other fields such as medicine and law react to this prospect in a perfectly rational way; just as they are hired for their expertise, they expect to need a professional financial advisor to guide them around the pitfalls. With a thorough understanding of the concepts in this book, they would find themselves quite capable of an enlightened discussion with such an advisor. By contrast, a representative of the accounting or financial profession would be far less comfortable discussing a legal case or operating procedure with the benefit of a single text on law or medicine.

This chapter introduces the environment of investing. Capital investment, with its need for funds, gives rise to capital markets. Fortunately, individuals have excess funds and regularly provide them to institutions that require those funds. The process is complex and highly organized. Capital markets exist for a diverse array of financial instruments that meet the precise needs of investors and users of capital; each of those instruments, starting with stocks and bonds, has evolved in response to those needs. We examine this system from all angles, the individuals and the institutions and their respective requirements, and the financial intermediaries which serve to bring the two together.

We begin with a short presentation of the turbulent history of North American markets. This is followed by an examination of the markets and their participants—the process of capital formation, the roles that the market plays, and individual investors and their investment-consumption patterns. After this, we describe the system of financial intermediaries and how these have created instruments responsive to the needs of the participants. Finally, we discuss how the market turbulence represents a failure of the financial system to fulfill its purpose—determining the value of financial assets through the sale and purchase of financial instruments.

1.1

A SHORT HISTORY OF INVESTING

Investing has been a priority for as long as individuals realized that current needs had to be balanced with future needs. Once society had progressed from a truly hand-to-mouth existence, food and other assets have been stored for later consumption. The creation of coinage as a means of exchange enabled individuals with surplus assets to store their wealth in a currency and transform it into an investment in assets of other varieties. Over the millennia, the economic system has developed to direct the surplus wealth of some individuals into needed areas of production.

By the twenty-first century, this evolution has culminated in a vast array of financial contracts made between individuals and institutions, each specifying how an initial investment will yield payment flows over a period of time. That period ranges from a day to eternity, even if neither party to the contract is likely to last very long. All of these contracts have evolved from more primitive forms that might have existed for centuries or more. The refinement of the contracts reflects the attempt to satisfy the specific needs of the one party requiring funds for a purpose and a time, and with a vision of when returns from the investment of those funds are likely to occur. On the other side, the investing party has needs for a specific pattern of payments for future consumption or for reinvestment in other contracts.

The fascination of the public with the investment world varies in intensity, with a general lack of interest in this poorly understood and not very newsworthy subject—except occasionally when stock market activity and results capture media attention. This was the case during the 1920s, as fortunes were rapidly made by supposedly brilliant investors; in those days, "elevator boys" and cab drivers overhearing the Wall Street financiers in their discussions participated in the public mania for investing. The result was a phenomenal rise in the stock market averages and the Crash of 1929, which appeared to precipitate the Great Depression.[1]

Near the end of the century, the crash of 1987 attracted universal interest by the one-day panic in the stock market. Unlike in 1929, however, no economic collapse followed. This may well have been due to more enlightened financial response by monetary officials; but the economic situation was markedly different. So was the financial environment, as 1987 turned out to be a neutral year for investors from January to December. Once out of the way, with confidence restored, the 1987 crash set the stage for the economic and financial boom of the 1990s.

The 1990s were also a period of public interest in the stock market, with nightly news reports on the levels of the market indices—the Dow and the TSX—on both television and radio. The last five years of the millennium witnessed another phenomenal rise in the markets, although the vast majority of this increase was confined to the technology arena. Small companies such as Dell Computer and Cisco Systems grew incredibly fast. The measurement of their sizes is a detail that needs to be examined. One measure is the value of sales, an indicator of the production of the company; another is the value of the share price and what we call the market capitalization, which indicate the investing public's appraisal of value of the current and future production and profits. The market capitalization of Dell grew by thousands of percentage points over the decade; such increases are relatively rare in history, though not unprecedented.

The problem with the rapid growth in share values in technology is that it spurred increasing attention by unsophisticated investors, individuals who had no experience with the stock market. Such individuals were seduced by the media attention revealing the fortunes that were being made so quickly, with results as high as 100 percent gains overnight. An indication of the media effect is that the U.S. financial news network CNBC apparently became the most watched program on television, outstripping all those soap operas, game shows, and sitcoms that used to be more entertaining.

---

[1]The Tulip Bulb Craze of the 1630s was a similar phenomenon. See www.investopedia.com for a guide to past crashes.

The growth in the technology companies, measured globally by the value of the Nasdaq market index, was being described as a "bubble," a term used many times before in history to describe the unwarranted inflation in asset values. Inevitably bubbles are punctured, and the most naïve investors lose the most money in the collapse, as they enter the bubbling market long after the initial gains have been made, just in time to watch their capital evaporate in the relentless return to pre-bubble prices. In this case, however, even experienced investors insisted on staying in the market, afraid to lose the opportunity to participate in the gains. By the time the euphoria of the new millennium had ended, the Nasdaq and its most overpriced stocks began their decline and the acceptance that it had indeed been a bubble became universal. What was surprising to many was the extent of the collapse; even those predicting a return to more rational and defensible valuation were amazed by the declines in the shares of highly profitable companies, Nortel being a prime example. As the market fell, the debate switched to whether the good companies were now bargains or still overpriced; those with the latter view proved to be correct for over a year. In market parlance, the great "bull market" of the 1990s turned into the "bear market" of the new millennium. The decline ended in October 2002, at a level more than 50 percent below the all-time high in 1999; by April 2006 the TSX had surpassed its prior record closing, and by July 2008 it had recorded a gain of over 180 percent on its 2002 bottom in one of the longest bull markets on record. The U.S. S&P 500 index had finally reached its previous record, gaining only 100 percent, reflecting the Canadian economy's benefit from the commodity boom. Commodity reliance is a two-edged sword, however; in 2013 the tables turned, as the U.S. market surged by another 30 percent while the TSX barely moved.

The first decade of the new millennium brought a new bubble, this time in real assets rather than financial assets; commodities such as copper and oil and many food staples rose drastically in price, but the significant inflation occurred in real estate. Due in some part to the miscalculations of the Federal Reserve about the risk of deflation leading to insufficiently high interest rates, mortgages soared; borrowers normally considered poor credit risks, with the compliance of mortgage officers and banks, were able to finance the purchase of homes that should have been unaffordable. The mortgages issued were resold by banks through mortgage-backed securities (which we discuss below); other instruments backed by credit obligations were devised and circulated. The trading in these instruments created immense leverage that resulted in trillions of dollars of securities being circulated. Small and large investors bought and sold these securities without understanding the risk entailed by them, much of it due to the poor credit risks in the mortgage market. At the end of 2007, the cracks appeared in the credit market and it became clear that many of the largest banks in the world, who were inextricably entangled in these instruments, were effectively bankrupt as they were owed billions by other institutions that could not honour their obligations. The concentration of these holdings was in U.S., British, and European banks; Canadian banks, which had earlier participated in the game, had largely divested themselves of these credit instruments by the time of the collapse. In fact, the problem was at first more of a failure of faith in the ability to repay debts, as it had become clear that the underlying securities were deficient. With the parties to these contracts unable to trust others, no matter how big, the credit system froze, because credit is by definition faith. The final straw was the collapse in September 2008 of Lehman Brothers, one of the largest and oldest investment banks, as no one could be persuaded to rescue it.

Stock markets plunged, as investors understood that the world was on the verge of a financial collapse because of frozen credit. Governments and central banks stepped in to guarantee banks and deposits. By dropping the rate of interest to near zero, monetary policy attempted to restart borrowing, but this alone was insufficient. Bank balance sheets were destroyed by the need to value their assets at realistic estimates of their true value rather than their nominal values; those estimates depended on what they could sell the assets for in an open market, and the answer to that question was too often a fraction of the nominal value. Hence the government guarantees

A NEW SCANDAL: LIBOR

Banking is a lucrative industry for the participants—not including customers. Yet recently the industry has suffered a few mishaps. Both investment and commercial bankers helped to create the greatest financial crisis in memory with the mortgage derivatives debacle that emerged in 2007. With the help of quite a few government bailouts, the industry survived, but it had to deal with the vast number of bad mortgages involved; that was mishandled by a practice of badly executed foreclosures leading to some extremely large fines. Not content with these blunders, banks were found to be colluding in a far more insidious practice that, while posing less of a threat to the financial system, indicates a lack of integrity that shatters banks' reputations as fitting custodians of the financial system. This was a case of fixing interest rates to their own benefit. Not that they don't already set rates for their own benefit, but manipulating a rate—specifically LIBOR—with international implications is different from setting prime.

LIBOR stands for **London Interbank Offered Rate**, which refers to short-term interest rates of 15 different periods in 10 currencies. The rates are calculated and published daily at 11:30 a.m. (GMT) by Thomson Reuters. Internationally, rates are set by other financial institutions, lenders, and credit card agencies relative to the published LIBOR, with more than $150 trillion of financial instruments affected.

In a process overseen by the British Bankers' Association, representatives of 7 to 18 banks report the rates they pay or would have to pay to borrow for short-term periods in various currencies from other banks. After removing outliers, the figures are averaged to arrive at a set of standards for borrowing and lending rates around the world. Loans are tied to those benchmarks similarly to the quote of a loan at "prime plus one-half." In consequence, organizations both public and private may have earned too little or paid too much in their financial dealings.

Investigations by British, American, and Canadian authorities revealed that the major international banks, including Barclays, UBS, Citigroup and Bank of America, had been either inflating or deflating (usually) the rate they reported. Lowering the rates allowed banks to appear healthier during the crisis with a lower cost of funds. At other times, a manipulated rate allowed investment bankers to profit from trading positions. The consequences of this discovery were significant. Barclays lost its chairman and its CEO by resignation and paid fines of about $450 million; UBS agreed to a fine of $1.5 billion, collected by U.S., British, and Swiss authorities. What next?

and purchases of bank equity. Fears of a new Great Depression were everywhere, but government action worked. By April 2009, markets round the world, which had collapsed by typically half their value, bottomed out, and a new bull market appeared to have started after only nine months of the bear market. The worldwide recession, more severe than any since the Great Depression, was still in effect, but by the end of 2009 economic statistics confirmed that it had ended by the third quarter in most countries.

Economists noted that, historically, recessions caused by financial crises, rather than by excess production and consumption leading to cyclical contractions, had far-longer-lasting effects. This proved to be the case, as world economies expanded slowly with less job creation and slipped back into recession in following years. Central banks engaged in the new practice of "quantitative easing," that is, expanding the money supply greatly through printing new money to purchase government securities. The ultimate effect of printing money is to spur inflation; inflation, however, was considered a far lesser evil than deflation, which has plagued Japan since the 1987 crash. Hence, policy strove to balance the two risks. (Bankers continued to create problems, however, as described in the nearby box.)

One factor blamed for the collapse was the use of complex derivative instruments, but the blame is misapplied. While derivatives were at the heart of the crisis, they were not themselves at fault. The ability to escape from the risk created by poor mortgages through derivatives was the culprit, but this was a failure of regulation, as was the excessive leverage in which financial institutions were able to engage. Also at fault was an excessive reliance on mathematical modelling that was not based on the underlying market realities. Models in general relied on the liquidity of the instruments they described, which liquidity disappeared far more rapidly than assumed; also, models failed to recognize the potential for rapid increases in volatility in the trading of these instruments and the resultant risk expansion.

Beneath this general account of the market's behaviour lies a complex subject that must be examined closely, with a variety of issues that will be addressed in this book. The end of the twentieth century revealed a number of major mistakes by individual investors and by professionals, mistakes in the sense of their not following the precepts of investment analysis. This book will present the major concerns in investing, and how those concerns should be addressed. Much of it is theory and much is practice. Very often, the market will appear to contradict theoretical predictions, but over the long run most of the theory holds up well. Even if investors appear to ignore theory, if fortunes can be made thereby and, what is worse, if some theories prove inaccurate, it is essential to understand the theories. Much of professional practice pays more than lip service to the theoretical results of academic research. Careers in finance require familiarity with the theories, if only to realize how and when they are not being followed.

1.2   THE ECONOMIC SYSTEM AND INVESTMENT

To many naïve observers of the market, professionals and individuals seem to be buying and selling shares in major corporations whose names are familiar because they provide well-known goods or services. They may then presume that every time such a trade occurs, on the other side of the transaction the shares are being sold or bought by those same corporations. However, if they thought it through, they might realize the enormity of such a process and begin to understand why something quite different is happening.

When investors buy or sell stocks, they are rarely trading with the company that issued the shares. Instead the trade is made with another investor, one who has an opposite idea of what the value of the company is—buyers think value is higher than the share price and sellers think the opposite. The price in the market is crucial to establishing a fair valuation of the shares. This ultimately becomes relevant to the corporation when it needs to issue new shares at a fair price, which only occurs when it requires new capital. The company itself is fairly remote from the trading, its interest lying only in what the trade price says about investor sentiment on its perceived financial prospects. The company gets involved only when it makes an issue of stock to the public to raise capital, or when, having excess capital, it decides to repurchase its shares.

Shares in companies exist because those companies need capital in order to expand and purchase physical assets. Companies must raise this capital from the investing public because they do not have sufficient funds to make all the investments in plant and equipment required for their growth. Investors have this capital because, in general, individuals have more funds than required for immediate needs; they can and wish to postpone their current consumption to save and build capital for later consumption.

In order to obtain capital, those with a deficit must issue securities, which are bought by those with excess funds. The types of securities or financial instruments involved will be defined formally in the following chapter, but we can begin by talking about stocks and bonds, issued by private corporations. Bonds are notes that acknowledge indebtedness and specify the terms of repayment; stocks are instruments that convey ownership rights to their holders, with no guarantee of any fixed, or even positive, return. Stocks enable investors to participate in business activities while being protected from the major drawbacks of individual ownership or partnership; they are relatively liquid, enabling the investor to extract the true value of the shares fairly quickly, and they offer limited liability, so that the greatest loss to be suffered is the investment itself, in the case of a catastrophe in the business.

Real Investment Versus Financial Investment

The investment by individuals in stocks and bonds of corporations is identified as **financial investment**. For the most part, this occurs as investors enter the securities markets and exchange cash for the financial instruments. Since the cash is exchanged between investors and no new capital reaches the corporations, no **real investment** occurs as a result of this activity. Real investment only occurs when a corporation takes capital and invests it in productive assets; this may come about as a result of reinvested profits, but major real investment requires the issuance of new debt or equity instruments.

Real investment is channelled into **real assets**, which determine the productive capacity of the economy. These real assets are the land, buildings, and machines, even the knowledge, necessary to produce goods, together with the workers and their skills in operating those resources. In contrast to real assets are **financial assets**, such as stocks or bonds. These assets, per se, do not represent a society's wealth. For example, shares of stock represent only ownership rights to assets; they do not directly contribute to the productive capacity of the economy. Financial assets instead contribute to the productive capacity of the economy *indirectly*, because they allow for separation of the ownership and management of the firm and facilitate the transfer of funds to enterprises with attractive investment opportunities. Financial assets certainly contribute to the wealth of the individuals or firms holding them, because they are claims on the income generated by real assets or on income from the government.

When the real assets used by a firm ultimately generate income, that income is allocated to investors according to their ownership of financial assets, or securities, issued by the firm. Bondholders, for example, are entitled to a flow of income based on the interest rate and par value of the bond. Equityholders or stockholders are entitled to any residual income after bondholders and other creditors are paid. In this way the values of financial assets are derived from and depend on the values of the underlying real assets of the firm.

Real assets are income-generating assets, whereas financial assets define the allocation of income or wealth among investors. Individuals can choose between consuming their current endowments of wealth today and investing for the future. When they invest for the future, they may choose to hold financial assets. The money a firm receives when it issues securities (sells them to investors) is used to purchase real assets. Ultimately, then, the returns on a financial asset come from the income produced by the real assets financed by the issuance of the security. In this way, it is useful to view financial assets as the means by which individuals hold their claims on real assets in well-developed economies. Most of us cannot personally own a bank, but we can hold shares of the Royal Bank or the Bank of Nova Scotia, which provide us with income derived from providing banking services.

An operational distinction between real and financial assets involves the balance sheets of individuals and firms in the economy. Real assets appear only on the asset side of the balance sheet. In contrast, financial assets always appear on both sides of balance sheets. Your financial claim on a firm is an asset for you, but the firm's issuance of that claim is the firm's liability. When we aggregate over all balance sheets, financial assets will cancel out, leaving only the sum of real assets as the net wealth of the aggregate economy. Another way of distinguishing between financial and real assets is to note that financial assets are created and destroyed in the ordinary course of doing business. For example, when a loan is paid off, both the creditor's claim (a financial asset) and the debtor's obligation (a financial liability) cease to exist. In contrast, real assets are destroyed only by accident or by wearing out over time.

CC 1

CONCEPT CHECK

Are the following assets real or financial?
a. Patents
b. Lease obligations
c. Customer goodwill
d. A university education
e. A $5 bill

Financial assets and the markets they trade in play several crucial roles that help ensure the efficient allocation of capital to real assets in the economy. One such function is the **informational role**. Stock prices reflect investors' collective assessment of a firm's current performance and future prospects. When the market is more optimistic about the firm, its share price will rise. That higher price makes it easier for the firm to raise capital and therefore encourages investment. In this manner, stock prices play a major role in the allocation of capital in market economies, directing capital to the firms and applications with the greatest perceived potential.

Do capital markets actually channel resources to the most efficient use? At times, they appear to fail miserably. Companies or whole industries can be "hot" for a period of time (think about the dot-com bubble that peaked in 2000), attract a large flow of investor capital, and then fail after only a few years. The process seems highly wasteful. But we need to be careful about our standard of efficiency. No one knows with certainty which ventures will succeed and which will fail. It is therefore unreasonable to expect that markets will never make mistakes. The market encourages allocation of capital to firms that seem to have prospects until such prospects no longer seem likely.

You may well be skeptical about resource allocation through markets. But if you are, then take a moment to think about the alternatives. Would a central planner make fewer mistakes? Would you prefer that politicians make these decisions? To paraphrase Winston Churchill's comment about democracy, markets may be the worst way to allocate capital except for all the others that have been tried.

Financial assets are also the vehicle enabling **consumption timing** by individuals. Some individuals in an economy are earning more than they currently wish to spend. Others, for example, retirees, spend more than they currently earn. How can you shift your purchasing power from high-earnings to low-earnings periods of life? One way is to "store" your wealth in financial assets. In high-earnings periods, you can invest your savings in financial assets such as stocks and bonds. In low-earnings periods, you can sell these assets to provide funds for your consumption needs. By so doing, you can "shift" your consumption over the course of your lifetime, thereby allocating your consumption to periods that provide the greatest satisfaction. Thus, financial markets allow individuals to separate decisions concerning current consumption from constraints that otherwise would be imposed by current earnings.

Financial assets provide the structure by which the **separation of ownership and management** occurs. With few exceptions large corporations are not owner-operated. Corporate executives are selected by boards of directors who oversee the management of the firm in accordance with the interests of the actual owners—the shareholders (some of whom will be the executives and directors themselves). This gives the firm a stability that the owner-managed firm cannot achieve. For example, if some stockholders decide they no longer wish to have holdings in the firm, they can sell their shares to other investors, with no impact on the management of the firm. Thus, financial assets and the ability to buy and sell those assets in the financial markets allow for easy separation of ownership and management.

How can all of the disparate owners of the firm, ranging from large pension funds holding hundreds of thousands of shares to small investors who may hold only a single share, agree on the objectives of the firm? Again, the financial markets provide some guidance. All may agree that the firm's management should pursue strategies that enhance the value of their shares. Such policies will make all shareholders wealthier and allow them all to better pursue their personal goals, whatever those might be.

Yet managers may not always attempt to maximize firm value. The possible substitution of personal interests for those of the owners is referred to as the **agency problem**. Several mechanisms have evolved to avoid such problems. First, compensation plans tie the income of managers to the success of the firm. A major part of the total compensation of top executives is typically in the form of stock options, which means that the managers will not do well unless the stock price increases, benefiting shareholders. (Of course, we've learned more recently that overuse of options can create its own agency problem. Options can create an incentive for managers to engage in excessively risky projects or manipulate information to prop up a stock price temporarily, giving them a chance to cash out before the price returns to a level reflective of the firm's true prospects.) Second, while boards of directors have sometimes been portrayed as defenders of top management, they can, and more recently have forced out management teams that are underperforming. The average tenure of CEOs fell from 8.1 years in 2006 to 6.6 years in 2011, and the percentage of incoming CEOs who also serve as chairman of the board of directors fell from 48 percent in 2002 to less than 12 percent in 2009. Third, outsiders such as security analysts or mutual funds and pension funds monitor the firm closely and make the life of poor performers at the least uncomfortable.

Finally, bad performers are subject to the threat of takeover. If the board of directors is lax in monitoring management, unhappy shareholders in principle can elect a different board. They can do this by launching a *proxy contest* in which they seek to obtain enough proxies (i.e., rights to vote the shares of other shareholders) to take control of the firm and vote in another board. However, this threat is usually minimal. Shareholders who attempt such a fight have to use their own funds, while management can defend itself using corporate coffers. Most proxy fights fail. The real takeover threat is from other firms. If one firm observes another underperforming, it can acquire the underperforming business and replace management with its own team. The stock price should rise to reflect the prospects of improved performance, which provides incentive for firms to engage in such takeover activity.

1.3   THE PARTICIPANTS: INDIVIDUALS AND FINANCIAL INTERMEDIARIES

Essentially, there are three types of participants in financial markets:

1. Households typically are net suppliers of capital as savers. They purchase the securities issued by firms that need to raise funds.
2. Firms are net demanders of capital. They raise capital now to pay for investments in plant and equipment. The income generated by those real assets provides the returns to investors who purchase the securities issued by the firm.
3. Governments can be either, depending on the relationship between tax revenue and government expenditures. Most of the time, they spend more than they raise through taxation, although occasionally they succeed in running small surpluses. The picture is complicated by spending for investment in infrastructure and incurring liabilities for future payments of pensions.

Individuals and Financial Objectives

The reader of a book on investments presumably has a good idea of what the objective of investing is—making a return on capital. This broad statement, however, encompasses a range of possibilities for the kind of return expected, as different kinds of investors will be attracted to strategies from the very conservative to the very risky, and at times to combinations of them, on the basis of their future needs. How much, how safely, and how quickly they want their return on capital, together with their personal tolerances for risk, will dictate the kinds of investments they are likely to make at different stages of their lives.

Investors are a very diverse group. Some of them are content with a fixed return if the principal is guaranteed; these investors usually place funds in a savings account. Others are looking for opportunities to double their investment in a matter of days. Neither of these extremes is of much interest to the subject of this book; some might label these individuals as "hoarders" or "speculators" rather than investors. There is a place, however, for both of these behaviours within the overall investment plan of an investor, provided this is part of a portfolio of investments. At times, cash may rightfully be hoarded in some safe form with virtually no return, while highly risky (speculative) investments offering extravagant returns might also be justified in other circumstances.

Saving means not spending all of your current income on consumption. Investing, on the other hand, is choosing what assets to hold. You may choose to invest in safe assets, risky assets, or a combination of both. In everyday English, however, the term *saving* is often taken to mean investing in safe assets such as an insured bank account. It is easy to get confused between saving and safe investing. To avoid confusion remember this example. Suppose you earn $100,000 a year from your job, and you spend $80,000 of it on consumption. You are saving $20,000. Suppose you decide to invest all $20,000 in risky assets. You are still saving $20,000, but you are not investing it safely.

The first significant investment decision for most individuals concerns education, building up their human capital. The major asset most people have during their early working years is the earning power that draws on their human capital. In these circumstances, the risk of illness or injury is far greater than the risk associated with their financial wealth. The most direct way of hedging human capital risk is to purchase insurance. Life insurance is a hedge against the complete loss of income as a result of the death of any of the family's income earners. Insurance is not limited to covering loss of life and income, however; besides insuring personal assets and health, insurance can be used to accumulate retirement savings and to do so in a way that has tax benefits.

The first major economic asset acquired by most people is a personal residence. This is a financial investment that requires an evaluation of potential appreciation in residential values in the light of rental expense. When we consider real estate investment as a diversifying alternative, it is important to recognize the degree of direct exposure from a personal residence; in many cases, a personal portfolio may be overweighted in real estate.

The risk in this area is correlated to risk in human capital. Individuals are first exposed to the risk of a downturn in their employer's industry or factors affecting the firm itself. Should the individual lose his or her job, the necessity of moving, with associated expenses and the risk of housing prices, presents itself. Hence, the investment portfolio should attempt to diversify away from the industry sector and real estate, if the latter is overweighted.

People save and invest money to provide for future consumption and leave an estate. The primary aim of lifetime savings is to allow maintenance of the customary standard of living after retirement. Life expectancy, when one makes it to retirement at age 65, approaches 85 years, so the average retiree needs to prepare a 20-year nest egg and sufficient savings to cover unexpected health care costs. Investment income also may increase the welfare of one's heirs, favourite charity, or both.

The consumption enabled by investment income depends on the degree of risk the household is willing to take with its investment portfolio. Empirical observation examines how life cycle affects risk tolerance. Studies have shown that almost 50 percent of young and middle-aged investors are willing to take some risk, but that barely a quarter of investors over 55 are willing to accept any risk in their portfolios. Questionnaires suggest that attitudes shift away from risk tolerance and toward risk aversion as investors near retirement age. With age, individuals lose the potential to recover from a disastrous investment performance. When they are young, investors can respond to a loss by working harder and saving more of their income. But as retirement approaches, investors realize there will be less time to recover; hence the shift to safe assets.

CC 3

CONCEPT CHECK

a. Think about the financial circumstances of your closest relative in your parents' generation (preferably your parents' household, if you are fortunate enough to have them around). Write down the objectives and constraints for their investment decisions.
b. Now consider the financial situation of your closest relative who is in his or her 30s. Write down the objectives and constraints that would fit his or her investment decision.
c. How much of the difference between the two statements is due to the age of the investors?

The Investment Process

An investor's *portfolio* is simply his collection of investment assets. Once the portfolio is established, it is updated or "rebalanced" by selling existing securities and using the proceeds to buy new securities, by investing additional funds to increase the overall size of the portfolio, or by selling securities to decrease the size of the portfolio.

Investment assets can be categorized into broad asset classes, such as stocks, bonds, real estate, commodities, and so on. Investors make two types of decisions in constructing their portfolios. The **asset allocation** decision is the choice among these broad asset classes, while the **security selection** decision is the choice of which particular securities to hold *within* each asset class.

Top-down portfolio construction starts with asset allocation. For example, an individual who currently holds all his or her money in a bank account would first decide what proportion of the overall portfolio ought to be moved into stocks, bonds, and so on. In this way, the broad features of the portfolio are established. While the average annual return on the common stock of large firms since 1926 has been about 11 percent per year, the average return on Treasury bills has been less than 7 percent. On the other hand, stocks are far riskier, with annual returns that have ranged as low as 225 percent and as high as 45 percent. In contrast, T-bill returns are effectively risk-free: you know what interest rate you will earn when you buy the bills. Therefore, the decision to allocate your investments to the stock market or to the money market where Treasury bills are traded will have great ramifications for both the risk and the return of your portfolio. A top-down investor first makes this and other crucial asset allocation decisions before turning to the decision of the particular securities to be held in each asset class.

Security analysis involves the valuation of particular securities that might be included in the portfolio. For example, an investor might ask whether Encana or Petro-Canada is more attractively priced. Both bonds and stocks must be evaluated for investment attractiveness, but valuation is far more difficult for stocks because a stock's performance usually is far more sensitive to the condition of the issuing firm.

In contrast to top-down portfolio management is the *bottom-up* strategy. In this process, the portfolio is constructed from the securities that seem attractively priced without as much concern for the resultant asset allocation. Such a technique can result in unintended bets on one or another sector of the economy. For example, it might turn out that the portfolio ends up with a very heavy representation of firms in one industry, from one part of the country, or with exposure to one source of uncertainty. However, a bottom-up strategy does focus the portfolio on the assets that seem to offer the most attractive investment opportunities.

Financial Intermediaries

Corporations and governments do not sell all or even most of their securities directly to individuals. For example, about half of all stock is held by large financial institutions such as pension funds, mutual funds, insurance companies, and banks. Similarly, corporations do not market their own securities to the public; instead they hire agents, called *investment bankers*, to represent them to the investing public. These institutions stand between the security issuer (the firm) and the ultimate owner of the security (the investor), and for this reason they are called **financial intermediaries**. Let's examine their roles.

Households want desirable investments for their savings, yet the small (financial) size of most households makes direct investment difficult. A small investor seeking to lend money to businesses that need to finance investments doesn't advertise in the local newspaper to find a willing and desirable borrower. Moreover, an individual lender would not be able to diversify across borrowers to reduce risk. Finally, an individual lender is not equipped to assess and monitor the credit risk of borrowers.

For these reasons, financial intermediaries have evolved to bring lenders and borrowers together: banks, investment companies, insurance companies, and credit unions. Financial intermediaries issue their own securities to raise funds to purchase the securities of other corporations.

For example, a bank raises funds by borrowing (taking deposits) and lending that money to other borrowers. The spread between the interest rates paid to depositors and the rates charged to borrowers is the source of the bank's profit. In this way, lenders and borrowers do not need to contact each other directly. Instead, each goes to the bank, which acts as an intermediary between the two. The problem of matching lenders with borrowers is solved when each comes independently to the common intermediary.

Other examples of financial intermediaries are investment companies, insurance companies, and credit unions. All these firms offer similar advantages in their intermediary role. First, by pooling the resources of many small investors, they are able to lend considerable sums to large borrowers. Second, by lending to many borrowers, intermediaries achieve significant diversification, so they can accept loans that individually might be too risky. Third, intermediaries build expertise through the volume of business they do and can use economies of scale and scope to assess and monitor risk.

Investment companies, which pool and manage the money of many investors, also arise out of economies of scale. Here, the problem is that most household portfolios are not large enough to be spread among a wide variety of securities. It is very expensive in terms of brokerage fees and research costs to purchase one or two shares of many different firms. Mutual funds have the advantage of large-scale trading and portfolio management, while participating investors are assigned a prorated share of the total funds according to the size of their investment. This system gives small investors advantages they are willing to pay for via a management fee to the mutual fund operator.

Investment companies can also design portfolios specifically for large investors with particular goals. In contrast, mutual funds are sold in the retail market, and their investment philosophies are differentiated mainly by strategies that are likely to attract a large number of clients.

Economies of scale also explain the proliferation of analytic services available to investors. Newsletters, databases, and brokerage house research services all engage in research to be sold to a large client base. This setup arises naturally. Investors clearly want information, but with small portfolios to manage, they do not find it economical to personally gather all of it. Hence, a profit opportunity emerges: a firm can perform this service for many clients and charge for it.

CC 4

CONCEPT CHECK

Computer networks have made it much cheaper and easier for small investors to trade for their own accounts and perform their own security analysis. What will be the likely effect on financial intermediation?

Investment Bankers   Just as economies of scale and specialization create profit opportunities for financial intermediaries, so too do these economies create niches for firms that perform specialized services for businesses. Firms raise much of their capital by selling securities such as stocks and bonds to the public. Because these firms do not do so frequently, however, investment banking firms that specialize in such activities can offer their services at a cost below that of maintaining an in-house security issuance division.

Investment bankers, also known in Canada as *investment dealers*, such as Scotia Capital, RBC Investments, or BMO Nesbitt, advise the issuing corporation on the prices it can charge for the securities issued, appropriate interest rates, and so forth. Ultimately, the investment banking firm handles the marketing of the security in the **primary market**, where new issues of securities are offered to the public. Later, investors can trade previously issued securities among themselves in the so-called **secondary market**.

Investment bankers can provide more than just expertise to security issuers. Because investment bankers are constantly in the market, assisting one firm or another in issuing securities, it is in the banker's own interest to protect and maintain its reputation for honesty. Their investment in reputation is another type of scale economy that arises from frequent participation in the capital markets. The investment banker will suffer along with investors if the securities it underwrites are marketed to the public with overly optimistic or exaggerated claims; the public will not be so trusting the next time that investment banker participates in a security sale. As we have seen, this lesson was relearned with considerable pain in the boom years of the late 1990s and the subsequent high-tech crash of 2000–2002. Too many investment bankers seemed to get caught up in the flood of money that could be made by pushing stock issues to an overly eager public. The failure of many of these offerings soured the public on both the stock market and the firms managing the IPOs. At least some on Bay Street belatedly recognize that they squandered a valuable asset—reputational capital—and there are signs that they recognize as well that the conflicts of interest that engendered these deals are not only wrong but bad for business as well. The investment banker's effectiveness and ability to command future business depend on the reputation it has established over time. (See nearby box.)

Although they too are financial intermediaries, hedge funds and private equity groups provide alternatives to the mutual funds and usual retail intermediaries. These pools of capital, which we discuss in Chapter 23, have become major players in capital markets and one of the most important new trends in investing in addition to those we next describe.

1.4   RECENT TRENDS

Four important trends have changed the contemporary investment environment: (1) globalization, (2) financial engineering, (3) securitization, and (4) information and computer networks.

Globalization

If a wider range of investment choices can benefit investors, why should we limit ourselves to purely domestic assets? Increasingly efficient communication technology and the dismantling of regulatory constraints have encouraged **globalization** in recent years.

Canadian investors commonly can participate in foreign (non-U.S.) investment opportunities in several ways by trading on U.S. markets to: (1) purchase foreign securities using **American Depository Receipts (ADRs)**, which are domestically traded securities that represent claims to shares of foreign stocks; (2) purchase foreign securities that are offered in dollars; (3) buy mutual funds or exchange-traded funds that invest internationally; and (4) buy derivative securities with payoffs that depend on prices in foreign security markets.

Brokers who act as intermediaries for ADRs purchase an inventory of stock from some foreign issuer. The broker then issues an ADR that represents a claim to some number of those foreign

The banking industry is conventionally separated into commercial and investment banking functions. From the Great Depression until near the end of the century, the two functions were practised by the chartered banks accepting deposits and granting loans, and the investment banks underwriting securities. In the U.S., this was mandated by the *Glass-Steagall Act* as a reaction to the financial calamities of the Depression, but this act was repealed in 1999. In both Canada and the United States, chartered banks expanded usually by swallowing investment dealers (such as BMO absorbing Nesbitt Burns and Chase Manhattan acquiring J. P. Morgan) to become "universal banks" offering a full range of commercial and investment banking services. In contrast, Europe had never forced the separation of commercial and investment banking, so their giant banks such as Credit Suisse, Deutsche Bank, HSBC, and UBS had long been universal banks. As well, giant corporations such as GE created huge financing arms that acted much like commercial banks in helping customers to finance their purchases; these needed to obtain funds by issuing securities.

The events of the financial crisis brought the trend of consolidation to a close. In order to obtain government backing, the remaining U.S. investment banking giants such as Goldman Sachs converted to bank holding companies, subjecting themselves to more stringent capital requirements. Citigroup found itself obliged to trim its portfolio composed of insurance, commercial, and investment banking. Public bodies debated whether to reinstate a *Glass-Steagall* regime, since insured citizens' deposits were unsupported by safe assets as a result of risky investment practices. By 2010, Congress had enacted legislation that prohibited banks from trading in many derivatives for their own accounts and had amended the regulatory framework for financial institutions. Nevertheless, the universal bank model is likely to persist albeit with greater regulation.

This history of the U.S. banking system and its regulatory environment is of little relevance to Canada of itself, where the banking sector operates in a much different context. The equivalent of the *Glass-Steagall Act* had been abolished many years before 1999, but at the same time, a 1987 act of parliament established the Office of the Superintendent of Financial Institutions (OSFI), which was given broad regulatory powers over the financial industry, namely banks, insurance, trust, loan and cooperative credit societies, and for supervising federally regulated private pension plans. The OSFI has maintained tight limits on allowable leverage ratios, to the point that the average Canadian bank leverage ratio was 18:1, as against 26:1 for U.S. commercial banks, and as much as 46:1 for U.S. investment banks before the crisis struck. The OSFI may also have pressed Canadian banks to refrain from loading their balance sheets with "too many" securitized assets. Additionally, Canadian mortgage lending practices are far more conservative than in the United States. Finally, Canadian banks were repeatedly rebuffed when they sought to merge with each other and become an even tighter oligopoly than they already are, implying that no financial institution was allowed to become too large so that its failure would jeopardize the stability of the entire system.

A recent debate considers whether increased regulation and supervision is the key to avoiding bank failures or if instead placing banks in an environment of less competition may help greatly to increase the safety of banks. It is suggested, and evidence has been advanced for the theory, that excessive competition causes banks to risk too much capital and lower their leverage ratios in an attempt to increase returns and profits.

Most economists would reject such arguments. Canada's "Big Five," the major banks, are often accused of noncompetitive pricing of services, but simultaneously they are profitable and safe. Canada's credit markets are dominated by these banks, and corporations wanting other financing arrangements must resort to U.S. and U.K. markets, which were virtually frozen by the crisis while Canadian banks were in far better shape to continue to provide credit to Canadian corporations. Although Canadian banks' share prices declined significantly as a result of the general financial meltdown, they had largely recovered by 2010 and traded sideways until late 2012, before beginning a strong advance due in part to generous dividends. The banking crisis largely bypassed Canada, and no bank failed.

(For a comprehensive account of the financial crisis in an international perspective, see "The Financial Crisis of 2008" in the Online Learning Centre.)

shares held in inventory. The ADR is denominated in U.S. dollars and can be traded on U.S. stock exchanges, but it is in essence no more than a claim on foreign shares. Thus, from the investor's point of view, there is no more difference between buying a British versus a Canadian stock than there is in holding an Ontario-based company as against an Alberta-based one. Of course, the investment implications may differ: ADRs still expose investors to exchange-rate risk.

World Equity Benchmark Shares (WEBS) are a variation on ADRs. WEBS use the same depository structure to allow investors to trade *portfolios* of foreign stocks in a selected country. Each WEBS security tracks the performance of an index of share returns for a particular country. WEBS can be traded by investors just like any other security (they trade on the American Stock Exchange) and thus enable U.S. investors to obtain diversified portfolios of foreign stocks in one fell swoop.

Figure 1.1

Globalization: A debt issue denominated in euros.

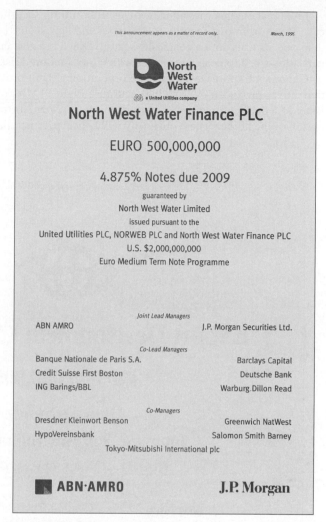

Source: North West Water Finance PLC, April 1999.

A giant step toward globalization took place when 11 European countries replaced their existing currencies with a new currency called the *euro*.[2] The idea behind the euro is that a common currency will facilitate trade and encourage integration of markets across national boundaries. Figure 1.1 is an announcement of a debt offering in the amount of 500 million euros.

Financial Engineering

Financial engineering is the use of mathematical models and computer-based trading technology to synthesize new financial products. A good example of a financially engineered investment product is the *principal-protected equity-linked note*. These are securities issued by financial intermediaries that guarantee a minimum fixed return plus an additional amount that depends on the performance of some specified stock index, such as the S&P TSX Composite.

[2]The 11 countries are Austria, Belgium, Finland, France, Germany, Ireland, Italy, Luxembourg, Netherlands, Portugal, and Spain. Since then, seven more nations that joined the European Union also adopted the euro, namely Cyprus, Estonia, Greece, Latvia, Malta, Slovakia, and Slovenia.

Financial engineering often involves **unbundling** securities—breaking up and allocating the cash flows from one security to create several new securities—or **bundling**—combining more than one security into a composite security. Such creative engineering of new investment products allows one to design securities with custom-tailored risk attributes.

Canada's Export Development Corporation (EDC) provides some interesting examples of derivatives produced by bundling securities. Figure 1.2 reproduces the announcement of EDC's issue of a dual-currency bond, with payment in either Australian dollars or Japanese yen, at the option of the holder. These obviously will appeal to Australian and Japanese investors; however,

Figure 1.2

Derivative securities: A dual-currency bond issue.

This announcement appears as a matter of record only.   *September, 1990*

Export Development Corporation

¥20,000,000,000

Dual Currency
Japanese Yen/Australian Dollar
Bonds—First Series (1990)

Issue Price: 99.3%   Coupon Rate: 8.0% (A$335.75)
Maturity Date: September 5, 2000

Daiwa Securities Co. Ltd.

The Nikko Securities Co., Ltd.   The Nomura Securities   Yamaichi Securities Company, Limited
                                              Co., Ltd.

New Japan Securities Co., Ltd.

KOKUSAI Securities Co., Ltd.   The Nippon Kangyo Kakumaru Securities Co., Ltd.

Sanyo Securities Co., Ltd.   Universal Securities Co., Ltd.

Cosmo Securities Co., Ltd.   Dai-ichi Securities Co., Ltd.   Marusan Securities Co., Ltd.

Okasan Securities Co., Ltd.   Taiheiyo Securities Co., Ltd.   Tokyo Securities Co., Ltd.

Toyo Securities Co., Ltd.   Wako Securities Co., Ltd.   Yamatane Securities Co., Ltd.

they also provide an opportunity to Canadian or other investors to speculate on the appreciation of either of the currencies against the dollar. EDC was also a pioneer in the principal-protected equity-linked note. In 1991, it was offering its PINs or protected index notes, as shown in Figure 1.3. Each PIN on issue cost $10 in U.S. dollars and promised, at the option of the holder, to repay the $10 upon maturity after five-and-a-half years, or, at any time up to

Figure 1.3

Derivative securities: Prospectus for a minimum-return index investment.

Offering Circular dated June 25, 1991

This Offering Circular constitutes a public offering of these securities only in those jurisdictions where they may be lawfully offered for sale. No securities commission nor similar authority in Canada has in any way passed upon the merits of the securities offered hereunder and any representation to the contrary is an offence.

Export Development Corporation

(An agent of Her Majesty in right of Canada)

Société pour l'expansion des exportations

(Mandataire de Sa Majesté du chef du Canada)

U.S.$75,000,000

S&P 500® Protected Index Notes Due 1997 ("PINS")

The S&P 500 Protected Index Notes Due 1997 (the "Notes") offered hereby will mature on January 3, 1997 (the "Stated Maturity"). The Notes may not be called for redemption by Export Development Corporation ("EDC") prior to Stated Maturity. Each Note will have a principal amount of U.S.$10 and all payments with respect to the Notes will be denominated in U.S. dollars. At Stated Maturity, a holder of each Note (a "Holder") will receive in respect of each Note held by such Holder the greater of (A) U.S.$10 or (B) the Repurchase Price which will be computed by reference to the Standard & Poor's 500 Composite Stock Price Index (the "S&P 500 Index"). The repurchase price of each Note (the "Repurchase Price") will equal U.S.$10 multiplied by the Spot S&P Index (as hereinafter defined) for the applicable Valuation Date (as hereinafter defined) divided by the Strike S&P Index (as hereinafter defined) (rounded down to the nearest cent). The Strike S&P Index will equal 105% of the Initial S&P Index (as hereinafter defined). No interest will be paid on the Notes, except to the extent that the Repurchase Price exceeds U.S.$10 upon exercise of the Repurchase Option or at Stated Maturity. The Repurchase Price will not exceed U.S.$10 unless the S&P 500 Index increases to a level greater than the Strike S&P Index. Prior to 10:00 a.m. on the sixteenth Business Day immediately preceding the Stated Maturity, a Holder will have the option (the "Repurchase Price") to require EDC to repurchase any Notes held by such Holder at the Repurchase Price. If a Holder exercises the Repurchase Option prior to January 3, 1992, the amount payable to the Holder will be equal to 95% of the Repurchase Price.

The valuation and payment of the Repurchase Price may be postponed as a result of a Market Disruption Event (as hereinafter defined). In such event the Holder will receive the Repurchase Price determined as of a later date, except that Notes tendered for repurchase that become subject to such postponed valuation and payment will not be repurchased if the Holder elects in the Repurchase Notice that the Note Agent withdraw the Repurchase Notice (a "Withdrawal Election") in the event of a Market Disruption Event (as hereinafter defined).

PRICE: U.S.$10.00 per Note
Minimum Subscription: 100 Notes

	Price to the Public (1)(2)	Agents' Commission	Proceeds to EDC (3)
Per Note	U.S.$10.00	U.S.$0.30	U.S.$9.70
Total Offering (4)	U.S.$75,000,000	U.S.$2,250,000	U.S.$72,750,000

Notes:

(1) The subscription price has been determined by negotiation between EDC and the Agents (as hereinafter defined).

(2) On June 24, 1991, the Canadian dollar purchase price of each Note would have been C$11.43 based on the noon exchange rate of C$1.1427 for each U.S.$1.00.

(3) The expenses of the issue of approximately C$350,000 are being borne by the Issuer and the Agents.

(4) EDC has granted to the Agents an overallotment option, exercisable from time to time up to the Date of Closing (as hereinafter defined) with the concurrence of EDC, to distribute an additional 1,000,000 Notes on the same terms and conditions as the other Notes offered hereby. To the extent such option is exercised, the Agents will offer to the public such additional Notes at the price shown above.

Investment in the Notes is speculative and a Holder may sustain a substantial loss of its investment if such Holder elects to exercise the Repurchase Option and the Notes are repurchased prior to Stated Maturity. Since the return to a Holder on exercise of the Repurchase Option or at Stated Maturity is determined solely by reference to the S&P 500 Index, the Notes are not suitable for persons unfamiliar with the risks of investing in equity securities. (See "Risk Factors".) In order for a Holder to avoid a loss of principal on the Notes, the level of the S&P 500 Index must increase to the Breakeven Point (as hereinafter defined) or the Notes must be held to Stated Maturity. (See "Description of Notes — Breakeven Point" and "Description of the Notes — Repurchase Price".) The Notes will constitute direct unsecured obligations of EDC and, as such, will constitute direct obligations of Her Majesty in right of Canada. (See "Description of the Notes — Status".)

The Repurchase Option will be exercisable on any Business Day (as hereinafter defined) after the Date of Closing and will expire at 10:00 a.m. on the sixteenth Business Day immediately preceding the Stated Maturity of the Notes. Any Holder who does not exercise the Repurchase Option will receive in respect of each Note held by such Holder the greater of (A) U.S.$10 or (B) the Repurchase Price, at the Stated Maturity. The Repurchase Option may not be exercised by or on behalf of any Holder in respect of fewer than 100 Notes or integral multiples thereof. (See "Description of the Notes — Repurchase Option".)

maturity, an amount based on the value of the S&P 500 index relative to its value at issue. The holder is guaranteed a minimum repayment of the initial investment without interest but also can participate in any appreciation in the U.S. equity market—in both cases speculating on the exchange rate.

Most examples of innovative instruments are responses to U.S. tax or regulatory restrictions, reflecting the dominance of the U.S. financial markets. Eurobonds and financial futures are products that have left their U.S. origins behind and become international, now serving a far more diverse purpose than escaping U.S. taxes or regulations. The process continues as unanticipated financial innovations are created to evade the government's efforts to obtain fiscal revenues; as the government reacts to these innovations, even more instruments are designed.

These innovations are a small sample of the product of financial engineering in recent decades. Essentially, they are derivatives of familiar instruments such as deposits, stocks, and bonds. The original derivatives, namely options and futures, are described in detail in Part Six. The creation of options and futures on stock indices and for interest rates has led to the development of techniques to hedge portfolios against market risk; this area, often known as **portfolio insurance**, is explored in Chapter 20, and again in Chapter 22, where the process of portfolio management is discussed.

Securitization

The process of **securitization** converts non-marketable assets, such as receivables held by a firm, into traded securities by issuing claims against the firm backed by the original assets. This process creates a new class of negotiable securities offering reliable credit quality to investors, and provides cash advances to the issuing firm, with financial intermediaries handling the issue.

Canada Mortgage and Housing Corporation www.cmhc-schl .gc.ca

One widely used but little-known instrument is the **mortgage-backed security (MBS)**. These were first created in the United States, then came to Canada in 1986 under the Canada Mortgage and Housing Corporation (CMHC), which insures and guarantees pools of mortgages issued by banks and trust companies; the securities granting an interest in the payments on the mortgages (both principal and interest) to their holders are MBSs. These were a tremendous innovation in mortgage markets.[3] The securitization of mortgages meant that mortgages could be traded just like other securities in national financial markets. Availability of funds no longer depended on local credit conditions; with mortgage **pass-through securities** trading in national markets, mortgage funds could flow from any region to wherever demand was greatest.

In contrast to the long-term MBS market, short-term loans are also subject to securitization by investment bankers. The major asset-backed securities are issued for credit card debt, automobile loans, home equity loans, and student loans. In these cases, the regular payments made by the borrowers to the original grantors of the credit are passed through to the holders of the securities. The security for the paper is the underlying pool of loans and the security associated with them. The pooling and issuing by the investment banker makes these illiquid small instruments negotiable. The process enables the borrower (the original holder of the paper) to enjoy the use of the funds, while the lenders receive a superior return on those funds. Another instrument at the heart of the credit crisis is the credit default swap (CDS), described in Chapter 20.

Information and Computer Networks

The Internet and other advances in computer networking are transforming many sectors of the economy, and few more so than the financial sector. These advances will be treated in greater

---

[3]These were followed by **collateralized mortgage obligations (CMOs)** with different effective times to maturity.

detail in Chapter 3, but for now we can mention a few important innovations: online trading, online information dissemination, and automated trade crossing.

Online trading connects a customer directly to a brokerage firm. Online brokerage firms can process trades more cheaply and therefore can charge lower commissions. The average commission for an online trade is now below $20, as against more than $100 at full-service brokers.

The Internet has also allowed vast amounts of information to be made cheaply and widely available to the public. Individual investors today can obtain data, investment tools, and even analyst reports that just a decade ago would have been available only to professionals.

Electronic communication networks that allow direct trading among investors have exploded in recent years. These networks allow members to post buy or sell orders and to have those orders automatically matched up or "crossed" with orders of other traders in the system without recourse to an intermediary such as a securities dealer.

CC 5

CONCEPT CHECK

How can tax motives contribute to the desire for unbundling?

1.5

THE AGENCY PROBLEM: EXECUTIVES, ANALYSTS, AND AUDITORS

The bubble and the ensuing collapse in the high-tech market at the end of the millennium are fundamentally the result of the age-old economic phenomenon of supply and demand. During the bubble, the demand for shares exceeded the supply and forced the price up, as investors saw increasing value behind the shares; subsequently, supply greatly exceeded demand, as cash appeared to hold more value. In financial market parlance, greed overcame fear, until the reverse occurred.

The underlying question is why. Why did investors believe that the potential profits of fibre optic technology could justify not just high P/E ratios, but price-to-operating-revenue ratios when earnings were negative, price-to-sales ratios when there were no operating earnings, and price-to-ideas when there were no sales? Why did the public embrace the "dot-com" mania so enthusiastically? Answers include naïveté, the herd instinct, and media attention; but a major factor was that respected analysts (of varying age and experience) recommended these and other stocks, and, in particular, placed one-year target prices that were 50 to 100 percent higher than the current price. Since their advice to buy these stocks had been so right in the recent past, it was presumed to be as good for the future. Since these stocks could rise by 500 or more percent in a year, it was hard to justify not owning them and "missing the boat."

On what analysis did the analysts base their opinions? As you will see in Chapter 16 on security analysis, it should have been a process consisting of the following:

1. Estimation of the potential size of the product market
2. Estimation of the potential share of the market for the company
3. Estimation of the profit margins
4. Estimation of an appropriate P/E ratio for when the earnings appeared
5. Discounting of the future price to the present

This process is not easy to accomplish under normal conditions; it becomes even more difficult when the technology and the growth are relatively unprecedented.

As the bubble inflated, it became apparent that the best source for growth projections was from the companies themselves. They would predict their sales in following quarters and inform the analysts; the analysts would adjust these predictions as they saw fit and pass on the good news. The analysts became expert at predicting extremely accurate sales and earnings figures for each quarter. Any time an event would cause the estimate to need revision, the companies would inform the analysts and their official estimates would be modified. The general result was that companies actually reported results that were right in line with expectations.

In selected cases, companies would regularly beat the predicted figures by a small percentage. Despite having informed analysts of their best predictions shortly before the official reports, they still managed to beat their best estimates; this caused a satisfactory jump in the price at the "surprise" good news. The investing public grew to expect the good news, and companies that failed to beat their own predictions, via the analysts, would be punished by a price fall.

Eventually, the story ended. The economic realism behind the past sales growth and the tightening by the Federal Reserve of the money supply to avoid inflation combined to impress the investing public, and even the analysts, that there could be no more such growth in the immediate future; and the market fell—sharply and relentlessly. Canada's Nortel was a major player in the collapse, as it continued to predict growth in sales after the inevitable slowdown in tech spending began, in defiance of the monetary actions of the Fed. That shares of small companies with no sales could lose most of their value in the market fall was no surprise; that Nortel and Cisco, market leaders and huge companies with real sales and operating profits, could also was a definite shock. Nortel fell from a high of $124 to 70 cents, an incredible loss of 99.4 percent in value in two years, finally going bankrupt in 2009, despite still being a major supplier of communications equipment. That represented a loss of some $400 billion in equity value. Cisco lost only 90 percent in value as it fell from $80 to $8, while maintaining a multibillion-dollar net income except in 2001. Even the realists who recognized the extreme overvaluation could not have predicted such a correction in value.

By 2002, the market continued to doubt the prospects for companies that had unique and valuable technologies. Analysts had reversed their enthusiastic appraisals, forecast continued depressed sales, and estimated that many high-tech shares had no bottoms. Those same analysts who found ABC shares a "strong buy" at $100 in 2000, reevaluated them as "holds" or "sells" at $20 two years later. For the future, one must hope that advisors will provide better service to investors.

How could investors have avoided these losses? The simple answer is by taking profits near the top—shortly after the millennium celebrations had ended. This is also a very incomplete answer; it implies that one can and should try to exit at the right time. A wealth of evidence indicates that this is impossible, and that trying to do so results in missing many of the market's gains. Conservative and experienced investors would have taken gains on companies such as Dell much earlier in the decade; younger companies would have been dropped after the first few doubles in value. Such early exits would have missed almost all of the stupendous gains that followed. In fact, buying early and staying in through the collapse still left many investors with more than 100 percent gains in less than five years in many cases; this record should be recognized as excellent in a historical context.

An even better scenario could have occurred. Seasoned advisors should have counselled investors to take their profits much earlier; the final year of bubble would then not have developed, and the magnitude of the collapse would have been avoided. Traditional evaluation methods certainly indicated the overpriced situation, and many advisors stressed this. Investors, however, were more interested in following the momentum of the market, believing either that it would never end, or, equally foolishly, that they would be able to recognize the top and take their profits then. Many analysts and advisors cautioned against the overvaluation and excess hopes, and the media presented the conservative view as well; but, on the whole, the public and the media preferred the positive note. Too few professionals did anything to correct the problem, and many happily participated in magnifying it.

Bill 198 was established by Ontario to effect *Sarbanes-Oxley* (SOX) changes for Canadian companies, by establishing rules and penalties for noncompliance. Canadian Securities Administrators (CSA), including the OSC, were to enforce the new regulations with specific reference to audit committees, management, and the applicable penalties. The major requirement for management was the personal certification by both the CEO and CFO of the reliability of the financial reports presented to the public, with civil and criminal prosecution potentially following false reporting. This certification was to be audited, but unlike the SOX standard, the internal controls mechanism did not require an independent audit. A precise definition of the internal control over financial reporting or IFCR process was stated, including that it be supervised by both the CFO and the CEO and effected by the board of directors, management,

and other personnel, in order to provide reasonable assurance concerning the reliability of financial reporting and preparation of financial statements.

Sarbanes-Oxley regulations have been blamed by American corporations for adding huge costs to the reporting and auditing process; in doing so, they have supposedly deterred companies from seeking to be listed on American exchanges, in contrast to easier compliance for European and Asian exchanges. Estimates as high as $200 billion for the additional cost of compliance have been made, while studies have pointed to a drop in new listing and some deregistering of companies; others claim that going private has been given a large boost. Those in favour claim that SOX has greatly increased the trust of investors in U.S. public firms. There is some acceptance that perhaps the complexity of the law is excessive.

After the collapse, fingers were pointed at three players: investment dealers and their analysts, multinational auditors, and corporate executives. A common term used was *disclosure*, or the failure of it. The accusation of inadequate disclosure was directed at

- Investment dealers who failed to disclose the conflict of interest between their banking divisions and their analyst sections, despite the potential for biased recommendations
- Accounting audits that failed to disclose enough information about the cash flows, the risky assets and the alternative definitions of income (before and after different potential writeoffs)
- Managers who failed to disclose their own investment or disinvestment in company shares through incentive plans based on stock options or loans

Fingers should also have been pointed at the investors themselves. Quite possibly, the disclosure was not so inadequate on the part of everyone; rather, the shareholders failed to inform themselves of the available facts, interpret them correctly, and act accordingly.

As the bear market ended in the new millennium and markets began their recovery, blame was fixed on greedy executives, compliant and negligent directors, discriminatory and criminal actions by investment bankers, and inadequate audits. Both prosecutions and regulation followed, with the U.S. enacting the *Sarbanes-Oxley Act* to control the presentation and audit of financial reports, as the public recognized the failure of directors and auditors to monitor and restrain the actions of corporate managers (see the boxed article here). Excessively generous compensation packages were awarded without question on the excuse of being competitive and needed for incentives. The following bull market dulled the public outrage until news of multibillion-dollar bonuses emerged along with the financial collapse. This time the bonuses for high-tech successes were replaced by rewards for arranging complicated financing and trading in derivatives. The response to tens of billions of dollars in bonuses paid to high- and mid-level employees of investment banks, at the same time as immense investments to rescue those same banks, was often proposals to tax away the bonuses or penalize the banks for awarding them. The losers in all these scandals have been the shareholders of the corporations, even if a few executives face fines and prison sentences. There is little indication that executive salaries are falling, although bonuses might be. A more thoughtful analysis indicates that the undeniable effect of the bonuses was to encourage high-risk behaviour; high-risk activity rewards the employees when it succeeds and costs the shareholders, and recently the taxpayers, when it fails. Nevertheless, corporate executives still strongly insist on the need to offer competitive (high) pay packages in order to attract employees. It apparently has not dawned on anyone that if everyone in the industry paid one-half or one-tenth of the compensation, then that amount would be sufficiently competitive.

The economic problem linked to both disclosure and compensation is analyzed under the name of **agency theory**. This refers to the principal–agent relationship when employees are hired to represent the interests of owners. Shareholders are principals in corporations; management is the agent of the owners. Auditors are agents of the shareholders; their duty is to ensure that management provides all the relevant information in a clear and unambiguous manner. Analysts are also agents, whose compensation comes from the salaries earned from firms that are paid commissions to engage in investment banking activities; but the ultimate payer is the investor who purchases shares.

The recognized problem is that the agent tends to further his or her own interests rather than those of the principal. Corporate executives are receiving regular compensation ranging from $100,000 in very small companies to the $10 million level at large corporations; this is augmented by performance bonuses on a similar scale and options as incentives for higher performance. (For the CEO of Nortel, this amounted to $100 million.) These incentives are designed to ensure that management takes actions "aligned with shareholder interests," that is, actions that will maximize share price; options clearly fulfill that objective—except to the extent that the aggregate resulting share issues are highly dilutive to the stock value. It is curious to consider that executives will not make all possible efforts to earn their base salary of $10 million, but require added inducement. If financial results are sufficiently poor, executives will lose all of these rewards.

Management pays the board of directors to watch over itself and the company. Director compensation includes an annual fee plus attendance fees, plus further payments for additional duties; it often includes a pension for service (i.e., after being a highly paid and successful executive elsewhere, with a pension, a director receives a further pension for the many years of valuable service on the board). Directors who do not cooperate with the executives on the board are likely to lose their seats; yet they can be held responsible if they do not protect their shareholders' interests.

The board of directors pays auditors to ensure that financial information is correctly presented to the investors. Auditors are highly paid to provide this service, but their firms also have derived large revenues from consulting services. Auditors do not want to jeopardize a relationship by displeasing the board with an audit that differs from the management view. At the same time, if an auditor's reputation suffers from inadequate representation of investors, the widespread loss of business is far greater. In order to tip the scale away from pleasing management, there has been strong pressure to separate the two lines of business.

Management pays investment dealers to issue securities on behalf of the firm. The commissions on these operations are extremely large. Yet these same investment dealers are in the retail business acting for individuals; besides trading for them, they advise on investment opportunities, with in-house analysis departments providing the information. This merging of the two sides of the securities industry gives rise to two problems. In order to serve their corporate clients, the investment bankers may not divulge an impending issue to the trading public; furthermore, keeping that corporate business involves not giving advice that would tend to lower the share price. This leads to the creation of an artificial barrier within the securities firm between the brokerage and investment banking departments; on the other hand, that barrier is breached to the extent that negative forecasts by the analysis department are likely to be softened. The absorption of most securities dealers by the chartered banks, who must satisfy the other financing needs of the same corporate clients, puts the banks in a unique position. It also limits the availability of independent financial advice.

Consequently, one may suspect that investors receive from management the true story on neither the operating and financial prospects nor results. Financial results are modified and presented, with the approval of the auditors, to satisfy management's wishes as to how the results should appear. Directors do not question the actions of the executive in presenting information, nor question the compensation paid to the executives. Analysts dispute neither management's projections nor their directions to avoid offending management by making negative recommendations and jeopardizing investment banking activities.

Such a bleak picture is grossly overstated most of the time, but it is all too likely an explanation for the end-of-century bubble. It probably serves to explain the failure of the financial industry to arrive at realistic estimates of stock values. In fact, the normal situation has analysts reacting quite skeptically to optimistic management projections. The regulators and securities industry itself in both Canada and the United States have taken aggressive steps to ensure better and ethical behaviour by the professionals, with regulations for analyst conflict disclosure, corporate announcements, and auditor independence.[4]

In compensation, the self-regulatory solution is favoured by business interests. An obvious solution is to create an alternative to awarding immediate rewards for performance of cash bonuses or options, which pay off as soon as the stock rises, too often on a failure of the market to recognize hidden risks that will be later revealed. There is increasing use of stock that must be held for a number of years, as a better guarantee of long-term effects of the actions taken. The value of the awards has not yet fallen appreciably.

Finally, the investor must be wary. "He who pays the piper, calls the tune." It appears here that the audience is using intermediaries to hire the musicians, buy the tickets, and broadcast the music. The impression left is that the concert is not quite what it should be, yet the audience cannot directly arrange for the performance. Individual investors ultimately pay for the concert and have the right to be satisfied with what they hear; to that end, they must learn to recognize the quality of the music. Unless individuals are capable of investigating their own company results, they must rely on those agents whose advice has proven fallible in the past.

1.6 ▸ LESSONS TO LEARN

The twenty-first-century investor plays the same role as always: to help determine the true current value of equities and bonds. This is part of the essential process of raising capital for real investment through the intermediation of several types of institutions. Compared to his or her twentieth-century predecessor, the modern investor faces a broader array of financial instruments with which to establish the value of the basic corporate issues. The derivative securities at hand present more choice and complicate the process to some degree. Yet all these are ultimately intended to suit more precisely the needs and tastes of the investor; and, fundamentally, the values of all of the available instruments depend on the individual's perception of the value of the firm that issues the primary instruments.

The lesson from the end of the century is that investors collectively and drastically failed in determining the firms' prospects for the near future. With the dubious benefit of professional advice, many investors found their portfolio values decimated after a concentration in high-risk assets whose prices soared and then collapsed. The attraction of these particular assets was their recent ascent in price. This approach to portfolio selection, described as "momentum investing," coincided with a focus on so-called "growth stocks." Analysts and fund managers with this style were paraded as heroes, and rewarded with substantial bonuses. Many other investors and portfolio managers rejected the temptation to follow the momentum and opted for the alternative of "value investing." These latter were usually disappointed in the last five years of the 1990s; what normal investment analysis would identify as bargain stocks became better bargains. Finally they had their vindication in the high-tech collapse. Yet even these could not escape the final market fall in 2001 and 2002. Nothing protected investors from the global collapse in 2008, where equities depended on economic performance which in turn required a stable financial industry.

---

[4]See the document "Setting Analyst Standards" published jointly by the TSE, Canadian Venture Exchange, and the Investment Dealers Association in 2001. Note also the SEC investigation of sources of audit conflict resulting from the Enron collapse and its business relationship to Andersen.

Free Lunches

Financial markets are highly competitive. Thousands of intelligent and well-backed analysts constantly scour securities markets searching for the best buys. This competition means that we should expect to find few, if any, "free lunches," securities that are so underpriced that they represent obvious bargains. Two significant principles follow from the absence of free lunches.

Investors invest for anticipated future returns, but those returns rarely can be predicted precisely. There will almost always be risk associated with investments. Actual or realized returns will almost always deviate from the expected return anticipated at the start of the investment period. For example, in 1931 (the worst calendar year for the market since 1926), the U.S. stock market lost 43 percent of its value. In 1933 (the best year), the market gained 54 percent. You can be sure that investors did not anticipate such extreme performance at the start of either of these years.

Naturally, if all else could be held equal, investors would prefer investments with the highest expected return.[5] However, the no-free-lunch rule tells us that all else cannot be held equal. If you want higher expected returns, you will have to pay a price in terms of accepting higher investment risk. If higher expected return can be achieved without bearing extra risk, there will be a rush to buy the high-return assets, with the result that their prices will be driven up. Individuals considering investing in the asset at the now-higher price will find the investment less attractive: If you buy at a higher price, your expected rate of return (i.e., profit per dollar invested) is lower. The asset will be considered attractive and its price will continue to rise until its expected return is no more than commensurate with risk. At this point, investors can anticipate a "fair" return relative to the asset's risk, but no more. Similarly, if returns were independent of risk, there would be a rush to sell high-risk assets. Their prices would fall (and their expected future rates of return rise) until they eventually were attractive enough to be included again in investor portfolios. We conclude that there should be a **risk–return tradeoff** in the securities markets, with higher-risk assets priced to offer higher expected returns than lower-risk assets.

The measurement of risk and the interplay between assets when diversified in a portfolio is a complex matter affecting the risk of that portfolio. The effect of diversification on portfolio risk, the implications for the proper measurement of risk, and the risk–return relationship are the topics of Part Two. These topics are the subject of what has come to be known as *modern portfolio theory*. The development of this theory earned two of its pioneers, Harry Markowitz and William Sharpe, Nobel Prizes.

Another implication of the no-free-lunch proposition is that we should rarely expect to find bargains in the security markets. We will spend all of Part Three examining the theory and evidence concerning the hypothesis that financial markets process all relevant information about securities quickly and efficiently, that is, that the security price usually reflects all the information available to investors concerning the value of the security. According to this hypothesis, as new information about a security becomes available, the price of the security quickly adjusts so that at any time, the security price equals the market consensus estimate of the value of the security. If this were so, there would be neither underpriced nor overpriced securities.

One interesting implication of this "efficient market hypothesis" concerns the choice between active and passive investment management strategies. **Passive management** calls for holding highly diversified portfolios without spending effort or other resources attempting to improve investment performance through security analysis. **Active management** is the attempt to improve performance either by identifying mispriced securities or by timing the performance of

---

[5]The "expected" return is not the return investors believe they necessarily will earn, or even their most likely return. It is instead the result of averaging across all possible outcomes, recognizing that some are more likely than others. It is the average rate of return across possible economic scenarios.

broad asset classes—for example, increasing one's commitment to stocks when one is bullish on the stock market. If markets are efficient and prices reflect all relevant information, perhaps it is better to follow passive strategies instead of spending resources in a futile attempt to outguess your competitors in the financial markets.

If the efficient market hypothesis were taken to the extreme, there would be no point in active security analysis; only fools would commit resources to actively analyze securities. Without ongoing security analysis, however, prices eventually would depart from "correct" values, creating new incentives for experts to move in. Therefore, even in environments as competitive as the financial markets, we may observe only *near*-efficiency, and profit opportunities may exist for especially diligent and creative investors. This motivates our discussion of active portfolio management in Part Seven. More importantly, our discussions of security analysis and portfolio construction generally must account for the likelihood of nearly efficient markets.

Diversification, Information, and Patience

The protection from the disappointment for value investors in the high-tech boom and from the calamity for growth investors that followed lies in the well-understood principle of diversification. By holding both kinds of stocks, investors could have mitigated the losses, or failures to gain, in one part of the portfolio with the other part's successes. Diversification entails the design of a portfolio that generally offsets some gains with other losses, and in the long run grows at a fairly predictable rate. This is achieved to a great extent by selecting assets with interests in different sectors of the economy, which react differently to economic conditions and cycles. Even a diversified portfolio, however, must rise and fall in value with the whole market trend. Hence an economic slowdown will be correlated with a portfolio loss.

Solutions to the macroeconomic vulnerability of a portfolio have emerged from two recent developments. One is the use of the financial derivatives previously mentioned; these are used to hedge the value of the portfolio and can greatly reduce the risk in a portfolio at the cost of lower returns. The second approach lies in further diversification. One method of this is by a balanced portfolio made up of both equities and bonds, a cash position, and other, less liquid assets. Another is to follow the trend toward globalization.

Investors can increase their diversification by taking positions in assets located in other countries. In this way, the effects of an economic downturn domestically can be offset by the continued boom in other parts of the world. This may occur when a foreign country benefits from increased export sales due to a better economic policy, leading to more competitive prices and increased production; this is quite possibly related to the mentioned decline in one's domestic economy. A portfolio with assets in the home and the foreign countries will find the combined effect less variable.

The drawback to international diversification is the increasing interconnection of the economies of the world. To the extent that a global economy develops, the effects of a slowdown in one major nation are felt globally. Already, the introduction of the euro as a currency and the development of a common economic policy for the Eurozone have reduced the diversification possibilities for European markets. There is increasing evidence of three zones of economic activity—American, European, and Asian—which are highly dependent internally, but also interdependent. This too is a manifestation of globalization. The technical measure of interdependence is the statistical correlation between returns in different markets. This has been steadily rising over the past decades. While China was held out as the last bastion of relative independence, its market plunged too as the prospect of sales in its major export market dove with the inevitable recession associated with the financial collapse. Global diversification was pointless for this "once in a lifetime" event. Yet China's own stimulatory intervention and its massive domestic market led to both its own market resurgence and those of its Asian neighbours (excluding Japan) in 2009; economic rebounds based on resumption of production fuelled market advances in the range of 100 percent.

One of the ironies of the 1990s bubble is that the result of constructing a portfolio by modern principles would have resulted in an uncomfortable concentration in stocks such as Nortel, Cisco, and Dell. The theory prescribes that a portfolio should be invested in stocks according to their market value. Since these three stocks rose from modest values to immense values, investors were supposed to have large holdings in them; those holdings would have then collapsed after the bubble burst. An alternative strategy would have prescribed reducing the holdings to maintain a more equally balanced portfolio. If that had been followed, the portfolio would never have risen to anything approaching the value of the buy-and-hold strategy at the end of the decade. No credible approach pretends to dictate that good stocks be held until they reach their maximum value, and then promptly sold. Such prescience, while it would be invaluable, is impossible. Hence no ideal resolution of the investor's dilemma exists.

The solution for investors is finally to be diversified, to be informed, and to be patient. A program of investing in a well-chosen portfolio, characterized by diverse asset holdings selected after consulting reliable sources of information, will lead in time to returns that are superior to alternatives. Concentrated investments, and those based on tips, may often lead to quick gains; over an extended period, the associated risk can be expected to cause major losses. Inexperienced investors tend to sell poor investments after losses are experienced and then fail to benefit from recoveries, if not having suffered irreparable losses to their wealth.

The purpose of a book on investing is to present the techniques that have the highest expectation of success, while showing the pitfalls of alternative approaches. One thing, however, should be clear. Chance plays a major role in any uncertain outcome such as investing. Someone must always come out ahead; after the fact, some investor who did not diversify will inevitably have a better return than the great majority that did. Finally, it is better to be lucky. Since one cannot count on good fortune, it is far wiser to be informed and diversified, and then let time work for you.

1.7   OUTLINE OF THE TEXT

The text has seven Parts, which are fairly independent and may be studied in a variety of sequences. Part One is an introduction to financial markets, instruments, and trading of securities.

Parts Two and Three contain the core of what has come to be known as "modern portfolio theory." We start in Part Two with a general discussion of risk and return and the lessons of capital market history. We then focus more closely on how to describe investors' risk preferences and progress to asset allocation, efficient diversification, and portfolio optimization.

In Part Three, we investigate the implications of portfolio theory for the equilibrium relationship between risk and return. We introduce the capital asset pricing model, its implementation using index models, and more advanced models of risk and return. This part also treats the efficient market hypothesis as well as behavioural critiques of theories based on investor rationality and closes with a chapter on empirical evidence concerning security returns.

Parts Four through Six cover security analysis and valuation. Part Four is devoted to debt markets and Part Five to equity markets. Part Six covers derivative assets, such as options and futures contracts.

Part Seven is an introduction to active investment management. It shows how different investors' objectives and constraints can lead to a variety of investment policies. This part discusses the role of active management in nearly efficient markets and considers how one should evaluate the performance of managers who pursue active strategies. It also shows how the principles of portfolio construction can be extended to the international setting and describes the use of managed funds.

SUMMARY

1. Real investment creates real assets that are used to produce the goods and services created by an economy. Financial investment is in financial assets, which are claims to the income generated by real assets. Securities are financial assets. Financial assets are part of an investor's wealth, but not part of national wealth. Instead, financial assets determine how the "national pie" is split up among investors.

2. Financial instruments such as stocks and bonds are issued by firms to investors who buy and sell them in markets; except on the initial issue, they do not directly affect the capital and production of the issuing firms.

3. Financial instruments play several roles in capital allocation: as a source of information about promising economic sectors and companies; as a vehicle of consumption timing; and as a means of separation of ownership and management of corporations.

4. The life-cycle approach to the management of an individual's investment portfolio views the individual as passing through a series of stages, becoming more risk-averse in later years. The rationale underlying this approach is that as we age, we use up our human capital and have less time remaining to recoup possible portfolio losses through increased labour supply.

5. Investors select investments that will provide them with the kind of returns that will suit their needs and preferences. Their investment opportunities correspond to the need for funds by corporations and governments. The after-tax returns that accompany the various types of financial instruments guide investors' choices.

6. The excess funds of investors are channelled to businesses for investment purposes through financial intermediaries such as banks, investment bankers, mutual funds, and insurance companies. Economies of scale and specialization are factors supporting the investment banking industry.

7. Recent trends in financial markets include private equity and hedge funds, globalization, financial engineering, securitization, and computer networks.

8. Overvaluation of financial assets occurs when information is not properly disclosed by insiders, or analyzed by investors and by financial advisors. Faulty disclosure is a prime example of a market failure due to the agency problem between principals and agents.

9. Successful investing requires diversification across domestic assets and internationally, in addition to efficient processing of information. Finally, the passage of time is necessary for expected results to follow from good investment techniques.

PROBLEMS

connect™ **Practise and learn online with Connect.**

1. Suppose housing prices across the world double.
   a. Is society any richer for the change?
   b. Are homeowners wealthier?
   c. Can you reconcile your answers to (a) and (b)? Is anyone worse off as a result of the discovery?
2. Lanni Products is a start-up computer software development firm. It currently owns computer equipment worth $30,000 and has cash on hand of $20,000 contributed by Lanni's owners. For each of the following transactions, identify the real and/or financial assets that trade hands. Are any financial assets created or destroyed in the transaction?
   a. Lanni takes out a bank loan. It receives $50,000 in cash and signs a note promising to pay back the loan over three years.
   b. Lanni uses the cash from the bank plus $15,000 of its own funds to finance the development of new financial planning software.

c. Lanni sells the software product to Microsoft, which will market it to the public under the Microsoft name. Lanni accepts payment in the form of 1,500 shares of Microsoft stock.

d. Lanni sells the shares of stock for $80 per share and uses part of the proceeds to pay off the bank loan.

3. Reconsider Lanni Products from problem 2.

   a. Prepare Lanni's balance sheet just after it gets the bank loan. What is the ratio of real assets to financial assets?

   b. Prepare the balance sheet after Lanni spends the $65,000 to develop the product. What is the ratio of real assets to total assets?

   c. Prepare the balance sheet after Lanni accepts payment of shares from Microsoft. What is the ratio of real assets to total assets?

4. Give an example of three financial intermediaries, and explain how they act as a bridge between small investors and large capital markets or corporations,

5. Why would you expect securitization to take place only in highly developed capital markets?

6. Firms raise capital from investors by issuing shares in the primary markets. Does this imply that corporate financial managers can ignore trading of previously issued shares in the secondary market?

7. What is the relationship between securitization and the role of financial intermediaries in the economy? What happens to financial intermediaries as securitization progresses?

8. Many investors would like to invest part of their portfolios in real estate, but obviously cannot on their own purchase office buildings or strip malls. Explain how this situation creates a profit incentive for investment firms that can sponsor REITs (real estate investment trusts).

9. Financial engineering has been disparaged as nothing more than paper shuffling. Critics argue that resources that go to *rearranging wealth* (i.e., bundling and unbundling financial assets) might better be spent on *creating* wealth (i.e., creating real assets). Evaluate this criticism. Are there any benefits realized by creating an array of derivative securities from various primary securities?

10. Although we stated that real assets make up the true productive capacity of an economy, it is hard to conceive of a modern economy without well-developed financial markets and security types. How would the productive capacity of the Canadian economy be affected if there were no markets in which one could trade financial assets?

11. Why does it make sense that the first futures markets introduced in nineteenth-century America were for trades in agricultural products? For example, why did we not see instead futures markets for goods such as paper or pencils?

12. Oversight by large institutional investors or creditors is one mechanism to reduce agency problems. Why don't individual investors in the firm have the same incentive to keep an eye on management?

13. Discuss the advantages and disadvantages of the following forms of managerial compensation in terms of mitigating agency problems, that is, potential conflicts of interest between managers and shareholders.

   a. A fixed salary

   b. Stock in the firm

   c. Call options on shares of the firm

14. Consider Figure 1.4, which describes an issue of American gold certificates.

   a. Is this issue a primary or secondary market transaction?

   b. Are the certificates primitive or derivative assets?

   c. What market niche is filled by this offering?

Figure 1.4

Announcement
of an issue of
American gold
certificates.

> *This announcement is neither an offer to sell nor a solicitation of an offer to buy any of these Certificates.
> This offer is made only by the Offering Memorandum.*
>
> NEW ISSUE   **$100,000,000**   July 7, 1987
>
> # AMERICAN
> # GOLD
> # CERTIFICATES
>
> **Due July 1, 1991**
>
> • *American Gold Certificates represent physical allocated gold bullion
> insured and held in safekeeping at Bank of Delaware.*
> • *Anytime during the four-year period, the certificate holder
> may request physical delivery of the gold.*
>
> *Copies of the Offering Memorandum may be obtained in any State from only such of the undersigned
> as may legally offer these certificates in such State.*
>
> J. W. KORTH CAPITAL MARKETS. INC.
>
> THE CHICAGO CORPORATION   COWEN & CO.   DOMINICK & DOMINICK
> FIRST ALBANY CORPORATION   INCORPORATED
> INTERSTATE SECURITIES CORPORATION   GRIFFIN, KUBIK, STEPHENS & THOMPSON, INC.
> MCDONALD & COMPANY   JANNEY MONTGOMERY SCOTT INC.
> SECURITIES, INC   STEPHENS INC.   PACIFIC SECURITIES, INC.
> RONEY & CO.   UMIC, INC.
> VINING-SPARKS SECURITIES, INC.   WESTCAP SECURITIES, INC.
> BAKER, WATTS & CO.   BARCLAY INVESTMENTS, INC.
> BIRR, WILSON SECURITIES, INC.   D. A. DAVIDSON & CO.
> INDEPENDENCE SECURITIES, INC.   INCORPORATED
> EMMETT A. LARKIN CO., INC.   JESUP & LAMONT SECURITIES CO., INC.
> SEIDLER AMDEC SECURITIES INC.   SCOTT & STRINGFELLOW, INC.
>   UNDERWOOD, NEUHAUS & CO.
>   INCORPORATED

15. The average rate of return on investments in stocks has outpaced that on investments in Treasury bills by over 4 percent since 1957. Why, then, does anyone invest in Treasury bills?

16. You see an advertisement for a book that claims to show how you can make $1 million with no risk and with no money down. Will you buy the book?

17. Bay Street firms have traditionally compensated their traders with a share of the trading profits that they generated. How might this practice have affected traders' willingness to assume risk? What is the agency problem this practice engendered?

Financial Markets and Instruments

This chapter covers a range of financial securities and the markets in which they trade. Our goal is to introduce you to the features of various security types. This foundation will be necessary to understand the more analytic material that follows in later chapters.

We refer to the traditional classification of securities into money market instruments or capital market instruments. The **money market** includes short-term, marketable, liquid, low-risk debt securities. Money market instruments are sometimes called *cash equivalents* because of their safety and liquidity. **Capital markets**, in contrast, include longer-term and riskier securities. Securities in the capital market are much more diverse than those found within the money market. For this reason, we will subdivide the capital market into four segments. This chapter therefore contains a discussion of five markets overall: the money market, longer-term fixed-income capital markets, equity markets, and the two so-called derivative markets: options and futures.

We first describe money market instruments and how to measure their yields. We then move on to fixed-income and equity securities. We explain the structure of various stock market indices in this chapter because market benchmark portfolios play an important role in portfolio construction and evaluation. Finally, we survey the derivative security markets for options and futures contracts.

THE MONEY MARKET

The money market is a subsector of the fixed-income market. It consists of very-short-term debt securities that usually are highly marketable. Many of these securities trade in large denominations and so are out of reach of individual investors. Money market funds, however, are easily accessible to small investors. These mutual funds pool the resources of many investors and purchase a wide variety of money market securities on their behalf. Table 2.1 is an extract of a money rates listing from the *Financial Post* Web site. It includes some of the various instruments of the money market that we will describe in detail.[1]

Treasury Bills

Treasury bills (T-bills) are the most marketable of all Canadian money market instruments. They represent the simplest form of borrowing: the government raises money by selling bills to the public. Investors buy the bills at a discount from the stated maturity value. At the bill's maturity, the holder receives from the government a payment equal to its face value. The difference between the purchase price and ultimate maturity value constitutes the investor's earnings.

T-bills with initial maturities of 3, 6, and 12 months are issued biweekly. Sales are conducted by auction, at which chartered banks and authorized dealers can submit only *competitive* bids. A competitive bid is an order for a given quantity of bills at a specific offered price. The order is filled only if the bid is high enough relative to other bids to be accepted. By contrast, a noncompetitive bid is an unconditional offer to purchase at the average price of the successful competitive bids; such bids can be submitted only for bonds. The government rank-orders bids by offering price and accepts bids in order of descending price until the entire issue is absorbed.

TABLE 2.1 Yields on Money Market Securities

Yields on 2013.05.13							
Canadian Yields	**Latest**	**U.S. Yields**	**Latest**	**Canadian Yields**	**Latest**	**U.S. Yields**	**Latest**
T-Bills				**Bankers' Acceptances (Ask Price)**			
1-month	0.96	1-month	0.008	1-month	1.15		
3-month	1.00	3-month	0.033	3-month	1.18		
6-month	1.01	6-month	0.07	6-month	1.28		
1-year	1.05					**Commercial Paper**	
						1-month	0.06
Bonds						3-month	0.11
2-year	1.01	2-year	0.23			6-month	0.20
5-year	1.34	5-year	0.81	**3-Mth Forward Rate Agreement**			
10-year	1.89	10-year	1.89	3-month	1.27	3-month	0.27
30-year	2.51	30-year	3.09	6-month	1.27	6-month	0.29
				9-month	1.29	9-month	0.31

Source: "Canadian and U.S. Yields," Financial Post Web site, http://www.financialpost.com/markets/market-data/money-yields-can_us .html, accessed May 10, 2013.

[1] An excellent overview and statistics of the money markets (and other debt and equity markets) are given by the Investment Industry Association of Canada's (IIAC) website, at http://iiac.ca/resources/publications.

Competitive bidders face two dangers: they may bid too high and overpay for the bills, or they may bid too low and be shut out of the auction.

T-bills are purchased primarily by chartered banks, by investment dealers, by the Bank of Canada (as part of its monetary policy), and by individuals who obtain them on the secondary market from a government securities dealer. T-bills are highly liquid; that is, they are easily converted to cash and sold at low transaction cost with not much price risk. Unlike most other money market instruments, which sell in minimum denominations of $100,000, T-bills are now offered in denominations of $1,000, $5,000, $25,000, $100,000, and $1 million.

Certificates of Deposit and Bearer Deposit Notes

A **certificate of deposit (CD)** is a time deposit with a chartered bank. Time deposits may not be withdrawn on demand. The bank pays interest and principal to the depositor only at the end of the fixed term of the deposit. A similar time deposit for smaller amounts is known as a **guaranteed investment certificate (GIC)**.

Although both CDs and GICs are nontransferable in Canada, some bank time deposits issued in denominations greater than $100,000 are negotiable; that is, they can be sold to another investor if the owner needs to cash in the deposit before its maturity date. In Canada these marketable CDs are known as **bearer deposit notes (BDNs)**. By contrast, a CD in the United States is a marketable instrument, similar to BDNs. Some trust companies also have issued transferable GICs as well as GICs with variable rates or with payoffs linked to equity indices. CDs and GICs are treated as bank deposits by the Canada Deposit Insurance Corporation (CDIC), so they are insured for up to $100,000 in the event of a bank insolvency.

Commercial Paper

Large, well-known companies often issue their own short-term unsecured debt notes rather than borrow directly from banks. These notes are called **commercial paper**. Very often, commercial paper is backed by a bank line of credit, which gives the borrower access to cash that can be used (if needed) to pay off the paper at maturity. Commercial paper maturities range up to one year; longer maturities would require registration under the *Ontario Securities Act* and so are almost never issued. Most often, commercial paper is issued with maturities of less than one or two months and minimum denominations of $50,000. Therefore, small investors can invest in commercial paper only indirectly, via money market mutual funds. Almost all commercial paper today is rated for credit quality by the major rating agencies.

Commercial paper is considered to be a fairly safe asset, because a firm's condition presumably can be monitored and predicted over a term as short as one month. Many firms issue commercial paper intending to roll it over at maturity, that is, issue new paper to obtain the funds necessary to retire the old paper. If in the meantime there are doubts raised about their creditworthiness, then the borrowers may be forced to turn to other, more expensive, sources of financing. For instance, in March 1992, Olympia and York was forced to retire its outstanding commercial paper several weeks before it became insolvent.

While nonfinancial firms issue most commercial paper, in recent years there was a sharp increase in *asset-backed commercial paper* issued by financial firms such as banks. This was short-term commercial paper typically used to raise funds for the institution to invest in other assets, most notoriously, subprime mortgages. These assets were in turn used as collateral for the commercial paper—hence the label "asset-backed." This practice led to many difficulties starting in the summer of 2007 when the subprime mortgages began defaulting. The banks found themselves unable to issue new commercial paper to refinance their positions as the old paper matured.

Bankers' Acceptances

A **bankers' acceptance** starts as an order to a bank by a bank's customer to pay a sum of money at a future date, typically within six months. At this stage, it is similar to a postdated cheque. In return for a stamping fee, the bank endorses the order for payment as "accepted"; it thereby assumes responsibility for ultimate payment to the holder of the acceptance, making the instrument second only to T-bills in terms of default security. At this point, the acceptance may be traded in secondary markets like any other claim on the bank. Bankers' acceptances are considered very safe assets, because traders can substitute the bank's credit standing for their own. They are used widely in foreign trade where the creditworthiness of one trader is unknown to the trading partner. Acceptances sell at a discount from the face value of the payment order, just as T-bills sell at a discount from par value, with a similar calculation for yield.

Eurodollars

Eurodollars are U.S. dollar–denominated deposits at foreign banks or foreign branches of American banks. By locating outside the United States, these banks escape regulation by the Federal Reserve Board. Despite the tag "Euro," these accounts need not be in European banks, although that is where the practice of accepting dollar-denominated deposits outside the United States began.

Most Eurodollar deposits are for large sums, and most are time deposits of less than six months' maturity. A variation on the Eurodollar time deposit is the Eurodollar certificate of deposit, which resembles a U.S. domestic bank CD, except that it is the liability of a non-U.S. branch of a bank (typically a London branch). The advantage of Eurodollar CDs over Eurodollar time deposits is that the holder can sell the asset to realize its cash value before maturity. Eurodollar CDs are considered less liquid and riskier than U.S. domestic CDs, however, and thus offer higher yields. Firms also issue Eurodollar bonds, which are dollar-denominated bonds in Europe, although bonds are not a money market investment because of their long maturities.

All of the above instruments—time deposits, CDs, and bonds—also exist denominated in all major currencies; these are labelled Eurocurrency instruments when located outside the country of currency. When issued in Canadian dollar denominations then they are referred to as *Euro-Canadian* dollars; these constitute a minor portion of the Eurocurrency market, which is dominated by Eurodollar trading.

Repos and Reverses

Dealers in government securities use **repurchase agreements** (also called **repos** or **RPs**) as a form of short-term, usually overnight, borrowing. The dealer sells government securities to an institutional investor on an overnight basis, with an agreement to buy back those securities the next day at a slightly higher price. The increase in the price is the overnight interest. The dealer thus takes out a one-day loan from the investor, and the securities serve as collateral.

A *term repo* is essentially an identical transaction, except that the term of the implicit loan can be 30 days or more. Repos are considered very safe in terms of credit risk, because the loans are backed by the government securities. A *reverse repo* is the mirror image of a repo. Here, the dealer finds an investor holding government securities and buys them, agreeing to sell them back at a specified higher price on a future date.

Federal Funds

Just as most of us maintain deposits at banks, many banks operating in the United States maintain deposits of their own at a Federal Reserve bank. Each member bank of the Federal Reserve System, or "the Fed," is required to maintain a minimum balance in a reserve account with the Fed. The required balance depends on the total deposits of the bank's customers. Funds in the bank's reserve account are called **federal funds**, or *fed funds*. At any time, some banks have more funds than required at the Fed. Other banks, primarily big banks in New York and other financial centers, tend to have a shortage of federal funds. In the federal funds market, banks with excess funds lend to those with a shortage. These loans, which are usually overnight transactions, are arranged at a rate of interest called the *federal funds rate*.

Although the fed funds market arose primarily as a way for banks to transfer balances to meet reserve requirements, today the market has evolved to the point that many large banks use federal funds in a straightforward way as one component of their total sources of funding. Therefore, the fed funds rate is simply the rate of interest on very short-term loans among financial institutions, including U.S. banks, foreign banks, and Canadian banks. While most investors cannot participate in this market, the fed funds rate commands great interest as a key barometer of monetary policy.

Brokers' Call Loans

Individuals who buy stocks on margin borrow part of the funds to pay for the stocks from their broker. The broker in turn may borrow the funds from a bank, agreeing to repay the bank immediately (on call) if the bank requests it. Chartered banks make such call loans to investment firms that use them to finance their inventory of securities. The rate paid on these loans is usually closely related to the rate on short-term T-bills.

The LIBOR Market

The London Interbank Offered Rate (LIBOR), mentioned in Chapter 1, is the rate at which large banks in London are willing to lend money among themselves. This rate has become the premier short-term interest rate quoted in the European money market, and it serves as a reference rate for a wide range of transactions. For example, a corporation might borrow at a rate equal to LIBOR plus 2 percent.

LIBOR interest rates may be tied to currencies other than the U.S. dollar. For example, LIBOR rates are widely quoted for transactions denominated in British pounds, yen, euros, and so on. There is also a similar rate called EURIBOR (European Interbank Offered Rate) at which banks in the Eurozone are willing to lend euros among themselves.

Yields on Money Market Instruments

Although most money market securities are of low risk, they are not risk-free. For example, in 1987, the U.S. commercial paper market was rocked by the Penn Central bankruptcy, which precipitated a default on $82 million of commercial paper. Money market investors in that country became more sensitive to creditworthiness after this episode, and the yield spread between low- and high-quality paper widened.

The securities of the money market do promise yields greater than those on default-free T-bills, at least in part because of greater relative riskiness. In addition, many investors require more liquidity; thus they will accept lower yields on securities such as T-bills that can be quickly and cheaply sold for cash. Figure 2.1 shows that commercial paper, for example, has consistently paid a risk premium over T-bills of approximately equal maturity. Moreover, that risk premium increased with economic crises, such as the energy price shocks associated with the two OPEC disturbances; except for the Asian and Russian crises of the 1990s and the recent financial crisis, the spread has been remarkably low since the early 1980s. It is significant that the spread for the financial crisis has not been as great as for the OPEC oil embargoes on an absolute basis, while it has been much greater on a relative basis.

T-Bill Yields   T-bill yields are not quoted in the financial pages as effective annual rates of return. Instead, the **bond equivalent yield** is used. To illustrate this method, consider a $1,000

Figure 2.1

Yield spread between 3-month corporate paper and T-bills.

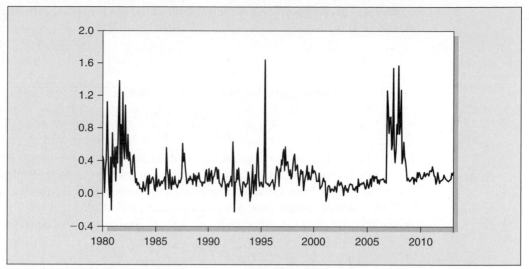

Source: Data from Scotia Capital and PC Bonds Analytics, *Debt Market Indices*, 2013, and Thomson Reuters.
©Thomson Reuters.

par value T-bill sold at $960 with a maturity of a half-year, or 182 days. With the bond equivalent yield method, the bill's discount from par value, which here equals $40, is "annualized" on the basis of a 365-day year. The $40 discount is annualized as

$$\$40 \times (365/182) = \$80.22$$

The result is divided by the $960 purchase price to obtain a bond equivalent yield of 8.356 percent per year. Rather than report T-bill prices, the financial pages report these bond equivalent yields.

The bond equivalent yield is not an accurate measure of the effective annual rate of return. To see this, note that the half-year holding period return on the bill is 4.17 percent: the $960 investment provides $40 in earnings, and 40/960 = .0417. The compound interest annualized rate of return, or **effective annual yield**, is therefore

$$(1.0417)^2 - 1 = .0851 = 8.51\%$$

We can highlight the source of the discrepancy between the bond equivalent yield and the effective annual yield by examining the bond equivalent yield formula:

$$r_{\text{BEY}} = \frac{1,000 - P}{P} \times \frac{365}{n} \tag{2.1}$$

where P is the bond price, n is the maturity of the bill in days, and r_{BEY} is the bond equivalent yield. The bond equivalent formula thus takes the bill's discount from par as a fraction of price and then annualizes by the factor $365/n$. The annualization technique uses simple interest rather than compound interest. Multiplication by $365/n$ does not account for the ability to earn interest on interest, which is the essence of compounding. The discrepancy is, therefore, greater for a 91-day bill and disappears for a one-year bill.

The quoted yields for U.S. T-bills use a formula similar to that in equation 2.1, with a 360-day year and the par value of 1,000 in the denominator instead of P. The resulting yield is known as the **bank discount yield**. As a result, the quoted U.S. rate for the example would have been 7.912 percent. Part of the difference in yields between Canadian and U.S. bills can thus be attributed to the method of quoting yields. A convenient formula relating the bond equivalent yield to the bank discount yield is

$$r_{BEY} = \frac{365 \times d}{360 - (d \times n)}$$

where d is the discount yield. Suppose $d = .07912$; then

$$r_{BEY} = \frac{365 \times .07912}{360 - (.07912 \times 182)} = .08356$$

which is the bond equivalent yield. Hence, in this case, about .4 percentage points of the differential between Canadian and U.S. quoted yields stem from the method of calculation.

In Table 2.1, the money market listings include Treasury bills for closing prices on May 10, 2013. Three-month T-bills show a bond equivalent yield of .033 percent. To determine a bill's true market price, we must solve equation 2.1 for P. Rearranging that equation, we obtain

$$P = 1,000/[1 + r_{BEY} \times (n/365)] \tag{2.2}$$

Equation 2.2 in effect first "deannualizes" the bond equivalent yield to obtain the actual proportional interest rate, then discounts the par value of $1,000 to obtain the T-bill's sale price. In the case at hand, $n = 91$ days, and the yield is .033 percent for the bill, so that the price is

$$\$1,000/[1 + .00033 \times (91/365)] = \$999.92$$

The bond equivalent yield is the bill's yield over its life, assuming that it is purchased for the auction bid price and annualized using simple interest techniques. Note that this yield uses a simple interest procedure to annualize, also known as *annual percentage rate* (APR), and so there are problems in comparing yields on bills with different maturities. Nevertheless, yields on most securities with less than a year to maturity are annualized using a simple interest approach.

Finally, the effective annual yield on the quoted bill based on the market price, $999.92, is .033 percent. The bond's 91-day return equals $(1,000 - \$999.92)/\$999.92$ or .008 percent. Annualizing this return, we obtain $(1.000424)^{365/91} = 1.00032$, implying an effective annual interest rate of .032 percent. This is not exactly equal to the quoted .033 percent; for larger and more normal rates, the difference is more significant.

CC 1

CONCEPT CHECK

Find the price of the Canadian six-month bill from Table 2.1. Also, find the effective annual rate if the bond equivalent yield were quoted at 3.94 percent.

2.2   THE BOND MARKET

The bond market is composed of longer-term borrowing instruments than those that trade in the money market. This market includes Government of Canada bonds, provincial and municipal bonds, corporate bonds, and mortgage securities. Bonds can be callable during a given period; this feature allows the issuer to redeem the bond at par value, or at a stated premium prior to maturity.

These instruments are sometimes said to make up the *fixed-income capital market*, because most of them promise either a fixed stream of income or a stream of income determined according to a specific formula. In practice, these formulas can result in a flow of income that is far from fixed. Therefore, the term "fixed income" is probably not fully appropriate. It is simpler and more straightforward to call these securities either *debt instruments* or *bonds*.

Government of Canada Bonds

The Canadian government borrows funds in large part by selling both nonmarketable and marketable debt securities. The nonmarketable securities are known as Canada Savings Bonds (CSBs) or Canada Premium Bonds (CPBs); they are issued every year starting November 1, with a sale period of a few months. Although these bonds are nontransferable, they bear little interest rate risk. The CSBs are perfectly liquid, since they can be cashed any time prior to maturity at face value plus accrued interest. The CPBs can only be cashed in November of succeeding years, so they are somewhat like 365-day term deposits; interest rates also rise if the realized holding period is longer. Because of the redemption feature, the valuation of CSBs is quite complex and transcends the level of this text. These instruments are more accurately described as savings certificates than bonds. See the boxed article for the latest twist.

Government of Canada bonds, also known as *Canadas* or *Canada bonds*, are longer-term marketable debt securities issued by the Canadian federal government. These bonds have varying maturities at issue date, ranging up to 40 years. They are considered part of the money market when their term becomes less than three years. Canada bonds are generally noncallable and make semiannual coupon payments that are set at a competitive level designed to ensure their issue at or near par value.

Figure 2.2 shows a listing of actively traded Canada bonds extracted from the Web site of CBID. In the "Government of Canada Benchmarks" section, note the bond that matures in

Canadian bond and fixed-income returns data
www.bankofcanada.ca/rates/interest-rates/canadian-bonds
http://pcbond.com

Figure 2.2

Bond market summary.

Closing Markets as of: 4:00 PM EST 14-May-2013

Government of Canada Benchmarks

	Coupon	Eff. Maturity	Price	Yield
2 Year	1.000	2015-May-01	99.97	1.02
5 Year	1.250	2018-Mar-01	99.38	1.38
10 Year	1.500	2023-Jun-01	96.00	1.94
20 Year	**5.750**	**2033-Jun-01**	**151.42**	**2.48**
30 Year	4.000	2041-Jun-01	128.86	2.55

Active Provincials and Agencies

	Coupon	Eff. Maturity	Price	Yield
Ontario	3.150	2022-Jun-02	103.99	2.65
Quebec	5.250	2013-Oct-01	101.56	1.06
Ontario	3.250	2014-Sep-08	102.70	1.17
Ontario	3.500	2043-Jun-02	99.17	3.55
Ontario	1.900	2017-Sep-08	100.55	1.77

Active Corporates

	Coupon	Eff. Maturity	Price	Yield
Cominar REIT	**4.274**	**2017-Jun-15**	**103.49**	**3.35**
Telus Corp	3.350	2024-Apr-01	99.86	3.37
Westn George	6.690	2033-Mar-01	118.20	5.21
Morgan Stnly	4.850	2016-Feb-03	106.04	2.53
Royal Bank	4.350	2020-Jun-15	105.11	1.83

Source: Perimeter Financial Web site, CanadianFixedIncome.ca, accessed May 14, 2013.

The first new product in five years was unveiled by the federal government's retail debt agency yesterday—Canada Investment Bonds (CIBs). Think of them as "locked-in Canada Savings Bonds," suggests Warren Baldwin, regional vice president for Toronto-based T. E. Financial Consultants Ltd. As a pilot project available only through investment dealers, CIBs pay a fixed 3% rate each year over a three-year term to maturity. While not redeemable, the 3% yields more than regular CSBs or Canada Premium Bonds over that time. Sadly, CIBs do nothing to protect investors from inflation or taxes.

A press backgrounder describes CIBs as "transferable but not redeemable before maturity." That means that, unlike the older bonds, ownership can be transferred to others. The government expects a secondary market to develop in them, says Jacqueline Orange, president of Canada Investing & Savings. However, they cannot be redeemed, except in cases of hardship. It's just as well these locked-in bonds pay more interest because the first-year rate on the new series of CSBs that went on sale yesterday is just 1.75%. That's low but better than the all-time low of 1.3% that CSBs paid in the first quarter of 2002.

CSBs should be considered an alternative to money market mutual funds, most of which also pay less than 2%. However, treasury bills pay 2.56%. Most high-yield savings accounts will beat the CSB and have equal liquidity, says Rob Whipp, branch manager for Toronto-based Fiscal Agents. ING Direct pays 2.5% and President's Choice 2.25%.

With CSBs for ready cash and CIBs as the higher-yielding locked-in version, CPBs become the middle-of-the-road compromise in yield and liquidity. Cashable once a year, they were introduced in 1998. The new series of CPBs which went on sale yesterday pay 2.45% in Year 1, rising each year to reach 5% in Year 5, for a blended yield of 3.34% over the five years.

However, CPBs pay slightly less than comparable bank escalator GICs, says David Newman, Fiscal Agents' director of information services. Thus, BMO's five-year Rate Riser GIC pays 3% in the first year, rises 25 basis points each year till Year 4, and pays 5.5% in the fifth, for a blended yield of 3.8%. TD Canada Trust's five-year Stepper GIC pays only 2.25% in

Year 1, but jumps to 3.3% in Year 2 and 6% in Year 5, for a blended yield of 3.81%.

CI&S does a better job of competing against the three-year GICs of the banks with its new CIBs. TD Canada Trust three-year GICs pay just 2.45%, while comparable products at three other big banks pay 2.35%, all less than the 3% of the CIB. However, the CIB pays less than some of the independents like ING Direct's 3.5% or Community Trust's 3.6%, Whipp says.

Questioned as to the accuracy of describing a savings vehicle as an investment, Orange says the banks use similar terminology in their Guaranteed Investment Certificates. Besides, the name Canada Investment Bonds tested well in focus groups. Orange laughs off the suggestion CIBs should be renamed the "Barely Break Even After Inflation Bonds." As predicted earlier this week, the new product does nothing to address taxes or inflation. There is some precedent for the former. The Ontario Opportunity Bonds issued in the spring paid 4.25% for a five-year term and are free of Ontario income taxes payable.

As for inflation, Orange's view is it will stay within the government-mandated range of 1% to 3% per year, which goes "hand in hand" with the low interest rates that have prevailed so far this century. Those concerned about inflation can buy Real Return Bonds from brokers, but something like America's Inflation Bonds would have been a welcome addition to the CI&S stable.

For many CSB investors, the year 2001 was a big shock as older maturing CSBs paying 5.5% were replaced by issues paying just 1.8%. "There was a lot of sticker shock there," Orange says. "I personally feel that, like it or not, we Canadians have become resigned to lower rates. They're not a flash in the pan." Even so, CSB sales have stayed steady the last four years. Sales to the first quarter of 2003 were $3.5-billion, up 29% from $2.8-billion to the first quarter of 2002. Total sales in fiscal 2001 were $3.3-billion and in 2000 [were] $2.9-billion.

For the well-heeled, the agency has raised the maximum which can be invested "per registration" to $500,000 from the previous $200,000. But it's hard to believe such clients wouldn't also welcome innovative new CSBs that protected them from the ravages of taxes and inflation.

Source: Jonathan Chevreau, "Personal Finance," Financial Post Investing, *National Post*, October 2, 2003, p. IN.01.F. © National Post 2003. Don Mills, ON.

June 2033 (*shown in bold*). The coupon income, or interest, paid by the bond is 5.750 percent of par value, meaning that for a $1,000 face value bond, $57.50 in annual interest payments will be made in two semiannual installments of $23.75 each. The price given here shows $151.42, denoting a percentage of par value. Thus, the price shown should be interpreted as 151.42 percent of par, or $1,514 for a $1,000 face value bond. Finally, the yield to maturity on the bond is 2.48 percent. More detailed listings are likely to show the change in yield and/or price from the previous close, as well as the bid and ask prices, which represent, respectively, the price at which an investor can sell or buy the asset on the market. Figure 2.3 is an example of such a listing from CanDeal, an online bond market created by the major investment dealers of Canada.

Figure 2.3

Benchmark
Canadian bond
and bill rates.

CanDeal Benchmarks							
Term	Security	Bid Yield	Ask Yield	Yield Change	Bid Price	Ask Price	Price Change
3 mo	CTB 08/15/2013	1.00	0.99	0.00	99.749	99.751	+0.003
6 mo	CTB 11/07/2013	1.02	1.01	0.00	99.511	99.515	+0.003
1 yr	CTB 05/08/2014	1.06	1.05	0.00	98.971	98.981	+0.003
2 yr	CAN 1.000 05/01/2015	1.04	1.03	0.00	99.924	99.937	−0.004
5 yr	CAN 1.250 03/01/2018	1.39	1.38	−0.01	99.369	99.401	+0.045
10 yr	CAN 1.500 06/01/2023	1.95	1.94	−0.01	95.961	96.010	+0.102
30 yr	CAN 4.000 06/01/2041	2.56	2.55	0.00	128.736	128.842	+0.134
Last Updated: 15 May 2013 1:00 ET							

Source: "Bonds & Rates," TMXmoney.com, http://www.tmxmoney.com/en/market_activity/bonds_rates.html, accessed February 20, 2014.

The quotations also highlight the benchmarks for standard-length Canada bonds and actively traded provincials, agencies, and corporates. The full CBID listing also shows real return bond and municipal issue quotations.

The **yield to maturity** reported in the financial pages is calculated by determining the semi-annual yield and then doubling it, rather than compounding it for two half-year periods. This use of a simple interest technique to annualize means that the yield is quoted on an annual percentage rate (APR) basis, rather than as an effective annual yield. The APR method in this context is also called the *bond equivalent yield*. From Figure 2.3 we can see that the yields on Government of Canada bonds are generally rising with term to maturity; this is not true uniformly, due to the different coupons of bonds with similar maturities. Listings for callable bonds trading at a premium (selling above par value) show the yield calculated to the first call date, while for discount bonds the yield is calculated to the redemption date. (No such callable bonds appear in Figure 2.3.)

CC 2

CONCEPT CHECK

Why does it make sense to calculate yields on discount bonds to maturity and yields on premium bonds to the first call date?

The current yield on a bond is annual coupon income per dollar invested in the bond. For this Canada 4.25 percent bond, the current yield is then

$$\text{Current yield} = \frac{\text{Annual coupon income}}{\text{Price}} = \frac{4.25}{100.27} = .0424 \text{ or } 4.24 \text{ percent}$$

Provincial and Municipal Bonds

Figure 2.2 showed a representative sample of bonds issued by provincial governments and by provincial Crown corporations; the latter are generally guaranteed by the corresponding provincial government (although no agency is shown in this sample). All these bonds are similar in their characteristics to federal government issues, with a variety of maturities and coupon rates, and are available to investors at any given time. These securities are considered extremely safe assets, even though not as safe as comparable Canada bonds. Consequently, a small yield spread can be observed in the figure between Canada bonds and provincial bonds, as well as between the bonds of the various provinces. For instance, Canada's bonds maturing in May 2015 yield 1.02 percent, while Ontario's September 2014 bonds 1.17 percent. Quebec's October 2013 bonds yield only 0.11 percentage points less than Ontario's September 2014 bonds, which is somewhat less than a one-year difference should command.

U.S. municipal bonds are exempt from federal income tax and from state and local tax in the issuing state. Hence, the quoted yield is an after-tax yield, which should be compared with after-tax yields on other bonds. This explains why the quoted yields on municipals are lower than the quoted (before-tax) yields on other, comparable bonds. Since the tax advantage is not available to Canadian investors, U.S. municipal bonds generally would not be attractive to them.

Corporate Bonds

Corporate bonds enable private firms to borrow money directly from the public. These bonds are similar in structure to government issues—they typically pay semiannual coupons over their lives and return the face value to the bondholder at maturity. They differ most importantly from government bonds in degree of risk. Default risk is a real consideration in the purchase of corporate bonds, and Chapter 12 discusses this issue in considerable detail. For now, we distinguish only between *secured bonds*, which have specific collateral backing them in the event of firm bankruptcy, unsecured bonds called **debentures**, which have no collateral, and **subordinated debentures**, which have a lower-priority claim to the firm's assets in the event of bankruptcy. Referring to Figure 2.2 again, we see a COMINAR REIT bond (*shown in bold*) maturing in 2017 and paying a coupon of 4.27 percent; its yield of 3.35 percent compares with the above-mentioned Canada and Alberta bonds with yields ranging from 1.02 to 1.17 percent. Figure 2.4 shows a sample of corporate bonds extracted from the Web site of CBID, which gives an extensive listing of actively traded bonds.

Corporate bonds usually come with options attached. **Callable bonds** give the firm the option to repurchase the bond from the holder at a stipulated call price. **Retractable** and **extendible bonds** give the holder the option, respectively, to redeem the bonds earlier and later than the stated maturity date. **Convertible bonds** give the bondholder the option to convert each bond into a stipulated number of shares of stock. These options can give rise to sophisticated trading strategies[2] and are treated in more detail in Chapter 12.

International Bonds

Many firms borrow abroad and many investors buy bonds from foreign issuers. In addition to national capital markets, there is a thriving international capital market, largely centred in London.

A *Eurobond* is a bond denominated in a currency other than that of the country in which it is issued. For example, a dollar-denominated bond sold in Britain would be called a Eurodollar

---

[2]See for example Frank Fabozzi, Jinlin Liu, and Lorne N. Switzer, "Market Efficiency and Returns from Convertible Bond Hedging and Arbitrage Strategies," *Journal of Alternative Investments* 11 (Winter 2009), pp. 37–46.

Figure 2.4 Canadian bond quotations.

	Coupon	Eff. Maturity	Price	Yield		Coupon	Eff. Maturity	Price	Yield
Alim C-T	2.861	2017-Nov-01	100.72	2.69	BMO CapTr	5.750	2017-Sep-26	114.18	2.31
Alim C-T	3.319	2019-Nov-01	101.39	3.08	BMO CapTr	4.633	2015-Dec-31	106.92	1.91
Alim C-T	3.899	2022-Nov-01	101.45	3.72	BNS	6.000	2013-Oct-03	101.70	1.48
Amex Cda Cr	4.853	2014-Oct-03	104.53	1.52	BNS	4.560	2013-Oct-30	101.47	1.29
Amex Cda Cr	3.600	2016-Jun-03	105.00	1.90	BNS	3.430	2014-Jul-16	102.33	1.41
Amex Cda Cr	2.310	2018-Mar-29	99.95	2.32	BNS	3.350	2014-Nov-18	102.72	1.52
BMO	5.050	2013-Sep-03	101.14	1.13	BNS	3.340	2015-Mar-25	103.25	1.56
BMO	4.780	2014-Apr-30	103.24	1.35	BNS	2.250	2015-May-08	101.27	1.59
BMO	4.870	2015-Apr-22	105.95	1.72	BNS	3.610	2016-Feb-22	104.94	1.77
BMO	3.930	2015-Apr-27	104.44	1.60	BNS	1.800	2016-May-09	99.83	1.86
BMO	5.180	2015-Jun-10	107.24	1.60	BNS	2.740	2016-Dec-01	102.59	1.98
BMO	1.890	2015-Oct-05	100.56	1.65	BNS	2.598	2017-Feb-27	101.91	2.07
BMO	3.103	2016-Mar-10	103.60	1.78	BNS	4.100	2017-Jun-08	107.66	2.12
BMO	3.490	2016-Jun-10	104.83	1.86	BNS	2.898	2017-Aug-03	102.17	2.35
BMO	2.960	2016-Aug-02	103.26	1.91	BNS	2.370	2018-Jan-11	100.68	2.21
BMO	2.390	2017-Jul-12	101.06	2.12	BNS	2.242	2018-Mar-22	99.96	2.25
BMO	5.450	2017-Jul-17	113.21	2.12	BNS	4.940	2014-Apr-15	102.92	1.70

Source: CanadianFixedIncome.ca, http://www.pfin.ca/canadianfixedincome/Default.aspx, accessed May 15, 2013.

bond. Similarly, investors might speak of Euroyen bonds, yen-denominated bonds sold outside Japan. Since the European currency is called the "euro," the term "Eurobond" may be confusing. It is best to think of them simply as international bonds.

In contrast to bonds that are issued in foreign currencies, many firms issue bonds in foreign countries but in the currency of the investor. For example, a Yankee bond is a dollar-denominated bond sold in the United States by a non-U.S. issuer. Similarly, Samurai bonds are yen-denominated bonds sold in Japan by non-Japanese issuers.

Mortgages and Mortgage-Backed Securities

An investments text of 30 years ago probably would not include a section on mortgage loans, since at that time investors could not invest in them. Now, because of the explosion in mortgage-backed securities, almost anyone can invest in a portfolio of mortgage loans, and these securities have become a major component of a fixed-income market.

Home mortgages are usually written with a long-term (25-to-30-year maturity) amortization of the principal. Until the 1970s, almost all such mortgages had a fixed interest rate over the life of the loan, with equal fixed monthly payments. Since then these so-called conventional mortgages have become renewable at one-to-five-year intervals, at which point their interest rates may be renegotiated. More recently, a diverse set of alternative mortgage designs has been developed.

Fixed-rate mortgages pose difficulties to banks in years of increasing interest rates because of the mismatching of the maturities of assets and liabilities. Banks commonly issue short-term liabilities (the deposits of their customers) and hold long-term assets such as fixed-rate mortgages. Hence, they suffer losses when interest rates increase: the rates they pay on deposits increase while their mortgage income remains fixed. The five-year renewal period helps to alleviate this problem.

A more recent introduction is the **variable-rate mortgage**. These mortgages require the borrower to pay an interest rate that varies with some measure of the current market interest rate. For example, the interest rate might be set at two points above the current rate on one-year Treasury bills and might be adjusted once a year. Often, a contract sets a limit, or cap, on the maximum size of an interest rate change within a year and over the life of the contract. The variable-rate contract shifts the risk of fluctuations in interest rates from the lender to the borrower.

Because of the shifting of interest rate risk to their customers, banks are willing to offer lower rates on variable-rate mortgages than on conventional fixed-rate mortgages. This proved to be a great inducement to borrowers during a period of high interest rates in the early 1980s. As interest rates fell, however, conventional mortgages appeared to regain popularity.

A *mortgage-backed security* (MBS) is either an ownership claim in a pool of mortgages or an obligation secured by such a pool. These claims represent securitization of mortgage loans. Mortgage lenders originate loans and then sell packages of these loans in the secondary market. Specifically, they sell their claim to the cash inflows from the mortgages as those loans are paid off. The mortgage originator continues to service the loan, collecting principal and interest payments, and passes these payments along to the purchaser of the mortgage. For this reason, these mortgage-backed securities are called **pass-throughs**.

For example, suppose that ten 30-year mortgages, each with a principal value of $100,000, are grouped into a million-dollar pool. If the mortgage rate is 10 percent, then the first month's payment for each loan would be $877.57, of which $833.33 would be interest and $44.24 would be principal repayment. The holder of the mortgage pool would receive a payment in the first month of $8,775.70, the total payments of all ten of the mortgages in the pool.[3] In addition, if one of the mortgages happens to be paid off in any month, the holder of the pass-through security also receives that payment of principal. In future months, of course, the pool will comprise fewer loans, and the interest and principal payments will be lower. The prepaid

---

[3]Actually, the institution that services the loan and the pass-through agency that guarantees the loan each retain a portion of the monthly payment as a charge for their services. Thus, the interest rate received by the pass-through investor is a bit less than the interest rate paid by the borrower. For example, although the ten homeowners together make total monthly payments of $8,775.70, the holder of the pass-through security may receive a total payment of only $8,740.

mortgage in effect represents a partial retirement of the pass-through holder's investment. Mortgage-backed pass-through securities were first introduced in Canada by the Canada Mortgage and Housing Corporation (CMHC, a federal Crown corporation) in 1987. CMHC pass-throughs carry a federal government guarantee under the *National Housing Act* (NHA), which ensures the timely payment of principal and interest. Thus, the cash flow can be considered risk-free even if individual borrowers default on their mortgages. This guarantee increases the marketability of the pass-through. Therefore, investors can buy or sell NHA MBSs like any other bond.

Although pass-through securities often guarantee payment of interest and principal, they do not guarantee the rate of return. Holders of mortgage pass-throughs therefore can be severely disappointed in their returns in years when interest rates drop significantly. This is because homeowners usually have an option to prepay, or pay ahead of schedule, up to 10 percent of the remaining principal outstanding on their mortgages.

2.3   EQUITY SECURITIES

Common Stock as Ownership Shares

Common stocks, also known as *equity securities* or **equities**, represent ownership shares in a corporation. Each share of common stock entitles its owner to one vote on any matters of corporate governance that are put to a vote at the corporation's annual meeting, as well as to a share in the financial benefits of ownership.

The corporation is controlled by a board of directors elected by the shareholders. The board, which meets only a few times each year, selects managers who actually run the corporation on a day-to-day basis. Managers have the authority to make most business decisions without the board's specific approval. The board's mandate is to oversee the management to ensure that it acts in the best interests of shareholders.

The members of the board are elected at the annual meeting. Shareholders who do not attend the annual meeting can vote by **proxy**, empowering another party to vote in their name. Management usually solicits the proxies of shareholders and normally gets a vast majority of these proxy votes. Thus, management usually has considerable discretion to run the firm as it sees fit—without daily oversight from the equityholders who actually own the firm.

We noted in Chapter 1 that such separation of ownership and control can give rise to "agency problems," in which managers pursue goals not in the best interests of shareholders. However, there are several mechanisms designed to alleviate these agency problems. Among these are: compensation schemes that link the success of the manager to that of the firm; oversight by the board of directors as well as outsiders such as security analysts, creditors, or large institutional investors; the threat of a proxy contest in which unhappy shareholders attempt to replace the current management team; and the threat of a takeover by another firm.

Several Canadian firms have at times issued a special type of common stock (**restricted shares**) that has no voting rights, or only restricted voting rights, but otherwise participates fully in the financial benefits of share ownership. For instance, a company may issue two classes of shares, only one of which has the right to vote; alternatively, the senior class may have five votes and the subordinate class only one vote per share. Such shares are issued by firms that want to expand without diluting the holdings of a controlling group. Occasionally, restricted shares are issued to comply with regulatory requirements, such as those restricting foreign ownership in Canadian broadcasting.

Restricted shares sometimes carry different (generally higher) financial benefits for their holders than regular common stock. Otherwise, the loss of the right to vote should be reflected in a lower market value for restricted than for ordinary shares; this loss is the market value of the right to vote. Restricted shareholders also have some legal protection in case of tender offers. Several studies have examined this value of the voting rights, as well as other implications of restricted shares.[4]

The common stock of most large corporations can be bought or sold freely on one or more stock exchanges. A corporation whose stock is not publicly traded is said to be *closely held*. In most closely held corporations, the owners of the firm also take an active role in its management. Takeovers, therefore, are generally not an issue.

Characteristics of Common Stock

The two most important characteristics of common stock as an investment are its **residual claim** and **limited liability** features.

"Residual claim" means that shareholders are last in line of all those who have a claim on the assets and income of the corporation. In a liquidation of the firm's assets, the shareholders have a claim to what is left after all other claimants, such as the tax authorities, employees, suppliers, bondholders, and other creditors, have been paid. For a firm not in liquidation, shareholders have a claim to the part of operating income left over after interest and taxes have been paid. Management either can pay this residual as cash **dividends** to shareholders or reinvest it in the business to increase the value of the shares.

Limited liability means that the greatest amount shareholders can lose in event of failure of the corporation is their original investment. Unlike owners of unincorporated businesses, whose creditors can lay claim to the personal assets of the owner (e.g., house, car, furniture), corporate shareholders may at worst have worthless stock. They are not personally liable for the firm's obligations.

CC 3

CONCEPT CHECK

a. If you buy 100 shares of Teck stock, to what are you entitled?

b. What is the most money you can make on this investment over the next year?

c. If you pay $50 per share, what is the most money you could lose over the year?

Stock Market Listings

Toronto Stock Exchange
www.tsx.ca

Figure 2.5 shows a partial listing of stocks traded on the Toronto Stock Exchange (TSX) in the form of a daily summary (which are also available annually, and weekly as well). The TSX is the major Canadian market in which investors may buy or sell shares of stock. We will examine securities markets in detail in Chapter 3. The summary gives examples of common stock of one or more classes, of warrants, and of units. Stock listings can be obtained from the TSX, from major Canadian business newspapers such as the *Financial Post*, or from the *Wall Street Journal* for U.S. and other markets.

---

[4]See, for instance, Vijay Jog and Allan Riding, "Price Effects of Dual-Class Shares," *Financial Analysts Journal*, January/February 1986, and "Market Reactions of Return, Risk, and Liquidity to the Creation of Restricted Voting Shares," *Canadian Journal of Administrative Sciences* 6, no. 1 (March 1989); Elizabeth Maynes, Chris Robinson, and Alan White, "How Much Is a Share Vote Worth?" *Canadian Investment Review* 3, no. 1 (Spring 1990); Chris Robinson and Alan White, "Empirical Evidence on the Relative Valuation of Voting and Restricted Voting Shares," *Canadian Journal of Administrative Sciences* 7, no. 4 (December 1990); and Elizabeth Maynes, "Evidence on the Value of a Stock Exchange Listing," *Canadian Journal of Administrative Sciences* 8, no. 3 (September 1991). More recently, see: "Corporate Governance Mechanisms and the Performance of Small Cap Firms in Canada," *International Journal of Business Governance and Ethics* 2 (2006), pp. 294–328 (with C. Kelly). There are also non-Canadian studies on restricted shares; see, for instance, M. Partch, "The Creation of a Class of Limited Voting Common Stock and Shareholder Wealth," *Journal of Financial Economics* 18, no. 2 (June 1987).

Figure 2.5 TSX listings: One-year summary, as of May 17, 2013.

Company	Symbol	Last Price	52 Wk. High	52 Wk. Low	Net Chg.	Vol.	P/E Ratio	Div. Yield
Argent Energy Trust	AET.UN	10.18	10.84	8.95	−0.12	112,275	NA	10.3
Aecon Group	ARE	11.22	13.35	9.48	+0.03	239,053	8.8	2.9
Agnico-Eagle Mines	AEM.WT.U	0.53	13.35	0.53	+0.10	2,200	NA	0
Agnico-Eagle Mines	AEM	29.91	56.99	28.50	+0.88	756,532	19.7	3.0
Ainsworth Lumber Co.	ANS	3.58	4.31	1.12	+0.07	495,591	8.5	0
Air Canada	AC.A	2.21	3.39	0.82	+0.03	42,005	4.4	0
Air Canada	AC.B	2.18	3.40	0.83	+0.02	1,954,616	4.4	0
Alimentation Couche-Tard	ATD.A	59.69	62.00	37.86	−0.04	1,288	20.0	0.5
Alimentation Couche-Tard	ATD.B	60.00	62.91	38.64	+0.25	162,126	20.1	0.5

Source: "Daily Market Summary," *Financial Post* Web site, http://www.financialpost.com/markets/data/market-tsx.html, accessed May 17, 2013.

To interpret the information provided for each traded stock, consider the two listings for Alimentation Couche-Tard, identified as ATD.A and ATD.B in the second column. These two shares are identical, except that the first or Class A listing has multiple voting rights, whereas Class B shares have only one vote. For the Class A shares, the next column gives the last or *closing* price for the stock in the period (in this case, one day), $59.69. The next two columns provide the highest and the lowest price at which the stock has traded in the last 52 weeks, $62 and $37.86, respectively. The next column shows the net decrease in the price from the previous close (one day here) of $.04. The number 1,288 indicates that 1,288 shares were traded during that day, in contrast to the 162,126 for Class B shares; this implies that the nonvoting shares are actively traded, while the voting shares are closely held and rarely traded. We can infer the dividend being paid by working with the yield in the last column; Akita Class A stock, which is selling at $59.69 (the last recorded price), has a dividend yield of $x/59.69 = .5$ percent, or a dividend of $x = .30$; this is higher than the yield on the non-voting shares due to the difference in price. Both classes are receiving the same dividend of $.30 per share on an annual basis. A cursory analysis of the stock listings shows that dividend yields vary widely across firms. It is important to recognize that high-yield dividend stocks are not necessarily better investments than low-yield stocks. Total return to an investor comes from dividends and **capital gains**, or appreciation in the value of the stock. Low-yield dividend firms presumably offer greater prospects for capital gains, or investors would not be willing to hold the low-yield firms in their portfolios. The majority of yields shown are either to trust units (usually higher—see below) or are zero for normal equities.

The P/E ratio, or **price–earnings ratio**, is the ratio of the closing stock price to last year's earnings per share. It tells us how much stock purchasers must pay per dollar of earnings that the firm generates. It also varies widely across firms. Where dividend yield or P/E ratio are not reported in the second-last column of Figure 2.5, the firms have zero dividends, or zero or negative earnings. We shall have much to say about P/E ratios in Chapter 16.

Shares commonly are traded in **board lots** of 100 shares each; however, a board lot consists of 1,000 shares for stocks selling below $5, while it falls to 25 shares for stocks above $100. Investors who wish to trade in smaller, odd lots may pay higher commissions to their stockbrokers, although many brokers are not charging an odd-lot differential in order to attract the small investor.

Preferred Stock

Preferred stock has features similar to those of both equity and debt. Like a bond, it promises to pay to its holder a fixed amount of income every year. In this sense, preferred stock is similar to an infinite-maturity bond, that is, a perpetuity. It also resembles a bond in that it does not convey voting power regarding the management of the firm. Preferred stock is an equity investment, however, in the sense that failure to pay the dividend does not precipitate corporate bankruptcy. Instead, preferred dividends are usually *cumulative*; that is, unpaid dividends cumulate and must be paid in full before any dividends may be paid to holders of common stock.

Preferred stock also differs from bonds in terms of its tax treatment for the firm. Because preferred stock payments are treated as dividends rather than interest, they are not tax-deductible expenses for the firm. This disadvantage is offset somewhat by the fact that corporations may exclude dividends received from domestic corporations in the computation of their taxable income. Preferred stocks, therefore, make desirable fixed-income investments for some corporations. Similarly, preferred dividends are taxed like common dividends for individual investors, which confers them a higher after-tax yield than bonds with the same pretax yield. Hence, even though they rank after bonds in the event of corporate bankruptcy, preferred stocks generally sell at lower yields than corporate bonds.

Preferred stock is issued in variations similar to those of corporate bonds. It can be callable by the issuing firm, in which case it is said to be *redeemable*. It also can be convertible into common stock at some specified conversion ratio. A firm often issues different series of preferreds, with different dividends, over time. One innovation in the market is variable-rate preferred stock, which, similarly to variable-rate mortgages, ties the dividend rate to current market interest rates.

Income Trusts

Income trusts also are instruments with debt and equity features. An income trust holds an underlying asset or group of assets that generate income, most of which is distributed to unitholders. This is a variation on the structure of an REIT or a royalty trust. REITs derive their income from holdings in real estate, while the source for royalty trusts is royalties in the oil and gas industry. The notion has been expanded to industries where income is considered to be reliable and predictable and there are minimal capital spending requirements that would act as a drain on cash flow; these might include the hotel or food service industries among others. The trusts are likely to be formed by an existing company that identifies an operating division as a source of revenue.

Instead of using alternatives such as equity carve-outs or spinoffs offered directly to investors, the parent corporation would cooperate in the creation of a trust that issues units to the public. Proceeds from the unit sales are used to purchase common shares and debt that represent the capital base of the operating division.

The principal motive for the creation of the trust is the tax treatment, which is favourable to both investors and the underlying operating division. The income generated is flowed through to investors virtually tax-free. Use of high leverage, and hence high-yield debt, is typically part of the design, implying a degree of risk that may not be recognized by investors. The issue of trust units is similar to that of equity issues, with a prospectus preceding the primary issue. Secondary trading occurs on stock exchanges, after the units are listed. The trust functions like a closed-end mutual fund (see Chapter 23), which protects against the need to sell assets to cover redemptions.[5]

---

[5]For a comprehensive analysis, see Vijay Jog and Liping Wang, "The Growth of Income Trusts in Canada and the Economic Consequences," *National Tax Journal* 52, no. 3 (2004).

The major attraction for investors is the promise of a high yield; recent low yields on debt instruments have increased the appeal of trust units, and investors' appetites have been strong. There were over 400 income trusts of various types available in Canada at the end of 2006. By mid-2005 about $140 billion had been raised through new issues of trust units, up from less than $2 billion in 1999.

Unfortunately, the structure that enabled corporations to pass along cash flows to be taxed in the hands of investors, many of whom were tax-exempt or tax-deferred, threatened to deprive the government of increasing tax revenues. When in 2006 Telus and BCE decided to adopt the structure, the federal government had had enough. The announcement by the Finance Minister of plans to phase out the tax treatment for income trusts triggered a one-day sell-off of 300 points in the TSX index. Income trusts lost up to 20 percent in a few days, even though many recovered greatly in subsequent weeks. Since then income trusts have been converting themselves to standard corporations, although their revenues and payouts are likely to be stabler than for typical firms.

Although there is a perception of guaranteed cash flow, the payouts depend on the operating results of the underlying business. Frequently, the cash flow involves also a repayment of capital to unitholders. For this reason, the initial level of payments may be impossible to maintain for a lengthy period and many income trusts have suffered losses on the order of 50 percent in a few years. One risky variety entails the trading of derivatives on the basis of an underlying portfolio in order to generate the promised payouts.

Depository Receipts

American Depository Receipts, or ADRs, are certificates traded in U.S. markets that represent ownership in shares of a foreign company. Each ADR may correspond to ownership of a fraction of a foreign share, one share, or several shares or the foreign corporation. ADRs were created to make it easier for foreign firms to satisfy U.S. security registration requirements. They are the most common way for U.S. investors to invest in and trade the shares of foreign corporations.

2.4 STOCK AND BOND MARKET INDICES

Stock Market Indices

The daily performance of the Dow Jones Industrial Average and the Toronto Stock Exchange (TSX) Composite Index are staple portions of the Canadian evening news report. Although these indices are, respectively, the best-known measures of the performances of the U.S. and Canadian stock markets, they are only two of several indicators of stock market performance in the two countries. Other indices are computed and published daily. In addition, several indices of bond market performance are widely available.

The ever-increasing role of international trade and investments has made indices of foreign financial markets part of the general news. Thus, foreign stock exchange indices, such as the Nikkei Average of Tokyo and the Financial Times Index of London, are fast becoming household names.

Toronto Stock Exchange Indices   The S&P/TSX Composite Index is Canada's best-known stock market indicator. It contains over 270 of the largest securities (in terms of market value) traded on the TSX, regardless of industry group, but excluding control blocks composed of more than 20 percent of outstanding shares. The TSX Composite is a **market-value-weighted index** based on a very broad set of companies. It is constructed to reflect an investment in each company proportional to its total market capitalization, giving considerably more weight to large, highly valued stocks.

TABLE 2.2   Stock Market Index Calculation

Stock	No. of Shares	Initial Price	Market Value	Final Price	Market Value
ABC	20M	$25	$500M	$30	$600M
XYZ	1M	$100	$100M	$90	$90M
Initial	Value-weighted average = (500 + 100)/10 = 60				
	Price-weighted average = (25 + 100)/2 = 62.5				
Final	Value-weighted average = (600 + 90)/10 = 69		Percentage gain = (69 − 60)/60 = 15%		
	Price-weighted average = (30 + 90)/2 = 60		Percentage gain = (60 − 62.5)/62.5 = −4%		

The TSX Composite is computed by calculating the total market value of the stocks in the index and the total market value of those stocks on the previous day of trading, always excluding the control blocks. The percentage increase in the total market value from one day to the next represents the increase in the index. The rate of return of the index therefore equals the rate of return that would be earned by an investor holding a portfolio of all stocks in the index in proportion to their market value, except that the index does not reflect cash dividends paid out by those stocks.

To illustrate, suppose that there are only two companies in the market—ABC with 20 million shares at $25 and XYZ with 1 million shares at $100; then the index would be set at the combined market values of the companies of $600 million divided by the arbitrary divisor of 10, giving a level of 60. (Initially an index is likely to be set at a round number such as 100 or 1,000, by dividing the opening value by 6, or .6 in this case.) ABC has five times the weight of XYZ in the index. Table 2.2 shows how the index changes value with the individual stock movements; as ABC rises to $30 and XYZ falls to $90, the index value changes to 69, and rising by 15 percent.

CC 4

CONCEPT CHECK

Suppose that shares of XYZ increase in price to $110 while shares of ABC fall to $20. Find the percentage change in the market-value-weighted average of these two stocks. Compare that to the percentage return of a portfolio that holds $500 of ABC for every $100 of XYZ, that is, an index portfolio.

S&P's
Institutional
Market Services
www.compustat.
com

Dow Jones
Indexes
indexes.dow
jones.com

The Toronto Stock Exchange is described by a variety of indices, all calculated by S&P, including capped indices and 14 indices based on narrow industry groupings, such as energy, financials, and gold, which are the constituents of the main index. The narrower TSX 60 represents the 60 most important companies, while the TSX MidCap and TSX SmallCap reflect the performance of smaller companies. Both the TSX 60 and the Composite index are recalculated as capped indices by limiting the contribution of each component to a maximum of 10 percent of the index value. The associated TSX Venture Exchange, for smaller Canadian companies not listed on the TSX, is described by the S&P/TSX Venture Index. Total return indices are also calculated; these include the value of dividends paid by constituent companies in the returns on the indices. In addition, Dow Jones has computed a DJ Canada 40 Index. Figure 2.6 shows an example of a summary of the performance of the various indices.

Suppose now that a two-for-one stock split occurs in XYZ, giving shareholders a total of two million shares valued at $50. Since the total market value of XYZ and of the market are unchanged,

Figure 2.6

Canadian stock indices, May 16, 2013.

Index	Last	Change
TSX	12,528.31	+54.66
TSX Venture	933.87	−3.00
Energy	247.87	+1.48
Financials	197.37	+0.68
Health care	70.59	−0.29
Industrials	141.64	+1.68
Information technology	33.18	+0.15
Metals and mining	843.52	+3.03
Telecommunications	121.78	+0.24
Utilities	225.92	+1.43

Market Summary

	Total Volume	Issues Traded	Advancing	Declining	Unchanged
Toronto Stock Exchange	212,545,688	1,817	826	690	301
TSX Venture Exchange	88,828,475	985	232	351	402

the value of the index remains unaffected, as can be seen by examining Table 2.3. This characteristic is a considerable advantage in the calculation and maintenance of a value-weighted index.

Market value weighting corresponds to the theoretical solution to portfolio construction presented in Chapter 6. It also corresponds to a buy-and-hold strategy based on an initial portfolio that is value-weighted. Unfortunately, it can have a very distorting effect on the index. The market appreciation of Nortel gave it a total capitalization of $367.2 billion in July 2000, representing 36.5 percent of the then TSE 300. For mutual funds limited to maximum holdings in a single security, this made matching the index performance impossible. By August 13, 2001 it had fallen to $35.6 billion in value, or 5.01 percent of the TSE 300; at this point it was passed by Royal Bank at $36 billion. For all but Nortel investors this was considered a much healthier scenario.

Investors today can purchase shares in mutual funds that hold shares in proportion to their representation in the S&P/TSX Composite. These **index funds** yield a return equal to that of the TSX index and so provide a low-cost passive investment strategy for equity investors. The topic of index funds and exchange-traded funds is developed in Chapter 23.

TABLE 2.3 Stock Market Index Calculation After a Stock Split

Stock	No. of Shares	Initial Price	Market Value	Final Price	Market Value
ABC	20M	$25	$500M	$30	$600M
XYZ	2M	$50	$100M	$45	$90M
Initial	Value-weighted average = (500 + 100)/10 = 60				
	Price-weighted average = (25 + 50)/1.2 = 62.5				
Final	Value-weighted average = (600 + 90)/10 = 69		Percentage gain = (69 − 60)/60 = 15%		
	Price-weighted average = (30 + 45)/1.2 = 62.5		Percentage gain = (62.5 − 62.5)/62.5 = 0		

Dow Jones
Indexes
indexes.
dowjones.com

Dow Jones Averages   The Dow Jones Industrial Average (DJIA) of 30 large blue-chip corporations has been computed since 1896. Its long history probably accounts for its preeminence in the public mind. (The average covered only 20 stocks until 1928.) The Dow is a **price-weighted average**, which means it is computed by adding the prices of the 30 companies and dividing by a certain number.

Originally, the divisor was simply 20 when 20 stocks were included in the index; thus, the index was no more than the average price of the 20 stocks. This makes the index performance a measure of the performance of a particular portfolio strategy that buys one share of each firm in the index. Therefore, the weight of each firm in the index is proportional to the share price rather than the total outstanding market value of the shares. In the case of the firms ABC and XYZ above, the "Dow portfolio" would have four times as much invested in XYZ as in ABC ($100 as against $25), as Table 2.2 also shows. Although the market-value-weighted index increased by 15 percent, the price-weighted average drops by 4 percent, due to the reliance on the high-priced XYZ that loses value. A price-weighted average reflects the performance of a portfolio that holds an equal number of shares in each of the companies in the index; unfortunately, the capital invested in each stock is arbitrarily determined by when and to what level each stock has last split.

> **CC 5**
>
> ### CONCEPT CHECK
>
> Consider again the changes to the stocks, as in Concept Check 4. Calculate the percentage change in the price-weighted index. Compare that to the rate of return of a portfolio that holds one share in each company.

As stocks are added to or dropped from the average, or stocks split over time, the Dow divisor is continually adjusted to leave the average unaffected by the change. The treatment of a stock split is more complicated, as we would not want the average to fall because of a company's decision to split when no change in actual value has occurred. Following a split, the divisor must be reduced to a value that leaves the average unaffected by the split. Table 2.3 illustrates this point. The initial share price of XYZ, which was $100 in Table 2.2, falls to $50 if the stock splits at the beginning of the period. Notice that the number of shares outstanding doubles, leaving the market value of total shares unaffected. The divisor, d, which originally was 2.0 when the two-stock average was initiated, must be reset to a value that leaves the average unchanged. Because the sum of the post-split stock price is 75 and the pre-split average price was 62.5, we calculate the new value of d by solving $75/d = 62.5$. The value of d therefore falls from its original value of 2.0 to $75/62.5 = 1.20$, and the initial value of the average is indeed unaffected by the split: $75/1.20 = 62.5$. At period-end, shares of ABC will sell for $30, while shares of XYZ will sell for $45, representing the same negative 10 percent return it was assumed to earn in Table 2.2. The new value of the price-weighted average is $(30 + 45)/1.20 = 62.5$, and the rate of return on the average is $62.5/62.5 - 1 = 0$. Notice that this return is greater than the –4 percent calculated in Table 2.2. The relative weight of XYZ, which is the poorer-performing stock, is lower after the split because its price is lower; the performance of the average therefore improves. This example illustrates again that the implicit weighting scheme of a price-weighted average is somewhat arbitrary, being determined by the prices rather than the outstanding market values of the shares in the average.

Just as the divisor is updated for stock splits, so if one firm is dropped from the average and another firm with a different price is added, the divisor has to be updated to leave the average unchanged by the substitution. By now, the divisor for the Dow Jones Industrial Average has fallen to a value of about .17.

Dow Jones also computes a Transportation Average of 20 airline, trucking, and railroad stocks; a Public Utility Average of 15 electric and natural gas utilities; and a Composite Average combining the 65 firms of the three separate averages. Each is a price-weighted average, and thus overweights the performance of high-priced stocks.

www.nyse.com

www.nasdaq. com

Other U.S. Market-Value Indices   Professionals pay more attention to the S&P 500 and 100 indices of the largest U.S. corporations, as they assess their performance with respect to these market-value standards. Like the TSX index, these and most others adjust for nontraded shares held by governments or in controlling blocks. The New York Stock Exchange publishes a market-value-weighted composite index of all NYSE-listed stocks, in addition to subindices for industrial, utility, transportation, and financial stocks. The National Association of Securities Dealers publishes an index of 3,000 over-the-counter (OTC) firms traded on the Nasdaq market.

The ultimate U.S. equity index so far computed is the Wilshire 5000 index of the market value of all NYSE and American Stock Exchange (Amex) stocks plus actively traded Nasdaq stocks. Despite its name, the index actually includes about 6,000 stocks. Figure 2.7 shows an example of a summary of U.S. stock index performance. Vanguard offers an index mutual fund, the Total Stock Market Portfolio that enables investors to match the performance of the Wilshire 5000 index, and a small stock portfolio that matches the MSCI (Morgan Stanley Capital International) U.S. small-capitalization 1750 index.

Equally Weighted Indices   Market performance sometimes is measured by an equally weighted average of the returns of each stock in an index. Such an averaging technique, by placing equal weight on each return, corresponds to an implicit portfolio strategy that places equal dollar values on each stock. This is in contrast to both price-weighting (which requires equal numbers of shares of each stock) and market-value-weighting (which requires investments in proportion to outstanding value).

Figure 2.7
U.S. stock indices, February 19, 2014.

US Major Stock Indexes, 2:35 P.M. EST 02/19/14			
	Last	**Change**	**% Change**
DJIA	16119.71	−10.69	−0.07
Nasdaq	4256.46	−16.32	−0.38
S&P 500	1837.79	−2.97	−0.16
Russell 2000	1158.86	−2.62	−0.23
Markets Diary			
Issues	**NYSE**	**Nasdaq**	**NYSE MKT**
Advances	1,543	975	168
Declines	1,570	1,608	219
Unchanged	86	79	15
Issues at			
New Highs	161	134	11
New Lows	15	8	0
Share Volume			
Total	2,421,330,301	1,309,848,926	88,325,202
Advancing	1,176,563,618	586,602,036	34,686,315
Declining	1,215,515,123	715,855,941	51,569,155

Source: "U.S. Stocks Overview," Markets Data Center, *The Wall Street Journal Online*, http://online.wsj.com/mdc/public/page/mdc_us_stocks.html, accessed February 20, 2014.

Unlike price- or market-value-weighted indices, equally weighted indices do not correspond to buy-and-hold portfolio strategies. Suppose that you start with equal-dollar investments in the two stocks of Table 2.2, ABC and XYZ. Because ABC increases in value by 20 percent over the year while XYZ increases by only 10 percent, your portfolio no longer is equally weighted; it is now more heavily invested in ABC. To reset the portfolio to equal weights, you would need to rebalance: sell off some ABC stock and/or purchase more XYZ stock. Such rebalancing would be necessary to align the return on your portfolio with that on the equally weighted index.

Foreign and International Stock Market Indices

Development in financial markets worldwide includes the construction of indices for these markets. The popular indices are broader than the Dow Jones average and most are value-weighted.

The most important are the Nikkei, FTSE (pronounced "footsie"), Hang Seng, and DAX. The Nikkei 225 is a price-weighted average of the largest Tokyo Stock Exchange (TSE) stocks. The Nikkei 300 is a value-weighted index. FTSE is published by *The Financial Times* of London and is a value-weighted index of 100 of the largest London Stock Exchange corporations. The Hang Seng tracks the Hong Kong market, while the DAX index is the premier German stock index. Table 2.4 shows the list of foreign stock exchange indices published by *The Globe and Mail*. More details on international indices are provided in Chapter 24.

On January 6, 2014, the Japan Exchange Group, Inc., Tokyo Stock Exchange, Inc. and Nikkei Inc. introduced a new index, the "JPX-Nikkei Index 400." The new index includes companies that meet requirements of global investment standards, such as efficient use of capital and investor-focused management perspectives. The aim is to attract new foreign investors in Japanese companies, to encourage improvements in corporate practices in Japan, and to help revitalize the Japanese stock market (see www.tse.or.jp/english/market/topix/jpx_nikkei.html).

The leading compendium of international indices is produced by MSCI (Morgan Stanley Capital International), which computes over 50 country indices and several regional indices. Table 2.5 presents a sample of MSCI indices.

www.theglobe
andmail.com

TABLE 2.4 Foreign Stock Exchange Indices

	High	Low	Last	Change
FTSE 100 INDEX				
	6,714.48	6,677.15	6,687.80	−5.75 / −0.09%
GERMANY DAX (TR)				
	8,401.28	8,324.23	8,369.87	+7.45 / +0.09%
DJ STOXX 50				
	2,822.27	2,793.65	2,820.94	+23.20 / +0.83%
JAPAN NIKKEI AVERAGE INDEX (225)				
	15,155.72	14,879.51	15,037.24	−58.79 / −0.39%
SPAIN IBEX 35				
	8,589.70	8,521.90	8,542.30	−40.20 / −0.47%
FRANCE CAC 40				
	3,984.28	3,957.77	3,979.07	−3.16 / −0.08%
FTSE MIB INDEX				
	17,492.97	17,207.52	17,492.97	+177.72 / +1.03%

Source: "World Indices, 05/16/2013," FXStreet.com, http://www.fxstreet.com/rates-charts/world-indices. Solution by TeleTrader; Data Source: Interactive Data.

TABLE 2.5

Sample of
MSCI Stock
Indices

Regional Indices		Countries	
Developed Markets	**Emerging Markets**	**Developed Markets**	**Emerging Markets**
EAFE (Europe, Australia, Far East)	Emerging Markets (EM)	Australia	Argentina
EASEA (EAFE ex Japan)	EM Asia	Austria	Brazil
Europe	EM Far East	Belgium	Chile
European Monetary Union (EMU)	EM Latin America	Canada	China
Far East	Emerging Markets Free (EMF)	Denmark	Colombia
Kokusai (World ex Japan)	EMF Asia	Finland	Czech Republic
Nordic Countries	EMF Eastern Europe	France	Egypt
North America	EMF Europe	Germany	Greece
Pacific	EMF Europe & Middle East	Hong Kong	Hungary
The World Index	EMF Far East	Ireland	India
G7 countries	EMF Latin America	Italy	Indonesia
World ex U.S.		Japan	Israel
		Netherlands	Jordan
		New Zealand	Korea
		Norway	Malaysia
		Portugal	Mexico
		Singapore	Morocco
		Spain	Pakistan
		Sweden	Peru
		Switzerland	Philippines
		U.K.	Poland
		U.S.	Russia
			South Africa
			Sri Lanka
			Taiwan
			Thailand
			Turkey
			Venezuela

Source: MSCI Barra Web site, http://www.mscibarra.com.

Bond Market Indicators

Just as stock market indices provide guidance concerning the performance of the overall stock market, bond market indicators measure the performance of various categories of bonds. Scotia Capital publishes the main Canadian bond market indices, while in the United States the three most well-known groups of indices are those of Merrill Lynch, Lehman Brothers, and Salomon Brothers.

The indices all are computed monthly, and all measure total returns as the sum of capital gains plus interest income derived from the bonds during the month. Any intramonth cash distributions received from the bonds are assumed to be reinvested weekly during the month back into the bond market.

The major problem with these indices is that true rates of return on many bonds are difficult to compute, because the infrequency with which the bonds trade make reliable up-to-date prices difficult to obtain. In practice, prices must often be estimated from bond valuation models. These "matrix" prices may differ substantially from true market values.

2.5   DERIVATIVE MARKETS

One of the most significant developments in financial markets in recent years has been the growth of futures and options markets. These instruments provide payoffs that depend on the values of other assets, such as commodity prices, bond and stock prices, or market index values. For this reason, these instruments sometimes are called **derivative assets**, or **contingent claims**. Their values derive from or are contingent on the values of other assets.

Options

A **call option** gives its holder the right to purchase an asset for a specified price, called the **exercise** or **strike price**, on or before a specified expiration date. For example, a February call option on Alcan Aluminum stock with an exercise price of $60 entitles its owner to purchase Alcan stock for a price of $60 at any time up to and including the expiration date in February. Each option contract is for the purchase of 100 shares. However, quotations are made on a per-share basis. The holder of the call need not exercise the option; it will be profitable to exercise only if the market value of the asset that may be purchased exceeds the exercise price.

When the market price exceeds the exercise price, the option holder may "call away" the asset for the exercise price and reap a profit equal to the difference between the stock price and the exercise price. Otherwise, the option will be left unexercised. If not exercised before the expiration date of the contract, the option simply expires and no longer has value. Calls therefore provide greater profits when stock prices increase and thus represent bullish investment vehicles.

In contrast, a **put option** gives its holder the right to sell an asset for a specified exercise price on or before a specified expiration date. A February put on Alcan with an exercise price of $40 thus entitles its owner to sell Alcan stock ("put the stock") to the put writer at a price of $40 at any time before expiration in February, even if the market price of Alcan is lower than $40. Whereas profits on call options increase when the asset increases in value, profits on put options increase when the asset value falls. The put is exercised only if its holder can deliver an asset worth less than the exercise price in return for the exercise price.

Canadian
Derivatives
Exchange
www.m-x.ca/
accueil_en.php

Figure 2.8 gives listed stock option quotations from the Web site of the Montréal Exchange. The quotations cover trading on the Montréal Exchange (also known as the Canadian Derivatives Exchange). Locate the option listed in the table for shares of Canadian Natural Resources (CNQ). The table notes the closing price of $29.79 per share, as well as the change and bid and ask prices; it also shows historical volatility which is compared with the implied volatilities listed lower in the table (this is a concept you will encounter in Chapter 19). Options were traded on CNQ with exercise prices ranging from $22 to $40. (Many other options with other exercise prices and maturity are given in the full table.) These values, the exercise price or strike price, are given in the first column of numbers, after the expiration month.

The next three columns of numbers provide the bid, ask, and last trade prices of call options on CNQ shares followed by the volume of options traded and implied volatility. The information is then repeated for puts The prices of call options decrease in successive rows for a given expiration date, corresponding to progressively higher exercise prices. This makes sense, because the right to purchase a share at a given exercise price is worth less as the exercise price increases. For example, with an exercise price of $24, the May call lists for $5.85 per share, whereas the option to purchase the stock for an exercise price of $34 is worth only $.05. The exercise price indicates the range of prices at which the stock has traded during the life of some options; examining the full listings, we see that CNQ has had a price in the $25–$40 range in the past 18 months. The volume column gives an indication of the liquidity of the options.

Put options have parallel strike prices and times to maturity; their prices, of course, increase with the exercise price. The right to sell a share of CNQ at a price of $24 is less valuable than the right to sell it at $34.

Figure 2.8   Canadian equity options market listings.

Last update:		May 15, 2013		17:30 ET	

Last Price	29.79	Net Change	−0.18	Bid Price	29.77	Ask Price	29.80	30-Day Historical Volatility: 25.9%

Calls						Puts					
Month/Strike	Bid Price	Ask Price	Last Price	Vol.	Impl. Vol.	Month/Strike	Bid Price	Ask Price	Last Price	Vol.	Impl. Vol.
MAY 22.000	7.700	7.850	7.850	49.4%	32	MAY 22.000	0	0.050	0.050	51.1%	12
MAY 23.000	6.700	6.850	6.850	49.4%	0	MAY 23.000	0	0.050	0.050	51.1%	54
MAY 24.000	5.700	5.850	5.850	49.4%	0	MAY 24.000	0	0.050	0.050	51.1%	49
MAY 25.000	4.700	4.850	4.850	49.4%	20	MAY 25.000	0	0.050	0.050	51.1%	57
MAY 26.000	3.700	3.850	3.850	49.4%	0	MAY 26.000	0	0.050	0.050	51.1%	377
MAY 27.000	2.740	2.840	2.840	50.1%	18	MAY 27.000	0	0.050	0.050	51.1%	262
MAY 28.000	1.730	1.840	1.840	49.9%	157	MAY 28.000	0	0.050	0.050	51.2%	404
MAY 29.000	0.760	0.860	0.860	51.7%	118	MAY 29.000	0.010	0.090	0.090	53.7%	547
MAY 30.000	0.120	0.170	0.170	63.4%	2,099	MAY 30.000	0.300	0.400	0.400	62.6%	1,089
MAY 31.000	0	0.060	0.060	59.1%	937	MAY 31.000	1.180	1.280	1.280	55.2%	0
MAY 32.000	0	0.050	0.050	77.2%	10,140	MAY 32.000	2.170	2.280	2.280	63.4%	494
MAY 33.500	0	0.040	0.040	—	286	MAY 33.500	3.650	3.800	3.800	—	146
MAY 34.000	0	0.050	0.050	—	2,784	MAY 34.000	4.150	4.300	4.300	—	153
MAY 36.000	0	0.050	0.050	—	1,717	MAY 36.000	6.150	6.300	6.300	—	89
MAY 38.000	0	0.050	0.050	—	35	MAY 38.000	8.150	8.300	8.300	—	2
MAY 40.000	0	0.050	0.050	—	0	MAY 40.000	10.15	10.300	10.300	—	0
JUN 23.000	6.750	6.900	6.900	51.0%	0	JUN 23.000	0.010	0.090	0.090	50.6%	0
JUN 24.000	5.750	5.900	5.900	51.0%	0	JUN 24.000	0.010	0.090	0.090	50.6%	0
JUN 25.000	4.800	4.900	4.900	51.3%	0	JUN 25.000	0.040	0.130	0.130	51.0%	0

Source: "CNQ—Canadian Natural Resources Limited," Montréal Exchange Web site, http://www.m-x.ca/nego_fin_jour_en.php?symbol=CNQ*&lang_txt=en&jj=08&mm=01&aa=10&jjF=08&mmF=01&aaF=10#cote, accessed May 15, 2013.

Note that option prices increase with time to expiration. Clearly, the right to buy CNQ at $24 (or sell at $24) until June is worth less than the same right until May. (Check the prices for calls with the same exercise price in successive months.)

Most options have relatively short expiration dates, that is, less than one year. There is also a class of options called LEAPS (long-term equity anticipation securities) with much longer expiration dates, of two to three years at issue.

CC 6

CONCEPT CHECK

What would be the profit or loss per share of stock to an investor who bought the June 2013 maturity CNQ call option with exercise price $24 on May 15, 2013 if the stock price at the expiration of the option was $35? What about a purchaser of a put option with the same exercise price ($24) and the same maturity (June 2013)?

Futures Contracts

The **futures contract** calls for delivery of an asset or its cash value at a specified delivery or maturity date for an agreed-upon price, called the **futures price**, to be paid at contract maturity. The *long position* is held by the trader who commits to purchasing the commodity on the delivery date. The trader who takes the *short position* commits to delivering the commodity at contract maturity.

Figure 2.9 illustrates the listing of several futures financial contracts as they appear on the Montréal Exchange Web site. The listings include futures on bankers' acceptances, bonds, stock indices, ETFs, and currencies. For the bankers' acceptances, there are five different maturities given for contracts traded. Each contract calls for delivery of $1 million in acceptances.

The five rows detail price data for contracts expiring on various dates. The June maturity contract's highest futures price during the day was 98.720, the lowest was 98.710, and the settlement price (a representative trading price during the last few minutes of trading) was 98.715, having opened at the same price. 14,326 contracts were traded during the day. Finally, open interest was 98,398. Corresponding information is given for the other maturity dates. Other information often given includes the change from the previous day in the settlement price; as well, the history of the highest and lowest futures prices over the contract's life to date is very useful.

The trader holding the long position profits from price increases. Suppose that at expiration acceptances are priced at 98.92. The long-position trader who entered the contract at the futures price of 98.715 on May 15 would pay the previously-agreed-upon 98.715 for each unit of the index, which at contract maturity would be worth 98.92. Because each contract calls for delivery of $1 million in acceptances, ignoring brokerage fees, the gain to the long position would equal $1 million $\times$ (.9892 − .9872) = $2,000. Conversely, the short position must deliver $1 million in acceptances for the previously-agreed-upon futures price. The short position's loss equals the long position's profit.

In addition to futures contracts, there are also stock index options. Several call and put option contracts are quoted on the S&P/TSX 60 stock index. Index options differ from stock options because they are **cash settlement** options. If the value of the index rises above the exercise price, then the holder of a call option on the S&P/TSX 60 index receives, upon exercise, a cash amount equal to $200 times the difference between the stock index and exercise price. Conversely, the put option holder would exercise the option only when the index falls below the exercise price.

Stock index options are listed as Canadian equity options. (There are also U.S. index options on the Dow, S&P 500, S&P 100, and Nasdaq 100.) Index options are not to be confused with index futures, shown in Figure 2.9, or with options on futures (which are more complex).

Figure 2.9 Montréal Exchange futures.

May 15, 2013

Volume by Product			
Name	**Volume**	**Trans.**	**Open Interest**
BAX	153,490	4,739	705,408
Options on BAX	10,000	22	122,751
ONX	0	0	0
OIS	0	0	0
CGZ	546	13	1,291
CGF	2,140	42	7,612
CGB	61,279	20,237	363,559
LGB	0	0	0
OGB	0	0	904
SXF	10,060	7,568	144,856
SXM	432	145	1,567
SCF	0	0	0
Sector index futures	0	0	0
SXO	430	7	121,688
Equity options	85,564	2,919	2,837,684
ETF options	16,605	134	572,770
USX	14	1	643
Total	340,560	35,827	4,880,733

Most Active Options Classes	
Class	**Volume**
ATH	15,170
XIU	15,056
RY	7,012
TD	6,013
NA	4,763
CM	4,254
IFC	3,016
TLM	2,877
BB	2,663
G	2,536

Three-Month Canadian Bankers' Acceptance Futures (BAX)						
Month	**Open**	**High**	**Low**	**Settle**	**Change**	**Volume**	**Open Int.**
JN 13	98.715	98.720	98.710	98.715	0.000	14,326	98,398
JL 13	0.000	0.000	0.000	98.720	0.000	0	0
AU 13	0.000	0.000	0.000	98.715	0.000	0	0
SE 13	98.690	98.700	98.690	98.690	0.000	20,659	120,668
DE 13	98.680	98.690	98.670	98.680	−0.010	29,909	163,899
MR 14	98.640	98.670	98.630	98.650	0.000	50,923	152,626

Ten-Year Government of Canada Bond Futures (CGB)						
Month	**Open**	**High**	**Low**	**Settle**	**Change**	**Volume**	**Open Int.**
JN 13	134.130	134.490	133.950	134.290	0.110	56,964	349,081

S&P/TSX 60™ Index Futures (SXF)						
Month	**Open**	**High**	**Low**	**Settle**	**Change**	**Volume**	**Open Int.**
JN 13	720.300	722.000	710.400	713.000	−7.800	10,060	144,856

Source: "Trading Activity Data—May 15, 2013," Montréal Exchange Web site, http://www.m-x.ca/revue_march_en.php?id=2837, accessed May 15, 2013.

Futures are also quoted on commodities such as grains, meats, fruits, fuels, and base and precious metals in Winnipeg, New York, Chicago, and other locations.

The right to purchase the asset at an agreed-upon price, as opposed to the obligation, distinguishes call options from long positions in futures contracts. A futures contract *obliges* the long position to purchase the asset at the futures price; the call option, in contrast, *conveys the right* to purchase the asset at the exercise price. The purchase will be made only if it yields a profit.

Clearly, a holder of a call has a better position than the holder of a long position on a futures contract with a futures price equal to the option's exercise price. This advantage, of course, comes only at a price. Call options must be purchased; futures investments may be entered into without cost. The purchase price of an option is called the **premium**. It represents the compensation the holder of the call must pay for the ability to exercise the option only when it is profitable to do so. Similarly, the difference between a put option and a short futures position is the right, as opposed to the obligation, to sell an asset at an agreed-upon price.

Other Derivative Assets: Warrants, Swaps, and Hybrid Securities

In addition to options and futures, other contingent claims are traded in Canadian financial markets. We list briefly the most important of them, which will be discussed in more detail in Chapters 18 to 20.

Warrants are like call options, with the difference being that the holder receives the shares upon exercise from the firm that issued them, rather than from another investor. For this reason, unlike call options, the exercise of warrants increases the number of outstanding shares of a corporation and its capital, while diluting the equity of its shareholders. Warrants also trade on the regular stock exchanges and have much longer expiration dates than normal stock options.

A **swap** is an agreement between two parties to exchange a set of liabilities, like the obligation to pay a stream of future interest payments in a given currency and rate. For instance, in an interest rate swap, one party trades its fixed interest payments against the other party's payments at a rate that varies with a benchmark rate, like LIBOR. Swaps are brokered by intermediaries, and the terms of representative agreements are quoted in the over-the-counter market.

Last, some firms have issued instruments that are essentially a combination of a bond and a call option on a stock index. Most such instruments are traded in the over-the-counter market, but a couple of them trade on the TSX. We shall return to them in Chapter 18.

SUMMARY

1. Money market securities are very-short-term debt obligations. They are usually highly marketable and have relatively low credit risk. Their low maturities and low credit risk ensure minimal capital gains or losses. These securities trade in large denominations but may be purchased indirectly through money market funds.

2. Much of the Canadian government borrowing is in the form of Canada bonds. These are coupon-paying bonds usually issued at or near par value. Canada bonds are similar in design to coupon-paying corporate bonds. Provincial governments and Crown corporations also issue similar default-free coupon-paying bonds.

3. Mortgage pass-through securities are pools of mortgages sold in one package. Owners of pass-throughs receive all principal and interest payments made by the borrower. The originator that issued the mortgage merely services the mortgage, simply "passing through" the payments to the purchasers of the mortgage. The government guarantees the timely payment of interest and principal on mortgages pooled into these pass-through securities.

4. Common stock is an ownership share in a corporation. Each voting share entitles its owner to a vote on matters of corporate governance and to a prorated share of the dividends paid to shareholders. Restricted shares have a lower number of votes, or no right to vote. Stock, or equity, owners are the residual claimants on the income earned by the firm.

5. Preferred stock usually pays fixed dividends for the life of the firm; it is a perpetuity. A firm's failure to pay the dividend due on preferred stock, however, does not precipitate corporate bankruptcy. Instead, unpaid dividends simply cumulate. New varieties of preferred stock include convertible and variable-rate issues.

6. Many stock market indices measure the performance of the overall market in Canada and the United States. The Dow Jones Averages, the oldest and best-known indicators, are U.S. price-weighted indices. Today, many broad-based market value-weighted indices are computed daily. These include the main Canadian index, S&P/TSX Composite stock index, as well as the S&P/TSX 60, the U.S. Standard & Poor's 500 stock index, the NYSE and AMEX indices, the Nasdaq index, and the Wilshire 5000 index.

7. A call option is a right to purchase an asset at a stipulated exercise price on or before a maturity date. A put option is the right to sell an asset at some exercise price. Calls increase in value while puts decrease in value as the value of the underlying asset increases.

8. A futures contract is an obligation to buy or sell an asset at a stipulated futures price on a maturity date. The long position, which commits to purchasing, gains if the asset value increases, while the short position, which commits to delivering the asset, loses.

KEY EQUATIONS

$$(2.1) \quad r_{BEY} = \frac{1,000 - P}{P} \times \frac{365}{n}$$

$$(2.2) \quad P = 1,000/[1 + r_{BEY} \times (n/365)]$$

PROBLEMS

 **Practise and learn online with Connect.**

1. Why are money market securities sometimes referred to as "cash equivalents"?

2. The investment manager of a corporate pension fund has purchased a Treasury bill with 182 days to maturity at a price of $9,600 per $10,000 face value. The manager has computed the bank discount yield at 8 percent.
   a. Calculate the bond equivalent yield for the Treasury bill. Show your calculations.
   b. Briefly state two reasons why a Treasury bill's bond equivalent yield is always different from the discount yield.

3. A T-bill has a bank discount yield of 6.81 percent based on the ask price, and 6.90 percent based on the bid price. The maturity of the bill (already accounting for skip-day settlement) is 61 days. Find the bid and ask prices of the bill.

4. Reconsider the T-bill of problem 3. Calculate its bond equivalent yield and effective annual yield on the basis of the ask price. Confirm that these yields exceed the discount yield.

5. The bond equivalent yield of a 91-day T-bill is 5 percent. What is the price of the bill for a $10,000 face value?

6. a. Which security offers a higher effective annual yield?
      i. A three-month bill selling at $9,764
      ii. A six-month bill selling at $9,539
   b. Calculate the bank discount yield on each bill.

7. A U.S. Treasury bill with 90-day maturity sells at a bank discount yield of 3 percent.

   a. What is the price of the bill?

   b. What is the 90-day holding period return of the bill?

   c. What is the bond equivalent yield of the bill?

   d. What is the effective annual yield of the bill?

8. Find the price of a six-month (180-day) U.S. T-bill with a par value of $100,000 and a bank discount yield of 9.18 percent.

9. Find the after-tax return to a corporation that buys a share of preferred stock at $40, sells it at year-end at $40, and receives a $4 year-end dividend. The firm is in the 25 percent tax bracket.

10. Consider the following data for the three stocks that make up the market:

Stock	P_0	Q_0	P_1
A	$60	200	$70
B	$80	500	$70
C	$20	600	$25

   a. What is the single-period return on the price-weighted index constructed from the three stocks?

   b. What is the single-period return on the value-weighted index constructed from the three stocks using a divisor of 100?

   c. What is the single-period return on the price-weighted index constructed from the three stocks if stocks A and B were to split 2 for 1 and 4 for 1, respectively, after period 0?

   d. What is the single-period return on the value-weighted index constructed from the three stocks if stocks A and B were to split 2 for 1 and 4 for 1, respectively, after period 0?

11. Consider the three stocks in the following table. P_t represents price at time t, and Q_t represents shares outstanding at time t. Stock C splits two for one in the last period.

	P_0	Q_0	P_1	Q_1	P_2	Q_2
A	90	100	95	100	95	100
B	50	200	45	200	45	200
C	100	200	110	200	55	400

   a. Calculate the rate of return on a price-weighted index of the three stocks for the first period ($t = 0$ to $t = 1$).

   b. What must happen to the divisor for the price-weighted index in year 2?

   c. Calculate the price-weighted index for the second period ($t = 1$ to $t = 2$).

12. Using the data in problem 11, calculate the first period rates of return on the following indices of the three stocks:

   a. A market-value-weighted index

   b. An equally weighted index

13. Which of the following securities should sell at a greater price?

   a. A 10-year Canada bond with a 9 percent coupon rate versus a 10-year Canada bond with a 10 percent coupon rate

   b. A three-month maturity call option with an exercise price of $40 versus a three-month call on the same stock with an exercise price of $35

c. A put option on a stock selling at $50, or a put option on another stock selling at $60 (all other relevant features of the stocks and options may be assumed to be identical)

d. A three-month T-bill with a discount yield of 6.1 percent versus a three-month T-bill with a discount yield of 6.2 percent

14. In what ways is preferred stock like long-term debt? In what ways is it like equity?

15. Both a call and a put currently are traded on stock XYZ; both have strike prices of $50 and maturities of six months. What will be the profit to an investor who buys the call for $4 in the following stock price scenarios in six months?

a. $40

b. $45

c. $50

d. $55

e. $60

16. Why do call options with exercise prices greater than the price of the underlying stock sell for positive prices?

17. Explain the difference between a call option and a long position in a futures contract.

18. Explain the difference between a put option and a short position in a futures contract.

19. Examine the first 25 stocks listed in the stock market listings for TSX stocks in your local newspaper. For how many of these stocks is the 52-week high price at least 50 percent greater than the 52-week low price? What do you conclude about the volatility of prices on individual stocks?

20. What would you expect to happen to the spread between yields on commercial paper and Treasury bills if the economy were to enter a steep recession?

21. Turn to Figure 2.8 and find the options for Canadian Natural Resources. Suppose you buy a June call option with exercise price $24, and the stock price in June is $28.

a. Will you exercise your call? What are the profit and rate of return on your position?

b. What, if you had bought the call with exercise price $25 and the stock price turns out to be $24, would be your revised answers?

c. Suppose you had bought a June put with exercise price $24. What would be your answers, if the share price in June is $22?

22. Turn to Figure 2.5 and find the listing for Aecon Group.

a. What was the closing price for Aecon?

b. How many shares could you buy for $5,000?

c. What would be your annual dividend income from those shares?

d. What must be Aecon's earnings per share?

23. Turn to Figure 2.9 and find the S&P 60 future.

a. Suppose you buy one contract for March delivery. If the contract closes in March at a price of 720, what will your profit be?

b. How many March contracts are outstanding? (*Hint:* Use the Montréal Exchange Web site for help.)

The following problems are based on questions that have appeared in past CFA examinations.

24. A firm's preferred stock often sells at yields below its bonds because

a. Preferred stock generally carries a higher agency rating.

b. Owners of preferred stock have a prior claim on the firm's earnings.

c. Owners of preferred stock have a prior claim on a firm's assets in the event of liquidation.

d. Corporations owning stock may exclude from income taxes most of the dividend income they receive.

25. Which is the *most risky* transaction to undertake in the stock index option markets if the stock market is expected to increase substantially after the transaction is completed?

   a. Write a call option.
   b. Write a put option.
   c. Buy a call option.
   d. Buy a put option.

E-INVESTMENTS **Security Prices and Returns**	Go to **www.marketwatch.com**. What was the return on the S&P/TSX today? Chart its value over the last day and the last year. What is the current yield on 10-year-maturity treasury bonds? At what price is Alcan stock selling? Find the price of the nearest-to-maturity Alcan call option with exercise price equal to Alcan stock price rounded down to the nearest $5. What was the return on the following indices: Nikkei 225, FTSE 100, DAX? (*Hint:* Find the appropriate symbol for US$ and C$ listings.)

Trading on Securities Markets

The buying and selling of securities is, to the ordinary investor, a fairly simple procedure. A telephone call to the broker is all that is needed to place an order and cause a given number of shares or bonds to be traded. Behind the execution of that order, however, lies a complicated and efficient system; and even the statement of the order must follow one of a variety of forms, so that it will follow the investor's actual wishes. The creation or issuance of securities, and the subsequent exchange of them between investors, requires the participation of a large number of financial professionals, who are subject to precise regulations in their actions.

We examine in this chapter the institutional details and mechanics of making investments in securities. We see how firms issue securities in the primary market and then how investors trade in these securities in the secondary market. The secondary market is further specified, depending on the type and structure of the exchange where trading takes place. How the trading is handled varies with the type of exchange, but the details seen by the investor are similar. The cost of trading in securities is an important factor affecting returns, and it is related to the services provided to the investor. We explain the notion of trading using margin, in which security is provided for borrowed money or short sales. Finally, we present the subject of how securities markets are regulated by various bodies to protect the interests of investors by guaranteeing a degree of openness and fairness in trading.

HOW FIRMS ISSUE SECURITIES

Firms regularly need to raise new capital to help pay for their many investment projects. Broadly speaking, they can raise funds either by borrowing money or by selling shares in the firm. Investment bankers are generally hired to manage the sale of these securities in what is called a **primary market** for newly issued securities. Once these securities are issued, however, investors might well wish to trade them among themselves. For example, you may decide to raise cash by selling some of your shares in Bombardier Inc. to another investor. This transaction would have no impact on the total outstanding number of Bombardier shares. Trades in existing securities take place in the **secondary market**.

Shares of *publicly listed* firms trade continually on well-known markets such as the Toronto or New York stock exchanges. There, any investor can choose to buy shares for his or her portfolio. These companies are also called *publicly traded*, *publicly owned*, or just *public companies*. Other firms, however, are *private corporations*, whose shares are held by small numbers of managers and investors. While ownership stakes in the firm are still determined in proportion to share ownership, those shares do not trade on public exchanges. While many private firms are relatively young companies that have not yet chosen to make their shares generally available to the public, others may be more established firms that are still largely owned by the company's founders or families, and others may simply have decided that private organization is preferable.

Privately Held Firms

A privately held company is owned by a relatively small number of shareholders. Privately held firms have fewer obligations to release financial statements and other information to the public. This saves money and frees the firm from disclosing information that might be helpful to its competitors. Some firms also believe that eliminating requirements for quarterly earnings announcements gives them more flexibility to pursue long-term goals free of shareholder pressure.

At the moment, however, privately held firms may have only up to 499 shareholders. This limits their ability to raise large amounts of capital from a wide base of investors. Thus, almost all of the largest companies in Canada are public corporations.

When private firms wish to raise funds, they sell shares directly to a small number of institutional or wealthy investors in a **private placement**. Rule 144A of the SEC allows them to make these placements without preparing the extensive and costly registration statements required of a public company (similar exemptions exist provincially in Canada). While this is attractive, shares in privately held firms do not trade in secondary markets such as a stock exchange, and this greatly reduces their liquidity and presumably reduces the prices that investors will pay for them. *Liquidity* has many specific meanings, but generally speaking it refers to the ability to buy or sell an asset at a fair price on short notice. Investors demand price concessions to buy illiquid securities.

As firms increasingly chafe at the informational requirements of going public, federal regulators have come under pressure to loosen the constraints entailed by private ownership, and they are currently reconsidering some of the restrictions on private companies. They may raise beyond 499 the number of shareholders that private firms can have before they are required to disclose financial information, and they may make it easier to publicize share offerings.

Trading in private corporations also has evolved in recent years. To get around the 499-investor restriction, middlemen have formed partnerships to buy shares in private companies; the partnership counts as only one investor, even though many individuals may participate in it.

Very recently, some firms have set up computer networks to enable holders of private-company stock to trade among themselves. However, unlike the public stock markets regulated by the SEC, these networks require little disclosure of financial information and provide correspondingly little oversight of the operations of the market. For example, in the runup to its 2012 IPO,

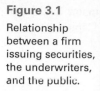

Figure 3.1

Relationship between a firm issuing securities, the underwriters, and the public.

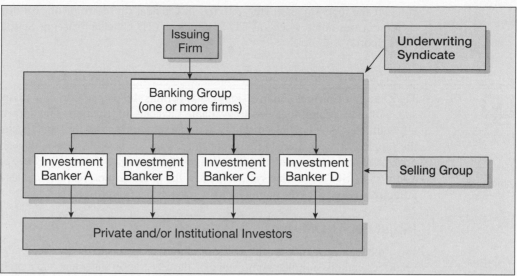

Facebook enjoyed huge valuations in these markets, but skeptics worried that investors in these markets could not obtain a clear view of the firm, the interest among other investors in the firm, or the process by which trades in the firm's shares were executed.

A **public offering** of stocks or bonds typically is marketed via an **underwriting** by investment bankers, often known in Canada as **investment dealers**. The major firms are subsidiaries of chartered banks such as Nesbitt Burns (BMO) or Scotia McLeod (Scotiabank). In fact, more than one investment dealer usually markets the securities. A lead firm forms an **underwriting syndicate** of other investment dealers to share the responsibility for the stock issue.

The bankers advise the firm regarding the terms, such as price and number of units, on which it should attempt to sell the securities. A preliminary registration statement describing the issue and the prospects of the company must be filed with the provincial securities commission in the provinces in which the securities will be offered for sale. When the statement is finalized and approved by the commission, it is called the **prospectus**. At this time, the price at which the securities will be offered to the public is announced.

In a typical underwriting arrangement the investment bankers purchase the securities from the issuing company and then resell them to the public. The issuing firm sells the securities to the underwriting syndicate for the public offering price less a spread that serves as compensation to the underwriters. This procedure is called a *firm commitment* (or *bought deal*). The underwriters receive the issue and assume the full risk that the shares cannot in fact be sold to the public at the stipulated offering price. Besides being compensated by the spread between the purchase price and the public offering price, the investment banker may receive shares of common stock or other securities of the firm. Figure 3.1 depicts the relationship between the firm issuing the security, the underwriting syndicate, and the public. By contrast, a *best efforts* agreement has the banker helping in the issue without risk of purchase.

Corporations engage investment bankers either by negotiation or by competitive bidding. Negotiation is more common. Besides being compensated by the spread between the purchase and public offering prices, an investment banker may receive shares of common stock or other securities of the firm. In the case of competitive bidding, a firm may announce its intent to issue securities and then invite investment bankers to submit bids for the underwriting. Such a bidding process may reduce the cost of the issue; however, it might also bring fewer services from the investment banker. The immensely profitable business of IPOs is prized by the companies that conduct the investment dealer activity. In Canada, these are primarily the major banks that own securities dealers such as TD Waterhouse (TD Canada Trust) or Scotia Capital (Bank of Nova Scotia).

Short Form Prospectus Distribution System (SFPDS)

Ontario Securities
Commission
www.osc.gov
.on.ca

The Ontario Securities Commission (OSC) permits the preparation of a prospectus for a new issue, with only minor additions to available financial information. This information, filed annually with the OSC, contains virtually all required information for a prospectus. The approval of the supplementary material requires only a few days instead of weeks, thus allowing the prompt placement of the issue with the underwriters; this is known as the *short form prospectus distribution system* (SFPDS).[1] This system reduces the underwriters' risk and makes bought deals more attractive. The sale to the public no longer requires a full prospectus.

Initial Public Offerings

Investment bankers manage the issuance of new securities to the public. Once the OSC (or other securities commission) has commented on the registration statement and a preliminary prospectus has been distributed to interested investors, the investment bankers organize road shows in which they travel around the country to publicize the imminent **initial public offering (IPO)**. These *road shows* serve two purposes. First, they attract potential investors and provide them information about the offering. Second, they collect for the issuing firm and its underwriters information about the price at which they will be able to market the securities. Large investors communicate their interest in purchasing shares of the IPO to the underwriters; these indications of interest are called a *book* and the process of polling potential investors is called *bookbuilding*. The book provides valuable information to the issuing firm because large institutional investors often will have useful insights about the market demand for the security as well as the prospects of the firm and its competitors. It is common for investment bankers to revise both their initial estimates of the offering price of a security and the number of shares offered based on feedback from the investing community.

Why would investors truthfully reveal their interest in an offering to the investment banker? Might they be better off expressing little interest in the hope that this will drive down the offering price? Truth is the better policy in this case because truth-telling is rewarded. Shares of IPOs are allocated to investors in part on the basis of the strength of each investor's expressed interest in the offering. If a firm wishes to get a large allocation when it is optimistic about the security, it needs to reveal its optimism. In turn, the underwriter needs to offer the security at a bargain price to these investors to induce them to participate in bookbuilding and share their information. Thus IPOs commonly are underpriced compared to the price at which they could be marketed. Such underpricing is reflected in price jumps on the date when the shares are first traded in public security markets. The IPO of Twitter Inc. incorporated is a recent example of such underpricing. The stock closed its first trading day on November 7, 2013 at $44.90 a share, up 73 percent from the initial public offering price of $26 set late on the previous day. This increase drove the seven-year-old company's value to $25 billion!

While the explicit costs of an IPO tend to be around 7 percent of the funds raised, such underpricing should be viewed as another cost of the issue. For example, if Twitter had sold its shares for the $44 that investors obviously were willing to pay for them, its IPO would have raised $1.6 billion more than it actually did. The money "left on the table" in this case far exceeded the explicit costs of the stock issue. Nevertheless, underpricing seems to be a universal phenomenon.

---

[1]The efficiency of the SFPD and the U.S. equivalent "shelf registration" have reduced the use of "rights" for secondary offerings since 1970; see Nancy D. Ursel and David J. Trepanier, "Securities Regulation Reform and the Decline of Rights Offerings," *Canadian Journal of Administrative Sciences* 18, no. 2 (June 2001), pp. 77–86.

Figure 3.2

Average initial returns for IPOs in various countries.

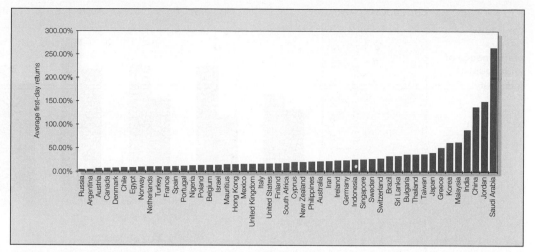

Source: Professor J. Ritter of the University of Florida, 2001. This is an updated version of the information contained in T. Loughran, J. Ritter, and K. Rydquist, "Initial Public Offerings," *Pacific-Basin Finance Journal* 2 (1994), pp. 165–99.

Figure 3.2 presents average first-day returns on IPOs of stocks across the world. The results consistently indicate that the IPOs are marketed to the investors at attractive prices. Underpricing of IPOs makes them appealing to all investors, yet institutional investors are allocated the bulk of a typical new issue. Some view this as unfair discrimination against small investors. However, our discussion suggests that the apparent discounts on IPOs may be no more than fair payments for a valuable service, specifically the information contributed by the institutional investors. The right to allocate shares in this way may contribute to efficiency by promoting the collection and dissemination of such information.[2]

Both views of IPO allocations probably contain some truth. IPO allocations to institutions do serve a valid economic purpose as an information-gathering tool. Nevertheless, the system can be—and has been—abused. Part of the Wall Street scandals of 2000–2002 centred on the allocation of shares in IPOs. Some investment bankers used IPO allocations to corporate insiders to curry favour, in effect as implicit kickback schemes. Underwriters apparently would award generous IPO allocations to executives of particular firms in return for the firm's future investment banking business. Pricing of IPOs is not trivial, and not all IPOs turn out to be underpriced. Some stocks do poorly after the initial issue and others cannot even be fully sold to the market. Underwriters left with unmarketable securities are forced to sell them at a loss on the secondary market. Therefore, the investment banker bears the price risk of an underwritten issue.

Interestingly, despite their dramatic initial investment performance, IPOs have been poor long-term investments. Figure 3.3 compares the stock price performance of IPOs with shares of other firms of the same size for each of the five years after issue of the IPO. The year-by-year underperformance of the IPOs is dramatic, suggesting that on average, the investing public may be too optimistic about the prospects of these firms. Such long-lived systematic errors on the part of investors would be surprising. An interesting study by Brav, Geczy, and Gompers,[3] however, suggests that apparent IPO underperformance may be illusory. When they carefully match firms on the basis of size and ratios of book values to market values, they find that IPO returns are actually similar to those of comparison firms.

---

[2]An elaboration of this point and a more complete discussion of the bookbuilding process is provided in Lawrence Benveniste and William Wilhelm, "Initial Public Offerings: Going by the Book," *Journal of Applied Corporate Finance* 9 (Spring 1997).

[3]Alon Brav, Christopher Geczy, and Paul A. Gompers, "Is the Abnormal Return Following Equity Issuances Anomalous?" *Journal of Financial Economics* 56 (2000), pp. 209–49.

Figure 3.3

Long-term relative performance of initial public offerings.

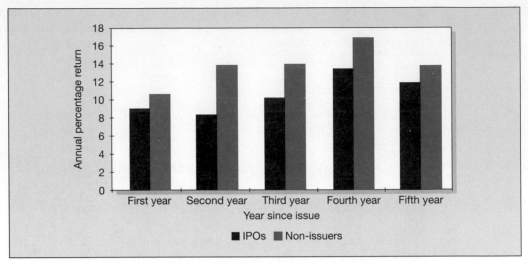

Source: Professor Jay R. Ritter, University of Florida, May 2005, http://bear.cba.ufl.edu/ritter/ipodata.htm. This is an updated version of the information contained in T. Loughran, J. Ritter, and K. Rydqvist, "Initial Public Offerings," *Pacific-Basin Journal* 2 (1994), pp. 165–199. Copyright 1994 with permission from Elsevier Science.

IPOs can be expensive, especially for small firms. In an attempt to gain their business, W. R. Hambrecht & Co. conducts IPOs on the Internet geared toward smaller, retail investors. Unlike typical investment bankers that tend to favour institutional investors in the allocation of shares and that determine an offer price through the bookbuilding process, Hambrecht conducts a "Dutch auction." In this procedure, which Hambrecht has dubbed "Open IPO," investors submit a price for a given number of shares. The bids are ranked in order of bid price, and shares are allocated to the highest bidders until the entire issue is absorbed.

To date, upstarts like Hambrecht have captured only a tiny share of the underwriting market. Their long-term prospects are still unclear. In fact, by 2004, most observers had written off the IPO auction model, when Google surprised the financial world by announcing that it would use such an auction in its multibillion-dollar IPO, assisted in part by Hambrecht. The mutual fund research company Morningstar also used Hambrecht to manage an IPO auction in 2005.

Canadian underwriters have faced increasing competition from U.S. investment bankers for large offerings. Yet evidence indicates that Canadian costs are lower than U.S. costs, for small firms especially.[4] A comprehensive examination of the price behaviour of Canadian IPOs was presented by Chung et al.,[5] while Jog and Wang[6] traced the evolution through the 1990s of IPO underpricing and its link to volatility, finding that the latter has increased while the former has not. Recent Canadian research has examined the IPO issue with regard to special factors. For instance, Boabang[7] investigated the pricing of *installment receipts*—share issues in which only a portion of the price is paid initially, and the remainder is paid on one or more later dates (in installments). He found that IPOs of this type had a significant level of underpricing, associated

---

[4]The relative cost structures are examined in M. Kooli and J.-M. Suret, "How Cost Effective Are Canadian IPO Markets?" *CIRANO Working Papers*, April 2002.

[5]R. Chung, L. Kryzanowski, and I. Rakita, "The Relationship Between Overallotment Options, Underwriting Fees and Price Stabilization for Canadian IPOs," *Multinational Finance Journal* 4, nos. 1–2 (June 2000).

[6]V. Jog and L. Wang, "Aftermarket Volatility and Underpricing of Canadian Initial Public Offerings," *Canadian Journal of Administrative Sciences* 19, no. 3 (September 2002), pp. 231–248.

[7]F. Boabang, "The IPOs of Canadian Firms via Installment Receipts: The Opening Performance and Implications for the Short-Run Efficiency of the Canadian Market," *Canadian Journal of Administrative Sciences* 20, no. 3 (September 2003).

with greater uncertainty about the underlying corporate value; the underpricing persisted throughout the first month of trading. Londerville[8] substantiated an earlier study showing evidence of underpricing of REITS using a Canadian sample from 1998.

3.2   TYPES OF MARKETS AND ORDERS

Once securities have been issued to the public, investors may trade among themselves. This occurs in markets that have evolved to meet the needs of investors; consider what would happen if the organized markets did not exist. Investors seeking to sell would have to find potential buyers. To avoid a buyers' market, there would need to be a meeting place, which also would serve buyers who did not want to be at the mercy of sellers. Hence buyers and sellers would meet and bargain for satisfactory prices, or agents would undertake to match potential buyers and sellers; ideally, competition among agents would drive down their fees. Eventually, the meeting place would evolve into a financial market, as was the case for a pub called Lloyd's in London and a Manhattan curb on Wall Street. Without this evolution of the secondary market, the costs of selling shares would be extremely detrimental to the purchase of shares in the primary market; so an efficient secondary market, which determines a fair and accurate price and allows the relatively quick and cheap transfer of shares, is crucial to the raising of investment capital by businesses.

Types of Markets

The markets that have evolved can be characterized as four types: direct search markets, brokered markets, dealer markets, and auction markets. The **direct search market** is what we have described above, where buyers and sellers must seek each other out directly. Such markets are characterized by sporadic participation and low-priced and nonstandard goods.

The next level of organization is a **brokered market**. If there is sufficient activity in trading a good, brokers can find it profitable to offer search services to buyers and sellers. Examples include the real estate market, as well as primary and secondary markets for security trading. Markets for large **block transactions** of shares have developed, since attempts to move them on the regular exchanges would cause major price movements; blocks are recorded as being "crossed" on the exchange by traders, who have located other large traders, even though the trade does not actually pass through the usual exchange process.

When trading activity in a particular type of asset increases, **dealer markets** arise. Here, dealers specialize in various commodities, purchase assets for their own accounts, and sell them for a profit from their inventory. The dealer's profit margin is the difference between the price at which the dealer buys for and sells from inventory. Dealer markets save traders on search costs because market participants are easily able to look up the prices at which they can buy from or sell to dealers. Obviously, a fair amount of market activity is required before dealing in a market is an attractive source of income. The over-the-counter securities market is one example of a dealer market.

The most integrated market is an **auction market**, in which all transactors in a good converge at one place to bid on or offer a good. The New York Stock Exchange (NYSE) is an example of an auction market, and so are all the major Canadian markets. An advantage of auction markets over dealer markets is that one need not search to find the best price for a good. If all participants converge, they can arrive at mutually agreeable prices and thus save the bid–asked spread. Notice that both over-the-counter dealer markets and stock exchanges are secondary markets. They are organized for investors to trade existing securities among themselves.

---

[8] J. Londerville, "Canadian Real Estate Investment Trusts: A Review of the IPO Literature and Preliminary Analysis of Canadian REIT IPO Pricing," *Canadian Journal of Administrative Sciences* 19, no. 4 (December 2002), pp. 359–368.

CC 1

CONCEPT CHECK

Many assets trade in more than one type of market. What types of markets do the following trade in?
a. Used cars
b. Paintings
c. Rare coins

Types of Orders

Market Orders   Market orders are buy or sell orders that are to be executed immediately at current market prices. For example, an investor might call his or her broker and ask for the market price of Goldcorp. The retail broker might reply that the current quotes are a **bid price** of $48 and an **ask price** of $48.20, and the investor might then direct the broker to buy 100 shares "at market," meaning he or she is willing to pay $48.20 per share for an immediate transaction. Similarly, an order to "sell at market" will result in stock sales at $48 per share.

There are two potential complications to this simple scenario, however. First, as noted earlier, the posted quotes of $48 and $48.20 actually represent commitments to trade up to a specified number of shares. If the market order is for more than this number of shares, the order may be filled at multiple prices. For example, if the asked price is good for orders of up to 600 shares, and the investor wishes to purchase 1,000 shares, it may be necessary to pay a slightly higher price for the last 400 shares than the quoted asked price.

The second complication arises from the possibility of trading "inside the quoted spread." If the broker who has received a market buy order for Goldcorp meets another broker who has received a market sell order for Goldcorp, they can agree to trade with each other at a price of $48.10 per share. By meeting in the middle of the quoted spread, both the buyer and the seller obtain "price improvement," that is, transaction prices better than the best quoted prices. Such "meetings" of brokers are more than accidental. Because all trading takes place at the specialist's post on the NYSE, floor brokers know where to look for counterparties to take the other side of a trade. One U.S. study[9] found that when the spread between the quoted bid and asked price was $.25 or greater, approximately one-half of trades on the NYSE were actually executed "inside the quotes."

Price-Contingent Orders   Investors also may place orders specifying prices at which they are willing to buy or sell a security. A limit buy order may instruct the broker to buy some number of shares if and when Goldcorp may be obtained *at or below* a stipulated price. Conversely, a limit sell instructs the broker to sell if and when the stock price rises above a specified limit. A collection of limit orders waiting to be executed is called a *limit order book*.

Figure 3.4 is an extract from the limit order book for shares in QSOLAR Ltd. (QSL) taken from the CNQ exchange (an electronic Canadian exchange now called the Canadian National Stock Exchange or CSNX). Orders are submitted to CNSX's platform via the Pure Trading system. The limit orders are ordered with the best orders first: the orders to buy at the highest price and to sell at the lowest price. The buy and sell orders at the top of the list—$.78 and $.80—are called the *inside quotes*. For QSOLAR Ltd., the inside spread is $.02. This is actually quite large as a percentage, but this is an illiquid stock, compared to large-cap companies trading on the TSX. Note, however, that the order sizes at the inside quotes are fairly small. Therefore, investors seeking larger trades view the effective spread as greater than the nominal spread; for example,

[9]K. Ross, J. Shapiro, and K. Smith, "Price Improvement of SuperDOT Market Orders on the NYSE," NYSE Working Paper 96-02, March 1996.

Figure 3.4   The limit order book for QSOLAR Ltd. (on the CNSX exchange, February 19, 2014).

Bid Broker	Bid Size	Bid Price	Ask Price	Ask Size	Ask Broker
MARKET BY ORDER—Price delayed at least 15 minutes					
National Bank Financial	2,000	0.780	0.800	2,000	RBC Dominion Securities Inc.
Leede Financial Markets Inc.	2,000	0.780	0.800	5,000	CIBC World Markets Inc.
Canaccord Genuity Corporation	1,000	0.750	0.810	10,000	National Bank Financial
Canaccord Genuity Corporation	17,000	0.700	0.830	6,500	Leede Financial Markets Inc.
Leede Financial Markets Inc.	5,000	0.660	0.850	1,000	RBC Dominion Securities Inc.
Canaccord Genuity Corporation	7,000	0.650	0.860	15,000	RBC Dominion Securities Inc.
National Bank Financial	2,000	0.650	0.930	20,000	Anonymous
Leede Financial Markets Inc.	5,000	0.630	0.940	19,500	TD Securities Inc.
Desjardins Securities	10,000	0.600	0.950	10,000	Anonymous
Questrade Inc.	500	0.600	0.950	2,000	Questrade Inc.

Source: Canadian Trading and Quotation System Inc., http://www.cnsx.ca.

to sell 17,000 shares, one would need to accept a price of $.70 for some, and to buy the same quantity the price would be $.83; for this quantity, the effective spread is $.13.

What happens if a limit order is placed between the quoted bid and ask prices? For example, suppose you have instructed your broker to buy Goldcorp at a price of $48.10 or better. The order may not be executed immediately, since the quoted asked price for the shares is $48.20, which is more than you are willing to pay. However, your willingness to buy at $48.10 is better than the quoted bid price of $48 per share. Therefore, you may find that there are traders who were unwilling to sell their shares at the $48 bid price but are happy to sell shares to you at your higher bid price of $48.10.

Stop-loss orders are similar to limit orders in that the trade is not to be executed unless the stock hits a price limit. In this case, however, the stock is to be sold if its price falls *below* a stipulated level. As the name suggests, the order lets the stock be sold to stop further losses from accumulating. Symmetrically, *stop-buy orders* specify that the stock should be bought when its price rises above a given limit. These trades often accompany short sales, and they are used to limit potential losses from the short position. (Short sales are discussed in greater detail in Section 3.5.) A stop-loss at $21.50 will be executed (a sale) if the price drops to $21.50; however, the sale may only realize $21.20 if that is the next limit-buy order. To prevent this a *stop limit* is needed; the arrival of the new low at $21.50 triggers a limit order to sell at $21.50. In this case, however, if the price immediately falls to $21, there is no sale. Figure 3.5 organizes the types of orders in a simple matrix.

Orders also can be limited by a time period. Day orders, for example, expire at the close of the trading day. If it is not executed on that day, the order is cancelled. *Open or good-till-cancelled orders*, in contrast, remain in force for up to six months unless cancelled by the customer. At the other extreme, *fill or kill orders* expire if the broker cannot fill them immediately.[10]

Trading Mechanisms

An investor who wishes to buy or sell shares will place an order with a brokerage firm. The broker charges a commission for arranging the trade on the client's behalf. Brokers have several

---

[10]For an analysis on how limit orders can lower the costs of trading, see Lorne N. Switzer and Haibo Fan, "Limit Orders, Trading Activity, and Transactions Costs in Equity Futures in an Electronic Trading Environment," *International Econometric Review* 2 (April 2010), pp. 1–25.

Figure 3.5

Limit orders.

	CONDITION		
ACTION	Price ≤ The limit	Price = The limit	Price ≥ The limit
Buy	Limit-buy order	Stop-limit (buy) order	Stop-buy order
Sell	Stop-loss order	Stop-limit (sell) order	Limit-sell order

avenues by which they can execute that trade, that is, find a buyer or seller and arrange for the shares to be exchanged.

In general, there are three types of trading systems for securities: over-the-counter dealer markets, electronic communication networks, and specialist markets. Well-known markets may use a variety of trading procedures, so it is essential to understand each form.

Dealer Markets   Dealer markets are commonly known as **over-the-counter (OTC) markets**. Several hundred issues are traded on the Canadian over-the-counter (OTC) market on a regular basis, and in fact any security may be traded there. The OTC market, however, is not a formal exchange; there are neither membership requirements for trading nor listing requirements for securities. In the OTC market, brokers registered with the provincial securities commission act as dealers in OTC securities. Security dealers quote prices at which they are willing to buy or sell securities. A broker can execute a trade by contacting a dealer listing an attractive quote. OTC trades do not require a centralized trading floor. Dealers can be located anywhere they can communicate effectively with other buyers and sellers.

The Canadian OTC market has developed similarly to that of the United States. Before 1971, all U.S. OTC quotations were recorded manually and published daily on so-called "pink sheets." In 1971, the National Association of Securities Dealers introduced its Automatic Quotations System, or **Nasdaq Stock Market** to link brokers and dealers in a computer network where price quotes could be displayed and revised. Dealers can use the network to display the bid price at which they are willing to purchase a security and the ask price at which they are willing to sell. The difference in these prices, the bid–asked spread, is the source of the dealer's profit. Brokers representing clients may examine quotes over the computer network, contact the dealer with the best quote, and execute a trade.

As originally organized, Nasdaq was more of a price-quotation system than a trading system. While brokers could survey bid and ask prices across the network of dealers in the search for the best trading opportunity, actual trades required direct negotiation (often over the phone) between the investor's broker and the dealer in the security. However, as we will see shortly, Nasdaq has progressed far beyond a pure price-quotation system. While dealers still post bid and ask prices over the network, Nasdaq now allows for electronic execution of trades at quoted prices without the need for direct negotiation, and the bulk of trades are executed electronically.

Electronic Communication Networks (ECNs)   **Electronic communication networks** are private computer networks that directly link buyers with sellers, and allow participants to post market and limit orders over computer networks. Since 2004, CNSX (originally CNQ) has offered an ECN for Canadian listings in competition with the TSX. The current CNSX display gives only the inside quotes for listings instead of the limit order book, yet its ten most active list includes iShares, Bombardier, and Manulife, indicating its growing business. CNSX claims that its "Trading Rules are designed to facilitate integrity, transparency, and efficiency." Orders that can be "crossed," that is, matched against another order, are crossed automatically without the intervention of a broker. For example, an order to buy a share at a price of $50 or lower will be immediately executed if there is an outstanding asked price of $50. Therefore, ECNs are true trading systems, not merely price-quotation systems.

ECNs offer several attractions. Direct crossing of trades without using a broker-dealer system eliminates the bid–asked spread that otherwise would be incurred. Instead, trades are automatically crossed at a modest cost, typically less than a penny per share. ECNs are attractive as well because of the speed with which a trade can be executed. Finally, these systems offer investors considerable anonymity in their trades.

Specialist Markets   In formal exchanges such as the Toronto Stock Exchange, trading in each security is managed by a **specialist** assigned responsibility for that security. Brokers who wish to buy or sell shares on behalf of their clients must bring the trade to the specialist's post on the floor of the exchange. The specialist may also be referred to as a "market-maker," since this aptly describes the function. While the NYSE uses "specialists," the Toronto Exchange calls them **registered traders**.

The Execution of Trades

The registered trader, who is the central figure in the execution of trades, makes a market in the shares of one or more firms. Part of this task is simply mechanical. It involves maintaining a "book" listing all outstanding unexecuted limit orders entered by brokers on behalf of clients. Actually, the book is now a computer console. When limit orders can be executed at market prices, the registered trader sees to the trade; in this role, he or she merely acts as a facilitator. As buy and sell orders at mutually agreeable prices cross the trading desk, the market-maker matches the two parties to the trade.

The registered trader is required to use the highest outstanding offered purchase price and lowest outstanding offered selling price when matching trades. Therefore, this system results in an auction market—all buy orders and all sell orders come to one location, and the best bids "win" the trades.

The more interesting function of the market-maker is to maintain a "fair and orderly market" by dealing personally in the stock. In return for the exclusive right to make the market in a specific stock on the exchange, the registered trader is required to maintain an orderly market by buying and selling shares from inventory. Registered traders maintain bid and asked prices, within a maximum spread specified by TSX regulations, at which they are obligated to meet at least a limited amount of market orders. If market buy orders come in, the registered traders must sell shares from their own accounts at the maintained asked price; if sell orders come in, they must be willing to buy at the listed bid price.

Ordinarily, in an active market registered traders can cross buy and sell orders without direct participation on their own accounts. That is, the trader's own inventory need not be the primary means of order execution. However, sometimes the market-maker's bid and asked prices will be better than those offered by any other market participant. Therefore, at any point, the effective asked price in the market is the lower of either the registered trader's offered asked price or the lowest of the unfilled limit-sell orders. Similarly, the effective bid price is the highest of unfilled limit-buy orders or the trader's bid. These procedures ensure that the registered trader provides liquidity to the market.

By standing ready to trade at quoted bid and asked prices, the market-maker is exposed somewhat to exploitation by other traders. Large traders with ready access to late-breaking news will trade with market-makers only if the latter's quoted prices are temporarily out of line with assessments based on the traders' (possibly superior) information. Registered traders who cannot match the information resources of large traders will be at a disadvantage when their quoted prices offer profit opportunities to better-informed traders.

You might wonder why market-makers do not protect their interests by setting a low bid price and a high asked price. A registered trader using that strategy would not suffer losses by maintaining a too-low asked price or a too-high bid price in a period of dramatic movements in the stock price. Traders who offer a narrow spread between the bid and the asked prices have little leeway for error and must constantly monitor market conditions to avoid offering other investors advantageous terms.

Large bid–asked spreads are not viable options for the specialist for two reasons. First, one source of the specialist's income is derived from frequent trading at the bid and asked prices, with the spread as the trading profit. A too-large spread would make the specialist's quotes noncompetitive with the limit orders placed by other traders. If the specialist's bid and asked quotes are consistently worse than those of public traders, it will not participate in any trades and will lose the ability to profit from the bid–asked spread.

An equally important reason that specialists cannot use large bid–asked spreads to protect their interests is that they are obligated to provide *price continuity* to the market. To illustrate the principle of price continuity, suppose that the highest limit-buy order for a stock is $30 while the lower limit-sell order is at $32. When a market buy order comes in, it is matched to the best limit-sell at $32. A market sell order would be matched to the best limit-buy at $30. As market buys and sells come to the floor randomly, the stock price would fluctuate between $30 and $32. The exchange would consider this excessive volatility, and the specialist would be expected to step in with bid and/or asked prices between these values to reduce the bid–asked spread to an acceptable level, typically less than $.05 for large firms.

Registered traders earn income both from commissions for acting as brokers for orders and from the spread between the bid and asked prices at which they buy and sell securities. It also appears that their "book" of limit orders gives them unique knowledge about the probable direction of price movement over short periods of time. For example, suppose the market-maker sees that a stock now selling for $45 has limit-buy orders for over 100,000 shares at prices ranging from $44.50 to $44.75. This latent buying demand provides a cushion of support, because it is unlikely that enough sell pressure could come in during the next few hours to cause the price to drop below $44.50. If there are very few limit-sell orders above $45, some transient buying demand could raise the price substantially. The trader in such circumstances realizes that a position in the stock offers little downside risk and substantial upside potential. Such unique access to the trading intentions of other market participants seems to allow a market-maker to earn substantial profits on personal transactions.

Specific regulations of the TSX govern the registered traders' ability to profit from their superior information and their responsibility to maintain an orderly market. Such a market should respond to changes in information affecting the value of the stock by adjusting the price without excessive fluctuations. The trader achieves this result by making *stabilizing* trades. As defined by the TSX, a stabilizing trade is one in which a purchase (sale) is made at a price lower (higher) than the last price on an *uptick* (*downtick*); an uptick is an upward move in the share price. Registered traders are required to make a minimum 70–30 superiority of stabilizing over destabilizing trades, where the latter is defined as the reverse of a stabilizing trade.[11]

---

[11] *Toronto Stock Exchange Members' Manual*, Division G, Part XIX, p. G19-3.

There are also **desk traders** who engage only in executing trades for clients by transmitting orders to the exchange. These are precluded from executing trades for their firms, although they may enter personal orders.

Settlement

Since June 1995, an order executed on the exchange must be settled within three working days. This requirement is often called *T + 3*, for "trade date plus three days." The purchaser must deliver the cash, and the seller must deliver the stock to his or her broker, who in turn delivers it to the buyer's broker. Transfer of the shares is made easier when the firm's clients keep their securities in **street name**, meaning that the broker holds the shares registered in the firm's own name on behalf of the client. This arrangement can speed security transfer. T + 3 settlement has made such arrangements more important: it can be quite difficult for a seller of a security to complete delivery to the purchaser within the three-day period if the stock is kept in a safety deposit box.

Settlement is simplified further by a clearinghouse. The trades of all exchange members are recorded each day, with members' transactions netted out, so that each member need only transfer or receive the net number of shares sold or bought that day. Each member settles only with the clearinghouse, instead of with each firm with whom trades were executed.

The Rise of Electronic Trading

When first established, Nasdaq was primarily an over-the-counter dealer market and the NYSE was a specialist market. But today both are primarily electronic markets.

These changes were driven by an interaction of new technologies and new regulations. New regulations allowed brokers to compete for business, broke the hold that dealers once had on information about best-available bid and ask prices, forced integration of markets, and allowed securities to trade in ever-smaller price increments (called *tick sizes*). Technology made it possible for traders to rapidly compare prices across markets and direct their trades to the markets with the best prices. The resulting competition drove down the cost of trade execution to a tiny fraction of its value just a few decades ago.

In 1975, fixed commissions on the NYSE were eliminated, which freed brokers to compete for business by lowering their fees. In that year also, Congress amended the *Securities Exchange Act* to create the National Market System to at least partially centralize trading across exchanges and enhance competition among different market-makers. The idea was to implement centralized reporting of transactions as well as a centralized price quotation system to give traders a broader view of trading opportunities across markets.

The aftermath of a 1994 scandal at Nasdaq turned out to be a major impetus in the further evolution and integration of markets. Nasdaq dealers were found to be colluding to maintain wide bid–asked spreads. For example, if a stock was listed at $30 bid–$30½ ask, a retail client who wished to buy shares from a dealer would pay $30½ while a client who wished to sell shares would receive only $30. The dealer would pocket the ½-point spread as profit. Other traders may have been willing to step in with better prices (e.g., they may have been willing to buy shares for $30⅛ or sell them for $30⅞), but those better quotes were not made available to the public, enabling dealers to profit from artificially wide spreads at the public's expense. When these practices came to light, an antitrust lawsuit was brought against Nasdaq.

In response to the scandal, the SEC instituted new order-handling rules. Published dealer quotes now had to reflect limit orders of customers, allowing them to effectively compete with dealers to capture trades. As part of the antitrust settlement, Nasdaq agreed to integrate quotes from ECNs into its public display, enabling the electronic exchanges to also compete for trades. Shortly after this settlement, the SEC adopted Regulation ATS (Alternative Trading Systems), giving ECNs the right to register as stock exchanges. Not surprisingly, they

Figure 3.6

The effective spread (measured in dollars per share) fell dramatically as the minimum tick size fell (value-weighted average of NYSE-listed shares).

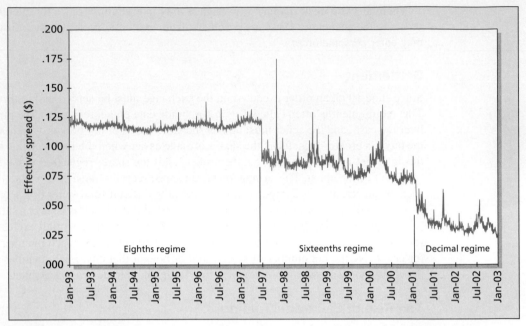

Source: Tarun Chordia, Richard Roll, and Avanidhar Subrahmanyam, "Liquidity and Market Efficiency, *Journal of Financial Economics* 87 (2008), 249–268. © February 2008, with permission from Elsevier.

captured an ever-larger market share, and in the wake of this new competition, bid–asked spreads narrowed.

Even more dramatic narrowing of trading costs came in 1997, when the SEC allowed the minimum tick size to fall from one-eighth of a dollar to one-sixteenth. Not long after, in 2001, "decimalization" allowed the tick size to fall to 1 cent. Bid–asked spreads again fell dramatically. Figure 3.6 shows estimates of the "effective spread" (the cost of a transaction) during three distinct time periods defined by the minimum tick size. Notice how dramatically effective spread falls along with the minimum tick size.

Technology was also changing trading practices. The first ECN, Instinet, was established in 1969. By the 1990s, exchanges around the world were rapidly adopting fully electronic trading systems. Europe led the way in this evolution, but eventually American exchanges followed suit. On April 23, 1997, the TSX's trading floor closed, making it the second-largest stock exchange in North America to choose a floorless, electronic (or virtual trading) environment. Canadian derivatives markets were soon to follow suit: on January 29, 2001, the Montréal Exchange completed its automation process with the transfer of stock options on SAM (Montreal Automated System). All derivatives were traded on SAM and the Trading Floor was closed. The results to date for Canada seem favourable: screen trading mitigates the extent of pricing errors in the markets, and decreases expected volatility.[12]

The National Association of Securities Dealers (NASD) spun off the Nasdaq Stock Market as a separate entity in 2000, which quickly evolved into a centralized limit-order matching system—effectively a large ECN. The NYSE acquired the electronic Archipelago Exchange in 2006 and renamed it NYSE Arca.

---

[12]For further details, see Lorne N. Switzer and Haibo Fan, "The Transactions Costs of Risk Management vs. Speculation in an Electronic Trading Environment: Evidence from the Montreal Exchange," *Journal of Trading* 2 (Fall 2007), pp. 82–100; Lorne N. Switzer and Haibo Fan, "Screen Based Trading, the Cost of Carry, and Futures Market Efficiency," *Risk and Decision Analysis* 1 (2009), pp. 57–71.

In 2005, the SEC adopted Regulation NMS or "Reg NMS" (for National Market System), which was fully implemented in 2007. The goal was to link exchanges electronically, creating in effect one integrated electronic market. The regulation required exchanges to honour quotes of other exchanges when they could be executed automatically. An exchange that could not handle a quote electronically would be labelled a "slow market" under Reg NMS and could be ignored by other market participants. The NYSE, which was still devoted to the specialist system, was particularly at risk of being passed over, and in response to this pressure, it moved aggressively toward automated execution of trades. Electronic trading networks and the integration of markets in the wake of Reg NMS made it much easier for exchanges around the world to compete; the NYSE lost its effective monopoly in the trading of its own listed stocks, and by the end of the decade, its share in the trading of NYSE-listed stocks fell from about 75 to 25 percent.

While specialists still exist, trading today is overwhelmingly electronic, at least for stocks. Bonds are still traded in more traditional dealer markets. In the United States, the share of electronic trading in equities rose from about 16 percent in 2000 to over 80 percent by the end of the decade. In the rest of the world, the dominance of electronic trading is even greater.

3.3 SECURITIES MARKETS

Montréal
Exchange
www.m-x.ca

Where previously there were five **stock exchanges** in Canada, the largest being in Toronto, Montreal, and Vancouver, there is now one major exchange for equities, the TSX, with the Canadian Derivatives Exchange (CDE) handling derivative securities. In 2000, the TSX became a for-profit organization rather than a mutual body of member firms. The major consolidation began in 1999 with the division of trading and listing of large firms on the TSX and small firms on the Canadian Venture Exchange or CDNX; stocks listed on the Montréal Exchange (ME) moved to the TSX, or to the CDNX if small. All trading in financial derivatives moved to the ME from Toronto and Vancouver. The CDNX was formed from the trading in small and regional issues in Vancouver, Alberta, and Winnipeg. In 2002, the Toronto Stock Exchange acquired the Canadian Venture Exchange, and renamed CDNX as the TSX Venture Exchange. In May 2008, the Montréal Exchange Inc. and TSX Group Inc. combined operations to create TMX Group Inc., a leading integrated exchange group. On October 30, 2012, a consortium of Canadian banks, pension funds, and investment firms known as the Maple Group Acquisition Corporation reached an agreement with TMX Group Inc. shareholders for the purchase of all outstanding TMX Group shares pursuant to an integrated two-step transaction valued at approximately $3.8 billion. The acquisition was completed on August 10, 2012. This is a case of a publicly listed firm going private!

Historically, an exchange provided a facility for its members to trade securities, with only members of the exchange allowed to trade there. Therefore memberships, or *seats*, on the exchange have been valuable assets. Brokerage firms are exchange members who own seats and advertise their willingness to execute trades for customers for a fee. The commissions that can be earned through this activity determine the market value of a seat. Hence, the price of a seat is taken as an indicator of the buoyancy of the market.

For instance, a seat on the New York Stock Exchange (NYSE), which sold for more than US$1 million prior to the October 1987 crash, was worth only US$625,000 by January 1988; in 2005 the price was $4 million. The highest price of a seat on the TSE was $370,000 in 1987, but by 1996 it had fallen to $52,000.

The Toronto Stock Exchange

Following its reorganization in 2000, the Toronto Stock Exchange has separated itself into the TSX, a platform for trading senior companies, and the Venture Exchange, for junior issues. In

2007, its parent, TSX Group, acquired the Montréal Exchange. Following the merger and other acquisitions, it is now called TMX Group.

Under its new structure, the TMX has no seats, only shares owned by participating organizations; these shares will sell at prices reflecting the buoyancy of the market. The realignment of the TMX is a consequence of the development of alternative trading systems (ATSs), particularly ECNs, by which traders can effect their investment decisions more efficiently or cheaply than under the traditional exchange-centred model. The TSX sees the NYSE, the Nasdaq, and the ATSs as its primary competition, and is trying to accommodate the ATSs within its new structure. Interlisting between exchanges exposes a stock to competition from both domestic and foreign equities, leading to greater efficiencies of pricing.[13] It may also cause trading to shift from the domestic to a foreign exchange if the trading time is comparable. In particular, sufficient interest in the United States will divert trading from Canadian exchanges if there is greater liquidity, or higher trading volume, that leads to tighter spreads.[14]

At the end of 2013, 1,525 companies were listed on the TSX, down marginally from the previous year. The total market capitalization of these companies exceeded $2 trillion. The value of trading of companies for 2013 on the TSX also exceeded $1.3 trillion. (See Table 3.1.)

The TSX is willing to list a stock (i.e., allow trading in that stock on the exchange) only if it meets certain criteria of size and stability. Table 3.2 gives the initial listing requirements of the TSX. Unlike the NYSE, the TSX has different requirements for the various kinds of companies. Besides industrials, the TSX also lists mining and energy companies; these are required to have both capital and either reserves of or potential for mineral production. These requirements ensure that a firm is of significant trading interest before the TSX will allocate facilities for it to be traded on the exchange. If a listed company suffers a decline and fails to meet the criteria in Table 3.2 (or those applicable), it may be "de-listed."

World Federation of Exchanges www.world-exchanges.org

The TSX Venture Exchange was taken over by the TSE in 2001 as a vehicle for trading in stocks that do not qualify for TSX listing. The exchange is described as being designed for "emerging" companies, with a focus on venture capital investment; two tiers are established for companies, corresponding to their stage of development. Both tiers have separate standards for five categories of firms: mining, oil and gas, technology or industrial, research and development, and real estate or investment. Requirements vary, but they cover such items as net tangible assets, property or reserves (O&G), prior expenditures (R&D), working capital, pretax earnings, share issues (distribution, market capitalization, and **float**), and availability of financial statements, with lighter requirements for second-tier companies. The Venture Exchange identifies two types of affiliates, "Member" brokerage firms and "Participating Organizations," the latter being defined as having trading access to the facilities of the Exchange.

Beyond the TSX Venture Exchange for true over-the-counter trading lie the NEX and the Canadian Unlisted Board (CUB—where dealers report their trading in unlisted securities). The TSX Venture Exchange, in fact, describes itself as an alternative exchange and not an OTC market. Technically, those stocks that previously traded on the Canadian Dealer Network (CDN) were moved to the TSX Venture Exchange at Tier 2 if qualified. Those that did not qualify were listed as Tier 3, now the NEX or the CUB, although the CUB is restricted to Ontario companies. All three tiers are cleared and settled through the Canadian Depository for Securities. It should be borne in mind that, often, stocks trading on the OTC market are subject to manipulation by some small brokerage houses and promoters.

---

[13]For a detailed explanation of the reorganization of the TSX, its strategies, and its trading systems, refer to their Web site at www.tsx.ca.
[14]For a discussion of the benefits of interlisting, see Usha Mittoo, "How Canadian Companies Win by Interlisting Shares on U.S. Exchanges," *Canadian Investment Review*, Winter 1993/1994. See also Lorne N. Switzer, "The Benefits and Costs of Listing Canadian Stocks in U.S. Markets," *Corporate Structure, Finance and Operations* 4 (1986), pp. 141–156, and John Doukas and Lorne N. Switzer, "Common Stock Returns and International Interlisting: Conditional Tests of the Mild Segmentation Hypothesis," *Journal of Banking and Finance* 24 (2000), pp. 471–502.

TABLE 3.1 The Top Ten Stock Exchanges in the World, December 2013

By Market Capitalization (in millions USD)

Exchange	End of Dec. 2012	End of Dec. 2013	% Change in USD	% Change in Local Currency
NYSE Euronext (US)	14,085,944.1	17,949,883.8	27.4%	27.4%
NASDAQ OMX	4,582,389.1	6,084,969.7	32.8%	32.8%
Japan Exchange Group—Tokyo	1,179,419.5	4,543,169.1	30.6%	58.7%
NYSE Euronext (Europe)	242,764.9	3,583,899.7	26.5%	21.1%
Hong Kong Exchanges	428,222.6	3,100,777.2	9.5%	9.5%
Shanghai SE	1,150,172.3	2,496,989.9	−2.0%	−4.7%
TMX Group	2,058,838.7	2,113,821.8	2.7%	9.6%
Deutsche Börse	59,182.0	1,936,106.3	30.3%	24.6%
SIX Swiss Exchange	161,855.5	1,540,699.8	24.9%	21.4%
Shenzhen SE	765,078.0	1,452,153.6	26.3%	22.7%

By Value of Trading (in millions USD)

Exchange	2012	2013	% Change in USD	% Change in Local Cur
NYSE Euronext (US)	13,442,719.6	13,700,450.5	1.9%	1.9%
NASDAQ OMX	9,784,206.2	9,584,742.2	−2.0%	−2.0%
Japan Exchange Group—Tokyo	1,517,896.9	6,304,927.5	82.1%	122.7%
Shenzhen SE	256,055.9	3,858,509.0	62.9%	58.5%
Shanghai SE	2,369,079.6	3,731,128.9	43.6%	39.8%
NYSE Euronext (Europe)	146,149.8	1,661,878.3	5.4%	2.4%
TMX Group	1,357,293.0	1,371,477.7	1.0%	4.5%
Deutsche Börse	17,855.7	1,334,544.9	4.6%	1.7%
Hong Kong Exchanges	94,585.7	1,323,373.3	19.6%	19.7%
Korea Exchange	526,162.7	1,284,599.3	−15.4%	−17.2%

Source: World Federation of Exchanges.

TABLE 3.2

Minimum Listing Requirements for the Toronto Stock Exchange (senior companies)

| | Financial Requirements | | |
	Industrials*	Mining	Oil and Gas
Pretax cash flow in last year	$700K	$700K	$700K
Earnings before taxes in last year	300K	Positive	Positive
Net tangible assets	7.5M	$7.5M	
Adequate working capital	✓	✓	
Sufficient capital funds	✓	✓	
Proven reserves	$7.5M		
	Public Distribution		
Market value of publicly held stock	$4M	$4M	$4M
Shares publicly held	1M	1M	1M
Number of holders of board lot or more	300	300	300

*Alternative, stricter requirements for technology companies.

Source: Toronto Stock Exchange.

The Bond Market

Although most common and preferred stocks are traded on the exchanges, bonds are not. Corporate and all federal, provincial, and municipal government bonds are traded only over the counter. Investors must submit orders to brokers who transmit these to, and obtain quotes from, the OTC market—a loosely organized network of dealers linked by a computer quotation system for a number of bellwether bonds. However, because these dealers do not carry extensive inventories of the wide range of bonds that have been issued to the public, they cannot necessarily offer to sell bonds from their inventory to clients or even buy bonds for their own inventory. They may instead work to locate an investor who wishes to take the opposite side of a trade. Candeal, operated by the TMX Group and the six largest Canadian banks, is the major electronic marketplace for fixed-income instruments. In 2005 it handled $148 billion of trading.

Markets depend ultimately on liquidity to establish themselves. If two markets compete and one has significantly greater liquidity, trading will migrate to that market, as the bid–asked spread will be lower. For that reason the United States has tended to dominate international bond markets. In recognition of the perversity that Asian issuers, both sovereign and corporate, must issue in the U.S. and then Asian investors with excess capital must buy these and other bonds through the U.S., there has been a recent initiative to develop an Asian bond market for issuance and trading. Yet the major impediment has been the inability to build a critical mass that brings liquidity. Likewise, Canadian issuers still use New York-based investment bankers, and send the underwriting profits there, because of the greater pool of investment capital, even though Canadian bonds trade OTC in Canada. The bond market in general is subject to liquidity risk, with difficulty in realizing quick sales of holdings. The corporate bond market, in particular, for both Canadian and U.S. bonds, is quite "thin," as few investors will be interested in trading any particular issue at a given time.

U.S. Markets

We have already sketched the three major trading mechanisms used in the United States: over-the-counter dealer markets, exchange trading managed by specialists, and direct trading among brokers or investors over electronic networks. The Nasdaq market is the most important dealer market in the United States, and the New York Stock Exchange is the most important formal equity exchange. As we will see, however, these markets have evolved in response to new information technology and both have dramatically increased their commitment to automated electronic trading.

Nasdaq
www.nasdaq.com

Nasdaq   The Nasdaq Stock Market lists about 3,000 firms. (Table 3.3 presents some of the requirements for a listing there.) It has steadily introduced ever-more-sophisticated trading platforms, which today handle the great majority of its trades. The current version, called the Nasdaq Market Center, consolidates Nasdaq's previous electronic markets into one integrated system. Nasdaq merged in 2008 with OMX, a Swedish-Finnish company that controls seven Nordic and Baltic stock exchanges to form Nasdaq OMX Group. In addition to maintaining the Nasdaq Stock Market, it also maintains several stock markets in Europe as well as an options and futures exchange in the United States.

Nasdaq has three levels of subscribers. The highest, level 3 subscribers, are registered market-makers—firms that make a market in securities, maintain inventories of securities, and post bid and ask prices at which they are willing to buy or sell shares. Level 3 subscribers can enter and change bid–asked quotes continually, and have the fastest execution of trades. They profit from the spread between bid and ask prices.

Level 2 subscribers receive all bid and ask quotes but cannot enter their own quotes. They can see which market-makers are offering the best prices. These subscribers tend to be brokerage firms that execute trades for clients but do not actively deal in stocks for their own account.

	Nasdaq National Market	Nasdaq Small Cap Market
Shareholders' equity	$15 million	$5 million
Shares in public hands	1.1 million	1 million
Market value of publicly traded shares	$8 million	$5 million
Minimum price of stock	$5	$4
Pretax income	$1 million	$750,000
Shareholders	400	300

Source: The Nasdaq Stock Market, www.nasdaq.com. © 2005, The Nasdaq Stock Market, Inc. Reprinted with permission.

Level 1 subscribers receive only inside quotes (i.e., the best bid and ask prices), but do not see how many shares are being offered. These subscribers tend to be investors who are not actively buying or selling but want information on current prices.

The New York Stock Exchange   The NYSE is the largest U.S. **stock exchange** as measured by the value of the stocks listed on the exchange. Daily trading volume on the NYSE is about a billion shares. In 2006 the NYSE merged with the Archipelago Exchange to form a publicly held company called the NYSE Group; then in 2007 it merged with the European exchange Euronext to form NYSE Euronext. The firm acquired the American Stock Exchange in 2008, since renamed NYSE Amex, which focuses on small firms. NYSE Arca is the firm's electronic communications network, where the bulk of exchange-traded funds trade.

Before 1976, the NYSE had long been committed to its specialist trading system, which in execution relied heavily on human participation. Then it began its transition to electronic trading for smaller trades with the introduction of its DOT (Designated Order Turnaround), and later Super-DOT systems, which could route orders directly to the specialist. In 2000, the exchange launched Direct+, which could automatically cross smaller trades (up to 1,099 shares) without human intervention, and in 2004, it began eliminating the size restrictions on Direct+ trades. The change of emphasis dramatically accelerated in 2006 with the introduction of the NYSE Hybrid Market, which allowed brokers to send orders either for immediate electronic execution or to the specialist, who could seek price improvement from another trader. The Hybrid system allowed the NYSE to qualify as a fast market for the purposes of Regulation NMS, but still offer the advantages of human intervention for more complicated trades. In contrast, NYSE's Arca marketplace is fully electronic.

ECNs   Over time, more fully automated markets have gained market share at the expense of less automated ones, in particular the NYSE. Some of the biggest ECNs today are Direct Edge, BATS, and NYSE Arca. Brokers with an affiliation with an ECN have computer access and can enter orders in the limit order book. As orders are received, the system determines whether there is a matching order, and if so the trade is immediately crossed.

Originally, ECNs were open only to other traders using the same system. But following the implementation of Reg NMS, ECNs began listing limit orders on other networks. Traders could use their computer systems to sift through the limit order books of many ECNs and instantaneously route orders to the market with the best prices. Those cross-market links have become the impetus for one of the more popular strategies of so-called high-frequency traders, which seek to profit from even small, transitory discrepancies in prices across markets. Speed is obviously of the essence here, and ECNs compete in terms of the speed they can offer. **Latency** refers to the time it takes to accept, process, and deliver a trading order. BATS, for example, advertises latency times of around 200 microseconds, that is, .0002 second.

New Trading Strategies

The marriage of electronic trading mechanisms with computer technology has had far-ranging impacts on trading strategies and tools. *Algorithmic trading* delegates trading decisions to computer programs. *High-frequency trading* is a special class of algorithmic trading in which computer programs initiate orders in tiny fractions of a second, far faster than any human could process the information driving the trade. Much of the market liquidity that once was provided by brokers making a market in a security has been displaced by these high-frequency traders. But when high-frequency traders abandon the market, as in the so-called flash crash of 2010, liquidity can likewise evaporate in a flash. *Dark pools* are trading venues that preserve anonymity, but also affect market liquidity. We will address these emerging issues later in this section.

Algorithmic Trading   **Algorithmic trading** is the use of computer programs to make trading decisions. Well more than half of all equity volume in the United States is believed to be initiated by computer algorithms. Many of these trades exploit very small discrepancies in security prices and entail numerous and rapid cross-market price comparisons well suited to computer analysis. These strategies would not have been feasible before decimalization of the minimum tick size.

Some algorithmic trades attempt to exploit very-short-term trends (as short as a few seconds) as new information about a firm becomes reflected in its stock price. Others use versions of *pairs trading* in which normal price relations between pairs (or larger groups) of stocks seem temporarily disrupted and offer small profit opportunities as they move back into alignment. Still others attempt to exploit discrepancies between stock prices and prices of stock-index futures contracts.

Some algorithmic trading involves activities akin to traditional market-making. The traders seek to profit from the bid–asked spread by buying a stock at the bid price and rapidly selling it at the ask price before the price can change. While this mimics the role of a market-maker who provides liquidity to other traders in the stock, these algorithmic traders are not registered market-makers and so do not have an affirmative obligation to maintain both bid and ask quotes. If they abandon a market during a period of turbulence, the shock to market liquidity can be disruptive. This seems to have been a problem during the flash crash of May 6, 2010, when the stock market encountered extreme volatility, with the Dow Jones average falling by 1,000 points before recovering around 600 points in intraday trading. The nearby box discusses this amazing and troubling episode.

High-Frequency Trading   It is easy to see that many algorithmic trading strategies require extremely rapid trade initiation and execution. **High-frequency trading** is a subset of algorithmic trading that relies on computer programs to make extremely rapid decisions. High-frequency traders compete for trades that offer very small profits. But if those opportunities are numerous enough, they can add up to big money.

We pointed out that one high-frequency strategy entails a sort of market-making, attempting to profit from the bid–asked spread. Another relies on cross-market arbitrage, in which even tiny price discrepancies across markets allow the firm to buy a security at one price and simultaneously sell it at a slightly higher price. The competitive advantage in these strategies lies with the firms that are quickest to identify and execute these profit opportunities. There is a tremendous premium on being the first to "hit" a bid or ask price.

Trade execution times for high-frequency traders are now measured in milliseconds, even microseconds. This has induced trading firms to "co-locate" their trading centres next to the computer systems of the electronic exchanges. When execution or latency periods are less than a millisecond, the extra time it takes for a trade order to travel from a remote location to a New York exchange would be enough to make it nearly impossible to win the trade.

At 2:42 New York time on May 6, 2010, the Dow Jones Industrial Average was already down about 300 points for the day. The market was demonstrating concerns about the European debt crisis, and nerves were already on edge. Then, in the next five minutes, the Dow dropped an *additional* 600 points. And only 20 minutes after that, it had recovered most of those 600 points. Besides the staggering intraday volatility of the broad market, trading in individual shares and ETFs was even more disrupted. The iShares Russell 1000 Value fund temporarily fell from $59 a share to 8 cents. Shares in the large consulting company Accenture, which had just sold for $38, traded at 1 cent only a minute or two later. At the other extreme, share prices of Apple and Hewlett-Packard momentarily increased to over $100,000. These markets were clearly broken.

The causes of the flash crash are still debated. An SEC report issued after the trade points to a $4 billion sale of market index futures contracts by a mutual fund. As market prices began to tumble, many algorithmic trading programs withdrew from the markets, and those that remained became net sellers, further pushing down equity prices. As more and more of these algorithmic traders shut down, liquidity in these markets evaporated: buyers for many stocks simply disappeared.

Finally, trading was halted for a short period. When it resumed, buyers decided to take advantage of many severely depressed stock prices, and the market rebounded almost as quickly as it had crashed. Given the intraday turbulence and the clearly distorted prices at which some trades had been executed, the NYSE and Nasdaq decided to cancel all trades that were executed more than 60 percent away from a "reference price" close to the opening price of the day. Almost 70 percent of those cancelled trades involved ETFs.

The SEC has since approved experimentation with new circuit breakers to halt trading for five minutes in large stocks that rise or fall by more than 10 percent in a five-minute period. The idea is to prevent trading algorithms from moving share prices quickly before human traders have a chance to determine whether those prices are moving in response to fundamental information.

The flash crash highlighted the fragility of markets in the face of huge variation in trading volume created by algorithmic traders. The potential for these high-frequency traders to withdraw from markets in periods of turbulence remains a concern, and many observers are not convinced that we are protected from future flash crashes.

To understand why co-location has become a key issue, consider this calculation. Even light can travel only 186 miles in one millisecond, so an order originating in Chicago transmitted at the speed of light would take almost five milliseconds to reach New York. But ECNs today claim latency periods considerably less than one millisecond, so an order from Chicago could not possibly compete with one launched from a co-located facility.

In some ways, co-location is a new version of an old phenomenon. Think about why, even before the advent of the telephone, so many brokerage firms originally located their headquarters in New York: they were "co-locating" with the NYSE so that their brokers could bring trades to the exchange quickly and efficiently. Today, trades are transmitted electronically, but competition among traders for fast execution means that the need to be near the market (now embodied in computer servers) remains.

Dark Pools Many large traders seek anonymity. They fear that if others see them executing a large buy or sell program, their intentions will become public and prices will move against them. Very large trades (called **blocks**, usually defined as trades of more than 10,000 shares) traditionally were brought to "block houses," brokerage firms specializing in matching block buyers and sellers. Part of the expertise of block houses is in identifying traders who might be interested in a large purchase or sale if given an offer. These brokers discreetly arrange large trades out of the public eye, and so avoid moving prices against their clients.

Block trading today has been displaced to a great extent by **dark pools**, trading systems in which participants can buy or sell large blocks of securities without showing their hand. Not only are buyers and sellers in dark pools hidden from the public; trades may not even be reported. Or if they are, they may be lumped with others to obscure information about the participants.

Dark pools are somewhat controversial, because they contribute to the fragmentation of markets. When many orders are removed from the consolidated limit order book, fewer orders are left to absorb fluctuations in demand for the security, and the public price may no longer be "fair" in the sense of reflecting all the potentially available information about security demand.

Another approach to dealing with large trades is to split them into many small ones, each of which can be executed on electronic markets, attempting to hide the fact that the total number of shares ultimately to be bought or sold is large. This trend has led to rapid decline in average trade size, which today is less than 300 shares.

CC 2

CONCEPT CHECK

In August 1999, a seat on the NYSE sold for a then-record $2.65 million. But prices then entered a steep descent, and in January 2005, a seat sold for as little as $.975 million, before dramatically surging in price later that year in response to the merger agreement with Archipelago. What factors might have contributed to the decline? Consider the impact of ECNs, decimalization of security prices, and the stock market decline of the early 2000s.

Foreign Markets

An important development in trading is the cross-listing of major corporations on exchanges around the world. In particular, listing on the London, Euronext, and Tokyo stock exchanges permits traders to trade virtually at any hour of the day, if so inclined. In fact, the Frankfurt Exchange has an active market in major U.S. corporations prior to the New York opening. This has implications for valuation, as news can be received and traded upon immediately, leading to more pricing efficiency.

The structure of security markets varies considerably from one country to another. A full cross-country comparison is far beyond the scope of this text. Instead we briefly review three of the biggest non-U.S. stock markets: the London, Euronext, and Tokyo exchanges.

London   The London Stock Exchange uses an electronic clearing system dubbed SETS (Stock Exchange Electronic Trading Service) for trading in large, liquid securities. This is an electronic clearing system similar to ECNs in which buy and sell orders are submitted via computer networks, and any buy and sell orders that can be crossed are executed automatically. Less-liquid shares are traded in a more traditional dealer market called the SEAQ (Stock Exchange Automated Quotations) system, in which market-makers enter bid and ask prices at which they are willing to transact.

Euronext   Euronext was formed in 2000 by a merger of the Paris, Amsterdam, and Brussels exchanges. Euronext, like most European exchanges, uses an electronic trading system. Its system, called NSC (for Nouveau Système de Cotation, or New Quotation System), has fully automated order routing and execution. In fact, investors can enter their orders directly without contacting their brokers. An order submitted to the system is executed immediately if it can be crossed against an order in the public limit-order book; if it cannot be executed, it is entered into the limit-order book.

Euronext is in the process of establishing cross-trading agreements with several other European exchanges such as Helsinki or Luxembourg. In 2001, it also purchased LIFFE, the London International Financial Futures and Options Exchange.

Tokyo   The Tokyo Stock Exchange (TSE) is among the largest in the world, measured by either trading volume or the market capitalization of its roughly 2,400 listed firms. It exemplifies many of the general trends that we have seen affecting stock markets throughout the world. In 1999, it closed its trading floor and switched to all-electronic trading. It switched from a membership form of organization to a corporate form in 2001.

The TSE maintains three "sections." The "First" section is for large companies, the "Second" for mid-sized firms, and the "Mothers" for emerging and high-growth stocks. About three-quarters of all listed firms trade on the First section, and about 200 trade in the Mothers section.

The two major stock market indices for the TSE are the Nikkei 225 index, which is a price-weighted average of the 225 top-tier Japanese firms, and the TOPIX index, which is a value-weighted index of the First-section companies.

Consolidation of Stock Markets   All stock markets have come under increasing pressure in recent years to make international alliances or mergers. Much of this pressure is due to the impact of electronic trading. To a growing extent, traders view stock markets as computer networks that link them to other traders, and there are increasingly fewer limits on the securities around the world that they can trade. Against this background, it becomes more important for exchanges to provide the cheapest and most efficient mechanism by which trades can be executed and cleared. This argues for global alliances that can facilitate the nuts and bolts of cross-border trading and can benefit from economies of scale. Moreover, in the face of competition from electronic networks, established exchanges feel that they eventually need to offer 24-hour global markets and platforms that allow trading of different security types, for example both stocks and derivatives. Finally, companies want to be able to go beyond national borders when they wish to raise capital.

These pressures have resulted in a broad trend toward market consolidation. In the past decade, most of the mergers were relatively "local," that is, involving exchanges operating in the same continent. In the United States, the NYSE merged with Archipelago ECN, and in 2008 it announced a deal to acquire the American Stock Exchange. Nasdaq acquired Instinet (which operated the other major ECN, INET) in 2005 and the Boston Stock Exchange in 2007; in the derivatives market, the Chicago Mercantile Exchange (CME) acquired the Chicago Board of Trade. In 2008, the New York Mercantile Exchange (NYMEX) agreed to be acquired by the CME, with full consolidation of NYMEX trading under the CME occurring in January 2010. As noted above, Euronext was formed similarly.

More recently, the trend has been to intercontinental mergers. In 2007, Euronext and the NYSE Group merged into a new company called NYSE Euronext. Germany's Deutsche Börse and the NYSE Euronext agreed to merge in late 2011. The merged firm would be able to support trading in virtually every type of investment. Although in early 2012 the proposed merger ran aground when European Union antitrust regulators recommended that the combination be blocked, the merger attempt indicates the thrust of market pressures, and other combinations continue to develop. The NYSE and the Tokyo stock exchange have announced their intention to link their networks to give customers of each access to both markets. In 2007, the Nasdaq stock market merged with OMX, which operates seven Nordic and Baltic stock exchanges, to form NASDAQ OMX Group. In 2008, Eurex took over International Securities Exchange (ISE), to form a major options exchange.

Derivatives Markets

ICE Futures U.S.
www.theice.com

Markets also exist in Canada for trading in options and futures. Unlike stocks, for which the primary markets exist to raise capital for the issuing firms, derivatives are created as contracts between investors; therefore, there is only a secondary market for them. Commodity futures for agricultural products are traded on the Winnipeg Commodity Exchange; options and financial futures trade on the Canadian Derivatives Exchange or the Montréal Exchange. In addition, a number of options and futures trade on U.S. or foreign exchanges. The world's largest equity options exchange is operated by the ISE. Because of the complexity of these derivatives, our discussion of these markets is given in Chapters 18 to 20. The mechanics of trading in derivatives are similar to those of stock trading, but there are far more complicated strategies.

3.4   ## TRADING COSTS

Part of the cost of trading is the explicit payment to the broker of a commission. The size of this commission depends mostly on the choice between a full-service or discount broker. *Full-service brokers* provide a variety of services. Besides carrying out the basic services of executing orders, holding securities for safekeeping, extending margin loans, and facilitating short sales, normally they also provide information and advice relating to investment alternatives. Full-service brokers usually are supported by a research staff that issues analyses and forecasts of general economic, industry, and company conditions and often makes specific buy or sell recommendations. Some customers take the ultimate leap of faith and allow a full-service broker to make buy and sell decisions for them by establishing a **discretionary account**.[15] In this account, the broker can buy and sell prespecified securities whenever this is deemed appropriate. This step requires an unusual degree of trust on the part of the customer, because an unscrupulous broker can "churn" an account, that is, trade securities excessively in order to generate commissions.

Discount brokers are able to charge much lower commissions by providing "no frills" services; they restrict their services to execution of orders, holding securities for safekeeping, offering margin loans, and facilitating short sales. They provide the basic information of price quotations about indices and individual securities. The more comprehensive discounters also will offer analytical services of online company research and software for an additional fee, these being provided by outside firms, and the opportunity to participate in IPOs.

In recent years, discount brokerage services have become increasingly available, offered by both mutual fund management companies and chartered banks. With the chartered banks having bought up most of the independent full-service banks as well, we have banks such as the Royal Bank offering both full-service and discount brokerage subsidiaries to customers in an attempt to provide a full range of financial services. Customers are able to deposit cash with their banks, transfer it to pay for securities, and have interest and dividends either transferred back to their bank accounts or deposited in money market funds.

With discount brokers offering trades as low as $10 compared to the $100–$300 commission charged by the full-service brokers, the latter are losing a lot of customers. Faced with this competition, full-service brokers have turned to converting commission-based accounts into managed accounts that are fee-based, known as *wrap accounts*. Annual fees typically are 2.5 to 3.5 percent of assets managed.

In addition to the explicit cost of commissions, there is an implicit cost deriving primarily from the **bid–asked spread**. If the broker for a trade is actually the dealer in the security, instead of a commission, the fee for purchase or sale will come entirely in the form of the bid–asked spread. With the dramatic reduction in commissions, the execution cost of the spread has become a far more significant component of trading costs. Another implicit cost of trading that some observers would distinguish is the price concession an investor may be forced to make for trading in any quantity that exceeds the quantity the dealer is willing to trade at the posted bid or asked price.

An ongoing controversy is the extent to which better execution on a traditional market such as the NYSE offsets the generally lower explicit costs of trading in other markets. Execution refers to the size of the effective bid–asked spread and the amount of price impact in a market. The NYSE believes that many investors focus too intently on the costs they can see, despite the fact that quality of execution can be a far more important determinant of total costs. Many trades on the NYSE are executed at a price inside the quoted spread. This can happen because floor brokers at the specialist's post can bid above or sell below the specialist's quote. In this way, two public orders cross without incurring the specialist's spread. This trading at a price between the bid and asked prices is known as "price improvement."

---

[15]Certain individuals, such as politicians, are often required to place their investment assets in blind trusts that are managed in discretionary accounts.

In contrast, in a dealer market such as Nasdaq, all trades go through the dealer, and all trades, therefore, are subject to a bid–asked spread. The client never sees the spread as an explicit cost, however. The price at which the trade is executed incorporates the dealer's spread, but this part of the trading cost is never reported to the investor.

Internet Investing

Almost any kind of information on investments can be found on the Internet. This includes analysts' recommendations, financial statements, an assortment of charts, and economic projections; these are available either free or for a stated charge. Much of the information is distributed freely by financial news providers and by brokers, while more can be downloaded in conjunction with a brokerage account from the online brokers' sites; typically the latter may be free in limited quantities, with additional amounts earned by trading. Services provide an opportunity to record one's portfolio and have its value updated daily.

The trading itself is conducted by establishing an online account with the major brokers (usually their discount operations) or with a variety of cut-rate brokers offering trades for less than $10 (in U.S. dollars, as that is where the great majority of these services operate). With a secure connection and a password, trading in stocks, options, and futures is limited only by the traffic. (This latter qualification may be significant, but access to human voices may also be difficult at times of heavy volume.) Orders may be entered during trading hours or after, for execution upon opening; they may be limit or market orders. Essentially, for an experienced trader there is only one difference in trading online from what has been experienced in using a broker: the cost of trading is much lower.

Pre-market and post-market trading on ECNs is also handled through the Internet. Unfortunately, the lack of integration and the current thinness of trading leads to poor execution of orders; prices are quite volatile and often not representative of the actual market.

3.5 TRADING WITH MARGIN

The concept of *margin* refers to the need for investors to provide security whenever they engage in a transaction in which the asset value of their accounts can fall beneath the value of the liabilities they have incurred. In this event, they—and failing them, their brokers—would be liable to pay the shortfall. This possibility arises if investors purchase shares without having the full purchase price available or if they short-sell shares or derivative securities.

Buying on Margin

Investors who purchase stocks on margin borrow part of the purchase price of the stock from their brokers. The **margin** in the account is the portion of the purchase price contributed by the investor. The brokers in turn borrow money from banks using *brokers' call loans* at the call money rate to finance these purchases, then charge their clients that rate plus a service charge for the loan. All securities purchased on margin must be left with the brokerage firm in street name, because the securities are used as collateral for the loan.

The regulators of the various exchanges set limits on the extent to which stock purchases can be financed via margin loans. Currently, the margin is 30 percent for the most marginable stocks, meaning that, at most, 70 percent of the purchase price may be borrowed; however, this margin rises to as much as 100 percent on low-price stocks. Brokers are likely to require a higher margin to open a margin position so as to avoid an immediate drop in value below 30 percent. In the United States, the initial margin requirement is 50 percent, with a 30 percent minimum level. The *percentage margin* is defined as the ratio of the net worth, or *equity value* of the account, to the market value of the securities.

EXAMPLE 3.1   Margin

Suppose that the investor initially pays $6,000 toward the purchase of $10,000 worth of stock (100 shares at $100 per share), borrowing the remaining $4,000 from the broker. The account will have a balance sheet as follows:

Assets		Liabilities and Owner's Equity	
Value of stock	$10,000	Loan from broker	$4,000
		Equity	$6,000

The initial percentage margin is

$$\text{Margin ratio} = \frac{\text{Equity}}{\text{Market value of assets}} = \frac{\text{Market value of assets} - \text{Loan}}{\text{Market value of assets}} \tag{3.1}$$

$$= \frac{\$10,000 - \$4,000}{\$10,000} = .6 = 60\%$$

If the stock's price declines to $70 per share, the account balance becomes:

Assets		Liabilities and Owner's Equity	
Value of stock	$7,000	Loan from broker	$4,000
		equity	$3,000

The equity in the account falls by the full decrease in the stock value, and the percentage margin is now

$$\text{Margin ratio} = \frac{\text{Equity}}{\text{Value of stock}} = \frac{\$3,000}{\$7,000} = .43, \text{ or } 43\%$$

If the stock value were to fall below $4,000, equity would become negative, meaning that the value of the stock is no longer sufficient collateral to cover the loan from the broker. To guard against this possibility, the margin must be maintained above the limit of 30 percent. If the percentage margin falls below this level, the broker will issue a *margin call*, requiring the investor to add new cash or securities to the margin account. If the investor does not act, the broker may sell the securities from the account to pay off enough of the loan to restore the percentage margin to an acceptable level.

Margin calls can occur with little warning. For example, on October 25, 2000, when the TSE index fell by 8.3 percent, the accounts of many investors who had purchased stock with borrowed funds fell afoul of their minimum margin requirements. Some brokerage houses, concerned about the incredible volatility in the market and the possibility that stock prices would fall below the point that remaining shares could cover the amount of the loan, gave their customers only a few hours or less to meet a margin call rather than the more typical notice of a few days. If customers could not come up with the cash, or were not at a phone to receive the notification of the margin call until later in the day, their accounts were sold out. In other cases, brokerage houses sold out accounts without notifying their customers.

EXAMPLE 3.2   **Minimum Margin Level and Margin Calls**

What price decrease could the investor survive without getting a margin call, given a 30 percent minimum?

Let P be the price of the stock. The value of the investor's 100 shares is then $100P$, and the equity in his or her account is $100P - \$4,000$. The percentage margin is therefore $(100P - \$4,000)/100P$. The price at which the percentage margin equals the minimum margin of .3 is found by solving the equation

$$\frac{100P - \$4,000}{100P} = .3$$

$$100P - \$4,000 = 30P$$

for

$$P = \$57.14$$

If the price of the stock were to fall below \$57.14 per share, the investor would get a margin call.

CC 3

CONCEPT CHECK

If the minimum margin in the above example were 40 percent, how far could the stock price fall before the investor would get a margin call?

Why do investors buy stock (or bonds) on margin? They do so when they wish to invest an amount greater than their own money alone would allow. Thus they can achieve greater upside potential, but they also expose themselves to greater downside risk.

EXAMPLE 3.3   **Using Margin for Leverage**

Let us suppose that an investor is bullish (optimistic) on SNC stock, which is currently selling at \$100 per share. The investor has \$10,000 to invest and expects SNC stock to go up in price by 30 percent during the next year. Ignoring any dividends, the expected rate of return would thus be 30 percent if the investor spent only \$10,000 to buy 100 shares.

But now let us assume that the investor also borrows another \$10,000 from the broker and invests it in SNC also. The total investment in SNC would thus be \$20,000 (for 200 shares). Assuming an interest rate on the margin loan of 9 percent per year, what will be the investor's rate of return now (again ignoring dividends) if SNC's stock does go up 30 percent by year's end?

The 200 shares will be worth \$26,000. Paying off \$10,900 of principal and interest on the margin loan leaves \$15,100 (\$26,000 − \$10,900). The rate of return therefore will be

$$\frac{\$15,100 - \$10,000}{\$10,000} = 51\%$$

The investor has parlayed a 30 percent rise in the stock's price into a 51 percent rate of return on the \$10,000 investment.

continued

Doing so, however, magnifies the downside risk. Suppose that instead of going up by 30 percent the price of SNC stock goes down by 30 percent to $70 per share. In that case, the 200 shares will be worth $14,000, and the investor is left with $3,100 after paying off the $10,900 of principal and interest on the loan. The result is a disastrous rate of return:

$$\frac{\$3,100 - \$10,000}{\$10,000} = -69\%$$

CC 4

CONCEPT CHECK

Suppose that in the previous example the investor borrows only $5,000 at the same interest rate of 9 percent per year. What will be the rate of return if the price of SNC stock goes up by 30 percent? If it goes down by 30 percent? If it remains unchanged?

Short Sales

In contrast to a purchase followed by a sale of stock, an investor can sell first and buy later, using a **short sale**, which allows investors to profit from a decline in a security's price. An investor borrows a share of stock from a broker and sells it. Later, the short-seller must purchase a share of the same stock in the market to replace the share that was borrowed. This is called *covering the short position*. Table 3.4 compares stock purchases to short sales.

The short-seller anticipates the stock price will fall, so that the share can be purchased at a lower price than it initially sold for; the short-seller will then reap a profit. Short-sellers must not only replace the shares but also pay the lender of the security any dividends paid during the short sale. See nearby box for a discussion on the market effects of short selling.

In practice, the shares loaned out for a short sale are typically provided by the short-seller's brokerage firm, which holds a wide variety of securities in street name. The owner of the shares will not even know that the shares have been lent to the short-seller. If the owner

TABLE 3.4

Cash Flows from Purchasing Versus Short Selling Shares of Stock

Time	Action	Cash Flow*
Purchase of Stock		
0	Buy share	− Initial price
1	Receive dividend, sell share	Ending price + Dividend
Profit = (Ending price + Dividend) − Initial price		
Short Sale of Stock		
0	Borrow share; sell it	+ Initial price
1	Repay dividend and buy share to replace the share originally borrowed	− (Ending price + Dividend)
Profit = Initial price − (Ending price + Dividend)		

*A negative cash flow implies a cash outflow.

Short selling has long been viewed with suspicion, if not outright hostility. England banned short sales for a good part of the eighteenth century. Napoleon called short-sellers enemies of the state. In the United States, short selling was widely viewed as contributing to the market crash of 1929, and in 2008, short-sellers were blamed for the collapse of the investment banks Bear Stearns and Lehman Brothers. With share prices of other financial firms collapsing in September 2008, the SEC instituted a temporary ban on short selling about 800 of those firms. Similarly, the Financial Services Authority, the financial regulator in the United Kingdom, prohibited short sales on about 30 financial companies, and Australia banned "shorting" altogether.

The motivation for these bans is that short sales put downward pressure on share prices that in some cases may be unwarranted: tales abound of investors who first put on a short sale and then spread negative rumours about the firm to drive down its price. More often, however, shorting is an innocent bet that a share price is too high and ripe to fall; despite this, during the market stresses of late 2008, the widespread feeling was that even so, regulators should do what they could to prop up the affected institutions.

Hostility to short selling may well stem from confusion between bad news and the bearer of that news. Shorting allows investors whose analysis indicates a firm is over-priced to take action on that belief—and to profit if they are correct. Rather than *causing* the stock price to fall, shorts may simply be *anticipating* a decline in the stock price. Their sales simply force the market to reflect the deteriorating prospects of troubled firms sooner than it might have otherwise. In other words, short selling is part of the process by which the full range of information and opinion—pessimistic as well as optimistic—is brought to bear on stock prices.

For example, short-sellers took large (negative) positions in firms such as WorldCom, Enron, and Tyco even before these firms were exposed by regulators. In fact, one might argue that these emerging short positions helped regulators identify the previously undetected scandals. And in the end, Lehman and Bear Stearns were brought down by their very real losses on their mortgage-related investments—not by unfounded rumours.

Academic research supports the conjecture that short sales contribute to efficient "price discovery." For example, the greater the demand for shorting a stock, the lower its future returns tend to be; moreover, firms that attack short-sellers with threats of legal action or bad publicity tend to have especially poor future returns.* Short sale bans may in the end be nothing more than an understandable, but nevertheless misguided, impulse to "shoot the messenger."[16]

*See, for example, C. Jones and O. A. Lamont, "Short Sale Constraints and Stock Returns," *Journal of Financial Economics*, November 2002, pp. 207–39; or O. A. Lamont, "Go Down Fighting: Short Sellers vs. Firms," Yale ICF Working Paper No. 04-20, July 2004.

wishes to sell the shares, the brokerage firm will simply borrow shares from another investor. Therefore, the short sale may have an indefinite term. However, if the brokerage firm cannot locate new shares to replace the ones sold, the short-seller will need to repay the loan immediately by purchasing shares in the market and turning them over to the brokerage firm to close out the loan.

Exchange rules permit short sales only when the last recorded change in the stock price is positive, that is, after an *uptick*. This rule apparently is meant to prevent waves of speculation against the stock. In other words, the votes of "no confidence" in the stock that short sales represent may be entered only after a price increase.

Finally, exchange rules require that proceeds from a short sale be kept on account with the broker. The short-seller, therefore, cannot invest these funds to generate income. However, large or institutional investors typically will receive some income from the proceeds of a short sale being held with the broker. In addition, short-sellers are required to post margin (which is essentially collateral) with the broker to ensure that the trader can cover any losses sustained should the stock price rise during the period of the short sale.[17]

[16]See for example Jonathan Karpoff and Xiaoxia Lu, "Short Selling and Financial Misconduct," *Journal of Finance* 65 (2010), pp. 1879–1913.
[17]We should note that although we have been describing a short sale of a stock, bonds also may be sold short.

EXAMPLE 3.4   Short Sales

To illustrate the actual mechanics of short selling, suppose that you are bearish (pessimistic) on SNC stock, and that its current market price is $50 per share. You tell your broker to sell short 1,000 shares. The broker borrows 2,000 shares either from another customer's account or from another broker.

The $100,000 cash proceeds from the short sale are credited to your account. Suppose the broker has a 50 percent margin requirement on short sales. This means that you must have other cash or securities in your account worth at least $50,000 that can serve as margin (i.e., collateral) on the sale. Let us suppose that you have $50,000 in Treasury bills. Your account with the broker after the short sale will then be:

Assets		Liabilities and Owner's Equity	
Cash	$100,000	Short position in SNC stock	$100,000
T-bills	$ 50,000	(1,000 shares owed)	
		Equity	$ 50,000

The 50 percent margin satisfies the requirement that your credit balance be at least 150 percent of the market value of borrowed stock, so that the margin ratio is the market value of assets in the account, $150,000, divided by the current value of the borrowed shares,

$$\text{Margin ratio} = \frac{\text{Market value of assets}}{\text{Value of stock owed}}$$

$$\frac{\$150,000}{\$100,000} = 150\%$$

(3.2)

If you are right, and SNC stock falls to $35 per share, you can close out your position at a profit. To cover the short sale, you buy 2,000 shares to replace the borrowed shares for $70,000. Because your account was credited by $100,000 at the time of the sale, your profit is $30,000, which is the decline in share price times the number of shares sold short.

On the other hand, if the price of SNC rises while you are short, you may get a margin call. Using the minimum margin requirement of 30 percent for short sales, the equity in your account must be at least 30 percent of the value of your short position at all times. How far can the price of SNC rise before you get a margin call?

Let P be the price of the stock; then the value of the shares you must repay is $2,000P$, and the asset value in your account is $150,000. The critical value of P for a margin ratio of 130 percent is

$$\frac{\text{Market value of assets}}{\text{Value of stock owed}} = \frac{\$150,000}{2,000P} = 1.3$$

or

$$P = \$57.69 \text{ per share}$$

If SNC stock should rise above $57.69 per share, you will get a margin call and you will have to either put up additional cash or cover your short position.

You can see now why stop-buy orders often accompany short sales. You short-sold SNC at $50 per share. If the share price falls, you will profit from the short sale. On the other hand, if the share price rises, let's say to $65, you will lose $15 per share. But suppose that when you initiate the short sale, you also enter a stop-buy order at $60. The stop-buy will be executed if the share price surpasses $60, limiting your losses to $10 per share. (If the stock price drops, the stop-buy will never be executed.) The stop-buy order thus provides protection to the short-seller if the share price moves up.

CC 5

CONCEPT CHECK

a. If the short-position minimum margin in the preceding example were 40 percent, how far could the stock price rise before the investor would get a margin call?

b. Construct the balance sheet if SNC goes up to $55.

3.6 **REGULATION OF SECURITIES MARKETS**

Trading in securities markets in Canada is regulated under a number of laws. Laws such as the federal *Canada Business Corporations Act* govern the conduct of business firms, while the various provincial securities acts regulate the trading of securities. Most legislation is at the provincial level, even though historically the first Canadian laws concerning securities were introduced at the federal level in the late nineteenth century. Provincial legislation in the Maritime provinces followed shortly thereafter, while the *Ontario Companies Act* was established in 1907. The *Ontario Securities Act*, Canada's first provincial securities act, was passed in 1945, and has been revised repeatedly since that time. Other provinces generally have tended to follow Ontario's lead. Although the federal government doesn't have a securities act, portions of the Criminal Code of Canada are specifically directed to securities trading.

In addition to the laws, there also is considerable self-regulation in the financial services industry. It takes place via regulations governing membership in various associations of professionals participating in the industry. Thus, the Investment Dealers Association of Canada encompasses stock exchange members and bond dealers, while the Mutual Fund Dealers Association is the association of Canadian mutual funds. Trading on the TSX is regulated by Market Regulation Services Inc.

The Investment Dealers Association and the stock exchanges have established the Canadian Investor Protection Fund (CIPF) to protect investors from losses if their brokerage firms fail. Just as the Canada Deposit Insurance Corporation provides federal protection to depositors against bank failure, the CIPF ensures that investors will receive the value of their accounts up to a maximum of $1 million. Securities held for their account in street name by the failed brokerage firm and cash balances will be replaced by equivalent securities, or by their cash value. The CIPF is financed by levying an "insurance premium" on its participating, or member, brokerage firms.

Provincial securities legislation exists in all Canadian provinces and territories, but not all have provincial securities commissions, which are responsible for administering and enforcing the provincial securities laws. In other cases, this responsibility is exercised within the justice departments. The key purpose of these laws is to protect investors from fraud. They achieve this by controlling (through registration) the people participating in the financial services industry and by ensuring that investors have all material facts at their disposal in order to make their own investment decisions. The approval, however, by a securities commission of a prospectus or financial report does not mean that it views the security as a good investment. The commission cares only that the relevant facts are disclosed; investors make their own evaluations of the security's value.

Relevant facts are revealed for prospective investors when a primary issue takes place, through the prospectus. Investors also must be kept informed, on a continuous basis, about all important changes to a company's status, such as changes in the control structure of the corporation, acquisitions or disposals of major assets, and proposed takeovers or mergers. Companies also must issue several financial reports on a quarterly basis and more complete reports annually.

Several problems are created by the fragmentation along provincial lines of the regulatory system for Canadian securities markets. Differences in provincial laws are an immediate cause, although the CSA (Canadian Securities Administrators) are taking steps to harmonize the legislation. Financial transactions in markets may involve parties residing in different provinces; for instance, a group of Ontario investors might purchase the shares of a Quebec company, traded on the TSX.

Such a transaction would fall under the jurisdiction of two provinces' regulatory bodies, implying that it should simultaneously comply with the Quebec and Ontario regulatory regimes. Apart from the fact that this may create multiple (and costly) investigations of the same transaction, it also would generate uncertainty among the investors about the set of rules governing their investment.

Securities and
Exchange
Commission
www.sec.gov

Such problems are avoided in the United States, where the securities industry is regulated by national agencies. The most important of these is the Securities and Exchange Commission (SEC), established by the 1934 *Securities Exchange Act*, to ensure the full disclosure of relevant information relating to the issue of new securities and the periodic release of financial information for secondary trading. The act also empowered the SEC to register and regulate securities exchanges, OTC trading, brokers, and dealers. It thus established the SEC as the administrative agency responsible for broad oversight of the securities markets. The SEC, however, shares oversight with other regulatory bodies. For example, the Commodity Futures Trading Commission (CFTC) regulates trading in futures markets, whereas the Federal Reserve Bank ("the Fed") has broad responsibility for the health of the U.S. financial system. In this role, the Fed sets margin requirements on stocks and stock options and regulates bank lending to the securities markets' participants. On the other hand, exchanges are delegated extensive self-regulatory functions by the SEC. The NYSE and NASD are attempting to merge parts of their regulatory arms into a single agency, so as to reduce costs of redundant and overlapping regulation.

Regulatory Responses to Recent Scandals and the 2008–09 Financial Crisis

The scandals of 2000–2002 centred largely on three broad practices: allocations of shares in initial public offerings, tainted securities research and recommendations put out to the public, and, probably most important, misleading financial statements and accounting practices. The regulatory response to these issues was captured rapidly by the *Sarbanes-Oxley Act (SOX)* of Congress passed in 2002. This act has been extremely controversial, with international ramifications, including Canadian firms listed in the United States;[18] business has found its demands highly expensive to satisfy. In Canada a more reflective response has resulted in three sets of rules which were enacted as Bill 198, and effective as of December 2005:

- The first set of rules enacted by Canadian regulators requires CEO/CFO certification of annual and quarterly reports. Canadian companies will also have to adopt disclosure controls and procedures with regard to financial reporting. The proposed national instrument for Canada is very similar to Section 302 of *Sarbanes-Oxley*, in both form and implementation.

- The second set of rules establishes new standards and an expanded role for the audit committee. Major Canadian public companies will be required to have fully independent and financially literate audit committees.

- The third set of rules relates to internal controls. Companies are now required to perform detailed tests of all their internal accounting processes, and their external auditors will have to examine and give an opinion on those tests. In addition, a new accounting supervision body, the Canadian Public Accountability Board, has been established.

In the wake of what has been labelled by the International Monetary Fund as "the largest financial shock since the Great Depression," policymakers in the United States responded to widespread calls for regulatory reform to address perceived supervisory deficiencies with the

---

[18] See for example Lorne Switzer and Hui Lin, "Corporate Governance, Compliance, and Valuation Effects of *Sarbanes Oxley* on U.S. and Foreign Firms," *International Journal of Business Governance and Ethics* 4 (2009), pp. 400–426 (with Hui Lin). The recent debate on the onerous costs of compliance with the *Sarbanes-Oxley Act* (SOX) has primarily focused on small firms. Lorne Switzer looks at the effects of SOX compliance on Canadian small firms and shows possible benefits of SOX in the form of increased accountability of managers to act in shareholders' interest outweigh the costs of increased disclosure and compliance. See Lorne Switzer, "Corporate Governance, *Sarbanes-Oxley*, and Small-Cap Firm Performance," *Quarterly Review of Economics and Finance* 47 (2007), pp. 651–666.

I. Professionalism

- *Knowledge of law.* Members must understand, have knowledge of, and comply with all applicable laws, rules, and regulations including the Code of Ethics and Standards of Professional Conduct.
- *Independence and objectivity.* Members shall maintain independence and objectivity in their professional activities.
- *Misrepresentation.* Members must not knowingly misrepresent investment analysis, recommendations, or other professional activities.

II. Integrity of Capital Markets

- *Non-public information.* Members must not exploit material non-public information.
- *Market manipulation.* Members shall not attempt to distort prices or trading volume with the intent to mislead market participants.

III. Duties to Clients

- *Loyalty, prudence, and care.* Members must place their clients' interests before their own and act with reasonable care on their behalf.
- *Fair dealing.* Members shall deal fairly and objectively with clients when making investment recommendations or taking actions.
- *Suitability.* Members shall make a reasonable inquiry into a client's financial situation, investment experience, and investment objectives prior to making appropriate investment recommendations.
- *Performance presentation.* Members shall attempt to ensure that investment performance is presented fairly, accurately, and completely.
- *Confidentiality.* Members must keep information about clients confidential unless the client permits disclosure.

IV. Duties to Employers

- *Loyalty.* Members must act for the benefit of their employer.
- *Compensation.* Members must not accept compensation from sources that would create a conflict of interest with their employer's interests without written consent from all involved parties.
- *Supervisors.* Members must make reasonable efforts to detect and prevent violation of applicable laws and regulations by anyone subject to their supervision.

V. Investment Analysis and Recommendations

- *Diligence.* Members must exercise diligence and have reasonable basis for investment analysis, recommendations, or actions.
- *Communication.* Members must distinguish fact from opinion in their presentation of analysis and disclose general principles of investment processes used in analysis.

VI. Conflicts of Interest

- *Disclosure of conflicts.* Members must disclose all matters that reasonably could be expected to impair their objectivity or interfere with their other duties.
- *Priority of transactions.* Transactions for clients and employers must have priority over transactions for the benefit of a member.

VII. Responsibilities as Member of CFA Institute

- *Conduct.* Members must not engage in conduct that compromises the reputation or integrity of the CFA Institute or CFA designation.

Dodd-Frank Wall Street Reform and Consumer Protection Act (Dodd-Frank). Dodd-Frank incorporates 235 rule-making projects involving 16 regulatory agencies represents the largest regulatory mandate since the Great Depression. From the earliest proposals outlining what would eventually become *Dodd-Frank*, opponents have argued that the proposed regulation would involve an overly burdensome cost of compliance, and would harm the competitiveness of U.S. financial firms relative to their foreign counterparts.

Since the implementation of *Dodd-Frank* is an ongoing process, research on the market reaction to that act's specific regulatory impact is ongoing.[19]

---

[19]See Lorne Switzer, Qianyin Shan, and Jean-Michel Sahut, "The Impact of Derivatives Regulations on the Liquidity and Pricing Efficiency of Exchange Traded Derivatives," *Review of Futures Markets* 21, March 2013, pp. 71–103; and Lorne Switzer and Easton Sheahan-Lee, "The Impact of Dodd-Frank Regulation of OTC Derivative Markets on International Versus US Banks: New Evidence," working paper.

Self-Regulation and Circuit Breakers

Much of the securities industry relies on self-regulation, which is conducted by bodies known as self-regulatory organizations (SROs). These comprise the various exchanges and the Investment Dealers Association (IDA) representing the member firms. The policies of the IDA are intended to foster efficient markets by encouraging participation and ensuring integrity of the marketplace and protection of investors. The Canadian Securities Institute (CSI) serves these SROs (and others) by providing educational programs. Among these programs are the Conduct and Professional Handbook (CPH) Course, which presents to students the regulations as well as ethical and professional responsibilities regarding dealing with investors. In addition, the CFA Institute has developed standards of professional conduct for members with the Chartered Financial Analyst designation (see the boxed article for an outline of those principles).

The collapse of markets around the world in October 1987 prompted a number of responses, starting with mechanisms to prevent panic selling exacerbated by program trading. "Circuit breakers" were instituted to close temporarily the markets when drastic losses occur as well as to limit extreme movements in either direction during periods of high volatility. These were imposed directly on the NYSE, but other exchanges have often chosen to key their regulations to the NYSE practice. Failing this, trading might easily move from the NYSE to other exchanges for products that might be expected to move in direct correlation with NYSE securities, as well as for securities actually traded on other exchanges. On the other hand, markets outside the United States might choose to observe more relaxed rules that would entice program trading away from the NYSE.

The NYSE response is keyed to the level of the Dow Jones Industrial Average (DJIA), with circuit breaker thresholds for trading halts, based on 10, 20, and 30 percent of the DJIA of the previous month, and rounded to the nearest 50 points; these levels are reset every quarter. (For example, as of January 2, 2004 the triggering DJIA drops at each level were 1,000, 2,000, and 3,050 points.)

These are implemented as follows: If the Dow Jones Industrial Average falls by 10 percent, trading will be halted for one hour if the drop occurs before 2:00 p.m. (Eastern Standard Time), for one half-hour if the drop occurs between 2:00 and 2:30, but not at all if the drop occurs after 2:30. If the Dow falls by 20 percent, trading will be halted for two hours if the drop occurs before 1:00 p.m., for one hour if the drop occurs between 1:00 and 2:00, and for the rest of the day if the drop occurs after 2:00. A 30 percent drop in the Dow would close the market for the rest of the day, regardless of the time.

For the TSX, Market Regulation Services Inc. determines the circuit breaker mechanism in conjunction with the thresholds announced by the New York Stock Exchange. The TSX responds to the same levels 1, 2, and 3 above by imposing corresponding halts to trading as defined for the NYSE.

The idea behind circuit breakers is that a temporary halt in trading during periods of very high volatility can mitigate informational problems that might contribute to excessive price swings. For example, even if a trader is unaware of any specific adverse economic news, if she sees the market plummeting, she will suspect that there might be a good reason for the price drop and will become unwilling to buy shares. In fact, the trader might decide to sell shares to avoid losses. Thus, feedback from price swings to trading behaviour can exacerbate market movements. Circuit breakers give participants a chance to assess market fundamentals while prices are temporarily frozen. In this way, they have a chance to decide whether price movements are warranted while the market is closed.

Insider Trading

One of the important restrictions on trading involves *insider trading*. It is illegal for anyone to transact in securities to profit from **inside information**, that is, private information held by officers, directors, or major stockholders that has not yet been divulged to the public. The difficulty is that the definition of *insiders* can be ambiguous. Although it is obvious that the chief financial officer of a firm is an insider, it is less clear whether the firm's biggest supplier can be considered an insider. However, the supplier may deduce the firm's near-term prospects from significant changes in orders. This gives the supplier a unique form of private information, yet the supplier does not necessarily qualify as an insider. These ambiguities plague security analysts, whose job is to uncover as much information as possible concerning the firm's expected prospects. The distinction between legal private information and illegal inside information can be fuzzy.

The OSC requires officers, directors, and major shareholders of all publicly held firms to report all of their transactions in their firm's stock within ten days of the occurrence of the transaction. A compendium of insider trades is published monthly in the OSC's insider trading bulletin, extracts of which are published promptly by *The Globe and Mail*. The idea is to inform the public of any implicit votes of confidence or no confidence made by insiders.

Do insiders exploit their knowledge? The answer seems to be: Yes, to a limited degree. Although the recent case of the celebrity Martha Stewart is better known, in 1988 the Premier of British Columbia was reported to have gained from inside information on Doman Industries; in both cases, the parties sold holdings prior to the release of adverse news. More formal evidence also supports this conclusion. First, there is massive evidence of "leakage" of useful information to some traders *before* any public announcement of that information. For example, share prices of firms announcing dividend increases (which the market interprets as good news concerning the firm's prospects) commonly increase in value a few days before the public announcement of the increase.[20] Clearly, some investors are acting on the good news before it is released to the public. Similarly, share prices tend to increase a few days before the public announcement of above-trend earnings growth.[21] At the same time, share prices still rise substantially on the day of the public release of good news, indicating that insiders, or their associates, have not fully bid up the price of the stock to the level commensurate with that news.

The second sort of evidence on insider trading is based on returns earned on trades by insiders. Researchers have examined the SEC's summary of insider trading to measure the performance of insiders. Muelbroek[22] investigated the contention by previous researchers that insider trading actually improves market efficiency by accelerating the price adjustment process, through the examination of SEC information on illegal trading activity. She found there to be no doubt that insider trading causes significant price adjustment to occur in advance of the public release of information and gave some support to the view that this "victimless crime" is actually beneficial. A Canadian study by Baesel and Stein[23] investigated the abnormal return on stocks over the months following purchases or sales by insiders. They found that a simulated policy of buying a portfolio of stocks purchased by insiders yielded an abnormal return in the following eight months of about 3.8 percent. If the insiders were also directors of Canadian banks (presumed to be even better informed), the abnormal return persisted for 12 months and rose to 7.8 percent. In both cases, the major part of the gain occurred after publication of the insiders' actions. Insider sales, however, did not generate information leading to abnormal gains.

---

[20]See, for example, J. Aharony and I. Swary, "Quarterly Dividend and Earnings Announcement and Stockholders' Return: An Empirical Analysis," *Journal of Finance* 35 (March 1980).

[21]See, for example, George Foster, Chris Olsen, and Terry Shevlin, "Earnings Releases, Anomalies, and the Behavior of Security Returns," *The Accounting Review*, October 1984.

[22]Lisa K. Muelbroek, "An Empirical Analysis of Illegal Insider Trading," *The Journal of Finance* 47, no. 5 (December 1992), pp. 1661–1699.

[23]Jerome Baesel and Garry Stein, "The Value of Information: Inferences from the Profitability of Insider Trading," *Journal of Financial and Quantitative Analysis*, September 1979. See also Jean-Marc Suret and Elise Cormier, "Insiders and the Stock Market," *Canadian Investment Review* 3, no. 2 (Fall 1990).

SUMMARY

1. Firms issue securities to raise the capital necessary to finance their investments. Investment bankers market these securities to the public on the primary market. Investment bankers generally act as underwriters who purchase the securities from the firm and resell them to the public at a markup. Before the securities may be sold to the public, the firm must publish a securities commission-approved prospectus that provides information on the firm's prospects.

2. Issued securities are traded on organized stock exchanges, on the over-the-counter market, and, for large traders, through direct negotiation. Only members of exchanges may trade on the exchange. Brokerage firms holding seats on the exchange sell their services to individuals, charging commissions for executing trades on their behalf. The TSX has fairly strict listing requirements; the TSX Venture Exchange is much less restrictive, being designed for firms who do not meet the requirements of the TSX.

3. Trading may take place in dealer markets, via electronic communication networks, or in specialist markets. In dealer markets, security dealers post bid and ask prices at which they are willing to trade. Brokers for individuals execute trades at the best available prices. In electronic markets, the existing book of limit orders provides the terms at which trades can be executed. Mutually agreeable offers to buy or sell securities are automatically crossed by the computer system operating the market. In specialist markets, the registered trader or market-maker acts to maintain an orderly market with price continuity. Registered traders maintain a limit order book, but also sell from or buy for their own inventories of stock. Thus, liquidity in specialist markets comes from both the limit order book and the registered trader's inventory.

4. Block transactions are a fast-growing segment of the securities market, which currently accounts for about one-half of trading volume. These trades often are too large to be handled readily by regular market-makers, and thus block houses have developed that specialize in these transactions, identifying potential trading partners for their clients.

5. Total trading costs consist of commissions, the dealer's bid–asked spread, and price concessions. These costs can represent as much as 30 percent of the value of the securities traded.

6. Buying on margin means borrowing money from a broker in order to buy more securities. By buying securities on margin, an investor magnifies both the upside potential and the downside risk. If the equity in a margin account falls below the required maintenance level, the investor will get a margin call from the broker.

7. Short selling is the practice of selling securities that the seller does not own. The short-seller borrows the securities sold through a broker and may be required to cover the short position at any time on demand. The cash proceeds of a short sale are always kept in escrow by the broker, and the broker usually requires that the short-seller deposit additional cash or securities to serve as margin (collateral) for the short sale.

8. Securities trading is regulated by the provincial securities commissions and by self-regulation of the exchanges and the dealer associations. Many of the important regulations have to do with full disclosure of relevant information concerning the securities in question. Insider trading rules also prohibit traders from attempting to profit from inside information.

KEY EQUATIONS

(3.1) $\text{Margin ratio} = \dfrac{\text{Equity value}}{\text{Market value of assets}} = \dfrac{\text{Market value of assets} - \text{Loan}}{\text{Market value of assets}}$

(3.2) $\text{Margin ratio} = \dfrac{\text{Market value of assets}}{\text{Value of stock owed}}$

PROBLEMS

Mc Graw Hill Education **connect**™ Practise and learn online with Connect.

1. Call one full-service broker and one discount broker and find out the transaction costs of implementing the following strategies:

   a. Buying 100 shares of BMO now and selling them six months from now.

   b. Investing an equivalent amount in six-month "at the-money" call options (calls with strike price equal to the stock price) on BMO stock now and selling them six months from now.

2. Suppose that you sell short 100 shares of Alcan, now selling at $70 per share.

   a. What is your maximum possible loss?

   b. What happens to the maximum loss if you simultaneously place a stop-buy order at $78?

3. Dee Trader opens a brokerage account, and purchases 300 shares of Internet Dreams at $40 per share. She borrows $4,000 from her broker to help pay for the purchase. The interest rate on the loan is 8 percent.

   a. What is the margin in Dee's account when she first purchases the stock?

   b. If the price falls to $30 per share by the end of the year, what is the remaining margin in her account? If the maintenance margin requirement is 30 percent, will she receive a margin call?

   c. What is the rate of return on her investment?

4. Old Economy Traders opened an account to short-sell 1,000 shares of Internet Dreams from the previous problem. The initial margin requirement was 50 percent. (The margin account pays no interest.) A year later, the price of Internet Dreams has risen from $40 to $50, and the stock has paid a dividend of $2 per share.

   a. What is the remaining margin in the account?

   b. If the maintenance margin requirement is 30 percent, will Old Economy receive a margin call?

   c. What is the rate of return on the investment?

5. An expiring put will be exercised and the stock will be sold if the stock price is below the exercise price. A stop-loss order causes a stock sale when the stock price falls below some limit. Compare and contrast the two strategies of purchasing put options versus issuing a stop-loss order.

6. Compare call options and stop-buy orders.

7. Here is some price information on Barrick:

   You have placed a stop-loss order to sell at $38.

	Bid	Asked
Barrick	37.80	38.10

   What are you telling your broker? Given market prices, will your order be executed?

8. You have placed a stop-loss order on Kinross at $38, and the current bid and asked prices are $37.85 and $38.12, respectively. What does your order instruct your broker to do? Given market prices, will your order be executed?

9. Consider the following limit-order book of a market-maker. The last trade in the stock took place at a price of $50.

Limit-Buy Orders		Limit-Sell Orders	
Price ($)	Shares	Price ($)	Shares
49.75	500	50.25	100
49.50	800	51.50	100
49.25	500	54.75	300
49.00	200	58.25	100
48.50	600		

    a. If a market-buy order for 100 shares comes in, at what price will it be filled?

    b. At what price would the next market-buy order be filled?

    c. If you were the specialist, would you desire to increase or decrease your inventory of this stock?

10. What purpose does the Designated Order Turnaround system (SuperDOT) serve on the New York Stock Exchange?

11. Who sets the bid and asked price for a stock traded over the counter? Would you expect the spread to be higher on actively or inactively traded stocks?

12. Suppose that Weston (WN) currently is selling at $80 per share. You buy 250 shares, using $15,000 of your own money and borrowing the remainder of the purchase price from your broker. The rate on the margin loan is 8 percent.

    a. What is the percentage increase in the net worth of your brokerage account if the price of WN *immediately* changes to (i) $88; (ii) $80; (iii) $72? What is the relationship between your percentage return and the percentage change in the price of WN?

    b. If the minimum margin is 30 percent, how low can WN's price fall before you get a margin call?

    c. How would your answer to (*b*) change if you had financed the initial purchase with only $10,000 of your own money?

    d. What is the rate of return on your margined position (assuming again that you invest $15,000 of your own money) if WN is selling *after one year* at (i) $88; (ii) $80; (iii) $72? What is the relationship between your percentage return and the percentage change in the price of WN? Assume that WN pays no dividends.

    e. Continue to assume that a year has passed. How low can WN price fall before you get a margin call?

13. Suppose that you sell short 250 shares of Weston (WN), currently selling for $80 per share, and give your broker $15,000 to establish your margin account.

    a. If you earn no interest on the funds in your margin account, what will be your rate of return after one year if WN stock is selling at (i) $88; (ii) $80; (iii) $72? Assume that WN pays no dividends.

    b. If the minimum margin is 30 percent, how high can WN's price rise before you get a margin call?

    c. Redo parts (*a*) and (*b*), now assuming that WN's dividend (paid at year-end) is $2 per share.

14. Here is some price information on Fincorp stock. Suppose first that Fincorp trades in a dealer market.

Bid	Asked
55.25	55.50

    a. Suppose you have submitted an order to your broker to buy at market. At what price will your trade be executed?

    b. Suppose you have submitted an order to sell at market. At what price will your trade be executed?

    c. Suppose an investor has submitted a limit order to sell at $55.40. What will happen?

    d. Suppose another investor has submitted a limit order to buy at $55.40. What will happen?

15. On May 1, you sold short one "round lot" (i.e., 100 shares) of Zenith stock at $14 per share. On July 1, a dividend of $2 per share was paid. On August 1, you covered the short sale by buying the stock at a price of $9 per share. You paid 50 cents per share in commissions for each transaction. What is the value of your account on August 1?

16. You are bullish on BCE stock. The current market price is $50 per share, and you have $5,000 of your own to invest. You borrow an additional $5,000 from your broker at an interest rate of 8 percent per year and invest $10,000 in the stock.

   a. What will be your rate of return if the price of BCE stock goes up by 10 percent during the next year? (Ignore the expected dividend.)

   b. How far does the price of BCE stock have to fall for you to get a margin call if the minimum margin is 30 percent?

17. You've borrowed $20,000 on margin to buy shares in Bombardier, which is now selling at $80 per share. Your account starts at the initial margin requirement of 50 percent. The minimum margin is 35 percent. Two days later, the stock price falls to $75 per share.

   a. Will you receive a margin call?

   b. How low can the price of Bombardier shares fall before you receive a margin call?

18. You are bearish on BCE stock and decide to sell short 100 shares at the current market price of $50 per share.

   a. How much in cash or securities must you put into your brokerage account if the broker's initial margin requirement is 50 percent of the value of the short position?

   b. How high can the price of the stock go before you get a margin call if the minimum margin is 30 percent of the value of the short position?

19. To cover the initial margin requirement of 60 percent, you deposited funds after short-selling 100 shares of common stock at $45 per share.

   a. What is your rate of return if you cover at $50, assuming no dividends and no addition or removal of funds from the account?

   b. At what price would you receive a margin call if the minimum margin requirement is 30 percent?

20. In Table 3.1, what is the leading exchange in terms of value of stocks listed? What is the leading exchange in terms of trading activity?

CFA®
PROBLEMS

The following questions are from past CFA examinations.

21. If you place a stop-loss order to sell 100 shares of stock at $55 when the current price is $62, how much will you receive for each share if the price drops to $50?

   a. $50

   b. $55

   c. $54.90

   d. Cannot be determined from the information given.

22. FBN, Inc. has just sold 100,000 shares in an initial public offering. The underwriter's explicit fees were $70,000. The offering price for the shares was $50, but immediately upon issue the share price jumped to $53.

   a. What is the total cost to FBN of the equity issue?

   b. Is the entire cost of the underwriting a source of profit to the underwriters?

23. Specialists on the New York Stock Exchange do all of the following except

   a. Act as dealers for their own accounts

   b. Execute limit orders

   c. Help provide liquidity to the marketplace

   d. Act as odd-lot dealers

24. You wish to sell short 100 shares of XYZ Corporation stock. If the last two transactions were at 34.10 followed by 34.15, you only can sell short on the next transaction at a price of

a. 34.10 or higher

b. 34.15 or higher

c. 34.15 or lower

d. 34.10 or lower

APPENDIX 3A: A DETAILED MARGIN POSITION

Examples 3.1, 3.2, and 3.3 in Section 3.5 show the basic margin analysis for buying and selling. The balance sheets showed a progression from the assets including only the purchased stock to having T-bills, which were needed for margin for the short position. Those T-bills could have been included in the first balance sheet, if you happened to hold them in your account. The assets provided for margin purposes can earn a return within the account. The balance sheet could, and would normally, also include other stocks in your portfolio. It is the aggregate value of the account that goes into the margin calculation. Table 3A.1 shows the balance sheet for a more complicated account, first at the time of opening the positions—a margin purchase of 500 shares of SNC at $100 and a short sale of 300 shares of ACE at $40—in addition to other assets, and then at a later date; we ignore any dividends or interest payments and suppose that no cash is advanced at the time of the opening trades.

If the margin position had come from all purchases or all short sales, the calculations would have been simple extensions of equations 3.1 and 3.2, where we aggregate long positions for

TABLE 3A.1   Illustration of a Margined Account

Initial Account Position			
Assets		**Liabilities**	
Cash	$ 12,000	ACE (300 @ $40) (short position)	$12,000
T-bills	30,000	Broker loan	50,000
SNC (500 @ $100)	50,000	Equity	72,500
CIBC (1,000 @ $30)	30,000		$134,500
Teck (500 @ $25)	12,500		
	$134,500		

Later Account Position			
Assets		**Liabilities**	
Cash	$ 12,000	ACE (300 @ $50) (short position)	$ 15,000
T-bills	30,000	Broker loan	50,000
SNC (500 @ $102)	51,000	Equity	71,000
CIBC (1,000 @ $28)	28,000		$136,000
Teck (500 @ $30)	15,000		
	$136,000		

market value, short positions for value owed, and the loan amounts. When we have both long and short positions, we have to calculate the exposure of the account on both long and short sides and sum the requirements to protect against both. If the equity in the account is sufficient to cover both sides, then margin has been met. The initial margin requirement for the margin purchase alone in this account is found by considering the market value of the account before the effect of the short sale, or $122,500 when we remove the $12,000 short sale and cash proceeds; the equity value is found by subtracting the $50,000 loan, which we then divide by the market value of the securities held long, or $122,500, for a margin ratio of .59. The investor needs $30,000 to establish margin of .3 and has $42,500 excess equity.

For the short position alone, we remove the effect of the margin purchase from the market value; so the investor has $84,500 as account value, which is divided by the short value of $12,000 for a margin ratio of 7; but we have counted the same equity twice in arriving at the two satisfactory ratios. To cover the short-sale margin requirement, the investor needs assets of V where $V/\$12,000$ must equal 1.3; solving for V yields $15,600 as the asset requirement. Separately, there is plenty of excess equity in the account, but combined, the investor needs $30,000 plus $15,600, or $45,600, equity in the account before making both the margin purchase and the short sale. There is an excess of only $26,900; without the T-bills, the investor would have needed to find another $3,100 to place on deposit.

In finding the amount of margin that the investor must provide, we have been using the following two formulas; for margin purchases, the market value of collateral required is

$$\text{Market value} = \text{Loan value}/(1 - \text{Margin ratio}) \tag{3A.1}$$

and for short sales, the value of collateral required is

$$\text{Market value} = \text{Short value} \times \text{Margin ratio} \tag{3A.2}$$

Using these equations, we can see that at the later date, the account easily satisfies the margin requirement of $50,000/(1 - .3) = \$71,429$ for the purchase plus $15,000 \times 1.3 = \$19,500$ for the short sale, summing to $90,929 against assets of $136,000.

CC 3A.1

CONCEPT CHECK

If at the later date in the preceding example the prices of Teck and CIBC were the same as given but SNC had fallen to $80, how high could ACE stock rise before a margin call would result? If instead ACE rose to $60, how low could SNC fall before triggering a margin call?

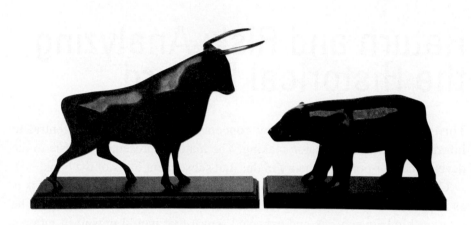

Return and Risk: Analyzing the Historical Record

This chapter introduces some key concepts and issues that are central to informed investment decision making. The material presented is basic to the development of portfolio theory in this and subsequent Parts of the book.

Casual observation and formal research both suggest that investment risk is as important to investors as expected return. While we have theories about the relationship between risk and expected return that would prevail in rational capital markets, there is no theory about the levels of risk we should find in the marketplace. We can at best estimate the level of risk likely to confront investors from historical experience.

This is to be expected, because prices of investment assets fluctuate in response to news about the fortunes of corporations and to macroeconomic developments that affect interest rates. There is no theory about the frequency and importance of such events; hence we cannot determine a "natural" level of risk.

The difficulty is compounded by the fact that neither expected returns nor risk are directly observable. We observe only *realized* rates of return. Hence, to make forecasts about future expected returns and risk, we first must learn how to "forecast" their *past* values, that is, the expected returns and risk that investors actually anticipated, from historical data. (There is an old saying that forecasting the future is even more difficult than forecasting the past.) Moreover, in learning from a historical record we face what has become known as the "black swan" problem.[1] No matter how long a historical record, there is never a guarantee that it exhibits the worst (and best) nature can throw at us in the future. This problem is particularly daunting when assessing the risk of long-run investments. In this chapter, we present the essential tools for estimating expected returns and risk from the historical record and consider implications for future investments.

---

[1]Black swans are a metaphor for highly improbable—but highly impactful—events. Until the discovery of Australia, Europeans, having observed only white swans, believed that a black swan was outside the realm of reasonable possibility or, in statistical jargon, an extreme "outlier" relative to their "sample" of observations.

We begin with interest rates and investments in safe assets and examine the history of risk-free investments in Canada over the past 56 years. Moving to risky assets, we begin with scenario analysis of risky investments and the data necessary to conduct it. With this in mind, we develop statistical tools needed to make inferences from historical time series of portfolio returns. We present a global view of the history of stock and bond returns worldwide. We end with implications of the historical record for future investments and risk measures commonly used in the industry.

4.1 DETERMINANTS OF THE LEVEL OF INTEREST RATES

Interest rates and forecasts of their future values are among the most important inputs into an investment decision.

For example, suppose you have $10,000 in a savings account. The bank pays you a variable interest rate tied to some short-term reference rate such as the 30-day Treasury bill rate. You have the option of moving some or all of your money into a longer-term *guaranteed investment certificate* (GIC) that offers a fixed rate over the term of the deposit.

Your decision depends critically on your outlook regarding interest rates. If you think rates will fall, you will want to lock in the current higher rates by investing in a relatively long-term GIC. If you expect rates to rise, you will want to postpone committing any funds to long-term GICs.

Forecasting interest rates is one of the most notoriously difficult parts of applied macroeconomics. Nonetheless, we do have a good understanding of the fundamental factors that determine the level of interest rates:

1. The supply of funds from savers, primarily households
2. The demand for funds from businesses to be used to finance physical investments in plant, equipment, and inventories (real assets or capital formation)
3. The government's net supply demand for funds as modified by actions of the monetary authority

Before we elaborate on these forces and resultant interest rates, we need to distinguish real from nominal interest rates.

Real and Nominal Rates of Interest

Rates and Statistics www.bankof-canada.ca/rates/interest-rates/

An interest rate is a promised rate of return denominated in some unit of account (dollars, yen, euros, or even purchasing power units) over some time period (a month, a year, 20 years, or longer). Thus, when we say the interest rate is 5 percent, we must specify both the unit of account and the time period.

Assuming there is no default risk, we can refer to the promised rate of interest as a risk-free rate for that particular unit of account and time period. But if an interest rate is risk-free for one unit of account and time period, it will not be risk-free for other units or periods. For example, interest rates that are absolutely safe in dollar terms will be risky when evaluated in terms of purchasing power because of inflation uncertainty.

Suppose exactly one year ago you deposited $1,000 in a one-year time deposit guaranteeing a rate of interest of 10 percent. You are about to collect $1,100 in cash.

Is your $100 return for real? That depends on what money can buy these days, relative to what you *could* buy a year ago. The consumer price index (CPI) measures purchasing power by averaging the prices of goods and services in the consumption basket of an average urban family of four.

Suppose the rate of inflation (percent change in the CPI, denoted by i) for the last year amounted to $i = 6$ percent. This tells you the purchasing power of money is reduced by 6 percent a year. The value of each dollar depreciates by 6 percent a year in terms of the goods it can buy. Therefore, part of your interest earnings are offset by the reduction in the purchasing power of the dollars you will receive at the end of the year. With a 10 percent interest rate, after you net out the 6 percent reduction in the purchasing power of money, you are left with a net increase in purchasing power of about 4 percent. Thus, we need to distinguish between a **nominal interest rate**—the growth rate of your money—and a **real interest rate**—the growth rate of your purchasing power. If we call R the nominal rate, r the real rate, and i the inflation rate, then we conclude

$$r \approx R - i \tag{4.1}$$

That is, the real rate of interest is the nominal rate reduced by the loss of purchasing power resulting from inflation.

In fact, the exact relationship between the real and nominal interest rate is given by

$$1 + r = \frac{1 + R}{1 + i} \tag{4.2}$$

This is because the growth factor of your purchasing power, $1 + r$, equals the growth factor of your money, $1 + R$, divided by the new price level, that is, $1 + i$ times its value in the previous period. The exact relationship can be rearranged to

$$r = \frac{R - i}{1 + i} \tag{4.3}$$

which shows that the approximation rule (equation 4.1) overstates the real rate by the factor $1/(1 + i)$.

EXAMPLE 4.1　　**The Real Rate of Interest**

If the interest rate on a one-year GIC is 8 percent, and you expect inflation to be 5 percent over the coming year, then using the approximation formula you expect the real rate to be $r = 8$ percent $- 5$ percent $= 3$ percent. Using the exact formula, the real rate is

$$r = \frac{.08 - .05}{1 + .05} = .0286$$

or 2.86 percent. Therefore, the approximation rule overstates the expected real rate by only .14 percent (14 basis points). The approximation rule is more exact for small inflation rates and is perfectly exact for continuously compounded rates. We discuss further details in the next section.

Note that conventional investment certificates offer a guaranteed *nominal* rate of interest. Thus, you can only infer the expected real rate by adjusting for your expectation of the rate of inflation.

Figure 4.1

Determination of the equilibrium real rate of interest.

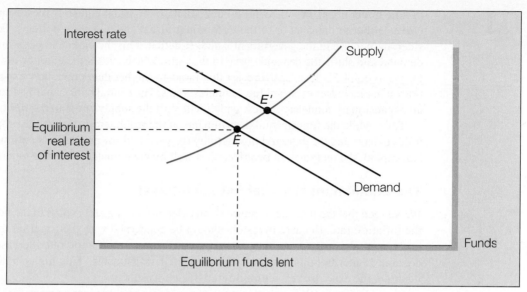

Interest rate

Supply

E'

Equilibrium real rate of interest

E

Demand

Funds

Equilibrium funds lent

Statistics Canada
www.statcan
.gc.ca

It is always possible to calculate the real rate after the fact. The inflation rate is published by Statistics Canada. The future real rate, however, is unknown, and one has to rely on expectations. In other words, because future inflation is risky, the real rate of return is risky even if the nominal rate is risk-free.[2]

The Equilibrium Real Rate of Interest

Three basic factors—supply, demand, and government actions—determine the *real* interest rate. The nominal interest rate is the real rate plus the expected rate of inflation. So a fourth factor affecting the interest rate is expected inflation.

Although there are many different interest rates economywide (as many as there are types of securities), economists frequently talk as if there were a single representative rate because these rates move together. We can use this abstraction to gain some insights into determining the real rate of interest if we consider the supply and demand curves for funds.

Figure 4.1 shows a downward-sloping demand curve and an upward-sloping supply curve. On the horizontal axis we measure the quantity of funds, and on the vertical axis we measure the real rate of interest.

The supply curve slopes up from left to right because the higher the real interest rate, the greater the supply of household savings. The assumption is that at higher real interest rates, households will choose to postpone some current consumption and set aside or invest more of their disposable income for future use.[3] The demand curve slopes down from left to right because the lower the real interest rate, the more businesses will want to invest in physical capital. Assuming that businesses rank projects by the expected real return on invested capital, firms will undertake more projects the lower the real interest rate on the funds needed to finance those projects.

Equilibrium is at the point of intersection of the supply and demand curves, point E in Figure 4.1.

---

[2]You can find the real rate for a desired maturity for inflation-indexed Canada bonds called real return bonds (see Chapter 12 for a full discussion). The difference between real return bond yields and yields on comparable ordinary Canada bonds provides an estimate of the market's expected future inflation.

[3]There is considerable disagreement among experts on the extent to which household saving does go up in response to an increase in the real interest rate.

Bank of Canada
www.bankof-
canada.ca

The government and the central bank (Bank of Canada) can shift these supply and demand curves either to the right or to the left through fiscal and monetary policies. For example, consider an increase in the government's budget deficit. This increases the government's borrowing demand and shifts the demand curve to the right, which causes the equilibrium real interest rate to rise to point E'. That is, a forecast that indicates higher than previously expected government borrowing increases expected future interest rates. The central bank can offset such a rise through an expansionary monetary policy, which will shift the supply curve to the right.

Thus, while the fundamental determinants of the real interest rate are the propensity of households to save and the expected productivity (or we could say profitability) of investment in physical capital, the real rate can be affected as well by government fiscal and monetary policies.

The Equilibrium Nominal Rate of Interest

We've seen that the real rate of return of an asset is approximately equal to the nominal rate minus the inflation rate. Because investors should be concerned with their real returns—the increase in their purchasing power—we would expect that as the inflation rate increases, investors will demand higher nominal rates of return on their investments. This higher rate is necessary to maintain the expected real return offered by an investment.

Irving Fisher in 1965 argued that the nominal rate ought to increase one for one with expected inflation, $E(i)$. The so-called Fisher equation is

$$R = r + E(i) \tag{4.4}$$

This relationship has been debated and empirically investigated. The equation implies that when real rates are reasonably stable, then changes in nominal rates ought to predict changes in inflation rates. The results are mixed; while the data do not strongly support the Fisher equation, nominal interest rates seem to predict inflation as well as alternative methods, in part because we are unable to forecast inflation well with any method.

It is difficult to determine the empirical validity of the Fisher hypothesis because real rates also change unpredictably over time. Nominal interest rates can be viewed as the sum of the required real rate on nominally risk-free assets, plus a "noisy" forecast of inflation.

In Chapter 13, we discuss the relationship between short- and long-term interest rates. Longer rates incorporate forecasts for long-term inflation. For this reason alone, interest rates on bonds of different maturities may diverge. In addition, we will see that prices of long-term bonds are more volatile than those of short-term bonds. This implies that expected returns on long-term bonds may include a risk premium, so that the expected real rate offered by bonds of varying maturity also may vary.

CC 1

CONCEPT CHECK

a. Suppose the real interest rate is 3 percent per year and the expected inflation rate is 8 percent. What is the nominal interest rate according to the Fisher hypothesis?
b. Suppose the expected inflation rate rises to 10 percent, but the real rate is unchanged. What happens to the nominal interest rate?

Taxes and the Real Rate of Interest

Tax liabilities are based on *nominal* income and the tax rate determined by the investor's tax bracket. Parliament has recognized the resultant "bracket creep" (when nominal income grows due to inflation and pushes taxpayers into higher brackets) and has partially indexed tax brackets and exemptions since 1975.

Index-linked tax brackets do not provide relief from the effect of inflation on the taxation of savings, however. Given a tax rate (*r*) and a nominal interest rate (*R*), the after-tax interest rate is $R(1 - t)$. The real after-tax rate is approximately the after-tax nominal rate minus the inflation rate:

$$R(1 - t) - i = (r + i)(1 - t) - i = r(1 - t) - it \qquad (4.5)$$

Thus the after-tax real rate of return falls as inflation rises. Investors suffer an inflation penalty equal to the tax rate times the inflation rate. If, for example, you are in a 30 percent tax bracket and your investments yield 12 percent, while inflation runs at the rate of 8 percent, then your before-tax real rate is 4 percent, and you *should*, in an inflation-protected tax system, net after taxes $4(1 - .3) = 2.8$ percent. But the tax code does not recognize that the first 8 percent of your return is just compensation for inflation—not real income—and hence your after-tax return is reduced by 8 percent $\times$ .3 = 2.4 percent, so that your after-tax real interest rate, at .4 percent, is almost wiped out.

4.2 COMPARING RATES OF RETURN FOR DIFFERENT HOLDING PERIODS

Consider an investor who seeks a safe investment, say in Canadian government securities. Suppose we observe zero-coupon government securities with several different maturities. Zero-coupon bonds, discussed more fully in Chapter 12, are bonds that are sold at a discount from par value and provide their entire return from the difference between the purchase price and the ultimate repayment of par value.[4] Given the price, $P(T)$, of a Canada bond with $100 par value and maturity of T years, we calculate the total risk-free return as the percentage increase in the value of the investment over the life of the bond.

$$r_f(T) = \frac{100}{P(T)} - 1 \qquad (4.6)$$

For $T = 1$, equation 4.6 provides the risk-free rate for an investment horizon of one year.

EXAMPLE 4.2   Annualized Rates of Return

Suppose prices of zero-coupon Canada bonds with $100 face value and various maturities are as follows. We find the total return of each security by using equation 4.6:

Horizon, *T*	Price, *P(T)*	[100/*P(T)*] − 1	Risk-Free Return
Half-year	$97.36	100/97.36 − 1 = .0271	$r_f(.5) = 2.71\%$
1 year	$95.52	100/95.52 − 1 = .0580	$r_f(1) = 5.80\%$
25 years	$23.30	100/23.30 − 1 = 3.2918	$r_f(25) = 329.18\%$

Not surprisingly, longer horizons in Example 4.2 provide greater total returns. How should we compare returns on investments with differing horizons? This requires that we re-express each

---

[4]The Canadian government issues T-bills, which are pure discount (or zero-coupon) securities with maturities of up to 1 year. However, financial institutions create zero-coupon Canada bonds called *Canada strips* with maturities up to 30 years by buying coupon-paying T-bonds, "stripping" off the coupon payments, and selling claims to the coupon payments and final payment of face value separately. See Chapter 12 for further details.

total return as a *rate* of return for a common period. We typically express all investment returns as an **effective annual rate (EAR)**, defined as the percentage increase in funds invested over a 1-year horizon.

For a 1-year investment, the EAR equals the total return, $r_f(1)$, and the gross return, $(1 + EAR)$, is the terminal value of a $1 investment. For investments that last less than 1 year, we compound the per-period return for a full year. For the 6-month bill in Example 4.2, we compound the 2.71 percent half-year return for two semiannual periods to obtain a terminal value of $1 + EAR = (1.0271)^2 = 1.0549$, implying that EAR = 5.49 percent.

For investments longer than a year, the convention is to express the EAR as the annual rate that would compound to the same value as the actual investment. For example, the investment in the 25-year bond in Example 4.2 grows by its maturity date by a factor of 4.2918, so its EAR is found by solving

$$(1 + EAR)^{25} = 4.2918$$

$$1 + EAR = 4.2918^{1/25} = 1.0600$$

In general, we can relate EAR to the total return, $r_f(T)$, over a holding period of length T by using the following equation:

$$1 + EAR = [1 + r_f(T)]^{1/T} \tag{4.7}$$

We illustrate with an example.

EXAMPLE 4.3   **Equivalent Annual Return Versus Total Return**

For the 6-month Canada bond in Example 4.2, $T = \frac{1}{2}$, and $1/T = 2$. Therefore,

$$1 + EAR = (1.0271)^2 = 1.0549 \quad and \quad EAR = 5.49\%$$

For the 25-year Canada bond in Example 4.2, $T = 25$. Therefore,

$$1 + EAR = 4.2918^{1/25} = 1.060 \quad and \quad EAR = 6.0\%$$

Annual Percentage Rates

Annualized rates on short-term investments (by convention, $T < 1$ year) often are reported using simple rather than compound interest. These are called **annual percentage rates**, or **APRs**. For example, the APR corresponding to a monthly rate such as that charged on a credit card is reported as 12 times the monthly rate. More generally, if there are n compounding periods in a year, and the per-period rate is $r_f(T)$, then the APR $= n \times r_f(T)$. Conversely, you can find the per-period rate from the APR as $r_f(T) = T \times APR$.

Using this procedure, the APR of the 6-month bond in Example 4.2 with a 6-month rate of 2.71 percent is $2 \times 2.71 = 5.42$ percent. To generalize, note that for short-term investments of length T, there are $n = 1/T$ compounding periods in a year. Therefore, the relationship among the compounding period, the EAR, and the APR is

$$1 + EAR = [1 + r_f(T)]^n = [1 + r_f(T)]^{1/T} = [1 + T \times APR]^{1/T} \tag{4.8}$$

Equivalently,

$$APR = \frac{(1 + EAR)^r - 1}{T}$$

EXCEL APPLICATIONS ⟋

To find r_{cc} from the effective annual rate, we solve equation 4.9 for r_{cc} as follows:

$$\ln(1 + EAR) = r_{cc}$$

where $\ln(\bullet)$ is the natural logarithm function, the inverse of $\exp(\bullet)$. Both the exponential and the logarithmic function are available in Excel; they are called LN() and EXP(), respectively.

TABLE 4.1 Annual Percentage Rate (APR) and Effective Annual Rates (EAR) ⟋

Compounding Period	T	EAR = $[1 + r_f(T)]^{1/T} - 1 = .058$		APR = $r_f(T)*(1/T) = .058$	
		$r_f(T)$	APR = $[(1 + EAR)^T - 1]/T$	$r_f(T)$	EAR = $(1 + APR*T)^{(1/T)} - 1$
1 year	1.0000	.0580	.05800	.0580	.05800
6 months	.5000	.0286	.05718	.0290	.05884
1 quarter	.2500	.0142	.05678	.0145	.05927
1 month	.0833	.0047	.05651	.0048	.05957
1 week	.0192	.0011	.05641	.0011	.05968
1 day	.0027	.0002	.05638	.0002	.05971
Continuous		$r_{cc} = \ln(1 + EAR) = .05638$		EAR = $\exp(r_{cc}) - 1 = .05971$	

EXAMPLE 4.4   EAR Versus APR

In Table 4.1 we use equation 4.8 to find the APR corresponding to an EAR of 5.8 percent with various compounding periods. Conversely, we find the values of EAR implied by an APR of 5.8 percent.

Continuous Compounding

It is evident from Table 4.1 (and equation 4.8) that the difference between APR and EAR grows with the frequency of compounding. This raises the question: How far will these two rates diverge as the compounding frequency continues to grow? Put differently, what is the limit of $[1 + T \times APR]^{1/T}$, as T gets ever smaller? As T approaches zero, we effectively approach *continuous compounding (CC)*, and the relation of EAR to the annual percentage rate, denoted by r_{cc} for the continuously compounded case, is given by the exponential function

$$1 + EAR = \exp(r_{cc}) = e^{r_{cc}} \tag{4.9}$$

where e is approximately 2.71828.

EXAMPLE 4.5   Continuously Compounded Rates

The continuously compounded annual percentage rate, r_{cc}, that provides an EAR of 5.8 percent is 5.638 percent (see Table 4.1). This is virtually the same as the APR for daily compounding. But for less frequent compounding, for example semiannually, the APR necessary to provide the same EAR is noticeably higher, 5.718 percent. With less frequent compounding, a higher APR is necessary to provide an equivalent effective return.

continued

While continuous compounding might at first seem to be a mathematical nuisance, working with such rates in many cases can simplify calculations of expected return and risk. For example, given a continuously compounded rate, the total return for any period T, $r_{cc}(T)$, is simply $\exp(T \times r_{cc})$.[5] In other words, the total return scales up in direct proportion to the time period, T. This is far simpler than working with the exponents that arise using discrete period compounding. As another example, look again at equation 4.1. There, the relationship between the real rate, r, the nominal rate R, and the inflation rate i, $r \approx R - i$, was only an approximation, as is demonstrated by equation 4.3. But if we express all rates as continuously compounded, then equation 4.3 is exact,[6] that is, $r_{cc}(\text{real}) = r_{cc}(\text{nominal}) - i_{cc}$.

CC 2

CONCEPT CHECK

A bank offers two alternative interest schedules for a savings account of $100,000 locked in for 3 years: (a) a monthly rate of 1 percent; (b) an annually, continuously compounded rate (r_{cc}) of 12 percent. Which alternative should you choose?

4.3

BILLS AND INFLATION, 1957–2012

Table 4.2 summarizes the historical record of short-term interest rates in Canada, the inflation rate, and the resultant real rate.[7] The annual rates on T-bills are computed from rolling over four 3-month bills during each year. The real rate is computed from the annual T-bill rate and the percent change in the CPI according to equation 4.2.

The average real rate for the whole 56-year period of 2.25 percent actually disguises the quite different experiences between the various subperiods. For the years 1957–1984 the average real rate was only 1.65 percent, but it rose to 2.85 percent over the second half, 19853–2012, of the period. In the more recent years of the current century, on the other hand, the rate fell to 0.59 percent, These rates fluctuated during each subperiod, with corresponding standard deviations of 2.28, 2/61, and 1.75, respectively.

TABLE 4.2   Short-Term Interest Rates, Inflation Rate, and Resultant Real Rate in Canada, 1957–2012

| | Bills and Inflation, 1957–2012 | | | | | |
| | Averages (%) | | | Standard Deviations (%) | | |
	T-Bills	Inflation	Real T-Bill	T-Bills	Inflation	Real T-Bill
All years, 1957–2012	6.22	3.89	2.25	3.89	3.13	2.76
First half, 1957–1984	7.04	5.32	1.65	4.13	3.71	2.82
Second half, 1985–2012	5.40	2.00	2.85	3.51	1.38	2.61
2001–2012	2.5	1.9	0.59	1.47	0.86	1.75

[5]This follows from equation 4.9. If $1 + \text{EAR} = e^{rcc}$, then $(1 + \text{EAR})^T = e^{rccT}$.

[6] $1 + r(\text{real}) = \dfrac{1 + r(\text{nominal})}{1 + \text{inflation}}$

$\Rightarrow \ln[1 + r(\text{real})] = \ln\left(\dfrac{1 + r(\text{nominal})}{1 + \text{inflation}}\right) = \ln[1 + r(\text{nominal})] - \ln(1 + \text{inflation})$

$\Rightarrow r_{cc}(\text{real}) = r_{cc}(\text{nominal}) - i_{cc}$

[7]You can find the entire post-1957 history of the annual rates of these series and other series as well on the text's Web site.

Figure 4.2

Interest and inflation rates, 1957–2012.

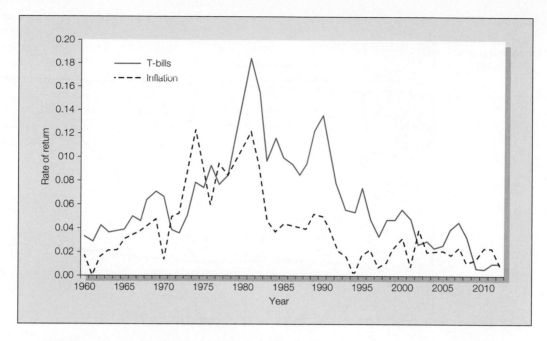

If the real rate remains approximately constant, the Fisher equation (4.4) predicts a close connection between inflation and the rate of returns on T-bills. This is apparent in Figure 4.2, which plots both time series on the same set of axes. With the exception of the most recent years, both series have tended to move together, which implies that inflation has been the driving force for the nominal rate of interest for most of the period.[8] Indeed, the correlation coefficient between the T-bill rate and the inflation rate is .68 for the entire 56-year history and .71 for the period 1985–2012, but falls to −.11 for 2001–2012.

A good part of these more recent trends may be attributed to economic thinking reflected in policies of the Bank of Canada that attempt to maintain a low rate of inflation. Whatever the reason may be, the fact is that the average rate of inflation has declined, from 5.32 percent in the first half of the period to 2 percent over the period 1985–2012. Stability is even more impressive if one concentrates on the last 12 years, in which the standard deviation of the rate of inflation was only .86 percent, down from 3.71 percent in 1957–1984. Of course, no one can rule out more extreme temporary fluctuations as a result of possible severe shocks to the economy.

Figure 4.3 shows the progression of the nominal and real value of $1 invested in T-bills at the beginning of 1957, accumulated to 2012. The progression of the value of a $1 investment is called a *wealth index*. The wealth index in a current year is obtained by compounding the portfolio value from the end of the previous year by $1 + r$, the gross rate of return in the current year. Deviations of the curve of the nominal wealth index in Figure 4.3 from a smooth exponential line are due to variation over time in the rate of return. The lines in the figure, which grow quite smoothly, clearly demonstrate that short-term interest rate risk (real as well as nominal) is small even for long-term horizons. It certainly is less risky by an order of magnitude than investments in stocks, as we will soon see.

One important lesson from this history is the effect of inflation when compounded over long periods. The average inflation rate was 3.89 percent between 1957 and 2012, and 2.0 percent between 1985 and 2012. These rates may not seem impressive, but are sufficient to reduce the terminal value of $1 invested in the beginning of 1981 from a nominal value of $7.18 in 2012 to a real (constant purchasing power) value of only $2.74.

---

[8]See Nabil T. Khoury and Guy McLeod, "The Relationship Between the Canadian Treasury Bill Rate and Expected Inflation in Canada and the United States," *Canadian Journal of Administrative Sciences* 2, no. 1 (June 1985).

Figure 4.3

Nominal and real wealth indices, 1957–2012.

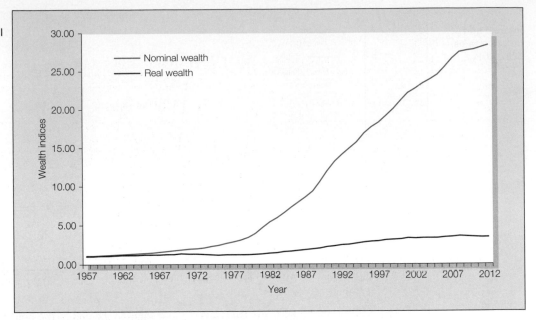

Investors presumably focus on the real returns they can earn on their investments. For them to realize an acceptable real rate, they must earn a higher nominal rate when inflation is expected to be higher. Therefore, the nominal T-bill rate observed at the beginning of a period should reflect anticipations of inflation over that period. When the expected real rate is stable and realized inflation matches initial expectations, the correlation between inflation and nominal T-bill rates will be close to perfect (1.0), while the correlation between inflation and the realized real rate will be close to zero. At the other extreme, if investors either ignored or were very poor at predicting inflation, its correlation with nominal T-bill rates would be zero and the correlation between inflation and real rates would be perfectly negative (-1.0), since the real rate would then fall one-for-one with any increase in inflation. We saw earlier that the correlation between inflation and nominal T-bill rates was approximately constant and quite high for most of the period, but that it declined dramatically for the most recent years. This is also reflected in the correlation between inflation and realized real rates, which was $-.58$ in 2001–2012. This may reflect the active intervention of the Bank of Canada in order to mitigate the financial crisis.

4.4   RISK AND RISK PREMIUMS

Holding-Period Returns

You are considering investing in a stock index fund. The fund currently sells for $100 per share, and your *time horizon* is one year. You expect the cash dividend during the year to be $4, so your expected **dividend yield** (i.e., dividends earned per dollar invested) is 4 percent.

Your total **holding-period return (HPR)** will depend on the price that will prevail one year from now. Suppose that it will be $110 per share. Then your *capital gain* will be $10 and your HPR 14 percent. The definition of the holding period return in this context is capital gain income plus dividend income per dollar invested in the stock at the start of the period:

$$\text{HPR} = \frac{\text{Ending price of a share} - \text{Beginning price} + \text{Cash dividend}}{\text{Beginning price}} \quad (4.10)$$

In our case we have

$$\text{HPR} = \frac{\$110 - \$100 + \$4}{\$100} = .14, \text{ or } 14\%$$

EXCEL SPREADSHEET 4.1

Distribution of HPR on the stock index fund.

	A	B	C	D	E	F	G	H	I
1									
2									
3	Purchase Price =		$100			T-bill Rate =	0.04		
4									
5							Squared		Squared
6	State of the		Year-end	Cash		Deviations	Deviations	Excess	Deviations
7	Market	Probability	Price	Dividends	HPR	from Mean	from Mean	Returns	from Mean
8	Excellent	0.25	126.50	4.50	0.3100	0.2124	0.0451	0.2700	0.0451
9	Good	0.45	110.00	4.00	0.1400	0.0424	0.0018	0.1000	0.0018
10	Poor	0.25	89.75	3.50	−0.0675	−0.1651	0.0273	−0.1075	0.0273
11	Crash	0.05	46.00	2.00	−0.5200	−0.6176	0.3815	−0.5600	0.3815
12	Expected Value (mean)	SUMPRODUCT(B8:B11, E8:E11) =			0.0976				
13	Variance of HPR			SUMPRODUCT(B8:B11, G8:G11) =			0.0380		
14	Standard Deviation of HPR				SQRT(G13) =		0.1949		
15	Risk Premium			SUMPRODUCT(B8:B11, H8:H11) =			0.0576		
16	Standard Deviation of Excess Return				SQRT(SUMPRODUCT(B8:B11, I8:I11)) =			0.1949	

This definition of the HPR treats the dividend as paid at the end of the holding period. When dividends are received earlier, the HPR ignores reinvestment income between the receipt of the payment and the end of the holding period. Recall also that the percent return from dividends is called the dividend yield, and so the dividend yield plus the capital gains yield equals the HPR.

Expected Return and Standard Deviation

There is considerable uncertainty about the price of a share a year from now, however, so you cannot be sure about your eventual HPR. We can try to quantify our beliefs about the state of the economy and the stock market, however, in terms of three possible scenarios with probabilities as presented in columns A through E of Spreadsheet 4.1.

How can we evaluate this probability distribution? To start, we characterize probability distributions of rates of return by their **expected** or **mean return**, $E(r)$, and their **standard deviation**, σ. The expected rate of return is a probability-weighted average of the rates of return in all scenarios. Calling $p(s)$ the probability of each scenario and $r(s)$ the HPR in each scenario, where scenarios are labelled or "indexed" by the variable s, we may write the expected return as

$$E(r) = \sum_s p(s)r(s) \tag{4.11}$$

Applying this formula to the data in Spreadsheet 4.1, we find that the expected rate of return on the index fund is

$$E(r) = .25 \times 31\% + .45 \times 14\% + .25 \times (-6.75\%) + .05 \times (-52\%) = 9.76\%$$

The standard deviation of the rate of return (σ) is a measure of risk. It is defined as the square root of the **variance**, which in turn is defined as the expected value of the squared deviations from the expected return. The higher the volatility in outcomes, the higher the average value of these squared deviations. Therefore, variance and standard deviation measure the uncertainty of outcomes. Symbolically,

$$\sigma^2 = \sum_s p(s)[r(s) - E(r)]^2 \tag{4.12}$$

Therefore, in our example,

$$\sigma^2 = .25(31 - 9.76)^2 + .45(14 - 9.76)^2 + .25(-6.75 - 9.76)^2 + .05 \times (-52 - 9.76)^2 = 380$$

and

$$\sigma = 19.49\%$$

Clearly, what would trouble potential investors in the index fund is the downside risk of a crash or poor market, not the upside potential of a good or excellent market. The standard deviation of the rate of return does not distinguish between these two; it treats both as deviations from the mean. As long as the probability distribution is more or less symmetric about the mean, however, σ is a reasonable measure of risk. In the special case where we can assume that the probability distribution is normal—represented by the well-known bell-shaped curve—$E(r)$ and σ completely characterize the distribution.

Excess Returns and Risk Premiums

Financial Risk
Management
www.contingency-
analysis.com

Getting back to the example, how much, if anything, should you invest in the index fund? First, you must ask how much of an expected reward is offered for the risk involved in investing money in stocks.

We measure the reward as the difference between the expected HPR on the index stock fund and the **risk-free rate**, that is, the rate you can earn by leaving money in risk-free assets such as T-bills, money market funds, or the bank. We call this difference the **risk premium** on common stocks. If the risk-free rate in the example is 4 percent per year, and the expected index fund return is 9.76 percent, then the risk premium on stocks is 5.76 percent per year. The difference between the actual rate of return on a risky asset and the risk-free rate is called **excess return**. Therefore, the risk premium is the expected excess return, and the standard deviation of the excess return is a measure of its risk. See Spreadsheet 4.1 for these calculations.

The degree to which investors are willing to commit funds to stocks depends on **risk aversion**. CFAs and financial analysts generally assume investors are risk-averse in the sense that, if the risk premium were zero, people would not be willing to invest any money in stocks. In theory then, there must always be a positive risk premium on stocks in order to induce risk-averse investors to hold the existing supply of stocks instead of placing all their money in risk-free assets. We explore their theory more systematically further on in this chapter.

Although this simple scenario analysis illustrates the concepts behind the quantification of risk and return, you might still wonder how to get a more realistic estimate of $E(r)$ and σ for common stocks and other types of securities. Here history has insights to offer. First, however, we introduce some important statistical tools and concepts.

CC 3

CONCEPT CHECK

You invest $27,000 in a corporate bond selling for $900 per $1,000 par value. Over the coming year, the bond will pay interest of $75 per $1,000 of par value. The price of the bond at year's end will depend on the level of interest rates that will prevail at that time. You construct the following scenario analysis:

Interest Rates	Probability	Year-End Bond Price
High	.2	$850
Unchanged	.5	915
Low	.3	985

Your alternative investment is a T-bill that yields a sure rate of return of 5 percent. Calculate the HPR for each scenario, the expected rate of return, and the risk premium on your investment. What is the expected end-of-year dollar value of your investment?

4.5   TIME SERIES ANALYSIS OF PAST RATES OF RETURN

Time Series Versus Scenario Analysis

In a forward-looking scenario analysis we determine a set of relevant scenarios and associated investment outcomes (rates of return), assign probabilities to each, and conclude by computing the risk premium (the reward) and standard deviation (the risk) of the proposed investment. In contrast, asset and portfolio return histories come in the form of time series of past realized returns that do not explicitly provide investors' original assessments of the probabilities of those observed returns; we observe only dates and associated HPRs. We have to infer from this limited data the probability distributions from which these returns might have been drawn, or at least some of its characteristics such as expected return and standard deviation.

Expected Returns and the Arithmetic Average

When we use historical data, we treat each observation as an equally likely "scenario." So if there are n observations, we substitute equal probabilities of magnitude $1/n$ for each $p(s)$ in equation 4.11. The expected return, $E(r)$, is then estimated by the arithmetic average of the sample rates of return:

$$E(r) = \sum_{s=1}^{n} p(s)r(s) = \frac{1}{n} \sum_{s=1}^{n} r(s) \tag{4.13}$$

$$= \text{Arithmetic average of rates of return}$$

EXAMPLE 4.6   **Arithmetic Average and Expected Return**

Spreadsheet 4.2 presents a (short) time series of annual holding-period returns for the S&P/TSX Composite index over the period 2005–2009. We treat each HPR of the $n = 5$ observations in the time series as an equally likely annual outcome during the sample years and assign it an equal probability of 1/5, or .2. Column B in Spreadsheet 4.2 therefore uses .2 as probabilities, and column C shows the annual HPRs. Applying equation 4.13 (using Excel's SUMPRODUCT function) to the time series in the spreadsheet demonstrates that adding up the products of probability times HPR amounts to taking the arithmetic average of the HPRs (compare cells C10 and C11).

EXCEL SPREADSHEET 4.2

Time series of HPR for the S&P/TSX Composite. ↗

	A	B	C	D	E	F
1						
2						
3		Implicitly Assumed		Squared	Gross HPR =	Wealth
4	Period	Probability = 1/5	HPR (decimal)	Deviation	1 + HPR	Index*
5	2005	.2	0.2413	0.0182	1.2413	1.2413
6	2006	.2	0.1726	0.0044	1.1726	1.4555
7	2007	.2	0.0983	0.0007	1.0983	1.5986
8	2008	.2	−0.3300	0.1906	0.6700	1.0710
9	2009	.2	0.3506	0.0595	1.3505	1.4465
10	Arithmetic average	AVERAGE(C5:C9) =	0.1065			
11	Expected HPR	SUMPRODUCT(B5:B9, C5:C9) =	0.1065			
12		Standard deviation	SUMPRODUCT(B5:B9, D5:D9)^.5 =	0.2335		Check:
13			STDEV(C5:C9) =	0.2611		1.0766^5=
14			Geometric average return	GEOMEAN(E5:E9) − 1 =	0.0766	=1.4465
15	*The value of $1 invested at the beginning of the sample period (1/1/2005).					

Example 4.6 illustrates the logic for the wide use of the arithmetic average in investments. If the time series of historical returns fairly represents the true underlying probability distribution, then the arithmetic average return from a historical period provides a good forecast of the investment's expected HPR.

The Geometric (Time-Weighted) Average Return

We saw that the arithmetic average provides an unbiased estimate of the *expected* rate of return. But what does the time series tell us about the *actual* performance of the portfolio over the full sample period? Column F in Spreadsheet 4.2 shows the wealth index from investing $1 in an S&P/TSX Composite index fund at the beginning of 2005. The value of the wealth index at the end of 2009, $1.4465, is the terminal value of the $1 investment, which implies a *5-year* holding period return (HPR) of 44.65 percent.

An intuitive measure of performance over the sample period is the (fixed) annual HPR that would compound over the period to the same terminal value as obtained from the sequence of actual returns in the time series. Denote this rate by g, so that

$$\text{Terminal value} = (1 + r_1) \times (1 + r_2) \times \cdots \times (1 + r_5) = 1.4465$$

$$(1 + g)^n = \text{Terminal value} = 1.4465 \text{ (cell F9 in Spreadsheet 4.2)} \tag{4.14}$$

$$g = \text{Terminal value}^{1/n} - 1 = (1.4465)^{1/5} - 1 - .07662 = 7.66\% \text{ (cell E14)}$$

where $1 + g$ is the geometric average of the gross returns $(1 + r)$ from the time series (which can be computed with Excel's GEOMEAN function) and g is the annual HPR that would replicate the final value of our investment.

Practitioners of investments also call g the *time-weighted* (as opposed to dollar-weighted) average return, to emphasize that each past return receives an equal weight in the process of averaging. This distinction is important because investment managers often experience significant changes in funds under management as investors purchase or redeem shares. Rates of return obtained during periods when the fund is large produce larger dollar profits than rates obtained when the fund is small. We discuss this distinction further in the chapter on performance evaluation.

EXAMPLE 4.7   **Geometric Versus Arithmetic Average**

The geometric average in Example 4.6 (7.66 percent) is substantially less than the arithmetic average (10.65 percent). This discrepancy is sometimes a source of confusion. It arises from the asymmetric effect of positive and negative rates of returns on the terminal value of the portfolio.

Observe the returns in years 2008 $(-.3300)$ and 2009 (.3506). The arithmetic average return over the 2 years is $(-.3300 + .3506)/2 = .0106$ (1.06 percent). However, if you had invested $100 at the beginning of 2008, you would have ended with only $67 at the end of 2008. In order to break even, you would then have needed to earn $33 in 2009, which would amount to a return of 49.25 percent (33.00/67.00). Why is such a rate necessary to break even, rather than the 33 percent you lost in 2008? Because your base for 2009 was smaller than $100; the lower base means that it takes a greater subsequent rate to just break even. Even a rate as high as the 35.06 percent realized in 2009 yields a portfolio value in 2009 of $67 \times 1.3506 = \$90.49$, which implies a 2-year annually compounded rate (the geometric average) of only -4.87 percent, significantly less than the arithmetic average of 1.06 percent.

The larger the swings in rates of return, the greater the discrepancy between the arithmetic and geometric averages, that is, between the compound rate earned over the sample period and the average of the annual returns. If returns come from a normal distribution, the difference exactly equals half the variance of the distribution, that is,

$$\text{Geometric average} = \text{Arithmetic average} - \frac{1}{2}\sigma^2 \tag{4.15}$$

(*Warning*: To use equation 4.15, you must express returns as decimals, not percentages.) When returns are approximately normal, equation 4.15 will be a good approximation.[9]

Variance and Standard Deviation

When thinking about risk, we are interested in the likelihood of deviations from the *expected* return. In practice, we usually cannot directly observe expectations, so we estimate the variance by averaging squared deviations from our estimate of the expected return, the arithmetic average, $\bar{r}$. Adapting equation 4.12 for historic data, we again use equal probabilities for each observation, and use the sample average in place of the unobservable $E(r)$.

$$\text{Variance} = \text{Expected value of squared deviations}$$

$$\sigma^2 = \sum p(s)[r(s) - E(r)]^2$$

Using historical data with n observations, we *estimate* variance as

$$\sigma^2 = \frac{1}{n}\sum_{s=1}^{n}[r(s) - \bar{r}]^2 \tag{4.16}$$

EXAMPLE 4.8   Variance and Standard Deviation

Take another look at Spreadsheet 4.2. Column D shows the squared deviations from the arithmetic average, and cell D12 gives the standard deviation as the square root of the sum of products of the (equal) probabilities times the squared deviations (.2335).

The variance estimate from equation 4.16 is downward-biased, however. The reason is that we have taken deviations from the sample arithmetic average, $\bar{r}$, instead of the unknown, true expected value, $E(r)$, and so have introduced a bit of estimation error. We can eliminate the bias by multiplying the arithmetic average of squared deviations by the factor $n/(n-1)$. The variance and standard deviation then become

$$\sigma^2 = \left(\frac{n}{n-1}\right) \times \frac{1}{n}\sum_{j=1}^{n}[r(s) - \bar{r}]^2 = \frac{1}{n-1}\sum_{j=1}^{n}[r(s) - \bar{r}]^2$$

$$\sigma = \sqrt{\frac{1}{n-1}\sum_{j=1}^{n}[r(s) - \bar{r}]^2} \tag{4.17}$$

Cell D13 shows that the unbiased estimate of the standard deviation is .2611, which is a bit higher than the .2335 value obtained in cell D12.

---

[9]We are told to measure historical performance over a particular sample period by the *geometric* average but to estimate expected future performance from that same sample as the *arithmetic* average. The question naturally arises: If the same sample were to recur in the future, performance would be measured by the *geometric* average, so isn't that the best estimator of expected return? Surprisingly, the answer is no. Future results will always contain both positive and negative surprises compared to prior expectations. When compounded, a run of positive surprises has greater impact on final wealth than a run of equal-sized negative ones. Because of this asymmetry, the sample geometric average is actually a downward-biased estimate of the future average return drawn from the same distribution. The bias turns out to be half the variance, and thus using the arithmetic average corrects for this bias.

Mean and Standard Deviation Estimates from Higher-Frequency Observations

Do more frequent observations lead to more accurate estimates? The answer to this question may be surprising: observation frequency has no impact on the accuracy of mean estimates. It is the *duration* of a sample time series (as opposed to the *number* of observations) that improves accuracy.

The total 10-year return divided by 10 is as accurate an estimate of the expected annual return as 12 times the average of 120 monthly returns. The average monthly return must be consistent with the average 10-year return, so the extra intrayear observations yield no additional information about average return. However, a longer sample, for example a 100-year return, will provide a more accurate estimate of the mean return than a 10-year return, *provided* the probability distribution of returns remains unchanged over the 100 years. This suggests a rule: Use the longest sample that you still believe comes from the same return distribution. Unfortunately, in practice, old data may be less informative. Are return data from the nineteenth century relevant to estimating expected returns in the twenty-first century? Quite possibly not, implying that we face severe limits to the accuracy of our estimates of mean returns.

For ease of comparison, it is customary to report the mean and other statistics on an annual basis. The monthly average return, $\bar{r}_M$, is annualized by compounding:

$$\bar{r}_A = (1 + \bar{r}_M)^{12} - 1$$

In contrast to the mean, the accuracy of estimates of the standard deviation and higher moments (all computed using *deviations from the average*) can be made more precise by increasing the number of observations. Thus, we can improve accuracy of estimates of SD and higher moments of the distribution by using more frequent observations.

Estimates of standard deviation begin with the variance. When monthly returns are uncorrelated from one month to another, monthly variances simply add up. Thus, when the variance is the same every month, we annualize by:[10] $\sigma_A^2 = 12\sigma_M^2$. In general, the T-month variance is T times the 1-month variance. Consequently, standard deviation grows at the rate of $\sqrt{T}$, that is, $\sigma_A = \sqrt{12}\sigma_M$. While the mean and the variance grow in direct proportion to time, SD grows at the rate of square root of time.

The Reward-to-Variability (Sharpe) Ratio

Finally, it is worth noting that investors presumably are interested in the expected *excess* return they can earn over the T-bill rate by replacing T-bills with a risky portfolio as well as the risk they would thereby incur. While the T-bill rate is not fixed each period, we still know with certainty what rate we will earn if we purchase a bill and hold it to maturity. Other investments typically entail accepting some risk in return for the prospect of earning more than the safe T-bill rate. Investors price risky assets so that the risk premium will be commensurate with the risk of that expected *excess* return, and hence it's best to measure risk by the standard deviation of excess, not total, returns.

The importance of the tradeoff between reward (the risk premium) and risk (as measured by standard deviation or SD) suggests that we measure the attraction of an investment portfolio by the ratio of its risk premium to the SD of its excess returns.

$$\text{Sharpe ratio (for portfolios)} = \frac{\text{Risk premium}}{\text{SD of excess return}} \tag{4.18}$$

This reward-to-volatility measure (first proposed by William Sharpe and hence called the *Sharpe ratio*) is widely used to evaluate the performance of investment managers.

---

[10]When returns are uncorrelated, we do not have to worry about covariances among them. Therefore, the variance of the sum of 12 monthly returns (i.e., the variance of the annual return) is the sum of the 12 monthly variances. If returns are correlated across months, annualizing is more involved and requires adjusting for the structure of serial correlation.

Notice that the Sharpe ratio divides the risk premium (which rises in direct proportion to time) by the standard deviation (which rises in direct proportion to square root of unit of time). Therefore, the Sharpe ratio will be higher when annualized from higher-frequency returns. For example, to annualize the Sharpe ratio (SR) from monthly rates, we multiply the numerator by 12 and the denominator by $\sqrt{12}$. Hence the annualized Sharpe ratio is $SR_A = SR_M\sqrt{12}$. In general, the Sharpe ratio of a long-term investment over T years will increase by a factor of $\sqrt{T}$ when T-period rates replace annual rates.

EXAMPLE 4.9   Sharpe Ratio

Take another look at Spreadsheet 4.1. The scenario analysis for the proposed investment in the stock index fund resulted in a risk premium of 5.76 percent, and standard deviation of excess returns of 19.49 percent. This implies a Sharpe ratio of .30, a value pretty much in line with past performance of stock index funds. We will see that while the Sharpe ratio is an adequate measure of the risk–return tradeoff for diversified portfolios (the subject of this chapter), it is inadequate when applied to individual assets such as shares of stock.

CC 4

CONCEPT CHECK

Using the annual returns for years 2007–2009 in Spreadsheet 4.2,
a. Compute the arithmetic average return.
b. Compute the geometric average return.
c. Compute the standard deviation of returns.
d. Compute the Sharpe ratio assuming the risk-free rate was 6 percent per year.

4.6   THE NORMAL DISTRIBUTION

The bell-shaped **normal distribution** appears naturally in many applications. For example, heights and weights of newborns are well described by the normal distribution. In fact, many variables that are the end result of multiple random influences will exhibit a normal distribution. By the same logic, if return expectations implicit in asset prices are rational, actual rates of return realized should be normally distributed around these expectations.

To see why the normal curve is "normal," consider a newspaper stand that turns a profit of $100 on a good day and breaks even on a bad day, with equal probabilities of .5. Thus, the mean daily profit is $50 dollars. We can build a tree that compiles all the possible outcomes at the end of any period. Here is an **event tree** showing outcomes after two days:

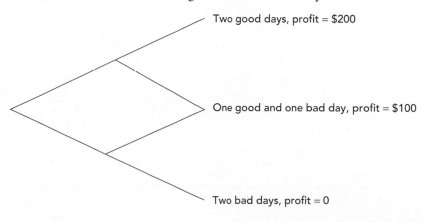

Two good days, profit = $200

One good and one bad day, profit = $100

Two bad days, profit = 0

Notice that two days can produce three different outcomes and, in general, n days can produce $n + 1$ possible outcomes. The most likely two-day outcome is "one good and one bad day," which can happen two ways (first a good day, or first a bad day). The probability of this outcome is .5. Less likely are the two extreme outcomes (both good days or both bad days) with probability .25 each.

What is the distribution of profits at the end of many business days? For example, after 200 days, there are 201 possible outcomes, and again, the midrange outcomes are the more likely because there are more sequences that lead to them. For example, while there is only one sequence that results in 200 consecutive bad days, there are an enormous number of sequences that result in 100 good days and 100 bad days. The probability distribution will eventually take on the familiar bell shape.[11]

Figure 4.4 is a graph of the normal curve with mean of 10 percent and standard deviation of 20 percent. It shows the theoretical probability of rates of return within various ranges given these parameters. A smaller SD means that possible outcomes cluster more tightly around the mean, while a higher SD implies more diffuse distributions. The likelihood of realizing any particular outcome when sampling from a normal distribution is fully determined by the number of standard deviations that separate that outcome from the mean. Put differently, the normal distribution is completely characterized by two parameters, the mean and SD.

Investment management is far more tractable when rates of return can be well approximated by the normal distribution. First, the normal distribution is symmetric, that is, the probability of any positive deviation above the mean is equal to that of a negative deviation of the same magnitude. Absent symmetry, measuring risk as the standard deviation of returns is inadequate. Second, the normal distribution belongs to a unique family of distributions characterized as "stable," because of the following property: When assets with normally distributed returns are mixed to construct a portfolio, the portfolio return also is normally distributed. Third, scenario analysis is greatly simplified when only two parameters (mean and SD) need to be estimated to obtain the probabilities of future scenarios. Fourth, when constructing portfolios of securities, we must account for the statistical dependence of returns across securities. Generally, such dependence is a complex, multilayered relationship. But when securities are normally distributed,

Figure 4.4

The normal distribution.

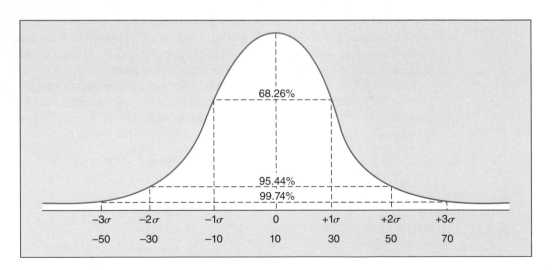

[11]As a historical footnote, early descriptions of the normal distribution in the eighteenth century were based on the outcomes of a binomial tree like the one we have drawn for the newspaper stand, extended out to many periods. This representation is used in practice to price many option contracts, as we will see in Chapter 18. For a nice demonstration of how the binomial distribution quickly approximates the normal, go to www.jcu.edu/math/isep/Quincunx/Quincunx.html.

the statistical relationships between returns can be summarized with a straightforward correlation coefficient. Thus we need to estimate only one parameter to summarize the dependence of any two securities.

How closely must actual return distributions fit the normal curve to justify its use in investment management? Clearly, the normal curve cannot be a perfect description of reality. For example, actual returns cannot be less than -100 percent, which the normal distribution would not rule out. But this does not mean that the normal curve cannot still be useful. A similar issue arises in many other contexts. For example, shortly after birth, a baby's weight is typically evaluated by comparing it to a normal curve of newborn weights. This may seem surprising, because a normal distribution admits values from minus to plus infinity, and surely no baby is born with a negative weight. The normal distribution is still useful in this application because the SD of the weight is small relative to its mean, and the likelihood of a negative weight would be too trivial to matter.[12] In a similar spirit, we must identify criteria to determine the adequacy of the normality assumption for rates of return.

EXAMPLE 4.10 Normal Distribution Function in Excel

Suppose the monthly rate of return on the S&P/TSX Composite is approximately normally distributed with a mean of 1 percent and standard deviation of 6 percent. What is the probability that the return on the index in any month will be negative? We can use Excel's built-in functions to quickly answer this question. The probability of observing an outcome less than some cutoff according to the normal distribution function is given as NORMDIST(cutoff, mean, standard deviation, TRUE). In this case, we want to know the probability of an outcome below zero, when the mean is 1 percent and the standard deviation is 6 percent, so we compute NORMDIST(0, 1, 6, TRUE) = .4338. We could also use Excel's built-in *standard* normal function and ask for the probability of an outcome 1/6 of a standard deviation below the mean. This would be the same: NORMSDIST($-1/6$) = .4338.

CC 5 CONCEPT CHECK

What is the probability that the return on the index in Example 4.10 will be below -15 percent?

4.7 DEVIATIONS FROM NORMALITY AND RISK MEASURES

As we noted earlier (but you can't repeat it too often!), normality of excess returns hugely simplifies portfolio selection. Normality assures us that standard deviation is a complete measure of risk and hence the Sharpe ratio is a complete measure of portfolio performance. Unfortunately, deviations from normality of asset returns are quite significant and difficult to ignore.

Deviations from normality may be discerned by calculating the higher moments of return distributions. The nth central moment of a distribution of excess returns, R, is estimated as the average value of $[R - E(R)]^n$. The first moment ($n = 1$) is necessarily zero (the average deviation from the sample average must be zero). The second moment ($n = 2$) is the estimate of the

[12]In fact, the standard deviation is 511 grams while the mean is 3,958 grams. A negative weight would therefore be 7.74 standard deviations below the mean, and according to the normal distribution would have probability of only 4.97×10^{-15}. The issue of negative birth weight clearly isn't a *practical* concern.

Figure 4.5a

Normal and skewed distributions (mean = 6%, SD = 17%).

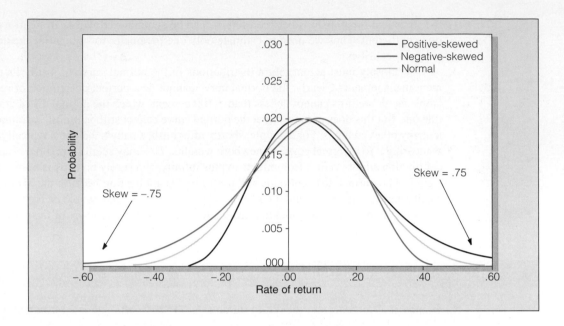

variance of returns.[13] Our first criterion is symmetry. A measure of asymmetry called **skew** uses the ratio of the average *cubed* deviations from the mean, called the third moment, to the cubed standard deviation to measure asymmetry or "skewness" of a distribution.

$$\text{Skew} = \frac{E[r(s) - E(r)]^3}{\sigma^3} \tag{4.19}$$

Cubing deviations maintain their sign (e.g., the cube of a negative number is negative). When a distribution is "skewed to the right," as in the dark curve of Figure 4.5a, the extreme positive values, when cubed, dominate the third moment, resulting in a positive skew. When a distribution is "skewed to the left," the cubed extreme negative values dominate, and the skew will be negative.

When the distribution is positively skewed (skewed to the right), the standard deviation overestimates risk, because extreme positive deviations from expectation (which do not concern investors) nevertheless increase the estimate of volatility. Conversely, and more importantly, when the distribution is negatively skewed, the SD will underestimate risk.

Another potentially important deviation from normality, *kurtosis*, concerns the likelihood of extreme values on either side of the mean at the expense of a smaller likelihood of moderate deviations. Graphically speaking, when the tails of a distribution are "fat," there is more probability mass in the tails of the distribution than predicted by the normal distribution, at the expense of "slender shoulders," that is, less probability mass near the centre of the distribution. Figure 4.5b superimposes a "fat-tailed" distribution on a normal with the same mean and SD. Although symmetry is still preserved, the SD will underestimate the likelihood of extreme events: large losses as well as large gains.

---

[13]For distributions that are symmetric about the average, as is the case for the normal distribution, all odd moments ($n = 1, 3, 5, \ldots$) have expectations of zero. For the normal distribution, the expectations of all higher even moments ($n = 4, 6, \ldots$) are functions *only* of the standard deviation, σ. For example, the expected fourth moment ($n = 4$) is $3\sigma^4$, and for $n = 6$, it is $15\sigma^6$. Thus, for normally distributed returns the standard deviation, σ, provides a complete measure of risk, and portfolio performance may be measured by the Sharpe ratio, $\bar{R}/\sigma$. For other distributions, however, asymmetry may be measured by higher nonzero odd moments. Higher even moments (in excess of those consistent with the normal distribution), combined with large, negative odd moments, indicate higher probabilities of extreme negative outcomes.

Figure 4.5b

Normal and fat-tailed distributions (mean = .1, SD = .2).

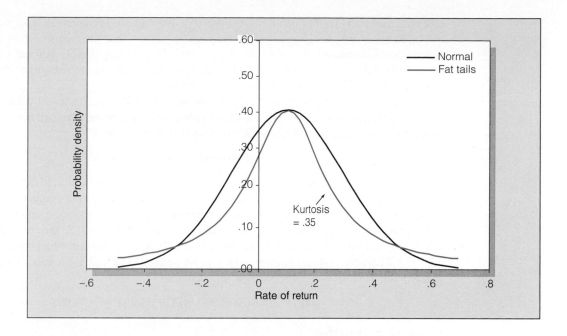

Kurtosis measures the degree of fat tails. We use the expectation of deviations from the mean raised to the *fourth* power, scaled by dividing by the fourth power of the SD,

$$\text{Kurtosis} = \frac{E[r(s) - E(r)]^4}{\sigma^4} - 3 \qquad (4.20)$$

We subtract 3 in equation 4.20 because the ratio for a normal distribution is 3. Thus, the kurtosis of a normal distribution is defined as zero, and any kurtosis above zero is a sign of fatter tails. The kurtosis of the distribution in Figure 4.5b, which has visible fat tails, is .36.

In addition to a shift of observations between the shoulders and the tails, kurtosis can be affected by a shift from the shoulders to the centre of the distribution (which decreases kurtosis), or vice versa. This element of kurtosis is called "peakedness," as it affects the height of the peak of the distribution at its centre. It is not shown in Figure 4.5b, but we often encounter peakedness in histograms of actual distributions. Notice that both skew and kurtosis are pure numbers. They do not change when annualized from higher frequency observations.

Higher frequency of extreme negative returns may result from negative skew and/or kurtosis (fat tails). Therefore, we would like a risk measure that indicates vulnerability to extreme negative returns. We discuss four such measures that are most frequently used in practice: value at risk, expected shortfall, lower partial standard deviation, and the frequency of extreme (3-sigma) returns.

CC 6

CONCEPT CHECK

Estimate the skew and kurtosis of the five rates in Spreadsheet 4.2.

Value at Risk

The **value at risk** (denoted **VaR** to distinguish it from *Var*, the abbreviation for variance) is the loss corresponding to a very low percentile of the entire return distribution, for example, the fifth or first percentile return. VaR is actually written into regulation of banks and closely watched by risk managers. It is another name for *quantile* of a distribution. The quantile, q, of a distribution is the value below which lies q percent of the possible values. Thus the median is $q = 50$th quantile. Practitioners commonly estimate the 5 percent VaR, meaning that 95 percent of returns will exceed the VaR, and 5 percent will be worse. Therefore, VaR may be viewed as the best rate of return out of the 5 percent *worst-case* future scenarios.

When portfolio returns are normally distributed, the VaR is determined by the mean and SD of the distribution. Recalling that -1.65 is the 5th percentile of the standard normal distribution (with mean $= 0$ and SD $= 1$), the VaR for a normal distribution is

$$\text{VaR}(.05, \text{normal}) = \text{Mean} - 1.65\text{SD}$$

To obtain a sample estimate of VaR, we sort the observations from high to low. The VaR is the return at the 5th percentile of the sample distribution. Almost always, 5 percent of the number of observations will not be an integer, and so we must interpolate. Suppose a sample comprises 56 annual returns, so that 5 percent of the number of observations is 2.8. We must interpolate between the second and the third observation from the bottom. Suppose the bottom three returns are -33.4 percent, -41.03 percent, and -45.64 percent. The VaR is therefore between -33.49 percent and -41.03 percent and would be calculated as

$$\text{VaR} = -41.03 + .8(41.03 - 33.49) = -34.998$$

Expected Shortfall

When we assess tail risk by looking at the 5 percent worst-case scenarios, the VaR is the most optimistic measure of risk, as it takes the highest return (smallest loss) of all these cases. A more realistic view of downside exposure would focus instead on the *expected* loss given that we find ourselves in one of the worst-case scenarios. This value, unfortunately, has two names: either **expected shortfall (ES)** or **conditional tail expectation (CTE)**; the latter emphasizes that this expectation is conditioned on being in the left tail of the distribution. ES is the more commonly used terminology.

Extending the previous VaR example, we assume equal probabilities for all values. Hence, we need to average across the bottom 5 percent of the observations. We sum the bottom 4 returns plus .2 of the fifth from the bottom, and divide by 4.2 to find ES $= -40.05$ percent, significantly less than the -34.998 percent VaR.[14]

Lower Partial Standard Deviation and the Sortino Ratio

The use of standard deviation as a measure of risk when the return distribution is nonnormal presents two problems: (1) the asymmetry of the distribution suggests we should look at negative outcomes separately; (2) because an alternative to a risky portfolio is a risk-free investment, we should look at deviations of returns from the risk-free rate rather than from the sample average, that is, at negative *excess* returns.

A risk measure that addresses these issues is the **lower partial standard deviation (LPSD)** of excess returns, which is computed like the usual standard deviation, but using only "bad" returns. Specifically, it uses only negative deviations from the risk-free rate (rather than negative deviations from the sample average), squares those deviations to obtain an analogue to variance,

---

[14]A formula for the ES in the case of normally distributed returns is given in Jonathan Treussard, "The Non-monotonicity of Value-at-Risk and the Validity of Risk Measures over Different Horizons," *IFCAI Journal of Financial Risk Management*, March 2007. The formula is

$$\text{ES} = \frac{1}{.05} \exp(\mu)N[-\sigma - F(.95)] - 1$$

where μ is the mean of the continuously compounded returns, σ is the SD, $N(\bullet)$ is the cumulative standard normal, and F is its inverse. In the sample above, μ and σ were estimated as 5.47 percent and 19.54 percent. Assuming normality, we would have ES $= -30.57$ percent, suggesting that this distribution has a larger left tail than the normal. It should be noted, however, that estimates of VaR and ES from historical samples, while unbiased, are subject to large estimation errors because they are estimated from a small number of extreme returns.

In 2008 a typical investment portfolio of 60% stocks and 40% bonds lost roughly a fifth of its value. Standard portfolio-construction tools assume that will happen only once every 111 years. Though mathematicians and many investors have long known market behavior isn't a pretty picture, standard portfolio construction assumes returns fall along a tidy, bell-curve-shaped distribution. With that approach, a 2008-type decline would fall near the skinny left tall, indicating its rarity.

Recent history would suggest such meltdowns aren't so rare. In a little more than two decades, investors have been buffeted by the 1987 market crash, the implosion of hedge fund Long-Term Capital Management, the bursting of the tech-stock bubble, and other crises.

Many of Wall Street's new tools assume market returns fall along a "fat-tailed" distribution, where, say, last year's nearly 40% stock-market decline would be more common than previously thought. These new assumptions present a far different picture of risk. Consider the 60% stock, 40% bond portfolio that fell about 20% last year. Under the fat-tailed distribution, that should occur once every 40 years, not once every 111 years as assumed under a bell-curve-type distribution. (The last year as bad as 2008 was 1931.)

One potential pitfall: Number-crunchers have a smaller supply of historical observations to construct models focused on rare events. "Data are intrinsically sparse," says Lisa Goldberg, executive director of analytic initiatives at MSCI Barra.

Many of the new tools also limit the role of conventional risk measures. Standard deviation, proposed as a risk measure by Nobel Prize–winning economist Harry Markowitz in the 1950s, can be used to gauge how much an investment's returns vary over time. But it is equally affected by upside and downside moves, whereas many investors fear losses much more than they value gains. And it doesn't fully gauge risk in a fat-tailed world.

A newer measure that has gained prominence in recent decades ignores potential gains and looks at downside risk. That measure, called "value at risk," might tell you that you have a 5% chance of losing 3% or more in a single day, but it doesn't home in on the worst downside scenarios.

To focus on extreme risk, many firms have begun using a measure called "expected shortfall" or "conditional value at risk," which is the expected portfolio loss when value at risk has been breached. Conditional value at risk helps estimate the magnitudes of expected loss on the very bad days. Firms such as J. P. Morgan and MSCI Barra are employing the measure.

Source: Eleanor Laise, "Some Funds Stop Grading on the Curve," *The Wall Street Journal*, September 8, 2009, p. C1. Reprinted by permission of The Wall Street Journal, © 2009.

and then takes the square root to obtain a "left-tail standard deviation." The LPSD is therefore the square root of the average squared deviation, *conditional* on a negative excess return. Notice that this measure ignores the frequency of negative excess returns—that is, portfolios with the same average squared negative excess returns will yield the same LPSD regardless of the relative frequency of negative excess returns.

Practitioners who replace standard deviation with this LPSD typically also replace the Sharpe ratio (the ratio of average excess return to standard deviation) with the ratio of average excess returns to LPSD. This variant on the Sharpe ratio is called the **Sortino ratio**.

Relative Frequency of Large, Negative 3-Sigma Returns

Here we concentrate on the relative frequency of large, negative returns compared with those frequencies in a normal distribution with the same mean and standard deviation. Extreme returns are often called *jumps*, as the stock price makes a big, sudden movement. We compare the fraction of observations with returns three or more standard deviations below the mean to the relative frequency of negative 3-sigma returns in the corresponding normal distribution.

This measure can be quite informative about downside risk, but in practice is most useful for large, high-frequency samples. Observe from Figure 4.4 that the relative frequency of negative 3-sigma jumps in a standard normal distribution is only .13 percent—that is, 1.3 observations per 1,000. Thus, in a small sample, it is hard to obtain a "representative" outcome, one that reflects true statistical expectations of extreme events.

In the analysis of the history of some popular investment vehicles in the next section we will show why practitioners need this plethora of statistics and performance measures to analyze risky investments. The nearby box discusses the growing popularity of these measures, and particularly the new focus on fat tails and extreme events.

4.8   THE HISTORICAL RECORD

Bills, Bonds, and Stocks, 1957–2012

We are now ready to examine the record of past rates of return for information about risk premiums and their standard deviations. Table 4.3 presents summary statistics extracted from annual and monthly data in our online centre on the annual HPRs on three asset classes for the period 1957–2012.

The first is the arithmetic mean or average HPR. For bills it is 6.19 percent, for bonds it is 8.92 percent, and for common stock it is 10.43 percent. These numbers imply an average risk premium of 2.73 percent per year on bonds and 4.24 percent on stocks (the average HPR less the risk-free rate of 6.19 percent).

Figure 4.6 gives a graphical representation of the relative variabilities of the annual HPR on the three different asset classes. We have plotted the three time series on the same set of axes. Clearly, the annual HPR on stocks is the most variable series. The standard deviations are shown in the third line of Table 4.3. For stock returns it has been 16.88 percent, in contrast to 9.71 percent for bonds and 3.90 percent for bills.

Comparable figures for U.S. stocks show that they have both a higher return and a higher risk than their Canadian counterparts. A study by Roll[15] that used daily data covering the period April 1988–March 1991 gives average annual HPRs of 4.20 percent and 12.27 percent for Canada and the United States, with corresponding standard deviations of 9.97 percent and 14.37 percent. Part of the Canada–U.S. difference is due to the different industrial composition of their respective economies. We provide more information on this topic in the next subsection.

Averages and standard deviations of raw annual returns should be interpreted with caution. First, standard deviations of total returns are affected by variation in the risk-free rate and thus do not measure the true source of risk, namely the uncertainty surrounding *excess* returns. Second, annual rates that compound over a whole year exhibit meaningful amounts of skewness, and estimates of kurtosis also may be misleading.

TABLE 4.3   Summary Statistics of Rates of Return, 1957–2012

	T-Bill	LT Bond	Stock	CPI Change	Real Rate
Arithmetic average	.061894	.089198	.1043433	.0389377	.022291
Geometric average	.082975	.071058	.0613919	.0317938	.034101
Standard deviation	.039033	.097116	.1688318	.0312613	.027531
Minimum	.005354	−.07387	−.330036	0	−.03987
Maximum	.184056	.458225	.4476979	.1232877	.081143
Average, excess return		.027304191	.042449718		
Standard deviation, excess return		.098001562	.174228069		
Serial correlation	.882642	.023443	−.176135		
Sharpe ratio		.27861	.2436445		
Skew		1.081128	−.31599		
Kurtosis		2.554986	−.241269		

Source: Data from Scotia Capital and PC Bonds Analytics, "Debt Market Indices," various years, and Thomson Reuters. Used by permission of Scotia Capital and PC Bonds Analytics, and Thomson Reuters. ©Thomson Reuters. Also, Bank of Canada, http://www.bankofcanada.ca. Reprinted with permission by the Bank of Canada.

[15]See R. Roll, "Industrial Structure and the Comparative Behavior of International Stock Market Indexes," *Journal of Finance* 47, no. 1 (March 1992).

Figure 4.6

Rates of return on bills, bonds, and stocks, 1957–2012.

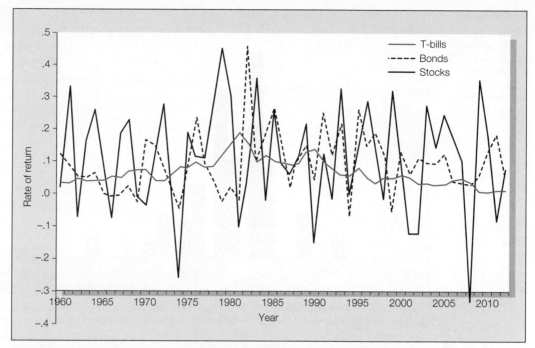

Source: Data from Scotia Capital and PC Bonds Analytics, "Debt Market Indices," various years, and Thomson Reuters. Used by permission of Scotia Capital and PC Bonds Analytics, and Thomson Reuters. ©Thomson Reuters.

Nevertheless, these simple statistics still reveal much about the nature of returns for these asset classes. For example, the asset classes with higher volatility (standard deviation) have provided higher average returns, supporting the idea that investors demand a risk premium to bear risk. Observe, for example, the consistently larger average return as well as standard deviations of stocks, compared to bond portfolios.

Other summary measures in Table 4.3 show the highest and lowest annual HPR (the range) for each asset over the period. The size of this range is another possible measure of the relative riskiness of each asset class. It too confirms the ranking of stocks as the riskiest and bills as the least risky of the three asset classes. The table also shows the Sharpe ratios for LT (long-term) bonds and stocks, and the skewness and kurtosis of the annual data, documenting possible deviations from normality. These will be examined more extensively with monthly return data in the next subsection.

Figures 4.7a and 4.7b present another view of the historical data, the actual frequency distribution of returns on various asset classes over the period 1957–2012. Notice the greater range of stock returns relative to bill or bond returns. Thus, the historical results are consistent with the risk–return tradeoff: riskier assets have provided higher expected returns.

Figure 4.8 presents graphs of wealth indices for investments in three asset classes over the period 1957–2012. The plot for each asset class assumes that you invest $1 at year-end 1956 and traces the value of your investment in following years. The inflation plot demonstrates that to achieve the purchasing power represented by $1 in year-end 1956 one would require $8.29 at year-end 2012. One dollar continually invested in T-bills starting at year-end 1956 would have grown to $28.26 by year-end 2012, representing 3.41 times the original purchasing power (28.26/8.29 = 3.41). That same dollar invested in stocks would have grown to $130.56, representing 15.75 times the original purchasing power of the dollar invested, more than four times as much as the investment in T-bills, despite the risk from sharp downturns during the period. Hence, the lesson of the past is that risk premiums can translate into vast increases in purchasing power over the long haul.

Figure 4.7a

Frequency distributions of the annual HPR on two asset classes: T-bills and long-term bonds.

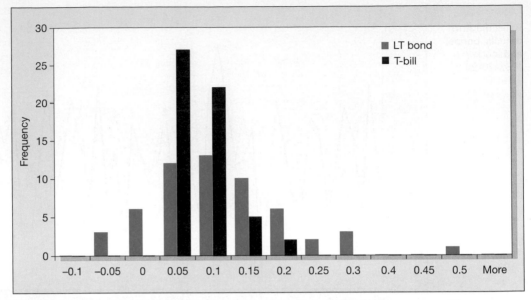

Source: Data from Scotia Capital and PC Bonds Analytics, "Debt Market Indices," various years, and Thomson Reuters. Used by permission of Scotia Capital and PC Bonds Analytics, and Thomson Reuters. © Thomson Reuters.

Figure 4.7b

Frequency distributions of the annual HPR on stocks and inflation.

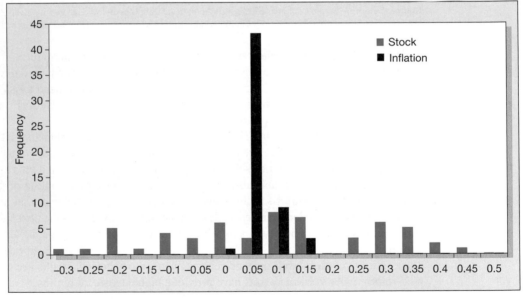

Source: Data from Scotia Capital and PC Bonds Analytics, "Debt Market Indices," various years, and Thomson Reuters. Used by permission of Scotia Capital and PC Bonds Analytics, and Thomson Reuters. © Thomson Reuters.

We should stress that variability of HPR in the past can be an unreliable guide to risk, at least in the case of the risk-free asset. For an investor with a holding period of one year, for example, a one-year T-bill is risk-free with a σ of zero, despite the fact that the standard deviation of the one-year T-bill rate estimated from historical data is not zero.

The risk of cash flows of real assets reflects both *business risk* (profit fluctuations due to business conditions) and *financial risk* (increased profit fluctuations due to leverage). This reminds us that an all-stock portfolio represents claims on leveraged corporations. Most corporations carry some debt, the service of which is a fixed cost. Greater fixed cost makes profits riskier; thus, leverage increases equity risk.

Figure 4.8

Wealth indices for investments in three asset classes and inflation, 1957–2012.

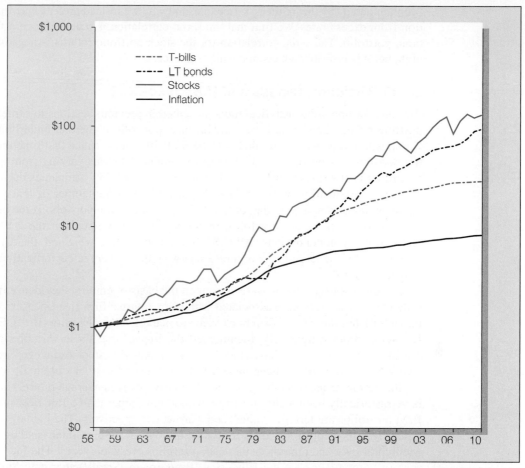

Source: Data from Scotia Capital and PC Bonds Analytics, "Debt Market Indices," various years, and Thomson Reuters. Used by permission of Scotia Capital and PC Bonds Analytics, and Thomson Reuters. ©Thomson Reuters.

> **CC 7**
>
> **CONCEPT CHECK**
>
> Compute the average excess return on stocks (over the T-bill rate) and its standard deviation for the years 1957–1975.

For the serial correlation we note that in well-functioning capital markets we would expect excess returns from successive years to be uncorrelated; that is, the serial correlation of excess returns should be zero. Suppose, for example, that the serial correlation of the annual rate of return on a stock index were negative and that the index fell last year. Investors therefore could predict that stock prices are more likely than usual to rise in the coming year. But armed with this insight, they would *immediately* buy shares and bid up stock prices, eliminating the prospect of an above-normal return in the coming year. We elaborate on this mechanism in the chapter on market efficiency.

Such a consideration does not apply to the T-bill rate, whose return is known in advance. The positive serial correlation of T-bill rates (.88 for the last 56 years) indicates that the short-term rate follows periods in which it predictably tends to rise or fall. However, this predictability in the baseline risk-free rate is not a source of abnormal profits (i.e., excessive profits relative to risk borne). This is a reason why the serial correlation of the *total* return on risky assets will be "contaminated" by that of the risk-free rate, and why we instead prefer to measure serial correlation from excess rates. We find that the serial correlation is practically zero for the long-term bond portfolio. The serial correlation for the stock portfolio returns is negative and somewhat high, but it is probably not economically significant.

Stock Portfolios, Canada and U.S., 1950–2012

We can now apply the analytical tools presented in previous sections to some interesting risky portfolios from Canada and the US. Our base portfolio is the one underlying the S&P/TSX Composite Index, which till 2002 was the S&P 300 index. Since that time the composition of the portfolio has become variable, with the number of firms varying from quarter to quarter according to the rules of inclusion. It contained around 250 companies during 2012, with an average capitalization of about $5,800 Can million in September of that year.[16] Its performance will be compared to that of five U.S. portfolios. One portfolio is the benchmark broadest possible U.S. equity portfolio, including all stocks listed on the NYSE, AMEX, and Nasdaq. We shall denote it as "All U.S." Because it is value-weighted, the All U.S. portfolio is dominated by the large-firm corporate sector, with an average capitalization of US$4,470 in September 2012.

The other four portfolios were chosen on the basis of empirical evidence that two variables (other than risk) have been associated with stock returns: firm size (measured by market capitalization) and the ratio of firm book value to market value of equity (B/M). Eugene Fama and Kenneth French extensively documented the impact that these variables have on realized returns, and these patterns have since been corroborated in stock exchanges around the world.[17] Average realized returns have generally been higher for stocks of small- rather than large-capitalization firms, other things equal. Similarly, realized average returns, other things equal, have historically been higher for firms with a high rather than a low B/M ratio; high and low B/M portfolios are termed "Value" and "Growth" respectively. The Fama-French database includes returns on portfolios of U.S. stocks sorted by size (Big; Small) and by B/M ratio (High; Medium; Low), and rebalances these six portfolios every midyear.[18] The four portfolios chosen for our comparisons are the Big/Value, Big/Growth, Small/Value, and Small/Growth, with respective average capitalizations (in $US million) of 13,325, 18,070, 297, and 582 as of September 2012.

Tables 4.4a, b, and c present summary statistics of the historical record of the excess return of the base Canadian portfolio during the 56 years of our data, continuously compounded and annualized from monthly returns; they also present similar statistics of the record broken down in two subperiods, the 44 years of the twentieth century and the 12 years of the twenty-first century. Figure 4.9, panel A, plots the histogram of the monthly data for the 1957–2012 period plotted in bins of 50 basis points over a range of −26.5 to 14.81 percent; annualized, this is equivalent to −95.84 to 591.33 percent. The vertical axis shows the fraction of the returns in each bin.

A first look at the excess returns on the Canadian stocks shows that they behaved in a very similar manner in both subperiods, with virtually identical means and standard deviations, as well as performance ratios. On the other hand, both the histogram of Figure 4.9 and the statistics of Tables 4.4a, b, and c document some deviations from normality, in the form of a

---

[16]See http://www.ratesupermarket.ca/blog/the-toronto-composite-index-sptsx-stats and http://www.standardandpoors.com/indices/sp-tsx-composite/en/us/?indexId=spcadntxc-caduf--p-ca----.

[17]This literature began in earnest with their 1992 publication "The Cross Section of Expected Stock Returns," *Journal of Finance* 47, 427–465.

[18]The database is available at http://mba.tuck.dartmouth.edu/pages/faculty/ken/french/data_library.html. A Canadian database containing similarly sorted portfolios compiled by Claude Francoeur of HEC Montreal is available at http://expertise.hec.ca/professorship_information_financiere_strategique/fama-french-canadian-factors; unfortunately, it contains too short a period for meaningful comparisons.

fatter left tail and more extreme negative events than would be observed in a normal distribution. Thus, although the actual and the normal VaR 5 percent are virtually identical, the expected shortfall is significantly lower in the actual data than in the normal approximation.

TABLE 4.4a

Annualized Statistics from the History of Monthly Excess Returns on Canadian Common Stocks, January 1957–December 2012

All 672 Months	
Average excess return (%)	4.04
Standard deviation (%)	16.47
Checks on Normality	
Lower partial SD (LPSD)	17.52
Skew	−0.295
Kurtosis	3.74
VaR 5%, actual (%)	−23.19
VaR 5%, normal (%)	−23.15
ES 5%, actual (%)	−37.25
ES 5%, normal (%)	−26.53
Negative 3-sigma observations, actual	7
Negative 3-sigma observations, normal	0.9
# months with more than 10% loss	16
1-month SD cond. on 10% loss (%)	5.05
# months with more than 10% gain	6
Positive 3-sigma observations, actual	1
Performance	
Sharpe ratio (annualized)	0.25
Sortino ratio (annualized)	0.23

TABLE 4.4b

Annualized Statistics from the History of Monthly Excess Returns on Canadian Common Stocks, January 1957–December 1999

All 528 Months	
Average excess return (%)	4.09
Standard deviation (%)	16.49
Checks on Normality	
Lower partial SD (LPSD)	17.57
Skew	−0.29
Kurtosis	4.19
VaR 5%, actual (%)	−22.65
VaR 5%, normal (%)	−23.14
ES 5%, actual (%)	−36.91
ES 5%, normal (%)	−26.53
Negative 3-sigma observations, actual	4
Negative 3-sigma observations, normal	0.7
# months with more than 10% loss (%)	13
1-month SD cond. on 10% loss (%)	5.5
# months with more than 10% gain (%)	5
Performance	
Sharpe ratio (annualized)	0.25
Sortino ratio (annualized)	0.24

TABLE 4.4c

Annualized Statistics from the History of Monthly Excess Returns on Canadian Common Stocks, January 2000– December 2012

All 144 Months	
Average excess return (%)	3.90
Standard deviation (%)	16.44
Checks on Normality	
Lower partial SD (LPSD)	19.05
Skew	−0.31
Kurtosis	2.36
VaR 5%, actual (%)	−25.51
VaR 5%, normal (%)	−23.28
ES 5%, actual (%)	−38.10
ES 5%, normal (%)	−23.28
Negative 3-sigma observations, actual	3
Negative 3-sigma observations, normal	0.19
1-month SD cond. on 10% loss, (%)	21.76
Performance	
Sharpe ratio (annualized)	0.24
Sortino ratio (annualized)	0.20

Source: From Scotia Capital and PC Bond Analytics, "Debt Market Indices," various years, and Thomson Reuters. Used by permission of Scotia Capital and PC Bond Analytics, and Thomson Reuters.

Figure 4.9

Return histograms of base portfolios, Canada and U.S.

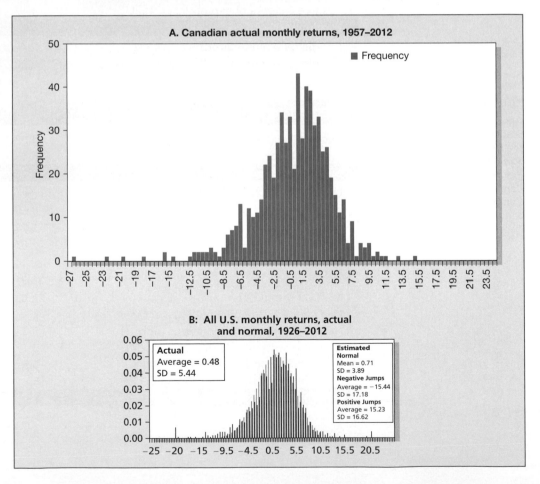

This is consistent with the far greater incidence of extreme events (defined as negative returns exceeding either −10 percent or three standard deviations) in the actual data than in the equivalent normal distribution. It is also clear that the incidence of positive extreme events is much lower (only one positive return larger than three standard deviations from the mean in the entire period).

Table 4.5 compares the Canadian stock portfolio to the five U.S. portfolios, All U.S., Big/Value, Big/Growth, Small/Value, and Small/Growth, during the two subperiods, the second half of the twentieth century and the 12 available years of the twenty-first century, roughly equivalent to the partition of the 56-year period of our data. Figure 4.9, panel B, shows the histogram of the All U.S. portfolio over the 1,026 monthly data points available in the U.S. database. Overall, the Canadian stock portfolio had significantly lower mean returns than the U.S. portfolios in most cases, but also similarly lower standard deviations. Nonetheless, the Sharpe ratios were significantly lower for the Canadian stocks. The difference between the United States and Canada is most striking during the twenty-first century, when the standard deviation of the Canadian returns remained virtually unchanged while that of all U.S. portfolios increased. Except for one case, the increase in standard deviations also resulted in lower Sharpe ratios for all U.S. portfolios. The statistics in the table offer also some support to the popularly held notion that Canadian stocks were more resilient to the financial crisis of the twenty-first century than their comparable U.S. counterparts: the All U.S. portfolio, the closest to the Canadian with respect to size, was the one most affected by the crisis, with its Sharpe ratio declining from .56 to .09.

Among the U.S. portfolios the Small/Value portfolio did in fact offer a higher average return in all periods, and the differences from the averages of the other portfolios are all statistically significant.[19] But before deeming these performances superior or inferior, it must be shown that the differences in their average returns cannot be explained by differences in risk. Table 4.5 shows that the standard deviations vary from about 15 percent to about twice that amount. Here, we must question the use of standard deviation as a measure of risk for any particular asset or portfolio. Standard deviation measures overall volatility, and hence is a legitimate risk measure only for portfolios considered appropriate for an investor's entire wealth at risk, that is, for broad capital allocation. Assets or portfolios considered to be *added* to the rest of an investor's entire-wealth portfolio must be judged on the basis of *incremental* risk. This distinction requires risk measures other than standard deviation, and we will return to this issue in great detail in later chapters.

Regardless of how we resolve the question of performance of these portfolios, we must determine whether SD is an adequate measure of risk in the first place, in view of deviations from normality. Table 4.5 shows that negative skew is present in most of the portfolios and positive kurtosis is present in *all* portfolios *all* the time. This implies that we must carefully evaluate the effect of these deviations on value at risk (VaR) and expected shortfall (ES), and also consider the evidence on negative 3-sigma frequencies where these are present.

We start with the difference between VaR and ES from the actual distribution of returns and the "equivalent normal distribution" (with the same mean and variance). Recall that the 5 percent VaR is the loss corresponding to the fifth percentile of the rate of return distribution and ES is the expected loss given a return less than the 5 percent VaR. It is one measure of the risk of extreme outcomes, often called *tail risk* because it focuses on outcomes in the far left tail of the distribution. We compare historical tail risk with that predicted by the normal distribution by comparing actual VaR and ES to the VaR and ES of the equivalent normal distribution. The "excess VaR" is the VaR of the historical distribution versus the VaR of the corresponding normal, where negative numbers indicate greater losses. The excess ES is presented in Table 4.5 as a fraction of the monthly standard deviation.

---

[19]The *t*-statistic of the difference in average return is (Average difference)/SD(Difference).

TABLE 4.5   Canada and U.S. Portfolios, Annualized Statistics from the History of Monthly Excess Returns, January 1950–December 2012

	Canadian Stocks		All U.S.		U.S., Big/ Value		U.S., Big/ Growth		U.S., Small/ Value		U.S., Small/ Growth	
	1957–1999	2000–2012	1950–1999	2000–2012	1950–1999	2000–2012	1950–1999	2000–2012	1950–1999	2000–2012	1950–1999	2000–2012
Average returns (%)	4.09	3.9	8.44	1.82	11.50	8.80	9.83	14.51	17.05	17.89	7.20	4.83
Standard deviations	16.49	16.44	14.99	20.08	17.21	24.08	16.51	20.93	21.41	28.93	25.60	29.49
Skew	−0.29	−0.31	−0.81	−0.74	−0.15	−0.59	−0.70	−0.34	−0.22	−0.32	−0.77	0.1
Kurtosis	4.19	2.36	3.5	1.21	2.28	2.6	3.76	1.23	5.09	1.62	4.23	1.72
Sharpe ratios	0.25	0.24	0.56	0.09	0.67	0.37	0.60	0.69	0.80	0.62	0.28	0.16
VaR excess over normal (%)	0.49	−2.23	−1.16	−1.02	−0.09	−1.71	0.08	0.34	−0.39	−0.67	0.18	−0.37
ES excess over normal (fraction of SD)	−2.28	−3.26	−0.77	−0.28	−0.59	−0.47	−0.77	−0.17	−0.37	−0.19	−0.26	−0.11

Source: U.S. data from author's calculations, using data from Professor Kenneth French's Web site, http://mba.tuck.dartmouth.edu/pages/faculty/ken.french/data_library.html. Canadian data from Scotia Capital and PC Bond Analytics, "Debt Market Indices," various years, and Thomson Reuters. Used by permission of Scotia Capital and PC Bond Analytics, and Thomson Reuters.

It is clear from the comparative data that the normal distribution is generally a good enough approximation for the U.S. portfolios' stock returns. The worst excess VaR compared to the normal (−1.71 percent for the Big/Value portfolio in the twenty-first century) is less than a third of the monthly SD of this portfolio, 6.01 percent. Similarly for the ES, while the negative signs tell us that while the most negative 5 percent of the actual observations are always worse than the equivalent normal, the differences are not substantial: the magnitudes are never larger than .77 of the portfolio SD.

By contrast, it is clear from Table 4.5 that the Canadian stock portfolio's returns present significantly larger probabilities of abnormally low returns than those that correspond to the normal distribution. In both periods the expected shortfall is larger than twice the monthly variance of the returns, and in the 144 months of the twenty-first century the ES was actually more than three times the SD. Tables 4.4a, b, and c also show that there were three observations in which the negative returns were larger in absolute value than three standard deviations, far in excess of what would have been expected for a normal distribution. We conclude that when analyzing investments in Canadian stocks we should be very careful about deriving inferences that rely on the normality of returns. For reasons that are probably related to the concentration of Canadian firms in the volatile resource sectors, the probability of extreme negative shocks is much higher than in well-diversified U.S. stock portfolios.

A Global View of the Historical Record

As financial markets around the world grow and become more regulated and transparent, Canadian investors look to improve diversification by investing internationally. Investors in many countries that traditionally used U.S. financial markets as a safe haven to supplement home-country investments also seek international diversification to reduce risk. The question arises of how historical the Canadian and U.S. experiences compare with those of stock markets around the world.

Figure 4.10 shows a century-long history (1900−2000) of average nominal and real returns in stock markets of 16 developed countries. We find the United States in fourth and Canada in fifth

Figure 4.10

Nominal and real equity returns around the world, 1900−2000.

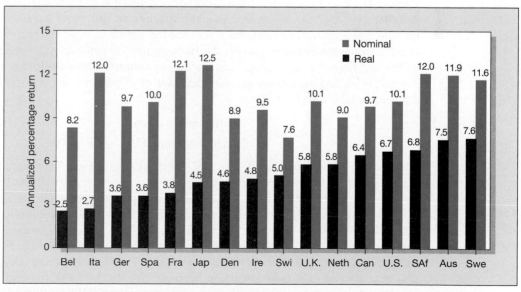

Source: Elroy Dimson, Paul Marsh, and Mike Staunton, *Triumph of the Optimists: 101 Years of Global Investment Returns* (Princeton, NJ: University Press, 2002).

Figure 4.11

Standard deviations of real equity and bond returns around the world, 1900–2000.

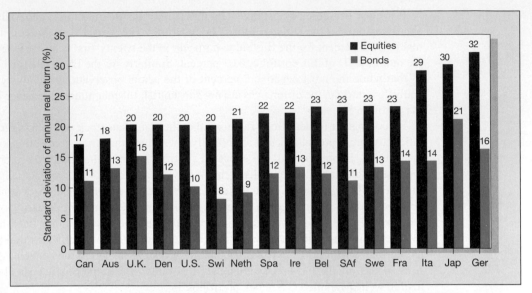

Source: Elroy Dimson, Paul Marsh, and Mike Staunton, *Triumph of the Optimists: 101 Years of Global Investment Returns* (Princeton, NJ: University Press, 2002).

place in terms of real, average returns, behind Sweden, Australia, and South Africa. Figure 4.11 shows the standard deviations of real stock and bond returns for these same countries. We find Canada in first place and the United States tied with four other countries for third place in terms of lowest standard deviation of real stock returns. So Canada has done well, but not abnormally so compared with these countries.

One interesting feature of these figures is that the countries with the worst results, measured by the ratio of average real returns to standard deviation, are Italy, Belgium, Germany, and Japan— the countries most devastated by World War II. The top-performing countries are Australia, Canada, and the United States, the countries least devastated by the wars of the twentieth century. Another, perhaps more telling feature is the insignificant difference between the real returns in the different countries. The difference between the highest average real rate (Sweden, at 7.6 percent) from the average return across the 16 countries (5.1 percent) is 2.5 percent. Similarly, the difference between the average and the lowest country return (Belgium, at 2.5 percent) is 2.6 percent. Using the average standard deviation of 23 percent, the *t*-statistic for a difference of 2.6 percent with 100 observations is

$$t\text{-statistic} = \frac{\text{Difference in mean}}{\text{Standard deviation}/\sqrt{n}} = \frac{2.6}{23/\sqrt{100}} = 1.13$$

which is far below conventional levels of statistical significance. We conclude that neither the Canadian nor the U.S. experience can be dismissed as an outlier case. Hence, using the large U.S. stock market as a yardstick for return characteristics may be reasonable.

These days, practitioners and scholars are debating whether the historical Canadian average risk premium of large stocks over T-bills of 4.24 percent (Table 4.3) is a reasonable forecast for the long term. This debate centres around two questions. First, do economic factors that prevailed over that historical period (1957–2012) adequately represent those that may prevail over the forecasting horizon? Second, is the arithmetic average from the available history a good yardstick for long-term forecasts? We take up some of these issues in the appendix.

SUMMARY

1. The economy's equilibrium level of real interest rates depends on the willingness of households to save, as reflected in the supply curve of funds, and on the expected profitability of business investment in plant, equipment, and inventories, as reflected in the demand curve for funds. It depends also on government fiscal and monetary policy.

2. The nominal rate of interest is the equilibrium real rate plus the expected rate of inflation. In general, we can directly observe only nominal interest rates; from them, we must infer expected real rates, using inflation forecasts.

3. The equilibrium expected rate of return on any security is the sum of the equilibrium real rate of interest, the expected rate of inflation, and a security-specific risk premium.

4. Investors face a tradeoff between risk and expected return. Historical data confirm our intuition that assets with low degrees of risk provide lower returns on average than do those of higher risk.

5. Assets with guaranteed nominal interest rates are risky in real terms because the future inflation rate is uncertain.

6. Historical rates of return over the twentieth century in developed capital markets suggest the Canadian history of stock returns is not an outlier compared to other countries.

7. Historical returns on stocks exhibit more frequent large negative deviations from the mean than would be predicted from a normal distribution. The lower partial standard deviation (LPSD), the skew and kurtosis of the actual distribution quantify the deviation from normality. The LPSD, instead of the standard deviation, is sometimes used by practitioners as a measure of risk.

8. Widely used measures of risk are value at risk (VaR) and conditional tail expectations or, equivalently, expected shortfall (ES). VaR measures the loss that will be exceeded with a specified probability such as 5 percent. The VaR does not add new information when returns are normally distributed. When negative deviations from the average are larger and more frequent than the normal distribution, the 5 percent VaR will be more than 1.65 standard deviations below the average return. Expected shortfall (ES) measure the expected rate of return conditional on the portfolio falling below a certain value. Thus, 1 percent ES is the expected return of all possible outcomes in the bottom 1 percent of the distribution.

KEY EQUATIONS

(4.1) $r \approx R - i$

(4.2) $1 + r = \dfrac{1 + R}{1 + i}$

(4.3) $r = \dfrac{R - i}{1 + i}$

(4.4) $R = r + E(i)$

(4.5) $R(1 - t) - i = (r + i)(1 - t) - i$
$= r(1 - t) - it$

(4.6) $r_f(T) = \dfrac{100}{P(T)} - 1$

(4.7) $1 + \text{EAR} = [1 + r_f(T)]^{1/T}$

(4.8) $1 + \text{EAR} = [1 + r_f(T)]^n = [1 + r_f(T)]^{1/T}$
$= [1 + T \times \text{APR}]^{1/T}$

(4.9) $1 + \text{EAR} = \exp(r_{cc}) = e^{r_{cc}}$

(4.10) $\text{HPR} = \dfrac{\begin{array}{c}\text{Ending price} \\ \text{of a share}\end{array} - \begin{array}{c}\text{Beginning} \\ \text{price}\end{array} + \begin{array}{c}\text{Cash} \\ \text{dividend}\end{array}}{\text{Beginning price}}$

(4.11) $E(r) = \sum_s p(s)r(s)$

(4.12) $\sigma^2 = \sum_s p(s)[r(s) - E(r)]^2$

(4.13) $E(r) = \sum_{s=1}^{n} p(s)r(s) = \dfrac{1}{n}\sum_{s=1}^{n} r(s)$

(4.14) Terminal value $= (1 + r_1) \times (1 + r_2) \times \cdots$
$\times (1 + r_5)$

(4.15) Geometric average = Arithmetic average $- \frac{1}{2}\sigma^2$

(4.16) $\sigma^2 = \dfrac{1}{n}\sum_{s=1}^{n} [r(s) - \bar{r}]^2$

(4.17) $\sigma^2 = \left(\dfrac{n}{n-1}\right) \times \dfrac{1}{n}\sum_{j=1}^{n}[r(s) - \bar{r}]^2$

(4.19)   Skew $= \dfrac{E[r(s) - E(r)]^3}{\sigma^3}$

$= \dfrac{1}{n-1}\sum_{j=1}^{n}[r(s) - \bar{r}]^2$

(4.20)   Kurtosis $= \dfrac{E[r(s) - E(r)]^4}{\sigma^4} - 3$

(4.18) Sharpe ratio (for portfolios) $= \dfrac{\text{Risk premium}}{\text{SD of excess return}}$

PROBLEMS

connect™   Practise and learn online with Connect.

1. You have $5,000 to invest for the next year and are considering the following three alternatives:
   a. A money market fund with an average maturity of 30 days offering a current yield of 6 percent per year
   b. A one-year savings deposit at a bank offering an interest rate of 7.5 percent
   c. A 20-year Canada bond offering a yield to maturity of 9 percent per year
   What role does your forecast of future interest rates play in your decision?

2. You are considering two alternative two-year investments. You can invest in a risky asset with a positive risk premium and returns in each of the two years that will be identically distributed and uncorrelated, or you can invest in the risky asset for only one year and then invest the proceeds in a risk-free asset. Which of the following statements about the first investment alternative (compared with the second) are true?
   a. Its two-year risk premium is the same as the second alternative.
   b. The standard deviation of its two-year return is the same.
   c. Its annualized standard deviation is lower.
   d. Its Sharpe ratio is higher.
   e. It is relatively more attractive to investors who have lower degrees of risk aversion.

3. Use Figure 4.1 to analyze the effect of the following on the level of real interest rates:
   a. Businesses become more optimistic about future demand for their products and decide to increase their capital spending.
   b. Households are induced to save more because of increased uncertainty about their future Canada Pension Plan benefits.
   c. The Bank of Canada undertakes open-market sales of Canada Treasury securities to reduce the supply of money.

4. You are considering the choice between investing $50,000 in a conventional one-year bank GIC offering an interest rate of 5 percent and a one-year inflation-plus GIC offering 1.5 percent per year plus the rate of inflation.
   a. Which is the safer investment?
   b. Which offers the higher expected return?
   c. If you expect the rate of inflation to be 3 percent over the next year, which is the better investment? Why?
   d. If we observe a risk-free nominal interest rate of 5 percent per year and a risk-free real rate of 1.5 percent, can we infer that the market's expected rate of inflation is 3.5 percent per year?

5. Suppose that you revise your expectations regarding the stock market (which were summarized in Spreadsheet 4.1) as follows:

State of Economy	Probability	Ending Price ($)	HPR (%)
Boom	.35	140	44
Normal growth	.30	110	14
Recession	.35	80	−16

Use equations 4.11 and 4.12 to compute the mean and standard deviation of the HPR on stocks. Compare your revised parameters with your previous ones.

6. Derive the probability distribution of the one-year holding period return on a 30-year Canada bond with an 8 percent coupon if it is currently selling at par and the probability distribution of its yield to maturity (YTM) a year from now is as follows:

State of Economy	Probability	YTM (%)
Boom	.20	11.0
Normal growth	.50	8.0
Recession	.30	7.0

For simplicity, assume that the entire 8 percent coupon is paid at the end of the year rather than every six months.

7. Using the historical risk premiums over the 1957–2012 period as your guide, if the current risk-free interest rate is 3 percent, what is your estimate of the expected annual HPR on the S&P/TSX Composite stock portfolio?

8. Compute the means and standard deviations of the annual holding period returns listed in our Web site data for this chapter using only the last 28 years, 1985–2012. How do they compare with these same statistics computed from data for the period 1957–1984? Which do you think are the most relevant statistics to use for projecting into the future?

9. During a period of severe inflation, a bond offered a nominal HPR of 80 percent per year. The inflation rate was 70 percent per year.

   a. What was the real HPR on the bond over the year?

   b. Compare this real HPR to the approximation $R = r - i$.

10. What is the standard deviation of a random variable q with the following probability distribution:

Value of q	Probability
0	.25
1	.25
2	.50

11. The continuously compounded annual return on a stock is normally distributed with a mean of 20 percent and standard deviation of 30 percent. With 95.44 percent confidence, we should expect its actual return in any particular year to be between which pair of values? *Hint:* Look again at Figure 4.4.

   a. −40.0 percent and 80.0 percent

   b. −30.0 percent and 80.0 percent

   c. −20.6 percent and 60.6 percent

   d. −10.4 percent and 50.4 percent

12. Suppose that the inflation rate is expected to be 3 percent in the near future. Using the historical data provided in this chapter, what would be your predictions for

  a. The T-bill rate?

  b. The expected rate of return on large stocks?

  c. The risk premium on the stock market?

13. An economy is making a rapid recovery from steep recession, and businesses foresee a need for large amounts of capital investment. Why would this development affect real interest rates?

Problems 14 and 15 represent a greater challenge. You may need to review the definitions of call and put options in Chapter 2.

14. You are faced with the probability distribution of the HPR on the stock market index fund given in Spreadsheet 4.1. Suppose the price of a put option on a share of the index fund with exercise price of $110 and maturity of one year is $12.

  a. What is the probability distribution of the HPR on the put option?

  b. What is the probability distribution of the HPR on a portfolio consisting of one share of the index fund and a put option?

  c. In what sense does buying the put option constitute a purchase of insurance in this case?

15. Take as given the conditions described in the previous question, and suppose the risk-free interest rate is 6 percent per year. You are contemplating investing $107.55 in a one-year CD and simultaneously buying a call option on the stock market index fund with an exercise price of $110 and a maturity of one year. What is the probability distribution of your dollar return at the end of the year?

16. Consider these long-term investment data:

  i. The price of a 10-year $100 par-zero coupon inflation-indexed bond is $84.49.

  ii. A real estate property is expected to yield 2 percent per quarter (nominal) with an SD of the (effective) quarterly rate of 10 percent.

  a. Compute the annual rate on the real bond.

  b. Compute the CC annual risk premium on the real-estate investment.

  c. Use the appropriate formula and Excel's Solver or its Goal Seek function to find the SD of the CC annual excess return on the real estate investment.

  d. What is the probability of loss or shortfall after 10 years?

The following questions are from past CFA examinations.

Use the following expectations on stocks X and Y to answer problems 17 through 19 (round to the nearest percent).

	Bear Market	Normal Market	Bull Market
Probability	0.2	0.5	0.3
Stock X	−20%	18%	50%
Stock Y	−15%	20%	10%

17. What is the expected return for stocks X and Y?

18. What is the standard deviation of returns on stocks X and Y?

19. Assume you invest your $10,000 portfolio in $9,000 of stock X and $1,000 of stock Y. What is the expected return on your portfolio?

20. Given $100,000 to invest, what is the expected risk premium in dollars of investing in equities versus risk-free T-bills based on the following table?

Action	Probability	Expected Return
Invest in equities	.6 _____	$50,000
	.4 _____	−$30,000
Invest in risk-free T-bills	1.0 _____	$ 5,000

21. Judging from the scenarios below, what is the expected return for a portfolio with the following return profile?

	Market Condition		
	Bear	Normal	Bull
Probability	.2	.3	.5
Rate of return	−25%	10%	24%

22. An analyst estimates that a stock has the following probabilities of return depending on the state of the economy:

State of Economy	Probability	Return
Good	.1	15%
Normal	.6	13%
Poor	.3	7%

What is the expected return of the stock?

23. Probabilities for three states of the economy, and probabilities for the returns on a particular stock in each state, are shown in the table below.

State of Economy	Probability of Economic State	Stock Performance	Probability of Stock Performance in Given Economic State
Good	.3	Good	.6
		Neutral	.3
		Poor	.1
Neutral	.5	Good	.4
		Neutral	.3
		Poor	.3
Poor	.2	Good	.2
		Neutral	.3
		Poor	.5

What is the probability that the economy will be neutral *and* the stock will experience poor performance?

E-INVESTMENTS
Inflation and Rates

The Federal Reserve Bank of St. Louis has information available on interest rates and economic conditions. A publication called *Monetary Trends* contains graphs and tables with information about current conditions in the capital markets. Go to the Web site **www.stls.frb.org** and click on "Economic Research" on the menu at the top of the page. Find the most recent issue of *Monetary Trends* in the "Recent Data Publications" section and answer these questions.

1. What is the professionals' consensus forecast for inflation for the next two years? (Use the "Federal Reserve Bank of Philadelphia" line on the graph to answer this.)
2. What do consumers expect to happen to inflation over the next two years? (Use the "University of Michigan" line on the graph to answer this.)
3. Have real interest rates increased, decreased, or remained the same over the last two years?
4. What has happened to short-term nominal interest rates over the last two years? What about long-term nominal interest rates?
5. How do recent U.S. inflation and long-term interest rates compare with those of the other countries listed?
6. What are the most recently available levels of 3-month and 10-year yields on Treasury securities?

APPENDIX 4A: LONG-TERM INVESTMENTS

Consider an investor saving $1 today toward retirement in 25 years, or 300 months. Investing the dollar in a risky stock portfolio (reinvesting dividends until retirement) with an expected rate of return of 1 percent per month, this retirement "fund" is expected to grow almost 20-fold to a terminal value of $(1 + .01)^{300} = \$19.79$ (providing total growth of 1,879 percent). Compare this impressive result with an investment in a 25-year Canada bond having a risk-free rate of 6 percent (.487 percent per month) that yields a retirement fund of $1.06^{25} = \$4.29$. We see that a monthly risk premium of just .593 percent produces a retirement fund that is more than four times that of the risk-free alternative. Such is the power of compounding. Why, then, would anyone invest in Canada bonds? Obviously, this is an issue of trading excess return for risk. What is the nature of this risk–return tradeoff? The risk of an investment that compounds at fluctuating rates over the long run is widely misunderstood, and it is important to figure it out.

We can construct the probability distribution of the stock-fund terminal value from a binomial tree just as we did earlier for the newspaper stand, except that instead of *adding* monthly profits, the portfolio value *compounds* monthly by a rate drawn from a given distribution. For example, suppose we can approximate the portfolio monthly distribution as follows: Each month the rate of return is either 5.54 percent or −3.54 percent, with equal probabilities of .5. This configuration generates an expected return of 1 percent per month. The portfolio risk is measured as the monthly standard deviation: $\sqrt{.5 \times (5.54 - 1)^2 + .5 \times (-3.54 - 1^2)} = 4.54$ percent. After two months, the event tree looks like this:

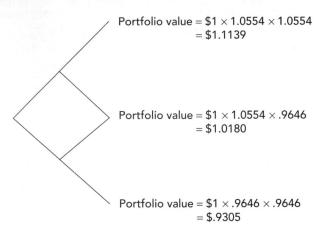

Portfolio value = $1 × 1.0554 × 1.0554
= $1.1139

Portfolio value = $1 × 1.0554 × .9646
= $1.0180

Portfolio value = $1 × .9646 × .9646
= $.9305

"Growing" the tree for 300 months will result in 301 different possible outcomes. The probability of each outcome can be obtained with Excel's BINOMDIST function. From the 301 possible outcomes and associated probabilities we compute the mean ($19.79) and the standard deviation ($18.09) of the terminal value. Can we use this standard deviation as a measure of risk to be weighed against the risk premium of $19.79 − 4.29 = 15.5$ (1,550 percent)? Recalling the effect of asymmetry on the validity of standard deviation as a measure of risk, we must first view the shape of the distribution at the end of the tree.

Figure 4A.1 plots the probability of possible outcomes against the terminal value. The asymmetry of the distribution is striking. The highly positive skewness suggests the standard deviation of terminal value will not be useful in this case. Indeed, the binomial distribution, when period outcomes compound, converges to a *lognormal*, rather than a normal, distribution. The lognormal describes the distribution of a variable whose *logarithm* is normally distributed.

Figure 4A.1

Probability of investment outcomes after 25 years with a lognormal distribution (approximated from a binomial tree).

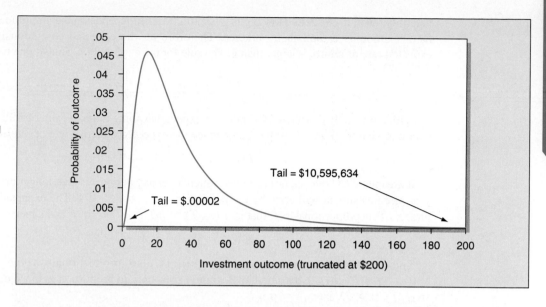

Normal and Lognormal Returns

As we mentioned earlier, one of the important properties of the normal distribution is its stability, in the sense that adding up normally distributed returns results in a return that also is normally distributed. This property does not extend to *multiplying* normally distributed returns; yet this is what we need to do to find returns over longer horizons. For example, even if two returns, r_1 and r_2, are normal, the two-period return will compound to $(1 + r_1)(1 + r_2) - 1$, which is *not* normally distributed. Perhaps the normal distribution does not qualify as the simplifying distribution we purported it to be. But the lognormal distribution does! What is this distribution?

Technically, a random variable X is lognormal if its logarithm, $\ln(X)$, is normally distributed. It turns out that if stock prices are "instantaneously" normal (i.e., returns over the shortest time intervals are normally distributed) then their longer-term compounded returns and the future stock price will be lognormal.[20] Conversely, if stock prices are distributed lognormally, then the continuously compounded rate of return will be normally distributed. Thus, if we work with continuously compounded (CC) returns rather than effective per-period rates of return, we can preserve the simplification provided by the normal distribution, since those CC returns will be normal regardless of the investment horizon.

Recall that the continuously compounded rate is $r_{CC} = \ln(1 + r)$, so if we observe effective rates of return, we can use this formula to compute the CC rate. With r_{CC} normally distributed, we can do all our analyses and calculations using the normally distributed CC rates. If needed, we can always recover the effective rate, r, from the CC rate from $r = e^{r_{CC}} - 1$.

Let's see what the rules are when a stock price is lognormally distributed. Suppose the log of the stock price is normally distributed with an expected annual growth rate of g and an SD of σ. When a normal rate compounds by random shocks from instant to instant, the fluctuations do not produce symmetric effects on price. A positive uptick raises the base, so the next tick is expected to be larger than the previous one. The reverse is true after a downtick: the base is smaller and the next tick is expected to be smaller. As a result, a sequence of positive shocks will have a larger upward effect than the downward effect of a sequence of negative shocks. Thus, an upward drift is created just by

---

[20]We see a similar phenomenon in the binomial tree example depicted in Figure 4A.1. Even with many bad returns, stock prices cannot become negative, so the distribution is bounded at zero. But many good returns can increase stock prices without limit, so the compound return after many periods has a long right tail, but a left tail bounded by a worst-case cumulative return of −100 percent. This gives rise to the asymmetric skewed shape characteristic of the lognormal distribution.

volatility, even if g is zero. How big is this extra drift? It depends on the amplitude of the ticks; in fact, it amounts to half their variance. Therefore m, the expected continuously compounded expected rate of return, is larger than g. The rule for the expected CC annual rate becomes

$$E(r_{CC}) = m = g + \frac{1}{2}\sigma^2 \qquad (4A.1)$$

With a normally distributed CC rate, we expect that some initial wealth of $\$W_0$ will compound over one year to $W_0 e^{g + \frac{1}{2}\sigma^2} = We^m$, and hence the expected effective rate of return is

$$E(r) = e^{g + \frac{1}{2}\sigma^2} - 1 = e^m - 1 \qquad (4A.2)$$

If an annual CC rate applies to an investment over any period T, either longer or shorter than one year, the investment will grow by the proportion $r(T) = e^{r_{CC}T} - 1$. The expected cumulative return, $r_{CC}T$, is proportional to T, that is, $E(r_{CC}T) = mT = gT + \frac{1}{2}\sigma^2 T$ and expected final wealth is

$$E(W_T) = W_0 e^{mT} = W_0 e^{(g + \frac{1}{2}\sigma^2)T} \qquad (4A.3)$$

The variance of the cumulative return is also proportional to the time horizon: $\text{Var}(r_{CC}T) = T\text{Var}(r_{CC})$, but standard deviation rises only in proportion to the square root of time: $\sigma(r_{CC}T) = \sqrt{T\text{Var}(r_{CC})} = \sigma\sqrt{T}$.

This *appears* to offer a mitigation of investment risk in the long run: since the expected return increases with horizon at a faster rate than the standard deviation, the expected return of a long-term, risky investment becomes ever larger relative to its standard deviation. Perhaps shortfall risk declines as investment horizon increases. We look at this possibility in Example 4A1.

EXAMPLE 4A.1   **Shortfall Risk in the Short Run and the Long Run**

An expected effective monthly rate of return 1 percent is equivalent to a CC rate of $\ln(1.01) = .00995$ (.995 percent per month). The risk-free rate is assumed to be .5 percent per month, equivalent to a CC rate of $\ln(1.005) = .4988$ percent. The effective SD of 4.54 percent implies a monthly SD of the CC rate of 4.4928 percent. Hence the monthly CC risk premium is $.995 - .4988 = .4963$ percent, with an SD of 4.4928 percent, and a Sharpe ratio of $.4963/4.4928 = .11$. In other words, returns would have to be .11 standard deviations below the mean before the stock portfolio underperformed T-bills. Using the normal distribution, we see that the probability of a rate of return shortfall relative to the risk-free rate is 45.6 percent. (You can confirm this by entering $-.11$ in Excel's NORMS-DIST function.)[21] This is the probability of investor "regret," after the fact, that the investor would have been better off in T-bills than investing in the stock portfolio.

For a 300-month horizon, however, the expected value of the cumulative excess return is .4963 percent $\times$ 300 = 148.9 percent and the standard deviation is $4.4928\sqrt{300} = 77.82$, implying a whopping Sharpe ratio of 1.91. Enter -1.91 in Excel's NORMSDIST function, and you will see that the probability of shortfall over a 300-month horizon is only .029.

Warning: The probability of a shortfall is an incomplete measure of investment risk. Such probability does not take into account the *size* of potential losses, which for some of the possible outcomes (however unlikely) amount to complete ruin. The worst-case scenarios for the 25-year investment are *far* worse than for the one-month investment. We demonstrate the buildup of risk over the long run graphically below.

---

[21]In some versions of Excel, the function is NORM.S.DIST(z,TRUE).

A better way to quantify the risk of a long-term investment would be the market price of insuring it against a shortfall. An insurance premium must take into account both the probability of possible losses and the magnitude of these losses. We show in later chapters how the fair market price of portfolio insurance can be estimated from option-pricing models.

Despite the low probability that a portfolio insurance policy would have to pay up (only 2.9 percent for the 25-year policy), the magnitude and timing[22] of possible losses would make such long-term insurance surprisingly costly. For example, standard option-pricing models suggest that the value of insurance against shortfall risk over a 10-year horizon would cost nearly 20 percent of the initial value of the portfolio. And contrary to any intuition that a longer horizon reduces shortfall risk, the value of portfolio insurance increases dramatically with the maturity of the contract. For example, a 25-year policy would be about 50 percent more costly, or about 30 percent of the initial portfolio value.

Simulation of Long-Term Future Rates of Return

The frequency distributions in Figures 4.7a and 4.7b provide only rough descriptions of the nature of the return distributions, and are even harder to interpret for long-term investments. A good way to use past history to learn about the distribution of long-term future returns is to simulate these future returns from the available sample. A popular method to accomplish this is *bootstrapping*.

Bootstrapping is a procedure that avoids any assumptions about the return distribution, except that all rates of return in the sample history are equally likely. For example, we could simulate a 25 years of possible future returns by sampling (with replacement) 25 randomly selected annual returns from our available 56-year history. We compound those 25 returns to obtain one 25-year holding-period return. This procedure is repeated thousands of times to generate a probability distribution of long-term total returns anchored in the historical frequency distribution.

The cardinal decision when embarking on a bootstrapping exercise is the choice of how far into the past we should go to draw observations for "future" return sequences. We will use our entire 56-year sample so that we are more likely to include low-probability events of extreme value.

At this point, it is well to bring up again Nassim Taleb's metaphor of the black swan.[23] Taleb uses this analogy as an example of events that may occur without any historical precedent. The black swan (an animal once unknown to Europeans) is a symbol of tail risk—highly unlikely but extreme and important outcomes that are all but impossible to predict from experience. The implication for bootstrapping is that limiting possible future returns to the range of past returns, or extreme returns to their historical frequency, may easily underestimate actual exposure to tail risk. Notice that when simulating from a normal distribution, we do allow for unbounded bad outcomes, although without allowing for fat tails we may greatly underestimate their probabilities. However, using *any* particular probability distribution determines the shape of future events based on measurements from the past.

The dilemma of how to describe uncertainty largely comes down to how investors should respond to the possibility of low-probability disasters. Those who argue that an investment is less risky in the long run implicitly downplay extreme events. The high price of portfolio insurance is proof positive that a majority of investors certainly do not ignore them. As far as the present exercise is concerned, we show that even a simulation based on generally benign past Canadian history will result in cases of investor ruin.

---

[22]By "timing," we mean that a decline in stock prices is associated with a bad economy when extra income would be most important to an investor. The fact that the insurance policy would pay off in these scenarios contributes to its market value.
[23]*The Black Swan: The Impact of the Highly Improbable* (New York: Random House, 2010).

One important objective of this exercise is to assess the potential effect of deviations from the normality assumption on the probability distribution of a long-term investment in Canadian stocks. For this purpose, we simulate a 25-year distribution of annual returns for stocks and contrast these samples to similar samples drawn from normal distributions that (due to compounding) result in lognormally distributed long-term total returns. Results are shown in Figure 4A.2, which shows the frequency distributions of the paired samples of Canadian stocks, constructed by sampling both from actual returns and from the normal distribution. The box inside Figure 4A.2 shows the statistics of the distributions.

Viewing the frequency distributions, the difference between the simulated history and the normal draw is small but distinct. Despite the very small differences between the averages of 1-year and 25-year annual returns, and between the standard deviations, the small differences in skewness and kurtosis combine to produce a significant difference in the probabilities of losses, and in the potential terminal loss.

What about risk for investors with other long-term horizons? Figure 4A.3 compares 25-year to 10-year investments in Canadian stocks. For an appropriate comparison, we must account for

Figure 4A.2   Annually compounded 25-year HPRs from bootstrapped history (all results based on 100,000 trials for nominal returns).

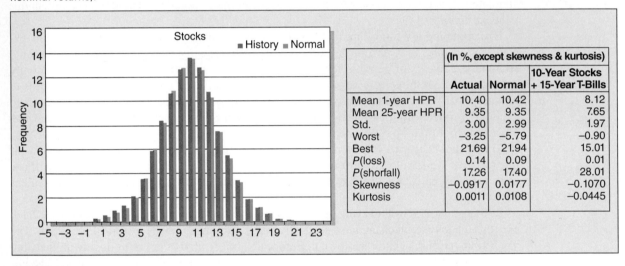

	Actual	Normal	10-Year Stocks + 15-Year T-Bills
	(In %, except skewness & kurtosis)		
Mean 1-year HPR	10.40	10.42	8.12
Mean 25-year HPR	9.35	9.35	7.65
Std.	3.00	2.99	1.97
Worst	−3.25	−5.79	−0.90
Best	21.69	21.94	15.01
P(loss)	0.14	0.09	0.01
P(shorfall)	17.26	17.40	28.01
Skewness	−0.0917	0.0177	−0.1070
Kurtosis	0.0011	0.0108	−0.0445

Figure 4A.3   Annually compounded 25-year HPRs from bootstrapped history.

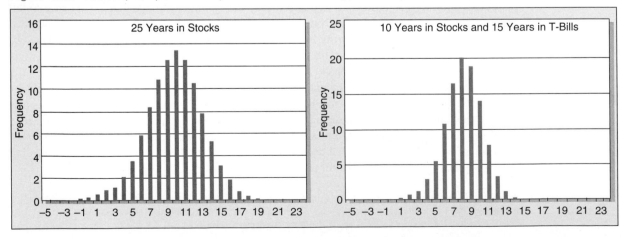

Figure 4A.4   Wealth indices of selected outcomes of large stock portfolios and the average T-bill portfolio.

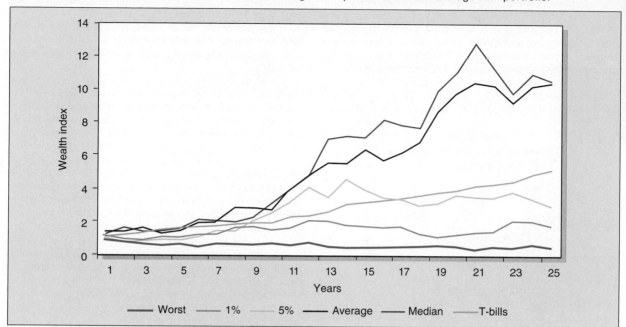

the fact that the 10-year investment will be supplemented with a 15-year investment in T-bills. To accomplish this comparison, we bootstrap 15-year samples from the 56-year history of T-bill rates and augment each sample with 10 annual rates drawn from the history of the risky investment. Panels A and B in Figure 4A.3 show the comparison for Canadian stocks. The frequency distributions reveal a substantial difference in the risks of the terminal portfolio. This difference is clearly manifested in the portfolio performance statistics, in which the probability of loss has virtually disappeared but the probability of shortfall increased significantly.

Figure 4A.4 shows the trajectories of the wealth indices of possible outcomes of a 25-year investment in stocks, compared with the wealth index of the average outcome of a T-bill portfolio. The outcomes of the stock portfolio in Figure 4A.4 range from the worst to the bottom 1 percent and 5 percent of terminal value, and up to the mean and median terminal values. While the probability of loss is only .14 percent in Figure 4A.2, the probability of shortfall is substantial. The bottom 5 percent of the distribution still results in a significant shortfall relative to the T-bill portfolio. From Figure 4A.2 the probability of this shortfall is 17.25 percent. In sum, the analysis clearly demonstrates that the notion that investments in stocks become less risky in the long run must be rejected.

Yet many practitioners hold onto the view that investment risk is less pertinent to long-term investors. A typical demonstration shown in the nearby box relies on the fact that the standard deviation (or range of likely outcomes) of *annualized* returns is lower for longer term horizons. But the demonstration is silent on the range of *total* returns.

Where Is Research of Rates of Return Headed?

In order to learn more about the distribution of returns, particularly the behaviour of relatively rare extreme events, we need a lot more data. The speed with which we accumulate even daily rates of return will not get us there; by the time we have a large enough sample, the distributions may well have changed. But help may be on the way.

Many beginning investors eye the stock market with a bit of suspicion. They view equity investing as an anxious game of Russian roulette: The longer they stay in, the greater their chance of experiencing more losses. In fact, history shows that the opposite is true. The easiest way to reduce the risk of investing in equities—and improve the gain—is to increase the time you hang on to your portfolio.

See for yourself. The demonstration below uses historical data from 1950 through 2005 to compare investment returns over different lengths of time for small-cap stocks, large caps, long-term bonds and T-bills.

The graph starts out showing results for investments held over one-year periods. There's no doubt about it: Over such short intervals, small-cap stocks are definitely the riskiest bet.

But what about investing for more than a year? If you move the slider at the bottom right of the graph, you can see the range of returns for longer time periods. Even investing for two years instead of one cuts your risk significantly. As the length of time increases, the volatility of equities decreases sharply—so much so that you may need to click the "zoom in" button to get a closer view. Over 10-year periods, government bonds look safer than large-cap equities on the downside. Click the "adjust for inflation" box, however, and you'll see that bond "safety" can be illusory. Inflation has an uncanny ability to erode the value of securities that don't grow fast enough.

Now move the slider all the way to the right to see the results of investing for 20-year intervals. Adjusting for inflation, the best 20-year gain a portfolio of long-term Treasury bonds could muster is much lower than that achieved by small- and large-cap stocks. And contrary to popular belief, over their worst 20-year period, long-term bonds actually *lost* money when adjusted for inflation. Meanwhile, small-cap investors still had gains over a 20-year-period, even when stocks were at their worst.

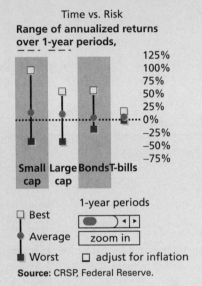

Source: CRSP, Federal Reserve.

Source: Abridged from http://www.marketwatch.com/(S(jpgxu155hzygvlzbebtr5r45))/retirement/tools/investment-comparison-time-vs-risk, accessed December 14, 2013.

The highest frequency we can obtain for rates of return comes from trade-by-trade data. Statistical methods recently developed by astrophysicists can glean from these observations the essential components of the return distributions. The return process might usefully be described as a sum of an instantaneous normal that develops into a lognormal compound return plus jumps that generate deviation from normality. The jump process itself can be decomposed to an aggregation of small jumps plus large jumps that dominate the tails of the distributions.[24]

We expect that before long practitioners will be able to purchase output of such research, and obtain accurate risk parameters of a large array of investments. These will add relevance to the insights and investment practices described in future chapters.

Forecasts for the Long Haul

We use arithmetic averages to forecast future rates of return because they are unbiased estimates of expected rates over equivalent holding periods. But the arithmetic average of short-term returns can be misleading when used to forecast long-term cumulative returns. This is because sampling errors in the estimate of expected return will have asymmetric impact when

---

[24]For an introduction to this approach, see Yacine Aït-Sahalia and Jean Jacod, "Analyzing the Spectrum of Asset Returns: Jump and Volatility Components in High Frequency Data," *Journal of Economic Literature* 50 (2012), pp. 1007–1050.

compounded over long periods. Positive sampling variation will compound to greater upward errors than negative variation.

Jacquier, Kane, and Marcus[25] how that an unbiased forecast of total return over long horizons requires compounding at a weighted average of the arithmetic and geometric historical averages. The proper weight applied to the geometric average equals the ratio of the length of the forecast horizon to the length of the estimation period. For example, if we wish to forecast the cumulative return for a 25-year horizon from a 80-year history, an unbiased estimate would be to compound at a rate of

$$\text{Geometric average} \times \frac{25}{80} = \text{Arithmetic average} \times \frac{(80 - 25)}{80}$$

This correction would take about .5 percent off the historical arithmetic average risk premium on stocks. A forecast for the next 50 years would require compounding at only the geometric average, and for longer horizons at an even lower number. The forecast horizons that are relevant for current investors would depend on their life expectancies.

[25]Eric Jacqier, Alex Kane, and Alan J. Marcus, "Geometric or Arithmetic Means: A Reconsideration," *Financial Analysts Journal*, November/December 2003.

5 CHAPTER

Capital Allocation to Risky Assets

The process of constructing an investor's overall portfolio includes the sequence: (1) select the composition of the risky portfolio and (2) decide how much to invest in it, directing the remaining investment budget to a risk-free investment. The second step is called *capital allocation to risky assets.*

Clearly, to decide on your capital allocation you need to know the risky portfolio and evaluate its attractiveness. Can the construction of that risky portfolio be delegated to an expert? An affirmative answer is necessary for a viable investments management industry. A negative answer would require every investor to learn and implement portfolio management for him- or herself.

To understand the existence of a portfolio management industry in the face of personal investor preferences, we need insight into the nature of risk aversion. We characterize a personal utility function that quantifies a score for the attractiveness of candidate overall portfolios on the basis of expected return and risk. By choosing the portfolio with the highest score, investors maximize their satisfaction with their choice of investments; that is, they achieve the optimal allocation of capital to risky assets.

The utility model also reveals the appropriate objective function for the construction of an optimal *risky* portfolio, and thus explains how an industry can serve investors of a wide range of preferences without the need to know each of them personally.

RISK AND RISK AVERSION

In Chapter 4 we introduced the concepts of the holding-period return (HPR) and the excess return over the risk-free rate. We also discussed estimation of the **risk premium** (the *expected excess return*) and the standard deviation of the rate of excess return, which we use as the measure of portfolio risk. We demonstrated these concepts with a scenario analysis of a specific risky portfolio (Spreadsheet 4.1). To emphasize that bearing risk typically must be accompanied by a reward in the form of a risk premium, we first distinguish between speculation and gambling.

Risk, Speculation, and Gambling

One definition of *speculation* is "the assumption of considerable business risk in obtaining commensurate gain." However, this definition is useless without first specifying what is meant by "commensurate gain" and "considerable risk."

By *commensurate gain* we mean a positive expected profit beyond the risk-free alternative. This is the risk premium, the incremental expected gain from taking on the risk. By *considerable risk* we mean that the risk is sufficient to affect the decision. An individual might reject a prospect that has a positive risk premium because the added gain is insufficient to make up for the risk involved.

To gamble is "to bet or wager on an uncertain outcome." The central difference between gambling and speculation is the lack of "commensurate gain." Economically speaking, a gamble is the assumption of risk for enjoyment of the risk itself, whereas speculation is undertaken because one perceives a favourable risk–return tradeoff. To turn a gamble into a speculative prospect requires an adequate risk premium for compensation to risk-averse investors for the risks that they bear. Hence *risk aversion and speculation are consistent.*

In some cases a gamble may *appear* as speculation. Suppose that two investors disagree sharply about the future exchange rate of the Canadian dollar against the British pound. They may choose to bet on the outcome: Paul will pay Mary $100 if the value of one pound exceeds $2 one year from now, whereas Mary will pay Paul if the pound is worth less than $2. There are only two relevant outcomes: (1) the pound will exceed $2 or (2) it will fall below $2. If Paul and Mary agree on the probabilities of the two possible outcomes, and if neither party anticipates a loss, it must be that they assign $p = .5$ to each outcome. In that case the expected profit to both is zero and each has entered one side of a gambling prospect.

What is more likely, however, is that Paul and Mary assign different probabilities to the outcome. Mary assigns it $p > .5$, whereas Paul's assessment is $p < .5$. They perceive, subjectively, two different prospects. Economists call this case of differing belief's *heterogeneous expectations*. In such cases investors on each side of a financial position see themselves as speculating rather than gambling.

Both Paul and Mary should be asking, "Why is the other willing to invest in the side of a risky prospect that I believe offers a negative expected profit?" The ideal way to resolve heterogeneous beliefs is for Paul and Mary to "merge their information," that is, for each party to verify that he or she possesses all relevant information and processes the information properly. Of course, the acquisition of information and the extensive communication that is required to eliminate all heterogeneity in expectations is costly, and thus, up to a point, heterogeneous expectations cannot be taken as irrational. If, however, Paul and Mary enter such contracts frequently, they would recognize the information problem in one of two ways: either they will realize that they are creating gambles when each wins half of the bets, or the consistent loser will admit that he or she has been betting on inferior forecasts.

CC 1

CONCEPT CHECK

Assume that Canadian-dollar-denominated T-bills in Canada and pound-denominated bills in the United Kingdom offer equal yields to maturity. Both are short-term assets, and both are free of default risk. Neither offers investors a risk premium. However, a Canadian investor who holds U.K. bills is subject to exchange rate risk since the pounds earned on the U.K. bills eventually will be exchanged for Canadian dollars at the future exchange rate. Is the Canadian investor engaging in speculation or gambling?

Risk Aversion and Utility Values

The history of rates of return on various asset classes, as well as elaborate empirical studies, leave no doubt that risky assets command a risk premium in the marketplace. This implies that most investors are risk averse.

A prospect that has a zero-risk premium is called a **fair game**. Investors who are *risk-averse* reject investment portfolios that are fair games or worse. Risk-averse investors consider only risk-free or speculative prospects with positive risk premiums. Loosely speaking, a risk-averse investor "penalizes" the expected rate of return of a risky portfolio by a certain percentage (or penalizes the expected profit by a dollar amount) to account for the risk involved. The greater the risk, the larger the penalty. We believe that most investors accept this view from simple introspection, but we discuss the question more fully in the appendix at the end of this chapter.

We can formalize this notion of a risk-penalty system. To do so, we will assume that each investor can assign a welfare, or **utility**, score to competing investment portfolios based on the expected return and risk of those portfolios. The **utility value** may be viewed as a means of ranking portfolios. Higher utility values are assigned to portfolios with more attractive risk–return profiles. Portfolios receive higher utility scores for higher expected returns and lower scores for higher volatility. Many particular "scoring" systems are legitimate. One reasonable function that is commonly employed by financial theorists and the CFA Institute assigns a portfolio with expected return $E(r)$ and variance of returns σ^2 the following utility score:

$$U = E(r) - \frac{1}{2}A\sigma^2 \tag{5.1}$$

where U is the utility value and A is an index of the investor's aversion to taking on risk. (The factor of ½ is a scaling convention that will simplify calculations in later chapters. It has no economic significance, and we could eliminate it simply by defining a "new" A with half the value of the A used here.)

Equation 5.1 is consistent with the notion that utility is enhanced by high expected returns and diminished by high risk. The extent to which variance lowers utility depends on A, the investor's degree of risk aversion. More risk-averse investors (who have the larger A's) penalize risky investments more severely. Investors choosing among competing investment portfolios will select the one providing the highest utility level. Notice in equation 5.1 that the utility provided by a risk-free portfolio is simply the rate of return on the portfolio, since there is no penalization for risk.

Risk aversion obviously will have a major impact on the investor's appropriate risk–return tradeoff. The nearby box discusses some techniques that financial advisors use to gauge the risk aversion of their clients.

EXAMPLE 5.1   **Evaluating Investments by Using Utility Scores**

Consider three investors with different degrees of risk aversion: $A_1 = 2$, $A_2 = 3.5$, and $A_3 = 5$, all of whom are evaluating the three portfolios in Table 5.1. Since the risk-free rate is assumed to be 5 percent, equation 5.1 implies that all three investors would assign a utility score of .05 to the risk-free alternative. Table 5.2 presents the utility scores that would be assigned by each investor to each portfolio. The portfolio with the highest utility score for each investor appears in bold. Notice that the high-risk portfolio, H, would be chosen only by the investor with the lowest degree of risk aversion, $A_1 = 2$, while the low-risk portfolio, L, would be passed over even by the most risk-averse of our three investors. All three portfolios beat the risk-free alternative for the investors with levels of risk aversion given in the table.

CC 2

CONCEPT CHECK

A portfolio has an expected rate of return of .20 and standard deviation of .20. Bills offer a sure rate of return of .07. Which investment alternative will be chosen by an investor whose $A = 4$? What if $A = 8$?

Because we can compare utility values to the rate offered on risk-free investments when choosing between a risky portfolio and a safe one, we may interpret a portfolio's utility value as its "certainty equivalent" rate of return to an investor. The **certainty equivalent rate** of a portfolio is the rate that risk-free investments would need to offer with certainty to be considered equally attractive to the risky portfolio.

Now we can say that a portfolio is desirable only if its certainty equivalent return exceeds that of the risk-free alternative. A sufficiently risk-averse investor may assign any risky portfolio, even one with a positive risk premium, a certainty equivalent rate of return that is below the risk-free rate, which will cause the investor to reject the portfolio. At the same time, a less risk-averse (more risk-tolerant) investor will assign the same portfolio a certainty equivalent rate that exceeds

TABLE 5.1

Available Risky Portfolios (risk-free rate = 5%)

Portfolio	Risk Premium	Expected Return	Risk (SD)
L (low risk)	2%	7%	5%
M (medium risk)	4	9	10
H (high risk)	8	13	20

TABLE 5.2   Utility Scores of Alternative Portfolios for Investors with Varying Degrees of Risk Aversion

Investor Risk Aversion (A)	Utility Score of Portfolio L [$E(r) = .07$; $\sigma = .05$]	Utility Score of Portfolio M [$E(r) = .09$; $\sigma = .10$]	Utility Score of Portfolio H [$E(r) = .13$; $\sigma = .20$]
2.0	$.07 - \frac{1}{2} \times 2 \times .05^2 = .0675$	$.09 - \frac{1}{2} \times 2 \times .1^2 = .0800$	$\mathbf{.13 - \frac{1}{2} \times 2 \times .2^2 = .09}$
3.5	$.07 - \frac{1}{2} \times 3.5 \times .05^2 = .0656$	$\mathbf{.09 - \frac{1}{2} \times 3.5 \times .1^2 = .0725}$	$.13 - \frac{1}{2} \times 3.5 \times .2^2 = .06$
5.0	$.07 - \frac{1}{2} \times 5 \times .05^2 = .0638$	$\mathbf{.09 - \frac{1}{2} \times 5 \times .1^2 = .0650}$	$.13 - \frac{1}{2} \times 5 \times .2^2 = .03$

Figure 5.1

The tradeoff between risk and return of a potential investment portfolio.

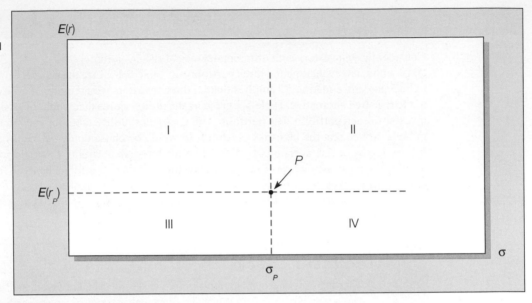

the risk-free rate and thus will prefer the portfolio to the risk-free alternative. If the risk premium is zero or negative to begin with, any downward adjustment to utility only makes the portfolio look worse. Its certainty equivalent rate will be below that of the risk-free alternative for all risk-averse investors.

In contrast to risk-averse investors, **risk-neutral** investors judge risky prospects solely by their expected rates of return. The level of risk is irrelevant to the risk-neutral investor, meaning that there is no penalization for risk. For this investor, a portfolio's certainty equivalent rate is simply its expected rate of return.

A **risk lover** is willing to engage in fair games and gambles; this investor adjusts the expected return upward to take into account the "fun" of confronting the prospect's risk. Risk lovers always will take a fair game because their upward adjustment of utility for risk gives the fair game a certainty equivalent that exceeds the alternative of the risk-free investment.

We can depict the individual's tradeoff between risk and return by plotting the characteristics of potential investment portfolios that the individual would view as equally attractive on a graph with axes measuring the expected value and standard deviation of portfolio returns. Figure 5.1 plots the characteristics of one portfolio.

Portfolio P, which has expected return $E(r_P)$ and standard deviation σ_P, is preferred by risk-averse investors to any portfolio in quadrant IV because it has an expected return equal to or greater than any portfolio in that quadrant and a standard deviation equal to or smaller than any portfolio in that quadrant. Conversely, any portfolio in quadrant I is preferable to portfolio P because its expected return is equal to or greater than P's and its standard deviation is equal to or smaller than P's.

This is the mean-standard deviation, or equivalently, **mean-variance (M-V) criterion**. It can be stated as: A dominates B if

$$E(r_A) \geq E(r_B)$$

and

$$\sigma_A \leq \sigma_B$$

and at least one inequality is strict (rules out indifference).

Figure 5.2

The indifference curve.

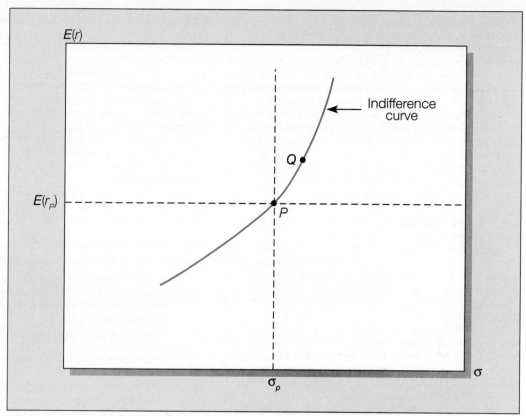

In the expected return–standard deviation graph, the preferred direction is northwest, because in this direction we simultaneously increase the expected return *and* decrease the variance of the rate of return. Any portfolio that lies northwest of *P* is superior to *P*.

What can be said about the portfolios in quadrants II and III? Their desirability, compared with *P*, depends on the exact nature of the investor's risk aversion. Suppose an investor identifies all portfolios that are equally as attractive as portfolio *P*. Starting at *P*, an increase in standard deviation lowers utility; it must be compensated for by an increase in expected return. Thus, point *Q* is equally desirable to this investor as *P*. Investors will be equally attracted to portfolios with high risk and high expected returns compared with other portfolios with lower risk but lower expected returns.

These equally preferred portfolios will lie on a curve in the mean-standard deviation graph that connects all portfolio points with the same utility value (Figure 5.2). This is called the **indifference curve**.

To determine some of the points that appear on the indifference curve, examine the utility values of several possible portfolios for an investor with *A* = 4, presented in Table 5.3. Note that

TABLE 5.3

Utility Values of Possible Portfolios for Investors with *A* = 4

Expected Return, $E(r)$	Standard Deviation, σ	Utility $= E(r) - \frac{1}{2}A\sigma^2$
.10	.200	$.10 - .5 \times 4 \times .04 = .02$
.15	.255	$.15 - .5 \times 4 \times .065 = .02$
.20	.300	$.20 - .5 \times 4 \times .09 = .02$
.25	.339	$.25 - .5 \times 4 \times .115 = .02$

TIME FOR INVESTING'S FOUR-LETTER WORD

What four-letter word should pop into mind when the stock market takes a harrowing nose dive?

No, not those. R-I-S-K.

Risk is the potential for realizing low returns or even losing money, possibly preventing you from meeting important objectives, like sending your kids to the college of their choice or having the retirement lifestyle you crave.

But many financial advisers and other experts say that these days investors aren't taking the idea of risk as seriously as they should, and they are overexposing themselves to stocks.

"The market has been so good for years that investors no longer believe there's risk in investing," says Gary Schatsky, a financial adviser in New York.

So before the market goes down and stays down, be sure that you understand your tolerance for risk and that your portfolio is designed to match it.

Assessing your risk tolerance, however, can be tricky. You must consider not only how much risk you can afford to take but also how much risk you can stand to take.

Determining how much risk you can stand—your temperamental tolerance for risk—is more difficult. It isn't quantifiable.

To that end, many financial advisers, brokerage firms and mutual-fund companies have created risk quizzes to help people determine whether they are conservative, moderate or aggressive investors. Some firms that offer such quizzes include Merrill Lynch, T. Rowe Price Associates Inc., Baltimore, Zurich Group Inc.'s Scudder Kemper Investments Inc., New York, and Vanguard Group in Malvern, Pennsylvania.

Typically, risk questionnaires include seven to 10 questions about a person's investing experience, financial security and tendency to make risky or conservative choices.

The benefit of the questionnaires is that they are an objective resource people can use to get at least a rough idea of their risk tolerance. "It's impossible for someone to assess their risk tolerance alone," says Mr. Bernstein. "I may say I don't like risk, yet will take more risk than the average person."

Many experts warn, however, that the questionnaires should be used simply as a first step to assessing risk tolerance. "They are not precise," says Ron Meier, a certified public accountant.

The second step, many experts agree, is to ask yourself some difficult questions, such as: How much you can stand to lose over the long term?

"Most people can stand to lose a heck of a lot temporarily," says Mr. Schatsky. The real acid test, he says, is how much of your portfolio's value you can stand to lose over months or years.

As it turns out, most people rank as middle-of-the-road risk-takers, say several advisers. "Only about 10% to 15% of my clients are aggressive," says Mr. Roge.

What's Your Risk Tolerance?

Circle the letter that corresponds to your answer.

1. Just 60 days after you put money into an investment its price falls 20 percent. Assuming none of the fundamentals have changed, what would you do?
   a. Sell to avoid further worry and try something else
   b. Do nothing and wait for the investment to come back
   c. Buy more. It was a good investment before; now it's a cheap investment too

2. Now look at the previous question another way. Your investment fell 20 percent, but it's part of a portfolio being used to meet investment goals with three different time horizons.

2A. What would you do if the goal were five years away?
   a. Sell
   b. Do nothing
   c. Buy more

each portfolio offers identical utility, since the high-return portfolios also have high risk (standard deviation). Although in practice the exact indifference curves of various investors cannot be known, this analysis can take us a long way in determining appropriate principles for portfolio selection strategy.

CC 3

CONCEPT CHECK

a. How will the indifference curve of a less risk-averse investor compare to the indifference curve drawn in Figure 5.2?

b. Draw both indifference curves passing through point P.

2B. What would you do if the goal were 15 years away?
   a. Sell
   b. Do nothing
   c. Buy more

2C. What would you do if the goal were 30 years away?
   a. Sell
   b. Do nothing
   c. Buy more

3. The price of your retirement investment jumps 25% a month after you buy it. Again, the fundamentals haven't changed. After you finish gloating, what do you do?
   a. Sell it and lock in your gains
   b. Stay put and hope for more gain
   c. Buy more; it could go higher

4. You're investing for retirement, which is 15 years away. Which would you rather do?
   a. Invest in a money-market fund or guaranteed investment contract, giving up the possibility of major gains, but virtually assuring the safety of your principal
   b. Invest in a 50-50 mix of bond funds and stock funds, in hopes of getting some growth, but also giving yourself some protection in the form of steady income
   c. Invest in aggressive growth mutual funds whose value will probably fluctuate significantly during the year, but have the potential for impressive gains over five or 10 years

5. You just won a big prize! But which one? It's up to you.
   a. $2,000 in cash
   b. A 50% chance to win $5,000
   c. A 20% chance to win $15,000

6. A good investment opportunity just came along. But you have to borrow money to get in. Would you take out a loan?
   a. Definitely not
   b. Perhaps
   c. Yes

7. Your company is selling stock to its employees. In three years, management plans to take the company public. Until then, you won't be able to sell your shares and you will get no dividends. But your investment could multiply as much as 10 times when the company goes public. How much money would you invest?
   a. None
   b. Two months' salary
   c. Four months' salary

Scoring Your Risk Tolerance

To score the quiz, add up the number of answers you gave in each category a–c, then multiply as shown to find your score.

(a) answers _____ × 1 = _____ points

(b) answers _____ × 2 = _____ points

(c) answers _____ × 3 = _____ points

YOUR SCORE _____ points

If you scored . . .	You may be a(n):
9–14 points	Conservative investor
15–21 points	Moderate investor
22–27 points	Aggressive investor

Estimating Risk Aversion

How can we estimate the levels of risk aversion of individual investors? A number of methods may be used. The questionnaire in the nearby box is of the simplest variety and, indeed, can distinguish only between high (conservative) and medium (moderate) or low (aggressive) levels of the coefficient of risk aversion. More complex questionnaires, allowing subjects to pinpoint specific levels of risk aversion coefficients, ask would-be investors to choose from various set of hypothetical lotteries.

Access to investment accounts of active investors would provide observations of how portfolio composition changes over time. Coupling this information with estimates of the risk–return combinations of these positions would in principle allow us to calculate investors' implied risk aversion coefficients.

Finally, researchers track behaviour of groups of individuals to obtain average degrees of risk aversion. These studies range from observed purchase of insurance policies and durables warranties to labor supply and aggregate consumption behaviour.

5.2 CAPITAL ALLOCATION ACROSS RISKY AND RISK-FREE PORTFOLIOS

History shows us that long-term bonds have been riskier investments than Treasury bills and that stocks have been riskier still. On the other hand, the riskier investments have offered higher average returns. Investors, of course, do not make all-or-nothing choices from these investment classes. They can and do construct their portfolios using securities from all asset classes. Some of the portfolio may be in risk-free Treasury bills, and some in high-risk stocks.

The most straightforward way to control the risk of the portfolio is through the fraction of the portfolio invested in Treasury bills and other safe money market securities versus risky assets. As *capital allocation decision* is an *asset allocation* choice among broad investment classes, rather than among the specific securities within each asset class. Most investment professionals consider asset allocation to be the most important part of portfolio construction (see the box here). Therefore, we start our discussion of the risk-return tradeoff available to investors by examining the most basic asset allocation choice: the choice of how much of the portfolio to place in risk-free money market securities versus in other risky asset classes.

We denote the investor's portfolio of risky assets as P, and the risk-free asset as F. We assume for the sake of illustration that the risky component of the investor's overall portfolio comprises two mutual funds: one invested in stocks and the other invested in long-term bonds. For now, we take the composition of the risky portfolio as given and focus only on the allocation between it and risk-free securities. In later sections, we turn to asset allocation and security selection across risky assets.

When we shift wealth from the risky portfolio to the risk-free asset, we do not change the relative proportions of the various risky assets within the risky portfolio. Rather, we reduce the relative weight of the risky portfolio as a whole in favour of risk-free assets.

For example, assume that the total market value of an initial portfolio is $300,000, of which $90,000 is invested in the Ready Asset money market fund, a risk-free asset for practical purposes. The remaining $210,000 is invested in risky equity securities—$113,400 in equities (E) and $96,600 in long-term bonds (B). The E and B holding is "the" risky portfolio, 54 percent in E and 46 percent in B:

$$\text{E:} \qquad w_1 = \frac{113,400}{210,000}$$

$$= .54$$

$$\text{B:} \qquad w_2 = \frac{96,600}{210,000}$$

$$= .46$$

The weight of the risky portfolio, P, in the **complete portfolio**, including risk-free investments, is denoted by y:

$$y = \frac{210,000}{300,000} = .7 \text{ (Risky assets)}$$

$$1 - y = \frac{90,000}{300,000} = .3 \text{ (Risk-free assets)}$$

If asset allocation explains nearly everything about variance, it logically follows that security selection explains nearly nothing. For about a decade, various investment firms have been cranking out marketing material quoting academic work done in the 1980s and 1990s by researchers led by Gary Brinson about asset allocation and variance for large U.S. pension funds. Most get it wrong.

It is perhaps the most misquoted and misunderstood research in the history of capital markets research. If the findings could be summed up in a sentence, it would likely be that asset allocation explains more than 90% of portfolio variability in returns on average.

Two observations pop up. One, the study's primary finding is about variability, sometimes called standard deviation and referred to as risk. Two, the phrase "on average" acknowledges there are times when the actual experience may be considerably better or considerably worse.

Mr. Brinson suggests active management (security selection) has no measurable impact on variance. Product manufacturers drone on about what asset allocation does explain without ever referencing what it doesn't.

Here's what Mr. Brinson has said: "Our study does not mean that if you got a return of 10%, then 9% is due to asset allocation. What it means is that if you looked at the ups and downs and zigs and zags of your portfolio across time, I could explain on average 90% of those zigs and zags if I know your asset allocation. But I can't tell you anything about the return you'll achieve."

This research is most often used in support of wrap account products that aim to optimize risk-adjusted returns

by assigning clients an off-the-shelf portfolio that offers an asset mix that is purportedly customized to the client's unique circumstances. Product manufacturers usually have four-to-eight model portfolios available and clients end up in one of them based on their answers to a relatively generic questionnaire.

These programs almost exclusively use higher-cost actively managed funds as the portfolio building blocks. Actively managed funds are not only more expensive, they also tend to have higher portfolio turnover and tend to be at least somewhat impure, so the prescribed asset allocation is often not the actual asset allocation. As such, active funds could materially compromise the asset mix.

Separate research by Bill Sharpe and others has repeatedly shown that most active managers lag their benchmarks. If the product manufacturers genuinely understood and believed both pieces of research, they would at least consider using cheap, pure and tax-effective index products in the construction of their portfolios. Instead, consumers are fed selective information that maximizes corporate profit (Brinson on variability) without being told about other material aspects that might harm profit (Sharpe on return).

In a court of law, people are required to tell the truth, the whole truth and nothing but the truth. We can now go to regulators and politicians and ask them to insist there be more complete disclosure in prospectuses, too. Cherrypicking material facts should not be tolerated in a profession where the practitioners are expected to put the client's interests first.

Source: John De Goey, "Why No Index-Based Asset Allocation Programs?" *National Post* [National Edition], April 25, 2005, p. FP 9. Copyright National Post 2005.

The weights of each stock in the complete portfolio are as follows:

$$E: \quad \frac{\$113,400}{\$300,000} = .378$$

$$B: \quad \frac{\$96,600}{\$300,000} = .322$$

$$\text{Risky portfolio} \quad = .700$$

The risky portfolio is 70 percent of the complete portfolio.

| EXAMPLE 5.2 | The Risky Portfolio |

Suppose that the owner of this portfolio wishes to decrease risk by reducing the allocation to the risky portfolio from $y = .7$ to $y = .56$. The risky portfolio would total only $168,000 ($.56 \times \$300,000 = \$168,000$), requiring the sale of $42,000 of the original $210,000 risky holdings, with the proceeds used to purchase more shares in Ready Asset (the money market

continued

fund). Total holdings in the risk-free asset will increase to $300,000(1 - .56) = \$132,000$, or the original holdings plus the new contribution to the money market fund:

$$\$90,000 + \$42,000 = \$132,000$$

The key point, however, is that we leave the proportions of each stock in the risky portfolio unchanged. Because the weights of E and B in the risky portfolio are .54 and .46, respectively, we sell $.54 \times \$42,000 = \$22,680$ of E and $.46 \times \$42,000 = \$19,320$ of B. After the sale, the proportions of each share in the risky portfolio are in fact unchanged:

$$\text{E:} \qquad w_1 = \frac{113,400 - 22,680}{210,000 - 42,000}$$

$$= .54$$

$$\text{B:} \qquad w_2 = \frac{96,600 - 19,320}{210,000 - 42,000}$$

$$= .46$$

Rather than thinking of our risky holdings as E and B stock separately, we may view our holdings as if they were in a single fund that holds E and B in fixed proportions. In this sense we treat the risky fund as a single risky asset, that asset being a particular bundle of securities. As we shift in and out of safe assets, we simply alter our holdings of that bundle of securities commensurately.

With this assumption, we turn to the desirability of reducing risk by changing the risky/risk-free asset mix, that is, reducing risk by decreasing the proportion y. As long as we do not alter the weights of each stock within the risky portfolio, the probability distribution of the rate of return on the risky portfolio remains unchanged by the asset reallocation. What will change is the probability distribution of the rate of return on the complete portfolio that consists of the risky asset and the risk-free asset.

CC 4

CONCEPT CHECK

What will be the dollar value of your position in E and its proportion in your overall portfolio if you decide to hold 50 percent of your investment budget in Ready Asset?

5.3   **THE RISK-FREE ASSET**

By virtue of its power to tax and control the money supply, only the government can issue default-free bonds. Actually, the default-free guarantee by itself is not sufficient to make the bonds risk-free in real terms. The only risk-free asset in real terms would be a perfectly price-indexed bond. Moreover, a default-free perfectly indexed bond offers a guaranteed real rate to an investor only if the maturity of the bond is identical to the investor's desired holding period. Even indexed bonds are subject to interest rate risk, because real interest rates change unpredictably through time. When future real rates are uncertain, so is the future price of perfectly indexed bonds.

Nevertheless, it is common practice to view Treasury bills as "the" risk-free asset. Their short-term nature makes their values insensitive to interest rate fluctuations. Indeed, an investor can lock in a short-term nominal return by buying a bill and holding it to maturity. The inflation uncertainty over the course of a few weeks, or even months, is negligible compared with the uncertainty of stock market returns.

Figure 5.3

Yield spread between three-month corporate paper and T-bills.

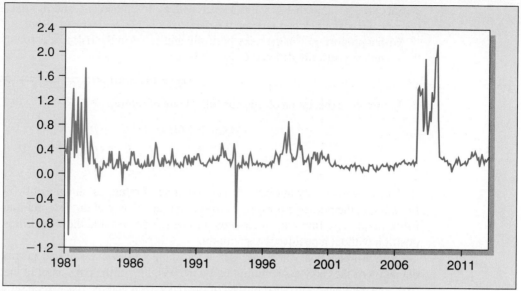

Source: Data from Scotia Capital and PC Bonds Analytics, Debt Market Indices, various years. Available www. canadianbondindices.com.

In practice, most investors use a broader range of money market instruments as a risk-free asset. All the money market instruments are virtually free of interest rate risk because of their short maturities and are fairly safe in terms of default or credit risk.

Most money market funds hold, for the most part, three types of securities: Treasury bills, bearer deposit notes (BDNs), and commercial paper (CP), differing slightly in their default risk. The yields to maturity on BDNs and CP for identical maturity, for example, are always slightly higher than those of T-bills. The pattern of this yield spread for short-term high-quality commercial paper is shown in Figure 5.3.

Money market funds have changed their relative holdings of these securities over time, but by and large, T-bills make up only about 15 percent of their portfolios.[1] Nevertheless, the risk of such blue-chip short-term investments as BDNs and CP is minuscule compared with that of most other assets, such as long-term corporate bonds, common stocks, or real estate. Hence, we treat money market funds as the most easily accessible risk-free asset for most investors.

5.4   PORTFOLIOS OF ONE RISKY ASSET AND ONE RISK-FREE ASSET

In this section, we examine the feasible risk-return combinations available to investors when the choice of the risky portfolio has already been made. This is the "technical" part of capital allocation. In the next section, we will address the "personal" part of the problem—the individual's choice of the best risk–return combination from the feasible set.

Suppose that the investor already has decided on the composition of the optimal risky portfolio P. Now the concern is with capital allocation, that is the proportion of the investment budget, y, to be allocated to P. The remaining proportion, $1 - y$, is to be invested in the risk-free asset, F.

Denote the risky rate of return by r_P and denote the expected rate of return on P by $E(r_P)$ and its standard deviation by σ_P. The rate of return on the risk-free asset is denoted r_f. In the numerical

---

[1]See http://www.icifactbook.org, Section 4 of "Data Tables."

example we assume that $E(r_P) = 15$ percent, $\sigma_P = 22$ percent, and the risk-free rate is $r_f = 7$ percent. Thus, the risk premium on the risky asset is $E(r_P) - r_f = 8$ percent.

With a proportion y in the risky portfolio and $1 - y$ in the risk-free asset, the rate of return on the *complete* portfolio, denoted C, is r_C where

$$r_C = yr_P + (1 - y)r_f \tag{5.2}$$

Taking the expectation of this portfolio's rate of return,

$$\begin{aligned} E(r_C) &= yE(r_P) + (1 - y)r_f \\ &= r_f + y[E(r_P) - r_f] \\ &= .07 + y(.15 - .07) \end{aligned} \tag{5.3}$$

This result is easily interpreted. The base rate of return for any portfolio is the risk-free rate. In addition, the portfolio is *expected* to earn a proportion y of the risk premium of the risky portfolio, $E(r_P) - r_f$. Investors are assumed to be risk-averse and thus unwilling to take on a risky position without a positive risk premium.

With a proportion y in a risky asset, the standard deviation of that portfolio is the standard deviation of the risky asset multiplied by the weight y of the risky asset in that portfolio.[2] In our case, the complete portfolio consists of the risky asset and the risk-free asset. Since the standard deviation of the risky portfolio is $\sigma_P = .22$,

$$\sigma_C = y\sigma_P = .22y \tag{5.4}$$

which makes sense, because the standard deviation of the portfolio is proportional to both the standard deviation of the risky asset and the proportion invested in it. In sum, the rate of return of the complete portfolio will have expected return $E(r_C) = r_f + y[E(r_P) - r_f] = .07 + .08y$ and standard deviation $\sigma_C = .22y$.

The next step is to plot the portfolio characteristics (as a function of y) in the expected return–standard deviation plane in Figure 5.4. The expected return–standard deviation combination for the risk-free asset, F, appears on the vertical axis because the standard deviation is zero. The risky asset, P, is plotted with a standard deviation, $\sigma_P = .22$, and expected return of .15. If an investor chooses to invest solely in the risky asset, then $y = 1.0$, and the resulting portfolio is P. If the chosen position is $y = 0$, then $1 - y = 1.0$, and the resulting portfolio is the risk-free portfolio F.

What about the more interesting midrange portfolios where y lies between zero and 1? These portfolios will graph on the straight line connecting points F and P. The slope of that line is simply $[E(r_P) - r_f]/\sigma_P$ (or rise/run), in this case .08/.22.

The conclusion is straightforward. Increasing the fraction of the overall portfolio invested in the risky asset increases expected return at a rate of 8 percent according to equation 5.3. It also increases portfolio standard deviation according to equation 5.4 at the rate of .22. The extra return per extra risk is thus .08/.22 = .36.

To derive the exact equation for the straight line between F and P, we rearrange equation 5.4 to find that $y = \sigma_C/\sigma_P$, and substitute for y in equation 5.3 to describe the expected return—standard deviation tradeoff:

$$\begin{aligned} E[r_C(y)] &= r_f + y[E(r_P) - r_f] \\ &= r_f + \frac{\sigma_C}{.22}[E(r_P) - r_f] \\ &= .07 + \frac{.08}{.22}\sigma_C \end{aligned} \tag{5.5}$$

---

[2]This is an application of a basic rule from statistics: If you multiply a random variable by a constant, the standard deviation is multiplied by the same constant. In our application, the random variable is the rate of return on the risky asset, and the constant is the fraction of that asset in the complete portfolio. We will elaborate on the rules for portfolio return and risk in the following chapter.

Figure 5.4

The investment opportunity set with a risky asset and a risk-free asset.

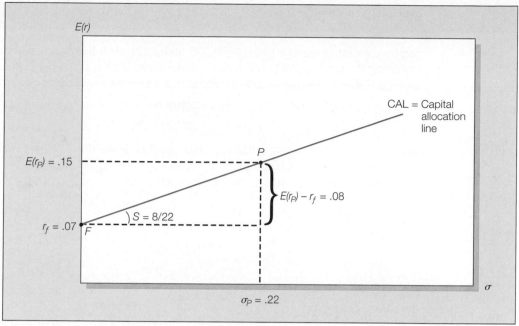

Thus, the expected return of the portfolio as a function of its standard deviation is a straight line, with intercept r_f and slope as follows:

$$S = \frac{E(r_P) - r_f}{\sigma_P} = \frac{.08}{.22} \tag{5.6}$$

Figure 5.4 graphs the *investment opportunity set*, which is the set of feasible expected return and standard deviation pairs of all portfolios resulting from different values of y. The graph is a straight line originating at r_f and going through the point labelled P.

This straight line is called the **capital allocation line (CAL)**. It depicts all the risk–return combinations available to investors. The slope of the CAL, S, equals the increase in the expected return of the chosen portfolio per unit of additional standard deviation—in other words, the measure of extra return per extra risk. For this reason, the slope also is called the **reward-to-volatility ratio**. It is also called the Sharpe ratio (see Chapter 4).

A portfolio equally divided between the risky asset and the risk-free asset, that is, where $y = .5$, will have an expected rate of return of $E(r_C) = .07 + .5 \times .08 = .11$, implying a risk premium of 4 percent, and a standard deviation of $\sigma_C = .5 \times 22 = .11$, or 11 percent. It will plot on the line FP midway between F and P. The reward-to-volatility ratio will be $S = .04/.11 = .36$, same as that of portfolio P.

CC 5

CONCEPT CHECK

Can the reward-to-volatility ratio, $S = [E(r_C) - r_f]/\sigma_C$, of any combination of the risky asset and the risk-free asset be different from the ratio for the risky asset taken alone, $[E(r_P) - r_f]/\sigma_P$, which in this case is .36?

What about points on the line to the right of portfolio P in the investment opportunity set? If investors can borrow at the (risk-free) rate of $r_f = 7$ percent, they can construct portfolios that may be plotted on the CAL to the right of P.

EXAMPLE 5.3   **Leverage**

Suppose the investment budget is $300,000, and our investor borrows an additional $120,000, investing the total available funds in the risky asset. This is a *levered* position in the risky asset; it is financed in part by borrowing. In that case

$$y = \frac{420,000}{300,000} = 1.4$$

and $1 - y = 1 - 1.4 = -.4$, reflecting a short position in the risk-free asset, which is a borrowing position. Rather than lending at a 7 percent interest rate, the investor borrows at 7 percent. The distribution of the portfolio rate of return still exhibits the same reward-to-variability ratio:

$$E(r_C) = .07 + (1.4 \times .08) = .182$$
$$\sigma_C = 1.4 \times .22 = .308$$
$$S = \frac{E(r_C) - r_f}{\sigma_C}$$
$$= \frac{.182 - .07}{.308} = .36$$

As one might expect, the levered portfolio has a higher standard deviation than does an unlevered position in the risky asset.

Of course, nongovernment investors cannot borrow at the risk-free rate. The risk of a borrower's default induces lenders to demand higher interest rates on loans. Therefore, the nongovernment investor's borrowing cost will exceed the lending rate of $r_f = 7$ percent. Suppose that the borrowing rate is $r^B_f = 9$ percent. Then, in the borrowing range the reward-to-variability ratio, the slope of the CAL, will be $[E(r_P) - r^B_f]/\sigma_P = .06/.22 = .27$. The CAL therefore will be "kinked" at point P as shown in Figure 5.5. To the left of P the investor is lending at 7 percent, and the slope of the CAL is .36. To the right of P, where $y > 1$, the investor is borrowing to finance extra investments in the risky asset, and the slope is .27.

In practice, borrowing to invest in the risky portfolio is easy and straightforward if you have a margin account with a broker. All you have to do is tell your broker that you want to buy "on margin." Margin purchases may not exceed 70 percent of the purchase value. Therefore, if your net worth in the account is $300,000, the broker is allowed to lend you up to $300,000 to purchase additional stock.[3] You would then have $600,000 on the asset side of your account and $300,000 on the liability side, resulting in $y = 2.0$.

CC 6

CONCEPT CHECK

Suppose that there is a shift upward in the expected rate of return on the risky asset, from 15 percent to 17 percent. If all other parameters remain unchanged, what will be the slope of the CAL for $y \leq 1$ and $y > 1$?

[3]Margin purchases require the investor to maintain the securities in a margin account with the broker. If the value of the securities declines below a maintenance margin, a margin call is sent out, requiring a deposit to bring the net worth of the account up to the appropriate level. If the margin call is not met, regulations mandate that some or all of the securities be sold by the broker and the proceeds used to reestablish the required margin. See Chapter 3, Section 3.5, for a further discussion. As we will see in Chapter 20, futures contracts also offer leverage if the risky portfolio is an index fund on which a contract trades.

Figure 5.5

The opportunity set with differential borrowing and lending rates.

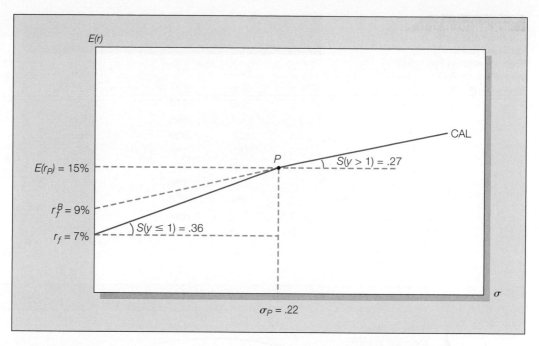

RISK TOLERANCE AND ASSET ALLOCATION

We have shown how to develop the CAL, the graph of all feasible risk–return combinations available for capital allocation. The investor confronting the CAL now must choose one optimal combination from the set of feasible choices. This choice entails a tradeoff between risk and return. Individual differences in risk aversion lead to different capital allocation choices even when facing an identical opportunity set (as described by a risk-free rate and a reward-to-variability ratio). In particular, more risk-averse investors will choose to hold less of the risky asset and more of the risk-free asset.

The expected return of the complete portfolio is given by equation 5.3:

$$E(r_C) = r_f + y[E(r_P) - r_f]$$

From equation 5.4, the variance of the overall portfolio is

$$\sigma_C^2 = y^2 \sigma_p^2$$

Investors choose the allocation to the risky asset, y, that maximizes their utility function given by equation 5.1: $U = E(r) - \frac{1}{2}A\sigma^2$. As the allocation to the risky asset increases (higher y), expected return increases, but so does volatility, so utility can increase or decrease. Table 5.4 shows utility levels corresponding to different values of y. Initially, utility increases as y increases, but eventually it declines.

Figure 5.6 is a plot of the utility function from Table 5.4. The graph shows that utility is highest at $y = .41$. When y is less than $.41$, investors are willing to assume more risk to increase expected return. But at higher levels of y, risk is higher, and additional allocations to the risky asset are undesirable—beyond this point, further increases in risk dominate the increase in expected return and reduce utility.

To solve the utility maximization problem more generally, we write the problem as follows:

$$\operatorname*{Max}_{y} U = E(r_C) - \frac{1}{2}A\sigma_C^2 = r_f + y[E(r_P) - r_f] - \frac{1}{2}Ay^2\sigma_P^2$$

TABLE 5.4

Utility Levels for Various Positions in Risky Assets (y) for Investor with Risk Aversion A = 4

(1) y	(2) $E(r_C)$	(3) σ_C	(4) $U = E(r) - \frac{1}{2}A\sigma^2$
0	.070	0	.0700
.1	.078	.022	.0770
.2	.086	.044	.0821
.3	.094	.066	.0853
.4	.102	.088	.0865
.5	.110	.110	.0858
.6	.118	.132	.0832
.7	.126	.154	.0786
.8	.134	.176	.0720
.9	.142	.198	.0636
1.0	.150	.220	.0532

Figure 5.6

Utility as a function of allocation to the risky asset, y.

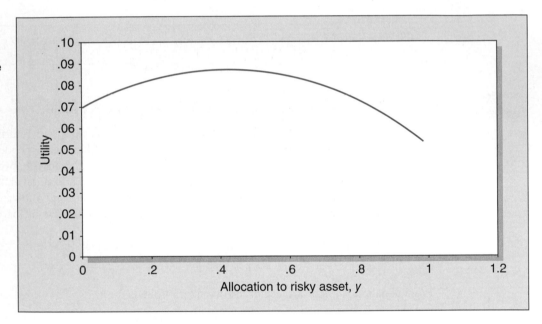

Students of calculus will remember that the maximization problem is solved by setting the derivative of this expression to zero. Doing so and solving for y yields the optimal position for risk-averse investors in the risky asset, y^*, as follows:[4]

$$y^* = \frac{E(r_P) - r_f}{A\sigma_P^2} \tag{5.7}$$

This solution shows that the optimal position in the risky asset is *inversely* proportional to the level of risk aversion and the level of risk (as measured by the variance) and directly proportional to the risk premium offered by the risky asset.

---

[4]The derivative with respect to y equals $E(r_P) - r_f - yA\sigma_P^2$. Setting this expression equal to zero and solving for y yields equation 5.7.

EXAMPLE 5.4   **Capital Allocation**

Using our numerical example ($r_f = 7\%$, $E(r_P) = 15\%$, and $\sigma_P = 22\%$), and expressing all returns as decimals, the optimal solution for an investor with a coefficient of risk aversion $A = 4$ is

$$y^* = \frac{.15 - .07}{4 \times .22^2} = .41$$

In other words, this particular investor will invest 41 percent of the investment budget in the risky asset and 59 percent in the risk-free asset. As we saw in Figure 5.6, this is the value of y at which utility is maximized.

With 41 percent invested in the risky portfolio, the expected return and standard deviation of the complete portfolio are

$$E(r_C) = 7 + [.41 \times (15 - 7)] = 10.28\%$$
$$\sigma_C = .41 \times 22 = 9.02\%$$

The risk premium of the complete portfolio is $E(r_C) - r_f = 3.28$ percent, which is obtained by taking on a portfolio with a standard deviation of 9.02 percent. Notice that 3.28/9.02 = .36, which is the reward-to-volatility (Sharpe) ratio assumed for this example.

A graphical way of presenting this decision problem is to use indifference curve analysis. To illustrate how to build an indifference curve, consider an investor with risk aversion $A = 4$ who currently holds all her wealth in a risk-free portfolio yielding $r_f = 5$ percent. Because the variance of such a portfolio is zero, equation 5.1 tells us that its utility value is $U = .05$. Now we find the expected return the investor would require to maintain the *same* level of utility when holding a risky portfolio, say with $\sigma = 1$ percent. We use equation 5.1 to find how much $E(r)$ must increase to compensate for the higher value of σ:

$$U = E(r) - \frac{1}{2}A\sigma^2$$

$$.05 = E(r) - \frac{1}{2} \times 4 \times .01^2$$

This implies that the necessary expected return increases to

$$\text{Required } E(r) = .05 + \frac{1}{2} \times A\sigma^2 \tag{5.8}$$

$$= .05 + \frac{1}{2} \times 4 \times .01^2 = .0502$$

We can repeat this calculation for many other levels of σ, each time finding the value of $E(r)$ necessary to maintain $U = .05$. This process will yield all combinations of expected return and volatility with utility level of .05; plotting these combinations gives us the indifference curve.

We can readily generate an investor's indifference curves using a spreadsheet. Table 5.5 contains risk–return combinations with utility values of .05 and .09 for two investors, one with $A = 2$ and the other with $A = 4$. The plot of these indifference curves appears in Figure 5.7. Notice that the intercepts of the indifference curves are at .05 and .09, exactly the level of utility corresponding to the two curves.

TABLE 5.5

Spreadsheet Calculations of Indifference Curves (entries in columns 2–4 are expected returns necessary to provide specified utility value)

σ	A = 2		A = 4	
	U = .05	U = .09	U = .05	U = .09
0	.0500	.0900	.050	.090
.05	.0525	.0925	.055	.095
.10	.0600	.1000	.070	.110
.15	.0725	.1125	.095	.135
.20	.0900	.1300	.130	.170
.25	.1125	.1525	.175	.215
.30	.1400	.1800	.230	.270
.35	.1725	.2125	.295	.335
.40	.2100	.2500	.370	.410
.45	.2525	.2925	.455	.495
.50	.3000	.3400	.550	.590

Any investor would prefer a portfolio on the higher indifference curve with a higher certainty equivalent (utility). Portfolios on higher indifference curves offer a higher expected return for any given level of risk. For example, both indifference curves for $A = 2$ have the same shape, but for any level of volatility, a portfolio on the curve with utility of .09 offers an expected return 4 percent greater than the corresponding portfolio on the lower curve, for which $U = .05$.

Figure 5.7 demonstrates that more risk-averse investors have steeper indifference curves than less risk-averse investors. Steeper curves mean that investors require a greater increase in expected return to compensate for an increase in portfolio risk.

Higher indifference curves correspond to higher levels of utility. The investor thus attempts to find the complete portfolio on the highest possible indifference curve. When we superimpose plots of indifference curves on the investment opportunity set represented by the capital

Figure 5.7

Indifference curves for $U = .05$ and $U = .09$ with $A = 2$ and $A = 4$.

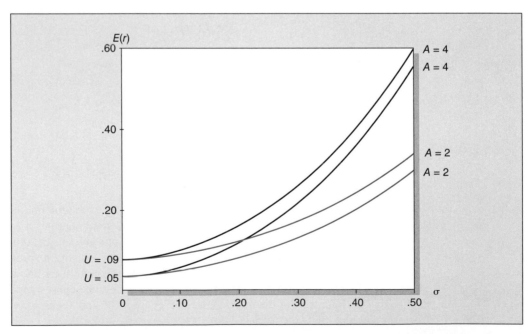

Figure 5.8

Finding the optimal complete portfolio by using indifference curves.

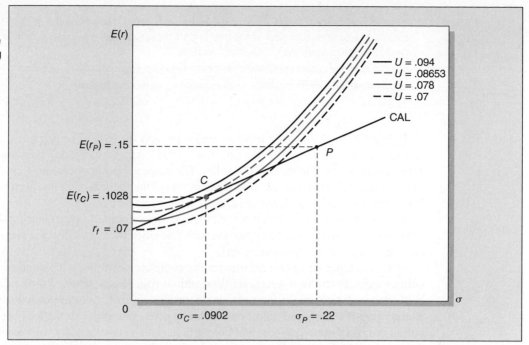

allocation line as in Figure 5.8, we can identify the *highest possible* indifference curve that still touches the CAL. That indifference curve is tangent to the CAL, and the tangency point corresponds to the standard deviation and expected return of the optimal complete portfolio.

To illustrate, Table 5.6 provides calculations for four indifference curves (with utility levels of .07, .078, .08653, and .094) for an investor with $A = 4$. Columns 2–5 use equation 5.8 to calculate the expected return that must be paired with the standard deviation in column 1 to provide the utility value corresponding to each curve. Column 6 uses equation 5.5 to calculate $E(r_C)$ on the CAL for the standard deviation σ_C in column 1:

$$E(r_C) = r_f + [E(r_P) - r_f]\frac{\sigma_C}{\sigma_P} = .07 + [.15 - .07]\frac{\sigma_C}{.22}$$

TABLE 5.6

Expected Returns on Four Indifference Curves and the CAL

σ	$U = .07$	$U = .078$	$U = .08653$	$U = .094$	CAL
0	.0700	.0780	.0865	.0940	.0700
.02	.0708	.0788	.0873	.0948	.0773
.04	.0732	.0812	.0897	.0972	.0845
.06	.0772	.0852	.0937	.1012	.0918
.08	.0828	.0908	.0993	.1068	.0991
.09	.0863	.0943	.1028	.1103	.1028
.10	.0900	.0980	.1065	.1140	.1064
.12	.0988	.1068	.1153	.1228	.1136
.14	.1092	.1172	.1257	.1332	.1209
.18	.1348	.1428	.1513	.1588	.1355
.22	.1668	.1748	.1833	.1908	.1500
.26	.2052	.2132	.2217	.2292	.1645
.30	.2500	.2580	.2665	.2740	.1791

Figure 5.8 graphs the four indifference curves and the CAL. The graph reveals that the indifference curve with $U = .08653$ is tangent to the CAL; the tangency point corresponds to the complete portfolio that maximizes utility. The tangency point occurs at $\sigma_C = 9.02$ percent and $E(r_C) = 10.28$ percent, the risk–return parameters of the optimal complete portfolio with $y^* = .41$. These values match our algebraic solution using equation 5.7.

We conclude that the choice for y^*, the fraction of overall investment funds to place in the risky portfolio, is determined by risk aversion (the slope of the indifference curve) and the Sharpe ratio (the slope of the opportunity set).

In sum, capital allocation determines the complete portfolio, which makes up the investor's entire wealth. Portfolio P represents all-wealth-at-risk. Hence, when returns are normally distributed, standard deviation is the appropriate measure of risk. In future chapters we will consider augmenting P with "good" additions, meaning assets that improve the feasible risk–return trade-off. The risk of these potential additions will have to be measured by their *incremental* effect on the standard deviation of P.

CC 7

CONCEPT CHECK

a. If an investor's coefficient of risk aversion is $A = 3$, how does the optimal asset mix change? What are the new $E(r_C)$ and σ_C?

b. Suppose that the borrowing rate, $r^B f = 9$ percent, is greater than the lending rate, $r_f = 7$ percent. Show, graphically, how the optimal portfolio choice of some investors will be affected by the higher borrowing rate. Which investors will not be affected by the borrowing rate?

Non-normal Returns

In the foregoing analysis we assumed normality of returns by taking the standard deviation as the appropriate measure of risk. But as we discussed in Chapter 4, departures from normality could result in extreme losses with far greater likelihood than would be plausible under a normal distribution. These exposures, which are typically measured by value at risk (VaR) or expected shortfall (ES), also would be important to investors.

Therefore, an appropriate extension of our analysis would be to present investors with forecasts of VaR and ES. Taking the capital allocation from the normal-based analysis as a benchmark, investors facing fat-tailed distributions might consider reducing their allocation to the risky portfolio in favour of an increase in the allocation to the risk-free vehicle.

There are signs of advances in dealing with extreme values (in addition to new techniques to handle transaction data mentioned in Chapter 4). Back in the early twentieth century, Frank Knight, one of the great economists of the time, distinguished *risk* from *uncertainty*, the difference being that risk is a known problem in which probabilities can be ascertained while uncertainty is characterized by ignorance even about probabilities (reminiscent of the black swan problem). Hence, Knight argued, we must use different methods to handle uncertainty and risk.

Probabilities of moderate outcomes in finance can be readily assessed from experience because of the high relative frequency of such observations. Extreme negative values are blissfully rare, but for that very reason, accurately assessing their probabilities is virtually impossible. However, the Bayesian statistics that took centre stage in decision making in later periods rejected Knight's approach on the basis of the argument that even if probabilities are hard to estimate objectively, investors nevertheless have a notion, albeit subjective, of what they may be, and must use those beliefs to make economic decisions. In the Bayesian framework, these so-called priors must be used even if they apply to unprecedented events that characterize "uncertainty." Accordingly, in this school of thought, the distinction between risk and uncertainty is deemed irrelevant.

Economists today are coming around to Knight's position. Advanced utility functions attempt to distinguish risk from uncertainty and give these uncertain outcomes a larger role in the choice of portfolios. These approaches have yet to enter everyday practice, but as they are developed, practical measures are certain to follow.

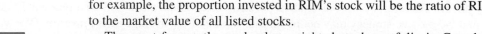

5.6 PASSIVE STRATEGIES: THE CAPITAL MARKET LINE

The CAL is derived with the risk-free asset and "the" risky portfolio P. Determination of the assets to include in P may result from a passive or an active strategy. A **passive strategy** describes a portfolio decision that avoids *any* direct or indirect security analysis.[5] At first blush, a passive strategy would appear to be naïve. As will become apparent, however, forces of supply and demand in large capital markets may make such a strategy a reasonable choice for many investors.

In Chapter 4, we presented a compilation of the history of rates of return on different portfolios. We can use the data underlying these portfolios to examine various passive strategies.

A natural candidate for a passively held risky asset would be a well-diversified portfolio of common stocks. Because a passive strategy requires that we devote no resources to acquiring information on any individual stock or group of stocks, we must follow a "neutral" diversification strategy. One way is to select a diversified portfolio of stocks that mirrors the value of the corporate sector of the Canadian economy. This results in a value-weighted portfolio in which, for example, the proportion invested in RIM's stock will be the ratio of RIM's total market value to the market value of all listed stocks.

Toronto Stock
Exchange
www.tsx.com

The most frequently used value-weighted stock portfolio in Canada is the Toronto Stock Exchange's composite index of the largest-capitalization Canadian corporations[6] (S&P/TSX Composite). Table 5.7 shows the historical record of this portfolio over the 1957–2012 period, as well as for the four subperiods. The last columns show the average risk premium over T-bills, its standard deviation, and the reward-to-volatility (Sharpe) ratio. The risk premium of 4.24 percent and standard deviation of 17.42 percent over the entire period correspond to the figures of 8 percent and 22 percent we assumed for the risky portfolio example in Section 5.4.

The Sharpe ratio is .24 for the entire 56-year period. It varies between .17 and .31 over the various subperiods. These numbers are clearly lower than the corresponding Sharpe ratios for the U.S. large stocks that make up the S&P 500 index. Over the 87-year 1926–2012 period, these stocks have a Sharpe ratio of .40, while over different subperiods it varies from a low of .21 to a high of .74.

We call the capital allocation line provided by one-month T-bills and a broad index of common stocks the **capital market line (CML)**. A passive strategy generates an investment opportunity set that is represented by the CML.

---

[5]By "indirect security analysis" we mean the delegation of that responsibility to an intermediary, such as a professional money manager.
[6]For the composition and capitalization of the S&P/TSX Composite index see http://www.standardandpoors.com/indices/sp-tsx-composite/en/us/?indexId=spcadntxc-caduf--p-ca----.

TABLE 5.7

Annual Rates of Return for Common Stock and Three-Month T-Bills, Standard Deviations, and Sharpe Ratios of Stock Risk Premiums over Time

	Stocks Mean	T-Bills Mean	Risk Premiums Mean	St. Dev.	Sharpe Ratio
1957–1970	8.53	4.47	4.06	16.61	.24
1971–1984	13.10	9.60	3.50	2.43	.17
1985–1998	11.20	7.82	3.38	14.03	.24
1999–2012	9.66	2.83	6.04	19.73	.31
1957–2012	1.43	6.19	4.24	17.42	.24

Source: Modified from Scotia Capital and PC Bonds Analytics, Debt Market Indices, various years.

How reasonable is it for an investor to pursue a passive strategy? Of course, we cannot answer such a question without comparing the strategy to the costs and benefits accruing to an active portfolio strategy. Some thoughts are relevant at this point, however.

First, the alternative active strategy is not free. Whether you choose to invest the time and cost to acquire the information needed to generate an optimal active portfolio of risky assets, or whether you delegate the task to a professional who will charge a fee, construction of an active portfolio is more expensive than construction of a passive one. The passive portfolio requires negligible cost to purchase T-bills and management fees to either an exchange-traded fund or a mutual fund company that operates a market index fund. First Canadian's Equity Index Fund, for example, mimics the S&P/TSX Composite index. It purchases shares of the firms constituting the Composite in proportion to the market values of the outstanding equity of each firm, and therefore essentially replicates it. The fund thus duplicates its performance. It has low operating expenses (as a percentage of assets) when compared to other mutual stock funds precisely because it requires minimal managerial effort.

A second reason supporting a passive strategy is the free-rider benefit. If we assume there are many active, knowledgeable investors who quickly bid up prices of undervalued assets and bid down overvalued assets (by selling), we have to conclude that at any time most assets will be fairly priced. Therefore, a well-diversified portfolio of common stock will be a reasonably fair buy, and the passive strategy may not be inferior to that of the average active investor. (We will explain this assumption and provide a more comprehensive analysis of the relative success of passive strategies in later chapters.) The box here points out that passive index funds have actually outperformed most actively managed funds in past decades and that investors are responding to the lower costs and better performance of the index funds by directing their investments into these products.

To summarize, a passive strategy involves investment in two passive portfolios: virtually risk-free, short-term T-bills (or, alternatively, a money market fund) and a fund of common stocks that mimics a broad market index. The capital allocation line representing such a strategy is called the *capital market line*. Historically, judging by data from 1957 to 2012, the passive risky portfolio offered an average risk premium of 4.24 percent and a standard deviation of 17.42 percent, resulting in a reward-to-volatility ratio of .24.

Passive investors allocate their investment budgets among instruments according to their degree of risk aversion. We can use our analysis to deduce a typical investor's risk-aversion parameter. Suppose, for instance, that we have estimated that approximately 66 percent of Canadians' net worth is invested in a broad array of risky assets.[7] We assume this portfolio has

---

[7]We include in the risky portfolio real assets, half of pension reserves, corporate and noncorporate equity, and half of mutual fund shares.

INVESTORS SOUR ON PRO STOCK PICKERS

Investors are jumping out of mutual funds managed by professional stock pickers and shifting massive amounts of money into lower-cost funds that echo the broader market. Through November 2012, investors pulled $119.3 billion from so-called actively managed U.S. stock funds according to the latest data from research firm Morningstar Inc. At the same time, they poured $30.4 billion into U.S. stock exchange–traded funds.

The move reflects the fact that many money managers of stock funds, which charge fees but also dangle the prospect of higher returns, have underperformed the benchmark stock indexes. As a result, more investors are choosing simply to invest in funds tracking the indexes, which carry lower fees and are perceived as having less risk.

The mission of stock pickers in a managed mutual fund is to outperform the overall market by actively trading individual stocks or bonds, with fund managers receiving higher fees for their effort. In an ETF (or indexed mutual fund), managers balance the share makeup of the fund so it accurately reflects the performance of its underlying index, charging lower fees.

Morningstar says that when investors have put money in stock funds, they have chosen low-cost index funds and ETFs. Some index ETFs cost less than 0.1% of assets a year, while many actively managed stock funds charge 1% a year or more.

While the trend has put increasing pressure lately on stock pickers, it is shifting the fortunes of some of the biggest players in the $14 trillion mutual-fund industry.

Fidelity Investments and American Funds, among the largest in the category, saw redemptions or weak investor interest compared with competitors, according to an analysis of mutual-fund flows done for *The Wall Street Journal* by research firm Strategic Insight, a unit of New York-based Asset International.

At the other end of the spectrum, Vanguard, the world's largest provider of index mutual funds, pulled in a net $141 billion last year through December, according to the company.

Many investors say they are looking for a way to invest cheaply, with less risk.

Source: Adapted from Kirsten Grind, "Investors Sour on Pro Stock Pickers," *The Wall Street Journal*, January 3, 2013.

---

the same reward–risk characteristics as the S&P/TSX Composite has exhibited since 1957, as is documented in Table 5.7. Substituting these values in equation 6.7, we obtain

$$y^* = \frac{E(r_M) - r_f}{A\sigma_M^2} = \frac{.0424}{.1742^2 \times A} = .66,$$

which implies a coefficient of risk aversion of

$$A = \frac{.0424}{.1742^2 \times .66} = 2.12$$

Of course, this calculation is highly speculative, even if our estimate of the risky asset proportion of net worth is correct. We have assumed that the average investor holds the naïve view that historical average rates of return and standard deviations are the best estimates of expected rates of return and risk, looking to the future. To the extent that the average investor takes advantage of contemporary information in addition to simple historical data, our estimate of $A = 2.12$ would be an unjustified inference. Nevertheless, a broad range of studies, taking into account the full range of available assets, puts the degree of risk aversion for the representative investor in the range of 2.0 to 4.0.[8]

CC 8

CONCEPT CHECK

Suppose that expectations about the S&P/TSX Composite index and the T-bill rate are the same as they were in 2012, but you find that today a greater proportion is invested in T-bills than in 2012. What can you conclude about the change in risk tolerance over the years since 2012?

---

[8]See, for example, I. Friend and M. Blume, "The Demand for Risky Assets," *American Economic Review* 64 (1974); or S. J. Grossman and R. J. Shiller, "The Determinants of the Variability of Stock Market Prices," *American Economic Review* 71 (1981).

SUMMARY

1. Speculation is the undertaking of a risky investment for its risk premium. The risk premium has to be large enough to compensate a risk-averse investor for the risk of the investment.

2. A fair game is a risky prospect that has a zero risk premium. It will not be undertaken by a risk-averse investor.

3. Investors' preferences toward the expected return and volatility of a portfolio may be expressed by a utility function that is higher for higher expected returns and lower for higher portfolio variances. More risk-averse investors will apply greater penalties for risk. We can describe these preferences graphically using indifference curves.

4. The desirability of a risky portfolio to a risk-averse investor may be summarized by the certainty equivalent value of the portfolio. The certainty equivalent rate of return is a value that, if it is received with certainty, would yield the same utility as the risky portfolio.

5. Shifting funds from the risky portfolio to the risk-free asset is the simplest way to reduce risk. Other methods involve diversification of the risky portfolio and hedging. We take up these methods in later chapters.

6. T-bills provide a perfectly risk-free asset in nominal terms only. Nevertheless, the standard deviation of real rates on short-term T-bills is small compared to that of other assets such as long-term bonds and common stocks, so for purposes of our analysis we consider T-bills to be the risk-free asset. Money market funds hold, in addition to T-bills, short-term relatively safe obligations such as CP and CDs. These entail some default risk, but again, the additional risk is small relative to most other risky assets. For convenience, we often refer to money market funds as *risk-free assets*.

7. An investor's risky portfolio (the risky asset) can be characterized by its reward-to-variability ratio, $S = [E(r_P) - r_f]/\sigma_P$. This ratio is also the slope of the CAL, the line that, when graphed, goes from the risk-free asset through the risky asset. All combinations of the risky asset and the risk-free asset lie on this line. Other things equal, an investor would prefer a steeper-sloping CAL, because that means higher expected return for any level of risk. If the borrowing rate is greater than the lending rate, the CAL will be "kinked" at the point of the risky asset.

8. The investor's degree of risk aversion is characterized by the slope of his or her indifference curve. Indifference curves show, at any level of expected return and risk, the required risk premium for taking on one additional percentage point of standard deviation. More risk-averse investors have steeper indifference curves; that is, they require a greater risk premium for taking on more risk.

9. The optimal position, y^*, in the risky asset, is proportional to the risk premium and inversely proportional to the variance and degree of risk aversion:

$$y^* = \frac{E(r_P) - r_f}{A\sigma_P^2}$$

Graphically, this portfolio represents the point at which the indifference curve is tangent to the CAL.

10. A passive investment strategy disregards security analysis, targeting instead the risk-free asset and a broad portfolio of risky assets such as the S&P/TSX Composite stock portfolio.

KEY EQUATIONS

(5.1) $U = E(r) - \dfrac{1}{2}A\sigma^2$

(5.2) $r_C = yr_P + (1 - y)r_f$

(5.3) $E(r_C) = yE(r_P) + (1 - y)r_f$

(5.4) $\sigma_C = y\sigma_P$

(5.5) $E[r_C(y)] = r_f + y[E(r_P) - r_f]$

(5.6) $S = \dfrac{E(r_P) - r_f}{\sigma_P}$

(5.7) $y^* = \dfrac{E(r_P) - r_f}{A\sigma_P^2}$

(5.8)   Required $E(r) = .05 + \dfrac{1}{2} \times A\sigma^2$

PROBLEMS

connect™ Practise and learn online with Connect.

1. Consider a risky portfolio. The end-of-year cash flow derived from the portfolio will be either $70,000 or $200,000 with equal probabilities of .5. The alternative risk-free investment in T-bills pays 6 percent per year.

   a. If you require a risk premium of 8 percent, how much will you be willing to pay for the portfolio?

   b. Suppose that the portfolio can be purchased for the amount you found in (a). What will be the expected rate of return on the portfolio?

   c. Now suppose that you require a risk premium of 12 percent. What is the price that you will be willing to pay?

   d. Comparing your answers to (a) and (c), what do you conclude about the relationship between the required risk premium on a portfolio and the price at which the portfolio will sell?

2. Consider a portfolio that offers an expected rate of return of 12 percent and a standard deviation of 18 percent. T-bills offer a risk-free 7 percent rate of return. What is the maximum level of risk aversion for which the risky portfolio is still preferred to bills?

3. Draw the indifference curve in the expected return–standard deviation plane corresponding to a utility level of .05 for an investor with a risk aversion coefficient of 3. *Hint:* Choose several possible standard deviations, ranging from .05 to .25, and find the expected rates of return providing a utility level of .05. Then plot the expected return–standard deviation points so derived.

4. Now draw the indifference curve corresponding to a utility level of .04 for an investor with risk aversion coefficient $A = 4$. Comparing your answers to problems 2 and 3, what do you conclude?

5. Draw an indifference curve for a risk-neutral investor providing a utility level of .05.

6. What must be true about the sign of the risk aversion coefficient, A, for a risk lover? Draw the indifference curve for a utility level of .05 for a risk lover.

   Consider the historical data of Table 5.7, showing that the average annual rate of return on the S&P/TSX Composite portfolio over the past 56 years has averaged about 4.24 percent more than the Treasury bill return and that the Composite standard deviation has been about 17.42 percent per year. Assume that these values are representative of investors' expectations for future performance and that the current T-bill rate is 5 percent. Use these values to answer problems 7 to 9.

7. The expected return on T-bills is 5 percent and the same on the Composite index is 9.24 percent. Calculate the expected return and standard deviation of portfolios invested in T-bills and the Composite index with weights as follows:

W_{bills}	W_{market}
0	1.0
.2	.8
.4	.6
.6	.4
.8	.2
1.0	0

8. Calculate the utility levels of each portfolio of problem 7 for an investor with $A = 3$. What do you conclude?

9. Repeat problem 8 for an investor with $A = 5$. What do you conclude?

   You manage a risky portfolio with an expected rate of return of 18 percent and a standard deviation of 28 percent. The T-bill rate is 8 percent. Use these data for problems 10–19.

10. Your client chooses to invest 70 percent of a portfolio in your fund and 30 percent in a T-bill money market fund. What is the expected value and standard deviation of the rate of return on your client's portfolio?

11. Suppose that your risky portfolio includes the following investments in the given proportions:

Stock A:	27 percent
Stock B:	33 percent
Stock C:	40 percent

    What are the investment proportions of your client's overall portfolio, including the position in T-bills?

12. What is the reward-to-volatility ratio (S) of your risky portfolio? Your client's?

13. Draw the CAL of your portfolio on an expected return–standard deviation diagram. What is the slope of the CAL? Show the position of your client on your fund's CAL.

14. Suppose that your client decides to invest in your portfolio a proportion y of the total investment budget so that the overall portfolio will have an expected rate of return of 16 percent.
    a. What is the proportion y?
    b. What are your client's investment proportions in your three stocks and the T-bill fund?
    c. What is the standard deviation of the rate of return on your client's portfolio?

15. Suppose that your client prefers to invest in your fund a proportion y that maximizes the expected return on the overall portfolio subject to the constraint that the overall portfolio's standard deviation will not exceed 18 percent.
    a. What is the investment proportion (y)?
    b. What is the expected rate of return on the overall portfolio?

16. Your client's degree of risk aversion is $A = 3.5$.
    a. What proportion (y) of the total investment should be invested in your fund?
    b. What is the expected value and standard deviation of the rate of return on your client's optimized portfolio?

    You estimate that a passive portfolio (i.e., one invested in a risky portfolio that mimics an index) yields an expected rate of return of 13 percent with a standard deviation of 25 percent. Continue to assume that $r_f = 8$ percent.

17. Draw the CML and your fund's CAL on an expected return–standard deviation diagram.
    a. What is the slope of the CML?
    b. Characterize in one short paragraph the advantage(s) of your fund over the passive fund.

18. Your client ponders whether to switch the 70 percent that is invested in your fund to the passive portfolio.
    a. Explain to your client the disadvantage(s) of the switch.
    b. Show your client the maximum fee you could charge (as a percentage of the investment in your fund deducted at the end of the year) that would still leave him or her at least as well off investing in your fund as in the passive one. (*Hint*: The fee will lower the slope of your client's CAL by reducing the expected return net of the fee.)

19. Consider the client in problem 16 with $A = 3.5$.

    a. If the client chose to invest in the passive portfolio, what proportion (y) would be selected?

    b. Is the fee (percentage of the investment in your fund, deducted at the end of the year) that you can charge to make the client indifferent between your fund and the passive strategy affected by her capital allocation decision?

Problems 20–23 are based on the following assumptions. Suppose that the lending rate is $r_f = 5$ percent, while the borrowing rate that your client faces is 9 percent. Continue to assume that the passive portfolio has an expected return of 13 percent and a standard deviation of 25 percent. Your fund here has $r_p = 11$ percent and $\sigma_p = 15$ percent.

20. Draw a diagram of the CML your client faces with the borrowing constraints. Superimpose on it two sets of indifference curves, one for a client who will choose to borrow, and one for a client who will invest in both the index fund and a money market fund.

21. What is the range of risk aversion for which the client will neither borrow nor lend, that is, for which $y = 1$?

22. Solve problems 20 and 21 for a client who uses your fund rather than an index fund.

23. Amend your solution to problem 19(b) for clients in the risk-aversion range that you found in problem 21.

24. Look at the data in Table 5.7 regarding the average risk premium of the S&P/TSX Composite over T-bills and the standard deviation of that risk premium. Suppose that the S&P/TSX Composite is your risky portfolio.

    a. If your risk-aversion coefficient is 2 and you believe that the entire 1957–2012 period is representative of future expected performance, what fraction of your portfolio should be allocated to T-bills and what fraction to equity?

    b. What if you believe that the most recent subperiod is representative?

    c. What do you conclude upon comparing your answers to (a) and (b)?

25. What do you think would happen to the expected return on stocks if investors perceived higher volatility in the equity market? Relate your answer to equation 5.8.

26. Consider the following information about a risky portfolio that you manage, and a risk-free asset: $E(r_P) = 11\%$, $\sigma_P = 15\%$, $r_f = 5\%$.

    a. Your client wants to invest a proportion of her total investment budget in your risky fund to provide an expected rate of return on her overall or complete portfolio equal to 8 percent. What proportion should she invest in the risky portfolio, P, and what proportion in the risk-free asset?

    b. What will be the standard deviation of the rate of return on her portfolio?

    c. Another client wants the highest return possible subject to the constraint that you limit his standard deviation to be no more than 12 percent. Which client is more risk-averse?

27. Investment Management Inc. (IMI) uses the capital market line to make asset allocation recommendations. IMI derives the following forecasts:

    - Expected return on the market portfolio: 12%

    - Standard deviation on the market portfolio: 20%

    - Risk-free rate: 5%

    Samuel Johnson seeks IMI's advice for a portfolio asset allocation. Johnson informs IMI that he wants the standard deviation of the portfolio to equal half of the standard deviation for the market portfolio. Using the capital market line, what expected return can IMI provide subject to Johnson's risk constraint?

28. The change from a straight to a kinked capital allocation line is a result of the

a. Reward-to-variability ratio increasing

b. Borrowing rate exceeding the lending rate

c. Investor's risk tolerance decreasing

d. Increase in the portfolio proportion of the risk-free asset

Use the following data in answering problems 29, 30, and 31.

Utility Formula Data		
Investment	Expected Return $E(r)$	Standard Deviation (σ)
1	12%	30%
2	15	50
3	21	16
4	24	21

$$U = E(r) - \frac{1}{2}A\sigma^2 \quad \text{where } A = 4.0$$

The following problems are based on questions that have appeared in past CFA examinations.

29. On the basis of the utility formula above, which investment would you select if you were risk-averse?

30. On the basis of the utility formula above, which investment would you select if you were risk-neutral?

31. The variable A in the utility formula represents the

a. Investor's return requirement

b. Investor's aversion to risk

c. Certainty-equivalent rate of the portfolio

d. Preference for one unit of return per four units of risk

Use the following graph in answering problems 32 to 37.

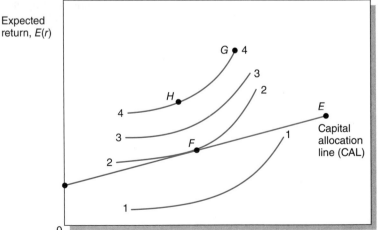

32. Which indifference curve represents the greatest level of utility that can be achieved by the investor?

33. Which point designates the optimal portfolio of risky assets?

34. Given $100,000 to invest, what is the expected risk premium in dollars of investing in equities versus risk-free T-bills on the basis of the following table?

Action	Probability	Expected Return
Invest in equities	.6	$50,000
	.4	−$30,000
Invest in risk-free T-bills	1.0	$ 5,000

35. The change from a straight to a kinked capital allocation line is a result of the
   a. Reward-to-volatility ratio increasing
   b. Borrowing rate exceeding the lending rate
   c. Investor's risk tolerance decreasing
   d. Increase in the portfolio proportion of the risk-free asset

36. You manage an equity fund with an expected risk premium of 10 percent and an expected standard deviation of 14 percent. The rate on Treasury bills is 6 percent. Your client chooses to invest $60,000 of her portfolio in your equity fund and $40,000 in a T-bill money market fund. What is the expected return and standard deviation of return on your client's portfolio?

37. What is the reward-to-volatility ratio for the *equity fund* in problem 36?

APPENDIX 5A: RISK AVERSION AND EXPECTED UTILITY

We digress here to examine the rationale behind our contention that investors are risk-averse. Recognition of risk aversion as central in investment decisions goes back at least to 1738. Daniel Bernoulli, one of a famous Swiss family of distinguished mathematicians, spent the years 1725 through 1733 in St. Petersburg, where he analyzed the following coin-toss game. To enter the game one pays an entry fee. Thereafter, a coin is tossed until the *first* head appears. The number of tails, denoted by n, that appear until the first head is tossed is used to compute the payoff, R, to the participant, as

$$R(n) = 2^n$$

The probability of no tails before the first head ($n = 0$) is ½ and the corresponding payoff is $2^0 = \$1$. The probability of one tail and then heads ($n = 1$) is ½ × ½ with payoff $2^1 = \$2$, the probability of two tails and then heads ($n = 2$) is ½ × ½ × ½, and so forth.

The following table illustrates the probabilities and payoffs for various outcomes:

Tails	Probability	Payoff = $R(n)	Probability × Payoff
0	$\frac{1}{2}$	$1	$1/2
1	$\frac{1}{4}$	$2	$1/2
2	$\frac{1}{8}$	$4	$1/2
3	$\frac{1}{16}$	$8	$1/2
—	—	—	—
—	—	—	—
n	$\left(\frac{1}{2}\right)^{n+1}$	2^n	$1/2

The expected payoff is therefore

$$E(R) = \sum_{n=0}^{\infty} Pr(n)R(n)$$

$$= \tfrac{1}{2} + \tfrac{1}{2} + \cdots$$

$$= \infty$$

This game is called the "St. Petersburg Paradox." Although the expected payoff is infinite, participants obviously will be willing to purchase tickets to play the game only at a finite, and possibly quite modest, entry fee.

Bernoulli resolved the paradox by noting that investors do not assign the same value per dollar to all payoffs. Specifically, the greater their wealth, the less their "appreciation" for each extra dollar. We can make this insight mathematically precise by assigning a welfare or utility value to any level of investor wealth. Our utility function should increase as wealth is higher, but each extra dollar of wealth should increase utility by progressively smaller amounts.[9] (Modern economists would say that investors exhibit "decreasing marginal utility" from an additional payoff dollar.) One particular function that assigns a subjective value to the investor from a payoff of R, which has a smaller value per dollar the greater the payoff, is the function $\log(R)$. If this function measures utility values of wealth, the subjective utility value of the game is indeed finite.[10] The certain wealth level necessary to yield this utility value is $2, because $\log(2.00) = .693$. Hence the certainty equivalent value of the risky payoff is $2, which is the maximum amount that this investor will pay to play the game.

Von Neumann and Morgenstern adapted this approach to investment theory in a complete axiomatic system in 1946. To avoid unnecessary technical detail, we will restrict ourselves here to an intuitive exposition of the rationale for risk aversion.

Imagine two individuals who are identical twins, except that one is less fortunate than the other. Peter has only $1,000 to his name while Paul has a net worth of $200,000. How many hours of work would each twin be willing to offer to earn one extra dollar? It is likely that Peter (the poor twin) has more essential uses for the extra money than does Paul. Therefore, Peter will offer more hours. In other words, Peter derives a greater personal welfare or assigns a greater "utility" value to the 1,001st dollar than Paul does to the 200,001st.

Figure 5A.1 depicts graphically the relationship between wealth and the utility value of wealth that is consistent with this notion of decreasing marginal utility.

Individuals have different rates of decrease in their marginal utility of wealth. What is constant is the *principle* that per-dollar utility decreases with wealth. Functions that exhibit the property of decreasing per-unit value as the number of units grows are called *concave*. A simple example is the log function, familiar from high school mathematics. Of course, a log function will not fit all investors, but it is consistent with the risk aversion that we assume for all investors.

Now consider the following simple prospect:

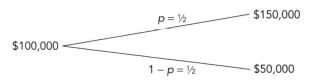

---

[9]This utility function is similar in spirit to the one that assigns a satisfaction level to portfolios with given risk-and-return attributes. However, the utility function here refers not to investors' satisfaction with alternative portfolio choices but only to the subjective welfare they derive from different levels of wealth.

[10]If we substitute the "utility" value, $\log(R)$, for the dollar payoff, R, to obtain an expected utility value of the game (rather than expected dollar value), we have, calling $V(R)$ the expected utility,

$$V(R) = \sum_{n=0}^{\infty} Pr(n) \log[R(n)] = \sum_{n=0}^{\infty} (\tfrac{1}{2})^{n+1} \log(2^n) = .693$$

Figure 5A.1

Utility of wealth with a log utility function.

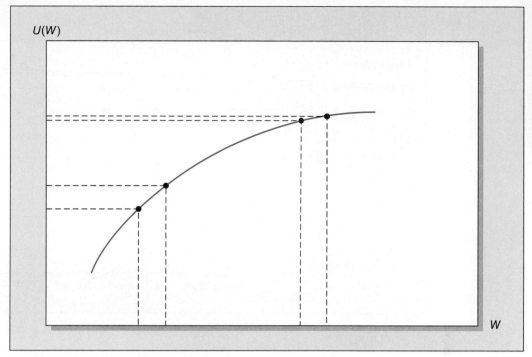

This is a fair game in that the expected profit is zero. Suppose, however, that the curve in Figure 5A.1 represents the investor's utility value of wealth, assuming a log utility function. Figure 5A.2 shows this curve with the numerical values marked.

Figure 5A.2 shows that the loss in utility from losing $50,000 exceeds the gain from winning $50,000. Consider the gain first. With probability $p = .5$, wealth goes from $100,000 to $150,000. Using the log utility function, utility goes from log(100,000) = 11.51 to log(150,000) = 11.92, the distance G on the graph. This gain is $G = 11.92 - 11.51 = .41$. In expected utility terms, then, the gain is $pG = .5 \times .41 = .21$.

Now consider the possibility of coming up on the short end of the prospect. In that case, wealth goes from $100,000 to $50,000. The loss in utility, the distance L on the graph, is $L = \log(100,000) - \log(50.000) = 11.51 - 10.82 = .69$. Thus the loss in expected utility terms is $(1 - p)L = .5 \times .69 = .35$, which exceeds the gain in expected utility from the possibility of winning the game.

We compute the expected utility from the risky prospect as follows:

$$E[U(W)] = pU(W_1) + (1 - p)U(W_2)$$
$$= \tfrac{1}{2}\log(50,000) + \tfrac{1}{2}\log(150,000)$$
$$= 11.37$$

If the prospect is rejected, the utility value of the (sure) $100,000 is log(100,000) = 11.51, which is greater than that of the fair game (11.37). Hence the risk-averse investor will reject the fair game.

Using a specific investor utility function (such as the log utility) allows us to compute the certainty equivalent value of the risky prospect to a given investor. This is the amount that, if received with certainty, the investor would consider equally attractive as the risky prospect.

Figure 5A.2

Fair games and
expected utility.

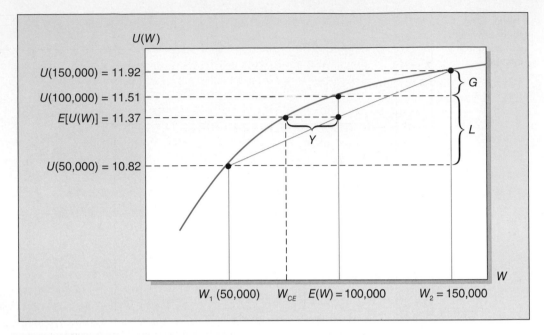

If log utility describes the investor's preferences toward wealth outcomes, then Figure 5A.2 also can tell us what is, for her, the dollar value of the prospect. We ask: What sure level of wealth has a utility value of 11.37 (which equals the expected utility from the prospect)? A horizontal line drawn at the level 11.37 intersects the utility curve at the level of wealth W_{CE}. This means that

$$\log(W_{CE}) = 11.37$$

which implies that

$$W_{CE} = e^{11.37}$$
$$= \$86,681.87$$

W_{CE} is therefore the certainty equivalent of the prospect. The distance Y in Figure 5A.2 is the penalty, or the downward adjustment, to the expected profit that is attributable to the risk of the prospect:

$$Y = E(W) - W_{CE}$$
$$= \$100,000 - \$86,681.87$$
$$= \$13,318.13$$

The investor views \$86,681.86 for certain as being equal in utility value as \$100,000 at risk. Therefore, she would be indifferent between the two.

APPENDIX 5B: UTILITY FUNCTIONS AND EQUILIBRIUM PRICES OF INSURANCE CONTRACTS

The utility function of an individual investor allows us to measure the subjective value the individual would place on a dollar at various levels of wealth. Essentially, a dollar in bad times (when wealth is low) is more valuable than a dollar in good times (when wealth is high).

Suppose that all investors hold the risky S&P/TSX Composite portfolio. Then, if the portfolio value falls in a worse-than-expected economy, all investors will, albeit to different degrees, experience a "low wealth" scenario. Therefore, the equilibrium value of a dollar in the low-wealth economy would be higher than the value of a dollar when the portfolio performs better than expected. This observation helps explain the apparently high cost of portfolio insurance that we encountered when considering long-term investments in the previous chapter. It also helps explain why an investment in a stock portfolio (and hence in individual stocks) has a risk premium that appears to be so high and results in probability of shortfall that is so low. Despite the low probability of shortfall risk, stocks still do not dominate the lower-return risk-free bond, because if an investment shortfall should transpire it will coincide with states in which the value of dollar returns is high.

Does revealed behaviour of investors demonstrate risk aversion? Looking at prices and past rates of return in financial markets, we can answer with a resounding yes. With remarkable consistency, riskier bonds are sold at lower prices than safer ones with otherwise similar characteristics. Riskier stocks also have provided higher average rates of return over long periods of time than less risky assets such as T-bills. For example, over the 1957–2012 period, the average rate of return on the S&P/TSX Composite portfolio exceeded the T-bill return by about 4.24 percent per year.

It is abundantly clear from financial data that the average, or representative, investor exhibits substantial risk aversion. For readers who recognize that financial assets are priced to compensate for risk by providing a risk premium and at the same time feel the urge for some gambling, we have a constructive recommendation: Direct your gambling desire to investment in financial markets. As Von Neumann once said, "The stock market is a casino with the odds in your favour." A small risk-seeking investor may provide all the excitement you want with a positive expected return to boot!

CC A1

CONCEPT CHECK

Suppose the utility function is $U(W) = \sqrt{w}$.
a. What is the utility level at wealth levels $50,000 and $150,000?
b. What is expected utility if p still equals .5?
c. What is the certainty equivalent of the risky prospect?
d. Does this utility function also display risk aversion?
e. Does this utility function display more or less risk aversion than the log utility function?

PROBLEMS

1. Suppose that your wealth is $250,000. You buy a $200,000 house and invest the remainder in a risk-free asset paying an annual interest rate of 6 percent. There is a probability of .001 that your house will burn to the ground and its value will be reduced to zero. With a log utility of end-of-year wealth, how much would you be willing to pay for insurance (at the beginning of the year)? (Assume that if the house does not burn down, its end-of-year value still will be $200,000.) Do not round your intermediate calculations, and round your final answer to the nearest cent.

2. If the cost of insuring your house is $1 per $1,000 of value, what will be the certainty equivalent of your end-of-year wealth if you insure your house at

   a. ½ its value?

   b. Its full value?

   c. 1½ times its value?

   Do not round your intermediate calculations, and round your final answer to the nearest dollar.

Optimal Risky Portfolios

The investment decision can be viewed as a top-down process: (1) *capital allocation* between the risky portfolio and risk-free assets, (2) *asset allocation* in the risky portfolio across broad asset classes (e.g., Canadian stocks, international stocks, and long-term bonds), and (3) *security selection* of individual assets within each asset class.

Capital allocation, as we saw in Chapter 5, determines the investor's exposure to risk. The optimal capital allocation is determined by risk aversion as well as expectations for the risk–return tradeoff of the optimal risky portfolio. In principle, asset allocation and security selection are technically identical; both aim at identifying that optimal risky portfolio, namely the combination of risky assets that provides the best risk–return tradeoff. In practice, however, asset allocation and security selection are typically separated into two steps, in which the broad outlines of the portfolio are established first (asset allocation), while details concerning specific securities are filled in later (security selection). After we show how the optimal risky portfolio may be constructed, we will consider the cost and benefits of pursuing this two-step approach.

We first motivate the discussion by illustrating the potential gains from simple diversification into many assets. We then proceed to examine the process of *efficient* diversification from the ground up, starting with an investment menu of only two risky assets, then adding the risk-free asset, and finally, incorporating the entire universe of available risky securities. We learn how diversification can reduce risk without affecting expected returns. This accomplished, we reexamine the hierarchy of capital allocation, asset allocation, and security selection. Finally, we offer insight into the power of diversification and we demonstrate how construction of the optimal risky portfolio can easily be accomplished with Excel, a spreadsheet package available to every investor.

The portfolios we discuss in this and the following chapters are of a short-term horizon—even if the overall investment horizon is long, portfolio composition can be rebalanced or updated almost continuously. For these short horizons, the assumption of normality is sufficiently accurate to describe holding-period returns, and we will be concerned only with portfolio means and variances.

In Appendix 6A, we draw an analogy between diversification and the workings of the insurance industry.

6.1

DIVERSIFICATION AND PORTFOLIO RISK

Suppose that your risky portfolio is composed of only one stock, Dominion Computing Corporation (DCC). What would be the sources of risk to this "portfolio"? You might think of two broad sources of uncertainty. First, there is the risk that comes from conditions in the general economy, such as the business cycle, the inflation rate, interest rates, and exchange rates. None of these macroeconomic factors can be predicted with certainty, and all affect the rate of return that DCC stock eventually will provide. In addition to these macroeconomic factors there are firm-specific influences, such as DCC's success in research and development, and personnel changes. These factors affect DCC without noticeably affecting other firms in the economy.

Now consider a naïve **diversification** strategy, in which you include additional securities in your risky portfolio. For example, suppose that you place half of your risky portfolio in an oil and minerals firm, Energy Resources Ltd. (ERL), leaving the other half in DCC. What should happen to portfolio risk? To the extent that the firm-specific influences on the two stocks differ, we should reduce portfolio risk. For example, when oil prices fall, hurting ERL, computer prices might rise, helping DCC. The two effects are offsetting and stabilize portfolio return.

But why end diversification at only two stocks? If we diversify into many more securities, we continue to spread out our exposure to firm-specific factors, and portfolio volatility should continue to fall. Ultimately, however, even if we include a large number of risky securities in our portfolio, we cannot avoid risk altogether, since virtually all securities are affected by the common macroeconomic factors. For example, if all stocks are affected by the business cycle, we cannot avoid exposure to business cycle risk no matter how many stocks we hold.

When all risk is firm-specific, as in Figure 6.1A, diversification can reduce risk to arbitrarily low levels. The reason is that with all risk sources independent, and with the portfolio spread across many securities, the exposure to any particular source of risk is reduced to a negligible level. The reduction of risk to very low levels in the case of independent risk sources is sometimes called the **insurance principle**, because of the conventional belief that an insurance company depends on the risk reduction achieved through diversification when it writes many policies insuring against many independent sources of risk, with each policy being a small part of the company's overall portfolio. (See Appendix 6A for a discussion of the insurance principle.)

When common sources of risk affect all firms, however, even extensive diversification cannot eliminate risk. In Figure 6.1B portfolio risk measured by variance or standard deviation, falls as

Figure 6.1

Portfolio risk as a function of the number of stocks in the portfolio. A: All risk is firm-specific. B: Some risk is systematic or marketwide.

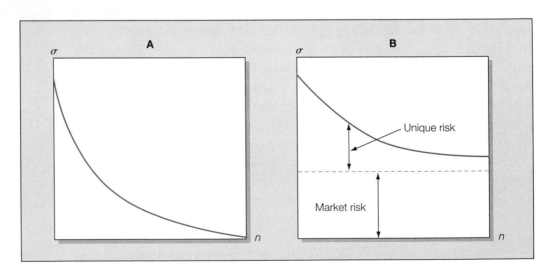

Figure 6.2 Portfolio diversification. The average standard deviation of returns of portfolios composed of only one stock was 49.2 percent. The average portfolio risk fell rapidly as the number of stocks included in the portfolio increased. In the limit, portfolio risk could be reduced to only 19.2 percent.

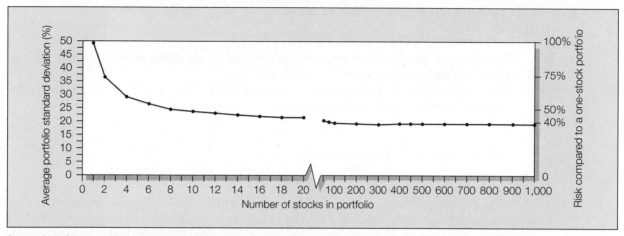

Source: Meir Stratman, "How Many Stocks Make a Diversified Portfolio?" *Journal of Financial and Quantitative Analysis* 22 (September 1987). Reprinted by permission.

the number of securities increases, but it cannot be reduced to zero. The risk that remains even after extensive diversification is called **market risk**, risk that is attributable to marketwide risk sources. Such risk also is called **systematic risk**, or **nondiversifiable risk**. In contrast, the risk that *can* be eliminated by diversification is called **unique risk**, **firm-specific risk**, **nonsystematic risk**, or **diversifiable risk**.

This analysis is borne out by empirical studies. Figure 6.2 shows the effect of portfolio diversification, using data on NYSE stocks. The figure shows the average standard deviation of equally weighted portfolios constructed by selecting stocks at random as a function of the number of stocks in the portfolio. On average, portfolio risk does fall with diversification, but the power of diversification to reduce risk is limited by systematic or common sources of risk.

6.2 PORTFOLIOS OF TWO RISKY ASSETS

In the last section, we analyzed naïve diversification, examining the risk of equally weighted portfolios composed of several securities. It is time now to study efficient diversification, whereby we construct risky portfolios to provide the lowest possible risk for any given level of expected return.

Portfolios of two risky assets are relatively easy to analyze, and they illustrate the principles and considerations that apply to portfolios of many assets. We will consider a portfolio comprising two mutual funds, a bond portfolio specializing in long-term debt securities, denoted D, and a stock fund that specializes in equity securities, E. Table 6.1 lists the parameters describing the

TABLE 6.1

Descriptive Statistics for Two Assets

	Debt (%)	Equity (%)
Expected return, $E(r)$	8	13
Standard deviation, σ	12	20
Covariance, $\text{Cov}(r_D, r_E)$	72	
Correlation coefficient, σ_{DE}	.30	

rate-of-return distribution of these funds. These parameters are representative of those that can be estimated from actual funds.

A proportion denoted by w_D is invested in the bond fund, and the remainder, $1 - w_D$, denoted w_E, is invested in the stock fund. The rate of return on this portfolio will be

$$r_P = w_D r_D + w_E r_E \tag{6.1}$$

where r_P stands for the rate of return on the portfolio, r_D the return on investment in the debt fund, and r_E the return on investment in the equity fund.

The expected rate of return on the portfolio is a weighted average of expected return on the component securities with portfolio proportions as weights:

$$E(r_P) = w_D E(r_D) + w_E E(r_E) \tag{6.2}$$

The variance of the two-asset portfolio is

$$\sigma^2{}_P = w^2{}_D \sigma^2{}_D + w^2{}_E \sigma^2{}_E + 2 w_D w_E \text{Cov}(r_D, r_E) \tag{6.3}$$

The first observation is that the variance of the portfolio, unlike the expected return, is *not* a weighted average of the individual asset variances. To understand the formula for the portfolio variance more clearly, recall that the covariance of a variable with itself (in this case the variable is the uncertain rate of return) is the variance of that variable; that is,

$$\text{Cov}(r_D, r_D) = \sum_{\text{scenarios}} \text{Pr(scenario)}[r_D - E(r_D)][r_D - E(r_D)] \tag{6.4}$$

$$= \sum_{\text{scenarios}} \text{Pr(scenario)}[r_D - E(r_D)]^2$$

$$= \sigma^2{}_D$$

Therefore, another way to write the variance of the portfolio is as follows:

$$\sigma^2{}_P = w_D w_D \text{Cov}(r_D, r_D) + w_E w_E \text{Cov}(r_E, r_E) + 2 w_D w_E \text{Cov}(r_D, r_E) \tag{6.5}$$

In words, the variance of the portfolio is a weighted sum of covariances, where each weight is the product of the portfolio proportions of the pair of assets in the covariance term.

Why do we double the covariance between the two *different* assets in the last term of equation 6.3? This should become clear in the covariance matrix, Table 6.2, which is bordered by the portfolio weights.

The diagonal (from top left to bottom right) of the covariance matrix is made up of the asset variances. The off-diagonal elements are the covariances. Note that

$$\text{Cov}(r_D, r_E) = \text{Cov}(r_E, r_D)$$

so that the matrix is symmetric. To compute the portfolio variance, we sum over each term in the matrix, first multiplying it by the product of the portfolio proportions from the corresponding row and column. Thus we have *one* term for each asset variance, but twice the term for each covariance pair because each covariance appears twice.

TABLE 6.2

Bordered
Covariance Matrix

Portfolio Weights	Covariances	
	w_D	w_E
w_D	$\sigma^2{}_D$	$\text{Cov}(r_D, r_E)$
w_E	$\text{Cov}(r_E, r_D)$	$\sigma^2{}_E$

Equation 6.3 reveals that variance is reduced if the covariance term is negative. It is important to recognize that, even if the covariance term is positive, the *portfolio* standard deviation still is less than the weighted average of the individual security standard deviations, unless the two securities are perfectly positively correlated.

To see this, notice that the covariance can be written as

$$\text{Cov}(r_D,r_E) = \rho_{DE}\sigma_D\sigma_E \tag{6.6}$$

Substituting into equation 6.3,

$$\sigma^2_P = w^2_D\sigma^2_D + w^2_E\sigma^2_E + 2w_Dw_E\sigma_D\sigma_E\sigma_{DE} \tag{6.7}$$

You can see from this information that the covariance term adds the most to the portfolio variance when the correlation coefficient, ρ_{DE}, is highest, that is, when it equals 1—as it would in the case of perfect positive correlation. In this case, the right-hand side of equation 6.7 is a perfect square, and simplifies to

$$\sigma^2_P = (w_D\sigma_D + w_E\sigma_E)^2$$

or

$$\sigma_P = w_D\sigma_D + w_E\sigma_E \tag{6.8}$$

In other words, the standard deviation of the portfolio with perfect positive correlation is just the weighted average of the component standard deviations. In all other cases, the correlation coefficient is less than 1, making the portfolio standard deviation *less* than the weighted average of the component standard deviations.

A hedge asset has negative correlation with the other assets in the portfolio. Equation 6.7 shows that such assets will be particularly effective in reducing total risk without affecting expected return. This equation adds the additional insight that the standard deviation of a portfolio of assets is less than the weighted average of the component security standard deviations, even when the assets are positively correlated. Because the portfolio expected return always is the weighted average of its component expected returns, while its standard deviation is less than the weighted average of the component standard deviations, *portfolios of less than perfectly correlated assets always offer some degree of diversification benefit*. The lower the correlation between assets, the greater the gain in efficiency.

How low can portfolio standard deviation be? The lowest possible value of the correlation coefficient is −1, representing perfect negative correlation, in which case equation 6.7 becomes a perfect square and the portfolio variance is as follows:

$$\sigma^2_P = (w_D\sigma_D - w_E\sigma_E)^2 \tag{6.9}$$

and the portfolio standard deviation is

$$\sigma_P = \text{Absolute value}(w_D\sigma_D - w_E\sigma_E) \tag{6.10}$$

Where $\rho = -1$, the investor has the opportunity of creating a perfectly hedged position. By setting equation 6.10 equal to zero and choosing the portfolio proportions as

$$w_D = \frac{\sigma_E}{\sigma_D + \sigma_E}$$

$$w_E = \frac{\sigma_D}{\sigma_D + \sigma_E} = 1 - w_D \tag{6.11}$$

The standard deviation of the portfolio will equal zero.

E-INVESTMENTS **Diversification**	Go to the **www.investopedia.com/articles/basics/03/050203.asp** Web site to learn more about diversification, the factors that influence investors' risk preferences, and the types of investments that fit into each of the risk categories. Then check out **www.investopedia.com/articles/pf/05/061505.asp** for asset allocation guidelines for various types of portfolios from conservative to very aggressive. What do you conclude about your own risk preferences and the best portfolio type for you? What would you expect to happen to your attitude toward risk as you get older? How might your portfolio composition change?

EXAMPLE 6.1   Portfolio Risk and Return

Let us apply this analysis to the data of the bond and stock funds as presented in Table 6.1. Using these data, the formulas for the expected return, variance, and standard deviation of the portfolio are

$$E(r_p) = 8w_D + 13w_E$$
$$\sigma^2_P = 12^2 w^2_D + 20^2 w^2_E + 2 \times 72 w_D w_E$$
$$\sigma_P = \sqrt{\sigma^2_P}$$

Now we are ready to experiment with different portfolio proportions to observe the effect on portfolio expected return and variance. Suppose we change the proportion invested in bonds. The effect on the portfolio's expected return is tabulated in Table 6.3 and plotted in Figure 6.3. When the proportion invested in debt varies from zero to one (so that the proportion in equity varies from one to zero), the portfolio expected return goes from 13 percent (the stock fund's expected return) to 8 percent (the expected return on bonds).

What happens to the left of this region, when $w_D > 1$ and $w_E < 0$? In this case, portfolio strategy would be to sell the stock fund short and invest the proceeds of the short sale in bonds. This will decrease the expected return of the portfolio. For example, when $w_D = 2$ and $w_E = -1$, expected portfolio return falls to 3 percent ($= 2 \times 8 + (-1) \times 13$). At this point, the value of the bond fund in the portfolio is twice the net worth of the account. This extreme position is financed in part by short-selling stocks equal in value to the portfolio's net worth.

The reverse happens when $w_D < 0$ and $w_E > 1$. This strategy calls for selling the bond fund short and using the proceeds to finance additional purchases of the equity fund.

Of course, varying investment proportions also has an effect on portfolio standard deviation. Table 6.3 presents portfolio standard deviations for different portfolio weights calculated from equation 6.7 for the assumed value of the correlation coefficient, .30, as well as for other values

TABLE 6.3

Expected Return and Standard Deviation with Various Correlation Coefficients

			Portfolio Standard Deviation for Given Correlation			
w_D	w_E	$E(r_P)$	$\rho = -1$	$\rho = 0$	$\rho = .30$	$\rho = 1$
.00	1.00	13.00	20.00	20.00	20.00	20.00
.10	.90	12.50	16.80	18.04	18.40	19.20
.20	.80	12.00	13.60	16.18	16.88	18.40
.30	.70	11.50	10.40	14.46	15.47	17.60
.40	.60	11.00	7.20	12.92	14.20	16.80
.50	.50	10.50	4.00	11.66	13.11	16.00
.60	.40	10.00	.80	10.76	12.26	15.20
.70	.30	9.50	2.40	10.32	11.70	14.40
.80	.20	9.00	5.60	10.40	11.45	13.60
.90	.10	8.50	8.80	10.98	11.56	12.80
1.00	.00	8.00	12.00	12.00	12.00	12.00
			Minimum Variance Portfolio			
		w_D	.6250	.7353	.8200	
		w_E	.3750	.2647	.1800	
		$E(r_p)$	9.8750	9.3235	8.9000	
		σ_p	.0000	10.2899	11.4473	

of ρ. Figure 6.4 shows the relationship between standard deviation and portfolio weights. Look first at the curve for $\rho = .30$. The graph shows that as the portfolio weight in the equity fund increases from zero to one, portfolio standard deviation first falls with the initial diversification from bonds into stocks but then rises again as the portfolio becomes heavily concentrated in stocks and again is undiversified.

Figure 6.3

Portfolio expected return as a function of investment proportions.

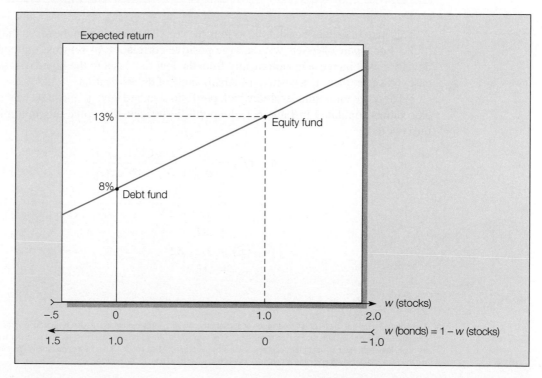

Figure 6.4

Portfolio standard deviation as a function of investment proportions.

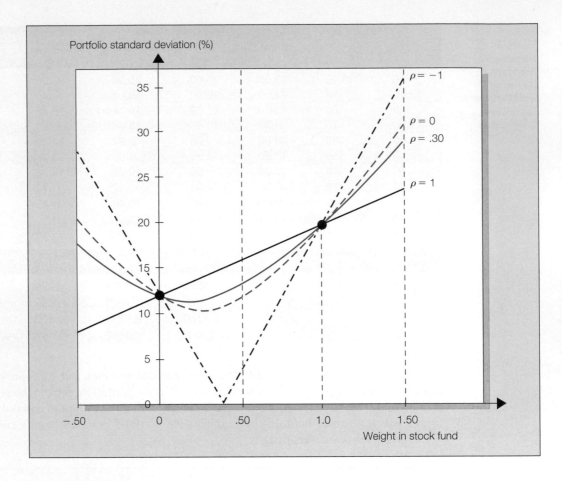

This pattern generally will hold as long the correlation coefficient between the funds is not too high.[1] For a pair of assets with a large positive correlation of returns, the portfolio standard deviation will increase monotonically from the low-risk asset to the high-risk asset. Even in this case, however, there is a positive (if small) value of diversification.

What is the minimum level to which portfolio standard deviation can be held? For the parameter values stipulated in Table 6.1, the portfolio weights that solve this minimization problem turn out to be[2]

$$w_{\min}(D) = \frac{\sigma^2_E - \text{Cov}(r_D, r_E)}{\sigma^2_D + \sigma^2_E - 2\text{Cov}(r_D, r_E)} \tag{6.12}$$

$$= \frac{20^2 - 72}{12^2 + 20^2 - 2 \times 72}$$

$$= .82$$

$$w_{\min}(E) = 1 - .82$$

$$= .18$$

---

[1]As long as $\rho < \dfrac{\sigma_D}{\sigma_E}$, volatility will initially fall when we start with all bonds and begin to move into stocks.

[2]This solution uses the minimization techniques of elementary calculus. Write out the expression for portfolio variance from equation 6.3, substitute $1 - w_D$ for w_E, differentiate the result with respect to w_D, set the derivative equal to zero, and solve for w_D. With a spreadsheet program, however, you can obtain an accurate solution by generating a fine grid for Table 6.3 and observing the minimum. You can also use the Excel Solver to minimize the variance.

This minimum variance portfolio has a standard deviation of

$$\sigma_{\min}(P) = [.82^2 \times 12^2 + .18^2 \times 20^2 + 2 \times .82 \times .18 \times 72]^{1/2}$$
$$= 11.45\%$$

as indicated in the last line of Table 6.3.

The curved solid coloured line in Figure 6.4 represents the portfolio standard deviation when $\rho = .30$ as a function of the investment proportions. It passes through the two undiversified portfolios of $w_D = 1$ and $w_E = 1$. Note that the **minimum-variance portfolio** has a standard deviation smaller than that of either of the individual component assets. This highlights the effect of diversification.

The other three lines in Figure 6.4 show how portfolio risk varies for other values of the correlation coefficient, holding the variances of each asset constant. These lines plot the values in the other three columns of Table 6.3.

The straight line connecting the undiversified portfolios of all-bonds or all-stocks, $w_D = 1$ or $w_E = 1$, demonstrates portfolio standard deviation with perfect positive correlation, $\rho = 1$. In this case, there is no advantage from diversification, and the portfolio standard deviation is the simple weighted average of the component asset standard deviations.

The dashed coloured curve depicts portfolio risk for the case of uncorrelated assets, $\rho = 0$. With lower correlation between the two assets, diversification is more effective and portfolio risk is lower (at least when both assets are held in positive amounts). The minimum portfolio standard deviation when $\rho = 0$ is 10.32 percent (see Table 6.3), which again is lower than the standard deviation of either assets.

Finally, the V-shaped broken line illustrates the perfect hedge potential when the two assets are perfectly negatively correlated ($\rho = -1$). In this case, the solution for the minimum-variance portfolio is

$$w_{\min}(D; \rho = -1) = \frac{\sigma_E}{\sigma_D + \sigma_E}$$
$$= \frac{20}{12 + 20}$$
$$= .625$$
$$w_{\min}(E; \rho = -1) = 1 - .625$$
$$= .375$$

and the portfolio variance (and standard deviation) is zero.

We can combine Figures 6.3 and 6.4 to demonstrate the relationship between the portfolio's level of risk (standard deviation) and the expected rate of return on that portfolio—given the parameters of the available assets. This is done in Figure 6.5. For any pair of investment proportions, w_D, w_E, we read the expected return from Figure 6.3 and the standard deviation from Figure 6.4. The resulting pairs of portfolio expected return and standard deviation are plotted in Figure 6.5.

The solid coloured curve in Figure 6.5 shows the **portfolio opportunity set** for $\rho = .30$, so called because it shows the combination of expected return and standard deviation of all the portfolios that can be constructed from the two available assets. The broken and dotted lines show the portfolio opportunity set for other values of the correlation coefficient. The line farthest to the right, which is the straight line connecting the undiversified portfolios, shows that there is no benefit from diversification when the correlation between the two assets is perfectly positive ($\rho = 1$). The opportunity set is not "pushed" to the northwest. The dashed curve shows that there is greater benefit from diversification when the correlation coefficient is zero than when it is positive.

Finally, the $\rho = -1$ lines show the effect of perfect negative correlation. The portfolio opportunity set is linear, but now it offers a perfect hedging opportunity and the maximum advantage from diversification.

Figure 6.5

Portfolio expected return as a function of standard deviation.

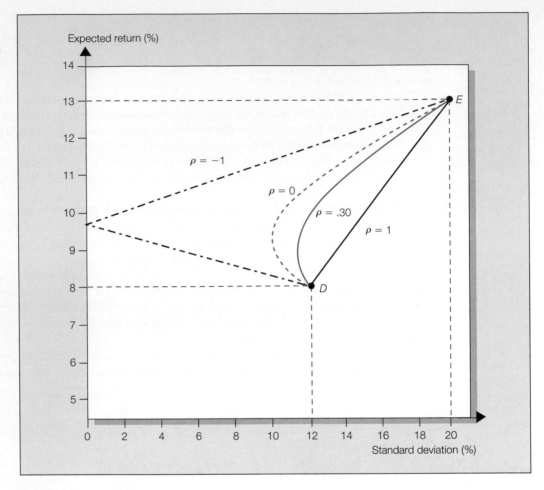

To summarize, although the expected rate of return of any portfolio is simply the weighted average of the asset expected return, this is not true of the portfolio standard deviation. Potential benefits from diversification arise when correlation is less than perfectly positive. The lower the correlation coefficient, the greater the potential benefit of diversification. In the extreme case of perfect negative correlation, we have a perfect hedging opportunity and can construct a zero-variance portfolio.

Suppose now that an investor wishes to select the optimal portfolio from the opportunity set. The best portfolio will depend on risk aversion. Portfolios to the northeast in Figure 6.5 provide higher rates of return, but they impose greater risk. The best tradeoff among these choices is a matter of personal preference. Investors with greater risk aversion will prefer portfolios to the southwest, with lower expected return, but lower risk.[3]

---

[3]Given a level of risk aversion, one can determine the portfolio that provides the highest level of utility. Recall from Chapter 5 that we were able to describe the utility provided by a portfolio as a function of its expected return, $E(r_P)$, and its variance, σ^2_P, according to the relationship $U = E(r_P) - .5A\sigma^2_P$. The portfolio mean and variance are determined by the portfolio weights in the two funds, w_E and w_D, according to equations 6.2 and 6.3. Using those equations, one can show, using elementary calculus, that the optimal investment proportions in the two funds are

$$w_D = \frac{E(r_D) - E(r_E) + A(\sigma^2_E - \sigma_D\sigma_E\rho_{DE})}{A(\sigma^2_D + \sigma^2_E - 2\sigma_D\sigma_E\rho_{DE})}, w_E = 1 - w_D$$

Here, too, Excel's Solver or similar software can be used to maximize utility subject to the constraints of equations 6.2 and 6.3, plus the portfolio constraint that $w_D + w_E = 1$ (i.e., that portfolio weights sum to 1).

CC 2

CONCEPT CHECK

Compute and draw the portfolio opportunity set for the debt and equity funds when the correlation coefficient between them is $\rho = .25$.

6.3 ASSET ALLOCATION WITH STOCKS, BONDS, AND BILLS

When optimizing capital allocation, we want to work with the capital allocation line (CAL) offering the highest slope or Sharpe ratio. In the previous section we saw how portfolio weights affect the portfolio's expected return and standard deviation. Now we proceed to asset allocation: constructing the optimal risky portfolio of major asset classes, here a bond and a stock fund.

The asset allocation decision requires that we consider T-bills or another safe asset along with the risky asset classes. The reason is that the Sharpe ratio we seek to maximize is defined as the risk premium in *excess of the risk-free rate*, divided by the standard deviation. We use T-bill rates as the risk-free rate in evaluating the Sharpe ratios of all possible portfolios. The portfolio that maximizes the Sharpe ratio is the solution to the asset allocation problem. Using only stocks, bonds, and bills is actually not so restrictive, as it includes all three major asset classes. As the nearby box emphasizes, most investment professionals recognize that "the really critical decision is how to divvy up your money among stocks, bonds, and supersafe investments such as Treasury bills."

Asset Allocation with Two Risky Assets

What if we were still confined to the bond and stock funds, but now could also invest in risk-free T-bills yielding 5 percent? We start with a graphical solution. Figure 6.6 shows the opportunity set generated from the joint probability distribution of the bond and stock funds, using the data from Table 6.1.

Figure 6.6

The opportunity set of the debt and equity funds and two feasible CALs.

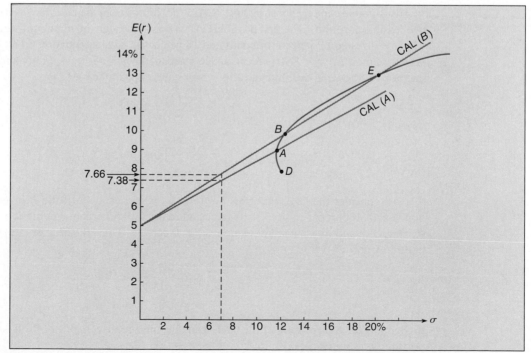

First things first.

If you want dazzling investment results, don't start your day foraging for hot stocks and stellar mutual funds. Instead, say investment advisers, the really critical decision is how to divvy up your money among stocks, bonds, and supersafe investments such as Treasury bills.

In Wall Street lingo, this mix of investments is called your asset allocation. "The asset-allocation choice is the first and most important decision," says William Droms, a finance professor at Georgetown University. "How much you have in [the stock market] really drives your results."

"You cannot get [stock market] returns from a bond portfolio, no matter how good your security selection is or how good the bond managers you use," says William John Mikus, a managing director of Financial Design, a Los Angeles investment adviser.

For proof, Mr. Mikus cites studies such as the 1991 analysis done by Gary Brinson, Brian Singer and Gilbert Beebower. That study, which looked at the 10-year results for 82 large pension plans, found that a plan's asset-allocation policy explained 91.5% of the return earned.

Designing a Portfolio

Because your asset mix is so important, some mutual fund companies now offer free services to help investors design their portfolios.

Gerald Perritt, editor of the *Mutual Fund Letter*, a Chicago newsletter, says you should vary your mix of assets depending on how long you plan to invest. The further away your investment horizon, the more you should have in stocks. The closer you get, the more you should lean toward bonds and money-market instruments, such as Treasury bills. Bonds and money-market instruments may generate lower returns than stocks. But for those who need money in the near future, conservative investments make more sense, because there's less chance of suffering a devastating short-term loss.

Summarizing Your Assets

"One of the most important things people can do is summarize all their assets on one piece of paper and figure out their asset allocation," says Mr. Pond.

Once you've settled on a mix of stocks and bonds, you should seek to maintain the target percentages, says Mr. Pond. To do that, he advises figuring out your asset allocation once every six months. Because of a stock-market plunge, you could find that stocks are now a far smaller part of your portfolio than you envisaged. At such a time, you should put more into stocks and lighten up on bonds.

When devising portfolios, some investment advisers consider gold and real estate in addition to the usual trio of stocks, bonds and money-market instruments. Gold and real estate give "you a hedge against hyperinflation," says Mr. Droms. "But real estate is better than gold, because you'll get better long-run returns."

Two possible capital allocation lines (CALs) are drawn from the risk-free rate ($r_f = 5$ percent) to two feasible portfolios. The first possible CAL is drawn through the minimum-variance portfolio A, which is invested 82 percent in bonds and 18 percent in stocks (equation 6.13). Portfolio A's expected return is $E(r_A) = 8.90$ percent, and its standard deviation is $\sigma_A = 11.45$ percent. With a T-bill rate of $r_f = 5$ percent, the **Sharpe ratio**, which is the slope of the CAL, is

$$S_A = \frac{E(r_A) - r_f}{\sigma_A}$$
$$= \frac{8.9 - 5}{11.45}$$
$$= .34$$

Now consider the CAL that uses portfolio B instead of A. Portfolio B invests 70 percent in bonds and 30 percent in stocks. Its expected return is 9.5 percent (giving it a risk premium of 4.5 percent), and its standard deviation is 11.70 percent. Thus, the Sharpe ratio on the CAL supported by portfolio B is

$$S_B = \frac{9.5 - 5}{11.7}$$
$$= .38$$

higher than the Sharpe ratio of the CAL using the minimum-variance portfolio and T-bills. Thus, portfolio B dominates portfolio A.

Figure 6.7

The opportunity set of the stock and bond funds with the optimal CAL and the optimal risky portfolio.

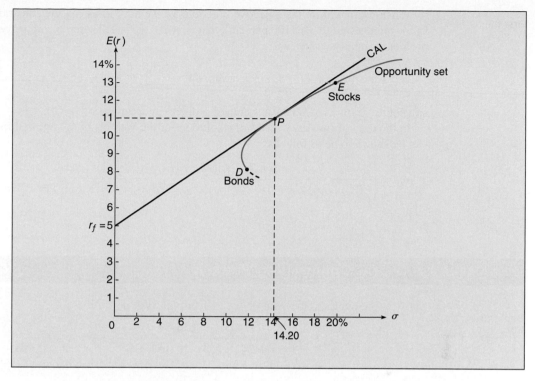

But why stop at portfolio B? We can continue to ratchet the CAL upward until it ultimately reaches the point of tangency with the investment opportunity set. This must yield the CAL with the highest feasible Sharpe ratio. Therefore, the tangency portfolio, P, drawn in Figure 6.7, is the **optimal risky portfolio** to mix with T-bills. We can read the expected return and standard deviation of portfolio P from the graph in the figure:

$$E(r_P) = 11\%$$
$$\sigma_P = 14.2\%$$

In practice, we obtain an algebraic solution to this problem with a computer program. The spreadsheet we present further on in this chapter can be used to construct efficient portfolios of many assets. Here we describe the process briefly, with only two risky assets.

The objective is to find the weights w_D, w_E that result in the highest slope of the CAL (i.e., the yield of the risky portfolio with the highest Sharpe ratio). Thus our *objective function* is the slope S_P:

$$S_P = \frac{E(r_p) - r_f}{\sigma_P}$$

For the portfolio with two risky assets, the expected return and standard deviation of portfolio P are

$$E(r_P) = w_D E(r_D) + w_E E(r_E)$$
$$= 8w_D + 13w_E$$
$$\sigma_p = [w^2_D \sigma^2_D + w^2_E \sigma^2_E + 2w_D w_E \text{Cov}(r_D, r_E)]^{1/2}$$
$$= [144w^2_D + 400w^2_E + 2 \times 72w_D w_E]^{1/2}$$

When we maximize the objective function, S_P, we have to satisfy the constraint that the portfolio weights sum to one (100 percent), that is, $w_D + w_E = 1$. Therefore, we solve a mathematical problem formally written as

$$\underset{w_i}{\text{Max }} S_P = \frac{E(r_p) - r_f}{\sigma_P}$$

subject to $\sum w_i = 1$. This is a standard problem in optimization.

In the case of two risky assets, the solution for the weights of the optimal risky portfolio, P, can be shown to be as follows:[4]

$$w_D = \frac{[E(r_D) - r_f]\sigma^2_E - [E(r_E) - r_f]\text{Cov}(r_D, r_E)}{[E(r_D) - r_f]\sigma^2_E + [E(r_E) - r_f]\sigma^2_D - [E(r_D) - r_f + E(r_E) - r_f]\text{Cov}(r_D, r_E)} \tag{6.13}$$

$$w_E = 1 - w_D$$

EXAMPLE 6.2   **The Optimal Risky Portfolio**

Substituting our data, the solution for the optimal risky portfolio is

$$w_D = \frac{(8 - 5)400 - (13 - 5)72}{(8 - 5)400 + (13 - 5)144 - (8 - 5 + 13 - 5)72}$$

$$= .40$$

$$w_E = 1 - .4$$

$$= .6$$

The expected return on this optimal risky portfolio is 11 percent ($= E(r_P) = .4 \times 8 + .6 \times 13$). The standard deviation is 14.2 percent:

$$\sigma_P = (.4^2 \times 144 + .6^2 \times 400 + 2 \times .4 \times .6 \times 72)^{1/2}$$

$$= 14.2\%$$

The CAL using this optimal portfolio has a slope of

$$S_P = \frac{11 - 5}{14.2} = .42$$

which is the Sharpe ratio of portfolio P. Notice that this slope exceeds the slope of any of the other feasible portfolios that we have considered, as it must if it is to be the slope of the best feasible CAL.

In Chapter 5 we found the optimal *complete* portfolio given an optimal risky portfolio and the CAL generated by a combination of this portfolio and T-bills. Now that we have constructed the optimal risky portfolio, P, we can use the individual investor's degree of risk aversion, A, to calculate the optimal proportion of the complete portfolio to invest in the risky component.

---

[4]The solution procedure is as follows. Substitute for $E(r_P)$ from equation 6.2 and for σ_P from equation 6.7. Substitute $1 - w_D$ for w_E. Differentiate the resulting expression for S_P with respect to w_D, set the derivative equal to zero, and solve for w_D.

Risk Aversion and an Investor's Optimal Portfolio

An investor with a coefficient of risk aversion $A = 4$, would take a position in portfolio P of

$$y = \frac{E(r_P) - r_f}{A\sigma^2_P} \qquad (6.14)$$

$$= \frac{.11 - .05}{4 \times .142^2}$$

$$= .7439$$

Thus, the investor will invest 74.39 percent of his or her wealth in portfolio P and 25.61 percent in T-bills. Portfolio P consists of 40 percent in bonds, so the percentage of wealth in bonds will be $yw_D = .4 \times .7439 = .2976$, or 29.76 percent. Similarly, the investment in stocks will be $yw_E = .6 \times .7439 = .4463$, or 44.63 percent. The graphical solution of this problem is presented in Figures 6.8 and 6.9.

Once we have reached this point, generalizing to the case of many risky assets is straightforward. Before we move on, let us briefly summarize the steps we followed to arrive at the complete portfolio.

1. Specify the return characteristics of all securities (expected returns, variances, covariances).
2. Establish the risky portfolio:
   a. Calculate the optimal risky portfolio, P (equation 6.13).
   b. Calculate the properties of portfolio P using the weights determined in step (*a*) and equations 6.2 and 6.3.

Figure 6.8

Determination of the optimal overall portfolio.

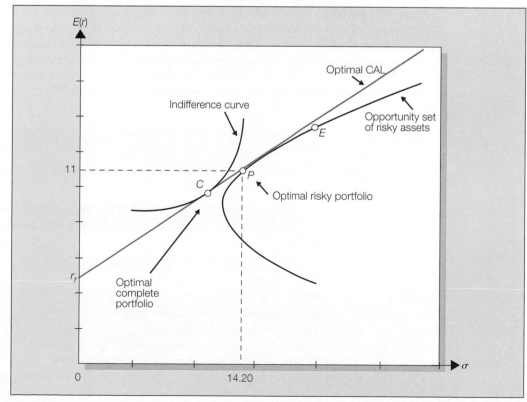

Figure 6.9

The proportions of the optimal overall portfolio.

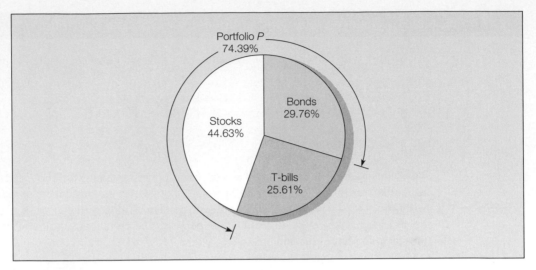

3. Allocate funds between the risky portfolio and the risk-free asset:
   a. Calculate the fraction of the complete portfolio allocated to portfolio P (the risky portfolio) and to T-bills (the risk-free asset) (equation 6.14).
   b. Calculate the share of the complete portfolio invested in each asset and in T-bills.

Recall that the two assets in the asset allocation problem are already diversified portfolios. The diversification *within* each of these portfolios must be credited for most of the risk reduction, compared to undiversified single securities. For example, the standard deviation of the rate of return on an average stock is about 50 percent. In contrast, the standard deviation of our hypothetical stock index fund is only 20 percent. This is evidence of the importance of diversification within the asset class. Asset allocation between bonds and stocks contributed incrementally to the improvement in the Sharpe ratio of the complete portfolio. The CAL with stocks, bonds, and bills (Figure 6.7) shows that the standard deviation of the complete portfolio can be further reduced to 18 percent, while maintaining the same expected return of 13 percent as the stock portfolio.

CC 3

CONCEPT CHECK

The universe of available securities includes two risky stock funds, *A* and *B*, and T-bills. The data for the universe are as follows:

	Expected Return	Standard Deviation
A	.10	.20
B	.30	.60
T-bills	.05	.00

The correlation coefficient between funds *A* and *B* is −.2.
a. Draw the opportunity set of funds *A* and *B*.
b. Find the optimal risky portfolio *P* and its expected return and standard deviation.
c. Find the slope of the CAL supported by T-bills and portfolio *P*.
d. How much will an investor with $A = 5$ invest in funds *A* and *B* and in T-bills?

6.4

THE MARKOWITZ PORTFOLIO OPTIMIZATION MODEL

Security Selection

We can generalize the portfolio construction problem to the case of many risky securities and a risk-free asset. As in the two risky assets example, the problem has three parts. First, we identify the risk–return combinations available from the set of risky assets. Next, we identify the optimal portfolio of risky assets by finding the portfolio that results in the steepest CAL. Finally, we choose an appropriate complete portfolio by mixing the risk-free asset, T-bills, with the optimal risky portfolio. Before describing the process in detail, let us first present an overview.

The first step is to determine the risk–return opportunities available to the investor. These are summarized by the **minimum-variance frontier** of risky assets. This frontier is a graph of the lowest possible portfolio variance that can be attained for a given portfolio expected return. Given the set of data for expected returns, variances, and covariances, we can calculate the minimum-variance portfolio (or equivalently, minimum-standard deviation portfolio) for any targeted expected return. The plot of these expected return–standard deviation pairs is presented in Figure 6.10.

Notice that all the individual assets lie to the right inside of the frontier, at least when we allow short sales in the construction of risky portfolios.[5] This tells us that risky portfolios composed of only a single asset are inefficient. Diversifying investments leads to portfolios with higher expected returns and lower standard deviations.

All the portfolios that lie on the minimum-variance frontier, from the global minimum variance portfolio and upward, provide the best risk–return combinations, and thus are candidates for the optimal portfolio. The part of the frontier that lies above the global minimum variance portfolio, therefore, is called the **efficient frontier**. For any portfolio on the lower portion of the minimum-variance frontier, there is a portfolio with the same standard deviation and a greater expected return positioned directly above it. Hence, the bottom part of the minimum-variance frontier is inefficient.

Figure 6.10

The minimum-variance frontier of risky assets.

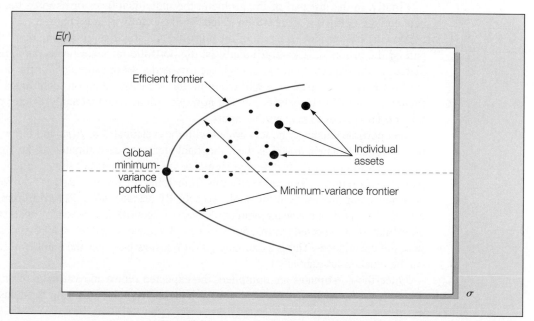

[5]When short sales are prohibited, single securities may lie on the frontier. For example, the security with the highest expected return must lie on the frontier, as that security represents the only way that one can obtain a return that high, and so it also must be the minimum-variance way to obtain that return. When short sales are feasible, however, portfolios can be constructed that offer the same expected return and lower variance. These portfolios typically will have short positions in low-expected-return securities.

Figure 6.11

The efficient frontier of risky assets with the optimal CAL.

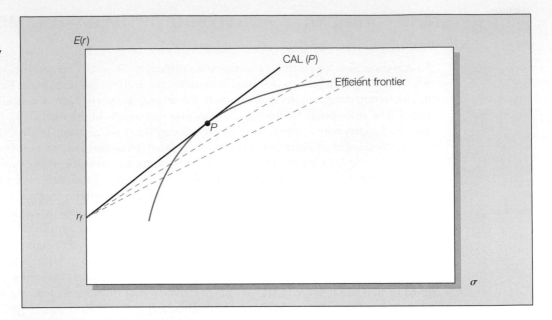

The second part of the optimization plan involves the risk-free asset. As before, we search for the capital allocation line with the highest Sharpe ratio (i.e., the steepest slope) as shown in Figure 6.11.

The CAL that is supported by the optimal portfolio, P, is, as before, the one that is tangent to the efficient frontier. This CAL dominates all alternative feasible lines that may be drawn through the frontier. Portfolio P, therefore, is the optimal risky portfolio.

Finally, in the last part of the problem, the individual investor chooses the appropriate mix between the optimal risky portfolio P and T-bills, exactly as in Figure 6.8.

Now let us consider each part of the portfolio construction problem in more detail. In the first part of the problem, risk–return analysis, the portfolio manager needs, as inputs, a set of estimates for the expected returns of each security and a set of estimates for the covariance matrix. (In Part Five, "Equities," we will examine the security valuation techniques and methods of financial analysis that analysts use. For now, we will assume that analysts have already spent the time and resources to prepare the inputs.)

The portfolio manager now is armed with the n estimates of $E(r_i)$ and the $n \times n$ estimates in the covariance matrix in which the n diagonal elements are estimates of the variances, $\sigma^2 i$, and the $n^2 - n = n(n - 1)$ off-diagonal elements are the estimates of the covariances between each pair of asset returns. (You can verify this from Table 6.2 for the case $n = 2$.) We know that each covariance appears twice in this table, so actually we have $n(n - 1)/2$ different covariance estimates. If our portfolio management unit covers 50 securities, our security analysts need to deliver 50 estimates of expected returns, 50 estimates of variances, and $50 \times 49/2 = 1{,}225$ different estimates of covariances. This is a daunting task! (We show later how the number of required estimates can be reduced substantially.)

Once these estimates are compiled, the expected return and variance of any risky portfolio with weights in each security, w_i, can be calculated from the following formulas:

$$E(r_P) = \sum_{i=1}^{n} w_i E(r_i) \tag{6.15}$$

$$\sigma^2_P = \sum_{i=1}^{n} w^2_i \sigma^2_i + \sum_{\substack{i=1 \\ i \neq j}}^{n} \sum_{j=1}^{n} w_i w_j \text{Cov}(r_i, r_j) \tag{6.16}$$

Figure 6.12
The efficient portfolio set.

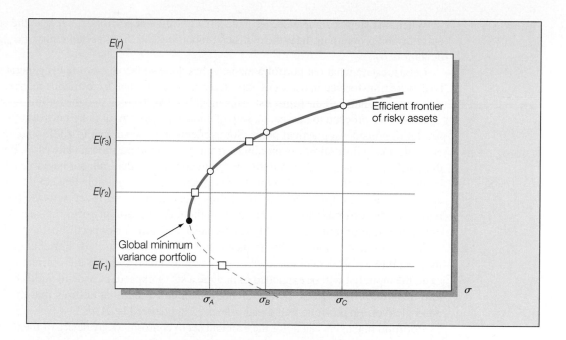

An extended worked example showing you how to do this on a spreadsheet is presented in the next section.

We mentioned earlier that the idea of diversification is age-old. The adage "Don't put all your eggs in one basket" existed long before modern finance theory. It was not until 1952, however, that Harry Markowitz published a formal model of portfolio selection embodying diversification principles, ultimately earning himself the 1990 Nobel prize for economics.[6] His model is precisely step one of portfolio management: the identification of the efficient set of portfolios, or, as it is often called, the efficient frontier of risky assets.

The principal idea behind the frontier set of risky portfolios is that, for any risk level, we are interested only in that portfolio with the highest expected return. Alternatively, the frontier is the set of portfolios that minimizes the variance for any target expected return.

Indeed, the two methods of computing the efficient set of risky portfolios are equivalent. To see this, consider the graphical representation of these procedures. Figure 6.12 shows the minimum-variance frontier.

The points marked by squares are the result of a variance-minimization program. We first draw the constraint, that is, a horizontal line at the level of required expected return. We then look for the portfolio with the lowest standard deviation that plots on this horizontal line—we look for the portfolio that will plot farthest to the left (smallest standard deviation) on that line. When we repeat this for various levels of required expected returns, the shape of the minimum-variance frontier emerges. We then discard the bottom part of the frontier, because it is inefficient.

In the alternative approach, we draw a vertical line that represents the standard deviation constraint. We then consider all portfolios that plot on this line (have the same standard deviation) and choose the one with the highest expected return, that is, that portfolio falling highest on this vertical line. Repeating this procedure for various vertical lines (levels of standard deviation) gives us the points marked by circles that trace the upper portion of the minimum-variance frontier, the efficient frontier.

---

[6]Harry Markowitz, "Portfolio Selection," *Journal of Finance*, March 1952.

When this step is completed, we have a list of efficient portfolios, because the solution to the optimization program includes the portfolio proportions, w_i, the expected return, $E(r_p)$, and standard deviation, σ_P.

Let us restate what our portfolio manager has done so far. The estimates generated by the analysts were transformed into a set of expected rates of return and a covariance matrix. This group of estimates we shall call the **input list**. This input list was then fed into the optimization program.

Before we proceed to the second step of choosing the optimal risky portfolio from the frontier set, let us consider a practical point. Some clients may be subject to additional constraints. For example, many institutions are prohibited from taking short positions in any asset. For these clients, the portfolio manager will add to the program constraints that rule out negative (short) positions in the search for efficient portfolios. In this special case it is possible that single assets may be, in and of themselves, efficient risky portfolios. For example, the asset with the highest expected return will be a frontier portfolio because, without the opportunity of short sales, the only way to obtain that rate of return is to hold the asset as one's entire risky portfolio.

Short-sale restrictions are by no means the only such constraints. For example, some clients may want to assure a minimal level of expected dividend yield on the optimal portfolio. In this case, the input list will be expanded to include a set of expected dividend yields $d_1, ..., d_n$ and the optimization program will include an additional constraint that ensures that the expected dividend yield of the portfolio will equal or exceed the desired level, d.

Portfolio managers can tailor the efficient set to conform to any desire of the client. Of course, any constraint carries a price tag in the sense that an efficient frontier constructed subject to extra constraints will offer a Sharpe ratio inferior to that of a less constrained one. The client should be made aware of this cost and should reconsider constraints that are not mandated by law.

Another type of constraint that has become increasingly popular is aimed at ruling out investments in industries or countries considered ethically or politically undesirable. This is referred to as *socially responsible investing*.

Capital Allocation and Separation Property

Now that we have the efficient frontier, we proceed to step two and introduce the risk-free asset. Figure 6.13 shows the efficient frontier plus three CALs representing various portfolios from the efficient set. As before, we ratchet up the CAL by selecting different portfolios until we reach

Figure 6.13

Capital allocation lines with various portfolios from the efficient set.

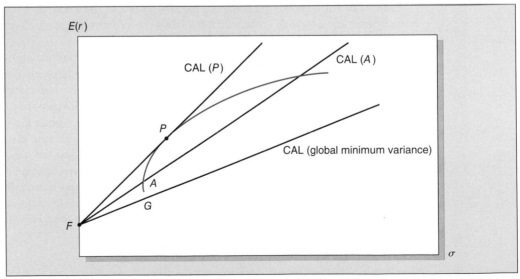

portfolio P, which is the tangency point of a line from F to the efficient frontier. Portfolio P maximizes the Sharpe ratio, the slope of the CAL from F to portfolios on the efficient frontier. At this point, our portfolio manager is done. Portfolio P is the optimal risky portfolio for the manager's clients. This is a good time to ponder our results and their implementation.

There is yet another way to find the best risky portfolio, achievable by introducing the risk-free (T-bill) rate from the outset. In this approach, we ask the spreadsheet program to maximize the Sharpe ratio of portfolio P. The reason this is worth mentioning is that we can skip the charting of the efficient frontier altogether, and proceed directly to find the portfolio that produces the steepest CAL. The program maximizes the Sharpe ratio with no constraint on expected return or variance at all (using just the feasibility constraint that portfolio weights sum to 1.0). Examination of Figure 6.13 shows that the solution strategy is to find the portfolio producing the highest slope of the CAL (Sharpe ratio) regardless of expected return or SD. Expected return and standard deviation are easily computed from the optimal portfolio weights applied to the input list in equations 6.15 and 6.16.

While this last approach does not immediately produce the entire minimum variance frontier, this shortcoming is rectified by directly identifying two portfolios on the frontier. The first is the already familiar global minimum variance portfolio, identified in Figure 6.12 as G. Portfolio G is achieved by minimizing variance without any constraint on the expected return; check this in Figure 6.13. The expected return on portfolio G is higher than the risk-free rate (its risk premium will be positive).

Another portfolio that will be of great interest to us later is the portfolio on the inefficient portion of the minimum-variance frontier with zero covariance (or correlation) with the optimal risky portfolio. We will call this portfolio Z. Once we identify portfolio P, we can find portfolio Z by solving in Excel for the portfolio that minimizes standard deviation subject to having zero covariance with P. In later chapters we will return to this portfolio.

An important property of frontier portfolios is that any portfolio formed by combining two portfolios from the minimum-variance frontier will also be on that frontier, with location along the frontier depending on the weights of that mix. Therefore, portfolio P plus either G or Z can be used to easily trace out the entire efficient frontier.

The most striking conclusion is that a portfolio manager will offer the same risky portfolio, P, to all clients regardless of their degree of risk aversion.[7] The degree of risk aversion of the client comes into play only in the selection of the desired point on the CAL. Thus, the only difference between clients' choices is that the more risk-averse client will invest more in the risk-free asset and less in the optimal risky portfolio, P, than will a less risk-averse client. However, both will use portfolio P as their optimal risky investment vehicle.

This result is called a **separation property**; it tells us that the portfolio choice problem may be separated into two independent tasks. The first task, determination of the optimal risky portfolio, P, is purely technical. Given the manager's input list, the best risky portfolio is the same for all clients, regardless of risk aversion. The second task, however, capital allocation, depends on personal preference. Here the client is the decision maker.

The crucial point is that the optimal portfolio P that the manager offers is the same for all clients. This result makes professional management more efficient and hence less costly. One management firm can serve any number of clients with relatively small incremental administrative costs.

In practice, however, different managers will estimate different input lists, thus deriving different efficient frontiers, and offer different "optimal" portfolios to their clients. The source of the disparity lies in the security analysis. It is worth mentioning here that the rule of GIGO (garbage

---

[7]Clients who impose special restrictions (constraints) on the manager, such as dividend yield, will obtain another optimal portfolio. Any constraint that is added to an optimization problem leads, in general, to a different and less desirable optimum compared to an unconstrained program.

in, garbage out) applies to security analysis, too. If the quality of the security analysis is poor, a passive portfolio such as a market index fund will result in a better CAL than an active portfolio that uses low-quality security analysis to tilt the portfolio weights toward seemingly favourable (seemingly mispriced) securities.

One particular input list that would lead to a worthless estimate of the efficient frontier is based on recent security average returns. If sample average returns over recent years are used as proxies for the true expected return on the security, the noise in those estimates will make the resultant efficient frontier virtually useless for portfolio construction.

Consider a stock with an annual standard deviation of 50 percent. Even if one were to use a 10-year average to estimate its expected return (and 10 years is almost ancient history in the life of a corporation), the standard deviation of that estimate would still be $50/\sqrt{10} = 15.8$ percent. The chances that this average represents expected returns for the coming year are negligible.[8] In Chapter 24, we see an example demonstrating that efficient frontiers constructed from past data may be wildly optimistic in terms of the *apparent* opportunities they offer to improve Sharpe ratios.

As we have seen, the optimal risky portfolios for different clients also may vary because of portfolio constraints such as dividend-yield requirements, tax considerations, or other client preferences. Nevertheless, this analysis suggests that only a very limited number of portfolios may be sufficient to serve the demands of a wide range of investors. This is the theoretical basis of the mutual fund industry.

The (computerized) optimization technique is the easiest part of the portfolio construction problem. The real arena of competition among portfolio managers is in sophisticated security analysis. This analysis, as well as its proper interpretation, is part of the art of portfolio construction.[9]

CC 4

CONCEPT CHECK

Suppose that two portfolio managers who work for competing investment management houses each employ a group of security analysts to prepare the input list for the Markowitz algorithm. When all is completed, it turns out that the efficient frontier obtained by portfolio manager A dominates that of manager B. By domination we mean that A's optimal risky portfolio lies northwest of B's. Hence, given a choice, investors will always prefer the risky portfolio that lies on the CAL of A.

a. What should be made of this outcome?

b. Should it be attributed to better security analysis by A's analysts?

c. Could it be that A's computer program is superior?

d. If you were advising clients (and had an advance glimpse at the efficient frontiers of various managers), would you tell them to periodically switch their money around to the manager with the most northwesterly portfolio?

The Power of Diversification

Section 6.1 introduced the concept of diversification and the limits to the benefits of diversification caused by systematic risk. Given the tools we have developed, we can reconsider this intuition more rigorously and at the same time sharpen our insight regarding the power of diversification.

---

[8]Moreover, you cannot avoid this problem by observing the rate of return on the stock more frequently. In Chapter 4 we pointed out that the accuracy of the sample average as an estimate of expected return depends on the length of the sample period, and is not improved by sampling more frequently within a given sample period.

[9]You can find a nice discussion of some practical issues in implementing efficient diversification in a white paper prepared by Wealthcare Capital Management, available at www.financeware.com/ruminations/WP_EfficiencyDeficiency.pdf.

Recall from equation 6.16, restated here, that the general formula for the variance of a portfolio is

$$\sigma^2_P = \sum_{i=1}^{n} w^2_i\sigma^2 i + \sum_{\substack{i=1 \\ i\neq j}}^{n} \sum_{j=1}^{n} w_iw_j \text{Cov}(r_i,r_f) \tag{6.16}$$

Consider now the naïve diversification strategy in which an equally weighted portfolio is constructed, meaning that $w_i = 1/n$ for each security. In this case, equation 6.16 may be rewritten as follows:

$$\sigma^2_P = \frac{1}{n}\sum_{i=1}^{n}\frac{1}{n}\sigma^2 i + \sum_{\substack{i=1 \\ i\neq j}}^{n} \sum_{j=1}^{n} \frac{1}{n^2} \text{Cov}(r_i,r_f) \tag{6.17}$$

Note that there are n variance terms and $n(n-1)$ covariance terms in equation 6.17.

If we define the average variance and average covariance of the securities as

$$\overline{\sigma^2} = \frac{1}{n}\sum_{i=1}^{n}\sigma^2 i$$

$$\overline{\text{Cov}} = \frac{1}{n(n-1)}\sum_{\substack{j=1 \\ j\neq i}}^{n}\sum_{j=1}^{n}\text{Cov}(r_i,r_f)$$

we can express portfolio variance as

$$\sigma^2_P = \frac{1}{n}\overline{\sigma^2} + \frac{n-1}{n}\overline{\text{Cov}} \tag{6.18}$$

Now examine the effect of diversification. When the average covariance among security returns is zero, as it is when all risk is firm-specific, portfolio variance can be driven to zero. We see this from equation 6.18: the second term on the right-hand side will be zero in this scenario, while the first term approaches zero as n becomes larger. Hence, when security returns are uncorrelated, the power of diversification to limit portfolio risk is unlimited.

However, the more important case is the one in which economywide risk factors impart positive correlation among stock returns. In this case, as the portfolio becomes more highly diversified (n increases), portfolio variance remains positive. While firm-specific risk, represented by the first term in equation 6.18, still is diversified away, the second term simply approaches $\overline{\text{Cov}}$ as n becomes greater. (Note that $(n-1)/n = 1 - 1/n$, which approaches 1 for large n.) Thus the irreducible risk of a diversified portfolio depends on the covariance of the returns of the component securities, which in turn is a function of the importance of systematic factors in the economy.

To see further the fundamental relationship between systematic risk and security correlations, suppose for simplicity that all securities have a common standard deviation, σ, and all security pairs have a common correlation coefficient ρ. Then the covariance between all pairs of securities is $\rho\sigma^2$, and equation 6.18 becomes

$$\sigma^2_P = \frac{1}{n}\sigma^2 + \frac{n-1}{n}\rho\sigma^2$$

The effect of correlation is now explicit. When $\rho = 0$, we again obtain the insurance principle, in which portfolio variance approaches zero as n becomes greater. For $\rho > 0$, however, portfolio variance remains positive. In fact, for $\rho = 1$, portfolio variance equals σ^2 regardless of n, demonstrating that diversification is of no benefit: in the case of perfect correlation, all risk is systematic. More generally, as n becomes greater, equation 6.19 shows that systematic risk becomes $\rho\sigma^2$.

Table 6.4 presents portfolio standard deviation as we include even greater numbers of securities in the portfolio for two cases: $\rho = 0$ and $\rho = .40$. The table takes σ to be 50 percent. As one

TABLE 6.4   Risk Reduction of Equally Weighted Portfolios in Correlated and Uncorrelated Universes

Universe Size n	Optimal Portfolio Proportion $1/n$ (%)	$\rho = 0$		$\rho = .4$	
		Standard Deviation (%)	Reduction in σ	Standard Deviation (%)	Reduction in σ
1	100	50.00	14.64	50.00	8.17
2	50	35.36		41.83	
5	20	22.36	1.95	36.06	.70
6	16.67	20.41		35.36	
10	10	15.81	.73	33.91	.20
11	9.09	15.08		33.71	
20	5	11.18	.27	32.79	.06
21	4.76	10.91		32.73	
100	1	5.00	.02	31.86	.00
101	.99	4.98		31.86	

would expect, portfolio risk is greater when $\rho = .40$. More surprising, perhaps, is that portfolio risk diminishes far less rapidly as n increases in the positive correlation case. The correlation among security returns limits the power of diversification.

Note that, for a 100-security portfolio, the standard deviation is 5 percent in the uncorrelated case—still significant when we consider the potential of zero standard deviation. For $\rho = .40$, the standard deviation is high, 31.86 percent, yet it is very close to undiversifiable systematic risk in the infinite-sized universe, $\sqrt{\rho\sigma^2} = \sqrt{.4 \times .50} = .3162$, or 31.62 percent. At this point, further diversification is of little value.

We also gain an important insight from this exercise. When we hold diversified portfolios, the contribution to portfolio risk of a particular security will depend on the *covariance* of that security's return with those of other securities, and *not* on the security's variance. As we shall see in Chapter 7, this implies that fair risk premiums also should depend on covariances rather than the total variability of returns.

CC 5

CONCEPT CHECK

Suppose that the universe of available risky securities consists of a large number of stocks, identically distributed with $E(r) = 15$ percent, $\sigma = 60$ percent, and a common correlation coefficient of $\rho = .5$.

a. What is the expected return and standard deviation of an equally weighted risky portfolio of 25 stocks?

b. What is the smallest number of stocks necessary to generate an efficient portfolio with a standard deviation equal to or smaller than 43 percent?

c. What is the systematic risk in this universe?

d. If T-bills are available and yield 10 percent, what is the slope of the CAL?

Asset Allocation and Security Selection

As we have seen, the theories of security selection and asset allocation are identical. Both activities call for the construction of an efficient frontier and the choice of a particular portfolio from along that frontier. The determination of the optimal combination of securities proceeds in the same manner as the analysis of the optimal combination of asset classes. Why, then, do we (and the investment community) distinguish between asset allocation and security selection?

Three factors are at work. First, as a result of greater need and ability to save (for college education, recreation, longer life in retirement and health care needs, etc.), the demand for sophisticated investment management has increased enormously. Second, the growing spectrum of financial markets and financial instruments have put sophisticated investment beyond the capacity of most amateur investors. Finally, there are strong economic returns to scale in investment management. The end result is that the size of a competitive investment company has grown with the industry, and efficiency in organization has become an important issue.

A large investment company is likely to invest both in domestic and international markets and in a broad set of asset classes, each of which requires specialized expertise. Hence, the management of each asset-class portfolio needs to be decentralized, and it becomes impossible to simultaneously optimize the entire organization's risky portfolio in one stage, although this would be prescribed as optimal on *theoretical* grounds. In future chapters we will see how optimization of decentralized portfolios can be mindful as well of the entire portfolio of which they are part.

The practice is therefore to optimize the security selection of each asset-class portfolio independently. At the same time, top management continually updates the asset allocation of the organization, adjusting the investment budget of each asset-class portfolio. When changed frequently in response to intensive forecasting activity, the reallocations are called *market timing*.

Optimal Portfolios and Non-normal Returns

The portfolio optimization techniques we have used so far assume normal distributions of returns in that standard deviation is taken to be a fully adequate measure of risk. However, potential non-normality of returns requires us to pay attention as well to risk measures that focus on worst-case losses such as value at risk (VaR) or expected shortfall (ES).

In Chapter 6 we suggested that capital allocation to the risky portfolio should be reconsidered in the face of fat-tailed distributions that can result in extreme values of VaR and ES. Specifically, forecasts of greater than normal VaR and ES should encourage more moderate capital allocations to the risky portfolio. Accounting for the effect of diversification on VaR and ES would be useful as well. Unfortunately, the impact of diversification on tail risk cannot be easily anticipated.

A practical way to estimate values of VaR and ES in the presence of fat tails is *bootstrapping* (described in Appendix 4A). We start with a historical sample of returns of each asset in our prospective portfolio. We compute the portfolio return corresponding to a draw of one return from each asset's history. We thus calculate as many of these random portfolio returns as we wish. 50,000 returns produced in this way can provide a good estimate of VaR and ES values. The forecasted values for VaR and ES of the mean-variance optimal portfolio can then be compared to other candidate portfolios. If these other portfolios yield sufficiently better VaR and ES values, we may prefer one of those to the mean-variance efficient portfolio.

6.5   A SPREADSHEET MODEL

Several software packages can be used to generate the efficient frontier. We will demonstrate the method using Microsoft Excel. Excel is far from the best program for this purpose, and it is limited in the number of assets it can handle; but working through a simple portfolio optimizer in Excel can illustrate concretely the nature of the calculations used in more sophisticated "black box" programs. You will find that even in Excel, the computation of the efficient frontier is fairly easy.

We apply the Markowitz portfolio optimization program to a practical problem of international diversification. We take the perspective of a portfolio manager serving U.S. clients, who wishes to construct for the next year an optimal risky portfolio of large stocks in the United States and six developed capital markets (Japan, Germany, the United Kingdom, France, Canada, and Australia). First we describe the input list: forecasts of risk premiums and the covariance matrix. Next, we describe Excel's Solver, and finally we show the solution to the manager's problem.

The Covariance Matrix

To capture recent risk parameters the manager compiles an array of the most recent 60 recent monthly (annualized) rates of return, as well as the monthly T-bill rates for the same period.

The standard deviations of excess returns are shown in Table 6.5 (column C). They range from 14.95 percent (U.S. large stocks) to 22.7 percent (Germany). For perspective on how these parameters can change over time, standard deviations for the period 1991–2000 are also shown (column B). In addition, we present the correlation coefficient between large stocks in the six foreign markets with U.S. large stocks for the same two periods. Here we see that correlations are higher in the more recent period, consistent with the process of globalization.

The covariance matrix shown in Table 6.6 was estimated from the array of 60 returns of the seven countries using the COVARIANCE.S function from the Formulas menu in Excel's most recent version.

Expected Returns

While estimation of the risk parameters (the covariance matrix) from excess returns is a simple technical matter, estimating the risk premium (the expected excess return) is a daunting task. As we discussed in Chapter 4, estimating expected returns using historical data is unreliable. Consider, for example, the negative average excess returns on U.S. large stocks over the period 2001–2005 (cell G6) and, more generally, the big differences in average returns between the 1991–2000 and 2001–2005 periods, as demonstrated in columns F and G.

In this example, we simply present the manager's forecasts of future returns as shown in column H. In Chapter 8 we will establish a framework that makes the forecasting process more explicit.

The Bordered Covariance Matrix and Portfolio Variance

The covariance matrix in Table 6.6 is bordered by the portfolio weights, as explained in Section 6.2 and Table 6.2. The values in cells A18–A24, to the left of the covariance matrix, will be selected by the optimization program. For now, we arbitrarily input 1.0 for the U.S. and zero for the others. Cells A16–I16, above the covariance matrix, must be set equal to the column of weights on the left, so that they will change in tandem as the column weights are changed by Excel's Solver. Cell A25 sums the column weights and is used to force the optimization program to set the sum of portfolio weights to 1.0.

Cells C25–I25, below the covariance matrix, are used to compute the portfolio variance for any set of weights that appears in the borders. Each cell accumulates the contribution to portfolio variance from the column above it. It uses the function SUMPRODUCT to accomplish this task. For example, row 33 shows the formula used to derive the value that appears in cell C25.

Finally, the short column A26–A28 below the bordered covariance matrix presents portfolio statistics computed from the bordered covariance matrix. First is the portfolio risk premium in cell A26, with formula shown in row 35, which multiplies the column of portfolio weights by the column of forecasts (H6–H12) from Table 6.5. Next is the portfolio standard deviation in cell A27. The variance is given by the sum of cells C25–I25 below the bordered covariance matrix. Cell A27 takes the square root of this sum to produce the standard deviation. The last statistic is the portfolio Sharpe ratio, cell A28, which is the slope of the CAL (capital allocation line) that runs through the portfolio constructed using the column weights (the value in cell A28 equals cell A26 divided by cell A27). The optimal risky portfolio is the one that maximizes the Sharpe ratio.

TABLES 6.5, 6.6, 6.7   Spreadsheet Model for International Diversification ⤴

6.5 Country Index Statistics and Forecasts of Risk Premiums

	A	B	C	D	E	F	G	H
	Country	Standard Deviation		Correlation with the U.S.		Average Excess Return		Forecast
		1991–2000	2001–2005	1991–2000	2001–2005	1991–2000	2001–2005	2006
6	US	0.1295	0.1495	1	1	0.1108	−0.0148	0.0600
7	UK	0.1466	0.1493	0.64	0.83	0.0536	0.0094	0.0530
8	France	0.1741	0.2008	0.54	0.83	0.0837	0.0247	0.0700
9	Germany	0.1538	0.2270	0.53	0.85	0.0473	0.0209	0.0800
10	Australia	0.1808	0.1617	0.52	0.81	0.0468	0.1225	0.0580
11	Japan	0.2432	0.1878	0.41	0.43	−0.0177	0.0398	0.0450
12	Canada	0.1687	0.1727	0.72	0.79	0.0727	0.1009	0.0590

6.6 The Bordered Covariance Matrix

	A	B	C	D	E	F	G	H	I
16	Portfolio Weights →		1.0000	0.0000	0.0000	0.0000	0.0000	0.0000	0.0000
17			US	UK	France	Germany	Australia	Japan	Canada
18	1.0000	US	0.0224	0.0184	0.0250	0.0288	0.0195	0.0121	0.0205
19	0.0000	UK	0.0184	0.0223	0.0275	0.0299	0.0204	0.0124	0.0206
20	0.0000	France	0.0250	0.0275	0.0403	0.0438	0.0259	0.0177	0.0273
21	0.0000	Germany	0.0288	0.0299	0.0438	0.0515	0.0301	0.0183	0.0305
22	0.0000	Australia	0.0195	0.0204	0.0259	0.0301	0.0261	0.0147	0.0234
23	0.0000	Japan	0.0121	0.0124	0.0177	0.0183	0.0147	0.0353	0.0158
24	0.0000	Canada	0.0205	0.0206	0.0273	0.0305	0.0234	0.0158	0.0298
25	1.0000		0.0224	0.0000	0.0000	0.0000	0.0000	0.0000	0.0000
26	0.0600	Mean							
27	0.1495	SD							
28	0.4013	Slope							
30	Cell A18 - A24		A18 is set arbitrarily to 1 while A19 to A24 are set to 0						
31	Formula in cell	C16	=A18	...	Formula in cell I16	= A24			
32	Formula in cell	A25	=SUM(A18:A24)						
33	Formula in cell	C25	=C16*SUMPRODUCT($A$18:$A$24,C18:C24)						
34	Formula in cell	D25-I25	Copied from C25 (note the absolute addresses)						
35	Formula in cell	A26	=SUMPRODUCT($A$18:$A$24,H6:H12)						
36	Formula in cell	A27	=SUM(C25:I25)^0.5						
37	Formula in cell	A28	=A26/A27						

6.7 The Efficient Frontier

	A	B	C	D	E	F	G	H	I	J	K	L
41	Cell to store constraint on risk premium				0.0400							
43			Min Var					Optimum				
44	Mean		0.0383	0.0400	0.0450	0.0500	0.0550	0.0564	0.0575	0.0600	0.0700	0.0800
45	SD	0.1	0.1132	0.1135	0.1168	0.1238	0.1340	0.1374	0.1401	0.1466	0.1771	0.2119
46	Slope		0.3386	0.3525	0.3853	0.4037	0.4104	0.4107	0.4106	0.4092	0.3953	0.3774
47	US		0.6112	0.6195	0.6446	0.6696	0.6947	0.7018	0.7073	0.7198	0.7699	0.8201
48	UK		0.8778	0.8083	0.5992	0.3900	0.1809	0.1214	0.0758	−0.0283	−0.4465	−0.8648
49	France		−0.2140	−0.2029	−0.1693	−0.1357	−0.1021	−0.0926	−0.0852	−0.0685	−0.0014	0.0658
50	Germany		−0.5097	−0.4610	−0.3144	−0.1679	−0.0213	0.0205	0.0524	0.1253	0.4185	0.7117
51	Australia		0.0695	0.0748	0.0907	0.1067	0.1226	0.1271	0.1306	0.1385	0.1704	0.2023
52	Japan		0.2055	0.1987	0.1781	0.1575	0.1369	0.1311	0.1266	0.1164	0.0752	0.0341
53	Canada		−0.0402	−0.0374	−0.0288	−0.0203	−0.0118	−0.0093	−0.0075	−0.0032	0.0139	0.0309
54	CAL*	0.0411	0.0465	0.0466	0.0480	0.0509	0.0550	0.0564	0.0575	0.0602	0.0727	0.0871
55	*Risk premium on CAL = SD * slope of optimal risky portfolio											

Using the Excel Solver

Excel's Solver is a user-friendly, but quite powerful, optimizer. It has three parts: (1) an objective function, (2) decision variables, and (3) constraints. Figure 6.14 shows three pictures of the Solver. For the current discussion we refer to picture A.

The top panel of the Solver lets you choose a target cell for the "objective function," that is, the variable you are trying to optimize. In picture A, the target cell is A27, the portfolio standard deviation. Below the target cell, you can choose whether your objective is to maximize, minimize, or set your objective function equal to a value that you specify. Here we choose to minimize the portfolio standard deviation.

The next panel contains the decision variables. These are cells that the Solver can change in order to optimize the objective function in the target cell. Here, we input cells A18–A24, the portfolio weights that we select to minimize portfolio volatility.

The bottom panel of the Solver can include any number of constraints. One constraint that must always appear in portfolio optimization is the "feasibility constraint," namely, that portfolio weights sum to 1.0. When we bring up the constraint dialogue box, we specify that cell A25 (the sum of weights) be set equal to 1.0.

Finding the Minimum Variance Portfolio

It is helpful to begin by identifying the global minimum variance portfolio (*G*). This provides the starting point of the efficient part of the frontier. Once we input the target cell, the decision variable cells, and the feasibility constraint, as in picture A, we can punch "solve" and the Solver returns portfolio *G*. We copy the portfolio statistics and weights to our output Table 6.7. Column C in Table 6.7 shows that the lowest standard deviation (SD) that can be achieved with our input list is 11.32 percent. Notice that the SD of portfolio *G* is considerably lower than even the lowest SD of the individual indices. From the risk premium of portfolio *G* (3.83 percent) we begin building the efficient frontier with ever-larger risk premiums.

Figure 6.14
Solver dialogue box.

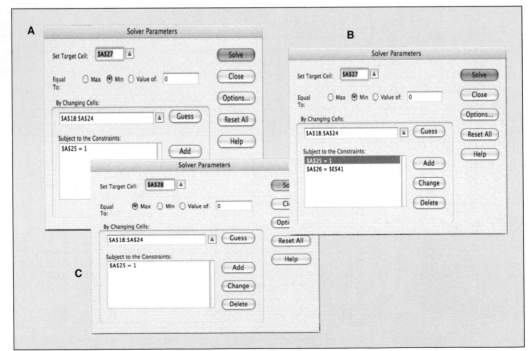

Charting the Efficient Frontier of Risky Portfolios

We determine the desired risk premiums (points on the efficient frontier) that we wish to use to construct the graph of the efficient frontier. It is good practice to choose more points in the neighbourhood of portfolio G because the frontier has the greatest curvature in that region. It is sufficient to choose for the highest point the highest risk premium from the input list (here, 8 percent for Germany). You can produce the entire efficient frontier in minutes following this procedure.

1. Input to the Solver a constraint that says: cell A26 (the portfolio risk premium) must equal the value in cell E41. The Solver at this point is shown in picture B of Figure 6.14. Cell E41 will be used to change the required risk premium and thus generate different points along the frontier.

2. For each additional point on the frontier, you input a different desired risk premium into cell E41, and ask the Solver to solve again.

3. Every time the Solver gives you a solution to the request in step 2, copy the results into Table 6.7, which tabulates the collection of points along the efficient frontier. For the next step, change cell E41 and repeat from step 2.

Finding the Optimal Risky Portfolio on the Efficient Frontier

Now that we have an efficient frontier, we look for the portfolio with the highest Sharpe ratio (i.e., reward-to-volatility ratio). This is the efficient frontier portfolio that is tangent to the CAL. To find it, we just need to make two changes to the Solver. First, change the target cell from cell A27 to cell A28, the Sharpe ratio of the portfolio, and request that the value in this cell be maximized. Next, eliminate the constraint on the risk premium that may be left over from the last time you used the Solver. At this point the Solver looks like picture C in Figure 6.14.

The Solver now yields the optimal risky portfolio. Copy the statistics for the optimal portfolio and its weights to your Table 6.7. In order to get a clean graph, place the column of the optimal portfolio in Table 6.7 so that the risk premiums of all portfolios in the table are steadily increasing from the risk premium of portfolio G (3.83 percent) all the way up to 8 percent.

The efficient frontier is graphed using the data in cells C45–I45 (the horizontal or *x*-axis is portfolio standard deviation) and C44–I44 (the vertical or *y*-axis is portfolio risk premium). The resulting graph appears in Figure 6.15.

Figure 6.15

Efficient frontier and CAL for country stock indices.

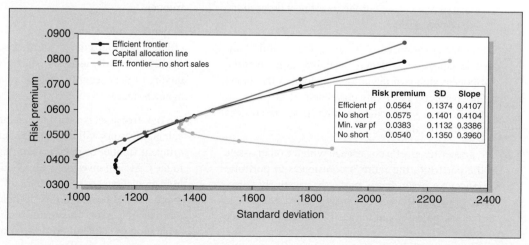

The Optimal CAL

It is instructive to superimpose on the graph of the efficient frontier in Figure 6.15 the CAL that identifies the optimal risky portfolio. This CAL has a slope equal to the Sharpe ratio of the optimal risky portfolio. Therefore, we add at the bottom of Table 6.7 a row with entries obtained by multiplying the SD of each column's portfolio by the Sharpe ratio of the optimal risky portfolio from cell H46. This results in the risk premium for each portfolio along the CAL efficient frontier. We now add a series to the graph with the standard deviations in B45–I45 as the *x*-axis and cells B54–I54 as the *y*-axis. You can see this CAL in Figure 6.15.

The Optimal Risky Portfolio and the Short-Sales Constraint

With the input list used by the portfolio manager, the optimal risky portfolio calls for significant short positions in the stocks of France and Canada (see column H of Table 6.7). In many cases the portfolio manager is prohibited from taking short positions. If so, we need to amend the program to preclude short sales.

To accomplish this task, we repeat the exercise, but with one change. We add to the Solver the following constraint: each element in the column of portfolio weights, A18–A24, must be greater than or equal to zero. You should try to produce the short-sale constrained efficient frontier in your own spreadsheet. The graph of the constrained frontier is also shown in Figure 6.15.

SUMMARY

1. The expected return of a portfolio is the weighted average of the component assets' expected returns with the investment proportions as weights.

2. The variance of a portfolio is the weighted sum of the elements of the covariance matrix with the product of the investment proportions as the weight. Thus, the variance of each asset is weighted by the square of its investment proportion. Each covariance of any pair of assets appears twice in the covariance matrix, and thus the portfolio variance includes twice each covariance weighted by the product of the investment proportions in each of two assets.

3. Even if the covariances are positive, the portfolio standard deviation is less than the weighted average of the component standard deviations, as long as the assets are not perfectly positively correlated. Thus, portfolio diversification is of value as long as assets are less than perfectly correlated.

4. The greater an asset's covariance with the other assets in the portfolio, the more it contributes to portfolio variance. An asset that is perfectly negatively correlated with a portfolio can serve as a perfect hedge. The perfect hedge asset can reduce the portfolio variance to zero.

5. The efficient frontier is the graphical representation of a set of portfolios that maximize expected return for each level of portfolio risk. Rational investors will choose a portfolio on the efficient frontier.

6. A portfolio manager identifies the efficient frontier by first establishing estimates for the asset expected returns and the covariance matrix. This input list then is fed into an optimization program that reports as outputs the investment proportions, expected returns, and standard deviations of the portfolios on the efficient frontier.

7. In general, portfolio managers will arrive at different efficient portfolios due to a difference in methods and quality of security analysis. Managers compete on the quality of their security analysis relative to their management fees.

8. If a risk-free asset is available and input lists are identical, all investors will choose the same portfolio on the efficient frontier of risky assets: the portfolio tangent to the CAL. All investors with identical input lists will hold an identical risky portfolio, differing only in how much each allocates to this optimal portfolio and to the risk-free asset. This result is characterized as the separation principle of portfolio construction.

KEY EQUATIONS

(6.1) $r_P = w_D r_D + w_E r_E$

(6.2) $E(r_P) = w_D E(r_D) + w_E E(r_E)$

(6.3) $\sigma^2_P = w^2_D \sigma^2_D + w^2_E \sigma^2_E + 2 w_D w_E \text{Cov}(r_D, r_E)$

(6.4) $\text{Cov}(r_D, r_D) = \sum_{\text{scenarios}} \text{Pr(scenario)}[r_D - E(r_D)][r_D - E(r_D)]$

(6.5) $\sigma^2_P = w_D w_D \text{Cov}(r_D, r_D) + w_E w_E \text{Cov}(r_E, r_E) + 2 w_D w_E \text{Cov}(r_D, r_E)$

(6.6) $\text{Cov}(r_D, r_E) = \rho_{DE} \sigma_D \sigma_E$

(6.7) $\sigma^2_P = w^2_D \sigma^2_D + w^2_E \sigma^2_E + 2 w_D w_E \sigma_D \sigma_E \sigma_{DE}$

(6.8) $\sigma_P = w_D \sigma_D + w_E \sigma_E$

(6.9) $\sigma^2_P = (w_D \sigma_D - w_E \sigma_E)^2$

(6.10) $\sigma_P = \text{Absolute value}(w_D \sigma_D - w_E \sigma_E)$

(6.11) $w_E = \dfrac{\sigma_D}{\sigma_D + \sigma_E} = 1 - w_D$

(6.12) $w_{\min}(D) = \dfrac{\sigma^2_E - \text{Cov}(r_D, r_E)}{\sigma^2_D + \sigma^2_E - 2\text{Cov}(r_D, r_E)}$

(6.13) $w_D = \dfrac{[E(r_D) - r_f]\sigma^2_E - [E(r_E) - r_f]\text{Cov}(r_D, r_E)}{[E(r_D) - r_f]\sigma^2_E + [E(r_E) - r_f]\sigma^2_D - [E(r_D) - r_f + E(r_E) - r_f]\text{Cov}(r_D, r_E)}$

(6.14) $y = \dfrac{E(r_P) - r_f}{A\sigma^2_P}$

(6.15) $E(r_P) = \sum_{i=1}^{n} w_i E(r_i)$

(6.16) $\sigma^2_P = \sum_{i=1}^{n} w^2_i \sigma^2_i + \sum_{\substack{i=1 \\ i \neq j}}^{n} \sum_{j=1}^{n} w_i w_j \text{Cov}(r_i, r_j)$

(6.17) $\sigma^2_P = \dfrac{1}{n}\sum_{i=1}^{n}\dfrac{1}{n}\sigma^2 i + \sum_{\substack{i=1 \\ i \neq j}}^{n}\sum_{j=1}^{n}\dfrac{1}{n^2}\text{Cov}(r_i, r_f)$

(6.18) $\sigma^2_P = \dfrac{1}{n}\overline{\sigma^2} + \dfrac{n-1}{n}\overline{\text{Cov}}$

PROBLEMS

Mc Graw Hill Education **connect**™   **Practise and learn online with Connect.**

1. Which of the following factors reflect *pure* market risk for a given corporation?

   a. Increased short-term interest rates

   b. Fire in the corporate warehouse

   c. Increased insurance costs

   d. Death of the CEO

   e. Increased labour costs

2. When adding real estate to an asset allocation program that currently includes only stocks, bonds, and cash, which of the properties of real estate returns affect portfolio *risk*? Explain.

   a. Standard deviation

   b. Expected return

   c. Correlation with returns of the other asset classes

3. Which of the following statements about the minimum variance portfolio of all risky securities are valid? (Assume short sales are allowed.) Explain.

   a. Its variance must be lower than those of all other securities or portfolios.

   b. Its expected return can be lower than the risk-free rate.

   c. It may be the optimal risky portfolio.

   d. It must include all individual securities.

The following data apply to problems 4–10: A pension fund manager is considering three mutual funds. The first is a stock fund, the second is a long-term government and corporate bond fund, and the third is a T-bill money market fund that yields a rate of 8 percent. The probability distribution of the risky funds is as follows:

	Expected Return	Standard Deviation
Stock fund (S)	.20	.30
Bond fund (B)	.12	.15

The correlation between the fund returns is .10.

4. What are the investment proportions of the minimum-variance portfolio of the two risky funds, and what is the expected value and standard deviation of its rate of return?

5. Tabulate and draw the investment opportunity set of the two risky funds. Use investment proportions for the stock fund of zero to 100 percent in increments of 20 percent.

6. Draw a tangent from the risk-free rate to the opportunity set. What does your graph show for the expected return and standard deviation of the optimal portfolio?

7. Solve numerically for the proportions of each asset and for the expected return and standard deviation of the optimal risky portfolio.

8. What is the reward-to-variability ratio of the best feasible CAL?

9. You require that your portfolio yield an expected return of 14 percent and be efficient on the best feasible CAL.

   a. What is the standard deviation of your portfolio?

   b. What is the proportion invested in the T-bill fund and each of the two risky funds?

10. If you were to use only the two risky funds and will require an expected return of 14 percent, what must be the investment proportions of your portfolio? Compare its standard deviation to that of the optimized portfolio in problem 9. What do you conclude?

11. Stocks offer an expected rate of return of 18 percent, with a standard deviation of 22 percent. Gold offers an expected return of 10 percent with a standard deviation of 30 percent.

    a. In the light of the apparent inferiority of gold with respect to both mean return and volatility, would anyone hold gold? If so, demonstrate graphically why one would do so.

    b. Given the data above, re-answer problem (*a*) with the additional assumption that the correlation coefficient between gold and stocks equals 1. Draw a graph illustrating why one would or would not hold gold in one's portfolio. Could this set of assumptions for expected returns, standard deviations, and correlation represent an equilibrium for the security market?

12. Suppose that there are many stocks in the market and that the characteristics of stocks *A* and *B* are as follows:

Stock	Expected Return	Standard Deviation
A	.10	.05
B	.15	.10
Correlation = −1		

Suppose that it is possible to borrow at the risk-free rate, r_f. What must be the value of the risk-free rate? (*Hint:* Think about constructing a risk-free portfolio from stocks *A* and *B*.)

13. Assume that expected returns and standard deviations for all securities (including the risk-free rate for borrowing and lending) are known. "In this case all investors will have the same optimal risky portfolio." True or false?

14. "The standard deviation of the portfolio always is equal to the weighted average of the standard deviations of the assets in the portfolio." True or false?

15. Suppose that you have a project that has a .7 chance of doubling your investment in a year and a .3 chance of halving your investment in a year. What is the standard deviation of the rate of return on this investment?

16. Suppose that you have $1 million and the following two opportunities from which to construct a portfolio:

    a. Risk-free asset earning .12 per year

    b. Risky asset earning .30 per year with a standard deviation of .40. If you construct a portfolio with a standard deviation of .30, what will be the rate of return?

17. The correlation coefficients between pairs of stocks is as follows:

$$\text{Corr}(A,B) = .85; \text{Corr}(A,C) = .60; \text{Corr}(A,D) = .45$$

Each stock has an expected return of 8 percent and a standard deviation of 20 percent. If your entire portfolio now comprises stock *A* and you can add only one more, which of the following would you choose, and why?

    a. B   *b. C*   *c. D*   *d.* Need more data

18. Would your answer to problem 17 change for more risk-averse or risk-tolerant investors? Explain.

19. Suppose that in addition to investing in one more stock you can invest in T-bills as well. Would you change your answers to problems 17 and 18 if the T-bill rate is 8 percent?

The table that appears next, "U.S. Compound Annual Returns by Decade," applies to problems 20 and 21.

U.S. Compound Annual Returns by Decade

	1920s*	1930s	1940s	1950s	1960s	1970s	1980s	1990s
Small company stocks	−3.72%	7.28%	20.63%	19.01%	13.72%	8.75%	12.46%	13.84%
Large company stocks	18.36	−1.25	9.11	19.41	7.84	5.90	17.60	18.20
Long-term government	3.98	4.60	3.59	0.25	1.14	6.63	11.50	8.60
Intermediate-term government	3.77	3.91	1.70	1.11	3.41	6.11	12.01	7.74
Treasury bills	3.56	0.30	0.37	1.87	3.89	6.29	9.00	5.02
Inflation	−1.00	−2.04	5.36	2.22	2.52	7.36	5.10	2.93

*Based on the period 1926–1929.

20. Input the data from the table into a spreadsheet. Compute the serial correlation in decade returns for each asset class and for inflation. Also find the correlation between the returns of various asset classes. What do the data indicate?

21. Convert the asset returns by decade presented in the table into real rates. Repeat the analysis of problem 20 for the real rates of return.

22. Abigail Grace has a $900,000 fully diversified portfolio. She subsequently inherits ABC Company common stock worth $100,000. Her financial advisor provided her with the following forecasted information:

Risk and Return Characteristics		
	Expected Monthly Returns	Standard Deviation of Monthly Returns
Original portfolio	0.67%	2.37%
ABC Company	1.25	2.95

The correlation coefficient of ABC stock returns with the original portfolio returns is .40.

a. The inheritance changes Grace's overall portfolio and she is deciding whether to keep the ABC stock. Assuming Grace keeps the ABC stock, calculate the

   i. Expected return of her new portfolio which includes the ABC stock

   ii. Covariance of ABC stock returns with the original portfolio returns

   iii. Standard deviation of her new portfolio which includes the ABC stock

b. If Grace sells the ABC stock, she will invest the proceeds in risk-free government securities yielding .42 percent monthly. Assuming Grace sells the ABC stock and replaces it with the government securities, calculate the

   i. Expected return of her new portfolio which includes the government securities

   ii. Covariance of the government security returns with the original portfolio returns

   iii. Standard deviation of her new portfolio which includes the government securities

c. Determine whether the systematic risk of her new portfolio which includes the government securities will be higher or lower than that of her original portfolio.

d. Based on conversations with her husband, Grace is considering selling the $100,000 of ABC stock and acquiring $100,000 of XYZ Company common stock instead. XYZ stock has the same expected return and standard deviation as ABC stock. Her husband comments, "It doesn't matter whether you keep all of the ABC stock or replace it with $100,000 of XYZ stock." State whether her husband's comment is correct or incorrect. Justify your response.

e. In a recent discussion with her financial advisor, Grace commented, "If I just don't lose money in my portfolio, I will be satisfied." She went on to say, "I am more afraid of losing money than I am concerned about achieving high returns."

   i. Describe *one* weakness of using standard deviation of returns as a risk measure for Grace.

   ii. Identify an alternative risk measure that is more appropriate under the circumstances.

The following information applies to problems 23 to 27:

Greta, an elderly investor, has a degree of risk aversion of $A = 2$ when applied to return on wealth over a three-year horizon. She is pondering two portfolios, the S&P 500 and a hedge fund, as well as a number of three-year strategies. (All rates are annual, continuously compounded.) The S&P 500 risk premium is estimated at 5 percent per year, with a SD of 20 percent. The hedge fund risk premium is estimated at 10 percent with a SD of 35 percent. The return on any of these portfolios in one year is uncorrelated with the return on any portfolios in any other year. The hedge fund management claims the correlation coefficient between the annual returns on the S&P 500 and the hedge fund is zero, but Greta believes this is far from certain.

23. Compute the estimated three-year risk premiums, SDs, and Sharpe ratios of the two portfolios.

24. Assuming the correlation between the annual returns is indeed zero, what would be the optimal asset allocation? What should be Greta's capital allocation?

25. If the correlation coefficient between annual returns is .3, what is the annual covariance?

26. With correlation of .3, what is the covariance between the three-year returns?

27. Repeat problem 24 using a correlation of .3. (If you cannot calculate the three-year covariance in problem 26, assume it is .005.)

The following data apply to problems 28–30:

Hennessy & Associates manages a $30 million equity portfolio for the multi-manager Wilstead Pension Fund. Jason Jones, financial vice-president of Wilstead, noted that Hennessy had rather consistently achieved the best record among Wilstead's six equity managers. Performance of the Hennessy portfolio had been clearly superior to that of the S&P 500 in four of the past five years. In the one less favourable year, the shortfall was trivial.

Hennessy is a "bottom-up" manager. The firm largely avoids any attempt to "time the market." It also focuses on selection of individual stocks, rather than the weighting of favoured industries.

There is no apparent conformity of style among the six equity managers. The five managers, other than Hennessy, manage portfolios aggregating $250 million made up of more than 150 individual issues.

Jones is convinced that Hennessy is able to apply superior skill to stock selection, but the favourable results are limited by the high degree of diversification in the portfolio. Over the years, the portfolio generally has held 40–50 stocks, with about 2 percent to 3 percent of total funds committed to each issue. The reason Hennessy seemed to do well most years was because the firm was able to identify each year 10 or 12 issues that registered particularly large gains.

On the basis of this overview, Jones outlined the following plan to the Wilstead pension committee:

Let's tell Hennessy to limit the portfolio to no more than 20 stocks. Hennessy will double the commitments to the stocks that it really favours and eliminate the remainder. Except for this one new restriction, Hennessy should be free to manage the portfolio exactly as before.

All the members of the pension committee generally supported Jones' proposal, because all agreed that Hennessy had seemed to demonstrate superior skill in selecting stocks. Yet the proposal was a considerable departure from previous practice, and several committee members raised questions. Respond to each of these questions:

28. Answer the following:

    a. Will the limitation of 20 stocks likely increase or decrease the risk of the portfolio? Explain.

    b. Is there any way Hennessy could reduce the number of issues from 40 to 20 without significantly affecting risk? Explain.

29. One committee member was particularly enthusiastic concerning Jones' proposal. He suggested that Hennessy's performance might benefit further from reduction in the number of issues to 10. If the reduction to 20 could be expected to be advantageous, explain why reduction to 10 might be less likely to be advantageous. (Assume that Wilstead will evaluate the Hennessy portfolio independently of the other portfolios in the fund.)

30. Another committee member suggested that, rather than evaluating each managed portfolio independently of other portfolios, it might be better to consider the effects of a change in the Hennessy portfolio on the total fund. Explain how this broader point of view could affect the committee decision to limit the holdings in the Hennessy portfolio to either 10 or 20 issues.

CFA®
PROBLEMS

The following problems are based on questions that have appeared in past CFA examinations.

31. Which *one* of the following portfolios *cannot* lie on the efficient frontier as described by Markowitz?

	Portfolio	Expected Return	Standard Deviation
a.	W	15%	36%
b.	X	12%	15%
c.	Z	5%	7%
d.	Y	9%	21%

32. Which of the following statements about portfolio diversification is *correct*?

a. Proper diversification can reduce or eliminate systematic risk.

b. Diversification reduces the portfolio's expected return because diversification reduces a portfolio's total risk.

c. As more securities are added to a portfolio, total risk typically would be expected to fall at a decreasing rate.

d. The risk-reducing benefits of diversification do not occur meaningfully until at least 30 individual securities are included in the portfolio.

33. The measure of risk for a security held in a diversified portfolio is

a. Specific risk

b. Standard deviation of returns

c. Reinvestment risk

d. Covariance

34. Portfolio theory as described by Markowitz is most concerned with

a. The elimination of systematic risk

b. The effect of diversification on portfolio risk

c. The identification of unsystematic risk

d. Active portfolio management to enhance return

35. Assume that a risk-averse investor owning stock in Miller Corporation decides to add the stock of either Mac or Green Corporation to her portfolio. All three stocks offer the same expected return and total variability. The covariance of return between Miller and Mac is $-.05$, and between Miller and Green $+.05$. Portfolio risk is expected to

a. Decline more when the investor buys Mac

b. Decline more when the investor buys Green

c. Increase when either Mac or Green is bought

d. Decline or increase, depending on other factors

36. Stocks A, B, and C have the same expected return and standard deviation. The following table shows the correlations between the returns on these stocks.

	Stock A	Stock B	Stock C
Stock A	+1.0		
Stock B	+0.9	+1.0	
Stock C	+0.1	−0.4	+1.0

Given these correlations, the portfolio constructed from these stocks having the lowest risk is a portfolio

a. Equally invested in stocks A and B

b. Equally invested in stocks A and C

     c. Equally invested in stocks *B* and *C*

     d. Totally invested in stock *C*

37. Statistics for three stocks, *A*, *B*, and *C*, are shown in the following tables.

Standard Deviations of Returns		
Stock		
A	*B*	*C*
.40	.20	.40

Correlations of Returns			
	Stock		
	A	*B*	*C*
A	1.00	.90	.50
B		1.00	.10
C			1.00

Only on the basis of the information provided in the tables, and given a choice between a portfolio made up of equal amounts of stocks *A* and *B* or a portfolio made up of equal amounts of stocks *B* and *C*, state which portfolio you would recommend. Justify your choice.

38. George Stephenson's current portfolio of $2 million is invested as follows:

Summary of Stephenson's Current Portfolio				
	Value	Percentage of Total	Expected Annual Return	Annual Standard Deviation
Short-term bonds	$ 200,000	10	4.6%	1.6%
Domestic large-cap equities	600,000	30	12.4	19.5
Domestic small-cap equities	1,200,000	60	16.0	29.9
Total portfolio	$2,000,000	100	13.8	23.1

Stephenson soon expects to receive an additional $2 million and plans to invest the entire amount in an index fund that best complements the current portfolio. Stephanie Coppa, CFA, is evaluating the four index funds shown in the following table for their ability to produce a portfolio that will meet two criteria relative to the current portfolio: (1) maintain or enhance expected return and (2) maintain or reduce volatility.

    Each fund is invested in an asset class that is not substantially represented in the current portfolio.

Index Fund Characteristics			
Index Fund	Expected Annual Return	Expected Annual Standard Deviation	Correlation of Returns with Current Portfolio
Fund *A*	15%	25%	+.80
Fund *B*	11	22	+.60
Fund *C*	16	25	+.90
Fund *D*	14	22	+.65

State which fund Coppa should recommend to Stephenson. Justify your choice by describing how your chosen fund *best* meets both of Stephenson's criteria. No calculations are required.

39. Dudley Trudy, CFA, recently met with one of his clients. Trudy typically invests in a master list of 30 equities drawn from several industries. As the meeting concluded, the client made the following statement: "I trust your stock-picking ability and believe that you should invest my funds in your five best ideas. Why invest in 30 companies when you obviously have stronger opinions on a few of them?" Trudy plans to respond to his client within the context of modern portfolio theory.

a. Contrast the concepts of systematic risk and firm-specific risk, and give an example of *each* type of risk.

b. Critique the client's suggestion. Discuss how both systematic and firm-specific risk change as the number of securities in a portfolio is increased.

APPENDIX 6A: RISK POOLING, RISK SHARING, AND THE RISK OF LONG-TERM INVESTMENTS

Diversification means that we spread our investment budget across a variety of assets and thus limit overall risk. Sometimes it is argued that spreading investments across time, so that the average performance reflects returns in several investment periods, offers an analogous benefit dubbed "time diversification." A common belief is that time diversification can make long-term investing safer.

Is this extension of diversification to investments over time valid? The question of how risk increases when the horizon of a risky investment lengthens is analogous to risk pooling, the process by which an insurance company aggregates a large portfolio (or pool) of uncorrelated risks. However, application of risk pooling to investment risk is widely misunderstood, as is the application of "the insurance principle" to long-term investments. In this appendix, we try to clarify these issues and explore the appropriate extension of the insurance principle to investment risk.

Risk Pooling and the Insurance Principle

Risk pooling means merging uncorrelated, risky projects as a means to reduce risk. Applied to the insurance business, risk pooling entails selling many uncorrelated insurance policies. This application of risk pooling has come to be known as the insurance principle. Conventional wisdom holds that risk pooling reduces risk, and that such pooling is the driving force behind risk management for the insurance industry.

But even brief reflection should convince you that risk pooling cannot be the entire story. How can *adding* bets that are independent of your other bets reduce your total exposure to risk? This would be little different from a gambler in Las Vegas arguing that a few more trips to the roulette table will reduce his total risk by diversifying his overall "portfolio" of wagers. You would immediately realize that the gambler now has more money at stake, and his overall potential swing in wealth is clearly wider: While his average gain or loss *per bet* may become more predictable as he repeatedly returns to the table, his total proceeds become less so. As we will see, the insurance principle is sometimes similarly misapplied to long-term investments by incorrectly extending what it implies about *average* returns to predictions about *total* returns.

Risk Pooling

Imagine a rich investor, Warren, who holds a \$1 billion portfolio, P. The fraction of the portfolio invested in a risky asset, A, is y, leaving the fraction $1 - y$ invested in the risk-free rate. Asset A's risk premium is R, and its standard deviation is σ. From equations 5.3 and 5.4, the risk premium of the complete portfolio P is $R_P = yR$, its standard deviation is $\sigma_P = y\sigma$, and the Sharpe ratio is $S_P = R/\sigma$. Now Warren identifies another risky asset, B, with the same risk premium and standard deviation as A. Warren estimates that the correlation (and therefore covariance) between the two investments is zero, and he is intrigued at the potential this offers for risk reduction through diversification.

Given the benefits that Warren anticipates from diversification, he decides to take a position in asset B equal in size to his existing position in asset A. He therefore transfers another fraction, y, of wealth from the risk-free asset to asset B. This leaves his total portfolio allocated as follows:

the fraction y is still invested in asset A, an additional investment of y is invested in B, and $1 - 2y$ is in the risk-free asset. Notice that this strategy is analogous to pure risk pooling; Warren has taken on additional risky (albeit uncorrelated) bets, and his risky portfolio is larger than it was previously. We will denote Warren's new portfolio Z.

We can compute the risk premium of portfolio Z from equation 6.2 and its variance from equation 6.3, and thus its Sharpe ratio. Remember that R denotes the risk premium of each asset and the risk premium of the risk-free asset is zero. When calculating portfolio variance, we use the fact that covariance is zero. Thus, for portfolio Z:

$$R_Z = yR + yR + (1 - 2y)0 = 2yR \qquad \text{(double } R_P\text{)}$$
$$\sigma_Z^2 = y^2\sigma^2 + y^2\sigma^2 + 0 = 2y^2\sigma^2 \qquad \text{(double the variance of } P\text{)}$$
$$\sigma_Z = y\sigma\sqrt{2} \qquad (\sqrt{2} = 1.41, \text{ times the standard deviation of } P)$$
$$S_Z = R_Z/\sigma_Z = 2yR/(y\sigma\sqrt{2}) = \sqrt{2}R/\sigma \quad (\sqrt{2} = 1.41, \text{ times the Sharpe ratio of } P)$$

The good news from these results is that the Sharpe ratio of Z is higher than that of P by the factor $\sqrt{2}$. Its excess rate of return is double that of P, yet its standard deviation is only $\sqrt{2}$ times larger. The bad news is that by increasing the scale of the risky investment, the standard deviation of the portfolio also increases by $\sqrt{2}$.

We might now imagine that instead of two uncorrelated assets, Warren has access to many. Repeating our analysis, we would find that with n assets the Sharpe ratio under strategy Z increases (relative to its original value) by a factor of $\sqrt{n}$ to $\sqrt{n}R/\sigma$. But the total risk of the pooling strategy Z will increase by the same multiple, to $\sigma\sqrt{n}$.

This analysis illustrates both the opportunities and limitations of pure risk pooling: pooling increases the scale of the risky investment (from y to $2y$) by adding an additional position in another, uncorrelated asset. This addition of another risky bet also increases the size of the risky budget. So risk pooling *by itself* does not reduce risk, despite the fact that it benefits from the lack of correlation across policies.

The insurance principle tells us only that risk increases less than proportionally to the number of policies insured when the policies are uncorrelated; hence profitability—in this application, the Sharpe ratio—increases. But this effect does not actually reduce risk.

This might limit the potential economies of scale of an ever-growing portfolio such as that of a large insurer. You can interpret each "asset" in our analysis as one insurance policy. Each policy written requires the insurance company to set aside additional capital to cover potential losses. The insurance company invests its capital until it needs to pay out on claims. Selling more policies entails increasing the total position in risky investments and therefore the capital that must be allocated to those policies. As the company invests in more uncorrelated assets (insurance policies), the Sharpe ratio continuously increases (which is good), but since more funds are invested in risky policies, the overall risk of the portfolio rises (which is bad). As the number of policies grows, the risk of the pool will certainly grow—despite "diversification" across policies. Eventually, that growing risk will overwhelm the company's available capital.

Insurance analysts often think in terms of probability of loss. Their mathematically correct interpretation of the insurance principle is that the probability of loss declines with risk pooling. This interpretation relates to the fact that the Sharpe ratio (profitability) increases with risk pooling. But to equate the declining probability of loss to reduction in total risk is erroneous; the latter is measured by overall standard deviation, which increases with risk pooling. (Again, think about the gambler in Las Vegas. As he returns over and over again to the roulette table, the probability that he will lose becomes ever more certain, and the magnitude of potential dollar gains or losses becomes ever greater.) Thus risk pooling allows neither investors nor insurance companies to shed risk. However, the increase in risk can be overcome when risk pooling is augmented by risk sharing, as discussed in the next subsection.

Risk Sharing

Now think about a variation on the risk pooling portfolio Z. Imagine that Warren has identified several attractive insurance policies and wishes to invest in all of them. For simplicity, we will look at the case of two policies, so the pool will have the same properties as portfolio Z. We saw that if Warren invested in this two-policy pool, his total risk would be $\sigma_Z = y\sigma\sqrt{2}$. But if this is more risk than he is willing to bear, what might he do?

His solution is **risk sharing**, the act of selling shares in an attractive risky portfolio to limit risk and yet maintain the Sharpe ratio (profitability) of the resultant position. Suppose that every time a new risky asset is added to the portfolio, Warren sells off a portion of his investment in the pool to maintain the total funds invested in risky assets unchanged. For example, when a second asset is added, he sells half of his position to other investors. While the total investment budget directed into risky assets is therefore unchanged, it is equally divided between assets A and B, with weights in each of $y/2$. In following this strategy, the risk-free component of his complete portfolio remains fixed with weight $1 - y$. We will call this strategy V.

If you compare the risk-pooling strategy Z with the risk-pooling-plus-risk-sharing strategy V, you will notice that they both entail an investment in the pool of two assets; the only difference between them is that the risk-sharing strategy sells off half the combined pool to maintain a risky portfolio of *fixed size*. While the weight of the total risky pool in strategy Z is $2y$, in the risk-sharing strategy the risky weight is only one-half that level. Therefore, we can find the properties of the risk-sharing portfolio by substituting y for $2y$ in each formula or, equivalently, substituting $y/2$ for y in the following table.

Risk Pooling: Portfolio Z	Risk Sharing: Portfolio V
$R_z = 2yR$	$R_v = 2(y/2)R = yR$
$\sigma^2_z = 2y^2\sigma^2$	$\sigma^2_v = 2(y/2)^2\sigma^2 = y^2\sigma^2/2$
$\sigma_z = \sqrt{\sigma^2_z} = y\sigma\sqrt{2}$	$\sigma_v = \sqrt{\sigma^2_v} = y\sigma/\sqrt{2}$
$S_z = R_z/\sigma_z = 2yR/(y\sigma\sqrt{2}) = \sqrt{2}R/\sigma$	$S_v = R_v/\sigma_v = \sqrt{2}R/\sigma$

We observe that portfolio V matches the attractive Sharpe ratio of portfolio Z, but with lower volatility. Thus risk sharing *combined* with risk pooling is the key to the insurance industry. True diversification means spreading a portfolio of *fixed size* across many assets, not merely adding more risky bets to an ever-growing risky portfolio.

To control his total risk, Warren had to sell off a fraction of the pool of assets. This implies that a portion of those assets must now be held by someone else. For example, if the assets are insurance policies, other investors must be sharing the risk, perhaps by buying shares in the insurance company. Alternatively, insurance companies commonly "reinsure" their risk by selling off portions of the policies to other investors or insurance companies, thus explicitly sharing the risk.

We can easily generalize Warren's example to the case of more than two assets. Suppose the risky pool has n assets. Then the volatility of the risk-sharing portfolio will be $\sigma_v = y\sigma/\sqrt{n}$, and its Sharpe ratio will be $\sqrt{n}R/\sigma$. Clearly, both of these improve as n increases. Think back to our gambler at the roulette wheel one last time. He was wrong to argue that diversification means that 100 bets are less risky than 1 bet. His intuition would be correct, however, if he shared those 100 bets with 100 of his friends. A 1/100 share of 100 bets is in fact less risky than one bet. Fixing the amount of his total money at risk as that money is spread across more independent bets is the way for him to reduce risk.[10]

---

[10]For the Las Vegas gambler, risk sharing makes the gambles ever more certain to produce a *negative* rate of return, highlighting the illness that characterizes compulsive gambling.

With risk sharing, one can set up an insurance company of any size, amassing a large portfolio of policies and limiting total risk by selling shares among many investors. As the Sharpe ratio steadily increases with the number of policies written, while the risk to each diversified shareholder falls, the size of ever-more-profitable insurance companies appears unlimited. In reality, however, two problems put a damper on this process. First, burdens related to problems of managing very large firms will sooner or later eat into the increased gross margins. More important, the issue of "too big to fail" may emerge. The possibility of error in assessing the risk of each policy or misestimating the correlations across losses on the pooled policies (or worse yet, intentional underestimation of risk) can cause an insurance company to fail. "Too big to fail" means that such failure can lead to related failures among the firm's trading partners. This is similar to what happened in the financial crisis of 2008. The jury is still out on the role of lack of scruples in this affair. It is hoped that future regulation will put real limits on exaggerated optimism concerning the power of diversification to limit risk, despite the appealing mitigation of risk sharing.

Investment for the Long Run

Now we turn to the implications of risk pooling and risk sharing for long-term investing. Think of extending an investment horizon for another period (which adds the uncertainty of that period's risky return) as analogous to adding another risky asset or insurance policy to a pool of assets.

Examining the impact of an extension of the investment horizon requires us to clarify what the alternative is. Suppose you consider an investment in a risky portfolio over the next two years, which we'll call the "long-term investment." How should you compare this decision to a "short-run investment"? We must compare these two strategies over the same period, that is, two years. The short-term investment therefore must be interpreted as investing in the risky portfolio over one year and in the risk-free asset over the other.

Once we agree on this comparison, and assuming the risky return on the first year is uncorrelated with that of the second, it becomes clear that the "long-term" strategy is analogous to portfolio Z. This is because holding on to the risky investment in the second year (rather than withdrawing to the risk-free rate) piles up more risk, just as selling another insurance policy does. Put differently, the long-term investment may be considered analogous to risk pooling. While extending a risky investment to the long run improves the Sharpe ratio (as does risk pooling), it also increases risk. Thus "time diversification" is not really diversification.

The more accurate analogy to risk sharing for a long-term horizon is to spread the risky investment budget across each of the investment periods. Compare the following three strategies applied to the whole investment budget over a two-year horizon:

1. Invest the whole budget at risk for one period, and then withdraw the entire proceeds, placing them in a risk-free asset in the other period. Because you are invested in the risky asset for only one year, the risk premium over the whole investment period is R, the two-year SD is σ, and the two-year Sharpe ratio is $S = R/\sigma$.

2. Invest the whole budget in the risky asset for both periods. The two-year risk premium is $2R$ (assuming CC rates), the two-year variance is $2\sigma^2$, the two-year SD is $\sigma\sqrt{2}$, and the two-year Sharpe ratio is $S = R\sqrt{2}/\sigma$. This is analogous to risk pooling, taking two "bets" on the risky portfolio instead of one (as in strategy 1).

3. Invest half the investment budget in the risky position in each of two periods, placing the remainder of funds in the risk-free asset. The two-year risk premium is R, the two-year variance is $2 \times (\frac{1}{2}\sigma)^2 = \sigma^2/2$, the SD is $\sigma/\sqrt{2}$, and the Sharpe ratio is $S = R\sqrt{2}/\sigma$. This is analogous to risk sharing, taking a fractional position in each year's investment return.

Strategy 3 is less risky than either alternative. Its expected total return equals strategy 1's, yet its risk is lower and therefore its Sharpe ratio is higher. It achieves the same Sharpe ratio as strategy 2 but with total risk reduced by a factor of 2. In summary, its Sharpe ratio is at least as good as either alternative and, more to the point, its total risk is less than either.

We conclude that risk does not fade in the long run. An investor who can invest in an attractive portfolio for only one period, and chooses to invest a given budget in that period, would find it preferable to put money at risk in that portfolio in as many periods as allowed *but will decrease the risky budget in each period*. Simple risk pooling, or in this case, time diversification, does not reduce risk.

PART **3**

The Capital Asset Pricing Model

The capital asset pricing model, almost always referred to as the CAPM, is a centrepiece of modern financial economics.

The model gives us a precise prediction of the relationship that we should observe between the risk of an asset and its expected return. This relationship serves two vital functions. First, it provides a benchmark rate of return for evaluating possible investments. For example, if we are analyzing securities, we might be interested in whether the expected return we forecast for a stock is more or less than its "fair" return, given risk. Second, the model helps us to make an educated guess as to the expected return on assets that have not yet been traded in the marketplace. For example, how do we price an initial public offering of stock? How will a major new investment project affect the return investors require on a company's stock? Although the CAPM does not fully withstand empirical tests, it is widely used both because of the insight if offers and because its accuracy suffices for many important applications.

THE CAPITAL ASSET PRICING MODEL

The **capital asset pricing model (CAPM)** is a set of predictions concerning equilibrium expected returns on risky assets. We intend to explain it in one short chapter, but do not expect this to be easy going. Harry Markowitz laid down the foundation of modern portfolio management in 1952. The CAPM was developed 12 years later in articles by William Sharpe,[1] John Lintner,[2] and Jan Mossin.[3] The time for this gestation indicates that the leap from Markowitz's portfolio selection model to the CAPM is not trivial.

Let us go straight to the heart of the CAPM. Suppose all investors optimized their portfolios á la Markowitz. That is, each investor uses an input list (expected returns and covariance matrix) to draw an efficient frontier employing all available risky assets and identifies an efficient risky portfolio, P, by drawing the tangent CAL (capital allocation line) to the frontier as in Figure 7.1, Panel A (which is just a reproduction of Figure 6.11). As a result, each investor holds securities in the investable universe with weights arrived at by the Markowitz optimization process.

The CAPM asks what would happen if all investors shared an identical investable universe and used the same input list to draw their efficient frontiers. Obviously, their efficient frontiers would be identical. Facing the same risk-free rate, they would then draw an identical tangent CAL and naturally would arrive at the same risky portfolio, P. All investors therefore would choose the same set of weights for each risky asset. What must these weights be?

A key insight of the CAPM is this: Because the market portfolio is the aggregation of all of these identical risky portfolios, it too will have the same weights. Therefore, if all investors choose the same risky portfolio, it must be the **market portfolio**, that is, the value-weighted portfolio of all assets in the investable universe. Therefore, the capital allocation line based on each investor's optimal risky portfolio will in fact also be the capital *market* line, as depicted in Figure 7.1, Panel B. This implication will allow us to say much about the risk–return tradeoff.

Why Do All Investors Hold the Market Portfolio?

What is the market portfolio? When we sum over, or aggregate, the portfolios of all individual investors, lending and borrowing will cancel out (since each lender has a corresponding borrower), and the value of the aggregate risky portfolio will equal the entire wealth of the economy. This is the market portfolio, M. The proportion of each stock in this portfolio equals the market value of the stock (price per share times number of shares outstanding) divided by the sum of the market value of all stocks.[4] This implies that if the weight of RIM stock, for example, in each common risky portfolio is 1 percent, then when we sum over all investors' portfolios to obtain the aggregate market portfolio, RIM also will make up 1 percent of the market portfolio. The same principle applies to the proportion of any stock in each investor's risky portfolio. As a result, the optimal risky portfolio of all investors is simply a share of the market portfolio, which we label M in Figure 7.1.

Now suppose that the optimal portfolio of our investors does not include the stock of some company such as Canadian Tire (CT). When all investors avoid CT stock, the demand is zero, and CT's price takes a free fall. As CT stock gets progressively cheaper, it becomes ever more attractive as an investment and all other stocks look (relatively) less attractive. Ultimately, CT reaches a price where it is profitable enough to include in the optimal stock portfolio.

Such a price adjustment process guarantees that all stocks will be included in the optimal portfolio. It shows that *all* assets have to be included in the market portfolio. The only issue is the price at which investors will be willing to include a stock in their optimal risky portfolio.

---

[1]William Sharpe, "Capital Asset Prices: A Theory of Market Equilibrium," *Journal of Finance*, September 1964.
[2]John Lintner, "The Valuation of Risk Assets and the Selection of Risky Investments in Stock Portfolios and Capital Budgets," *Review of Economics and Statistics*, February 1965.
[3]Jan Mossin, "Equilibrium in a Capital Asset Market," *Econometrica*, October 1966.
[4]As noted previously, we use the term "stock" for convenience; the market portfolio properly includes all assets in the economy.

Figure 7.1

The efficient frontier and the capital market line. **Panel A:** The efficient frontier of risky assets with the optimal CAL. **Panel B:** The efficient frontier and the capital market line.

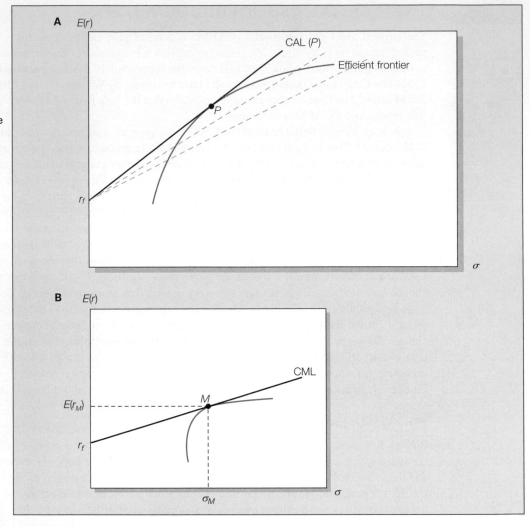

Efficient Frontier
www
.efficientfrontier
.com

The Passive Strategy Is Efficient

In Chapter 6 we defined the CML (capital market line) as the CAL (capital allocation line) that is constructed from either a money market account or T-bills and the market portfolio. Perhaps now you can fully appreciate why the CML is an interesting CAL. In the simple world of the CAPM, M is the optimal tangency portfolio on the efficient frontier.

In this scenario, the market portfolio, M, that all investors hold is based on the common input list, thereby incorporating all relevant information about the universe of securities. This means an investor can skip the trouble of doing specific analysis and obtain an efficient portfolio simply by holding the market portfolio. (Of course, if everyone were to follow this strategy, no one would perform security analysis, and this result would no longer hold. We discuss this issue in depth in Chapter 9 on market efficiency.)

Thus, the passive strategy of investing in a market index portfolio is efficient. For this reason, we sometimes call this result a **mutual fund theorem**. The mutual fund theorem is another incarnation of the separation property discussed in Chapter 6. If all investors would freely choose to hold a common risky portfolio identical to the market portfolio, they would not object if all stocks in the market were replaced with shares of a single mutual fund holding that market portfolio. In

THE PARABLE OF THE MONEY MANAGERS

Some years ago, in a land called Indicia, revolution led to the overthrow of a socialist regime and the restoration of a system of private property. Former government enterprises were reformed as corporations, which then issued stocks and bonds. These securities were given to a central agency, which offered them for sale to individuals, pension funds, and the like (all armed with newly printed money).

Almost immediately a group of money managers came forth to assist these investors. Recalling the words of a venerated elder, uttered before the previous revolution ("Invest in Corporate Indicia"), they invited clients to give them money, with which they would buy a cross-section of all the newly issued securities. Investors considered this a reasonable idea, and soon everyone held a piece of Corporate Indicia.

Before long the money managers became bored because there was little for them to do. Soon they fell into the habit of gathering at a beachfront casino where they passed the time playing roulette, craps, and similar games, for low stakes, with their own money.

After a while, the owner of the casino suggested a new idea. He would furnish an impressive set of rooms which would be designated the Money Managers' Club. There the members could place bets with one another about the fortunes of various corporations, industries, the level of the Gross National Product, foreign trade, etc. To make the betting more exciting, the casino owner suggested that the managers use their clients' money for this purpose.

The offer was immediately accepted, and soon the money managers were betting eagerly with one another. At the end of each week, some found that they had won money for their clients, while others found that they had lost. But the losses always exceeded the gains, for a certain amount was deducted from each bet to cover the costs of the elegant surroundings in which the gambling took place.

Before long a group of professors from Indicia U. suggested that investors were not well served by the activities being conducted at the Money Managers' Club. "Why pay people to gamble with your money? Why not just hold your own piece of Corporate Indicia?" they said.

This argument seemed sensible to some of the investors, and they raised the issue with their money managers. A few capitulated, announcing that they would henceforth stay away from the casino and use their clients' money only to buy proportionate shares of all the stocks and bonds issued by corporations.

The converts, who became known as managers of Indicia funds, were initially shunned by those who continued to frequent the Money Managers' Club, but in time, grudging acceptance replaced outright hostility. The wave of puritan reform some had predicted failed to materialize, and gambling remained legal. Many managers continued to make their daily pilgrimage to the casino. But they exercised more restraint than before, placed smaller bets, and generally behaved in a manner consonant with their responsibilities. Even the members of the Lawyers' Club found it difficult to object to the small amount of gambling that still went on.

And everyone but the casino owner lived happily ever after.

Source: William F. Sharpe, "The Parable of the Money Managers," *The Financial Analysts' Journal* 32 (July/August 1976), p. 4. Copyright 1976, CFA Institute. Reproduced from *The Financial Analysts' Journal* with permission from the CFA Institute. All rights reserved.

reality different investment managers do create risky portfolios that differ from the market index. We attribute this in part to the use of different input lists in the formation of their optimal risky portfolio. Nevertheless, the significance of the mutual fund theorem is that a passive investor may view the market index as a reasonable first approximation of an efficient risky portfolio.

The boxed article here contains a parable illustrating the argument for indexing. If the passive strategy is efficient, then attempts to beat it simply generate trading and research costs with no offsetting benefit, and ultimately inferior results.

CC 1

CONCEPT CHECK

If there are only a few investors who perform security analysis, and all others hold the market portfolio *M*, would the CML still be the efficient CAL for investors who do not engage in security analysis? Why or why not?

The Risk Premium of the Market Portfolio

In Chapter 5 we discussed how individual investors go about deciding capital allocation. If all investors choose to invest in portfolio *M* and the risk-free asset, what can we deduce about the equilibrium risk premium of portfolio *M*?

We asserted earlier that the equilibrium risk premium on the market portfolio, $E(r_M) - r_f$, will be proportional to the average degree of risk aversion of the investor population and the risk of the market portfolio, σ^2_M. Now we can explain this result.

Recall that each individual investor chooses a proportion, y, allocated to the optimal portfolio M, such that

$$y = \frac{E(r_M) - r_f}{A\sigma^2_M} \tag{7.1}$$

where $E(r_M) - r_f = E(R_M)$ is the risk premium (expected excess return) on the market portfolio.

In the simplified CAPM economy, risk-free investments involve borrowing and lending among investors. Any borrowing position must be offset by the lending position of the creditor. This means that net borrowing and lending across all investors must be zero and, therefore, the average position in the risky portfolio is 100 percent, or $y = 1$. Setting $\bar{y} = 1$ in equation 7.1 and rearranging, we find that the risk premium on the market portfolio is related to its variance by the average degree of risk aversion:

$$E(r_M) - r_f = \bar{A}\sigma^2_M \tag{7.2}$$

CONCEPT CHECK

CC 2

Data from the period 1957–2012 for the S&P/TSX Composite index yield the following statistics: average excess return, 4.24 percent; standard deviation, 17.42 percent.
a. To the extent that these averages approximated investor expectations for the period, what must have been the average coefficient of risk aversion?
b. If the coefficient of risk aversion were actually 1.5, what risk premium would have been consistent with the market's historical standard deviation?

Expected Returns on Individual Securities

The CAPM is built on the insight that the appropriate risk premium of an asset will be determined by its contribution to the risk of investors' overall portfolios. Portfolio risk is what matters to investors and governs the risk premiums they demand.

Remember that all investors use the same input list, that is, the same estimates of expected returns, variances, and covariances. To calculate the variance of the market portfolio, we use the covariance matrix bordered by market portfolio weights, as discussed in Chapter 6. We highlight Bell Canada (BCE) in this depiction of the n stocks in the market portfolio so that we can measure the contribution of BCE to the risk of the market portfolio.

Portfolio Weights:	w_1	w_2	...	w_B	...	w_n
w_1	$Cov(r_1,r_1)$	$Cov(r_1,r_2)$	...	$Cov(r_1,r_B)$	...	$Cov(r_1,r_n)$
w_2	$Cov(r_2,r_1)$	$Cov(r_2,r_2)$	...	$Cov(r_2,r_B)$	...	$Cov(r_2,r_n)$
.	.	.		.		.
.	.	.		.		.
w_B	$Cov(r_B,r_1)$		...	$Cov(r_B,r_B)$	...	$Cov(r_B,r_n)$
.	.	.		.		.
w_n	$Cov(r_n,r_1)$	$Cov(r_n,r_2)$	...	$Cov(r_n,r_B)$	...	$Cov(r_n,r_n)$

Recall that we calculate the variance of the portfolio by summing over all the elements of the covariance matrix and multiplying each element by the portfolio weights from the row and the column. The contribution of one stock to portfolio variance therefore can be expressed as the sum of all the covariance terms in the row corresponding to the stock where each covariance is multiplied by both the portfolio weight from its row and the weight from its column.[5]

For example, the contribution of BCE's stock to the variance of the market portfolio is

$$w_B[w_1\text{Cov}(r_1,r_B) + w_2\text{Cov}(r_2,r_B) + \ldots + w_B\text{Cov}(r_B,r_B) + \ldots + w_n\text{Cov}(r_n,r_B)] \quad (7.3)$$

Notice that every term in the square brackets can be slightly rearranged as follows: $w_i\text{Cov}(R_i, R_B) = \text{Cov}(w_iR_i, R_B)$, with $R_B = r_B - r_f$, the excess return on BCE stock. Moreover, because covariance is additive, the sum of the terms in the square brackets is

$$\sum_{i=1}^{n} w_i\text{Cov}(R_i,R_B) = \sum_{i=1}^{n} \text{Cov}(w_iR_i,R_B) = \text{Cov}\left(\sum_{i=1}^{n} w_iR_i, R_B\right) \quad (7.4)$$

But because $\sum_{i=1}^{n} w_iR_i = R_M$, equation 7.4 implies that

$$\sum_{i=1}^{n} w_i\text{Cov}(R_i,R_B) = \text{Cov}(R_M,R_B)$$

and therefore, BCE's contribution to variance (equation 7.3) may be more simply stated as $w_B\text{Cov}(R_M,R_B)$.

This should not surprise us. For example, if the covariance between BCE and the rest of the market is negative, then BCE makes a "negative contribution" to portfolio risk: by providing excess returns that move inversely with the rest of the market, BCE stabilizes the return on the overall portfolio. If the covariance is positive, BCE makes a positive contribution to overall portfolio risk because its returns amplify swings in the rest of the portfolio.[6] We also observe that the contribution of BCE to the risk premium of the market portfolio is $w_BE(R_B)$.

Therefore, the reward-to-risk ratio for investments in BCE can be expressed as

$$\frac{\text{BCE's contribution to risk premium}}{\text{BCE's contribution to variance}} = \frac{w_B[E(r_B) - r_f]}{w_B\text{Cov}(r_B,r_M)} = \frac{E(r_B) - r_f}{\text{Cov}(r_B,r_M)} = \frac{E(R_B)}{\text{Cov}(R_B,R_M)}$$

The market portfolio is the tangency (efficient mean-variance) portfolio. The reward-to-risk ratio for investment in the market portfolio is

$$\frac{\text{Market risk premium}}{\text{Market variance}} = \frac{E(r_M) - r_f}{\sigma^2_M} = \frac{E(R_M)}{\sigma^2_M} \quad (7.5)$$

The ratio in equation 7.5 is often called the **market price of risk**[7] because it quantifies the extra return that investors demand to bear portfolio risk. Notice that for *components* of the

---

[5]An alternative and equally valid approach would be to measure BCE's contribution to market variance as the sum of the elements in the row *and* the column corresponding to BCE. In this case, BCE's contribution would be twice the sum in equation 7.3. The approach that we take in the text allocates contributions to portfolio risk among securities in a convenient manner in that the sum of the contributions of each stock equals the total portfolio variance, whereas the alternative measure of contribution would sum to twice the portfolio variance. This results from a type of double-counting, because adding both the rows and the columns for each stock would result in each entry in the matrix being added twice.

[6]A positive contribution to variance doesn't imply that diversification isn't beneficial. Excluding BCE from the portfolio would require that its weight be assigned to the remaining stocks, and that reallocation would increase variance even more. Variance is reduced by including more stocks and reducing the weight of all (i.e., diversifying), despite the fact that each positive-covariance security makes some contribution to variance.

[7]Unfortunately the market portfolio's Sharpe ratio

$$\frac{E(r_M) - r_f}{\sigma_M}$$

is sometimes referred to as "the market price of risk." Note, however, that the true unit of risk is variance, and the price of risk relates risk premium to variance (or to covariance for incremental risk).

efficient portfolio, such as shares of BCE, we measure risk as the *contribution* to portfolio variance. In contrast, for the efficient portfolio itself, variance is the appropriate measure of risk.

A basic principle of equilibrium is that all investments should offer the same reward-to-risk ratio. If the ratio were better for one investment than another, investors would rearrange their portfolios, tilting toward the alternative with the better tradeoff and shying away from the other. Such activity would impart pressure on security prices until the ratios were equalized. Therefore we conclude that the reward-to-risk ratios of BCE and the market portfolio should be equal:

$$\frac{E(r_B) - r_f}{\text{Cov}(r_B, r_M)} = \frac{E(r_M) - r_f}{\sigma^2_M}, \text{ or } \frac{E(R_B)}{\text{Cov}(R_B, r_M)} = \frac{E(R_M)}{\sigma^2_M} \tag{7.6}$$

To determine the fair risk premium of BCE stock, we rearrange equation 7.6 slightly to obtain

$$E(r_B) - r_f = \frac{\text{Cov}(r_B, r_M)}{\sigma^2_M}[E(r_M) - r_f] \text{ or } E(R_B) = \frac{\text{Cov}(R_B, r_M)}{\sigma^2_M}E(R_M) \tag{7.7}$$

The ratio $\text{Cov}(r_B, r_M)/\sigma^2_M$ measures the contribution of BCE stock to the variance of the market portfolio as a fraction of the total variance of the market portfolio. The ratio is called **beta** and is denoted by β. Using this measure, we can restate equation 7.7 as

$$E(r_B) = r_f + \beta_B[E(r_M) - r_f] \tag{7.8}$$

This **expected return–beta (or mean–beta) relationship** is the most familiar expression of the CAPM to practitioners.

If the expected return–beta relationship holds for any individual asset, it must hold for any combination of assets. Suppose that some portfolio P has weight w_k for stock k, where k takes on values $1, \ldots, n$. Writing out the CAPM equation 7.7 for each stock and multiplying each equation by the weight of the stock in the portfolio, we obtain these equations, one for each stock:

$$
\begin{aligned}
w_1 E(r_1) &= w_1 r_f + w_1 \beta_1 [E(r_M) - r_f] \\
+ \ w_2 E(r_2) &= w_2 r_f + w_2 \beta_2 [E(r_M) - r_f] \\
+ \ \ldots &= \ldots \\
+ \ w_n E(r_n) &= w_n r_f + w_n \beta_n [E(r_M) - r_f] \\
E(r_p) &= r_f + \beta_P [E(r_M) - r_f]
\end{aligned}
$$

Summing each column shows that the CAPM holds for the overall portfolio because $E(r_p) = \Sigma_k w_k E(r_k)$ is the expected return on the portfolio and $\beta_p = \Sigma_k w_k \beta_k$ is the portfolio beta. Incidentally, this result has to be true for the market portfolio itself.

$$E(r_M) = r_f + \beta_M[E(r_M) - r_f]$$

Indeed, this is a tautology, because $\beta_M = 1$, as we can verify by demonstrating that

$$\beta_M = \frac{\text{Cov}(r_M, r_M)}{\sigma^2_M} = \frac{\sigma^2_M}{\sigma^2_M}$$

This also establishes 1 as the weighted average value of beta across all assets. If the market beta is 1, and the market is a portfolio of all assets in the economy, the weighted average beta of all assets must be 1. Hence betas greater than 1 are considered aggressive in that investment in high-beta stocks entails above-average sensitivity to market swings. Betas below 1 can be described as defensive.

CC 3

CONCEPT CHECK

Suppose that the risk premium on the market portfolio is estimated at 8 percent with a standard deviation of 22 percent. What is the risk premium on a portfolio invested 25 percent in BCE and 75 percent in RIM, if they have betas of 1.10 and 1.25, respectively?

A word of caution: We often hear that well-managed firms will provide high rates of return. We agree this is true if one measures the *firm's* return on investments in plant and equipment. The CAPM, however, predicts returns on investments in the *securities* of the firm.

Let us say that everyone knows a firm is well run. Its stock price will therefore be bid up and, consequently, returns to shareholders who buy at those high prices will not be excessive. Security prices, in other words, reflect public information about a firm's prospects, but only the risk of the company (as measured by beta in the context of the CAPM) should affect expected returns. In a rational market investors receive high expected returns only if they are willing to bear risk.

Investors do not directly observe or determine expected returns on securities. Rather, they observe security prices and bid those prices up or down. Expected rates of return are determined by the prices investors must pay compared to the cash flows those investments might garner.

The Security Market Line

We can view the expected return–beta relationship as a reward–risk equation. The beta of a security is the appropriate measure of its risk because beta is proportional to the risk that the security contributes to the optimal risky portfolio.

Risk-averse investors measure the risk of the optimal risky portfolio by its variance. Hence, we would expect the risk premium on individual assets, to depend on the *contribution* of the asset to the portfolio. The beta of a stock measures its contribution to the variance of the market portfolio and therefore the required risk premium is a function of beta. The CAPM confirms this intuition, stating further that the security's risk premium is directly proportional to both the beta and the risk premium of the market portfolio; that is, the risk premium equals

$$\beta[E(r_M) - r_f]$$

The expected return–beta relationship can be portrayed graphically as the **security market line (SML)** in Figure 7.2. Its slope is the risk premium of the market portfolio. At the point where $\beta = 1$ on the horizontal axis (which is the market portfolio's beta), we can read off the vertical axis the expected return on the market portfolio.

It is useful to compare the security market line to the capital market line. The CML graphs the risk premiums of efficient portfolios (i.e., portfolios composed of the market and the risk-free asset) as a function of portfolio standard deviation. This is appropriate because standard deviation is a valid measure of risk for efficiently diversified portfolios that are candidates for an investor's overall portfolio. The SML, in contrast, graphs *individual asset* risk premiums as a function of asset risk. The relevant measure of risk for individual assets held as parts of well-diversified portfolios is not the asset's standard deviation or variance; it is, instead, the contribution of the asset to the portfolio variance, which we measure by the asset's beta. The SML is valid for both efficient portfolios and individual assets.

The security market line provides a benchmark for the evaluation of investment performance. Given the risk of an investment, as measured by its beta, the SML provides the required rate of return from that investment to compensate investors for risk, as well as the time value of money.

Because the security market line is the graphical representation of the expected return–beta relationship, "fairly priced" assets plot exactly on the SML; that is, their expected returns

Figure 7.2

The security
market line.

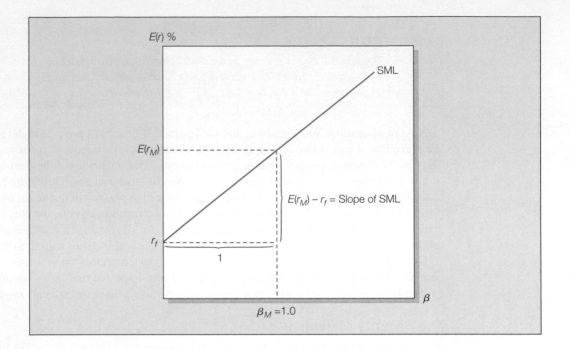

are commensurate with their risk. All securities must lie on the SML in market equilibrium. We see here how the CAPM may be of use in the money management industry. Suppose that the SML relation is used as a benchmark to assess the fair expected return on a risky asset. Then security analysis is performed to calculate the return actually expected. (Notice that we depart here from the simple CAPM world in that some investors now apply their own unique analysis to derive an "input list" that may differ from their competitors'.) If a stock is perceived to be a good buy, or underpriced, it will provide an expected return in excess of the fair return stipulated by the SML. Underpriced stocks, therefore, plot above the SML: given their betas, their expected returns are greater than dictated by the CAPM. Overpriced stocks plot below the SML.

The difference between the fair and actually expected rates of return on a stock is called the stock's **alpha**, denoted α. For example, if the market is expected to be 14 percent, a stock has a beta of 1.2, and the T-bill rate is 6 percent, the SML would predict an expected return on the stock of $6 + 1.2 (14 - 6) = 15.6$ percent. If one believed the stock would provide a return of 17 percent, the implied alpha would be 1.4 percent (see Figure 7.3). One could say that security analysis, which we cover in Part Five, is about uncovering securities with non-zero alphas.

CC 4

CONCEPT CHECK

Stock XYZ has an expected return of 12 percent and risk of $\beta = 1$. Stock ABC has expected return of 13 percent and $\beta = 1.5$. The market's expected return is 11 percent and $r_f = 5$ percent.

a. According to the CAPM, which stock is a better buy?

b. What is the alpha of each stock? Plot the SML and each stock's risk return point on one graph. Show the alphas graphically.

Figure 7.3

The SML and a positive-alpha stock.

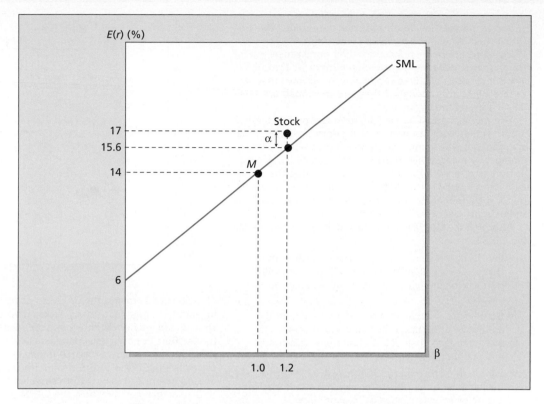

The CAPM is also useful in capital budgeting decisions. For a firm considering a new project, the CAPM can provide the return that the project needs to yield, based on its beta, to be acceptable to investors. Managers can use the CAPM to obtain this cutoff internal rate of return (IRR) or "hurdle rate" for the project.

The boxed article describes how the CAPM can be used in capital budgeting. It also discusses some empirical anomalies concerning the model, which we address in detail in Chapters 8, 9, and 10.

CC 5

CONCEPT CHECK

The risk-free rate is 8 percent and the expected return on the market portfolio is 16 percent. A firm considers a project that is expected to have a beta of 1.3.
a. What is the required rate of return on the project?
b. If the expected IRR of the project is 19 percent, should it be accepted?

EXAMPLE 7.1   **Using the CAPM**

Yet another use of the CAPM is in utility rate-making cases. In this case, the issue is the rate of return that a regulated utility should be allowed to earn on its investment in plant and equipment. Suppose that the equityholders have invested $100 million in the firm and that the beta of the equity is .6. If the T-bill rate is 6 percent and the market risk premium is 4 percent, then the fair profits to the firm would be assessed as $6 + .6(4) = 8.4$ percent of the $100 million investment, or $8.4 million. The firm would be allowed to set prices at a level expected to generate these profits.

TALES FROM THE FAR SIDE

Financial markets' evaluation of risk determines the way firms invest. What if the markets are wrong?

Investors are rarely praised for their good sense. But for the past two decades a growing number of firms have based their decisions on a model which assumes that people are perfectly rational. If they are irrational, are businesses making the wrong choices?

The model, known as the "capital-asset pricing model," or CAPM, has come to dominate modern finance. Almost any manager who wants to defend a project—be it a brand, a factory or a corporate merger—must justify his decision partly based on the CAPM. The reason is that the model tells a firm how to calculate the return that its investors demand. If shareholders are to benefit, the returns from any project must clear this "hurdle rate."

Although the CAPM is complicated, it can be reduced to five simple ideas:

- Investors can eliminate some risks—such as the risk that workers will strike, or that a firm's boss will quit—by diversifying across many regions and sectors.

- Some risks, such as that of a global recession, cannot be eliminated though diversification. So even a basket of all of the stocks in a stockmarket will still be risky.

- People must be rewarded for investing in such a risky basket by earning returns above those that they can get on safer assets, such as Treasury bills.

- The rewards on a specific investment depend only on the extent to which it affects the market basket's risk.

- Conveniently, that contribution to the market basket's risk can be captured by a single measure—dubbed "beta"—which expresses the relationship between the investment's risk and the market's.

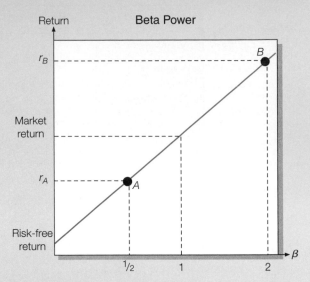

Beta is what makes the CAPM so powerful. Although an investment may face many risks, diversified investors should care only about those that are related to the market basket. Beta not only tells managers how to measure those risks, but it also allows them to translate them directly into a hurdle rate. If the future profits from a project will not exceed that rate, it is not worth shareholders' money.

The diagram shows how the CAPM works. Safe investments, such as Treasury bills, have a beta of zero. Riskier investments should earn a premium over the risk-free rate which increases with beta. Those whose risks roughly match the market's have a beta of one, by definition, and should earn the market return.

So suppose that a firm is considering two projects, A and B. Project A has a beta of $\frac{1}{2}$: when the market rises or falls by 10%, its returns tend to rise or fall by 5%. So its risk

7.2 ASSUMPTIONS AND EXTENSIONS OF THE CAPM

Now that we understand the basic insights of the CAPM, we can more explicitly identify the set of simplifying assumptions on which it relies. A model consists of (1) a set of assumptions, (2) logical/mathematical development of the model through manipulation of those assumptions, and (3) a set of predictions. Assuming the logical/mathematical manipulations are free

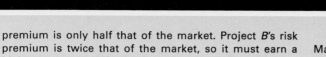

premium is only half that of the market. Project *B*'s risk premium is twice that of the market, so it must earn a higher return to justify the expenditure.

Never Knowingly Underpriced

But there is one small problem with the CAPM: Financial economists have found that beta is not much use for explaining rates of return on firms' shares. Worse, there appears to be another measure which explains these returns quite well.

That measure is the ratio of a firm's book value (the value of its assets at the time they entered the balance sheet) to its market value. Several studies have found that, on average, companies that have high book-to-market ratios tend to earn excess returns over long periods, even after adjusting for the risks that are associated with beta.

The discovery of this book-to-market effect has sparked a fierce debate among financial economists. All of them agree that some risks ought to carry greater rewards. But they are now deeply divided over how risk should be measured. Some argue that since investors are rational, the book-to-market effect must be capturing an extra risk factor. They conclude, therefore, that managers should incorporate the book-to-market effect into their hurdle rates. They have labeled this alternative hurdle rate the "new estimator of expected return," or NEER.

Other financial economists, however, dispute this approach. Since there is no obvious extra risk associated with a high book-to-market ratio, they say, investors must be mistaken. Put simply, they are underpricing high book-to-market stocks, causing them to earn abnormally high returns. If managers of such firms try to exceed those inflated hurdle rates, they will forgo many profitable investments. With economists now at odds, what is a conscientious manager to do?

In a new paper, Jeremy Stein, an economist at the Massachusetts Institute of Technology's business school, offers a paradoxical answer.* If investors are rational, then beta cannot be the only measure of risk, so managers should stop using it. Conversely, if investors are irrational, then beta is still the right measure in many cases. Mr. Stein argues that if beta captures an asset's fundamental risk—that is, its contribution to the market basket's risk—then it will often make sense for managers to pay attention to it, even if investors are somehow failing to.

Often, but not always. At the heart of Mr. Stein's argument lies a crucial distinction—that between (*a*) boosting a firm's long-term value and (*b*) trying to raise its share price. If investors are rational, these are the same thing: any decision that raises long-term value will instantly increase the share price as well. But if investors are making predictable mistakes, a manager must choose.

For instance, if he wants to increase today's share price—perhaps because he wants to sell his shares, or to fend off a takeover attempt—he must usually stick with the NEER approach, accommodating investors' misperceptions. But if he is interested in long-term value, he should usually continue to use beta. Showing a flair for marketing, Mr. Stein labels this farsighted alternative to NEER the "fundamental asset risk"—or FAR—approach.

Mr. Stein's conclusions will no doubt irritate many company bosses, who are fond of denouncing their investors' myopia. They have resented the way in which CAPM—with its assumption of investor infallibility—has come to play an important role in boardroom decision-making. But it now appears that if they are right, and their investors are wrong, then those same far-sighted managers ought to be the CAPM's biggest fans.

---

*Jeremy Stein, "Rational Capital Budgeting in an Irrational World," *The Journal of Business*, October 1996.

Source: "Tales from the FAR Side," *The Economist*, November 16, 1996, p. 8.

of errors, we can test a model in two ways, *normative* and *positive*. Normative tests examine the assumptions of the model, while positive tests examine the predictions.

If a model's assumptions are valid, and the development is error-free, the predictions of the model must be true. In this case, testing the assumptions is synonymous with testing the model. But few, if any, models can pass the normative test. In most cases, as with the CAPM, the assumptions are admittedly invalid—we recognize that we have simplified reality, and therefore to this extent are relying on "untrue" assumptions. The motivation for invoking unrealistic assumptions is clear; we simply cannot solve a model that is perfectly consistent with the full complexity of real-life markets. As we've noted, the need to use simplifying assumptions is not peculiar to economics—it characterizes all of science.

Assumptions are chosen first and foremost to render the model solvable. But we prefer assumptions to which the model is "robust." A model is robust with respect to an assumption if its predictions are not highly sensitive to violation of the assumption. If we use only assumptions to which the model is robust, the model's predictions will be reasonably accurate despite its shortcomings. The upshot of all this is that tests of models are almost always positive—we judge a model on the success of its empirical predictions. This standard brings statistics into any science and requires us to take a stand on what are acceptable levels of

TABLE 7.1

The Assumptions
of the CAPM

1. Individual behaviour
   a. Investors are rational, mean-variance optimizers.
   b. Their planning horizon is a single period.
   c. Investors have homogenous expectations (identical input lists).
2. Market structure
   a. All assets are publicly held and trade on public exchanges, short positions
       are allowed, and investors can borrow or lend at a common risk-free rate.
   b. All information is publicly available.
   c. No taxes.
   d. No transaction costs.

significance and power.[8] Because the nonrealism of the assumptions precludes a normative test, the positive test is really a test of the robustness of the model to its assumptions.

Assumptions of the CAPM

Table 7.1 enumerates the list of assumptions underlying the CAPM. In our discussion so far, we have cited explicitly only these three assumptions:

1. *a.* Investors are rational, mean-variance optimizers.
1. *c.* Investors use identical input lists, referred to as "homogenous expectations."
2. *a.* All assets are publicly traded (short positions are allowed) and investors can borrow or
        lend at a common risk-free rate.

The first assumption is far-reaching. Its "visible" part is that investors are not concerned with higher moments (skew and kurtosis) that may "fatten" the left tail of the return distribution. We can ascertain the validity of this assumption from statistical tests of the normality of return distributions as we did in Chapter 4.

Less visible is that assumption 1*a* rules out investor concern with the correlation of asset returns with inflation or with prices of important consumption items such as housing or energy. The extra demand for assets that can be used to hedge these "extra market" risks would increase their prices and reduce their risk premiums in violation of the CAPM.

A similar effect would apply to events farther in the future and requires the addition of assumption 1*b*, which limits investors to a common single-period horizon. Consider a possible decline in future interest rates. Investors would be unhappy about this event to the extent that it would reduce the expected income their investments could throw off in the future. Assets whose returns are negatively correlated with interest rates (e.g., long-term bonds) would hedge this risk and thus command higher prices and lower risk premiums. Because of such hedging demands, correlation with any parameter describing future investment opportunities can result in violations

[8]To illustrate the meanings of significance and power, consider a test of the efficacy of a new drug. The agency testing the drug may make two possible errors. The drug may be useless (or even harmful), but the agency may conclude that it is useful. This is called a "Type I" error. The *significance level* of a test is the probability of a Type I error. Typical practice is to fix the level of significance at some low level, for example 5 percent. In the case of drug testing, for example, the first goal is to avoid introducing ineffective or harmful treatments. The other possible error is that the drug is actually useful, but the testing procedure concludes it is not. This mistake, called "Type II" error, would lead us to discard a useful treatment. The *power* of the test is the probability of avoiding Type II error (i.e., one minus the probability of making such an error), that is, the probability of accepting the drug if it is indeed useful. We want tests that, at a given level of significance, have the most power, so we will admit effective drugs with high probability. In social sciences in particular, available tests often have low power, in which case they are susceptible to Type II error and will reject a correct model (a "useful drug") with high frequency. "The drug is useful" is analogous in the CAPM to alphas being zero. When the test data reject the hypothesis that observed alphas are zero at the desired level of significance, the CAPM fails. However, if the test has low power, the probability that we accept the model when true is not all that high.

of the CAPM mean beta equation (and therefore with the efficiency of the market portfolio). A single-period investor horizon eliminates these possibilities.

Interestingly, assumption 1c (investors optimize with the same input list) looks ominously restrictive, but it is actually not all that problematic. With the addition of assumption 2b (all information is public), investors will generally be close to agreement. Moreover, trades of investors who derive different input lists will offset and prices will reflect consensus expectations. We will later allow for the likelihood that some investors expend resources to obtain private information and exploit prices that don't reflect the insights derived from this information. But regardless of their success, it is reasonable to assert that, absent private information, investors should assume alpha values are zero.

The assumption that all assets are tradable (2a) is essential for identical input lists. It allows us to ignore federal and state assets and liabilities. More importantly, privately held but non-traded assets such as human capital and private business can create large differences in investor portfolios. Consider owners of a family business. Prudence dictates that they avoid assets that are highly correlated with their businesses. Similarly, investors should avoid stock returns that are positively correlated with their personal income; for example, Boeing employees should avoid investing in the airline and related businesses. Differential demands arising from this consideration can lead to violation of the mean-beta equation and derail the mean-variance efficiency of the index portfolio.

Restrictions on borrowing (or significantly higher rates on borrowed funds), which violates assumption 2a, also can create problems for the CAPM, because borrowers and lenders will arrive at different tangency portfolios and thus different optimal risky portfolios.

Taxes create conditions in which two investors can realize different after-tax returns from the same stock. Such distortions might, in principle, lead to different after-tax optimal risky portfolios to different investors—hence assumption 2c (no taxes).

Despite an extension to the CAPM that incorporates personal taxes on dividends and capital gains,[9] there is no decisive evidence that taxes are a major factor in stock returns. A plausible explanation for this negative finding relies on "clientele" and supply effects. If high-tax-bracket investors shy away from high-yield (dividend paying) stocks and thus force down their prices, this will lead tax-exempt investors to view the stocks as a bargain and take up the slack in demand. On the other end, if corporations see that high dividend yields reduce stock prices, they will simply substitute stock repurchases for dividends, reinforcing the clientele effect in neutralizing tax effects.

Finally, transaction costs inhibit trades and thus the reaction to changes in information—hence assumption 2d (no transaction costs). While in reality trading costs have fallen, remaining differentials in trading costs may still play an important role in stock returns.

Challenges and Extensions to the CAPM

Which assumptions are most worrisome? We start with the fact that short positions are not as easy to take as long ones for three reasons:

1. The liability of investors who hold a short position in an asset is potentially unlimited, since the price may rise without limit. Hence a large short position requires large collateral, and proceeds cannot be used to invest in other risky assets.

2. There is a limited supply of shares of any stock to be borrowed by would-be short sellers. It often happens that investors simply cannot find shares to borrow in order to short.

3. Many investment companies are prohibited from short sales. The United States and other countries further restrict short sales by regulation.

---

[9]Michael J. Brennan, "Taxes, Market Valuation, and Corporate Finance Policy," *National Tax Journal*, December 1973.

Why are short sales important? Notice that assumption 1*a* begins with "investors are rational. . . ." When investors exhibit "irrational exuberance" (excessive optimism) about an asset and, as a result, prices rise above intrinsic values, rational investors will take short positions, thus holding down the price. But with effective restrictions, short sales can fail to prevent prices rising to unsustainable levels that are precursors to a correction or even a crash. This really defines a "bubble."

Three unrealistic assumptions, 2*a* (all assets trade) and 2*d* (there are no transaction costs), combined with 1*b* (single-period horizon), generate the major challenges to the model. These challenges have motivated a set of extensions that, even today, are "under construction" in one way or another. For this reason, none of the extensions has decisively superseded the simple CAPM in the industry. It is an impressive phenomenon that, despite failing many empirical tests, the compelling logic of the CAPM keeps it at the centre of the investment industry. However, for better insight into the CAPM, it is useful to understand the extensions of the model.

The Zero-Beta Model

Efficient frontier portfolios have a number of interesting characteristics, independently derived by Merton and Roll.[10] Three of these are:

1. Any portfolio that is a combination of two frontier portfolios is itself on the efficient frontier.

2. The expected return of any asset can be expressed as an exact linear function of the expected return on any two efficient frontier portfolios P and Q according to the following equation:

$$E(r_i) - E(r_Q) = [E(r_P) - E(r_Q)]\frac{\text{Cov}(r_i,r_P) - \text{Cov}(r_P,r_Q)}{\sigma^2_P - \text{Cov}(r_P,r_Q)} \tag{7.9}$$

3. Every portfolio on the efficient frontier, except for the global minimum-variance portfolio, has a "companion" portfolio on the bottom (inefficient) half of the frontier with which it is uncorrelated. Because it is uncorrelated, the companion portfolio is referred to as the **zero-beta portfolio** of the efficient portfolio. If we choose the market portfolio M and its zero-beta companion portfolio Z, then equation 7.9 simplifies to the CAPM-like equation

$$E(r_i) - E(r_z) = [E(R_M) - E(R_z)]\frac{\text{Cov}(r_i,r_M)}{\sigma^2_M} = \beta_i[E(r_M) - E(r_z)] \tag{7.10}$$

Equation 7.10 resembles the SML of the CAPM, except that the risk-free rate is replaced with the expected return on the zero-beta companion of the market index portfolio.

Fischer Black used these properties to show that equation 7.10 is the CAPM equation that results when investors face restrictions on borrowing and/or investment in the risk-free asset.[11] In this case, at least some investors will choose portfolios on the high-risk portion of the efficient frontier that are not necessarily the market index portfolio. Put differently, investors who wish to borrow and leverage their portfolios but find it impossible or costly will instead tilt their portfolios toward high-beta stocks and away from low-beta ones. As a result, prices of high-beta stocks will rise, and their risk premium will fall. The SML will be flatter than in the simple CAPM. You

[10]Robert C. Merton, "An Analytic Derivation of the Efficient Portfolio Frontier," *Journal of Financial and Quantitative Analysis*, 1972; Richard Roll, "A Critique of the Asset Pricing Theory's Tests: Part I: On Past and Potential Testability of the Theory," *Journal of Financial Economics* 4 (1977).

[11]Fischer Black, "Capital Market Equilibrium with Restricted Borrowing," *Journal of Business*, July 1972.

can see from equation 7.10 that the risk premium on the market portfolio is smaller (because the expected return on the zero-beta portfolio is greater than the risk-free rate) and therefore the reward for bearing beta risk is smaller.

Labour Income and Nontraded Assets

Two important asset classes that are *not* traded are human capital and privately held businesses. The discounted value of future labour income exceeds the total market value of traded assets. The market value of privately held corporations and businesses is of the same order of magnitude. Human capital and private enterprises are different types of assets with possibly different implications for equilibrium returns on traded securities.

Privately held business may be the lesser of the two sources of departures from the CAPM. Suppose that privately held business have similar risk characteristics as those of traded assets. In this case, individuals can partially offset the diversification problems posed by their nontraded entrepreneurial assets by reducing their portfolio demand for securities of similar, traded assets. Thus, the CAPM expected return–beta equation may not be greatly disrupted by the presence of entrepreneurial income.

To the extent that private enterprises have different risk characteristics from traded securities, a portfolio of traded assets that best hedges the risk of typical private business would enjoy excess demand from the population of private business owners. The price of assets in this portfolio will be bid up relative to the CAPM considerations, and the expected returns on these securities will be lower in relation to their systematic risk. Conversely, securities highly correlated with such risk will have high equilibrium risk premiums and may appear to exhibit positive alphas relative to the conventional SML. In fact, Heaton and Lucas show that adding proprietary income to a standard linear asset-pricing model improves its predictive performance.[12]

The size of labour income and its special nature is of greater concern for the validity of the CAPM. The possible effect of labour income on equilibrium returns can be appreciated from its important effect on personal portfolio choice. Despite the fact that an individual can borrow against labour income (via a home mortgage) and reduce some of the uncertainty about future labour income via life insurance, human capital is less "portable" across time and may be more difficult to hedge using traded securities than nontraded business. This may put pressure on security prices and result in departures from the CAPM expected return–beta equation. Thus, the demand for stocks of labour-intensive firms may be reduced, and these stocks may require a higher expected return than predicted by the CAPM.

Mayers[13] derives the equilibrium expected return–beta equation for an economy in which individuals are endowed with labour income of varying size relative to their nonlabour capital. The resultant SML equation is

$$E(R_i) = E(R_M) \frac{\text{Cov}(R_i,R_M) + \dfrac{P_H}{P_M}\text{Cov}(R_i,R_M)}{\sigma^2_M + \dfrac{P_H}{P_M}\text{Cov}(R_M,R_H)} \tag{7.11}$$

where

P_H = value of aggregate human capital

P_M = market value of traded assets (market portfolio)

R_H = excess rate of return on aggregate human capital

---

[12]John Heaton and Deborah Lucas, "Portfolio Choice and Asset Prices: The Importance of Entrepreneurial Risk," *Journal of Finance* 55 (June 2000). This paper offers evidence of the effect of entrepreneurial risk on both portfolio choice and the risk–return relationship.
[13]David Mayers, "Nonmarketable Assets and Capital Market Equilibrium Under Uncertainty," in M. C. Jensen, ed., *Studies in the Theory of Capital Markets* (New York: Praeger, 1972).

The CAPM measure of systematic risk, beta, is replaced in the extended model by an adjusted beta that also accounts for covariance with the portfolio of aggregate human capital. Notice that the ratio of human capital to market value of all traded assets, $\frac{P_H}{P_M}$, may well be greater than 1.0, and hence the effect of the covariance of a security with labour income, $\text{Cov}(R_i, R_H)$, relative to the average, $\text{Cov}(R_M, R_H)$, is likely to be economically significant. Since we expect the average covariance to be positive, the adjusted beta of the average security will be smaller than the CAPM beta. The model thus predicts a security market line that is less steep than that of the standard CAPM. This may help explain the average negative alpha of high-beta securities and positive alpha of low-beta securities that lead to the statistical failure of the CAPM equation. In Chapter 11 on empirical evidence we present additional results along these lines.

A Multiperiod Model and Hedge Portfolios

Robert C. Merton revolutionized financial economics by using continuous-time models to extend models of asset pricing.[14] While his contributions to option-pricing theory and financial engineering (along with those of Fischer Black and Myron Scholes) may have had greater impact on the investment industry, his solo contribution to portfolio theory was equally important for our understanding of the risk–return relationship.

In his basic model, Merton relaxes the "single-period" myopic assumptions about investors. He envisions individuals who optimize a lifetime consumption/investment plan, and who continually adapt consumption/investment decisions to current wealth and planned retirement age. When uncertainty about portfolio returns is the only source of risk and investment opportunities remain unchanged through time, that is, there is no change in the risk-free rate or the probability distribution of the return on the market portfolio or individual securities, Merton's so-called intertemporal capital asset pricing model (ICAPM) predicts the same expected return–beta relationship as the single-period equation.[15]

But the situation changes when we include additional sources of risk. These extra risks are of two general kinds. One concerns changes in the parameters describing investment opportunities, such as future risk-free rates, expected returns, or the risk of the market portfolio. Suppose that the real interest rate may change over time. If it falls in some future period, one's level of wealth will now support a lower stream of real consumption. Future spending plans, for example, for retirement spending, may be put in jeopardy. To the extent that returns on some securities are correlated with changes in the risk-free rate, a portfolio can be formed to hedge such risk, and investors will bid up the price (and bid down the expected return) of those hedge assets. Investors will sacrifice some expected return if they can find assets whose returns will be higher when other parameters (in this case, the risk-free rate) change adversely.

The other additional source of risk concerns the prices of the consumption goods that can be purchased with any amount of wealth. Consider inflation risk. In addition to the expected level and volatility of their nominal wealth, investors must be concerned about the cost of living—what those dollars can buy. Therefore, inflation risk is an important extramarket source of risk, and investors may be willing to sacrifice some expected return to purchase securities whose returns will be higher when the cost of living changes adversely. If so, hedging demands for securities that help to protect against inflation risk would affect portfolio choice and thus expected return. One can push this conclusion even further, arguing that empirically significant hedging demands may arise for important subsectors of consumer expenditures; for example, investors may bid up share prices of energy companies that will hedge energy price uncertainty. These sorts of effects may characterize any assets that hedge important extramarket sources of risk.

---

[14]Merton's classic works are collected in *Continuous-Time Finance* (Oxford, UK: Basil Blackwell, 1992).

[15]Eugene F. Fama also made this point in "Multiperiod Consumption–Investment Decisions," *American Economic Review* 60 (1970).

More generally, suppose we can identify K sources of extramarket risk and find K associated hedge portfolios. Then, Merton's ICAPM expected return–beta equation would generalize the SML to a multi-index version:

$$E(R_i) = \beta_{iM}E(R_M) + \sum_{t=1}^{K} \beta_{ik}E(R_k) \tag{7.12}$$

where β_{iM} is the familiar security beta on the market-index portfolio, and β_{ik} is the beta on the kth hedge portfolio.

Other multifactor models using additional factors that do not arise from extramarket sources of risk have been developed and lead to SMLs of a form identical to that of the ICAPM. These models also may be considered extensions of the CAPM in the broad sense. We examine these models in the next chapter.

A Consumption-Based CAPM

The logic of the CAPM together with the hedging demands noted in the previous subsection suggests that it might be useful to centre the model directly on consumption. Such models were first proposed by Mark Rubinstein, Robert Lucas, and Douglas Breeden.[16]

In a lifetime consumption plan, the investor must in each period balance the allocation of current wealth between today's consumption and the savings and investment that will support future consumption. When optimized, the utility value from an additional dollar of consumption today must be equal to the utility value of the expected future consumption that can be financed by that additional dollar of wealth.[17] Future wealth will grow from labour income, as well as returns on that dollar when invested in the optimal complete portfolio.

Suppose risky assets are available and you wish to increase expected consumption growth by allocating some of your savings to a risky portfolio. How would we measure the risk of these assets? As a general rule, investors will value additional income more highly during difficult economic times (when resources are scarce) than in affluent times (when consumption is already abundant). An asset will therefore be viewed as riskier in terms of consumption if it has positive covariance with consumption growth—in other words, if its payoff is higher when consumption is already high and lower when consumption is relatively restricted. Therefore, equilibrium risk premiums will be greater for assets that exhibit higher covariance with consumption growth. Developing this insight, we can write the risk premium on an asset as a function of its "consumption risk" as follows:

$$E(R_i) = \beta_{iC}RP_C \tag{7.13}$$

where portfolio C may be interpreted as a *consumption-tracking portfolio* (also called a *consumption-mimicking portfolio*), that is, the portfolio with the highest correlation with consumption growth; β_{iC} is the slope coefficient in the regression of asset i's excess returns, R_i, on those of the consumption-tracking portfolio; and, finally, RP_C is the risk premium associated with consumption uncertainty, which is measured by the expected excess return on the consumption-tracking portfolio:

$$RP_C = E(R_C) = E(r_C) - r_f \tag{7.14}$$

[16]Mark Rubinstein, "The Valuation of Uncertain Income Streams and the Pricing of Options," *Bell Journal of Economics and Management Science* 7 (1976), pp. 407–25; Robert Lucas, "Asset Prices in an Exchange Economy," *Econometrica* 46 (1978), pp. 1429–45; Douglas Breeden, "An Intertemporal Asset Pricing Model with Stochastic Consumption and Investment Opportunities," *Journal of Financial Economics* 7 (1979), pp. 265–96.

[17]Wealth at each point in time equals the market value of assets in the balance sheet plus the present value of future labour income. These models of consumption and investment decisions are often made tractable by assuming investors exhibit constant relative risk aversion, or CRRA. CRRA implies that an individual invests a constant proportion of wealth in the optimal risky portfolio regardless of the level of wealth. You might recall that our prescription for optimal capital allocation in Chapter 5 also called for an optimal investment proportion in the risky portfolio regardless of the level of wealth. The utility function we employed there also exhibited CRRA.

Notice how similar this conclusion is to the conventional CAPM. The consumption-tracking portfolio in the CCAPM plays the role of the market portfolio in the conventional CAPM. This is in accord with its focus on the risk of *consumption* opportunities rather than the risk und return of the *dollar* value of the portfolio. The excess return on the consumption-tracking portfolio plays the role of the excess return on the market portfolio, M. Both approaches result in linear, single-factor models that differ mainly in the identity of the factor they use.

In contrast to the CAPM, the beta of the market portfolio on the market factor of the CCAPM is not necessarily 1. It is perfectly plausible and empirically evident that this beta is substantially greater than 1. This means that in the linear relationship between the market index risk premium and that of the consumption portfolio,

$$E(R_M) = \alpha_M + \beta_{MC}E(R_C) + \varepsilon_M \tag{7.15}$$

where α_M and ε_M allow for empirical deviation from the exact model in equation 7.15, and β_{MC} is not necessarily equal to 1.

Because the CCAPM is so similar to the CAPM, one might wonder about its usefulness. Indeed, just as the CAPM is empirically flawed because not all assets are traded, so is the CCAPM. The attractiveness of this model is in that it compactly incorporates consumption hedging and possible changes in investment opportunities, that is, in the parameters of the return distributions in a single-factor framework. There is a price to pay for this compactness, however. Consumption growth figures are published infrequently (monthly at most) compared with financial assets, and are measured with significant error. Nevertheless, recent empirical research[18] indicates that this model is more successful in explaining realized returns than the CAPM, which is a reason why students of investments should be familiar with it. We return to this issue, as well as empirical evidence concerning the CCAPM, in Chapter 11.

Liquidity and the CAPM

Despite assumption 2*d* saying that that securities can be traded costlessly, the CAPM has little to say about trading activity. In the equilibrium of the CAPM, all investors share all available information and demand identical portfolios of risky assets. The awkward implication of this result is that there is no reason for trade. If all investors hold identical portfolios of risky assets, then when new (unexpected) information arrives, prices will change commensurately, but each investor will continue to hold a piece of the market portfolio, which requires no exchange of assets. How do we square this implication with the observation that on a typical day trading volume amounts to several billion shares? One obvious answer is heterogeneous expectations, that is, beliefs not shared by the entire market. Diverse beliefs will give rise to trading as investors attempt to profit by rearranging portfolios in accordance with their now-heterogeneous demands. In reality, trading (and trading costs) will be of great importance to investors.

The **liquidity** of an asset is the ease and speed with which it can be sold at fair market value in a timely fashion. Part of liquidity is the cost of engaging in a transaction, particularly the bid–asked spread. Another part is price impact—the adverse movement in price one would encounter when attempting to execute a larger trade. Yet another component is immediacy—the ability to sell the asset quickly without reverting to fire-sale prices. Conversely, **illiquidity** can be measured in part by the discount from fair market value a seller must accept if the asset is to be sold quickly. A perfectly liquid asset is one that would entail no illiquidity discount.

Liquidity (or the lack of it) has long been recognized as an important characteristic that affects asset values. In legal cases, courts have routinely applied very steep discounts to the values of

---

[18]Ravi Jagannathan and Yong Wang, "Lazy Investors, Discretionary Consumption, and the Cross-Section of Stock Returns," *Journal of Finance* 62 (August 2007), pp. 1633–61.

businesses that cannot be publicly traded. But liquidity has not always been appreciated as an important factor in security markets, presumably due to the relatively small trading cost per transaction compared with the large costs of trading assets such as real estate. The breakthrough came in the work of Amihud and Mendelson,[19] and today liquidity is increasingly viewed as an important determinant of prices and expected returns. We supply only a brief synopsis of this important topic here and provide empirical evidence in Chapter 11.

One important component of trading cost is the bid–asked spread. For example, in electronic markets, the limit-order book contains the "inside spread," that is, the difference between the highest price at which some investor will purchase any shares and the lowest price at which another investor is willing to sell. The effective bid–asked spread will also depend on the size of the desired transaction. Larger purchases will require a trader to move deeper into the limit-order book and accept less-attractive prices. While inside spreads on electronic markets often appear extremely low, effective spreads can be much larger, because the limit orders are good for only small numbers of shares.

There is greater emphasis today on the component of the spread that is due to asymmetric information. Asymmetric information is the potential for one trader to have private information about the value of the security that is not known to the trading partner. To see why such an asymmetry can affect the market, think about the problems facing someone buying a used car. The seller knows more about the car than the buyer, so the buyer naturally wonders if the seller is trying to get rid of the car because it is a "lemon." At the least, buyers worried about overpaying will shave the prices they are willing to pay for a car of uncertain quality. In extreme cases of asymmetric information, trading may cease altogether.[20] Similarly, traders who post offers to buy or sell at limit prices need to be worried about being picked off by better-informed traders who hit their limit prices only when they are out of line with the intrinsic value of the firm.

Broadly speaking, we may envision investors trading securities for two reasons. Some trades are driven by "noninformational" motives, for example, selling assets to raise cash for a big purchase, or even just for portfolio rebalancing. These sorts of trades, which are not motivated by private information that bears on the value of the traded security, are called *noise trades*. Security dealers will earn a profit from the bid–asked spread when transacting with noise traders (also called *liquidity traders* since their trades may derive from needs for liquidity, i.e., cash).

Other transactions are initiated by traders who believe they have come across information that a security is mispriced. But if that information gives them an advantage, it must be disadvantageous to the other party in the transaction. In this manner information traders impose a cost on both dealers and other investors who post limit orders. Although on average dealers make money from the bid–asked spread when transacting with liquidity traders, they will absorb losses from information traders. Similarly, any trader posting a limit order is at risk from information traders. The response is to increase limit-ask prices and decrease limit-bid orders—in other words, the spread must widen. The greater the relative importance of information traders, the greater the required spread to compensate for the potential losses from information traders. In the end, therefore, liquidity traders absorb most of the cost of the information trades because the bid–asked spread that they must pay on their "innocent" trades widens when informational asymmetry is more severe.

The discount in a security price that results from illiquidity can be surprisingly large, far larger than the bid–asked spread. Consider a security with a bid–asked spread of 1 percent.

---

[19]Yakov Amihud and Haim Mendelson, "Asset Pricing and the Bid–Ask Spread," *Journal of Financial Economics* 17 (1986). A summary of the ensuing large body of literature on liquidity can be found in Yakov Amihud, Haim Mendelson, and Lasse Heje Pedersen, "Liquidity and Asset Prices," *Foundations and Trends in Finance* 1, no. 4 (2005).

[20]The problem of informational asymmetry in markets was introduced by the 2001 Nobel laureate George A. Akerlof and has since become known as the *lemons problem*. A good introduction to Akerlof's contributions can be found in George A. Akerlof, *An Economic Theorist's Book of Tales* (Cambridge, UK: Cambridge University Press, 1984).

Suppose it will change hands once a year for the next three years and then will be held forever by the third buyer. For the last trade, the investor will pay for the security 99.5 percent or .995 of its fair price; the price is reduced by half the spread that will be incurred when the stock is sold. The second buyer, knowing the security will be sold a year later for .995 of fair value, and having to absorb half the spread upon purchase, will be willing to pay .995 − .005/1.05 = .9902 (i.e., 99.02 percent of fair value), if the cost of trading is discounted at a rate of 5 percent. Finally, the current buyer, knowing the loss next year, when the stock will be sold for .9902 of fair value (a discount of .0098), will pay for the security only .995 − .0098/1.05 = .9857. Thus the discount has ballooned from .5 percent to 1.43 percent. In other words, the present values of all three future trading costs (spreads) are discounted into the current price.[21] Extending this logic, if the security will be traded once a year forever, its current illiquidity cost will equal immediate cost plus the present value of a perpetuity of .5 percent at an annual discount rate of 5 percent, that is, .005 + .005/.05 = .105, or 10.5 percent! Obviously, liquidity is of potentially large value and should not be ignored in deriving the equilibrium value of securities.

As trading costs are higher, the illiquidity discount will be greater. Of course, if someone can buy a share at a lower price, the expected rate of return will be higher. Therefore, we should expect to see less-liquid securities offer higher average rates of return. But this **illiquidity premium** need not rise in direct proportion to trading cost. If an asset is less liquid, it will be shunned by frequent traders and held instead by longer term traders who are less affected by high trading costs. Hence in equilibrium, investors with long holding periods will, on average, hold more of the illiquid securities, while short-horizon investors will more strongly prefer liquid securities. This "clientele effect" mitigates the effect of the bid–asked spread for illiquid securities. The end result is that the liquidity premium should increase with trading costs (measured by the bid–asked spread) at a decreasing rate. Figure 7.4 confirms this prediction.

Figure 7.4

The relationship between illiquidity and average returns.

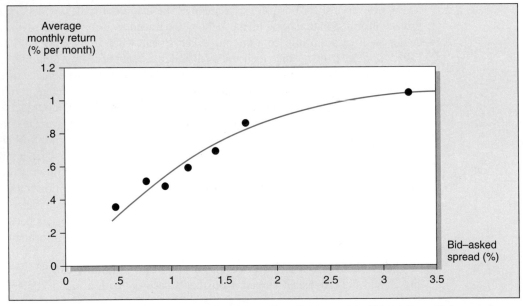

Source: Derived from Yakov Amihud and Haim Mendelson, "Asset Pricing and the Bid–Ask Spread," *Journal of Financial Economics* 17 (1986), pp. 223–49.

[21]We will see another instance of such capitalization of trading costs in Chapter 11, where one explanation for large discounts on closed-end funds is the substantial present value of a *stream* of apparently small per-period expenses.

So far, we have shown that the expected level of liquidity can affect prices, and therefore expected rates of return. What about unanticipated *changes* in liquidity? In some circumstances, liquidity can unexpectedly dry up. For example, in the financial crisis of 2008, as many investors attempted to reduce leverage and cash out their positions, finding buyers for some assets became difficult. Many mortgage-backed securities stopped trading altogether. Liquidity had evaporated. Nor was this an unheard-of phenomenon. The market crash of 1987, as well as the failure of Long-Term Capital Management in 1998, also saw large declines in liquidity across broad segments of the market.

In fact, several studies have investigated variation in a number of measures of liquidity for large samples of stocks and found that when liquidity in one stock decreases, it tends to decrease in other stocks at the same time; thus liquidity across stocks shows significant correlation.[22] In other words, variation in liquidity has an important systematic component. Not surprisingly, investors demand compensation for exposure to *liquidity risk*. The extra expected return they demand for bearing liquidity risk modifies the CAPM expected return–beta relationship.

Following up on this insight,[23] Amihud demonstrates that firms with greater liquidity uncertainty have higher average returns. Later studies focus on exposure to *marketwide* liquidity risk, as measured by a "liquidity beta." Analogously to a traditional market beta, the liquidity beta measures the sensitivity of a firm's returns to changes in market liquidity (whereas the traditional beta measures return sensitivity to the market return). Firms that provide better returns when market liquidity falls offer some protection against liquidity risk, and thus should be priced higher and offer lower expected returns. In fact, we will see in Chapter 11 that firms with high liquidity betas have offered higher average returns, just as theory predicts.[24] Moreover, the liquidity premium that emerges from these studies appears to be of roughly the same order of magnitude as the market risk premium, suggesting that liquidity should be a first-order consideration when thinking about security pricing.

7.3 THE CAPM AND THE ACADEMIC WORLD

The thorn in the side of academic researchers is Assumption 1a (all assets trade) that leads to the result that the efficient portfolio must include all risky assets in the economy. In reality, we cannot even observe all the assets that do trade, let alone properly account for those that do not. The theoretical market portfolio, which is central to the CAPM, is impossible to pin down in practice.

Since the theoretical CAPM market portfolio cannot be observed, tests of the CAPM must be directed at the mean-beta relationship as applied to all observed assets with respect to an observed, but perhaps inefficient, stock index portfolio. These tests face surprisingly difficult hurdles.

The objective is to test the SML equation $E(R_i) = \beta_i\, RM$. We do so with a regression of excess returns of a sample of stocks ($i = 1, \ldots, N$) over a given period, t, against the betas of each stock:

$$R_{i,t} = \lambda_0 + \lambda_1 \beta_i + \lambda_2 \sigma_{ei}^2 + \eta_{i,t} \tag{7.16}$$

The CAPM predicts that (i) $\lambda_0 = 0$, that is, the average alpha in the sample will be zero; (ii) $\lambda_1 = R_M$, that is, the slope of the SML equals the market index risk premium; and (iii) $\lambda_2 = 0$, that is, unique risk, σ_{ei}^2, doesn't earn a risk premium. $\eta_{i,t}$ is the zero-mean residual of this regression.

---

[22]See, for example, Tarun Chordia, Richard Roll, and Avanidhar Subrahmanyam, "Commonality in Liquidity," *Journal of Financial Economics* 56 (2000), pp. 3–28, or J. Hasbrouck and D. H. Seppi, "Common Factors in Prices, Order Flows and Liquidity," *Journal of Financial Economics* 59 (2001), pp. 383–411.

[23]Yakov Amihud, "Illiquidity and Stock Returns: Cross-Section and Time-Series Effects," *Journal of Financial Markets* 9 (2002), pp. 31–56.

[24]See L. Pástor and R. F. Stambaugh, "Liquidity Risk and Expected Stock Returns," *Journal of Political Economy* 111 (2003), pp. 642–685, or V. V. Acharya and L. H. Pedersen, "Asset Pricing with Liquidity Risk," *Journal of Financial Economics* 77 (2005), pp. 375–410.

Where, you may ask, do we obtain the beta coefficients and residual variances for the N stocks in the regression? We have to estimate this pair for each stock from a time series of stock returns. And therein lies the snag: we estimate these parameters with large errors. Moreover, these errors may be correlated: First, beta may be correlated with the residual variance of each stock (as well as errors in these estimates), and second, the error terms in the regression may be correlated across stocks. These measurement errors can result in a downward bias in the slope of the SML (λ_1), and an upward bias in the average alpha (λ_0). We can't even predict the sign of the bias in (λ_2).

An example of this hazard was pointed out in an early paper by Miller and Scholes,[25] who demonstrated how econometric problems could lead one to reject the CAPM even if it were perfectly valid. They considered a checklist of difficulties encountered in testing the model and showed how these problems potentially could bias conclusions. To prove the point, they simulated rates of return that were constructed to satisfy the predictions of the CAPM and used these rates to "test" the model with standard statistical techniques of the day. The result of these tests was a rejection of the model that looks surprisingly similar to what we find in tests of returns from actual data—this despite the fact that the "data" were constructed to satisfy the CAPM. Miller and Scholes thus demonstrated that econometric technique alone could be responsible for the rejection of the model in actual tests.

Moreover, both coefficients, alpha and beta, as well as residual variance, are likely time varying. There is nothing in the CAPM that precludes such time variation, but standard regression techniques rule it out and thus may lead to false rejection of the model. There are now well-known techniques to account for time-varying parameters. In fact, Robert Engle won the Nobel Prize for his pioneering work on econometric techniques to deal with time-varying volatility, and a good portion of the applications of these new techniques have been in finance.[26] Moreover, betas may vary not purely randomly over time, but in response to changing economic conditions. A "conditional" CAPM allows risk and return to change with a set of "conditioning variables."[27] As importantly, Campbell and Vuolteenaho[28] find that the beta of a security can be decomposed into two components, one of which measures sensitivity to changes in corporate profitability and another which measures sensitivity to changes in the market's discount rates. These are found to be quite different in many cases. Improved econometric techniques such as those proposed in this short survey may help resolve part of the empirical failure of the simple CAPM.

A strand of research that has not yet yielded fruit is the search for portfolios that hedge the price risk of specific consumption items, as in Merton's equation 7.12. But the jury is still out on the empirical content of this equation with respect to future investment opportunities.

As mentioned in Chapter 4, Fama and French documented the explanatory power of size and book-to-market ratios (B/M). They interpret portfolios formed to align with these characteristics as hedging portfolios in the context of equaiton 7.12. Following their lead, other papers have now suggested a number of other extramarket risk factors (discussed in the next chapter). But we don't really know what uncertainties in future investment opportunities are hedged by these factors, leading many to be skeptical of empirically driven identification of extramarket hedging portfolios.

---

[25]Merton H. Miller and Myron Scholes, "Rates of Return in Relations to Risk: A Reexamination of Some Recent Findings," in *Studies in the Theory of Capital Markets*, Michael C. Jensen, ed. (New York: Praeger, 1972).

[26]Engle's work gave rise to the widespread use of so-called ARCH models. ARCH stands for *autoregressive conditional heteroskedasticity*, which is a fancy way of saying that volatility changes over time, and that recent levels of volatility can be used to form optimal estimates of future volatility.

[27]There is now a large literature on conditional models of security market equilibrium. Much of it derives from Ravi Jagannathan and Zhenyu Wang, "The Conditional CAPM and the Cross-Section of Expected Returns," *Journal of Finance* 51 (March 1996), pp. 3–53.

[28]John Campbell and Tuomo Vuolteenaho, "Bad Beta, Good Beta," *American Economic Review* 94 (December 2004), pp. 1249–75.

The bottom line is that in the academic world the single-index CAPM is considered passé. We don't yet know, however, what shape the successful extension to replace it will take. Stay tuned for future editions of this text.

7.4 THE CAPM AND THE INVESTMENT INDUSTRY

While academics have been riding multiple-index models in search of a CAPM that best explains returns, the industry has steadfastly stayed with the single-index CAPM.

This interesting phenomenon can be explained by a "test of the non-testable." Presumably, the CAPM tenet that the market portfolio is efficient cannot be tested because the true market portfolio cannot be observed in the first place. But as time has passed, it has become ever more evident that consistently beating a (not very broad) index portfolio such the S&P/TSX Composite or the S&P 500 appears to be beyond the power of most investors.

Indirect evidence on the efficiency of the market portfolio can be found in a study by Burton Malkiel,[29] who examined the alphas realized by a large sample of equity mutual funds over the period 1972 to 1991. Figure 7.5 shows the frequency distribution of these alphas, which is roughly bell-shaped with a mean that is slightly negative but statistically indistinguishable from zero. On average it does not appear that mutual funds outperform the market index on a risk-adjusted basis.[30]

Figure 7.5

Estimates of individual mutual fund alphas, 1972–1991.

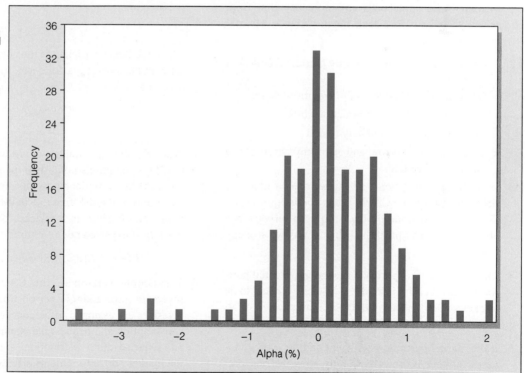

Source: Burton G. Malkiel, "Returns from Investing in Equity Mutual Funds 1972–1991," *Journal of Finance* 50 (June 1995). Reprinted by permission of the publisher, Blackwell Publishing Inc.

---

[29]Burton G. Malkiel, "Returns from Investing in Equity Mutual Funds 1971–1991," *Journal of Finance* 50 (June 1995), pp. 549–72.
[30]Notice that the study included all mutual funds with at least 10 years of continuous data. This suggests that the average alpha is upward-biased, since funds that failed after less than 10 years were ignored and omitted from the left tail of the distribution. This *survivorship bias*, which we discuss further in Chapter 11, makes the finding that the average fund underperformed the index even more telling.

This result is quite meaningful. While we might expect realized alphas of individual securities to centre around zero, professionally managed mutual funds might be expected to demonstrate average positive alphas. Funds with superior performance, which are supposed to exist, should tilt the sample average to a positive value. The small impact of superior funds on this distribution suggests the difficulty in beating the passive strategy that the CAPM deems to be optimal.

From the standpoint of the industry, an index portfolio that can be beaten by only a small fraction of professional managers over a 10-year period may well be taken as ex ante efficient for all practical purposes, that is, to be used as: (1) a diversification vehicle to mix with an active portfolio from security analysis (discussed in Chapter 8); (2) a benchmark for performance evaluation and compensation (discussed in Chapter 20); (3) a means to adjudicate law suits about fair compensation to various risky enterprises; and (4) a means to determine proper prices in regulated industries, allowing shareholders to earn a fair rate of return on their investments, but no more.

SUMMARY

1. The CAPM assumes that investors are single-period planners who agree on a common input list from security analysis and seek mean-variance optimal portfolios.

2. The CAPM assumes that security markets are ideal in the sense that
   a. They are large, and investors are price-takers.
   b. There are no taxes or transaction costs.
   c. All risky assets are publicly traded.
   d. Investors can borrow and lend any amount at a fixed risk-free rate.

3. With these assumptions, all investors hold identical risky portfolios. The CAPM holds that in equilibrium the market portfolio is the unique mean-variance efficient tangency portfolio. Thus, a passive strategy is efficient.

4. The CAPM market portfolio is a value-weighted portfolio. Each security is held in a proportion equal to its market value divided by the total market value of all securities.

5. If the market portfolio is efficient and the average investor neither borrows nor lends, then the risk premium on the market portfolio is proportional to its variance, σ^2_M, and to the average coefficient of risk aversion across investors $\overline{A}$:

$$E(r_M) - r_f = 1.0 \times \overline{A}\sigma^2_M$$

6. The CAPM implies that the risk premium on any individual asset or portfolio is the product of the

risk premium on the market portfolio and the beta coefficient:

$$E(r) - r_f = \beta[E(r_M) - r_f]$$

where the beta coefficient is the covariance of the asset with the market portfolio as a fraction of the variance of the market portfolio:

$$\beta = \frac{\text{Cov}(r,r_M)}{\sigma^2_M}$$

7. When risk-free investments are restricted but all other CAPM assumptions hold, then the simple version of the CAPM is replaced by its zero-beta version. Accordingly, the risk-free rate in the expected return–beta relationship is replaced by the zero-beta portfolio's expected rate of return:

$$E(r_i) = E[r_{Z(M)}] + \beta_i E[r_M - r_{Z(M)}]$$

8. The simple version of the CAPM assumes that investors have a single-period time horizon. When investors are assumed to be concerned with lifetime consumption and bequest plans, but investors' tastes and security return distributions are stable over time, the market portfolio remains efficient and the simple version of the expected return–beta relationship holds. But if those distributions change unpredictably, or if investors seek to hedge nonmarket sources of risk to their consumption, simple CAPM will give way to a multifactor version in which the security's exposure to these nonmarket sources of risk command risk premiums.

9. The consumption-based capital asset pricing model (CCAPM) is a single-factor model in which the market portfolio excess return is replaced by that of a consumption-tracking portfolio. By appealing directly to consumption, the model naturally incorporates consumption-hedging considerations and changing investment opportunities within a single-factor framework.

10. The security market line of the CAPM must be modified to account for labour income and other significant nontraded assets.

11. Liquidity costs and liquidity risk can be incorporated into the CAPM relationship. Investors demand compensation for both expected costs of illiquidity as well as the risk surrounding those costs.

KEY EQUATIONS

(7.1) $y = \dfrac{E(r_M) - r_f}{A\sigma^2_M}$

(7.2) $E(r_M) - r_f = \bar{A}\sigma^2_M$

(7.3) $w_B[w_1\text{Cov}(r_1,r_B) + w_2\text{Cov}(r_2,r_B) + \ldots$
$\qquad + w_B\text{Cov}(r_B,r_B) + \ldots + w_n\text{Cov}(r_n,r_B)]$

(7.4) $\displaystyle\sum_{i=1}^{n} w_i\text{Cov}(R_i,R_B) = \sum_{i=1}^{n}\text{Cov}(w_iR_i,R_B)$
$\qquad = \text{Cov}\left(\displaystyle\sum_{i=1}^{n} w_iR_i, R_B\right)$

(7.5) $\dfrac{\text{Market risk premium}}{\text{Market variance}} = \dfrac{E(r_M) - r_f}{\sigma^2_M} = \dfrac{E(R_M)}{\sigma^2_M}$

(7.6) $\dfrac{E(r_B) - r_f}{\text{Cov}(r_B,r_M)} = \dfrac{E(r_M) - r_f}{\sigma^2_M}$, or $\dfrac{E(R_B)}{\text{Cov}(R_B,r_M)}$
$\qquad = \dfrac{E(R_M)}{\sigma^2_M}$

(7.7) $E(r_B) - r_f = \dfrac{\text{Cov}(r_B,r_M)}{\sigma^2_M}[E(r_M) - r_f]$ or $E(R_B)$
$\qquad = \dfrac{\text{Cov}(R_B,r_M)}{\sigma^2_M}E(R_M)$

(7.8) $E(r_B) = r_f + \beta_B[E(r_M) - r_f]$

(7.9) $E(r_i) - E(r_Q)$
$\qquad = [E(r_P) - E(r_Q)]\dfrac{\text{Cov}(r_i,r_P) - \text{Cov}(r_P,r_Q)}{\sigma^2_P - \text{Cov}(r_P,r_Q)}$

(7.10) $E(r_i) - E(r_z) = [E(R_M) - E(R_Z)]\dfrac{\text{Cov}(r_i,r_M)}{\sigma^2_M}$
$\qquad = \beta_i[E(r_M) - E(r_z)]$

(7.11) $E(R_i) = E(R_M)\dfrac{\text{Cov}(R_i,R_M) + \dfrac{P_H}{P_M}\text{Cov}(R_i,R_M)}{\sigma^2_M + \dfrac{P_H}{P_M}\text{Cov}(R_M,R_H)}$

(7.12) $E(R_i) = \beta_{iM}E(R_M) + \displaystyle\sum_{t=1}^{K}\beta_{ik}E(R_k)$

(7.13) $E(R_i) = \beta_{iC}\text{RP}_C$

(7.14) $\text{RP}_C = E(R_C) = E(r_C) - r_f$

(7.15) $E(R_M) = \alpha_M + \beta_{MC}E(R_C) + \varepsilon_M$

(7.16) $R_{i,t} = \lambda_0 + \lambda_1\beta_i + \lambda_2\sigma^2_{ei} + \eta_{i,t}$

PROBLEMS

connect™   **Practise and learn online with Connect.**

1. What is the beta of a portfolio with $E(r_p) = 18$ percent, if $r_f = 6$ percent and $E(r_M) = 14$ percent?

2. The market price of a security is $50. Its expected rate of return is 14 percent. The risk-free rate is 6 percent and the market risk premium is 8.5 percent. What will be the market price of the security if its covariance with the market portfolio doubles (and all other variables remain unchanged)?

3. You are a consultant to a large manufacturing corporation that is considering a project with the following net after-tax cash flows (in millions of dollars):

Years from Now	After-Tax Cash Flow
0	−40
1–10	15

The project's beta is 1.7. Assuming that $r_f = 8$ percent and $E(r_M) = 16$ percent, what is the net present value of the project? What is the highest possible beta estimate for the project before its NPV becomes negative?

4. Are the following statements true or false?

   a. Stocks with a beta of zero offer an expected rate of return of zero.

   b. The CAPM implies that investors require a higher return to hold highly volatile securities.

   c. You can construct a portfolio with a beta of .75 by investing .75 of the budget in bills and the remainder in the market portfolio.

5. Here are data on two companies. The T-bill rate is 4 percent and the market risk premium is 6 percent.

Company	$1 Discount Store	Everything $5
Forecasted return	12%	11%
Standard deviation of returns	8%	10%
Beta	1.5	1.0

What would be the fair return for each company, according to the capital asset pricing model (CAPM)?

6. Characterize each company in the previous problem as underpriced, overpriced, or properly priced.

7. What is the expected rate of return for a stock that has a beta of 1.0 if the expected return on the market is 15 percent?

   a. 15 percent

   b. More than 15 percent

   c. Cannot be determined without the risk-free rate

8. Kaskin, Inc. stock has a beta of 1.2 and Quinn, Inc. stock has a beta of .6. Which of the following statements is *most* accurate?

   a. The expected rate of return will be higher for the stock of Kaskin, Inc. than that of Quinn, Inc.

   b. The stock of Kaskin, Inc. has more total risk than Quinn, Inc.

   c. The stock of Quinn, Inc. has more systematic risk than that of Kaskin, Inc.

9. Consider the following table, which gives a security analyst's expected return on two stocks for two particular market returns:

Market Return	Aggressive Stock	Defensive Stock
.05	−.02	.06
.25	.38	.12

   a. What are the betas of the two stocks?

   b. What is the expected rate of return on each stock if the market return is equally likely to be 5 percent or 25 percent?

c. If the T-bill rate is 6 percent and the market return is equally likely to be 5 percent or 25 percent, draw the SML for this economy.

d. Plot the two securities on the SML graph. What is the alpha of each?

e. What hurdle rate should be used by the management of the aggressive firm for a project with the risk characteristics of the defensive firm's stock?

If the simple CAPM is valid, which of the following situations in problems 10–16 are possible? Explain. Consider each situation independently.

10.

Portfolio	Expected Return	Beta
A	.20	1.4
B	.25	1.2

11.

Portfolio	Expected Return	Standard Deviation
A	.30	.35
B	.40	.25

12.

Portfolio	Expected Return	Beta
Risk-free	.10	0
Market	.18	1.0
A	.16	1.5

13.

Portfolio	Expected Return	Beta
Risk-free	.10	0
Market	.18	1.0
A	.16	.9

14.

Portfolio	Expected Return	Standard Deviation
Risk-free	.10	0
Market	.18	.24
A	.16	.22

15.

Portfolio	Expected Return	Standard Deviation
Risk-free	.10	0
Market	.18	.24
A	.16	.12

16.

Portfolio	Expected Return	Standard Deviation
Risk-free	.10	0
Market	.18	.24
A	.20	.22

In problems 17–19, assume that the risk-free rate of interest is 6 percent and the expected rate of return on the market is 16 percent.

17. A share of stock sells for $50 today. It will pay a dividend of $6 per share at the end of the year. Its beta is 1.2. What do investors expect the stock to sell for at the end of the year?

18. I am buying a firm with an expected cash flow of $1,000 but am unsure of its risk. If I think the beta of the firm is 0.5, when in fact the beta is really 1, how much *more* will I offer for the firm than it is truly worth?

19. A stock has an expected rate of return of 4 percent. What is its beta?

20. Two investment advisors are comparing performance. One averaged a 19 percent rate of return and the other a 16 percent rate of return. However, the beta of the first investor was 1.5, whereas that of the second was 1.

    a. Can you tell which investor was a better predictor of individual stocks (aside from the issue of general movements in the market)?

    b. If the T-bill rate were 6 percent and the market return during the period were 14 percent, which investor would be the superior stock selector?

    c. What if the T-bill rate were 3 percent and the market return were 15 percent?

21. Suppose the rate of return on short-term government securities (perceived to be risk-free) is about 5 percent. Suppose the expected rate of return required by the market for a portfolio with a beta measure of 1 is 12 percent. According to the capital asset pricing model (security market line),

    a. What is the expected rate of return on the market portfolio?

    b. What would be the expected rate of return on a stock with $\beta = 0$?

    c. Suppose you consider buying a share of stock at $40. The stock is expected to pay $3 in dividends next year and to sell then for $41. The stock risk has been evaluated by $\beta = -.5$. Is the stock overpriced or underpriced?

22. Suppose that borrowing is restricted so that the zero-beta version of the CAPM holds. The expected return on the market portfolio is 17 percent, and on the zero-beta portfolio it is 8 percent. What is the expected return on a portfolio with a beta of .6?

23. a. A mutual fund with beta of .8 has an expected rate of return of 14 percent. If $r_f = 5$ percent, and you expect the rate of return on the market portfolio to be 15 percent, should you invest in this fund? What is the fund's alpha?

    b. What passive portfolio comprising a market-index portfolio and a money market account would have the same beta as the fund? Show that the difference between the expected rate of return on this passive portfolio and that of the fund equals the alpha from part (a).

24. Outline how you would incorporate the following into the CCAPM:

    a. Liquidity

    b. Nontraded assets (Do you have to worry about labour income?)

The following problems are based on questions that have appeared in past CFA examinations.

25. a. John Wilson is a portfolio manager at Austin & Associates. For all of his clients, Wilson manages portfolios that lie on the Markowitz efficient frontier. Wilson asks Mary Regan, CFA, a managing director at Austin, to review the portfolios of two of his clients, the Eagle Manufacturing Company and the Rainbow Life Insurance Co. The expected returns of the two portfolios are substantially different. Regan determines that the Rainbow portfolio is virtually identical to the market portfolio and concludes that the Rainbow portfolio must be superior to the Eagle portfolio. Do you agree or disagree with Regan's conclusion that the Rainbow portfolio is superior to the Eagle portfolio? Justify your response with reference to the capital market line.

    b. Wilson remarks that the Rainbow portfolio has a higher expected return because it has greater unsystematic risk than Eagle's portfolio. Define unsystematic risk and explain why you agree or disagree with Wilson's remark.

26. Wilson is now evaluating the expected performance of two common stocks, Furhman Labs Inc. and Garten Testing Inc. He has gathered the following information:

    • The risk-free rate is 5 percent.

    • The expected return on the market portfolio is 11.5 percent.

- The beta of Furhman stock is 1.5.
- The beta of Garten stock is .8.

On the basis of his own analysis, Wilson's forecasts of the returns on the two stocks are 13.25 percent for Furhman stock and 11.25 percent for Garten stock. Calculate the required rate of return for Furhman Labs stock and for Garten Testing stock. Indicate whether *each* stock is undervalued, fairly valued, or overvalued.

27. The security market line depicts
    a. A security's expected return as a function of its systematic risk
    b. The market portfolio as the optimal portfolio of risky securities
    c. The relationship between a security's return and the return on an index
    d. The complete portfolio as a combination of the market portfolio and the risk-free asset

28. Within the context of the capital asset pricing model (CAPM), assume:
    - Expected return on the market = 15 percent
    - Risk-free rate = 8 percent
    - Expected rate of return on XYZ security = 17 percent
    - Beta of XYZ security = 1.25

    Which *one* of the following is *correct*?
    a. XYZ is overpriced.
    b. XYZ is fairly priced.
    c. XYZ's alpha is $-.25$ percent.
    d. XYZ's alpha is .25 percent.

29. What is the expected return of a zero-beta security?
    a. Market rate of return
    b. Zero rate of return
    c. Negative rate of return
    d. Risk-free rate of return

30. The capital asset pricing model asserts that portfolio returns are best explained by
    a. Economic factors
    b. Specific risk
    c. Systematic risk
    d. Diversification

31. According to the CAPM, the expected rate of return of a portfolio with a beta of 1.0 and an alpha of 0 is
    a. Between r_M and r_f
    b. The risk-free rate, r_f
    c. $\beta(r_M(-r_f))$
    d. The expected return on the market, r_M

Solve problems 32–33, referring to the following table showing risk and return measures of two portfolios.

Portfolio	Average Annual Rate of Return	Standard Deviation	Beta
R	11%	10%	0.5
S&P 500	14%	12%	1.0

32. When plotting portfolio *R* on the preceding table relative to the SML, portfolio *R* lies
  a. On the SML
  b. Below the SML
  c. Above the SML
  d. Insufficient data given

33. When plotting portfolio *R* relative to the capital market line, portfolio *R* lies
  a. On the CML
  b. Below the CML
  c. Above the CML
  d. Insufficient data given

34. Briefly explain whether investors should expect a higher return from holding portfolio *A* versus portfolio *B* under the CAPM. Assume that both portfolios are fully diversified.

	Portfolio *A*	Portfolio *B*
Systematic risk (beta)	1.0	1.0
Specific risk for each individual security	High	Low

35. Joan McKay is a portfolio manager for a bank trust department. McKay meets with two clients, Kevin Murray and Lisa York, to review their investment objectives. Each client expresses an interest in changing his or her individual investment objectives. Both clients currently hold well-diversified portfolios of risky assets.

  a. Murray wants to increase the expected return of his portfolio. State what action McKay should take to achieve Murray's objective. Justify your response in the context of the capital market line.

  b. York wants to reduce the risk exposure of her portfolio but does not want to engage in borrowing or lending activities to do so. State what action McKay should take to achieve York's objective. Justify your response in the context of the security market line.

36. Karen Kay, a portfolio manager at Collins Asset Management, is using the capital asset pricing model for making recommendations to her clients. Her research department has developed the information shown in the following exhibit.

	Forecast Return	Standard Deviation	Beta
Stock *X*	14.0%	36%	.8
Stock *Y*	17.0	25	1.5
Market index	14.0	15	1.0
Risk-free rate	5.0		

  a. Calculate expected return and alpha for each stock.
  b. Identify and justify which stock would be more appropriate for an investor who wants to
    i. Add this stock to a well-diversified equity portfolio
    ii. Hold this stock as a single-stock portfolio

Index Models and the Arbitrage Pricing Theory

The exploitation of security mispricing in such a way that risk-free economic profits may be earned is called **arbitrage**. It involves the simultaneous purchase and sale of equivalent securities in order to profit from discrepancies in their price relationship. The concept of arbitrage is central to the theory of capital markets. This chapter discusses the nature, and illustrates the use, of arbitrage.

Perhaps the most basic principle of capital market theory is that equilibrium market prices are rational: they rule out arbitrage opportunities. If actual security prices allow for arbitrage, the result will be strong pressure on security prices to restore equilibrium. Therefore, security markets ought to satisfy a "no arbitrage condition."

In this chapter, we show how such no-arbitrage conditions allow us to generalize the security market line of the CAPM to gain richer insight into the risk–return relationship.

We show how the decomposition of risk into market versus firm-specific influences introduced in the chapter can be extended to deal with the multifaceted nature of systematic risk. Multifactor models of security returns can be used to measure and manage exposure to each of many economywide factors such as business-cycle risk, interest or inflation rate risk, energy price risk, and so on. These models also lead us to a multifactor version of the security market line in which each factor is a separate source of risk with its own risk premium. This approach to the risk–return tradeoff is called *arbitrage pricing theory* or *APT*. We derive the APT and show why it implies a multifactor security market line. We also discuss the relation of the APT to a multifactor version of the CAPM.

A single-factor APT is based on the assumption that only one systematic common factor affects the returns of all securities. This assumption, however, was also at the origin of another class of models, known as *index* or *market models*, that predate the APT by several years. These models are initially introduced in order to simplify the computations of the Markowitz portfolio selection model. Since they also offer significant new insights into the nature of systematic risk versus firm-specific risk and constitute a good introduction to the concept of factor models of security returns, they will be examined in the first sections of this chapter.

8.1   A SINGLE-FACTOR SECURITY MARKET

The Input List of the Markowitz Model

The success of a portfolio selection rule depends on the quality of the input list, that is, the estimates of expected security returns and the covariance matrix. In the long run, efficient portfolios will beat portfolios with less reliable input lists and consequently inferior reward-to-risk tradeoffs.

Suppose your security analysts can thoroughly analyze 50 stocks. This means that your input list will include the following:

$$n = 50 \text{ estimates of expected returns}$$
$$n = 50 \text{ estimates of variances}$$
$$(n^2 - n)/2 = 1{,}225 \text{ estimates of covariances}$$
$$1{,}325 \text{ total estimates}$$

This is a formidable task, particularly in the light of the fact that a 50-security portfolio is relatively small. Doubling n to 100 will nearly quadruple the number of estimates to 5,150. If $n = 1{,}516$, roughly the number of TSX-listed stocks in 2014, we need almost 2.3 *million* estimates.

Introducing a model that simplifies the way we describe the sources of security risk allows us to use a smaller set of estimates of parameters. The simplification emerges because positive covariances among security returns arise from common economic forces that affect most firms. Some examples of such common factors are business cycles, interest rates, and the cost of natural resources. The unexpected changes in these variables cause simultaneous unexpected changes in the rates of return of the entire stock market. By decomposing uncertainty into these systemwide versus firm-specific sources, we vastly simplify the problem of estimating covariance and correlation.

Another difficulty in applying the Markowitz model to portfolio optimization is that errors in the assessment or estimation of correlation coefficients can lead to nonsensical results. This can happen because some sets of correlation coefficients are mutually inconsistent, as the following example demonstrates:[1]

Asset	Standard Deviation (%)	Correlation Matrix		
		A	**B**	**C**
A	20	1.00	.90	.90
B	20	.90	1.00	.00
C	20	.90	.00	1.00

Suppose that you construct a portfolio with weights 1.00, 1.00, and 1.00 for assets A, B, and C respectively, and calculate the portfolio variance. You will find that the portfolio variance appears to be negative $(-.200)$. This of course is not possible, because portfolio variances cannot be negative: we conclude that the inputs in the estimated correlation matrix must be mutually inconsistent. Of course, *true* correlation coefficients are always consistent.[2] But we do not know these true correlations and can only estimate them with some imprecision. Unfortunately, it is difficult to determine at a quick glance whether a correlation matrix is inconsistent, providing another motivation to seek a model that is easier to implement.

---

[1]We are grateful to Andrew Kaplin and Ravi Jagannathan, Kellogg Graduate School of Management, Northwestern University, for this example.
[2]The mathematical term for a correlation matrix that cannot generate negative portfolio variance is "positive definite."

Normality of Returns and Systematic Risk

Suppose that we group all relevant factors into one macroeconomic indicator and assume that it moves the security market as a whole. We further assume that, beyond this common effect, all remaining uncertainty in stock returns is firm-specific; that is, there is no other source of correlation between securities. Firm-specific events would include new inventions, deaths of key employees, and other factors that affect the fortune of the individual firm without affecting the broad economy in a measurable way.

We can summarize the distinction between macroeconomic and firm-specific factors by writing the return, r_i, realized on any security during some holding period as

$$r_i = E(r_i) + m_i + e_i \qquad (8.1)$$

where $E(r_i)$ is the expected return on the security as of the beginning of the holding period, m_i is the impact of unanticipated macroevents on the security's return during the period, and e_i is the impact of unanticipated firm-specific events. Both m_i and e_i have zero expected values because each represents the impact of unanticipated events, which by definition must average out to zero; m_i and e_i are also uncorrelated.

We can gain further insight by recognizing that different firms have different sensitivities to macroeconomic events. Thus, if we denote the unanticipated component of the macro factor by m, and denote the responsiveness of security i to macroevents by beta, β_i, then equation 8.1 becomes[3]

$$r_i = E(r_i) + \beta_i m_i + e_i \qquad (8.2)$$

Equation 8.2 is known as a **single-factor model** for stock returns. It is easy to imagine that a more realistic decomposition of security returns would require more than one factor in equation 8.2. We treat this issue in subsequent sections. For now, let us examine the easy case with only one macro factor.

The variance σ^2_i arises from two uncorrelated sources, systematic and firm-specific. Equation 8.2 tells us the systematic risk of security i is determined by its beta coefficient. "Cyclical" firms have greater sensitivity to the market and therefore higher systematic risk. The systematic risk of security i is $\beta^2_i \sigma^2_m$, and its total risk is

$$\sigma^2_i = \beta^2_i \sigma^2_m + \sigma^2(e_i) \qquad (8.3)$$

The covariance between any pair of securities also is determined by their betas:

$$\text{Cov}(r_i, r_j) = \text{Cov}(\beta_i m + e_i, \beta_j m + e_j) = \beta_i \beta_j \sigma^2_m \qquad (8.4)$$

In terms of systematic risk and market exposure, this equation tells us that firms are close substitutes. Equivalent beta securities give equivalent market positions.

Up to this point we have used only statistical implications from the joint normality of security returns. Normality of security returns alone guarantees that portfolio returns are also normal (from the "stability" of the normal distribution discussed in Chapter 4) and that there is a linear relationship between security returns and the common factor. This greatly simplifies portfolio analysis. Statistical analysis, however, does not identify the common factor, nor does it specify how that factor might operate over a longer investment period. However, it seems plausible (and can be empirically verified) that the variance of the common factor changes relatively slowly through time, as do the variances of individual securities and the covariances among them. We seek a variable that can proxy for this common factor. To be useful, this variable must be observable, so that we will be able to estimate its volatility as well as the sensitivity of individual securities returns to variation in its value.

---

[3]You might wonder why we choose the notation β for the responsiveness coefficient, since β has already been defined in Chapter 7 in the context of the CAPM. The choice is deliberate, however. Our reason will be obvious shortly.

THE SINGLE-INDEX MODEL

A reasonable approach to making the single-factor model operational is to assert that the rate of return on a broad index of securities such as the S&P/TSX Composite is a valid proxy for the common macroeconomic factor. This approach leads to an equation similar to the single-factor model, which is called a **single-index model** because it uses the market index to proxy for the common factor.

The Regression Equation of the Single-Index Model

Since the S&P/TSX Composite is a portfolio of stocks whose prices and rates of return can be observed, we have a considerable amount of past data with which to estimate systematic risk. We denote the market index by M, with excess return of $R_M = r_M - r_f$, and standard deviation of σ_M. Because the index model is linear, we can estimate the sensitivity (or beta) coefficient of a security on the index using a single-variable linear regression. We regress the excess return of a security, $R_i = r_i - r_f$, on the excess return of the index, R_M. To estimate the regression, we collect a historical sample of paired observations, $R_i(t)$ and $R_M(t)$, where t denotes the date of each pair of observations (e.g., the excess returns on the stock and the index in a particular month).[4] The **regression equation** is

$$R_i(t) = \alpha_i + \beta_i R_M(t) + e_i(t) \tag{8.5}$$

We write the index model in terms of excess returns over r_f rather than in terms of total returns, because the level of the stock market return represents the state of the macroeconomy only to the extent that it exceeds or falls short of the rate of return on risk-free T-bills. For example, in the 1950s, when T-bills were yielding only a 3 percent or 4 percent rate of return, a return of 8 percent or 9 percent on the stock market would be considered good news. In contrast, in the early 1980s, when bills were yielding over 10 percent, that same 8 percent or 9 percent stock market return would signal disappointing macroeconomic news.

The intercept of equation 8.5 (denoted by the Greek letter alpha, or α) is the security's expected excess return *when the market excess return is zero*. The slope coefficient, β_i, is the security beta. Beta is the security's sensitivity to the index: it is the amount by which the security return tends to increase or decrease for every 1 percent increase or decrease in the return on the index. e_i is the zero-mean, firm-specific surprise in the security return in time t, also called the residual.

The Expected Return–Beta Relationship

Because $E(e_i) = 0$, if we take the expected value of $E(R_i)$ in equation 8.5, we obtain the expected return–beta relationship of the single-index model:

$$E(R_i) = \alpha_i + \beta_i E(R_M) \tag{8.6}$$

The second term in equation 8.6 tells us that part of a security's risk premium is due to the risk premium of the index. The market risk premium is multiplied by the relative sensitivity, or beta, of the individual security. We call this the systematic risk premium because it derives from the risk premium that characterizes the entire market, which proxies for the condition of the full economy or economic system.

The remainder of the risk premium is given by the first term in the equation α. Alpha is a *nonmarket* premium. For example, α may be large if you think a security is underpriced and therefore offers an attractive expected return. Later on, we will see that when security prices are

---

[4]Practitioners often use a "modified" index model that is similar to equation 8.5 but that uses total rather than excess returns. This practice is most common when daily data are used. In this case the rate of return on T-bills is on the order of only about .01 percent per day, so total and excess returns are almost indistinguishable.

in equilibrium, such attractive opportunities ought to be competed away, in which case α will be driven to zero. But for now, let's assume that each security analyst comes up with his or her own estimates of alpha. If managers believe that they can do a superior job of security analysis, then they will be confident in their ability to find stocks with nonzero values of alpha.

We will see in Chapter 22 that the index model decomposition of an individual security's risk premium to market and nonmarket components greatly clarifies and simplifies the operation of macroeconomic and security analysis within an investment company.

Risk and Covariance in the Single-Index Model

Remember that one of the problems with the Markowitz model is the overwhelming number of parameter estimates required to implement it. Now we will see that the index model simplification vastly reduces the number of parameters that must be estimated.

Equation 8.5 says that each security has two sources of risk: *market* or *"systematic" risk*, attributable to its sensitivity to macroeconomic factors as reflected in R_M, and *firm-specific risk* as reflected in e. If we denote the variance of the excess return on the market, R_M, as σ^2_M, then we can break the variance of the rate of return on each stock into two components:

	Symbol
1. The variance attributable to the uncertainty of the common macroeconomic factors	$\beta^2_i\sigma^2_M$
2. The variance attributable to firm-specific uncertainty	$\sigma^2(e_i)$

The covariance between R_M and e_i is zero because e_i is defined as firm-specific, that is, independent of movements in the market. Hence, the variance of the rate of return on security i is

$$\sigma^2_i = \beta^2_i\sigma^2_M + \sigma^2(e_i)$$

The covariance between the excess rates of return on two stocks, for example R_i and R_j, derives only from the common factor, R_M, because e_i and e_j are each firm-specific and therefore presumed to be uncorrelated. Hence, the covariance between two stocks is

$$\text{Cov}(R_i, R_j) = \text{Cov}(\beta_i R_M, \beta_j R_M) = \beta_i\beta_j\sigma^2_M \qquad (8.7)$$

CC 1

CONCEPT CHECK

The data below describe a three-stock financial market that satisfies the single-index model.

Stock	Capitalization	Beta	Mean Excess Return	Standard Deviation
A	$3,000	1.0	10%	40%
B	$1,940	.2	2	30
C	$1,360	1.7	17	50

The standard deviation of the market index portfolio is 25.

a. What is the mean excess return of the index portfolio?

b. What is the covariance between stock A and stock B?

c. What is the covariance between stock B and the index?

d. Break down the variance of stock B into its systematic and firm-specific components.

The Set of Estimates Needed for the Single-Index Model

We summarize the results for the single index model in the table below.

	Symbol
1. The stock's expected return if the market is neutral, that is, if the market's excess return, $rM - rf$, is zero	α_i
2. The component of return due to movements in the overall market; β_i is the security's responsiveness to market movements	$\beta_i(r_M - r_f)$
3. The unexpected component of return due to unexpected events that are relevant only to this security (firm-specific)	e_i
4. The variance attributable to the uncertainty of the common macroeconomic factor	$\beta^2_i\sigma^2_m$
5. The variance attributable to firm-specific uncertainty	$\sigma^2(e_i)$

These calculations show that if we have

n estimates of the expected returns, $E(R_i)$

n estimates of the sensitivity coefficients, β_i

n estimates of the firm-specific variances, $\sigma^2(e_i)$

1 estimate for the market risk premium $E(R_M)$

1 estimate for the variance of the (common) macroeconomic factor, σ^2_M

then these $(3n + 2)$ estimates will enable us to prepare the input list for this single-index security universe. Thus, for a 50-security portfolio we will need 152 estimates, rather than 1,325, and for the entire TSX market with its 1,516 securities we will need only 4.550 estimates, rather than close to 2.3 million.

It is easy to see why the index model is such a useful abstraction. For large universes of securities, the data estimates required for this model are only a small fraction of what otherwise would be needed.

Another advantage is less obvious but equally important. The index model abstraction is crucial for specialization of effort in security analysis. If a covariance term had to be calculated directly for each security pair, then security analysts could not specialize by industry. For example, if one group were to specialize in the retail industry and another in the banking industry, who would have the common background necessary to estimate the covariance *between* Canadian Tire and CIBC? Neither group would have the deep understanding of other industries necessary to make an informed judgment of co-movements among industries. In contrast, the index model suggests a simple way to compute covariances. Covariances among securities are due to the influence of the single common factor, represented by the market index return, and can be easily estimated using equation 8.7.

The simplification derived from the index model assumption is, however, not without cost. The "cost" of the model lies in the restrictions it places on the structure of asset return uncertainty. The classification of uncertainty into a simple dichotomy—macro versus micro risk—oversimplifies sources of real-world uncertainty and misses some important sources of dependence in stock returns. For example, this dichotomy rules out industry events, events that may affect many firms within an industry without substantially affecting the broad macroeconomy.

Statistical analysis shows that the firm-specific components of some firms are correlated. Examples are the nonmarket components of stocks in a single industry, such as retail stocks or banking stocks. At the same time, statistical significance does not always correspond to economic significance. Economically speaking, the question more relevant to the assumption of a single-index model is whether portfolios constructed using covariances estimated on the basis of the single-factor or single-index assumption are significantly different from, and less efficient than, portfolios constructed using covariances estimated directly for each pair of stocks. We will demonstrate the effect of correlations in firm-specific components in the spreadsheet example in this chapter. In Part Seven, which deals with active portfolio management, we explore this issue further.

CC 2

CONCEPT CHECK

Suppose that the index model for stocks A and B is estimated with the following results:

$$R = .01 + .9R_M + e_A$$
$$R_B = -.02 + 1.1R_M + e_B$$
$$\sigma_M = .20$$
$$\sigma(e_A) = .3$$
$$\sigma(e_B) = .1$$

Find the standard deviation of each stock and the covariance between them.

The Index Model and Diversification

The index model, which was first suggested by Sharpe,[5] also offers insight into portfolio diversification. Suppose that we choose an equally weighted portfolio of n securities. The excess rate of return on each security is given by

$$R_i = \alpha_i + \beta_i R_M + e_i$$

Similarly, we can write the excess return on the portfolio of stocks as

$$R_P = \alpha_P + \beta_P R_M + e_P \qquad (8.8)$$

We now show that, as the number of stocks included in this portfolio increases, the part of the portfolio risk attributable to nonmarket factors becomes ever smaller. This part of the risk is diversified away. In contrast, the market risk remains, regardless of the number of firms combined into the portfolio.

To understand these results, note that the excess rate of return on this equally weighted portfolio, for which $w_i = 1/n$, is

$$R_P = \sum_{i=1}^{n} w_i R_i = \frac{1}{n} \sum_{i=1}^{n} R_i = \frac{1}{n} \sum_{i=1}^{n} (\alpha_i + \beta_i R_M + e_i)$$

$$= \frac{1}{n} \sum_{i=1}^{n} \alpha_i + \left(\frac{1}{n} \sum_{i=1}^{n} \beta_i \right) R_M + \frac{1}{n} \sum_{i=1}^{n} e_i \qquad (8.9)$$

Comparing equations 8.8 and 8.9, we see that the portfolio has a sensitivity to the market given by

$$\beta_P = \frac{1}{n} \sum_{i=1}^{n} \beta_i$$

[5]William F. Sharpe, "A Simplified Model of Portfolio Analysis," *Management Science*, January 1963.

(which is the average of the individual β_i's), and it has a nonmarket return component of a constant (intercept)

$$\alpha_P = \frac{1}{n}\sum_{i=1}^{n}\alpha_i$$

(which is the average of the individual alphas), plus the zero mean variable

$$e_P = \frac{1}{n}\sum_{i=1}^{n}e_i$$

which is the average of the firm-specific components. Hence the portfolio's variance is

$$\sigma_P^2 = \beta_p^2\sigma_M^2 + \sigma^2(e_P) \tag{8.10}$$

The systematic risk component of the portfolio variance, which we defined as the part that depends on marketwide movements, is $\beta_P^2\sigma_M^2$ and depends on the sensitivity coefficients of the individual securities. This part of the risk depends on portfolio beta and σ_M^2 and will persist regardless of the extent of portfolio diversification. No matter how many stocks are held, their common exposure to the market will be reflected in portfolio systematic risk.[6]

In contrast, the nonsystematic component of the portfolio variance is $\sigma^2(e_P)$ and is attributable to firm-specific components, e_i. Because these e_i's are independent, and all have zero expected value, the law of averages can be applied to conclude that as more and more stocks are added to the portfolio, the firm-specific components tend to cancel out, resulting in ever-smaller nonmarket risk. Such risk is thus termed *diversifiable*. To see this more rigorously, examine the formula for the variance of the equally weighted "portfolio" of firm-specific components. Because the e_i's are all uncorrelated,

$$\sigma^2(e_P) = \sum_{i=1}^{n}\left(\frac{1}{n}\right)^2\sigma^2(e_i) = \frac{1}{n}\overline{\sigma}^2(e)$$

where $\overline{\sigma}^2(e)$ is the average of the firm-specific variances. Since this average is independent of n, when n gets large, $\overline{\sigma}^2(e_P)$ becomes negligible.

To summarize, as diversification increases, the total variance of a portfolio approaches the systematic variance, defined as the variance of the market factor multiplied by the square of the portfolio sensitivity coefficient β_P. This is shown in Figure 8.1.

The figure shows that, as more and more securities are combined into a portfolio, the portfolio variance decreases because of the diversification of firm-specific risk. However, the power of diversification is limited. Even for very large n, risk remains because of the exposure of virtually all assets to the common, or market, factor. Therefore this systematic risk is said to be nondiversifiable.

This analysis is borne out by empirical analysis. We saw the effect of portfolio diversification on portfolio standard deviations in Figure 6.2. These empirical results are similar to the theoretical graph presented in Figure 8.1.

The assumption that all security returns can be represented by equation 8.1 is the main assumption of the index model. It can be combined with other assumptions in order to lead to the CAPM. Alternatively, it can be used as the basis of the single-factor APT, examined in later sections.

---

[6]One can always construct a portfolio with zero systematic risk by mixing negative β and positive β assets. The point of our discussion is that the vast majority of securities have a positive β, implying that well-diversified portfolios with small holdings in large numbers of assets will indeed have positive systematic risk.

Figure 8.1

The variance of a portfolio with β in the single-index model.

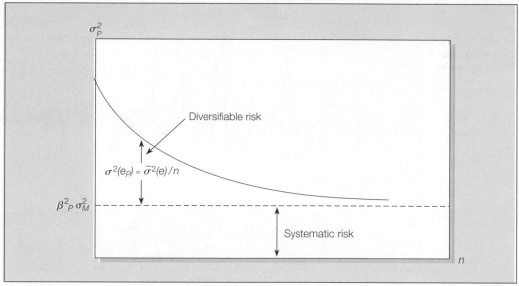

CC 3

CC 3

CONCEPT CHECK

Reconsider the two stocks in Concept Check 2. Suppose we form an equally weighted portfolio of A and B. What will be the nonsystematic standard deviation of that portfolio?

8.3   ESTIMATING THE SINGLE-INDEX MODEL

Equation 8.5 also suggests how we might go about actually measuring market and firm-specific risk. Suppose we observe the excess return on the market index and six specific firms belonging to different sectors over a number of holding periods. We use as an example hypothetical monthly excess returns on the S&P/TSX Composite index and firms XA and XB, both information technology (IT) stocks, as well as the pairs of firms YA and YB from the retailing sector and ZA and ZB from the energy sector.

 We work with monthly observations of rates of return for the six stocks, the S&P/TSX Composite portfolio, and T-bills over a 60-month period. As a first step, the excess returns on the seven risky assets are computed. We start with a detailed look at the preparation of the input list for XA Corporation, and then proceed to display the entire input list. Later in the chapter, we will show how these estimates can be used to construct the optimal risky portfolio.

The Security Characteristic Line for XA Corporation

The index model regression equation 8.5, restated for XA Corporation, is

$$R_{XA}(t) = \alpha_{XA} + \beta_{XA}R_M(t) + e_{XA}(t)$$

 The equation describes the (linear) dependence of XA's excess return on changes in the state of the economy as represented by the excess returns of the market index portfolio (denoted M). The regression estimates describe a straight line with intercept α_{XA} and slope β_{XA}, which we call the **security characteristic line (SCL)** for XA.

Figure 8.2

Excess returns on XA and S&P/TSX Composite over a 60-month period.

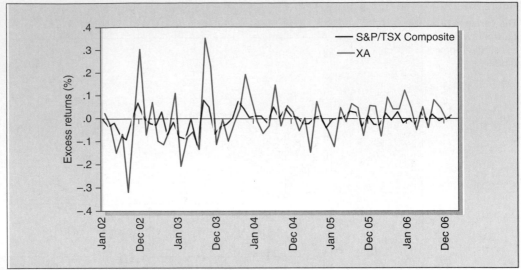

Figure 8.2 shows a graph of the excess returns on XA and the market portfolio over the 60-month period. The graph shows that XA returns generally follow those of the index, but with much larger swings. Indeed, the annualized standard deviation of the excess return on the market portfolio over the period was 13.58 percent, while that of XA was 38.17 percent. The swings in XA's excess returns suggest a larger-than-average sensitivity to the index, that is, a beta greater than 1.0.

The relationship between the returns of XA and the market index is made clearer by the **scatter diagram** in Figure 8.3, where the regression line is drawn through the scatter. The vertical distance of each point from the regression line is the value of XA's residual $e_X(t)$, corresponding to that particular date. The rates in Figures 8.2 and 8.3 are not annualized, and the scatter diagram shows monthly swings of over 30 percent for XA, but returns in the range of -11 to 8.5 percent for the S&P/TSX Composite index. The regression analysis output obtained by using Excel is shown in Table 8.1.

Figure 8.3

Scatter diagram of XA, the S&P/TSX Composite, and the security characteristic line (SCL) for XA.

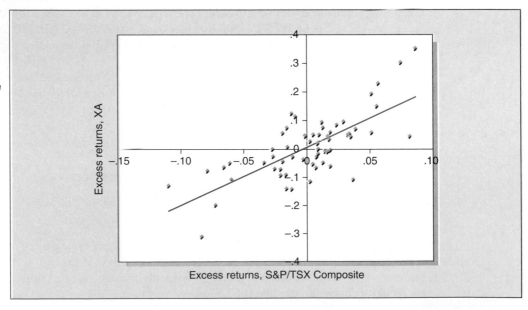

TABLE 8.1

Excel Output: Regression Statistics for the SCL of XA Corporation

Regression Statistics				
Multiple R	.7238			
R-squared	.5239			
Adjusted R-squared	.5157			
Standard error	.0767			
Observations	60			

ANOVA				
	df	**SS**	**MS**	
Regression	1	.3752	.3752	
Residual	58	.3410	.0059	
Total	59	.7162		

	Coefficients	**Standard Error**	**t-Stat**	**p-Value**
Intercept	.0086	.0099	.8719	.3868
S&P/TSX Composite	2.0348	.2547	7.9888	.0000

The Explanatory Power of the SCL for XA

Considering the top panel of Table 8.1 first, we see that the correlation of XA with the market index is quite high (.7238), telling us that XA tracks changes in the returns of the market fairly closely. The R-squared (.5239) tells us that variation in the market excess returns explains about 52 percent of the variation in the XA series. The adjusted R-squared (which is slightly smaller) corrects for an upward bias in R-squared that arises because we use the fitted values of two parameters,[7] the slope (beta) and intercept (alpha), rather than their true but unobservable values. With 60 observations, this bias is small. The standard error of the regression is the standard deviation of the residual, which we discuss in more detail shortly. This is a measure of the slippage in the average relationship between the stock and the index due to the impact of firm-specific factors. This measure, of course, is based on *in-sample* data. A more severe test is to look at returns from periods later than the one covered by the regression sample and test the power of the independent variable (the S&P/TSX Composite) to predict the dependent variable (the return on XA). Correlation between regression forecasts and realizations of *out-of-sample* data is almost always considerably lower than in-sample correlation.

Analysis of Variance

The next panel of Table 8.1 shows the analysis of variance (ANOVA) for the SCL. The sum of squares (SS) of the regression (.3752) is the portion of the variance of the dependent variable (XA's return) that is explained by the independent variable (the S&P/TSX Composite return); it is equal to $\beta_{XA}^2 \sigma_{S\&P/TSX}^2$. The MS column for the residual (.0059) shows the variance of the *unexplained* portion of XA's return, that is, the portion of return that is independent of the market index. The square root of this value is the standard error (SE) of the regression (.0767) reported in the first panel. If you divide the total SS of the regression (.7162) by 59, you will obtain the estimate of the variance of the dependent variable (XA), .012 per month, equivalent to a monthly

---

[7]In general, the adjusted R-squared (R_A^2) is derived from the unadjusted by $R_A^2 = 1 - (1 - R^2)\dfrac{n-1}{n-k-1}$, where k is the number of independent variables (here, $k = 1$). An additional degree of freedom is lost to the estimate of the intercept.

standard deviation of 11 percent. When annualized,[8] we obtain an annualized standard deviation of 38.17 percent, as reported earlier. Notice that the R-squared (the ratio of explained to total variance) equals the explained (regression) SS divided by the total SS.[9]

The Estimate of Alpha

Moving to the bottom panel, the intercept (.0086 = .86 percent per month) is the estimate of XA's alpha for the sample period. Although this is an economically large value (10.32 percent on an annual basis), it is statistically insignificant. This can be seen from the three statistics next to the estimated coefficient. The first is the standard error of the estimate (.0099).[10] This is a measure of the imprecision of the estimate. If the standard error is large, the range of likely estimation error is correspondingly large.

The t-statistic reported in the bottom panel is the ratio of the regression parameter to its standard error. This statistic equals the number of standard errors by which our estimate exceeds zero, and therefore can be used to assess the likelihood that the true but unobserved value might actually equal zero rather than the estimate derived from the data.[11] The intuition is that if the true value were zero, we would be unlikely to observe estimated values far away (many standard errors) from zero. So large t-statistics imply low probabilities that the true value is zero.

In the case of alpha, we are interested in the average value of XA's return net of the impact of market movements. Suppose we define the nonmarket component of XA's return as its actual return minus the return attributable to market movements during any period. Call this XA's firm-specific return, which we abbreviate as R_{fs}.

$$R_{\text{firm-specific}} = R_{fs} = R_{\text{XA}} - \beta_{\text{XA}} R_M$$

If R_{fs} were normally distributed with a mean of zero, the ratio of its estimate to its standard error would have a t-distribution. From a table of the t-distribution (or using Excel's TINV function) we can find the probability that the true alpha is actually zero or even lower given the positive estimate of its value and the standard error of the estimate. This is called the *level of significance* or, as in Table 8.1, the probability or *p-value*. The conventional cutoff for statistical significance is a probability of less than 5 percent, which requires a t-statistic of about 2.0. The regression output shows the t-statistic for XA's alpha to be .8719, indicating that the estimate is not significantly different from zero. That is, we cannot reject the hypothesis that the true value of alpha equals zero with an acceptable level of confidence. The p-value for the alpha estimate (.3868) indicates that if the true alpha were zero, the probability of obtaining an estimate as high as .0086 (given the large standard error of .0099) would be .3868, which is not so unlikely. We conclude that the sample average of R_{fs} is too low to reject the hypothesis that the true value of alpha is zero.

---

[8]When annualizing monthly data, average return and variance are multiplied by 12. However, because variance is multiplied by 12, standard deviation is multiplied by $\sqrt{12}$.

[9]R-squared $= \dfrac{\beta^2_{\text{XA}}\sigma^2_{\text{S\&P/TSX}}}{\beta^2_{\text{XA}}\sigma^2_{\text{S\&P/TSX}} + \sigma^2(e_{\text{XA}})} = \dfrac{.3752}{.7162} = .5239$

Equivalently, R-squared equals 1 minus the fraction of variance that is *not* explained by market returns, that is, 1 minus the ratio of firm-specific risk to total risk. For XA, this is

$$1 - \frac{\sigma^2(e_{\text{XA}})}{\beta^2_{\text{XA}}\sigma^2_{\text{S\&P/TSX}} + \sigma^2(e_{\text{XA}})} = 1 - \frac{.3410}{.7162} = .5239$$

[10]We can relate the standard error of the alpha estimate to the standard error of the residuals as follows:

$$\text{SE}(\alpha_{\text{XA}}) = \sigma(e_{\text{XA}})\sqrt{\frac{1}{n} + \frac{(\text{Avg S\&P/TSX})^2}{\text{Var(S\&P/TSX)} \times (n-1)}}$$

[11]The t-statistic is based on the assumption that returns are normally distributed. In general, if we standardize the estimate of a normally distributed variable by computing its difference from a hypothesized value and dividing by the standard error of the estimate (to express the difference as a number of standard errors), the resulting variable will have a t-distribution. With a large number of observations, the bell-shaped t-distribution approaches the normal distribution.

But even if the alpha value were both economically *and* statistically significant *within the sample*, we still would not use that alpha as a forecast for a future period. Overwhelming empirical evidence shows that five-year alpha values do not persist over time, that is, there seems to be virtually no correlation between estimates from one sample period to the next. In other words, while the alpha estimated from the regression tells us the average return on the security when the market was flat during that estimation period, it does *not* forecast what the firm's performance will be in future periods. This is why security analysis is so hard. The past does not readily foretell the future. We elaborate on this issue in Chapter 9 on market efficiency.

The Estimate of Beta

The regression output in Table 8.1 shows the beta estimate for XA to be 2.0348, more than twice that of the S&P/TSX. Such high market sensitivity is not unusual for technology stocks. The standard error (SE) of the estimate is .2547.[12]

The value of beta and its SE produce a large *t*-statistic (7.9888), and a *p*-value of practically zero. We can confidently reject the hypothesis that XA's true beta is zero. A more interesting *t*-statistic might test a null hypothesis that XA's beta is greater than the marketwide average beta of 1.0. This *t*-statistic would measure how many standard errors separate the estimated beta from a hypothesized value of 1. Here too, the difference is easily large enough to achieve statistical significance:

$$\frac{\text{Estimated value} - \text{Hypothesized value}}{\text{Standard error}} = \frac{2.03 - 1}{.2547} = 4.00$$

However, we should bear in mind that, even here, the precision is not what we might like it to be. For example, if we wanted to construct a confidence interval that includes the true but unobserved value of beta with 95 percent probability, we would take the estimated value as the centre of the interval and then add and subtract about two standard errors. This produces a range between 1.43 and 2.53, which is quite wide.

Firm-Specific Risk

The monthly standard deviation of XA's residual is 7.67 percent, or 26.6 percent annually. This is quite large, on top of XA's high-level systematic risk. The standard deviation of systematic risk is $\beta \times \sigma(\text{S\&P/TSX}) = 2.03 \times 13.58 = 27.57$ percent. Notice that XA's firm-specific risk is as large as its systematic risk, a common result for individual stocks.

Correlation and Covariance Matrix

Figure 8.4 graphs the excess returns of the pairs of securities from each of the three sectors with the S&P/TSX Composite index on the same scale. We see that the IT sector is the most variable, followed by the retail sector, and then the energy sector, which has the lowest volatility.

Panel 1 in Spreadsheet 8.1 shows the estimates of the risk parameters of the S&P/TSX Composite portfolio and the six analyzed securities. You can see from the high residual standard deviations (column E) how important diversification is. These securities have tremendous firm-specific risk. Portfolios concentrated in these (or other) securities would have unnecessarily high volatility and inferior Sharpe ratios.

---

[12] $\text{SE}(\beta) = \dfrac{\sigma(e_{\text{XA}})}{\text{Var}(R_{\text{XA}}) \times (n - 1)}$

Figure 8.4

Excess returns on portfolio assets.

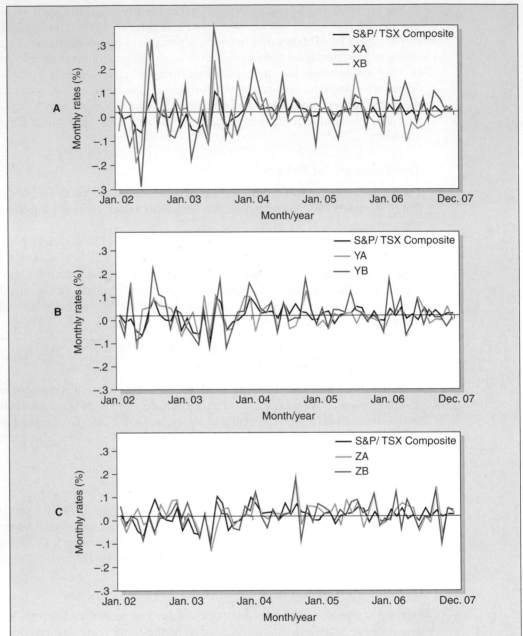

Panel 2 shows the correlation matrix of the residuals from the regressions of excess returns on the S&P/TSX Composite. The shaded cells show correlations of same-sector stocks, which are as high as .7 for the two energy stocks (ZA and ZB). This is in contrast to the assumption of the index model that all residuals are uncorrelated. Of course, these correlations are, to a great extent, high by design, because we selected pairs of firms from the same industry. Cross-industry correlations are typically far smaller, and the empirical estimates of correlations of residuals for industry indices (rather than individual stocks in the same industry) would be far more in accord with the model. In fact, a few of the stocks in this sample actually seem to have negatively correlated residuals. Of course, correlation is also subject to statistical sampling error, and this may be a fluke.

EXCEL SPREADSHEET 8.1

Implementing the index model.

	A	B	C	D	E	F	G	H	I	J
1	Panel 1: Risk Parameters of the Investable Universe (annualized)									
2										
3		SD of Excess Return	Beta	SD of Systematic Component	SD of Residual	Correlation with the S&P 500				
4	S&P/TSX	0.1358	1.00	0.1358	0	1				
5	XA	0.3817	2.03	0.2762	0.2656	0.72				
6	XB	0.2901	1.23	0.1672	0.2392	0.58				
7	YA	0.1935	0.62	0.0841	0.1757	0.43				
8	YB	0.2611	1.27	0.1720	0.1981	0.66				
9	ZA	0.1822	0.47	0.0634	0.1722	0.35				
10	ZB	0.1988	0.67	0.0914	0.1780	0.46				
11										
12	Panel 2: Correlation of Residuals									
13										
14		XA	XB	YA	YB	ZA				
15	XA	1								
16	XB	0.08	1							
17	YA	−0.34	0.17	1						
18	YB	−0.10	0.12	0.50	1					
19	ZA	−0.20	−0.28	−0.19	−0.13	1				
20	ZB	−0.06	−0.19	−0.24	−0.22	0.70				
21										
22	Panel 3: The Index Model Covariance Matrix									
23										
24			S&P/TSX	XA	XB	YA	YB	ZA	ZB	
25		Beta	1.00	2.03	1.23	0.62	1.27	0.47	0.67	
26	S&P/TSX	1.00	0.0184	0.0375	0.0227	0.0114	0.0234	0.0086	0.0124	
27	XA	2.03	0.0375	0.1457	0.0462	0.0232	0.0475	0.0175	0.0253	
28	XB	1.23	0.0227	0.0462	0.0842	0.0141	0.0288	0.0106	0.0153	
29	YA	0.62	0.0114	0.0232	0.0141	0.0374	0.0145	0.0053	0.0077	
30	YB	1.27	0.0234	0.0475	0.0288	0.0145	0.0682	0.0109	0.0157	
31	ZA	0.47	0.0086	0.0175	0.0106	0.0053	0.0109	0.0332	0.0058	
32	ZB	0.67	0.0124	0.0253	0.0153	0.0077	0.0157	0.0058	0.0395	
33										
34	Cells on the diagonal (shadowed) equal to variance									
35			formula in cell C26	= B4^2						
36	Off-diagonal cells equal to covariance									
37			formula in cell C27	= C$25*$B27*$B$4^2						
38			multiplies beta from row and column by index variance							
39										
40	Panel 4: Macro Forecast and Forecasts of Alpha Values									
41										
42										
43		S&P/TSX	XA	XB	YA	YB	ZA	ZB		
44	Alpha	0	0.0150	−0.0100	−0.0050	0.0075	0.012	0.0025		
45	Risk premium	0.0600	0.1371	0.0639	0.0322	0.0835	0.0400	0.0429		
46										
47	Panel 5: Computation of the Optimal Risky Portfolio									
48										
49		S&P/TSX	Active Pf A	XA	XB	YA	YB	ZA	ZB	Overall Pf
50	$\sigma^2(e)$			0.0705	0.0572	0.0309	0.0392	0.0297	0.0317	
51	$\alpha/\sigma^2(e)$		0.5505	0.2126	−0.1748	−0.1619	0.1911	0.4045	0.0789	
52	$w^0(i)$		1.0000	0.3863	−0.3176	−0.2941	0.3472	0.7349	0.1433	
53	$[w^0(i)]^2$			0.1492	0.1009	0.0865	0.1205	0.5400	0.0205	
54	α_A		0.0222							
55	$\sigma^2(e_A)$		0.0404							
56	w^0_A		0.1691							
57	w^*(Risky portf)	0.8282	0.1718							
58	Beta	1	1.0922	2.0348	1.2315	0.6199	1.2672	0.4670	0.6736	1.0158
59	Risk premium	0.06	0.0878	0.1371	0.0639	0.0322	0.0835	0.0400	0.0429	0.0648
60	SD	0.1358	0.2497							0.1422
61	Sharpe ratio	0.44	0.35							0.46

Panel 3 produces covariances derived from equation 8.10 of the single-index model. Variances of the S&P/TSX Index and the individual covered stocks appear on the diagonal. The variance estimates for the individual stocks equal $\beta^2{}_i\sigma^2{}_M + \sigma^2(e_i)$. The off-diagonal terms are covariance values and equal $\beta_i\beta_j\sigma^2{}_M$.

8.4   PORTFOLIO CONSTRUCTION AND THE SINGLE-INDEX MODEL

In this section, we look briefly at the implications of the index model for portfolio construction.[13] We will see that the model offers several advantages, not only in terms of parameter estimation, but also for the analytic simplification and organizational decentralization that it makes possible. A detailed analysis of the use of the single-index model in selecting optimal portfolios is in Chapter 22.

Alpha and Security Analysis

Perhaps the most important advantage of the single-index model is the framework it provides for macroeconomic and security analysis in the preparation of the input list that is so critical to the efficiency of the optimal portfolio. The Markowitz model requires estimates of risk premiums for each security. The estimate of expected return depends on both macroeconomic and individual-firm forecasts. But if many different analysts perform security analysis for a large organization such as a mutual fund company, a likely result is inconsistency in the macroeconomic forecasts that partly underlie expectations of returns across securities. Moreover, the underlying assumptions for market-index risk and return are often not explicit in the analysis of individual securities.

The single-index model creates a framework that separates these two quite different sources of return variation and makes it easier to ensure consistency across analysts. We can lay down a hierarchy of the preparation of the input list using the framework of the single-index model.

1. Macroeconomic analysis is used to estimate the risk premium and risk of the market index.
2. Statistical analysis is used to estimate the beta coefficients of all securities and their residual variances, $\sigma^2(e_i)$.
3. The portfolio manager uses the estimates for the market-index risk premium and the beta coefficient of a security to establish the expected return of that security *absent* any contribution from security analysis. The market-driven expected return is conditional on information common to all securities, not on information gleaned from security analysis of particular firms. This market-driven expected return can be used as a benchmark.
4. Security-specific expected return forecasts (specifically, security alphas) are derived from various security-valuation models (such as those discussed in Part Five). Thus, the alpha value distills the incremental risk premium attributable to private information developed from security analysis.

In the context of equation 8.6, the risk premium on a security not subject to security analysis would be $\beta_i E(R_M)$. In other words, the risk premium would derive solely from the security's

---

[13]The use of the index model to construct optimal risky portfolios was originally developed in Jack Treynor and Fischer Black, "How to Use Security Analysis to Improve Portfolio Selection," *Journal of Business*, January 1973.

tendency to follow the market index. Any expected return beyond this benchmark risk premium (the security alpha) would be due to some nonmarket factor that would be uncovered through security analysis.

The end result of security analysis is the list of alpha values. Statistical methods of estimating beta coefficients are widely known and standardized; hence, we would not expect this portion of the input list to differ greatly across portfolio managers. In contrast, macro and security analysis are far less of an exact science and therefore provide an arena for distinguished performance. Using the index model to disentangle the premiums due to market and nonmarket factors, a portfolio manager can be confident that macro analysts compiling estimates of the market-index risk premium and security analysts compiling alpha values are using consistent estimates for the overall market.

In the context of portfolio construction, alpha is more than just one of the components of expected return. It is the key variable that tells us whether a security is a good or a bad buy. Consider an individual stock for which we have a beta estimate from statistical considerations and an alpha value from security analysis. We easily can find many other securities with identical betas and therefore identical systematic components of their risk premiums. Therefore, what really makes a security attractive or unattractive to a portfolio manager is its alpha value. In fact, we've suggested that a security with a positive alpha is providing a premium over and above the premium it derives from its tendency to track the market index. This security is a bargain and therefore should be over-weighted in the overall portfolio compared to the passive alternative of using the market-index portfolio as the risky vehicle. Conversely, a negative-alpha security is overpriced and, other things equal, its portfolio weight should be reduced. In more extreme cases, the desired portfolio weight might even be negative, that is, a short position (if permitted) would be desirable.

The Index Portfolio as an Investment Asset

The process of charting the efficient frontier using the single-index model can be pursued much like the procedure we used in Chapter 7, where we used the Markowitz model to find the optimal risky portfolio. Here, however, we can benefit from the simplification the index model offers for deriving the input list. Moreover, portfolio optimization highlights another advantage of the single-index model, namely, a simple and intuitively revealing representation of the optimal risky portfolio. Before we get into the mechanics of optimization in this setting, however, we start by considering the role of the index portfolio in the optimal portfolio.

Suppose the prospectus of an investment company limits the universe of investable assets to only stocks included in the S&P/TSX Composite portfolio. In this case, the S&P/TSX Composite index captures the impact of the economy on the large stocks the firm may include in its portfolio. Suppose that the resources of the company allow coverage of only a relatively small subset of this so-called *investable universe*. If these analyzed firms are the only ones allowed in the portfolio, the portfolio manager may well be worried about limited diversification.

A simple way to avoid inadequate diversification is to include the S&P/TSX Composite portfolio as one of the assets of the portfolio. Examination of equations 8.5 and 8.6 reveals that if we treat the S&P/TSX Composite portfolio as the market index, it will have a beta of 1.0 (its sensitivity to itself), no firm-specific risk, and an alpha of zero—there is no nonmarket component in its expected return. Equation 8.3 shows that the covariance of any security, i, with the index is $\beta_i \sigma^2_M$. To distinguish the S&P/TSX Composite from the n securities covered by the firm, we will designate it the $(n + 1)$th asset. We can think of the S&P/TSX Composite as a *passive portfolio* that the manager would select in the absence of security analysis. It gives broad market exposure without the need for expensive security analysis. However, if the manager is willing to engage in such research, she may devise an *active portfolio* that can be mixed with the index to provide an even better risk–return tradeoff.

8.5

PORTFOLIO MANAGEMENT WITH THE SINGLE-INDEX MODEL

The tone of our discussions in this chapter indicates that the index model may be preferred for the practice of portfolio management. Switching from the Markowitz to an index model is an important decision and hence the first question is whether the index model is really inferior to the Markowitz full-covariance model.

Is the Index Model Inferior to the Full-Covariance Model?

This question is partly related to a more general question of the value of parsimonious models. As an analogy, consider the question of adding additional explanatory variables in a regression equation. We know that adding explanatory variables will in most cases increase R-squared, and in no case will R-squared fall. But this does not necessarily imply a better regression equation.[14] A better criterion is contribution to the predictive power of the regression. The appropriate question is whether inclusion of a variable that contributes to in-sample explanatory power is likely to contribute to out-of-sample forecast precision. Adding variables, even ones that may appear significant, sometimes can be hazardous to forecast precision. Put differently, a parsimonious model that is stingy about inclusion of independent variables is often superior. Predicting the value of the dependent variable depends on two factors, the precision of the coefficient estimates and the precision of the forecasts of the independent variables. When we add variables, we introduce errors on both counts.

This problem applies as well to replacing the single-index with the full-blown Markowitz model, or even a multi-index model of security returns. To add another index, we need both a forecast of the risk premium of the additional index portfolio and estimates of security betas with respect to that additional factor. The Markowitz model allows far more flexibility in our modelling of asset covariance structure than the single-index model. But that advantage may be illusory if we can't estimate those covariances with a sufficient degree of accuracy. Using the full-covariance matrix invokes estimation risk of thousands of terms. Even if the full Markowitz model would be better in principle, it is quite possible that the cumulative effect of so many estimation errors will result in a portfolio that is actually inferior to that derived from the single-index model.

Against the potential superiority of the full-covariance model, we have the clear practical advantage of the single-index framework. Its aid in decentralizing macro and security analysis is another decisive advantage.

The Industry Version of the Index Model

Not surprisingly, the index model has attracted the attention of practitioners. To the extent that it is approximately valid, it provides a convenient benchmark for security analysis. Also, it can generate instruments that allow investors to invest in the entire market.

A modern practitioner using the CAPM who has no special information about a security and no insight unavailable to the general public will conclude that the security is "properly" priced. By this, the analyst means that the expected return on the security is fair, given its risk, and therefore plots on the security market line. For instance, if one has no private information about Bell Canada's (BCE) stock, then one should expect

$$E(r_{\mathrm{BCE}}) = r_f + \beta_{\mathrm{BCE}}[E(r_M) - r_f]$$

---

[14]In fact, the adjusted R-squared may fall if the additional variable does not contribute enough explanatory power to compensate for the extra degree of freedom it uses.

A portfolio manager who has a forecast for the market index, $E(r_M)$, and observes the risk-free T-bill rate, r_f, can use the model to determine the benchmark expected return for any stock. The beta coefficient, the market risk, σ^2_M, and the firm-specific risk, $\sigma^2(e)$, can be estimated from historical SCLs, that is, from regressions of security excess returns on market index excess returns.

There are many sources for such regression results. For instance, the Quantitative Analysis division of BMO Capital Markets publishes periodic estimates of stock betas. It uses the S&P/TSX Composite index as the proxy for the market portfolio.[15] It relies on the 54 most recent monthly observations to calculate the regression parameters. BMO Capital Markets and most services[16] use total returns, rather than excess returns (deviations from T-bill rates), in their regressions. In this way they estimate a variant of our index model, which is

$$r = a + br_M + e \tag{8.11}$$

instead of

$$r - r_f = \alpha + \beta(r_M - r_f) + e \tag{8.12}$$

To see the effect of this departure, we can rewrite equation 8.12 as

$$r = r_f + \alpha + \beta r_M - \beta r_f + e = \alpha + r_f(1 - \beta) + \beta r_M + e \tag{8.13}$$

Comparing equations 8.11 and 8.13, you can see that if r_f is constant over the sample period, both equations have the same independent variable, r_M, and residual, e. Therefore the slope coefficient will be the same in the two regressions.[17]

However, the intercept that BMO Capital Markets calls alpha is really, using the parameters of the CAPM, an estimate of $\alpha + r_f(1 - \beta)$. The apparent justification for this procedure is that, on a monthly basis, $r_f(1 - \beta)$ is small and is apt to be swamped by the volatility of actual stock returns. However, it is worth noting that for $\beta \neq 1$, the regression intercept in equation 8.11 will not equal the CAPM alpha as it does when excess returns are used as in equation 8.12.

Company Beta Estimates

Table 8.2 illustrates some Morningstar CPMS estimates of equation 8.11 for a number of important Canadian firms (based on market capitalization) using 60 months of data ending in April 2014, as well as these beta estimates relative to the industry averages. For each period, after the company name, the next two columns show the beta and alpha coefficients. Remember that BMO Capital Markets' alpha is actually $a + r_f(1 - \beta)$. The next column, "% Expl. by Market," shows the R-squared statistic. As we saw in Section 8.3, the R-squared the coefficient of determination also may be expressed as

$$R\text{-squared} = 1 - \frac{\sigma^2(e)}{\sigma^2} \tag{8.14}$$

The American brokerage firm Merrill Lynch provides another estimate of beta, called *adjusted beta*. The motivation for adjusting beta estimates is the observation that, on average, the beta coefficients of stocks seem to move toward 1 over time. One explanation for this phenomenon is intuitive. A business enterprise usually is established to produce a specific product or service, and a

---

[15]Although the S&P/TSX Composite is the most easily available and most often used proxy for the market portfolio, it clearly does not include all stocks available for investment to Canadian investors. In addition to many Canadian stocks, it also ignores Canadians' opportunity to invest in foreign stocks. This should be taken in account when interpreting the results.

[16]Value Line is a well-known source of U.S. betas; Bloomberg and Morningstar CPMS are useful sources of Canadian betas. The latter uses five years of monthly data to estimate company betas.

[17]Actually, r_f does vary over time and so should not be grouped casually with the constant term in the regression. However, variations in r_f are tiny compared with swings in the market return. The actual volatility in the T-bill rate has only a small impact on the estimated value of beta.

TABLE 8.2

Estimates of
Stock Return
Betas

Company	Alpha	Beta	Beta Rel. to Industry	Mkt. Cap in $Billions
Royal Bank of Canada	.38	.80	1.18	105.51126
Toronto-Dominion Bank	.69	.94	1.38	97.197859
Bank of Nova Scotia	.47	.94	1.38	80.932102
Suncor Energy Inc.	−.55	1.75	1.20	62.140152
Cdn. National Railway	1.39	.41	.56	52.934145
Valeant Pharmaceutical	4.04	.62	.63	48.803402
Cdn. Natural Resources	−.31	1.68	1.15	48.778117
Bank of Montreal	.46	.90	1.32	48.7335
Imperial Oil Limited	−.19	.85	.58	45.3635
Enbridge Inc.	1.67	.20	.14	44.141535
Cdn. Imperial Bank	.40	.86	1.27	38.86073
Manulife Financial Corp	−.66	1.40	2.06	38.144152
BCE Inc.	.99	.19	.66	37.912129
TransCanada Corporation	.68	.36	.25	36.149887
Husky Energy Inc.	−.45	1.21	.83	35.229102
Potash Corp. of Sask.	−.32	1.31	.65	33.505758
Thomson Reuters Corp.	.10	.31	.66	32.267834
Great-West Lifeco Inc.	−.07	1.12	1.65	30.814053
Cdn. Pacific Railway Ltd	1.78	.94	1.31	29.975906
Brookfield Asset Mgmt.	1.11	.69	1.02	28.829912
Power Financial Corp.	−.03	.99	1.45	24.763068
Telus Corporation	1.38	.42	1.50	23.942119
Magna Intl. Inc.	2.93	.33	.69	23.550625
Sun Life Financial Inc.	.17	.72	1.06	22.652807
Rogers Communications, B	.48	.35	1.23	22.406771
Barrick Gold Corp.	−1.43	1.24	.62	22.280127
Loblaw Companies Ltd.	.51	.39	1.24	19.67

Source: Morningstar CPMS, accessed May 1, 2014.

new firm may be more unconventional than an older one in many ways, from technology to management style. As it grows, however, a firm diversifies, first expanding to similar products and later to more diverse operations. As the firm becomes more conventional, it starts to resemble the rest of the economy even more. Thus, its beta coefficient will tend to change in the direction of 1.

Another explanation for this phenomenon is statistical. We know that the average beta over all securities is 1. Thus, before estimating the beta of a security our guess would be that it is 1. When we estimate this beta coefficient over a particular sample period, we sustain some unknown sampling error of the estimated beta. The greater the difference between our beta estimate and 1, the greater is the chance that we incurred a large estimation error and that, when we estimate this same beta in a subsequent sample period, the new estimate will be closer to 1.

The sample estimate of the beta coefficient is the best guess for the sample period. Given that beta has a tendency to evolve toward 1, however, a forecast of the future beta coefficient should adjust the sample estimate in that direction.

Merrill Lynch adjusts beta estimates in a simple way. It takes the sample estimate of beta and averages it with 1, using the weights of two-thirds and one-third:

$$\text{Adjusted beta} = \frac{2}{3}(\text{sample beta}) + \frac{1}{3}(1)$$

For example, consider BCE, an actively traded stock on both the TSX and NYSE. Its beta estimated for the 60-month period ending in April 2014 is .19. Its adjusted beta is .53, taking it one-third of the way toward 1.

The sample period regression estimate for BCE for 2014 is .19. Since BCE's beta is *less* than 1, we know that this means that the index model alpha estimate is smaller. As we did in equation 8.13, we have to subtract $(1 - \beta)r_f$ from the regression alpha to obtain the index model alpha.

CC 4

CONCEPT CHECK

What was BCE's CAPM alpha per month during the period covered by Morningstar CPMS Markets' 2014 regression if during this period the average monthly rate of return of T-bills was .1 percent?

More importantly, these alpha estimates are *ex post* (after the fact) measures. They do not mean that anyone could have forecast these alpha values *ex ante* (before the fact). In fact, the name of the game in security analysis is to forecast alpha values ahead of time. A well-constructed portfolio that includes long positions in future positive alpha stocks and short positions in future negative alpha stocks will outperform the market index. The key term here is *well constructed*, meaning that the portfolio has to balance concentration on high alpha stocks with the need for risk-reducing diversification. The beta and residual variance estimates from the index model regression make it possible to achieve this goal. (We examine this technique in more detail in Part Seven on active portfolio management.)

In the absence of special information concerning BCE, if our forecast for the market index is 10 percent and T-bills pay 1 percent, we learn from Morningstar CPMS Markets' estimates that the CAPM forecast for the rate of return on BCE stock is

$$E(r_{BCE}) = r_f + \beta \times [E(r_M) - r_f]$$
$$= .001 + .19(.10 - .001)$$
$$= .0198 = 1.98\%$$

Index Models and Tracking Portfolios

Suppose a portfolio manager believes she has identified an underpriced portfolio. Her security analysis team estimates the index model equation for this portfolio (using the S&P/TSX Composite index) in excess return form and obtains the following estimates:

$$R_P = .04 + 1.4R_{S\&P/TSX} + e_P \tag{8.15}$$

Therefore, *P* has an alpha value of 4 percent (which measures the extent of mispricing) and a beta of 1.4. The manager is confident in the quality of her security analysis but is wary about the performance of the broad market in the near term. If she buys the portfolio, and the market as a whole turns down, she still could lose money on her investment (which has a large positive beta) even if her team is correct that the portfolio is underpriced on a relative basis. She would like a position that takes advantage of her team's analysis but is independent of the performance of the overall market.

To this end, a **tracking portfolio** (*T*) can be constructed. A tracking portfolio for portfolio *P* is a portfolio designed to match the systematic component of *P*'s return. The idea is for the portfolio to "track" the market-sensitive component of *P*'s return. This means the tracking portfolio must have the same beta on the index portfolio as *P* and as little nonsystematic risk as possible.

ALPHA BETTING

It has never been easier to pay less to invest. No fewer than 136 exchange-traded funds (ETFs) were launched in the first half of 2006, more than in the whole of 2005.

For those who believe in efficient markets, this represents a triumph. ETFs are quoted securities that track a particular index, for a fee that is normally just a fraction of a percentage point. They enable investors to assemble a low-cost portfolio covering a wide range of assets from international equities, through government and corporate bonds, to commodities.*

But as fast as the assets of ETFs and index-tracking mutual funds are growing, another section of the industry seems to be flourishing even faster. Watson Wyatt, a firm of actuaries, estimates that "alternative asset investment" (ranging from hedge funds through private equity to property) grew by around 20% in 2005, to $1.26 trillion. Investors who take this route pay much higher fees in the hope of better performance. One of the fastest-growing assets, funds of hedge funds, charge some of the highest fees of all.

Why are people paying up? In part, because investors have learned to distinguish between the market return, dubbed beta, and managers' outperformance, known as alpha. "Why wouldn't you buy beta and alpha separately?" asks Amo Kitts of Henderson Global Investors, a fund-management firm. "Beta is a commodity and alpha is about skill."

Clients have become convinced that no one firm can produce good performance in every asset class. That has led to a "core and satellite" model, in which part of the portfolio is invested in index trackers with the rest in the hands of specialists. But this creates its own problems. Relations with a single balanced manager are simple. It is much harder to research and monitor the performance of specialists. That has encouraged the middlemen—managers of managers (in the traditional institutional business) and funds-of-funds (in the hedge-fund world), which are usually even more expensive.

That their fees endure might suggest investors can identify outperforming fund managers in advance. However, studies suggest this is extremely hard. And even where you can spot talent, much of the extra performance may be siphoned off into higher fees. "A disproportionate amount of the benefits of alpha go to the manager, not the client," says Alan Brown at Schroders, an asset manager.

In any event, investors will probably keep pursuing alpha, even though the cheaper alternatives of ETFs and tracking funds are available. Craig Baker of Watson Wyatt says that, although above market returns may not be available to all, clients who can identify them have a "first mover" advantage. As long as that belief exists, managers can charge high fees.

*See, for example, Lorne N. Switzer and Rana Zoghaib, "Index Participation Units, Market Tracking Risk, and Equity Market Demand," *Canadian Journal of Administrative Sciences* 16 (1999), pp. 243–255, and Lorne N. Switzer, Paula Varson, and Samia Zghidi, "Standard and Poor's Depository Receipts and the Performance of the S&P 500 Index Futures Market," *Journal of Futures Markets* 20 (2000), pp. 705–716.

Source: *The Economist*, September 14, 2006. © 2007 The Economist Newspaper and The Economist Group. All rights reserved.

A tracking portfolio for P will have a levered position in the S&P/TSX to achieve a beta of 1.4. Therefore, T includes positions of 1.4 in the Composite and $-.4$ in T-bills. Because T is constructed from the index and bills, it has an alpha value of zero.

Now consider buying portfolio P but at the same time offsetting systematic risk by assuming a short position in the tracking portfolio. The short position in T cancels out the systematic exposure of the long position in P: the overall combined position is thus *market-neutral*. Therefore, even if the market does poorly, the combined position should not be affected. But the alpha on portfolio P will remain intact. The combined portfolio, C, provides a return per dollar of

$$R_C = R_P - R_T = (.04 + 1.4R_{S\&P/TSX} + e_P) - 1.4R_{S\&P/TSX} = .04 + e_P \qquad (8.16)$$

While this portfolio is still risky (due to the residual risk, e_P), the systematic risk has been eliminated, and if P is reasonably well diversified, the remaining nonsystematic risk will be small. Thus the objective is achieved: the manager can take advantage of the 4 percent alpha without inadvertently taking on market exposure. The process of separating the search for alpha from the choice of market exposure is called *alpha transport*.

This "long-short strategy" is characteristic of the activity of many *hedge funds*. Hedge fund managers identify an underpriced security and then try to attain a "pure play" on the perceived underpricing. They hedge out all extraneous risk, focusing the bet only on the perceived "alpha." Tracking funds are the vehicle used to hedge the exposures to which they do *not* want exposure. Hedge fund managers use index regressions such as those discussed here, as well as more sophisticated variations, to create the tracking portfolios at the heart of their hedging strategies.

8.6 MULTIFACTOR MODELS

The index model's decomposition of returns into systematic and firm-specific components is compelling, but confining systematic risk to a single factor is not. Indeed, when we introduced the single-index model, we noted that the systematic or macro factor summarized by the market return arises from a number of sources, for example, uncertainty about the business cycle, interest rates, and inflation. Asset risk premiums may also depend on correlations with extramarket risk factors, such as inflation, or changes in the parameters describing future investment opportunities: interest rates, volatility, market risk premiums, and betas. For example, returns on an asset whose return increases when inflation increases can be used to hedge uncertainty in the future inflation rate. Its risk premium may fall as a result of investors' extra demand for this asset.

Risk premiums of individual securities should reflect their sensitivities to changes in extramarket risk factors just as their betas on the market index determine their risk premiums in the simple CAPM. When securities can be used to hedge these factors, the resulting hedging demands will make the SML "multifactor," with each risk source that can be hedged adding an additional factor to the SML. Risk factors can be represented either by returns on these hedge portfolios (just as the index portfolio represents the market factor), or more directly by changes in the risk factors themselves, for example, changes in interest rates or inflation.

Factor Models of Security Returns

To illustrate the approach, let's start with a two-factor model. Suppose the two most important macroeconomic sources of risk are uncertainties surrounding the state of the business cycle, which we will measure by gross domestic product, denoted GDP, and interest rates, denoted IR. The return on any stock will respond to both sources of macro risk as well as to its own firm-specific risks. We therefore can generalize the single-index model into a two-factor model describing the excess rate of return on a stock in some time period as follows:

$$R_t = \alpha + \beta_{\text{GDP}}\text{GDP}_t + \beta_{\text{IR}}\text{IR}_t + e_t \tag{8.17}$$

The two macro factors on the right-hand side of the equation are the systematic factors in the economy; thus they play the role of the market index in the single-index model. Their coefficients are sometimes called *factor sensitivities*, *factor loadings*, or, equivalently, *factor betas*. As before, e_t reflects firm-specific influences.

Now consider two firms, one a regulated utility, the other an airline. Because its profits are controlled by regulators, the utility is likely to have a low sensitivity to GDP risk, that is, a "low GDP beta." But it may have a relatively high sensitivity to interest rates: when rates rise, its stock price will fall; this will be reflected in a large (negative) interest rate beta. Conversely, the performance of the airline is very sensitive to economic activity, but it is not very sensitive to interest rates. It will have a high GDP beta and a small interest rate beta. Suppose that on a particular day, a news item suggests that the economy will expand. GDP is expected to increase, but so are interest rates. Is the "macro news" on this day good or bad? For the utility this is bad news, since its dominant sensitivity is to rates. But for the airline, which responds more to GDP, this is good news. Clearly a one-factor or single-index model cannot capture such differential responses to varying sources of macroeconomic uncertainty.

Of course the market return reflects macro factors as well as the average sensitivity of firms to those factors. When we estimate a single-index regression, therefore, we implicitly impose an (incorrect) assumption that each stock has the same relative sensitivity to each risk factor. If stocks actually differ in their betas relative to the various macroeconomic factors, then lumping all systematic sources of risk into one variable such as the return on the market index will ignore the nuances that better explain individual-stock returns. Once you see why a two-factor model can better explain stock returns, it is easy to see that models with even more factors—**multifactor models**—can provide even better descriptions of returns.

EXAMPLE 8.1   **Two-Factor Models**

Suppose we estimate the two-factor model in equation 8.17 for Dominion Airlines and find the following result:

$$r = .10 + 18(\text{GDP}) + .7(\text{IR}) + e$$

This tells us that on the basis of currently available information, the expected rate of return for Dominion is 10 percent, but that for every percentage point increase in GDP beyond current expectations, the return on Dominion shares increases on average by 1.8 percent, while for every unanticipated percentage point that interest rates decrease, Dominion's shares rise on average by .7 percent.

Another reason that multifactor models can improve on the descriptive power of the index model is that betas seem to vary over the business cycle. Therefore, it makes sense that we can improve the single-index model by including variables that are related to the business cycle.

The factor betas can provide a framework for a hedging strategy. The idea for an investor who wishes to hedge a source of risk is to establish an opposite factor exposure to offset that particular source of risk. Often, futures contracts can be used to hedge particular factor exposures. We explore this application in Chapter 20.

However, the multifactor model is no more than a *description* of the factors that affect security returns. There is no "theory" in the equation. The obvious question left unanswered by a factor model like equation 8.17 is where $E(r)$ comes from, in other words, what determines a security's expected rate of return. This is where we need a theoretical model of equilibrium security returns.

In the previous chapter we developed one example of such a model: the security market line of the capital asset pricing model. The CAPM asserts that securities will be priced to give investors an expected return comprising two components: the risk-free rate, which is compensation for the time value of money, and a risk premium, determined by multiplying a benchmark risk premium (i.e., the risk premium offered by the market portfolio) times the relative measure of risk, beta:

$$E(r) = r_f + \beta[E(r_M) - r_f] \tag{8.18}$$

If we denote the risk premium of the market portfolio by RP_M, then a useful way to rewrite equation 8.18 is as follows:

$$E(r) = r_f + \beta\text{RP}_M \tag{8.19}$$

We pointed out in Section 8.1 that you can think of beta as measuring the exposure of a stock or portfolio to marketwide or macroeconomic risk factors. Therefore, one interpretation of the SML is that investors are rewarded with a higher expected return for their exposure to macro risk, based on both the sensitivity to that risk (beta) as well as the compensation for bearing each unit of that source of risk (i.e., the risk premium, RP_M), but are *not* rewarded for exposure to firm-specific uncertainty.

How might this single-factor view of the world generalize once we recognize the presence of multiple sources of systematic risk? We will work out the details of the argument in the next section, but before getting lost in the trees, we will start with the lay of the forest, motivating intuitively the results that are to come. Perhaps not surprisingly, a multifactor index model gives rise to a multifactor security market line in which the risk premium is determined by the exposure to *each* systematic risk factor, and by a risk premium associated with each of those factors.

For example, in a two-factor economy in which risk exposures can be measured by equation 8.17, we would conclude that the expected rate of return on a security would be the sum of

1. The risk-free rate of return
2. The sensitivity to GDP risk (i.e., the GDP beta) times the risk premium for GDP risk
3. The sensitivity to interest rate risk (i.e., the interest rate beta) times the risk premium for interest rate risk

This assertion is expressed as follows in equation 8.20. In that equation, for example, β_{GDP} denotes the sensitivity of the security return to unexpected changes in GDP growth, and RP_{GDP} is the risk premium associated with "one unit" of GDP exposure, that is, the exposure corresponding to a GDP beta of 1.0. Here then is a two-factor security market line.

$$E(r) = r_f + \beta_{GDP}RP_{GDP} + \beta_{IR}RP_{IR} \tag{8.20}$$

If you look back at equation 8.19, you will see that equation 8.20 is a generalization of the simple security market line. In the usual SML, the benchmark risk premium is given by the market portfolio, $RP_M = E(r_M) - r_f$, but once we generalize to multiple risk sources, each with its own risk premium, we see that the insights are highly similar.

However, one difference between a single- and a multiple-factor economy is that a factor risk premium can be negative. For example, a security with a positive interest rate beta performs better when rates increase, and thus would hedge the value of a portfolio against interest rate risk. Investors might well accept a lower rate of return, that is, a negative risk premium, as the cost of this hedging attribute. In contrast, a more typical security that does worse when rates increase (a negative IR beta) adds to interest rate exposure, and therefore has a higher required rate of return. Equation 8.20 shows that the contribution of interest rate risk to required return for such a security would then be positive, the product of a negative-factor beta times a negative-factor risk premium.

We still need to specify how to estimate the risk premium for each factor. Analogously to the simple CAPM, the risk premium associated with each factor can be thought of as the risk premium of a portfolio that has a beta of 1.0 on that particular factor and a beta of zero on all other factors. In other words, it is the risk premium one might expect to earn by taking a "pure play" on that factor. We will return to this below, but for now, let's just take the factor risk premiums as given and see how a multifactor SML might be used.

EXAMPLE 8.2   A Multifactor SML

Think about our regression estimates for our earlier example of Dominion Airlines. Dominion has a GDP beta of 1.8 and an interest rate beta of .7. Suppose the risk premium for one unit of exposure to GDP risk is 6 percent, while the risk premium for one unit of exposure to interest rate risk is 3 percent. Then the overall risk premium on the Dominion portfolio should equal the sum of the risk premiums required as compensation for each source of systematic risk.

The risk premium attributable to GDP risk should be the stock's exposure to that risk multiplied by the risk premium of the first factor portfolio, 6 percent. Therefore, the portion of the firm's risk premium that is compensation for its exposure to the first factor is $1.8 \times 6\% = 10.8\%$. Similarly, the risk premium attributable to interest rate risk is $.7 \times 3\% = 2.1\%$. The continued

continued

total risk premium should be $10.8 + 2.1 = 12.9$ percent. Therefore, if the risk-free rate is 4 percent, the total return on the portfolio should be

4.0%	Risk-free rate
$+10.8$	$+$ Risk premium for exposure to GDP risk
$+\underline{\ 2.1}$	$+$ Risk premium for exposure to interest rate risk
16.9%	Total expected return

More concisely,

$$E(r) = 4\% + 1.8 \times 6\% + .7 \times 3\% = 16.9\%$$

The multifactor model clearly gives us a much richer way to think about risk exposures and compensation for those exposures than the single-index model or CAPM. Let us now fill in some of the gaps in the argument and more carefully explore the link between multifactor models of security returns and multifactor security market lines.

CC 5

CONCEPT CHECK

Suppose the risk premiums in the above example were $RP_{GDP} = 4$ percent and $RP_{IR} = 2$ percent. What would be the new value for the equilibrium expected rate of return on Dominion Airlines?

8.7   **ARBITRAGE PRICING THEORY**

Stephen Ross developed the **arbitrage pricing theory (APT)** in 1976.[18] Like the CAPM, the APT predicts a security market line linking expected returns to risk, but the path it takes to its SML is quite different. Ross's APT relies on three key propositions: (1) security returns can be described by a factor model; (2) there are sufficient securities to diversify away idiosyncratic risk; and (3) well-functioning security markets do not allow for the persistence of arbitrage opportunities. We begin with a simple version of Ross's model, which assumes that only one systematic factor affects security returns. However, the usual discussion of the APT is concerned with the multifactor case, so we treat this more general case as well.

Arbitrage, Risk Arbitrage, and Equilibrium

An arbitrage opportunity arises when an investor can earn riskless profits without making a net investment. A trivial example of an arbitrage opportunity would arise if shares of a stock sold for different prices on two different exchanges. For example, suppose IBM sold for $60 on the NYSE but only $58 on Nasdaq. Then you could buy the shares on Nasdaq and simultaneously sell them on the NYSE, clearing a riskless profit of $2 per share without tying up any of your own capital. The **Law of One Price** states that if two assets are equivalent in all economically relevant respects, then they should have the same market price. The Law of One Price is enforced by arbitrageurs: if they observe a violation of the law, they will engage in *arbitrage*

---

[18]Stephen A. Ross, "Return, Risk and Arbitrage," in I. Friend and J. Bicksler, eds., *Risk and Return in Finance* (Cambridge, MA: Ballinger, 1976).

activity—simultaneously buying the asset where it is cheap and selling where it is expensive. In the process, they will bid up the price where it is low and force it down where it is high until the arbitrage opportunity is eliminated.

The idea that market prices will move to rule out arbitrage opportunities is perhaps the most fundamental concept in capital market theory. Violation of this restriction would indicate the grossest form of market irrationality.

The critical property of a risk-free arbitrage portfolio is that any investor, regardless of risk aversion or wealth, will want to take an infinite position in it. Because those large positions will quickly force prices up or down until the opportunity vanishes, security prices should satisfy a "no-arbitrage condition," that is, a condition that rules out the existence of arbitrage opportunities.

There is an important difference between arbitrage and risk–return dominance arguments in support of equilibrium price relationships. A dominance argument holds that when an equilibrium price relationship is violated, many investors will make limited portfolio changes, depending on their degree of risk aversion. Aggregation of these limited portfolio changes is required to create a large volume of buying and selling, which in turn restores equilibrium prices. By contrast, when arbitrage opportunities exist each investor wants to take as large a position as possible; hence it will not take many investors to bring about the price pressures necessary to restore equilibrium. Therefore, implications for prices derived from no-arbitrage arguments are stronger than implications derived from a risk-return dominance argument.

The CAPM is an example of a dominance argument, implying that all investors hold mean variance efficient portfolios. If a security is mispriced, then investors will tilt their portfolios toward the underpriced and away from the overpriced securities. Pressure on equilibrium prices results from many investors shifting their portfolios, each by a relatively small dollar amount. The assumption that a large number of investors are mean-variance optimizers is critical. In contrast, the implication of a no-arbitrage condition is that a few investors who identify an arbitrage opportunity will mobilize large dollar amounts and quickly restore equilibrium.

Practitioners often use the terms "arbitrage" and "arbitrageurs" more loosely than our strict definition. "Arbitrageur" often refers to a professional searching for mispriced securities in specific areas such as merger-target stocks, rather than to one who seeks strict (risk-free) arbitrage opportunities. Such activity is sometimes called **risk arbitrage** to distinguish it from pure arbitrage.

Well-Diversified Portfolios

We start by examining a single-factor model similar in spirit to the index model introduced in Section 8.1. As in that model, uncertainty in asset returns has two sources: a common or macroeconomic factor and a firm-specific or microeconomic cause. The common factor is assumed to have zero expected value, since it measures new information concerning the macroeconomy, which, by definition, has zero expected value. There is no need, however, to assume that the factor can be proxied by the return on a market index portfolio. The return r_i on firm i is given by equation 8.2.

Now we look at the risk of a portfolio of stocks. We first show that if a portfolio is well diversified, its firm-specific or nonfactor risk can be diversified away. Only factor (or systematic) risk remains. If we construct an n-stock portfolio with weights w_i $\Sigma w_i = 1$, then the rate of return on this portfolio is as follows:

$$R_P = E(R_P) + \beta_P F + e_P \tag{8.21}$$

where

$$\beta_P = \sum w_i \beta_i$$

is the weighted average of the β_i of the n securities. The portfolio nonsystematic component (which is uncorrelated with F) is

$$e_P = \sum w_i e_i$$

which similarly is a weighted average of the e_i of the n securities.

We can divide the variance of this portfolio into systematic and nonsystematic sources, as we saw in Section 8.2 (equation 8.10). The portfolio variance is

$$\sigma^2{}_P = \beta^2{}_P \sigma^2{}_F + \sigma^2(e_P)$$

where $\sigma^2{}_F$ is the variance of the factor F, and $\sigma^2(e_P)$ is the nonsystematic risk of the portfolio, which is given by

$$\sigma^2(e_P) = \text{Variance}\left(\sum w_i e_i\right) = \sum w_i^2 \sigma^2(e_i)$$

Note that, in deriving the nonsystematic variance of the portfolio, we depend on the fact that the firm-specific e_i's are uncorrelated and hence that the variance of the "portfolio" of nonsystematic e_i's is the weighted sum of the individual nonsystematic variances with the square of the investment proportions as weights.

If the portfolio were equally weighted, $w_i = 1/n$, then the nonsystematic variance would be

$$\sigma^2\left(e_P; w_i = \frac{1}{n}\right) = \sum \left(\frac{1}{n}\right)^2 \sigma^2(e_i) = \frac{1}{n} \sum \frac{\sigma^2(e_i)}{n} = \frac{1}{n}\overline{\sigma^2}(e_i)$$

In this case, we divide the average nonsystematic variance, $\overline{\sigma^2}(e_i)$ by n, so that when the portfolio gets large (in the sense that n is large and the portfolio remains equally weighted across all n stocks), the nonsystematic variance approaches zero.

CC 6

CONCEPT CHECK

What will be the nonsystematic standard deviation of the equally weighted portfolio if the average value of $\sigma^2(e_i)$ equals .30, and (a) $n = 10$, (b) $n = 100$, (c) $n = 1,000$, and (d) $n = 10,000$? What do you conclude about the nonsystematic risk of large, diversified portfolios?

The set of portfolios for which the nonsystematic variance approaches zero as n gets large consists of more portfolios than just the equally weighted portfolio. Any portfolio for which each w_i becomes consistently smaller as n gets large (specifically where each $w^2{}_i$ approaches zero as n gets large) will satisfy the condition that the portfolio nonsystematic risk will approach zero as n gets large.

In fact, this property motivates us to define a **well-diversified portfolio** as one that is diversified over a large enough number of securities with proportions, w_i, each small enough that for practical purposes the nonsystematic variance, $\sigma^2(e_P)$, is negligible. Because the expected return of e_P is zero, if its variance also is zero, we can conclude that any realized value of e_P will be virtually zero. Rewriting equation 8.2, we conclude that for a well-diversified portfolio for all practical purposes

$$R_P = E(R_p) + \beta_P F$$

and

$$\sigma^2{}_P = \beta^2{}_P \sigma^2{}_F; \; \sigma_P = \beta_P \sigma_F$$

CC 7

CONCEPT CHECK

a. A portfolio is invested in a very large number of shares (n is large). However, one-half of the portfolio is invested in stock 1, and the rest of the portfolio is equally divided among the other $n - 1$ shares. Is this portfolio well diversified?

b. Another portfolio also is invested in n shares, where n is very large. Instead of equally weighting with portfolio weights of $1/n$ in each stock, the weights in half the securities are $1.5/n$ while the weights in the other shares are $.5/n$. Is this portfolio well diversified?

The solid line in Figure 8.5, panel A, plots the return of a well-diversified portfolio (A) with $\beta_A = 1$ for various realizations of the systematic factor. The expected return of portfolio A is 10 percent: this is where the solid line crosses the vertical axis. At this point, the systematic factor is zero, implying no macro surprises. If the macro factor is positive, the portfolio's return exceeds its expected value; if it is negative, the portfolio's return falls short of its mean. The return on the portfolio is therefore

$$E(r_A) + \beta_A F = .10 + 1.0 \times F$$

Compare panel A with panel B, which is a similar graph for a single stock (S) with $\beta_S = 1$. The undiversified stock is subject to nonsystematic risk, which is seen in a scatter of points around the line. The well-diversified portfolio's return, in contrast, is determined completely by the systematic factor.

In a single-factor world, all pairs of well-diversified portfolios are perfectly correlated: Their risk is fully determined by the same systematic factor. Consider a second well-diversified portfolio, portfolio Q, with $R_Q = E(R_Q) + \beta_Q F$. We can compute the standard deviations of P and Q, as well as the covariance and correlation between them:

$$\sigma_P = \beta_P \sigma_F; \, \sigma_Q = \beta_Q \sigma_F$$

$$\text{Cov}(R_P, R_Q) = \text{Cov}(\beta_P F, \beta_Q F) = \beta_P, \beta_Q \sigma^2_F$$

$$\rho_{PQ} = \frac{\text{Cov}(R_P, R_Q)}{\sigma_P \sigma_Q} = 1$$

Figure 8.5

Returns as a function of the systematic factor. **Panel A:** Well-diversified portfolio (A). **Panel B:** Single stock (S).

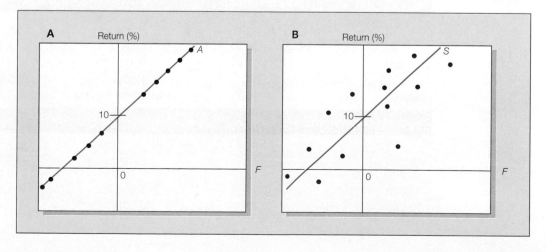

Perfect correlation means that in a plot of expected return versus standard deviation any two well-diversified portfolios lie on straight line. We will see later that this common line is the CML.

Diversification and Residual Risk in Practice

What is the effect of diversification on portfolio residual SD *in practice*, where portfolio size is not unlimited? In reality, we may find (annualized) residual SDs as high as 50 percent for large stocks and even 100 percent for small stocks. To illustrate the impact of diversification, we examine portfolios of two configurations. One portfolio is equally weighted; this achieves the highest benefits of diversification with equal-SD stocks. For comparison, we form the other portfolio using far-from-equal weights. We select stocks in groups of four, with relative weights in each group of 70 percent, 15 percent, 10 percent and 5 percent. The highest weight is 14 times greater than the lowest, which will severely reduce potential benefits of diversification. However, extended diversification in which we add to the portfolio more and more groups of four stocks with the same relative weights will overcome this problem because the highest portfolio weight still falls with additional diversification. In an equally weighted 1,000-stock portfolio, each weight is .1 percent; in the "unequally weighted portfolio," with $1,000/4 = 250$ groups of four stocks, the highest and lowest weights are $70\%/250 = .28$ percent, and $5\%/250 = .02$ percent, respectively.

What is a large portfolio? Hundreds of widely held ETFs each include hundreds of stocks, and some funds such as the Wilshire 5000 hold thousands. These portfolios are accessible to the public since the annual expense ratios of investment companies that offer such funds are on the order of only 10 basis points. Thus a portfolio of 1,000 stocks is not highly unusual, but a portfolio of 10,000 stocks is.

Table 8.3 shows portfolio residual SD as a function of the number of stocks. Equally weighted, 1,000-stock portfolios achieve small but not negligible standard deviations of 1.58 percent when residual risk is 50 percent and 3.16 percent when residual risk is 100 percent. The SDs for the unbalanced portfolios are about double these values. For 10,000-stock portfolios,

TABLE 8.3
Residual Variance with Even and Uneven Portfolio Weights

Equal Weights: $w_i = 1/N$			
Residual SD of Each Stock = 50%		**Residual SD of Each Stock = 100%**	
N	**SD(e) Portfolio**	**N**	**SD(e) Portfolio**
4	25.00	4	50.00
60	6.45	60	12.91
200	3.54	200	7.07
1,000	1.58	1,000	3.16
10,000	.50	10,000	1.00
Sets of Four Weights: $w_1 = .65$, $w_2 = .2$, $w_3 = .1$, $w_4 = .05$			
4	36.23	4	72.46
60	9.35	60	18.71
200	5.12	200	10.25
1,000	2.29	1,000	4.58
10,000	.72	10,000	1.45

the SDs are negligible, verifying that diversification can eliminate risk even in very unbalanced portfolios, at least in principle, if the investment universe is large enough.

Executing Arbitrage

Imagine a single-factor market where the well-diversified portfolio, M, represents the market factor, F, of equation 8.18. The excess return on any security is given by

$$R_i = \alpha_i + \beta_i R_M + e_i$$

and that of a well-diversified (therefore zero residual) portfolio, P, is

$$R_P = \alpha_p + \beta_p R_M \tag{8.22}$$

$$E(R_P) = \alpha_p + \beta_p E(R_M) \tag{8.23}$$

Now suppose that security analysis reveals that portfolio P has a positive alpha.[19] We also estimate the risk premium of the index portfolio, M, from macro analysis.

Since neither M nor portfolio P has residual risk, the only risk to the returns of the two portfolios is systematic, derived from their betas on the common factor (the beta of the index is 1.0). Therefore, you can eliminate the risk of P altogether. Construct a zero-beta portfolio, called Z, from P and M by appropriately selecting weights w_P and $_{wM} = 1 - w_P$ on each portfolio:

$$\beta_Z = w_p \beta_p + (1 - w_p)\beta_M = 0$$
$$\beta_M = 1 \tag{8.24}$$
$$w_p = \frac{1}{1 - \beta_p}; w_M = 1 - w_p = \frac{\beta_p}{1 - \beta_p}$$

Therefore, the alpha of portfolio Z is

$$\alpha_Z = w_p \alpha_p + (1 - w_p)\alpha_m = w_p \alpha_p \tag{8.25}$$

The risk premium on Z must be zero, because the risk of Z is zero. If its risk premium were not zero, you could earn arbitrage profits. Here is how.

Since the beta of Z is zero, equation 8.23 implies that its risk premium is just its alpha. Using equation 8.25, its alpha is $w_p \alpha_p$, so

$$E(R_Z) = w_p \alpha_p = \frac{1}{1 - \beta_P}\alpha_P \tag{8.26}$$

You now form a zero-net-investment arbitrage portfolio: If $\beta_P < 1$ and the risk premium of Z is positive (implying that Z returns more than the risk-free rate), borrow and invest the proceeds in Z. For every borrowed dollar invested in Z, you get a net return (i.e., net of paying the interest on your loan) of $\frac{1}{1 - \beta_P}\alpha_P$. This is a money machine, which you would work as hard as you can.[20] Similarly if $\beta_P > 1$, equation 8.26 tells us that the risk premium is negative; therefore, sell Z short and invest the proceeds at the risk-free rate. Once again, a money machine has been created. Neither situation can persist, as the large volume of trades from arbitrageurs pursuing these strategies will push prices until the arbitrage opportunity disappears.

---

[19]If the portfolio alpha is negative, we can still pursue the following strategy. We would simply switch to a short position in P, which would have a positive alpha of the same absolute value as P's, and a beta that is the negative of P's.

[20]The function in equation 8.26 becomes unstable at $\beta_P = 1$. For values of β_P near 1, it becomes infinitely large with the sign of α_P. This isn't an economic absurdity, since in that case, the sizes of your long position in P and short position in M will be almost identical, and the arbitrage profit you earn *per dollar invested* will be nearly infinite.

Figure 8.6

Returns as a function of the systematic factor: An arbitrage opportunity.

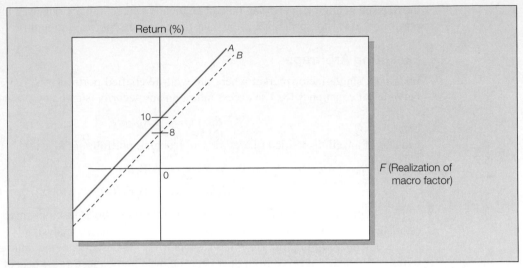

The No-Arbitrage Equation of the APT

We've seen that arbitrage activity will quickly pin the risk premium of any zero-beta well-diversified portfolio to zero.[21] Setting the expression in equation 8.26 to zero implies that the alpha of *any* well-diversified portfolio must also be zero. From equation 8.23, this means that for any well-diversified P,

$$E(R_P) = \beta_P E(R_M) \tag{8.27}$$

In other words, the risk premium (expected excess return) on portfolio P is the product of its beta and the market-index risk premium. Equation 8.27 thus establishes that the SML of the CAPM applies to well-diversified portfolios simply by virtue of the "no-arbitrage" requirement of the APT.

Another demonstration that the APT results in the same SML as the CAPM is more graphical in nature. First we show why all well-diversified portfolios with the same beta must have the same expected return. Figure 8.6 plots the returns on two such portfolios, A and B, both with betas of 1, but with differing expected returns: $E(rA) = 10$ percent and $E(rB) = 8$ percent.

Could portfolios A and B coexist with the return pattern depicted? Clearly not: no matter what the systematic factor turns out to be, portfolio A outperforms portfolio B, leading to an arbitrage opportunity.

If you sell short \$1 million of B and buy \$1 million of A, a zero net investment strategy, your return would be \$20,000, as follows:

$(.10 + 1.0 \times F) \times \$1\text{ million}$	(From long position in A)
$-(.08 + 1.0 \times F) \times \$1\text{ million}$	(From short position in B)
$.02 \times \$1\text{ million} = \$20,000$	(Net proceeds)

You make a risk-free profit because the factor risk cancels out across the long and short positions. Moreover, the strategy requires zero net investment. You should pursue it on an infinitely large scale until the return discrepancy between the two portfolios disappears. Portfolios with equal betas must have equal expected returns in market equilibrium, or arbitrage opportunities exist.

---

[21]As an exercise, show that when $\alpha_P < 0$ you reverse the position of P in Z, and the arbitrage portfolio will still earn a riskless excess return.

Figure 8.7
An arbitrage opportunity.

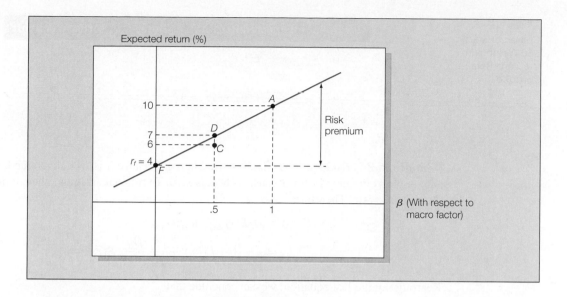

What about portfolios with different betas? Their risk premiums must be proportional to beta. To see why, consider Figure 8.7. Suppose that the risk-free rate is 4 percent and that well-diversified portfolio C, with a beta of .5, has an expected return of 6 percent. Portfolio C plots below the line from the risk-free asset to portfolio A. Consider therefore a new portfolio, D, composed of half of portfolio A and half of the risk-free asset. Portfolio D's beta will be $(\frac{1}{2} \times 0 + \frac{1}{2} \times 1.0) = .5$, and its expected return will be $\frac{1}{2} \times 4 + \frac{1}{2} \times 10 = 7$ percent. Now portfolio D has an equal beta but a greater expected return than portfolio C. From our analysis in the previous paragraph we know that this constitutes an arbitrage opportunity.

We conclude that, to preclude arbitrage opportunities, the expected return on all well-diversified portfolios must lie on the straight line from the risk-free asset in Figure 8.7.

Notice in Figure 8.7 that risk premiums are indeed proportional to portfolio betas. The risk premium is depicted by the vertical arrow, which measures the distance between the risk-free rate and the expected return on the portfolio. As in the simple CAPM, the risk premium is zero for $\beta = 0$, and rises in direct proportion to β.

More formally, suppose that two well-diversified portfolios are combined into a zero-beta portfolio, Z, by choosing the weights shown in Table 8.4. The weights of the two assets in portfolio Z sum to 1, and the portfolio beta is zero:

$$\beta_Z = w_U\beta_U + w_V\beta_V = \frac{\beta_V}{\beta_V - \beta_U}\beta_U + \frac{-\beta_U}{\beta_V - \beta_U}\beta_V = 0$$

Portfolio	Expected Return	Beta	Portfolio Weight
U	$E(r_U)$	β_U	$\dfrac{\beta_V}{\beta_V - \beta_U}$
V	$E(r_V)$	β_V	$\dfrac{-\beta_U}{\beta_V - \beta_U}$

Portfolio Z is riskless: it has no diversifiable risk because it is well diversified, and no exposure to the systematic factor because its beta is zero. To rule out arbitrage, then, it must earn only the risk-free rate. Therefore,

$$E(r_Z) = w_U E(r_U) + w_V E(r_V)$$
$$= \frac{\beta_V}{\beta_V - \beta_U} E(r_U) + \frac{-\beta_U}{\beta_V - \beta_U} E(r_V) = r_f$$

Rearranging the last equation, we can conclude that

$$\frac{E(r_U) - r_f}{\beta_U} = \frac{E(r_V) - r_f}{\beta_V} \tag{8.28}$$

which implies that risk premiums be proportional to betas, as in Figure 8.7.

8.8

THE APT, THE CAPM, AND THE INDEX MODEL

Equation 8.27 raises three questions:

1. Does the APT also apply to less-than-well-diversified portfolios?
2. Is the APT as a model of risk and return superior or inferior to the CAPM? Do we need both models?
3. Suppose a security analyst identifies a positive-alpha portfolio with some remaining residual risk: Don't we already have a prescription for this case from the Treynor-Black (TB) procedure applied to the index model? Is this procedure preferred to the APT?

The APT and the CAPM

The APT is built on the foundation of well-diversified portfolios. However, we've seen, for example in Table 8.3, that even large portfolios may have non-negligible residual risk. Some indexed portfolios may have hundreds or thousands of stocks, but active portfolios generally cannot, as there is a limit to how many stocks can be actively analyzed in search of alpha. How does the APT stand up to these limitations?

Suppose we order all portfolios in the universe by residual risk. Think of Level 0 portfolios as having zero residual risk—in other words, they are the theoretically well-diversified portfolios of the APT. Think of Level 1 portfolios as having very small residual risk, say up to .5 percent; Level 2 portfolios yet greater residual SD, say up to 1 percent; and so on.

If equation 8.27 applies to all well-diversified Level 0 portfolios, it must at least approximate the risk premiums of Level 1 portfolios. Even more importantly, while Level 1 risk premiums may deviate slightly from equation 8.27, such deviations should be "unbiased," with alphas equally likely to be positive or negative. Deviations should be uncorrelated with beta or residual SD and should average to zero.

We can apply the same logic to portfolios of slightly higher Level 2 residual risk.

Since all Level 1 portfolios are still well approximated by equation 8.27, so must be risk premiums of Level 2 portfolios, albeit with slightly less accuracy. Here too, we may take comfort in the lack of bias and zero average deviations from the risk premiums predicted by the equation. But still, the precision of predictions of risk premiums from the equation consistently deteriorates with increasing residual risk. (One might ask why we don't transform Level 2 portfolios into Level 1 or even Level 0 portfolios by further diversifying; but as we've pointed out, this may not be feasible in practice for assets with considerable residual risk when active portfolio size or the size of the investment universe is limited.) If residual risk is sufficiently high and the impediments to complete diversification are too onerous, we cannot have full confidence in the APT and the arbitrage activities that underpin it.

Despite this shortcoming, the APT is valuable. First, recall that the CAPM requires that almost all investors be mean-variance optimizers. We may well suspect that they are not. The APT frees us of this assumption. It is sufficient that a small number of sophisticated arbitrageurs scour the market for arbitrage opportunities. This alone produces a mean return–beta equation (8.27) that is a good and unbiased approximation for all assets but those with significant residual risk.

Perhaps even more important is the fact that the APT is anchored by observable portfolios such as the market index. The CAPM is not even testable because it relies on an unobserved, all-inclusive portfolio. The reason that the APT is not fully superior to the CAPM is that at the level of individual assets and high residual risk, pure arbitrage may be insufficient to enforce equation 8.27. Therefore, we need to turn to the CAPM as the theoretical construct behind equilibrium risk premiums.

It should be noted, however, that when we replace the unobserved market portfolio of the CAPM with an observed, broad index portfolio that may not be efficient, we no longer can be sure that the CAPM predicts risk premiums of all assets with no bias. Neither model therefore is free of limitations. Comparing the APT arbitrage strategy to maximization of the Sharpe ratio in the context of an index model may well be the more useful framework for analysis.

The APT and Portfolio Optimization in a Single-Index Market

The APT is couched in a single-factor market,[22] and applies with perfect accuracy to *well-diversified* portfolios. It shows arbitrageurs how to generate infinite profits if the risk premium of a well-diversified portfolio deviates from equation 8.27. The trades executed by these arbitrageurs are the enforcers of the accuracy of this equation.

In effect, the APT shows how to take advantage of security mispricing when diversification opportunities are abundant. When you lock in and scale up an arbitrage opportunity, you're sure to be as rich as Croesus, regardless of the composition of the rest of your portfolio—but only if the arbitrage portfolio is truly risk-free! However, if the arbitrage position is not perfectly well diversified, an increase in its scale (borrowing cash, or borrowing shares to go short) will increase the risk of the "arbitrage" position, potentially without bound. But if you limit the scale of the risky arbitrage, the composition of your overall risky portfolio then becomes relevant. The APT ignores this fact.

Now consider an investor who confronts the same single-factor market, and whose security analysis reveals an underpriced asset (or portfolio), that is, one whose risk premium implies a positive alpha. This investor can follow the advice weaved throughout Chapters 6 to 8 to construct an optimal risky portfolio. The optimization process will consider both the potential profit

---

[22]The APT is easily extended to a multifactor market as we show later.

from a position in the mispriced asset, as well as the risk of the overall portfolio and efficient diversification. As we have seen, the TB procedure can be summarized as follows:[23]

1. Estimate the risk premium and standard deviation of the benchmark (index) portfolio, RP_M and σ_M.

2. Place all the assets that are mispriced into an active portfolio. Call the alpha of the active portfolio α_A, its systematic-risk coefficient β_A, and its residual risk $\sigma(e_A)$. Your optimal risky portfolio will allocate to the active portfolio a weight w_A*:

$$w_A^0 = \frac{\alpha_A/\sigma^2(e_A)}{RP_M/\sigma_M^2}; \; w_A^* = \frac{w_A^0}{1 + w_A^0(1 - \beta_A)}$$

The allocation to the passive portfolio is then, $w_M^* = 1 - w_A^*$. With this allocation, the increase in the Sharpe ratio of the optimal portfolio, S_P, over that of the passive portfolio, S_M, depends on the size of the information ratio of the active portfolio, IR $= \alpha_A/\sigma(e_A)$. The optimized portfolio can attain a Sharpe ratio of $S_P = \sqrt{S_M^2 + IR_A^2}$.

3. To maximize the Sharpe ratio of the risky portfolio, you maximize the IR of the active portfolio. This is achieved by allocating to each asset with a nonzero alpha a portfolio weight proportional to $w_{Ai} = \alpha_i/\sigma^2(e_i)$. When this is done, the square of the information ratio of the active portfolio will be the sum of the squared individual information ratios: $IR_A^2 = \sum IR_i^2$.

Now see what happens in the TB model when the residual risk of the active portfolio is zero. This is essentially the assumption of the APT, that a well-diversified portfolio (with zero residual risk) can be formed. When the residual risk of the active portfolio goes to zero, the position in it goes to infinity. This is the precisely the same implication as the APT: when portfolios are well diversified, you will scale up an arbitrage position without bound. Similarly, when the residual risk of an asset in the active TB portfolio is zero, it will displace all other assets from that portfolio, and thus the residual risk of the active portfolio will be zero and elicit the same extreme portfolio response.

When residual risks are nonzero, the TB procedure produces the optimal risky portfolio, which is a compromise between seeking alpha and shunning potentially diversifiable risk. The APT ignores residual risk altogether, prescribing the same arbitrage position as it would with no residual risk. Obviously, we have no use for the APT in this context. When residual risk can be made small through diversification, the TB model prescribes very aggressive (large) positions in mispriced securities that exert great pressure on equilibrium risk premiums to eliminate nonzero alpha values. The TB model does what the APT is meant to do, but with more flexibility in terms of accommodating the practical limits to diversification. In this sense, Treynor and Black anticipated the development of the APT.

EXAMPLE 8.3   **Exploiting Alpha**

Table 8.5 summarizes a rudimentary experiment that compares the prescriptions and predictions of the APT and TB model in the presence of realistic values of residual risk. We use relatively small alpha values (1 and 3 percent), three levels of residual risk (2, 3, and 4 percent), and two levels of beta (.5 and 2) to span the likely range of reasonable parameters.

The first set of columns, titled "Active Portfolio," show the parameter values in each example. The second set of columns, titled "Zero Net Investment, Arbitrage (Zero-Beta) Portfolio,"

continued

---

[23]The tediousness of some of the expressions involved in the TB method should not deter anyone. The calculations are pretty straightforward, especially in a spreadsheet. The estimation of the risk parameters also is a relatively straightforward statistical task. The real difficulty is to uncover security alphas and the macro-factor risk premium, RP_M.

TABLE 8.5   Performance of APT Versus Index Model When Diversification of Residual SD is Incomplete

Index Risk Premium = 7			Index SD = 20		Index Sharpe Ratio = .35			
Active Portfolio			Zero Net Investment, Arbitrage (Zero-Beta) Portfolio		Treynor-Black Procedure			
Alpha (%)	Residual SD (%)	Beta	w in Active	Info Ratio	w (beta = 0)	w (beta)	Sharpe Ratio	Incremental Sharpe Ratio
1	4	.5	2	.25	3.57	1.28	.43	.18
1	4	2	1	.25	3.57	1.00	.43	.18
1	3	.5	2	.33	6.35	1.52	.48	.15
1	3	2	1	.33	6.35	1.00	.48	.15
1	2	.5	2	.50	14.29	1.75	.61	.11
1	2	2	1	.50	14.29	1.00	.61	.11
3	4	.5	2	.75	10.71	1.69	.83	.08
3	4	2	1	.75	10.71	1.00	.83	.08
3	3	.5	2	1.00	19.05	1.81	1.06	.06
3	3	2	1	1.00	19.05	1.00	1.06	.06
3	2	.5	2	1.50	42.86	1.91	1.54	.04
3	2	2	1	1.50	42.86	1.00	1.54	.04

shows the weight in the active portfolio and resultant information ratio of the active portfolio. This would be the Sharpe ratio if the arbitrage position (the positive-alpha, zero-beta portfolio) made up the entire risky portfolio (as would be prescribed by the APT). The last set of columns shows the TB position in the active portfolio that maximizes the Sharpe ratio of the overall risky portfolio. The final column of that group shows the increment to the Sharpe ratio of the TB portfolio relative to the APT portfolio.

Keep in mind that even when the two models call for a similar weight in the active portfolio, they prescribe a different overall risky portfolio. The APT assumes zero investment beyond what is necessary to hedge out the market risk of the active portfolio. In contrast, the TB procedure chooses a mix of active and index portfolios to maximize the Sharpe ratio. With identical investment in the active portfolio, the TB portfolio can still include additional investment in the index portfolio.

To obtain the Sharpe ratio of the risky portfolio, we need the Sharpe ratio of the index portfolio. Suppose the average return of the broad market index is 7 percent, and the standard deviation of the broad market index is 20 percent per year. The top row (over the column titles) shows an annual Sharpe ratio of .35 (7/20). The rows of the table (the experiments) are ordered by the information ratio of the active portfolio.

The results in Table 8.5 show that the TB procedure noticeably improves the Sharpe ratio beyond the information ratio of the APT (for which IR is also the Sharpe ratio). However, as the information ratio of the active portfolio increases, the difference in the TB and APT active portfolio positions declines, as does the difference between their Sharpe ratios. Put differently, the higher the information ratio, the closer we are to a risk-free arbitrage opportunity, and the closer are the results of using the APT and TB models. Notice that the beta of the active portfolio affects the composition of the portfolios but not the Sharpe ratio. The APT zeros it out, while the TB procedure accounts for it in determining portfolio composition.

8.9

A MULTIFACTOR APT

For simplicity we have assumed so far that there is only one systematic factor affecting stock returns. This assumption is in fact too simple. We've noted that it is easy to think of several factors driven by the business cycle that might affect stock returns: interest rate fluctuations, inflation rates, and so on. Presumably, exposure to any of these factors will affect a stock's risk and hence its expected return. We can derive a multifactor version of the APT to accommodate these multiple sources of risk.

Suppose that we generalize the factor model expressed in equation 8.2 to a two-factor model:

$$R_i = E(R_i) + \beta_{i1}F_1 + \beta_{i2}F_2 + e_i \qquad (8.29)$$

In Example 8.1, factor 1 was the departure of GDP growth from expectations, and factor 2 was the unanticipated decline in interest rates. Each factor has zero expected value because each measures the *surprise* in the systematic variable rather than the level of the variable. Similarly, the firm-specific component of unexpected return, e_i, also has zero expected value. Extending such a two-factor model to any number of factors is straightforward.

Establishing a multifactor APT is similar to the one-factor case. But first we must introduce the concept of a **factor portfolio**—a well-diversified portfolio constructed to have a beta of 1 on one of the factors and a beta of 0 on any other factor. We can think of a factor portfolio as a tracking portfolio; that is, the returns on such a portfolio track the evolution of particular sources of macroeconomic risk, but are uncorrelated with other sources of risk. It is possible to form such portfolios because we have a large number of securities to choose from, and a relatively small number of factors. Factor portfolios will serve as the benchmark portfolios for a multifactor security market line.

EXAMPLE 8.4   **Multifactor SML**

Suppose that the two-factor portfolios, portfolios 1 and 2, have expected returns $E(r_1) = 10\%$ and $E(r_2) = 12\%$. Suppose further that the risk-free rate is 4 percent. The risk premium on the first factor portfolio is $10\% - 4\% = 6\%$, whereas that on the second factor portfolio is $12\% - 4\% = 8\%$.

Now consider a well-diversified portfolio, portfolio A, with beta on the first factor, $\beta_{A1} = .5$, and beta on the second factor, $\beta_{A2} = .75$. The multifactor APT states that the overall risk premium on this portfolio must equal the sum of the risk premiums required as compensation for each source of systematic risk. The risk premium attributable to risk factor 1 should be the portfolio's exposure to factor 1, β_{A1}, multiplied by the risk premium earned on the first factor portfolio, $E(r_1) - r_f$. Therefore, the portion of portfolio A's risk premium that is compensation for its exposure to the first factor is $\beta_{A1}[E(r_1) - r_f] = .5(10\% - 4\%) = 3\%$, whereas the risk premium attributable to risk factor 2 is $\beta_{A2}[E(r_2) - r_f] = .75(12\% - 4\%) = 6\%$. The total risk premium on the portfolio should be $3 + 6 = 9\%$ and the total return on the portfolio should be $4\% + 9\% = 13\%$.

To generalize the argument in the above example, note that the factor exposures of any portfolio, P, are given by its betas, β_{P1} and β_{P2}. A competing portfolio, Q, can be formed by investing in factor portfolios with the following weights: β_{P1} in the first factor portfolio, β_{P2} in the second factor portfolio, and $1 - \beta_{P1} - \beta_{P2}$ in T-bills. By construction, portfolio Q will have betas equal to those of portfolio P and expected return of

$$\begin{aligned} E(r_Q) &= \beta_{P1}E(r_1) + \beta_{P2}E(r_2) + (1 - \beta_{P1} - \beta_{P2})r_f \\ &= r_f + \beta_{P1}[E(r_1) - r_f] + \beta_{P2}[E(r_2) - r_f] \end{aligned} \qquad (8.30)$$

Using the numbers in the example:

$$E(r_Q) = 4 + .5 \times (10 - 4) + .75 \times (12 - 4) = 13\%$$

Because portfolio Q has precisely the same exposures as portfolio A to the two sources of risk, their expected returns also ought to be equal. So portfolio A also ought to have an expected return of 13 percent. If it does not, there will be an arbitrage opportunity.

EXAMPLE 8.5 **Mispricing and Arbitrage**

Suppose that the expected return on portfolio A were 12 percent rather than 13 percent. This would give rise to an arbitrage opportunity. Form a portfolio from the factor portfolios with the same betas as portfolio A. This requires weights of .5 on the first factor portfolio, .75 on the second factor portfolio, and $-.25$ on the risk-free asset. This portfolio has exactly the same factor betas as portfolio A: it has a beta of .5 on the first factor because of its .5 weight on the first factor portfolio, and a beta of .75 on the second factor. (The weight of $-.25$ on risk-free T-bills does not affect the sensitivity to either factor.)

Now invest $1 in portfolio Q and sell (short) $1 in portfolio A. Your net investment is zero, but your expected dollar profit is positive and equal to

$$\$1 \times E(r_Q) - \$1 \times E(r_A) = \$1 \times .13 - \$1 \times .12 = \$.01$$

Moreover, your net position is riskless. Your exposure to each risk factor cancels out because you are long $1 in portfolio Q and short $1 in portfolio A, and these two well-diversified portfolios have exactly the same factor betas. Thus, if portfolio A's expected return differs from that of portfolio Q, you can earn positive risk-free profits on a zero net investment position. This is an arbitrage opportunity.

CC 9

CONCEPT CHECK

Using the factor portfolios of the above example, find the equilibrium rate of return on a portfolio with $\beta_1 = .2$ and $\beta_2 = 1.4$.

We conclude that any well-diversified portfolio with betas β_{P1} and β_{P2} must have the return given in equation 8.25 if arbitrage opportunities are to be precluded. If you compare equations 8.23 and 8.25, you will see that equation 8.25 is simply a generalization of the one-factor SML.

Finally, the extension of the multifactor SML of equation 8.25 to individual assets is precisely the same as for the one-factor APT. Equation 8.25 cannot be satisfied by every well-diversified portfolio unless it is satisfied by virtually every security taken individually. Equation 8.25 thus represents the multifactor SML for an economy with multiple sources of risk.

We pointed out earlier that one application of the CAPM is to provide "fair" rates of return for regulated utilities. The multifactor APT can be used to the same ends. The nearby box summarizes a study in which the APT was applied to find the cost of capital for regulated electric companies.

8.10 WHERE SHOULD WE LOOK FOR FACTORS?

One shortcoming of the multifactor APT is that it gives no guidance concerning the determination of the relevant risk factors or their risk premiums. Two principles guide us when we specify a reasonable list of factors. First, we want to limit ourselves to systematic factors with considerable ability to explain security returns. If our model calls for hundreds of explanatory variables, it does little to simplify our description of security returns. Second, we wish to choose factors that seem likely to be important risk factors, that is, factors that concern investors sufficiently that they will demand meaningful risk premiums to bear exposure to those sources of risk.

Elton, Gruber, and Mei* use the APT to derive the cost of capital for electric utilities. They assume that the relevant risk factors are unanticipated developments in the term structure of interest rates, the level of interest rates, inflation rates, the business cycle (measured by GDP), foreign exchange rates, and a summary measure they devise to measure other macro factors.

Their first step is to estimate the risk premium associated with exposure to each risk source. They accomplish this in a two-step strategy. . . :

1. *Estimate "factor loadings" (i.e., betas) of a large sample of firms.* Regress returns of 100 randomly selected stocks against the systematic risk factors. They use a time-series regression for each stock (e.g., 60 months of data), therefore estimating 100 regressions, one for each stock.

2. *Estimate the reward earned per unit of exposure to each risk factor.* For each month, regress the return of each stock against the five betas estimated. The coefficient on each beta is the extra average return earned as beta increases, that is, it is an estimate of the risk premium for that risk factor from that month's data. These estimates are of course subject to sampling error. Therefore, average the risk premium estimates across the 12 months in each year. The *average* response of return to risk is less subject to sampling error.

The risk premiums found for 1990 are in the second column of the table here.

Notice that some risk premiums are negative. The interpretation of this result is that risk premium should be positive for risk factors you don't want exposure to, but *negative* for factors you *do* want exposure to. For example, you should desire securities that have higher returns when inflation increases and be willing to accept lower expected returns on such securities; this shows up as a negative risk premium.

Therefore, the expected return on any security should be related to its factor betas as follows:

$$r_f + .425\beta_{\text{term strue}} - .051\beta_{\text{int rate}} - .049\beta_{\text{ex rate}} + .041\beta_{\text{bus cycle}}$$
$$- .069\beta_{\text{inflation}} + .530\beta_{\text{other}}$$

Finally, to obtain the cost of capital for a particular firm, the authors estimate the firm's betas against each source of risk, multiply each factor beta by the "cost of factor risk" from the table above, sum over all risk sources to obtain the total risk premium, and add the risk-free rate.

For example, the beta estimates for Niagra Mohawk appear in the last column of the table. Therefore its cost of capital is

$$\text{Cost of capital} = r_f + .425 \times 1.0615 - .051(2.4167)$$
$$- .049(1.3235) + .041(.1292)$$
$$- .069(2.5220) + .530(.3046)$$
$$= r_f + .712$$

In other words, the monthly cost of capital for Niagra Mohawk is .712 percent above the monthly risk-free rate. Its annualized risk premium is therefore .712% × 12 = 8.544 percent.

Factor	Factor Risk Premium	Factor Betas for Niagra Mohawk
Term structure	.425	1.0615
Interest rates	−.051	−2.4167
Exchange rates	−.049	1.3235
Business cycle	.041	.1292
Inflation	−.069	−.5220
Other macro factors	.530	.3046

*Edwin J. Elton, Martin J. Gruber, and Jianping Mei, "Cost of Capital Using Arbitrage Pricing Theory: A Case Study of Nine New York Utilities," *Financial Markets, Institutions, and Instruments* 3 (August 1994), pp. 46–68.

One example of the multifactor approach is the work of Chen, Roll, and Ross,[24] who chose the following set of factors on the basis of the ability of these factors to paint a broad picture of the macroeconomy. Their set is obviously but one of many possible sets that might be considered.

IP = % change in industrial production

EI = % change in expected inflation

UI = % change in unanticipated inflation

CG = excess return of long-term corporate bonds over long-term government bonds

GB = excess return of long-term government bonds over T-bills

This list gives rise to the following five-factor model of security returns during holding period t as a function of the change in the set of macroeconomic indicators:

$$r_{it} = \alpha_i + \beta_{i\text{IP}}\text{IP}_t + \beta_{i\text{EI}}\text{EI}_t + \beta_{i\text{UI}}\text{UI}_t + \beta_{i\text{CG}}\text{CG}_t + \beta_{i\text{GB}}\text{GB}_t + e_{it} \tag{8.31}$$

[24]N. Chen, R. Roll, and S. Ross, "Economic Forces and the Stock Market," *Journal of Business* 59 (1986), pp. 383–403.

Equation 8.31 is a multidimensional security characteristic line (SCL), with five factors. As before, to estimate the betas of a given stock we can use regression analysis. Here, however, because there is more than one factor, we estimate a *multiple* regression of the returns of the stock in each period on the five macroeconomic factors. The residual variance of the regression estimates the firm-specific risk. We discuss the results of this model in Chapter 11, which focuses on empirical evidence on security pricing.

An alternative approach to specifying macroeconomic factors as candidates for relevant sources of systematic risk uses firm characteristics that seem on empirical grounds to proxy for exposure to systematic risk. In other words, the factors are chosen as variables that on past evidence seem to predict high average returns and therefore may be capturing risk premiums. One example of this approach is the so-called Fama and French (FF) three-factor model,[25]

$$r_{it} = \alpha_i + \beta_{iM}R_{Mt} + \beta_{iSMB}\text{SMB}_t + \beta_{iHML}\text{HML}_t + e_{it} \tag{8.32}$$

where

SMB = *small minus big*, that is, the return of a portfolio of small stocks in excess of the return on a portfolio of large stocks

HML = *high minus low*, that is, the return of a portfolio of stocks with a high book-to-market ratio in excess of the return on a portfolio of stocks with a low book-to-market ratio

Note that in this model the market index does play a role and is expected to capture systematic risk originating from macroeconomic factors.

These two firm-characteristic variables are chosen because of long-standing observations that corporate capitalization (firm size) and book-to-market ratio seem to be predictive of average stock returns. Fama and French justify this model on empirical grounds: while SMB and HML are not themselves obvious candidates for relevant risk factors, the hope is that these variables proxy for yet-unknown more-fundamental variables. For example, Fama and French point out that firms with high ratios of book to market value are more likely to be in financial distress and that small stocks may be more sensitive to changes in business conditions. Thus, these variables may capture sensitivity to risk factors in the macroeconomy. Evidence on the FF model also appears in Chapter 11.

The problem with empirical approaches such as the FF model, which use proxies for extramarket sources of risk, is that none of the factors in the proposed models can be clearly identified as hedging a significant source of uncertainty. Black[26] points out that when researchers scan and rescan the database of security returns in search of explanatory factors (an activity often called "data snooping"), they may eventually uncover past "patterns" that are due purely to chance. Black observes that return premiums to factors such as firm size have largely vanished since first discovered. However, Fama and French point out that size and book-to-market ratios have predicted average returns in various time periods and in markets all over the world, thus mitigating potential effects of data snooping.

The firm-characteristic basis of the FF factors raises the question of whether they reflect an APT model or an approximation to a multi-index ICAPM based on extramarket hedging demands. This is an important distinction for the debate over the proper interpretation of the model, because the validity of FF-style models may constitute either a deviation from rational equilibrium (as there is no rational reason to prefer one or another of these firm characteristics per se), or that firm characteristics identified as empirically associated with average returns are correlated with other (yet unknown) risk factors.

The issue is still unresolved and is discussed in Chapter 11.

---

[25]Eugene F. Fama and Kenneth R. French, "Multifactor Explanations of Asset Pricing Anomalies," *The Journal of Finance* 51 (1996), pp. 55–84. Several studies also include a fourth factor, based on price momentum, for example the previous year's price change. See, for example, Mark Carhart, "On Persistence in Mutual Fund Performance," *Journal of Finance* 52 (1997), pp. 57–82.
[26]Fischer Black, "Beta and Return," *Journal of Portfolio Management* 20 (1993), pp. 8–18.

8.11   THE MULTIFACTOR CAPM AND THE APT

It is important to distinguish the multifactor APT from the multi-index CAPM. In the latter, the factors are derived from a multiperiod consideration of a stream of consumption as well as randomly evolving investment opportunities pertaining to the distributions of rates of return. Hence, the hedge index portfolios must be derived from considerations of the utility of consumption, nontraded assets, and changes in investment opportunities.

A multi-index CAPM will therefore inherit its risk factors from sources of risk that a broad group of investors deem important enough to hedge. If hedging demands are common to many investors, the prices of securities with desirable hedging characteristics will be bid up and their expected return reduced. This process requires a multifactor model to explain expected returns, wherein each factor arises from a particular hedging motive. Risk sources that are "priced" in market equilibrium (i.e., are sufficiently important to result in detectable risk premiums) presumably will be systematic sources of uncertainty that affect investors broadly.

In contrast, the APT is largely silent on where to look for priced sources of risk. This lack of guidance is problematic, but by the same token, it accommodates a less structured search for relevant risk factors. These may reflect the concerns of a broader set of investors, including institutions such as endowment or pension funds that may be concerned about exposures to risks that would not be obvious from an examination of individual consumption/investment decisions.

> **CC 10**
>
> **CONCEPT CHECK**
>
> Consider the following regression results for stock X:
>
> $$r_X = 2\% + 1.2 \text{ (percentage change in oil prices)}$$
>
> a. If I live in Alberta, where the local economy is heavily dependent on oil industry profits, does stock X represent a useful asset to hedge my overall economic well-being?
> b. What if I live in Nova Scotia, where most individuals and firms are energy consumers?
> c. If energy consumers are far more numerous than energy producers, will high-oil-beta stocks have higher or lower expected rates of return in market equilibrium than low-oil-beta stocks?

SUMMARY

1. A single-factor model of the economy classifies sources of uncertainty as systematic (macroeconomic) factors or firm-specific (microeconomic) factors. The index model assumes that the macro factor can be represented by a broad index of stock returns.

2. The single-index model drastically reduces the necessary inputs into the Markowitz portfolio selection procedure. It also aids in specialization of labour in security analysis.

3. If the index model specification is valid, then the systematic risk of a portfolio or asset equals $\beta^2 \sigma^2_M$, and the covariance between two assets equals $\beta_i \beta_j \sigma^2_M$.

4. The index model is estimated by applying regression analysis to excess rates of return. The slope of the regression curve is the beta of an asset, whereas the intercept is the asset's alpha during the sample period. The regression line also is called the security characteristic line.

5. Optimal active portfolios constructed from the index model include analyzed securities in proportion to their information ratios. The full risky portfolio is a mixture of the active portfolio and the passive market index portfolio. The index portfolio is used to enhance the diversification of the overall risky position.

6. Practitioners routinely estimate the index model using total rather than excess rates of return. This makes their estimate of alpha equal to $\alpha + r_f(1 - \beta)$.

7. Betas show a tendency to evolve toward 1 over time. Beta forecasting rules attempt to predict this drift. Moreover, other financial variables can be used to help forecast betas.

8. Multifactor models seek to improve the explanatory power of single-factor models by explicitly accounting for the various systematic components of security risk. These models use indicators intended to capture a wide range of macroeconomic risk factors.

9. Once we allow for multiple risk factors, we conclude that the security market line also ought to be multidimensional, with exposure to each risk factor contributing to the total risk premium of the security.

10. A risk-free arbitrage opportunity arises when two or more security prices enable investors to construct a zero net investment portfolio that will yield a sure profit. Rational investors will want to take infinitely large positions in arbitrage portfolios regardless of their degree of risk aversion. This will create pressure on security prices that will continue until prices reach levels that preclude arbitrage.

11. When securities are priced so that there are no risk-free arbitrage opportunities, we say that they satisfy the no-arbitrage condition. Price relationships that satisfy the no-arbitrage condition are important, because we expect them to hold in real-world markets.

12. Portfolios are called *well diversified* if they include a large number of securities and the investment proportion in each is sufficiently small. The proportion of a security in a well-diversified portfolio is small enough so that, for all practical purposes, a reasonable change in that security's rate of return will have a negligible effect on the portfolio rate of return.

13. In a single-factor security market, all well-diversified portfolios have to satisfy the expected return–beta relationship of the security market line in order to satisfy the no-arbitrage condition. If all well-diversified portfolios satisfy the expected return–beta relationship, then all but a small number of securities also satisfy this relationship.

14. The APT does not require the restrictive assumptions of the CAPM and its (unobservable) market portfolio. The price of this generality is that the APT does not guarantee this relationship for all securities at all times.

15. A multifactor APT generalizes the single-factor model to accommodate several sources of systematic risk. The multidimensional security market line predicts that exposure to each risk factor contributes to the security's total risk premium by an amount equal to the factor beta times the risk premium of the factor portfolio that tracks that source of risk.

16. A multifactor extension of the single-factor CAPM, the ICAPM, is a model of the risk–return tradeoff that predicts the same multidimensional security market line as the APT. The ICAPM suggests that priced risk factors will be those sources of risk that lead to significant hedging demand by a substantial fraction of investors.

KEY EQUATIONS

(8.1) $\quad r_i = E(r_i) + m_i + e_i$

(8.2) $\quad r_i = E(r_i) + \beta_i m_i + e_i$

(8.3) $\quad \sigma^2_i = \beta^2_i \sigma^2_m + \sigma^2(e_i)$

(8.4) $\quad \text{Cov}(r_i, r_j) = \text{Cov}(\beta_i m + e_i, \beta_j m + e_j)$
$\quad\quad\quad\quad\quad = \beta_i \beta_j \sigma^2_m$

(8.5) $\quad R_i(t) = \alpha_i + \beta_i R_M(t) + e_i(t)$

(8.6) $\quad E(R_i) = \alpha_i + \beta_i E(R_M)$

(8.7) $\quad \text{Cov}(R_i, R_j) = \text{Cov}(\beta_i R_M, \beta_j R_M) = \beta_i \beta_j \sigma^2_M$

(8.8) $\quad R_P = \alpha_P + \beta_P R_M + e_P$

(8.9) $\quad = \dfrac{1}{n}\sum_{i=1}^{n} \alpha_i + \left(\dfrac{1}{n}\sum_{i=1}^{n} \beta_i\right) R_M + \dfrac{1}{n}\sum_{i=1}^{n} e_i$

(8.10) $\quad \sigma^2_P = \beta^2_P \sigma^2_M + \sigma^2(e_P)$

(8.11) $\quad r = a + b r_M + e$

(8.12) $\quad r - r_f = \alpha + \beta(r_M - r_f) + e$

(8.13) $\quad r = r_f + \alpha + \beta r_M - \beta r_f + e$
$\quad\quad\quad = \alpha + r_f(1 - \beta) + \beta r_M + e$

(8.14) $\quad R\text{-squared} = 1 - \dfrac{\sigma^2(e)}{\sigma^2}$

(8.15) $\quad R_P = .04 + 1.4 R_{\text{S\&P/TSX}} + e_P$

(8.16) $\quad R_C = R_P - R_r = (.04 + 1.4 R_{\text{S\&P/TSX}} + e_P)$
$\quad\quad\quad\quad - 1.4 R_{\text{S\&P/TSX}} = .04 + e_P$

(8.17) $\quad R_t = \alpha + \beta_{\text{GDP}} \text{GDP}_t + \beta_{\text{IR}} \text{IR}_t + e_t$

(8.18) $\quad E(r) = r_f + \beta[E(r_M) - r_f]$

(8.19) $\quad E(r) = r_f + \beta \text{RP}_M$

(8.20) $\quad E(r) = r_f + \beta_{\text{GDP}} \text{RP}_{\text{GDP}} + \beta_{\text{IR}} \text{RP}_{\text{IR}}$

(8.21) $\quad R_P = E(R_P) + \beta_P F + e_P$

(8.22) $\quad R_P = \alpha_p + \beta_p R_M$

(8.23) $\quad E(R_P) = \alpha_p + \beta_p E(R_M)$

(8.24) $\quad \beta_Z = w_p \beta_p + (1 - w_p)\beta_M = 0$
$\quad\quad\quad \beta_M = 1$
$\quad\quad\quad w_p = \dfrac{1}{1 - \beta_p}; w_M = 1 - w_p = \dfrac{\beta_p}{1 - \beta_p}$

(8.25) $\quad \alpha_Z = w_p \alpha_p + (1 - w_p)\alpha_m = w_p \alpha_p$

(8.26) $\quad E(R_Z) = w_P \alpha_P = \dfrac{1}{1 - \beta_P} \alpha_P$

(8.27) $E(R_P) = \beta_P E(R_M)$

(8.28) $\dfrac{E(r_U) - r_f}{\beta_U} = \dfrac{E(r_V) - r_f}{\beta_V}$

(8.29) $R_i = E(R_i) + \beta_{i1}F_1 + \beta_{i2}F_2 + e_i$

(8.30) $E(r_Q) = \beta_{P1}E(r_1) + \beta_{P2}E(r_2) + (1 - \beta_{P1} - \beta_{P2})r_f$
$= r_f + \beta_{P1}[E(r_1) - r_f] + \beta_{P2}[E(r_2) - r_f]$

(8.31) $r_{it} = \alpha_i + \beta_{iIP}IP_t + \beta_{iEI}EI_t + \beta_{iUI}UI_t$
$+ \beta_{iCG}CG_t + \beta_{iGB}GB_t + e_{it}$

(8.32) $r_{it} = \alpha_i + \beta_{iM}R_{Mt} + \beta_{iSMB}SMB_t$
$+ \beta_{iHML}HML_t + e_{it}$

PROBLEMS

Mc Graw Hill Education **connect**™   **Practise and learn online with Connect.**

1. A portfolio management organization analyzes 60 stocks and constructs a mean-variance efficient portfolio that is constrained to these 60 stocks.

   a. How many estimates of expected returns, variances, and covariances are needed to optimize this portfolio?

   b. If one could safely assume that stock market returns closely resemble a single-index structure, how many estimates would be needed?

2. The following are estimates for two of the stocks in problem 1.

Stock	Expected Return	Beta	Firm-Specific Standard Deviation
A	.13	.8	.30
B	.18	1.2	.40

   The market index has a standard deviation of .22 and the risk-free rate is .08.

   a. What is the standard deviation of stocks A and B?

   b. Suppose that we were to construct a portfolio with the following proportions:

Stock A	.30
Stock B	.45
T-bills	.25

   Compute the expected return, standard deviation, beta, and nonsystematic standard deviation of the portfolio.

3. Consider the following two regression curves for stocks A and B.

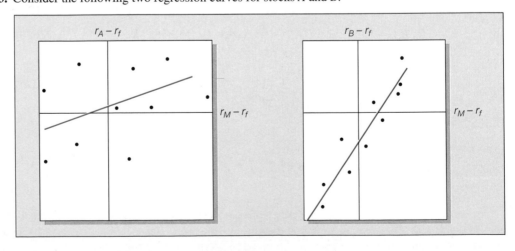

    a. Which stock has higher firm-specific risk?

    b. Which stock has greater systematic (market) risk?

    c. Which stock has higher R-squared?

    d. Which stock has higher alpha?

    e. Which stock has higher correlation with the market?

4. Consider the two (excess return) index model regression results for stocks A and B:

$$R_A = .01 + 1.2R_M$$
$$R\text{-squared} = .576$$
$$\sigma(e) = 10.3\%$$
$$R_B = -.02 + .8R_M$$
$$R\text{-squared} = .436$$
$$\sigma(e) = 9.1\%$$

    a. Which stock has more firm-specific risk?

    b. Which has greater market risk?

    c. For which stock does market movement explain a greater fraction of return variability?

    d. Which stock had an average return in excess of that predicted by the CAPM?

    e. If r_f were constant at 6 percent and the regression had been run using total rather than excess returns, what would have been the regression intercept for stock A?

Use the following data for problems 5–11. Suppose that the index model for stocks A and B is estimated with the following results:

$$R_A = .03 + .70R_M + e_A$$
$$R_B = -.02 + 1.20R_M + e_B$$
$$\sigma_M = .20; R_A\text{-squared} = .20; R_B\text{-squared} = .12$$

  5. What is the standard deviation of each stock?

  6. Break down the variance of each stock to the systematic and firm-specific components.

  7. What is the covariance and correlation coefficient between the two stocks?

  8. What is the covariance between each stock and the market index?

  9. Are the intercepts of the two regressions consistent with the CAPM? Interpret their values.

10. For portfolio P with investment proportions of .60 in A and .40 in B, rework problems 5, 6, and 8.

11. Rework problem 10 for portfolio Q with investment proportions of .50 in P, .30 in the market index, and .20 in T-bills.

12. A stock recently has been estimated to have a beta of 1.24:

    a. What will Merrill Lynch compute as the "adjusted beta" of this stock?

    b. Suppose that you estimate the following regression describing the evolution of beta over time:

$$\beta_t = .3 + 7\beta_{t-1}$$

What would your predicted beta be for next year?

13. Based on current dividend yields and expected growth rates, the expected rates of return on stocks A and B are 11 percent and 14 percent, respectively. The beta of stock A is .8, while that of stock B is 1.5. The T-bill rate is currently 6 percent, while the expected rate of return on the S&P/TSX index is 12 percent. The standard deviation of stock A is 10 percent annually, while that of stock B is 11 percent. If you currently hold a passive index portfolio, would you choose to add either of these stocks to your holdings?

14. The correlation between the Charlottesville International Fund and the EAFE Market Index is 1.0. The expected return on the EAFE Index is 11 percent, the expected return on Charlottesville International Fund is 9 percent, and the risk-free return in EAFE countries is 3 percent. Based on this analysis, what is the implied beta of Charlottesville International?

15. The concept of beta is most closely associated with
    a. Correlation coefficients
    b. Mean-variance analysis
    c. Nonsystematic risk
    d. Systematic risk

16. Suppose that the following factors have been identified for the Canadian economy: the growth rate of industrial production, IP, and the inflation rate, IR. IP is expected to be 3 percent, and IR 5 percent. A stock with a beta of 1 on IP and .5 on IR currently is expected to provide a rate of return of 12 percent. If industrial production actually grows by 5 percent while the inflation rate turns out to be 8 percent, what is your revised estimate of the expected rate of return on the stock?

17. Suppose that there are two independent economic factors, F_1 and F_2. The risk-free rate is 6 percent, and all stocks have independent firm-specific components with a standard deviation of 45 percent. The following are well-diversified portfolios:

Portfolio	Beta on F_1	Beta on F_2	Expected Return
A	1.5	2.0	31%
B	2.2	−.2	27%

What is the expected return–beta relationship in this economy?

18. Consider the following data for a one-factor economy. All portfolios are well diversified.

Portfolio	E(r)	Beta
A	12%	1.2
F	6%	0

Suppose that portfolio B is well diversified with a beta of .6 and expected return of 8 percent. Would an arbitrage opportunity exist? If so, what would be the arbitrage strategy?

19. The following is a scenario for three stocks constructed by the security analysts of Pf Inc.

		Scenario Rate of Return (%)		
Stock	Price ($)	Recession	Average	Boom
A	10	−15	20	30
B	15	25	10	−10
C	50	12	15	12

Construct an arbitrage portfolio using these stocks.

20. Assume that both portfolios A and B are well diversified, that $E(r_A) = .12$, and $E(r_B) = .09$. If the economy has only one factor, and $\beta_A = 1.2$ whereas $\beta_B = .8$, what must the risk-free rate be?

21. Assume that stock market returns have the market index as a common factor, and that all stocks in the economy have a beta of 1 on the market index. Firm-specific returns all have a standard deviation of .30.

Suppose that an analyst studies 20 stocks and finds that one-half have an alpha of 2 percent, and the other half an alpha of −2 percent. Suppose the analyst buys $1 million of an equally weighted portfolio of the positive alpha stocks and shorts $1 million of an equally weighted portfolio of the negative alpha stocks.

a. What is the expected profit (in dollars) and standard deviation of the analyst's profit?

b. How does your answer change if the analyst examines 50 stocks instead of 20 stocks? 100 stocks instead of 20 stocks?

22. Assume that security returns are generated by the single-index model

$$R_i = \alpha_i + \beta_i R_M + e_i$$

where R_i is the excess return for security i, and R_M is the market's excess return. The risk-free rate is 2 percent. Suppose also that there are three securities, A, B, and C, characterized by the following data:

Security	β_i	$E(R_i)$	$\sigma(e_i)$
A	.8	.10	.25
B	1.0	.12	.10
C	1.2	.14	.20

a. If $\sigma_M = .20$, calculate the variance of returns of securities A, B, and C.

b. Now assume that there are an infinite number of assets with return characteristics identical to those of A, B, and C, respectively. If one forms a well-diversified portfolio of type A securities, what will be the mean and variance of the portfolio's excess returns? What about portfolios composed only of type B or C stocks?

c. Is there an arbitrage opportunity in this market? What is it? Analyze the opportunity graphically.

23. The SML relationship states that the expected risk premium on a security in a one-factor model must be directly proportional to the security's beta. Suppose that this were not the case. For example, suppose that expected return rises more than proportionately with beta as in the following figure.

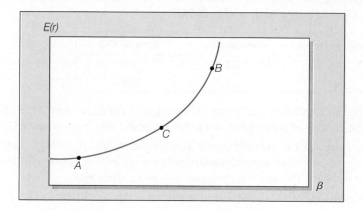

a. How could you construct an arbitrage portfolio? (*Hint:* Consider combinations of portfolios A and B, and compare the resultant portfolio to C.)

b. Some researchers have examined the relationship between average return on diversified portfolios and the β and β^2 of those portfolios. What should they have discovered about the effect of β^2 on portfolio return?

24. As a finance intern at Pork Products, Jennifer Wainwright's assignment is to come up with fresh insights concerning the firm's cost of capital. She decides that this would be a good opportunity to try out the new material on the APT that she learned last semester. She decides that three promising factors would be (i) the return on a broad-based index such as the S&P/TSX; (ii) the level of interest rates, as represented by the yield to maturity on 10-year Treasury bonds; and (iii) the price of hogs,

which are particularly important to her firm. Her plan is to find the beta of Pork Products against each of these factors by using a multiple regression and to estimate the risk premium associated with each exposure factor. Comment on Jennifer's choice of factors. Which are most promising with respect to the likely impact on her firm's cost of capital? Can you suggest improvements to her specification?

25. Assume a universe of n (large) securities for which the largest residual variance is of an order not larger than $n\sigma^2_M$. Construct as many different weighting schemes as you can that generate well-diversified portfolios.

26. Derive a more general (than the numerical example in the chapter) demonstration of the APT security market line

   a. For a single-factor market

   b. For a multifactor market

27. When the annualized monthly percentage rates of return for a stock market index were regressed against the returns for ABC and XYZ stocks over a five-year period ending in 2009 in an ordinary least squares regression, the following results were obtained:

Statistic	ABC	XYZ
Alpha	−3.20%	7.3%
Beta	.60	.97
R-squared	.35	.17
Residual standard deviation	13.02%	21.45%

Explain what these regression results tell the analyst about risk–return relationships for each stock over the 2005–2009 period. Comment on their implications for future risk–return relationships, assuming both stocks were included in a diversified common stock portfolio, especially in view of the following additional data obtained from two brokerage houses, which are based on two years of weekly data ending in December 2009.

Brokerage House	Beta of ABC	Beta of XYZ
A	.62	1.45
B	.71	1.25

28. Assume the correlation coefficient between Baker Fund and the S&P/TSX stock index is .70. What percentage of Baker Fund's total risk is specific (i.e., nonsystematic)?

29. Jeffrey Bruner, CFA, uses the capital asset pricing model (CAPM) to help identify mispriced securities. A consultant suggests Bruner use arbitrage pricing theory (APT) instead. In comparing CAPM and APT, the consultant made the following arguments:

   a. Both the CAPM and the APT require a mean-variance efficient market portfolio.

   b. Neither the CAPM nor APT assumes normally distributed security returns.

   c. The CAPM assumes that one specific factor explains security returns but APT does not.

   State whether each of the consultant's arguments is correct or incorrect. Indicate, for each incorrect argument, why the argument is incorrect.

30. Consider the following multifactor (APT) model of security returns for a particular stock:

Factor	Factor Beta	Factor Risk Premium (%)
Inflation	1.2	6
Industrial production	.5	8
Oil prices	.3	3

a. If T-bills currently offer a 6 percent yield, find the expected rate of return on this stock if the market views the stock as fairly priced.

b. Suppose that the market expected the values for the three macro factors given in the middle column below, but that the actual values turn out as given in the last column. Calculate the revised expectations for the rate of return on the stock once the "surprises" become known.

Factor	Expected Rate of Change (%)	Actual Rate of Change (%)
Inflation	5	4
Industrial production	3	6
Oil prices	2	0

31. Suppose that the market can be described by the following three sources of systematic risk with associated risk premiums:

Factor	Risk Premium (%)
Industrial production (I)	6
Interest rates (R)	2
Consumer confidence (C)	4

The return on a particular stock is generated according to the following equation:

$$r = 15\% + 1.0I + .5R + .75C + e$$

Find the equilibrium rate of return on this stock using the APT. The T-bill rate is 6 percent. Is the stock over- or underpriced? Explain.

The following problems are based on questions that have appeared in past CFA examinations.

32. Assume that both X and Y are well-diversified portfolios and the risk-free rate is 8 percent.

Portfolio	Expected Return (%)	Beta
X	16	1.00
Y	12	.25

In this situation, you would conclude that portfolios X and Y

a. Are in equilibrium

b. Offer an arbitrage opportunity

c. Are both underpriced

d. Are both fairly priced

33. According to the theory of arbitrage,

a. High-beta stocks are consistently overpriced

b. Low-beta stocks are consistently overpriced

c. Positive alpha stocks will quickly disappear

d. Rational investors will arbitrage consistent with their risk tolerance

34. A zero investment portfolio with a positive alpha could arise if

a. The expected return of the portfolio equals zero

b. The capital market line is tangent to the opportunity set

c. The law of one price remains unviolated

d. A risk-free arbitrage opportunity exists

35. The arbitrage pricing theory (APT) differs from the capital asset pricing model (CAPM) because the APT

    a. Puts more emphasis on market risk

    b. Minimizes the importance of diversification

    c. Recognizes multiple unsystematic risk factors

    d. Recognizes multiple systematic risk factors

36. An investor will take as large a position as possible when an equilibrium price relationship is violated. This is an example of

    a. A dominance argument

    b. The mean-variance efficient frontier

    c. A risk-free arbitrage

    d. The capital asset pricing model

37. The feature of APT that offers the greatest potential advantage over the simple CAPM is the

    a. Identification of anticipated changes in production, inflation, and term structure of interest rates as key factors explaining the risk–return relationship

    b. Superior measurement of the risk-free rate of return over historical time periods

    c. Variability of coefficients of sensitivity to the APT factors for a given asset over time

    d. Use of several factors instead of a single market index to explain the risk–return relationship

38. In contrast to the capital asset pricing model, arbitrage pricing theory

    a. Requires that markets be in equilibrium

    b. Uses risk premiums based on micro variables

    c. Specifies the number and identifies specific factors that determine expected returns

    d. Does not require the restrictive assumptions concerning the market portfolio

---

**E-INVESTMENTS
Beta Estimates**

Go to **http://finance.yahoo.com** and click on *Stocks* link under the *Investing* tab. Look for the *Stock Screener* link under *Research Tools*. The *Java Yahoo! Finance Screener* lets you create your own screens. In the *Click to Add Criteria* box, find *Trading* and *Volume* on the menu and choose *Beta*. In the *Conditions* box, choose < = and in the *Values* box enter 1. Hit the *Enter* key and then request the top 200 matches in the *Return Top Matches* box. Click on the *Run Screen* button.

Select the *View Table* tab and sort the results to show the lowest betas at the top of the list by clicking on the *Beta* column header. Which firms have the lowest betas? In which industries do they operate?

Select the *View Histogram* tab and when the histogram appears, look at the bottom of the screen to see the *Show Histogram for* box. Use the menu that comes up when you click on the down arrow to select *beta*. What pattern(s), if any, do you see in the distributions of betas for firms that have betas less than 1?

**E-INVESTMENTS
Unanticipated
Inflation**

One of the factors in the APT model of Chen, Roll, and Ross is the percent change in unanticipated inflation. Who gains and who loses when inflation changes? Go to **http://hussmanfunds.com/rsi/infsurprises.htm** to see the graphs of "Inflation Surprise Index" and "Economist's Inflation Forecast."

Market Efficiency

In the 1950s, an early application of computers in economics was for analysis of economic time series. Business cycle theorists felt that tracing the evolution of several economic variables over time would clarify and predict the progress of the economy through boom and bust periods. A natural candidate for analysis was the behaviour of stock market prices over time. Assuming that stock prices reflect the prospects of the firm, recurrent patterns of peaks and troughs in economic performance ought to show up in those prices.

Maurice Kendall examined this proposition in 1953.[1] He found to his great surprise that he could identify *no* predictable patterns in stock prices. Prices seemed to evolve randomly. They were as likely to go up as they were to go down on any particular day, regardless of past performance. The data provided no way to predict price movements.

At first blush, Kendall's results were disturbing to some financial economists. They seemed to imply that the stock market is dominated by erratic market psychology, or "animal spirits"—that it follows no logical rules. In short, the results appeared to confirm the irrationality of the market. On further reflection, however, economists came to reverse their interpretation of Kendall's study.

It soon became apparent that random price movements indicated a well-functioning or efficient market, not an irrational one. In this chapter we will explore the reasoning behind what may seem a surprising conclusion. We show how competition among analysts leads naturally to market efficiency, and we examine the implications of the efficient market hypothesis for investment policy. We consider empirical evidence that supports and contradicts the notion of market efficiency.

---

[1]Maurice Kendall, "The Analysis of Economic Time Series, Part I: Prices," *Journal of the Royal Statistical Society* 96 (1953).

9.1   RANDOM WALKS AND THE EFFICIENT MARKET HYPOTHESIS

Suppose Kendall had discovered that stock price changes are predictable. What a gold mine this would have been for investors! If they could use Kendall's equations to predict stock prices, investors would reap unending profits simply by purchasing stocks that the computer model implied were about to increase in price and by selling those stocks about to fall in price.

A moment's reflection should be enough to convince yourself that this situation could not persist for long. For example, suppose that the model predicts with great confidence that XYZ's stock price, currently at $100 per share, will rise dramatically in three days to $110. What would all investors with access to the model's prediction do today? Obviously, they would place a great wave of immediate buy orders to cash in on the prospective increase in stock price. No one holding XYZ, however, would be willing to sell. The net effect would be an *immediate* jump in the stock price to $110. The forecast of a future price increase will lead instead to an immediate price increase. In other words, the stock price will immediately reflect the "good news" implicit in the model's forecast.

This simple example illustrates why Kendall's attempt to find recurrent patterns in stock price movements was doomed to failure. A forecast about favourable *future* performance leads instead to favourable *current* performance, as market participants all try to get in on the action before the price jump.

More generally, one might say that any information that could be used to predict stock performance must already be reflected in stock prices. As soon as there is any information indicating that a stock is underpriced and therefore offers a profit opportunity, investors flock to buy the stock and immediately bid up its price to a fair level, where only ordinary rates of return can be expected.

These "ordinary rates" are simply rates of return commensurate with the risk of the stock.

However, if prices are bid immediately to fair levels, given all available information, it must be that they increase or decrease only in response to new information. New information, by definition, must be unpredictable; if it could be predicted, then the prediction would be part of today's information. Thus stock prices that change in response to new (i.e., previously unpredictable) information also must move unpredictably.

This is the essence of the argument that stock prices should follow a **random walk**, that is, that price changes should be random and unpredictable.[2] Far from a proof of market irrationality, randomly evolving stock prices are the necessary consequence of intelligent investors competing to discover relevant information on which to buy or sell stocks before the rest of the market becomes aware of that information. Indeed, if stock price movements were predictable, that would be damning evidence of stock market inefficiency, because the ability to predict prices would indicate that all available information was not already reflected in stock prices. Therefore, the notion that stocks already reflect all available information is referred to as the **efficient market hypothesis (EMH)**.[3]

Figure 9.1 illustrates the response of stock prices to new information in an efficient market. The graph plots the price response of a sample of 172 firms in which a controlling shareholder offered to buy out the minority shareholders. In most such buyouts, the acquiring shareholder pays a substantial premium over current market prices. Therefore, announcement of a buyout attempt should cause the stock price to jump. The figure shows that stock prices jump dramatically on the day the

---

[2]Actually, we are being a little loose with terminology here. Strictly speaking, we should characterize stock prices as following a *submartingale*, meaning that the expected change in the price can be positive, presumably as compensation for the time value of money and systematic risk. Moreover, the expected return may change over time as risk factors change. A random walk is more restrictive in that it constrains successive stock returns to be independent *and* identically distributed. Nevertheless, the term *random walk* is commonly used in the looser sense that price changes are essentially unpredictable. We will follow this convention.

[3]Market efficiency should not be confused with the idea of efficient portfolios introduced in Chapter 6. An informationally efficient *market* is one in which information is rapidly disseminated and reflected in prices. An efficient *portfolio* is one with the highest expected return for a given level of risk.

Figure 9.1

Cumulative abnormal returns before/after minority buyout attempts: Target companies.

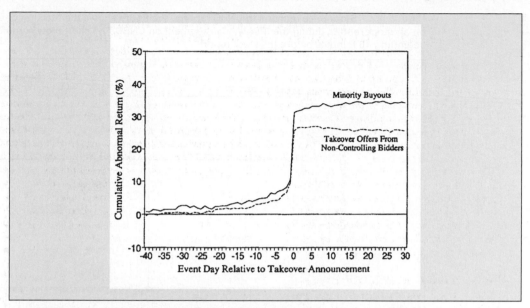

Source: Brian F. Smith and Ben Amoako-Adu, "Minority Buyouts and Ownership Characteristics: Evidence from the Toronto Stock Exchange," *Financial Management*, Summer 1992. Reprinted by permission.

news becomes public. However, there is no further drift in prices *after* the announcement date, suggesting that prices reflect the new information, including the likely magnitude of the buyout premium, by the end of the trading day.

Even more dramatic evidence of rapid response to new information may be found in intraday prices. For example, Patell and Wolfson show that most of the stock price response to corporate dividend or earnings announcements occurs within 10 minutes of the announcement.[4] A nice illustration of such rapid adjustment is provided in a study by Busse and Green, who track minute-by-minute stock prices of firms that are featured on CNBC's *Morning Call* or *Midday Call* segments.[5] Minute 0 in Figure 9.2 is the time at which the stock is mentioned on the midday show. The top line is the average price movement of stocks that receive positive reports, while the bottom line reports returns on stocks with negative reports. Notice that the top line levels off, indicating that the market has fully digested the news, within 5 minutes of the report. The bottom line levels off within about 12 minutes.

Competition as the Source of Efficiency

Why should we expect stock prices to reflect "all available information"? After all, if you are willing to spend time and money gathering information, it might seem reasonable that you could turn up something that has been overlooked by the rest of the investment community. When information is costly to uncover and analyze, one would expect investment analysis calling for such expenditures to result in an increased expected return. This point has been stressed by Grossman and Stiglitz.[6] They argue that investors will have an incentive to spend time and resources to analyze and uncover new information only if such activity is likely to generate

---

[4]J. M. Patell and M. A. Wolfson, "The Intraday Speed of Adjustment of Stock Prices to Earnings and Dividend Announcements," *Journal of Financial Economics* 13 (June 1984), pp. 223–52.

[5]J. A. Busse and T. C. Green, "Market Efficiency in Real Time," *Journal of Financial Economics* 65 (2002), pp. 415–37.

[6]Sanford J. Grossman and Joseph E. Stiglitz, "On the Impossibility of Informationally Efficient Markets," *American Economic Review* 70 (June 1980).

Figure 9.2   Stock price reaction to CNBC reports. The figure shows the reaction of stock prices to on-air stock reports during the *Midday Call* segment on CNBC. The chart plots cumulative returns beginning 15 minutes before the stock report.

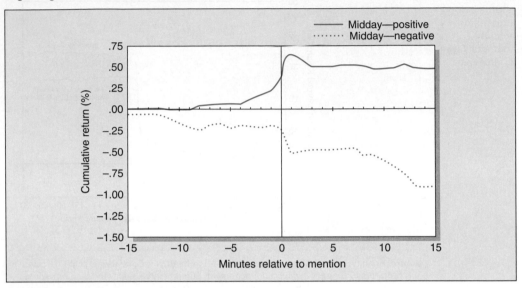

Source: Reprinted from J. A. Busse and T. C. Green, "Market Efficiency in Real Time," *Journal of Financial Economics* 65 (2002), p. 422. Copyright 2002 with permission from Elsevier Science.

higher investment returns. Thus, in market equilibrium efficient information-gathering activity should be fruitful. Moreover, it would not be surprising to find that the degree of efficiency differs across various markets. For example, emerging markets that are less intensively analyzed than U.S. or Canadian markets and in which accounting disclosure requirements are much less rigorous may be less efficient than U.S. or Canadian markets. Small stocks which receive relatively little coverage by analysts may be less efficiently priced than large ones. Still, while we would not go so far as to say that you absolutely cannot come up with new information, it makes sense to consider and respect your competition.

EXAMPLE 9.1   **Rewards for Incremental Performance**

Consider an investment management fund currently managing a $5 billion portfolio. Suppose that the fund manager can devise a research program that could increase the portfolio rate of return by one-tenth of one percent per year, a seemingly modest amount. This program would increase the dollar return to the portfolio by $5 billion × .001, or $5 million. Therefore, the fund would be willing to spend up to $5 million per year on research to increase stock returns by a mere one-tenth of one percent per year. With such large rewards for such small increases in investment performance, it should not be surprising that professional portfolio managers are willing to spend large sums on industry analysts, computer support, and research effort and therefore that price changes are, generally speaking, difficult to predict.

With so many well-backed analysts willing to spend considerable resources on research, there will not be many easy pickings in the market. Moreover, the incremental rates of return on research activity are likely to be so small that only managers of the largest portfolios will find them worth pursuing.

The most precious commodity on Wall Street is information, and informed players can charge handsomely for providing it. An industry of so-called *expert network providers* has emerged to sell access to experts with unique insights about a wide variety of firms and industries to investors who need that information to make decisions. These firms have been dubbed matchmakers for the information age. Experts can range from doctors who help predict the release of block-buster drugs to meteorologists who forecast weather that can affect commodity prices to business executives who can provide specialized insight about companies and industries.

But it's turned out that some of those experts have ped-dled prohibited inside information. In 2011, Winifred Jiau, a consultant for Primary Global Research, was convicted of selling information about Nvidia and Marvell Technologies to the hedge fund SAC Capital Advisors. Several other employ-ees of Primary Global also were charged with insider trading.

Expert firms are supposed to provide only public infor-mation, along with the expert's insights and perspective. But the temptation to hire experts with inside information and charge handsomely for access to them is obvious. The SEC

has raised concerns about the boundary between legitimate and illegal services, and several hedge funds in 2011 shut down after raids searched for evidence of such illicit activity.

In the wake of increased scrutiny, compliance efforts of both buyers and sellers of expert information have mush-roomed. The largest network firm is Gerson Lehrman Group with a stable of 300,000 experts. It now maintains records down to the minute of which of its experts talks to whom and the topics they have discussed.* These records could be turned over to authorities in the event of an in-sider trading investigation. For their part, some hedge funds have simply ceased working with expert-network firms or have promulgated clearer rules for when their em-ployees may talk with consultants.

Even with these safeguards, however, there remains room for trouble. For example, an investor may meet an expert through a legitimate network and then the two may establish a consulting relationship on their own. This legal matchmaking becomes the precursor to the illegal selling of insider tips. Where there is a will to cheat, there will usu-ally be a way.

*"Expert Networks Are the Matchmakers for the Information Age," *The Economist*, June 16, 2011.

Source: Adapted from: "Expert Networks are the Matchmakers for the Information Age," *The Economist*, June 16, 2011; several other articles from *The Economist*.

Although it may not literally be true that "all" relevant information will be uncovered, it is virtually certain that there are many investigators hot on the trail of any leads that may improve investment performance. Competition among these many well-backed, highly paid, aggressive analysts ensures that, as a general rule, stock prices ought to reflect available information regard-ing their proper levels.

A concrete illustration of this point appears in the box here. In another notorious case, in 2011 Raj Rajaratnam, the head of the Galleon Group hedge fund, which once managed $6.5 billion, was convicted on insider trading charges for soliciting tips from a network of corporate insiders and traders. Rajaratnam's was only one of several major insider trading cases working their way through the courts in 2011. While Galleon's practices were egregious, it often can be difficult to draw a clear line separating legitimate and prohibited sources of information. For example, a large industry of *expert network* firms has emerged in the last decade to connect (for a fee) inves-tors to industry experts who can provide unique perspective on a company. As the box discusses, this sort of arrangement can easily cross the line into insider trading.

Versions of the Efficient Market Hypothesis

It is common to distinguish among three versions of the EMH: the weak, semistrong, and strong forms of the hypothesis. These versions differ by their notions of what is meant by the term *all available information.*

The **weak-form** hypothesis asserts that stock prices already reflect all information that can be derived by examining market trading data, such as the history of past prices, trading volume, or short interest. This version of the hypothesis implies that trend analysis is fruitless. Past stock price data are publicly available and virtually costless to obtain. The weak-form hypothesis holds that if such data ever conveyed reliable signals about future performance, all investors would have learned already to exploit the signals. Ultimately, the signals lose their value as they become widely known because a buy signal, for instance, would result in an immediate price increase.

The **semistrong-form** hypothesis states that all publicly available information regarding the prospects of a firm must be reflected already in the stock price. Such information includes, in addition to past prices, fundamental data on the firm's product line, quality of management, balance sheet composition, patents held, earning forecasts, and accounting practices. Again, if any investor has access to such information from publicly available sources, one would expect it to be reflected in stock prices.

Finally, the **strong-form** version of the efficient market hypothesis states that stock prices reflect all information relevant to the firm, even including information available only to company insiders. This version of the hypothesis is quite extreme. Few would argue with the notion that corporate officers have access to pertinent information long enough before public release to enable them to profit from trading on that information. Indeed, much of the activities of the provincial securities commissions is directed toward preventing insiders from profiting by exploiting their privileged situation. In Ontario, corporate officers, directors, and substantial owners are required to report trades in their firms' shares within ten days of the end of the month in which the trade took place. These insiders, their relatives, and any associates who trade on information supplied by insiders are considered in violation of the law.

Defining insider trading is not always easy, however. After all, stock analysts are in the business of uncovering information not already widely known to market participants. As we saw in Chapter 3, the distinction between private and inside information is sometimes murky.

CC 1

CONCEPT CHECK

a. Suppose you observed that high-level managers make superior returns on investments in their company's stock. Would this be a violation of weak-form market efficiency? Would it be a violation of strong-form market efficiency?

b. If the weak form of the efficient market hypothesis is valid, must the strong form also hold? Conversely, does strong-form efficiency imply weak-form efficiency?

9.2 IMPLICATIONS OF THE EMH FOR INVESTMENT POLICY

Technical Analysis

Technical analysis is essentially the search for recurring and predictable patterns in stock prices. Although technicians recognize the value of information that has to do with future economic prospects of the firm, they believe such information is not necessary for a successful trading strategy. Whatever the fundamental reason for a change in stock price, if the stock price responds slowly enough, the analyst will be able to identify a trend that can be exploited during the adjustment period. Technical analysis assumes a sluggish response of stock prices to fundamental supply and demand factors. This assumption is diametrically opposed to the notion of an efficient market.

Technical analysts sometimes are called *chartists* because they study records or charts of past stock prices, hoping to find patterns they can exploit to make a profit. As an example of technical analysis, consider the *relative strength* approach. The chartist compares stock performance over a recent period to performance of the market or other stocks in the same industry. A simple version of relative strength takes the ratio of the stock price to a market indicator, such as the S&P/TSX Composite index. If the ratio increases over time, the stock is said to exhibit relative strength, because its price performance is better than that of the broad market. Such strength presumably may continue for a long enough period to offer profit opportunities. We will explore this technique as well as several other tools of technical analysis further in Chapter 10.

The efficient market hypothesis predicts that technical analysis is without merit. The past history of prices and trading volume is publicly available at minimal cost. Therefore, any information that was ever available from analyzing past prices has already been reflected in stock prices. As investors compete to exploit their common knowledge of a stock's price history, they necessarily drive stock prices to levels where expected rates of return are commensurate with risk. At those levels, stocks are neither bad nor good buys. They are just fairly priced, meaning one should not expect abnormal returns.

Despite these theoretical considerations, some technically oriented trading strategies would have generated abnormal profits in the past. We will consider these strategies, and technical analysis more generally, in Chapter 10.

Fundamental Analysis

Fundamental analysis uses earnings and dividend prospects of the firm, expectations of future interest rates, and risk evaluation of the firm to determine proper stock prices. Ultimately, it represents an attempt to determine the present discounted value of all the payments a shareholder will receive from each share of stock. If that value exceeds the stock price, the fundamental analyst will recommend purchasing the stock.

Fundamental analysts usually start with a study of past earnings and an examination of company balance sheets. They supplement this analysis with further detailed economic analysis, ordinarily including an evaluation of the quality of the firm's management, the firm's standing within its industry, and the prospects for the industry as a whole. The hope is to attain some insight into the future performance of the firm that is not yet recognized by the rest of the market. Chapters 15–17 provide a detailed discussion of the types of analyses that underlie fundamental analysis.

Once again, the efficient market hypothesis predicts that *most* fundamental analysis adds little value. If analysts rely on publicly available earnings and industry information, one analyst's evaluation of the firm's prospects is not likely to be significantly more accurate than another's. There are many well-informed, well-financed firms conducting such market research, and in the face of such competition it will be difficult to uncover data not also available to other analysts. Only analysts with unique insight will be rewarded.

Fundamental analysis is much more difficult than merely identifying well-run firms with good prospects. Discovery of good firms does an investor no good in and of itself if the rest of the market also knows those firms are good: if the knowledge is already public, the investor will be forced to pay a high price for those firms and will not realize a superior rate of return. The trick is not to identify firms that are good, but to find firms that are *better* than everyone else's estimate. Similarly, poorly run firms can be great bargains if they are not quite as bad as their stock prices suggest. This is why fundamental analysis is difficult. It is not enough to do a good analysis of a firm; you can make money only if your analysis is better than that of your competitors, because the market price is expected already to reflect all commonly recognized information.

Active Versus Passive Portfolio Management

By now it is apparent that casual efforts to pick stocks are not likely to pay off. Competition among investors ensures that any easily implemented stock evaluation technique will be used widely enough so that any insights derived will be reflected in stock prices. Only serious, time-consuming, and expensive techniques are likely to generate the *differential* insight necessary to generate trading profits.[7]

---

[7]See for example Bala Arshanapalli, Lorne N. Switzer, and Loretta Hung, "Active Versus Passive Strategies for EAFE and the S&P 500," *Journal of Portfolio Management* 30 (Summer 2004), pp. 51–60; and Bala Arshanapalli, Lorne N. Switzer, and Karim Panju, "Equity Style Timing: A Multi-Style Rotation Model for the Russell Large-Cap and Small-Cap Growth and Value Style Indexes," *Journal of Asset Management* 8 (2007), pp. 9–23.

Moreover, these techniques are economically feasible only for managers of large portfolios. If you have only $100,000 to invest, even a 1 percent per year improvement in performance generates only $1,000 per year, hardly enough to justify herculean efforts. The billion-dollar manager, however, reaps extra income of $10 million annually from the same 1 percent increment.

If small investors are not in a favoured position to conduct active portfolio management, what are their choices? The small investor probably is better off placing funds in a mutual fund. By pooling resources in this way, small investors can gain from economies of scale.

More difficult decisions remain, though. Can investors be sure that even large mutual funds have the ability or resources to uncover mispriced stocks? Further, will any mispricing be sufficiently large to repay the costs entailed in active portfolio management?

Proponents of the efficient market hypothesis believe that active management is largely wasted effort and unlikely to justify the expenses incurred. Therefore, they advocate a **passive investment strategy** that makes no attempt to outsmart the market. A passive strategy aims only at establishing a well-diversified portfolio of securities without attempting to find under- or overvalued stocks. Passive management usually is characterized by a buy-and-hold strategy. Because the efficient market theory indicates that stock prices are at fair levels, given all available information, it makes no sense to buy and sell securities frequently, which generates large brokerage fees without increasing expected performance.

TD Bank Group
www.td.com

One common strategy for passive management is to create an **index fund**. Such a fund aims to mirror the performance of a broad-based index of stocks. For example, TD Canada Trust sponsors a mutual fund called the TD Canadian Index Fund, which holds stocks in direct proportion to their weight in the S&P/TSX Composite Total Return index. The performance of the fund therefore replicates the performance of the Composite. Investors in this fund obtain broad diversification with relatively low management fees. The fees can be kept to a minimum because there is no need to pay analysts for assessing stock prospects or to incur transaction costs from high portfolio turnover.

Similarly, in the United States Vanguard's Index 500 Portfolio holds stocks in direct proportion to their weight in the Standard & Poor's 500 stock price index. The performance of the Index 500 fund therefore replicates the performance of the S&P 500. Today, Vanguard's Index 500 Portfolio is among the largest equity mutual funds with over $100 billion of assets in May 2012, and about 10 percent of equity funds are indexed.

Indexing need not be limited to the major stock indices, however. For example, some of the funds offered by the Vanguard Group track the broader-based CRSP[8] index of the total U.S. equity market, the Barclays U.S. Aggregate, the CRSP index of small-capitalization U.S. companies, and the *Financial Times* indices of the European and Pacific Basic equity markets. Several other mutual fund complexes have introduced indexed portfolios, but Vanguard dominates the retail market for indexed products. In Canada, TD Canada Trust offers funds tracking, among others, the Canadian T-Bill and the Canadian Bond Index.

Exchange-traded funds, or ETFs, are a close (and usually lower-expense) alternative to indexed mutual funds. As will be noted in Chapter 23, these are shares in diversified portfolios that can be bought or sold just like shares of individual stock. ETFs matching several broad stock market indices such as the S&P 500 or S&P/TSX 60 indices and dozens of international and industry stock indices are available to investors who want to hold a diversified sector of a market without attempting active security selection.

CC 2

CONCEPT CHECK

What would happen to market efficiency if *all* investors attempted to follow a passive strategy?

---

[8]CRSP is the Center for Research in Security Prices at the University of Chicago.

The Role of Portfolio Management in an Efficient Market

If the market is efficient, why not throw darts at a stock quotations page instead of trying rationally to choose a stock portfolio? This is a tempting conclusion to draw from the notion that security prices are fairly set, but it is far too facile. There is a role for rational portfolio management, even in perfectly efficient markets.

You have learned that a basic principle in portfolio selection is diversification. Even if all stocks are priced fairly, each still poses firm-specific risks that can be eliminated through diversification. Therefore, rational security selection, even in an efficient market, calls for the selection of a well-diversified portfolio providing the systematic risk level that the investor wants.

Rational investment policy also requires that tax considerations be reflected in security choice. High tax-bracket investors generally will not want the same securities that low-bracket investors find favourable. For instance, high-bracket investors might want to tilt their portfolios in the direction of capital gains as opposed to dividend or interest income, because the option to defer the realization of capital gains income is more valuable the higher the current tax bracket. Hence these investors may prefer stocks that yield lower dividends yet offer greater expected capital gains income. They also will be more attracted to investment opportunities for which returns are sensitive to tax benefits, such as real estate ventures.

A third argument for rational portfolio management relates to the particular risk profile of the investor. For example, an executive for an auto parts firm whose annual bonus depends on his firm's profits generally should not invest additional amounts in auto stocks. To the extent that his or her compensation already depends on the auto industry's well-being, the executive already is overinvested in that industry and should not exacerbate the lack of diversification.

Investors of varying ages also might warrant different portfolio policies with regard to risk bearing. For example, older investors who are essentially living off savings might choose to avoid long-term bonds whose market values fluctuate dramatically with changes in interest rates (discussed in Part Four). Because these investors are living off accumulated savings, they require conservation of principal. In contrast, younger investors might be more inclined toward long-term bonds. The steady flow of income over long periods of time that is locked in with long-term bonds can be more important than preservation of principal to those with long life expectancies.

In conclusion, there is a role for portfolio management even in an efficient market. Investors' optimal positions will vary according to factors such as age, tax bracket, risk aversion, and employment. The role of the portfolio manager in an efficient market is to tailor the portfolio to these needs, rather than to beat the market.

Resource Allocation

We've focused so far on the investments implications of the efficient market hypothesis. Deviations from efficiency may offer profit opportunities to better-informed traders at the expense of less-informed traders.

However, deviations from informational efficiency would also result in a large cost that will be borne by all citizens, namely, inefficient resource allocation. Recall that in a capitalist economy, investments in *real* assets such as plant, equipment, and know-how are guided in large part by the prices of financial assets. For example, if the values of biotech assets as reflected in the stock market prices of biotech firms exceed the cost of acquiring those assets, the managers of such firms have a strong signal that further investments in the firm will be regarded by the market as a positive net present value venture. In this manner, capital market prices guide resource allocation. Security mispricing thus could entail severe social costs by fostering inappropriate investments on the real side of the economy.

Corporations with overpriced securities will be able to obtain capital too cheaply and corporations with undervalued securities might forgo investment opportunities because the cost of raising capital will be too high. Therefore, inefficient capital markets would diminish one of the most potent benefits of a market economy.

9.3   EVENT STUDIES

The notion of informationally efficient markets leads to a powerful research methodology. If security prices reflect all currently available information, then price changes must reflect new information. Therefore it seems that one should be able to measure the importance of an event of interest by examining price changes during the period in which the event occurs.

An **event study** describes a technique of empirical financial research that enables an observer to assess the impact of a particular event on a firm's stock price. A stock market analyst might want to study the impact of dividend changes on stock prices, for example. An event study would quantify the relationship between dividend changes and stock returns.

Analyzing the impact of any particular event is more difficult than it might first appear. On any particular day stock prices respond to a wide range of economic news, such as updated forecasts for GNP, inflation rates, interest rates, or corporate profitability. Isolating the part of a stock price movement that is attributable to a specific event is not a trivial exercise.

The statistical approach that researchers commonly use to measure the impact of a particular information release, such as the announcement of a merger or a dividend change, is a marriage of efficient market theory with the index model discussed in Chapter 8. We want to measure the unexpected return that results from an event. This is the difference between the actual stock return and the "normal" return that might have been expected given the performance of the market. This expected return can be calculated using the index model. Another approach estimates normal returns using an asset pricing model such as the CAPM or one of its multifactor generalizations such as the Fama-French three-factor model.

Recall that the index model holds that stock returns are determined by a market factor and a firm-specific factor. The stock return, r_t, during a given period, t, would be expressed mathematically as

$$r_t = a + br_{Mt} + e_t \tag{9.1}$$

where r_{Mt} is the market's excess rate of return during the period and e_t is the part of a security's return resulting from firm-specific events. The parameter b measures sensitivity to the market return, and a is the average rate of return the stock would realize in a period with a zero market return. Equation 9.1 therefore provides a decomposition of r_t into market and firm-specific factors. The firm-specific return may be interpreted as the unexpected return that results from the event.

Determination of the firm-specific return in a given period requires that we obtain an estimate of the term e_t. Therefore, we rewrite equation 9.1:

$$e_t = r_t - (a + br_{Mt}) \tag{9.2}$$

Equation 9.2 has a simple interpretation: to determine the firm-specific component of a stock's return, subtract the return that the stock ordinarily would earn for a given level of market performance from the actual rate of return on the stock. The residual, e_t, is the stock's return over and above what one would predict from broad market movements in that period, given the stock's sensitivity to the market. We sometimes refer to e_t as the **abnormal return**—the return beyond what would be predicted from market movements alone. More generally, the abnormal return is the difference between the stock's actual return and the return that the stock would have had in the absence of the event. To estimate the latter, the index model can be generalized to include richer models of benchmark returns. For instance, industry returns or returns on indices constructed to match characteristics such as firm size can be included on the right-hand side of equation 9.1.

EXAMPLE 9.2   **Abnormal Returns**

Suppose that the analyst has estimated that $a = .5\%$ and $b = .8$. On a day that the market goes up by 1 percent, you would predict from equation 9.1 that the stock should rise by an expected value of $.5\% + .8 \times 1\% = 1.3\%$.[9] If the stock actually rises by 2 percent, the analyst would infer that firm-specific news that day caused an additional stock return of $2\% - 1.3\% = .7\%$.

The general strategy in event studies is to estimate the abnormal return around the date that new information about a stock is released to the market and attribute the abnormal stock performance to the new information. The first step in the study is to estimate parameters a and b for each security in the study. These typically are calculated using index model regressions, as described in Chapter 8, in a period before that in which the event occurs. The prior period is used for estimation so that the impact of the event will not affect the estimates of the parameters. Next, the information release dates for each firm are recorded. For example, in a study of the impact of merger attempts on the stock prices of target firms, the **announcement date** is the date on which the public is informed that a merger is to be attempted. Finally, the abnormal returns of each firm surrounding the announcement date are computed, and the statistical significance and magnitude of the typical abnormal return is assessed to determine the impact of the newly released information.

One concern that complicates event studies arises from *leakage* of information. Leakage occurs when information regarding a relevant event is released to a small group of investors before official public release. In this case, the stock price might start to increase (in the case of a "good news" announcement) days or weeks before the official announcement date. Any abnormal return on the announcement date is then a poor indicator of the total impact of the information release. A better indicator would be the **cumulative abnormal return**, which is simply the sum of all abnormal returns over the time period of interest. The cumulative abnormal return thus captures the total firm-specific stock movement for an entire period when the market might be responding to new information.

Figure 9.1 earlier on in this chapter presents the results from a fairly typical event study. The authors of this study were interested in leakage of information before minority buyout[10] announcements and constructed a sample of 172 firms that were targets of a minority buyout attempt. In most buyouts, shareholders of the acquired firms sell their shares to the acquirer at substantial premiums over market value. Announcement of a buyout attempt is good news for shareholders of the target firm and therefore should cause stock prices to jump.

Figure 9.1 confirms the good-news nature of the announcements. On the announcement day, called day 0, the average cumulative abnormal return (CAR) for the sample of buyout candidates increases substantially, indicating a large and positive abnormal return on the announcement date. Notice that immediately after the announcement date the CAR no longer increases or decreases significantly. This is in accord with the efficient market hypothesis. Once the new information became public, the stock prices jumped almost immediately in response to the good news. With prices once again fairly set, reflecting the effect of the new information, further abnormal returns on any particular day are equally likely to be positive or negative. In fact, for a sample of many firms, the average abnormal return will be extremely close to zero, and thus the CAR will show neither upward nor downward drift. This is precisely the pattern shown in the figure.

[9]We know from Chapter 7, Section 7.1, that the CAPM implies that the intercept a in equation 9.1 should equal $r_f(1 - b)$. Nevertheless, it is customary to estimate the intercept in this equation empirically rather than imposing the CAPM value. One justification for this practice is the empirically fitted security market lines seem flatter than predicted by the CAPM (see Chapter 11), which would make the intercept implied by the CAPM too small.

[10]A minority buyout occurs when a controlling shareholder purchases the remaining shares of the firm from the minority shareholders.

The pattern of returns for the days preceding the public announcement date yields some interesting evidence about efficient markets and information leakage. If insider trading rules were perfectly obeyed and perfectly enforced, stock prices should show no abnormal returns on days before the public release of relevant news, because no special firm-specific information would be available to the market before public announcement. Instead, we should observe a clean jump in the stock price only on the announcement day. In fact, the prices of these buyout or, more generally, takeover targets clearly start an upward drift 30 days before the public announcement. There are two possible interpretations of this pattern. One is that information is leaking to some market participants who then purchase the stocks before the public announcement. At least some abuse of insider trading rules is occurring.

Another interpretation is that in the days before a takeover attempt the public becomes suspicious of the attempt as it observes someone buying large blocks of stock. As acquisition intentions become more evident, the probability of an attempted merger is gradually revised upward so that we see a gradual increase in CARs. Although this interpretation is certainly a valid possibility, evidence of leakage appears almost universally in event studies, even in cases where the public's access to information is not gradual. It appears as if insider trading violations do occur.

Actually, securities commissions can take some comfort from patterns such as that in Figure 9.1. If insider trading rules were widely and flagrantly violated, we would expect to see abnormal returns earlier than they appear in these results. The CAR would turn positive as soon as the minority buyout is decided, because insiders would start trading immediately. By the time of the public announcement, the insiders would have bid up the stock price to levels reflecting the buyout attempt, and the abnormal returns on the actual public announcement date would be close to zero. The dramatic increase in the CAR that we see on the announcement date indicates that a good deal of these announcements were indeed news to the market and that stock prices did not already reflect complete knowledge about the buyouts. It would appear, therefore, that securities commission enforcement does have a substantial effect on restricting insider trading, even if some amount of it persists.

Early Canadian studies had painted a less optimistic picture of the contribution of securities trading regulation to market efficiency. For instance, the event study methodology was applied by Kryzanowski[11] to investigate the effectiveness of trading suspensions in the three major Canadian stock exchanges (TSE, ME, and VSE) in arresting manipulative activities (mostly through dissemination of misleading information) on stock returns. The study identified stocks suspended from floor trading in these three exchanges over the period 1967–1973 because of alleged manipulation. It then examined the CARs in the weeks before and after the suspension event. These were significantly positive before, and significantly negative after, for up to ten weeks around the suspension date. Hence, it appeared that disseminating and exploiting misleading information about stocks is profitable. It also seemed that investors were slow to react to the unfavourable information conveyed by the trading suspension.

Fortunately these inefficiencies seem to have disappeared in recent years. Two more recent studies by Kryzanowski and Nemiroff[12] found that post-trading-halt price adjustments of suspended firms were very quick, and the CARs reached their post-event level within the same day that trading resumed, in both Canadian exchanges. Canadian investors seem to have become more sophisticated in assimilating and reacting to relevant information, thus enhancing market efficiency.

---

[11]Lawrence Kryzanowski, "Misinformation and Regulatory Actions in the Canadian Capital Markets: Some Empirical Evidence," *The Bell Journal of Economics* 9, no. 2 (Fall 1978); and "The Efficacy of Trading Suspensions: A Regulatory Action Designed to Prevent the Exploitation of Monopoly Information," *Journal of Finance* 34 (December 1979).

[12]L. Kryzanowski and Howard Nemiroff, "Price Discovery Around Trading Halts on the Montreal Exchange Using Trade Data" and "Market Quote and Spread Component Cost Behaviour Around Trading Halts for Stocks Inter-listed on the Toronto Stock Exchange," both in the *Financial Review*, 1998, pp. 195–212 and 2001, pp. 115–138.

Event study methodology has become a widely accepted tool to measure the economic impact of a wide range of events. For example, three Canadian studies have used the event methodology to investigate the impact of banking merger failures, the announcements of business relocation decisions, and the impact of changes in the taxation of corporate dividends and income trust distributions.[13] The U.S. SEC regularly uses event studies to measure illicit gains captured by traders who may have violated insider trading or other securities laws.[14] Event studies are also used in fraud cases, in which the courts must assess damages caused by a fraudulent activity.

EXAMPLE 9.3   **Using Abnormal Returns to Infer Damages**

Suppose the stock of a company with market value of $100 million falls by 4 percent on the day that news of an accounting scandal surfaces. The rest of the market, however, generally did well that day. The market indices were up sharply, and assuming the usual relationship between the stock and the market, one would have expected a 2 percent gain on the stock. We would conclude that the impact of the scandal was a 6 percent drop in value, the difference between the 2 percent gain we would have expected and the 4 percent drop actually observed. One might then infer that the damages sustained from the scandal were $6 million, because the value of the firm (after adjusting for general market movements) fell by 6 percent of $100 million when investors became aware of the news and reassessed the value of the stock.

CC 3

CONCEPT CHECK

Suppose that we see negative abnormal returns (declining CARs) after an announcement date. Is this a violation of efficient markets?

9.4   **ARE MARKETS EFFICIENT?**

The Issues

Not surprisingly, the efficient market hypothesis does not exactly arouse enthusiasm in the community of professional portfolio managers. It implies that a great deal of the activity of portfolio managers—the search for undervalued securities—is at best wasted effort and quite probably harmful to clients because it costs money and leads to imperfectly diversified portfolios. Consequently, the EMH has never been widely accepted among professionals, and debate continues today on the degree to which security analysis can improve investment performance. Before discussing empirical tests of the hypothesis, we want to note three factors that together imply that the debate will probably never be settled: the *magnitude* issue, the *selection bias* issue, and the *lucky event* issue.

The Magnitude Issue   Consider an investment manager overseeing a $5 billion portfolio. If she can improve performance by only one-tenth of one percent per year, that effort will be worth .001 × $5 billion = $5 million annually. This manager clearly would be worth her

---

[13]Ramon Baltazar and Michael Santos, "The Benefits of Banking Mega-mergers: Event Study Evidence from the 1998 Failed Mega-merger Attempts in Canada"; H. Bhabra, U. Lel, and D. Tirtiroglu, "Stock Market's Reaction to Business Relocations: Canadian Evidence"; and Ben Amoako-Adu and B. F. Smith, "Valuation Effects of Recent Dividend and Income Trust Distribution Tax Changes," in *Canadian Journal of Administrative Sciences*, September 2003, December 2002, and March 2008.

[14]For a review of SEC applications of this technique, see Mark Mitchell and Jeffry Netter, "The Role of Financial Economics in Securities Fraud Cases: Applications at the Securities and Exchange Commission," *The Business Lawyer* 49 (February 1994), pp. 545–90.

salary! Yet can we, as observers, statistically measure her contribution? Probably not: a one-tenth-of-one-percent contribution would be swamped by the yearly volatility of the market. Remember, the annual standard deviation of the well-diversified S&P/TSX Composite index has been more than 17 percent per year. Against these fluctuations, a small increase in performance would be hard to detect. Nevertheless, $5 million remains an extremely valuable improvement in performance.

All might agree that stock prices are very close to fair values, and that only managers of large portfolios can earn enough trading profits to make the exploitation of minor mispricing worth the effort. According to this view, the actions of intelligent investment managers are the driving force behind the constant evolution of market prices to fair levels. Rather than ask the qualitative question "Are markets efficient?" we ought to instead ask a more quantitative question "How efficient are markets?"

Wall Street
Journal Online
http://online.wsj
.com

The Selection Bias Issue

Suppose that you discover an investment scheme that could really make money. You have two choices: either publish your technique in *The Wall Street Journal* or *The Globe and Mail* to win fleeting fame, or keep your technique secret and use it to earn millions of dollars. Most investors would choose the latter option, which presents us with a conundrum. Only investors who find that an investment scheme cannot generate abnormal returns will be willing to report their findings to the whole world. Hence, opponents of the efficient-market view of the world always can use evidence that various techniques do not provide investment rewards as proof that the techniques that do work simply are not being reported to the public. This is a problem in *selection bias*: the outcomes we are able to observe have been preselected in favour of failed attempts. Therefore, we cannot fairly evaluate the true ability of portfolio managers to generate winning stock market strategies.

The Lucky Event Issue

In virtually any month it seems we read an article about some investor or investment company with a fantastic investment performance over the recent past. Surely the superior records of such investors disprove the efficient market hypothesis.

Yet this conclusion is far from obvious. As an analogy to the investment game, consider a contest to flip the most number of heads out of 50 trials using a fair coin. The expected outcome for any person is, of course, 50 percent heads and 50 percent tails. If 10,000 people, however, compete in this contest, it would not be surprising if at least one or two contestants flipped more than 75 percent heads. In fact, elementary statistics tells us that the expected number of contestants flipping 75 percent or more heads would be two. It would be silly, though, to crown these people the "head-flipping champions of the world." Obviously, they are simply the contestants who happened to get lucky on the day of the event. (See the boxed article here.)

The analogy to efficient markets is clear. Under the hypothesis that any stock is fairly priced given all available information, any bet on a stock is simply a coin toss. There is equal likelihood of winning or losing the bet. However, if many investors using a variety of schemes make fair bets, statistically speaking, *some* of those investors will be lucky and win a great majority of the bets. For every big winner, there may be many big losers, but we never hear of these managers. The winners, though, turn up in the financial press as the latest stock market gurus; then they can make a fortune publishing market newsletters.

Our point is that after the fact there will have been at least one successful investment scheme. A doubter will call the results luck; the successful investor will call it skill. The proper test would be to see whether the successful investors can repeat their performance in another period, yet this approach is rarely taken.

With these caveats in mind, we now turn to some of the empirical tests of the efficient markets hypothesis.

HOW TO GUARANTEE A SUCCESSFUL MARKET NEWSLETTER

Suppose you want to make your fortune publishing a market newsletter. You need first to convince potential subscribers that you have talent worth paying for. Ah, but what if you have no talent? The solution is simple: start eight newsletters.

In year 1, let four of your newsletters predict an up-market and four a down-market. In year 2, let half of the originally optimistic group of newsletters continue to predict an up-market and the other half a down-market. Do the same for the originally pessimistic group. Continue in this manner to obtain the pattern of predictions shown in the table here (U = prediction of an up-market, D = prediction of a down-market).

After three years, no matter what has happened to the market, one of the newsletters would have had a perfect prediction record. This is because after three years there are $2^3 = 8$ outcomes for the market, and we have covered all eight possibilities with the eight newsletters. Now, we simply slough off the seven unsuccessful newsletters, and market the eighth newsletter on its perfect track record. If we want to establish a newsletter with a perfect track record over a four-year period, we need $2^4 = 16$

newsletters. A five-year period requires 32 newsletters, and so on.

After the fact, the one newsletter that was always right will attract attention for your uncanny foresight and investors will rush to pay large fees for its advice. Your fortune is made, and you never even researched the market!

Warning: This scheme is illegal! The point, however, is that with hundreds of market newsletters, you can find one that has stumbled onto an apparently remarkable string of successful predictions without any real degree of skill. After the fact, *someone's* prediction history can seem to imply great forecasting skill. This person is the one we will read about in *The Wall Street Journal* and *The Globe and Mail*; the others will be forgotten.

	Newsletter Predictions							
Year	1	2	3	4	5	6	7	8
1	U	U	U	U	D	D	D	D
2	U	U	D	D	U	U	D	D
3	U	D	U	D	U	D	U	D

CC 4

CONCEPT CHECK

Legg Mason's Value Trust, managed by Bill Miller, outperformed the S&P 500 in each of the 15 years ending in 2005. Is Miller's performance sufficient to dissuade you from a belief in efficient markets? If not, would *any* performance record be sufficient to dissuade you?

Weak-Form Tests: Patterns in Stock Returns

Returns over Short Horizons Early tests of efficient markets were tests of the weak form. Could speculators find trends in past prices that would enable them to earn abnormal profits? This is essentially a test of the efficacy of technical analysis.

One way of discerning trends in stock prices is by measuring the *serial correlation* of stock market returns. Serial correlation refers to the tendency for stock returns to be related to past returns. Positive serial correlation means that positive returns tend to follow positive returns (a momentum type of property). Negative serial correlation means that positive returns tend to be followed by negative returns (a reversal or "correction" property). Both Conrad and Kaul[15] and Lo and MacKinlay[16] examine weekly returns of NYSE stocks and find positive serial correlation over short horizons. However, the correlation coefficients of weekly returns tend to be fairly small, at least for large stocks for which price data are the most reliably up to date. Thus, while these studies demonstrate weak price trends over short periods,[17] the evidence does not clearly suggest the existence of trading opportunities.

---

[15]Jennifer Conrad and Gautam Kaul, "Time-Variation in Expected Returns." *Journal of Business* 61 (October 1988), pp. 409–425.

[16]Andrew W. Lo and A. Craig MacKinlay, "Stock Market Prices Do Not Follow Random Walks: Evidence from a Simple Specification Test," *Review of Financial Studies* 1 (1988), pp. 41–66.

[17]On the other hand, there is evidence that share prices of individual securities (as opposed to broad market indices) are more prone to reversals than continuations at very short horizons. See, for example, B. Lehmann, "Fads, Martingales and Market Efficiency," *Quarterly Journal of Economics* 105 (February 1990), pp. 1–28; and N. Jegadeesh, "Evidence of Predictable Behavior of Security Returns," *Journal of Finance* 45 (September 1990), pp. 881–98. However, as Lehmann notes, this is probably best interpreted as due to liquidity problems after big movements in stock prices as market makers adjust their positions in the stock.

While broad market indices demonstrate only weak serial correlation, there appears to be stronger momentum in performance across market sectors exhibiting the best and worst recent returns. In an investigation of intermediate-horizon stock price behaviour (using 3-to-12-month holding periods), Jegadeesh and Titman[18] found a **momentum effect** in which good or bad recent performance of particular stocks continues over time. They conclude that while the performance of individual stocks is highly unpredictable, *portfolios* of the best-performing stocks in the recent past appear to outperform other stocks with enough reliability to offer profit opportunities. Thus, it appears that there is evidence of short-to-intermediate-horizon price momentum both in the aggregate market and cross-sectionally (i.e., across particular stocks).

The momentum property has also been documented in Canada by several studies.[19] As in the United States, momentum was found for both good and bad recent performance, but the excess returns that it generated may not have been sufficient to overcome transaction costs of a magnitude of about 100 basis points.

Returns over Long Horizons

While studies of short-horizon returns have detected modest positive serial correlation in stock market prices, tests of long-horizon returns (i.e., returns over multiyear periods) have found suggestions of pronounced negative long-term serial correlation.[20, 21] The latter result has given rise to a "fads hypothesis," which asserts that stock prices might overreact to relevant news. Such overreaction leads to positive serial correlation (momentum) over short time horizons. Subsequent correction of the overreaction leads to poor performance following good performance and vice versa. The corrections mean that a run of positive returns eventually will tend to be followed by negative returns, leading to negative serial correlation over longer horizons. These episodes of apparent overshooting followed by correction give stock prices the appearance of fluctuating around their fair values.

These long-horizon results are dramatic, but are still not conclusive. First, the study results need not be interpreted as evidence for stock market fads. An alternative interpretation of these results holds that they indicate only that market risk premiums vary over time. The response of market prices to variation in the risk premium can lead one to incorrectly infer the presence of mean reversion and excess volatility in prices. For example, when the risk premium and the required return on the market rises, stock prices will fall. When the market then rises (on average) at this higher rate of return, the data convey the impression of a stock price recovery. The impression of overshooting and correction is in fact no more than a rational response of market prices to changes in discount rates.

In addition to studies suggestive of overreaction in overall stock market returns over long horizons, many other studies suggest that over long horizons, extreme performance in particular securities also tends to reverse itself: the stocks that have performed best in the recent past seem

---

[18]Narasimhan Jegadeesh and Sheridan Titman, "Returns to Buying Winners and Selling Losers: Implications for Stock Market Efficiency," *Journal of Finance* 48 (March 1993), pp. 65–91.

[19]S. Cleary and M. Inglis, "Momentum in Canadian Stock Returns," *Canadian Journal of Administrative Sciences* 15 (1998), pp. 279–291; M. Cao and J. Wei, "Uncovering Sector Momentums," *Canadian Investment Review*, Winter 2002, pp. 14–22; and R. Deaves and P. Miu, "Refining Momentum Strategies by Conditioning on Prior Long-Term Returns: Canadian Evidence," *Canadian Journal of Administrative Sciences* 24 (2007), pp. 135–145. The last study finds superior returns net of transaction costs. See also S. Foerster, "Back to the Future—Again," and R. Kan and G. Kirikos, "Now You See Them, Now You Don't," both in the Fall 1996 issue of the *Canadian Investment Review*, and the survey articles by V. Jog, "Canadian Stock Pricing Anomalies: Revisited," *Canadian Investment Review*, Winter 1998, and G. Athanassakos and S. Foerster, "Canadian Security Market Anomalies," in W. Ziemba and D. Keim, eds., *Security Market Imperfections in Worldwide Equity Markets* (Cambridge University Press, 1999).

[20]Eugene F. Fama and Kenneth R. French, "Permanent and Temporary Components of Stock Prices," *Journal of Political Economy* 96 (April 1988), pp. 246–273.

[21]James Poterba and Lawrence Summers, "Mean Reversion in Stock Prices: Evidence and Implications," *Journal of Financial Economics* 22 (October 1988), pp. 27–59.

to underperform the rest of the market in following periods, while the worst past performers tend to offer above-average future performance. DeBondt and Thaler[22] and Chopra, Lakonishok, and Ritter[23] find strong tendencies for poorly performing stocks in one period to experience sizable reversals over the subsequent period, while the best-performing stocks in a given period tend to follow with poor performance in the following period.

For example, the DeBondt and Thaler study found that if one were to rank order the performance of stocks over a five-year period and then group stocks into portfolios based on investment performance, the base-period "loser" portfolio (defined as the 35 stocks with the worst investment performance) outperformed the "winner" portfolio (the top 35 stocks) by an average of 25 percent (cumulative return) in the following three-year period. This **reversal effect**, in which losers rebound and winners fade back, suggests that the stock market overreacts to relevant news. After the overreaction is recognized, extreme investment performance is reversed. This phenomenon would imply that a *contrarian* investment strategy—investing in recent losers and avoiding recent winners—should be profitable. Moreover, these returns seem pronounced enough to be exploited profitably.

Thus it appears that there may be short-run momentum but long-run reversal patterns in price behaviour both for the market as a whole and across sectors of the market. One interpretation of this pattern is that short-run overreaction (which causes momentum in prices) may lead to long-term reversals (when the market recognizes its past error).

Predictors of Broad Market Returns

Several studies have documented the ability of easily observed variables to predict market returns. For example, Fama and French[24] show that the return on the aggregate stock market tends to be higher when the dividend/price ratio, the dividend yield, is high. Campbell and Shiller[25] find that the earnings yield can predict market returns. Keim and Stambaugh[26] show that bond market data, such as the spread between yields on high- and low-grade corporate bonds, also help predict broad market returns.

Again, the interpretation of these results is difficult. On the one hand, they may imply that abnormal stock returns can be predicted, in violation of the efficient market hypothesis. More probably, however, these variables are proxying for variation in the market risk premium. For example, given a level of dividends or earnings, stock prices will be lower and dividend and earnings yields will be higher when the risk premium (and therefore the expected market return) is larger. Thus, a high dividend or earnings yield will be associated with higher market returns. This does not indicate a violation of market efficiency—the predictability of market returns is due to predictability in the risk premium, not in risk-adjusted abnormal returns.

Fama and French[27] show that the yield spread between high- and low-grade bonds has greater predictive power for returns on low-grade bonds than for returns on high-grade bonds and greater predictive power for stock returns than for bond returns, suggesting that the predictability in returns is in fact a risk premium rather than evidence of market inefficiency. Similarly, the fact that the dividend yield on stocks helps to predict bond market returns suggests that the yield captures a risk premium common to both markets rather than mispricing in the equity market.

[22]Werner F. M. DeBondt and Richard Thaler, "Does the Stock Market Overreact?" *Journal of Finance* 40 (1985), pp. 793–805.

[23]Navin Chopra, Josef Lakonishok, and Jay R. Ritter, "Measuring Abnormal Performance: Do Stocks Overreact?" *Journal of Financial Economics* 31 (1992), pp. 235–268.

[24]Eugene F. Fama and Kenneth R. French, "Dividend Yields and Expected Stock Returns," *Journal of Financial Economics* 22 (October 1988), pp. 3–25.

[25]John Y. Campbell and Robert Shiller, "Stock Prices, Earnings and Expected Dividends," *Journal of Finance* 43 (July 1988), pp. 661–676.

[26]Donald B. Keim and Robert F. Stambaugh, "Predicting Returns in the Stock and Bond Markets," *Journal of Financial Economics* 17 (1986), pp. 357–390.

[27]Eugene F. Fama and Kenneth R. French, "Business Conditions and Expected Returns on Stocks and Bonds," *Journal of Financial Economics* 25 (November 1989), pp. 3–22.

Semistrong Tests: Market Anomalies

Fundamental analysis calls on a much wider range of information to create portfolios than does technical analysis, and tests of the value of fundamental analysis are thus correspondingly more difficult to evaluate. They have, however, revealed a number of so-called **anomalies**, that is, evidence that seems inconsistent with the efficient market hypothesis. We will review several such anomalies in the following pages.

We must note before starting that one major problem with these tests is that most require risk adjustments to portfolio performance and most use the CAPM to make the risk adjustments. Although beta seems to be a relevant descriptor of stock risk, the empirically measured quantitative tradeoff between risk as measured by beta and expected return differs from the predictions of the CAPM. (We review this evidence in Chapter 11.) If we use the CAPM to adjust portfolio returns for risk, inappropriate adjustments may lead to the conclusion that various portfolio strategies can generate superior returns, when in fact it simply is the risk-adjustment procedure that has failed.

Another way to put this is to note that tests of risk-adjusted returns are *joint tests* of the efficient market hypothesis *and* the risk-adjustment procedure. If it appears that a portfolio strategy can generate superior returns, we must then decide whether this is due to a failure of the EMH or to an inappropriate risk-adjustment technique. Usually, the risk-adjustment technique is based on more questionable assumptions than is the EMH; by opting to reject the procedure, we are left with no conclusion about market efficiency.

An example of this issue is the discovery by Basu[28] that portfolios of low-price-earnings-ratio stocks have higher average returns than do high-P/E portfolios. The **P/E effect** holds up even if returns are adjusted for portfolio beta. Is this a confirmation that the market systematically misprices stocks according to P/E ratios? This would be an extremely surprising and, to us, disturbing conclusion, because analysis of P/E ratios is such a simple procedure. Although it may be possible to earn superior returns using hard work and much insight, it hardly seems possible that such a simplistic technique is enough to generate abnormal returns. One possible interpretation of these results is that the model of capital market equilibrium is at fault in that the returns are not properly adjusted for risk.

This makes sense, because if two firms have the same expected earnings, then the riskier stock will sell at a lower price and lower P/E ratio. Because of its higher risk, the low P/E stock also will have higher expected returns. Therefore, unless the CAPM beta fully adjusts for risk, P/E will act as a useful additional descriptor of risk, and will be associated with abnormal returns if the CAPM is used to establish benchmark performance.

The Small-Firm-in-January Effect The so-called "size effect," or **small-firm effect**, originally documented by Banz,[29] is illustrated in Figure 9.3. It shows the historical performance of portfolios formed by dividing the NYSE stocks into ten portfolios each year according to firm size (i.e., the total value of outstanding equity). Average annual returns are consistently higher on the small-firm portfolios. The difference in average annual return between portfolio 10 (with the largest firms) and portfolio 1 (with the smallest firms) is 7.73 percent. Of course, the smaller-firm portfolios tend to be riskier. But even when returns are adjusted for risk using the CAPM, there is still a consistent premium for the smaller-sized portfolios, especially for Canada.[30]

Imagine earning a premium of this size on a billion-dollar portfolio. Yet it is remarkable that following a simple (even simplistic) rule such as "invest in low capitalization stocks" should

[28]Sanjoy Basu, "The Investment Performance of Common Stocks in Relation to Their Price-Earnings Ratios: A Test of the Efficient Market Hypothesis," *Journal of Finance* 32 (June 1977), pp. 663–682; and "The Relationship Between Earnings Yield, Market Value, and Return for NYSE Common Stocks: Further Evidence," *Journal of Financial Economics* 12 (June 1983). See also J. Bourgeois and J. Lussier, "P/E's and Performance in the Canadian Market," *Canadian Investment Review*, Spring 1994.
[29]Rolf Banz, "The Relationship Between Return and Market Value of Common Stocks," *Journal of Financial Economics* 9 (March 1981).
[30]See for example Lorne N. Switzer and Haibo Fan, "Spanning Tests for Replicable Small Cap Indexes as Separate Asset Classes: Evidence for G-7 Countries," *Journal of Portfolio Management* 33 (Summer 2007), pp. 102–110.

Figure 9.3

Returns in excess of risk-free rate and in excess of the Security Market Line for ten size-based portfolios, 1926–2012.

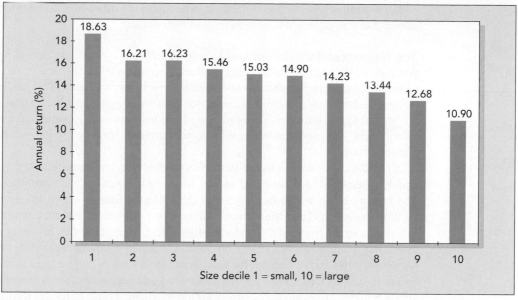

Source: Authors' calculations, using data from Professor Ken French's data library at http://mba.tuck.dartmouth.edu/pages/faculty/ken.french/data_library.html.

enable an investor to earn excess returns. After all, any investor can measure firm size at little cost. One would not expect such minimal effort to yield such large rewards.

Later studies (Keim,[31] Reinganum,[32] and Blume and Stambaugh[33]) showed that the small-firm effect occurs virtually entirely in January, in fact, in the first two weeks of January. The size effect is in fact a "small firm in January" effect.

Despite these theoretical objections, some empirical evidence supports the belief that the January effect is connected to tax-loss selling. For example, Reinganum found that, within size class, firms that had declined more severely in price had larger January returns.

The January effect was also found in several Canadian studies. Berges, McConnell, and Schlarbaum[34] found a significant January effect in Canadian stock returns, and this effect was more pronounced for firms with smaller values. A subsequent study by Tinic, Barone-Adesi, and West[35] found some influence of the tax laws on the seasonality of returns. More recent Canadian work[36] attributes the January effect to portfolio rebalancing by professional portfolio managers in the securities industry.

A 1998 survey article by Jog[37] confirms that the January effect still exists in Canada, albeit in a somewhat reduced form, a conclusion reinforced by two more recent studies.[38]

---

[31]Donald B. Keim, "Size Related Anomalies and Stock Return Seasonality: Further Empirical Evidence," *Journal of Financial Economics* 12 (June 1983).

[32]Marc R. Reinganum, "The Anomalous Stock Market Behavior of Small Firms in January: Empirical Tests for Tax-Loss Effects," *Journal of Financial Economics* 12 (June 1983).

[33]Marshall E. Blume and Robert F. Stambaugh, "Biases in Computed Returns: An Application to the Size Effect," *Journal of Financial Economics* 12 (1983), pp. 387–404.

[34]Angel Berges, John J. McConnell, and Gary G. Schlarbaum, "The Turn-of-the-Year in Canada," *Journal of Finance* 39, no. 1 (March 1984).

[35]Seha M. Tinic, Giovanni Barone-Adesi, and Richard R. West, "Seasonality in Canadian Stock Prices: A Test of the 'Tax-Loss-Selling' Hypothesis," *Journal of Financial and Quantitative Analysis* 21, no. 1 (March 1986).

[36]G. Athanassakos, "Portfolio Rebalancing and the January Effect in Canada," *Financial Analysts Journal* 48 (November/December 1992); and "The January Effect: Solving the Mystery," *Canadian Investment Review*, Spring 1995. See also G. Athanassakos and L. Ackert, "Institutional Investors, Analyst Following, and the January Anomaly," *Journal of Business Finance and Accounting* 27, nos. 3–4 (April/May 2000).

[37]V. Jog, "Canadian Stock Pricing Anomalies: Revisited," *Canadian Investment Review*, Winter 1998.

[38]The small-firm-in-January effect appears in a recent Canadian study by K. Assoé and O. Sy, "Profitability of the Short-Run Contrarian Strategy in Canadian Stock Markets," *Canadian Journal of Administrative Sciences* 20, no. 4 (December 2003). See also G. Althanassakos, "Happy New Year: The Persistence and Causes of the January Effect," *Canadian Investment Review*, Summer 2006.

Some studies have looked at the time variation in the small-firm effect. More recent work has shown that it is closely linked to the risk of firm default.[39]

The Neglected-Firm Effect and Liquidity Effects   Arbel and Strebel[40] give another interpretation of the small-firm-in-January effect. Because small firms tend to be neglected by large institutional traders, information about such firms is less available. This information deficiency makes smaller firms riskier investments that command higher returns. "Brand name" firms, after all, are subject to considerable monitoring from institutional investors that assures high-quality information, and presumably investors do not purchase "generic" stocks without the prospect of greater returns.

As evidence for the **neglected-firm effect**, Arbel[41] divided firms into highly researched, moderately researched, and neglected groups based on the number of institutions holding the stock. The January effect was in fact largest for the neglected firms.

Work by Amihud and Mendelson[42] on the effect of liquidity on stock returns might be related to both the small-firm and the neglected-firm effect. They argue that investors will demand a rate of return premium to invest in less-liquid stocks, which entail higher trading costs (see Chapter 7 for details). Indeed, spreads for the least-liquid stocks easily can be more than 5 percent of stock value. In accord with their hypothesis, Amihud and Mendelson show that these stocks show a strong tendency to exhibit abnormally high risk-adjusted rates of return. Because small and less-analyzed stocks as a rule are less liquid, the liquidity effect might be a partial explanation of their abnormal returns. However, this theory does not explain why the abnormal returns of small firms should be concentrated in January. In any case, exploiting these effects can be more difficult than it would appear. The trading costs on small stocks can easily wipe out any apparent abnormal profit opportunity.

Book-to-Market Ratios   Fama and French show that a very powerful predictor of returns across securities is the ratio of the book value of the firm's equity to the market value of equity.[43] They stratify firms into ten groups according to book-to-market ratios and examine the average monthly rate of return of each of the ten groups. Figure 9.4 gives an updated version of their results. The decile with the highest book-to-market ratio had an average annual return of 17.54 percent, while the lowest-ratio decile averaged only 10.78 percent. The dramatic dependence of returns on book-to-market ratio is independent of beta, suggesting either that low-book-to-market-ratio firms are relatively underpriced or that the book-to-market ratio is serving as a proxy for a risk factor that affects equilibrium-expected returns.

In fact, Fama and French found that after controlling for the size and **book-to-market effects**, beta seemed to have no power to explain average security returns.[44] This finding is an important challenge to the notion of rational markets, since it seems to imply that a factor that should affect

---

[39]See for example Lorne N. Switzer, "The Behaviour of Small Cap vs. Large Cap Stocks in Recessions: Empirical Evidence for the United States and Canada," *North American Journal of Economics and Finance* 21 (2010), pp. 332–346; and Lorne N. Switzer, "Domestic vs. US Default Risk and the Small-Cap Premium," *La Revue du Financier* 35 (2013), pp. 59–80.
[40]Avner Arbel and Paul J. Strebel, "Pay Attention to Neglected Firms," *Journal of Portfolio Management*, Winter 1983.
[41]Avner Arbel, "Generic Stocks: An Old Product in a New Package," *Journal of Portfolio Management*, Summer 1985.
[42]Yakov Amihud and Haim Mendelson, "Asset Pricing and the Bid–Ask Spread," *Journal of Financial Economics* 17 (December 1987), pp. 223–250; and "Liquidity, Asset Prices, and Financial Policy," *Financial Analysts Journal* 47 (November/December 1991), pp. 56–66.
[43]Eugene F. Fama and Kenneth R. French, "The Cross Section of Expected Stock Returns," *Journal of Finance* 47 (1992), pp. 427–465.
[44]However, a study by S. P. Kothari, Jay Shanken, and Richard G. Sloan, "Another Look at the Cross-Section of Expected Stock Returns," *Journal of Finance* 50 (March 1995), pp. 185–224 finds that when betas are estimated using annual rather than monthly returns, securities with high beta values do in fact have higher average returns. Moreover, the authors find a book-to-market effect that is attenuated compared with the results in Fama and French and that furthermore is inconsistent across different samples of securities. They conclude that the empirical case for the importance of the book-to-market ratio may be somewhat weaker than the Fama and French study would suggest. This conclusion is also supported by a recent Canadian study by T. Hou and P. McKnight, "An Explanation of Momentum in Canadian Stocks," *Canadian Journal of Administrative Sciences* 21 (December 2004), pp. 334–343.

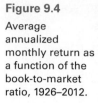

Figure 9.4

Average annualized monthly return as a function of the book-to-market ratio, 1926–2012.

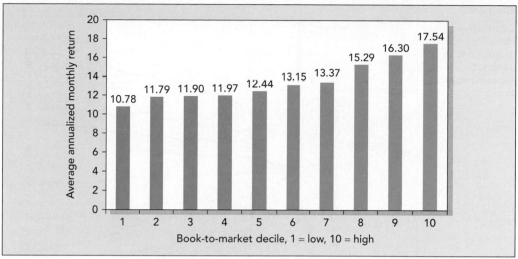

Source: Web site of Prof. Kenneth French, http://mba.tuck.dartmouth.edu/pages/faculty/ken.french/data_library.html.

returns—systematic risk—seems not to matter, while a factor that should not matter—the book-to-market ratio—seems capable of predicting future returns. We will return to the interpretation of this anomaly.

Post-Earnings-Announcement Price Drift   A fundamental principle of efficient markets is that any new information ought to be reflected in stock prices very rapidly. When good news is made public, for example, the stock price should jump immediately. A puzzling anomaly, therefore, is the apparently sluggish response of stock prices to firms' earnings announcements, as uncovered by Ball and Brown.[45] Their results were later confirmed and extended in many other papers.[46]

The "news content" of an earnings announcement can be evaluated by comparing the announcement of actual earnings to the value previously expected by market participants. The difference is the "earnings surprise." (Market expectations of earnings can be roughly measured by averaging the published earnings forecasts of Wall Street analysts or by applying trend analysis to past earnings.) Rendleman, Jones, and Latané[47] provide an influential study of sluggish price response to earnings announcements. They calculate earnings surprises for a large sample of firms, rank the magnitude of the surprise, divide firms into ten deciles based on the size of the surprise, and calculate abnormal returns for each decile. Figure 9.5 plots cumulative abnormal returns by decile.

Their results are dramatic. The correlation between ranking by earnings surprise and abnormal returns across deciles is as predicted. There is a large abnormal return (a jump in cumulative abnormal return) on the earnings announcement day (time 0). The abnormal return is positive for positive-surprise firms and negative for negative-surprise firms.

The more remarkable, and interesting, result of the study concerns stock price movement *after* the announcement date. The cumulative abnormal returns of positive-surprise stocks continue to rise—in other words, exhibit momentum—even after the earnings information becomes public,

[45]R. Ball and P. Brown, "An Empirical Evaluation of Accounting Income Numbers," *Journal of Accounting Research* 9 (1968), pp. 159–78.
[46]There is a voluminous literature on this phenomenon, often referred to as post-earnings-announcement price drift. For more recent papers that focus on why such drift may be observed, see V. Bernard and J. Thomas, "Evidence That Stock Prices Do Not Fully Reflect the Implications of Current Earnings for Future Earnings," *Journal of Accounting and Economics* 13 (1990), pp. 305–40; or R. H. Battalio and R. Mendenhall, "Earnings Expectation, Investor Trade Size, and Anomalous Returns Around Earnings Announcements," *Journal of Financial Economics* 77 (2005), pp. 289–319.
[47]Richard J. Rendleman Jr., Charles P. Jones, and Henry A. Latané, "Empirical Anomalies Based on Unexpected Earnings and the Importance of Risk Adjustments," *Journal of Financial Economics* 10 (November 1982), pp. 269–87.

Figure 9.5
Cumulative abnormal returns in response to earnings announcements.

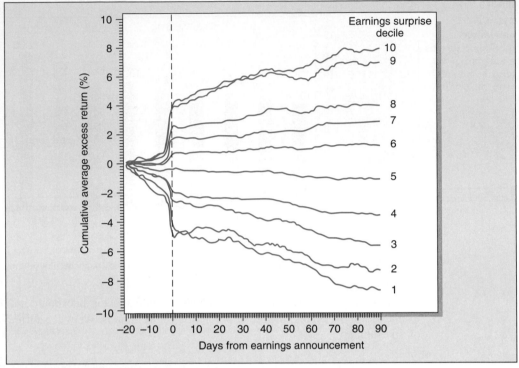

Source: Reprinted from R. J. Rendleman Jr., C. P. Jones, and H. A. Latané, "Empirical Anomalies Based on Unexpected Earnings and the Importance of Risk Adjustments," *Journal of Financial Economics* 10 (1982), pp. 269–287. Copyright 1982 with permission from Elsevier Science.

while the negative-surprise firms continue to suffer negative abnormal returns. The market appears to adjust to the earnings information only gradually, resulting in a sustained period of abnormal returns.

Evidently, one could have earned abnormal profits simply by waiting for earnings announcements and purchasing a stock portfolio of positive-earnings-surprise companies. These are precisely the types of predictable continuing trends that ought to be impossible in an efficient market.

E-INVESTMENTS
Earnings
Surprises

Several Web sites list information on earnings surprises. Much of the information supplied is from Zacks.com. Every day the largest positive and negative surprises are listed. Go to **www.zacks.com/research/earnings/today_eps.php** and identify the top positive and the top negative earnings surprises for the day. The table will list the time and date of the announcement. Do you notice any difference between the times of day positive announcements tend to be made versus negative announcements?

Identify the tickers for the top three positive surprises. Once you have identified the top surprises, go to **finance.yahoo.com**. Enter the ticker symbols and obtain quotes for these securities. Examine the five-day charts for each of the companies. Is the information incorporated into price quickly? Is there any evidence of prior knowledge or anticipation of the disclosure in advance of the trading?

Choose one of the stocks listed and click on its symbol to follow the link for more information. Click on the link for *Interactive Java Charting* that appears under the graph. In the *Graph Control* dialogue box choose a period of five years and check the box that says *EPS Surprise*. The resulting chart will show positive earnings surprises as green bars and negative surprises as red bars. You can move the cursor over various parts of the graph to investigate what happened to the price and trading volume of the stock around each of the surprise events. Do you notice any patterns?

Strong-Form Tests: Inside Information

It would not be surprising if insiders were able to make superior profits trading in their firm's stock. The ability of insiders to trade profitably in their own stock has been documented in U.S. studies by Jaffe,[48] Seyhun,[49] Givoly and Palmon,[50] and others. Jaffe's was one of the earlier studies that documented the tendency for stock prices to rise after insiders intensively bought shares and to fall after intensive insider sales.

Similar results also were found in Canadian studies by Masse, Hanrahan, and Kushner[51] and Eckbo,[52] who examined the daily returns to companies targeted for mergers or acquisitions prior to the date of public announcement. They found evidence of significant abnormally high returns, which is consistent with the use of inside information to trade profitably in the market.

To enhance fairness, securities commissions require all insiders to register the changes in their holdings of company stock within ten days of the end of the month in which the changes take place. Once the insiders file the required statements, the knowledge of their trades becomes public information. At that point, if markets are efficient, fully and immediately processing the released information, an investor should no longer be able to profit from following the pattern of those trades.

The U.S. study by Seyhun, which carefully tracked the public release dates of the insider trading information, found that following **insider transactions** would be of no avail. Although there is some tendency for stock prices to increase even after public reports of insider buying, the abnormal returns are not of sufficient magnitude to overcome transaction costs.

The Canadian evidence yields mixed conclusions. Baesel and Stein[53] investigated the performance of two insider groups on the TSX, ordinary insiders and insiders who were bank directors. Although both groups earned significant positive abnormal returns, the second group's such returns were higher. Fowler and Rorke[54] used monthly returns of firms listed on the TSE during the period 1967–1977 to investigate whether an outsider could realize abnormal returns by following insider transactions after they were publicly reported. They found that abnormal returns following "intense" buying or selling activity by insiders persisted for at least 12 months after the official release of the insider trading information. Moreover, the size of the returns indicated that trading profits could have been realized even after paying reasonable transactions costs. Similar results were also found in subsequent studies by Lee and Bishara,[55] for the period 1975–1983, and Suret and Cormier,[56] for the period May 1986–July 1988. These findings seem to indicate a clear violation of market efficiency for the TSX, at least for the periods covered by these studies.

On the other hand, a study by Heinkel and Kraus[57] on the Vancouver Stock Exchange[58] (VSE) found rather weak evidence of the ability of insider trading to generate abnormal returns for

---

[48]Jeffrey F. Jaffe, "Special Information and Insider Trading," *Journal of Business* 47 (July 1974).

[49]H. Nejat Seyhun, "Insiders' Profits, Costs of Trading and Market Efficiency," *Journal of Financial Economics* 16 (1986).

[50]Dan Givoly and Dan Palmon, "Insider Trading and Exploitation of Inside Information: Some Empirical Evidence," *Journal of Business* 58 (1985).

[51]Isidore Masse, Robert Hanrahan, and Joseph Kushner, "Returns to Insider Trading: The Canadian Evidence," *Canadian Journal of Administrative Sciences* 5, no. 3 (September 1988).

[52]B. Espen Eckbo, "Mergers and the Market for Corporate Control: The Canadian Evidence," *Canadian Journal of Economics* 19, no. 2 (May 1986).

[53]Jerome Baesel and Garry Stein, "The Value of Information Inferences from the Profitability of Insider Trading," *Journal of Financial and Quantitative Analysis* 14 (September 1979).

[54]David J. Fowler and C. Harvey Rorke, "Insider Trading Profits on the Toronto Stock Exchange, 1967–1977," *Canadian Journal of Administrative Sciences* 5, no. 1 (March 1988).

[55]M. H. Lee and H. Bishara, "Recent Canadian Experience on the Profitability of Insider Trades," *The Financial Review* 24, no. 2 (May 1989).

[56]Jean-Marc Suret and Elise Cormier, "Insiders and the Stock Market," *Canadian Investment Review* 3, no. 2 (Fall 1990).

[57]Robert Heinkel and Alan Kraus, "The Effect of Insider Trading on Average Rates of Return," *Canadian Journal of Economics* 20, no. 3 (August 1987).

[58]The VSE is now part of the TSX Venture Exchange.

insiders. The sample of firms that Heinkel and Kraus examined over the period June 1979–June 1, 1981 was rather atypical. It consisted of small resource companies listed on the VSE, for which insiders are by far the largest shareholders. Thus, although the results could be interpreted as evidence of market efficiency of the strong form, they cannot be extrapolated to other situations. A more recent Canadian study also found little evidence of insiders profiting from mergers and acquisitions in Canada between 1985 and 2002.[59] However, in a later study, King shows evidence of pre-bid runups of the prices of Canadian takeover targets that are consistent with informational leakages and *illegal* insider trading.[60]

Interpreting the Evidence

Risk Premiums or Anomalies?
The price-earnings, small-firm, market-to-book, momentum, and long-term reversal effects are currently among the most puzzling phenomena in empirical finance. There are several interpretations of these effects. First note that to some extent, these three phenomena may be related. The feature that small firms, low-market-to-book firms, and recent "losers" seem to have in common is a stock price that has fallen considerably in recent months or years. Indeed, a firm can become a small firm, or a low-market-to-book firm by suffering a sharp drop in price. These groups therefore may contain a relatively high proportion of distressed firms that have suffered recent difficulties.

Fama and French[61] argue that these effects can be explained as manifestations of risk premiums. Using their three-factor model, introduced in the previous chapter, they show that stocks with higher "betas" (also known as factor loadings) on size or market-to-book factors have higher average returns; they interpret these returns as evidence of a risk premium associated with the factor.

This model does a much better job than the one-factor CAPM of explaining security returns. While size or book-to-market ratios per se are obviously not risk factors, they perhaps might act as proxies for more fundamental determinants of risk. Fama and French argue that these patterns of returns may therefore be consistent with an efficient market in which expected returns are consistent with risk. In this regard, it is worth noting that returns to "style factors," for example the return on portfolios constructed based on the ratio of book to market value (specifically, the Fama-French high minus low book-to-market portfolio) or firm size (the return on the small minus big firm portfolio), do indeed seem to predict business cycles in many countries. Figure 9.6 shows that returns on these portfolios tend to have positive returns in years prior to rapid growth in gross domestic product. We examine the Fama-French paper in more detail in Chapter 11.

The opposite interpretation is offered by Lakonishok, Shleifer, and Vishny,[62] who argue that these phenomena are evidence of inefficient markets—more specifically, of systematic errors in the forecasts of stock analysts. They believe that analysts extrapolate past performance too far into the future and therefore overprice firms with recent good performance and underprice firms with recent poor performance. Ultimately, when market participants recognize their errors, prices reverse. This explanation is obviously consistent with the reversal effect and also, to a degree, consistent with the small-firm and market-to-book effects because firms with sharp price drops may tend to be small or have low market-to-book ratios.

If Lakonishok, Shleifer, and Vishny are correct, we ought to find that analysts systematically err when forecasting returns of recent "winner" versus "loser" firms. A study by La Porta[63] is consistent with this pattern. He finds that equity of firms for which analysts predict low growth

[59]M. R. King and M. Padalko, "Outing Insiders," *Canadian Investment Review*, Spring 2007.

[60]M. R. King, "Prebid Run-ups Ahead of Canadian Takeovers: How Big Is the Problem?" *Financial Management*, Winter 2009.

[61]Eugene F. Fama and Kenneth R. French, "Common Risk Factors in the Returns on Stocks and Bonds," *Journal of Financial Economics* 33 (1993) pp. 3–56.

[62]Josef Lakonishok, Andrei Shleifer, and Robert W. Vishny, "Contrarian Investment, Extrapolation, and Risk," *Journal of Finance* 49 (1994), pp. 1541–1578.

[63]Raphael La Porta, "Expectations and the Cross Section of Stock Returns," *Journal of Finance* 51 (December 1996), pp. 1715–1742.

Figure 9.6   Return to style portfolio (SMB, HML) as a predictor of GDP growth. Average difference in the return on the style portfolio in years before good GDP growth versus in years with bad GDP growth. Positive value means the style portfolio does better in years prior to good macroeconomic performance. HML = high minus low portfolio, sorted on ratio of book to market value. SMB = small minus big portfolio, sorted on firm size.

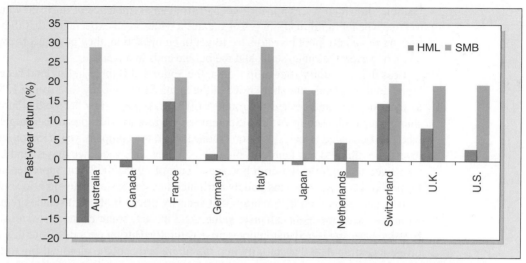

Source: Reprinted from J. Liew and M. Vassalou, "Can Book-to-Market, Size, and Momentum Be Risk Factors That Predict Economic Growth?" *Journal of Financial Economics* 57 (2000), pp. 221–45. Copyright 2000 with permission from Elsevier Science.

rates of earnings actually perform better than those with high expected earnings growth. Analysts seem overly pessimistic about firms with low growth prospects and overly optimistic about firms with high growth prospects. When these too-extreme expectations are "corrected," the low-expected-growth firms outperform high-expected-growth firms.

Anomalies or Data Mining?   We have covered many of the so-called anomalies cited in the literature, but our list could go on and on. Some wonder whether these anomalies really are unexplained puzzles in financial markets, or whether they instead are an artifact of data mining. After all, if one reruns the computer database of past returns over and over and examines stock returns along enough dimensions, simple chance will cause some criteria to *appear* to predict returns.

In this regard, it is noteworthy that some anomalies have not shown much staying power after being reported in the academic literature. For example, after the small-firm effect was published in the early 1980s, it promptly disappeared for much of the rest of the decade. Similarly, the book-to-market strategy, which commanded considerable attention in the early 1990s, was ineffective for the rest of that decade.

Still, even acknowledging the potential for data mining, a common thread seems to run through many of the anomalies we have considered, lending support to the notion that there is a real puzzle to explain. Value stocks—defined by low P/E ratio, high book-to-market ratio, or depressed prices relative to historic levels—seem to have provided higher average returns than "glamour" or growth stocks.

One way to address the problem of data mining is to find a data set that has not already been researched and see whether the relationship in question shows up in the new data. Such studies have revealed size, momentum, and book-to-market effects in other security markets around the world. While these phenomena may be a manifestation of a systematic risk premium, the precise nature of that risk is not fully understood.

Bubbles and Market Efficiency

Every so often, asset prices seem (at least in retrospect) to lose their grounding in reality. For example, in the tulip mania in seventeenth-century Holland, tulip prices peaked at several times the annual income of a skilled worker. This episode has become the symbol of a speculative "bubble" in which prices appear to depart from any semblance of intrinsic value. Bubbles seem to arise when a rapid runup in prices creates a widespread expectation that they will continue to rise. As more and more investors try to get in on the action, they push prices even further. Inevitably, however, the runup stalls and the bubble ends in a crash.

Less than a century after tulip mania, the South Sea Bubble in England became almost as famous. In this episode, the share price of the South Sea Company rose from £128 in January 1720 to £550 in May, and peaked at around £1,000 in August—just before the bubble burst and the share price collapsed to £150 in September, leading to widespread bankruptcies among those who had borrowed to buy shares on credit. In fact, the company was a major lender of money to investors willing to buy (and thus bid up) its shares. This sequence may sound familiar to anyone who lived through the dot-com boom and bust of 1995–2002[64] or, more recently, the financial turmoil of 2008, with origins widely attributed to a collapsing housing price bubble.

It is hard to defend the position that security prices in these instances represented rational, unbiased assessments of intrinsic value. And in fact, some economists, most notably Hyman Minsky, have suggested that bubbles arise naturally. During periods of stability and rising prices, investors extrapolate that stability into the future and become more willing to take on risk. Risk premiums shrink, leading to further increases in asset prices, and expectations become even more optimistic in a self-fulfilling cycle. But in the end, pricing and risk taking become excessive and the bubble bursts. Ironically, the initial period of stability fosters behaviour that ultimately results in instability.

But beware of jumping to the conclusion that asset prices may generally be thought of as arbitrary and obvious trading opportunities abundant. First, most bubbles become "obvious" only in retrospect. At the time, the price runup often seems to have a defensible rationale. In the dot-com boom, for example, many contemporary observers rationalized stock price gains as justified by the prospect of a new and more profitable economy, driven by technological advances. Even the irrationality of the tulip mania may have been overblown in its later retelling. In addition, security valuation is intrinsically difficult. Given the considerable imprecision of estimates of intrinsic value, large bets on perceived mispricing may entail hubris.

Moreover, even if you suspect that prices are in fact "wrong," taking advantage of them can be difficult. We explore these issues in more detail in the following chapter. For now, we simply point out some impediments to making aggressive bets against an asset—among them the costs of short selling overpriced securities, potential problems obtaining the securities to sell short, and the possibility that, even if you are ultimately correct, the market may disagree and prices can still move dramatically against you in the short term, wiping out your portfolio.

The "Noisy Market Hypothesis" and Fundamental Indexing

The efficient market hypothesis argues in favour of capitalization-weighted indexed portfolios that provide broad diversification with minimal trading costs. But several researchers and practitioners have forcefully argued that such "cap-weighted" indexing is necessarily inferior to a strategy they call *fundamental indexing*.[65] The rationale for their argument goes by the name "noisy market hypothesis."

---

[64]The dot-com boom gave rise to the term *irrational exuberance*. In this vein, consider that one company going public in the investment boom of 1720 described itself simply as "a company for carrying out an undertaking of great advantage, but nobody to know what it is."

[65]See, for example, Robert Arnott, "Orthodoxy Overwrought," *Institutional Investor*, December 18, 2006.

The hypothesis begins with the observation that market prices may well contain pricing errors or "noise" relative to the intrinsic or "true" value of a firm. Even if prices are correct on average, at any time some stocks will be overvalued and others undervalued. Overpriced stocks have inflated market values relative to intrinsic value, while the market values of underpriced stocks are too low. Because indexed portfolios invest in proportion to market capitalization, portfolio weights will track these pricing errors, with greater amounts invested in overpriced stocks (which have poor expected returns) and lesser amounts invested in underpriced stocks (which have high expected returns). The conclusion is that a capitalization-weighted strategy is destined to overweight precisely the firms with the worst return prospects. In contrast, a fundamental index that invests in proportion to intrinsic value would avoid the detrimental association between portfolio weights and the market's pricing errors, and would therefore outperform a capitalization-weighted index.

However, while this conclusion is correct, it invites the crucial question: How can we find the intrinsic values necessary to form a fundamental index? The necessary inputs are in fact the holy grail of all active managers: true stock values or, equivalently, market pricing errors. Clearly, *given* the errors in market prices, we could outperform passive cap-weighted portfolios by tilting toward undervalued stocks and away from overpriced ones. This is hardly a surprise. The problem is finding a guide to these pricing errors. Unfortunately, market capitalization by itself tells us *nothing* about potential mispricing (indeed, this is the starting assumption of the noisy market hypothesis), and therefore, gives us no guidance on how to tilt our portfolio.[66]

Advocates of fundamental indexing propose that portfolio weights determined by indicators of intrinsic value such as dividends or earnings be used to construct an alternative to a cap-weighted index. These rules would result in allocations that are skewed (compared to cap weighting) toward firms with high value indicators. But notice that these indicators are precisely the tools used in the value-investing strategies we discussed earlier in this section (e.g., dividend yield or price-earnings ratios). There may be good reasons to pursue value investing, chiefly the evidence reviewed earlier that value stocks have typically outperformed growth stocks over long periods in many countries. But we've also noted that there may be other, risk-premium-based, explanations for that performance. Regardless of your interpretation of the value premium, you should recognize that fundamental indexing is at heart nothing more than a value tilt, a point emphasized by Asness.[67] It is therefore, despite its name, *not* indexing, but rather a form of active investing, and it is hardly a radical new approach to either indexation or investment policy.

9.5 MUTUAL FUND AND ANALYST PERFORMANCE

We have documented some of the apparent chinks in the armour of efficient market proponents. For investors, the issue of market efficiency boils down to whether skilled investors can make consistent abnormal trading profits. The best test is to look at the performance of market professionals to see if they can generate performance superior to that of a passive index fund that buys and holds the market. We will look at two facets of professional performance: that of stock market analysts who recommend investment positions and that of mutual fund managers who actually manage portfolios.

Stock Market Analysts

Stock market analysts historically have worked for brokerage firms, which presents an immediate problem in interpreting the value of their advice: analysts have tended to be overwhelmingly

---

[66]For a more rigorous demonstration of this point and an insightful discussion of fundamental indexing, see André Perold, "Fundamentally Flawed Indexing," *Financial Analysts Journal* 63 (November/December 2007), pp. 31–37.
[67]Cliff Asness, "The Value of Fundamental Indexing," *Institutional Investor*, October 16, 2006, pp. 94–99.

positive in their assessment of the prospects of firms.[68] For example, on a scale of 1 (strong buy) to 5 (strong sell), the average recommendation for 5,628 covered firms in 1996 was 2.04.[69] As a result, one cannot take positive recommendations (e.g., to buy) at face value. Instead, we must look at either the enthusiasm of analyst recommendations compared to those for other firms, or at the change in consensus recommendations.

Womack[70] focuses on changes in analysts' recommendations and finds that positive changes are associated with increased stock prices of about 5 percent, and negative changes result in average price decreases of 11 percent. One might wonder whether these price changes reflect the market's recognition of analysts' superior information or insight about firms or, instead, simply result from new buy or sell pressure brought on by the recommendations themselves. Womack argues that price impact seems to be permanent, and therefore consistent with the hypothesis that analysts do in fact reveal new information. Jegadeesh, Kim, Krische, and Lee[71] also find that changes in consensus recommendations are associated with price changes, but that the *level* of consensus recommendations is an inconsistent predictor of future stock performance.

Barber, Lehavy, McNichols, and Trueman focus on the level of consensus recommendations and show that firms with the most-favourable recommendations outperform those with the least-favourable recommendations. While their results seem impressive, the authors note that portfolio strategies based on analyst consensus recommendations would result in extremely heavy trading activity with associated costs that would probably wipe out the potential profits from the strategy. Similar results emerge from Canadian studies by Dutta et al.[72] and Brown, Richardson, and Trzcinka.[73] In the latter study the authors found that use of the Research Evaluation Service of *The Financial Post Information Service* in a trading strategy led to significant excess returns, net of transactions costs. They also tested the significance of the benchmark for risk adjustment, and concluded that the result was independent of the choice of a CAPM or APT approach; hence, they demonstrated that use of the simpler CAPM methodology was justified in this context.

Financial Post
www.canada.
com/nationalpost/
financialpost

In another Canadian study L'Her and Suret[74] examined the reaction to earnings revisions by measuring abnormal returns. Although most of the price reaction occurred in anticipation of the announcement, the extreme cases showed that abnormal returns persisted for nine months following release for upward revisions, but for only three months for downward revisions. (On the other hand, the reaction to unfavourable revisions was much more pronounced over the 18-month period.) Findings such as these may lead one to suspect the causality; it is possible that analysts revise their forecasts in response to price changes, which they interpret as inside information.

In sum, the literature suggests some value is added by analysts, but some ambiguity remains. Are superior returns following analyst upgrades due to new information or to changes in investor demand in response to the changed outlook? Also, are these results exploitable by investors who necessarily incur trading costs?

---

[68]This problem may be less severe in the future; as noted in Chapter 3, one recent reform intended to mitigate the conflict of interest in having brokerage firms that sell stocks also provide investment advice is to separate analyst coverage from the other activities of the firm.

[69]B. Barber, R. Lehavy, M. McNichols, and B. Trueman, "Can Investors Profit from the Prophets? Security Analyst Recommendations and Stock Returns," *Journal of Finance* 56 (April 2001), pp. 531–63.

[70]K. L. Womack, "Do Brokerage Analysts' Recommendations Have Investment Value?" *Journal of Finance* 51 (March 1996), pp. 137–67.

[71]N. Jegadeesh, J. Kim, S. D. Krische, and C. M. Lee, "Analyzing the Analysts: When Do Recommendations Add Value?" *Journal of Finance* 59 (June 2004), pp. 1083–124.

[72]Barber et al., op. cit.; and S. Dutta, K. Macaulay, T. Hynes, and M. Oxner, "Curbing Their Enthusiasm," *Canadian Investment Review*, Spring 2008.

[73]Lawrence Brown, Gordon Richardson, and Charles Trzcinka, "Strong-Form Efficiency on the Toronto Stock Exchange: An Analysis of Analyst Price Forecasts," *Contemporary Accounting Research*, Spring 1991.

[74]Jean-François L'Her and Jean-Marc Suret, "The Reaction of Canadian Securities to Revisions of Earnings," *Contemporary Accounting Research*, Spring 1991.

Mutual Fund Managers

Casual evidence does not support the claim that professionally managed portfolios can consistently beat the market. Between 1972 and 2011 the returns of a passive portfolio indexed to the Wilshire 5000 typically would have been better than those of the average equity fund. On the other hand, there was some (admittedly inconsistent) evidence of persistence in performance, meaning that the better managers in one period tended to be better managers in following periods. Such a pattern would suggest that the better managers can with some consistency outperform their competitors, and it would be inconsistent with the notion that market prices already reflect all relevant information. In this section we examine the question of mutual fund performance, paying attention to the benchmark against which performance ought to be evaluated.

As a first pass, we can examine the risk-adjusted returns (i.e., the alpha, or return in excess of required return based on beta and the market return in each period) of a large sample of mutual funds.

One problem in interpreting these alphas is that the S&P 500 may not be an adequate benchmark against which to evaluate mutual fund returns. Because mutual funds tend to maintain considerable holdings in equity of small firms, whereas the S&P 500 exclusively comprises large firms, mutual funds as a whole will tend to outperform the S&P when small firms outperform large ones and underperform when small firms fare worse. Thus a better benchmark for the performance of funds would be an index that incorporates the stock market performance of smaller firms.

The importance of the benchmark can be illustrated by examining the returns on small stocks in various subperiods.[75] In the 20-year period between 1945 and 1964, a small-stock index underperformed the S&P 500 by about 4 percent per year (i.e., the alpha of the small-stock index after adjusting for systematic risk was −4 percent). In the more recent 20-year period between 1965 and 1984, small stocks outperformed the S&P index by 10 percent. Thus if one were to examine mutual fund returns in the earlier period, they would tend to look poor, not necessarily because small-fund managers were poor stock pickers, but simply because mutual funds as a group tend to hold more small stocks than are represented in the S&P 500. In the later period, funds would look better on a risk-adjusted basis relative to the S&P 500 because small funds performed better. The "style choice," that is, the exposure to small stocks (which is an asset allocation decision) would dominate the evaluation of performance even though it has little to do with managers' stock-picking ability.[76]

Consistently with Figure 9.7, Fama and French[77] use the four-factor model to assess the performance of equity mutual funds and show that, while they may exhibit positive alphas *before* fees, after the fees charged to their customers, alphas were negative. Likewise, Wermers,[78] who uses both style portfolios and the characteristics of the stocks held by mutual funds to control for performance, also finds positive gross alphas but negative net alphas after controlling for fees and risk.

Carhart[79] reexamined the issue of consistency in mutual fund performance and finds that there is persistence in relative performance across managers. However, much of that persistence seems due to expenses and transactions costs rather than gross investment returns. This last point is important; although there can be no consistently superior performers in a fully efficient market, there *can* be consistently inferior performers. Repeated weak performance would not be due to an ability to pick bad stocks consistently (that would be impossible in an efficient market!) but could result from a

---

[75]This illustration and the statistics cited are based on E. J. Elton, M. J. Gruber, S. Das, and M. Hlavka, "Efficiency with Costly Information: A Reinterpretation of Evidence from Managed Portfolios," *Review of Financial Studies* 6 (1993), pp. 1–22, which is discussed shortly.
[76]Remember that the asset allocation decision is usually in the hands of the individual investor. Investors allocate their investment portfolios to funds in asset classes they desire to hold, and they can reasonably expect only that mutual fund portfolio managers will choose stocks advantageously *within* those asset classes.
[77]Eugene F. Fama and Kenneth R. French, "Luck Versus Skill in the Cross-Section of Mutual Fund Returns," *Journal of Finance* 65 (2010), pp. 1915–47.
[78]R. R. Wermers, "Mutual Fund Performance: An Empirical Decomposition into Stock-Picking Talent, Style, Transaction Costs, and Expenses," *Journal of Finance* 55 (2000), pp. 1655–1703.
[79]Mark M. Carhart, "On Persistence in Mutual Fund Performance," *Journal of Finance* 52 (1997), pp. 57–82.

Figure 9.7　Mutual fund alphas computed using a four-factor model of expected return, 1993–2007. (The best and worst 2.5 percent of observations are excluded from this distribution.)

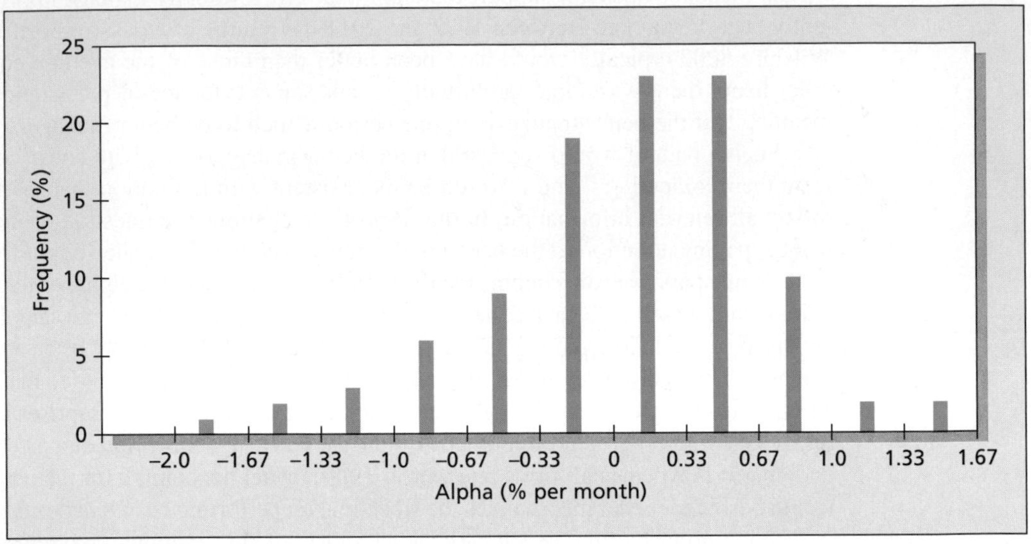

Source: Professor Richard Evans, University of Virginia, Darden School of Business.

consistently high expense ratio and consistently high portfolio turnover with the resulting trading costs. Nevertheless, even allowing for expenses, some amount of performance persistence seems to be due to differences in investment strategy. Carhart found, however, that the evidence of persistence is concentrated at the two extremes. This suggests that there may be a small group of exceptional managers who can with some consistency outperform a passive strategy, but that for the majority of managers, over- or underperformance in any period is largely a matter of chance.

Del Guercio and Reuter[80] offer a finer interpretation of mutual fund performance and the Berk and Green hypothesis. They split mutual fund investors into those who buy funds directly for themselves versus those who purchase funds through brokers, reasoning that the direct-sold segment may be more financially literate while the broker-sold segment is less comfortable making financial decisions without professional advice. Consistent with this hypothesis, they show that direct-sold investors direct their assets to funds with positive alphas (consistent with the Berk-Green model), but broker-sold investors generally do not. This provides an incentive for direct-sold funds to invest relatively more in alpha-generating inputs such as talented portfolio managers or analysts than in broker-sold funds. Moreover, they show that the after-fee performance of direct-sold funds is as good as that of index funds (again, consistently with Berk-Green), while the performance of broker-sold funds is considerably worse. It thus appears that the average underperformance of actively managed mutual funds is driven largely by broker-sold funds and that this underperformance may be interpreted as an implicit cost that less informed investors pay for the advice they get from their brokers.

In contrast to the extensive studies of equity fund managers, there have been very few studies on the performance of bond fund managers. Blake, Elton, and Gruber[81] examined the performance of fixed-income mutual funds. They found that, on average, bond funds underperform passive fixed-income indices by an amount roughly equal to expenses, and that there is no evidence that past performance can predict future performance.

---

[80]Diane Del Guercio and Jonathan Reuter, "Mutual Fund Performance and the Incentive to Generate Alpha," *Journal of Finance*, forthcoming, 2014.
[81]Christopher R. Blake, Edwin J. Elton, and Martin J. Gruber, "The Performance of Bond Mutual Funds," *Journal of Business* 66 (July 1993), pp. 371–404.

A Canadian study by Jog[82] confirms these findings for a sample of Canadian pension fund managers. The study used several different performance measures, which included the alphas, and four different benchmark portfolios, one of which was the S&P/TSX Composite index. The results, however, were virtually identical for all measures and benchmark portfolios: managers of pension funds included in the sample failed to exhibit any significant or consistent ability to achieve superior risk-adjusted performance of the portfolios that they managed. Pension funds would have achieved a better risk–return combination by using combinations of suitable index funds.

Thus, the evidence on the risk-adjusted performance of professional managers is mixed at best. We conclude that the performance of professional managers is broadly consistent with market efficiency. The amounts by which professional managers as a group beat or are beaten by the market fall within the margin of statistical uncertainty. In any event, it is quite clear that performance superior to passive strategies is far from routine. Studies show either that most managers cannot outperform passive strategies or that if there is a margin of superiority, it is small.

On the other hand, a small number of investment superstars—Peter Lynch (formerly of Fidelity's Magellan Fund), Warren Buffett (of Berkshire Hathaway), John Templeton (of Templeton Funds), and John Neff (of Vanguard's Windsor Fund) among them—have compiled career records that show a consistency of superior performance hard to reconcile with absolutely efficient markets. Nobel Prize winner Paul Samuelson[83] reviews this investment hall of fame but points out that the records of the vast majority of professional money managers offer convincing evidence that there are no easy strategies to guarantee success in the securities markets.

Survivorship Bias in Mutual Fund Studies

In any period, some managers may be lucky, and others unlucky. We will argue in Chapter 23 that a good way to separate skill from luck is to see whether the managers who perform well in one period tend to be above-average performers in subsequent periods. If they are, we should be more willing to ascribe their success to skill. Unfortunately, studies of mutual fund performance can be affected by *survivorship bias*, the tendency for less successful funds to go out of business over time, thus leaving the sample. This can give rise to the appearance of persistence in performance, even if there is none in reality.

Define a "winner" fund as one in the top half of the distribution of returns in a given period and a "loser" fund as one in the bottom half of the sample. If performance is due solely to chance, the probability of being a winner or loser in the next period is the same regardless of first-period performance. A 2×2 tabulation of performance in two consecutive periods would look like this:

First Period	Second Period	
	Winners	**Losers**
Winners	.25	.25
Losers	.25	.25

For example, the first-period winners (50 percent of the sample) are equally likely to be winners or losers in the second period, so 25 percent of total outcomes fall in each cell in the first row.

But what happens if losing funds or managers are removed from the sample because they are shut down by their management companies? This can lead to the appearance of performance

[82]Vijay M. Jog, "Investment Performance of Pension Funds—A Canadian Study," *Canadian Journal of Administrative Sciences* 3, no. 1 (June 1986).

[83]Paul Samuelson, "The Judgment of Economic Science on Rational Portfolio Management," *Journal of Portfolio Management* 16 (Fall 1989), pp. 4–12.

TABLE 9.1

Two-Way Table of Managers Classified by Risk-Adjusted Returns over Successive Intervals

	Second-Period Winners	Second-Period Losers
A. No cutoff (*n* = 600)		
First-period winners	150.09	149.51
First-period losers	149.51	150.09
B. 5% cutoff (*n* = 494)		
First-period winners	127.49	119.51
First-period losers	119.51	127.49
C. 10% cutoff (*n* = 398)		
First-period winners	106.58	92.42
First-period losers	92.42	106.58

Source: S. J. Brown, W. Goetzmann, and S. A. Ross, "Survivorship Bias in Performance Studies," *Review of Financial Studies* 5 (1992).

persistence. Brown, Goetzmann, Ibbotson, and Ross[84] use a sample of mutual fund returns to simulate the potential import of survivorship bias. They simulate annual returns over a four-year period for 600 managers drawing from distributions constructed to mimic historical equity and fund returns in the United States, compute performance over two two-year periods, and construct 2×2 tables of winner/loser performance like the one above. Their results appear in Table 9.1. If all 600 managers remain in the simulated sample, the results look much like the ones above (see panel A). But if the bottom 5 percent of first-period performers are removed from the sample each year (5 percent cutoff, panel B), the diagonal terms are larger than the off-diagonal terms: winners seem more likely to remain winners, and losers to remain losers. If a higher fraction of poor performers are removed from the sample (panel C), there is even greater appearance of performance persistence.

The appearance of persistence in the simulation is due to survivorship bias. Average alphas are constructed to be zero for all groups. These results serve as a warning that data sets used to assess performance of professional managers must be free of survivorship bias. Unfortunately, many are not.

So Are Markets Efficient?

There is a telling joke about two economists walking down the street. They spot a $20 bill on the sidewalk. One starts to pick it up, but the other one says, "Don't bother; if the bill were real someone would have picked it up already."

The lesson is clear. An overly doctrinaire belief in efficient markets can paralyze the investor and make it appear that no research effort can be justified. This extreme view is probably unwarranted. There are enough anomalies in the empirical evidence to justify the search for underpriced securities that clearly goes on.

The bulk of the evidence, however, suggests that any supposedly superior investment strategy should be taken with many grains of salt. The market is competitive *enough* that only differentially superior information or insight will earn money; the easy pickings have been picked. In the end it is likely that the margin of superiority that any professional manager can add is so slight that the statistician will not be able to detect it.

For the United States, we can safely conclude that markets are very efficient, but that rewards to the especially diligent, intelligent, or creative may in fact be waiting. In Canada, the anomalies are stronger and last longer. However, Canadian professional investment managers as a whole have shown no evidence of having exploited such inefficiencies.

[84]S. J. Brown, W. Goetzmann, R. G. Ibbotson, and S. A. Ross, "Survivorship Bias in Performance Studies," *Review of Financial Studies* 5 (1992).

SUMMARY

1. Statistical research has shown that stock prices seem to follow a random walk with no discernible predictable patterns that investors can exploit. Such findings are now taken to be evidence of market efficiency, that is, of evidence that market prices reflect all currently available information. Only new information will move stock prices, and this information is equally likely to be good news or bad news.

2. Market participants distinguish among three forms of the efficient market hypothesis. The weak form asserts that all information to be derived from past stock prices already is reflected in stock prices. The semistrong form claims that all publicly available information is already reflected. The strong form, usually taken only as a straw man, asserts that all information, including insider information, is reflected in prices.

3. Technical analysis focuses on stock price patterns and on proxies for buy or sell pressure in the market. Fundamental analysis focuses on the determinants of the underlying value of the firm, such as current profitability and growth prospects. Since both types of analysis are based on public information, neither should generate excess profits if markets are operating efficiently.

4. Proponents of the efficient market hypothesis often advocate passive as opposed to active investment strategies. The policy of passive investors is to buy and hold a broad-based market index. They expend resources neither on market research nor on the frequent purchase and sale of stocks. Passive strategies may be tailored to meet individual investor requirements.

5. Event studies are used to evaluate the economic impact of events of interest, using abnormal stock returns. Such studies usually show that there is some leakage of inside information to some market participants before the public announcement date. Therefore insiders do seem to be able to exploit their access to information to at least a limited extent.

6. Empirical studies of technical analysis do not support the hypothesis that such analysis can generate superior trading profits. One notable exception to this conclusion over intermediate-term horizons is the apparent success of momentum-based strategies over intermediate-term horizons.

7. Several anomalies regarding fundamental analysis have been uncovered. These include the P/E effect, the small-firm-in-January effect, the neglected-firm effect, post-earnings-announcement price drift, the book-to-market effect, and the insider trading effect in Canada. Whether these anomalies represent market inefficiency or poorly understood risk premiums is still a matter of debate.

8. By and large, the performance record of professionally managed funds lends little credence to claims that most professionals can consistently beat the market.

KEY EQUATIONS

(9.1) $r_t = a + br_{Mt} + e_t$

(9.2) $e_t = r_t - (a + br_{Mt})$

PROBLEMS

connect™ **Practise and learn online with Connect.**

1. If markets are efficient, what should be the correlation coefficient between stock returns for two nonoverlapping time periods?

2. Which of the following most appears to contradict the proposition that the stock market is *weakly* efficient? Explain.
   a. Over 25 percent of mutual funds outperform the market on average.
   b. Insiders earn abnormal trading profits.
   c. Every January, the stock market earns above-normal returns.

3. Suppose that, after conducting an analysis of past stock prices, you come up with the following observations. Which would appear to *contradict* the *weak* form of the efficient market hypothesis? Explain.

   a. The average rate of return is significantly greater than zero.

   b. The correlation between the return during a given week and the return during the following week is zero.

   c. One could have made superior returns by buying stock after a 10 percent rise in price and selling after a 10 percent fall.

   d. One could have made higher than average capital gains by holding stock with low dividend yields.

4. Which of the following statements are true if the efficient market hypothesis holds?

   a. Future events can be forecast with perfect accuracy.

   b. Prices reflect all available information.

   c. Security prices change for no discernible reason.

   d. Prices do not fluctuate.

5. Which of the following observations would provide evidence *against* the *semistrong-form* version of the efficient market theory? Explain.

   a. Mutual fund managers do not on average make superior returns.

   b. You cannot make superior profits by buying (or selling) stocks after the announcement of an abnormal rise in dividends.

   c. Low P/E stocks tend to have positive abnormal returns.

   d. In any year, approximately 50 percent of pension funds outperform the market.

6. The shares of Magna International Inc. (MG/TSX) rose by over 50 percent in the first half of 2013. They also rose by over 40 percent in 2012. Is this a violation of the EMH?

7. Suppose you find that prices of stocks before large dividend increases show on average consistently positive abnormal returns. Is this a violation of the EMH?

8. "If the business cycle is predictable, and a stock has a positive beta, the stock's returns also must be predictable." Respond.

9. Which of the following phenomena would be either consistent with or a violation of the efficient market hypothesis? Explain briefly.

   a. Nearly half of all professionally managed mutual funds are able to outperform the S&P/TSX Composite in a typical year.

   b. Money managers that outperform the market (on a risk-adjusted basis) in one year are likely to outperform it in the following year.

   c. Stock prices tend to be predictably more volatile in January than in other months.

   d. Stock prices of companies that announce increased earnings in January tend to outperform the market in February.

   e. Stocks that perform well in one week perform poorly in the following week.

10. "If all securities are fairly priced, all must offer equal market rates of return." Comment.

11. An index model regression applied to past monthly excess returns in ABC Corporation's stock price produces the following estimates, which are believed to be stable over time:

$$R_{ABC} = .10\% + 1.1R_M$$

If the market index subsequently rises by 8 percent and ABC's stock price rises by 7 percent, what is the abnormal change in ABC's stock price? The T-bill return during the month is 1 percent.

12. The monthly rate of return on T-bills is 1 percent. The market went up this month by 1.5 percent. In addition, AmbChaser, Inc., which has an equity beta of 2, surprisingly just won a lawsuit that awards it $1 million immediately.

   a. If the original value of AmbChaser equity were $100 million, what would you guess was the rate of return of its stock this month?

   b. What is your answer to (a) if the market had expected AmbChaser to win $2 million?

13. In a recent, closely contested lawsuit, Apex sued Bpex for patent infringement. The jury came back today with its decision. The rate of return on Apex was $r_A = 3.1$ percent. The rate of return on Bpex was only $r_B = 2.5$ percent. The market today responded to very encouraging news about the unemployment rate, and $r_M = 3$ percent. The historical relationship between returns on these stocks and the market portfolio has been estimated from index model regressions as

   Apex: $r_A = .2\% + 1.4r_M$

   Bpex: $r_B = -.1\% + .6r_M$

   Judging from these data, which company do you think won the lawsuit?

14. Dollar cost averaging means that you buy equal dollar amounts of a stock every period, for example, $500 per month. The strategy is based on the idea that when the stock price is low, your fixed monthly purchase will buy more shares, and when the price is high, it will buy fewer shares. Averaging over time, you will end up buying more shares when the stock is cheaper and fewer when it is relatively expensive. Therefore, by design, you will exhibit good market timing. Evaluate this strategy.

15. Steady Growth Industries has never missed a dividend payment in its 94-year history. Does this make it more attractive to you as a possible purchase for your stock portfolio?

16. We know that the market should respond positively to good news and that good-news events, such as the end of a recession, can be predicted with at least some accuracy. Why, then, can we not predict the market will go up as the economy recovers?

17. If prices are as likely to increase as decrease, why do investors earn positive returns from the market on average?

18. You know that firm XYZ is very poorly run. On a scale of 1 (worst) to 10 (best), you would give it a score of 3. The market consensus evaluation is that the management score is only 2. Should you buy or sell the stock?

19. Good News Inc. just announced an increase in its annual earnings, yet its stock price fell. Is there a rational explanation for this phenomenon?

20. Investors *expect* the market rate of return in the coming year to be 12 percent. The T-bill rate is 4 percent. Changing Fortunes Industries' stock has a beta of .5. The market value of its outstanding equity is $100 million.

   a. What is your best guess currently as to the expected rate of return on Changing Fortunes' stock? You believe that the stock is fairly priced.

   b. If the market return in the coming year actually turns out to be 10 percent, what is your best guess as to the rate of return that will be earned on Changing Fortunes' stock?

   c. Suppose now that Changing Fortunes wins a major lawsuit during the year. The settlement is $5 million. Changing Fortunes' stock return during the year turns out to be 10 percent. What is your best guess as to the settlement the market previously *expected* Changing Fortunes to receive from the lawsuit? (Continue to assume that the market return in the year turned out to be 10 percent.) The magnitude of the settlement is the only unexpected firm-specific event during the year.

21. Examine the figure[85] that follows, which presents cumulative abnormal returns both before and after dates on which insiders buy or sell shares in their firms. How do you interpret it? What are we to make of the pattern of CARs before and after the event date?

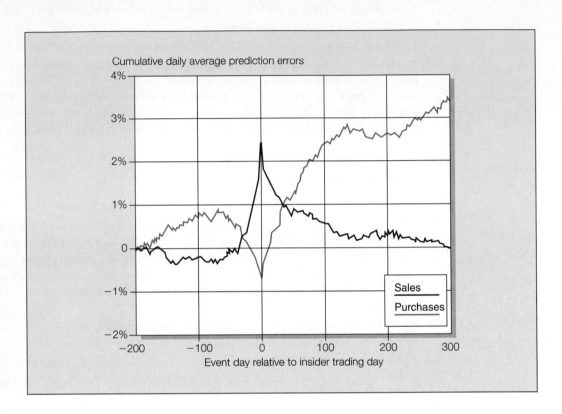

22. Suppose that during a certain week the Fed in the U.S. announces a new monetary growth policy. Congress surprisingly passes legislation restricting imports of foreign automobiles, and Ford comes out with a new car model that it believes will increase profits substantially. How might you go about measuring the market's assessment of Ford's new model?

23. When technical analysts say a stock has good "relative strength," they mean

    a. The ratio of the price of the stock to a market or industry index has trended upward

    b. The recent trading volume in the stock has exceeded the normal trading volume

    c. The total return on the stock has exceeded the total return on T-bills

    d. The stock has performed well recently compared to its past performance

The following problems are based on questions that have appeared in past CFA examinations.

24. The semistrong form of the efficient market hypothesis asserts that stock prices

    a. Fully reflect all historical price information

    b. Fully reflect all publicly available information

    c. Fully reflect all relevant information including insider information

    d. May be predictable

25. Assume that a company announces an unexpectedly large cash dividend to its shareholders. In an efficient market *without* information leakage, one might expect

    a. An abnormal price change at the announcement

    b. An abnormal price increase before the announcement

    c. An abnormal price decrease after the announcement

    d. No abnormal price change before or after the announcement

26. Which one of the following would provide evidence *against* the *strong form* of the efficient market theory?

    a. About 50 percent of pension funds outperform the market in any year.

    b. All investors have learned to exploit signals about future performance.

    c. Trend analysis is worthless in determining stock prices.

    d. Low-P/E stocks tend to have positive abnormal returns over the long run.

27. According to the efficient market hypothesis,

    a. High-beta stocks are consistently overpriced

    b. Low-beta stocks are consistently overpriced

    c. Positive alphas on stocks will quickly disappear

    d. Negative-alpha stocks consistently yield low returns for arbitrageurs

28. A "random walk" occurs when

    a. Stock price changes are random but predictable

    b. Stock prices respond slowly to both new and old information

    c. Future price changes are uncorrelated with past price changes

    d. Past information is useful in predicting future prices

29. Two basic assumptions of technical analysis are that security prices adjust

    a. Gradually to new information, and study of the economic environment provides an indication of future market movements

    b. Rapidly to new information, and study of the economic environment provides an indication of future market movements

    c. Rapidly to new information, and market prices are determined by the interaction between supply and demand

    d. Gradually to new information, and market prices are determined by the interaction between supply and demand

30. Your investment client asks for information concerning the benefits of active portfolio management. She is particularly interested in the question of whether or not active managers can be expected to consistently exploit inefficiencies in the capital markets to produce above-average returns without assuming higher risk.

    The semistrong form of the efficient market hypothesis asserts that all publicly available information is rapidly and correctly reflected in securities prices. This implies that investors cannot expect to derive above-average profits from purchases made after information has become public because security prices already reflect the information's full effects.

    a. Identify and explain two examples of empirical evidence that tend to support the EMH implication stated above.

    b. Identify and explain two examples of empirical evidence that tend to refute the EMH implication stated above.

    c. Discuss reasons why an investor might choose not to index even if the markets were, in fact, semi-strong form efficient.

31. *a.* Briefly explain the concept of the efficient market hypothesis (EMH) and each of its three forms—weak, semistrong, and strong—and briefly discuss the degree to which existing, empirical evidence supports each of the three forms of the EMH.

b. Briefly discuss the implications of the efficient market hypothesis for investment policy as it applies to

   i. Technical analysis in the form of charting

   ii. Fundamental analysis

c. Briefly explain the roles or responsibilities of portfolio managers in an efficient market environment.

32. Growth and value can be defined in several ways. "Growth" usually conveys the idea of a portfolio emphasizing or including only issues believed to possess above-average future rates of per-share earnings growth. Low current yield, high price-to-book ratios, and high price-to-earnings ratios are typical characteristics of such portfolios. "Value" usually conveys the idea of portfolios emphasizing or including only issues currently showing low price-to-book ratios, low price-to-earnings ratios, above-average levels of dividend yield, and market prices believed to be below the issues' intrinsic values.

a. Identify and provide reasons why, over an extended period of time, value-stock investing might outperform growth-stock investing.

b. Explain why the outcome suggested in (*a*) should not be possible in a market widely regarded as being highly efficient.

Behavioural Finance and Technical Analysis

The efficient market hypothesis makes two important predictions. First, it implies that security prices properly reflect whatever information is available to investors. A second implication follows immediately: active traders will find it difficult to outperform passive strategies such as holding market indices. To do so would require differential insight; this in a highly competitive market is very hard to come by.

Unfortunately, it is hard to devise measures of the "true" or intrinsic value of a security, and correspondingly difficult to test directly whether prices match those values. Therefore, most tests of market efficiency have focused on the performance of active trading strategies. These tests have been of two kinds. The anomalies literature has examined strategies that apparently *would* have provided superior risk-adjusted returns (e.g., investing in stocks with momentum or in value rather than glamour stocks). Other tests have looked at the results of actual investments by asking whether professional managers have been able to beat the market.

Neither class of tests has proven fully conclusive. The anomalies literature suggests that several strategies would have provided superior returns. But there are questions as to whether some of these apparent anomalies reflect risk premiums not captured by simple models of risk and return, or even if they merely reflect data mining. Moreover, the apparent inability of the typical money manager to turn these anomalies into superior returns on actual portfolios casts additional doubt on their "reality."

A relatively new school of thought dubbed *behavioural finance* argues that the sprawling literature on trading strategies has missed a larger and more important point by overlooking the first implication of efficient markets—the correctness of security prices. This may be the more important implication, since market economies rely on prices to allocate resources efficiently. The behavioural school argues that even if security prices are wrong, it still can be difficult to exploit them, and therefore that the failure to uncover obviously successful trading rules or traders cannot be taken as proof of market efficiency.

Whereas conventional theories presume that investors are rational, behavioural finance starts with the assumption that they are not. We will examine some of the information-processing and behavioural irrationalities uncovered by psychologists in other contexts and show how these tendencies applied to financial markets might result in some of the anomalies discussed in the previous chapter. We then consider the limitations of strategies designed to take advantage of behaviourally induced mispricing. If the limits to such arbitrage activity are severe, mispricing can survive even if some rational investors attempt to exploit it. We turn next to technical analysis and show how behavioural models give some support to techniques that clearly would be useless in efficient markets. We close the chapter with a brief survey of some of these technical strategies.

10.1 THE BEHAVIOURAL CRITIQUE

The premise of **behavioural finance** is that conventional financial theory ignores how real people make decisions and that people make a difference.[1] A growing number of economists have come to interpret the anomalies literature as consistent with several "irrationalities" that seem to characterize individuals making complicated decisions. These irrationalities fall into two broad categories: first, that investors do not always process information correctly and therefore infer incorrect probability distributions about future rates of return; and second, that even given a probability distribution of returns, they often make inconsistent or systematically suboptimal decisions.

Of course, the existence of irrational investors would not by itself be sufficient to render capital markets inefficient. If such irrationalities did affect prices, then sharp-eyed arbitrageurs taking advantage of profit opportunities might be expected to push prices back to their proper values. Thus, the second leg of the behavioural critique is that in practice the actions of such arbitrageurs are limited and therefore insufficient to force prices to match intrinsic value.

This leg of the argument is important. Virtually everyone agrees that if prices are right (i.e., price = intrinsic value), there are no easy profit opportunities. But the reverse is not necessarily true. If behaviourists are correct about limits to arbitrage activity, the absence of profit opportunities does not necessarily imply that markets are efficient. We've noted that most tests of the efficient market hypothesis have focused on the existence of profit opportunities, often as reflected in the performance of money managers. But their failure to systematically outperform passive investment strategies need not imply that markets are in fact efficient.

We will start our summary of the behavioural critique with the first leg of the argument, surveying a sample of the informational processing errors uncovered by psychologists in other areas. We next examine a few of the behavioural irrationalities that seem to characterize decision makers. Finally, we look at limits to arbitrage activity, and conclude with a tentative assessment of the import of the behavioural debate.

---

[1]The discussion in this section is based on two excellent survey articles: Nicholas Barberis and Richard Thaler, "A Survey of Behavioral Finance," in G. M. Constantinides, M. Harris, and R. Stulz, eds., *Handbook of the Economics of Finance* (Amsterdam: Elsevier, 2003); and W.F.M. De Bondt and R. H. Thaler, "Financial Decision Making in Markets and Firms," in R. A. Jarrow, V. Maksimovic, and W. T. Ziemba, eds., *Handbooks in Operations Research and Management Science, Volume 9: Finance* (Amsterdam: Elsevier, 1995).

Information Processing

Errors in information processing can lead investors to misestimate the true probabilities of possible events or associated rates of return. Several such biases have been uncovered. Here are four of the more important ones.

Forecasting Errors   A series of experiments by Kahneman and Tversky[2] indicate that people give too much weight to recent experience as against prior beliefs when making forecasts (sometimes dubbed a *memory bias*) and tend to make forecasts that are too extreme given the uncertainty inherent in their information. DeBondt and Thaler[3] argue that the P/E effect can be explained by earnings expectations that are too extreme. In this view, when forecasts of a firm's future earnings are high, perhaps due to favourable recent performance, they tend to be *too* high relative to the objective prospects of the firm. This results in a high initial P/E (due to the optimism built into the stock price) and poor subsequent performance when investors recognize their error. Thus, high-P/E firms tend to be poor investments.

Overconfidence   People tend to overestimate the precision of their beliefs or forecasts, and they tend to overestimate their abilities. In one famous survey, 90 percent of drivers in Sweden ranked themselves as better-than-average drivers. Such overconfidence may be responsible for the prevalence of active versus passive investment management—itself an anomaly to adherents of the efficient market hypothesis. Despite the growing popularity of indexing, only about 15 percent of the equity in the mutual fund industry is held in indexed accounts. The dominance of active management in the face of the typical underperformance of such strategies (consider the disappointing performance of actively managed mutual funds reviewed in Chapter 23 and in the previous chapter) is consistent with a tendency to overestimate ability.

An interesting example of overconfidence in financial markets is provided by Barber and Odean,[4] who compare trading activity and average returns in brokerage accounts of men and women. They find that men (in particular single men) trade far more actively than women, consistent with the generally greater overconfidence among men well documented in the psychology literature. They also find that trading activity is highly predictive of poor investment performance. The top 20 percent of accounts ranked by portfolio turnover had average returns 7 percentage points lower than the 20 percent of the accounts with the lowest turnover rates. As they conclude, "trading [and by implication, overconfidence] is hazardous to your wealth."

Overconfidence appears to be a widespread phenomenon, also showing up in many corporate finance contexts. For example, overconfident CEOs are more likely to overpay for target firms when making corporate acquisitions.[5] Just as overconfidence can degrade portfolio investments, so can it lead such firms to make poor investments in real assets.

Conservatism   A **conservatism** bias means that investors are too slow (too conservative) in updating their beliefs in response to new evidence. This means that they might initially underreact to news about a firm, so that prices will fully reflect new information only gradually. Such a bias would give rise to momentum in stock market returns.

---

[2]D. Kahneman and A. Tversky, "On the Psychology of Prediction," *Psychology Review* 80 (1973), pp. 237–51; and "Subjective Probability: A Judgment of Representativeness," *Cognitive Psychology* 3 (1972), pp. 430–54.

[3]W.F.M. De Bondt and R. H. Thaler, "Do Security Analysts Overreact?" *American Economic Review* 80 (1990), pp. 52–57.

[4]Brad Barber and Terrance Odean, "Boys Will Be Boys: Gender, Overconfidence, and Common Stock Investment," *Quarterly Journal of Economics* 16 (2001), pp. 262–92; and "Trading Is Hazardous to Your Wealth: The Common Stock Investment Performance of Individual Investors," *Journal of Finance* 55 (2000), pp. 773–806.

[5]U. Malmendier and G. Tate. "Who Makes Acquisitions? CEO Overconfidence and the Market's Reaction," *Journal of Financial Economics* 89 (July 2008), pp. 20–43.

Sample Size Neglect and Representativeness   The notion of **representativeness** holds that people commonly do not take into account the size of a sample, apparently reasoning that a small sample is just as representative of a population as a large one. They may therefore infer a pattern too quickly based on a small sample and extrapolate apparent trends too far into the future. It is easy to see how such a pattern would be consistent with overreaction and correction anomalies. A short-lived run of good earnings reports or high stock returns would lead such investors to revise their assessments of likely future performance, and thus generate buying pressure that exaggerates the price runup. Eventually, the gap between price and intrinsic value becomes glaring and the market corrects its initial error. Interestingly, stocks with the best recent performance suffer reversals precisely in the few days surrounding earnings announcements, suggesting that the correction occurs just as investors learn that their initial beliefs were too extreme.[6]

> **CC 1**
>
> ### CONCEPT CHECK
>
> We saw in the previous chapter that stocks seem to exhibit a pattern of short-to-middle-term momentum, along with long-term reversals. How might this pattern arise from an interplay between the conservatism and representativeness biases?

Behavioural Biases

Even if information processing were perfect, many studies conclude that individuals would tend to make less-than-fully-rational decisions using that information. These behavioural biases largely affect how investors frame questions of risk versus return, and therefore make risk–return tradeoffs.

Framing   Decisions seem to be affected by how choices are **framed**. For example, an individual may reject a bet when it is posed in terms of the risk surrounding possible gains but may accept that same bet when described in terms of the risk surrounding potential losses. In other words, individuals may act risk-averse in terms of gains but risk-seeking in terms of losses. But in many cases, the choice of how to frame a risky venture—as involving gains or losses—can be arbitrary.

EXAMPLE 10.1   **Framing**

Consider a coin toss with a payoff of $50 for tails. Now consider a gift of $50 that is bundled with a bet that imposes a loss of $50 if that coin toss comes up heads. In both cases, you end up with zero for heads and $50 for tails. But the former description frames the coin toss as posing a risky gain while the latter frames the coin toss in terms of risky losses. The difference in framing can lead to different attitudes toward the bet.

Mental Accounting   **Mental accounting** is a specific form of framing in which people segregate certain decisions. For example, an investor may take a lot of risk with one investment account but establish a very conservative position with another account that is dedicated to her child's education. Rationally, it might be better to view both accounts as part of the investor's overall portfolio with the risk–return profiles of each integrated into a unified framework.

---

[6]N. Chopra, J. Lakonishok, and J. Ritter, "Measuring Abnormal Performance: Do Stocks Overreact?" *Journal of Financial Economics* 31 (1992), pp. 235–68.

Statman[7] argues that mental accounting is consistent with some investors' irrational preference for stocks with high cash dividends (they feel free to spend dividend income, but would not "dip into capital" by selling a few shares of another stock with the same total rate of return) and with a tendency to ride losing stock positions for too long (since "behavioural investors" are reluctant to realize losses). In fact, investors are more likely to sell stocks with gains than those with losses, precisely contrary to a tax-minimization strategy.[8]

Mental accounting effects also can help explain momentum in stock prices. The *house money effect* refers to gamblers' greater willingness to accept new bets if they are currently ahead. They think of (i.e., frame) the bet as being made with their "winnings account," that is, with the casino's and not with their own money, and thus are more willing to accept risk. Analogously, after a stock market runup, individuals may view investments as largely funded out of a "capital gains account," become more tolerant of risk, discount future cash flows at a lower rate, and thus further push up prices.

Regret Avoidance   Psychologists have found that individuals who make decisions that turn out badly have more regret (blame themselves more) when that decision was more unconventional. For example, buying a blue-chip portfolio that turns down is not as painful as experiencing the same losses on an unknown start-up firm. Any losses on the blue-chip stocks can be more easily attributed to bad luck rather than bad decision making and cause less regret. De Bondt and Thaler[9] argue that such **regret avoidance** is consistent with both the size and the book-to-market effect. Higher-book-to-market firms tend to have depressed stock prices. They are "out of favour" and more likely to be in a financially precarious position. Similarly, smaller, less-well-known firms are also less conventional investments. Such firms require more "courage" on the part of the investor, which increases the required rate of return. Mental accounting can add to this effect. If investors focus on the gains or losses of individual stocks, rather than on broad portfolios, they can become more risk-averse concerning stocks with recent poor performance, discount their cash flows at a higher rate, and thereby create a value-stock risk premium.

CC 2

CONCEPT CHECK

How might the P/E effect (discussed in the previous chapter) also be explained as a consequence of regret avoidance?

Prospect Theory   **Prospect theory** modifies the analytic description of rational risk-averse investors found in standard financial theory.[10] Figure 10.1, panel A, illustrates the conventional description of a risk-averse investor. Higher wealth provides higher satisfaction or "utility," but at a diminishing rate (the curve flattens as the individual becomes wealthier). This gives rise to risk aversion: a gain of $1,000 increases utility by less than a loss of $1,000 reduces it; therefore, investors will reject risky prospects that don't offer a risk premium.

---

[7]Meir Statman, "Behavioral Finance," *Contemporary Finance Digest* 1 (Winter 1997), pp. 5–22.

[8]H. Shefrin and M. Statman, "The Disposition to Sell Winners Too Early and Ride Losers Too Long: Theory and Evidence," *Journal of Finance* 40 (July 1985), pp. 777–90; and T. Odean, "Are Investors Reluctant to Realize Their Losses?" *Journal of Finance* 53 (1998), pp. 1775–98.

[9]W.F.M. De Bondt and R. H. Thaler, "Further Evidence on Investor Overreaction and Stock Market Seasonality," *Journal of Finance* 42 (1987), pp. 557–81.

[10]Prospect theory originated with a highly influential paper about decision making under uncertainty by D. Kahneman and A. Tversky, "Prospect Theory: An Analysis of Decision Under Risk," *Econometrica* 47 (1979), pp. 263–91.

Figure 10.1

Prospect theory. **Panel A:** A conventional utility function is defined in terms of wealth and is concave, resulting in risk aversion. **Panel B:** Under loss aversion, the utility function is defined in terms of losses relative to current wealth. It is also convex to the left of the origin, giving rise to risk-seeking behaviour in terms of losses.

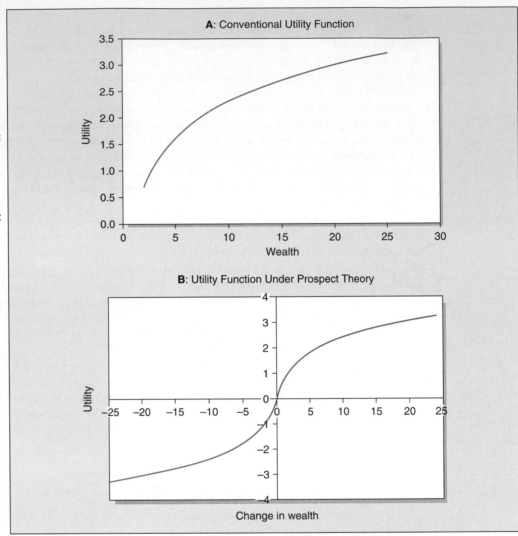

Panel B shows a competing description of preferences characterized by "loss aversion." Utility depends not on the *level* of wealth, as in panel A, but on *changes* in wealth from current levels. Moreover, to the left of zero (zero denotes no change from current wealth), the curve is convex rather than concave. This has several implications. Whereas many conventional utility functions imply that investors may become less risk-averse as wealth increases, the function in panel B always re-centres on current wealth, ruling out such decreases in risk aversion and possibly helping to explain high average historical equity risk premiums. Moreover, the convex curvature to the left of the origin in panel B will induce investors to be risk-seeking rather than risk-averse when it comes to losses. Consistently with loss aversion, traders in the T-bond futures contract have been observed to assume significantly greater risk in afternoon sessions following morning sessions in which they have lost money.[11]

[11] J. D. Coval and T. Shumway, "Do Behavioral Biases Affect Prices?" *Journal of Finance* 60 (February 2005), pp. 1–34.

If your portfolio is out of whack, you could ask an investment adviser for help. But you might have better luck with your therapist.

It's a common dilemma: You know you have the wrong mix of investments, but you cannot bring yourself to fix the mess. Why is it so difficult to change? At issue are three mental mistakes.

Chasing Winners

Looking to lighten up on bonds and get back into stocks? Sure, you know stocks are a long-term investment and, sure, you know they are best bought when cheap.

Yet it's a lot easier to pull the trigger and buy stocks if the market has lately been scoring gains. "People are influenced by what has happened most recently, and then they extrapolate from that," says Meir Statman, a finance professor at Santa Clara University in California. "But often, they end up being optimistic and pessimistic at just the wrong time."

Consider some results from the UBS Index of Investor Optimism, a monthly poll conducted by UBS and the Gallup Organization. Each month, the poll asks investors what gain they expect from their portfolio during the next 12 months. Result? You guessed it: The answers rise and fall with the stock market.

For instance, during the bruising bear market, investors grew increasingly pessimistic, and at the market bottom they were looking for median portfolio gains of just 5%. But true to form, last year's rally brightened investors' spirits and by January they were expecting 10% returns.

Getting Even

This year's choppy stock market hasn't scared off just bond investors. It has also made it difficult for stock investors to rejigger their portfolios.

Blame it on the old "get even, then get out" syndrome. With stocks treading water, many investors are reluctant to sell, because they are a long way from recovering their bear-market losses. To be sure, investors who bought near the peak are underwater, whether they sell or not. But selling losers is still agonizing, because it means admitting you made a mistake.

"If you're rational and you have a loss, you sell, take the tax loss and move on," Prof. Statman says. "But if you're a normal person, selling at a loss tears your heart out."

Mustering Courage

Whether you need to buy stocks or buy bonds, it takes confidence to act. And right now, investors just aren't confident. "There's this status-quo bias," says John Nofsinger, a finance professor at Washington State University in Pullman, Washington. "We're afraid to do anything, because we're afraid we'll regret it."

Once again, it's driven by recent market action. When markets are flying high, folks attribute their portfolio's gains to their own brilliance. That gives them the confidence to trade more and to take greater risks. Overreacting to short-term market results is, of course, a great way to lose a truckload of money. But with any luck, if you are aware of this pitfall, maybe you will avoid it.

Or maybe [this is] too optimistic. "You can tell somebody that investors have all these behavioral biases," says Terrance Odean, a finance professor at the University of California at Berkeley. "So what happens? The investor thinks, 'Oh, that sounds like my husband.' I don't think many investors say, 'Oh, that sounds like me.'"

These are only a sample of many behavioural biases uncovered in the literature. Many have implications for investor behaviour. The boxed article here offers some good examples.

Limits to Arbitrage

Behavioural biases would not matter for stock pricing if rational arbitrageurs could fully exploit the mistakes of behavioural investors. Trades of profit-seeking investors would correct any misalignment of prices. However, behavioural advocates argue that, in practice, several factors limit the ability to profit from mispricing.[12]

Fundamental Risk Suppose that a share of Weston is underpriced. Buying it may present a profit opportunity, but it is hardly risk-free, since the presumed market underpricing can get worse. While price eventually should converge to intrinsic value, this may not happen until after

---

[12]Some of the more influential references on limits to arbitrage are J. B. DeLong, A. Schleifer, L. Summers, and R. Waldmann, "Noise Trader Risk in Financial Markets," *Journal of Political Economy* 98 (August 1990), pp. 704–38; and A. Schleifer and R. Vishny, "The Limits of Arbitrage," *Journal of Finance* 52 (March 1997), pp. 35–55.

the trader's investment horizon. For example, the investor may be a mutual fund manager who may lose clients (not to mention a job!) if short-term performance is poor, or a trader who may run through her capital if the market turns against her, even temporarily. The **fundamental risk** incurred in exploiting the apparent profit opportunity presumably will limit the activity of the traders.

EXAMPLE 10.2   Fundamental Risk

In the spring of 2013, the Nasdaq index had regained the level of 3300, higher than before the 2008 bottom. From that perspective, the value the index had reached 13 years earlier, around 5000, seemed obviously crazy. Surely some investors living through the Internet "bubble" of the late 1990s must have identified the index as grossly overvalued, suggesting a good selling opportunity. But this hardly would have been a riskless arbitrage opportunity. Consider that Nasdaq may also have been overvalued in 1999 when it first crossed above 3300 (its value in 2013). An investor in 1999 who believed (as it turns out, quite correctly) that Nasdaq was over-valued at 3300 and decided to sell it short would have suffered enormous losses as the index increased by another 1700 points before finally peaking at 5000. While the investor might have derived considerable satisfaction from eventually being proven right about the overpricing, by entering a year before the market "corrected" he or she might also have gone broke.

Implementation Costs   Exploiting overpricing can be particularly difficult. Short-selling a security entails costs; short-sellers may have to return the borrowed security on little notice, rendering the horizon of the short sale uncertain; other investors such as many pension or mutual fund managers face strict limits on their discretion to short securities. This can limit the ability of arbitrage activity to force prices to fair value.

Model Risk   One always has to worry that an apparent profit opportunity is more apparent than real. Perhaps you are using a faulty model to value the security, and the price actually is right. Mispricing may make a position a good bet, but it is still a risky one, which limits the extent to which it will be pursued.

The Law of One Price

While one can debate the implications of much of the anomalies literature, surely the Law of One Price (positing that effectively identical assets should have identical prices) should be satisfied in rational markets. Yet there are several instances where the law seems to have been violated. These instances are good case studies of the limits to arbitrage.

"Siamese Twin" Companies[13]   In 1907, Royal Dutch Petroleum and Shell Transport merged their operations into one firm. The two original companies, which continued to trade separately, agreed to split all profits from the joint company on a 60/40 basis. Shareholders of Royal Dutch receive 60 percent of the cash flow, and those of Shell receive 40 percent. One would therefore expect that Royal Dutch should sell for exactly 60/40 = 1.5 times the price of Shell. But this is not the case. Figure 10.2 shows that the relative value of the two firms has departed considerably from this "parity" ratio for extended periods of time.

---

[13]This discussion is based on K. A. Froot and E. M. Dabora, "How Are Stock Prices Affected by the Location of Trade?" *Journal of Financial Economics* 53 (1999), pp. 189–216.

Figure 10.2 Pricing of Royal Dutch relative to Shell (deviation from parity).

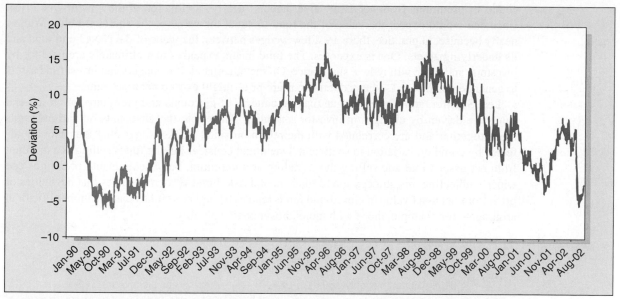

Source: O. A. Lamont and R. H. Thaler, "Anomalies: The Law of One Price in Financial Markets," *Journal of Economic Perspectives* 17 (Fall 2003), pp. 191–202.

Doesn't this mispricing give rise to an arbitrage opportunity? If Royal Dutch sells for more than 1.5 times Shell, why not buy relatively underpriced Shell and short-sell overpriced Royal? This seems like a reasonable strategy, but if you had followed it in February 1993 when Royal sold for about 10 percent more than its parity value, the figure shows that you would have lost a lot of money as the premium widened to about 17 percent before finally reversing after 1999. As in Example 10.2, this opportunity posed fundamental risk.

Equity Carve-outs   Several equity carve-outs have also violated the Law of One Price.[14] To illustrate, consider the case of 3Com, which in 1999 decided to spin off its Palm division. It first sold 5 percent of its stake in Palm in an IPO, announcing that it would distribute the remaining 95 percent of its Palm shares to 3Com shareholders six months later in a spinoff. Each 3Com shareholder would receive 1.5 shares of Palm in the spinoff.

Once Palm shares began trading, but prior to the spinoff, the share price of 3Com should have been *at least* 1.5 times that of Palm. After all, each share of 3Com entitled its owner to 1.5 shares of Palm *plus* an ownership stake in a profitable company. Instead, Palm shares at the IPO actually sold for *more* than the 3Com shares. The *stub value* of 3Com (i.e., the value of each 3Com share net of the value of the claim to Palm represented by that share) could be computed as the price of 3Com minus 1.5 times the price of Palm. This calculation, however, implies that 3Com's stub value was negative, this despite the fact that it was a profitable company with cash assets alone of about $10 per share.

Again, an arbitrage strategy seems obvious. Why not buy 3Com and sell Palm? The limit to arbitrage in this case was the inability of investors to sell Palm short. Virtually all available shares in Palm were already borrowed and sold short, and the negative stub values persisted for more than two months.

---

[14]O. A. Lamont and R. H. Thaler, "Can the Market Add and Subtract? Mispricing in Tech Carve-outs," *Journal of Political Economy* 111 (2003), pp. 227–68.

Closed-End Funds We shall see later that closed-end funds often sell for substantial discounts or premiums from net asset value. This is "nearly" a violation of the Law of One Price, since one would expect the value of the fund to equal the value of the shares it holds. We say nearly because, in practice, there are a few wedges between the value of the closed-end fund and its underlying assets. One is expenses. The fund incurs expenses that ultimately are paid for by investors, and these will reduce share price. On the other hand, if managers can invest fund assets to generate positive risk-adjusted returns, share price might exceed net asset value.

Lee, Shleifer, and Thaler[15] argue that the patterns of discounts and premiums on closed-end funds are driven by changes in investor sentiment. They note that discounts on various funds move together and are correlated with the return on small stocks, suggesting that they are affected by common variation in sentiment. One might consider buying funds selling at a discount from net asset value and selling those trading at a premium, but discounts and premiums can widen, subjecting this strategy too to fundamental risk. Pontiff[16] demonstrates that deviations of price from net asset value in closed-end funds tend to be higher in funds that are more difficult to arbitrage—for example, those with more idiosyncratic volatility.

CC 3

CONCEPT CHECK

Fundamental risk may be limited by a "deadline" that forces a convergence between price and intrinsic value. What do you think would happen to a closed-end fund's discount if the fund announced that it plans to liquidate in six months, at which time it will distribute NAV to its shareholders?

Closed-end fund discounts are a good example of apparent anomalies that also may have rational explanations. Ross demonstrates that they can be reconciled with rational investors even if expenses or fund abnormal returns are modest.[17] He shows that if a fund has a dividend yield of δ, an alpha (risk-adjusted abnormal return) of α, and expense ratio of ε, using the constant-growth dividend discount model (see Chapter 19) the premium of the fund over its net asset value will be

$$\frac{\text{Price} - \text{NAV}}{\text{NAV}} = \frac{\alpha - \varepsilon}{\delta + \varepsilon - \alpha}$$

If the fund manager's performance more than compensates for expenses (i.e., if a $\alpha > \varepsilon$), the fund will sell at a premium to NAV; otherwise it will sell at a discount. For example, suppose $\alpha = .015$, the expense ratio is $\varepsilon = .0125$, and the dividend yield is $\delta = .02$. Then the premium will be .14, or 14 percent. But if the market turns sour on the manager and revises its estimate of a downward to .005, that premium quickly turns into a discount of 43 percent.

This analysis might explain why the public is willing to purchase closed-end funds at a premium; if investors do not expect α to exceed ε, they won't purchase shares in the fund. But the fact that most premiums eventually turn into discounts indicates how difficult it is for management to fulfill these expectations.[18]

[15]C. M. Lee, A. Shleifer, and R. H. Thaler, "Investor Sentiment and the Closed-End Fund Puzzle," *Journal of Finance* 46 (March 1991), pp. 75–109.
[16]Jeffrey Pontiff, "Costly Arbitrage: Evidence from Closed-End Funds," *Quarterly Journal of Economics* 111 (November 1996), pp. 1135–51.
[17]S. A. Ross, "Neoclassical Finance, Alternative Finance and the Closed End Fund Puzzle," *European Financial Management* 8 (2002), pp. 129–37, http://ssrn.com/abstract=313444.
[18]We might ask why this logic of discounts and premiums does not apply to open-end mutual funds since they incur similar expense ratios. Because investors in these funds can redeem shares for NAV, the shares cannot sell at a discount to NAV. Expenses in open-end funds reduce returns in each period rather than being capitalized into price and inducing a discount.

Bubbles and Behavioural Economics

In Example 10.2, we pointed out that the stock market runup of the late 1990s, and, even more spectacularly, the runup of the technology-heavy Nasdaq market, seems in retrospect to have been an obvious bubble. In a six-year period beginning in 1995, the Nasdaq index increased by a factor of more than 6. Former Fed Chairman Alan Greenspan famously characterized the dot-com boom as an example of "irrational exuberance," and his assessment turned out to be correct: by October 2002, the index fell to less than one-fourth the peak value it had reached only 2½ years earlier. This episode seems to be a case in point for advocates of the behavioural school, exemplifying a market moved by irrational investor sentiment. Moreover, in accord with behavioural patterns, as the dot-com boom developed, it seemed to feed on itself, with investors increasingly confident of their investment prowess (overconfidence bias) and apparently willing to extrapolate short-term patterns into the distant future (representativeness bias).

On the other hand, bubbles are a lot easier to identify as such once they are over. While they are going on, it is not as clear that prices are irrationally exuberant and, indeed, many financial commentators at the time justified the boom as consistent with glowing forecasts for the "new economy." A simple example shows how hard it can be to tie down the fair value of stock investments.[19]

EXAMPLE 10.3   A Stock Market Bubble?

In 2000 near the peak of the dot-com boom, the dividends paid by the firms included in the S&P 500 totalled $154.6 billion. If the discount rate for the index was 9.2 percent and the expected dividend growth rate was 8 percent, the value of these shares according to the constant-growth dividend discount model (see Chapter 19 for more on this model) would be

$$\text{Value} = \frac{\text{Dividend}}{\text{Discount rate} - \text{Growth rate}} = \frac{\$154.6}{.092 - .08} = \$12{,}883 \text{ billion}$$

This was quite close to the actual total value of those firms at the time. But the estimate is highly sensitive to the input values, and even a small reassessment of their prospects would result in a big revision of price. Suppose the expected dividend growth rate fell to 7.4 percent. This would reduce the value of the index to

$$\text{Value} = \frac{\text{Dividend}}{\text{Discount rate} - \text{Growth rate}} = \frac{\$154.6}{.092 - .074} = \$8{,}589 \text{ billion}$$

which was about the value to which the S&P 500 firms had fallen by October 2002. In the light of this example, the runup and crash of the 1990s seems easier to reconcile with rational behaviour.

Still, other evidence seems to tag the dot-com boom as at least partially irrational. Consider, for example, the results of a study documenting that firms adding ".com" to the end of their names during this period enjoyed a meaningful stock price increase.[20] That doesn't sound like rational valuation.

---

[19]The following example is taken from R. A. Brealey, S. C. Myers, and F. Allen, *Principles of Corporate Finance*, 8th ed. (Burr Ridge, IL: McGraw-Hill Irwin, 2006).

[20]P. R. Rau, O. Dimitrov, and M. Cooper, "A Rose.com by Any Other Name," *Journal of Finance* 56 (2001), pp. 2371–88.

For forty years, economist Eugene Fama argued that financial markets were highly efficient in reflecting the underlying value of stocks. His longtime intellectual nemesis, Richard Thaler, a member of the "behaviorist" school of economic thought, contended that markets can veer off course when individuals make stupid decisions.

This long-running argument has big implications for real-life problems, ranging from the privatization of Social Security to the regulation of financial markets to the way corporate boards are run. Mr. Fama's ideas helped foster the free-market theories of the 1980s and spawned the $1 trillion index-fund industry. Mr. Thaler's theory suggests policymakers have an important role to play in guiding markets and individuals where they're prone to fail.

Behavioral economists argue that markets are imperfect because people often stray from rational decisions. They believe this behavior creates market breakdowns and also buying opportunities for savvy investors.

Small Anomalies

Even before the late 1990s, Mr. Thaler and a growing legion of behavioral finance experts were finding small anomalies that seemed to fly in the face of efficient-market theory. For example, researchers found that value stocks, companies that appear undervalued relative to their profits or assets, tended to outperform growth stocks, ones that are perceived as likely to increase profits rapidly. If the market was efficient and impossible to beat, why would one asset class outperform another? (Mr. Fama says there's a rational explanation: Value stocks

come with hidden risks and investors are rewarded for those risks with higher returns.)

Moreover, in a rational world, share prices should move only when new information hits the market. But with more than one billion shares a day changing hands on the New York Stock Exchange, the market appears overrun with traders making bets all the time.

Robert Shiller, a Yale University economist, has long argued that efficient-market theorists made one huge mistake: Just because markets are unpredictable doesn't mean they are efficient. The leap in logic, he wrote in the 1980s, was one of "the most remarkable errors in the history of economic thought." Mr. Fama says behavioral economists made the same mistake in reverse: The fact that some individuals might be irrational doesn't mean the market is inefficient.

Mr. Thaler's views have seeped into the mainstream through the support of a number of prominent economists who have devised similar theories about how markets operate. In 2002, Daniel Kahneman won a Nobel Prize for pioneering research in the field of behavioral economics. Even [former] Federal Reserve Chairman Alan Greenspan, a firm believer in the benefits of free markets, famously adopted the term "irrational exuberance" in 1996.

Defending efficient markets has gotten harder, but it's probably too soon for Mr. Thaler to declare victory. He concedes that most of his retirement assets are held in index funds, the very industry that Mr. Fama's research helped to launch. And despite his research on market inefficiencies, he also concedes that "it is not easy to beat the market, and most people don't."

Source: Jon E. Hilsenrath, *The Wall Street Journal*, October 18, 2004, p. A1. © 2004 Dow Jones & Company, Inc. All rights reserved.

Evaluating the Behavioural Critique

As investors, we are concerned with the existence of profit opportunities. The behavioural explanations of efficient market anomalies do not give guidance on how to exploit any irrationality. For investors, the question is still whether there is money to be made from mispricing, and the behavioural literature is largely silent on this point.

However, as we emphasized above, one of the important implications of the efficient market hypothesis is that security prices serve as reliable guides to the allocation of real assets. If prices are distorted, then capital markets will give misleading signals (and incentives) as to where the economy may best allocate resources. In this crucial dimension, the behavioural critique of the efficient market hypothesis is certainly important irrespective of any implication for investment strategies.

There is considerable debate among financial economists concerning the strength of the behavioural critique. Many believe that the behavioural approach is too unstructured, in effect allowing virtually any anomaly to be explained by some combination of irrationalities chosen from a laundry list of behavioural biases. While it is easy to "reverse-engineer" a behavioural explanation for any particular anomaly, these critics would like to see a consistent or unified behavioural theory that can explain a *range* of behavioural anomalies.

More fundamentally, others are not convinced that the anomalies literature as a whole is a convincing indictment of the efficient market hypothesis. Fama[21] reviews the anomalies literature

[21]E. F. Fama, "Market Efficiency, Long-Term Returns, and Behavioral Finance," *Journal of Financial Economics* 49 (September 1998), pp. 283–306.

and mounts a counterchallenge to the behavioural school. He notes that the anomalies are inconsistent in terms of their support for one type of irrationality versus another. For example, some papers document long-term corrections (consistent with overreaction), while others document long-term continuations of abnormal returns (consistent with underreaction). Moreover, the statistical significance of many of these results is difficult to assess. Even small errors in choosing a benchmark against which to compare returns can cumulate to large apparent abnormalities in long-term returns. Therefore, many of the results in these studies are sensitive to small benchmarking errors, and Fama argues that seemingly minor changes in methodology can have big impacts on conclusions.

The behavioural critique of full rationality in investor decision making is well taken, but the extent to which limited rationality affects asset pricing remains controversial. It is probably still too early to pass judgment on the behavioural approach, specifically, which behavioural models will "stick" and become part of the standard tool kit of financial analysts. The boxed article here discusses the ongoing debate between stock market "rationalists" and "behaviourists."

10.2   THE APPEAL OF TECHNICAL ANALYSIS

Technical analysis is, in most instances, an attempt to exploit recurring and predictable patterns in stock prices to generate abnormal trading profits. Technicians do not necessarily deny the value of fundamental information; rather, they believe stock prices eventually "close in" on their fundamental values. Technicians believe, nevertheless, that shifts in market fundamentals can be discerned before the impact of those shifts is fully reflected in prices. As the market adjusts to a new equilibrium, astute traders can exploit these price trends.

For example, one of the best-documented behavioural tendencies is the *disposition effect*, which refers to the tendency of investors to hold on to losing investments. Behavioural investors seem reluctant to realize losses. This disposition effect can lead to momentum in stock prices even if fundamental values follow a random walk.[22] The fact that the demand of "disposition investors" for a company's shares depends on the price history of those shares means that prices close in on fundamental values only over time, consistent with the central motivation of technical analysis.

Behavioural biases may also be consistent with technical analysts' use of volume data. An important behavioural trait noted above is overconfidence, a systematic tendency to overestimate one's abilities. As traders become overconfident, they may trade more, inducing an association between trading volume and market returns.[23] Technical analysis thus uses volume data as well as price history to direct trading strategy.

Technicians also believe that market fundamentals can be perturbed by irrational factors. More or less random fluctuations in price will accompany any underlying trend. If these fluctuations dissipate slowly, they can be taken advantage of for abnormal profits.

These presumptions, of course, clash head-on with those of the efficient market hypothesis (EMH) and with the logic of well-functioning capital markets. According to the EMH, a shift in market fundamentals should be reflected in prices immediately. According to technicians, though, that shift will lead to a gradual price change that can be recognized as a trend. Such easily exploited trends in stock market prices would be damning evidence against the EMH, as they would indicate profit opportunities that market participants had left unexploited.

The essence of the conflict between the EMH and technical analysis lies in the weak-form statement given in Section 9.1—that the price reflects all information that can be extracted from trading data. Hence, all statistics about price and volume, all trends, all charts must be useless in

---

[22]Mark Grinblatt and Bing Han, "Prospect Theory, Mental Accounting, and Momentum," *Journal of Financial Economics* 78 (November 2005), pp. 311–39.
[23]S. Gervais and T. Odean, "Learning to Be Overconfident," *Review of Financial Studies* 14 (2001), pp. 1–27.

Figure 10.3

U.S. GDP growth and the term spread between 10-year Treasuries and 3-month T-bills; smoothed data (4-quarter moving average), lagged term spread (4 quarters).

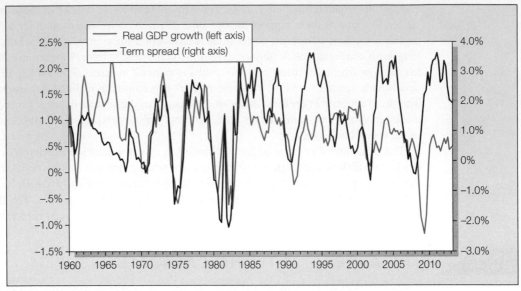

predicting future movements. Similarly the semistrong form claims that all publicly available fundamental information is equally useless; this in particular includes economic data that would affect the entire market, an industry or certain companies in an industry. This is not to say that interpreting data in a particular way may not lead to correct forecasts; rather, the balance of interpretations of information has led to the current price levels, and no randomly selected forecast is expected to be better than another.

The line between fundamental analysis and some technical analysis is hard to draw. If certain economic signals suggest that the market will rise (or fall), then the EMH states that the market index should already reflect that view. Betting on that signal should yield no expectable profit. As we shall see in Chapter 15, there are leading indicators for the economy, but the market index itself is one of them. As an example of economic predictors, consider Figure 10.3, which shows a smoothed graph of the U.S. GDP growth and of the spread between 10-year Treasuries and 3-month T-bills; note that this is a proxy for the spread between 10-year bonds and the Fed funds rate, itself one of the official leading indicators for the U.S. GDP. In the graph, the real GDP growth series is calculated quarterly from a four-quarter moving average; then the series of quarterly averaged term spreads is lagged four quarters and placed concurrently with the GDP series. There is a clear coincidence of the rise and fall of the two series, most obviously at major turning points. A low or negative term spread is associated with the negative growth periods in the GDP (recessions). (The term spread has been lagged in the graph to indicate more clearly the concurrence of the two series.) The four-quarter lag implies that the bond data predicts the economic performance by one year; as long as the stock market does not also precede the GDP changes by as much as a year, then the term spread indicator would lead the market also. The interpretation is that when the spread falls to almost nothing, one should be selling the market before it too anticipates the recession. This response very much agrees with the street maxim "Don't fight the Fed"—the time to buy is not when the Federal Reserve is raising interest rates to restrain the economy, but when it is loosening the strings to stimulate growth. A negative spread corresponds to an inverted yield curve—long-term rates are lower than short-term—another sign of better times ahead. In fact, economists have recognized the predictive power of the term spread for some time.[24]

---

[24]See David C. Wheelock and Mark E. Wohar, "Can the Term Spread Predict Output Growth and Recessions? A Survey of the Literature," *Federal Reserve Bank of St. Louis Review* 91, no. 5 (Part 1) (September/October 2009), pp. 419–40.

How does the indicator rate as a predictor of the stock market? Examining the major instances of negative spreads, the 1973–1974 dip corresponds to the oil crisis that lasted from October 1973 to March 1974. The next dips in 1980–1981 occurred while inflation worries were extreme. The 1990 dip corresponded to the sharp recession of 1990–1991 (a delayed reaction to the 1987 crash) and another oil price spike associated with the first Gulf War; this preceded the greatest bull market of the century throughout the 1990s. Note, however, that the spread was trending lower from 1995 on but didn't bottom until well into 2000, even though the run from 1995 to 2000 was the extreme bubble in the market. For the two greatest recent crashes, the spread in 2000 was an excellent warning, while in 2006 reaction to it would have missed the peak of the market, but saved a 50 percent drop in the S&P 500 by the end of its fall. One might conclude that the steeply falling spread is a good indicator of trouble ahead, except that over the 1995–2000 period it anticipated an earlier collapse; for both the 1991 and 2009 dips, the term spread had as much as a six-to-eight-quarter lead. In the credit crisis, the indicator suggested in early 2007 that trouble was once again around the corner. All of the negative spreads and the positive .25 percent spread of late 1989 have predicted excellent occasions to enter the market. An economic graph such as Figure 10.3 would be part of the arsenal of some technicians.

Another time series that has strong correlation is the so-called VIX indicator. The VIX refers to the implied volatility of index options (as discussed in Chapter 19), reflecting the premium that option traders are willing to pay for options on the market index; the premium rises when they perceive increased volatility in the market. Historically, the VIX is inversely correlated with the general market; when the VIX is falling the market rises, and conversely. Charting the VIX for the S&P index (VXO) or for the Nasdaq index (VXN) and superimposing the corresponding index gives a very convincing picture of the inverse correlation. (Similarly, the VIX correlates negatively with the term spread series.) Hence, technicians will observe these two volatility indices as possible confirmations of their market predictions; since they are coincident rather that leading or lagging, the patterns they observe that indicate a rise or fall in the VIX can only be used to confirm the analogous pattern in the market.

In Chapter 16, we discuss the Value Line methodology. Much of its analysis is fundamental, referring to financial data; but ultimately, it produces an index as a function of observable, realized data, and recommends purchase or not on this basis. Similarly, new, rigorously tested filters have been devised to identify firms that should yield superior risk-adjusted returns. These might include the Fama-French identification of ratios that offer further explanatory power for returns than given by traditional beta, or patterns of return persistence or price reversal that lead to trading rules. Economic rationalization of the plausibility of these rules makes them appear acceptable strategies. Even if the pricing defies the CAPM, the EMH would argue that investors should react and re-price these securities so that the pattern no longer prevails. If not, then this is technical analysis that works.

A more subtle version of technical analysis holds that there are patterns in stock prices that can be exploited, but that once investors identify and attempt to profit from these patterns their trading activity affects prices, thereby altering price patterns. This means the patterns that characterize market prices will be constantly evolving, and only the best analysts who can identify new patterns earliest will be rewarded. We call this phenomenon *self-destructing* patterns and explore it further later in this chapter.

The notion of evolving patterns is consistent with almost but not quite efficient markets. It allows for the possibility of temporarily unexploited profit opportunities, but it also views market participants as aggressively exploiting those opportunities once they are uncovered. The market is continually groping toward full efficiency, but it is never quite there.

This is in some ways an appealing middle position in the ongoing debate between technicians and proponents of the EMH. Ultimately, however, it is an untestable hypothesis. Technicians will always be able to identify trading rules that would have worked in the past but need not work any longer. Is this evidence of a once-viable trading rule that has not been eliminated by competition? Perhaps. But it is far more likely that the trading rule could have been identified only after the fact.

Until technicians can show rigorous evidence that their trading rules provide *consistent* trading profits, we must doubt the viability of those rules. As you saw in the chapter on the efficient market hypothesis, the evidence on the performance of professionally managed funds does not support the efficacy of technical analysis.

10.3 TRENDS AND CHARTING

Technical analysts are sometimes called *chartists*, because they study records or charts of past stock prices and trading volume, hoping to find patterns they can exploit to make a profit. In this section, we examine several specific charting strategies. Much of technical analysis seeks to uncover trends in market prices. This is in effect a search for momentum. Momentum can be absolute, in which case one searches for upward price trends, or relative, in which case the analyst looks to invest in one sector over another (or even take on a long–short position in the two sectors). Relative-strength statistics are designed to reveal these potential opportunities.

Trends and Corrections

The **Dow theory**, named after its creator Charles Dow (of Dow Jones fame), is the ancestor of technical analyses. The aim of the Dow theory is to identify long-term trends in stock market prices. Many of today's more technically sophisticated methods are essentially variants of Dow's approach.

The Dow theory has many aspects, including the identification of three forces simultaneously affecting stock prices:

1. The *primary trend* is the long-term movement of prices, lasting from several months to several years.
2. *Secondary* or *intermediate trends* are caused by short-term deviations of prices from the underlying trend line. These deviations are eliminated via *corrections* when prices revert back to trend values.
3. *Tertiary* or *minor trends* are daily fluctuations of little importance.

The Dow theory incorporates notions of support and resistance levels in stock prices. A **support level** is a value below which the market is relatively unlikely to fall. A **resistance level** is a value above which it is difficult to rise. Support and resistance levels are determined by the recent history of prices.

CC 4

CONCEPT CHECK
Describe how technicians might explain support levels.

More recent variations on the Dow theory are the Elliott wave theory and the theory of Kondratieff waves. Like the Dow theory, the idea behind Elliott waves is that stock prices can be described by a set of wave patterns. Long-term and short-term wave cycles are superimposed and result in a complicated pattern of price movements; but by interpreting the cycles, one can, according to the theory, predict broad movements. Similarly, Kondratieff waves are named after a Russian economist who asserted that the macroeconomy (and therefore the stock market) moves in broad waves lasting between 48 and 60 years. The Kondratieff waves are therefore analogous

Figure 10.4   Actual and simulated levels for stock market prices of 52 weeks.

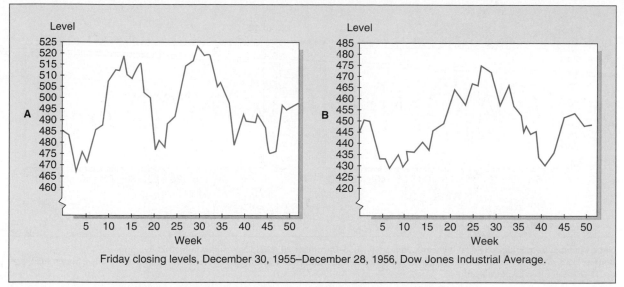

Friday closing levels, December 30, 1955–December 28, 1956, Dow Jones Industrial Average.

Note: Friday closing levels, December 30, 1955–December 28, 1956, Dow Jones Industrial Average.
Source: Harry Roberts, "Stock Market 'Patterns' and Financial Analysis: Methodological Suggestions," *Journal of Finance*, March 1959, pp. 11–25. Reprinted by permission.

to Dow's primary trend, although they are of far longer duration. Kondratieff's assertion is hard to evaluate empirically, however, because cycles that last about 50 years provide only two full data points per century, which is hardly enough data to test the predictive power of the theory.

A Warning

The search for patterns in stock market prices is nearly irresistible, and the ability of the human eye to discern apparent patterns is remarkable. Unfortunately, it is possible to perceive patterns that really don't exist. Consider Figure 10.4, which presents simulated and actual values of the Dow Jones Industrial Average during 1956 taken from a famous study by Harry Roberts.[25] In panel B, it appears as though the market presents a classic head-and-shoulders pattern where the middle hump (the head) is flanked by two shoulders. When the price index "pierces the right shoulder"—a technical trigger point—it is believed to be heading lower, and it is time to sell your stocks. Panel A also looks like a "typical" stock market pattern. Can you tell which of the two graphs is constructed from the real value of the Dow and which from the simulated data? Panel A is based on the real data. The graph in B was generated using "returns" created by a random number generator. These returns *by construction* were patternless, but the simulated price path that is plotted appears to follow a pattern much like that of A.

Figure 10.5 shows the weekly price changes behind the two panels in Figure 10.4. Here the randomness in both series—the stock price as well as the simulated sequence—is obvious.

A problem related to the tendency to perceive patterns where they don't exist is data mining. After the fact, you can always find patterns and trading rules that would have generated enormous profits. If you test enough rules, some will have worked in the past. Unfortunately, picking a theory that would have worked after the fact carries no guarantee of future success.

---

[25]Harry Roberts, "Stock Market 'Patterns' and Financial Analysis: Methodological Suggestions," *Journal of Finance* 14 (March 1959), pp. 701–717.

Figure 10.5   Actual and simulated changes in weekly stock prices for 52 weeks.

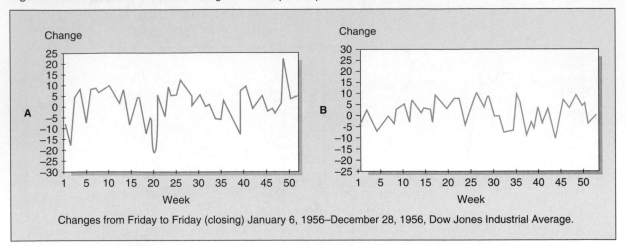

Changes from Friday to Friday (closing) January 6, 1956–December 28, 1956, Dow Jones Industrial Average.

Note: Changes from Friday to Friday (closing) January 6, 1956–December 28, 1956, Dow Jones Industrial Average.
Source: Harry Roberts, "Stock Market 'Patterns' and Financial Analysis: Methodological Suggestions," *Journal of Finance,* March 1959, pp. 11–25. Reprinted by permission.

There are a couple of rules with strong statistical support and credible economic rationales. One is based on the presidential cycle. Statistically, it has been amply verified that the stock market performs significantly worse in the second year of the U.S. president's term and better in the third year. It is explained that government economic policy is manipulated to deliver bitter and necessary medicine early in the term to effect improvements later. In the third year, policy is eased to suggest that a healthy economy has resulted from good administration. The market apparently responds in kind. Surprisingly, there is evidence that the phenomenon is not restricted to the U.S. market, but is visible in most other developed markets, obviously including Canada's.

Also, evidence based on decades of observations indicates that the U.S. market's gains come in the period between the beginning of October and the beginning of March; in the other six months the returns are negligible.

In evaluating trading rules, you should always ask whether the rule would have seemed reasonable *before* you looked at the data. If not, you might be buying into the one arbitrary rule among many that happened to have worked in the recent past. The hard but crucial question is whether there is reason to believe that what worked in the past should continue to work in the future.

Moving Averages

The **moving average** of a stock index is the average level of the index over a given interval of time. For example, a 50-day moving average tracks the average index value over the most recent 50 days. Each week, the moving average is recomputed by dropping the oldest observation and adding the latest. After a period in which prices have generally been falling, the moving average will be above the current price (because the moving average "averages in" the older and higher prices). When prices have been rising, the moving average will be below the current price.

When the market price breaks through the moving average line from below, it is taken as a bullish signal because it signifies a shift from a falling trend (with prices below the moving average) to a rising trend (with prices above the moving average). Conversely, when prices fall below the moving average, it's considered time to sell.

There is some variation in the length of the moving average considered most predictive of market movements. Two popular measures are 100-day and 50-day moving averages. When the

TABLE 10.1
Price Data

Week	S&P/TSX	5-Week Moving Average	Week	S&P/TSX	5-Week Moving Average
1	14,290		11	14,590	14,555
2	14,380		12	14,652	14,586
3	14,399		13	14,625	14,598
4	14,379		14	14,657	14,624
5	14,450	14,380	15	14,699	14,645
6	14,513	14,424	16	14,647	14,656
7	14,500	14,448	17	14,610	14,648
8	14,565	14,481	18	14,595	14,642
9	14,524	14,510	19	14,499	14,610
10	14,597	14,540	20	14,466	14,563

shorter moving average breaks through the longer one, this is a stronger signal than the original price action. Thus, if the 50-day moving average crosses the 100-day moving average from below, it's a buy signal.

Consider the price data in Table 10.1. Each observation represents the closing level of the S&P/TSX Composite on the last trading day of the week. The five-week moving average for each week is the average of the index over the previous five weeks. For example, the first entry, for week 5, is the average of the index value between weeks 1 and 5: 14,290, 14,380, 14,399, 14,379, and 14,450. The next entry is the average of the index values between weeks 2 and 6, and so on.

Figure 10.6 plots the level of the index and the five-week moving average. Notice that while the index itself moves up and down rather abruptly, the moving average is a relatively smooth series, since the impact of each week's price movement is averaged with that of the previous weeks. Week 16 is a bearish point according to the moving average rule. The price series crosses from above the moving average to below it, signifying the beginning of a downward trend in stock prices.

A study by Brock, Lakonishok, and LeBaron[26] actually supports the efficacy of moving-average strategies. They find that stock returns following buy signals from the moving-average rule are

Figure 10.6
Moving averages.

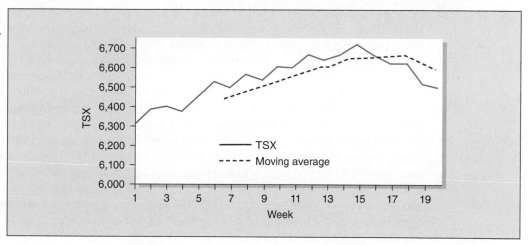

[26]William Brock, Josef Lakonishok, and Blake LeBaron, "Simple Technical Trading Rules and the Stochastic Properties of Stock Returns," *The Journal of Finance* 47 (December 1992), pp. 1731–1764.

higher and less volatile than those after sell signals. However, a more recent paper by Ready,[27] which uses intraday price data, finds that the moving-average rule would not be able to provide profits in practice because of trading costs and the fact that stock prices would already have moved adversely by the time the trader could act on the signal.

Many online sources offer charting services, with a variety of associated charts based on the primary price charts. Volume analyses, price envelopes, and moving averages are all available as desired. Almost any time period can be graphed. Simple high-low-close and open charts are shown; the scale can be modified to show logarithmic price, in order to produce a linear rather than exponential trend. Virtually any analysis is now available.

Charts can be tailored to individual preferences with popular indicators such as 50-day and 200-day moving averages, MACD, Bollinger bands, the stochastic, and volume. Moving averages, associated with the MACD, indicate the trend over shorter or longer periods. The MACD (moving average convergence–divergence) chart helps one to visualize the difference between and the change in two short-term moving averages. The MACD graph is positive for a rising moving average and becomes negative as the average falls; when the two are historically high and turning down, a change from a bullish to a bearish pattern emerges (and vice versa). Bollinger bands provide a form of confidence interval for the price range. The bands are typically drawn on the basis of a 20-day moving average of the price, plus and minus two standard deviations, thereby implying a 95 percent confidence interval of the possible price fluctuations. (A further refinement is to use exponential averages.) Chartists look at the stochastic as a sign of an overbought or oversold condition in the market trading; extreme high (low) levels are associated with local peaks (troughs) in the price, although both high and low levels can persist with the market continuing to rise (fall) while the stochastic is high (low).[28]

EXAMPLE 10.4   **Using Moving Averages**

Examine Figure 10.7, which is a price chart of Teck Resources. It shows first the daily price ranges for Teck for a period of one year. (Other periods, from a day to five or more years, are available, with different intervals such as one minute or one month.) Each vertical bar represents the daily price range, with the open and closing prices on the left and right, respectively, of the bar. The two brown lines bracketing the price ranges are the Bollinger bands; note that the price tends to follow the upper band while the price trend is rising, and the lower band while falling. The dashed and dotted lines are the moving averages, with the smoother dashed line representing a 100-day exponential moving average (EMA) and the more extreme dotted line being the 50-day EMA. Note how the EMAs change direction with a lag after the price trend changes, and the EMA(100) lags the change in the EMA(50). Between points A and B, the price trend is generally falling, while the two EMAs are clearly declining. Around point B the price breaks through the two EMAs and then falls back, before beginning a very clear uptrend. At point C the EMA(100) crosses the EMA(50) from below; this is considered to be confirmation of the reversal of the declining trend. At point D, the uptrend appears to have ended, and the price falls precipitously through the two EMAs; approximately one month later, at point E, the EMA(50) breaks through the EMA(100) from above, signifying a downtrend. Finally, the price rises to the level of the EMAs, which are both appearing to level off, and perhaps . . . beginning a new uptrend. This description should make very obvious that the confirmation by the crossing of EMAs of a trend occurs only after a lot of the trend has

---

[27]M. J. Ready, "Profits from Technical Trading Rules," University of Wisconsin working paper.
[28]We would like to have given a sample chart, but the preferred source does not authorize reproduction.

Figure 10.7 Enhanced price chart of Teck Resources.

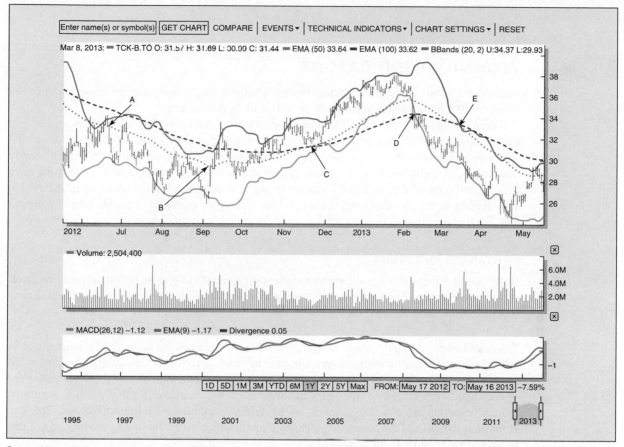

Source: Yahoo Finance Online, http://finance.yahoo.com; an alternative source with similar advanced charting capabilities is available at www.marketwatch.com.

already occurred; if one waits for the confidence of that confirmation, one has lost a lot of trading benefit already. The changing direction, say turning up, of the EMA(50) is often followed by another resumption of trend (down) if the EMA(100) has not also turned.

Either one must be patient and less greedy by waiting for confirmation or one must take more chances. Some help in this is provided by the MACD chart in Figure 10.7. Here the MACD is given with a nine-day moving average; as the MACD crosses its average, the rising and falling values indicate minor trends in the chart. The MACD can be positive but declining as the trend above is still rising but "running out of steam" (and vice versa). One tries to use this graph to predict changes in the general trend. Barely visible are the vertical bars showing the difference between the MACD and its moving average.

The reliance by technicians on these charts cannot provide a very good guarantee of success in trading. Yet technicians feel that the charts give them an edge. They definitely identify the trends that are taking place but cannot give any assurance of which way the future price will go. On the other hand, there are many instances of charts showing stocks with an undeniable trend indicated by an almost linear EMA, usually rising, for periods of a year or longer. One can certainly feel some confidence in buying such stocks, with no guarantee that the trend will continue but a simple rule to follow: the moment the price breaks through the EMA from above, that long-term trend is broken and a sale is probably the right answer. The stock may in fact recover, but that undeniable uptrend is no longer visible.

10.4 TECHNICAL INDICATORS

Technical analysts use other indicators besides charts to assess prospects for market declines or advances. We will examine some popular indicators in this section.

There are three types of technical indicators: sentiment indicators, flow of funds indicators, and market structure indicators. *Sentiment indicators* are intended to measure the expectations of various groups of investors, for example mutual fund issues. *Flow of funds* indicators are intended to measure the potential for various investor groups to buy or sell stocks in order to predict the price pressure from those actions. Finally, *market structure indicators* monitor price trends and cycles. The charting techniques described in the previous section are examples of market structure indicators. We will examine a few more market structure indicators in this section.

Sentiment Indicators

Behavioural finance devotes considerable attention to market "sentiment," which may be interpreted as the general level of optimism among investors. Technical analysts have devised several measures of sentiment; we review a few of them.

Trin Statistic Market volume is sometimes used to measure the strength of a market rise or fall. Increased investor participation in a market advance or retreat is viewed as a measure of the significance of the moment. Technicians consider market advances to be a more favourable omen of continued price increases when they are associated with increased trading volume. Similarly, market reversals are considered more bearish when associated with higher volume. The **trin statistic** is the ratio of the number of advancing to declining issues divided by the ratio of volume in advancing versus declining issues:

$$\text{Trin} = \frac{\text{Number advancing/Number declining}}{\text{Volume advancing/Volume declining}}$$

This expression can be rearranged as

$$\text{Trin} = \frac{\text{Volume declining/Number declining}}{\text{Volume advancing/Number advancing}}$$

Therefore, trin is the ratio of average volume in declining issues to average volume in advancing issues. Ratios above 1.0 are considered bearish because the falling stocks would then have higher average volume than the advancing stocks, indicating net selling pressure. Trin can be calculated from data in the *Financial Post* reports of the market diary section.

Note, however, that for every buyer of stock there must a seller. Rising volume in a rising market should not necessarily indicate a larger imbalance of buyers versus sellers. For example, a trin statistic above 1.0, which is considered bearish, might equally well be interpreted as indicating that there is more *buying* activity in declining issues.

Odd-Lot Trading Just as short-sellers tend to be larger institutional traders, odd-lot traders are almost always small individual traders. (An odd lot is a transaction of fewer than 100 shares; 100 shares is one board lot.) The **odd-lot theory** holds that these small investors tend to miss key market turning points, typically buying stock after a bull market has already run its course and selling too late into a bear market. Therefore, the theory suggests that when odd-lot traders are widely buying, you should sell, and vice versa.

The Wall Street Journal publishes odd-lot trading data every day. You can construct an index of odd-lot trading by computing the ratio of odd-lot purchases to sales. A ratio substantially above 1.0 is bearish because it implies small traders are net buyers.

Confidence Index   *Barron's* computes a confidence index using data from the bond market. The presumption is that actions of bond traders reveal trends that will emerge soon in the stock market.

The **confidence index** is the ratio of the average yield on 10 top-rated corporate bonds divided by the average yield on 10 intermediate-grade corporate bonds. The ratio will always be below 100 percent, because higher-rated bonds will offer lower promised yields to maturity. When bond trades are optimistic about the economy, however, they might require smaller default premiums on lower-rated debt. Hence, the yield spread will narrow, and the confidence index will approach 100 percent. Therefore, higher values of the confidence index are bullish signals.

CC 5

CONCEPT CHECK

Yields on lower-rated debt will rise after fears of recession have spread through the economy. This will reduce the confidence index. Should the stock market now be expected to fall or will it already have fallen?

Put/Call Ratio   Call options give investors the right to buy a stock at a fixed "exercise" price and therefore are a way of betting on stock price increases. Put options give the right to sell a stock at a fixed price and therefore are a way of betting on stock price decreases.[29] The ratio of outstanding put options to outstanding call options is called the **put/call ratio**. Typically, the put/call ratio hovers around 65 percent. Because put options do well in falling markets while call options do well in rising markets, deviations of the ratio from historical norms are considered to be a signal of market sentiment and therefore predictive of market movements.

Interestingly, however, a change in the ratio can be given a bullish or a bearish interpretation. Many technicians see an increase in the ratio as bearish, as it indicates growing interest in put options as a hedge against market declines. Thus, a rising ratio is taken as a sign of broad investor pessimism and a coming market decline. Contrarian investors, however, believe that a good time to buy is when the rest of the market is bearish because stock prices are then unduly depressed. Therefore, they would take an increase in the put/call ratio as a signal of a buy opportunity.

Flow of Funds

Short Interest   **Short interest** is the total number of shares of stock currently sold short in the market. Some technicians interpret high levels of short interest as bullish, some as bearish. The bullish perspective is that, because all short sales must be covered (i.e., short-sellers eventually must purchase shares to return the ones they have borrowed), short interest represents latent future demand for the stocks. As short sales are covered, the demand created by the share purchase will force prices up.

The bearish interpretation of short interest is based on the fact that short-sellers tend to be larger, more sophisticated investors. Accordingly, increased short interest reflects bearish sentiment by those investors "in the know," which would be a negative signal of the market's prospects.

---

[29]Puts and calls are defined in Chapter 2, Section 2.5.

The stock market's recent wiggles and wobbles have many people rethinking their views. For example, not long ago Peter Bernstein, a sober and respected researcher and money manager, criticized buy-and-hold investing and said positive things about market timing. That was a shocker, so what's next, legitimate technical analysis?

Academics and others proponents of orthodox stock market theory say that technical analysis doesn't work. There is no incremental investment information in the behaviour of share prices, so no system that attempts to systematically exploit price behaviour will earn investors any money. Resistance levels, Bollinger Bands, moving averages, stochastics . . . the whole bestiary of technical analysis greeblies are all worthless.

Followers of technical analysis disagree, of course. They point to traders that have made a great deal of money using technical analysis, and they say that it works for them. There are patterns in how stocks behave, and understanding those patterns can make you money.

Who Is Right?

In its purest form, efficient market theory says that all available public and private information is reflected in stock prices. In other words, research is useless because as quickly as new information comes out—whether changing stock prices, or information about markets and earnings—that data is assimilated into stocks. You can't make money from technical analysis (or fundamental analysis, for that matter) and you are wasting time trying. This has become known as the "strong" form of efficient market theory. And it doesn't work. For example, studies have shown disproportionate gains from tracking insider (executives, directors, etc.) buying behaviour. There is information out there that works, much of it private.

But violating strong-form efficiency doesn't mean that technical analysts get a free pass. If markets successfully assimilate all public information, from prices to earnings data, then we have what is called "semi-strong" efficiency. Academics tests of semi-strong efficiency have had much success. For example, repeated studies have shown that traditional technical analysis price patterns (e.g., head-and-shoulders, break-outs, etc.) don't work in any consistent, systematic way that can be tested repeatedly with data.

It is, of course, possible that markets are not even semistrong efficient. This would be a full-employment act for technical analysts, and for pretty much anyone else who wanted to hang out a shingle and call themselves money managers. You could make money from everything from price patterns to earnings releases, and it would be happy days indeed.

Credit Balances in Brokerage Accounts   Investors with brokerage accounts will often leave credit balances in those accounts when they plan to invest in the near future. Thus, credit balances may be viewed as measuring the potential for new stock purchases. As a result, a buildup of balances is viewed as a bullish indicator for the market.

Market Structure

Breadth   The **breadth** of the market is a measure of the extent to which movement in a market index is reflected widely in the price movements of all the stocks in the market. The most common measure of breadth is the spread between the number of stocks that advance and decline in price. If advances outnumber declines by a wide margin, then the market is viewed as being stronger because the rally is widespread. These breadth numbers also are reported daily in *The Financial Post* (see Figure 10.8).

Some analysts cumulate breadth data each day as in Table 10.2. The cumulative breadth for each day is obtained by adding that day's net advances (or declines) to the previous day's total. The direction of the cumulated series is then used to discern broad market trends. Analysts might use a moving average of cumulative breadth to gauge broad trends.

Figure 10.8   Market breadth.

Market breadth									
	TRADING (1000s)	ADVANCE (1000s)	DECLINE (1000s)	TRANS	ISSUES	ADV.	DECL.	UNCH	N.HIGH	N.LOW
TSX	408,419	164,545	236,326	425,156	1,770	743	798	229	96	12
Venture	192,441	79,786	82,879	32,843	1,472	528	581	363	40	15

Source: *Financial Post*, February 8, 2007, p. B20.

The problem is, it is clearly not the case. We all know from our own experience, if not from many credible studies, that most money managers can't consistently make money; and left to our own devices we are no better, at least not consistently. So the market is efficient, it is just a question of how efficient it us. And that is the slim post where technical analysts hang their collective hats. The less sophisticated among them argue that simple patterns like candlesticks and so on work and can make money. More sophisticated technical analysts argue that simple charts and models are over-used, so they don't work, but more sophisticated models do make money.

Generally speaking, most work in the area shows that successful technical investors don't follow their own rules, and they lose money if they do. Instead, they seemingly use their indicators as guides, signposts along the way, and then make buy/sell decisions through some other process that has little do with what they say they are doing.

But these naive and ill-explained processes aside, is it possible that more sophisticated models can detect complex, systematic patterns in the market? Sure, and billions of dollars are being managed that way as I type these words. But those models are exceedingly costly, using a myriad of indicators, and require many PhDs skulking about at hothouses in New York and Chicago. Their relationship to what passes for technical analysis in everyday chatter is akin to an aeronautics debate that mixes talk of jumbo jets with leaping off a cliff with paper taped to your arms.

So who is right? Strangely enough, it partly comes down to what people believe and how they act. To the extent that many people invest following technical analysis's charts and patterns, then some stocks will sometimes behave as if technical analysis works. So if technical analysts convert the rest of us to their creed, they win. But they haven't done that so far. And that leaves one twig left for technical analysts to grasp at. To the extent that market participants believe the market is highly efficient, and act accordingly, the market is likely somewhat inefficient and there will be opportunities to make money.

But most of the money in the market is invested as if markets aren't efficient. Mutual funds, technical analysts and others all think they can make money from public information. To the extent that the bulk of people believe the market is inefficient then, perversely enough, there is a darn good chance that the market is at least semi-strong efficient. It augurs ill for technical analysis.

Source: Paul Kedrosky, *National Post*, September 10, 2003, p. FP.19.

Ford Motor
Company
www.ford.ca

Relative Strength **Relative strength** measures the extent to which a security has outperformed or underperformed either the market as a whole or its particular industry. Relative strength is computed by calculating the ratio of the price of the security to a price index for the industry. For example, the relative strength of Ford versus the auto industry would be measured by movements in the ratio of the price of Ford divided by the level of an auto industry index. A rising ratio implies Ford has been outperforming the rest of the industry. If relative strength can be assumed to persist over time, then this would be a signal to buy Ford.

Similarly, the relative strength of an industry relative to the whole market can be computed by tracking the ratio of the industry price index to the market price index.

Some evidence in support of the relative strength strategy is provided in a study by Jegadeesh and Titman (1993).[30] They ranked firms according to stock market performance in a six-month base period and then examined returns in various followup periods ranging from 1 to

TABLE 10.2

Market Breadth

Day	Advances	Declines	Net Advances	Cumulative Breadth
1	802	748	54	54
2	917	640	277	331
3	703	772	−69	262
4	512	1,122	−610	−348
5	633	1,004	−371	−719

Note: The sum of advances plus declines varies across days because some stock prices are unchanged.

[30]Narasimhan Jegadeesh and Sheridan Titman, "Returns to Buying Winners and Selling Losers: Implications for Stock Market Efficiency," *Journal of Finance* 48 (March 1993).

Figure 10.9

Cumulative difference in returns of previously best-performing and worst-performing stocks in subsequent months.

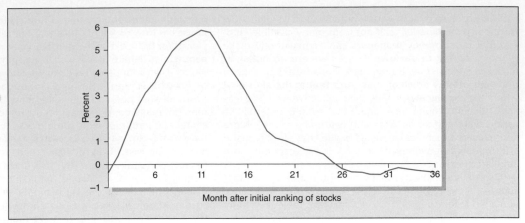

Source: Narasimhan Jegadeesh and Sheridan Titman, "Returns to Buying Winners and Selling Losers: Implications for Stock Market Efficiency," *Journal of Finance* 48 (March 1993).

36 months. They found that the best performers in the base period continued to outperform other stocks for several months. This pattern is consistent with the notion of persistent relative strength. Ultimately, however, the pattern reverses, with the best base-period performers giving up their initial superior returns. Figure 10.9 illustrates this pattern. The graph shows the cumulative difference in return between the 10 percent of the sample of stocks with the best base-period returns and the 10 percent with the worst base-period returns. Initially, the curve trends upward, indicating that the best performers continue to outperform the initial laggards. After about a year, however, the curve turns down, suggesting that abnormal returns on stocks with momentum are ultimately reversed.

The middle two columns of Table 10.3 present data on the levels of an auto industry index and a broad market index. Does the auto industry exhibit relative strength? That can be determined by examining the last column, showing the ratio of the two indices. Despite the fact that the auto industry as a whole has exhibited positive returns, reflected in the rising level of the industry index, the industry has *not* shown relative strength. The market ratio of the auto industry index to the market index shows that the auto industry has underperformed the broad market.

Some final thoughts on the practice of technical analysis are given in the preceding boxed article.

TABLE 10.3

Relative Strength Assessment

Week	Auto Industry	Market Index	Ratio
1	165.6	447.0	.370
2	166.7	450.1	.370
3	168.0	455.0	.369
4	166.9	459.9	.363
5	170.2	459.1	.371
6	169.2	463.0	.365
7	171.0	469.0	.365
8	174.1	473.2	.368
9	173.9	478.8	.363
10	174.2	481.0	.362

10.5   CAN TECHNICAL ANALYSIS WORK IN EFFICIENT MARKETS?

Self-Destructing Patterns   It should be abundantly clear from our presentation that most of technical analysis is based on ideas totally at odds with the foundations of the efficient market hypothesis. The EMH follows from the idea that rational profit-seeking investors will act on new information so quickly that prices will nearly always reflect all publicly available information. Technical analysis, on the other hand, posits the existence of long-lived trends that play out slowly and predictably. Such patterns, if they exist, would violate the EMH notion of essentially unpredictable stock price changes.

An interesting question is whether a technical rule that seems to work will continue to work in the future once it becomes widely recognized. A clever analyst may occasionally uncover a profitable trading rule, but the real test of efficient markets is whether the rule itself becomes reflected in stock prices once its value is discovered.

Suppose, for example, the Dow theory predicts an upward primary trend. If the theory is widely accepted, it follows that many investors will attempt to buy stocks immediately in anticipation of the price increase; the effect would be to bid up prices sharply and immediately rather than at the gradual, long-lived pace initially expected. The Dow theory's predicted trend would be replaced by a sharp jump in prices. It is in this sense that price patterns ought to be *self-destructing*. Once a useful technical rule (or price pattern) is discovered, it ought to be invalidated once the mass of traders attempts to exploit it.

For the prediction of a technical indicator to work, enough believers must trade correspondingly to bring about the anticipated price behaviour. In this sense, the trading rule may become self-fulfilling. If everyone were to believe, however, the necessary anticipation of the price movement would eliminate any potential gain. Technicians are happy to admit that they rely on enough believers to produce the effect, but enough skeptics to allow it to continue; alternatively, smaller investors can follow the rules, but institutional investors moving large blocks of stock are unable to profit from technical strategies. Indeed, there are plenty of examples of irrational purchase and sale at prices that are not efficient; often these are caused by traders lacking current information, whose orders are exploited by more observant participants. Even professionals are caught by false rumours or by program trading excesses. These occasions are infrequent or of low value, but their existence supports the case for occasional market inefficiency that can be exploited by those following charts.

The case of self-destruction for technical analysis requires that the techniques must be practicable by large numbers; if the analysis were available only to a few, then trading opportunities would exist for them. This would be the situation for a highly sophisticated technique such as the *chaos theory* approach. Chaos is the name given to nonlinear patterns in variables that are not observable by conventional (especially mean-variance) analysis. There are a few analysts with mathematical backgrounds who use this approach in forecasting prices. Additionally, the use of *neural networks*—advanced artificial intelligence programs that search for possible patterns—has become popular. There is not yet any reliable evidence on the success of these recent techniques.[31]

An instructive example is the evidence by Jegadeesh[32] and Lehmann[33] that stock prices seem to obey a reversal effect; specifically, the best-performing stocks in one week or month

---

[31]For an analysis that notes some success and a warning, see Vijay Jog, Wojtek Michalowski, Atul Srivastava and Roland Thomas, "Are Artificial Neural Networks Worth Considering?" *Canadian Investment Review* XI, no. 2 (Spring 1998); also, L. Kryzanowski, M. Galler, and D. W. Wright, "Using Artificial Neural Networks to Pick Stocks," *Financial Analysts Journal* 49 (1993), pp. 21–27.

[32]Narasimhan Jegadeesh, "Evidence of Predictable Behavior of Security Prices," *Journal of Finance* 45 (September 1990), pp. 881–898.

[33]Bruce Lehmann, "Fads, Martingales and Market Efficiency," *Quarterly Journal of Economics* 105 (February 1990), pp. 1–28.

tend to fare poorly in the following period, while the worst performers follow up with good performance. Such a phenomenon can be used to form a straightforward technically based trading strategy: Buy shares that recently have done poorly and sell shares that recently have done well. Lehmann shows such a strategy would have been extremely profitable in the past. Lehmann notes that Rosenberg Institutional Equity Management and the College Retirement Equity Fund now use return reversal strategies in their actively managed portfolios. These activities presumably should eliminate existing profit opportunities by forcing prices to their "correct" levels.

On the other hand, Foerster, Prihar, and Schmitz[34] report evidence of testing for return persistence in Canadian equities. Identifying superior returns in previous quarters, they show that the top performing decile of the data set continues to outperform the market on a risk-adjusted basis. Both before and after transaction costs, a policy of investing in a portfolio of that top decile (revised quarterly) yields extremely high returns—approximately three times those of the TSX. The results of quarterly persistence in Canada appear to contradict the above-mentioned monthly reversals in the United States.[35] They find, however, that the bottom decile has quite average returns, which might indicate reversal for poor performers.

Yet another study[36] offers conclusive evidence that even the simplest of technical trading strategies can be profitable, especially before transaction costs. The charting practices discussed earlier in the chapter, such as determining moving averages and price breakouts, were subjected to more sophisticated statistical analyses (including the GARCH technique) and shown to offer significantly better returns than trading on the basis of no technical signals. These effects are at odds with market efficiency and at the same time, consistent with the viability of technical analysis. The real test of these trading rules will come now that the potential of the strategies has been uncovered.

Thus, technical analysis is a continual search for profitable trading rules, followed by destruction by overuse of those rules found to be successful, followed by more search for yet-undiscovered rules.

Information and Signalling

Brown and Jennings[37] offer a rigorous foundation for the potential efficacy of technical analysis. They envision an economy where many investors have private information regarding the ultimate value of a stock. Moreover, as time passes, each investor acquires additional information. Each investor can infer something of the information possessed by other traders by observing the price at which securities trade. The entire sequence of past prices can turn out to be useful in the inference of the information held by other traders. In this sense, technical analysis can be useful to traders even if all traders rationally use all information available to them.

Most discussions of the EMH envision public information commonly available to all traders and ask only if prices reflect that information. In this sense, the Brown and Jennings framework is more complex. Here, different individuals receive different private signals regarding the value of a firm. As prices unfold, each trader infers the good-news or bad-news nature of the signals received by other traders and updates assessments of the firm accordingly. Prices *reveal* as well as *reflect* information and become useful data to traders. Without addressing

---

[34]Steven Foerster, Anoop Prihar, and John Schmitz, "Price Momentum Models and How They Beat the Canadian Equity Markets," *Canadian Investment Review* VII, no. 4 (Winter 1995), pp. 9–13.

[35]N. Jegadeesh and S. Titman, "Returns to Buying Winners and Selling Losers: Implications for Stock Market Efficiency," *The Journal of Finance* 48 (March 1993), pp. 65–91.

[36]William Brock, Josef Lakonishok, and Blake LeBaron, "Simple Technical Trading Rules and the Stochastic Properties of Stock Returns," *The Journal of Finance* 47 (December 1992), pp. 1731–1764.

[37]David Brown and Robert H. Jennings, "On Technical Analysis," *Review of Financial Studies* 2 (1989), pp. 527–552.

specific technical trading rules, the Brown and Jennings model is an interesting and innovative attempt to reconcile technical analysis with the usual assumption of rational traders participating in efficient markets.

Under the area of market microstructure studies, Blume, Easley, and O'Hara[38] have investigated the importance of analyzing trading volume in determining the underlying pressure on price. Increased volume is likely to be an indication of superior information possessed by some investors. This information as to the true equilibrium value of the stock will cause an increase in buying or selling by insiders. Uninformed investors must take account of the volume information in order to restore strong-form efficiency. Recognition of the volume may allow technical traders to trade and profit before the equilibrium value is identified.

---

[38]Marshall Blume, David Easley, and Maureen O'Hara, "Market Statistics and Technical Analysis: The Role of Volume," *The Journal of Finance* 49 (March 1994), pp. 153–182.

SUMMARY

1. Behavioural finance focuses on systematic irrationalities that characterize investor decision making. These "behavioural shortcomings" may be consistent with several efficient market anomalies.

2. Among the information processing errors uncovered in the psychology literature are memory bias, overconfidence, conservatism, and representativeness. Behavioural tendencies include framing, mental accounting, regret avoidance, and loss-aversion.

3. Limits to arbitrage activity impede the ability of rational investors to exploit pricing errors induced by behavioural investors. For example, fundamental risk means that even if a security is mispriced, it still can be risky to attempt to exploit the mispricing. This limits the actions of arbitrageurs who take positions in mispriced securities. Other limits to arbitrage are implementation costs, model risk, and costs to short-selling. Occasional failures of the Law of One Price suggest that limits to arbitrage are sometimes severe.

4. The various limits to arbitrage mean that even if prices do not equal intrinsic value, it still may be difficult to exploit the mispricing. As a result, the failure of traders to beat the market may not be proof that markets are in fact efficient, with prices equal to intrinsic value.

5. Technical analysis is the search for recurring and predictable patterns in stock prices. It is based on the premise that prices only gradually close in on intrinsic value. As fundamentals shift, astute traders can exploit the adjustment to a new equilibrium.

6. The Dow theory is the earliest chart-based version of technical analysis. The theory posits the existence of primary, intermediate, and minor trends that can be identified on a chart and acted on by an analyst before the trends fully dissipate.

7. Moving averages superimposed on price charts, with Bollinger bands as confidence intervals, are used to help identify changes in minor and major trends.

8. Technicians believe high volume and market breadth accompanying market trends add weight to the significance of a trend.

9. Odd-lot traders are viewed as uninformed, which suggests informed traders should pursue trading strategies in opposition to their activity. In contrast, short-sellers are viewed as informed traders, lending credence to their activity.

10. Relative strength measures performance of a stock against its industry or the market; anomalies based on momentum or reversals support or refute use of this measure.

11. New theories of information dissemination in the market suggest there may be a role for the examination of past prices in formulating investment strategies. They do not, however, support the specific charting patterns currently relied on by technical analysts.

PROBLEMS

connect Practise and learn online with Connect.

1. Explain how some of the behavioural biases discussed in the chapter might contribute to the success of technical trading rules.

2. Why would an advocate of the efficient market hypothesis believe that even if many investors exhibit the behavioural biases discussed in the chapter, security prices might still be set efficiently?

3. What sorts of factors might limit the ability of rational investors to take advantage of any "pricing errors" that result from the actions of "behavioural investors"?

4. Even if behavioural biases do not affect equilibrium asset prices, why might it still be important for investors to be aware of them?

5. Some advocates of behavioural finance agree with efficient market advocates that indexing is the optimal investment strategy for most investors. But their reasons for this conclusion differ greatly. Compare and contrast the rationale for indexing according to both of these schools of thought.

6. Jill Davis tells her broker that she does not want to sell her stocks that are below the price she paid for them. She believes that if she just holds on to them a little longer they will recover, at which time she will sell them. What behavioural characteristic does Davis have as the basis for her decision making?

   a. Loss aversion   *c.* Representativeness

   b. Conservatism

7. After Polly Shrum sells a stock, she avoids following it in the media. She is afraid that it may subsequently increase in price. What behavioural characteristic does Shrum have as the basis for her decision making?

   a. Fear of regret   *c.* Mental accounting

   b. Representativeness

8. All of the following actions are consistent with feelings of regret *except*

   a. Selling losers quickly   *c.* Holding onto losers too long

   b. Hiring a full-service broker

9. Match each example to one of the behavioural characteristics.

	Example	Behavioural Characteristic
a.	Investors are slow to update their beliefs when given new evidence.	i. Disposition effect
b.	Investors are reluctant to bear losses caused by their unconventional decisions.	ii. Representativeness bias
c.	Investors exhibit less risk tolerance in their retirement accounts versus their other stock accounts.	iii. Regret avoidance
d.	Investors are reluctant to sell stocks with "paper" losses.	iv. Conservatism bias
e.	Investors disregard sample size when forming views about the future from the past.	v. Mental accounting

10. What do we mean by fundamental risk, and why might such risk allow behavioural biases to persist for long periods of time?

11. What is meant by data mining, and why must technical analysts be careful not to engage in it?

12. Even if prices follow a random walk, they still may not be informationally efficient. Explain why this may be true, and why it matters for the efficient allocation of capital in our economy.

13. Use the data from *The Financial Post* in Figure 10.8 to construct the trin ratio for the TSX. Is the trin ratio bullish or bearish?

14. Collect data on the S&P/TSX Composite for a period covering a few months. Try to identify primary trends. Can you tell whether the market currently is in an upward or downward trend?

15. Go to Marketwatch.com and obtain a chart for CA:XIU. Add 50- and 200-day moving averages, Bollinger bands, MACD, and slow stochastic. What direction would you predict for the XIU? (Assess your prediction one month later.)

16. The ratio of put to call options outstanding is viewed by some as a technical indicator. Do you think a high ratio is viewed as bullish or bearish? Should it be?

17. Table 10.4 presents price data for Computers, Inc. and a computer industry index. Does Computers, Inc. show relative strength over this period?

TABLE 10.4   Computers, Inc. Stock Price History

Trading Day	Computers, Inc.	Industry Index	Trading Day	Computers, Inc.	Industry Index
1	19.64	50.0	21	19.64	54.1
2	20	50.1	22	21.5	54.0
3	20.5	50.5	23	22	53.9
4	22	50.4	24	23.13	53.7
5	21.13	51.0	25	24	54.8
6	22	50.7	26	25.25	54.5
7	21.88	50.5	27	26.25	54.6
8	22.5	51.1	28	27	54.1
9	23.13	51.5	29	27.5	54.2
10	23.88	51.7	30	28	54.8
11	24.5	51.4	31	28.5	54.2
12	23.25	51.7	32	28	54.8
13	22.13	52.2	33	27.5	54.9
14	22	52.0	34	29	55.2
15	20.64	53.1	35	29.25	55.7
16	20.25	53.5	36	29.5	56.1
17	19.75	53.9	37	30	56.7
18	18.75	53.6	38	28.5	56.7
19	17.5	52.9	39	27.75	56.5
20	19	53.4	40	28	56.1

18. Use the data in Table 10.4 to compute a five-day moving average for Computers, Inc. Can you identify any buy or sell signals?

19. Table 10.5 contains data on market advances and declines. Calculate cumulative breadth and decide whether this technical signal is bullish or bearish.

TABLE 10.5   Market Advances and Declines

Day	Advances	Declines	Day	Advances	Declines
1	906	704	6	970	702
2	653	986	7	1,002	609
3	721	789	8	903	722
4	503	968	9	850	748
5	497	1,095	10	766	766

20. If the trading volume in advancing shares on day 1 in the previous problem was 330 million shares, while the volume in declining issues was 240 million shares, what was the trin statistic for that day? Was trin bullish or bearish?

21. Yesterday, the S&P/TSX 60 gained 54 points. However, 580 issues declined in price while 436 advanced. Why might a technical analyst be concerned even though the market index rose on this day?

22. Baa-rated bonds currently yield 9 percent, while Aa-rated bonds yield 8 percent. Suppose that due to an increase in the expected inflation rate, the yields on both bonds increase, by 1 percent. What would happen to the confidence index? Would this be interpreted as bullish or bearish by a technical analyst? Does this make sense to you?

23. Using Figure 10.10, determine whether market price movements and volume patterns were bullish or bearish around the following dates: September 17, November 5, and January 5. In each instance, compare your prediction to the subsequent behaviour of the DJIA in the following few weeks.

Figure 10.10

Dow Jones Industrial Average and market volume.

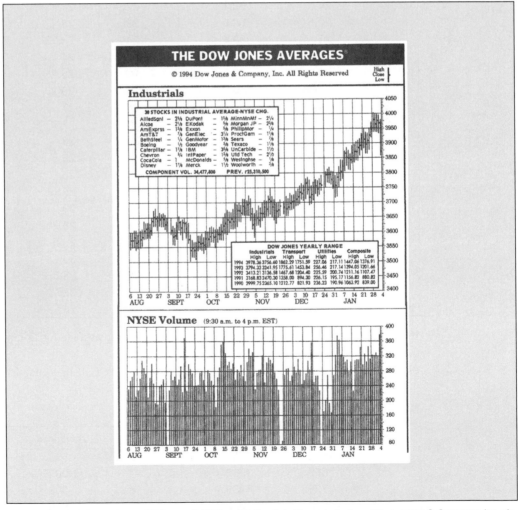

24. Is the confidence index rising or falling, given the following information?

	This Year (%)	Last Year (%)
Yield on top-rated corporate bonds	8	8.5
Yield on intermediate-grade corporate bonds	10.5	10

The following problems are based on questions that have appeared in past CFA examinations.

25. One seeming violation of the Law of One Price is the pervasive discrepancy of closed-end fund prices from their net asset values. Would you expect to observe greater discrepancies on diversified or less-diversified funds? Why?

26. Don Sampson begins a meeting with his financial advisor by outlining his investment philosophy as shown below:

Statement Number	Statement
1	Investments should offer strong return potential but with very limited risk. I prefer to be conservative and to minimize losses, even if I miss out on substantial growth opportunities.
2	All nongovernmental investments should be in industry-leading and financially strong companies.
3	Income needs should be met entirely through interest income and cash dividends. All equity securities held should pay cash dividends.
4	Investment decisions should be based primarily on consensus forecasts of general economic conditions and company-specific growth.
5	If an investment falls below the purchase price, that security should be retained until it returns to its original cost. Conversely, I prefer to take quick profits on successful investments.
6	I will direct the purchase of investments, including derivative securities, periodically. These aggressive investments result from personal research and may not prove consistent with my investment policy. I have not kept records on the performance of similar past investments, but I have had some "big winners."

Select the statement from this table that best illustrates each of the following behavioural finance concepts. Justify your selection.

a. Mental accounting

b. Overconfidence (illusion of control)

c. Reference dependence (framing)

27. Monty Frost's tax-deferred retirement account is invested entirely in equity securities. Because the international portion of his portfolio has performed poorly in the past, he has reduced his international equity exposure to 2 percent. Frost's investment adviser has recommended an increased international equity exposure. Frost responds with the following comments:

a. "Based on past poor performance, I want to sell all my remaining international equity securities once their market prices rise to equal their original cost."

b. "Most diversified international portfolios have had disappointing results over the past five years. During that time, however, the market in Country XYZ has outperformed all other markets, even our own. If I do increase my international equity exposure, I would prefer that the entire exposure consist of securities from Country XYZ."

c. "International investments are inherently more risky. Therefore, I prefer to purchase any international equity securities in my "speculative" account, my best chance at becoming rich. I do not want them in my retirement account, which has to protect me from poverty in my old age."

Frost's advisor is familiar with behavioural finance concepts but prefers a traditional or standard finance approach (modern portfolio theory) to investments.

Indicate the behavioural finance concept that Frost most directly exhibits in each of his three comments. Explain how each of Frost's comments can be countered by using an argument from standard finance.

28. Louise and Christopher Maclin live in London, United Kingdom and currently rent an apartment in the metropolitan area. During an initial discussion of the Maclins' financial plans, Christopher Maclin makes the following statements to the Maclins' financial advisor, Grant Webb:

a. "I have used the Internet extensively to research the outlook for the housing market over the next five years, and I believe now is the best time to buy a house."

b. "I do not want to sell any bond in my portfolio for a lower price than I paid for the bond."

c. "I will not sell any of my company stock because I know my company and I believe it has excellent prospects for the future."

For each statement (a)–(c) identify the behavioural finance concept most directly exhibited. Explain how each behavioural finance concept is affecting Maclin's investment decision making.

29. During an interview with her investment adviser, a retired investor made the following two statements:

a. "I have been very pleased with the returns I've earned on Petrie stock over the past two years and I am certain that it will be a superior performer in the future."

b. "I am pleased with the returns from the Petrie stock because I have specific uses for that money. For that reason, I certainly want my retirement fund to continue owning the Petrie stock."

Identify which principle of behavioural finance is most consistent with each of the investor's two statements.

30. Claire Pierce comments on her life circumstances and investment outlook:

I must support my parents who live overseas on Pogo Island. The Pogo Island economy has grown rapidly over the past two years with minimal inflation, and consensus forecasts call for a continuation of these favourable trends for the foreseeable future. Economic growth has resulted from the export of a natural resource used in an exciting new technology application.

I want to invest 10 percent of my portfolio in Pogo Island government bonds. I plan to purchase long-term bonds because my parents are likely to live more than ten years. Experts uniformly do not foresee a resurgence of inflation on Pogo Island, so I am certain that the total returns produced by the bonds will cover my parents' spending needs for many years to come. There should be no exchange rate risk because the bonds are denominated in local currency. I want to buy the Pogo Island bonds, but am not willing to distort my portfolio's long-term asset allocation to do so. The overall mix of stocks, bonds, and other investments should not change. Therefore, I am considering selling one of my U.S. bond funds to raise cash to buy the Pogo Island bonds. One possibility is my High Yield Bond Fund, which has declined 5 percent in value year to date. I am not excited about this fund's prospects; in fact I think it is likely to decline more, but there is a small probability that it could recover very quickly. So I have decided instead to sell my Core Bond Fund that has appreciated 5 percent this year. I expect this investment to continue to deliver attractive returns, but there is a small chance this year's gains might disappear quickly.

Once that shift is accomplished, my investments will be in great shape. The sole exception is my Small Company Fund, which has performed poorly. I plan to sell this investment as soon as the price increases to my original cost.

Identify three behavioural finance concepts illustrated in Pierce's comments and describe each of the three concepts. Discuss how an investor practising standard or traditional finance would challenge each of the three concepts.

E-INVESTMENTS **Charting and** **Technical** **Analysis**	Yahoo! Finance (**http://finance.yahoo.com**) offers significant capabilities in charting and other technical indicators. Under the charting function, you can specify comparisons between companies by choosing the technical analysis tab. Short interest ratios are found under the company profile report. Prepare charts of moving averages and obtain short interest ratios for GE and SWY. Prepare a one-year chart of the 50- and 100-day average price of BAM-A.TO, C, and the S&P 500 index. Which, if either, of the companies is priced above its 50- and 100-day averages? Would you consider their charts as bullish or bearish? Why? What are the short interest ratios for the two companies? Has short interest displayed any significant trend?

Empirical Evidence on Security Returns

In this chapter, we turn to the vast literature about testing models of risk and return. The very existence of such a vast literature suggests a serious problem is involved—testing these models is not trivial. Indeed, an important part of the work here is to understand the challenges in doing so.

All models of capital asset pricing have two parts. First, they derive the optimal portfolio of an individual investor, conditional on a utility function (describing how an investor trades off risk against expected return) and an input list that includes estimates of portfolio expected returns and risk. Second, they derive predictions about expected returns on capital assets in equilibrium, when investors complete the trades necessary to arrive at their personal optimal portfolios.

Obviously, the flow of new information alone will change input lists and thus desired portfolios. Here is where the efficient market hypothesis (EMH) kicks in. If asset prices reflect all available information, then *changes* of asset prices resulting from new information will have zero means, that is, prices will follow random walks.[1] The response to new information will introduce noise around the predictions of the model, but by itself this should not cause any difficulty that cannot be overcome with appropriate statistical methods and lots of data. But when the EMH is off, even temporarily, by economically significant margins, changes in prices and expected returns will not change randomly and model predictions can be affected. This is why a test of an asset pricing model is of necessity a joint test of the EMH.

The single-factor CAPM has one key inference that can be expressed in either of two ways: the market portfolio is mean-variance efficient, and (equivalently) the risk premium on each individual asset is proportional to its beta, $E(R_i) = \beta_i E(R_M)$. The first statement is, in practice, untestable, because we do

---

[1]Actually, prices will show an upward drift since expected rates of return are positive. But over short time horizons, this drift is trivial compared to volatility. For example, at a daily horizon, the expected rate of return is around 5 basis points (corresponding to an annual return of 12 percent). The daily standard deviation of stock prices is an order of magnitude higher, typically exceeding 2 percent for individual stocks.

not observe the market portfolio. However, if a broad index is sufficiently well diversified, even if not mean-variance-efficient, it may nevertheless support the mean–beta relationship (the SML) using the arguments of the APT.

A test of the ex ante mean-variance efficiency of a particular market index can never be a conclusive test of the CAPM. In any sample, there is always an ex post efficient portfolio that will never be identical to the index. How do we measure distance from efficiency, and what would constitute a rejection of the model? Given these difficulties, the mean-beta equation has been the test arena of most research. However, most of these tests are better interpreted as tests of the APT (rather than the CAPM), since we know from the outset that the index may not be mean-variance-efficient but may nevertheless be well diversified.

We begin with tests of the single-factor security market line, the theatre where the basic methodologies have been developed, and then proceed to multifactor models with emphasis on the empirically motivated Fama-French three-factor model. We show how this research may be interpreted as tests of Merton's multifactor ICAPM. We end this part of the chapter with a section that brings liquidity into the empirical framework. We devote a section to the theoretically appealing consumption CAPM in order to present the equity premium puzzle, and end with an assessment of where research into asset pricing is headed.

11.1   THE INDEX MODEL AND THE SINGLE-FACTOR APT

The Expected Return–Beta Relationship

Recall that if the expected return–beta relationship holds with respect to an observable ex ante efficient index, M, the expected rate of return on any security i is

$$E(r_i) = r_f + \beta_i[E(r_M) - r_f] \tag{11.1}$$

where β_i is defined as $\text{Cov}(r_i, r_M)/\sigma^2_M$.

This is the most commonly tested implication of the CAPM. Early simple tests followed three basic steps: establishing sample data, estimating the SCL (security characteristic line), and estimating the SML (security market line).

Setting Up the Sample Data   Determine a sample period of, for example, 60 monthly holding periods (five years). For each of the 60 holding periods, collect the rates of return on 100 stocks, a market portfolio proxy (e.g., the S&P 500 or the S&P/TSX Composite), and one-month (risk-free) T-bills. Your data thus consist of:

r_{it} 6,000 returns on the 100 stocks over the 60-month sample period; $i = 1, \ldots, 100$, and $t = 1, \ldots, 60$

r_{Mt} 60 observations of the returns on the S&P 500 index over the sample period

r_{ft} 60 observations of the risk-free rate (one each month)

This constitutes a table of $102 \times 60 = 6{,}120$ rates of return.

Estimating the SCL View equation 11.1 as a security characteristic line (SCL), as in Chapter 7. For each stock i, you estimate the beta coefficient as the slope of a **first-pass regression** equation. (The terminology *first-pass* regression is due to the fact that the estimated coefficients will be used as input into a **second-pass regression**.)

$$r_{it} - r_{ft} = a_i + b_i(r_{Mt} - r_{ft}) + e_{it}$$

You will use the following statistics in later analysis:

$\overline{r_i - r_f}$	Sample averages (over the 60 observations) of the excess return on each of the 100 stocks
b_i	Sample estimates of the beta coefficients of each of the 100 stocks
$\overline{r_M - r_f}$	Sample average of the excess return of the market index
$\sigma^2(e_i)$	Estimates of the variance of the residuals for each of the 100 stocks

The sample average excess returns on each stock and the market portfolio are taken as estimates of expected excess returns, and the values of b_i are estimates of the true beta coefficients for the 100 stocks during the sample period. $\sigma^2(e_i)$ estimates the nonsystematic risk of each of the 100 stocks. It is understood that all three statistics include estimation errors.

CC 1

CONCEPT CHECK

a. How many regression estimates of the SCL do we have from the sample?
b. How many observations are there in each of the regressions?
c. According to the CAPM, what should be the intercept in each of these regressions?

Estimating the SML Now view equation 11.1 as a security market line (SML) with 100 observations for the stocks in your sample. You can estimate γ_0 and γ_1 in the following second-pass regression equation with the estimates b_i from the first pass as the independent variable:

$$\overline{r_i - r_f} = \gamma_0 + \gamma_1 b_i \qquad i = 1, \dots, 100 \tag{11.2}$$

Compare equations 11.1 and 11.2; you should conclude that if the CAPM is valid, then γ_0 and γ_1 should satisfy

$$\gamma_0 = 0 \qquad \gamma_1 = \overline{r_M - r_f}$$

In fact, however, you can go a step further and argue that the key property of the expected return–beta relationship described by the SML is that the expected excess return on securities is determined *only* by the systematic risk (as measured by beta) and should be independent of the nonsystematic risk, as measured by the variance of the residuals, $\sigma^2(e_i)$, which also were estimated from the first-pass regression. These estimates can be added as a variable in equation 11.2 of an expanded SML that now looks like this:

$$\overline{r_i - r_f} = \gamma_0 + \gamma_1 b_i + \gamma_2 \sigma^2(e_i) \tag{11.3}$$

This *second-pass* regression is estimated with the hypotheses

$$\gamma_0 = 0 \qquad \gamma_1 = \overline{r_M - r_f} \qquad \gamma_2 = 0$$

The hypothesis that $\gamma_2 = 0$ is consistent with the notion that nonsystematic risk should not be "priced," that is, that there is no risk premium earned for bearing nonsystematic risk. More generally, according to the CAPM, the risk premium depends only on beta. Therefore, *any* additional right-hand-side variable in equation 11.3 beyond beta should have a coefficient that is insignificantly different from zero in the second-pass regression.

Tests of the CAPM

Early tests of the CAPM performed by John Lintner,[2] later replicated by Merton Miller and Myron Scholes,[3] used annual data on 631 NYSE stocks for ten years, 1954 to 1963, and produced the following estimates (with returns expressed as decimals rather than percentages):

Coefficient:	$\gamma_0 = .127$	$\gamma_1 = .042$	$\gamma_2 = .310$
Standard error:	.006	.006	.026
Sample average:		$\overline{r_M - r_f} = .165$	

These results are inconsistent with the CAPM. First, the estimated SML is "too flat"; that is, the γ_1 coefficient is too small. The slope should be $\overline{r_M - r_f} = .165$ (16.5 percent per year), but it is estimated at only .042. The difference, .122, is about 20 times the standard error of the estimate, .006, which means that the measured slope of the SML is less than it should be by a statistically significant margin. At the same time, the intercept of the estimated SML, γ_0, which is hypothesized to be zero, in fact equals .127, which is more than 20 times its standard error of .006.

CC 2

CONCEPT CHECK

a. What is the implication of the empirical SML being "too flat"?
b. Do high- or low-beta stocks tend to outperform the predictions of the CAPM?
c. What is the implication of the estimate of γ_2?

The two-stage procedure employed by these researchers (i.e., first estimate security betas using a time series regression and then use those betas to test the SML relationship between risk and average return) seems straightforward, and the rejection of the CAPM using this approach is disappointing. However, it turns out that there are several difficulties with this approach. First and foremost, stock returns are extremely volatile, which lessens the precision of any tests of average return. For example, the average standard deviation of annual returns of the stocks in the S&P 500 is about 40 percent; the average standard deviation of annual returns of the stocks included in these tests is probably even higher.

In addition, there are fundamental concerns about the validity of the tests. First, the market index used in the tests is surely not the "market portfolio" of the CAPM. Second, in light of asset volatility, the security betas from the first-stage regressions are necessarily estimated with substantial sampling error and therefore cannot readily be used as inputs to the second-stage regression. Finally, investors cannot borrow at the risk-free rate, as assumed by the simple version of the CAPM. Let us investigate the implications of these problems after examining the empirical studies in the Canadian context.

Estimating Index Models for Canadian Stocks

Studies on the SML along the lines of the previous section have been done using Canadian data since 1980.[4] Overall, the empirical results turned out to be unsatisfactory. The return–beta relationship turned out to be weak, erratic, and nonlinear, and implied unreasonably high estimates of the returns on low-risk assets.

---

[2]John Lintner, "Security Prices, Risk and Maximal Gains from Diversification," *Journal of Finance* 20 (December 1965).
[3]Merton H. Miller and Myron Scholes, "Rate of Return in Relation to Risk: A Reexamination of Some Recent Findings," in Michael C. Jensen, ed., *Studies in the Theory of Capital Markets* (New York: Praeger, 1972).
[4]Roger A. Morin, "Market Line Theory and the Canadian Equity Market," *Journal of Business Administration* 12, no. 1 (Fall 1980).

Similarly, later SML studies using Canadian data[5] reached conclusions that seem to confirm the basic outcome observed in the United States, namely that the single-variable expected return–beta relationship is, at best, only weakly supported by empirical work. Although a significant linear relationship between systematic risk and portfolio returns was found almost always, the introduction of unsystematic risk and of the squared beta coefficient in the regression showed both to be significant and more important than the beta.

Empirical research in Canadian financial markets is hindered by two effects that are not present to the same extent in the United States. The first is the existence of seasonal abnormal returns at variance with market efficiency as documented in the previous chapter. The second is the persistent problem of **thin trading** in a majority of Canadian securities.

Thin Trading

If transactions for many securities listed on the TSX are irregular and infrequent, then the prices quoted as closing by the exchange are unreliable and may also reflect situations that are no longer current. For instance, if a stock did not trade at all during a given month, then its recorded rate of return is zero during that month (in the absence of dividends). If many such securities and months occur in our database, then the statistical estimations of the SML will yield biased results.[6]

In addition to biases in the estimated coefficients, thinness of trading also causes heteroskedasticity,[7] that is, different variances of the residuals in the regressions. There are a number of procedures for correcting the biases arising out of thinness of trading, of which the one developed by Dimson[8] is perhaps the most popular. The Dimson method augments the single simultaneous market index term in the regression by two other terms, one with a lagged and one with a leading value of the index, each one with its own beta; an unbiased estimate of the "true" beta is equal to the sum of three estimated betas. Another bias-correcting method also was developed by Scholes and Williams,[9] but the small-sample properties of both methods are somewhat questionable.[10]

The Market Index

The CAPM and the Market Model www.msci.com/ products/risk management analytics/ barra_integrated model

In what has become known as *Roll's critique*, Richard Roll[11] pointed out that:

1. There is a single testable hypothesis associated with the CAPM: the market portfolio is mean-variance-efficient.

2. All the other implications of the model, the best known being the linear relation between expected return and beta, follow from the market portfolio's efficiency and therefore are not independently testable. There is an "if and only if" relation between the expected return–beta relationship and the efficiency of the market portfolio.

3. In any sample of observations of individual returns there will be an infinite number of ex post (i.e., after-the-fact) mean-variance-efficient portfolios using the sample period returns and covariances (as opposed to the ex ante expected returns and covariances).

[5]For instance, J. D. Jobson and R. M. Korkie, "Some Tests of Linear Asset Pricing with Multivariate Normality," *Canadian Journal of Administrative Sciences* 2, no. 1 (June 1985). See also M. J. Robinson, "Univariate Canadian CAPM Tests," in M. J. Robinson and B. F. Smith, eds., *Canadian Capital Markets* (London, ON: 1993), and A. L. Calvet and J. Lefoll, "Risk and Return on Canadian Capital Markets," *Canadian Journal of Administrative Sciences* 5, no. 1 (March 1988).

[6]David J. Fowler, C. Harvey Rorke, and V. M. Jog, "Thin Trading and Beta Estimation Problems on the Toronto Stock Exchange," *Journal of Business Administration* 12, no. 1 (Fall 1980).

[7]David J. Fowler, C. Harvey Rorke, and V. M. Jog, "Heteroscedasticity, R^2 and Thin Trading on the Toronto Stock Exchange," *Journal of Finance* 34, no. 5 (December 1979).

[8]E. Dimson, "Risk Measurement When Shares Are Subject to Infrequent Trading," *Journal of Financial Economics* 7 (1979).

[9]M. Scholes and J. Williams, "Estimating Betas from Nonsynchronous Data," *Journal of Financial Economics* 5 (1977).

[10]See Fowler, Rorke, and Jog, "Thin Trading and Beta Estimation Problems."

[11]Richard Roll, "A Critique of the Asset Pricing Theory's Tests: Part I: On Past and Potential Testability of the Theory," *Journal of Financial Economics* 4 (1977).

Sample betas of individual assets estimated against each such ex-post-efficient portfolio will be exactly linearly related to the sample average returns of these assets. In other words, if betas are calculated against such portfolios, they will satisfy the SML relation exactly whether or not the true market portfolio is mean-variance-efficient in an ex ante sense.

4. The CAPM is not testable unless we know the exact composition of the true market portfolio and use it in the tests. This implies that the theory is not testable unless *all* individual assets are included in the sample.

5. Using a proxy such as the S&P 500 for the market portfolio is subject to two difficulties. First, the proxy itself might be mean-variance-efficient even when the true market portfolio is not. Conversely, the proxy may turn out to be inefficient, but obviously this alone implies nothing about the true market portfolio's efficiency. Furthermore, most reasonable market proxies will be very highly correlated with each other and with the true market portfolio whether or not they are mean-variance-efficient. Such a high degree of correlation will make it seem that the exact composition of the market portfolio is unimportant, whereas the use of different proxies can lead to quite different conclusions. This problem is referred to as **benchmark error**, because it refers to the use of an incorrect benchmark (market proxy) portfolio in the tests of the theory.

Roll and Ross[12] and Kandel and Stambaugh[13] expanded Roll's critique. Essentially, they argued that tests that reject a positive relationship between average return and beta point to inefficiency of the market proxy used in those tests, rather than refuting the theoretical expected return–beta relationship. Their work demonstrates that it is plausible that even highly diversified portfolios, such as the value- or equally weighted portfolios of all stocks in the sample, will fail to produce a significant average return–beta relationship.

Kandel and Stambaugh (KS) considered the properties of the usual two-pass test of the CAPM in an environment in which borrowing is restricted but the zero-beta version of the CAPM holds. In this case, you will recall that the expected return–beta relationship describes the expected returns on a stock, a portfolio E on the efficient frontier, and that portfolio's zero-beta companion, Z (see equation 7.10):

$$E(r_i) - E(r_Z) = \beta_i[E(r_E) - E(r_Z)] \tag{11.4}$$

where β_i denotes the beta of security i on efficient portfolio E.

We cannot construct or observe the efficient portfolio E (since we do not know expected returns and covariances of all assets), and so we cannot estimate equation 11.4 directly. KS asked what would happen if we followed the common procedure of using a market proxy portfolio M in place of E, and used as well the more efficient generalized least squares (GLS) regression procedure in estimating the second-pass regression for the zero-beta version of the CAPM, that is,

$$r_i - r_Z = \gamma_0 + \gamma_1 \times \text{Estimated } \beta_i$$

They showed that the estimated values of γ_0 and γ_1 will be biased by a term proportional to the relative efficiency of the market proxy. If the market index used in the regression is fully efficient, the test will be well specified. But the second-pass regression will provide a poor test of the CAPM if the proxy for the market portfolio is not efficient. Thus, we still cannot test the model in a meaningful way without a reasonably efficient market proxy. Unfortunately, it is impossible to determine how efficient our market index is, so we cannot tell how good our tests are.

---

[12]Richard Roll and Stephen A. Ross, "On the Cross-Sectional Relation Between Expected Return and Betas," *Journal of Finance* 49 (1994), pp. 101–121.

[13]Schmuel Kandel and Robert F. Stambaugh, "Portfolio Inefficiency and the Cross-Section of Expected Returns," *Journal of Finance* 50 (1995), pp. 185–224; "A Mean-Variance Framework for Tests of Asset Pricing Models," *Review of Financial Studies* 2 (1989), pp. 125–156; "On Correlations and Inferences About Mean-Variance Efficiency," *Journal of Financial Economics* 18 (1987), pp. 61–90.

Given the impossibility of testing the CAPM directly, we can retreat to testing the APT, which produces the same mean-beta equation (the security market line).[14] This model depends only on the index portfolio being well diversified. Choosing a broad market index allows us to test the SML as applied to the chosen index.

Measurement Error in Beta

It is well known in statistics that if the right-hand-side variable of a regression equation is measured with error (in our case, beta is measured with error and is the right-hand-side variable in the second-pass regression), then the slope coefficient of the regression equation will be biased downward and the intercept biased upward. This is consistent with the findings cited above; γ_0 was higher than predicted by the CAPM and γ_1 was lower than predicted.

Indeed, a well-controlled simulation test by Miller and Scholes[15] confirms these arguments. In this test a random-number generator simulated rates of return with covariances similar to observed ones. The average returns were made to agree exactly with the CAPM. Miller and Scholes then used these randomly generated rates of return in the tests we have described as if they were observed from a sample of stock returns. The results of this "simulated" test were virtually identical to those reached using real data, despite the fact that the simulated returns were *constructed* to obey the SML, that is, the true γ coefficients were $\gamma_0 = 0$, $\gamma_1 = \overline{r_M - r_f}$, and $\gamma_2 = 0$.[16]

This post mortem of the early test gets us back to square one. We can explain away the disappointing test results, but we have no positive results to support the CAPM-APT implications.

The next wave of tests was designed to overcome the measurement error problem that led to biased estimates of the SML. The innovation in these tests, pioneered by Black, Jensen, and Scholes (BJS),[17] was to use portfolios rather than individual securities. Combining securities into portfolios diversifies away most of the firm-specific part of returns, thereby enhancing the precision of the estimates of beta and the expected rate of return of the portfolio of securities. This mitigates the statistical problems that arise from measurement error in the beta estimates.

Testing the model with diversified portfolios rather than individual securities completes our retreat to the APT. Additionally, combining stocks into portfolios reduces the number of observations left for the second-pass regression. Suppose we group the 100 stocks into five portfolios of 20 stocks each. If the residuals of the 20 stocks in each portfolio are practically uncorrelated the variance of the portfolio residual will be about one-twentieth the residual variance of the average stock. Thus the portfolio beta in the first-pass regression will be estimated with far better accuracy. However, with portfolios of 20 stocks each we are left with only five observations for the second-pass regression.

To get the best of this tradeoff, we need to construct portfolios with the largest possible dispersion of beta coefficients. Other things equal, a regression yields more accurate estimates the more widely spaced the observations of the independent variables. We therefore will attempt to maximize the range of the independent variable of the second-pass regression, the portfolio betas. Rather than allocate 20 stocks to each portfolio randomly, we first rank stocks by betas.

---

[14]Although the APT strictly applies only to well-diversified portfolios, the discussion in Chapter 8 shows that optimization in a single-index market will generate strong pressure on single securities to satisfy the mean-beta equation as well.

[15]Merton H. Miller and Myron Scholes, "Rate of Return in Relation to Risk: A Reexamination of Some Recent Findings," in Michael C. Jensen, ed., *Studies in the Theory of Capital Markets* (New York: Praeger, 1972).

[16]In statistical tests, there are two possible errors: Type I and Type II. A Type I error means that you reject a null hypothesis (e.g., a hypothesis that beta does not affect expected returns) when it is actually true. This is sometimes called a "false positive," in which you incorrectly decide that a relationship exists when it actually does not. The probability of this error is called the *significance* level of the test statistic. Thresholds for rejection of the null hypothesis are usually chosen to limit the probability of Type I error to below 5 percent. Type II error is a "false negative," in which a relationship actually does exist, but you fail to detect it. The *power* of a test equals (1 − probability of Type II). Miller and Scholes's experiment showed that early tests of the CAPM had low power.

[17]Fischer Black, Michael C. Jensen, and Myron Scholes, "The Capital Asset Pricing Model: Some Empirical Tests," in Michael C. Jensen, ed., *Studies in the Theory of Capital Markets* (New York: Praeger, 1972).

Portfolio 1 is formed from the 20 highest-beta stocks and portfolio 5 the 20 lowest-beta stocks. A set of portfolios with small nonsystematic components, e_P, and widely spaced betas will yield reasonably powerful tests of the SML.

Fama and MacBeth[18] (FM) used this methodology to verify that the observed relationship between average excess returns and beta is indeed linear and that nonsystematic risk does not explain average excess returns. Using 20 portfolios constructed according to the BJS methodology, FM expanded the estimation of the SML equation to include the square of the beta coefficient (to test for linearity of the relationship between returns and betas) and the estimated standard deviation of the residual (to test for the explanatory power of nonsystematic risk). For a sequence of many subperiods they estimated for each subperiod the equation

$$r_i = \gamma_0 + \gamma_1\beta_i + \gamma_1\beta_i^2 + \gamma_3\sigma(e_i) \tag{11.5}$$

The term γ_2 measures potential nonlinearity of return, and γ_3 measures the explanatory power of nonsystematic risk, $\sigma(e_i)$. According to the CAPM, both γ_2 and γ_3 should have coefficients of zero in the second-pass regression.

FM estimated equation 11.5 for every month of the period January 1935 through June 1968. The results are summarized in Table 11.1, which shows average coefficients and t-statistics for the overall period as well as for three subperiods. FM observed that the coefficients on residual standard deviation (nonsystematic risk), denoted by γ_3, fluctuated greatly from month to month and its t-statistics were insignificant despite large average values. Thus, the overall test results were reasonably favourable to the security market line of the CAPM (or perhaps more accurately of the APT that FM actually tested). But time has not been favourable to the CAPM since.

CC 3

CONCEPT CHECK

a. According to the CAPM, what are the predicted values of γ_0, γ_1, γ_2, and γ_3 in the Fama and MacBeth regressions for the period 1946–1955?

b. What would you conclude if you performed the Fama and MacBeth tests and found that the coefficients on β^2 and $\sigma(e)$ were positive?

TABLE 11.1

Summary of Fama and MacBeth (1973) Study (all rates in basis points per month)

Period	1935–1968	1935–1945	1946–1955	1956–June 1968
Av. r_f	13	2	9	26
Av. $\gamma_0 - r_f$	8	10	8	5
Av. $t(\gamma_0 - r_f)$	.20	.11	.20	.10
Av. $r_M - r_f$	130	195	103	95
Av. γ_1	114	118	209	34
Av. $t(\gamma_1)$	1.85	.94	2.39	.34
Av. γ_2	−26	−9	−76	0
Av. $t(\gamma_2)$	−.86	−.14	−2.16	0
Av. γ_3	516	817	−378	960
Av. $t(\gamma_3)$	1.11	.94	−.67	1.11
Av. R-squared	.31	.31	.32	.29

Source: Eugene Fama and James MacBeth, "Risk, Return, and Equilibrium: Empirical Tests," *Journal of Political Economy* 81 (March 1973).

---

[18]Eugene Fama and James MacBeth, "Risk, Return, and Equilibrium: Empirical Tests," *Journal of Political Economy* 81 (March 1973).

Recent replications of the FM test show that results deteriorate in later periods (since 1968). Worse, even for the FM period, 1935–1968, when the equally weighted NYSE-stock portfolio they used as the market index is replaced with the more appropriate value-weighted index, results turn against the model. In particular, the slope of the SML is clearly too flat. Thus, although the CAPM seems *qualitatively* correct in that β matters and $\sigma(e_i)$ does not, empirical tests do not validate its *quantitative* predictions. Nonetheless, some recent studies suggest that the CAPM can be rejected neither theoretically nor empirically, even though some of its theoretical foundations might be shaky.[19]

11.2   TESTS OF THE MULTIFACTOR CAPM AND APT

Three types of factors are likely candidates to augment the market risk factor in a multifactor SML: (1) factors that hedge consumption against uncertainty in prices of important consumption categories (e.g., housing or energy) or general inflation; (2) factors that hedge future investment opportunities (e.g., interest rates or the market risk premium); and (3) factors that hedge missing assets from the market index (e.g., labour income or private business).

As we learned from Merton's ICAPM (Chapter 7), these extramarket sources of risk will command a risk premium if there is significant demand to hedge them. We begin with the third source because there is little doubt that nontraded assets in the personal portfolios of investors affect demand for traded risky assets. Hence, a factor representing these assets, that is, one correlated with their returns, should affect risk premiums.

Labour Income

The major factors in the omitted asset category are labour income and private business. Taking on labour income first, Mayers[20] viewed each individual as being endowed with labour income, but able to trade only securities and an index portfolio. His model creates a wedge between betas measured against the traded, index portfolio, and betas measured against the true market portfolio, which includes aggregate labour income. The result of his model is an SML that is flatter than the simple CAPM's. Most of this income is positively correlated with the market index, and it has substantial value compared to the market value of the securities in the market index. Its absence from the index pushes the slope of the observed SML (return vs. beta measured against the index) below the return of the index portfolio.[21]

If the value of labour income is not perfectly correlated with the market-index portfolio, then the possibility of negative returns to labour will represent a source of risk not fully captured by the index. But suppose investors can trade a portfolio that is correlated with the return on aggregate human capital. Then their hedging demands against the risk to the value of their

---

[19]See H. Levy, "The CAPM: Alive and Well, A Review and Synthesis," *European Financial Management* 16 (2010), 43–71. Also, a recent study by Levy and Roll shows that slight variations in estimated parameters, well within estimation error bounds, are sufficient to make the market proxy efficient. Thus, many conventional market proxies could be perfectly consistent with the CAPM and useful for estimating expected returns. See M. Levy and R. Roll, "The Market Portfolio May Be Mean-Variance Efficient After All," *Review of Financial Studies* 23 (2010), 2464–2491.

[20]David Mayers, "Nonmarketable Assets and Capital Market Equilibrium Under Uncertainty," in *Studies in the Theory of Capital Markets*, ed. Michael C. Jensen (New York: Praeger, 1972), pp. 223–48.

[21]Asset betas on the index portfolio are likely positively correlated with their betas on the omitted asset (e.g., aggregate labour income). Therefore, the coefficient on asset beta in the SML regression (of returns on index beta) will be downward-biased, resulting in a slope smaller than average R_M. In equation 7.11 the observed beta of most assets will be larger than the true beta whenever $\beta_{iM} > \beta_{iH}\dfrac{\sigma_H^2}{\sigma_M^2}$.

human capital might meaningfully influence security prices and risk premiums. If so, human capital risk (or some empirical proxy for it) can serve as an additional factor in a multifactor SML. Stocks with a positive beta on the value of labour exaggerate exposure to this risk factor; therefore, they will command lower prices, or, equivalently, provide a larger-than-CAPM risk premium. Thus, by adding this factor, the SML becomes multidimensional.

Jagannathan and Wang (JW)[22] used the rate of change in aggregate labour income as a proxy for changes in the value of human capital. In addition to the standard security betas estimated using the value-weighted stock market index, which we denote β^{vw}, JW also estimated the betas of assets with respect to labour income growth, which we denote β^{labour}. Finally, they considered the possibility that business cycles affect asset betas, an issue that has been examined in a number of other studies.[23] These may be viewed as *conditional* betas, as their values are conditional on the state of the economy. JW used the spread between the yields on low- and high-grade corporate bonds as a proxy for the state of the business cycle and estimate asset betas relative to this business cycle variable; we denote this beta as β^{prem}.

With the estimates of these three betas for several stock portfolios, JW estimated a second-pass regression that includes firm size (market value of equity, denoted ME):

$$E(R_i) = c_0 + c_{size} \log(ME) + c_{vw}\beta^{vw} + c_{prem}\beta^{prem} + c_{labour}\beta^{labour} \tag{11.6}$$

Jagannathan and Wang test their model with 100 portfolios that are designed to spread securities on the basis of size and beta. Stocks are sorted to 10 size portfolios, and the stocks within each size portfolio are further sorted by beta into 10 subportfolios, resulting in 100 portfolios in total. Table 11.2 shows a subset of the various versions of the second-pass estimates. The first two lines in the table show the coefficients and t-statistics of a test of the CAPM along the lines of the Fama and MacBeth tests introduced in the previous section. The result is a sound rejection of the model, as the coefficient on beta is negative, albeit not significant.

The next two lines show that the model is not helped by the addition of the size factor. The dramatic increase in R-squared (from 1.35 percent to 57 percent) shows that size explains variations in average returns quite well while beta does not. Substituting the default premium and labour income for size results in a similar increase in explanatory power (R-squared of 55 percent), but the CAPM expected return–beta relationship is not redeemed. The default premium is significant, while labour income is borderline significant. When we add size as well, in the last two lines, we find it is no longer significant and only marginally increases explanatory power.

Despite the clear rejection of the CAPM, we do learn two important facts from Table 11.2. First, conventional first-pass estimates of security betas are greatly deficient. They clearly do not fully capture the cyclicality of stock returns and thus do not accurately measure the systematic risk of stocks. This can actually be interpreted as good news for the CAPM, in that it may be possible to replace the simple beta with better estimates of systematic risk and transfer the explanatory power of instrumental variables such as size and the default premium to the index rate of return. Second, and more relevant to the work of Jagannathan and Wang, is the conclusion that human capital will be important in any version of the CAPM that better explains the systematic risk of securities.

---

[22]Ravi Jagannathan and Zhenyu Wang, "The Conditional CAPM and the Cross-Section of Expected Returns," *Journal of Finance* 51 (March 1996), pp. 3–54.

[23]For example, Campbell Harvey, "Time-Varying Conditional Covariances in Tests of Asset Pricing Models," *Journal of Financial Economics* 24 (October 1989), pp. 289–317; Wayne Ferson and Campbell Harvey, "The Variation of Economic Risk Premiums," *Journal of Political Economy* 99 (April 1991), pp. 385–415; and Wayne Ferson and Robert Korajczyk, "Do Arbitrage Pricing Models Explain the Predictability of Stock Returns?" *Journal of Business* 68 (July 1995), pp. 309–49.

TABLE 11.2

Evaluation of
Various CAPM
Specifications

Coefficient	c_0	c_{vw}	c_{prem}	c_{labour}	c_{size}	R-Squared
A. The Static CAPM Without Human Capital						
Estimate	1.24	−.10				1.35
t-value	5.16	−.28				
Estimate	2.08	−.32			.11	57.56
t-value	5.77	−.94			−2.30	
B. The Conditional CAPM with Human Capital						
Estimate	1.24	−.40	.34	.22		55.21
t-value	4.10	−.88	1.73	2.31		
Estimate	1.70	−.40	.20	.10	−.07	64.73
t-value	4.14	−1.06	2.72	2.09	−1.30	

Note: This table gives the estimates for the cross-sectional regression model.

$$E(R_{it}) = c_0 + c_{size} \log(ME_i) + c_{vw}\beta_\gamma^{vw} + c_{prem}\beta_\gamma^{prem} + c_{labour}\beta_i^{labour}$$

with either a subset or all of the variables. Here, R_{it} is the return on portfolio i ($i = 1, 2, \ldots, 100$) in month t (July 1963–December 1990), R_t^{vw} is the return on the value-weighted index of stocks, R_{t-1}^{prem} is the yield spread between low- and high-grade corporate bonds, and R_{t-1}^{labour} is the growth rate in per capita labour income. The β_γ^{vw} is the slope coefficient in the OLS regression of R_{it} on a constant and R_γ^{vw}. The other betas are estimated in a similar way. The portfolio size, $\log(ME_i)$, is calculated as the equally weighted average of the logarithm of the market value (in millions of dollars) of the stocks in portfolio i. The regression models are estimated by using the Fama-MacBeth procedure. The "corrected t-values" take sampling errors in the estimated betas into account. All R-squareds are reported as percentages.

Private (Nontraded)

Whereas Jagannathan and Wang focus on labour income, Heaton and Lucas[24] combine various data sets to estimate the importance of proprietary business. We expect that private-business owners will reduce demand for traded securities that are positively correlated with their specific entrepreneurial income and increase holdings of securities that provide a hedge against negative shocks to their entrepreneurial income. If this effect is sufficiently important, aggregate demand for traded securities will be determined in part by the covariance with aggregate noncorporate business income. The risk premium on securities with high covariance with noncorporate business income should be commensurately higher.

Consistently with theory, Heaton and Lucas find that households with higher investments in private business do in fact reduce the fraction of total wealth invested in equity. Table 11.3 presents excerpts from their regression analysis, in which allocation of the overall portfolio to stocks is the dependent variable. The share of private business in total wealth (labelled "relative business") receives negative and statistically significant coefficients in these regressions. Notice also the negative and significant coefficient on risk attitude based on a self-reported degree of risk aversion.

Finally, Heaton and Lucas extend Jagannathan and Wang's equation to include the rate of change in proprietary-business wealth. They find that this variable also is significant and improves the explanatory power of the regression. Here, too, the market rate of return does not help explain the rate of return on individual securities and, hence, this implication of the CAPM must still be rejected.

---

[24] John Heaton and Debora Lucas, "Portfolio Choice and Asset Prices: The Importance of Entrepreneurial Risk," *Journal of Finance* 55, no. 3 (June 2000), pp. 1163–98.

TABLE 11.3
Determinants of
Stock Holdings

	Share of Stock in Assets		
	Stock Relative to Liquid Assets	**Stock Relative to Financial Assets**	**Stock Relative to Total Assets**
Intercept	.71 (14.8)	.53 (21.28)	.24 (10.54)
Total income $\times\ 10^{-10}$	−1.80 (−.435)	−.416 (−.19)	−1.72 (−.85)
Net worth $\times\ 10^{-10}$	2.75 (.895)	5.04 (3.156)	7.37 (5.02)
Relative business	−.14 (−4.34)	−.50 (−29.31)	−.32 (−20.62)
Age of respondent	-7.94×10^{-4} (−1.26)	-6.99×10^{-5} (−.21)	2.44×10^{-3} (−4.23)
Risk attitude	−.05 (−4.74)	−.02 (−3.82)	−.02 (−4.23)
Relative mortgage	.05 (1.31)	.43 (20.90)	.30 (16.19)
Relative pension	.07 (1.10)	−.41 (−11.67)	−.31 (−9.60)
Relative real estate	−.04 (−1.41)	−.44 (−27.00)	−.31 (−20.37)
Adjusted R-squared	.03	.48	.400

Note: *t*-statistics in parentheses.

Source: John Heaton and Debora Lucas, "Portfolio Choice and Asset Prices: The Importance of Entrepreneurial Risk," *Journal of Finance* 55, no. 3 (June 2000), pp. 1163–98. Reprinted by permission of the publisher, Blackwell Publishing, Inc.

11.3   EARLY VERSIONS OF THE MULTIFACTOR CAPM AND APT

The multifactor CAPM and APT are elegant theories of how exposure to systematic risk factors should influence expected returns, but they provide little guidance concerning which factors (sources of risk) ought to result in risk premiums. A test of this hypothesis would require three stages:

1. Specification of risk factors
2. Identification of portfolios that hedge these fundamental risk factors
3. Test of the explanatory power and risk premiums of the hedge portfolios

A Macro Factor Model

Chen, Roll, and Ross[25] identify several possible variables that might proxy for systematic factors:

IP = growth rate in industrial production

EI = changes in expected inflation measured by changes in short-term (T-bill) interest rates

UI = unexpected inflation defined as the difference between actual and expected inflation

---

[25]Nai-Fu Chen, Richard Roll, and Stephen Ross, "Economic Forces and the Stock Market," *Journal of Business* 59 (1986).

CG = unexpected changes in risk premiums measured by the difference between the returns on corporate Baa-rated bonds and long-term government bonds

GB = unexpected changes in the term premium measured by the difference between the returns on long- and short-term government bonds

With the identification of these potential economic factors, Chen, Roll, and Ross skipped the procedure of identifying factor portfolios (the portfolios that have the highest correlation with the factors). Instead, by using the factors themselves, they implicitly assumed that factor portfolios exist that can proxy for the factors. They use these factors in a test similar to that of Fama and MacBeth.

A critical part of the methodology is the grouping of stocks into portfolios. Recall that in the single-factor tests, portfolios were constructed to span a wide range of betas to enhance the power of the test. In a multifactor framework the efficient criterion for grouping is less obvious. Chen, Roll, and Ross chose to group the sample stocks into 20 portfolios by size (market value of outstanding equity), a variable known to be associated with stock returns.

They first used five years of monthly data to estimate the factor betas of the 20 portfolios in 20 first-pass regressions:

$$r = a + \beta_M r_M + \beta_{IP}IP + \beta_{EI}EI + \beta_{UI}UI + \beta_{CG}CG + \beta_{GB}GB + e \qquad (11.7a)$$

where M stands for the stock market index. Chen, Roll, and Ross used as the market index both the value-weighted NYSE index (VWNY) and the equally weighted NYSE index (EWNY).

Using the 20 sets of first-pass estimates of factor betas as the independent variables, they now estimated the second-pass regression (with 20 observations):

$$r = \gamma_0 + \gamma_M\beta_M + \gamma_{IP}\beta_{IP} + \gamma_{EI}\beta_{EI} + \gamma_{UI}\beta_{UI} + \gamma_{CG}\beta_{CG} + \gamma_{GB}\beta_{CG} + e \qquad (11.7b)$$

where the gammas become estimates of the risk premiums on the factors.

Chen, Roll, and Ross ran this second-pass regression for every month of their sample period, reestimating the first-pass factor betas once every 12 months. The estimated risk premiums (the values for the parameters γ) were averaged over all the second-pass regressions.

Note in Table 11.4 that the two market indices EWNY (equally weighted index of NYSE) and VWNY (value-weighted NYSE index) are not significant (their t-statistics of 1.218 and $-.633$ are less than 2). Note also that the VWNY factor has the wrong sign in that it seems to imply a negative market-risk premium. Industrial production (IP), the risk premium on corporate bonds (CG), and unanticipated inflation (UI) are the factors that appear to have significant explanatory power.

TABLE 11.4

Economic Variables and Pricing, Multivariate Approach (percent per month × 10)

A	EWNY	IP	EI	UI	CG	GB	Constant
	5.021	14.009	−.128	−.848	.130	−5.017	6.409
	(1.218)	(3.774)	(−1.666)	(−2.541)	(2.855)	(−1.576)	(1.848)
B	VWNY	IP	EI	UI	CG	GB	Constant
	−2.403	11.756	−.123	−.795	8.274	−5.905	10.713
	(−.633)	(3.054)	(−1.600)	(−2.376)	(2.972)	(−1.879)	(2.755)

Note: VWNY = return on the value-weighted NYSE index; EWNY = return on the equally weighted NYSE index; IP = monthly growth rate in industrial production; EI = change in expected inflation; UI = unanticipated inflation; CG = unanticipated change in the risk premium (Baa and under return − long-term government bond return); GB = unanticipated change in the term structure (long-term government bond return − Treasury-bill rate). Note that t-statistics are in parentheses.

Source: Modified from Nai-Fu Chen, Richard Roll, and Stephen Ross, "Economic Forces and the Stock Market," *Journal of Business* 59 (1986). Reprinted by permission of the publisher, The University of Chicago.

A variant of the Chen, Roll, and Ross study was replicated with Canadian data by Otuteye,[26] but the results were not as satisfactory. While the exogenous variables were more or less similar to the ones used by Chen, Roll, and Ross, the market index (the return on a value-weighted portfolio of Canadian stocks) turned out to be highly significant, in contrast to the U.S. results.

<table>
<tr><td>**11.4**</td><td></td></tr>
</table>

THE FAMA-FRENCH-TYPE FACTOR MODELS

The multifactor models that currently occupy centre stage are the three-factor model introduced by Fama and French (FF) and its close relatives. The systematic factors in the FF model are firm size and book-to-market ratio (B/M) as well as the market index.[27] These additional factors are empirically motivated by the observations that historical-average returns on stocks of small firms and on stocks with high ratios of book equity to market equity (B/M) are higher than predicted by the security market line of the CAPM. However, FF did more than document the empirical role of size and B/M in explaining rates of return. They also introduced a general method to generate factor portfolios, and applied their method to these firm characteristics. Exploring this innovation is a useful way to understand the empirical building blocks of a multifactor asset pricing model.

Suppose you find, as FF did, that stock market capitalization (or market cap) seems to predict alpha values in a CAPM equation. On average, the smaller the market cap, the greater the alpha of a stock. This finding would add size to the list of anomalies that refute the CAPM.

But suppose you believe that size varies with sensitivity to changes in future investment opportunities. Then, what appears as alpha in a single factor CAPM is really an extramarket source of risk in a multifactor CAPM. If this sounds far-fetched, here's a story: When investors anticipate a market downturn, they adjust their portfolios to minimize their exposure to losses. Suppose that small stocks generally are harder hit in down markets, akin to a larger beta in bad times. Then investors will avoid such stocks in favour of the less-sensitive stocks of larger firms. This would explain a risk premium to small size beyond the beta on contemporaneous market returns. An "alpha" for size may instead be an ICAPM risk premium for assets with greater sensitivity to deterioration in future investment opportunities.

The FF innovation is a method to quantify the size risk premium. Recall that the distribution of corporate size is asymmetric: a few big and many small corporations. Since the NYSE is the exchange where bigger stocks trade, FF first determine the median size of NYSE stocks. They use this median to classify all traded U.S. stocks (NYSE + AMEX + Nasdaq) as big or small and create one portfolio from big stocks and another from small stocks. Finally, each of these portfolios is value-weighted for efficient diversification.

As in the APT, FF construct a zero-net-investment size-factor portfolio by going long the small- and going short the big-stock portfolio. The return of this portfolio, called SMB (small minus big), is simply the return on the small-stock portfolio minus the return on the big-stock portfolio. If size is priced, then this portfolio will exhibit a risk premium. Because the SMB is practically well diversified (on the order of 4,000 stocks), it joins the market index portfolio in a two-factor APT model with size as the extramarket source of risk. In the two-factor SML, the risk premium on any asset should be determined by its loadings (betas) on the two factor portfolios. This is a testable hypothesis.

---

[26]E. Otuteye, "How Economic Forces Explain Canadian Stock Returns," *Canadian Investment Review* 4 (Spring 1991), pp. 93–99; and "The Arbitrage Pricing Dichotomy," *Canadian Investment Review*, Winter 1998.

[27]A four-factor model that also accounts for recent stock returns (a *momentum factor*) is also widely used. This factor is examined in a Canadian study by S. Desrosiers, J.-F. L'Her, and W. Hached, "Seize the Momentum of Global Equity Industries," *Canadian Investment Review*, Spring 2006, pp. 18–24.

FF use this approach to form both size and book-to-market ratio (B/M) factors. To create these two extramarket risk factors, they double-sort stocks, by both size and B/M. They break the U.S. stock population into three groups according to B/M ratio: the bottom 30 percent (low), the middle 40 percent (medium), and the top 30 percent (high).[28] Now six portfolios are created on the basis of the intersections of the size and B/M sorts: Small/Low; Small/Medium; Small/High; Big/Low; Big/Medium; Big/High. Each of these six portfolios is value-weighted.

The returns on the Big and Small portfolio are

$$R_S = \frac{1}{3}(R_{S/L} + R_{S/M} + R_{S/H}); \quad R_B = \frac{1}{3}(R_{B/L} + R_{B/M} + R_{B/H})$$

Similarly, the returns on the high and low (Value and Growth[29]) portfolios are

$$R_H = \frac{1}{2}(R_{S/H} + R_{B/H}); \quad R_L = \frac{1}{2}(R_{S/L} + R_{B/L})$$

The returns of the zero-net-investment factors SMB (small minus big, i.e., Long Small and Short Big), and HML (high minus low, i.e., Long High B/M and Short Low B/M) are created from these portfolios:

$$R_{SMB} = R_S - R_B; \quad R_{HML} = R_H - R_L$$

We measure the sensitivity of individual stocks to the factors by estimating the factor betas from first-pass regressions of stock excess returns on the excess return of the market index as well as on RSMB and RHML. These factor betas should, as a group, predict the total risk premium.

Therefore, the Fama-French three-factor asset pricing model is[30]

$$E(r_i) - r_f = a_i + b_i[E(r_M) - r_f] + s_i E[\text{SMB}] + h_i E[\text{HML}] \tag{11.8}$$

The coefficients b_i, s_i, and h_i are the betas (also called *loadings* in this context) of the stock on the three factors. If these are the only risk factors, excess returns on all assets should be fully explained by risk premiums due to these factor loadings. In other words, if these factors fully explain asset returns, the intercept of the equation should be zero.

Goyal[31] surveys asset pricing tests. He applies equation 11.8 to the returns of 25 portfolios of all U.S. stocks sorted by size and B/M ratio. Figure 11.1 shows the average actual return of each portfolio over the period 1946–2010 against returns predicted by the CAPM (panel A) and by the FF three-factor model. In this test, the FF model provides a clear improvement over the CAPM.

Notice in panel A that the predicted returns are almost the same for all portfolios. This is indeed a weakness of tests with portfolios that are sorted on size and B/M, but not on beta. As a result, all portfolios have betas near 1.0. Adding a sort on beta to a 5 × 5 sort on size and B/M will raise the number of portfolios from 25 to 125. This is unwieldy; but advances in econometrics and computing power will allow these types of tests to advance.

---

[28]FF could have experimented with "optimal" break points for the three B/M groups, but such an approach might quickly give way to data mining.

[29]High-B/M stocks are called "value" assets because, for the large part, their market values derive from assets already in place. Low-B/M stocks are called "growth" stocks because their market values derive from expected growth in future cash flows. One needs to assume high growth to justify the prices at which the assets trade. At the same time, however, a firm that falls on hard times will see its market price fall and its B/M ratio rise. So some of the so-called value firms may actually be distressed firms. This subgroup of the value-firm portfolio might well account for the value premium of the B/M factor.

[30]You might wonder why we subtract the risk-free rate from the return on the market portfolio, but not from the SMB and HML returns. The reason is that the SMB and HML factors are *already* differences in returns between two assets. They are return premiums of one portfolio relative to another (small minus big or high minus low), just as the market risk premium is the excess return of the index relative to the risk-free asset.

[31]Amit Goyal, "Empirical Cross Sectional Asset Pricing: A Survey," *Financial Markets and Portfolio Management* 26 (2012), pp. 3–38.

Figure 11.1

CAPM versus the Fama and French model. The figure plots the average actual returns against returns predicted by CAPM and the FF model for 25 size- and book-to-market double-sorted portfolios.

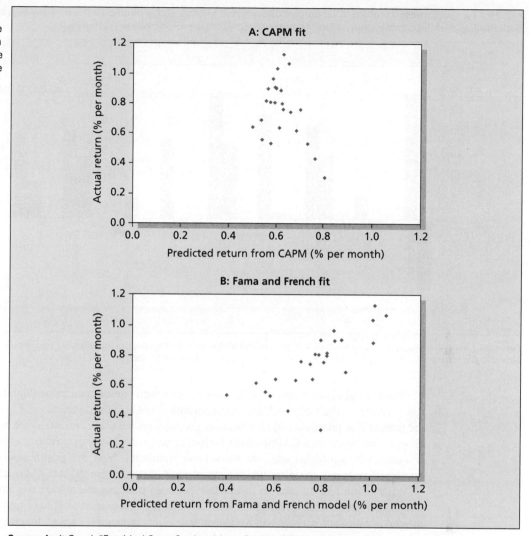

Source: Amit Goyal, "Empirical Cross Sectional Asset Pricing: A Survey," *Financial Markets and Portfolio Management* (2012) 26: 3–38.

Size and B/M as Risk Factors

Liew and Vassalou[32] show that returns on style portfolios (HML or SMB) seem to predict GDP growth, and thus may in fact capture some aspects of business cycle risk. Each bar in Figure 11.2 is the average difference in the return on the HML or SMB portfolio in years before good GDP growth versus in years with poor GDP growth. Positive values mean the portfolio does better in years prior to good macroeconomic performance. The predominance of positive values leads them to conclude that the returns on the HML and SMB portfolios are positively related to future growth in the macroeconomy, and so may be proxies for business cycle risk. Thus, at least part of the size and value premiums may reflect rational rewards for greater risk exposure.

---

[32]J. Liew and M. Vassalou, "Can Book-to-Market, Size and Momentum Be Risk Factors That Predict Economic Growth?" *Journal of Financial Economics* 57 (2000), pp. 221–45.

Figure 11.2 Difference in return to factor portfolios in year prior to above-average versus below-average GDP growth. Both SMB and HML portfolio returns tend to be higher in years preceding better GDP growth.

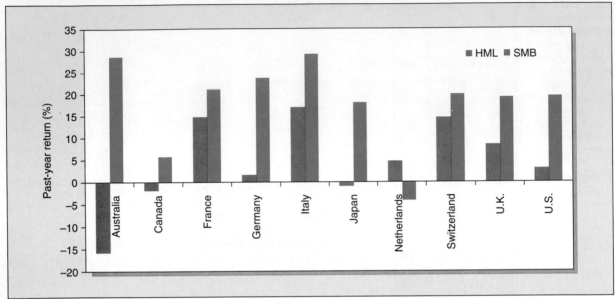

Source: J. Liew and M. Vassalou, "Can Book-to-Market, Size and Momentum Be Risk Factors That Predict Economic Growth?" *Journal of Financial Economics* 57 (2000), pp. 221–45. © 2000 with permission from Elsevier Science.

Petkova and Zhang[33] also try to tie the average return premium on value (high B/M) portfolios to risk premiums. Their approach uses a conditional CAPM. In the conventional CAPM, we treat both the market risk premium and firm betas as given parameters. In contrast, as we noted earlier in the chapter, the conditional CAPM allows both of these terms to vary over time, and possibly to covary. If a stock's beta is higher when the market risk premium is high, this positive association leads to a "synergy" in its risk premium, which is the product of its incremental beta and market risk premium.

What might lead to such an association between beta and the market risk premium? Zhang[34] focuses on irreversible investments. He notes that firms classified as value firms (with high book-to-market ratios) on average will have greater amounts of tangible capital. Investment irreversibility puts such firms more at risk for economic downturns, because in a severe recession they will suffer from excess capacity from assets already in place. In contrast, growth firms are better able to deal with a downturn by deferring investment plans. The greater exposure of high-book-to-market firms to recessions will result in higher down-market betas. Moreover, some evidence suggests that the market risk premium also is higher in down markets, when investors are feeling more economic pressure and anxiety. The combination of these two factors might give rise to a positive correlation between the beta of high-B/M firms and the market risk premium.

To quantify these notions, Petkova and Zhang attempt to fit both beta and the market risk premium to a set of "state variables," that is, variables that summarize the state of the economy. These are:

$$\text{DIV} = \text{market dividend yield}$$
$$\text{DEFLT} = \text{default spread on corporate bonds (Baa} - \text{Aaa rates)}$$
$$\text{TERM} = \text{term structure spread (10-year} - \text{1-year Treasury rates)}$$
$$\text{TB} = \text{1-month T-bill rate}$$

[33]Ralitsa Petkova and Lu Zhang, "Is Value Riskier Than Growth?" *Journal of Financial Economics* 78 (2005), pp. 187–202.
[34]Lu Zhang, "The Value Premium," *Journal of Finance* 60 (2005), pp. 67–103.

They estimate a first-pass regression, but first substitute these state variables for beta as follows:

$$r_{HML} = \alpha + \beta r_{Mt} + e_i$$
$$= \alpha + \underbrace{[b_0 + b_1 DIV_t + b_2 DEFLT_t + b_3\,TERM_t + b_4\,TB_t]}r_{Mt} + e_i$$
$$= \beta_t \ \leftarrow \textit{Time-varying beta}$$

The strategy is to estimate parameters b_0 through b_4 and then fit beta using the values of the four state variables at each date. In this way, they can estimate beta in each period.

Similarly, one can estimate directly the determinants of a time-varying market risk premium, using the same set of state variables:

$$r_{Mkt,t} - r_{ft} = c_0 + c_1 DIV_t + c_2 DEFLT_t + c_3 TERM_t + c_4 TB_t + e_t$$

The fitted value from this regression is the estimate of the market risk premium.

Finally, Petkova and Zhang examine the relationship between beta and the market risk premium. They define the state of economy by the size of the premium. A peak is defined as the periods with the 10 percent lowest risk premiums; a trough has the 10 percent highest risk premiums. The results, presented in Figure 11.3, support the notion of a countercyclical value beta: the beta of the HML portfolio is negative in good economies, meaning that the beta of value stocks (high B/M) is less than that of growth stocks (low B/M), but the reverse is true in recessions. While the covariance between the HML beta and the market risk premium is not sufficient to explain by itself the average return premium on value portfolios, it does suggest that at least part of the explanation may be a rational risk premium.

Behavioural Explanations

On the other side of the debate, several authors make the case that the value premium is a manifestation of market irrationality. The essence of the argument is that analysts tend to extrapolate recent performance too far into the future, and thus to overestimate the value of firms with good recent performance. When the market realizes its mistake, the prices of these firms fall. Thus, on average, "glamour firms," characterized by recent good performance, high prices, and lower book-to-market ratios, tend to underperform "value firms" because their high prices reflect excessive optimism relative to those lower book-to-market firms.

Figure 11.3

HML beta in different economic states. The beta of the HML portfolio is higher when the market risk premium is higher.

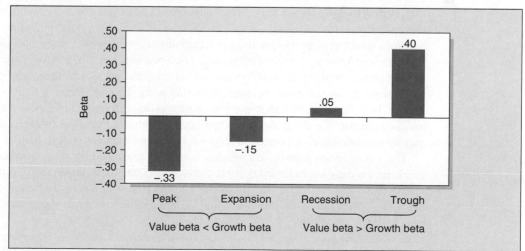

Source: Ralitsa Petkova and Lu Zhang, "Is Value Riskier Than Growth?" *Journal of Financial Economics* 78 (2005), pp. 187–202. © 2005 with permission from Elsevier Science.

Figure 11.4 The book-to-market ratio reflects past growth, but not future growth prospects. B/M tends to fall with income growth experienced at the end of a five-year period, but actually increases slightly with future income growth rates.

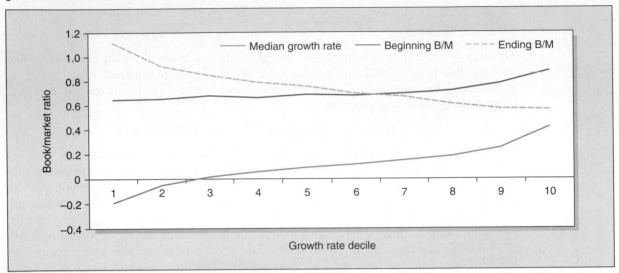

Source: L.K.C. Chan, J. Karceski, and J. Lakonishok, "The Level and Persistence of Growth Rates," *Journal of Finance* 58 (April 2003), pp. 643–84. Reprinted by permission of the publisher, Blackwell Publishing, Inc.

Figure 11.4, from a study by Chan, Karceski, and Lakonishok,[35] makes the case for overreaction. Firms are sorted into deciles based on income growth in the past five years. By construction, the growth rates uniformly increase from the first through the tenth quintile. The book-to-market ratio for each decile at the *end* of the five-year period (the dashed line) tracks recent growth very well. B/M falls steadily with growth over past five years. This is evidence that *past* growth is extrapolated and then impounded in price. High past growth leads to higher prices and lower B/M ratios.

But B/M at the *beginning* of a five-year period shows little or even an opposite relationship to subsequent growth (the solid coloured line). In other words, the firms with lower B/M (glamour firms) experience no better average future income growth than other firms. The implication is that the market ignores evidence that past growth cannot be extrapolated far into the future. Book-to-market may reflect past growth better than future growth, consistently with extrapolation error.

More direct evidence supporting extrapolation error is provided by La Porta, Lakonishok, Shleifer, and Vishny,[36] who examine stock price performance when actual earnings are released to the public. Firms are classified as growth versus value stocks, and the stock price performance at earnings announcements for four years following the classification date is then examined. Figure 11.5 demonstrates that growth stocks underperform value stocks surrounding these announcements. We conclude that when news of actual earnings is released to the public, the market is relatively disappointed in stocks it has been pricing as growth firms.

The value-versus-growth contrast has been also examined by Athanassakos with Canadian stock return data for 1985–2005.[37] He finds that value stocks consistently outperform growth stocks in bull as well as in bear markets. The difference in returns between value and growth stocks is termed the "value premium" and is shown to be strong and significant.

[35]L.K.C. Chan, J. Karceski, and J. Lakonishok, "The Level and Persistence of Growth Rates," *Journal of Finance* 58 (April 2003), pp. 643–84.
[36]R. La Porta, J. Lakonishok, A. Shleifer, and R. W. Vishny, "Good News for Value Stocks," *Journal of Finance* 51 (1997), pp. 1715–42.
[37]G. Athanassakos, "Value Versus Growth Stock Returns and the Value Premium: The Canadian Experience 1985–2005," *Canadian Journal of Administrative Sciences* 26 (2009), pp. 109–121.

Figure 11.5

Value minus glamour returns surrounding earnings announcements, 1971–1992. Announcement effects are measured for each of four years following classification as a value versus a growth firm.

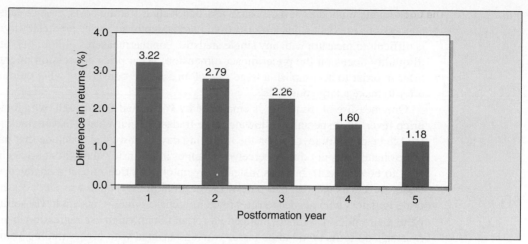

Source: R. La Porta, J. Lakonishok, A. Shleifer, and R. W. Vishny, "Good News for Value Stocks," *Journal of Finance* 51 (1997), pp. 1715–42. Reprinted by permission of the publisher, Blackwell Publishing, Inc.

Momentum: A Fourth Factor

Since the seminal Fama-French three-factor model was introduced, a fourth factor has come to be added to the standard controls for stock return behaviour: a momentum factor. As we first saw in Chapter 9, Jegadeesh and Titman uncovered a tendency for good or bad performance of stocks to persist over several months, a sort of momentum property.[38] Carhart added this momentum effect to the three-factor model as a tool to evaluate mutual fund performance.[39] He found that much of what appeared to be the alpha of many mutual funds could in fact be explained as due to their loadings or sensitivities to market momentum. The original Fama-French model augmented with a momentum factor has become a common four-factor model used to evaluate abnormal performance of a stock portfolio.

Of course, this additional factor presents further conundrums of interpretation. To characterize the original Fama-French factors as reflecting obvious sources of risk is already a bit of a challenge. A momentum factor seems even harder to position as reflecting a risk–return tradeoff.

11.5   LIQUIDITY AND ASSET PRICING

In Chapter 7 we saw that an important extension of the CAPM incorporates considerations of asset liquidity. Unfortunately, measuring liquidity is far from trivial. The effect of liquidity on an asset's expected return is composed of two factors:

1. Transaction costs that are dominated by the bid–asked spread that dealers set to compensate for losses incurred when trading with informed traders.

2. Liquidity *risk* resulting from covariance between *changes* in asset liquidity cost with both *changes* in market-index liquidity cost and with market-index rates of return.

Both of these factors are unobservable and their effect on equilibrium rates of return is difficult to estimate.

---

[38]Narasimhan Jegadeesh and Sheridan Titman, "Returns to Buying Winners and Selling Losers: Implications for Stock Market Efficiency," *Journal of Finance* 48 (March 1993), pp. 65–91.

[39]Mark M. Carhart, "On Persistence in Mutual Fund Performance," *Journal of Finance* 52 (March 1997), pp. 57–82.

Liquidity embodies several characteristics such as trading costs, ease of sale, necessary price concessions to effect a quick transaction, market depth, and price predictability. Consequently, it is difficult to measure with any single statistic. Popular measures of liquidity, or, more precisely, illiquidity, focus on the price impact dimension: What price concession might a seller have to offer in order to accomplish a large sale of an asset or, conversely, what premium must a buyer offer to make a large purchase?

One measure of illiquidity is employed by Pástor and Stambaugh, who look for evidence of price reversals, especially following large trades.[40] Their idea is that if stock price movements tend to be partially reversed on the following day, then we can conclude that part of the original price change was not due to perceived changes in intrinsic value (these price changes would not tend to be reversed), but was instead a symptom of price impact associated with the original trade. Reversals suggest that part of the original price change was a concession on the part of trade initiators who needed to offer higher purchase prices or accept lower selling prices to complete their trades in a timely manner. Pástor and Stambaugh use regression analysis to show that reversals do in fact tend to be larger when associated with higher trading volume—exactly the pattern that one would expect if part of the price move is a liquidity phenomenon. They run a first-stage regression of returns on lagged returns and trading volume. The coefficient on the latter term measures the tendency of high-volume trades to be accompanied by larger reversals.

Another measure of illiquidity, proposed by Amihud, also focuses on the association between large trades and price movements.[41] His measure is

$$\text{ILLIQ} = \text{Monthly average of daily} \left[\frac{\text{Absolute value(Stock return)}}{\text{Dollar volume}} \right]$$

This measure of illiquidity is based on the price impact per dollar of transactions in the stock and can be used to estimate both liquidity cost and liquidity risk.

Finally, Sadka uses trade-by-trade data to devise a third measure of liquidity.[42] He begins with the observation that part of price impact, a major component of illiquidity cost, is due to asymmetric information. (Turn back to our discussion of liquidity in Chapter 7 for a review of asymmetric information and the bid–asked spread.) He then uses regression analysis to break out the component of price impact that is due to information issues. The liquidity of firms can wax or wane as the prevalence of informationally motivated trades varies, giving rise to liquidity risk.

Any of these liquidity measures can be averaged over stocks to devise measures of market-wide illiquidity. Given market illiquidity, we can then measure the "liquidity beta" of any individual stock (the sensitivity of returns to changes in market liquidity) and estimate the impact of liquidity risk on expected return. If stocks with high-liquidity betas have higher average returns, we conclude that liquidity is a "priced factor," meaning that exposure to it offers higher expected return as compensation for the risk.

Pástor and Stambaugh conclude that liquidity risk is in fact a priced factor, and that the risk premium associated with it is quantitatively significant. They sort portfolios into deciles based on liquidity beta and then compute the average alphas of the stocks in each decile using two models that *ignore* liquidity: the CAPM and the Fama-French three-factor model. Figure 11.6 shows that the alpha computed under either model rises substantially across liquidity–beta deciles, clear evidence that when controlling for other factors, average return rises along with liquidity risk. Not surprisingly, the relationship between liquidity risk and alpha across deciles is more regular for the Fama-French model, as it controls for a wider range of other influences on average return.

Pástor and Stambaugh also test the impact of the liquidity beta on alpha computed from a four-factor model (that also controls for momentum), with results extremely similar to those in

---

[40]L. Pástor and R. F. Stambaugh, "Liquidity Risk and Expected Stock Returns," *Journal of Political Economy* 111 (2003), pp. 642–85.

[41]Yakov Amihud, "Illiquidity and Stock Returns: Cross-Section and Time-Series Effects," *Journal of Financial Markets* 5 (2002), pp. 31–56.

[42]Ronnie Sadka, "Momentum and Post-Earnings Announcement Drift Anomalies: The Role of Liquidity Risk," *Journal of Financial Economics* 80 (2006), pp. 309–49.

Figure 11.6

Alphas of value-weighted portfolios sorted on liquidity betas.

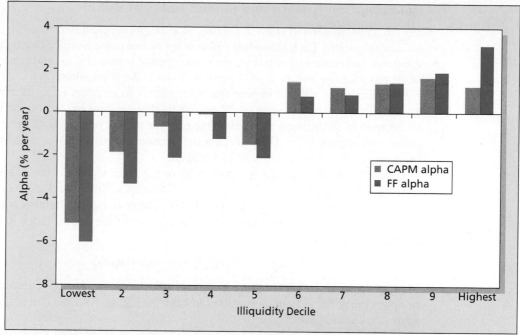

Source: L. Pástor and R. F. Stambaugh, "Liquidity Risk and Expected Stock Returns," *Journal of Political Economy* 111 (2003), pp. 642–85, Table 4.

Figure 7.4 in Chapter 7. In fact, they suggest that liquidity risk factor may account for a good part of the apparent profitability of the momentum strategy.

Acharya and Pedersen use Amihud's measure to test for price effects associated with the average *level* of illiquidity as well as a liquidity risk premium.[43] They demonstrate that expected stock returns depend on the average level of illiquidity. (Figure 7.4 shows a similar result.) But Acharya and Pedersen demonstrate that stock returns depend on several liquidity betas as well: the sensitivity of individual stock illiquidity to market illiquidity; the sensitivity of stock returns to market illiquidity; and the sensitivity of stock illiquidity to market return. They conclude that adding these liquidity effects to the conventional CAPM increases our ability to explain expected asset returns.[44]

11.6   CONSUMPTION-BASED ASSET PRICING AND THE EQUITY PREMIUM PUZZLE

In a classic article, Mehra and Prescott observed that historical excess returns on risky assets in the United States are too large to be consistent with economic theory and reasonable levels of risk aversion.[45] This observation has come to be known as the *equity premium puzzle*. The debate about the equity premium puzzle suggests that forecasts of the market risk premium should be lower than historical averages. The question of whether past returns provide a guideline to future returns is sufficiently important to justify stretching the scope of our discussions of equilibrium in capital markets.

---

[43]V. V. Acharya and L. H. Pedersen, "Asset Pricing with Liquidity Risk," *Journal of Financial Economics* 77 (2005), pp. 375–410.
[44]The increase in liquidity is often cited as one of the major motivations for cross-listing Canadian stocks in the United States. For a skeptical view of the benefits of cross-listing, see the two studies by Usha Mittoo, "Globalization and the Value of U.S. Listing: Revisiting Canadian Evidence," *Journal of Banking and Finance* 27 (2003), pp. 1629–1661, and "The Value of U.S. Listing," *Canadian Investment Review*, Fall 2003, pp. 31–37.
[45]Jarnish Mehra and Edward Prescott, "The Equity Premium: A Puzzle," *Journal of Monetary Economics*, March 1985.

Consumption Growth and Market Rates of Return

The ICAPM is derived from a lifetime consumption/investment plan of a representative consumer/investor. Each individual's plan is set to maximize a utility function of lifetime consumption, and consumption/investment in each period is based on age and current wealth, as well as the risk-free rate and the market portfolio's risk and risk premium.

The consumption model implies that what matters to investors is not their wealth per se, but their lifetime flow of consumption. There can be slippage between wealth and consumption due to variation in factors such as the risk-free rate, the market portfolio risk premium, or prices of major consumption items. Therefore, a better measure of consumer well-being than wealth is the consumption flow that such wealth can support.

Given this framework, the generalization of the basic CAPM is that instead of measuring security risk on the basis of the covariance of returns with the market return (a measure that focuses only on wealth), we are better off using the covariance of returns with aggregate consumption. Hence, we would expect the risk premium of the market index to be related to that covariance as follows:

$$E(r_M) - r_f = A\text{Cov}(r_M, r_C) \tag{11.9}$$

where A depends on the average coefficient of risk aversion and r_C is the rate of return on a consumption-tracking portfolio constructed to have the highest possible correlation with growth in aggregate consumption.[46]

The first wave of attempts to estimate consumption-based asset pricing models used consumption data directly rather than returns on consumption-tracking portfolios. By and large, these tests found the CCAPM no better than the conventional CAPM in explaining risk premiums. Looked at another way, the term "equity premium puzzle" refers to the fact that using reasonable estimates of A, the covariance of consumption growth with the market-index return, $\text{Cov}(r_M, r_C)$, is far too low to justify observed historical-average excess returns on the market-index portfolio, shown on the left hand of equation 11.9.[47] The risk premium puzzle says in effect that historical excess returns are too high and/or our inferences about risk aversion are too low.

Recent research improves the quality of estimation in several ways. First, rather than using consumption growth directly, it uses consumption-tracking portfolios. The available (infrequent) data on aggregate consumption is used only to construct the consumption-tracking portfolio. The frequent and accurate data on the return on these portfolios may then be used to test the asset pricing model. (On the other hand, any inaccuracy in the construction of the consumption-mimicking portfolios will muddy the relationship between asset returns and consumption risk.)

For example, a recent study by Jagannathan and Wang focuses on year-over-year fourth-quarter consumption and employs a consumption-tracking portfolio.[48] Table 11.5, excerpted from their study, shows that the Fama-French factors are in fact associated with consumption betas as well as excess returns. The top panel contains familiar results: moving across each row, we see that higher book-to-market ratios are associated with higher average returns. Similarly, moving down each column, we see that larger size generally implies lower average returns. The novel results are in the lower panel: a high book-to-market ratio is associated with higher consumption

---

[46]This equation is analogous to that for the risk premium in the conventional CAPM, that is, $E(r_M) - r_f = A\text{Cov}(r_M, r_M) = A\text{Var}(r_M)$. In the one-factor version of Merton's ICAPM, this equation for the market risk premium would also be valid. In the multifactor version of the ICAPM, however, the market is no longer mean-variance-efficient, so the risk premium of the market index will not be proportional to its variance. The APT also implies a linear relationship between risk premium and covariance with relevant factors, but it is silent about the slope of the relationship because it avoids assumptions about utility.

[47]Notice that the conventional CAPM does not pose such problems. In the CAPM, $E(r_M) - r_f = A\text{Var}(r_M)$. A risk premium of .085 (8.5 percent) and a standard deviation of .20 (20 percent, or variance of .04) imply a coefficient of risk aversion of .085/.04 = 2.125, which is quite plausible.

[48]Ravi Jagannathan and Yong Wang, "Lazy Investors, Discretionary Consumption, and the Cross-Section of Stock Returns," *Journal of Finance* 62 (August 2006), pp. 1623–61.

TABLE 11.5

Annual Excess Returns and Consumption Betas

	Book-to-Market		
Size	Low	Medium	High
Average annual excess returns*(%)			
Small	6.19	12.24	17.19
Medium	6.93	10.43	13.94
Big	7.08	8.52	9.50
Consumption beta*			
Small	3.46	4.26	5.94
Medium	2.88	4.35	5.71
Big	3.39	2.83	4.41

*Average annual excess returns on the 25 Fama-French portfolios from 1954 to 2003. Consumption betas estimated by the time series regression

$$R_{i,t} = \alpha_i + \beta_{i,c}g_{ct} + \varepsilon_{i,t}$$

where R_{it} is the excess return over the risk-free rate and g_{ct} is annual consumption growth calculated using fourth-quarter consumption data.

Source: Ravi Jagannathan and Yong Wang, "Lazy Investors, Discretionary Consumption, and the Cross-Section of Stock Returns," *Journal of Finance* 62 (August 2006), pp. 1623–61.

beta, and larger firm size is associated with lower consumption beta. The suggestion is that the explanatory power of the Fama-French factors for average returns may in fact reflect differences in consumption risk of those portfolios. Figure 11.7 shows that the average returns of the 25 Fama-French portfolios are strongly associated with their consumption betas. Other tests reported by Jagannathan and Wang show that the CCAPM explains returns even better than the Fama-French three-factor model, which in turn is superior to the single-factor CAPM.

Moreover, the standard CCAPM focuses on a representative consumer/investor, thereby ignoring information about heterogeneous investors with different levels of wealth and consumption habits. To improve the model's power to explain returns, some newer studies allow for several classes of

Figure 11.7 Cross-section of stock returns: Fama-French 25 portfolios, 1954–2003. Annual excess returns and consumption betas. This figure plots the average annual excess returns on the 25 Fama-French portfolios and their consumption betas. Each two-digit number represents one portfolio. The first digit refers to the size quintile (1 = smallest, 5 = largest), and the second digit refers to the book-to-market quintile (1 = lowest, 5 = highest).

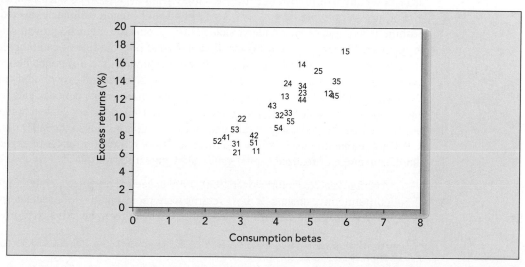

investors with differences in wealth and consumption behavior. For example, the covariance between market returns and consumption is far higher when we focus on the consumption risk of households that actually hold financial securities.[49] This observation mitigates the equity risk premium puzzle.

Expected Versus Realized Returns

Fama and French[50] offer one possible interpretation of the puzzle. They work with an expanded sample period, 1872–1999, and report the average risk-free rates, average return on equity (represented by the S&P 500 index), and the resultant risk premium for the overall period and subperiods:

Period	Risk-Free Rate	S&P 500 Return	Equity Premium
1872–1999	4.87	10.97	6.10
1872–1949	4.05	8.67	4.62
1950–1999	6.15	14.56	8.41

The big increase in the average excess return on equity after 1949 suggests that the equity premium puzzle is really a creature of modern times.

Fama and French (FF) suspect that estimating the risk premium from average realized returns may be the problem. They use the constant-growth dividend discount model (see an introductory finance text or Chapter 16) to estimate expected returns and find that for the period 1872–1949, the dividend discount model (DDM) yields similar estimates of the *expected* risk premium as the average *realized* excess return. But for the period 1950–1999, the DDM yields a much smaller risk premium, which suggests that the high average excess return in this period may have exceeded the returns investors actually expected to earn at the time.

In the constant-growth DDM, the expected capital gains rate on the stock will equal the growth rate of dividends. As a result, the expected total return on the firm's stock will be the sum of dividend yield (dividend/price) plus the expected dividend growth rate, g:

$$E(r) = \frac{D_1}{P_0} + g \tag{11.10}$$

where D_1 is end-of-year dividends and P_0 is the current price of the stock. FF treat the S&P 500 as representative of the average firm, and use equation 11.10 to produce estimates of $E(r)$.

For any sample period, $t = 1, \ldots, T$, Fama and French estimate expected return from the arithmetic average of the dividend yield (D_t/P_{t-1}) plus the dividend growth rate ($g_t = D_t/D_{t-1}$). In contrast, the *realized* return is the dividend yield plus the rate of capital gains ($P_t/P_{t-1} - 1$). Because the dividend yield is common to both estimates, the difference between the expected and realized return equals the difference between the dividend growth and capital gains rates. While dividend growth and capital gains were similar in the earlier period, capital gains significantly exceeded the dividend growth rate in modern times. Hence, FF conclude that the equity premium puzzle may be due at least in part to unanticipated capital gains in the latter period.

FF argue that dividend growth rates produce more reliable estimates of expected capital gains than the average of realized capital gains. They give three reasons:

1. Average realized returns over 1950–1999 exceeded the internal rate of return on corporate investments. If those returns were representative of expectations, we would have to conclude that firms were willingly engaging in negative NPV investments.

---

[49]C. J. Malloy, T. Moskowitz, and A. Vissing-Jørgensen, "Long-Run Stockholder Consumption Risk and Asset Returns," *Journal of Finance* 64 (December 2009), pp. 2427–80.

[50]Eugene Fama and Kenneth French, "The Equity Premium," *Journal of Finance* 57, no. 2 (2002).

2. The statistical precision of estimates from the DDM are far higher than those using average historical returns. The standard error of the estimates of the risk premium from realized returns is about 2.5 times the standard error from the dividend discount model (see table below).

3. The **reward-to-variability ratio** derived from the DDM is far more stable than that derived from realized returns. If risk aversion remains the same over time, we would expect the Sharpe ratio to be stable.

The evidence for the second and third points is shown in the table below, in which estimates from the dividend model ("DDM") and from realized returns ("Realized") are shown side by side.

Period	Mean Return		Standard Error		t-Statistic		Share Ratio	
	DDM	Realized	DDM	Realized	DDM	Realized	DDM	Realized
1872–1999	4.03	6.10	1.14	1.65	3.52	3.70	.22	.34
1872–1949	4.35	4.62	1.76	2.20	2.47	2.10	.23	.24
1950–1999	3.54	8.41	1.03	2.45	3.42	3.43	.21	.51

FF's study provides a simple explanation of the equity premium puzzle, namely that observed rates of return in the recent half-century were unexpectedly high. It also implies that forecasts of future excess returns will be lower than past averages. (Coincidentally, their study was published in 1999 and so far appears prophetic in the light of the results since then.)

Work by Goetzmann and Ibbotson[51] lends support to Fama and French's argument. Goetzmann and Ibbotson combine research that extends data on rates of return on stocks and long-term corporate bonds back to 1792. Summary statistics for these values between 1792 and 1925 are as follows:

	Arithmetic Average	Geometric Average	Standard Deviation
NYSE total return	7.93%	6.99%	14.64%
U.S. bond yields	4.17%	4.16%	4.17%

These statistics suggest a risk premium much lower than the historical average for 1926–2005 (much less 1950–1999), the period that produces the equity premium puzzle.[52] Thus, the period for which Fama and French claim realized rates were unexpected is actually relatively short in historical perspective.

Survivorship Bias

The equity premium puzzle emerged from long-term averages of U.S. stock returns. There are reasons to suspect that these estimates of the risk premium are subject to **survivorship bias**, as the United States has arguably been the most successful capitalist system in the world, an outcome that probably would not have been anticipated several decades ago. Jorion and Goetzmann[53] assembled a database of capital appreciation indices for the stock markets of 39 countries over the period 1926–1996. Figure 11.8 shows that U.S. equities had the highest real return of all countries, at 4.3 percent annually, versus a median of .8 percent for other countries. Moreover,

[51]William N. Goetzmann and Roger G. Ibbotson, "History and the Equity Risk Premium," working paper, Yale University, October 18, 2005.
[52]The short-term risk-free rate is a lot more difficult to assess, because short-term bonds in this period were quite risky and average rates exceeded the yields on long-term corporate bonds.
[53]Philippe Jorion and William N. Goetzmann, "Global Stock Markets in the Twentieth Century," *Journal of Finance* 54, no. 3 (June 1999).

Figure 11.8
Real returns on global stock markets. The figure displays average real returns for 39 markets over the period 1921 to 1996. Markets are sorted by years of existence. The graph shows that markets with long histories typically have higher returns. An asterisk indicates that the market suffered a long-term break.

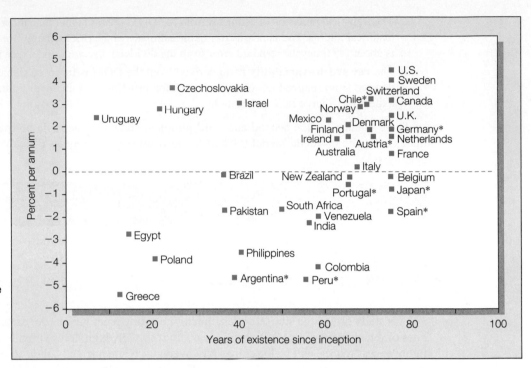

unlike the United States, many other countries have had equity markets that actually closed, either permanently or for extended periods.

The implication of these results is that using average U.S. data may induce a form of survivorship bias to our estimate of expected returns, since unlike many other countries the United States has never been a victim of such extreme problems. Estimating risk premiums from the experience of the most successful country and ignoring the evidence from stock markets that did not survive for the full sample period will impart an upward bias in estimates of expected returns. The high realized equity premium obtained for the United States may not be indicative of required returns.

As an analogy, think of the effect of survivorship bias in the mutual fund industry. We know that some companies regularly close down their worst-performing mutual funds. If performance studies include only mutual funds for which returns are available during an entire sample period, the average returns of the funds that make it into the sample will be reflective of the performance of long-term survivors only. With the failed funds excluded from the sample, the average measured performance of mutual fund managers will be better than one could reasonably expect from the full sample of managers. Think back to the boxed article in Chapter 9, "How to Guarantee a Successful Market Newsletter." If one starts many newsletters with a range of forecasts, and continues only the newsletters that turned out to have successful advice, then it will *appear* from the sample of survivors that the average newsletter had forecasting skill.

Extensions to the CAPM May Resolve the Equity Premium Puzzle

Constantinides[54] argues that the standard CAPM can be extended to account for observed excess returns by relaxing some of its assumptions, in particular by recognizing that consumers face uninsurable and idiosyncratic income shocks—for example, loss of employment. The prospect of such events is higher in economic downturns, which goes a long way toward explaining both the

---

[54]George M. Constantinides, "Understanding the Equity Risk Premium Puzzle," working paper, University of Chicago, August 2005.

unconditional moments (means and variances) of asset returns and their variation along the business cycle.

In addition, life-cycle considerations are important and often overlooked. Borrowing constraints grow important when put in the context of the life cycle. The imaginary "representative consumer" who holds all stock and bond market wealth does not face borrowing constraints. Young consumers, however, do face meaningful ones. Constantinides traces their impact on the equity premium, the demand for bonds, and on the limited participation of many consumers in the capital markets. Finally, he shows that adding habit formation to the conventional utility function helps explain higher risk premiums than those that would be justified by the covariance of stock returns with aggregate consumption growth. He argues that integrating the notions of habit formation, incomplete markets, the life cycle, borrowing constraints, and other sources of limited stock market participation is a promising approach to the study of the prices of assets and their returns, both theoretically and empirically, within the class of rational asset-pricing models.

Liquidity and the Equity Premium Puzzle

We've seen that liquidity risk is potentially important in explaining the cross-section of stock returns. The illiquidity premium may be on the same order of magnitude as the market risk premium. Therefore, the common practice of treating the average excess return on a market index as an estimate of a risk premium per se is almost certainly too simplistic. Part of that average excess return is almost certainly compensation for *liquidity* risk rather than just the (systematic) *volatility* of returns. If this is recognized, the equity premium puzzle may be less of a puzzle than it seems at first.

Behavioural Explanations of the Equity Premium Puzzle

Barberis and Huang[55] explain the puzzle as an outcome of irrational investor behaviour. The key elements of their approach are loss aversion and narrow framing, two well-known features of decision making under risk in experimental settings. Narrow framing is the idea that investors evaluate every risk they face in isolation. Thus, investors will ignore low correlation of the risk of a stock portfolio with other components of wealth, and therefore require a higher risk premium than rational models would predict. Combined with loss aversion, investor behaviour will generate large risk premiums despite the fact that traditionally measured risk aversion is plausibly low. (See Chapter 10 for more discussion of such behavioural biases.)

Models that incorporate these effects can generate a large equilibrium equity risk premium and a low and stable risk-free rate, even when consumption growth is smooth and only weakly correlated with the stock market. Moreover, they can do so for parameter values that correspond to plausible predictions about attitudes to independent monetary gambles. The analysis for the equity premium also has implications for a closely related portfolio puzzle, the *stock market participation puzzle*. They suggest some possible directions for future research.

The approach of Barberis and Huang, when accounting for heterogeneity of preferences, can explain why a segment of the population that predictably would participate in the stock market despite frictions and other rational explanations, still avoids it. Narrow framing also explains the disconnect between consumption growth and market rates of return. The assessment of stock market return in isolation ignores the limited impact on consumption via smoothing and other hedges. Loss aversion that exaggerates disutility of losses relative to a reference point magnifies this effect. The development of empirical literature on the tenets of these theories may determine the validity and implications of the equity premium puzzle.

---

[55]Nicholas Barberis and Ming Huang, "The Loss Aversion/Narrow Framing Approach to the Equity Premium Puzzle," in *Handbook of Investments: Equity Risk Premium*, Rajnish Mehra, ed. (Amsterdam: Elsevier, 2008), pp. 199–229.

SUMMARY

1. Although the single-factor expected return–beta relationship has not yet been confirmed by scientific standards, its use is already commonplace in economic life.

2. Early tests of the single-factor CAPM rejected the SML, finding that nonsystematic risk did explain average security returns.

3. Later tests controlling for the measurement error in beta found that nonsystematic risk does not explain portfolio returns but also that the estimated SML is too flat compared with what the CAPM would predict.

4. Roll's critique implied that the usual CAPM test is a test only of the mean-variance efficiency of a prespecified market proxy and therefore that tests of the linearity of the expected return–beta relationship do not bear on the validity of the model.

5. Tests of the mean-variance efficiency of professionally managed portfolios against the benchmark of a prespecified market index conform with Roll's critique in that they provide evidence of the efficiency of the prespecified market index.

6. Empirical evidence suggests that most professionally managed portfolios are outperformed by market indices, which lends weight to acceptance of the efficiency of those indices and hence the CAPM.

7. Work with economic factors suggests that factors such as unanticipated inflation do play a role in the expected return–beta relationship of security returns.

8. Tests of the single-index model, accounting for human capital and cyclical variations in asset betas, are far more consistent with the single-index CAPM and APT. These tests suggest that macroeconomic variables are not necessary to explain expected returns. Moreover, anomalies such as effects of size and book-to-market ratios disappear once these variables are accounted for.

9. The equity premium puzzle originates from the observation that equity returns exceeded the risk-free rate to an extent that is inconsistent with reasonable levels of risk aversion—at least when average rates of return are taken to represent expectations. Fama and French show that the puzzle emerges from excess returns over the last 50 years. Alternative estimates of expected returns using the dividend growth model instead of average returns suggest that excess returns on stocks were high because of unexpected large capital gains. The study implies that future excess returns will be lower than realized in recent decades.

10. Early research on consumption-based capital asset pricing models was disappointing, but more recent work is far more encouraging. In some studies, consumption betas explain average portfolio returns as well as the Fama-French three-factor model. These results support Fama and French's conjecture that their factors proxy for more fundamental sources of risk.

KEY EQUATIONS

(11.1) $E(r_i) = r_f + \beta_i[E(r_M) - r_f]; \qquad r_{it} - r_{ft} = a_i + b_i(r_{Mt} - r_{ft}) + e_{it}$

(11.2) $\overline{r_i - r_f} = \gamma_0 + \gamma_1 b_i \qquad i = 1, \ldots, 100; \qquad \gamma_0 = 0 \qquad \gamma_1 = \overline{r_M - r_f}$

(11.3) $\overline{r_i - r_f} = \gamma_0 + \gamma_1 b_i + \gamma_2 \sigma^2(e_i); \qquad \gamma_0 = 0 \qquad \gamma_1 = \overline{r_M - r_f} \qquad \gamma_2 = 0$

(11.4) $E(r_i) - E(r_Z) = \beta_i[E(r_E) - E(r_Z)]; \qquad r_i - r_Z = \gamma_0 + \gamma_1 \times \text{Estimated } \beta_i$

(11.5) $r_i = \gamma_0 + \gamma_1 \beta_i + \gamma_1 \beta_i^2 + \gamma_3 \sigma(e_i)$

(11.6) $E(R_i) = c_0 + c_{\text{size}} \log(\text{ME}) + c_{\text{vw}} \beta^{\text{vw}} + c_{\text{prem}} \beta^{\text{prem}} + c_{\text{labour}} \beta^{\text{labour}}$

(11.7a) $r = a + \beta_M r_M + \beta_{\text{IP}} \text{IP} + \beta_{\text{EI}} \text{EI} + \beta_{\text{UI}} \text{UI} + \beta_{\text{CG}} \text{CG} + \beta_{\text{GB}} \text{GB} + e$

(11.7b) $r = \gamma_0 + \gamma_M \beta_M + \gamma_{\text{IP}} \beta_{\text{IP}} + \gamma_{\text{EI}} \beta_{\text{EI}} + \gamma_{\text{UI}} \beta_{\text{UI}} + \gamma_{\text{CG}} \beta_{\text{CG}} + \gamma_{\text{GB}} \beta_{\text{CG}} + e$

(11.8) $E(r_i) - r_f = a_i + b_i[E(r_M) - r_f] + s_i E[\text{SMB}] + h_i E[\text{HML}]$

(11.9) $E(r_M) - r_f = A\text{Cov}(r_M, r_C)$

(11.10) $E(r) = \dfrac{D_1}{P_0} + g$

PROBLEMS

Mc Graw Hill Education **connect**™   **Practise and learn online with Connect.**

1. Suppose you find, as research indicates, that in the cross-section regression of the CCAPM, the coefficients of factor loadings on the Fama-French model are significant predictors of average return factors (in addition to consumption beta). How would you explain this phenomenon?

2. Search the Internet for a recent graph of market volatility. What does this history suggest about the history of consumption growth?

The following annual excess rates of return (%) were obtained for nine individual stocks and a market index:

		Stocks								
Year	Market Index	A	B	C	D	E	F	G	H	I
1	29.65	33.88	−25.20	36.48	42.89	−39.89	39.67	74.57	40.22	90.19
2	−11.91	−49.87	24.70	−25.11	−54.39	44.92	−54.33	−79.76	−71.58	−26.64
3	14.73	65.14	−25.04	18.91	−39.86	−3.91	−5.69	26.73	14.49	18.14
4	27.68	14.46	−38.64	−23.31	−.72	−3.21	92.39	−3.82	13.74	.09
5	5.18	15.67	61.93	63.95	−32.82	44.26	−42.96	101.67	24.24	8.98
6	25.97	−32.17	44.94	−19.56	69.42	90.43	76.72	1.72	77.22	72.38
7	10.64	−31.55	−74.65	50.18	74.52	15.38	21.95	−43.95	−13.40	28.95
8	1.02	−23.79	47.02	−42.28	28.61	−17.64	28.83	98.01	28.12	39.41
9	18.82	−4.59	28.69	−.54	2.32	42.36	18.93	−2.45	37.65	94.67
10	23.92	−8.03	48.61	23.65	26.26	−3.65	23.31	15.36	80.59	52.51
11	−41.61	78.22	−85.02	−.79	−68.70	−85.71	−45.64	2.27	−72.47	−80.26
12	−6.64	4.75	42.95	−48.60	26.27	13.24	−34.34	−54.47	−1.50	−24.46

3. Perform the first-pass regressions and tabulate the summary statistics.

4. Specify the hypotheses for a test of the second-pass regression for the SML.

5. Perform the second-pass SML regression by regressing the average excess return of each portfolio on its beta.

6. Summarize your test results and compare them to the reported results in the text.

7. Group the nine stocks into three portfolios, maximizing the dispersion of the betas of the three resultant portfolios. Repeat the test and explain any changes in the results.

8. Explain Roll's critique as it applies to the tests performed in problems 3 to 7.

9. Plot the capital market line (CML), the nine stocks, and the three portfolios on a graph of average returns versus standard deviation. Compare the mean-variance efficiency of the three portfolios and the market index. Does the comparison support the CAPM?

Suppose that, in addition to the market factor that has been considered in problems 3 to 9, a second factor is considered. The values of this factor for years 1 to 12 were as follows:

Year	% Change in Factor Value	Year	% Change in Factor Value
1	−9.84	7	−3.52
2	6.46	8	8.43
3	16.12	9	8.23
4	−16.51	10	7.06
5	17.82	11	−15.74
6	−13.31	12	2.03

10. Perform the first-pass regressions as Chen, Roll, and Ross did and tabulate the relevant summary statistics. (*Hint*: Use a multiple regression as in a standard spreadsheet package. Estimate the betas of the 12 stocks on the two factors.)

11. Specify the hypothesis for a test of a second-pass regression for the two-factor SML.

12. Do the data suggest a two-factor economy?

13. Can you identify a factor portfolio for the second factor?

14. Suppose you own your own business, which now makes up about half your net worth. On the basis of what you have learned in this chapter, how would you structure your portfolio of financial assets?

The following problems are based on questions that have appeared in past CFA examinations.

15. Identify and briefly discuss three criticisms of beta as used in the capital asset pricing model.

16. Richard Roll, in an article on using the CAPM to evaluate portfolio performance, indicated that it may not be possible to evaluate portfolio management ability if there is an error in the benchmark used.

    a. In evaluating portfolio performance, describe the general procedure, with emphasis on the benchmark employed.

    b. Explain what Roll meant by the benchmark error and identify the specific problem with this benchmark.

    c. Draw a graph that shows how a portfolio that has been judged as superior relative to a "measured" security market line (SML) can be inferior relative to the "true" SML.

    d. Assume that you are informed that a given portfolio manager has been evaluated as superior when compared to the Dow Jones Industrial Average, the S&P 500, and the NYSE Composite Index. Explain whether this consensus would make you feel more comfortable regarding the portfolio manager's true ability.

    e. Although conceding the possible problem with benchmark errors as set forth by Roll, some contend this does not mean the CAPM is incorrect, but only that there is a measurement problem when implementing the theory. Others contend that because of benchmark errors the whole technique should be scrapped. Take and defend one of these positions.

17. Bart Campbell, CFA is a portfolio manager who has recently met with a prospective client, Jane Black. After conducting a survey market line (SML) performance analysis using the Dow Jones Industrial Average as her market proxy, Black claims that her portfolio has experienced superior performance. Campbell uses the capital asset pricing model as an investment performance measure and finds that Black's portfolio plots below the SML. Campbell concludes that Black's apparent superior performance is a function of an incorrectly specified market proxy, not superior investment management. Justify Campbell's conclusion, by addressing the likely effects of an incorrectly specified market proxy on both beta and the slope of the SML.

Bond Prices and Yields

In the previous chapters on risk and return relationships, we have treated securities at a high level of abstraction. We have assumed implicitly that a prior, detailed analysis of each security had already been performed, and that its risk and return features have been assessed.

We turn now to specific analyses of particular security markets. We examine valuation principles, determinants of risk and return, and portfolio strategies commonly used within and across the various markets.

We begin by analyzing **debt securities**. A debt security is a claim on a specified periodic stream of income. Debt securities are often called *fixed-income securities* because they promise either a fixed stream of income or one that is determined according to a specified formula. These securities have the advantage of being relatively easy to understand because the payment formulas are specified in advance. Uncertainty about their cash flows is minimal as long as the issuer of the security is sufficiently creditworthy. That makes these securities a convenient starting point for our analysis of the universe of potential investment vehicles.

The bond is the basic debt security, and this chapter starts with an overview of the universe of bond markets, including Canada, provincial, corporate, and international bonds. We turn next to bond pricing, showing how bond prices are set in accordance with market interest rates and why bond prices change with those rates. Given this background, we can compare the myriad measures of bond returns such as yield to maturity, yield to call, holding-period return, or realized compound rate of return. We show how bond prices evolve over time, discuss certain tax rules that apply to debt securities, and show how to calculate after-tax returns. Finally, we consider the impact of default or credit risk on bond pricing and look at the determinants of credit risk and the default premium built into bond yields. Credit risk is central to both collateralized debt obligations and credit default swaps, so we examine these instruments as well.

12.1 BOND CHARACTERISTICS

A **bond** is a borrowing arrangement in which the borrower issues (sells) an IOU to the investor. The arrangement obligates the issuer to make specified payments to the bondholder on specified dates. A typical *coupon bond* obligates the issuer to make semiannual payments of interest, called coupon payments, to the bondholder for the life of the bond, and then to pay in addition the bond's **par value** (equivalently, **face value**) at the bond's maturity date. The **coupon rate** of the bond is the coupon payment divided by the bond's par value. The coupon rate, maturity date, and par value of the bond are part of the **bond indenture** contract between the issuer and the bondholder.

To illustrate, a bond with a par value of $1,000 and a coupon rate of 8 percent might be sold to a buyer for $1,000. The bondholder is then entitled to a payment of 8 percent of $1,000, or $80 per year, for the stated life of the bond, say 30 years. The $80 payment typically comes in two semiannual installments of $40 each. At the end of the 30-year life of the bond, the issuer also pays the $1,000 par value to the bondholder.

Bonds are usually issued with coupon rates set high enough to induce investors to pay par value to buy the bond. Sometimes, however, **zero-coupon bonds** are issued that make no coupon payments. In this case, investors receive par value at the maturity date, but they receive no interest payments until then: the bond has a coupon rate of zero. These bonds are issued at prices considerably below par value, and the investor's return comes solely from the difference between the issue price and the payment of par value at maturity. We will return to these bonds later.

Canada Bonds[1]

Bond Market Canada www.bondcan. com

Figure 12.1 is an excerpt from the listing of bond issues available online from the Web site CanadianFixedIncome.ca. Canada bond maturities range up to 30 years. The bonds are issued in denominations of $1,000 or more and make semiannual coupon payments.[2]

Some bonds are callable. These are easily identified in a listing such as Figure 12.1, because of a range of years appearing in the maturity date column. The first date is the time at which the bond is first callable; the second date is the maturity date of the bond. The bond may be called by the issuer at any coupon date in the call period, but it must be retired by the maturity date. No callable bonds appear in the figure.

The bond in Figure 12.1 (*bolded*) matures in September 1, 2017. Its coupon rate is 1.5 percent. Par value is $1,000; thus, the bond pays interest of $15 per year in two semiannual payments of $7.5. Payments are made in March and September of each year. The quote represents the best ask price available to investors at the closing of December 7, 2012.[3]

Although bonds are sold in denominations of $1,000 par value, the prices are quoted as a percentage of par value. Therefore, the ask price of the bond is 101.02 percent of par value or $1,010.20.

The columns labelled "Yield" show the yield to maturity on the bond. The yield to maturity is a measure of the average rate of return to an investor who purchases the bond for the quoted price and holds it until its maturity date. We will have much to say about yield to maturity below.

Bonds are generally traded over the counter, meaning that the market for the bonds is a loosely organized network of bond dealers linked by a computer quotation system. (See Chapter 3 for a comparison of exchange and OTC trading.) In practice, the bond market can be quite "thin," in that there are few investors interested in trading a particular bond at any particular time. On any day it

---

[1]Bonds issued by the U.S. government, the U.S. counterpart of Canada bonds, are known as *U.S. Treasury bonds*.
[2]Since 1995 all new issues of Canada bonds and T-bills are only in denominations of $1,000.
[3]Recall that the bid price is the price at which you can sell the bond to a dealer. The asked price, which is slightly higher, is the price at which you can buy the bond from a dealer.

Figure 12.1

Listings of
Canadian
bonds.

Closing Markets as of: 4:00 PM EST 07-December-12

Government of Canada Benchmarks

	Coupon	Eff. Maturity	Price	Yield
2 Year	1.000	2014 Nov 01	99.91	1.05
5 Year	**1.500**	**2017 Sep 01**	**101.02**	**1.28**
10 Year	2.750	2022 Jun 01	109.18	1.70
20 Year	5.750	2033 Jun 01	156.82	2.27
30 Year	4.000	2041 Jun 01	135.25	2.30

Active Corporates

	Coupon	Eff. Maturity	Price	Yield
Fairfax FinH	5.840	2022-Oct-14	105.74	5.09
GenwrthMIInc	5.680	2020-Jun-15	108.56	4.33
Royal Bank	**3.180**	**2020-Nov-02**	**103.12**	**2.06**
G-W Lifeco	5.691	2067-Jun-21	110.70	3.13
Sherrit Intl	7.500	2020-Sep-24	103.00	6.94

Active Provincials and Agencies

	Coupon	Eff. Maturity	Price	Yield
Ontario	4.750	2013-Jun-02	101.74	1.04
Ontario	3.150	2022-Jun-02	103.83	2.69
BC	3.700	2020-Dec-18	110.10	2.31
Ontario	1.900	2017-Sep-08	100.38	1.81
Alberta	1.750	2017-Jun-15	100.45	1.65

Active Strips

	Coupon	Eff. Maturity	Price	Yield
Manitoba	0.000	2014-Mar-05	98.52	1.22
TD Bank	0.000	2018-Jun-03	99.23	1.63
Bell CDA	0.000	2021-Apr-15	76.32	3.27
Bell CDA	0.000	2023-May-15	68.13	3.71
Hydro-Quebec	0.000	2020-Aug-15	81.28	2.72

Real Returns

	Coupon	Eff. Maturity	Price	Yield
CMHC	4.250	2016-Feb-01	108.86	1.36
Canada	1.750	2013-Mar-01	100.18	0.97
Canada	3.500	2013-Jun-01	101.17	1.00
Canada	5.250	2013-Jun-01	102.00	0.99
Canada	2.000	2013-Aug-01	100.63	1.01
Canada	2.500	2013-Sep-01	101.06	1.03

Source: Perimeter Financial site, http://www.pfin.ca/canadianfixedincome, accessed December 8, 2012.

might be difficult to find a buyer or seller for a particular issue, which introduces some "liquidity risk" into the bond market. It may be difficult to sell one's holdings quickly if the need arises.

Investing in
Bonds
www.investing
inbonds.com

Accrued Interest and Quoted Bond Prices The bond prices that you see quoted in the financial pages are not actually the prices that investors pay for the bond. This is because the quoted price does not include the interest that accrues between coupon payment dates.

If a bond is purchased between coupon payments, the buyer must pay the seller for accrued interest, the prorated share of the upcoming semiannual coupon. For example, if 40 days have passed since the last coupon payment, the seller is entitled to a payment of accrued interest of 40/365 of the annual coupon.[4] The sale, or *invoice price*, of the bond would equal the stated price plus the accrued interest.

EXAMPLE 12.1   Accrued Interest

Suppose that the coupon rate is 8 percent. Then the annual coupon payment is $80. Because 40 days have passed since the last coupon payment, the accrued interest on the bond is $80 × (40/365) = $8.76. If the quoted price of the bond is $990, then the invoice price will be $990 + $8.76 = $998.76.

The practice of quoting bond prices net of accrued interest explains why the price of a maturing bond is listed at $1,000 rather than $1,000 plus one coupon payment. A purchaser of an 8 percent coupon bond one day before the bond's maturity would receive $1,040 on the following day and so should be willing to pay a total price of $1,040 for the bond. In fact, $40 of that total payment constitutes the accrued interest for the preceding half-year period. The bond price is quoted net of accrued interest in the financial pages and thus appears as $1,000.

Corporate Bonds

Like the government, corporations borrow money by issuing bonds. Figure 12.1 also shows a sample of corporate bond listings from CanadianFixedIncome.ca. The data presented follow the same format as Government of Canada and provincial bond listings. For example, the Royal Bank 3.180 bond (*bolded*) pays a coupon rate of 3.180 percent and matures in 2020. Like government bonds, corporate bond listings quote the ask prices as well as the yield to maturity. Like government bonds, corporate bonds sell in units of $1,000 par value but are quoted as a percentage of par value.

Bonds issued in Canada today can be either *registered bonds* or *bearer bonds*. For registered bonds, the issuing firm keeps records of the owner of the bond and can mail interest cheques to him or her. Registration of bonds is clearly helpful to tax authorities in the enforcement of tax collection. In contrast, bearer bonds are traded without any record of ownership. The investor's physical possession of the bond certificate is the only evidence of ownership.

TD Bank
www.tdbank.com

Call Provisions on Corporate Bonds Many corporate bonds are issued with call provisions. The call provision allows the issuer to repurchase the bond at a specified *call price* before the maturity date. For example, if a company issues a bond with a high coupon rate when

---

[4]Alternatively, the accrued interest may be estimated by the formula

$$\text{Accrued interest} = \frac{\text{Annual coupon payment}}{2} \times \frac{\text{Days since last coupon payment}}{\text{Days separating coupon payments}}$$

market interest rates are high and interest rates later fall, the firm might like to retire the high coupon debt and issue new bonds at a lower coupon rate to reduce interest payments. This is called *refunding*.

The call price of a bond is commonly set at an initial level near par value plus one annual coupon payment. The call price falls as time passes, gradually approaching par value. Callable bonds typically come with a period of call protection, an initial time during which the bonds are not callable. Such bonds are referred to as *deferred callable bonds*.

The option to call the bond is valuable to the firm, allowing it to buy back the bonds and refinance at a lower interest rate when market rates fall. Of course, the firm's benefit is the bondholder's burden. Holders of called bonds forfeit their bonds for the call price, thereby giving up the prospect of an attractive rate of interest on their original investment. To compensate investors for this risk, callable bonds are issued with higher coupons and promised yields to maturity than noncallable bonds.

CC 1

CONCEPT CHECK

Suppose that a corporation issues two bonds with identical coupon rates and maturity dates. One bond is callable, however, whereas the other is not. Which bond will sell at a higher price?

Convertible Bonds   **Convertible bonds** give bondholders an option to exchange each bond for a specified number of shares of common stock of the firm. The *conversion ratio* gives the number of shares for which each bond may be exchanged. To see the value of this right, suppose a convertible bond that is issued at par value of $1,000 is convertible into 40 shares of a firm's stock. The current stock price is $20 per share, so the option to convert is not profitable now. Should the stock price later rise to $30, however, each bond may be converted profitably into $1,200 worth of stock. The *market conversion value* is the current value of the shares for which the bonds may be exchanged. At the $20 stock price, for example, the bond's conversion value is $800. The *conversion premium* is the excess of the bond value over its conversion value. If the bond were selling currently for $950, its premium would be $150.

Convertible bonds give their holders the ability to share in the price appreciation of the company's stock. Again, this benefit comes at a price; convertible bonds offer lower coupon rates and stated or promised yields to maturity than do nonconvertible bonds. At the same time, the actual return on the convertible bond may exceed the stated yield to maturity if the option to convert becomes profitable.

We discuss convertible and callable bonds further in Chapter 18.

Retractable and Extendible Bonds   Whereas the callable bond gives the issuer the option to retire the bond at the call date or to continue to the maturity date, the **retractable bond** gives the option to the bondholder. Thus, if the bond's coupon rate is below current market yields, the bondholder will choose to redeem the bond early, through retraction. An **extendible bond**, on the other hand, allows the bondholder to retain the bond for an additional period beyond maturity, which he or she will do if the coupon exceeds current rates. Retractable and extendible bonds are known as *puttable bonds* in the United States. These additional privileges granted to the bondholders are paid for by a slightly lower coupon.

There have also been retractable and extendible bond issues where the option to extend or retract rests with the issuer. In such a case it would be exercised in the diametrically opposite scenario from the case where the option lies with the investor.

Floating-Rate Bonds **Floating-rate bonds** make interest payments that are tied to some measure of current market rates. For example, the rate might be adjusted annually to the current T-bill rate plus 2 percent. If the one-year T-bill rate at the adjustment date is 4 percent, the bond's coupon rate over the next year would then be 6 percent. This arrangement means that the bond always pays approximately current market rates.

The major risk involved in floaters has to do with changes in the firm's financial strength. The yield spread is fixed over the life of the security, which may be many years. If the financial health of the firm deteriorates, then a greater yield premium would be required than is offered by the security. In this case, the price of the bond would fall. Although the coupon rate on floaters adjusts to changes in the general level of market interest rates, it does not adjust to changes in the financial condition of the firm.

Preferred Stock

Although preferred stock strictly speaking is considered to be equity, it often is included in the fixed-income universe. This is because, like bonds, preferred stock promises to pay a specified stream of dividends. However, unlike bonds, the failure to pay the promised dividend does not result in corporate bankruptcy. Instead, the dividends owed simply cumulate, and the common shareholders may not receive any dividends until the preferred shareholders have been paid in full. In the event of bankruptcy, the claims of preferred shareholders to the firm's assets have lower priority than those of bondholders, but higher priority than those of common shareholders.

Most preferred stock pays a fixed dividend. Therefore, it is in effect a perpetuity, providing a level cash flow indefinitely. In the last few years, however, adjustable or floating-rate preferred stock has become popular. Floating-rate preferred stock is much like floating-rate bonds. The dividend rate is linked to a measure of current market interest rates and is adjusted at regular intervals.

Other Issuers

There are, of course, several issuers of bonds in addition to the federal government and private corporations. For example, provinces, Crown corporations, and local governments issue bonds. Several such issues appear in the listings of Figure 12.1.

International Bonds

International bonds are commonly divided into two categories, *foreign bonds* and *Eurobonds*. Foreign bonds are issued by a borrower from a country other than the one in which the bond is sold. The bond is denominated in the currency of the country in which it is marketed. For example, if a Canadian firm sells a U.S.-dollar-denominated bond in the United States, the bond is considered a foreign bond. Such U.S.-dollar-denominated bond issues sold in the United States by Canadian firms have grown up significantly in recent years, especially for high-yield (risky) bonds.[5] These international bonds are given colourful names based on the countries in which they are marketed. For example, foreign bonds sold in the United States are called *Yankee bonds*. Like other bonds sold in the United States, they are registered with the Securities and Exchange Commission. Yen-denominated bonds sold in Japan by non-Japanese issuers are called *Samurai bonds*. British pound-denominated foreign bonds sold in the United Kingdom are called *bulldog bonds*.

In contrast to foreign bonds, Eurobonds are bonds issued in the currency of one country but sold in other national markets. For example, the Eurodollar market refers to U.S.-dollar-denominated bonds sold outside the United States (not just in Europe), although London is the largest market for

U.S. Securities
and Exchange
Commission
www.sec.gov

---

[5]See C. Freedman and W. Engert, "Financial Developments in Canada: Past Trends and Future Challenges," *Bank of Canada Review*, Summer 2003.

Eurodollar bonds. Because the Eurodollar market falls outside U.S. jurisdiction, these bonds are not regulated by U.S. federal agencies. Similarly, *Euroyen* bonds are yen-denominated bonds selling outside of Japan. *Eurosterling* bonds are pound-denominated Eurobonds selling outside the United Kingdom, *Euro-Canadian dollar bonds* are Canadian-dollar-denominated bonds selling outside Canada, and so on.

Innovation in the Bond Market

Bond design can be extremely flexible. Issuers constantly develop innovative bonds with unusual features. The following examples should give you a sense of the possible variety in security design.

Reverse Floaters   These are similar to the floating-rate bonds we described earlier, except that the coupon rate on these bonds *falls* when the general level of interest rates rises. Investors in these bonds suffer doubly when rates rise. Not only does the present value of each dollar of cash flow from the bond fall as the discount rate rises, but the level of those cash flows falls as well. Of course, investors in these bonds benefit doubly when rates fall.

Asset-Backed Bonds   Miramax issued bonds with coupon rates tied to the financial performance of several films. Similarly, Domino's Pizza has issued bonds with payments backed with revenue from its franchises. These are examples of asset-backed securities. The income from a specified group of assets is used to service the debt. More conventional asset-backed securities are mortgage-backed securities or securities backed by auto or credit card loans, as we discussed in Chapter 2.

Catastrophe Bonds   Oriental Land Company, which manages Tokyo's Disneyland, issued a bond in 1999 with a final payment that depended on whether there had been an earthquake near the park. More recently FIFA (the Fédération Internationale de Football Association) issued catastrophe bonds with payments that would be halted if terrorism forced the cancellation of the 2006 World Cup. These bonds are a way to transfer "catastrophe risk" from the firm to the capital markets. They represent a novel way of obtaining insurance from the capital markets against specified disasters. Investors in these bonds receive compensation for taking on the risk in the form of higher coupon rates. But in the event of a catastrophe, the bondholders will give up all or part of their investment. "Disaster" can be defined by total insured losses or by criteria such as wind speed in a hurricane or Richter level in an earthquake. Issuance of catastrophe bonds has grown in recent years as insurers sought to spread their risks across a wider spectrum of the capital market.

Indexed Bonds   Indexed bonds make payments that are tied to a general price index or the price of a particular commodity. For example, Mexico has issued 20-year bonds with payments that depend on the price of oil. Some bonds are tied to the general price level. The United States Treasury started issuing such inflation-indexed bonds in January 1997. They are called *Treasury Inflation Protected Securities (TIPS)*. In Canada such bonds are known as *real return bonds (RRBs)*. Six such bonds are quoted in Figure 12.1. By tying the par value of the bond to the general level of prices, coupon payments as well as the final repayment of par value on these bonds will increase in direct proportion to the consumer price index. Therefore, the interest rate on these bonds is a risk-free real rate.

To illustrate how RRBs work, consider a newly issued bond with a three-year maturity, a par value of $1,000, and a coupon rate of 4 percent. For simplicity, we will assume the bond makes annual coupon payments. Assume also that inflation turns out to be 2 percent, 3 percent, and 1 percent in the next three years. Table 12.1 shows how the bond cash flows will be calculated.

		Inflation in Year			Coupon		Principal		Total
TABLE 12.1	**Time**	**Just Ended**	**Par Value**		**Payment**	**+**	**Repayment**	**=**	**Payment**
Principal and	0		$1,000.00						
Interest	1	2%	1,020.00		$40.80		$0		$40.80
Payments for a	2	3	1,050.60		42.02		0		42.02
Real Return	3	1	1,061.11		42.44		1,061.11		1,103.55
Bond									

The first payment comes at the end of the first year, at $t = 1$. Because inflation over the year was 2 percent, the par value of the bond is increased from $1,000 to $1,020; since the coupon rate is 4 percent, the coupon payment is 4 percent of this amount, or $40.80. Notice that principal value increases in tandem with inflation, and, because the coupon payments are 4 percent of principal, they too increase in proportion to the general price level. Therefore, the cash flows paid by the bond are fixed in *real* terms. When the bond matures, the investor receives a final coupon payment of $42.44 plus the (price-level-indexed) repayment of principal, $1,061.11.[6]

The *nominal* rate of return on the bond in the first year is

$$\text{Nominal return} = \frac{\text{Interest} + \text{Price appreciation}}{\text{Initial price}} = \frac{40.80 + 20}{1000} = 6.08\%$$

The real rate of return is precisely the 4 percent real yield on the bond:

$$\text{Real return} = \frac{1 + \text{Nominal return}}{1 + \text{Inflation}} - 1 = \frac{1.0608}{1.02} - 1 = .04, \text{ or } 4\%$$

One can show in a similar manner (see problem 16 in the end-of-chapter problems) that the rate of return in each of the three years is 4 percent as long as the real yield on the bond remains constant. If real yields do change, there will be capital gains or losses on the bond.

12.2   BOND PRICING

Review of the Present Value Relationship

Because a bond's coupon payments and principal repayment all occur months or years in the future, the price an investor would be willing to pay for a claim to those payments depends on the value of dollars to be received in the future compared to dollars in hand today.

This "present value" calculation depends in turn on market interest rates. As we saw in Chapter 4, the nominal risk-free interest rate equals the sum of (1) a real risk-free rate of return and (2) a premium above the real rate to compensate for expected inflation. In addition, because most bonds are not riskless, the discount rate will embody an additional premium that reflects bond-specific characteristics such as default risk, liquidity, tax attributes, call risk, and so on.

We simplify for now by momentarily assuming there is a single interest rate appropriate for discounting cash flows of any maturity. In practice, there may be different discount rates for cash flows accruing in different periods.

To value a security, we discount its expected cash flows by the appropriate rate. The cash flows from a bond consist of coupon payments until the maturity date plus the final payment of par value. Therefore

$$\text{Bond value} = \text{Present value of coupons} + \text{Present value of par value}$$

---

[6]By the way, total nominal income (i.e., coupon plus that year's increase in principal) is treated as taxable income in each year.

If we call the maturity date T and the interest rate r, the bond value can be written as

$$\text{Bond value} = \sum_{t=1}^{T} \frac{\text{Coupon}}{(1+r)^t} + \frac{\text{Par value}}{(1+r)^T} \tag{12.1}$$

The summation sign in this equation directs us to add the present value of each coupon payment; each coupon is discounted on the basis of the time until it will be paid. The first term on the right-hand side is the present value of an annuity. The second term is the present value of a single amount, the final payment of the bond's par value.

You may recall from an introductory finance class that the present value of a \$1 annuity that lasts for T periods when the interest rate equals r is $\frac{1}{r}(1 - \frac{1}{(1+r)^T})$. We call this expression the *T-period annuity factor* for an interest rate of r.[7] Similarly, we call $\frac{1}{(1+r)^T}$ the *PV factor*, that is, the present value of a single payment of \$1 to be received in T periods. Therefore, we can write the price of the bond as

$$\text{Price} = \text{Coupon} \times \frac{1}{r}\left(1 - \frac{1}{(1+r)^T}\right) + \text{Par value} \times \frac{1}{(1+r)^T} \tag{12.2}$$

$$= \text{Coupon} \times \text{Annuity factor}(r,T) + \text{Par value} \times \text{PV factor}(r,T)$$

EXAMPLE 12.2   **Bond Pricing**

We discussed earlier an 8 percent coupon, 30-year-maturity bond with par value of \$1,000 paying 60 semiannual coupon payments of \$40 each. Suppose that the interest rate is 8 percent annually, or 4 percent per six-month period. Then the value of the bond can be written as

$$\text{Price} = \sum_{t=1}^{60} \frac{\$40}{(1.04)^t} + \frac{\$1,000}{(1.04)^{60}} \tag{12.3}$$

For notational simplicity, we can write this equation as

$$\text{Price} = \$40 \times \text{PA}(4\%,60) + \$1,000 \times \text{PF}(4\%,60)$$

where PA(4%,60) represents the present value of an annuity of \$1 when the interest rate is 4 percent and the annuity lasts for 60 six-month periods, and PF(4%,60) is the present value of a single payment of \$1 to be received in 60 periods.

It is easy to confirm that the present value of the bond's 60 semiannual coupon payments of \$40 each is \$904.94, whereas the \$1,000 final payment of par value has a present value of \$95.06, for a total bond value of \$1,000. You can perform these calculations from this equation on any financial calculator or use a set of present value tables.

In this example, the coupon rate equals yield to maturity, and the bond price equals par value. If the interest rate were not equal to the bond's coupon rate, the bond would not sell at par value. For example, if the interest rate were to rise to 10 percent (5 percent per six months), the bond's price would fall by \$189.29, to \$810.71, as follows:

$$\$40 \times \text{PA}(5\%,60) + \$1,000 \times \text{PF}(5\%,60)$$

$$= \$757.17 + \$53.54$$

$$= \$810.71$$

---

[7]Here is a quick derivation of the formula for the present value of an annuity. An annuity lasting T periods can be viewed as equivalent to a perpetuity whose first payment comes at the end of the current period *less* another perpetuity whose first payment comes at the end of the $(T+1)$th period. The immediate perpetuity net of the delayed perpetuity provides exactly T payments. We know that the value of a \$1 per period perpetuity is \$1/r. Therefore, the present value of the delayed perpetuity is \$1/r discounted for T additional periods, or $\frac{1}{r} \times \frac{1}{(1+r)^T}$. The present value of the annuity is the present value of the first perpetuity minus the present value of the delayed perpetuity, or $\frac{1}{r}(1 - \frac{1}{(1+r)^T})$.

Figure 12.2
The inverse relationship between bond prices and yields.

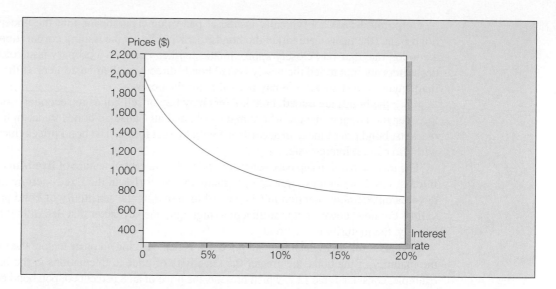

At a higher interest rate, the present value of the payments to be received by the bondholder is lower. Therefore, the bond price will fall as market interest rates rise. This illustrates a crucial general rule in bond valuation. When interest rates rise, bond prices must fall because the present values of the bond's payments are obtained by discounting at a higher interest rate.

Figure 12.2 shows the price of the 30-year, 8 percent coupon bond for a range of interest rates. The negative slope illustrates the inverse relationship between prices and yields. Note also from the figure (and from Table 12.2) that the shape of the curve implies that an increase in the interest rate results in a price decline that is smaller than the price gain resulting from a decrease of equal magnitude in the interest rate. This property of bond prices is called *convexity* because of the convex shape of the bond price curve. This curvature reflects the fact that progressive increases in the interest rate result in progressively smaller reductions in the bond price.[8] Therefore, the price curve becomes flatter at higher interest rates. We return to the issue of convexity in Chapter 14.

CC 2

CONCEPT CHECK

Calculate the price of the bond for a market interest rate of 3 percent per half-year. Compare the capital gains for the interest rate decline to the losses incurred when the rate increases to 5 percent.

TABLE 12.2

Bond Prices at Different Interest Rates (8% coupon bond, coupons paid semiannually)

| Time to Maturity | Bond Price at Given Market Interest Rate | | | | |
	4%	6%	8%	10%	12%
1 year	1,038.83	1,019.13	1,000.00	981.41	963.33
10 years	1,327.03	1,148.77	1,000.00	875.38	770.60
20 years	1,547.11	1,231.15	1,000.00	828.41	699.07
30 years	1,695.22	1,276.76	1,000.00	810.71	676.77

[8]The progressively smaller impact of interest increases results from the fact that at higher rates the bond is worth less. Therefore, an additional increase in rates operates on a smaller initial base, resulting in a smaller price reduction.

Corporate bonds are typically issued at par value. This means that the underwriters of the bond issue (the firms that market the bonds to the public for the issuing corporation) must choose a coupon rate that very closely approximates market yields. In a primary issue of bonds, the underwriters attempt to sell the newly issued bonds directly to their customers. If the coupon rate is inadequate, investors will not pay par value for the bonds.

After the bonds are issued, bondholders may buy or sell bonds in secondary markets, such as the over-the-counter market, where many U.S. and all Canadian bonds trade. In these secondary markets, bond prices move in accordance with market forces. The bond prices fluctuate inversely with the market interest rate.

The inverse relationship between price and yield is a central feature of **fixed-income securities**. Interest rate fluctuations represent the main source of risk in the fixed-income market, and we devote considerable attention in Chapter 14 to assessing the sensitivity of bond prices to market yields. For now, however, it is sufficient to highlight one key factor that determines that sensitivity, namely, the maturity of the bond.

A general rule in evaluating bond price risk is that, keeping all other factors the same, the longer the maturity of the bond, the greater the sensitivity of price to fluctuations in the interest rate. For example, consider Table 12.2, which presents the price of an 8 percent coupon bond at different market yields and times to maturity. For any departure of the interest rate from 8 percent (the rate at which the bond sells at par value), the change in the bond price is smaller for shorter times to maturity.

This makes sense. If you buy the bond at par with an 8 percent coupon rate, and market rates subsequently rise, you suffer a loss: you have tied up your money earning 8 percent when alternative investments offer higher returns. This is reflected in a capital loss on the bond—a fall in its market price. The longer the period for which your money is tied up, the greater the loss, and, correspondingly, the greater the drop in the bond price. In Table 12.2, the row for one-year-maturity bonds shows little price sensitivity—that is, with only one year's earnings at stake, changes in interest rates are not too threatening. But for 30-year-maturity bonds, interest rate swings have a large impact on bond prices.

That is why short-term government securities such as T-bills are considered the safest. They are free not only of default risk, but also largely of price risk attributable to interest rate volatility.

Bond Pricing Between Coupon Dates

Equation 12.2 for bond prices assumes that the next coupon payment is in precisely one payment period, either a year for an annual payment bond or six months for a semiannual payment bond. But you probably want to be able to price bonds all 365 days of the year, not just on the one or two dates each year that it makes a coupon payment!

We apply the same principles to pricing regardless of the date: we simply compute the present value of the remaining payments. However, if we are between coupon dates, there will be fractional periods remaining until each payment. Even if the principles are no more complicated, this certainly complicates the arithmetic computations.

Fortunately, bond pricing functions are included in most spreadsheet programs such as Excel. The spreadsheet allows you to enter today's date as well as the maturity date of the bond, and so can provide prices for bonds at any date. The Excel Applications box here shows you how.

As we pointed out earlier, bond prices are typically quoted net of accrued interest. These prices, which appear in the financial press, are called *flat prices*. The actual *invoice price* that a buyer pays for the bond includes accrued interest. Thus,

$$\text{Invoice price} = \text{Flat price} + \text{Accrued interest}$$

When a bond pays its coupon, flat price equals invoice price, since at that moment accrued interest reverts to zero. However, this will be the exceptional case, not the rule.

Bond Pricing

Excel and most other spreadsheet programs provide built-in functions to compute bond prices and yields. They typically ask you to input both the date you buy the bond (called the *settlement date*) and the maturity date of the bond. The Excel function for bond price is

=PRICE(settlement date, maturity date, annual coupon rate, yield to maturity, redemption value as percent of par value, number of coupon payments per year)

For the 1.5 percent coupon 2017 maturity bond highlighted in Figure 12.1, we would enter the values in the following spreadsheet. Alternatively, we could simply enter the following function in Excel:

=PRICE(DATE(2012,12,7), DATE (2017,9,1),.015,.0128,100,2)

The DATE function in Excel, which we use for both the settlement and the maturity date, uses the format DATE(year, month, day). The first date is December 7, 2012, when the bond is purchased, and the second is September 1, 2017, when it matures. Most bonds pay coupons on the 15th of the month.

Notice that the coupon rate and yield to maturity are expressed as decimals, not percentages. In most cases, redemption value is 100 (i.e., 100 percent of par value), and the resulting price similarly is expressed as a percent of par value. Occasionally, however, you may encounter bonds that pay off at a premium or discount to par value. One example would be callable bonds.

The value of the bond returned by the pricing function is 101.02 (cell B12), which matches the price reported in Figure 12.1 to the nearest second decimal. This bond paid a coupon on June 15, so adjustment for accrued interest is necessary.

Rows 13 through 16 make the necessary adjustments for the bond's invoice price. The function described in cell C13 counts the days since the last coupon. This day count is based on the bond's settlement date, maturity date, coupon period (1 = annual; 2 = semiannual), and day count convention (choice 1 uses actual days). The function described in cell C14 counts the total days in each coupon payment period. Therefore, the entries for accrued interest in row 15 are the semiannual coupon multiplied by the fraction of a coupon period that has elapsed since the last payment. Finally, the invoice prices in row 16 are the sum of flat price plus accrued interest.

As a final example, suppose you wish to find the price of the bond in Example 12.2. It is a 30-year-maturity bond with a coupon rate of 8 percent (paid semiannually). The market interest rate given in the latter part of the example is 10 percent. However, you are not given a specific settlement or maturity date. You can still use the PRICE function to value the bond. Simply choose an *arbitrary* settlement date (January 1, 2000 is convenient) and let the maturity date be 30 years hence. The appropriate inputs appear in column F of the spreadsheet, with the resulting price, 81.071 percent of face value, appearing in cell F16.

	A	B	C	D	E	F	G
1		1.5% coupon bond,				8% coupon bond,	
2		maturing September 2017	Formula in column B			30-year maturity	
3							
4	Settlement date	7/12/2012	= DATE (2012,12,7)			1/1/2000	
5	Maturity date	1/9/2017	= DATE (2017,9,1)			1/1/2030	
6	Annual coupon rate	0.015				0.08	
7	Yield to maturity	0.0128				0.1	
8	Redemption value (% of face value)	100				100	
9	Coupon payments per year	2				2	
10							
11							
12	**Flat price (% of par)**	**101.02**	=PRICE(B4,B5,B6,B7,B8,B9)			**81.071**	
13	Days since last coupon	97	=COUPDAYBS(B4,B5,2,1)			0	
14	Days in coupon period	181	=COUPDAYS(B4,B5,2,1)			182	
15	Accrued interest	0.4019	=(B13/B14)*B6*100/2			0	
16	**Invoice price**	**101.41**	=B12+B15			**81.071**	

The Excel pricing function provides the flat price of the bond. To find the invoice price, we need to add accrued interest. Fortunately, Excel also provides functions that count the days since the last coupon payment date and thus can be used to compute accrued interest. The Excel box also illustrates how to use these functions. It provides examples using bonds that have just paid a coupon and so have zero accrued interest, as well as a bond that is between coupon dates.

12.3 BOND YIELDS

The *current yield* of a bond measures only the cash income provided by the bond as a percentage of bond price and ignores any prospective capital gains or losses. We would like a measure of rate of return that accounts for both current income as well as the price increase or decrease over the bond's

Canadian bond
yields: 10-year
lookup
www
.bankofcanada.ca/
rates/interest-
rates/lookup-
bond-yields

life. The yield to maturity is the standard measure of the total rate of return of the bond over its life. However, it is far from a perfect measure, and we will explore several variations of this statistic.

Yield to Maturity

In practice, an investor considering the purchase of a bond is not quoted a promised rate of return. Instead, the investor must use the bond price, maturity date, and coupon payments to infer the return offered by the bond over its life. The **yield to maturity (YTM)** is a measure of the average rate of return that will be earned on a bond if it is bought now and held until maturity. To calculate the yield to maturity, we solve the bond price equation for the interest rate given the bond's price.

EXAMPLE 12.3   Yield to Maturity

Suppose an 8 percent coupon, paid semiannually, 30-year bond is selling at $1,276.76. What average rate of return would be earned by an investor purchasing the bond at this price? To answer this question, we find the interest rate at which the present value of the remaining bond payments equals the bond price. This is the rate consistent with the observed price of the bond. Therefore, we solve for r in the following equation:

$$\$1,276.76 = \sum_{t=1}^{60} \frac{\$40}{(1+r)^t} + \frac{\$1,000}{(1+r)^{60}}$$

or, equivalently,

$$1,276.76 = 40 \times PA(r,60) + 1,000 \times PF(r,60)$$

These equations have only one unknown variable, the interest rate, r. You can use a financial calculator to confirm that the solution to the equation is $r = .03$, or 3 percent per half-year.[9] This is considered the bond's yield to maturity.

The financial press reports yields on an annualized basis and annualizes the bond's semiannual yield using simple interest techniques, resulting in an annual percentage rate, or APR. Yields annualized using simple interest are also called "bond equivalent yields." Therefore, the semiannual yield would be doubled and reported in the newspaper as a bond equivalent yield of 6 percent. The *effective* annual yield of the bond, however, accounts for compound interest. If one earns 3 percent interest every six months, then after one year every dollar invested grows with interest to $1 \times (1.03)^2 = 1.0609$, and the effective annual interest rate on the bond is 6.09 percent.

The bond's yield to maturity is the internal rate of return on an investment in the bond. The yield to maturity can be interpreted as the compound rate of return over the life of the bond under the assumption that all bond coupons can be reinvested at an interest rate equal to the bond's yield to maturity.[10] Yield to maturity is widely accepted as a proxy for average return.

Yield to maturity is different from the *current yield* of a bond, which is the bond's annual coupon payment divided by the bond price. For example, for the 8 percent, 30-year bond currently selling at $1,276.76, the current yield would be $80/$1,276.76 = .0627, or 6.27 percent per year. In contrast, recall that the effective annual yield to maturity is 6.09 percent. For this bond, which is selling at a premium over par value ($1,276 rather than $1,000), the coupon rate (8 percent) exceeds the current yield (6.27 percent), which exceeds the yield to maturity

[9]Without a financial calculator, you still could solve the equation, but you would need to use a trial-and-error approach.
[10]If the reinvestment rate does not equal the bond's yield to maturity, the compound rate will differ from YTM. This is illustrated in Examples 12.5 and 12.6.

(6.09 percent). The coupon rate exceeds current yield because the coupon rate divides the coupon payments by par value ($1,000) rather than by bond price ($1,276). In turn, the current yield exceeds yield to maturity because the yield to maturity accounts for the built-in capital loss on the bond; the bond bought today for $1,276 will eventually fall in value to $1,000 at maturity.

Example 12.3 illustrates a general rule: for **premium bonds** (bonds selling above par value), coupon rate is greater than current yield, which in turn is greater than yield to maturity. For **discount bonds** (bonds selling below par value), these relationships are reversed (see Concept Check 3).

It is common to hear people speak loosely of "the yield on a bond," when almost always they are referring to the yield to maturity.

CC 3

CONCEPT CHECK

What will be the relationship among coupon rate, current yield, and yield to maturity for bonds selling at discounts from par? Illustrate using the 8 percent (semiannual payment) coupon bond assuming it is selling at a yield to maturity of 10 percent.

Excel also provides a function for yield to maturity:

=YIELD(settlement date, maturity date, annual coupon rate, bond price, redemption value as percent of par value, number of coupon payments per year)

The bond price used in the function should be the reported flat price, without accrued interest. For example, to find the yield to maturity of the 30-year 8 percent bond in Example 12.3, we would use column E of Spreadsheet 12.1. If the coupons were paid only annually, we would change the entry for payments per year to 1 (see cell G12), and the yield would fall slightly to 5.99 percent.

Yield to Call

Yield to maturity is calculated on the assumption that the bond will be held until maturity. What if the bond is callable, however, and may be retired prior to the maturity date? How should we measure average rate of return for bonds subject to a call provision?

Figure 12.3 illustrates the risk of call to the bondholder. The upper line is the value at various market interest rates of a "straight" (i.e., noncallable) bond with par value $1,000, an 8 percent

---

EXCEL SPREADSHEET 12.1

Finding yield to maturity in Excel.

	A	B	C	D	E	F	G	H
1								
2								
3								
4					Semiannual		Annual	
5					coupons		coupons	
6								
7	Settlement date				31/07/2012		02/01/2000	
8	Maturity date				31/07/2018		02/01/2030	
9	Annual coupon rate				0.0225		0.08	
10	Bond price (flat)				108.5391		127.676	
11	Redemption value (% of face value)				100		100	
12	Coupon payments per year				2		1	
13								
14	**Yield to maturity (decimal)**				**0.0079**		**0.0599**	
15								
16								
17		The formula entered here is: =YIELD(B3,B4,B5,B6,B7,B8)						

Figure 12.3

The inverse relationship between bond prices and yields for a callable bond.

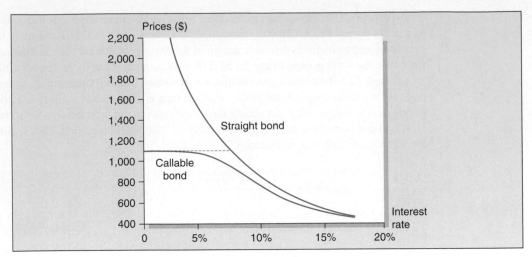

coupon rate, and a 30-year time to maturity. If interest rates fall, the bond price, which equals the present value of the promised payments, can rise substantially.

Now consider a bond that has the same coupon rate and maturity date but is callable at 110 percent of par value, or $1,100. When interest rates fall, the present value of the bond's *scheduled* payments rises, but the call provision allows the issuer to repurchase the bond at the call price. If the call price is less than the present value of the scheduled payments, the issuer can call the bond at the expense of the bondholder.

The lower line in Figure 12.3 is the value of the callable bond. At high interest rates, the risk of call is negligible, and the values of the straight and callable bonds converge. At lower rates, however, the values of the bonds begin to diverge, with the difference reflecting the value of the firm's opinion to reclaim the callable bond at the call price. At very low rates, the bond is called, and its value is simply the call price, $1,100.

This analysis suggests that bond market analysts might be more interested in a bond's yield to call rather than yield to maturity if the bond is especially vulnerable to being called. The yield to call is calculated just like the yield to maturity except that the time until call replaces the time until maturity, and the call price replaces the par value.

EXAMPLE 12.4 **Yield to Call**

Suppose the 8 percent coupon, paid semiannually, 30-year-maturity bond sells for $1,150 and is callable in 10 years at a call price of $1,100. Its yield to maturity and yield to call would be calculated using the following inputs:

	Yield to Call	Yield to Maturity
Coupon payment	$40	$40
Number of semiannual periods	20 periods	60 periods
Final payment	$1,100	$1,000
Price	$1,150	$1,150

The yield to call is then 6.64 percent, whereas yield to maturity is 6.82 percent.

We have noted that most callable bonds are issued with an initial period of call protection. In addition, an implicit form of call protection operates for bonds selling at deep discounts from their call prices. Even if interest rates fall a bit, deep-discount bonds still will sell below the call price and thus will not be subject to a call.

Premium bonds that might be selling near their call prices, however, are especially apt to be called if rates fall further. If interest rates fall, a callable premium bond is likely to provide a lower return than could be earned on a discount bond whose potential price appreciation is not limited by the likelihood of a call. As a consequence, investors in premium bonds often are more interested in the bond's yield to call than its yield to maturity, because it may appear to them that the bond will be retired at the call date.

Realized Compound Yield Versus Yield to Maturity

We have noted that yield to maturity will equal the rate of return realized over the life of the bond if all coupons are reinvested at an interest rate equal to the bond's yield to maturity. Consider, for example, a two-year bond selling at par value paying a 10 percent coupon once a year. The yield to maturity is 10 percent. If the $100 coupon payment is reinvested at an interest rate of 10 percent, the $1,000 investment in the bond will grow after two years to $1,210, as illustrated in Figure 12.4, panel A. The coupon paid in the first year is reinvested and grows with interest to a second-year value of $110, which, together with the second coupon payment and payment of par value in the second year, results in a total value of $1,210. The compound growth rate of invested funds, therefore, is calculated from

$$\$1,000(1 + y_{\text{realized}})^2 = \$1,210$$

$$y_{\text{realized}} = .10 = 10\%$$

With a reinvestment rate equal to the 10 percent yield to maturity, the **realized compound return** equals yield to maturity.

But what if the reinvestment rate is not 10 percent? If the coupon can be invested at more than 10 percent, funds will grow to more than $1,210, and the realized compound return will exceed 10 percent. If the reinvestment rate is less than 10 percent, so will be the realized compound return.

Figure 12.4
Growth of
invested funds.

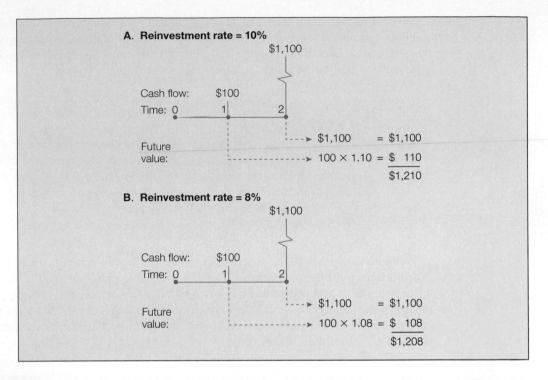

EXAMPLE 12.5   **Realized Compound Return**

Suppose that the interest rate at which the coupon can be invested equals 8 percent. The following calculations are illustrated in panel B of Figure 12.4:

Future value of first coupon payment with interest earnings	$100 × 1.08 = $ 108
Cash payment in second year (final coupon plus par value)	$1,100
Total value of investment with reinvested coupons	$1,208

The realized compound yield is computed by calculating the compound rate of growth of invested funds, assuming that all coupon payments are reinvested. The investor purchased the bond for par at $1,000, and this investment grew to $1,208.

$$\$1,000(1 + y_{realized})^2 = \$1,208$$

$$y_{realized} = .0991 = 9.91\%$$

This example highlights the problem with conventional yield to maturity when reinvestment rates can change over time. Conventional yield to maturity will not equal realized compound return. However, in an economy with future interest rate uncertainty, the rates at which interim coupons will be reinvested are not yet known. Therefore, although realized compound yield can be computed *after* the investment period ends, it cannot be computed in advance without a forecast of future reinvestment rates. This reduces much of the attraction of the realized yield measure.

Forecasting the realized compound yield over various holding periods or investment horizons is called **horizon analysis**. The forecast of total return depends on your forecasts of *both* the price of the bond when you sell it at the end of your horizon *and* the rate at which you are able to reinvest coupon income. The sales price depends in turn on the yield to maturity at the horizon date. With a longer investment horizon, however, reinvested coupons will be a larger component of your final proceeds.

EXAMPLE 12.6   Horizon Analysis

Suppose that you buy a 30-year, 7.5 percent (annual payment) coupon bond for $980 (when its yield to maturity is 7.67 percent) and plan to hold it for 20 years. Your forecast is that the bond's yield to maturity will be 8 percent when it is sold and that the reinvestment rate on the coupons will be 6 percent. At the end of your investment horizon, the bond will have 10 years remaining until expiration, so the forecast sales price (using a yield to maturity of 8 percent) will be $966.45. The 20 coupon payments will grow with compound interest to $2,758.92. (This is the future value of a 20-year $75 annuity with an interest rate of 6 percent.)

On the basis of these forecasts, your $980 investment will grow in 20 years to $966.45 + $2,758.92 = $3,725.37. This corresponds to an annualized compound return of 6.90 percent, calculated by solving for r in the equation $980(1 + r)^{20} = \$3,725.37$.

Examples 12.5 and 12.6 demonstrate that as interest rates change, bond investors are actually subject to two sources of offsetting risk. On the one hand, when rates rise, bond prices fall, which reduces the value of the portfolio. On the other hand, reinvested coupon income will compound more rapidly at those higher rates. This **reinvestment rate risk** will offset the impact of price risk. In Chapter 14, we will explore this tradeoff in more detail and will discover that by carefully tailoring their bond portfolios, investors can precisely balance these two effects for any given investment horizon.

12.4 BOND PRICES OVER TIME

As we noted earlier, a bond will sell at par value when its coupon rate equals the market interest rate. In these circumstances, the investor receives fair compensation for the time value of money in the form of the recurring interest payments. No further capital gain is necessary to provide fair compensation.

When the coupon rate is lower than the market interest rate, the coupon payments alone will not provide investors as high a return as they could earn elsewhere in the market. To receive a fair return on such an investment, investors also need to earn price appreciation on their bonds. The bonds, therefore, would have to sell below par value to provide a "built-in" capital gain on the investment.

EXAMPLE 12.7   Fair Holding-Period Return

To illustrate this point, suppose a bond was issued several years ago when the interest rate was 7 percent. The bond's annual coupon rate was thus set at 7 percent. (We will suppose for simplicity that the bond pays its coupon annually.) Now, with three years left in the bond's life, the interest rate is 8 percent per year. The bond's fair market price is the present value of the remaining annual coupons plus payment of par value. That present value is

$$\$70 \times \text{PA}(8\%,3) + \$1,000 \times \text{PF}(8\%,3) = \$974.23$$

which is less than par value.

In another year, after the next coupon is paid, the bond would sell at

$$\$70 \times \text{PA}(8\%,2) + \$1,000 \times \text{PF}(8\%,2) = \$982.17$$

thereby yielding a capital gain over the year of $7.94. If an investor had purchased the bond at $974.23, the total return over the year would equal the coupon payment plus capital gain, or $70 + $7.94 = $77.94. This represents a rate of return of $77.94/$974.23, or 8 percent, exactly the current rate of return available elsewhere in the market.

CC 6

CONCEPT CHECK

What will the bond price in Example 12.7 be in yet another year, when only one year remains until maturity? What is the rate of return to an investor who purchases the bond at $982.17 and sells it one year hence?

When bond prices are set according to the present value formula, any discount from par value provides an anticipated capital gain that will augment a below-market coupon rate just sufficiently to provide a fair total rate of return. Conversely, if the coupon rate exceeds the market interest rate, the interest income by itself is greater than that available elsewhere in the market. Investors will bid up the price of these bonds above their par values. As the bonds approach maturity, they will fall in value because fewer of these above-market coupon payments remain. The resulting capital losses offset the large coupon payments so that the bondholder again receives only a fair rate of return.

Problem 8 at the end of the chapter asks you to work through the case of the high-coupon bond. Figure 12.5 traces out the price paths of high- and low-coupon bonds (net of accrued interest) as time to maturity approaches. The low-coupon bond enjoys capital gains, whereas the high-coupon bond suffers capital losses.[11]

We use these examples to show that each bond offers investors the same total rate of return. Although the capital gain versus income components differ, the price of each bond is set to provide competitive rates, as we should expect in well-functioning capital markets. Security returns all should be comparable on an after-tax risk-adjusted basis. If they are not, investors will try to sell low-return securities, thereby driving down the prices until the total return at the now-lower price is competitive with other securities. Prices should continue to adjust until all securities are fairly priced, in that expected returns are comparable (given appropriate risk and tax adjustments).

Yield to Maturity Versus Holding-Period Return

In Example 12.7 the holding-period return and the yield to maturity were equal. In our example, the bond yield started and ended the year at 8 percent, and the bond's holding-period return also equalled 8 percent. This turns out to be a general result. When the yield to maturity is unchanged over the period, the rate of return on the bond will equal that yield. As we noted, this should not

Figure 12.5

Price paths of coupon bonds.

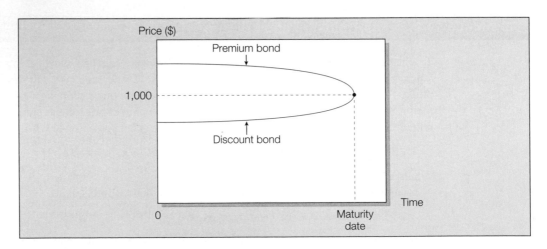

---

[11]If interest rates are volatile, the price path will oscillate around the path shown in Figure 12.5, reflecting capital gains or losses as interest rates fall or rise. Ultimately, however, the price path must reach par value at the maturity date, implying that the price of the premium bond will fall over time while that of the discount bond will rise.

be a surprising result: the bond must offer a rate of return competitive with those available on other securities.

However, when yields fluctuate, so will a bond's rate of return. Unanticipated changes in market rates will result in unanticipated changes in bond returns, and after the fact, a bond's holding-period return can be better or worse than the yield at which it initially sells. An increase in the bond's yield acts to reduce its price, which means that the holding-period return will be less than the initial yield.[12] Conversely, a decline in yield will result in a holding-period return greater than the initial yield.

EXAMPLE 12.8 **Yield to Maturity Versus Holding-Period Return**

Consider a 30-year bond paying an annual coupon of $80 and selling at par value of $1,000. The bond's initial yield to maturity is 8 percent. If the yield remains at 8 percent over the year, the bond price will remain at par, so the holding-period return also will be 8 percent. But if the yield falls below 8 percent, the bond price will increase. Suppose the price increases to $1,050. Then the holding-period return is greater than 8 percent:

$$\text{Holding-period return} = \frac{\$80 + (\$1,050 - \$1,000)}{\$1,000} = .13 \text{ or } 13\%$$

Here is another way to think about the difference between yield to maturity and holding period return. Yield to maturity depends only on the bond's coupon, *current* price, and par value at maturity. All of these values are observable today, so yield to maturity can be easily calculated. Yield to maturity can be interpreted as a measure of the *average* rate of return if the investment in the bond is held until the bond matures. In contrast, holding-period return is the rate of return over a particular investment period, and depends on the market price of the bond at the end of that holding period; of course this price is *not* known today. Since bond prices over the holding period will respond to unanticipated changes in interest rates, holding-period return can at most be forecasted.

Zero-Coupon Bonds

Original issue discount bonds are less common than coupon bonds issued at par. These are bonds that are issued intentionally with low coupon rates that cause the bond to sell at a discount from par value. An extreme example of this type of bond is the *zero-coupon bond*, which carries no coupons and must provide all its return in the form of price appreciation. Zeroes provide only one cash flow to their owners, and that is on the maturity date of the bond.

Bank of Canada
www.
bankofcanada.ca

Government of Canada Treasury bills are examples of short-term zero-coupon instruments. The Bank of Canada issues or sells a bill for some amount ranging from $1,000 to $1 million, agreeing to repay that amount at the bill's maturity. All of the investor's return comes in the form of price appreciation over time.

Longer-term zero-coupon bonds are commonly created synthetically. Several investment banking firms buy coupon-paying Government of Canada or provincial bonds and sell rights to single payments backed by the bonds. These bonds are said to be *stripped* of coupons, and are often called *strips*. The single payments are, in essence, zero-coupon bonds collateralized by the original securities and so are virtually free of default risk. Several such strips are shown in Figure 12.1.[13]

---

[12]Note, however, that when yields increase, coupon income can be reinvested at higher rates, partially offsetting the price decline. The offset can be important for long holding periods, but for short horizons the price impact will always dominate the reinvestment effect. See also Chapter 14.

[13]In the United States, strips are created directly by the U.S. Treasury upon request from dealers who purchase coupon bonds. The payments to strips are considered obligations of the U.S. Treasury.

Figure 12.6

The price of a 30-year zero-coupon bond over time. Price equals $1,000/(1.10)^T$ where T is time until maturity.

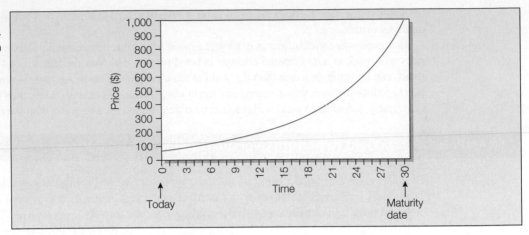

What should happen to prices of zeroes as time passes? On their maturity date, zeroes must sell for par value. Before maturity, however, they should sell at discounts from par, because of the time value of money. As time passes, price should approach par value. In fact, if the interest rate is constant, a zero's price will increase at exactly the rate of interest.

To illustrate this property, consider a zero with 30 years until maturity, and suppose the market interest rate is 10 percent per year. The price of the bond today will be $1,000/(1.10)^{30} = \$57.31$. Next year, with only 29 years until maturity, the price will be $1,000/(1.10)^{29} = \$63.04$, a 10 percent increase over its previous-year value. Because the par value of the bond is now discounted for one fewer year, its price has increased by the one-year discount factor.

Figure 12.6 presents the price path of a 30-year zero-coupon bond until its maturity date for an annual market interest rate of 10 percent. The bond's price rises exponentially, not linearly, until its maturity.

After-Tax Returns

Canada Revenue Agency
www.cra-arc.gc.ca

The tax authorities recognize that the "built-in" price appreciation on original issue discount (OID) bonds such as zero-coupon bonds represents an implicit interest payment to the holder of the security. The Canada Revenue Agency (CRA), therefore, calculates a price appreciation schedule to impute taxable interest income for the built-in appreciation during a tax year, even if the asset is not sold or does not mature until a future year. Any additional gains or losses that arise from changes in market interest rates are treated as capital gains or losses if the OID bond is sold during the tax year.

EXAMPLE 12.9 **Taxation of OID Bonds**

If the interest rate originally is 10 percent, the 30-year zero would be issued at a price of $1,000/(1.10)^{30} = \$57.31$. The following year, CRA calculates what the bond price would be if the yield remains at 10 percent. This is $1,000/(1.10)^{29} = \$63.04$. Therefore, the tax authorities impute interest income of $\$63.04 - \$57.31 = \$5.73$. This amount is subject to tax. Notice that the imputed interest income is based on a "constant-yield method" that ignores any changes in market interest rates.

If interest rates actually fall, say to 9.9 percent, the bond price actually will be $1,000/(1.099)^{29} = \$64.72$. If the bond is sold, the difference between $64.72 and $63.04 will be treated as capital gains income and taxed at the capital gains tax rate. If the bond is not sold, the price difference is an unrealized capital gain and does not result in taxes in that year. In either case, the investor has to pay taxes on the $5.73 of imputed interest at the rate of ordinary income.

The procedure illustrated in the above example is also applied to the taxation of other original issue discount bonds, even if they are not zero-coupon bonds. Consider, as an example, a 30-year-maturity bond that is issued with a coupon rate of 4 percent and a yield to maturity of 8 percent. For simplicity, we will assume that the bond pays coupons once annually. Because of the low coupon rate, the bond will be issued at a price far below par value, specifically at a price of $549.69. If the bond's yield to maturity remains at 8 percent, then its price in one year will rise to $553.66. (Confirm this for yourself.) This provides a pretax holding-period return of exactly 8 percent.

$$\text{HPR} = \frac{\$40 + (\$553.66 - \$549.69)}{\$549.69} = .08$$

The increase in the bond price based on a constant yield, however, is treated as interest income, so the investor is required to pay taxes on imputed interest income of $553.66 - $549.69 = $3.97. If the bond's yield actually changes during the year, the difference between the bond's price and the "constant-yield value" of $553.66 will be treated as capital gains income if the bond is sold.

CC 7

CONCEPT CHECK

Suppose that the yield to maturity of the 4 percent coupon, 30-year-maturity bond actually falls to 7 percent by the end of the first year, and that the investor sells the bond after the first year. If the investor's tax rate on interest income is 36 percent and the tax rate on capital gains is 20 percent, what is the investor's after-tax rate of return?

12.5   DEFAULT RISK

Although bonds generally *promise* a fixed flow of income, that income stream is not riskless unless the investor can be sure the issuer will not default on the obligation. While government bonds may be treated as free of default risk, this is not true of corporate bonds. If the company goes bankrupt, the bondholders will not receive all the payments they have been promised. Therefore, the actual payments on these bonds are uncertain, for they depend to some degree on the ultimate financial status of the firm.

Dominion Bond
Rating Service
www.dbrs.com

Bond default risk is measured by both Moody's Investor Services and Standard & Poor's Corporation in the United States and Dominion Bond Rating Service (DBRS) in Canada; the two U.S. rating services also rate several Canadian issues. All rating agencies assign letter grades to the bonds of corporations and municipalities to reflect their assessment of the safety of the bond issue. The top rating is AAA (Standard & Poor's and DBRS) and Aaa (Moody's). Moody's modifies each class with a 1, 2, or 3 suffix (e.g., Aaa1, Aaa2, Aaa3) to provide a finer gradation. S&P uses a + or - modification, and the Canadian service uses the terms "(high)" and "(low)" as modifiers.

Bonds rated BBB or above (S&P, DBRS) or Baa and above (Moody's) are considered **investment-grade bonds**, whereas lower-rated bonds are classified as **speculative-grade** or **junk bonds**. Defaults on low-grade issues are not uncommon. For example, almost half of the bonds that were rated CCC by Standard & Poor's at issue have defaulted within 10 years. Highly rated bonds rarely default, but even these bonds are not free of credit risk. For example, in May 2001 WorldCom sold $11.8 billion of bonds with an investment grade rating. Only a year later, the firm filed for bankruptcy and its bondholders lost more than 80 percent of their investment. Certain regulated institutional investors such as insurance companies have not always been allowed to invest in speculative-grade bonds.

Figure 12.7 provides the definition of each bond rating classification and the equivalences between rating agencies.

Figure 12.7 Definitions of bond rating classes.

	Bond Ratings				
	Very High Quality	High Quality	Speculative	Very Poor	
DBRS	AAA AA	A BBB	BB B	CCC D	
Standard & Poor's	AAA AA	A BBB	BB B	CCC D	
Moody's	Aaa Aa	A Baa	Ba B	Caa C	

At times all services have used adjustments to these ratings. S&P uses plus and minus signs: A+ is the strongest A rating and A− the weakest. Moody's uses a 1, 2, or 3 designation—with 1 indicating the strongest. DBRS uses a (high) for the strongest and a (low) for the weakest designations.

DBRS	Moody's	S&P	
AAA	Aaa	AAA	Debt rated Aaa and AAA has the highest rating. Capacity to pay interest and principal is extremely strong.
AA	Aa	A	Debt rated Aa and AA has a very strong capacity to pay interest and repay principal. Together with the highest rating, this group makes up the high-grade bond class.
A	A	A	Debt rated A has a strong capacity to pay interest and repay principal, although it is somewhat more susceptible to the adverse effects of changes in circumstances and economic conditions than debt in higher-rated categories.
BBB	Baa	BBB	Debt rated Baa and BBB is regarded as having an adequate capacity to pay interest and repay principal. Whereas it normally exhibits adequate protection parameters, adverse economic conditions or changing circumstances are more likely to lead to a weakened capacity to pay interest and repay principal for debt in this category than in higher-rated categories. These bonds are medium-grade obligations.
BB B CCC CC	Ba B Caa Ca	BB B CCC CC	Debt rated in these categories is regarded, on balance, as predominantly speculative with respect to capacity to pay interest and repay principal in accordance with the terms of the obligation. BB and Ba indicate the lowest degree of speculation, and CC and Ca the highest degree of speculation. Although such debt will likely have some quality and protective characteristics, these are outweighed by large uncertainties or major risk exposures to adverse conditions. Some issues may be in default.
C	C	C	This rating is reserved for income bonds on which no interest is being paid.
D	D	D	Debt rated D is in default, and payment of interest and/or repayment of principal is in arrears.

Source: Various editions of *Standard & Poor's Bond Guide*, *Moody's Bond Guide*, and *DBRS Bond Rating*.

Junk bonds
www.efmoody.
com/investments/
Junk

Junk Bonds

Junk bonds, also known as *high-yield bonds*, are nothing more than speculative-grade (low-rated or unrated) bonds. Before 1977, almost all junk bonds were "fallen angels," that is, firm-issued bonds that originally had investment-grade ratings but that had since been downgraded. In 1977, however, firms began to issue "original issue junk."

Much of the credit for this innovation is given to Drexel Burnham Lambert and especially its trader, Michael Milken. Drexel had long enjoyed a niche as a junk bond trader and had established a network of potential investors in junk bonds. Firms not able to muster an investment-grade rating were happy to have Drexel (and other investment bankers) market their bonds directly to the public, as this opened up a new source of financing. Junk issues were a lower-cost financing alternative than borrowing from banks.

High-yield bonds gained considerable notoriety in the 1980s when they were used as financing vehicles in leveraged buyouts and hostile takeover attempts. Shortly thereafter, however, the junk bond market suffered. The legal difficulties of Drexel and Michael Milken in connection with Wall Street's insider trading scandals of the late 1980s tainted the junk bond market.

At the height of Drexel's difficulties, the high-yield bond market nearly dried up. Since then, the market has rebounded dramatically. However, it is worth noting that the average credit quality of high-yield debt issued today is higher than the average quality in the boom years of the 1980s. Of course, junk bonds are more vulnerable to economic distress than investment-grade bonds. During the financial crisis of 2008–2009, prices on these bonds fell dramatically, and their yields to maturity rose equally dramatically. The spread between yields on B-rated bonds and Treasuries widened from around 3 percent in early 2007 to an astonishing 19 percent by the beginning of 2009.

Determinants of Bond Safety

Bond rating agencies base their quality ratings largely on an analysis of the level and trend of some of the issuer's financial ratios. The key ratios used to evaluate safety are as follows:

1. *Coverage ratios.* Ratios of company earnings to fixed costs. For example, the *times-interest-earned ratio* is the ratio of earnings before interest payments and taxes to interest obligations. The *fixed-charge coverage ratio* adds lease payments and sinking fund payments to interest obligations to arrive at the ratio of earnings to all fixed cash obligations. Low or falling coverage ratios signal possible cash flow difficulties.

2. *Leverage ratio.* Debt-to-equity ratio. A too-high leverage ratio indicates excessive indebtedness, signalling the possibility the firm will be unable to earn enough to satisfy the obligations on its bonds.

3. *Liquidity ratios.* The two common liquidity ratios are the *current ratio* (current assets/current liabilities) and the *quick ratio* (current assets excluding inventories/current liabilities). These ratios measure the firm's ability to pay bills coming due with cash currently being collected.

4. *Profitability ratio.* Measures of rates of return on assets or equity. Profitability ratios are indicators of a firm's overall financial health. The *return on assets* (earnings before interest and taxes divided by total assets) is the most popular of these measures. Firms with higher return on assets should be better able to raise money in security markets because they offer prospects for better returns on the firm's investments.

5. *Cash-flow-to-debt ratio.* This is the ratio of total cash flow to outstanding debt.

Standard & Poor's periodically computes median values of selected ratios for firms in several rating classes, which we present in Table 12.3. Of course, ratios must be evaluated in the context of industry standards, and analysts differ in the weights they put on particular ratios. Nevertheless, the table demonstrates the tendency of ratios to improve along with the firm's rating class. And default rates vary dramatically with bond rating. Historically, only about 1 percent of industrial bonds originally rated AA or better at issuance had defaulted after 15 years. That ratio is around 7.5 percent for BBB-rated bonds, and 40 percent for B-rated bonds. Credit risk clearly varies dramatically across rating classes.

TABLE 12.3

Financial Ratios
and Default Risk
by Rating Class,
Long-Term Debt

	Three-Year (2002 to 2004) Medians						
	AAA	AA	A	BBB	BB	B	CCC
EBIT interest coverage multiple	23.8	19.5	8.0	4.7	2.5	1.2	.4
EBITDA interest coverage multiple	25.5	24.6	10.2	6.5	3.5	1.9	.9
Funds from operations/total debt (%)	203.3	79.9	48.0	35.9	22.4	11.5	5.0
Free operating cash flow/total debt (%)	127.6	44.5	25.0	17.3	8.3	2.8	(2.1)
Total debt/EBITDA multiple	.4	.9	1.6	2.2	3.5	5.3	7.9
Return on capital (%)	27.6	27.0	17.5	13.4	11.3	8.7	3.2
Total debt/total debt + equity (%)	12.4	28.3	37.5	42.5	53.7	75.9	113.5
Historical default rate (%)	.5	1.3	2.3	6.6	19.5	35.8	54.4

Note: EBITDA: Earnings before interest, taxes, depreciation, and amortization.

Source: *Corporate Rating Criteria*, Standard & Poor's, 2006. Historical default rates from "Static Pools Cumulative Average Default Rates (%)," Standard & Poor's. Reproduced by permission of Standard & Poor's, a division of The McGraw-Hill Companies, Inc.

Many studies have tested the ability of financial ratios to predict bond ratings. For instance, such tests were conducted for the ratings of the Canadian Bond Rating Service[14] (CBRS) in a study by Barnes and Byng.[15] The researchers examined 27 financial variables that included ratios similar to those in Table 12.3, as well as variables representing the size and earnings stability of the firm. The results showed that the observed ratings assigned by CBRS in the years 1972, 1978, and 1983 could be predicted fairly accurately by an appropriate set of weights applied to the 27 variables for each year. These weights, though, tended to change from year to year, and the accuracy of one year's predictors tended to deteriorate with time.

Other studies have tested whether financial ratios can in fact be used to predict default risk. One of the best-known series of tests has been conducted by Edward Altman, who has used discriminant analysis to predict bankruptcy.[16] With this technique, a firm is assigned a score based on its financial characteristics. If its score exceeds a cutoff value, the firm is deemed creditworthy. A score below the cutoff value indicates significant bankruptcy risk in the near future.

To illustrate the technique, suppose that we were to collect data on the return on equity (ROE) and coverage ratios of a sample of firms and then keep records of any corporate bankruptcies. In Figure 12.8 we plot the ROE and coverage ratios for each firm using *X* for firms that eventually went bankrupt and *O* for those who remained solvent. Clearly, the *X* and *O* firms show different patterns of data, with the solvent firms typically showing higher values for the two ratios.

---

[14]CBRS was bought up by Standard & Poor's in 2000.

[15]Tom Barnes and Tom Byng, "The Prediction of Corporate Bond Ratings: The Canadian Case," *Canadian Journal of Administrative Sciences* 5, no. 3 (September 1988).

[16]Altman's original work was published in Edward I. Altman, "Financial Ratios, Discriminant Analysis, and the Prediction of Corporate Bankruptcy," *Journal of Finance* 23 (September 1968). This equation is from his updated study, *Corporate Financial Distress and Bankruptcy*, 2nd ed. (New York: Wiley, 1993), p. 29. Altman's original work was published in Edward I. Altman, "Financial Ratios, Discriminant Analysis, and the Prediction of Corporate Bankruptcy," *Journal of Finance* 23 (September 1968). This equation is from his updated study, *Corporate Financial Distress and Bankruptcy*, 2nd ed. (New York: Wiley, 1993), p. 29. Altman's analysis Is updated and extended in W. H. Beaver, M. F. McNichols, and J. W. Rhie, "Have Financial Statements Become Less Informative? Evidence from the Ability of Financial Ratios to Predict Bankruptcy," *Review of Accounting Studies* 10 (2005), 93–122.

Figure 12.8
Discriminant
analysis.

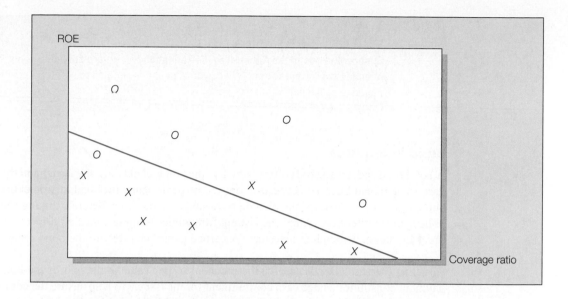

The discriminant analysis determines the equation of the line that best separates the X and O observations. Suppose that the equation of the line is $.75 = .9 \times \text{ROE} + .4 \times \text{Coverage}$. Each firm is assigned a "Z-score" equal to $.9 \times \text{ROE} + .4 \times \text{Coverage}$, using the firm's ROE and coverage ratios. If the Z-score exceeds .75, the firm plots above the line and is considered a safe bet; Z-scores below .75 foretell financial difficulty.

The discriminant analysis method was applied to a sample of Canadian firms in a study by Altman and Lavallee,[17] who found the following equation to best separate failing and nonfailing firms:

$$Z = .234\frac{\text{Sales}}{\text{Total assets}} + .972\frac{\text{Net after-tax profits}}{\text{Total debt}}$$

$$+ 1.002\frac{\text{Current assets}}{\text{Current liabilities}} - .531\frac{\text{Total debt}}{\text{Total assets}}$$

$$+ .612(\text{Rate of equity growth} - \text{Rate of asset growth})$$

Firms with Z-scores above 1.626 were deemed safe; 81.5 percent of these were still in business in the next year. In contrast, 85.2 percent of bankrupt firms had Z-scores below 1.626 the year before they failed.

A rather more skeptical view of the ability of financial ratios to predict default risk emerges from a Canadian study of *small-business* debt (mainly bank loans) by Kryzanowski and To.[18] They found that default risk depended on variables such as the firm's size and age, the type of loan, and the project performance assessment made by the lending institution. Several important financial ratios were examined, and none of them were found to be a significant determinant of default risk. It seems, therefore, that financial ratios are not good indicators of such risk for small businesses.

[17]Edward I. Altman and Marion Y. Lavallee, "Business Failure Classification in Canada," *Journal of Business Administration* 12, no. 1 (Fall 1980).
[18]Lawrence Kryzanowski and Minh Chau To, "Small-Business Debt Financing: An Empirical Investigation of Default Risk," *Canadian Journal of Administrative Sciences* 2, no. 1 (June 1985).

CC 8

CONCEPT CHECK

Suppose we add to the Altman-Lavallee equation a new variable equal to market value of equity/book value of debt. Would you expect this variable to receive a positive or negative coefficient?

Bond Indentures

A bond is issued with an **indenture**, which is the contract between the issuer and the bondholder. Part of the indenture is a set of restrictions on the firm issuing the bond to protect the rights of the bondholders. Such restrictions include provisions relating to collateral, sinking funds, dividend policy, and further borrowing. The issuing firm agrees to these so-called *protective covenants* in order to market its bonds to investors concerned about the safety of the bond issue.

Sinking Funds   Bonds call for the payment of par value at the end of the bond's life. This payment constitutes a large cash commitment for the issuer. To help ensure the commitment does not create a cash flow crisis, the firm agrees to establish a **sinking fund** to spread the payment burden over several years. The fund may operate in one of two ways:

1. The firm may repurchase a fraction of the outstanding bonds in the open market each year.

2. The firm may purchase a fraction of outstanding bonds at a special call price associated with the sinking fund provision. The firm has an option to purchase the bonds at either the market price or the sinking fund price, whichever is lower. To allocate the burden of the sinking fund call fairly among bondholders, the bonds chosen for the call are selected at random on the basis of serial numbers.[19]

The sinking fund call differs from a conventional bond call in two important ways. First, the firm can repurchase only a limited fraction of the bond issue at the sinking fund call price. At best, some indentures allow firms to use a *doubling option*, which allows repurchase of double the required number of bonds at the sinking fund call price. Second, the sinking fund call price generally is lower than the call price established by other call provisions in the indenture. The sinking fund call price usually is set at the bond's par value.

Although sinking funds ostensibly protect bondholders by making principal repayment more likely, they can hurt the investor. If interest rates fall and bond prices rise, firms will benefit from the sinking fund provision that enables them to repurchase their bonds at below-market prices. In these circumstances, the firm's gain is the bondholder's loss.

One bond issue that does not require a sinking fund is a *serial bond issue*. In a serial bond issue, the firm sells bonds with staggered maturity dates. As bonds mature sequentially, the principal repayment burden for the firm is spread over time just as it is with a sinking fund. Serial bonds do not include call provisions. A disadvantage of serial bonds is that bonds of different maturities are not interchangeable, which reduces the liquidity of the issue.

Subordination of Further Debt   One of the factors determining bond safety is total outstanding debt of the issuer. If you bought a bond today, you would be understandably distressed to see the firm tripling its outstanding debt tomorrow. Your bond would be of

---

[19]Although it is uncommon, the sinking fund provision also may call for periodic payments to a trustee, with the payments invested so that the accumulated sum can be used for retirement of the entire issue at maturity.

lower quality than it appeared when you bought it. To prevent firms from harming bondholders in this manner, **subordination clauses** restrict the amount of additional borrowing. Additional debt might be required to be subordinated in priority to existing debt; that is, in the event of bankruptcy, *subordinated* or *junior* debtholders will not be paid unless and until the prior senior debt is fully paid off. For this reason, subordination is sometimes called a "me-first rule," meaning the senior (earlier) bondholders are to be paid first in the event of bankruptcy.

Dividend Restrictions   Covenants also limit firms in the amount of dividends they are allowed to pay. These limitations protect the bondholders because they force the firm to retain assets rather than paying them out to shareholders. A typical restriction disallows payments of dividends if cumulative dividends paid since the firm's inception exceed cumulative net income plus proceeds from sales of stock.

Collateral   Some bonds are issued with specific collateral behind them. **Collateral** can take several forms, but it represents a particular asset of the firm that the bondholders receive if the firm defaults on the bond. If the collateral is property, the bond is called a *mortgage bond*. If the collateral takes the form of other securities held by the firm, the bond is a *collateral trust bond*. In the case of equipment, the bond is known as an *equipment obligation bond*. This last form of collateral is used most commonly by firms such as railroads, where the equipment is fairly standard and can be easily sold to another firm should the firm default and the bondholders acquire the collateral.

Because of the specific collateral that backs them, collateralized bonds generally are considered the safest variety of corporate bonds. General **debenture** bonds by contrast do not provide for specific collateral; they are *unsecured* bonds. The bondholder relies solely on the general earning power of the firm for the bond's safety. If the firm defaults, debenture owners become general creditors of the firm. Because they are safer, collateralized bonds generally offer lower yields than general debentures.

Figure 12.9 shows the terms of a bond issued by Mobil as described in *Moody's Industrial Manual*. The terms of the bond are typical and illustrate many of the indenture provisions we have mentioned. The bond is registered and listed on the NYSE. Although it was issued in 1991, it was not callable until 2002. Although the call price started at 105.007 percent of par value, it falls gradually until it reaches par after 2020.

Yield to Maturity and Default Risk

Because corporate bonds are subject to default risk, we must distinguish between the bond's promised yield to maturity and its expected yield. The promised or stated yield will be realized only if the firm meets the obligations of the bond issue. Therefore, the stated yield is the *maximum possible* yield to maturity of the bond. The expected yield to maturity must take into account the possibility of a default.

For example, at the height of the financial crisis, in October 2008, as Ford Motor Company struggled, its bonds due in 2028 were rated CCC and were selling at about 33 percent of par value, resulting in a yield to maturity of about 20 percent. Investors did not really expect these bonds to provide a 20 percent rate of return. They recognized that there was a decent chance bondholders would not receive all the payments promised in the bond contract and that the yield based on *expected* cash flows was far less than the yield based on *promised* cash flows. As it turned out, of course, Ford weathered the storm, and investors who purchased its bonds made a very nice profit: the bonds were selling in mid-2012 for about 110 percent of par value, more than triple their value in 2008.

Figure 12.9

Callable bond
issued by Mobil.

Mobil Corp. debenture 8s, due 2032:
Rating—Aa2

AUTH—$250,000,000.

OUTSTG—Dec. 31, 1993, $250,000,000.

DATED—Oct. 30, 1991.

INTEREST—F&A 12.

TRUSTEE—Chemical Bank.

DENOMINATION—Fully registered, $1,000 and integral multiples thereof.
Transferable and exchangeable without service charge.

CALLABLE—As a whole or in part, at any time, on or after Aug. 12, 2002, at the option
of Co. on at least 30 but not more than 60 days' notice to each Aug. 11 as follows:

2003.....105.007	2004.....104.756	2005.....104.506
2006.....104.256	2007.....104.005	2008.....103.755
2009.....103.505	2010.....103.254	2011 .....103.004
2012 .....102.754	2013.....102.503	2014 .....102.253
2015 .....102.003	2016.....101.752	2017 .....101.502
2018 .....101.252	2019 .....101.001	2020.....100.751
2021 .....100.501	2022.....100.250	

and thereafter at 100 plus accrued interest.

SECURITY—Not secured. Ranks equally with all other unsecured and unsubordinated
indebtedness of Co. nor any Affiliate will not incur any indebtedness; provided that Co.
will not create as security for any indebtedness for borrowed money, any mortgage,
pledge, security interest or lien on any stock or indebtedness is directly owned by Co.,
without effectively providing that the debt securities shall be secured equally and
ratably with such indebtedness, so long as such indebtedness shall be so secured.

INDENTURE MODIFICATION—Indenture may be modified, except as provided with,
consent of 66⅔% of debs. outstg.

RIGHTS ON DEFAULT—Trustee, or 25% of debs. outstg., may declare principal due
and payable (30 days' grace for payment of interest).

LISTED—On New York Stock Exchange.

PURPOSE—Proceeds used for general corporate purposes.

OFFERED—($250,000,000) at 99.51 plus accrued interest (proceeds to Co., 99.11)
on Aug. 5 1992 thru Merrill Lynch & Co., Donaldson, Lufkin & Jenerette Securities
Corp., PaineWebber Inc., Prudential Securities Inc., Smith Barney, Harris Upham &
Co. Inc. and associates.

Source: *Moody's Industrial Manual*, Moody's Investor Services, 1994.

EXAMPLE 12.10   Expected Versus Promised Yield to Maturity

Suppose a firm issued a 9 percent coupon bond 20 years ago. The bond now has 10 years left
until its maturity date but the firm is having financial difficulties. Investors believe that the firm
will be able to make good on the remaining interest payments, but that at the maturity date, the
firm will be forced into bankruptcy, and bondholders will receive only 70 percent of par value.
The bond is selling at $750.

continued

Yield to maturity (YTM) would then be calculated using the following inputs:

	Expected YTM	Stated YTM
Coupon payment	$45	$45
Number of semiannual periods	20 periods	20 periods
Final payment	$700	$1,000
Price	$750	$750

The yield to maturity based on promised payments is 13.7 percent. On the basis of the expected payment of $700 at maturity, however, the yield to maturity would be only 11.6 percent. The stated yield to maturity is greater than the yield investors actually expect to receive.

Example 12.10 suggests that when a bond becomes more subject to default risk, its price will fall, and therefore its promised yield to maturity will rise. Similarly, the default premium, the spread between the stated yield to maturity and that on otherwise-comparable Treasury bonds, will rise. However, its expected yield to maturity, which ultimately is tied to the systematic risk of the bond, will be far less affected. Let's continue the example.

EXAMPLE 12.11   **Default Risk and the Default Premium**

Suppose that the condition of the firm in Example 12.10 deteriorates further, and investors now believe that the bond will pay off only 55 percent of face value at maturity. Investors now demand an expected yield to maturity of 12 percent (i.e., 6 percent semiannually), which is .4 percent higher than in Example 12.10. But the price of the bond will fall from $750 to $688 ($n = 20$; $i = 6$; FV = 550; PMT = $45). At this price, the stated yield to maturity based on promised cash flows is 15.2 percent. While the expected yield to maturity has increased by .4 percent, the drop in price has caused the promised yield to maturity (and the default premium) to rise by 1.5 percent.

CC 9

CONCEPT CHECK

What is the expected yield to maturity if the firm is in even worse condition? Investors expect a final payment of only $500, and the bond price has fallen to $650.

To compensate for the possibility of default, corporate bonds must offer a **default premium**. The default premium is the difference between the promised yield on a corporate bond and the yield of an otherwise-identical government bond that is riskless in terms of default. If the firm remains solvent and actually pays the investor all of the promised cash flows, the investor will realize a higher yield to maturity than would be realized from the government bond. If, however, the firm goes bankrupt, the corporate bond is likely to provide a lower return than the

Figure 12.10   Yields on long-term bonds, 1977–2012.

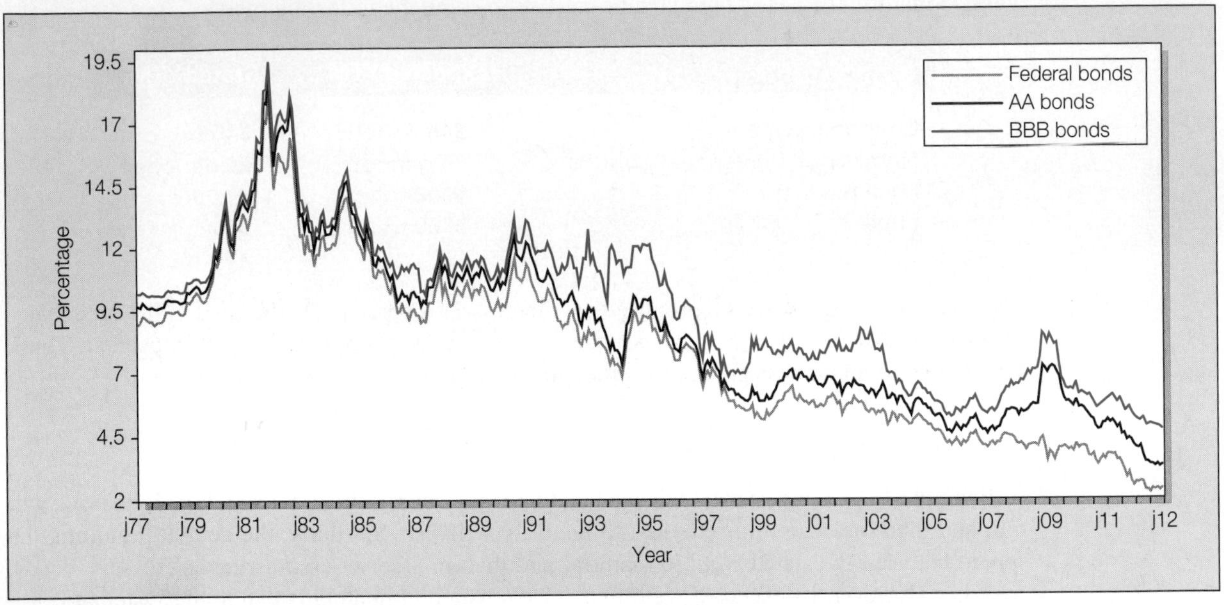

Source: Scotia Capital and PC Bonds Analytics, *Debt Market Indices*, various years.

government bond. The corporate bond has the potential for both better and worse performance than the default-free Treasury bond. In other words, it is riskier.

The pattern of default premiums offered on risky bonds is sometimes called the *risk structure of interest rates*. The greater the default risk, the higher the default premium. Figure 12.10 shows yield to maturity of bonds of different risk classes since 1977. You can see here clear evidence of credit-risk premiums on promised yields. Note, for instance, the credit spreads during the 2008–2009 financial crisis.

Credit Default Swaps

A **credit default swap (CDS)** is in effect an insurance policy on the default risk of a corporate bond or loan. To illustrate, the annual premium in July 2012 on a five-year German government CDS was about .75 percent, meaning that the CDS buyer would pay the seller an annual premium of $.75 for each $100 of bond principal. The seller collects these annual payments for the term of the contract but has to compensate the buyer for loss of bond value in the event of a default.[20]

As originally envisioned, credit default swaps were designed to allow lenders to buy protection against default risk. The natural buyers of CDSs would then be large bondholders or banks that wished to enhance the creditworthiness of their outstanding loans. Even if the borrower had shaky credit standing, the "insured" debt would be as safe as the issuer of the CDS. An investor holding a bond with a BB rating could, in principle, raise the effective quality of the debt to AAA by buying a CDS on the issuer.

This insight suggests how CDS contracts should be priced. If a BB-rated bond bundled with insurance via a CDS is effectively equivalent to a AAA-rated bond, then the premium on the

---

[20]Actually, credit default swaps may pay off even short of an actual default. The contract specifies the particular "credit events" that will trigger a payment. For example, restructuring (rewriting the terms of a firm's outstanding debt as an alternative to formal bankruptcy proceedings) may be defined as a triggering credit event.

Figure 12.11

Prices of five-year credit default swaps.

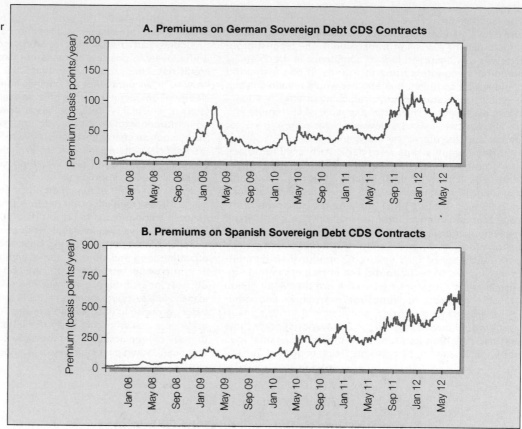

Source: Bloomberg, August 1, 2012, http://www.bloomberg.com/quote/CDBR1U5:IND/chart.

swap ought to approximate the yield spread between AAA-rated and BB-rated bonds.[21] The risk structure of interest rates and CDS prices ought to be tightly aligned.

Figure 12.11, panel A, shows the prices of five-year CDSs on German government debt between mid-2008 and 2012. Even as the strongest economy in the Eurozone, German CDS prices nevertheless reflect financial strain, first in the deep recession of 2009 and then again in 2011 as the prospects of defaults (and German-led bailouts) of Greece and other Eurozone countries worsened. As its perceived credit risk increased, so did the price of insuring its debt.

Panel B shows the prices of five-year CDS contracts on Spanish government debt. Spain's economy was far shakier than Germany's, and its CDS prices reflected this fact. By the summer of 2012, its five-year CDS prices were around 600 basis points, about eight times the price to insure German debt.

While CDSs were conceived as a form of bond insurance, it wasn't long before investors realized that they could be used to speculate on the financial health of particular issues. As Figure 12.11 makes clear, someone in early 2011 wishing to bet against Spain might have purchased CDS contracts on its sovereign debt and would have profited as CDS prices spiked over the next 18 months. The box here discusses the role of credit default swaps in the financial crisis of 2008–2009.

---

[21]We say "approximate" because there are some differences between highly rated bonds and bonds synthetically enhanced with credit default swaps. For example, the term of the swap may not match the maturity of the bond. Tax treatment of coupon payments versus swap payments may differ, as may the liquidity of the bonds. Finally, some CDSs may entail one-time up-front payments as well as annual premiums.

CREDIT DEFAULT SWAPS, SYSTEMIC RISK, AND THE CRISIS OF 2008–2009

The credit crisis of 2008–2009, when lending among banks and other financial institutions effectively seized up, was in large measure a crisis of transparency. The biggest problem was a widespread lack of confidence in the financial standing of counterparties to a trade. If one institution could not be confident that another would remain solvent, it would understandably be reluctant to offer it a loan. When doubt about the credit exposure of customers and trading partners spiked to levels not seen since the Great Depression, the market for loans dried up.

Credit default swaps were particularly cited for fostering doubts about counterparty reliability. By August 2008, $63 trillion of such swaps were reportedly outstanding. (By comparison, U.S. gross domestic product in 2008 was about $14 trillion.) As the subprime mortgage market collapsed and the economy entered a deep recession, the potential obligations on these contracts ballooned to levels previously considered unimaginable and the ability of CDS sellers to honour their commitments looked to be in doubt. For example, the huge insurance firm AIG alone had sold more than $400 billion of CDS contracts on subprime mortgages and other loans and was days from insolvency. But AIG's insolvency would have triggered the insolvency of other firms that had relied on its promise of protection against loan defaults. These in turn might have triggered further

defaults. In the end, the government felt compelled to rescue AIG to prevent a chain reaction of insolvencies.

Counterparty risk and lax reporting requirements made it effectively impossible to tease out firms' exposures to credit risk. One problem was that CDS positions do not have to be accounted for on balance sheets. And the possibility of one default setting off a sequence of further defaults means that lenders may be exposed to the default of an institution with which they do not even directly trade. Such knock-on effects create *systemic risk*, in which the entire financial system can freeze up. With the ripple effects of bad debt extending in ever-widening circles, lending to anyone can seem imprudent.

In the aftermath of the credit crisis the *Dodd-Frank Act* called for new regulation and reforms. One proposal is for a central clearing house for credit derivatives such as CDS contracts. Such a system would foster transparency of positions, would allow the clearing house to replace traders' offsetting long and short positions with a single net position, and would require daily recognition of gains or losses on positions through a margin or collateral account. If losses were to mount, positions would have to be unwound before growing to unsustainable levels. Allowing traders to accurately assess counterparty risk, and limiting such risk through margin accounts and the extra backup of the clearinghouse, would go a long way in limiting systemic risk.

Credit Risk and Collateralized Debt Obligations

Collateralized debt obligations, or **CDOs**, emerged in the last decade as a major mechanism to reallocate credit risk in the fixed-income markets. To create a CDO, a financial institution, commonly a bank, first establishes a legally distinct entity to buy and later resell a portfolio of bonds or other loans. A common vehicle for this purpose is the so-called *structured investment vehicle (SIV)*.[22] The SIV raises funds, often by issuing short-term commercial paper, and uses the proceeds to buy corporate bonds or other forms of debt such as mortgage loans or credit card debt. These loans are first pooled together and then split into a series of classes known as *tranches*. (*Tranche* is the French word for "slice.")

Each tranche is given a different level of seniority in terms of its claims on the underlying loan pool, and each can be sold as a stand-alone security. As the loans in the underlying pool make their interest payments, the proceeds are distributed to pay interest to each tranche in order of seniority. This priority structure implies that each tranche has a different exposure to credit risk.

Figure 12.12 illustrates a typical setup. The senior tranche is on top. Its investors may account for perhaps 80 percent of the principal of the entire pool. But it has first claim on *all* the debt service, and therefore bears little credit exposure. For example, using our numbers, even if 20 percent of the debt pool defaults, the senior tranche can be paid in full. Once the highest-seniority tranche is paid off, the next-lower class (e.g., the mezzanine 1 tranche in Figure 12.12) receives the proceeds from the pool of loans until its claims also are satisfied.

---

[22]The legal separation of the bank from the SIV allows the ownership of the loans to be conducted off the bank's balance sheet, and thus avoids capital requirements the bank would otherwise encounter.

Figure 12.12

Collateralized debt obligations.

		Senior-Subordinated Tranche Structure	Typical Terms
		Senior tranche	70–90% of notional principal, coupon similar to Aa-Aaa–rated bonds
		Mezzanine 1	5–15% of principal, investment-grade rating
Bank	Structured investment vehicle (SIV)		
		Mezzanine 2	5–15% of principal, higher-quality junk rating
		Equity/first loss/ residual tranche	<2%, unrated, coupon rate with 20% credit spread

Of course, shielding senior tranches from default risk means that the risk is concentrated on the lower tranches. The bottom tranche—called variously the *equity, first-loss,* or *residual* tranche—has last call on payments from the pool of loans, or, put differently, is at the head of the line in terms of absorbing default or delinquency risk. Using junior tranches to insulate senior tranches from credit risk in this manner, one can create Aaa-rated bonds even from a junk-bond portfolio. And, in fact, while Aaa-rated bonds are extremely few and far between, Aaa-rated CDO tranches are common.

Not surprisingly, investors in tranches with the greatest exposure to credit risk demand the highest coupon rates. Therefore, while the lower mezzanine and equity tranches bear the most risk, they will provide the highest returns if credit experience turns out favourably. Ideally, investors with greater expertise in evaluating credit risk are the natural investors in these securities. Often, the originating bank holds the residual tranche. This arrangement makes sense, because it provides incentives to the originator to perform careful credit analysis of the bonds included in the structure. The bank therefore retains significant interest in the management of the relationship with the borrowers.

Mortgage-backed CDOs were an investment disaster in 2007 and 2008. These CDOs are formed by pooling, not corporate debt, but subprime mortgage loans made to individuals whose credit standing did not allow them to qualify for conventional mortgages. When home prices stalled in 2007 and interest rates on these typically adjustable-rate loans reset to market levels, mortgage delinquencies and home foreclosures soared, and investors in these securities lost billions of dollars. Even investors in highly rated tranches experienced large losses. Not surprisingly, the rating agencies that had certified these tranches as investment-grade came under considerable fire. Questions were raised concerning conflicts of interest: because the rating agencies are paid by bond issuers, the agencies were accused of responding to pressure to ease their standards.

SUMMARY

1. Fixed-income securities are distinguished by their promise to pay a fixed or specified stream of income to their holders. The coupon bond is a typical fixed income security.

2. Government bonds have original maturities greater than one year. They are issued at or near par value, with their prices quoted net of accrued interest.

3. Callable bonds should offer higher promised yields to maturity to compensate investors for the fact that they will not realize full capital gains should the interest rate fall and the bonds be called away from them at the stipulated call price. Bonds often are issued with a period of call protection. In addition, discount bonds selling significantly below their call price offer implicit call protection.

4. Retractable and extendible bonds give the bondholder rather than the issuer the option to terminate or extend the life of the bond.

5. Convertible bonds may be exchanged, at the bondholder's discretion, for a specified number of shares of stock. Convertible bondholders "pay" for this option by accepting a lower coupon rate on the security.

6. Floating-rate bonds pay a fixed premium over a reference short-term interest rate. Risk is limited because the rate paid is tied to current market conditions.

7. The yield to maturity is the single interest rate that equates the present value of a security's cash flows to its price. Bond prices and yields are inversely related. For premium bonds, the coupon rate is greater than the current yield, which is greater than the yield to maturity. The order of these inequalities is reversed for discount bonds.

8. The yield to maturity often is interpreted as an estimate of the average rate of return to an investor who purchases a bond and holds it until maturity. This interpretation is subject to error, however. Related measures are yield to call, realized compound yield, and expected (versus promised) yield to maturity.

9. Prices of zero-coupon bonds rise exponentially over time, providing a rate of appreciation equal to the interest rate. CRA treats this price appreciation as imputed taxable interest income to the investor.

10. When bonds are subject to default, the stated yield to maturity is the maximum possible yield to maturity that can be realized by the bondholder. In the event of default, however, that promised yield will not be realized. To compensate bond investors for default risk, bonds must offer default premiums, that is, promised yields in excess of those offered by default-free government securities. If the firm remains healthy, its bonds will provide higher returns than government bonds. Otherwise the returns may be lower.

11. Bond safety is often measured using financial ratio analysis. Bond indentures are another safeguard to protect the claims of bondholders. Common indentures specify sinking fund requirements, collateralization of the loan, dividend restrictions, and subordination of future debt.

12. Credit default swaps provide insurance against the default of a bond or loan. The swap buyer pays an annual premium to the swap seller, but collects a payment equal to lost value if the loan later goes into default.

13. Collateralized debt obligations are used to reallocate the credit risk of a pool of loans. The pool is sliced into tranches, with each tranche assigned a different level of seniority in terms of its claims on the cash flows from the underlying loans. High-seniority tranches are usually quite safe, with credit risk concentrated on the lower level tranches. Each tranche can be sold as a stand-alone security.

KEY EQUATIONS

(12.1) $\text{Bond value} = \sum_{t=1}^{T} \dfrac{\text{Coupon}}{(1 + r)^t} + \dfrac{\text{Par value}}{(1 + r)^T}$

(12.2) $\text{Price} = \text{Coupon} \times \dfrac{1}{r}\left(1 - \dfrac{1}{(1 + r)^T}\right) + \text{Par value} \times \dfrac{1}{(1 + r)^T}$
   $= \text{Coupon} \times \text{Annuity factor}(r, T) + \text{Par value} \times \text{PV factor}(r, T)$

(12.3) $\text{Price} = \sum_{t=1}^{60} \dfrac{\$40}{(1.04)^t} + \dfrac{\$1,000}{(1.04)^{60}}$

PROBLEMS

connect Practise and learn online with Connect.

1. Define the following types of bonds:
   a. Catastrophe bond
   b. Eurobond
   c. Zero-coupon bond
   d. Samurai bond
   e. Junk bond
   f. Convertible bond
   g. Serial bond
   h. Equipment obligation bond
   i. Original issue discount bond
   j. Indexed bond
   k. Callable bond
   l. Puttable bond

2. Which security has a higher *effective* annual interest rate?
   a. A three-month T-bill selling at $97,645 with par value $100,000
   b. A coupon bond selling at par and paying a 10 percent per year coupon semiannually

3. Treasury bonds paying an 8 percent coupon rate with *semiannual* payments currently sell at par value. What coupon rate would they have to pay in order to sell at par if they paid their coupons *annually*?

4. Two bonds have identical times to maturity and coupon rates. One is callable at 105, the other at 110. Which should have the higher yield to maturity? Why?

5. Consider a bond with a 10 percent coupon and a yield to maturity of 8 percent. If the bond's yield to maturity remains constant, then in one year, will the bond price be higher, lower, or unchanged? Why?

6. Consider an 8 percent coupon bond selling for $953.10 with three years until maturity making *annual* coupon payments. The interest rates in the next three years will be, with certainty, $r_1 = 8$ percent, $r_2 = 10$ percent, and $r_3 = 12$ percent. Calculate the yield to maturity and realized compound yield of the bond.

7. Assume you have a one-year investment horizon and are trying to choose among three bonds. All have the same degree of default risk and mature in 10 years. The first is a zero-coupon bond that pays $1,000 at maturity. The second has an 8 percent coupon rate and pays the $80 coupon once per year. The third has a 10 percent coupon rate and pays the $100 coupon once per year.
   a. If all three bonds are now priced to yield 8 percent to maturity, what are their prices?
   b. If you expect their yields to maturity to be 8 percent at the beginning of next year, what will their prices be then? What is your before-tax holding period return on each bond? If your tax bracket is 30 percent on ordinary income and 20 percent on capital gains income, what will your after-tax rate of return be on each?
   c. Recalculate your answer to (b) under the assumption that you expect the yields to maturity on each bond to be 7 percent at the beginning of next year.

8. Consider a bond paying a coupon rate of 10 percent per year semiannually when the market interest rate is only 4 percent per half-year. The bond has three years until maturity.
   a. Find the bond's price today and six months from now after the next coupon is paid.
   b. What is the total rate of return on the bond?

9. A 20-year-maturity bond with par value of $1,000 makes semiannual coupon payments at a coupon rate of 8 percent. Find the bond equivalent and effective annual yield to maturity of the bond if the bond price is

   a. $950

   b. $1,000

   c. $1,050

10. Repeat problem 9 using the same data, but assuming that the bond makes its coupon payments annually. Why are the yields you compute lower in this case?

11. Fill in the table below for the following zero-coupon bonds, all of which have par values of $1,000.

Price ($)	Maturity (years)	Bond-Equivalent Yield to Maturity (%)
400	20	—
500	20	—
500	10	—
—	10	10
—	10	8
400	—	8

12. A newly issued bond pays its coupons once annually. Its coupon rate is 5 percent, its maturity is 20 years, and its yield to maturity is 8 percent.

    a. Find the holding-period return for a one-year investment period if the bond is selling at a yield to maturity of 7 percent by the end of the year.

    b. If you sell the bond after one year, what taxes will you owe if the tax rate on interest income is 40 percent and the tax rate on capital gains income is 30 percent? The bond is subject to original issue discount tax treatment.

    c. What is the after-tax holding-period return on the bond?

    d. Find the realized compound yield *before taxes* for a two-year holding period, assuming that (1) you sell the bond after two years, (2) the bond yield is 7 percent at the end of the second year, and (3) the coupon can be reinvested for one year at a 3 percent interest rate.

    e. Use the tax rates in part (b) to compute the *after-tax* two-year realized compound yield. Remember to take account of OID tax rules.

13. A bond with a coupon rate of 7 percent makes semiannual coupon payments on January 15 and July 15 of each year. The quoted price for the bond on January 30 at 100.125. What is the invoice price of the bond? The coupon period has 182 days.

14. A bond has a current yield of 9 percent and a yield to maturity of 10 percent. Is the bond selling above or below par value? Explain.

15. Is the coupon rate of the bond in problem 14 more or less than 9 percent?

16. Return to Table 12.1 and calculate the real and nominal rates of return on the RRB bond in the second and third years.

17. A newly issued 20-year-maturity, zero-coupon bond is issued with a yield to maturity of 8 percent and a face value of $1,000. Find the imputed interest income in the first, second, and last year of the bond's life.

18. A newly issued 10-year-maturity, 4 percent coupon bond making *annual* coupon payments is sold to the public at a price of $800. What will be an investor's taxable income from the bond over the coming year? The bond will not be sold at the end of the year. The bond is treated as an original issue discount bond.

19. A 30-year-maturity, 8 percent coupon bond paying coupons semiannually is callable in five years at a call price of $1,100. The bond currently sells at a yield to maturity of 7 percent (3.5 percent per half-year).

    a. What is the yield to call?

    b. What is the yield to call if the call price is only $1,050?

    c. What is the yield to call if the call price is $1,100, but the bond can be called in two years instead of five years?

20. A 10-year bond of a firm in severe financial distress has a coupon rate of 14 percent and sells for $900. The firm is currently renegotiating the debt, and it appears that the lenders will allow the firm to reduce coupon payments on the bond to one-half the originally contracted amount. The firm can handle these lower payments. What is the stated and expected yield to maturity of the bonds? The bond makes its coupon payments annually.

21. A two-year bond with a par value of $1,000 making annual coupon payments of $100 is priced at $1,000. What is the yield to maturity of the bond? What will be the realized compound yield to maturity if the one-year interest rate next year turns out to be (*a*) 8 percent, (*b*) 10 percent, (*c*) 12 percent?

22. The stated yield to maturity and realized compound yield to maturity of a (default-free) zero-coupon bond always will be equal. Why?

23. Suppose that today's date is April 15. A bond with a 10 percent coupon paid semiannually every January 15 and July 15 is listed as selling at an ask price of 101.25. If you buy the bond from a dealer today, what price will you pay for it?

24. Assume that two firms issue bonds with the following characteristics. Both bonds are issued at par.

	ABC Bonds	XYZ Bonds
Issue size	$1.2 billion	$150 million
Maturity	10 years*	20 years
Coupon	9%	10%
Collateral	First mortgage	General debenture
Callable	Not callable	In 10 years
Call price	None	110
Sinking fund	None	Starting in 5 years

*Bond is extendible at the discretion of the bondholder for an additional 10 years.

Ignoring credit quality, identify four features of these issues that might account for the lower coupon on the ABC debt. Explain.

25. An investor believes that a bond may temporarily increase in credit risk. Which of the following would be the most liquid method of exploiting this?

    a. The purchase of a credit default swap

    b. The sale of a credit default swap

    c. The short sale of the bond

26. Which of the following *most accurately* describes the behavior of credit default swaps?

    a. When credit risk increases, swap premiums increase.

    b. When credit and interest rate risk increases, swap premiums increase.

    c. When credit risk increases, swap premiums increase, but when interest rate risk increases, swap premiums decrease.

27. What would be the likely effect on the yield to maturity of a bond resulting from

    a. An increase in the issuing firm's times-interest-earned ratio

    b. An increase in the issuing firm's debt-to-equity ratio

    c. An increase in the issuing firm's quick ratio

28. A large corporation issued both fixed- and floating-rate notes five years ago, with terms given in the following table:

	9% Coupon Notes	Floating-Rate Note
Issue size	$250 million	$280 million
Maturity	20 years	10 years
Current price (% of par)	93	98
Current coupon	9%	8%
Coupon adjusts	Fixed coupon	Every year
Coupon reset rule	—	1-year T-bill rate +2%
Callable	10 years after issue	10 years after issue
Call price	106	102
Sinking fund	None	None
Yield to maturity	9.9%	—
Price range since issued	$85–$112	$97–$102

    a. Why is the price range greater for the 9 percent coupon bond than the floating-rate note?

    b. What factors could explain why the floating-rate note is not always sold at par value?

    c. Why is the call price for the floating-rate note not of great importance to investors?

    d. Is the probability of call for the fixed-rate note high or low?

    e. If the firm were to issue a fixed-rate note with a 15-year maturity, what coupon rate would it need to offer to issue the bond at par value?

    f. Why is an entry for yield to maturity for the floating-rate note not appropriate?

29. Masters Corp. issues two bonds with 20-year maturities. Both are callable at $1,050. The first bond is issued at a deep discount with a coupon rate of 4 percent and a price of $580 to yield 8.4 percent. The second bond is issued at par value with a coupon rate of 8¾ percent.

    a. What is the yield to maturity of the par bond? Why is it higher than the yield of the discount bond?

    b. If you expect rates to fall substantially in the next two years, which bond would you prefer to hold?

    c. In what sense does the discount bond offer "implicit call protection"?

The following problems are based on questions that have appeared in past CFA examinations.

30. Bonds of Zello Corporation with a par value of $1,000 sell for $960, mature in five years, and have a 7 percent annual coupon rate paid semiannually.

    a. Calculate the

        i. Current yield

        ii. Yield to maturity (to the nearest whole percent, i.e., 3 percent, 4 percent, 5 percent, etc.)

        iii. Realized compound yield for an investor with a three-year holding period and a reinvestment rate of 6 percent over the period; at the end of three years the 7 percent coupon bonds with two years remaining will sell to yield 7 percent

   b. Cite one major shortcoming for each of the following fixed-income yield measures:

      i. Current yield

      ii. Yield to maturity

      iii. Realized compound yield

31. Leaf Products may issue a 10-year-maturity fixed-income security, which might include a sinking fund provision and either refunding or call protection.

   a. Describe a sinking fund provision.

   b. Explain the impact of a sinking fund provision on

      i. The expected average life of the proposed security

      ii. Total principal and interest payments over the life of the proposed security

   c. From the investor's point of view, explain the rationale for demanding a sinking fund provision.

32. In June 1982, when the yield to maturity on long-term bonds was about 14 percent, many observers were projecting an eventual decline in these rates. It was not unusual to hear of customers urging portfolio managers to "lock in" these high rates by buying some new issues with these high coupons. You recognize that it is not possible to really lock in such returns for coupon bonds because of the potential reinvestment rate problem if rates decline. Assuming the following expectations for a five-year bond bought at par, compute the total realized compound yield (without taxes) for the bond below.

        Coupon   14% (assume annual interest payments at end of each year)

        Maturity   Five years

       One-year reinvestment rates during:

                 Year 2, 3: 10%

                 Year 4, 5: 8%

33. On May 30, 2012, Janice Kerr is considering one of the newly issued 10-year AAA corporate bonds:

Description	Coupon	Price	Callable	Call Price
Sentinel, due May 30, 2022	6.00%	100	Noncallable	NA
Colina, due May 30, 2022	6.20%	100	Currently callable	102

   a. Suppose that market interest rates decline by 100 basis points (i.e., 1 percent). Contrast the effect of this decline on the price of each bond.

   b. Should Kerr prefer the Colina over the Sentinel bond when rates are expected to rise or to fall?

   c. What would be the effect, if any, of an increase in the *volatility* of interest rates on the prices of each bond?

34. A convertible bond has the following features:

Coupon	5.25%
Maturity	June 15, 2030
Market price of bond	$775.00
Market price of underlying common stock	$28
Annual dividend	$1.20
Conversion ratio	20.83 shares

Calculate the conversion premium for this bond.

35. *a.* Explain the impact on the offering yield of adding a call feature to a proposed bond issue.

   b. Explain the impact on the bond's expected life of adding a call feature to a proposed bond issue.

   c. Describe *one* advantage and *one* disadvantage of including callable bonds in a portfolio.

36. *a.* An investment in a coupon bond will provide the investor with a return equal to the bond's yield to maturity at the time of purchase if

   i. The bond is not called for redemption at a price that exceeds its par value.

   ii. All sinking fund payments are made in a prompt and timely fashion over the life of the issue.

   iii. The reinvestment rate is the same as the bond's yield to maturity and the bond is held until maturity.

   iv. All of the above.

   b. The market risk of an AAA-rated preferred stock relative to an AAA-rated bond is

   i. Lower

   ii. Higher

   iii. Equal

   iv. Unknown

   c. A bond with a call feature

   i. Is attractive because the immediate receipt of principal plus premium produces a high return

   ii. Is more apt to be called when interest rates are high because the interest saving will be greater

   iii. Will usually have a higher yield than a similar noncallable bond

   iv. None of the above

   d. The yield to maturity on a bond is

   i. Below the coupon rate when the bond sells at a premium, and above the coupon rate when the bond sells at a discount

   ii. The discount rate that will set the present value of the payments equal to the bond price

   iii. The current yield plus the average annual capital gains rate

   iv. Based on the assumption that any payments received are reinvested at the coupon rate

   e. A particular bond has a yield to maturity on an APR basis of 12.00 percent but makes equal quarterly payments. What is the effective annual yield to maturity?

   i. 11.45 percent

   ii. 12.00 percent

   iii. 12.55 percent

   iv. 37.35 percent

   f. In which *one* of the following cases is the bond selling at a discount?

   i. Coupon rate is greater than current yield, which is greater than yield to maturity.

   ii. Coupon rate, current yield, and yield to maturity are all the same.

   iii. Coupon rate is less than current yield, which is less than yield to maturity.

   iv. Coupon rate is less than current yield, which is greater than yield to maturity.

   g. Consider a five-year bond with a 10 percent coupon that has a present yield to maturity of 8 percent. If interest rates remain constant, one year from now the price of this bond will be

   i. Higher

   ii. Lower

   iii. The same

   iv. Par

h. The call feature of a bond means the

    i. Investor can call for payment on demand

    ii. Investor can only call if the firm defaults on an interest payment

    iii. Issuer can call the bond issue before the maturity date

    iv. Issuer can call the issue during the first three years

i. Which *one* of the following statements about convertible bonds is *false*?

    i. The yield on the convertible typically will be higher than the yield on the underlying common stock.

    ii. The convertible bond will likely participate in a major upward movement in the price of the underlying common stock.

    iii. Convertible bonds typically are secured by specific assets of the issuing company.

    iv. A convertible bond can be valued as a straight bond with an attached option.

j. All else being equal, which *one* of the following bonds would be *most likely* to sell at the highest yield?

    i. Callable debenture

    ii. Puttable mortgage bond

    iii. Callable mortgage bond

    iv. Puttable debentures

k. Yields on nonconvertible preferred stock usually are lower than yields on bonds of the same company because of differences in

    i. Marketability

    ii. Risk

    iii. Taxation

    iv. Call protection

l. The yield to maturity on a bond is

    i. Below the coupon rate when the bond sells at a discount and above the coupon rate when the bond sells at a premium

    ii. The interest rate that makes the present value of the payments equal to the bond price

    iii. Based on the assumption that all future payments received are reinvested at the coupon rate

    iv. Based on the assumption that all future payments received are reinvested at future market rates

E-INVESTMENTS

1. Go to the website of Standard & Poor's at **www.standardandpoors.com**. Look for Rating Services (Find a Rating). Find the ratings on bonds of at least 10 companies. Try to choose a sample with a wide range of ratings. Then go to a website such as **http://money.msn.com** or **http://finance.yahoo.com** and obtain, for each firm, as many of the financial ratios tabulated in Table 12.3 as you can find. Which ratios seem to best explain credit ratings?

2. At **www.bondsonline.com** review the *Industrial Spreads* for various ratings (at the menu under *Today's Market—Corporate Bond Spreads*). These are spreads above U.S. Treasuries of comparable maturity. What factors tend to explain the yield differences? How might these yield spreads differ during an economic boom versus a recession? From *Today's Market—Corporate Bond Yields*, compare the historical bond spreads and current yield curves for U.S. Treasury, municipal, and corporate bonds.

The Term Structure of Interest Rates

In Chapter 13 we assumed for the sake of simplicity that the same constant interest rate is used to discount cash flows of any maturity. In the real world this is rarely the case. We have seen, for example, that in 2012 short-term Canada bonds and notes carried yields to maturity of less than 1 percent while the longest-term bonds offered yields of about 2.3 percent. At the time when these bond prices were quoted, anyway, the longer-term securities had higher yields. This, in fact, is a common empirical pattern, but as we shall see below, the relationship between time to maturity and yield to maturity can vary dramatically from one period to another.

In this chapter we explore the pattern of interest rates for different-term assets. We attempt to identify the factors that account for that pattern and determine what information may be derived from an analysis of the so-called **term structure of interest rates**, if the structure of interest rates for discounting cash flows of different maturities.

We demonstrate how the prices of Canada bonds may be derived from prices and yields of stripped zero-coupon Government of Canada securities. We also examine the extent to which the term structure reveals market-consensus forecasts of future interest rates and how the presence of interest rate risk may affect those inferences. Finally, we show how traders can use the term structure to compute forward rates that represent interest rates on "forward" or deferred loans, and consider the relationship between forward rates and future interest rates.

13.1   THE YIELD CURVE

Figure 13.1 demonstrates that bonds of different maturities typically sell at different yields to maturity. When these bond prices and yields were compiled, long-term bonds sold at slightly higher yields than short-term bonds. Practitioners commonly summarize the relationship between yield and maturity graphically in a **yield curve**, which is a plot of yield to maturity as a function of time to maturity. The yield curve is one of the key concerns of fixed-income investors. It is central to bond valuation and, as well, allows investors to gauge their expectations for future interest rates against those of the market. Such a comparison is often the starting point in the formulation of a fixed-income portfolio strategy.

Figure 13.1

Government of Canada yield curves.

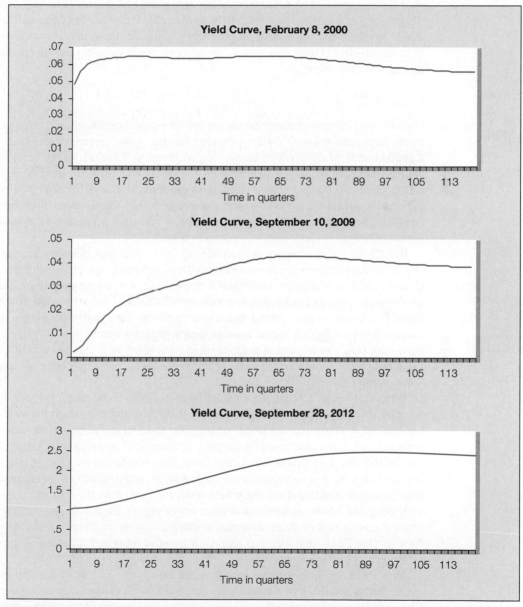

Source: Royal Bank of Canada. Data from "Yield Curves for Zero-Coupon Bonds," Bank of Canada site, http://www.bank-banque-canada.ca/en/rates/yield_curve.html.

Maturity (years)	Yield to Maturity (%)	Price
1	5	$952.38 = $1,000/1.05
2	6	$890.00 = $1,000/1.06^2
3	7	$816.30 = $1,000/1.07^3
4	8	$735.03 = $1,000/1.08^4

In 2012, the yield curve was rising, with long-term bonds offering yields higher than those of short-term bonds. But the relationship between yield and maturity can vary widely. Figure 13.1 illustrates yield curves of several different shapes. Panel A is an almost-flat curve. Panels B and C are more typical upward-sloping and slightly humped curves from September 2009 and September 2012. Other dates show an initially downward-sloping or "inverted" curve, first falling and then rising.

Bond Pricing

If yields on different-maturity bonds are not all equal, how should we value coupon bonds that make payments at many different times? For example, suppose that yields on zero-coupon Canada bonds of different maturities are as given in Table 13.1. The table tells us that zero-coupon bonds with one-year maturity sell at a yield to maturity of $y_1 = 5$ percent, two-year zeros sell at yields of $y_2 = 6$ percent, and three-year zeros sell at yields of $y_3 = 7$ percent. Which of these rates should we use to discount bond cash flows? The answer: all of them. The trick is to consider each bond cash flow—either coupon or principal payment—as at least potentially sold off separately as a stand-alone zero-coupon bond.

Recall the strips program we introduced in the previous chapter (Section 12.4). Stripped bonds are zero-coupon bonds created by selling each coupon or principal payment from a whole Canada bond as a separate cash flow. For example, a one-year-maturity Canada bond paying semiannual coupons can be split into a six-month-maturity zero (by selling the first coupon payment as a stand-alone security) and a twelve-month zero (corresponding to payment of final coupon and principal). Coupon bond stripping suggests exactly how to value a coupon bond. If each cash flow can be (and in practice often is) sold off as a separate security, then the value of the whole bond should be the same as the value of its cash flows bought piece by piece in the strips market.

What if it weren't? Then there would be easy profits to be made. For example, if investment bankers ever noticed a bond selling for less than the amount at which the sum of its parts could be sold, they would buy the bond, strip it into stand-alone zero-coupon securities, sell off the stripped cash flows, and profit by the price difference. If the bond were selling for *more* than the sum of the values of its individual cash flows, they would run the process in reverse: buy the individual zero-coupon securities in the strips market, *reconstitute* (i.e., reassemble) the cash flows into a coupon bond, and sell the whole bond for more than the cost of the pieces. Both **bond stripping** and **bond reconstitution** offer opportunities for *arbitrage*—the exploitation of mispricing among two or more securities to clear a riskless economic profit. Any violation of the Law of One Price, that identical cash flow bundles must sell for identical prices, gives rise to arbitrage opportunities.

Now, we know how to value each stripped cash flow. We simply look up its appropriate discount rate at the Bank of Canada Web site. Since each coupon payment matures at a different time, we discount by using the yield appropriate to its particular maturity—this is the yield on a strip maturing at the time of that cash flow. We can illustrate with an example.

EXAMPLE 13.1 **Valuing Coupon Bonds**

Suppose the yields on stripped Canada bonds are given in Table 13.1, and we wish to value a 10 percent coupon bond with a maturity of three years. For simplicity, assume the bond makes its payments annually. Then the first cash flow, the $100 coupon paid at the end of the first year, is discounted at 5 percent; the second cash flow, the $100 coupon at the end of the second year, is discounted at 6 percent; and the final cash flow consisting of the final coupon plus par value, or $1,100, is discounted at 7 percent. The value of the coupon bond is therefore

$$\frac{100}{1.05} + \frac{100}{1.06^2} + \frac{1100}{1.07^3} = 95.238 + 89.000 + 897.928 = \$1,082.17$$

Calculate the yield to maturity of the coupon bond in Example 13.1, and you may be surprised. Its yield to maturity is 6.88 percent; so while its maturity matches that of the three-year zero in Table 13.1, its yield is a bit lower.[1] This reflects the fact that the three-year coupon bond may usefully be thought of as a *portfolio* of three implicit zero-coupon bonds, one corresponding to each cash flow. The yield on the coupon bond is then an amalgam of the yields on each of the three components of the "portfolio." Think about what this means: if their coupon rates differ, bonds of the same maturity generally will not have the same yield to maturity.

What then do we mean by "the" yield curve? In fact, in practice, traders refer to several yield curves. The **pure yield curve** refers to the curve for stripped, or zero-coupon, Canada bonds. In contrast, the **on-the-run yield curve** refers to the plot of yield as a function of maturity for recently issued coupon bonds selling at or near par value. As we've just seen, there may be significant differences in these two curves. Several yield curves published in the financial press are typically on-the-run curves. On-the-run Canada bonds have the greatest liquidity, so traders have keen interest in their yield curve. One might also consider other yield curves—for instance, the real yield curve, that is, the yield curve for inflation-indexed bonds such as the real return bonds introduced in the previous chapter. This would be a plot of real interest rates as a function of maturity.

CC 1

CONCEPT CHECK

Calculate the price and yield to maturity of a three-year bond with a coupon rate of 4 percent making annual coupon payments. Does its yield match that of either the three-year zero or the 10 percent coupon bond considered in Example 13.1? Why is the yield spread between the 4 percent bond and the zero smaller than the yield spread between the 10 percent bond and the zero?

13.2

THE YIELD CURVE AND FUTURE INTEREST RATES

We've told you what the yield curve is, but we haven't yet had much to say about where it comes from. For example, why is the curve sometimes upward-sloping and sometimes downward-sloping? How do expectations for the evolution of interest rates affect the shape of today's yield curve?

---

[1] Remember that the yield to maturity of a coupon bond is the *single* interest rate at which the present value of cash flows equals market price. To calculate the bond's yield to maturity on your calculator or spreadsheet, set $n = 3$; price $= 1,082.17$; future value $= 1,000$; payment $= 100$. Then compute the interest rate.

These questions do not have simple answers, so we will begin with an admittedly idealized framework, and then extend the discussion to more realistic settings. To start, consider a world with no uncertainty—specifically, one in which all investors already know the path of future interest rates.

The Yield Curve Under Certainty

If interest rates are certain, what should we make of the fact that the yield on the two-year zero coupon bond in Table 13.1 is greater than that on the one-year zero? It can't be that one bond is expected to provide a higher rate of return than the other. This would not be possible in a certain world—with no risk, all bonds (in fact, all securities!) must offer identical returns, or investors will bid up the price of the high-return bond until its rate of return is no longer superior to that of other bonds.

Instead, the upward-sloping yield curve is evidence that short-term rates are going to be higher next year than they are now. To see why, consider two two-year bond strategies. The first strategy entails buying the two-year zero offering a two-year yield to maturity of $y_2 = 6$ percent, and holding it until maturity. The zero with face value $1,000 is purchased today for $1,000/1.06^2 = $890 and matures in two years to $1,000. The total two-year growth factor for the investment is therefore $1,000/$890 = 1.06^2 = 1.1236$.

Now consider an alternative two-year strategy. Invest the same $890 in a one-year zero-coupon bond with a yield to maturity of 5 percent. When that bond matures, reinvest the proceeds in another one-year bond. Figure 13.2 illustrates these two strategies. The interest rate that one-year bonds will offer next year is denoted as r_2.

Remember, both strategies must provide equal returns—neither entails any risk. Therefore, the proceeds after two years to either strategy must be equal:

$$\text{Buy and hold two-year zero} = \text{Roll over one-year bonds}$$
$$\$890 \times 1.06^2 = \$890 \times 1.05 \times (1 + r_2)$$

We find next year's interest rate by solving $1 + r_2 = 1.06^2/1.05 = 1.0701$, or $r_2 = 7.01$ percent. So while the one-year bond offers a lower yield to maturity than the two-year bond (5 percent as

Figure 13.2

Two two-year investment programs.

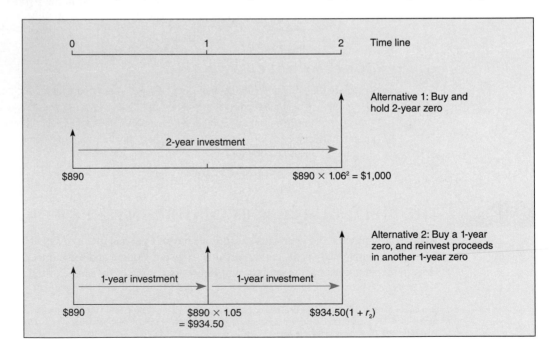

against 6 percent), we see that it has a compensating advantage: it allows you to roll over your funds into another short-term bond next year when rates will be higher. Next year's interest rate is higher than today's by just enough to make rolling over one-year bonds equally attractive as investing in the two-year bond.

To distinguish between yields on long-term bonds versus short-term rates that will be available in the future, practitioners use the following terminology. They call the yield to maturity on zero-coupon bonds the **spot rate**, meaning the rate that prevails *today* for a time period corresponding to the zero's maturity. In contrast, the **short rate** for a given time interval (e.g., 1 year) refers to the interest rate for that interval available at different points in time. In our example, the short rate today is 5 percent, and the short rate next year will be 7.01 percent.

Not surprisingly, the two-year spot rate is an average of today's short rate and next year's short rate. But because of compounding, that average is a geometric one.[2] We see this by again equating the total return on the two competing two-year strategies:

$$(1 + y_2)^2 = (1 + r_1) \times (1 + r_2)$$
$$1 + y_2 = [(1 + r_1) \times (1 + r_2)]^{1/2}$$

(13.1)

Equation 13.1 begins to tell us why the yield curve might take on different shapes at different times. When next year's short rate, r_2, is greater than this year's short rate, r_1, the average of the two rates is higher than today's rate, so $y_2 > r_1$ and the yield curve slopes upward. If next year's short rate were less than r_1, the yield curve would slope downward. Thus, at least in part, the yield curve reflects the market's assessments of coming interest rates. The following example uses a similar analysis to find the short rate that will prevail in year 3.

EXAMPLE 13.2   Finding a Future Short Rate

Now we compare two three-year strategies. One is to buy a three-year zero, with a yield to maturity from Table 13.1 of 7 percent, and hold it until maturity. The other is to buy a two-year zero yielding 6 percent, and roll the proceeds into a one-year bond in year 3, at the short rate r_3. The growth factor for the invested funds under each policy will be

Buy and hold 3-year zero = Buy 2-year zero; roll proceeds into one-year bond
$$(1 + y_3)^3 = (1 + y_2)^2 \times (1 + r_3)$$
$$1.07^3 = 1.06^2 \times (1 + r_3)$$

which implies that $r_3 = 1.07^3/1.06^2 - 1 = .09028 = 9.028$ percent. Again, notice that the yield on the three-year bond reflects a geometric average of the discount factors for the next three years:

$$1 + y_3 = [(1 + r_1) \times (1 + r_2) \times (1 + r_3)]^{1/3}$$
$$1.07 = (1.05 \times 1.0701 \times 1.09028)^{1/3}$$

We conclude that the yield or spot rate on a long-term bond reflects the path of short rates anticipated by the market over the life of the bond.

CC 2

CONCEPT CHECK

Use Table 13.1 to find the short rate that will prevail in the fourth year. Confirm that the yield on the four-year zero is a geometric average of the short rates in the next four years.

[2]In an arithmetic average, we add n numbers and divide by n. In a geometric average, we multiply n numbers and take the nth root.

Figure 13.3

Short rates versus spot rates.

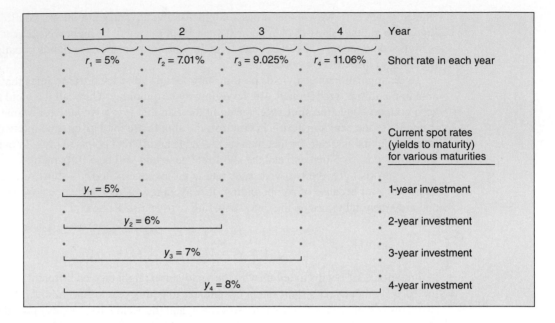

Figure 13.3 summarizes the results of our analysis and emphasizes the difference between short rates and spot rates. The top line presents the short rates for each year. The lower lines present spot rates—or, equivalently, yields to maturity on zero-coupon bonds for different holding periods—extending from the present to each relevant maturity date.

Holding-Period Returns

We've argued that the multiyear cumulative returns on all of our competing bonds ought to be equal. What about holding-period returns over shorter periods such as a year? You might think that bonds selling at higher yields to maturity will offer higher one-year returns, but this is not the case. In fact, once you stop to think about it, it's clear that this *cannot* be true. In a world of certainty, all bonds must offer identical returns, or investors will flock to the higher-return securities, bidding up their prices, and reducing their returns. We can illustrate by using the bonds in Table 13.1.

EXAMPLE 13.3   Holding-Period Returns on Zero-Coupon Bonds

The one-year bond in Table 13.1 can be bought today for $1,000/1.05 = $952.38 and will mature to its par value in one year. It pays no coupons, so total investment income is just its price appreciation, and its rate of return is ($1,000 − $952.38)/$952.38 = .05. The two-year bond can be bought for $1,000/1.06^2 = $890. Next year, the bond will have a remaining maturity of one year and the one-year interest rate will be 7.01 percent. Therefore, its price next year will be $1,000/1.0701 = $934.49, and its one-year holding-period rate of return will be ($934.49 − $890)/$890 = .05, for an identical 5 percent rate of return.

CC 3

CONCEPT CHECK

Show that the rate of return on the three-year zero in Table 13.1 also will be 5 percent. *Hint:* Next year, the bond will have a maturity of 2 years. Use the short rates derived in Figure 13.3 to compute the two-year spot rate that will prevail a year from now.

Forward Rates

The following equation generalizes our approach to inferring a future short rate from the yield curve of zero-coupon bonds. It equates the total return on two n-year investment strategies: buying and holding an n-year zero-coupon bond versus buying an $(n - 1)$-year zero and rolling over the proceeds into a one-year bond.

$$(1 + y_n)^n = (1 + y_{n-1})^{n-1} \times (1 + r_n) \tag{13.2}$$

where n denotes the number of periods, and y_n is the yield to maturity of a zero-coupon bond with an n-period maturity. Given the observed yield curve, we can solve equation 13.2 for the short rate in the last period:

$$(1 + r_n) = \frac{(1 + y_n)^n}{(1 + y_{n-1})^{n-1}} \tag{13.3}$$

Equation 13.3 has a simple interpretation. The numerator on the right-hand side is the total growth factor of an investment in an n-year zero held until maturity. Similarly, the denominator is the growth factor of an investment in an $(n - 1)$-year zero. Because the former investment lasts for one more year than the latter, the difference in these growth factors must be the rate of return available in year n when the $(n - 1)$-year zero can be rolled over into a one-year investment.

Of course, when future interest rates are uncertain, as they are in reality, there is no meaning to inferring "the" future short rate. No one knows today what the future interest rate will be. At best, we can speculate as to its expected value and associated uncertainty. Nevertheless, it still is common to use equation 13.3 to investigate the implications of the yield curve for future interest rates. In recognition of the fact that future interest rates are uncertain, we call the interest rate that we infer in this matter the **forward interest rate** rather than the *future short rate*, because it need not be the interest rate that actually will prevail at the future date.

If the forward rate for period n is denoted f_n, we then define f_n by the equation

$$(1 + f_n) = \frac{(1 + y_n)^n}{(1 + y_{n-1})^{n-1}} \tag{13.4}$$

We may rewrite this equation as

$$(1 + y_n)^n = (1 + y_{n-1})^{n-1}(1 + f_n) \tag{13.5}$$

In this formulation, the forward rate is *defined* as the "breakeven" interest rate that equates the return on an n-period zero-coupon bond to that of an $(n - 1)$-period zero-coupon bond rolled over into a one-year bond in year n. The actual total returns on the two n-year strategies will be equal if the short interest rate in year n turns out to equal f_n.

EXAMPLE 13.4   Forward Rates

Suppose a bond trader uses the data presented in Table 13.1. The forward rate for year 4 would be computed as

$$1 + f_4 = \frac{(1 + y_4)^4}{(1 + y_3)^3} = \frac{1.08^4}{1.07^3} = 1.1106$$

Therefore, the forward rate is $f_4 = .1106$, or 11.06 percent.

Spot and Forward Yields

The spreadsheet here can be used to estimate prices and yields of coupon bonds and to calculate the forward rates for both single-year and multiyear periods. Spot yields are derived for the yield curve of bonds that are selling at their par value, also referred to as the current coupon or "on-the-run" bond yield curve.

The spot rates for each maturity date are used to calculate the present value of each period's cash flow. The sum of these cash flows is the price of the bond. Given its price, the bond's yield to maturity can then be computed. If you were to err and use the yield to maturity of the on-the-run bond to discount each of the bond's coupon payments, you could find a significantly different price. That difference is calculated in the worksheet.

Excel Questions

1. Change the spot rate in the spreadsheet to 8 percent for all maturities. The forward rates will all be 8 percent. Why is this not surprising?

2. The spot rates in column B decrease for longer maturities, and the forward rates decrease even more rapidly with maturity. What happens to the pattern of forward rates if you input spot rates that increase with maturity? Why?

	A	B	C	D	E	F	G	H
56		**Forward Rate Calculations**						
57								
58		**Spot Rate**	**1-yr for.**	**2-yr for.**	**3-yr for.**	**4-yr for.**	**5-yr for.**	**6-yr for.**
59	**Period**							
60	1	8.0000%	7.9792%	7.6770%	7.2723%	6.9709%	6.8849%	6.7441%
61	2	7.9896%	7.3757%	6.9205%	6.6369%	6.6131%	6.4988%	6.5520%
62	3	7.7846%	6.4673%	6.2695%	6.3600%	6.2807%	6.3880%	6.1505%
63	4	7.4537%	6.0720%	6.3065%	6.2186%	6.3682%	6.0872%	6.0442%
64	5	7.1760%	6.5414%	6.2920%	6.4671%	6.0910%	6.0387%	5.8579%
65	6	7.0699%	6.0432%	6.4299%	5.9413%	5.9134%	5.7217%	5.6224%
66	7	6.9227%	6.8181%	5.8904%	5.8701%	5.6414%	5.5384%	5.3969%
67	8	6.9096%	4.9707%	5.3993%	5.2521%	5.2209%	5.1149%	5.1988%

We emphasize that the interest rate that actually will prevail in the future need not equal the forward rate, which is calculated from today's data. Indeed, it is not even necessarily the case that the forward rate equals the expected value of the future short interest rate. This is an issue that we address in the next section. For now, however, we note that forward rates equal future short rates in the *special case* of interest rate certainty.

CC 4

CONCEPT CHECK

You've been exposed to many "rates" in the last few pages. Explain the differences between spot rates, short rates, and forward rates.

13.3 INTEREST RATE UNCERTAINTY AND FORWARD RATES

Let us turn now to the more difficult analysis of the term structure when future interest rates are uncertain. We have argued so far that, in a certain world, different investment strategies with common terminal dates must provide equal rates of return. For example, two consecutive one-year investments in zeros would need to offer the same total return as an equal-sized investment in a two-year zero. Therefore, under certainty,

$$(1 + r_1)(1 + r_2) = (1 + y_2)^2 \tag{13.6}$$

What can we say when r_2 is not known today? For example, suppose that today's rate is $r_1 = 5$ percent and that the *expected* short rate for the following year is $E(r_2) = 6$ percent. If investors cared only about the expected value of the interest rate, then the yield to maturity on a two-year zero would be determined by using the expected short rate in equation 13.6:

$$(1 + y_2)^2 = (1 + r_1) \times [1 + E(r_2)] = 1.05 \times 1.06$$

The price of a two-year zero would be $\$1,000/(1 + y_2)^2 = \$1,000/(1.05 \times 1.06) = \$898.47$.

But now consider a short-term investor who wishes to invest only for one year. She can purchase the one-year zero and lock in a riskless 5 percent return because she knows that at the end of the year, the bond will be worth its maturity value of $1,000. She can also purchase the two-year zero. Its *expected* rate of return also is 5 percent: next year, the bond will have one year to maturity, and we expect that the one-year interest rate will be 6 percent, implying a price of $909.09 and a holding-period return of 5 percent.

But the rate of return on the two-year bond is risky. If next year's interest rate turns out to be above expectations, that is, greater than 6 percent, the bond price will be below $943.40, and conversely, if r_2 turns out to be less than 6 percent, the bond price will exceed $943.40. Why should this short-term investor buy the risky two-year bond when its expected return is 5 percent, no better than that of the risk-free one-year bond? Clearly, she would not hold the two-year bond unless it offered an expected rate of return greater than the riskless 5 percent return available on the competing one-year bond. This requires that the two-year bond sell at a price lower than the $898.47 value we derived when we ignored risk.

EXAMPLE 13.5   **Bond Prices and Forward Rates with Interest Rate Risk**

Suppose that most investors have short-term horizons and are willing to hold the two-year bond only if its price falls to $881.83. At this price, the expected holding-period return on the two-year bond is 7 percent (because $943.40/881.83 = 1.07$). The risk premium of the two-year bond, therefore, is 2 percent; it offers an expected rate of return of 7 percent versus the 5 percent risk-free return on the one-year bond. At this risk premium, investors are willing to bear the price risk associated with interest rate uncertainty.

In this environment, the forward rate, f_2, no longer equals the expected short rate, $E(r_2)$. Although we have assumed that $E(r_2) = 6$ percent, it is easy to confirm that $f_2 = 8$ percent. The yield to maturity on the two-year zero selling at $881.83 is 6.49 percent, and

$$1 + f_2 = \frac{(1 + y_2)^2}{1 + y_1} = \frac{1.0649^2}{1.05} = 1.08$$

The result in Example 13.5—that the forward rate exceeds the expected short rate—should not surprise us. We defined the forward rate as the interest rate that would need to prevail in the second year to make the long- and short-term investments equally attractive, ignoring risk. When we account for risk, it is clear that short-term investors will shy away from the long-term bond unless it offers an expected return greater than that offered by the one-year bond. Another way of putting this is to say that investors will require a risk premium to hold the longer-term bond. The risk-averse investor would be willing to hold the long-term bond only if $E(r_2)$ is less than the breakeven value, f_2, because the lower the expectation of r_2, the greater the anticipated return on the long-term bond.

Therefore, if most individuals are short-term investors, bonds must have prices that make f_2 greater than $E(r_2)$. The forward rate will embody a premium compared with the expected future short-interest rate. This **liquidity premium** compensates short-term investors for the uncertainty about the price at which they will be able to sell their long-term bonds at the end of the year.[3]

Perhaps surprisingly, we also can imagine scenarios in which long-term bonds can be perceived by investors to be *safer* than short-term bonds. To see how, we now consider a "long-term" investor, who wishes to invest for a full two-year period. Suppose that the investor can purchase a two-year $1,000 par value zero-coupon bond for $890 and lock in a guaranteed yield to maturity of $y_2 = 6$ percent. Alternatively, the investor can roll over two one-year investments. In this case an investment of 890 would grow in two years to $890 \times (1.05)(1 + r_2)$, which is an uncertain amount today because r_2 is not yet known. The breakeven year 2 interest rate is, once again, the forward rate, 7.01 percent, because the forward rate is defined as the rate that equates the terminal value of the two investment strategies.

The expected value of the payoff of the rollover strategy is $890(1.05)[1 + E(r_2)]$. If $E(r_2)$ equals the forward rate, f_2, then the expected value of the payoff from the rollover strategy will equal the *known* payoff from the two-year-maturity bond strategy.

Is this a reasonable presumption? Once again, it is only if the investor does not care about the uncertainty surrounding the final value of the rollover strategy. Whenever that risk is important, however, the long-term investor will not be willing to engage in the rollover strategy unless its expected return exceeds that of the two-year bond. In this case, the investor would require that

$$(1.05)[1 + E(r_2)] > (1.06)^2 = (1.05)(1 + f_2)$$

which implies that $E(r_2)$ exceeds f_2. The investor would require that the expected period-two interest rate exceed the forward rate.

Therefore, if all investors were long-term investors, no one would be willing to hold short-term bonds unless those bonds offered a reward for bearing interest rate risk. In this situation, bond prices would be set at levels such that rolling over short bonds would result in greater expected returns than holding long bonds. This would cause the forward rate to be less than the expected future spot rate.

For example, suppose that in fact $E(r_2) = 8$ percent. The liquidity premium therefore is negative: $f_2 - E(r_2) = 7.01\% - 8\% = -.99$ percent. This is exactly opposite of the conclusion we drew in the first case of the short-term investor. Clearly, whether forward rates will equal expected future short rates depends on investors' readiness to bear interest rate risk, as well as their willingness to hold bonds that do not correspond to their investment horizons.

13.4

THEORIES OF THE TERM STRUCTURE

The Expectations Hypothesis

The simplest theory of the term structure is the **expectations hypothesis**. A common version of this hypothesis states that the forward rate equals the market consensus expectation of the future short interest rate—in other words, that $f_2 = E(r_2)$, and that liquidity premiums are zero. Because $f_2 = E(r_2)$, we may relate yields on long-term bonds to expectations of future interest rates. In addition, we can use the forward rates derived from the yield curve to infer market expectations of future short rates.

---

[3]*Liquidity* refers to the ability to sell an asset easily at a predictable price. Because long-term bonds have greater price risk, they are considered less liquid in this context and thus must offer a premium.

Forward rates derived from conventional bonds are nominal interest rates. But using price-level-indexed bonds such as TIPS, we can also calculate forward *real* interest rates. Recall that the difference between the real rate and the nominal rate is approximately the expected inflation rate. Therefore, comparing real and nominal forward rates might give us a glimpse of the market's expectation of future inflation rates. The real versus nominal spread is a sort of forward inflation rate.

In September 2007, the U.S. Federal Reserve Board reduced its target federal funds rate in an attempt to stimulate the economy. The page capture shown here, from a Bloomberg screen, shows the minute-by-minute spread between the five-year forward nominal interest rate and forward real rate on September 18, the day the Fed announced its policy change. The spread immediately widened at the announcement, signifying that the market expected the more expansionary monetary policy to eventually result in an increased inflation rate. The increase in the inflation rate implied by the graph is fairly mild, about

.05 percent, from about 2.53 to 2.58 percent, but the impact of the announcement is very clear, and the speed of adjustment to the announcement was impressive.

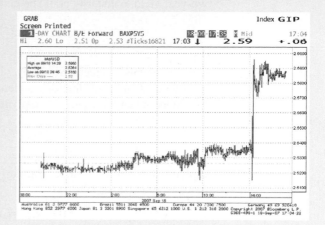

For example, with $(1 + y_2)^2 = (1 + r_1)(1 + f_2)$ from equation 13.5, we may also write that $(1 + y_2)^2 = (1 + r_1)[1 + E(r_2)]$ if the expectations hypothesis is correct. The yield to maturity would thus be determined solely by current and expected future one-period interest rates. An upward-sloping yield curve would be clear evidence that investors anticipate increases in interest rates.

CC 6

CONCEPT CHECK

If the expectations hypothesis is valid, what can we conclude about the premiums necessary to induce investors to hold bonds of different maturities from their investment horizons?

By the way, there is nothing that limits us to nominal bonds when using the expectations hypothesis. The boxed article points out that we can apply the theory to the term structure of real interest rates as well, and thereby learn something about market expectations of coming inflation rates.

Liquidity Preference

We noted earlier that short-term investors will be unwilling to hold long-term bonds unless the forward rate exceeds the expected short interest rate, $f_2 > E(r_2)$, whereas long-term investors will be unwilling to hold short bonds unless $E(r_2) > f_2$. In other words, both groups of investors require a premium to hold bonds with maturities different from their investment horizons. Advocates of the **liquidity preference theory** of the term structure believe that short-term investors dominate the market so that, generally speaking, the forward rate exceeds the expected short rate. The excess of f_2 over $E(r_2)$, the liquidity premium, is predicted to be positive.

CC 7

CONCEPT CHECK

The liquidity premium hypothesis also holds that *issuers* of bonds prefer to issue long-term bonds. How would this preference contribute to a positive liquidity premium?

To illustrate the differing implications of these theories for the term structure of interest rates, suppose the short interest rate is expected to be constant indefinitely. Suppose that $r_1 = 5$ percent and that $E(r_2) = 5$ percent, $E(r_3) = 5$ percent, and so on. Under the expectations hypothesis, the two-year yield to maturity could be derived from the following:

$$(1 + y_2)^2 = (1 + r_1)[1 + E(r_2)]$$
$$= (1.05)(1.05)$$

so that y_2 equals 5 percent. Similarly, yields on all-maturity bonds would equal 5 percent.

In contrast, under the liquidity preference theory, f_2 would exceed $E(r_2)$. For the sake of illustration, suppose that f_2 is 6 percent, implying a 1 percent liquidity premium. Then, for two-year bonds,

$$(1 + y_2)^2 = (1 + r_1)(1 + f_2)$$
$$= (1.05)(1.06) = 1.113$$

implying that $1 + y_2 = 1.055$. Similarly, if f_3 also equals 6 percent, then the yield on three-year bonds would be determined by

$$(1 + y_3)^3 = (1 + r_1)(1 + f_2)(1 + f_3)$$
$$= (1.05)(1.06)(1.06) = 1.17978$$

implying that $1 + y_3 = 1.0567$. The plot of the yield curve in this situation would be given as in Figure 13.4, panel A. Such an upward-sloping yield curve is commonly observed in practice.

If interest rates are expected to change over time, the liquidity premium may be overlaid on the path of expected spot rates to determine the forward interest rate. Then the yield to maturity for each date will be an average of the single-period forward rates. Several such possibilities for increasing and declining interest rates appear in panels B to D.

13.5　INTERPRETING THE TERM STRUCTURE

If the yield curve reflects expectations of future short rates, it offers a potentially powerful tool for fixed-income investors. If we can use the term structure to infer the expectations of other investors in the economy, we can use those expectations as benchmarks for our own analysis. For example, if we are relatively more optimistic than other investors that interest rates will fall, we will be more willing to extend our portfolios into longer-term bonds. Therefore, in this section, we will take a careful look at what information can be gleaned from a careful analysis of the term structure. Unfortunately, while the yield curve does reflect expectations of future interest rates, it also reflects other factors such as liquidity premiums. Moreover, forecasts of interest rate changes may have different investment implications depending on whether those changes are driven by changes in the expected inflation rate or the real rate, and this adds another layer of complexity to the proper interpretation of the term structure.

We have seen that under certainty, one plus the yield to maturity on a zero-coupon bond is simply the geometric average of one plus the future short rates that will prevail over the life of the bond. This is the meaning of equation 13.1, which we repeat here in a more general form:

$$1 + y_n = [(1 + r_1)(1 + r_2) \ldots (1 + r_n)]^{1/n}$$

When future rates are uncertain, we modify this equation by replacing future short rates with forward rates:

$$1 + y_n = [(1 + r_1)(1 + f_2)(1 + f_3) \ldots (1 + f_n)]^{1/n} \qquad (13.7)$$

Thus, there is a direct relationship between yields on various-maturity bonds and forward interest rates.

Figure 13.4
Yield curves.

Panel A:
Constant
expected short
rate. Liquidity
premium of 1
percent. Result
is a rising yield
curve.

Panel B:
Declining
expected short
rates.
Increasing
liquidity
premiums.
Result is a
rising yield
curve despite
falling expected
interest rates.

Panel C:
Declining
expected short
rates. Constant
liquidity
premiums.
Result is a
hump-shaped
yield curve.

Panel D:
Increasing
expected short
rates.
Increasing
liquidity
premiums.
Result is a
sharply rising
yield curve.

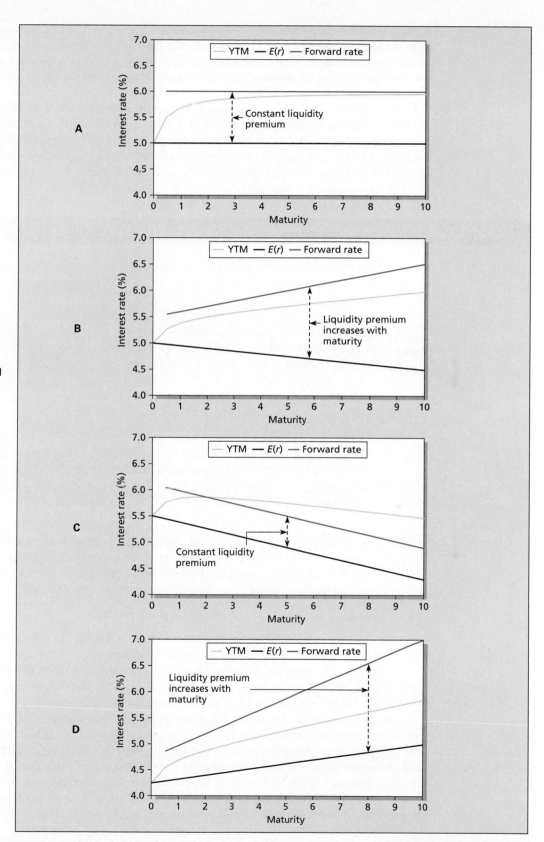

First, we ask what factors can account for a rising yield curve. Mathematically, if the yield curve is rising, f_{n+1} must exceed y_n. In words, the yield curve is upward-sloping at any maturity date, n, for which the forward rate for the coming period is greater than the yield at that maturity. This rule follows from the notion of the yield to maturity as an average (albeit a geometric average) of forward rates.

If the yield curve is to rise as one moves to longer maturities, it must be the case that extension to a longer maturity results in the inclusion of a "new" forward rate that is higher than the average of the previously observed rates. This is analogous to the observation that if a new student's test score is to increase the class average, that student's score must exceed the class's average without her score. To raise the yield to maturity, an above-average forward rate must be added to the other rates used in the averaging computation.

EXAMPLE 13.6   **Forward Rates and the Slopes of the Yield Curve**

If the yield to maturity on three-year bonds is 7 percent, the yield on four-year bonds will satisfy the following equation:

$$(1 + y_4)^4 = (1.07)^3(1 + f_4)$$

If $f_4 = .07$, then y_4 also will equal .07. (Confirm this!) If f_4 is greater than 7 percent, y_4 will exceed 7 percent, and the yield curve will slope upward. For example, if $f_4 = 8$ percent, then $(1 + y_4)^4 = (1.07)^3(1.08) = 1.3230$ and $y_4 = 7.25$ percent.

CC 8

CONCEPT CHECK

Look back at Table 13.1. Show that y_4 would exceed y_3 if and only if the interest rate for period 4 had been greater than 7 percent, which was the yield to maturity on the three-year bond, y_3.

Given that an upward-sloping yield curve is always associated with a forward rate higher than the spot, or current, yield, we need to ask next what can account for that higher forward rate. Unfortunately, there always are two possible answers to this question. Recall that the forward rate can be related to the expected future short rate according to the equation

$$f_n = E(r_n) + \text{Liquidity premium} \tag{13.8}$$

where the liquidity premium might be necessary to induce investors to hold bonds of maturities that do not correspond to their preferred investment horizons.

By the way, the liquidity premium need not be positive, although that is the position generally taken by advocates of the liquidity premium hypothesis. We showed previously that if most investors have long-term horizons, the liquidity premium could be negative.

In any case, equation 13.8 shows that there are two reasons why the forward rate might be high. Either investors expect rising interest rates, meaning that $E(r_n)$ is high, or they require a large premium for holding longer-term bonds. Although it is tempting to infer from a rising yield curve that investors believe that interest rates will eventually increase, this is not a valid inference. Indeed, Figure 13.4, panel A provides a simple counterexample to this line of reasoning. There, the spot rate is expected to stay at 5 percent forever. Yet there is a constant 1 percent liquidity premium so that all forward rates are 6 percent. The result is that the yield curve continually rises, starting at a level of 5 percent for one-year bonds, but eventually approaching 6 percent for long-term bonds as more and more forward rates at 6 percent are averaged into the yields to maturity.

Therefore, although it is true that expectations of increases in future interest rates can result in a rising yield curve, the converse is not true: a rising yield curve does not in and of itself imply expectations of higher future interest rates. The effects of possible liquidity premiums confound any simple attempt to extract expectations from the term structure. But estimating the market's expectations is a crucial task, because only by comparing your own expectations to those reflected in market prices can you determine whether you are relatively bullish or bearish on interest rates.

One very rough approach to deriving expected future spot rates is to assume that liquidity premiums are constant. An estimate of that premium can be subtracted from the forward rate to obtain the market's expected interest rate. For example, again making use of the example plotted in Figure 13.4, panel A, the researcher would estimate from historical data that a typical liquidity premium in this economy is 1 percent. After calculating the forward rate from the yield curve to be 6 percent, the expectation of the future spot rate would be determined to be 5 percent.

This approach has little to recommend it for two reasons. First, it is next to impossible to obtain precise estimates of a liquidity premium. The general approach to doing so would be to compare forward rates and eventually realized future short rates and to calculate the average difference between the two. However, the deviations between the two values can be quite large and unpredictable because of unanticipated economic events that affect the realized short rate. The data do not contain enough information to calculate a reliable estimate of the expected premium. Second, there is no reason to believe that the liquidity premium should be constant. Figure 13.5 shows the rate of return variability of Canada long-term bonds since 1977. Interest rate risk fluctuated dramatically during the period. So we should expect risk premiums on various-maturity bonds to fluctuate, and empirical evidence suggests that term premiums do in fact fluctuate over time.

Figure 13.5

Yield volatility of long-term bonds, 1977–2012.

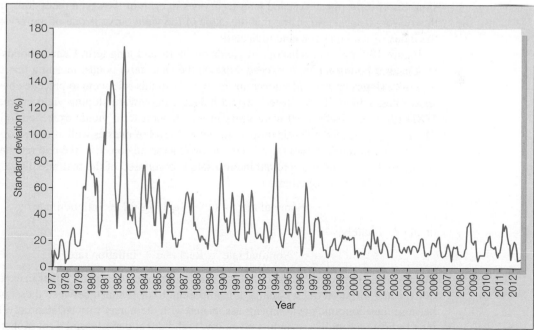

Source: Scotia Capital and PC Bonds Analytics, *Debt Market Indices*, various years, and Thomson Reuters. © Thomson Reuters.

Figure 13.6　Yields on long-term versus short-term government securities: Term spread, 1980–2012.

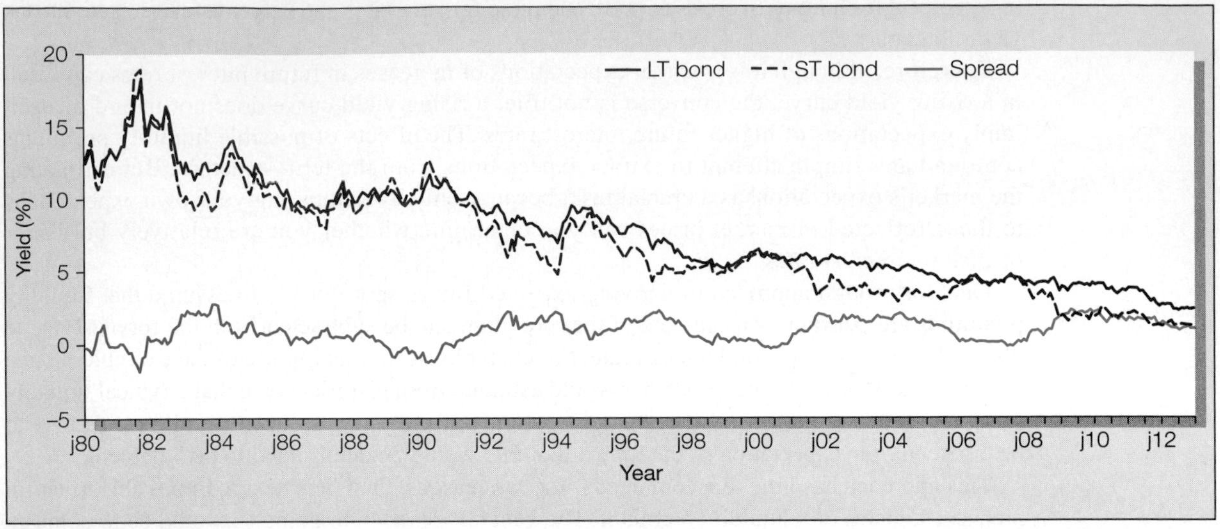

Source: Scotia Capital and PC Bonds Analytics, *Debt Market Indices*, various years, and Thomson Reuters. © Thomson Reuters.

Still, very steep yield curves are interpreted by many market professionals as warning signs of impending rate increases. In fact, the yield curve is a good predictor of the business cycle as a whole, because long-term rates tend to rise in anticipation of an expansion in economic activity.

The usually observed upward slope of the yield curve, especially for short maturities, is the empirical basis for the liquidity premium doctrine that long-term bonds offer a positive liquidity premium. Because the yield curve normally has an upward slope due to risk premiums, a downward sloping yield curve is taken as a strong indication that yields are more likely than not to fall. The prediction of declining interest rates is in turn often interpreted as a signal of a coming recession. Short-term rates exceeded long-term ones in each of the seven recessions since 1970. For this reason, it is not surprising that the slope of the yield curve is one of the key components of the index of leading economic indicators.

Figure 13.6 presents a history of yields on short- and long-term Canada bonds. Yields on the longer-term bonds *generally* exceed those on the short-term bonds, meaning that the yield curve generally slopes upward. Moreover, the exceptions to this rule seem to precede episodes of falling short rates, which, if anticipated, would induce a downward-sloping yield curve. For example, 1981–1982 and 1989–1990 were years in which short-term yields exceeded long-term yields. These years preceded a drastic drop in the general level of rates as well as two steep recessions.

Why might interest rates fall? There are two factors to consider: the real rate and the inflation premium. Recall that the nominal interest rate is composed of the real rate plus a factor to compensate for the effect of inflation:

$$1 + \text{Nominal rate} = (1 + \text{Real rate})(1 + \text{Inflation rate})$$

or, approximately,

$$\text{Nominal rate} = \text{Real rate} + \text{Inflation rate}$$

Therefore, an expected change in interest rates can be due to changes either in expected real rates or expected inflation rates. Usually, it is important to distinguish between these two possibilities because the economic environments associated with them may vary substantially. High real rates may indicate a rapidly expanding economy, high budget deficits, and tight monetary policy. Although high inflation rates also can arise out of a rapidly expanding economy, inflation also may be caused by rapid expansion of the money supply or supply-side shocks to the economy, such as interruptions in oil supplies. These factors have very different implications for investments. Even if we conclude from an analysis of the yield curve that rates will fall, we need to analyze the macroeconomic factors that might cause such a decline.

13.6 FORWARD RATES AS FORWARD CONTRACTS

We have seen that forward rates may be derived from the yield curve, using equation 13.5. In general, forward rates will not equal the eventually realized short rate, or even today's expectation of what that short rate will be. But there is still an important sense in which the forward rate is a market interest rate. Suppose that you wanted to arrange *now* to make a loan at some future date. You would agree today on the interest rate that will be charged, but the loan would not commence until some time in the future. How would the interest rate on such a "forward loan" be determined? Perhaps not surprisingly, it would be the forward rate of interest for the period of the loan. Let's use an example to see how this might work.

EXAMPLE 13.7   Forward Interest Rate Contracts

Suppose the price of one-year-maturity zero-coupon bonds with face value $1,000 is $952.38 and the price of two-year zeros with $1,000 face value is $890. The yield to maturity on the one-year bond is therefore 5 percent, while that on the two-year bond is 6 percent. The forward rate for the second year is thus

$$f_2 = \frac{(1 + y_2)^2}{(1 + y_1)} - 1 = \frac{1.06^2}{1.05} - 1 = .0701, \text{ or } 7.01\%$$

Now consider the strategy laid in out the following table. In the first column we present data for this example, and in the last column we generalize. We denote by $B_0(T)$, today's price of a zero maturing at time T.

	Initial Cash Flow	In General
Buy a one-year zero coupon bond	−952.38	−$B_0(1)$
Sell 1.1001 2-year zeros	+890 × 1.0701 = 952.38	+$B_0(2) \times (1 + f_2)$
	0	0

The initial cash flow (at time 0) is zero. You pay $952.38, or in general $B_0(1)$, for a zero maturing in one year, and you receive $890, or in general $B_0(2)$, for each zero you sell maturing in two years. By selling 1.0701 of these bonds, you set your initial cash flow to zero.[4]

At time 1, the one-year bond matures and you receive $1,000. At time 2, the two-year-maturity zero-coupon bonds that you sold mature, and you have to pay 1.0701 × $1,000 = $1,070.10. Your cash flow stream is shown in Figure 13.7, panel A. Notice that you have created a "synthetic" forward loan: you effectively *will* borrow $1,000 a year from now, and repay $1,070.10 a year later. The rate on this forward loan is therefore 7.01 percent, precisely equal to the forward rate for the second year.

---

[4]Of course, in reality one cannot sell a fraction of a bond, but you can think of this part of the transaction as follows. If you sold one of these bonds, you would effectively be borrowing $890 for a two-year period. Selling 1.0701 of these bonds means simply that you are borrowing $890 × 1.0701 = $952.38.

Figure 13.7

Engineering a synthetic forward loan.

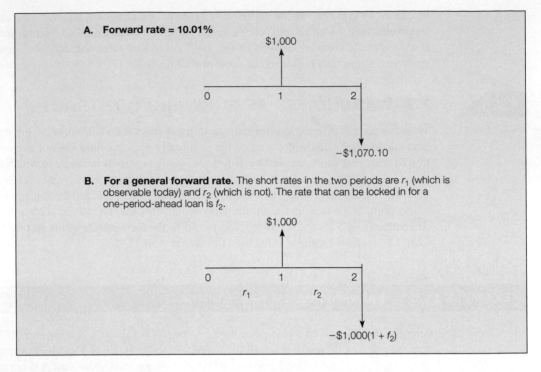

A. Forward rate = 10.01%

$1,000

0   1   2

−$1,070.10

B. For a general forward rate. The short rates in the two periods are r_1 (which is observable today) and r_2 (which is not). The rate that can be locked in for a one-period-ahead loan is f_2.

$1,000

0   1   2
      r_1 r_2

−$1,000(1 + f_2)

In general, to construct the synthetic forward loan, you sell $1 + f_2$ two-year zeros for every one-year zero that you buy. This makes your initial cash flow zero because the prices of the one- and two-year zeros differ by the factor $(1 + f_2)$; notice that

$$B_0(1) = \frac{\$1,000}{(1 + y_1)} \quad \text{while} \quad B_0(2) = \frac{\$1,000}{(1 + y_2)^2} = \frac{\$1,000}{(1 + y_1)(1 + f_2)}$$

Therefore, when you sell $(1 + f_2)$ two-year zeros you generate just enough cash to buy one one-year zero. Both zeros mature to a face value of $1,000, so the difference between the cash inflow at time 1 and the cash outflow at time 2 is the same factor, $1 + f_2$, as illustrated in panel B. As a result, f_2 is the rate on the forward loan.

Obviously, you can construct a synthetic forward loan for periods beyond the second year, and you can construct such loans for multiple periods. Problems 18 and 19 at the end of the chapter lead you through some of these variants.

CC 9

CONCEPT CHECK

Suppose that the price of three-year zero coupon bonds is $816.30. What is the forward rate for the third year? How would you construct a synthetic one-year forward loan that commences at $t = 2$ and matures at $t = 3$?

SUMMARY

1. The *term structure of interest rates* refers to the interest rates for various terms to maturity embodied in the prices of default-free zero-coupon bonds.

2. In a world of certainty all investments must provide equal total returns for any investment period. Short-term holding-period returns on all bonds would be equal in a risk-free economy, and all would be equal to the rate available on short-term bonds. Similarly, total returns from rolling over short-term bonds over longer periods would equal the total returns available from long-maturity bonds.

3. The *forward rate of interest* is the breakeven future interest rate that would equate the total return from a rollover strategy to that of a longer-term zero-coupon bond. It is defined by the equation

$$(1 + y_n)^n(1 + f_{n+1}) = (1 + y_{n+1})^{n+1}$$

where *n* is a given number of periods from today. This equation can be used to show that yields to maturity and forward rates are related by the equation

$$(1 + y_n)^n = (1 + r_1)(1 + f_2)(1 + f_3) \ldots (1 + f_n)$$

4. A common version of the expectations hypothesis holds that forward interest rates are unbiased estimates of expected future interest rates. However, there are good reasons to believe that forward rates differ from expected short rates by a risk premium known as a *liquidity premium*. A positive liquidity premium can cause the yield curve to slope upward even if no increase in short rates is anticipated.

5. The existence of liquidity premiums makes it extremely difficult to infer expected future interest rates from the yield curve. Such an inference would be made easier if we could assume the liquidity premium remained reasonably stable over time. However, both empirical and theoretical insights cast doubt on the constancy of that premium.

6. Forward rates are market interest rates in the important sense that commitments to forward (i.e., deferred) borrowing or lending arrangements can be made at these rates.

KEY EQUATIONS

(13.1) $1 + y_2 = [(1 + r_1) \times (1 + r_2)]^{1/2}$

(13.2) $(1 + y_n)^n = (1 + y_{n-1})^{n-1} \times (1 + r_n)$

(13.3) $(1 + r_n) = \dfrac{(1 + y_n)^n}{(1 + y_{n-1})^{n-1}}$

(13.4) $(1 + f_n) = \dfrac{(1 + y_n)^n}{(1 + y_{n-1})^{n-1}}$

(13.5) $(1 + y_n)^n = (1 + y_{n-1})^{n-1}(1 + f_n)$

(13.6) $(1 + r_1)(1 + r_2) = (1 + y_2)^2$

(13.7) $1 + y_n = [(1 + r_1)(1 + f_2)(1 + f_3) \ldots (1 + f_n)]^{1/n}$

(13.8) $f_n = E(r_n) +$ Liquidity premium

E-INVESTMENTS The Yield Curves and Economic Conditions	Go to **www.bank-banque-canada.ca/en/rates/yield_curve.html**. Look at Figure 13.6 during the 2007–2008 recession, when the term spread was zero or negative. Select a few dates around that time and plot in Excel the yield curves, as in Figure 13.1. Can you observe the inversion of the yield curve? Then select later dates and again plot the yield curves. What happened to them? What does this say about the economy? Which varies more: short-term or long-term rates? Can you explain why?

PROBLEMS

McGraw Hill Education **connect™**   **Practise and learn online with Connect.**

1. What is the relationship between forward rates and the market's expectation of future short rates? Explain in the context of both the expectations and liquidity preference theories of the term structure of interest rates.

2. "Under the expectations hypothesis, if the yield curve is upward-sloping, the market must expect an increase in short-term interest rates." Is this statement true, false, or uncertain? Why?

3. "Under the liquidity preference theory, if inflation is expected to be falling over the next few years, long-term interest rates will be higher than short-term rates." Is this statement true, false, or uncertain? Why?

4. The following is a list of prices for zero-coupon bonds of various maturities. Calculate the yields to maturity of each bond and the implied sequence of forward rates.

Maturity (years)	Price of Bond ($)
1	943.40
2	898.47
3	847.62
4	792.16

5. Assuming that the expectations hypothesis is valid, compute the expected price path of the four-year bond in problem 4 as time passes. What is the rate of return of the bond in each year? Show that the expected return equals the forward rate for each year.

6. If the liquidity preference hypothesis is true, what shape should the term structure curve have in a period where interest rates are expected to be constant?

  a. Upward-sloping

  b. Downward-sloping

  c. Flat

7. Which of the following is *true* according to the pure expectations theory? Forward rates

  a. Exclusively represent expected future spot rates

  b. Are biased estimates of market expectations

  c. Always overestimate future short rates

8. Assuming the pure expectations theory is correct, an upward-sloping yield curve implies

  a. Interest rates are expected to increase in the future.

  b. Longer-term bonds are riskier than short-term bonds.

  c. Interest rates are expected to decline in the future.

9. Would you expect the yield on a callable bond to lie above or below a yield curve fitted from noncallable bonds?

10. The current yield curve for default-free zero-coupon bonds is as follows:

Maturity (years)	YTM (%)
1	10
2	11
3	12

  a. What are the implied one-year forward rates?

  b. Assume that the pure expectations hypothesis of the term structure is correct. If market expectations are accurate, what will the pure yield curve, that is, the yields to maturity on one- and two-year zero-coupon bonds, be next year?

  c. If you purchase a two-year zero-coupon bond now, what is the expected total rate of return over the next year? What if it were a three-year zero-coupon bond? (*Hint:* Compute the current and expected future prices.) Ignore taxes.

  d. What should be the current price of a three-year-maturity bond with a 12 percent coupon rate paid annually? If you purchased it at that price, what would your total expected rate of return be over the next year (coupon plus price change)? Ignore taxes.

11. The term structure for zero-coupon bonds is currently:

Maturity (years)	YTM (%)
1	4
2	5
3	6

Next year at this time, *you* expect it to be:

Maturity (years)	YTM (%)
1	5
2	6
3	7

a. What do *you* expect the rate of return to be over the coming year on a three-year zero-coupon bond?

b. Under the expectations theory, what yield to maturity does the market expect to observe on one- and two-year zeroes next year? Is the market's expectation of the return on the three-year bond more or less than yours? Assume the face value of the bond is $100.

12. The yield to maturity on one-year zero-coupon bonds is currently 7 percent; the YTM on two-year zeroes is 8 percent. The federal government plans to issue a two-year-maturity *coupon* bond, paying coupons once per year with a coupon rate of 9 percent. The face value of the bond is $100.

a. At what price will the bond sell?

b. What will be the yield to maturity on the bond?

c. If the expectations theory of the yield curve is correct, what is the market expectation of the price that the bond will sell for next year?

d. Recalculate your answer to (*c*) if you believe in the liquidity preference theory and you believe that the liquidity premium is 1 percent.

13. Below is a list of prices for zero-coupon bonds of various maturities.

Maturity (years)	Price of $1,000 Par Bond (zero-coupon)
1	943.40
2	873.52
3	816.37

a. An 8.5 percent coupon $1,000 par bond pays an annual coupon and will mature in three years. What should be the yield to maturity on the bond?

b. If at the end of the first year the yield curve flattens out at 8 percent, what will be the one-year holding-period return on the coupon bond?

14. Prices of zero-coupon bonds reveal the following pattern of forward rates:

Year	Forward Rate (%)
1	5
2	7
3	8

In addition to the zero-coupon bond, investors also may purchase a three-year bond making annual payments of $60 with a par value of $1,000.

a. What is the price of the coupon bond?

b. What is the yield to maturity of the coupon bond?

c. Under the expectations hypothesis, what is the expected realized compound yield of the coupon bond?

d. If you forecast that the yield curve in one year will be flat at 7 percent, what is your forecast for the expected rate of return on the coupon bond for the one-year holding period?

15. You observe the following term structure:

	Effective Annual YTM (%)
1-year zero-coupon bond	6.1
2-year zero-coupon bond	6.2
3-year zero-coupon bond	6.3
4-year zero-coupon bond	6.4

a. If you believe that the term structure next year will be the same as today's, will the one-year or the four-year zeroes provide a greater expected one-year return?

b. What if you believe in the expectations hypothesis?

16. The yield to maturity (YTM) on one-year-maturity zero-coupon bonds is 5 percent and the YTM on two-year-maturity zero-coupon bonds is 6 percent. The yield to maturity on two-year-maturity coupon bonds with coupon rates of 12 percent (paid annually) is 5.8 percent. What arbitrage opportunity is available for an investment banking firm? What is the profit on the activity?

17. Suppose that a one-year zero-coupon bond with a face value of $100 currently sells at $94.34, while a two-year zero sells at $84.99. You are considering the purchase of a two-year-maturity bond making *annual* coupon payments. The face value of the bond is $100, and the coupon rate is 12 percent per year.

a. What is the yield to maturity of the two-year zero? The two-year coupon bond?

b. What is the forward rate for the second year?

c. If the expectations hypothesis is accepted, what are (i) the expected price of the coupon bond at the end of the first year and (ii) the expected holding period return on the coupon bond over the first year?

d. Will the expected rate of return be higher or lower if you accept the liquidity preference hypothesis?

18. Suppose that the prices of zero-coupon bonds with various maturities are given in the following table. The face value of each bond is $1,000.

Maturity (years)	Price ($)
1	925.93
2	853.39
3	782.92
4	715.00
5	650.00

a. Calculate the forward rate of interest for each year.

b. How could you construct a one-year forward loan beginning in year 3? Confirm that the rate on that loan equals the forward rate.

c. Repeat (b) for a one-year forward loan beginning in year 4.

19. Continue to use the data in the preceding problem. Suppose that you want to construct a *two-year-maturity* forward loan commencing in *three* years.

a. Suppose that you buy *today* one three-year-maturity zero-coupon bond. How many five-year-maturity zeros would you have to sell to make your initial cash flow equal to zero?

b. What are the cash flows on this strategy in each year?

c. What is the effective two-year interest rate on the effective three-year-ahead forward loan?

d. Confirm that the effective two-year interest rate equals $(1 + f_4) \times (1 + f_5) - 1$. You therefore can interpret the two-year loan rate as a two-year forward rate for the last two years. Alternatively, show that the effective two-year forward rate equals

$$\frac{(1 + y_5)^5}{(1 + y_3)^3} - 1$$

20. The following are the current coupon yields to maturity and spot rates of interest for six Canada bonds. Assume all securities pay interest annually.

Yields to Maturity and Spot Rates of Interest

Term to Maturity	Current Coupon Yield to Maturity (%)	Spot Rate of Interest (%)
1-year	5.25	5.25
2-year	5.75	5.79
3-year	6.15	6.19
5-year	6.45	6.51
10-year	6.95	7.10
30-year	7.25	7.67

Compute, under the expectations theory, the two-year implied forward rate three years from now, given the information provided in the preceding table. State the assumption underlying the calculation of the implied forward rate.

The following problems are based on questions that have appeared in past CFA examinations.

21. The six-month Treasury bill spot rate is 4 percent, and the one-year Treasury bill spot rate is 5 percent. What is the implied six-month forward rate for six months from now?

22. Briefly explain why bonds of different maturities have different yields in terms of the expectations and liquidity preferences hypotheses.

Briefly describe the implications of each hypothesis when the yield curve is (a) upward-sloping and (b) downward-sloping.

23. Which one of the following statements about the term structure of interest rates is true?

a. The expectations hypothesis indicates a flat yield curve if anticipated future short-term rates exceed current short-term rates.

b. The expectations hypothesis contends that the long-term rate is equal to the anticipated short-term rate.

    c. The liquidity premium theory indicates that, all else being equal, longer maturities will have lower yields.

    d. The liquidity preference theory contends that lenders prefer to buy securities at the short end of the yield curve.

24. The following table shows yields to maturity of U.S. Treasury securities:

Term to Maturity (in years)	Yield to Maturity (%)
1	3.50
2	4.50
3	5.00
4	5.50
5	6.00
10	6.60

    a. Using the data in the table, calculate the forward one-year rate of interest for year 3.

    b. Describe the conditions under which the calculated forward rate would be an unbiased estimate of the one-year spot rate of interest for that year.

    c. Assume that a few months earlier, the forward one-year rate of interest for that year had been significantly higher than it is now. What factors might account for such a decline in the forward rate?

25. The tables that follow show, respectively, the characteristics of two annual-pay bonds from the same issuer with the same priority in the event of default, and spot interest rates. Neither bond's price is consistent with the spot rates. Using the information in these tables, recommend either bond *A* or bond *B* for purchase. Justify your choice. Assume the face value of the bond is $100.

Bond Characteristics

	Bond A	Bond B
Coupons	Annual	Annual
Maturity	3 years	3 years
Coupon rate	10%	6%
Yield to maturity	10.65%	10.75%
Price	$98.40	$88.34

Spot Interest Rates

Term (years)	Spot Rates (zero-coupon) (%)
1	5
2	8
3	11

26. Sandra Kapple is a fixed-income portfolio manager who works with large institutional clients. Kapple is meeting with Maria VanHusen, consultant to the Star Hospital Pension Plan, to discuss management of the fund's approximately $100 million Treasury bond portfolio. The current U.S. Treasury yield curve is given in the following exhibit. VanHusen states, "Given the large differential between two- and ten-year yields, the portfolio would be expected to experience a higher

return over a ten-year horizon by buying ten-year Treasuries, rather than buying two-year Treasuries and reinvesting the proceeds into two-year T-bonds at each maturity date."

Maturity (years)	Yield (%)	Maturity (years)	Yield (%)
1	2.00	6	4.15
2	2.90	7	4.30
3	3.50	8	4.45
4	3.80	9	4.60
5	4.00	10	4.70

a. Indicate whether VanHusen's conclusion is correct, based on the pure expectations hypothesis.

b. VanHusen discusses with Kapple alternative theories of the term structure of interest rates and gives her the following information about the U.S. Treasury market:

Maturity (years)	2	3	4	5	6	7	8	9	10
Liquidity premium (%)	.55	.55	.65	.75	.90	1.10	1.20	1.50	1.60

Use this additional information and the liquidity preference theory to determine what the slope of the yield curve implies about the direction of future expected short-term interest rates.

27. A portfolio manager at Superior Trust Company is structuring a fixed-income portfolio to meet the objectives of a client. The portfolio manager compares coupon U.S. Treasuries with zero-coupon stripped U.S. Treasuries and observes a significant yield advantage for the stripped bonds:

Term (years)	Coupon U.S. Treasuries (%)	Zero-Coupon Stripped U.S. Treasuries (%)
3	5.50	5.80
7	6.75	7.25
10	7.25	7.60
30	7.75	8.20

Briefly discuss why zero-coupon stripped U.S. Treasuries could yield more than coupon U.S. Treasuries with the same final maturity.

28. The shape of the U.S. Treasury yield curve appears to reflect two expected Federal Reserve reductions in the Federal Funds rate. The current short-term interest rate is 5 percent. The first reduction of approximately 50 basis points (bp) is expected six months from now and the second reduction of approximately 50 bp is expected one year from now. The current U.S. Treasury term premiums are 10 bp per year for each of the next three years (out through the three-year benchmark).

However, the market also believes that the Federal Reserve reductions will be reversed in a single 100-bp increase in the Federal Funds rate 2½ years from now. You expect liquidity premiums to remain 10 bp per year for each of the next three years (out through the three-year benchmark).

Describe or draw the shape of the Treasury yield curve out through the three-year benchmark. Which term structure theory supports the shape of the U.S. Treasury yield curve you've described?

29. Canada bonds represent a significant holding in many pension portfolios. You decide to analyze the yield curve for Canada bonds.

    a. Using the data in the table below, calculate the five-year spot and forward rates assuming annual compounding. Show your calculations.

    Canada Bond Yield Curve Data

Maturity (years)	Maturity (%)	Rates (%)	Rates (%)
1	5.00	5.00	5.00
2	5.20	5.21	5.42
3	6.00	6.05	7.75
4	7.00	7.16	10.56
5	7.00	—	—

    b. Define and describe each of the following three concepts:

    - Yield to maturity
    - Spot rate
    - Forward rate

    Explain how these *three* concepts are related.

    c. You are considering the purchase of a zero-coupon Canada bond with four years to maturity. On the basis of above yield curve analysis, calculate both the expected yield to maturity and the price for the security. Show your calculations.

30. The spot rates of interest for five Canada bonds are shown in the following table. Assume all securities pay interest annually.

    Spot Rates of Interest

Term to Maturity (years)	Spot Rate of Interest (%)
1	13.00
2	12.00
3	11.00
4	10.00
5	9.00

    a. i. Compute the two-year implied forward rate for a deferred loan beginning in three years.

       ii. Explain your answer by using the expectations theory.

    b. Compute the price of a five-year annual-pay Canada bond with a coupon rate of 9 percent by using the information in the table.

E-INVESTMENTS   Go to **www.smartmoney.com**. Access the *Living Yield Curve* (look for the *Economy and Bonds* tab), a moving picture of the yield curve. Is the yield curve usually upward- or downward-sloping? What about today's yield curve? How much does the slope of the curve vary? Which varies more: short-term or long-term rates? Can you explain why this might be the case?

Managing Bond Portfolios

In this chapter we turn to various strategies that bond portfolio managers can pursue, making a distinction between passive and active strategies. A *passive investment strategy* takes market prices of securities as fairly set. Rather than attempting to beat the market by exploiting superior information or insight, passive managers act to maintain an appropriate risk–return balance given market opportunities. One special case of passive management is an immunization strategy that attempts to insulate or immunize the portfolio from interest rate risk. In contrast, an *active investment strategy* attempts to achieve returns greater than those commensurate with the risk borne. In the context of bond management this style of management can take two forms. Active managers either use interest rate forecasts to predict movements in the entire fixed-income market, or they employ some form of intramarket analysis to identify particular sectors of the fixed-income market or particular bonds that are relatively mispriced.

Because interest rate risk is crucial to formulating both active and passive strategies, we begin our discussion with an analysis of the sensitivity of bond prices to interest rate fluctuations. This sensitivity is measured by the duration of the bond, and we devote considerable attention to what determines bond duration. We discuss several passive investment strategies, and show how duration-matching techniques can be used to immunize the holding-period return of a portfolio from interest rate risk. After examining the broad range of applications of the duration measure, we consider refinements in the way that interest rate sensitivity is measured, focusing on the concept of bond convexity. Duration is important in formulating active investment strategies as well, and we next explore several of these strategies. We consider strategies based on intramarket analysis as well as on interest rate forecasting. We also show how interest rate swaps may be used in bond portfolio management. We conclude the chapter with a discussion of financial engineering and derivatives in the bond market, and the novel risk profiles that can be achieved through such techniques.

14.1 INTEREST RATE RISK

We have seen already that an inverse relationship exists between bond prices and yields, and we know that interest rates can fluctuate substantially. As interest rates rise and fall, bondholders experience capital losses and gains. These gains or losses make fixed-income investments risky, even if the coupon and principal payments are guaranteed, as in the case of government obligations. Interest rates reflect current and prospective economic conditions, and their changes across the yield curve have profound implications for the design of a bond portfolio. The boxed article here indicates some of the factors affecting rates, and their strategic implications for investors in bonds.

Why do bond prices respond to interest rate fluctuations? Remember that in a competitive market all securities must offer investors fair expected rates of return. If a bond is issued with an 8 percent coupon when competitive yields are 8 percent, then it will sell at par value. If the market rate rises to 9 percent, however, who would purchase an 8 percent coupon bond at par value? The bond price must fall until its expected return increases to the competitive level of 9 percent. Conversely, if the market rate falls to 7 percent, the 8 percent coupon on the bond is attractive compared to yields on alternative investments. In response, investors eager for that return would bid up the bond price until the total rate of return for someone purchasing at that higher price is no better than the market rate.

Interest Rate Sensitivity

Interest Rate Risk
www.investing
inbonds.com

The sensitivity of bond prices to changes in market interest rates is obviously of great concern to investors. To gain some insight into the determinants of interest rate risk, look at Figure 14.1, which presents the percentage change in price corresponding to changes in yield to maturity for four bonds that differ according to coupon rate, initial yield to maturity, and time to maturity. All four bonds illustrate that bond prices decrease when yields rise, and that the price curve is

Figure 14.1

Change in bond price as a function of change in yield to maturity.

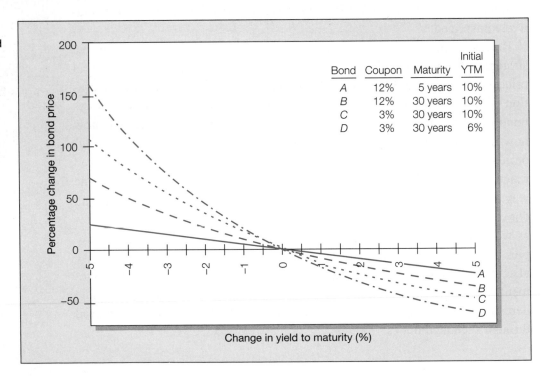

Bond	Coupon	Maturity	Initial YTM
A	12%	5 years	10%
B	12%	30 years	10%
C	3%	30 years	10%
D	3%	30 years	6%

Change in yield to maturity (%)

On June 1, 2007, the difference between a ten-year yield and a two-year yield was a single basis point; that is what is described as flat! On September 20, the ten-year yield at 4.70 percent was 59 basis points higher than the two-year rate. The Federal Reserve chairman, Ben Bernanke, had added liquidity to the banking system to help it deal with the asset-backed securities problem that was unfolding. But at the same time, it added to the risk of inflation as it lowered the yield on short-term securities. A lower-yielding market is less attractive to foreign capital, so the action puts downward pressure on the U.S. dollar, which, by making foreign goods and international commodities like oil more expensive, fuels inflation. The market response was to bid up the yield on longer-term securities.

In November 2010, Bernanke again infused cash into the banking system, this time by a resumption of *quantitative easing*—that is, purchases by the Fed of a number of financial assets not normally held by it. This represented a major departure from traditional monetary policy for lowering (or raising) interest rates. The process had already been used as an early response to the banking crisis in order to make cash available to the commercial banks. The intent was to help solve their shortage of funds for lending and to induce them to restart lending to businesses starved for loans. In 2010, the purpose was simply to lower long-term rates, again to make the cost of borrowing for businesses lower.

Once again, the backdrop for the Fed action included international aspects. The lower rates were expected to lead to a weakening of the dollar. Currency exchange rates were a touchy topic for the major international players, such as the Japanese and the Chinese. The yen had been appreciating, while the Chinese were resisting pressures to allow the yuan to appreciate against the dollar and thereby reduce their trade surplus.

convex, meaning that decreases in yields have bigger impacts on price than increases in yields of equal magnitude. These observations can be summarized in two propositions:

1. Bond prices and yields are inversely related: as yields increase, bond prices fall; as yields fall, bond prices rise.

2. An increase in a bond's yield to maturity results in a smaller price decline than the price gain associated with a decrease of equal magnitude in yield.

Now compare the interest rate sensitivity of bonds A and B, which are identical except for maturity. Figure 14.1 shows that bond B, which has a longer maturity than bond A, exhibits greater sensitivity to interest rate changes. This illustrates another general property:

3. Prices of long-term bonds tend to be more sensitive to interest rate changes than prices of short-term bonds.

Although bond B has six times the maturity of bond A, it has less than six times the interest rate sensitivity. Although interest rate sensitivity seems to increase with maturity, it does so less than proportionally as bond maturity increases. Therefore, our fourth property is that:

4. The sensitivity of bond prices to changes in yields increases at a decreasing rate as maturity increases. In other words, interest rate risk is less than proportional to bond maturity.

Bonds B and C, which are alike in all respects except for coupon rate, illustrate another point. The lower-coupon bond exhibits greater sensitivity to changes in interest rates. This turns out to be a general property of bond prices:

5. Interest rate risk is inversely related to the bond's coupon rate. Prices of high-coupon bonds are less sensitive to changes in interest rates than prices of low-coupon bonds.

Finally, bonds C and D are identical except for the yield to maturity at which the bonds currently sell. Yet bond C, with a higher yield to maturity, is less sensitive to changes in yields. This illustrates our final property:

6. The sensitivity of a bond's price to a change in its yield is inversely related to the yield to maturity at which the bond currently is selling.

TABLE 14.1

Prices of 8 Percent
Coupon Bond
(coupons paid
semiannually)

Yield to Maturity (APR)	T = 1 Year	T = 10 Years	T = 20 Years
8%	1,000.00	1,000.00	1,000.00
9%	990.64	934.96	907.99
Change in price (%)*	.94%	6.50%	9.20%

*Equals value of bond at a 9 percent yield to maturity divided by value of bond at (the original)
8 percent yield, minus 1.

The first five of these general properties were described by Malkiel[1] and are sometimes known as *Malkiel's bond-pricing relationships*. The last property was demonstrated by Homer and Liebowitz.[2]

These six propositions confirm that maturity is a major determinant of interest rate risk. However, they also show that maturity alone is not sufficient to measure interest rate sensitivity. For example, bonds *B* and *C* in Figure 14.1 have the same maturity, but the higher-coupon bond has less price sensitivity to interest rate changes. Obviously, we need to know more than a bond's maturity to quantify its interest rate risk.

To see why bond characteristics such as coupon rate or yield to maturity affect interest rate sensitivity, let's start with a simple numerical example. Table 14.1 gives bond prices for 8 percent semiannual coupon bonds at different yields to maturity and times to maturity, *T*. (The interest rates are expressed as annual percentage rates [APRs], meaning that the true six-month yield is doubled to obtain the stated annual yield.) The shortest-term bond falls in value by less than 1 percent when the interest rate increases from 8 percent to 9 percent. The 10-year bond falls by 6.5 percent, and the 20-year bond by over 9 percent.

Now look at a similar computation using a zero-coupon bond rather than the 8 percent coupon bond. The results are shown in Table 14.2. Notice that for each maturity, the price of the zero-coupon bond falls by a greater proportional amount than the price of the 8 percent coupon bond. Because we know that long-term bonds are more sensitive to interest rate movements than are short-term bonds, this observation suggests that in some sense a zero-coupon bond must represent a longer-term bond than an equal-time-to-maturity coupon bond.

In fact, this insight about effective maturity is a useful one that we can make mathematically precise. To start, note that the times to maturity of the two bonds in this example are not perfect measures of the long- or short-term nature of the bonds. The 20-year 8 percent bond makes many coupon payments, most of which come years before the bond's maturity date. Each of these payments may be considered to have its own "maturity." In the previous chapter, we pointed out that it can be useful to view a coupon bond as a "portfolio" of coupon payments. The effective maturity of the bond is therefore some sort of average of the maturities of *all* the cash flows. The zero-coupon bond, by contrast, makes only one payment at maturity. Its time to maturity is, therefore, a well-defined concept.

TABLE 14.2

Prices of Zero-
Coupon Bond
(semiannual
compounding)

Yield to Maturity (APR)	T = 1 Year	T = 10 Years	T = 20 Years
8%	924.56	456.39	208.29
9%	915.73	414.64	171.93
Change in price (%)*	.96%	9.15%	17.46%

*Equals value of bond at a 9 percent yield to maturity divided by value of bond at (the original)
8 percent yield, minus 1.

[1] Burton G. Malkiel, "Expectations, Bond Prices, and the Term Structure of Interest Rates," *Quarterly Journal of Economics* 76 (May 1962), pp. 197–218.
[2] Sidney Homer and Martin L. Liebowitz, *Inside the Yield Book: New Tools for Bond Market Strategy* (Englewood Cliffs, NJ: Prentice Hall, 1972).

Duration

To deal with the ambiguity of the "maturity" of a bond making many payments, we need a measure of the average maturity of the bond's promised cash flows to serve as a useful summary statistic of the effective maturity of the bond. We would like also to use the measure as a guide to the sensitivity of a bond to interest rate changes, because we have noted that price sensitivity tends to increase with time to maturity.

Frederick Macaulay[3] termed the effective maturity concept the **duration** of the bond and suggested that duration be computed as the weighted average of the times to each coupon or principal payment made by the bond. His method relates the weight associated with each payment time to the "importance" of that payment to the value of the bond. Specifically, the weight applied to each payment time is the proportion of the total value of the bond accounted for by that payment; that is, the proportion is the present value of the payment divided by the bond price.

In calculating the weighted average, we define the weight, w_t, associated with the cash flow made at time t (denoted CF_t) as

$$w_t = \frac{CF_t/(1 + y)^t}{\text{Bond price}}$$

where y is the bond's yield to maturity. The numerator on the right-hand side of this equation is the present value of the cash flow occurring at time t while the denominator is the value of all the payments forthcoming from the bond. These weights sum to 1.0 because the sum of the cash flows discounted at the yield to maturity equals the bond price.

Using these values to calculate the weighted average of the times until the receipt of each of the bond's payments, we obtain Macaulay's duration formula:

$$D = \sum_{t=1}^{T} t \times w_t \tag{14.1}$$

EXAMPLE 14.1   **Calculating Duration**

As an application of equation 14.1, we derive in Table 14.3 the durations of an 8 percent coupon and zero-coupon bond, each with two years to maturity. We assume that the yield to maturity on each bond is 10 percent, or 5 percent per half-year. The present value of each payment is discounted at 5 percent per period for the number of (semiannual) periods shown in column 1. The weight associated with each payment time (column 4) is the present value of the payment for that period (column 3) divided by the bond price (the sum of the present values in column 3). The numbers in column 5 are the products of time to payment and payment weight. Each of these products corresponds to one of the terms in equation 14.1. According to that equation, we can calculate the duration of each bond by adding the numbers in column 5.

The duration of the zero-coupon bond is exactly equal to its time to maturity, two years. This makes sense, because with only one payment, the average time until payment must be the bond's maturity. In contrast, the two-year coupon bond has a shorter duration of 1.8853 years.

continued

---

[3]Frederick Macaulay, *Some Theoretical Problems Suggested by the Movements of Interest Rates, Bond Yields, and Stock Prices in the United States Since 1856* (New York: National Bureau of Economic Research, 1938).

TABLE 14.3   Calculating the Duration of Two Bonds

	(1) Time Until Payment (years)	(2) Payment	(3) Payment Discounted at 5% Semiannually	(4) Weight*	(5) Column 1 Multiplied by Column 4
Bond A					
8% bond	.5	$ 40	$ 38.095	.0395	.0198
	1.0	40	36.281	.0376	.0376
	1.5	40	34.553	.0358	.0537
	2.0	1,040	855.611	.8871	1.7742
Sum			$964.540	1.0000	1.8853
Bond B					
Zero-coupon bond	.5–1.5	$ 0	$ 0	0	0
	2.0	1,000	822.70	1.0	2
Sum			$822.70	1.0	2

*Weight = Present value of each payment (column 3) divided by the bond price, $964.54 for bond A and $822.70 for bond B.

Figure 14.2 shows the spreadsheet formulas used to produce the entries in Table 14.3. The inputs in the spreadsheet—specifying the cash flows the bond will pay—are given in columns B–D. In column E we calculate the present value of each cash flow using the assumed yield to maturity, in column F we calculate the weights for equation 14.1, and in column G we compute the product of time to payment and payment weight. Each of these terms corresponds to one of the values that are summed in the equation. The sums computed in cells G8 and G14 are therefore the durations of each bond. Using the spreadsheet, you can easily answer several "what if" questions such as the one in Concept Check 1.

Figure 14.2   Spreadsheet formulas for calculating duration.

	A	B	C	D	E	F	G
1			Time Until		PV of CF		Column (C)
2			Payment		(discount rate =		Times
3		Period	(years)	Cash Flow	5% per period)	Weight	Column (F)
4	**A.** 8% coupon bond	1	0.5	40	=D4/(1+$B$16)^B4	=E4/E$8	=F4*C4
5		2	1	40	=D5/(1+$B$16)^B5	=E5/E$8	=F5*C5
6		3	1.5	40	=D6/(1+$B$16)^B6	=E6/E$8	=F6*C6
7		4	2	1040	=D7/(1+$B$16)^B7	=E7/E$8	=F7*C7
8	Sum:				=SUM(E4:E7)	=SUM(F4:F7)	=SUM(G4:G7)
9							
10	**B.** Zero-coupon	1	0.5	0	=D10/(1+$B$16)^B10	=E10/E$14	=F10*C10
11		2	1	0	=D11/(1+$B$16)^B11	=E11/E$14	=F11*C11
12		3	1.5	0	=D12/(1+$B$16)^B12	=E12/E$14	=F12*C12
13		4	2	1000	=D13/(1+$B$16)^B13	=E13/E$14	=F13*C13
14	Sum:				=SUM(E10:E13)	=SUM(F10:F13)	=SUM(G10:G13)
15							
16	Semiannual int rate:	0.05					

CC 1

CONCEPT CHECK

Suppose the interest rate decreases to 9 percent at an annual percentage rate. What will happen to the prices and durations of the two bonds in Table 14.3?

Duration is a key concept in fixed-income portfolio management for at least three reasons. First, it is a simple summary statistic of the effective average maturity of the portfolio. Second, it turns out to be an essential tool in immunizing portfolios from interest rate risk. We explore this application in Section 14.3. Third, duration is a measure of the interest rate sensitivity of a portfolio, which we explore here.

We have seen that a bond's price sensitivity to interest rate changes generally increases with maturity. Duration enables us to quantify this relationship. Specifically, it can be shown that when interest rates change, the proportional change in a bond's price can be related to the change in its yield to maturity, y, according to the rule

$$\frac{\Delta P}{P} = -D \times \left[\frac{\Delta(1 + y)}{1 + y} \right] \tag{14.2}$$

The proportional price change equals the proportional change in 1 plus the bond's yield times the bond's duration. Therefore, bond price volatility is proportional to the bond's duration, and duration becomes a natural measure of interest rate exposure.

Practitioners commonly use equation 14.2 in a slightly different form. They define **modified duration** as $D^* = D/(1 + y)$, note that $\Delta(1 + y) = \Delta y$, and rewrite the equation as

$$\frac{\Delta P}{P} = -D^* \Delta y \tag{14.3}$$

The percentage change in bond price is just the product of modified duration and the change in the bond's yield to maturity. Because the percentage change in the bond price is proportional to modified duration, modified duration is a natural measure of the bond's exposure to changes in interest rates.[4] (A related concept of *effective duration* is presented in this chapter's Appendix 14A.)

EXAMPLE 14.2   **Duration and Interest Rate Risk**

Consider the two-year-maturity, 8 percent coupon bond in Table 14.3 making semiannual coupon payments and selling at a price of $964.540, for a yield to maturity of 10 percent. The duration of this bond is 1.8852 years. For comparison, we will also consider a zero-coupon bond with maturity *and duration* of 1.8852 years. As we found in Table 14.3, because the coupon bond makes payments semiannually, it is best to treat one "period" as a half-year. So the duration of each bond is $1.8852 \times 2 = 3.7704$ (semiannual) periods, with a per-period interest rate of 5 percent. The modified duration of each bond is therefore $3.7704/1.05 = 3.591$ periods.

continued

---

[4]Actually, equation 14.2, or equivalently 14.3, is only approximately valid for large changes in the bond's yield. The approximation becomes exact as one considers smaller, or localized, changes in yields. Students of calculus will recognize that modified duration is proportional to the derivative of the bond's price with respect to changes in the bond's yield:

$$D^* = -\frac{1}{P} \frac{dP}{dy}$$

As such, it gives a measure of the slope of the bond price curve only in the neighbourhood of the current price.

Suppose the semiannual interest rate increases from 5 percent to 5.01 percent. According to equation 14.3, the bond prices should fall by

$$\Delta P/P = -D^*\Delta y = -3.591 \times .01\% = -03591\%$$

Now compute the price change of each bond directly. The coupon bond, which initially sells at \$964.540, falls to \$964.1942 when its yield increases to 5.01 percent, which is a decline of .0359 percent. The zero-coupon bond initially sells for $\$1,000/1.05^{3.7704} = 831.9704$. At the higher yield, it sells for $\$1,000/1.0501^{3.7704} = 831.6717$. This price also falls by .0359 percent.

We conclude that bonds with equal durations do in fact have equal interest rate sensitivity and that (at least for small changes in yields) the percentage price change is the modified duration times the change in yield.[5]

CC 2

CONCEPT CHECK

a. In Concept Check 1, you calculated the price and duration of a two-year-maturity, 8 percent coupon bond making semiannual coupon payments when the market interest rate is 9 percent. Now suppose the interest rate increases to 9.05 percent. Calculate the new value of the bond and the percentage change in the bond's price.

b. Calculate the percentage change in the bond's price predicted by the duration formula in equation 14.2 or 14.3. Compare this value to your answer for (a).

What Determines Duration?   Malkiel's bond price relations, which we laid out in the previous section, characterize the determinants of interest rate sensitivity. Duration allows us to quantify that sensitivity. For example, if we wish to speculate on interest rates, duration tells us how strong a bet we are making. Conversely, if we wish to remain "neutral" on rates, and simply match the interest rate sensitivity of a chosen bond-market index, duration allows us to measure that sensitivity and mimic it in our own portfolio. For these reasons, it is crucial to understand the determinants of duration, and convenient to have formulas to calculate the duration of some commonly encountered securities. Therefore, in this section, we present several "rules" that summarize most of the important properties of duration.

Duration Properties   The sensitivity of a bond's price to changes in market interest rates is influenced by three key factors: time to maturity, coupon rate, and yield to maturity. These determinants of price sensitivity are important to fixed-income portfolio management. Therefore, we summarize some of the important relationships in the following five rules. These rules are also illustrated in Figure 14.3, where durations of bonds of various coupon rates, yields to maturity, and times to maturity are plotted.

We have already established:

Rule 1 for Duration   The duration of a zero-coupon bond equals its time to maturity.

---

[5]Notice another implication of Example 14.2. We see from the example that when the bond makes payments semiannually, it is convenient to treat each payment period as a half-year. This implies that when we calculate modified duration, we divided Macaulay's duration by (1 + semiannual yield to maturity). It is more common to write this divisor as 1 + bond equivalent yield/2. In general, if a bond were to make n payments a year, modified duration would be related to Macaulay's duration by $D^* = D/(1 + y_{BEV}/n)$.

Figure 14.3

Bond duration versus bond maturity.

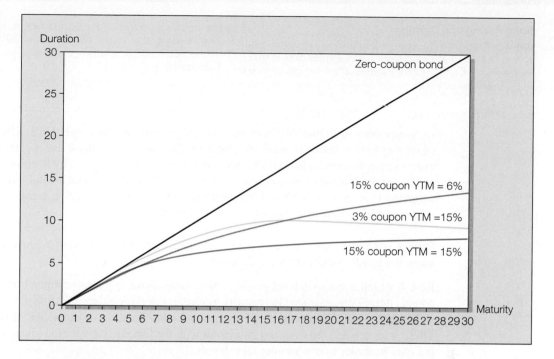

We have also seen that the two-year coupon bond has a lower duration than the two-year zero because coupons early in the bond's life lower the bond's weighted average time until payments. This illustrates another general property:

Rule 2 for Duration   Holding maturity constant, a bond's duration is higher when the coupon rate is lower.

This property corresponds to Malkiel's fifth relationship and is attributable to the impact of early coupon payments on the average maturity of a bond's payments. The higher these coupons, the higher the weights on the early payments and the lower the weighted average maturity of the payments. Compare the plots in Figure 14.3 of the durations of the 3 percent coupon and 15 percent coupon bonds, each with identical yields of percent. The plot of the duration of the 15 percent coupon bond lies below the corresponding plot for the 3 percent coupon bond.

Rule 3 for Duration   Holding the coupon rate constant, a bond's duration generally increases with its time to maturity. Duration always increases with maturity for bonds selling at par or at a premium to par.

This property of duration corresponds to Malkiel's third relationship, and it is fairly intuitive. What is surprising is that duration need not always increase with time to maturity. It turns out that for some deep-discount bonds, duration may eventually fall with increases in maturity. However, for virtually all traded bonds it is safe to assume that duration increases with maturity.

Notice in Figure 14.3 that for the zero-coupon bond, maturity and duration are equal. However, for coupon bonds duration increases by less than a year with a year's increase in maturity. The slope of the duration graph is less than 1.

Although long-maturity bonds generally will be high-duration bonds, duration is a better measure of the long-term nature of the bond because it also accounts for coupon payments. Time to maturity is an adequate statistic only when the bond pays no coupons; then, maturity and duration are equal.

Bond Pricing and Duration

Bond pricing and duration calculations can be cumbersome. The calculations are set up in a spreadsheet that is available on Connect. The models allow you to calculate the price and duration for bonds of different maturities. The models also allow you to examine the sensitivity of the calculations to changes in coupon rate and yield to maturity.

Notice also in Figure 14.3 that the two 15 percent coupon bonds have different durations when they sell at different yields to maturity. The lower-yield bond has greater duration. This makes sense, because at lower yields the more distant payments made by the bond have relatively greater present values and account for a greater share of the bond's total value. Thus in the weighted-average calculation of duration the distant payments receive greater weights, which results in a higher duration measure. This establishes rule 4:

Rule 4 for Duration Holding other factors constant, the duration of a coupon bond is higher when the bond's yield to maturity is lower.

Rule 4, which is the sixth bond-pricing relationship above, applies to coupon bonds. For zeros, of course, duration equals time to maturity, regardless of the yield to maturity.

Finally, we develop some algebraic rules for the duration of securities of special interest. These rules are derived from and consistent with the formula for duration given in equation 14.1 but may be easier to use for long-term bonds.

Rule 5 for Duration The duration of a level perpetuity is $(1 + y)/y$. For example, at a 10 percent yield, the duration of a perpetuity that pays \$100 once a year forever will equal $1.10/.10 = 11$ years, but at an 8 percent yield it will equal $1.08/.08 = 13.5$ years.

Rule 5 makes it obvious that maturity and duration can differ substantially. The maturity of the perpetuity is infinite, whereas the duration of the instrument at a 10 percent yield is only 11 years. The present-value-weighted cash flows early on in the life of the perpetuity dominate the computation of duration.

Notice from Figure 14.3 that as their maturities become ever longer, the durations of the two coupon bonds with yields of 15 percent converge to the duration of the perpetuity with the same yield, 7.67 years.

CC 3

CONCEPT CHECK

Show that the duration of the perpetuity increases as the interest rate decreases in accordance with rule 4.

More complex formulas exist for annuities and coupon bonds. For an annuity, the perpetuity formula is adjusted to

$$\frac{1 + y}{y} - \frac{T}{(1 + y)^T - 1} \tag{14.4}$$

where T is the number of payments and y is the annuity's yield per payment period. The duration of a coupon bond equals

$$\frac{1 + y}{y} - \frac{(1 + y) + T(c - y)}{c[(1 + y)^T - 1] + y} \tag{14.5}$$

Figure 14.4

Using Excel to compute duration.

	A	B	C
1			
2			
3	**Inputs**		**Formula in column B**
4	Settlement date	1/1/2000	=DATE(2000,1,1)
5	Maturity date	1/1/2008	=DATE(2008,1,1)
6	Coupon rate	0.09	0.09
7	Yield to maturity	0.1	0.1
8	Coupons per year	1	1
9			
10	**Outputs**		
11	Macaulay Duration	5.9735	=DURATION(B4,B5,B6,B7,B8)
12	Modified Duration	5.4304	=MDURATION(B4,B5,B6,B7,B8)

where c is the coupon rate per payment period, T is the number of payment periods, and y is the bond's yield per payment period; this simplifies for coupon bonds selling at par value to

$$\frac{1 + y}{y}\left[1 - \frac{1}{(1 + y)^T} \right] \tag{14.6}$$

The equations for the durations of coupon bonds are somewhat tedious. Moreover, they assume that the bond is at the beginning of a coupon payment period. Fortunately, spreadsheet programs such as Excel come with generalizations of these equations that can accommodate bonds between coupon payment dates. Figure 14.4 illustrates how to use Excel to compute duration. The spreadsheet uses many of the same conventions as the bond-pricing spreadsheets described in Chapter 13.

The settlement date (i.e., today's date) and maturity date are entered in cells B4 and B5 using Excel's date function, DATE(year, month, day). The coupon and maturity rates are entered as decimals in cells B6 and B7, and the payment periods per year are entered in cell B8. Macaulay and modified duration appear in cells B11 and B12. The spreadsheet shows that the duration of the bond in Figure 14.4 is indeed 5.97 years. For this eight-year-maturity bond, we don't have a specific settlement date. We arbitrarily set the settlement date to January 1, 2000, and use a maturity date precisely eight years later.

Durations can vary widely among traded bonds. Table 14.4 presents durations computed from Figure 14.4 for several bonds all assumed to pay semiannual coupons and to yield 4 percent per half-year. Notice that duration decreases as coupon rates increase, and duration generally increases with time to maturity. According to Table 14.4 and equation 14.2, if the interest rate were to increase from 8 percent to 8.1 percent, the 6 percent coupon 20-year bond would fall in

TABLE 14.4

Bond Durations (initial bond yield = 8 percent APR)

	Coupon Rates (per year)			
Years to Maturity	6%	8%	10%	12%
1	.985	.980	.976	.972
5	4.361	4.218	4.095	3.990
10	7.454	7.067	6.772	6.541
20	10.922	10.292	9.870	9.568
Infinite (perpetuity)	13.000	13.000	13.000	13.000

value by about 1.01 percent ($10.922 \times 1\%/1.08$), whereas the 10 percent coupon one-year bond would fall by only .090 percent. Notice also from Table 14.4 that duration is independent of coupon rate only for the perpetual bond.

CONVEXITY

Duration is clearly a key tool in fixed-income portfolio management. Yet the duration rule for the impact of interest rates on bond prices is only an approximation. Equation 14.2, or its equivalent, 14.3, which we repeat here, states that the percentage change in the value of a bond approximately equals the product of modified duration times the change in the bond's yield:

$$\frac{\Delta P}{P} = -D^* \Delta y$$

   This equation asserts that the percentage price change is directly proportional to the change in the bond's yield. If this were *exactly* so, however, a graph of the percentage change in bond price as a function of the change in its yield would plot as a straight line, with slope equal to $-D^*$. Yet we know from Figure 14.1, and more generally from Malkiel's five rules (specifically rule 2), that the relationship between bond prices and yields is *not* linear. The duration rule is a good approximation for small changes in bond yield, but it is less accurate for larger changes.

   Figure 14.5 illustrates this point. Like Figure 14.1, the figure presents the percentage change in bond price in response to a change in the bond's yield to maturity. The curved line is the percentage price change for a 30-year-maturity, 8 percent coupon bond, selling at an initial yield to maturity of 8 percent. The straight line is the percentage price change predicted by the duration rule: the modified duration of the bond at its initial yield is 11.26 years, so the straight line is a plot of $-D^* \Delta y = -11.26 \times \Delta y$. Notice that the two plots are tangent at the initial yield. Thus for small changes in the bond's yield to maturity, the duration rule is quite accurate. However, for larger changes in yield, there is progressively more "daylight" between the two plots, demonstrating that the duration rule becomes progressively less accurate.

Figure 14.5

Bond price convexity.

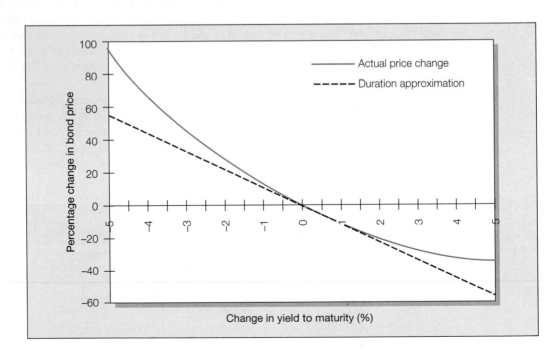

Notice from Figure 14.5 that the duration approximation (the straight line) always understates the value of the bond; it underestimates the increase in bond price when the yield falls, and it overestimates the decline in price when the yield rises. This is due to the curvature of the true price–yield relationship. Curves with shapes such as that of the price–yield relationship are said to be *convex*, and the curvature of the price–yield curve is called the **convexity** of the bond.

We can quantify convexity as the rate of change of the slope of the price–yield curve, expressed as a fraction of the bond price.[6] As a practical rule, you can view bonds with higher convexity as exhibiting higher curvature in the price–yield relationship. The convexity of noncallable bonds such as that in Figure 14.5 is positive: the slope increases (i.e., becomes less negative) at higher yields.

Convexity allows us to improve the duration for modified duration approximation for bond price changes. Accounting for convexity, equation 14.3 for modified duration can be adjusted as follows:[7]

$$\frac{\Delta P}{P} = -D^*\Delta y + \frac{1}{2} \times \text{Convexity} \times (\Delta y)^2 \tag{14.7}$$

The first term on the right-hand side is the same as the duration rule, equation 14.3. The second term is the adjustment for convexity. Notice that for a bond with positive convexity, the second term is positive, regardless of whether the yield rises or falls. This insight corresponds to the fact noted just above that the duration rule always underestimates the new value of a bond following a change in its yield. The more accurate equation 14.3, which accounts for convexity, always predicts a higher bond price than equation 14.2. Of course, if the change in yield is small, the convexity term, which is multiplied by $(\Delta y)^2$ in equation 14.3, will be extremely small and will add little to the approximation. In this case, the linear approximation given by the duration rule will be sufficiently accurate. Thus convexity is more important as a practical matter when potential interest rate changes are large.

EXAMPLE 14.2   **Convexity**

The bond in Figure 14.5 has a 30-year maturity and an 8 percent coupon, and sells at an initial yield to maturity of 8 percent. Because the coupon rate equals yield to maturity, the bond sells at par value, or $1,000. The modified duration of the bond at its initial yield is 11.26 years, and its convexity is 212.4 (which can be verified using the formula in footnote 6). If the bond's yield increases from 8 percent to 10 percent, the bond price will fall to $811.46, a decline of 18.85 percent. The duration rule, equation 14.3, would predict a price decline of

$$\frac{\Delta P}{P} = -D^*\Delta y = -11.26 \times .02 = -.2252, \text{ or } -22.52\%$$

continued

---

[6]We pointed out in footnote 4 that equation 14.2 for modified duration can be written as $dP/P = -D^*dy$. Thus $D^* = -1/P \times dP/dy$ is the slope of the price–yield curve expressed as a fraction of the bond price. Similarly, the convexity of a bond equals the second derivative (the rate of change of the slope) of the price–yield curve divided by bond price: $1/P \times d^2P/dy^2$. The formula for the convexity of a bond with a maturity of n years making annual coupon payments is

$$\text{Convexity} = \frac{1}{P \times (1 + y)^2} \sum_{t=1}^{n} \left[\frac{CF_t}{(1 + y)^t}(t^2 + t) \right]$$

where CF_t is the cash flow paid to the bondholder at date t; CF_t represents either a coupon payment before maturity or final coupon plus par value at the maturity date.

[7]To use the convexity rule, you must express interest rates as decimals rather than percentages.

which is considerably more than the bond price actually falls. The duration-with-convexity rule, equation 14.7, is more accurate:[8]

$$\frac{\Delta P}{P} = -D^*\Delta y + \frac{1}{2} \times \text{Convexity} \times (\Delta y)^2$$

$$= -11.26 \times 0.2 + \frac{1}{2} \times 212.4 \times (.02)^2 = -.1827, \text{ or } -18.27\%$$

which is far closer to the exact change in bond price.

Notice that if the change in yield were smaller, say .1 percent, convexity would matter less. The price of the bond actually would fall to $988.85, a decline of 1.115 percent. Without accounting for convexity, we would predict a price decline of

$$\frac{\Delta P}{P} = -D^*\Delta y = -11.26 \times .001 = .01126, \text{ or } 1.126\%$$

Accounting for convexity, we get almost the precisely correct answer:

$$\frac{\Delta P}{P} = -11.26 \times .001 + \frac{1}{2} \times 212.4 \times (.001)^2 = .01115, \text{ or } 1.115\%$$

Nevertheless, the duration rule is quite accurate in this case, even without accounting for convexity.

Why Do Investors Like Convexity?

Convexity is generally considered a desirable trait. Bonds with greater curvature gain more in price when yields fall than they lose when yields rise. For example in Figure 14.6 bonds *A* and *B* have the same duration at the initial yield. The plots of their proportional price changes as a function of

Figure 14.6

Convexity of two bonds.

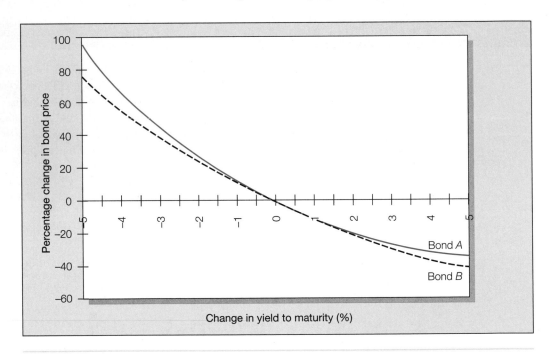

[8]Notice that when we use equation 14.3, we express interest rates as decimals rather than percentages. The change in rates from 8 percent to 10 percent is represented as $\Delta y = .02$.

interest-rate changes are tangent, meaning that their sensitivities to changes in yields at that point are equal. However, bond *A* is more convex than bond *B*. It enjoys greater price increases and smaller price decreases when interest rates fluctuate by larger amounts. If interest rates are volatile, this is an attractive asymmetry that increases the expected return on the bond, since bond *A* will benefit more from rate decreases and suffer less from rate increases. Of course, if convexity is desirable, it will not be available for free: investors will have to pay more and accept lower yields on bonds with greater convexity.

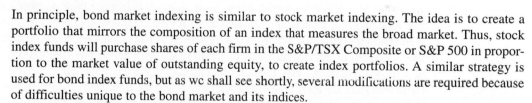

PASSIVE BOND MANAGEMENT

Passive managers take bond prices as fairly set and seek to control only the risk of their fixed-income portfolio. Two broad classes of passive management are pursued in the fixed-income market. The first is an indexing strategy that attempts to replicate the performance of a given bond index. The second broad class of passive strategies are known as **immunization** techniques and are used widely by financial institutions such as insurance companies and pension funds. These are designed to shield the overall financial status of the institution from exposure to interest rate fluctuations. While both indexing and immunization strategies are alike in that they accept market prices as correctly set, they are very different in terms of risk exposure. A **bond index portfolio** will have the same risk–reward profile as the bond market index to which it is tied. In contrast, immunization strategies seek to establish a virtually-zero-risk profile, in which interest rate movements have no impact on the value of the firm.

Bond Index Funds

TMX Group
www.tmx.com

In principle, bond market indexing is similar to stock market indexing. The idea is to create a portfolio that mirrors the composition of an index that measures the broad market. Thus, stock index funds will purchase shares of each firm in the S&P/TSX Composite or S&P 500 in proportion to the market value of outstanding equity, to create index portfolios. A similar strategy is used for bond index funds, but as we shall see shortly, several modifications are required because of difficulties unique to the bond market and its indices.

The major indices of the Canadian bond market are compiled by Scotia Capital, its Universe Index being the relevant one. In the United States, there are three: the Barclays Capital U.S. (formerly Lehman) Aggregate Bond Index, the Salomon Brothers Broad Investment Grade (BIG) Index, and the Merrill Lynch Domestic Master Index. These bond indices are market-value-weighted indices of total returns on (U.S.) government, corporate, mortgage-backed, and Yankee (foreign issuer, U.S.-dollar-denominated) bonds with maturities greater than one year; as time passes and the maturity of a bond falls below one year, the bond is dropped from the indices.

Bank of Nova
Scotia
www.gbm.
scotiabank.com

The Scotia Capital bond indices actually are based only on those bonds that are considered to be available for public investment. Those bonds held by the Bank of Canada in particular and other institutions that buy on issue to hold to maturity are not included in calculating the value weighting. This realization points up the well-known illiquidity of the Canadian bond market, which has a bearing on the subject of index funds. In the late 1980s, ScotiaMcLeod created a Canadian bond index fund but was disappointed with the results. The same problems that make an index portfolio difficult to maintain in the U.S. market were exaggerated in Canada, so that the fund became infeasible. There also proved to be very little interest in the fund from Canadian institutional and professional investors.

The first problem that arises in the formation of a bond index portfolio is that the index includes a vast number of securities (the U.S. indices include more than 5,000); hence, it is quite difficult to purchase each security in the index in proportion to its market value. Moreover, many bonds are very thinly traded, especially in Canada.

Bond index funds also present more difficult rebalancing problems than do stock index funds. Bonds are continually dropped from the index as their maturities fall below one year. Moreover, as new bonds are issued, they are added to the index. Therefore, in contrast to equity indices, the securities used to compute bond indices constantly change. As they do, the manager must update or rebalance the portfolio to ensure a close match between the composition of the portfolio and the bonds included in the index. The fact that bonds generate considerable interest income that must be reinvested further complicates the job of the index fund manager.

In practice, it is infeasible to achieve a precise replication of the broad bond indices. Instead, a stratified sampling or *cellular* approach is often pursued. Figure 14.7 illustrates the idea behind the cellular approach. First, the bond market is stratified into several subclasses. The figure shows a simple two-way breakdown by maturity and issuer; in practice, however, such criteria as the bond's coupon rate or the credit risk of the issuer also would be used to form cells. Bonds falling within each cell are then considered reasonably homogeneous. Next, the percentages of the entire universe (i.e., the bonds included in the index that is to be matched) falling within each cell are computed and reported, as we have done for a few cells in Figure 14.7. Finally, the portfolio manager establishes a bond portfolio with representation for each cell that matches the representation of that cell in the bond universe. In this way, the characteristics of the portfolio in terms of maturity, coupon rate, credit risk, industrial representation, and so on will match the characteristics of the index, and the performance of the portfolio likewise should match the index.

Retail investors can buy mutual funds or exchange-traded funds that track the broad bond market. ETFs with various focuses on the bond market are increasingly popular.

Immunization

In contrast to indexing strategies, many institutions try to insulate their portfolios from interest rate risk altogether. Generally, there are two ways of viewing this risk, depending on the circumstances of the particular investor. Some institutions, such as banks, are concerned with protecting the current net worth or net market value of the firm against interest rate fluctuations. Other investors, such as pension funds, may face an obligation to make payments after a given number of years. These investors are more concerned with protecting the future values of their portfolios.

What is common to all investors, however, is interest rate risk. The net worth of the firm or the ability to meet future obligations fluctuates with interest rates. We will see that, by properly adjusting the maturity structure of their portfolios, investors can shed their interest rate risk.

Figure 14.7

Stratification of bonds into cells.

Sector / Term to Maturity	Canada	Agency	Mortgage-Backed	Industrial	Finance	Utility	Yankee
<1 year	12.1%						
1–3 years	5.4%						
3–5 years			4.1%				
5–7 years							
7–10 years		0.1%					
10–15 years							
15–30 years			9.2%			3.4%	
30+ years							

Immunization techniques refer to strategies used by such investors to shield their overall financial status from interest rate risk.

Many banks and credit unions have a natural mismatch between asset and liability maturity structures. Bank liabilities are primarily the deposits owed to customers, most of which are very short-term in nature and, consequently, of low duration. Bank assets by contrast are composed largely of outstanding commercial and consumer loans or mortgages. These assets are of longer duration than are deposits, and their values are correspondingly more sensitive to interest rate fluctuations. In periods when interest rates increase unexpectedly, banks can suffer serious decreases in net worth—their assets fall in value by more than their liabilities.

The watchword in bank portfolio strategy has become asset and liability management. Techniques called *gap management* were developed to limit the "gap" between asset and liability durations. Adjustable-rate mortgages are one way to reduce the duration of bank asset portfolios. Unlike conventional mortgages, adjustable-rate mortgages do not fall in value when market interest rates rise, because the rates they pay are tied to an index of the current market rate. Even if the indexing is imperfect or entails lags, indexing greatly diminishes sensitivity to interest rate fluctuations. On the other side of the balance sheet, the introduction of bank certificates of deposit with fixed terms to maturity increases the duration of bank liabilities, also reducing the duration gap.

One way to view gap management is that the bank is attempting to equate the durations of assets and liabilities to effectively immunize its overall position from interest rate movements. Because bank assets and liabilities are roughly equal in size, if their durations also are equal, any change in interest rates will affect the values of assets and liabilities equally. Interest rates would have no effect on net worth, in other words. Therefore, net worth immunization requires a portfolio duration of zero. This will result if assets and liabilities are equal in both magnitude and duration.

CC 4

CONCEPT CHECK

If assets and liabilities are not equal, then immunization requires that $D_A A = D_L L$ where D denotes duration and A and L denote assets and liabilities, respectively. Explain why the simpler condition, $D_A = D_L$, is no longer valid in this case.

Similarly, a pension fund may have a mismatch between the interest rate sensitivity of the assets held in the fund and the present value of its liabilities—the obligation to make payments to retirees. Hence, pension funds think more in terms of future commitments than current net worth. As interest rates fluctuate, both the value of the assets held by the fund and the rate at which those assets generate income fluctuate. As interest rates have fallen to historically low levels, pension portfolios have gained in value on their fixed income holdings; yet the present value of the pension payment streams has risen even more, causing the net value to drop. The lesson is that funds should match the interest rate exposure of assets and liabilities so that the value of assets will track the value of liabilities whether rates rise or fall. The pension fund manager, therefore, may want to protect, or "immunize," the future accumulated value of the fund at some target date against interest rate movements.

Pension funds are not alone in this concern. Any institution with a future fixed obligation might consider immunization a reasonable risk management policy. Insurance companies, for example, also pursue immunization strategies. Indeed, the notion of immunization was introduced by F. M. Redington,[9] an actuary for a life insurance company. The idea behind immunization is that duration-matched assets and liabilities let the asset portfolio meet the firm's obligations despite interest rate movements. Consider, for example, an insurance company that issues a guaranteed investment contract, or GIC, for $10,000. (Essentially, GICs are zero-coupon bonds issued by the insurance

---

[9]F. M. Redington, "Review of the Principle of Life-Office Valuations," *Journal of the Institute of Actuaries* 78 (1952).

company to its customers. They are popular products for individuals' retirement-saving accounts.) If the GIC has a five-year maturity and a guaranteed interest rate of 8 percent, the insurance company is obligated to pay $10,000 \times (1.08)^5 = \$14,693.28$ in five years.

Suppose that the insurance company chooses to fund its obligation with $10,000 of 8 percent *annual* coupon bonds, selling at par value, with six years to maturity. As long as the market interest rate stays at 8 percent, the company has fully funded the obligation, as the present value of the obligation exactly equals the value of the bonds.

Table 14.5, panel A shows that if interest rates remain at 8 percent, the accumulated funds from the bond will grow to exactly the $14,693.28 obligation. Over the five-year period, the year-end coupon income of $800 is reinvested at the prevailing 8 percent market interest rate. At the end of the period, the bonds can be sold for $10,000; they still will sell at par value because the coupon rate still equals the market interest rate. Total income after five years from reinvested coupons and the sale of the bond is precisely $14,693.28.

If interest rates change, however, two offsetting influences will affect the ability of the fund to grow to the targeted value of $14,693.28. If interest rates rise, the fund will suffer a capital loss, impairing its ability to satisfy the obligation. The bonds will be worth less in five years than if interest rates had remained at 8 percent. However, at a higher interest rate, reinvested coupons will grow

TABLE 14.5

Terminal Value of a Bond Portfolio After Five Years (all proceeds reinvested)

Payment Number	Years Remaining Until Obligation	Accumulated Value of Invested Payment		
A. Rates remain at 8%				
1	4	$800 \times (1.08)^4$	=	1,088.39
2	3	$800 \times (1.08)^3$	=	1,007.77
3	2	$800 \times (1.08)^2$	=	933.12
4	1	$800 \times (1.08)^1$	=	864.00
5	0	$800 \times (1.08)^0$	=	800.00
Sale of bond	0	10,800/1.08	=	10,000.00
				14,693.28
B. Rates fall to 7%				
1	4	$800 \times (1.07)^4$	=	1,048.64
2	3	$800 \times (1.07)^3$	=	980.03
3	2	$800 \times (1.07)^2$	=	915.92
4	1	$800 \times (1.07)^1$	=	856.00
5	0	$800 \times (1.07)^0$	=	800.00
Sale of bond	0	10,800/1.07	=	10,093.46
				14,694.05
C. Rates increase to 9%				
1	4	$800 \times (1.09)^4$	=	1,129.27
2	3	$800 \times (1.09)^3$	=	1,036.02
3	2	$800 \times (1.09)^2$	=	950.48
4	1	$800 \times (1.09)^1$	=	872.00
5	0	$800 \times (1.09)^0$	=	800.00
Sale of bond	0	10,800/1.09	=	9,908.26
				14,696.03

Note: The sale price of the bond portfolio equals the portfolio's final payment ($10,800) divided by $1 + r$, because the time to maturity of the bonds will be one year at the time of sale.

at a faster rate, offsetting the capital loss. In other words, fixed-income investors face two offsetting types of interest rate risk: *price risk* and *reinvestment rate risk*. Increases in interest rates cause capital losses but at the same time increase the rate at which reinvested income will grow. If the portfolio duration is chosen appropriately, these two effects will cancel out exactly. When the portfolio duration is set equal to the investor's horizon date, the accumulated value of the investment fund at the horizon date will be unaffected by interest rate fluctuations. *For a horizon equal to the portfolio's duration, price risk and reinvestment risk are precisely offsetting.*

In this example, the duration of the six-year-maturity bonds used to fund the GIC is five years. Because the fully funded plan has equal duration for its assets and liabilities, the insurance company should be immunized against interest rate fluctuations. To confirm that this is the case, let us see whether the bond can generate enough income to pay off the obligation five years from now regardless of interest rate movements.

Panels B and C in Table 14.5 illustrate two possible interest rate scenarios: rates either fall to 7 percent, or increase to 9 percent. In both cases, the annual coupon payments from the bond are reinvested at the new interest rate, which is assumed to change before the first coupon payment, and the bond is sold in year 5 to help satisfy the obligation of the GIC.

Panel B shows that if interest rates fall to 7 percent, the total funds will accumulate to $14,694.05, providing a small surplus of $.77. If rates increase to 9 percent as in panel C, the fund accumulates to $14,696.02, providing a small surplus of $2.74.

Several points are worth highlighting. First, duration matching balances the difference between the accumulated value of the coupon payments (reinvestment rate risk) and the sale value of the bond (price risk). That is, when interest rates fall, the coupons grow less than in the base case, but the gain on the sale of the bond offsets this. When interest rates rise, the resale value of the bond falls, but the coupons more than make up for this loss because they are reinvested at the higher rate. Figure 14.8 illustrates this case. The solid curve traces the accumulated value of the bonds if interest rates remain at 8 percent. The dashed curve shows that value if interest rates happen to increase. The initial impact is a capital loss, but this loss eventually is offset by the now-faster growth rate of reinvested funds. At the five-year horizon date, the two effects just cancel each other out, leaving the company able to satisfy its obligation with the accumulated proceeds from the bond.

Figure 14.8 Growth of invested funds. The solid coloured curve represents the growth of portfolio value at the original interest rate. If interest rates increase at time t^*, the portfolio value initially falls but increases thereafter at the faster rate represented by the broken curve. At time D (duration) the curves cross.

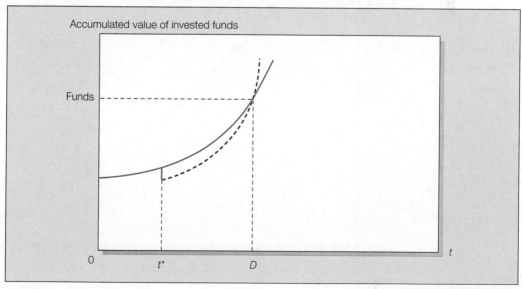

TABLE 14.6

Market Value
Balance Sheet

Assets		Liabilities	
A. Interest rate = 8%			
Bonds	$10,000	Obligation	$10,000.00
B. Interest rate = 7%			
Bonds	$10,476.65	Obligation	$ 10,476.11
C. Interest rate = 9%			
Bonds	$ 9,551.41	Obligation	$ 9,549.62

Notes:

Value of bonds = 800 × Annuity factor(r,6) + 10,000 × PV factor(r,6)

$$\text{Value of obligation} = \frac{14,693.28}{(1 + r)^5} = 14,693.28 \times \text{PV factor}(r,5)$$

We can also analyze immunization in terms of present as opposed to future values. Table 14.6, panel A shows the initial balance sheet for the insurance company's GIC account. Both assets and the obligation have market values of $10,000, so that the plan is just fully funded. Panels B and C in the table show that whether the interest rate increases or decreases, the value of the bonds funding the GIC and the present value of the company's obligation change by virtually identical amounts. Regardless of the interest rate change, the plan remains fully funded, with the surplus in panels B and C just about zero. The duration-matching strategy has ensured that both assets and liabilities react equally to interest rate fluctuations.

Figure 14.9 is a graph of the present values of the bond and the single-payment obligation as a function of the interest rate. At the current rate of 8 percent, the values are equal, and the obligation is fully funded by the bond. Moreover, the two present value curves are tangent at

Figure 14.9

Immunization.

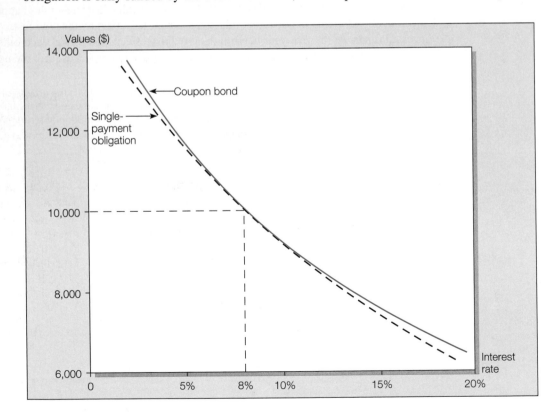

Holding-Period Immunization

The Connect site for this book contains a spreadsheet that is useful in understanding the concept of holding-period immunization. The spreadsheet calculates duration and holding-period returns on bonds of any maturity. The spreadsheet shows how price risk and reinvestment risk offset if a bond is sold at its duration.

Questions

1. When rates increase by 100 basis points (bp), what is the change in the future sales price of the bond? The value of reinvested coupons?

2. What if rates increase by 200 bp?

3. What is the relation between price risk and reinvestment rate risk as we consider larger changes in bond yields?

	A	B	C	D	E	F	
1	Holding-Period Immunization						
2	Example:						
3	YTM	0.1158	Mar Price	1111.929			
4	Coupon R	0.14					
5	Maturity	7					
6	Par Value	1000					
7	Holding P	5					
8	Duration	5.000251					
9							
10							
11	If Rates Increase by 200 Basis Points				If Rates Increase by 100 Basis Points		
12	Rate	0.1358			Rate	0.1258	
13	FV of CPS	917.739			FV of CPS	899.7046	
14	SalesP	1006.954			SalesP	1023.817	
15	Total	1924.693			Total	1923.522	
16	IRR	0.115981			IRR	0.115845	
17							
18							

$y = 8$ percent. As interest rates change, the change in value of both the asset and the obligation is equal, so the obligation remains fully funded. For greater changes in the interest rate, however, the present value curves diverge. This reflects the fact that the fund actually shows a small surplus at market interest rates other than 8 percent.

If the obligation was immunized, why is there *any* surplus in the fund? The answer is convexity. Figure 14.9 shows that the coupon bond has greater convexity than the obligation it funds. Hence, when rates move substantially, the bond value exceeds the present value of the obligation by a noticeable amount. Another way to think about it is that although the duration of the bond is indeed equal to 5 years at a yield to maturity of 8 percent, it rises to 5.02 years when its yield falls to 7 percent and drops to 4.97 years at $y = 9$ percent; that is, the bond and the obligation were not duration-matched *across* the interest rate shift.

This example highlights the importance of **rebalancing** immunized portfolios. As interest rates and asset durations change, a manager must rebalance the portfolio to realign its duration with the duration of the obligation. Moreover, even if interest rates do not change, asset durations *will* change solely because of the passage of time. Recall from Figure 14.3 that duration generally decreases less rapidly than does maturity. Thus, even if an obligation is immunized at the outset, as time passes the durations of the asset and liability will fall at different rates. Without portfolio rebalancing, durations will become unmatched and the goals of immunization will not be realized. Obviously, immunization is a passive strategy only in the sense that it does not involve attempts to identify undervalued securities. Immunization managers still actively update and monitor their positions.

EXAMPLE 14.3   **Constructing An Immunized Portfolio**

An insurance company must make a payment of $19,487 in 7 years. The market interest rate is 10 percent, so the present value of the obligation is $10,000. The company's portfolio manager wishes to fund the obligation using 3-year zero-coupon bonds and perpetuities paying annual coupons. (We focus on zeros and perpetuities to keep the algebra simple.) How can the manager immunize the obligation?

Immunization requires that the duration of the portfolio of assets equal the duration of the liability. We can proceed in four steps:

1. *Calculate the duration of the liability.* In this case, the liability duration is simple to compute. It is a single-payment obligation with duration of 7 years.

2. *Calculate the duration of the asset portfolio.* The portfolio duration is the weighted average of duration of each component asset, with weights proportional to the funds placed in each asset. The duration of the zero-coupon bond is simply its maturity, 3 years. The duration of the perpetuity is $1.10/.10 = 11$ years. Therefore, if the fraction of the portfolio invested in the zero is called w, and the fraction invested in the perpetuity is $(1 - w)$, the portfolio duration will be

$$\text{Asset duration} = w \times 3 \text{ years} + (1 - w) \times 11 \text{ years}$$

3. *Find the asset mix that sets the duration of assets equal to the 7-year duration of liabilities.* This requires us to solve for w in the following equation:

$$w \times 3 \text{ years} + (1 - w) \times 11 \text{ years} = 7 \text{ years}$$

This implies that $w = \frac{1}{2}$. The manager should invest half the portfolio in the zero and half in the perpetuity. This will result in an asset duration of 7 years.

4. *Fully fund the obligation.* Since the obligation has a present value of $10,000, and the fund will be invested equally in the zero and the perpetuity, the manager must purchase $5,000 of the zero-coupon bond and $5,000 of the perpetuity. (Note that the *face value* of the zero will be $5,000 \times (1.10)^3 = $6,655.)

Even if a position is immunized, however, the portfolio manager still cannot rest. This is because of the need for rebalancing in response to changes in interest rates. Moreover, even if rates do not change, the passage of time also will affect duration and require rebalancing. Let us continue Example 14.3 and see how the portfolio manager can maintain an immunized position.

EXAMPLE 14.4   **Rebalancing**

Suppose that 1 year has passed, and the interest rate remains at 10 percent. The portfolio manager of Example 14.3 needs to reexamine her position. Is the position still fully funded? Is it still immunized? If not, what actions are required?

First, examine funding. The present value of the obligation will have grown to $11,000, as it is 1 year closer to maturity. The manager's funds also have grown to $11,000: the zero-coupon bonds have increased in value from $5,000 to $5,500 with the passage of time, while the perpetuity has paid its annual $500 coupons and remains worth $5,000. Therefore, the obligation is still fully funded.

continued

The portfolio weights must be changed, however. The zero-coupon bond now will have a duration of 2 years, while the perpetuity duration remains at 11 years. The obligation is now due in 6 years. The weights must now satisfy the equation

$$w \times 2 + (1 - w) \times 11 = 6$$

which implies that $w = 5/9$. To rebalance the portfolio and maintain the duration match, the manager now must invest a total of $\$11,000 \times 5/9 = \$6,111.11$ in the zero-coupon bond. This requires that the entire $\$500$ coupon payment be invested in the zero, with an additional $\$111.11$ of the perpetuity sold and invested in the zero-coupon bond.

Of course, rebalancing of the portfolio entails transaction costs as assets are bought or sold, so one cannot rebalance continuously. In practice, an appropriate compromise must be established between the desire for perfect immunization, which requires continual rebalancing, and the need to control trading costs, which dictates less frequent rebalancing.

CC 5

CONCEPT CHECK

What would be the immunizing weights in the second year if the interest rate had fallen to 8 percent?

Cash Flow Matching and Dedication

The problems associated with immunization seem to have a simple solution. Why not simply buy a zero-coupon bond with face value equal to the projected cash outlay? If we follow the principle of **cash flow matching** we automatically immunize the portfolio from interest rate risk because the cash flow from the bond and the obligation exactly offset each other.

Cash flow matching on a multiperiod basis is referred to as a **dedication strategy**. In this case, the manager selects either zero-coupon or coupon bonds with total cash flows in each period that match a series of obligations. The advantage of dedication is that it is a once-and-for-all approach to eliminating interest rate risk. Once the cash flows are matched, there is no need for rebalancing. The dedicated portfolio provides the cash necessary to pay the firm's liabilities regardless of the eventual path of interest rates.

Cash flow matching is not more widely pursued probably because of the constraints it imposes on bond selection. Immunization-dedication strategies are appealing to firms that do not wish to bet on general movements in interest rates, but these firms may want to immunize using bonds that they perceive are undervalued. Cash flow matching, however, places so many more constraints on the bond selection process that it can be impossible to pursue a dedication strategy using only "underpriced" bonds. Firms looking for underpriced bonds give up exact and easy dedication for the possibility of achieving superior returns from the bond portfolio.

Sometimes, cash flow matching is not possible. To cash-flow-match for a pension fund that is obligated to pay out a perpetual flow of income to current and future retirees, the pension fund would need to purchase fixed-income securities with maturities ranging up to hundreds of years. Such securities do not exist, making exact dedication infeasible.

CC 6

CONCEPT CHECK

How would an increase in trading costs affect the attractiveness of dedication versus immunization?

In 2009, an S&P 500 gain of almost 25 percent was accompanied by historically low yields on bonds. This recovery in was a repeat of the bad news for pension funds in 2003. With the S&P 500 providing a rate of return in excess of 25 percent, 2003 was a banner year for the stock market. Not surprisingly, this performance showed up in the balance sheets of U.S. pension funds: assets in these funds rose by more than $100 billion. Despite this boost, pension funds actually lost ground in 2003, with the gap between assets and liabilities growing by about $45 billion.

How could this happen? Blame the decline in interest rates during the year that were in large part the force behind the stock market gains. As rates fell during the year, the present value of pension obligations to retirees rose even faster than the value of the assets backing those promises. It turns out that the value of pension liabilities is more sensitive to interest rate changes than the value of the typical assets held in those funds. So even though falling rates tend to pump up asset returns, they pump up liabilities even more so. In other words, the duration of fund investments tends to be shorter than the duration of its obligations. This duration mismatch makes funds vulnerable to interest rate declines.

Why don't funds better manage asset and liability durations? One reason is that fund managers are often evaluated based on their performance relative to standard bond market indices. Those indices tend to have far shorter durations that pension fund liabilities. So to some extent, managers may be keeping their eyes on the wrong ball, one with the wrong interest rate sensitivity.

Other Problems with Conventional Immunization

If you look back at the definition of duration in equation 14.1, you note that it uses the bond's yield to maturity to calculate the weight applied to the time until each coupon payment. Given this definition and limitations on the proper use of yield to maturity, it is perhaps not surprising that this notion of duration is strictly valid only for a flat yield curve for which all payments are discounted at a common interest rate.

If the yield curve is not flat, the definition of duration must be modified and $CF_t/(1 + y)^t$ replaced with the present value of CF_t, where the present value of each cash flow is calculated by discounting with the appropriate interest rate from the yield curve corresponding to the date of the *particular* cash flow, instead of by discounting with the *bond's* yield to maturity. Moreover, even with this modification, duration matching will immunize portfolios only for parallel shifts in the yield curve. Clearly, this sort of restriction is unrealistic. As a result, much work has been devoted to generalizing the notion of duration. Multifactor duration models have been developed to allow for tilts and other distortions in the shape of the yield curve, in addition to shifts in its level. However, it does not appear that the added complexity of such models pays off in terms of substantially greater effectiveness.[10]

There is an extensive literature on the design and testing of immunization strategies. Gagnon and Johnson[11] investigated the success of duration- versus convexity-based strategies for asset–liability matching to solve the problem of fluctuating interest rates, finding the duration-based approach more effective. Bierwag, Fooladi, and Roberts[12] analyzed a sophisticated strategy known as *M*-squared minimization and found it to perform less well than anticipated, while Fooladi and Roberts[13] also conducted an empirical study of Canadian bond portfolio management. These analyses point up the complexity of bond trading and the difficulties in attaining the objectives stated for various types of portfolios.

---

[10]G. O. Bierwag, G. C. Kaufman, and A. Toevs, eds., *Innovations in Bond Portfolio Management: Duration Analysis and Immunization* (Greenwich, CT: JAI Press, 1983). See also G. O. Bierwag and G. S. Roberts, "Single-Factor Duration Models," *The Journal of Financial Research* 13, no. 1 (Spring 1990), pp. 23–38.

[11]Louis Gagnon and Lewis D. Johnson, "Dynamic Immunization Under Stochastic Interest Rates," *Journal of Portfolio Management* 20, no. 3 (Spring 1994), pp. 48–54. Johnson has also written a series of articles on extending the notion of duration to equity portfolios, which appeared in *Financial Analysts Journal* in 1989, 1990, and 1992 and in *Canadian Journal of Administrative Sciences* in March 1991.

[12]G. O. Bierwag, I. Fooladi, and G. S. Roberts, "Designing an Immunized Portfolio—Is *M*-Squared the Key?" *Journal of Banking and Finance* 17 (December 1993), pp. 1147–1170.

[13]I. Fooladi and G. S. Roberts, "Bond Portfolio Immunization: Canadian Tests," *Journal of Economics and Business* 44 (February 1992), pp. 3–17.

Finally, immunization can be an inappropriate goal in an inflationary environment. Immunization is essentially a nominal notion and makes sense only for nominal liabilities. It makes no sense to immunize a projected obligation that will grow with the price level using nominal assets, such as bonds. For example, if your child will attend college in 15 years and if the annual cost of tuition is expected to be $15,000 at that time, immunizing your portfolio at a locked-in terminal value of $15,000 is not necessarily a risk-reducing strategy. The tuition obligation will vary with the realized inflation rate, whereas the asset portfolio's final value will not. In the end, the tuition obligation will not necessarily be matched by the value of the portfolio.

Loblaw Companies
Limited
www.loblaw.com

14.4 ACTIVE BOND MANAGEMENT

Sources of Potential Profit

Broadly speaking, there are two sources of potential value in active bond management. The first is interest rate forecasting, which tries to anticipate movements across the entire spectrum of the fixed-income market. If interest rate declines are anticipated, managers will increase portfolio duration (and vice versa). The second source of potential profit is identification of relative mispricing within the fixed-income market. An analyst, for example, might believe that the default premium on one particular bond is unnecessarily large and therefore that the bond is underpriced.

These techniques will generate abnormal returns only if the analyst's information or insight is superior to that of the market. You cannot profit from knowledge that rates are about to fall if everyone else in the market is aware of this. You know this from our discussion of market efficiency.

Valuable information is differential information. In this context it is worth noting that interest rate forecasters have a notoriously poor track record. If you consider this record, you will approach attempts to time the bond market with caution.

Homer and Liebowitz coined a popular taxonomy of active bond portfolio strategies. They characterize portfolio rebalancing activities as one of four types of *bond swaps*. In the first two swaps the investor typically believes that the yield relationship between bonds or sectors is only temporarily out of alignment. When the aberration is eliminated, gains can be realized on the underpriced bond. The period of realignment is called the *workout period*.

1. The **substitution swap** is an exchange of one bond for a nearly identical substitute. The substituted bonds should be of essentially equal coupon, maturity, quality, call features, sinking fund provisions, and so on. This swap would be motivated by a belief that the market has temporarily mispriced the two bonds, and that the discrepancy between the prices of the bonds represents a profit opportunity.

   An example of a substitution swap would be a sale of a 20-year-maturity, 5 percent coupon Weston bond callable after five years at $1,050 that is priced to provide a yield to maturity of 5.05 percent, coupled with a purchase of a 5 percent coupon Loblaw bond with the same call provisions and time to maturity that yields 5.15 percent. If the bonds have about the same credit rating, there is no apparent reason for the Loblaw bonds to provide a higher yield. Therefore, the higher yield actually available in the market makes the Loblaw bond seem relatively attractive. Of course, the equality of credit risk is an important condition. If the Loblaw bond is in fact riskier, then its higher yield does not represent a bargain.

2. The **intermarket spread swap** is pursued when an investor believes that the yield spread between two sectors of the bond market is temporarily out of line. For example, if the current spread between corporate and government bonds is considered too wide and is

expected to narrow, the investor will shift from government bonds into corporate bonds. If the yield spread does in fact narrow, corporates will outperform governments. For example, if the yield spread between 20-year Canada bonds and 20-year Baa-rated corporate bonds is now 3 percent, and the historical spread has been only 2 percent, an investor might consider selling holdings of Canada bonds and replacing them with corporates. If the yield spread eventually narrows, the Baa-rated corporate bonds will outperform the Canadas.

Of course, the investor must consider carefully whether there is a good reason that the yield spread seems out of alignment. For example, the default premium on corporate bonds might have increased because the market is expecting a severe recession. In this case, the wider spread would not represent attractive pricing of corporates relative to Canadas, but would simply be an adjustment for a perceived increase in credit risk.

3. The **rate anticipation swap** is pegged to interest rate forecasting. In this case if investors believe that rates will fall, they will swap into bonds of longer duration. Conversely, when rates are expected to rise, they will swap into shorter duration bonds. For example, the investor might sell a 5-year-maturity Canada bond, replacing it with a 25-year-maturity Canada bond. The new bond has the same lack of credit risk as the old one, but has longer duration.

4. The **pure yield pickup swap** is pursued not in response to perceived mispricing, but as a means of increasing return by holding higher-yield bonds. This must be viewed as an attempt to earn an expected term premium in higher-yield bonds. The investor is willing to bear the interest rate risk that this strategy entails.

A yield pickup swap can be illustrated using the Canada bond listings in Chapter 12, Figure 12.1. You can see from that figure that a Canada bond maturing in five years yields 1.28 percent, whereas one maturing in 10 years yields 1.70 percent. The investor who swaps the shorter- for the longer-term bond will earn an extra .42 percent rate of return as long as the yield curve does not shift up during the holding period. Of course, if it does, the longer-duration bond will suffer a greater capital loss.

We can add a fifth swap, called a **tax swap**, to this list. This simply refers to a swap to exploit some tax advantage. For example, an investor may swap from one bond that has decreased in price to another if realization of capital losses is advantageous for tax purposes.

Horizon Analysis

One form of interest rate forecasting is called **horizon analysis**. The analyst using this approach selects a particular holding period and predicts the yield curve at the end of that period. Given a bond's time to maturity at the end of the holding period, its yield can be read from the predicted yield curve and its end-of-period price calculated. Then the analyst adds the coupon income and prospective capital gain of the bond to obtain the total return on the bond over the holding period.

EXAMPLE 14.5   Horizon Analysis

Suppose a 20-year-maturity bond with a 10 percent coupon rate (paid annually) currently sells at a yield to maturity of 9 percent. A portfolio manager with a two-year horizon needs to forecast the total return on the bond over the coming two years. In two years, the bond will have an 18-year maturity. The analyst forecasts that two years from now, 18-year bonds will sell at yields to maturity of 8 percent, and that coupon payments can be reinvested in short-term securities over the coming two years at a rate of 7 percent.

continued

To calculate the two-year return on the bond, the analyst would perform the following calculations:

1. Current price = $100 × Annuity factor (9%, 20 years) + $1,000 × PV factor (9%, 20 years) = $1,091.29.

2. Forecast price = $100 × Annuity factor (8%, 18 years) + $1,000 × PV factor (8%, 18 years) = $1,187.44.

3. The future value of reinvested coupons will be ($100 × 1.07) + $100 = $207.

4. The two-year return is $\dfrac{\$207 + (\$1,187.44 - \$1,091.29)}{\$1,091.29} = .278$, or 27.8%.

The annualized rate of return over the two-year period would then be $(1.278)^{1/2} - 1 = .13$, or 13 percent.

CC 7

CONCEPT CHECK

Consider a 30-year, annual-pay 8 percent coupon bond currently selling at $925. The analyst believes that in two years the yield on 28-year bonds will be 8.3 percent. Should she purchase the 20-year bond of the above example or the 30-year bond?

Contingent Immunization

Contingent immunization is a mixed passive-active strategy suggested by Liebowitz and Weinberger.[14] To illustrate, suppose that interest rates currently are 10 percent and that a manager's portfolio is worth $10 million right now. At current rates the manager could lock in, via conventional immunization techniques, a future portfolio value of $12.1 million after two years. Now suppose that the manager wishes to pursue active management but is willing to risk losses only to the extent that the terminal value of the portfolio would not drop lower than $11 million. Because only $9.09 million ($11 million/1.10²) is required to achieve this minimum acceptable terminal value, and the portfolio currently is worth $10 million, the manager can afford to risk some losses at the outset and might start off with an active strategy rather than immediately immunizing.

The key is to calculate the funds required to lock in via immunization a future value of $11 million at current rates. If T denotes the time left until the horizon date, and r is the market interest rate at any particular time, then the value of the fund necessary to guarantee an ability to reach the minimum acceptable terminal value is $11 million/$(1 + r)^T$, because this size portfolio, if immunized, will grow risk-free to $11 million by the horizon date. This value becomes the trigger point: if and when the actual portfolio value dips to the trigger point, active management will cease. *Contingent* upon reaching the trigger, an immunization strategy is initiated instead, guaranteeing that the minimal acceptable performance can be realized.

Figure 14.10 illustrates two possible outcomes in a contingent immunization strategy. In panel A, the portfolio falls in value and hits the trigger at time t^*. At that point, immunization is pursued and the portfolio rises smoothly to the $11 million terminal value. In panel B, the portfolio does well, never reaches the trigger point, and is worth more than $11 million at the horizon date.

[14]Martin L. Liebowitz and Alfred Weinberger, "Contingent Immunization—Part I: Risk Control Procedures," *Financial Analysts Journal* 38 (November/December 1982).

Figure 14.10
Contingent
immunization.

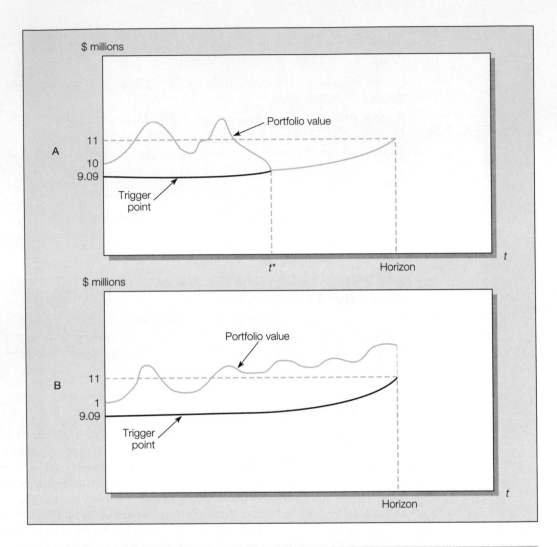

CC 8

CONCEPT CHECK

What would be the trigger point with a three-year horizon, an interest rate of 12 percent, and a minimum acceptable terminal value of $10 million?

14.5

FINANCIAL ENGINEERING AND INTEREST RATE DERIVATIVES

New financial instruments created through financial engineering can have highly unusual risk and return characteristics that offer both opportunities and challenges for fixed-income portfolio managers. To illustrate the possibilities opened up by financial engineering, consider the inverse floater, which is a bond that pays a *lower* coupon payment when a reference interest rate rises. For example, an inverse floater may pay a coupon rate equal to 10 percent *minus* the rate on one-year Treasury bills. Therefore, if the T-bill rate is 4 percent, the bond will pay interest income equal to $10\% - 4\% = 6$ percent of par value. You can see that such a bond will have an interest rate sensitivity much greater than that of a fixed-rate bond with comparable maturity. If the T-bill rate rises, say to 7 percent, the inverse floater's coupon payments fall to 3 percent of par value; in addition, as other interest rates rise along with the T-bill rate, the bond price falls as well for the usual reason that future cash flows are discounted at higher rates. Therefore, there is a dual impact on value and these securities perform especially poorly when interest rates rise. Conversely, inverse floaters perform especially well when rates fall: coupon payments rise, even as the discount rate falls.

While firms do not commonly issue inverse floaters, they may be created synthetically by allocating the cash flows from a fixed-rate security into two *derivative* securities. An investment banking firm can buy a bond issue and carve the original security into a floating-rate note and an inverse floater. The floater will receive interest payments that rise when the T-bill rate rises; the inverse floater will receive interest payments that fall when the T-bill rate rises. The sum of the interest payments due to the two classes of securities is fixed and equal to the interest from the original bond, the primary asset.

EXAMPLE 14.6 **Inverse Floater**

Consider a $100 million par value, 20-year-maturity bond with a coupon rate of 8 percent. The bond issue therefore pays total interest of $8 million annually. An investment banking firm might arrange to use the cash flows from the underlying bond to support issues of a floating-rate note and an inverse floater. The floating-rate notes might be issued with aggregate par value of $60 million and a coupon level equal to the T-bill rate plus 1 percent. If the T-bill rate currently is 6 percent, therefore, the coupon rate on the floater would be 7 percent and total interest payments would be .07 × $60 million = $4.2 million. This leaves $8 million − $4.2 million = $3.8 million available to pay interest on the interest floater. The coupon rate on the inverse floater might be set at 18.5% − 1.5 × (T-bill rate), which at the current T-bill rate equals 9.5 percent. Therefore, the coupon income flowing to the inverse floater is 9.5 percent of $40 million, or $3.8 million, which just absorbs the remaining interest flowing from the original bond.

Now suppose that in one year, the T-bill rate has increased by 1 percent. The coupon rate on the floater increases to 8 percent, while the coupon rate on the inverse floater falls to 18.5% − 1.5 × 7% = 8 percent. Again, total interest paid on the two derivative securities sums to $8 million: .08 × $60 million + .08 × $40 million = $8 million. However, the value of the inverse floater falls precipitously: not only are market interest rates higher (which makes the present value of any future cash flow lower), but the coupon rate on the bond has fallen from 9.5 percent to 8 percent.[15] Therefore, the inverse floater will have extreme interest rate sensitivity. When rates fall, its performance will be spectacular, but when rates rise, its performance will be disastrous.

The inverse floater is an example of an interest rate derivative product created by financial engineering in which the cash flows from the original bond are unbundled and reallocated to the floater and inverse floater. Because of the impact of interest rates on its coupon rate, the inverse floater will have a very large effective duration,[16] in fact much longer than the maturity of the bond.

---

[15]If the T-bill rate increases beyond 12.33 percent, the formula for the inverse floater's coupon would call for a negative coupon rate. However, in practice, the inverse floater provides that the coupon may never fall below zero. This floor on the coupon rate of the inverse floater necessitates a ceiling on the coupon rate of the floater. The total interest paid by the two securities is constrained to equal the interest provided by the underlying bond.

[16]Strictly speaking, the Macaulay duration (i.e., the weighted average of the times until payment of each cash flow) of an inverse floater is not well defined, since the cash flows accruing from the bond are not fixed but instead vary with the level of interest rates. The effective duration of a security therefore does not have the interpretation of an average maturity; it is defined instead as the percentage change in the price of a security given a one-percentage-point increase in yield. Therefore, effective duration, like Macaulay duration, measures interest rate sensitivity.

This property can be useful to investors who wish to immunize very-long-duration liabilities; it is also obviously useful to investors who wish to speculate on decreases in interest rates.

Inverse floaters are not the only financially engineered products with dramatic dependence on interest rates. In Chapters 1 and 2, we introduced you to derivative securities created by allocating the cash flows from mortgage-backed securities into various CMO (collateralized mortgage obligation) tranches. Some of the more popular mortgage derivative products are interest-only (IO) and principal-only (PO) strips. The IO strip gets all the interest payments from the mortgage pool and the PO strip gets all the principal payments. Both have extreme and interesting interest rate exposures. In both cases, the sensitivity is due to the effect of mortgage prepayments on the cash flows accruing to the security holder.

PO securities, like inverse floaters, exhibit very long effective durations; that is, their values are very sensitive to interest rate fluctuations. When interest rates fall and mortgage holders prepay their mortgages, PO holders receive their principal payments much earlier than initially anticipated. Therefore, the payments are discounted for fewer years than expected and have much higher present value. Hence PO strips perform extremely well when rates fall. Conversely, interest rate increases slow mortgage prepayments and reduce the value of PO strips.

The prices of interest-only strips, on the other hand, fall when interest rates fall. This is because mortgage prepayments abruptly end the flow of interest payments accruing to IO security holders. Because rising rates discourage prepayments, they increase the value of IO strips. Thus IOs have effective *negative* durations. They are good investments for an investor who wishes to bet on an increase in rates, or they can be useful for hedging the value of a conventional fixed-income portfolio.

There are still other ways to make highly sensitive bets on the direction of interest rates. Some of these are custom-designed swaps in which the cash flow paid by one party to the swap varies dramatically with the level of some reference interest rate. Such swaps made news in 1994 when Procter & Gamble lost more than $100 million in an interest rate swap that obligated it to make payments that exploded when interest rates increased. In the wake of its losses, P&G sued Bankers Trust, which sold it the swap, claiming that it was misled about the risks of the swap.

Interest rate derivatives are not necessarily bad, or even dangerous, investments. The dramatic sensitivity of their prices to interest rate fluctuations can be useful for hedging as well as for speculation. They can be potent risk management as well as risk-increasing tools. One Wall Street observer has compared them to power tools: when used well by a trained expert, they can serve a valuable function; but in untrained hands, they can lead to severe damage. Unfortunately, this observer was ignoring the other source of risk—**counterparty risk**, the risk of default by the other party to the derivative contract. When in 2008 financial corporations such as Lehman Brothers went bankrupt, they were unable to fulfill their side of the contract, leaving the other party involved in a position that could not be unwound. This lay at the heart of the financial collapse.

Procter & Gamble
www.pg.com

SUMMARY

1. Even default-free bonds such as government issues are subject to interest rate risk. Longer-term bonds generally are more sensitive to interest rate shifts than are short-term bonds. A measure of the average life of a bond is Macaulay's duration, defined as the weighted average of the times until each payment made by the security, with weights proportional to the present value of the payment.

2. Duration is a direct measure of the sensitivity of a bond's price to a change in its yield. The proportional change in a bond's price equals the negative of duration multiplied by the proportional change in $1 + y$.

3. Convexity refers to the curvature of a bond's price–yield relationship. Accounting for convexity can substantially improve on the accuracy of the duration approximation for bond price sensitivity to changes in yields.

4. Immunization strategies are characteristic of passive fixed-income portfolio management. Such strategies attempt to render the individual or firm immune from movements in interest rates. This may take the form of immunizing net worth or, instead, immunizing the future accumulated value of a fixed-income portfolio.

5. Immunization of a fully funded plan is accomplished by matching the durations of assets and liabilities. To maintain an immunized position as time passes and interest rates change, the portfolio must be periodically rebalanced. Classic immunization also depends on parallel shifts in a flat yield curve. Given that this assumption is unrealistic, immunization generally will be less than complete. To mitigate the problem, multifactor duration models can be used to allow for variation in the shape of the yield curve.

6. A more direct form of immunization is dedication, or cash flow matching. If a portfolio is perfectly matched

in cash flow with projected liabilities, rebalancing will be unnecessary.

7. Active bond management consists of interest rate forecasting techniques and intermarket spread analysis. One popular taxonomy classifies active strategies as substitution swaps, intermarket spread swaps, rate anticipation swaps, and pure yield pickup swaps.

8. Horizon analysis is a type of interest rate forecasting. In this procedure the analyst forecasts the position of the yield curve at the end of some holding period, and from that yield curve predicts corresponding bond prices. Bonds then can be ranked according to expected total returns (coupon plus capital gain) over the holding period.

9. Financial engineering has created many new fixed-income derivative assets with novel risk characteristics.

KEY EQUATIONS

(14.1) $\quad D = \sum_{t=1}^{T} t \times w_t$

(14.2) $\quad \dfrac{\Delta P}{P} = -D \times \left[\dfrac{\Delta(1 + y)}{1 + y} \right]$

(14.3) $\quad \dfrac{\Delta P}{P} = -D^* \Delta y$

(14.4) $\quad \dfrac{1 + y}{y} - \dfrac{T}{(1 + y)^T - 1}$

(14.5) $\quad \dfrac{1 + y}{y} - \dfrac{(1 + y) + T(c - y)}{c[(1 + y)^T - 1] + y}$

(14.6) $\quad \dfrac{1 + y}{y} \left[1 - \dfrac{1}{(1 + y)^T} \right]$

(14.7) $\quad \dfrac{\Delta P}{P} = -D^* \Delta y + \dfrac{1}{2} \times \text{Convexity} \times (\Delta y)^2$

PROBLEMS

Mc Graw Hill Education connect™ **Practise and learn online with Connect.**

1. A nine-year bond has a yield of 10 percent and a duration of 7.194 years. If the market yield changes by 50 basis points, what is the percentage change in the bond's price?

2. Find the duration of a 6 percent coupon bond making *annual* coupon payments if it has three years until maturity and has a yield to maturity of 6 percent. What is the duration if the yield to maturity is 10 percent?

3. Find the duration of the bond in problem 2 if the coupons are paid semiannually.

4. Rank the durations of the following pairs of bonds:

    a. Bond *A* is an 8 percent coupon bond, with a 20-year time to maturity selling at par value. Bond *B* is an 8 percent coupon bond, with a 20-year maturity time selling below par value.

    b. Bond *A* is a 20-year noncallable coupon bond with a coupon rate of 8 percent, selling at par. Bond *B* is a 20-year callable bond with a coupon rate of 9 percent, also selling at par.

5. How can a perpetuity, which has an infinite maturity, have a duration as short as 10 or 20 years?

6. Prices of long-term bonds are more volatile than prices of short-term bonds. However, yields to maturity of short-term bonds fluctuate more than yields of long-term bonds. How do you reconcile these two empirical observations?

7. a. Use a spreadsheet to answer this question. Calculate the convexity of a "bullet" fixed income portfolio, that is, a portfolio with a single cash flow. Suppose a single $1,000 cash flow is paid in year 5.

    b. Now calculate the convexity of a "barbell" fixed income portfolio, that is, a portfolio with equal cash flows over time. Suppose the security makes $100 cash flows in each of years 1–9, so that its duration is close to the bullet in part (*a*).

    c. Do barbells or bullets have greater convexity?

8. The historical yield spread between AAA bonds and Treasury bonds widened dramatically during the financial crisis in 2008. If you believed that the spread would soon return to more typical historical levels, what should you have done? This would be an example of what sort of bond swap?

9. An insurance company must make payments to a customer of $10 million in one year and $4 million in five years. The yield curve is flat at 10 percent.

    a. If it wants to fully fund and immunize its obligation to this customer with a *single* issue of a zero-coupon bond, what maturity bond must it purchase?

    b. What must be the face value and market value of that zero-coupon bond?

10. Long-term Canada bonds currently are selling at yields to maturity of nearly 6 percent. You expect interest rates to fall. The rest of the market thinks that they will remain unchanged over the coming year. In each question below, choose the bond that will provide the higher holding-period return over the next year if you are correct. Briefly explain your answer.

    a. i. A Baa-rated bond with coupon rate 6 percent and time to maturity 20 years

    ii. An Aaa-rated bond with coupon rate of 6 percent and time to maturity 20 years

    b. i. An A-rated bond with coupon rate 3 percent and maturity 20 years, callable at 105

    ii. An A-rated bond with coupon rate 6 percent and maturity 20 years, callable at 105

    c. i. A 4 percent coupon noncallable T-bond with maturity 20 years and YTM = 6 percent

    ii. A 7 percent coupon noncallable T-bond with maturity 20 years and YTM = 6 percent

11. Currently, the term structure is as follows: one-year bonds yield 7 percent, two-year bonds yield 8 percent, three-year bonds and greater maturity bonds all yield 9 percent. An investor is choosing between one-, two-, and three-year-maturity bonds all paying annual coupons of 8 percent, once a year. Which bond should you buy if you strongly believe that at year-end the yield curve will be flat at 9 percent?

12. You will be paying $10,000 a year in education expenses at the end of the next two years. Bonds currently yield 8 percent.

    a. What is the present value and duration of your obligation?

    b. What maturity zero-coupon bond would immunize your obligation?

    c. Suppose you buy a zero-coupon bond with value and duration equal to your obligation. Now suppose that rates immediately increase to 9 percent. What happens to your net position, that is, to the difference between the value of the bond and that of your education obligation? What if rates fall to 7 percent?

13. Pension funds pay lifetime annuities to recipients. If a firm will remain in business indefinitely, the pension obligation will resemble a perpetuity. Suppose, therefore, that you are managing a pension fund with obligations to make perpetual payments of $2 million per year to beneficiaries. The yield to maturity on all bonds is 16 percent.

    a. If the duration of 5-year-maturity bonds with coupon rates of 12 percent (paid annually) is 4 years and the duration of 20-year-maturity bonds with coupon rates of 6 percent (paid annually) is 11 years, how much of each of these coupon bonds (in market value) will you want to hold to both fully fund and immunize your obligation?

    b. What will be the par value of your holdings in the 20-year coupon bond?

14. You are managing a portfolio of $1 million. Your target duration is 10 years, and you can choose from two bonds: a zero-coupon bond with maturity of 5 years, and a perpetuity, each currently yielding 5 percent.

    a. How much of each bond will you hold in your portfolio?

    b. How will these fractions change *next year* if target duration is now nine years?

15. My pension plan will pay me $10,000 once a year for a 10-year period. The first payment will come in exactly five years. The pension fund wants to immunize its position.

    a. What is the duration of its obligation to me? The current interest rate is 10 percent per year.

    b. If the plan uses 5-year and 20-year zero-coupon bonds to construct the immunized position, how much money ought to be placed in each bond? What will be the *face value* of the holdings in each zero?

16. A 30-year-maturity bond making annual coupon payments with a coupon rate of 12 percent has duration of 11.54 years and convexity of 192.4. The bond currently sells at a yield to maturity of 8 percent. Use a financial calculator to find the price of the bond if its yield to maturity falls to 7 percent or rises to 9 percent. What prices for the bond at these new yields would be predicted by the duration rule and the duration-with-convexity rule? What is the percentage error for each rule? What do you conclude about the accuracy of the two rules?

17. A 12.75-year-maturity zero-coupon bond selling at a yield to maturity of 8 percent (effective annual yield) has convexity of 150.3 and modified duration of 11.81 years. A 30-year-maturity 6 percent coupon bond making annual coupon payments also selling at a yield to maturity of 8 percent has nearly identical duration, 11.79 years, but considerably higher convexity of 231.2.

    a. Suppose the yield to maturity on both bonds increases to 9 percent. What will be the actual percentage capital loss on each bond? What percentage capital loss would be predicted by the duration-with-convexity rule?

    b. Repeat part (a), but this time assume the yield to maturity decreases to 7 percent.

    c. Compare the performance of the two bonds in the two scenarios, one involving an increase in rates, the other a decrease. Based on the comparative investment performance, explain the attraction of convexity.

    d. In view of your answer to (c), do you think it would be possible for two bonds with equal duration but different convexity to be priced initially at the same yield to maturity if the yields on both bonds always increased or decreased by equal amounts, as in this example? Would anyone be willing to buy the bond with lower convexity under these circumstances?

18. A newly issued bond has a maturity of 10 years and pays a 7 percent coupon rate (with coupon payments coming once annually). The bond sells at par value.

    a. What are the convexity and the duration of the bond? Use the formula for convexity in footnote 6.

    b. Find the actual price of the bond assuming that its yield to maturity immediately increases from 7 percent to 8 percent (with maturity still 10 years).

c. What price would be predicted by the duration rule (equation 14.2)? What is the percentage error of that rule?

d. What price would be predicted by the duration-with-convexity rule? What is the percentage error of that rule?

19. A 30-year-maturity bond has a 7 percent coupon rate, paid annually. It sells today for $867.42. A 20-year-maturity bond has 6.5 percent coupon rate, also paid annually. It sells today for $879.50. A bond market analyst forecasts that in 5 years, 25-year-maturity bonds will sell at yields to maturity of 8 percent and 15-year-maturity bonds will sell at yields of 7.5 percent. Because the yield curve is upward-sloping, the analyst believes that coupons will be invested in short-term securities at a rate of 6 percent. Which bond offers the higher expected rate of return over the five-year period?

20. A fixed-income portfolio manager is unwilling to realize a rate of return of less than 3 percent annually over a five-year investment period on a portfolio currently valued at $1 million. Three years later, the interest rate is 8 percent. What is the trigger point of the portfolio at this time—that is, how low can the value of the portfolio fall before the manager will be forced to immunize to be assured of achieving the minimum acceptable return?

21. *a.* Use a spreadsheet to calculate the durations of the two bonds in Table 14.3 if the annual interest rate increases to 12 percent. Why does the duration of the coupon bond fall while that of the zero remains unchanged? (*Hint:* Examine what happens to the weights computed in column F.)

   b. Use the same spreadsheet to calculate the duration of the coupon bond if the coupon were 12 percent instead of 8 percent and the semiannual interest rate is again 5 percent. Explain why duration is lower than in Table 14.3. (Again, start by looking at column F.)

22. *a.* Footnote 6 presents the formula for the convexity of a bond. Build a spreadsheet to calculate the convexity of a five-year, 8 percent coupon bond making annual payments at the initial yield to maturity of 10 percent.

   b. What is the convexity of a five-year zero-coupon bond?

The following problems are based on questions that have appeared in past CFA examinations.

23. *a.* Explain the impact on the offering yield of adding a call feature to a proposed bond issue.

   b. Explain the impact on *both* bond duration and convexity of adding a call feature to a proposed bond issue.

24. *a.* A 6 percent coupon bond paying interest annually has a modified duration of 10 years, sells for $800, and is priced at a yield to maturity of 8 percent. If the YTM increases to 9 percent, what is the predicted change in price, using the duration concept?

   b. A 6 percent coupon bond with semiannual coupons has a convexity (in years) of 120, sells for 80 percent of par, and is priced at a yield to maturity of 8 percent. If the YTM increases to 9.5 percent, what is the predicted contribution to the percentage change in price, due to convexity?

   c. A bond with annual coupon payments has a coupon rate of 8 percent, yield to maturity of 10 percent, and Macaulay duration of 9. What is the bond's modified duration?

   d. When interest rates decline, the duration of a 30-year bond selling at a premium

      i. Increases

      ii. Decreases

      iii. Remains the same

      iv. Increases at first, then declines

   e. If a bond manager swaps a bond for one that is identical in terms of coupon rate, maturity, and credit quality but offers a higher yield to maturity, the swap is

      i. A substitution swap   iii. A tax swap

      ii. An interest rate anticipation swap   iv. An intermarket spread swap *f.* Which bond has the longest duration?

        i. 8-year maturity, 6 percent coupon

        ii. 8-year maturity, 11 percent coupon

        iii. 15-year maturity, 6 percent coupon

        iv. 15-year maturity, 11 percent coupon

25. A newly issued bond has the following characteristics:

Coupon	Yield to Maturity	Maturity	Macaulay Duration
8%	8%	15 years	10 years

    a. Calculate modified duration using the information above.

    b. Explain why modified duration is a better measure than maturity when calculating the bond's sensitivity to changes in interest rates.

    c. Identify the direction of change in modified duration if

        i. The coupon of the bond were 4 percent, not 8 percent

        ii. The maturity of the bond were 7 years, not 15 years

    d. Define convexity and explain how modified duration and convexity are used to approximate the bond's percentage change in price, given a change in interest rates.

26. Bonds of Zello Corporation with a par value of $1,000 sell for $960, mature in 5 years, and have a 7 percent annual coupon rate paid semiannually.

    a. Calculate each of these:

        i. Current yield

        ii. Yield to maturity (to the nearest whole percent, i.e., 3 percent, 4 percent, 5 percent, etc.)

        iii. Horizon yield (also called *total compound return*) for an investor with a 3-year holding period and a reinvestment rate of 6 percent over the period; at the end of 3 years the 7 percent coupon bonds with 2 years remaining will sell to yield 7 percent

    b. Cite *a* major shortcoming for *each* of the following fixed-income yield measures:

        i. Current yield

        ii. Yield to maturity

        iii. Horizon yield (also called *total compound return*)

27. Sandra Kapple presents Maria VanHusen with a description, given in the table below, of the bond portfolio held by the Star Hospital Pension Plan. All securities in the bond portfolio are noncallable U.S. Treasury securities.

Par Value (US$)	Treasury Security	Market Value (US$)	Current Price	Price If Yields Change: Up 100 Basis Points	Down 100 Basis Points	Effective Duration
48,000,000	2.375% due 2006	48,667,680	101.391	99.245	103.595	2.15
50,000,000	4.75% due 2031	50,000,000	100.000	86.372	116.887	—
98,000,000	Total bond portfolio	98,667,680	—	—	—	—

    a. Calculate the "effective duration" (see Appendix 14A) of *each* of the following:

        i. The 4.75 percent Treasury security due 2031

        ii. The total bond portfolio

b. VanHusen remarks to Kapple, "If you changed the maturity structure of the bond portfolio to result in a portfolio duration of 5.25, the price sensitivity of that portfolio would be identical to the price sensitivity of a single, noncallable Treasury security that has a duration of 5.25." In what circumstance would VanHusen's remark be correct?

28. One common goal among fixed-income portfolio managers is to earn high incremental returns on corporate bonds versus government bonds of comparable durations. The approach of some corporate-bond portfolio managers is to find and purchase those corporate bonds having the largest initial spreads over comparable-duration government bonds. John Ames, HFS's fixed-income manager, believes that a more rigorous approach is required if incremental returns are to be maximized.

    The table below presents data relating to one set of corporate/government spread relationships present in the market at a given date.

Current and Expected Spreads and Durations of High-Grade Corporate Bonds (one-year horizon)

Bond Rating	Initial Spread over Governments	Expected Horizon Spread	Initial Duration	Expected Duration One Year from Now
Aaa	31 bp	31 bp	4 years	3.1 years
Aa	40 bp	50 bp	4 years	3.1 years

Note: 1 bp means 1 basis point, or .01 percent.

a. Recommend purchase of *either* Aaa or Aa bonds for a one-year investment horizon given a goal of maximizing incremental returns.

b. Ames chooses not to rely *solely* on initial spread relationships. His analytical framework considers a full range of other key variables likely to impact realized incremental returns, including call provisions and potential changes in interest rates. Describe variables, *in addition to those identified* above, that Ames should include in his analysis *and* explain how *each* of these could cause realized incremental returns to differ from those indicated by initial spread relationships.

29. Patrick Wall is considering the purchase of one of the two bonds described in the following table. Wall realizes his decision will depend primarily on effective duration, and he believes that interest rates will decline by 50 basis points at all maturities over the next six months.

Characteristic	CIC	PTR
Market price	101.75	101.75
Maturity date	June 1, 2018	June 1, 2018
Call date	Noncallable	June 1, 2013
Annual coupon	6.25%	7.35%
Interest payment	Semiannual	Semiannual
Effective duration	7.35	5.40
Yield to maturity	6.02%	7.10%
Credit rating	A	A

a. Calculate the percentage price change forecasted by effective duration for *both* the CIC and PTR bonds if interest rates decline by 50 basis points over the next six months.

b. Calculate the six-month horizon return (in percent) for *each* bond, if the actual CIC bond price equals 105.55 and the actual PTR bond price equals 104.15 at the end of six months. Assume you purchased the bonds to settle on June 1, 2008.

Wall is surprised by the fact that although interest rates fell by 50 basis points, the actual price change for the CIC bond was greater than the price change forecasted by effective duration, whereas the actual price change for the PTR bond was less than the price change forecasted by effective duration.

c. Explain why the actual price change would be greater for the CIC bond and the actual price change would be less for the PTR bond.

30. You are the manager for the bond portfolio of a pension fund. The policies of the fund allow for the use of active strategies in managing the bond portfolio.

It appears that the economic cycle is beginning to mature, inflation is expected to accelerate, and in an effort to contain the economic expansion, central bank policy is moving toward constraint. For each of the situations below, state which one of the two bonds you would prefer. Briefly justify your answer in each case.

a. Government of Canada (Canadian pay) 7 percent due in 2012 and priced at 98.75 to yield 10.50 percent to maturity

or

Government of Canada (Canadian pay) 7 percent due in 2020 and priced at 91.75 to yield 11.19 percent to maturity

b. Texas Power and Light Co., $6\frac{1}{2}$ due in 2012, rated AAA, and priced at 95 to yield 8.02 percent to maturity

or

Arizona Public Service Co. 6.45 due in 2012, rated A−, and priced at 85 to yield 9.05 percent to maturity

c. Commonwealth Edison $2\frac{3}{4}$ due in 2012, rated Baa, and priced at 81 to yield 9.2 percent to maturity

or

Commonwealth Edison $12\frac{3}{8}$ due in 2012, rated Baa, and priced at 114.40 to yield 9.2 percent to maturity

d. Shell Oil Co. $7\frac{1}{2}$ sinking fund debentures due in 2025, rated AAA (sinking fund begins September 2009 at par), and priced at 78 to yield 10.91 percent to maturity

or

Warner-Lambert $7\frac{7}{8}$ sinking fund debentures due in 2025, rated AAA (sinking fund begins April 2014 at par), and priced at 84 to yield 10.31 percent to maturity.

e. Bank of Montreal (Canadian pay) 5 percent certificates of deposit due in 2014, rated AAA, and priced at 100 to yield 5 percent to maturity

or

Bank of Montreal (Canadian pay) floating-rate note due in 2017, rated AAA. Coupon currently set at 4.1 percent and priced at 100 (coupon adjusted semiannually to .5 percent above the three-month Government of Canada Treasury bill rate)

31. A member of a firm's investment committee is very interested in learning about the management of fixed-income portfolios. He would like to know how fixed-income managers position portfolios to capitalize on their expectations concerning three factors that influence interest rates:

a. Changes in the level of interest rates

b. Changes in yield spreads across/between sectors

c. Changes in yield spreads as to a particular instrument.

Assuming that no investment policy limitations apply, formulate and describe a fixed-income portfolio management strategy for each of these factors that could be used to exploit a portfolio manager's expectations about that factor. (*Note:* Three strategies are required, one for each of the listed factors.)

32. Carol Harrod is the investment officer for a $100 million U.S. pension fund. The fixed-income portion of the portfolio is actively managed, and a substantial portion of the fund's large-capitalization U.S. equity portfolio is indexed and managed by Webb Street Advisors.

    Harrod has been impressed with the investment results of Webb Street's equity index strategy and is considering asking Webb Street to index a portion of the actively managed fixed-income portfolio.

    a. Describe advantages and disadvantages of bond indexing relative to active bond management.

    b. Webb Street manages indexed bond portfolios. Discuss how an indexed bond portfolio is constructed under stratified sampling (cellular) methods.

    c. Describe the main source of tracking error for the cellular method.

33. Noah Kramer, a fixed-income portfolio manager based in the country of Sevista, is considering the purchase of a Sevista government bond. Kramer decides to evaluate two strategies for implementing his investment in Sevista bonds. Table 14.7 gives the details of the two strategies, and Table 14.8 contains the assumptions that apply to both strategies.

TABLE 14.7 Investment Strategies (amounts are market-value-invested)

Strategy	5-Year Maturity (modified duration = 4.83)	15-Year Maturity (modified duration = 14.35)	25-Year Maturity (modified duration = 23.81)
I	$5 million	0	$5 million
II	0	$10 million	0

TABLE 14.8
Investment
Strategy
Assumptions

Market value of bonds	$10 million
Bond maturities	5 and 25 years or 15 years
Bond coupon rates	.00%
Target modified duration	15 years

Before choosing one of the two bond investment strategies, Kramer wants to analyze how the market value of the bonds will change if an instantaneous interest rate shift occurs immediately after his investment. The details of the interest rate shift are shown in Table 14.9. Calculate, for the instantaneous interest rate shift shown in Table 14.9, the percent change in the market value of the bonds that will occur under each strategy.

TABLE 14.9
Instantaneous
Interest Rate Shift
Immediately
After Investment

Maturity	Interest Rate Change
5 years	Down 75 bp
15 years	Up 25 bp
25 years	Up 50 bp

E-INVESTMENTS
Bond
Calculations

Go to **www.derivativesmodels.com**. First, establish a (free) user account. This site has a wealth of calculators. Find the *Bond Calculator*. This tool provides yield to maturity, modified duration, and bond convexity as the bond's price changes. Experiment with different inputs. What happens to duration and convexity as coupon increases? As maturity increases? As price increases (holding coupon fixed)?

APPENDIX 14A: DURATION AND CONVEXITY OF CALLABLE BONDS AND MORTGAGE-BACKED SECURITIES

Callable Bonds

Look at Figure 14A.1, which depicts the price–yield curve for a callable bond. When interest rates are high, the curve is convex, as it would be for a straight bond. For example, at an interest rate of 10 percent, the price–yield curve lies above its tangency line. But as rates fall, there is a ceiling on the possible price: the bond cannot be worth more than its call price. So as rates fall, we sometimes say that the bond is subject to price compression—its value is "compressed" to the call price. In this region, for example at an interest rate of 5 percent, the price–yield curve lies *below* its tangency line, and the curve is said to have *negative convexity*.[17]

Notice that in the region of negative convexity, the price–yield curve exhibits an *unattractive* asymmetry. Interest rate increases result in a larger price decline than the price gain corresponding to an interest rate decrease of equal magnitude. The asymmetry arises from the fact that the bond issuer has retained an option to call back the bond. If rates rise, the bondholder loses, as would be the case for a straight bond. But if rates fall, rather than reaping a large capital gain, the investor may have the bond called back from her. The bondholder is thus in a "Heads I lose, tails I don't win" position. Of course, she was compensated for this unattractive situation when she purchased the bond. Callable bonds sell at lower initial prices (higher initial yields) than otherwise comparable straight bonds.

The effect of negative convexity was highlighted in equation 14.4. When convexity is negative, the second term on the right-hand side is necessarily negative, meaning that bond price performance will be worse than would be predicted by the duration approximation. However, callable bonds, or more generally, bonds with "embedded options," are difficult to analyze in

Figure 14A.1

Price–yield curve for a callable bond.

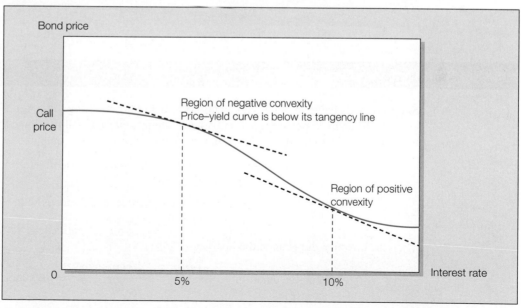

---

[17]If you've ever taken a calculus course, you will recognize that the curve is concave in this region. However, rather than saying that these bonds exhibit "concavity," bond traders prefer to say "negative convexity."

terms of Macaulay's duration. This is because in the presence of such options, the future cash flows provided by the bonds are no longer known. If the bond may be called, for example, its cash flow stream may be terminated and its principal repaid earlier than was initially anticipated. Because cash flows are random, we can hardly take a weighted average of times until each future cash flow, as would be necessary to compute Macaulay's duration.

The convention on Wall Street is to compute the *effective duration* of bonds with embedded options. Effective duration cannot be computed with a simple formula such as equation 14.1 for Macaulay's duration. Instead, more complex bond valuation approaches that account for the embedded options are used, and effective duration is *defined* as the proportional change in the bond price per unit change in market interest rates:

$$\text{Effective duration} = \frac{\Delta P/P}{\Delta r} \tag{14A.1}$$

This equation *seems* merely like a slight manipulation of the modified duration formula 15.3. However, there are important differences. First, note that we do not compute effective duration relative to a change in the bond's own yield to maturity. (The denominator is Δr, not Δy.) This is because for bonds with embedded options, which may be called early, the yield to maturity is often not a relevant statistic. Instead, we calculate price change relative to a shift in the level of the term structure of interest rates. Second, the effective duration formula relies on a pricing methodology that accounts for embedded options. In contrast, modified or Macaulay duration can be computed directly from the promised bond cash flows and yield to maturity.

CC 9

CONCEPT CHECK

What are the differences between Macaulay duration, modified duration, and effective duration?

EXAMPLE 14A.1   Effective Duration

Suppose that a callable bond with a call price of $1,050 is selling today for $980. If the yield curve shifts up by .5 percent, the bond price will fall to $930. If it shifts down by .5 percent, the bond price will rise to $1,010. To compute effective duration, we compute:

$$\Delta r = \text{Assumed increase in rates} - \text{Assumed decrease in rates}$$
$$= .5\% - (-.5\%) = 1\% = .01$$
$$\Delta P = \text{Price at .5\% increase in rates} - \text{Price at .5\% decrease in rates}$$
$$= \$930 - \$1,010 = -\$80$$

Then the effective duration of the bond is

$$\text{Effective duration} = -\frac{\Delta P/P}{\Delta r} = -\frac{-\$80/\$980}{.01} = 8.16 \text{ years}$$

In other words, the bond price changes by 8.16 percent for a 1 percentage point swing in rates around current values.

Mortgage-Backed Securities

In practice, the biggest market for which call provisions are important is the market for mortgage-backed securities. In recent years, firms have been less apt to issue bonds with call provisions, and the number of outstanding callable corporate bonds has steadily declined. In contrast, the mortgage-backed market has enjoyed rapid growth over the two decades preceding the financial crisis. Even in 2012, the two largest U.S. mortgage agencies (Fannie Mae and Freddie Mac) together issued more than $1 trillion of new mortgage-backed securities.

Lenders that originate mortgage loans commonly sell those loans to federal agencies such as the Canada Mortgage and Housing Corporation (CMHC), the Federal National Mortgage Association (FNMA, or Fannie Mae), or the Federal Home Loan Mortgage Corporation (FHLMC, or Freddie Mac). The original borrowers (the homeowners) continue to make their monthly payments to their lenders, but the lenders pass these payments along to the agency that has purchased the loan. In turn, the agencies may combine many mortgages into a pool called a *mortgage-backed security*, and then sell that security in the fixed-income market. These securities are called *pass-throughs*, because the cash flows from the borrowers are first passed through to the agency (CMHC) and then passed through again to the ultimate purchaser of the mortgage-backed security. CMHC, Fannie, and Freddie together hold the lion's share of the market for so-called conforming loans that satisfy size limitations and various standards for creditworthiness of the borrower.

For example, suppose that ten 30-year mortgages, each with principal value of $100,000, are grouped into a million-dollar pool. If the mortgage rate is 8 percent, the monthly payment on each loan would be $733.76. (The interest component of the first payment is $.08 \times 1/12 \times \$100,000 = \$666.67$; the remaining $67.09 is "amortization," or scheduled repayment of principal. In later periods, with a lower principal balance, less of the monthly payments goes to interest and more to amortization.) The owner of the mortgage-backed security would receive $7,337.60, the total payment from the 10 mortgages in the pool.[18]

But now recall that the homeowner has the right to prepay the loan at any time. For example, if mortgage rates go down, the homeowner may very well decide to take a new loan at a lower rate, using the proceeds to pay off the original loan. The right to prepay the loan is, of course, precisely analogous to the right to refund a callable bond. The call price is simply the remaining principal balance on the loan. Therefore, the mortgage-backed security is best viewed as a portfolio of *callable* amortizing loans.

Mortgage-backs are subject to the same negative convexity as other callable bonds. When rates fall and homeowners prepay their mortgages, the repayment of principal is passed through to the investors. Rather than enjoying capital gains on their investment, they simply receive the outstanding principal balance on the loan. Therefore, the value of the mortgage-backed security as a function of interest rates, presented in Figure 14A.2, looks much like the plot for a callable bond.

There are some differences between the mortgage-backeds and callable corporate bonds, however. For example, you will commonly find mortgage-backeds selling for more than their principal balance. This is because homeowners do not refinance their loans as soon as interest rates drop. Some homeowners do not want to incur the costs or hassles of refinancing unless the benefit is great enough, others may decide not to refinance if they are planning to move shortly, and others may simply be unsophisticated in making the refinancing decision. Therefore, while the mortgage-backed security exhibits negative convexity at low rates, its implicit call price (the principal balance on the loan) is not a firm ceiling on its value.

---

[18]Actually, the original lender that continues to service the loan and the pass-through agency that guarantees the loan each retain a portion of the monthly payment as a charge for their services. Thus, the monthly payment received by the investor is a bit less than the amount paid by the borrower.

Figure 14A.2

Price–yield curve for a mortgage-backed security.

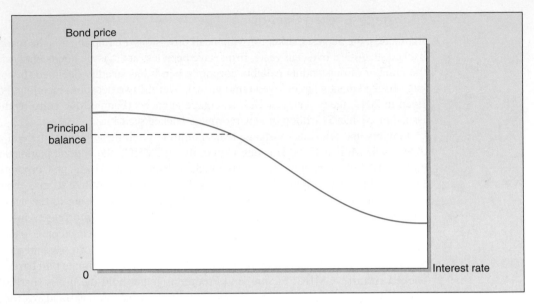

Mortgage-backed securities are among the most successful examples of financial engineering, the repackaging of cash flows from one security (in this case, the original mortgage) into new securities (the mortgage pass-through security). They have become the model for many other asset-backed securities and illustrate other important aspects of this market. For example, *credit enhancement* is a common feature of the asset-backed market. In the mortgage market, the credit risk of the underlying borrower is enhanced by the guarantee of CMHC, Freddie, or Fannie that any mortgage default will be treated from the point of view of the investor as if the mortgage had been prepaid. Rather than resulting in a loss of principal, the loan is in effect treated as if it has been paid off with the principal balance passed through to the investor. But remember that while the securities are thereby guaranteed in terms of payment of interest and principal, their rates of return are not guaranteed. They still are subject to the interest rate risk that is the topic of this chapter.

Simple mortgage-backs have also given rise to a rich set of mortgage-backed derivatives that can be used to help investors manage interest rate risk. For example, a CMO (collateralized mortgage obligation) further redirects the cash flow stream of the mortgage-backed security to several classes of derivative securities called *tranches*. These tranches may be designed to allocate interest rate risk to investors most willing to bear that risk.

The following table is an example of a very simple CMO structure. The underlying mortgage pool is divided into three tranches, each with a different effective maturity and therefore interest rate risk exposure. Suppose the original pool has $10 million of 15-year-maturity mortgages, each with an interest rate of 10.5 percent, and is subdivided into three tranches as follows:

Tranche A = $4 million principal	"Short-pay" tranche
Tranche B = $3 million principal	"Intermediate-pay" tranche
Tranche C = $3 million principal	"Long-pay" tranche

Suppose further that in each year, 8 percent of outstanding loans in the pool prepay. Then total cash flows in each year to the whole mortgage pool are given in panel A of

Figure 14A.3 **Panel A:** Cash flows to whole mortgage pool. **Panels B–D:** Cash flows to three tranches.

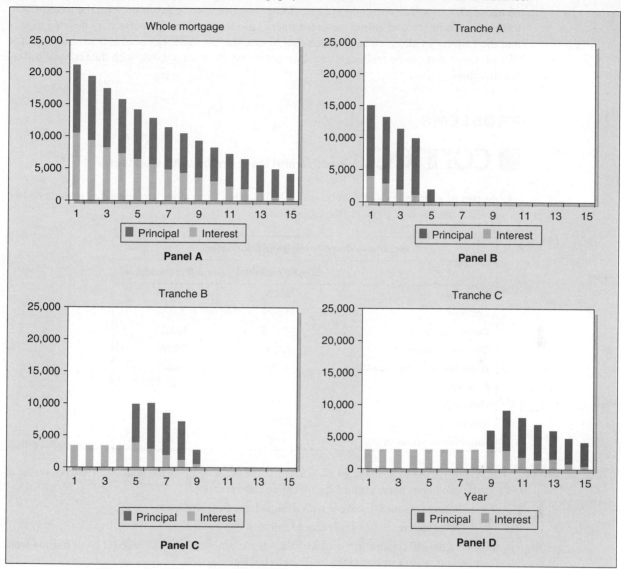

Figure 14A.3. Total payments shrink by 8 percent each year, as that percentage of the loans in the original pool is paid off. The light portions of each bar represent interest payments, while the dark-coloured portions are principal payments, comprising both loan amortization and prepayments.

In each period, each tranche receives the interest owed it based on the promised interest rate and outstanding principal balance. But initially, *all* principal payments, both prepayments and amortization, go to tranche A (Figure 14A.3, panel B). Notice from panels C and D that tranches B and C receive only interest payments until tranche A is retired. Once tranche A is fully paid off, all principal payments go to tranche B. Finally, when B is retired, all principal payments go to C. This makes tranche A a "short-pay" class, with the lowest effective duration, while tranche C is the longest-pay tranche. This is therefore a relatively simple way to allocate interest rate risk among tranches.

Many variations on the theme are possible and employed in practice. Different tranches may receive different interest or coupon rates. Some tranches may be given preferential treatment in terms of uncertainty over mortgage prepayment speeds. Complex formulas may be used to dictate the cash flows allocated to each tranche. In essence, the mortgage pool is treated as a source of cash flows that can be reallocated to different investors in accordance with the tastes of different investors.

PROBLEMS

 Practise and learn online with Connect.

1. As part of your analysis of debt issued by Monticello Corporation, you are asked to evaluate two specific bond issues, shown in the table below.

Monticello Corporation Bond Information		
	Bond *A* (callable)	Bond *B* (noncallable)
Maturity	2005	2005
Coupon	11.50%	7.25%
Current price	125.75	100.00
Yield to maturity	7.70%	7.25%
Modified duration to maturity	6.20	6.80
Call date	1999	—
Call price	105	—
Yield to call	5.10%	—
Modified duration to call	3.10	—

a. Using the duration and yield information in the table, compare the price and yield behaviour of the two bonds under each of the following two scenarios:

  i. Strong economic recovery with rising inflation expectations

  ii. Economic recession with reduced inflation expectations

b. Using the information in the table, calculate the projected price change for bond *B* if the yield to maturity for this bond falls by 75 basis points.

c. Describe the shortcoming of analyzing bond *A* strictly to call or to maturity.

The following problems are based on questions that have appeared in past CFA examinations.

2. Janet Meer is a fixed-income portfolio manager. Noting that the current shape of the yield curve is flat, she considers the purchase of a newly issued, 7 percent coupon, 10-year-maturity, option-free corporate bond priced at par. The bond has the following features:

	Change in Yield	
	Up 10 Basis Points	Down 10 Basis Points
Price	99.29	100.71
Convexity measure	35.00	
Convexity adjustment	.0035	

a. Calculate the duration of the bond.

b. Meer is also considering the purchase of a newly issued, 7.25 percent coupon, 12-year-maturity option-free corporate bond. She wants to evaluate this second bond's price sensitivity to an instantaneous, downward parallel shift in the yield curve of 200 basis points. Based on the following data, what will be its price change in this yield-curve scenario?

Original issue price	Par value, to yield 7.25%
Modified duration (at original price)	7.90
Convexity measure	41.55
Convexity adjustment (yield change of 200 basis points)	1.66

c. Meer asks her assistant to analyze several callable bonds, given the expected downward parallel shift in the yield curve. Meer's assistant argues that if interest rates fall enough, both modified convexity and effective convexity for a callable bond will become negative. Is the assistant's argument correct or incorrect?

15

Macroeconomic and Industry Analysis

The dilemma for the portfolio manager and the investor is whether to follow the implication of the empirical evidence and the theory of market efficiency or to ignore it. Should one accept a passive investment strategy of an index fund or will the effort and expense of active management provide a superior portfolio? You saw in our discussion of market efficiency that finding undervalued securities is hardly easy. At the same time, there are enough doubts about the accuracy of the efficient market hypothesis that the search for such securities should not be dismissed out of hand. Moreover, it is the continuing search for mispriced securities that maintains a nearly efficient market. Even infrequent discoveries of minor mispricing justify the salary of a stock market analyst.

The area of security analysis can be divided into fundamental analysis and technical analysis, which we have earlier discussed. **Fundamental analysis** refers to the search for information concerning the current and prospective profitability of a company in order to discover its fair market value; this is in direct contrast to the use of information contained in stock market data by technical analysis. Empirical evidence suggests that neither of these approaches, especially the latter, is fruitful on the whole, but both are widely practised and hence must be understood.

The intrinsic value of a stock depends on the dividend and earnings that can be expected from the firm. This is the heart of fundamental analysis—that is, the analysis of the determinants of value such as earnings prospects. Ultimately, the business success of the firm determines the dividends it can pay to shareholders and the price it will command in the stock market. Because the prospects of the firm are tied to those of the broader economy, however, fundamental analysis must consider the business environment in which the firm operates. For some firms, macroeconomic and industry circumstances might have a greater influence on profits than the firm's relative performance within its industry. In other words, investors need to keep the big economic picture in mind. Therefore, in analyzing a firm's prospects it often makes sense to start with the broad economic environment, examining the state of the aggregate economy and even the international economy. From there, one considers the implications of the outside environment on the industry in which the firm operates. Finally, the firm's position within the industry is examined. These factors affect the flow of earnings that the firm can generate. The analyst then must consider how the valuation of the firm is determined from the earnings, in particular looking at the cash flows. By using valuation models and by examining the financial results of the firm, the analyst attempts to discover unrecognized value.

This chapter treats the broad-based aspects of fundamental analysis—macroeconomic and industry analysis. The two chapters following cover firm-specific analysis. We begin with a discussion of international factors relevant to firm performance, and move on to an overview of the significance of the key variables usually used to summarize the state of the macroeconomy. We then discuss government macroeconomic policy. We conclude the analysis of the macro-environment with a discussion of business cycles. Finally, we move to industry analysis, treating issues concerning the sensitivity of the firm to the business cycle, the typical life cycle of an industry, and strategic issues that affect industry performance.

15.1 ► THE GLOBAL ECONOMY

Bureau of
Economic
Analysis
www.bea.gov

A top-down analysis of a firm's prospects must start with the global economy. The international economy might affect a firm's export prospects, the price competition it faces from competitors, or the profits it makes on investments abroad. Table 15.1 shows the importance of the global or regional macroeconomy to firms' prospects. Much of Europe, for example, was still mired in the Eurozone crisis and was expected to show anaemic or even negative growth. In contrast, other broad regions such as Asia were expected to exhibit healthy growth rates. The so-called BRIC countries (Brazil, Russia, India, and China), often grouped because of their rapid recent development, were by and large expected to continue that performance, although India's potential has been called into question, and China's growth is likely to shrink to single digits with changing labour conditions.

In addition to the variation in regional macroeconomic conditions, there is also considerable variation in economic performance across countries even within regions. In Europe, the Greek economy was expected to continue its painful contraction, with a forecasted decline in GDP of 5.0 percent in 2013, while Germany was expected to show positive, albeit modest, growth.

Perhaps surprisingly, the best stock market returns did not align with the best macroeconomic expectations. This reflects the impact of near-market-efficiency. China's growth was the highest in the Table 15.1 sample, but its growth was already expected to be high at the start of the year; with actual growth actually a bit lower than expectations, stock market performance was lacklustre. In contrast, German growth was tepid, but its stock market shone, as its risks from the Eurozone difficulties seemed to subside.

These data illustrate that the national economic environment can be a crucial determinant of industry performance. It is far harder for businesses to succeed in a contracting economy than in an expanding one. This observation highlights the role of a big-picture macroeconomic analysis as a fundamental part of the investment process. In addition, the global environment presents

TABLE 15.1

Economic
Performance

	Stock Market Return, 2012 (%)		Forecasted Growth in GDP, 2013 (%)
	In Local Currency	in U.S. Dollars	
Brazil	10.2	.8	3.5
Britain	8.2	13.3	1.0
Canada	4.9	8.6	2.0
China	3.1	4.2	8.5
France	18.2	20.5	.0
Germany	31.9	34.5	.7
Greece	38.3	41.1	−5.0
Hong Kong	26.5	26.7	2.6
India	27.6	26.7	6.5
Italy	12.0	14.2	−.9
Japan	18.0	4.2	.8
Mexico	19.5	30.9	3.7
Russia	3.7	10.5	3.7
Singapore	21.0	28.5	2.9
South Korea	11.2	20.5	3.4
Spain	−.6	1.4	−1.7
Thailand	37.3	42.7	4.2
U.S.	9.8	9.8	1.0

Source: *The Economist*, January 5, 2013.

political risks of considerable magnitude. The euro crisis offers a compelling illustration of the interplay between politics and economics. The prospect of a bailout for Greece, and support for struggling but much larger economies such as Spain and potentially Italy, have been in large part political issues, but with enormous consequences for the world economy. Similarly, the 2012 debate over the so-called "fiscal cliff" in the United States was the stage for pitched political battles with huge economic consequences. The ongoing battle over government budget deficits and how to address them is of tremendous import for the economy. At this level of analysis, it is clear that politics and economics are intimately entwined.

Other political issues, less sensational but still extremely important to economic growth and investment returns, are issues of protectionism and trade policy, the free flow of capital, and the status of a nation's work force.

One obvious factor that affects the international competitiveness of a country's industries is the exchange rate between that country's currency and other currencies. The **exchange rate** is the rate at which domestic currency can be converted into foreign currency. For example, in mid-2013, it took about 100 Japanese yen to purchase one Canadian dollar; that is, the exchange rate was ¥100 per dollar or, equivalently, $.01 per yen.

As exchange rates fluctuate, the dollar value of goods priced in foreign currency similarly fluctuates. For example, in 1980, the dollar–yen exchange rate was about $.005 per yen. Because the exchange rate today is $.01 per yen, a Canadian would need twice as many dollars in 2013 to buy a product selling for ¥10,000 than would have been required in 1980. If the Japanese producer were to maintain a fixed yen price for its product, the price expressed in Canadian dollars would than double. This would make Japanese products more expensive to Canadian consumers, however, and result in lost sales. Obviously, appreciation of the yen creates a problem for Japanese producers that have to compete with Canadian producers.

HONDA REVS UP OUTSIDE JAPAN

Honda Motor Co. plans to shift a major chunk of its manufacturing to North America over the next two years, bulking up production capacity in the region by as much as 40% to combat a strengthening yen that has made Japanese cars too expensive to export around the world.

The drive to bulk up In North America is led by the yen's strength against the U.S. dollar, a change that is causing Honda and other Japanese auto makers to lose money on many of the vehicles they now export from Japan. A stronger yen erodes the value of dollar-denominated profit and makes exports less price competitive.

Honda, which produced 1.29 million vehicles in North America in 2010, plans to build a new plant in Celaya, Mexico, and expand all seven of its existing assembly plants, aiming to build just short of 2 million cars and trucks a year, Tetsuo Iwamura, president of American Honda, the company's North American arm, said in an interview with *The Wall Street Journal*.

The strategic shift is "directly linked to the yen," Mr. Iwamura said. "It is virtually impossible to make money [on exporting vehicles from Japan] in the short and medium term."

Honda's shift is indicative of the broad impact the yen is having on Japanese auto makers facing a currency that has strengthened by nearly 40% in the last four years. The yen was trading at 77.89 to the dollar Tuesday and as recently as 2007 was at 120 to the dollar.

The dramatic strengthening of the yen makes it particularly hard to make money on small cars because profit margins are already thin. To help reduce the number of Fits that Honda exports from Japan, the company recently began shipping Fit cars from China to Canadian dealers as a stopgap measure.

Source: Mike Ramsey and Neal E. Boudette, *The Wall Street Journal*, December 21, 2011.

Recent changes in Japanese monetary policy have resulted in a 25 percent depreciation of the yen in the past year, in order to try to reestablish a more competitive basis. Planning for real investment, however, requires a long-range view; hence Honda's response to the dramatic increase in the value of the yen, as described in the box here. It is moving a good part of its manufacturing operations to North America to take advantage of the reduced cost of production (as measured in yen) in the U.S. and Mexico. Moreover, by locating some production to North America, Honda diversifies its exposure to future exchange rate fluctuations.

Figure 15.1 shows the change in the purchasing power of the Canadian dollar relative to the purchasing power of the currencies of several major industrial countries in the decade between 2001 and 2011. The ratio of purchasing powers is called the "real," or inflation-adjusted, exchange rate. The change in the real exchange rate measures how much more or less expensive foreign goods have become to Canadians, accounting for both exchange rate fluctuations and inflation differentials across countries. A positive value in Figure 15.1 means that the dollar has gained purchasing power relative to another currency. Therefore, the figure shows that goods priced in terms of U.S. dollars have become far less expensive to Canadian consumers. Conversely, goods priced in Canadian dollars have become less affordable to all but European consumers.

Figure 15.1

Change in real exchange rate: dollar versus major currencies, 2001–2011.

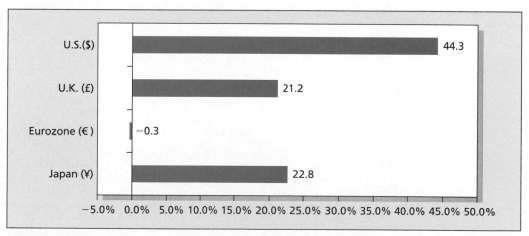

Source: Adapted from data in *Economic Report of the President*, 2012.

15.2 ▸ THE DOMESTIC MACROECONOMY

The macroeconomy is the environment in which all firms operate. The importance of the macro-economy in determining investment performance is illustrated in Figure 15.2, which compares the level of the S&P 500 stock price index to forecasts of earnings per share (EPS) of the S&P 500 companies over a 40-year period. The EPS series for the S&P 500 is multiplied by three different factors concurrently with the value of the S&P 500 index. The graph shows that stock prices tend to rise and fall with earnings. While the exact ratio of stock price to earnings varies with factors such as interest rates, risk, inflation rates, and other variables, the graph does illustrate that as a general rule the ratio has tended to be in the range of 12 to 25. Given "normal" price–earnings ratios, we would expect the S&P 500 index to fall within these boundaries. While the earnings-multiplier rule clearly is not perfect—note the dramatic increase in the price–earnings multiple during the dot-com boom of the late 1990s—it also seems clear that the level of the broad market and aggregate earnings do trend together. Thus the first step in forecasting the performance of the broad market is to assess the status of the economy as a whole, in order to predict corporate earnings.

The ability to forecast the macroeconomy can translate into spectacular investment performance. Yet it is not enough to forecast the macroeconomy well. You must forecast it *better* than your competitors to earn abnormal profits. In this section, we will review some of the key economic statistics used to describe the state of the macroeconomy.

Gross Domestic Product   Gross domestic product (GDP), is the measure of the economy's total production of goods and services. Rapidly growing GDP indicates an expanding economy with ample opportunity for a firm to increase sales. Another popular measure of the economy's output is *industrial production*. This statistic provides a measure of economic activity more narrowly focused on the manufacturing side of the economy.

Employment   The **unemployment rate** is the percentage of the total labour force (i.e., those who are either working or actively seeking employment) who have yet to find work. It measures the extent to which the economy is operating at full capacity. The unemployment rate is a factor related to workers only, but further insight into the strength of the economy can be gleaned from the unemployment rate for other factors of production. Analysts also look at the factory *capacity utilization rate*, which is the ratio of actual output from factories to potential output.

Figure 15.2

S&P 500 index versus earnings per share.

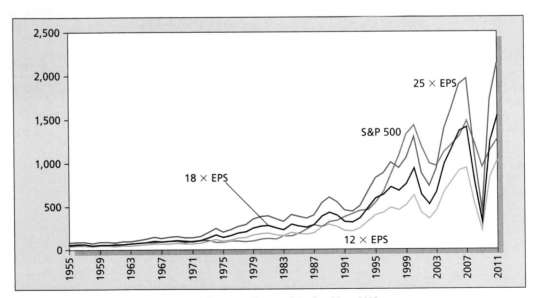

Source: Authors' calculations using data in *Economic Report of the President*, 2012.

Inflation   The rate at which the general level of prices rise is called **inflation**. High rates of inflation are often associated with "overheated" economies, that is, economies in which the demand for goods and services is outstripping productive capacity, which leads to upward pressure on prices. Most governments walk a fine line in their economic policies. They hope to stimulate their economies enough to maintain nearly full employment, but not so much as to bring on inflationary pressures. The perceived tradeoff between inflation and unemployment is at the heart of many macroeconomic policy disputes. There is considerable room for disagreement on the relative costs of these policies and the economy's relative vulnerability to these pressures at any particular time.

Interest Rates   High interest rates reduce the present value of future cash flows, reducing the attractiveness of investment opportunities. For this reason, real interest rates are key determinants of business investment expenditures. Demand for housing and high-priced consumer durables such as automobiles, which are commonly financed, is also highly sensitive to interest rates, because interest rates affect interest payments. (In Chapter 4, Section 4.1, we examined the determinants of interest rates.)

Budget Deficit   The **budget deficit** of the federal government is the difference between government spending and revenues. Any budgetary shortfall must be offset by government borrowing. Large amounts of government borrowing can force interest rates up by increasing the total demand for credit in the economy. Economists generally believe excessive government borrowing will "crowd out" private borrowing and investing by forcing up interest rates and choking off business investment.

Sentiment   Consumers' and producers' optimism or pessimism concerning the economy is an important determinant of economic performance. If consumers have confidence in their future income levels, for example, they will be more willing to spend on big-ticket items. Similarly, businesses will increase production and inventory levels if they anticipate higher demand for their products. In this way, beliefs influence how much consumption and investment will be pursued and affect the aggregate demand for goods and services.

In an export-dependent economy, such as Canada's, the international variables of the *exchange rate* and the *current account* are crucial. Exchange rates, primarily against the U.S. dollar, determine the balance between exports and imports; they also affect inflation through the domestic cost of imported goods. The current account is determined by the difference between the value of imports and exports and by international transfers of investment funds; these transfers depend greatly on the investment decisions of foreigners holding Canadian assets and Canadians holding foreign assets. Persistent trade deficits and payments to foreign-held debt will cause the dollar to depreciate. Thus, we have a complex interplay of forces affecting interest rates, inflation, and exchange rates resulting from government policies and private investment and production decisions.

CC 1

CONCEPT CHECK

Consider an economy in which the dominant industry is automobile production for domestic consumption as well as export. Now suppose the auto market is hurt by an increase in the length of time people use their cars before replacing them. Describe the probable effects of this change on
a. GDP
b. unemployment
c. the government budget deficit
d. interest rates

15.3   DEMAND AND SUPPLY SHOCKS AND GOVERNMENT POLICY

A useful way to organize the analysis of the factors that might influence the macroeconomy is to classify any impact as a demand or supply shock. A **demand shock** is an event that affects the demand for goods and services. Examples of positive demand shocks are reductions in tax rates, increases in the money supply, increases in government spending, or increases in foreign export demand. A **supply shock** is an event that influences production capacity and costs. Examples of supply shocks are changes in the price of oil and other raw materials; freezes, floods, or droughts that might destroy large quantities of agricultural crops; changes in the educational level of an economy's work force; or changes in the wage rates at which the labour force is willing to work.

Demand shocks are usually characterized by aggregate output moving in the same direction as interest rates and inflation. For example, a big increase in government spending will tend to stimulate the economy and increase GDP. It might also increase interest rates by increasing the demand for borrowed funds by the government and by businesses that might desire to borrow to finance new ventures. Finally, it might increase the inflation rate if the demand for goods and services is raised to a level at or beyond the total productive capacity of the economy.

Supply shocks are usually characterized by aggregate output moving in the opposite direction from inflation and interest rates. For example, a big increase in the price of imported oil will be inflationary because costs of production will rise, which eventually will lead to increases in prices of finished goods. The increase in inflation rates over the near term can lead to higher nominal interest rates. Against this background, aggregate output will be falling. With raw materials more expensive, the productive capacity of the economy is reduced, as is the ability of individuals to purchase goods at now-higher prices. GDP, therefore, tends to fall. How can we relate this framework to investment analysis? You want to identify the industries that will be most helped or hurt in any macroeconomic scenario you envision. For example, if you forecast a tightening of the money supply, you might want to avoid industries such as lumber producers that might be hurt by the likely increase in interest rates. We caution you again that these forecasts are no easy task. Macroeconomic predictions are notoriously unreliable. And again, you must be aware that in all likelihood your forecast will be made using only publicly available information. Any investment advantage you have will be a result only of better analysis—not better information.

15.4   FEDERAL GOVERNMENT POLICY

As the previous section would suggest, the government has two broad classes of macroeconomic tools—those that affect the demand for goods and services and those that affect the supply. For much of postwar history, demand-side policy was of primary interest. The focus was on government spending, tax levels, and monetary policy. Since the 1980s, however, increasing attention has been focused on supply-side economics. Broadly interpreted, supply-side concerns have to do with enhancing the productive capacity of the economy, rather than increasing the demand for the goods and services the economy can produce.

In practice, supply-side economists have focused on the appropriateness of the incentives to work, innovate, and take risks that result from our system of taxation. However, issues such as national policies on education, infrastructure (such as communication and transportation systems), and research and development also are properly regarded as part of supply-side macroeconomic policy.

Fiscal Policy

Fiscal policy refers to the government's spending and tax actions and is part of "demand-side management." Fiscal policy is probably the most direct way to either stimulate or slow the

The so-called fiscal cliff crisis at the end of 2012 came close to being an unintended experiment in extreme fiscal policy. The seed of the crisis was planted in August 2011 when Congress, until then unable to agree on an expansion of the federal debt ceiling, passed an interim compromise. The debt ceiling would be allowed to rise, but with the provision that Congress would, by the end of 2012, pass legislation reducing the federal budget deficit by $1.2 trillion over 10 years. A bipartisan "super-committee" would be formed to propose a package of tax increases and spending reductions. If no agreement were reached, 2013 tax rates would automatically revert to the higher levels prevailing during the Clinton presidency, and across-the-board annual spending cuts or "sequestrations" of about $110 billion would be split equally between domestic and defense programs.

This compromise was intended to create a sword of Damocles to hang over Congress's head, ensuring it would be forced to arrive at a legislative compromise. If not, the resulting contractionary fiscal policy, entailing both steep spending cuts and dramatic tax increases, was widely regarded as sure to lead to another recession. The Congressional Budget Office estimated that the threatened tax increases and spending reductions would act to reduce GDP growth in 2013 from around 1.7 percent to −.5 percent and increase the unemployment rate by more than a percentage point. This was the fiscal cliff Congress risked jumping from.

In the end, Congress narrowly avoided jumping by enacting yet another stopgap compromise. It delayed sequestration by two months, allowing budgetary negotiations to continue, and it paid for the cost of that delay by raising some tax rates, including those on capital gains and household income above $450,000. But the fiscal fight is far from over. The tax increases agreed to at the end of 2012 were far from enough to meet the original target of a $1.2 trillion reduction in the 10-year deficit; and the government was to bump up against the new debt ceiling in early 2013. In fact, Republicans deferred to political pressure and agreed to raise the ceiling ahead of the deadline, much as in 2011. Spending cut discussions are still contentious, and the fiscal debate continues unabated.

economy. Decreases in government spending directly deflate the demand for goods and services. Similarly, increases in tax rates immediately siphon income from consumers and result in fairly rapid decreases in consumption.

Ironically, although fiscal policy has the most immediate impact on the economy, the formulation and implementation of such policy is complicated. Canada's federal system involves federal transfers to the provinces, which also tax and spend according to their own choices. In the United States, disputes between the executive and legislative branches lead to inertia. The "fiscal cliff" had immense consequences for the U.S., and by extension global economies. (See the boxed article here.) Many social programs are fairly inflexible, so that the effect of changes to more discretionary spending may be muted. In short, fiscal policy may not be very effective as a tool to fine-tune the economy.

A common way to summarize the net impact of government fiscal policy is to look at the government's budget deficit or surplus, which is simply the difference between revenues and expenditures. A large deficit means the government is spending considerably more than it is taking in by way of taxes. The net effect is to increase the demand for goods (via spending) by more than it reduces the demand for goods (via taxes), thereby stimulating the economy.

Monetary Policy

Monetary policy refers to the manipulation of the money supply to affect the macroeconomy and is the other main leg of demand-side policy. Monetary policy works largely through its impact on interest rates. Increases in the money supply lower short-term interest rates, ultimately encouraging investment and consumption demand. Over longer periods, however, most economists believe a higher money supply leads only to a higher price level and does not have a permanent effect on economic activity. Thus the monetary authorities face a difficult balancing act. Expansionary monetary policy probably will lower interest rates and thereby stimulate investment and some consumption demand in the short run, but these circumstances ultimately will lead only to higher prices. The stimulation/inflation tradeoff is implicit in all debate over proper monetary policy.

Fiscal policy is cumbersome to implement but has a fairly direct impact on the economy, whereas monetary policy is easily formulated and implemented but has a less immediate impact.

Monetary policy is determined by the Governing Council of the Bank of Canada. The council is small enough that policy can be formulated and modulated relatively easily. Implementation of monetary policy also is quite direct. The council determines to raise or lower its *key policy rate*; this is the overnight rate, or the interest rate at which major financial institutions borrow and lend one-day (or "overnight") funds among themselves. These loans occur because some banks need to borrow funds to meet reserve requirements, while other banks have excess funds. In this way, the Bank sets the short-term interest rate that affects the cost of borrowing for corporations.

In the United States, the Federal Reserve also sets rates through the federal funds rate, an overnight rate, and through the discount rate, at which it lends short-term to banks. It can also modify requirements for reserves held by banks at the "Fed" so that a decrease in the requirement affords banks more money to lend and increases the money supply. A further tool, much in effect in the U.S., the U.K., Europe, and Japan, is the purchase of bonds currently under the policy of quantitative easing mentioned in Chapter 1.

Monetary policy affects the economy in a more roundabout way than fiscal policy. Whereas fiscal policy directly stimulates or dampens the economy, monetary policy works largely through its impact on interest rates. Increases in the money supply lower interest rates, which stimulates investment demand. As the quantity of money in the economy increases, investors will find that their portfolios of assets include too much money. They will rebalance their portfolios by buying securities such as bonds, forcing bond prices up and interest rates down. In the longer run, individuals may increase their holdings of stocks as well and ultimately buy real assets, which stimulates consumption demand directly. The ultimate effect of monetary policy on investment and consumption demand, however, is less immediate than that of fiscal policy.

CC 2

CONCEPT CHECK

Suppose the government wants to stimulate the economy without increasing interest rates. What combination of fiscal and monetary policy might accomplish this goal?

Supply-Side Policies

Fiscal policy and monetary policy are demand-oriented tools that affect the economy by stimulating the total demand for goods and services. The implicit belief is that the economy will not by itself arrive at full-employment equilibrium, and that macroeconomic policy can push the economy toward this goal. In contrast, supply-side policies treat the issue of the productive capacity of the economy. The goal is to create an environment in which workers and owners of capital have the maximum incentive and ability to produce and develop goods.

Supply-side economists also pay considerable attention to tax policy. Whereas demand-siders look at the effect of taxes on consumption demand, supply-siders focus on incentives and marginal tax rates. They argue that lowering tax rates will elicit more investment and improve incentives to work, thereby enhancing economic growth. Some go so far as to claim that reductions in tax rates can lead to increases in tax revenues because the lower tax rates will cause the economy and the revenue tax base to grow by more than the tax rate is reduced.

CC 3

CONCEPT CHECK

Large tax cuts in the past were followed by rapid growth in GDP. How would demand-side and supply-side economists differ in their interpretations of this phenomenon?

15.5   BUSINESS CYCLES

We've looked at the tools the government uses to fine-tune the economy, attempting to maintain low unemployment and low inflation. Despite these efforts, economies repeatedly seem to pass through good and bad times. One determinant of the broad asset allocation decision of many analysts is a forecast of whether the macroeconomy is improving or deteriorating. A forecast that differs from the market consensus can have a major impact on investment strategy.

The Business Cycle

The economy recurrently experiences periods of expansion and contraction, although the length and depth of those cycles can be irregular. This recurring pattern of recession and recovery is called the **business cycle**. The transition points across cycles are called *peaks* and *troughs*. A *peak* is the transition from the end of an expansion to the start of a contraction. A *trough* occurs at the bottom of a recession just as the economy enters a recovery.

As the economy passes through different stages of the business cycle, the relative performance of different industry groups might be expected to vary. For example, at a trough, just before the economy begins to recover from a recession, one would expect that *cyclical industries*, those with above-average sensitivity to the state of the economy, would tend to outperform other industries. Examples of cyclical industries are producers of durable goods such as automobiles or washing machines. Because purchases of these goods can be deferred during a recession, sales are particularly sensitive to macroeconomic conditions. Other cyclical industries are producers of capital goods, that is, goods used by other firms to produce their own products. When demand is slack, few companies will be expanding and purchasing capital goods. Therefore, the capital goods industry bears the brunt of a slowdown but does well in an expansion.

In contrast to cyclical firms, *defensive industries* produce goods for which sales and profits are least sensitive to the state of the economy, and will outperform other industries when the economy enters a recession. Examples are food producers and processors and pharmaceutical firms.

If your assessments of the state of the business cycle were reliably more accurate than those of other investors, you would simply choose cyclical industries when relatively optimistic about the economy and defensive firms when relatively pessimistic. Unfortunately, it is not so easy to determine when the economy is passing through a peak or a trough. If it were, choosing between cyclical and defensive industries would be easy. As we know from our discussion of efficient markets, however, attractive investment choices will rarely be obvious. It is usually not apparent that a recession or expansion has started or ended until several months after the fact. In hindsight, the transitions from expansion to recession and back might be apparent, but it is often quite difficult to say whether the economy is heating up or slowing down at any given moment.

The cyclical/defensive classification corresponds well to the notion of systematic or market risk introduced in our discussion of portfolio theory. When perceptions about the health of the economy become more optimistic, for example, the prices of most stocks will increase as forecasts of profitability rise. Because the cyclical firms are most sensitive to such developments, their stock prices will rise the most. Thus firms in cyclical industries will tend to have high-beta stocks. In general, then, stocks of cyclical firms will show the best results when economic news is positive but the worst results when that news is bad. Conversely, defensive firms will have low betas and performance that is relatively unaffected by overall market conditions.

TABLE 15.2	Retail Sales	Manufacturing
Components of Leading Economic Indicators' Composite Index	Furniture and appliances Other durable sales **Financial** Real money supply Toronto stock market (S&P/TSX Composite index) U.S. Leading index	New orders—durables Ratio of shipments to stocks Average work week Business and personnel services employment **House Spending** Residential construction

Economic Indicators

It is not surprising that the cycle can be predicted. Statistics Canada has developed a set of cyclical indicators to help forecast and measure short-term fluctuations in economic activity. **Leading economic indicators** are those economic series that tend to rise or fall in advance of the rest of the economy.

Ten series are grouped into a widely followed composite index of leading economic indicators, as specified in Table 15.2. Figure 15.3 graphs percent changes in the composite leading indicator series against changes in the GDP for the years 1962–2012. The leading indicator series appears to anticipate major changes of direction in GDP quite well.

The stock market price index is a leading indicator.[1] Unfortunately, this makes the series of leading indicators much less useful for investment policy—by the time the series predicts an upturn, the market already has made its move. While the business cycle may be somewhat predictable, the stock market may not be. This is one more manifestation of the efficient market hypothesis. Various industries, however, respond early or late in the cycle, while others are more insensitive. Forest products encompass two subsectors: lumber, which responds to home construction as interest rates fall, and pulp and paper, which follows business activity as advertising and packaging increase. Since interest rates fall as a recession deepens, lumber company profits pick up earlier than pulp and paper do; the efficient market anticipates the increased profits by raising the equity prices. You might miss the gains in forest product companies specializing in lumber operations, but still have time to invest in the pulp and paper companies.

Figure 15.3

Composite leading indicator and GDP for Canada.

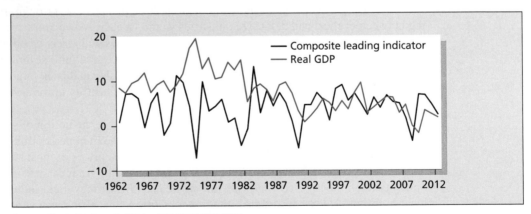

Source: Statistics Canada, Tables 377-0003, 379-0031.

[1]See, for example, Stanley Fischer and Robert C. Merton, "Macroeconomics and Finance: The Role of the Stock Market," *Carnegie-Rochester Conference Series on Public Policy* 21 (1984).

15.6 INDUSTRY ANALYSIS

Industry analysis is important for the same reason as macroeconomic analysis is. Just as it is difficult for an industry to perform well when the macroeconomy is ailing, it is unusual for a firm in a troubled industry to perform well. Similarly, just as we have seen that economic performance can vary widely across countries, performance also can vary widely across industries. For U.S. industry groupings, in 2012 ROE ranged from 6.7 percent for money centre banks to 29.6 percent for the restaurant industry; five-year expected growth rates ranged from 3 percent for closed-end equity funds to 40 percent for Internet service providers. Figure 15.4 illustrates this diversity of performance, showing the ROE of a number of U.S. major industry groups in 2012.

Given the wide variation in profitability, it is not surprising that industry groups exhibit considerable dispersion in their stock market performance. Figure 15.5 presents the stock market performance of the same industries included in Figure 15.4. The spread in performance is remarkable, ranging from a 57.3 percent gain in the home improvement industry to only 2.6 percent in the oil and gas industry.

Another perspective is given by the gain in equity value for the capped indices traded on the TSX in 2012. Figure 15.6 presents these values, ranging from −8.6 percent for metals and mining to 21.5 percent for consumer staples.

Even small investors can easily take positions in industry performance by using mutual funds or exchange-traded funds with an industry focus. One can invest directly in the TSX capped indices; for U.S. industry participation, Fidelity offers about 40 Select Funds, each of which is invested in a particular industry, and there are dozens of industry-specific ETFs available to retail investors.

Figure 15.4

Return on equity by industry, 2012.

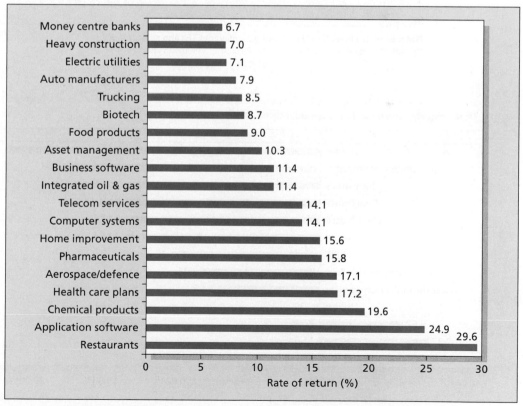

Source: Yahoo Finance, September 12, 2012, http://finance.yahoo.com.

Figure 15.5

Industry
stock price
performance,
2012.

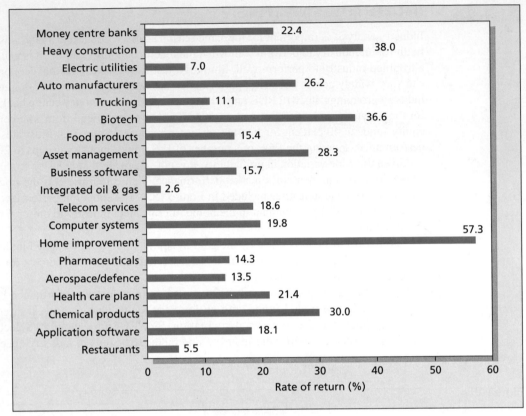

Note: Stock return is based on returns to relevant ETFs and select funds.
Source: Yahoo Finance, September 12, 2012, http://finance.yahoo.com.

Figure 15.6   Equity return for TSX capped indices, 2012.

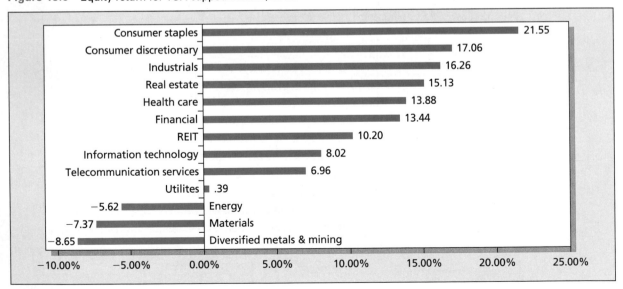

Source: TMX website.

Figure 15.7   Equity return across the Consumer Staples Index.

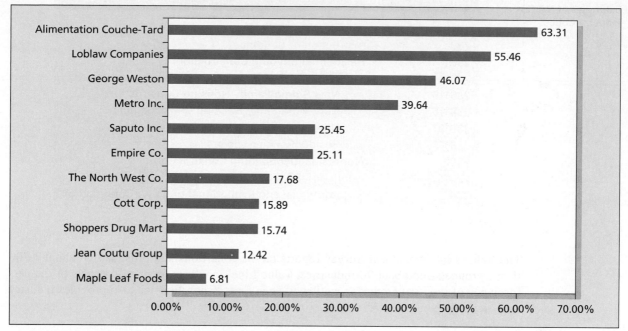

Source: TMX website.

Defining an Industry

Although we know what we mean by an "industry," it can be difficult in practice to decide where to draw the line between one industry and another. The consumer staples classification includes drug stores, grocery chains, meat packing, and bottling. We can see the considerable dispersion in financial performance as we look at the individual 2012 equity gains given in Figure 15.7 for the members in the Consumer Staples Index.

A useful way to define industry groups in practice is given by the North American Industry Classification System, or **NAICS codes**.[2] These are codes assigned to group firms for statistical analysis. The first two digits in the codes denote very broad industry classifications. For example, Table 15.3 shows that the codes for all construction firms start with 23. The next digits define the industry grouping more narrowly. Codes starting with 236 denote *building* construction, 2361 denotes *residential* construction, and 236115 denotes *single-family* construction. Firms with the same four-digit NAICS codes are commonly considered to be in the same industry.

NAICS industry classifications are not perfect. For example, both Walmart and Holt Renfrew might be classified as "Department Stores." Yet the former is a high-volume "value" store, whereas the latter is a high-margin elite retailer. Are they really in the same industry? Still, these classifications are a tremendous aid in conducting industry analysis, because they provide a means of focusing on very broadly or fairly narrowly defined groups of firms.

Several other industry classifications are provided by other analysts, for example Standard & Poor's reports on the performance of about 100 industry groups. S&P computes stock price indices for each group, which is useful in assessing past investment performance.

---

[2]These codes are used for firms operating inside the NAFTA (North American Free Trade Agreement) region, which includes the United States, Mexico, and Canada. NAICS codes replaced the Standard Industry Classification or SIC codes previously used.

TABLE 15.3

Examples of NAICS Industry Codes

Code	Title
23	Construction
236	Construction of Buildings
2361	Residential Building Construction
23611	Residential Building Construction
236115	New Single-Family Housing Construction
236116	New Multifamily Housing Construction
236117	New Housing Operative Builders
236118	Residential Remodelers
2362	Nonresidential Building Construction
23621	Industrial Building Construction
23622	Commercial and Institutional Building Construction

The Value Line Investment Survey reports on the conditions and prospects of about 1,700 firms, grouped into about 90 industries. Value Line's analysts prepare forecasts of the performance of industry groups as well as of each firm. Yahoo Finance also provides industry statistics online.

Sensitivity to the Business Cycle

Once the analyst forecasts the state of the macroeconomy, it is necessary to determine the implication of that forecast for specific industries. Not all industries are equally sensitive to the business cycle. For example, Figure 15.8 plots annual changes in retail sales for jewellery and grocery stores. Sales of jewellery, as a luxury good and discretionary purchase, fluctuate more widely than for a staple such as groceries. Jewellery sales actually fall in a recession, as in 2001, 2008, and 2009. In contrast, sales growth in the grocery industry is relatively stable, with no years in which sales meaningfully decline.

Figure 15.8

Industry cyclicality.

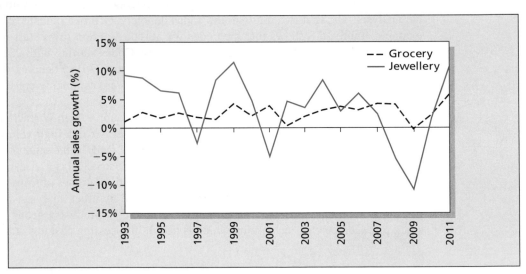

Source: "Retail Sales," *Economic Time Series,* http://economagic.com.

Three factors determine the sensitivity of a firm's earnings to the business cycle. First is the sensitivity of sales. Necessities such as food, drugs, and medical services will show little sensitivity to business conditions. Other industries with low sensitivity would be those for which income is not a crucial determinant of demand, such as tobacco products. In contrast, firms in industries such as machine tools, steel, autos, and transportation are highly sensitive.

The second factor determining business cycle sensitivity is operating leverage, which refers to the division between fixed and variable costs. (Fixed costs are those the firm incurs regardless of its production levels. Variable costs are those that rise or fall as the firm produces more or less product.) Firms with greater amounts of variable as opposed to fixed costs will be less sensitive to business conditions, because in economic downturns these firms can reduce costs as output falls in response to falling sales. Profits for firms with high fixed costs will swing more widely with sales, because costs do not move to offset revenue variability. Firms with high fixed costs are said to have *high operating leverage*, as small swings in business conditions can have large impacts on profitability.

EXAMPLE 15.1   Operating Leverage

Consider two firms operating in the same industry with identical revenues in all phases of the business cycle: recession, normal, and expansion. Firm A has short-term leases on most of its equipment and can reduce its lease expenditures when production slackens. It has fixed costs of $5 million and variable costs of $1 per unit of output. Firm B has long-term leases on most of its equipment and must make lease payments regardless of economic conditions. Its fixed costs are higher, $8 million, but its variable costs are only $.50 per unit. Table 15.4 shows that firm A will do better in recessions than firm B, but not as well in expansions. A's costs move in conjunction with its revenues to help performance in downturns and impede performance in upturns.

We can quantify operating leverage by measuring how sensitive profits are to changes in sales. The **degree of operating leverage**, or **DOL**, is defined as

$$DOL = \frac{\text{Percentage change in profits}}{\text{Percentage change in sales}}$$

DOL greater than 1 indicates some operating leverage. For example, if DOL = 2, then for every 1 percent change in sales, profits will change by 2 percent in the same direction, either up or down.

TABLE 15.4

Operating Leverage

	Recession Scenario		Normal Scenario		Expansion Scenario	
	Firm A	Firm B	Firm A	Firm B	Firm A	Firm B
Sales (million units)	5	5	6	6	7	7
Price per unit	$ 2	$ 2	$ 2	$ 2	$ 2	$ 2
Revenue ($ million)	10	10	12	12	14	14
Fixed costs ($ million)	5	8	5	8	5	8
Variable costs ($ million)	5	2.5	6	3	7	3.5
Total costs ($ million)	$10	$10.5	$11	$11	$12	$11.5
Profits	$ 0	$ (.5)	$ 1	$ 1	$ 2	$ 2.5

We have seen that the degree of operating leverage increases with a firm's exposure to fixed costs. In fact, one can show that DOL depends on fixed costs in the following manner:[3]

$$DOL = 1 + \frac{\text{Fixed costs}}{\text{Profits}}$$

EXAMPLE 15.2   **Degree of Operating Leverage**

Return to the two firms illustrated in Table 15.4 and compare profits and sales in the "normal" scenario for the economy with those in a recession. Profits of firm A fall by 100 percent (from $1 million to zero) when sales fall by 16.7 percent (from $6 million to $5 million):

$$DOL \text{ (firm A)} = \frac{\text{Percentage change in profits}}{\text{Percentage change in sales}} = \frac{-100\%}{-16.7\%} = 6$$

We can confirm the relationship between DOL and fixed costs as follows:

$$DOL \text{ (firm A)} = 1 + \frac{\text{Fixed costs}}{\text{Profits}} = 1 + \frac{\$5 \text{ million}}{\$1 \text{ million}} = 6$$

Firm B has higher fixed costs, and its operating leverage is higher. Again, compare data for a normal scenario to a recession. Profits for firm B fall by 150 percent, from $1 million to −$.5 million. Operating leverage for firm B is therefore

$$DOL \text{ (firm B)} = \frac{\text{Percentage change in profits}}{\text{Percentage change in sales}} = \frac{-150\%}{-16.7\%} = 9$$

which reflects its higher level of fixed costs:

$$DOL \text{ (firm B)} = 1 + \frac{\text{Fixed costs}}{\text{Profits}} = 1 + \frac{\$8 \text{ million}}{\$1 \text{ million}} = 9$$

The third factor influencing business cycle sensitivity is financial leverage, which is the use of borrowing. Interest payments on debt must be paid regardless of sales. They are fixed costs that also increase the sensitivity of profits to business conditions. We will have more to say about financial leverage in Chapter 17.

Investors should not always prefer industries with lower sensitivity to the business cycle. Firms in sensitive industries will have high-beta stocks and are riskier. But while they swing lower in downturns, they also swing higher in upturns. As always, the issue you need to address is whether the expected return on the investment is fair compensation for the risks borne.

CC 4

CONCEPT CHECK

In Table 15.4, what will be profits in the three scenarios for a firm C with fixed costs of $2 million and variable costs of $1.50 per unit? What are your conclusions regarding operating leverage and business risk?

[3]Operating leverage and DOL are treated in more detail in most corporate finance texts.

Figure 15.9

A stylized depiction of the business cycle.

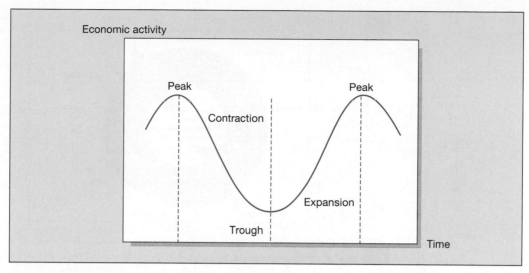

Sector Rotation

One way that many analysts think about the relationship between industry analysis and the business cycle is the notion of **sector rotation**. The idea is to shift the portfolio more heavily into industry or sector groups that are expected to outperform based on one's assessment of the state of the business cycle.

Figure 15.9 is a stylized depiction of the business cycle. Near the peak of the cycle, the economy might be overheated with high inflation and interest rates, and price pressures on basic commodities. This might be a good time to invest in firms engaged in natural resource extraction and processing such as minerals or petroleum.

Following a peak, when the economy enters a contraction or recession, one would expect defensive industries—for example, pharmaceuticals, food, and other necessities—to be the best performers. At the height of the contraction, financial firms will be hurt by shrinking loan volume and higher default rates. Toward the end of the recession, however, contractions induce lower inflation and interest rates, which favour financial firms.

At the trough of a recession, the economy is poised for recovery and subsequent expansion. Firms might thus be spending on purchases of new equipment to meet anticipated increases in demand. This, then, would be a good time to invest in capital goods industries, such as equipment, transportation, or construction.

Finally, in an expansion, the economy is growing rapidly. Cyclical industries such as consumer durables and luxury items will be most profitable in this stage of the cycle. Banks might also do well in expansions, since loan volume will be high and default exposure low when the economy is growing rapidly.

Figure 15.10 illustrates sector rotation. When investors are relatively pessimistic about the economy, they will shift into noncyclical industries such as consumer staples or health care. When anticipating an expansion, they will prefer more cyclical industries such as materials and technology.

Let us emphasize again that sector rotation, like any other form of market timing, will be successful only if one anticipates the next stage of the business cycle better than other investors. The business cycle depicted in Figure 15.9 is highly stylized. In real life, it is never as clear how long each phase of the cycle will last, nor how extreme it will be. These forecasts are where analysts need to earn their keep.

Figure 15.10
Sector rotation.

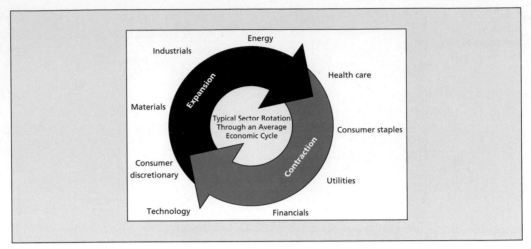

CC 5

CONCEPT CHECK

In which phase of the business cycle would you expect the following industries to enjoy their best performance?
a. Newspapers
b. Machine tools
c. Beverages
d. Timber

Industry Life Cycles

Examine the biotechnology industry and you will find many firms with high rates of investment, high rates of return on investment, and low dividend payout rates. Do the same for the public utility industry and you will find lower rates of return, lower investment rates, and higher dividend payout rates. Why should this be?

The biotech industry is still new. Recently, available technologies have created opportunities for highly profitable investment of resources. New products are protected by patents, and profit margins are high. With such lucrative investment opportunities, firms find it advantageous to put all profits back into the firm. The companies grow rapidly on average.

Eventually, however, growth must slow. The high profit rates will induce new firms to enter the industry. Increasing competition will hold down prices and profit margins. New technologies become proven and more predictable, risk levels fall, and entry becomes even easier. As internal investment opportunities become less attractive, a lower fraction of profits is reinvested in the firm. Cash dividends increase.

Ultimately, in a mature industry, we observe "cash cows," firms with stable dividends and cash flows and little risk. Growth rates might be similar to that of the overall economy. Industries in early states of their life cycles offer high-risk/high-potential-return investments. Mature industries offer lower-risk, lower-return profiles.

This analysis suggests that a typical **industry life cycle** might be described by four stages: a start-up stage, characterized by extremely rapid growth; a consolidation stage, characterized by growth that is less rapid but still faster than that of the general economy; a maturity stage, characterized by growth no faster than the general economy; and a stage of relative decline, in which the industry grows less rapidly than the rest of the economy, or actually shrinks. Let us turn to an elaboration of each of these stages.

Start-up Stage   The early stages of an industry are often characterized by a new technology or product such as desktop personal computers in the 1980s, cellphones in the 1990s, or the new generation of smartphones introduced more recently. At this stage, it is difficult to predict which firms will emerge as industry leaders. Some firms will turn out to be wildly successful, and others will fail altogether. Therefore, there is considerable risk in selecting one particular firm within the industry. For example, in the smartphone industry, there is still a battle among competing technologies, such as Google's Android phones and Apple's iPhone, and it is difficult to predict the winner or ultimate market shares.

At the industry level, however, sales and earnings will grow very rapidly, because the new product has not yet saturated its market. For example, in 2010 very few households had smartphones. The potential market for the product therefore was huge. In contrast, consider the market for a mature product such as refrigerators. Almost all households in the United States already have them, so the market for this good primarily comprises households replacing old ones. Obviously, the growth rate in this market in the next decade will be far lower than that for smartphones.

Consolidation Stage   After a product becomes established, industry leaders begin to emerge. The survivors from the start-up stage are more stable, and market share is easier to predict. Therefore, the performance of the surviving firms will more closely track the performance of the overall industry. The industry still grows faster than the rest of the economy as the product penetrates the marketplace and becomes more commonly used.

Maturity Stage   At this point, the product has reached its full potential for use by consumers. Further growth might merely track growth in the general economy. The product has become far more standardized, and producers are forced to compete to a greater extent on the basis of price. This leads to narrower profit margins and further pressure on profits. Firms at this stage sometimes are characterized as "cash cows," having reasonably stable cash flow but offering little opportunity for profitable expansion. These firms are best "milked" rather than reinvesting in the company.

We pointed to desktop PCs as a start-up industry in the 1980s. By the 1990s, desktops were progressively giving way to laptops, which were in their own start-up stage. Within a dozen years, laptops had in turn entered the maturity stage, with standardization, considerable market penetration, and dramatic price competition. Today, tablet computers are in the start-up stage.

Relative Decline   In this stage, the industry might grow at less than the rate of the overall economy, or it might even shrink. This might be due to obsolescence of the product, competition from new, low-cost suppliers, or competition from new products as is the case with laptops and tablet computers.

At which stage in the life cycle are investments in an industry most attractive? Conventional wisdom says that investors should seek firms in high-growth industries. This recipe for success is simplistic, however. If the security prices already reflect the likelihood for high growth, it is too late to make money from that knowledge. Moreover, high growth and fat profits encourage competition from other producers. The exploitation of profit opportunities brings about new sources of supply that eventually reduce prices, profits, investment returns, and finally growth. This is the dynamic behind the progression from one stage of the industry life cycle to another. The famous portfolio manager Peter Lynch makes this point in *One Up on Wall Street*:

> Many people prefer to invest in a high-growth industry, where there's a lot of sound and fury. Not me. I prefer to invest in a low-growth industry. . . . In a low-growth industry,

especially one that's boring and upsets people [such as funeral homes or the oil-drum retrieval business], there's no problem with competition. You don't have to protect your flanks from potential rivals . . . and this gives you the leeway to continue to grow.[4]

In fact, Lynch uses an industry classification system in a very similar spirit to the lifecycle approach we have described. He places firms in the following six groups:

- *Slow growers.* Large and aging companies that will grow only slightly faster than the broad economy. These firms have matured from their earlier fast-growth phase. They usually have steady cash flow and pay a generous dividend, indicating that the firm is generating more cash than can be profitably reinvested in the firm.
- *Stalwarts.* Large, well-known firms like Coca-Cola, Hershey's, or Colgate-Palmolive. They grow faster than the slow growers, but are not in the very rapid growth start-up stage. They also tend to be in noncyclical industries that are relatively unaffected by recessions.
- *Fast growers.* Small and aggressive new firms with annual growth rates in the neighbourhood of 20 to 25 percent. Company growth can be due to broad industry growth or to an increase in market share in a more mature industry.
- *Cyclicals.* These are firms with sales and profits that regularly expand and contract along with the business cycle. Examples are auto companies, steel companies, or the construction industry.
- *Turnarounds.* These are firms that are in bankruptcy or soon might be. If they can recover from what might appear to be imminent disaster, they can offer tremendous investment returns. A good example of this type of firm would be Chrysler in 1982, when it required a government guarantee on its debt to avoid bankruptcy. The stock price rose 15-fold in the next five years.
- *Asset plays.* These are firms that have valuable assets not currently reflected in the stock price. For example, a company may own or be located on valuable real estate that is worth as much as or more than the company's business enterprises. Sometimes the hidden asset can be tax-loss carry forwards. Other times the assets may be intangible. For example, a cable company might have a valuable list of cable subscribers. These assets do not immediately generate cash flow, and so may be more easily overlooked by other analysts attempting to value the firm.

Industry Structure and Performance

The maturation of an industry involves regular changes in the firm's competitive environment. As a final topic, let us examine the relationship between industry structure and profitability. Returns are limited in a competitive structure, which can be characterized by the following:

- *Threat of entry.* Barriers to entry deter new entrants who put pressure on price and profits. Such barriers take the form of distribution channels, experience, brand loyalty and proprietary knowledge or patent protection.
- *Rivalry between existing competitors.* Slow industry growth, high fixed costs, and homogeneous products all lead to price pressure (such as in the airline industry); in these cases, there will generally be more price competition and lower profit margins as competitors seek to expand their share of the market.
- *Pressure from substitute products.* The existence of substitute products means the industry faces competition from firms in related industries. For example, sugar producers compete with corn syrup producers. Wool producers compete with synthetic fibre producers. The availability of substitutes limits the prices that can be charged to customers.

---

[4]Peter Lynch with John Rothchild, *One Up on Wall Street* (New York: Penguin), p. 131.

- *Bargaining power of buyers.* Industries such as auto parts manufacturing have limited outlets for their products and little opportunity to demand higher profit margins.
- *Bargaining power of suppliers.* Profits also can be squeezed when there is little competition or substitutability among suppliers, as in the case of a unionized labour force.

Analysts seeking unrecognized value must be familiar with the response of industries to the business cycle and with the relative strengths of firms within the different industries. Experience and intelligent appraisal of the economic factors and financial statements can be combined in the process of investing based on timing and security selection. The auto industry is notoriously cyclical as both industry and consumers postpone decisions to replace existing vehicles during recessions. A vehicle that is one year older is a little bit rustier and less reliable than before and more needful of replacement. Therefore, the pressure to purchase increases, leading to relatively high auto sales following the low sales due to postponement. *When* the inevitable purchasing will start is a timing decision. Whether Japanese cars or the Big Three—and which of them—will get more of those sales is a question of customer preference; and whether Magna International, perhaps the leading Canadian parts supplier, will have more leverage to increased sales is a further question. The analyst is paid to resolve these questions.

Magna
International Inc.
www.magna.com

15.7   THE AGGREGATE STOCK MARKET

It has been well documented that the stock market is a leading economic indicator. This means that it tends to fall before a recession and rise before an economic recovery. Its collapse in the crash of 1987, however, did not foretell a recession at all, so the relationship is far from perfect. A well-known joke, often attributed to Paul Samuelson, is that the market has forecast eight of the last five recessions. Nevertheless, a prediction of corporate earnings in the expected economic conditions can be used to estimate the overall level of the market.

Figure 15.11 shows the behaviour of the earnings-to-price ratio (i.e., the earnings yield) of the TSX Composite Index versus the yield to maturity on long-term Canada bonds since 1956. The two series track each other quite closely, in terms of falling and rising trends. This is to be expected: the two variables that affect a firm's value are earnings (and implicitly the dividends they can support) and the discount rate, which "translates" future income into present value. Thus, it should not be surprising that the ratio of earnings to stock price (the inverse of the

Figure 15.11

Ten-year bond and TSX earnings yield.

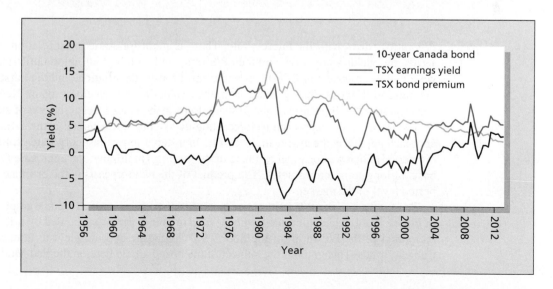

Recent academic study seriously undermines a popular reason for not worrying about the high price-to-earnings ratio of the stock market today: the idea that the ratios should be high when interest rates are low. The theoretical basis for this claim is the so-called Fed Model, which compares the interest rate on the U.S. government's 10-year treasury note with the inverse of the stock market's P/E ratio—known as the market's earnings yield. The stock market is considered undervalued when its earnings yield is greater than the treasury note rate.

According to this model, the stock market is significantly undervalued right now. The P/E ratio of the Standard & Poor's 500-stock index is 18.2, based on companies' estimated operating earnings for 2004. That translates into an earnings yield of 5.5%, much higher than the current yield of 4.09% for the 10-year treasury note.

The Fed Model was constructed by Edward E. Yardeni, now the chief investment strategist at the Prudential Equity Group, who based it on comments in the Fed's Monetary Policy Report to Congress in July, 1997. The Federal Reserve has not endorsed the model.

If the Fed Model held true, earnings growth should be slower when treasury note rates are high and faster when those rates are low. Historically, however, that has not been the case, according to the new study, "Inflation Illusion and Stock Prices," by the Harvard finance professors John Y. Campbell and Tuomo Vuolteenaho. The study has circulated this month as a National Bureau of Economic Research working paper and is at www.nber.org/papers.

A similar conclusion was reached in a study by the finance professors Jay R. Ritter of the University of Florida and Richard S. Warr, now at North Carolina State. That study, published in 2002, covered 1978 to 1999, but the new one covered a much longer period: 1927 through 2002. The government's 10-year treasury note has not traded during all those 75 years, but according to the professors, interest and inflation rates are highly correlated. And during those 75 years, earnings growth has tended to be higher during periods of high inflation and lower when inflation is low.

Put another way, the professors conclude that stocks are a good long-term hedge against inflation. They found that the growth rate of real, or inflation-adjusted, earnings is relatively constant when measured over several-year periods. That means the growth rate of nominal earnings tends to rise and fall with inflation.

Many investors overlook that point, because they assume that changes in inflation will not affect nominal earnings growth. Economists call that assumption an "inflation illusion." If it were true, real earnings growth should be faster in periods of low inflation, justifying higher P/E ratios. But the assumption has not been true over time, according to Messrs Campbell and Vuolteenaho. As a result, they found that the stock market has tended to become significantly undervalued in times of high inflation and overvalued in times of low inflation.

Consider equity valuations during the late 1970s and early 1980s, when interest rates and inflation were high. Investors used the equivalent of the Fed Model to justify a low P/E ratio for the overall market. The late Franco Modigliani, who was a finance professor at the Massachusetts Institute of Technology during that time and in 1985 would be the Nobel laureate in economics, recognized the inflation illusion that was implicit in this argument. In a 1979 article, he argued that stocks were significantly undervalued—a view that was vindicated in the 1980s and '90s by the strong bull market in stocks.

The situation today is the mirror opposite of what prevailed in the late 1970s, suggesting that stocks may be as overvalued today as they were undervalued then.

Source: Mark Hulbert, "A Time-Tested Sign of an Overvalued Market: Recent Research Sets Fed Model on Its Ear," *National Post*, February 24, 2004, p. IN.01.

P/E ratio) varies with the interest rate. There is room for some interpretation; until the early 1970s, the yields were close, and then P/E ratios fell with high inflation until 1980. Yields then were higher on bonds until 2004, as enthusiasm for the disinflation, and the burst dot-com bubble, raised P/E ratios sharply. Since then, their values have been closer again. Keep in mind that spikes in inverse P/E ratios are due to sharp drops in the index level at the end of market declines.

The most popular approach to forecasting the overall stock market is the earnings multiplier approach applied at the aggregate level. The first step is to forecast corporate profits for the coming period. Then we derive an estimate of the earnings multiplier, the aggregate P/E ratio, on the basis of long-term interest rates. The product of the two forecasts is the estimate of the end-of-period level of the market.

The forecast of the P/E ratio of the market is sometimes derived from a graph similar to that in Figure 15.11, which plots the *earnings yield* (earnings per share divided by price per share, the reciprocal of the P/E ratio) of the S&P/TSX Composite and the yield to maturity on 10-year Canada Bonds. This graph is the subject of the boxed article here on the Fed Model.

The *earnings yield* or earnings per share divided by price per share is the reciprocal of the P/E ratio; this can be calculated for the full S&P/TSX Composite Index. Since this value is linked to the interest rate, one can use this relationship and the current yield on 10-year Canada bonds to forecast the earnings yield on the TSX Composite. Given that earnings yield, a forecast of earnings could be used to predict the level of the TSX in some future period.

EXAMPLE 15.3   Forecasting the Aggregate Stock Market

The mid 2013 forecast for 2013 earnings per share for the TSX portfolio was about $725. The 10-year bond yield was about 2.2 percent, with yields expected to remain low but modest tightening was anticipated; that meant a fairly narrow range of 2.2 to 3.00 percent with perhaps 2.5 percent the consensus. Because the earnings yield on the Composite has been about 3.5 percentage points above the 10-year bond yield in recent quarters, a first guess for the earnings yield on the Composite might be 6.0 percent. This would imply a P/E ratio of 1/.06 = 16.67. Our forecast for the index would then be 16.67 × 725 = 12,083.

Of course, there is uncertainty regarding all three inputs into this analysis: the actual earnings on the S&P/TSX Composite stocks, the level of bond yields at year-end, and the spread between the bond yield and the earnings yield. One would wish to perform sensitivity or scenario analysis to examine the impact of changes in all of these variables. To illustrate, consider Table 15.5, which shows a simple scenario analysis treating possible effects of variation in the Canada bond yield and EPS forecast. The scenario analysis shows that forecasted level of the stock market varies with dramatic sensitivity to both estimates. The Composite was trading about 12,600 near the end of May, and sentiment suggested that the markets were somewhat overvalued by this time.

Other analysts use an aggregate version of the discounted dividend model rather than an earnings multiplier approach. Those models, however, rely heavily on forecasts of such macroeconomic variables as GDP, interest rates, and the rate of inflation, which are themselves very difficult to predict accurately.

TABLE 15.5

S&P/TSX Composite Price Targets Under Various Scenarios

Scenario	Most Likely	Pessimistic	Optimistic
Long-bond yield	2.5%	3.0%	2.2%
Earnings yield	6.0%	6.5%	5.7%
Resulting P/E	16.67	15.38	17.54
EPS forecast	$725	$675	$775
Forecast S&P/TSX Composite	12,083	10,385	13,596

Note: Forecast for the earnings yield on the S&P/TSX Composite equals the long-bond rate plus 3.5 percent. The P/E ratio is the reciprocal of the forecast earnings yield.

SUMMARY

1. Macroeconomic policy aims to maintain the economy near full employment without aggravating inflationary pressures. The proper tradeoff between these two goals is a source of ongoing debate.

2. Macroeconomic analysis plays a major role in fundamental analysis; economists identify supply and demand shocks to the macroeconomy and the business cycle and use these in predicting future returns in the markets.

3. The traditional tools of macro policy are government spending and tax collection, which comprise fiscal policy, and manipulation of the money supply via monetary policy. Expansionary fiscal policy can stimulate the economy and increase GDP but tends to increase interest rates. Expansionary monetary policy works by lowering interest rates.

4. The business cycle is the economy's recurring pattern of expansions and recessions. Leading economic indicators can be used to anticipate the evolution of the business cycle because their values tend to change before those of other key economic variables.

5. Industries differ in their sensitivity to the business cycle, in both the degree and the timing of their response. Operating leverage and financial leverage increase sensitivity to the business cycle. More sensitive industries tend to be those producing high-priced durable goods for which the consumer has considerable discretion as to the timing of purchase. Examples are jewellery, automobiles, and consumer durables. Other sensitive industries are those that produce capital equipment for other firms.

6. Industry analysis examines aspects of performance, such as cyclical sensitivity, stages within an industry's life cycle, and competitive pressures.

7. The key macroeconomic variables that determine the level of stock prices in the aggregate are interest rates and corporate profits.

PROBLEMS

Mc Graw Hill Education **connect**™   **Practise and learn online with Connect.**

1. What monetary and fiscal policies might be prescribed for an economy in a deep recession?

2. If you believe the U.S. dollar will depreciate more dramatically than other currencies do, what will be your stance on investments in U.S. auto producers?

3. Choose an industry and identify the factors that will determine its performance in the next three years. What is your forecast for performance in that time period?

4. What are the differences between bottom-up and top-down approaches to security valuation? What are the advantages of a top-down approach?

5. What characteristics will give firms greater sensitivity to business cycles?

6. Unlike other investors, you believe the Fed is going to loosen monetary policy. What would be your recommendations about investments in the following industries?

   a. Gold mining

   b. Construction

7. According to supply-side economists, what will be the long-run impact on prices if there is a reduction in income tax rates?

8. Which of the following is consistent with a steeply upwardly sloping yield curve?

   a. Monetary policy is expansive and fiscal policy is expansive.

   b. Monetary policy is expansive while fiscal policy is restrictive.

   c. Monetary policy is restrictive and fiscal policy is restrictive.

9. Which of the following is not a governmental structural policy that supply-side economists believe would promote long-term growth in an economy?

   a. A redistributive tax system

   b. A promotion of competition

   c. Minimal government interference in the economy

10. Consider two firms producing smartphones. One uses a highly automated robotics process, whereas the other uses workers on an assembly line and pays overtime when there is heavy production demand.

    a. Which firm will have higher profits in a recession? In a boom?

    b. Which firm's stock will have a higher beta?

11. Here are four industries and four forecasts for the macroeconomy. Match the industry to the scenario in which it is likely to be the best performer.

    Industry

    a. Housing construction

    b. Health care

    c. Gold mining

    d. Steel production

    Economic Forecast

    1. *Deep recession.* Falling inflation, falling interest rates, falling GDP

    2. *Superheated economy.* Rapidly rising GDP, increasing inflation and interest rates

    3. *Healthy expansion.* Rising GDP, mild inflation, low unemployment

    4. *Stagflation.* Falling GDP, high inflation

12. At which stage of the industry life cycle would you place each of the following industries? (*Note:* There is considerable room for disagreement about the answers to this question.)

    a. Oil well equipment

    b. Computer hardware

    c. Computer software

    d. Genetic engineering

    e. Railroads

13. For each pair of firms, choose the one you think would be more sensitive to the business cycle.

    a. General Autos or General Pharmaceuticals

    b. Friendly Airlines or Happy Cinemas

14. General Weedkillers dominates the chemical weed control market with its patented product Weed-ex. The patent is about to expire, however. What are your forecasts for changes in the industry? Specifically, what will happen to industry prices, sales, the profit prospects of General Weedkillers, and the profit prospects of its competitors? What stage of the industry life cycle do you think is relevant for the analysis of this market?

15. Your business plan for your proposed start-up firm envisions first-year revenues of $120,000, fixed costs of $30,000, and variable costs equal to one-third of revenue.

    a. What are expected profits based on these expectations?

    b. What is the degree of operating leverage based on the estimate of fixed costs and expected profits?

    c. If sales are 10 percent below expectation, what will be the decrease in profits?

    d. Show that the percentage decrease in profits equals DOL times the 10 percent drop in sales.

    e. Based on the DOL, what is the largest percentage shortfall in sales relative to original expectations that the firm can sustain before profits turn negative? What are breakeven sales at this point?

    f. Confirm that your answer to (*e*) is correct by calculating profits at the breakeven level of sales.

Use the following case in answering problems 16–19.

Institutional Advisors for All Inc., or IAAI, is a consulting firm that primarily advises all types of institutions such as foundations, endowments, pension plans, and insurance companies. IAAI also provides advice to a select group of individual investors with large portfolios.

    One of the claims the firm makes in its advertising is that IAAI devotes considerable resources to forecasting and determining long-term trends; then it uses commonly accepted investment models to determine how these trends should affect the performance of various investments.

    The members of the research department of IAAI recently reached conclusions concerning some important macroeconomic trends. For instance, they have seen an upward trend in job creation and consumer confidence and predict that this should continue for the next few years. Other domestic leading indicators that the research department at IAAI wishes to consider are industrial production, average weekly hours in manufacturing, S&P 500 stock prices, M2 money supply, and the index of consumer expectations.

    In the light of the predictions for job creation and consumer confidence, the investment advisors at IAAI want to make recommendations for their clients. They use established theories that relate job creation and consumer confidence to inflation and interest rates, and then incorporate the forecasted movements in inflation and interest rates into established models for explaining asset prices. Their primary concern is to forecast how the trends in job creation and consumer confidence should affect bond prices and how those trends should affect stock prices. The members of the research department at IAAI also note that stocks have been trending up in the past year, and this information is factored into the forecasts of the overall economy that they deliver. The researchers consider an upward-trending stock market a positive economic indicator in itself; however, they disagree about why this should be the case.

16. The researchers at IAAI have forecasted positive trends for both job creation and consumer confidence. Which, if either, of these trends should have a positive effect on stock prices?

17. Stock prices are useful as a leading indicator. To explain this phenomenon, which of the following is *most* accurate? Stock prices

    a. Predict future interest rates and reflect the trends in other indicators

    b. Do not predict future interest rates, nor are they correlated with other leading indicators; the usefulness of stock prices as a leading indicator is a mystery

    c. Reflect the trends in other leading indicators only, and do not have predictive power of their own

18. Which of the domestic series that the IAAI research department listed for use as leading indicators is *least* appropriate?

    a. Industrial production

    b. Manufacturing average weekly hours

    c. M2 money supply

19. IAAI uses primarily historical data in its calculations and forecasts. Which of the following regarding the actions of IAAI is *most* accurate?

    a. Credit risk premiums may be useful to IAAI because they are based on actual market expectations.

    b. IAAI should use a moving average of recent stock returns when times are bad because it will result in a high expected equity risk premium.

    c. Long time spans should be used so that regime changes can be factored into the forecasts.

Use the following case in answering problems 20–23.

Mary Smith, a Level II CFA candidate, was recently hired for an analyst position at the Bank of Ireland. Her first assignment is to examine the competitive strategies employed by various French wineries.

Smith's report identifies four wineries that are the major players in the French wine industry. Key characteristics of each are cited in Table 15A. In the body of Smith's report, she includes a discussion of the competitive structure of the French wine industry. She notes that over the past five years, the French wine industry has not responded to changing consumer tastes. Profit margins have declined steadily and the number of firms representing the industry has decreased from 10 to 4. It appears that participants in the French wine industry must consolidate in order to survive.

Smith's report notes that French consumers have strong bargaining power over the industry. She supports this conclusion with five key points, which she labels "Bargaining Power of Buyers":

- Many consumers are drinking more beer than wine with meals and at social occasions.
- Increasing sales over the Internet have allowed consumers to better research the wines, read opinions from other customers, and identify which producers have the best prices.
- The French wine industry is consolidating and consists of only 4 wineries today, as against 10 five years ago.
- More than 65 percent of the business for the French wine industry consists of purchases from restaurants. Restaurants typically make purchases in bulk, buying four to five cases of wine at a time.
- Land where the soil is fertile enough to grow grapes necessary for the wine production process is scarce in France. After completing the first draft of her report, Smith takes it to her boss, Ron VanDriesen, to review. VanDriesen tells her that he is a wine connoisseur himself, and often makes purchases from the South Winery. Smith tells VanDriesen, "In my report I have classified the South Winery as a stuck-in-the-middle firm. It tries to be a cost leader by selling its wine at a price that is slightly below the other firms, but it also tries to differentiate itself from its competitors by producing wine in bottles with curved necks, which increases its cost structure. The end result is that the South Winery's profit margin gets squeezed from both sides." VanDriesen replies, "I have met members of the management team from the South Winery at a couple of the wine conventions I have attended. I believe that the South Winery could succeed at following both a cost leadership and a differentiation strategy if its operations were separated into distinct operating units, with each unit pursuing a different competitive strategy." Smith makes a note to do more research on generic competitive strategies to verify VanDriesen's assertions before publishing the final draft of her report.

20. If the French home currency were to greatly appreciate in value compared to the English currency, what is the likely impact on the competitive position of the East Winery?

   a. Make the firm less competitive in the English market

   b. No impact, since the major market for East Winery is England, not France

   c. Make the firm more competitive in the English market

TABLE 15A   Characteristics of Four Major French Wineries

	South Winery	North Winery	East Winery	West Winery
Founding date	1750	1903	1812	1947
Generic competitive strategy	?	Cost leadership	Cost leadership	Cost leadership
Major customer market (more than 80% concentration)	France	France	England	U.S.
Production site	France	France	France	France

21. Which of Smith's points effectively support the conclusion that consumers have strong bargaining power over the industry?

22. Smith notes in her report that the West Winery might differentiate its wine product on attributes that buyers perceive to be important. Which of the following attributes would be the most likely area of focus for the West Winery to create a differentiated product?

    a. The method of delivery of the product

    b. The price of the product

    c. A focus on customers aged 30 to 45

23. Smith knows that a firm's generic strategy should be the centrepiece of a firm's strategic plan. On the basis of a compilation of research and documents, Smith makes three observations about the North Winery and its strategic planning process:

    i. North Winery's price and cost forecasts account for future changes in the structure of the French wine industry.

    ii. North Winery puts each of its business units into one of three categories: build, hold, or harvest.

    iii. North Winery uses market share as the key measure of its competitive position.

    Which of these observation(s) *least* support(s) the conclusion that the North Winery's strategic planning process is guided and informed by its generic competitive strategy?

24. You are trying to forecast the expected level of the aggregate Toronto stock market for the next year. Suppose the current three-month Treasury bill rate is 4 percent, the yield to maturity on 10+-year Canada bonds is 5 percent per year, the expected rate of inflation is 2 percent per year, and the expected EPS for the S&P/TSX Composite is $450. What is your forecast, and why?

 The following problems are based on questions that have appeared in past CFA examinations.

25. Briefly discuss what actions the Bank of Canada would probably take in pursuing an *expansionary* monetary policy using each of the following three monetary tools:

    a. Reserve requirements

    b. Open market operations

    c. Discount rate

26. An unanticipated expansionary monetary policy has been implemented. Indicate the impact of this policy on each of the following four variables:

    a. Inflation rate

    b. Real output and employment

    c. Real interest rate

    d. Nominal interest rate.

27. Universal Auto is a large multinational corporation headquartered in the United States. For segment reporting purposes, the company is engaged in two businesses: production of motor vehicles and information processing services. The motor vehicle business is by far the larger of Universal's two segments. It consists mainly of domestic U.S. passenger car production, but it also includes small truck manufacturing operations in the United States and passenger car production in other countries. This segment of Universal has had weak operating results for the past several years, including a large loss in 2013. Although the company does not reveal the operating results of its domestic passenger car segments, that part of Universal's business is generally believed to be primarily responsible for the weak performance of its motor vehicle segment. Idata, the information processing services segment of Universal, was started by Universal about 15 years ago. This business has shown strong, steady growth that has been entirely internal; no acquisitions have been made.

An excerpt from a research report on Universal prepared by Paul Adams, a CFA candidate, states: "Based on our assumption that Universal will be able to increase prices significantly on U.S. passenger cars in 2014, we project a multibillion-dollar profit improvement."

a. Discuss the concept of an industrial life cycle by describing each of its four phases.

b. Identify where each of Universal's two primary businesses—passenger cars and information processing—is in such a cycle.

c. Discuss how product pricing should differ between Universal's two businesses, on the basis of the location of each in the industrial life cycle.

28. Adams's research report (see the preceding problem) continued as follows: "With a business recovery already under way, the expected profit surge should lead to a much higher price for Universal Auto stock. We strongly recommend purchase."

a. Discuss the business cycle approach to investment timing. (Your answer should describe actions to be taken on both stocks and bonds at different points over a typical business cycle.)

b. Assuming Adams's assertion is correct (that a business recovery is already under way), evaluate the timeliness of his recommendation to purchase Universal Auto, a cyclical stock, on the basis of the business cycle approach to investment timing.

29. Janet Ludlow is preparing a report on U.S. manufacturers in the electric toothbrush industry, and has gathered the information shown in Tables 15B and 15C. Ludlow's report concludes that the electric toothbrush industry is in the maturity (i.e., late) phase of its industry life cycle.

a. Select and justify three factors from Table 15B that *support* Ludlow's conclusion.

b. Select and justify three factors from Table 15C that *refute* Ludlow's conclusion.

30. As a securities analyst you have been asked to review a valuation of a closely held business, Wigham Autoparts Heaven, Inc. (WAH), prepared by the Red Rocks Group (RRG). You are to give an opinion on the valuation and to support your opinion by analyzing each part of the valuation. WAH's sole business is automotive parts retailing. The RRG valuation includes a section called "Analysis of the Retail Auto Parts Industry," based completely on the data in Table 15D and the following additional information:

- WAH and its principal competitors each operated more than 150 stores at year-end 1999.
- The average number of stores operated per company engaged in the retail auto parts industry is 5.3.
- The major customer base for auto parts sold in retail stores consists of young owners of old vehicles. These owners do their own automotive maintenance out of economic necessity.

TABLE 15B Ratios for Electric Toothbrush Industry Index and Broad Stock Market Index

	2007	2008	2009	2010	2011	2012
Return on Equity						
Electric toothbrush industry index	12.5%	12.0%	15.4%	19.6%	21.6%	21.6%
Market index	10.2	12.4	14.6	19.9	20.4	21.2
Average P/E						
Electric toothbrush industry index	28.5	23.2	19.6	18.7	18.5	16.2
Market index	10.2	12.4	14.6	19.9	18.1	19.1
Dividend Payout Ratio						
Electric toothbrush industry index	8.8%	8.0%	12.1%	12.1%	14.3%	17.1%
Market index	39.2	40.1	38.6	43.7	41.8	39.1
Average Dividend Yield						
Electric toothbrush industry index	.3%	.3%	.6%	.7%	.8%	1.0%
Market index	3.8	3.2	2.6	2.2	2.3	2.1

TABLE 15C Characteristics of the Electric Toothbrush Manufacturing Industry

- *Industry sales growth.* Industry sales have grown at 15–20 percent per year in recent years and are expected to grow at 10–15 percent per year over the next three years.
- *Non-U.S. markets.* Some U.S. manufacturers are attempting to enter fast-growing non-U.S. markets, which remain largely unexploited.
- *Mail order sales.* Some manufacturers have created a new niche in the industry by selling electric toothbrushes directly to customers through mail order. Sales for this industry segment are growing at 40 percent per year.
- *U.S. market penetration.* The current penetration rate in the United States is 60 percent of households and will be difficult to increase.
- *Price competition.* Manufacturers compete fiercely on the basis of price, and price wars within the industry are common.
- *Niche markets.* Some manufacturers are able to develop new, unexploited niche markets in the United States based on company reputation, quality, and service.
- *Industry consolidation.* Several manufacturers have recently merged, and it is expected that consolidation in the industry will increase.
- *New entrants.* New manufacturers continue to enter the market.

    a. One of RRG's conclusions is that the retail auto parts industry as a whole is in the maturity stage of the industry life cycle. Discuss three relevant items of data from Table 15D that support this conclusion.

    b. Another RRG conclusion is that WAH and its principal competitors are in the consolidation stage of their life cycle.

        i. Cite three relevant items of data from Table 15D that support this conclusion.

        ii. Explain how WAH and its principal competitors can be in a consolidation stage while their industry as a whole is in the maturity stage.

31. *a.* If the exchange rate value of the British pound goes from US$1.75 to US$1.55, the pound has

        i. Appreciated and the British will find U.S. goods cheaper.

        ii. Appreciated and the British will find U.S. goods more expensive

        iii. Depreciated and the British will find U.S. goods more expensive

        iv. Depreciated and the British will find U.S. goods cheaper

    b. Changes in which of the following are likely to affect interest rates?

        i. Inflation expectations

        ii. Size of the federal deficit

        iii. Money supply

        iv. All of the above

    c. According to the supply-side view of fiscal policy, if the impact on total tax revenues is the same, does it make any difference whether the government cuts taxes by either reducing marginal tax rates or increasing the personal exemption allowance?

        i. No, both methods of cutting taxes will exert the same impact on aggregate supply.

        ii. No, people in both cases will increase their saving, expecting higher future taxes, and thereby offset the stimulus effect of lower current taxes.

        iii. Yes, the lower marginal tax rates alone will increase the incentive to earn marginal income and thereby stimulate aggregate supply.

        iv. Yes, interest rates will increase if marginal tax rates are lowered, whereas they will tend to decrease if the personal exemption allowance is raised.

TABLE 15D   Selected Retail Auto Parts Industry Data

	1999	1998	1997	1996	1995	1994	1993	1992	1991	1990
Population 18–29 years old (percentage change)	−1.8%	−2.0%	−2.1%	−1.4%	−.8%	−.9%	−1.1%	−.9%	−.7%	−.3%
Number of households with income more than $35,000 (percentage change)	6.0%	4.0%	8.0%	4.5%	2.7%	3.1%	1.6%	3.6%	4.2%	2.2%
Number of households with income less than $35,000 (percentage change)	3.0%	−1.0%	4.9%	2.3%	−1.4%	2.5%	1.4%	−1.3%	.6%	.1%
Number of cars 5–15 years old (percentage change)	.9%	−1.3%	−6.0%	1.9%	3.3%	2.4%	−2.3%	−2.2%	−8.0%	1.6%
Automotive aftermarket industry retail sales (percentage change)	5.7%	1.9%	3.1%	3.7%	4.3%	2.6%	1.3%	.2%	3.7%	2.4%
Consumer expenditures on automotive parts and accessories (percentage change)	2.4%	1.8%	2.1%	6.5%	3.6%	9.2%	1.3%	6.2%	6.7%	6.5%
Sales growth of retail auto parts companies with 100 or more stores	17.0%	16.0%	16.5%	14.0%	15.5%	16.8%	12.0%	15.7%	19.0%	16.0%
Market share of retail auto parts companies with 100 or more stores	19.0%	18.5%	18.3%	18.1%	17.0%	17.2%	17.0%	16.9%	15.0%	14.0%
Average operating margin of retail auto parts companies with 100 or more stores	12.0%	11.8%	11.2%	11.5%	10.6%	10.6%	10.0%	10.4%	9.8%	9.0%
Average operating margin of all retail auto parts companies	5.5%	5.7%	5.6%	5.8%	6.0%	6.5%	7.0%	7.2%	7.1%	7.2%

32. Dynamic Communication dominates a segment of the consumer electronics industry. A small competitor in that segment is Wade Goods & Co. Wade has just introduced a new product, the Carrycom, which will replace the existing Wade product line and could significantly affect the industry segment. Mike Brandreth is preparing an industry research update that focuses on Wade, including an analysis that makes extensive use of the five competitive forces (see list in the subsection "Industry Structure and Performance"). Wade's President, Toby White, makes the following statements:

   • "Wade has an exclusive three-year production licence for Carrycom technology from the patent owners of the new technology. This will provide us a window of opportunity to establish a leading position with this new product before competitors enter the market with similar products."

   • "A vital component in all existing competitive products is pari-copper, an enriched form of copper; production of pari-copper is limited and is effectively controlled by Dynamic. The Carrycom is manufactured with ordinary copper, thus overcoming the existing dependence on pari-copper. All other Carrycom components can be purchased from numerous sources."

- "Existing products based on pari-copper are designed to work in a single geographic region that is predetermined during the manufacturing process. The Carrycom will be the only product on the market that can be reset by the user for use in different regions. We expect other products within our industry segment to incorporate this functionality at the end of our exclusive licence period."

- "The Carrycom and similar, competitive products have recently added the function of automatic language conversion. This elevates these products to a superior position within the broader electronics market, ahead of personal digital assistants, personal computers, and other consumer electronics. We expect that the broader electronics market will not be able to integrate automatic language conversion for at least one year."

- "We intend to replace Dynamic as the market leader within the next three years. We expect ordinary copper-based products with automatic language conversion to be the industry standard in three years. This will result in a number of similar products and limited pricing power after the three-year licence expires."

Brandreth has adequately researched two of Porter's competitive forces—the bargaining power of buyers and the bargaining power of suppliers—and now turns his attention to the remaining competitive forces needed to complete his analysis of Wade.

Identify the three remaining competitive forces. Determine, with respect to each of the remaining competitive forces, whether Wade's position in the industry is likely to be strong or weak, both one year and five years from now.

33. Judging from historical data and assuming less-than-full employment, periods of sharp acceleration in the growth rate of the money supply tend to be associated *initially* with

   i. Periods of economic recession

   ii. An increase in the velocity of money

   iii. A rapid growth of gross domestic product

   iv. Reductions in real gross domestic product

E-INVESTMENTS
The
Macroeconomy

1. Go to the Bank of Canada's site at **www.bankofcanada.ca**. Click on the link for the most recent *Monetary Policy Report*. How has growth been recently relative to the Bank's targets and predictions? How is inflation being managed relative to target? What is forecast for the near future, and what risks are there?

2. Go to Canada's Policy Horizons site (**www.horizons.gc.ca**) and retrieve the paper "How Does International Trade Affect Business Cycle Synchronization in North America?" How correlated are U.S. and Canadian business cycles? Is this correlation increasing or decreasing? Why?

3. Look again at the Policy Horizons site and paper in question 2. What are the implications of trade treaties with Europe or East Asia for synchronization of their business cycles? How do economic shocks affect domestic and international business cycles?

Equity Evaluation Models

The dilemma for the portfolio manager and the investor is whether to follow the implication of the empirical evidence and the theory of market efficiency or to ignore it. Should one accept a passive investment strategy of an index fund or will the effort and expense of active management provide a superior portfolio? We saw in our discussion of market efficiency that finding undervalued securities is hardly easy. At the same time, there are enough doubts about the accuracy of the efficient market hypothesis that the search for such securities should not be dismissed out of hand. Moreover, it is the continuing search for mispriced securities that maintains a nearly efficient market. Even infrequent discoveries of minor mispricing justify the salary of a stock market analyst.

Fundamental analysis has various aspects to it, including an economic analysis of how the firm will react to potential future conditions that will affect earnings; alternatively, the analyst can examine the recent financial results of the firm in the hope of finding unrecognized value. In this chapter, we see how valuation based on cash flow can be estimated from earnings; earnings themselves are predicted by examining economic conditions. We describe the valuation models that stock market analysts use to uncover mispriced securities. The models presented are those used by fundamental analysts, those analysts who use information concerning the current and prospective profitability of a company to assess its fair market value.

We start with a discussion of alternative measures of the value of a company. From there, we review *dividend discount models*, from the simple growth model to compound variants that security analysts commonly use to measure the value of a firm as an ongoing concern; this leads to an examination of how earnings and dividend payouts are related to growth. Next, we turn to price-earnings (or P/E) ratios, explaining why they are of such interest to analysts but also highlighting some of their shortcomings. We explain how P/E ratios are tied to dividend valuation models and, more generally, to the growth prospects of the firm. At this point, we discuss two alternative strategies, growth investing and value investing. We then present a discussion and extended example of free cash flow models used by analysts to value firms based on forecasts of the cash flows that will be generated from the firms' business endeavours. Finally, we apply the several valuation tools covered in the chapter to a real firm and find some disparity in their conclusions—a conundrum that will confront any security analyst—and consider reasons for these discrepancies.

16.1 VALUATION BY COMPARABLES

The purpose of fundamental analysis is to identify securities that are mispriced in the market relative to some measure of "true" value that can be derived from observable financial and company specific data. The Law of One Price mentioned in Chapter 8 notes that two assets paying the same cash flow in the future must trade at the same price; more generally, any two assets promising the same expected cash flows with the same risks should also trade at the same price. Fundamental analysis works to estimate the predictable cash flows and determine a discount factor by comparison with other known asset values. Part of this process involves examining various items in the financial statements, together with market price and perceptions of growth; these are combined in simple ratios to compare against benchmarks for similar companies.

Financial data for publicly traded companies is available in increasingly complete form on the Internet. One source is Standard & Poor's Market Insight service, including COMPUSTAT. Table 16.1 shows some COMPUSTAT output of financial data for one of Canada's largest gold miners, Kinross, as of December 31, 2012. We use this to assess some of Kinross' financial ratios.

The market price of a share of Kinross is shown as $5.51, and the total market capitalization of $6.29 billion results from multiplying the share price times the 1.14 billion shares outstanding. The **book value** of equity is calculated as the net value of total assets less total liabilities and preferred shares, divided by the number of common shares outstanding—items given by the annual balance sheet. Under the heading "Valuation," Table 16.1 reports the ratios of Kinross'

CFA Institute
www.cfainstitute.org

TABLE 16.1

Financial Highlights for Kinross Gold, December 31, 2012

Price per share	$5.51	
Common shares outstanding (billion)	1.14	
Market capitalization ($ billion)	$6.29	
Latest 12 Months		**Quarterly Growth**
Revenues ($ billion)	$4.36	5.30%
EBITDA ($ billion)	$3.20	
Net income ($ billion)	($2.49)	
Earnings per share	($2.18)	51.80%
Valuation	**Kinross**	**Industry Avg.**
Price/earnings (forward)	10.40	18.45
Price/book	0.66	
Price/sales	1.51	4.34
Price/cash flow	5.35	
PEG	2.09	1.04
Profitability		
ROE (%)	−21.98	
ROA (%)	4.87	
Gross margin	0.57	0.48
Operating profit margin (%)	27.80	21
Net profit margin (%)	−56.14	

Source: Yahoo Finance, http://finance.yahoo.com, June 19, 2013.

stock price to four different items taken from its latest financial statements (each divided by the number of outstanding shares): net earnings (in this case forward estimated due to the annual loss), book value, sales revenue, and cash flow. Kinross' forward price-to-earnings (P/E) ratio is 10.4, the price-to-book-value is .66, price-to-sales is 1.51, and price-to-cash-flow is 5.35; there is also a calculation of the PEG, the quotient of the P/E ratio, and the earnings growth rate; in this case, analysts have adjusted the given numbers to arrive at an estimate of 2.09. Such comparative valuation ratios are used to assess the valuation of one firm versus others in the same industry. In the column to the right in Table 16.1 there appear some comparable ratios for the average firm in the North American gold mining industry. For example, an analyst might compare the forward price-to-earnings ratio for Kinross, 10.4, to the industry average ratio of 18.456. By comparison with this standard, Kinross appears to be relatively underpriced. The other comparisons appear to be quite favourable to Kinross. The price-to-sales ratio is useful for firms and industries that are in a start-up phase. Earnings figures for start-up firms are often negative and not reported, so analysts shift their focus from earnings per share to sales revenue per share in young industries.

The Balance Sheet Approach

Underlying all valuation approaches, there must be an appeal to the fundamental accounting relationship between total assets and liabilities. This would suggest that the book value of equity should approximate market value; yet the example shows market value at .66 times book value. Does book value represent a floor at least for market value? Apparently not, as frequently there are examples of stocks with market prices lower than book value per share.

The book value is established by applying a set of arbitrary accounting rules to spread the acquisition cost of assets over a specified number of years, whereas the market price of a stock takes account of the firm's value as a going concern. In other words, the market price reflects the present value of its expected future cash flows. It would be unusual if the market price of a stock were exactly equal to its book value.

A better measure of a floor for the stock price is the **liquidation value** per share of the firm. This represents the amount of money that could be realized by breaking up the firm, selling its assets, repaying its debt, and distributing the remainder to the shareholders. The reasoning behind this concept is that if the market price of equity drops below the liquidation value of the firm, the firm becomes attractive as a takeover target. A corporate raider would find it profitable to buy enough shares to gain control and then actually to liquidate, because the liquidation value exceeds the value of the business as a going concern.

Another measure of firm value is the **replacement cost** of its assets less its liabilities. Some analysts believe the market value of the firm cannot remain for long too far above its replacement cost because if it did, competitors would try to enter the market. The resulting competitive pressure would drive down the market value of all firms until they fell to replacement cost.

This idea is popular among economists, and the ratio of market price to replacement cost is known as **Tobin's q**, after the Nobel Prize–winning economist James Tobin. In the long run, according to this view, the ratio of market price to replacement cost will tend toward 1, but the evidence is that this ratio can differ significantly from 1 for very long periods of time.

A market valuation model accepts the accounting relationship as implicitly recognized by investors. They can proceed from the balance sheet and calculate the market value of equity as the present value of net operating revenues (after tax), less the market value of any debt claims; the latter value is itself a discounted valuation of the cash flows to the liabilities. Or they can find equity value by discounting net cash flows available to equityholders, after subtracting debt payments from operating revenues. (We have ignored noncash items such as depreciation in talking about revenues and cash flows.)

Assessment of the value of the equity of a going concern is based on the return that a stock-holder expects to receive, namely cash dividends and capital gains or losses. Assume that an investor will hold one share of ABC stock for a year, at the end of which is expected a dividend $E(D_1)$ of $4; suppose also that the forecast price at that time will be $E(P_1) = 52, with the current price being $P_0 = 48. The *expected* holding-period return is $E(D_1)$ plus the expected price appreciation, $E(P_1) - P_0$, all divided by the current price, P_0:

$$\text{Expected HPR} = E(r) = \frac{E(D_1) + [E(P_1) - P_0]}{P_0}$$

$$= \frac{4 + (52 - 48)}{48} = .167, \text{ or } 16.7\%$$

Thus, the stock's expected holding-period return is the sum of the expected dividend yield, $E(D_1)/P_0$, and the expected rate of price appreciation, the capital gains yield, $[E(P_1) - P_0]/P_0$.

But what is the required rate of return for ABC stock? We know from the CAPM that when stock market prices are at equilibrium levels, the rate of return that investors can expect to earn on a security is $r_f + \beta [E(r_M) - r_f]$. Thus, the CAPM may be viewed as providing the rate of return an investor can expect to earn on a security given its risk as measured by beta. This is the return that investors will require of any other investment with equivalent risk. We will denote this required rate of return as k. If a stock is priced "correctly," its *expected* return will equal the *required* return. Of course, the goal of a security analyst is to find stocks that are mispriced. For example, an underpriced stock will provide an expected return greater than the "fair," or required, return.

Suppose that $r_f = 6\%$, $E(r_M) - r_f = 5\%$, and the beta of ABC is 1.2. Then the value of k is

$$k = 6\% + 1.2 \times 5\% = 12\%$$

The rate of return the investor expects exceeds the required rate based on ABC's risk by a margin of 4.7 percent. Naturally, the investor will want to include more of ABC stock in the port-folio than a passive strategy would indicate.

16.2 INTRINSIC VALUE VERSUS MARKET PRICE

Another way to see this is to compare the intrinsic value of a share of stock to its market price. The **intrinsic value**, denoted V_0, of a share of stock is defined as the present value of all cash payments to the investor in the stock, including dividends as well as the proceeds from the ulti-mate sale of the stock, discounted at the appropriate risk-adjusted interest rate, k. Whenever the intrinsic value, or the investor's own estimate of what the stock is really worth, exceeds the mar-ket price, the stock is considered undervalued and a good investment. In the case of ABC, using a one-year investment horizon and a forecast that the stock can be sold at the end of the year at price $P_1 = 52, the intrinsic value is

$$V_0 = \frac{E(D_1) + E(P_1)}{1 + k} = \frac{\$4 + \$52}{1.12} = \$50$$

Equivalently, at a price of $50, the investor would derive a 12 percent rate of return—just equal to the required rate of return—on an investment in the stock. However, at the current price of $48, the stock is underpriced compared to intrinsic value. At this price, it provides better than a fair rate of return relative to its risk. In other words, using the terminology of the CAPM, it is a positive-alpha stock, and investors will want to buy more of it than they would following a passive strategy.

In market equilibrium, the current market price will reflect the intrinsic value estimates of all market participants. This means the individual investor whose V_0 estimate differs from the market price, P_0, in effect must disagree with some or all of the market consensus estimates of $E(D_1)$, $E(P_1)$, or k. A common term for the market consensus value of the required rate of return, k, is the **market capitalization rate**, which we use often throughout this chapter.

The aggregate equity value is the product of the number of shares times the price determined in the market. The total of dividends paid to shareholders comes from the cash flows earned by the firm, after the payment of interest and retained earnings for future growth. In the balance sheet, the sum of the equity value and the liabilities must be the value of total assets, which is the present value of the cash flows derived from the firm's operation of its assets.

To extend the preceding example to the firm level, let's assume that there are one million shares of ABC stock trading at $50 per share and $25 million ($B$) of 10 percent coupon perpetual debt, with no income tax and no depreciation. ABC is a no-growth firm and investors want a 12 percent rate of return on investment. The dividend per share of D each year must be $k = 12$ percent times the share price ($P = \$50$). Total dividend payments ($n \times D$) are the residual of operating income (OI) less interest payments ($I = 10\% \times \$25$ million); hence, reversing the process, we can conclude that operating income in millions is

$$\text{OI} = I + n \times D = \$2.5 + 1 \times .12 \times \$50 = \$8.5 \text{ (million)}$$

Therefore, $8.5 million of earnings are generated by the assets of the firm, which must be worth $75 million; we recognize this by observing the share price and using the balance sheet equation:

$$V = B + S = B + n \times P = \$25 + 1 \times \$50 = \$75 \text{ (million)}$$

In arriving at the price $P = \$50$, the market must have predicted operating earnings of $8.5 million and subtracted interest payments to get net income of $6 million, or $6 per share. Alternatively, we can capitalize operating income, estimated as $8.5 million, at an overall cost of $11\frac{1}{3}$ percent (the weighted average cost of capital) to find asset value of $75 million. Subtracting the debt of $25 million and dividing by the number of shares, we derive the share price of $50. In a simplified way, this is what analysts must do: estimate earnings, determine cash flows to equity, and capitalize them. As we shall see, a more realistic case would also require an estimate of growth in earnings.

In a perfect and simple economic setting, we might expect all of these accounting-based and market values to be about the same. Realistic depreciation rules applied to assets bought at competitive prices should yield values that equate to replacement values; and in a competitive environment, this also would equal capitalized values of earnings from those assets. In reality, market prices will differ from simple accounting-based values. Understanding why these differences occur is part of the analyst's job.

CC 1

CONCEPT CHECK

You expect the price of IBX stock to be $59.77 per share a year from now. Its current market price is $50, and you expect it to pay a dividend one year from now of $2.15 a share.

a. What is the stock's expected dividend yield, rate of price appreciation, and holding-period return?

b. If the stock has a beta of 1.15, the risk-free rate is 6 percent per year, and the expected rate of return on the market portfolio is 14 percent per year, what is the required rate of return on IBX stock?

c. What is the intrinsic value of IBX stock, and how does it compare to the current market price?

d. If there are one million shares and debt is $20 million paying 8 percent, what are the operating earnings and the value?

16.3   DIVIDEND DISCOUNT MODELS

Elementary financial mathematics provides us with some simple formulas for the value of the share price based on cash flows.[1] Under the **dividend discount model (DDM)**, we can consider the infinite flow of dividends or the payment of a dividend and sale of the share at the end of a single period; these can be shown to be consistent. Thus, for a stream of dividends D_t, a discount rate k, and future price P_1, we see that

$$V_0 = \frac{D_1}{1 + k} + \frac{D_2}{(1 + k)^2} + \frac{D_3}{(1 + k)^3} + \cdots = \frac{D_1 + P_1}{1 + k} \tag{16.1}$$

This model appears to give problems in the case of a company paying no dividends; but either the company will eventually decide to pay dividends—even a single liquidating dividend—or it never will and its value will be zero. Predicting an infinite stream of dividends could be challenging, and that is still needed in order to calculate P_1 recursively from future dividends; consequently, we usually move to a model for some growth pattern in dividends.

The basic model is known as the **constant-growth DDM** or the *Gordon model*, after its formulator, Myron J. Gordon. A constant growth rate in dividends, g, leads to the simple formula for the *intrinsic value*

$$V_0 = \frac{D_1}{k - g} \tag{16.2}$$

EXAMPLE 16.1   Valuation with the Constant-Growth DDM

High Flyer Industries has just paid its annual dividend of $3 per share. The dividend is expected to grow at a constant rate of 8 percent indefinitely. The beta of High Flyer stock is 1.0, the risk-free rate is 6 percent, and the market risk premium is 8 percent. What is the *intrinsic* value of the stock? What would be your estimate of intrinsic value if you believed that the stock was riskier, with a beta of 1.25?

Because a $3 dividend has just been paid and the growth rate of dividends is 8 percent, the forecast for the year-end dividend is $3 \times 1.08 = \$3.24$. The market capitalization rate according to the CAPM is $6\% + 1.0 \times 8\% = 14$ percent. Therefore, the value of the stock is

$$V_0 = \frac{D_1}{k - g} = \$3.24/(.14 - .08) = \$54$$

If the stock is perceived to be riskier, its value must be lower. At the higher beta, the market capitalization rate is $6\% + 1.25 \times 8\% = 16$ percent, and the stock is worth only $3.24/(.16 − .08) = \$40.50$.

When the market price, P_0, is presumed to be the value, equation 16.2 can be inverted to yield the intuitive result

$$E(r) = k = \frac{D_1}{P_0} + g \tag{16.3}$$

which states that the required return equals the current dividend yield plus the capital gain (the growth in the price). By observing the dividend yield, D_1/P_0, and estimating the growth rate of

---

[1]These elementary results are derived in standard corporation finance texts; for those not familiar with them or those needing a review, Appendix 16A to this chapter gives the details.

dividends, we can compute k. This equation is also known as the *discounted cash flow (DCF) formula*. This model also predicts that, for any time t, $P_t = (1 + g)P_{t-1}$; furthermore, $P_t + D_t = (1 + k)P_{t-1}$ (i.e., the return is always expected to be k).

This is an approach often used in rate hearings for regulated public utilities. The regulatory agency responsible for approving utility pricing decisions is mandated to allow the firms to charge just enough to cover costs plus a "fair" profit, that is, one that allows a competitive return on the investment the firm has made in its productive capacity. In turn, that return is taken to be the expected return investors require on the stock of the firm. The $D_1/P_0 + g$ formula provides a means to infer that required return.

The analyst or investor using this formula again must escape the circularity trap if an investment opportunity is to be found. Given the market price and a consensus on k, we infer the presumed growth rate. Analysis of financial results and market conditions may lead to the conclusion of a higher growth rate than implied by price. If the assumed k is accepted, then equation 16.2 will lead to a higher price estimate and a buy recommendation. By contrast, acceptance of the growth rate, combined with a feeling that the risk assessment implied by the discount rate k is too low, would imply that the price is too high, with sale recommended.

Convergence of Price to Intrinsic Value

Suppose that the current market price of ABC stock is only $48 per share and you estimate the true value is $50 with a growth rate of $g = 4$ percent. In this case the expected rate of price appreciation depends on an additional assumption about whether the discrepancy between the intrinsic value and the market price will disappear, and if so, when.

One fairly common assumption is that the discrepancy will never disappear and that the market price will trend upward at rate g forever. This implies that the discrepancy between intrinsic value and market price also will grow at the same rate. In our example:

Now	Next Year
$V_0 = \$50$	$V_1 = 50 \times 1.04 = \$52$
$P_0 = \$48$	$P_1 = \$48 \times 1.04 = \$49.92$
$V_0 - P_0 = \$2$	$V_1 - P_1 = \$2 \times 1.04 = \$2.08$

Under this assumption the expected HPR will exceed the required rate, because the dividend yield is higher than it would be if P_0 were equal to V_0. In our example the dividend yield would be 8.33 percent instead of 8 percent, so that the expected HPR would be 12.33 percent rather than 12 percent:

$$E(r) = D_1/P_0 + g = \$4/\$48 + .04 = .0833 + .04 = .1233$$

An investor who identifies this undervalued stock can get an expected dividend that exceeds the required yield by 33 basis points. This excess return is earned *each year*, and the market price never catches up to intrinsic value.

An alternative assumption is that the gap between market price and intrinsic value will disappear by the end of the year. In that case we would have

$$P_1 = V_1 = \$52, \text{ and } E(r) = D_1/P_0 + (P_1 - P_0)/P_0$$
$$= 4/48 + (52 - 48)/48 = .0833 + .0833 = .1667$$

The assumption of complete catch-up to intrinsic value produces a much larger one-year HPR. In future years, however, the stock is expected to generate only fair rates of return. Many stock analysts assume that a stock's price will approach its intrinsic value gradually over time—for example, over a five-year period. This puts their expected one-year HPR somewhere between the bounds of 12.33 and 16.67 percent.

Stock Prices and Investment Opportunities

The major practical issue in evaluating stocks is forecasting the cash flows. Generally firms expand, leading to growth in sales, earnings, and dividends. As we develop this issue, let us start with a simple case that illustrates the growth issue.

Consider two companies, Cash Cow and Prospects, each with expected earnings in the coming year of $5 per share. Both companies could in principle pay out all of these earnings as dividends, maintaining a perpetual dividend flow of $5 per share. If the market capitalization rate were $k = 12.5$ percent, both companies would then be valued at $D_1/k = \$5/.125 = \$40$ per share. Neither firm would grow in value, because with all earnings paid out as dividends, and no earnings reinvested in the firm, both companies' capital stock and earnings capacity would remain unchanged over time; earnings and dividends would not grow.

Actually, we are referring here to earnings net of the funds necessary to maintain the productivity of the firm's capital, that is, earnings net of "economic depreciation." In other words, the earnings figure should be interpreted as the maximum amount of money the firm could pay out each year in perpetuity without depleting its productive capacity. For this reason, the net earnings number may be quite different from the accounting earnings figure that the firm reports in its financial statements. (We explore this further in the next chapter.)

Now suppose one of the firms, Prospects, engages in projects that generate a return on investment of 15 percent, which is greater than the required rate of return, $k = 12.5$ percent. It would be foolish for such a company to pay out all of its earnings as dividends. If Prospects retains or plows back some of its earnings into its highly profitable projects, it can earn a 15 percent rate of return for its shareholders, whereas if it pays out all earnings as dividends, it forgoes the projects, leaving shareholders to invest the dividends in other opportunities at a fair market rate of only 12.5 percent. Suppose, therefore, that Prospects lowers its **dividend payout ratio** (the fraction of earnings paid out as dividends) from 100 percent to 40 percent, maintaining a **plowback ratio** (the fraction of earnings reinvested in the firm) at 60 percent. The plowback ratio is also referred to as the **earnings retention ratio**.

The dividend of the company, therefore, will be $2 (40 percent of $5 earnings) instead of $5. Will share price fall? No—it will rise! Although dividends initially fall under the earnings reinvestment policy, subsequent growth in the assets of the firm because of reinvested profits will generate growth in future dividends, which will be reflected in today's share price.

Figure 16.1 illustrates the dividend streams generated by Prospects under two dividend policies. A low-investment-rate plan allows the firm to pay higher initial dividends, but results in a lower dividend growth rate. Eventually, a high-reinvestment-rate plan will provide higher dividends.

Figure 16.1

Dividend growth for two earnings reinvestment policies.

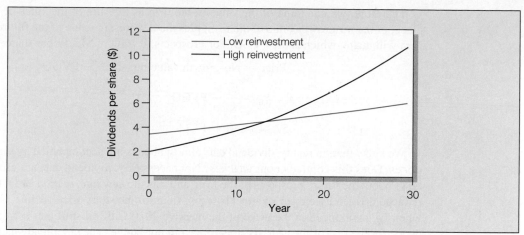

If the dividend growth generated by the reinvested earnings is high enough, the stock will be worth more under the high-reinvestment strategy.

How much growth will be generated? Suppose Prospects starts with plant and equipment of $100 million and is all equity-financed. With a return on investment or equity (ROE) of 15 percent, total earnings are ROE × $100 million = .15 × $100 million = $15 million. There are 3 million shares of stock outstanding, so earnings per share are $5, as posited above. If 60 percent of the $15 million in this year's earnings is reinvested, then the value of the firm's capital stock will increase by .60 × $15 million = $9 million, or by 9 percent. The percentage increase in the capital stock is the rate at which income was generated (ROE) times the plowback ratio (the fraction of earnings reinvested in more capital), which we will denote b.

Now endowed with 9 percent more capital, the company earns 9 percent more income, and pays out 9 percent higher dividends. The growth rate of the dividends, therefore, is[2]

$$g = ROE \times b = .15 \times .60 = .09$$

If the stock price equals its intrinsic value, it should sell at

$$P_0 = \frac{D_1}{k - g} = \frac{\$2}{.125 - .09} = \$57.14$$

When Prospects pursued a no-growth policy and paid out all earnings as dividends, the stock price was only $40. Therefore, you can think of $40 as the value per share of the assets the company already has in place.

When Prospects decided to reduce current dividends and reinvest some of its earnings in new investments, its stock price increased. The increase in the stock price reflects the fact that the planned investments provide an expected rate of return greater than the required rate. In other words, the investment opportunities have positive net present value. The value of the firm rises by the NPV of these investment opportunities. This net present value is also called the **present value of growth opportunities**, or **PVGO**.

---

[2]We can derive this relationship more generally by noting that with a fixed ROE, earnings (which equal ROE × book value) will grow at the same rate as the book value of the firm. Abstracting from issuance of new shares of stock, we find the growth rate of book value equals reinvested earnings/book value. Therefore,

$$g = \frac{\text{Reinvested earnings}}{\text{Book value}} = \frac{\text{Reinvested earnings}}{\text{Total earnings}} \times \frac{\text{Total earnings}}{\text{Book value}} = b \times ROE$$

Therefore, we can think of the value of the firm as the sum of the value of assets already in place, or the no-growth value of the firm, plus the net present value of the future investments the firm will make, which is the PVGO. For Prospects, PVGO = $17.14 per share:

$$\text{Price} = \text{No-growth value per share} + \text{PVGO} \qquad (16.4)$$

$$P_0 = \frac{E_1}{k} + \text{PVGO}$$

$$57.14 = 40 + 17.14$$

We know that, in reality, dividend cuts almost always are accompanied by steep drops in stock prices. Does this contradict our analysis? Not necessarily: dividend cuts are usually taken as bad news about the future prospects of the firm, and it is the *new information* about the firm—not the reduced dividend yield per se—that is responsible for the stock price decline. On the other hand, when BP announced in the wake of the massive 2010 Gulf oil spill that it would suspend dividends for the rest of the year, its stock price did not budge. The cut already had been widely anticipated, so it was not new information.

It is important to recognize that growth per se is not what investors desire. Growth enhances company value only if it is achieved by investment in projects with attractive profit opportunities (i.e., with ROE > k). To see why, let's now consider Prospects' unfortunate sister company, Cash Cow, Inc. Cash Cow's ROE is only 12.5 percent, just equal to the required rate of return, k. The net present value of its investment opportunities is zero. We've seen that following a zero-growth strategy with b = 0 and g = 0, the value of Cash Cow will be $E_1/k = \$5/.125 = \$40$ per share. Now suppose Cash Cow chooses a plowback ratio of b = .60, the same as Prospects' plowback. Then g would increase to

$$g = \text{ROE} \times b = .125 \times .60 = .075$$

but the stock price is still

$$P_0 = \frac{D_1}{k - g} = \frac{\$2}{.125 - .075} = \$40$$

which is no different from the no-growth strategy.

In the case of Cash Cow, the dividend reduction used to free funds for reinvestment in the firm generates only enough growth to maintain the stock price at the current level. This is as it should be: if the firm's projects yield only what investors can earn on their own, shareholders cannot be made better off by a high-reinvestment-rate policy. This demonstrates that "growth" is not the same as growth opportunities. To justify reinvestment, the firm must engage in projects with better prospective returns than those shareholders can find elsewhere. Notice also that the PVGO of Cash Cow is zero: PVGO = $P_0 - E_1/k = 40 - 40 = 0$. With ROE = k, there is no advantage to plowing funds back into the firm; this shows up as PVGO of zero. In fact, this is why firms with considerable cash flow but limited investment prospects are called "cash cows." The cash these firms generate is best taken out of, or "milked" from, the firm.

EXAMPLE 16.2   Growth Opportunities

Takeover Target is run by entrenched management that insists on reinvesting 60 percent of its earnings in projects that provide an ROE of 10 percent, despite the fact that the firm's capitalization rate is k = 15 percent. The firm's year-end dividend will be $2 per share, paid out of earnings of $5 per share. At what price will the stock sell? What is the present value of growth opportunities? Why would such a firm be a takeover target for another firm?

continued

Given current management's investment policy, the dividend growth rate will be

$$g = \text{ROE} \times b = .10\% \times .6 = .6\%$$

and the stock price should be

$$P_0 = \frac{\$2}{.15 - .06} = \$22.22$$

The present value of growth opportunities is

$$\text{PVGO} = \text{Price per share} - \text{No-growth value per share}$$

$$= \$22.22 - E_1/k = \$22.22 - \$5/.15 = -\$11.11$$

PVGO is *negative*. This is because the net present value of the firm's projects is negative: the rate of return on those assets is less than the opportunity cost of capital.

Such a firm would be subject to takeover, because another firm could buy the firm for the market price of $22.22 per share and increase the value of the firm by changing its investment policy. For example, if the new management simply paid out all earnings as dividends, the value of the firm would increase to its no-growth value, $E_1/k = \$5/.15 = \$33.33$.

CC 3

CONCEPT CHECK

a. Calculate the price of a firm with a plowback ratio of .60 if its ROE is 20 percent. Current earnings, E_1, will be $5 per share, and $k = 12.5$ percent. Find the PVGO for this firm. Why is PVGO so high?

b. Suppose ROE is only 10 percent and the capitalization rate is $k = 15$ percent. At what price will the stock sell? What is the PVGO? Why would such a firm be a target for a takeover by another firm?

Life Cycles and Multistage Growth Models

As useful as the constant-growth DDM formula is, you need to remember that it is based on a simplifying assumption, namely, that the dividend growth rate will be constant forever. In fact, firms typically pass through life cycles with very different dividend profiles in different phases. In early years, there are ample opportunities for profitable reinvestment in the company. Payout ratios are low, and growth is correspondingly rapid. In later years, the firm matures, production capacity is sufficient to meet market demand, competitors enter the market, and attractive opportunities for reinvestment may become harder to find. In this mature phase, the firm may choose to increase the dividend payout ratio, rather than retain earnings. The dividend level increases, but thereafter it grows at a slower rate because of fewer growth opportunities.

Table 16.2 illustrates this pattern. It gives Value Line's forecasts of return on capital dividend payout ratio, and three-year growth rate in earnings per share of a sample of the firms included in the computer software industry versus those in the electric utility group. Note that we present data from 2007, as current data for these companies would be meaningless due to recession results; note also the forecast is meaningless in terms of actual results, but the predictions illustrate normal expectations. (We compare return on capital rather than return on equity because the latter is affected by leverage, which tends to be far greater in the electric utility industry than in the software industry. Return on capital measures operating income per dollar of total long-term financing regardless of whether the source of the capital supplied is debt or equity. We will return to this issue in the next chapter.)

By and large, the software firms as a group have had attractive investment opportunities. The median return on capital of these firms is forecast to be 16.5 percent, and the firms have

TABLE 16.2
Financial Ratios in
Two Industries

	Ticker	Return on Capital	Payout Ratio (%)	Growth Rate 2014–2016
Computer Software				
Adobe Systems	ADBE	12.0	0	13.2%
Cognizant	CTSH	18.5	0	20.5%
Compuware	CPWR	13.5	0	16.6%
Intuit	INTU	20.0	22	10.9%
Microsoft	MSFT	31.5	34	11.7%
Oracle	ORCL	20.5	12	7.0%
Red Hat	RHT	13.0	0	18.2%
Parametric Tech	PMTC	15.0	0	16.0%
SAP	SAP	16.5	28	9.1%
Median		16.5%	0%	13.2%
Electric Utilities (East Coast)				
Central Hudson G&E	CHG	6.0	66	2.0%
Consolidated Edison	ED	6.5	58	2.9%
Duke Energy	DUK	5.5	66	4.0%
Northeast Utilities	NU	6.0	53	7.7%
Pennsylvania Power	PPL	7.0	58	7.7%
Public Service Enterprise	PEG	7.5	53	6.3%
South Carolina E & G	SCG	6.0	57	3.8%
Southern Company	SO	7.0	69	5.1%
Tampa Electric	TE	7.5	59	8.3%
United Illuminating	UIL	6.0	71	2.1%
Median		6.3%	58.5%	4.5%

Source: Value Line Investment Survey, July and August, 2012. Reprinted with permission of Value Line Investment Survey. © 2012 Value Line Publishing, Inc. All rights reserved.

responded with high plowback ratios. Many of these firms pay no dividends at all. The high return on capital and high plowback result in rapid growth. The median growth rate of earnings per share in this group is projected at 13.2 percent.

In contrast, the electric utilities are more representative of mature firms. Their return on capital is lower, 6.3 percent; dividend payout is higher, 58.5 percent; and median growth rate is lower 4.5 percent. We conclude that the higher payouts of the electric utilities reflect their more limited opportunities to reinvest earnings at attractive rates of return. Consistently with this view, Apple's announcement in 2013 that it would sharply increase its dividend and initiate multibillion-dollar stock buybacks was widely seen as an indication that the firm was maturing into a lower-growth stage. It was generating far more cash than it had the opportunity to invest attractively, and so was paying out that cash to its shareholders.

To value companies with temporarily high growth, analysts use a multistage version of the dividend discount model. Dividends in the early high-growth period are forecast and their combined present value is calculated. Then, once the firm is projected to settle down to a steady-growth phase, the constant-growth DDM is applied to value the remaining stream of dividends.

We can illustrate this with a real-life example. Figure 16.2 is a Value Line Investment Survey report on Honda Motor Co. Some of the relevant information for 2012 is labelled.

Figure 16.2   Value Line Investment Survey report on Honda Motor Co.

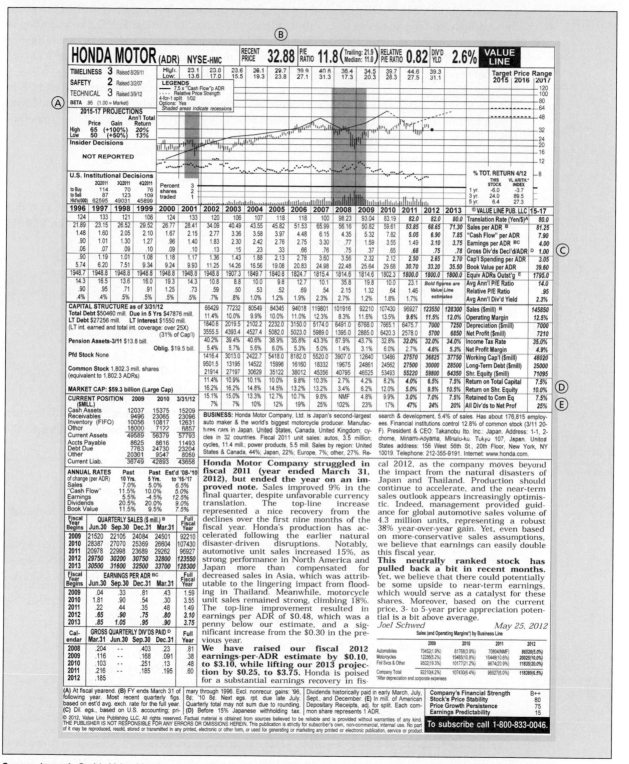

Source: Jason A. Smith, Value Line Investment Survey, May 25, 2012. Reprinted with permission of Value Line Investment Survey © 2012 Value Line Publishing, Inc. All rights reserved.

Honda's beta appears at the circled A, its recent stock price at the B, the per-share dividend payments at the C, the ROE (referred to as "return on shareholder equity") at the D, and the dividend payout ratio (referred to as "all dividends to net profits") at the E.[3] The rows ending at C, D, and E are historical time series. The boldfaced, italicized entries under 2013 are estimates for that year. Similarly, the entries in the far right column (labelled 15–17) are forecasts for some time between 2015 and 2017, which we will take to be 2016.

Value Line projects fairly rapid growth in the near term, with dividends rising from $.78 in 2013 to $1.00 in 2016. This growth rate cannot be sustained indefinitely. We can obtain dividend inputs for this initial period by using the explicit forecasts for 2013 and 2016 and linear interpolation for the years between:

| 2013 | $.78 | 2015 | $ .92 |
| 2014 | $.85 | 2016 | $1.00 |

Now let us assume the dividend growth rate levels off in 2016. What is a good guess for that steady-state growth rate? Value Line forecasts a dividend payout ratio of .25 and an ROE of 10 percent, implying long-term growth will be

$$g = \text{ROE} \times b = 10.0\% \times (1 - .25) = 7.5\%$$

Our estimate of Honda's intrinsic value using an investment horizon of 2016 is therefore obtained from equation 16.1, which we restate here:

$$V_{2012} = \frac{D_{2013}}{1 + k} + \frac{D_{2014}}{(1 + k)^2} + \frac{D_{2015}}{(1 + k)^3} + \frac{D_{2016} + P_{2016}}{(1 + k)^4}$$

$$= \frac{.78}{1 + k} + \frac{.85}{(1 + k)^2} + \frac{.92}{(1 + k)^3} + \frac{1.00 + P_{2016}}{(1 + k)^4}$$

Here, P_{2016} represents the forecast price at which we can sell our shares at the end of 2016, when dividends are assumed to enter their constant-growth phase. That price, according to the constant-growth DDM, should be

$$P_{2016} = \frac{D_{2017}}{k - g} = \frac{D_{2016}(1 + g)}{k - g} = \frac{1.00 \times 1.075}{k - .075}$$

The only variable remaining to be determined to calculate intrinsic value is the market capitalization rate, k.

One way to obtain k is from the CAPM. Observe from the Value Line report that Honda's beta is .95. The risk-free rate on long-term Treasury bonds in 2012 was about 2.0 percent.[4] Suppose that the market risk premium were forecast at 8 percent, roughly in line with its historical average. This would imply that the forecast for the market return was

$$\text{Risk-free rate} + \text{Market risk premium} = 2\% + 8\% = 10\%$$

Therefore, we can solve for the market capitalization rate as

$$k = r_f + \beta[E(r_M) - r_f] = 2\% + .95(10\% - 2\%) = 9.6\%$$

---

[3]Because Honda is a Japanese firm, Canadians (and Americans) would hold its shares via ADRs, or American Depository Receipts. ADRs are not shares of the firm, but are *claims* to shares of the underlying foreign stock that are then traded in U.S. security markets. Value Line notes that each Honda ADR is a claim on one common share, but in other cases, each ADR may represent a claim to multiple shares or even fractional shares.

[4]When valuing long-term assets such as stocks, it is common to treat the long-term Treasury bond, rather than short-term T-bills, as the risk-free asset.

Our forecast for the stock price in 2016 is thus

$$P_{2016} = \frac{\$1.00 \times 1.075}{.096 - .075} = \$51.19$$

And today's estimate of intrinsic value is

$$V_{2012} = \frac{.78}{1.096} + \frac{.85}{(1.096)^2} + \frac{.92}{(1.096)^3} + \frac{1.00 + 51.19}{(1.096)^4} = \$38.29$$

We know from the Value Line report that Honda's actual price was $32.88 (at the circled B). Our intrinsic value analysis indicates that the stock was underpriced. Should we increase our holdings?

Perhaps. But before betting the farm, stop to consider how firm our estimate is. We've had to guess at dividends in the near future, the ultimate growth rate of those dividends, and the appropriate discount rate. Moreover, we've assumed Honda will follow a relatively simple two-stage growth process. In practice, the growth of dividends can follow more complicated patterns. Even small errors in these approximations could upset a conclusion.

For example, suppose that we have overestimated Honda's growth prospects and that the actual ROE in the post-2016 period will be 9 percent rather than 10 percent. Using the lower return on equity in the dividend discount model would result in an intrinsic value in 2012 of only $28.77, which is *less* than the stock price. Our conclusion regarding intrinsic value versus price is reversed.

The exercise also highlights the importance of performing sensitivity analysis when you attempt to value stocks. Your estimates of stock values are no better than your assumptions. Sensitivity analysis will highlight the inputs that need to be most carefully examined. For example, even modest changes in the estimated ROE for the post-2016 period can result in big changes in intrinsic value. Similarly, small changes in the assumed capitalization rate would change intrinsic value substantially. On the other hand, reasonable changes in the dividends forecast between 2013 and 2016 would have a small impact on intrinsic value.

CC 4

CONCEPT CHECK

Confirm that the intrinsic value of Honda using ROE = 9% is $28.77. (*Hint:* First calculate the stock price in 2016. Then calculate the present value of all interim dividends plus the present value of the 2016 sales price.)

Multistage Growth Models

The two-stage growth model that we just considered for Honda is a good start toward realism, but clearly we could do even better if our valuation model allowed for more-flexible patterns of growth. Multistage growth models allow dividends per share to grow at several different rates as the firm matures. Many analysts use three-stage growth models. They may assume an initial period of high dividend growth (or instead make year-by-year forecasts of dividends for the short term), a final period of sustainable growth, and a transition period between, during which dividend growth rates taper off from the initial rapid rate to the ultimate sustainable rate. These models are conceptually no harder to work with than a two-stage model, but they require many more calculations and can be tedious to do by hand. It is easy, however, to build an Excel spreadsheet for such a model.

Spreadsheet 16.1 is an example of such a model. Column B contains the inputs we have used so far for Honda. Column E contains dividend forecasts. In cells E2 through E5 we present the Value Line estimates for the next four years. Dividend growth in this period is about 8.6 percent

EXCEL SPREADSHEET 16.1 📐

A three-stage growth model for Honda.

	A	B	C	D	E	F	G	H	I
1	Inputs			Year	Dividend	Div growth	Term value	Investor CF	
2	beta	0.95		2012	0.78			0.78	
3	mkt_prem	0.08		2013	0.85			0.85	
4	rf	0.02		2014	0.92			0.92	
5	k_equity	0.0960		2015	1.00			1.00	
6	plowback	0.75		2016	1.09	0.0863		1.09	
7	roe	0.1		2017	1.18	0.0852		1.18	
8	term_gwth	0.075		2018	1.28	0.0841		1.28	
9				2019	1.38	0.0829		1.38	
10				2020	1.50	0.0818		1.50	
11				2021	1.62	0.0807		1.62	
12	Value line			2022	1.75	0.0795		1.75	
13	forecasts of			2023	1.88	0.0784		1.88	
14	annual dividends			2024	2.03	0.0773		2.03	
15				2025	2.18	0.0761		2.18	
16				2026	2.35	0.0750		2.35	
17	Transitional period			2027	2.52	0.0750	129.18	131.71	
18	with slowing dividend								
19	growth							40.29	= PV of CF
20		Beginning of constant-			E17*(1+F17)/(B5−F17)				
21		growth period						NPV(B5,H2:H17)	

annually. Rather than assume a sudden transition to constant dividend growth starting in 2016, we assume instead that the dividend growth rate in 2016 will be 8.6 percent and that it will decline steadily through 2027, finally reaching the constant terminal growth rate of 7.5 percent (see column F). Each dividend in the transition period is the previous year's dividend times that year's growth rate. Terminal value once the firm enters a constant-growth stage (cell G17) is computed from the constant-growth DDM. Finally, investor cash flow in each period (column H) equals dividends in each year plus the terminal value in 2027. The present value of these cash flows is computed in cell H19 as $40.29, about 5 percent higher than the value we found from the two-stage model. We obtain a greater intrinsic value in this case because we assume that dividend growth only gradually declines to its steady-state value.

16.4 EARNINGS, GROWTH, AND PRICE-EARNINGS RATIOS

Much of the real-world discussion of stock market valuation concentrates on the firm's **price-earnings multiple**, the ratio of price per share to earnings per share, commonly called the P/E ratio.

Our discussion of growth opportunities shows why stock market analysts focus on the P/E ratio. Both companies considered, Cash Cow and Prospects, had earnings per share (EPS) of $5, but Prospects reinvested 60 percent of earnings in prospects with an ROE of 15 percent, whereas Cash Cow paid out all earnings as dividends. Cash Cow had a price of $40, giving it a P/E multiple of 40/5 = 8.0, whereas Prospects sold for $57.14, giving it a multiple of 57.14/5 = 11.4. This observation suggests the P/E ratio might serve as a useful indicator of expectations of growth opportunities. We can see this explicitly by rearranging equation 16.4 to

$$\frac{P_0}{E_1} = \frac{1}{k}\left(1 + \frac{\text{PVGO}}{E/k}\right) \tag{16.5}$$

When PVGO = 0, this equation shows that $P_0 = E_1/k$. The stock is valued like a non-growing perpetuity of EPS_1. The P/E ratio is just $1/k$. However, as PVGO becomes an increasingly dominant contributor to price, the P/E ratio can rise dramatically.

The ratio of PVGO to E/k has a straightforward interpretation. It is the ratio of the component of firm value due to growth opportunities to the component of value due to assets already in place (i.e., the no-growth value of the firm, E/k). When future growth opportunities dominate the estimate of total value, the firm will command a high price relative to current earnings. Thus a high P/E multiple appears to indicate a firm is endowed with ample growth opportunities.

Let's see if P/E multiples do vary with growth prospects. Consider CNQ and Magna International (an auto parts manufacturer). Between 1991 and 2012, CNQ's P/E ratio averaged about 18 while Magna's average P/E was only about two-thirds that. These numbers do not necessarily imply that CNQ was overpriced compared to Magna. If investors believed CNQ would grow faster than Magna, the higher price per dollar of earnings would be justified. That is, an investor might well pay a higher price per dollar of *current* earnings if he or she expects that earnings stream to grow more rapidly. In fact, CNQ's growth rate has been consistent with its higher P/E multiple. Between 1999 and 2012, its earnings per share grew at about 16 percent per year, while Magna's earnings had a rate of 8 percent; 2008 and 2009 results were off trend. Figure 16.3 shows the EPS history of the two companies.

Clearly, it is differences in expected growth opportunities that justify particular differentials in P/E ratios across firms. We conclude that the P/E ratio reflects the market's optimism concerning a firm's growth prospects. Analysts must decide whether they are more or less optimistic than the belief implied by the market multiple. If they are more optimistic, they will recommend buying the stock.

There is a way to make these insights more precise. Look again at the constant-growth DDM formula, $P_0 = D_1/(k - g)$. Now recall that dividends equal the earnings that are *not* reinvested in the firm: $D_1 = E_1(1 - b)$. Recall also that $g = \text{ROE} \times b$. Hence, substituting for D_1 and g, we find that

$$P_0 = \frac{E_1(1 - b)}{k - \text{ROE} \times b}$$

implying the P/E ratio is

$$\frac{P_0}{E_1} = \frac{1 - b}{k - \text{ROE} \times b} \qquad (16.6)$$

Figure 16.3

Earnings growth for two companies.

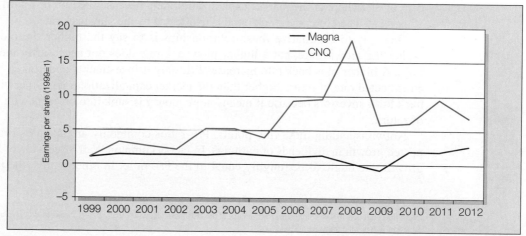

TABLE 16.3

Effect of ROE and Plowback on Growth and the P/E Ratio

	Plowback Rate (*b*)			
	0	.25	.50	.75
ROE (%)		**A. Growth rate, *g* (%)**		
10	0	2.5%	5.0%	7.5%
12	0	3.0	6.0	9.0
14	0	3.5	7.0	10.5
		B. P/E ratio (%)		
10	8.33	7.89	7.14	5.56
12	8.33	8.33	8.33	8.33
14	8.33	8.82	10.00	16.67

Note: Assumption: $k = 12\%$ per year.

It is easy to verify that the P/E ratio increases with ROE. This makes sense, because high-ROE projects give the firm good opportunities for growth.[5] We also can verify that the P/E ratio increases for higher b as long as ROE exceeds k. This too makes sense. When a firm has good investment opportunities, the market will reward it with a higher P/E multiple if it exploits those opportunities more aggressively by plowing back more earnings into those opportunities.

Remember, however, that growth is not desirable for its own sake. Examine Table 16.3, where we use equation 16.6 to compute both growth rates and P/E ratios for different combinations of ROE and b. Although growth always increases with the plowback rate (move across the rows in Table 16.3, panel A), the P/E ratio does not (move across the rows in panel B). In the top row of panel B, the P/E falls as the plowback rate increases. In the middle row, it is unaffected by plowback. In the third row, it increases.

This pattern has a simple interpretation. When the expected ROE is less than the required return, k, investors prefer that the firm pay out earnings as dividends rather than reinvest earnings in the firm at an inadequate rate of return. That is, for ROE lower than k, the value of the firm falls as plowback increases. Conversely, when ROE exceeds k, the firm offers attractive investment opportunities, so the value of the firm is enhanced as those opportunities are more fully exploited by increasing the plowback rate.

Finally, where ROE just equals k, the firm offers "breakeven" investment opportunities with a fair rate of return. In this case, investors are indifferent between reinvestment of earnings in the firm or elsewhere at the market capitalization rate, because the rate of return in either case is 12 percent. Therefore, the stock price is unaffected by the plowback rate.

One way to summarize these relationships is to say the higher the plowback rate, the higher the growth rate, but a higher plowback rate does not necessarily mean a higher P/E ratio. A higher plowback rate increases P/E only if investments undertaken by the firm offer an expected rate of return higher than the market capitalization rate. Otherwise, higher plowback hurts investors because it means more money is sunk into projects with inadequate rates of return.

Notwithstanding these fine points, P/E ratios commonly are taken as proxies for the expected growth in dividends or earnings. In fact, a common Wall Street rule of thumb is that the growth rate ought to be roughly equal to the P/E ratio. In other words, the ratio of P/E to g,

---

[5]Note that equation 16.6 is a simple rearrangement of the DDM formula, with ROE $\times$ b = g. Because that formula requires that $g < k$, equation 16.6 is valid only when ROE $\times$ $b < k$.

often called the *PEG ratio*, should be about 1.0. Peter Lynch, the famous portfolio manager, puts it this way in his book *One Up on Wall Street* (p. 198):

> The P/E ratio of any company that's fairly priced will equal its growth rate. I'm talking here about growth rate of earnings here. . . . If the P/E ratio of Coca Cola is 15, you'd expect the company to be growing at about 15% per year, etc. But if the P/E ratio is less than the growth rate, you may have found yourself a bargain.

EXAMPLE 16.3   P/E Ratio Versus Growth Rate

Let's try Lynch's rule of thumb. Assume

$r_f = 8\%$ (Roughly the value when Peter Lynch was writing)
$r_M - r_f = 8\%$ (About the historical average market risk premium)
$b = .4$ (A typical value for the plowback ratio in the United States)

Therefore, $r_M = r_f +$ market risk premium $= 8\% + 8\% = 16$ percent, and $k = 16$ percent for an average ($\beta = 1$) company. If we also accept as reasonable that ROE $= 16$ percent (the same value as the expected return on the stock), we conclude that

$$g = \text{ROE} \times b = 16\% \times .4 = 6.4\%$$

and

$$\frac{P}{E} = \frac{1 - .4}{.16 - .064} = 6.25$$

Thus the P/E ratio and g are about equal using these assumptions, which obeys the rule of thumb.

However, note that this rule of thumb, like almost all others, will not work in all circumstances. For example, the value of r_f today is more like 2 percent, so a comparable forecast of r_M today would be

$$r_f + \text{Market risk premium} = 2\% + 8\% = 10\%$$

If we continue to focus on a firm with $\beta = 1$, and if ROE still is about the same as k, then

$$g = 10\% \times .4 = 4.0\%$$

while

$$\text{P/E} = (1 - .4)/(.10 - .04) = 10$$

The P/E ratio and g now diverge and the PEG ratio is now 2.5. In fact, the P/E $= g$ rule can only apply when they are close and moderate; a look at *P/E* $= 2$ or 200 will illustrate. Nevertheless, it still is the case that high P/E stocks are almost invariably expected to show rapid earnings growth, even if the expected growth rate does not equal the P/E ratio.

The importance of growth opportunities is nowhere more evident than in the valuation of start-up firms. For example, in the dot-com boom of the late 1990s, many companies that had yet to turn a profit were valued by the market at billions of dollars. The perceived value of these companies was *exclusively* as growth opportunities. For example, the online auction firm eBay had 1998 profits of $2.4 million, far less than the $45 million profit earned by the traditional auctioneer Sotheby's; yet eBay's market value was more than 10 times greater: $22 billion versus

As investors dug into the company's freshly released financials Wednesday, analysts and investors began circulating a range of values—from as little as $50 billion to as much as $125 billion—for the social-networking website.

It will be months before the market sets a final price, but already the valuation question has become a tug of war over two essential questions: Just how fast can the company continue to grow? And can it extract value from advertising in the way it plans?

Facebook's revenue grew 88% in 2011, and net income grew 65%. Facebook's growth has already decelerated from 154% from 2009 to 2010, to the 88% it experienced last year.

Francis Gaskins, president of IPOdesktop.com, which analyzes IPOs for investors, says he doesn't believe Facebook is worth more than $50 billion—50 times its reported profits for 2011 of $1 billion, or more than triple the market's average price-to-earnings ratio. Google Inc.'s profits are 10 times that of Facebook, but its stock-market value is $190 billion, he notes.

A $100 billion valuation "would have us believe that Facebook is worth 53% of Google, even though Google's sales and profits are 10 times that of Facebook," he said.

Martin Pyykkonen, an analyst at Denver banking boutique Wedge Partners, is more bullish, saying the value could top $100 billion. He says Facebook could trade at 15 to 18 times next year's expected earnings before interest, taxes and certain non-cash charges, a cash-flow measure known as EBITDA. By comparison, he says, mature companies trade at eight to 10 times EBITDA. Microsoft Corp. trades at seven times, and Google about 10 times.

While that math only justifies an $81 billion valuation, he says Facebook may be able to unlock faster growth in ad spending and reach $5.5 billion in EBITDA, which could justify a higher multiple of 20 times, implying a $110 billion valuation.

Source: Randall Smith, "Facebook's $100 Billion Question," *Wall Street Journal*, February 3, 2012. Reprinted by permission of *The Wall Street Journal*, © 2012 Dow Jones & Company, Inc. All rights reserved worldwide.

$1.9 billion. (As it turns out, the market was quite right to value eBay so much more aggressively than Sotheby's. In 2011, eBay's net income was $1.8 billion, more than 10 times that of Sotheby's.)

Of course, when company valuation is determined primarily by growth opportunities, those values can be very sensitive to reassessments of such prospects. When the market became more skeptical of the business prospects of most Internet retailers at the close of the 1990s, that is, as it revised the estimates of growth opportunities downward, their stock prices plummeted.

As perceptions of future prospects wax and wane, share price can swing wildly. Growth prospects are intrinsically difficult to tie down; ultimately, however, those prospects drive the value of the most dynamic firms in the economy.

The nearby box contains a simple valuation analysis. As Facebook headed toward its highly anticipated IPO in 2012, there was widespread speculation about the price at which it would eventually trade in the stock market. Notice that the discussion in the article focused on two key questions. First, what was a reasonable projection of the growth rate of Facebook's profits? Second, what multiple of earnings was appropriate to translate an earnings forecast into a price forecast? These are precisely the questions addressed by our stock valuation models.

CC 5

CONCEPT CHECK

ABC stock has an expected ROE of 12 percent per year, expected earnings per share of $2, and expected dividends of $1.50 per share. Its market capitalization rate is 10 percent per year.

a. What are its expected growth rate, its price, and its P/E ratio?

b. If the plowback rate were .4, what would be the expected dividend per share, the growth rate, price, and the P/E ratio?

Growth or Value Investing

Many investment advisors express their approach to portfolio building as either "value investing" or "growth investing." The former is considered to be more conservative and the latter more rewarding, as it entails more risk. Others insist that all investing must be value-based, and that when growth opportunities are undervalued they become value opportunities. The two terms are generally accepted as implying a choice between companies for which there are superior growth prospects and those where fundamental analysis reveals unrecognized value. A more formal definition states that a **growth company** is one for which the growth rate is greater than the market average due to the opportunity to reinvest earnings at a rate greater than the market's required rate of return. (Note that this definition fits with the three stages of company life cycles.) Value is found in companies that can invest only at the market capitalization rate; the value is there because investors overlook these firms as they bid up the price of growth companies.

In fact, value investors rely upon misperceptions as to the real growth prospects of so-called growth companies, leaving true value in stable companies. There is considerable evidence to justify this approach. Growth investing assumes that there is a degree of persistence in growth trends such that superior returns can be generated from investing in companies with a record of growth; this return must justify the risk that actively growing firms often experience financial setbacks during downturns in the economy. More established, stable firms have greater financial resources to weather these difficulties. A famous study by I.M.D. Little in 1962 showed that, for British firms, those identified as growth companies in the first period were no more likely than other firms to be so identified in the second period; that is, there was no persistence of the growth characteristic. Subsequent studies of American firms showed the same results; growth could be identified only ex post.

Investors pay a premium price for future earnings of growth companies, captured by the high P/E ratio; should that growth fail to materialize, they will have inferior returns. Therefore, value investing in companies whose future earnings are much easier to predict should have a higher payoff. On the other hand, surely companies in growing industries with unique products to sell—the Microsofts and Cisco Systems of tomorrow—can be identified as growth companies. Ex post, they are easy to spot; the skill of being an analyst lies in finding them before their success occurs.

P/E Ratios and Stock Risk

One important implication of any stock valuation model is that (holding all else equal) riskier stocks will have lower P/E multiples. We can see this quite easily in the context of the constant-growth model by examining the formula for the P/E ratio (equation 16.6):

$$\frac{P}{E} = \frac{1-b}{k-g}$$

Riskier firms will have higher required rates of return, that is, higher values of k. Therefore, the P/E multiple will be lower. This is true even outside the context of the constant-growth model. For *any* expected earnings and dividend stream, the present value of those cash flows will be lower when the stream is perceived to be riskier. Hence the stock price and the ratio of price to earnings will be lower.

Of course, if you scan the financial pages, you will observe many small, risky, start-up companies with very high P/E multiples. This does not contradict our claim that P/E multiples should fall with risk; instead it is evidence of the market's expectations of high growth rates for those companies. This is why we said that high-risk firms will have lower P/E ratios *holding all else equal*. Holding the projection of growth fixed, the P/E multiple will be lower when risk is perceived to be higher.

Pitfalls in P/E Analysis

No description of P/E analysis is complete without mentioning some of its pitfalls. First, consider that the denominator in the P/E ratio is accounting earnings, which are influenced by somewhat arbitrary accounting rules such as the use of historical cost in depreciation and inventory valuation. In times of high inflation, historic cost depreciation and inventory costs will tend to underrepresent true economic values, because the replacement cost of both goods and capital equipment will rise with the general level of prices. As Figure 16.4 demonstrates, P/E ratios generally have been inversely related to the inflation rate. In part, this reflects the market's assessment that earnings in high inflation periods are of "lower quality," artificially distorted by inflation, and warranting lower P/E ratios.

Earnings management is the practice of using flexibility in accounting rules to improve the apparent profitability of the firm. We will have much to say on this topic in the next chapter on interpreting financial statements. A version of earnings management that became common in the 1990s was the reporting of "pro forma earnings" measures.

Pro forma earnings are calculated ignoring certain expenses, for example, restructuring charges, stock-option expenses, or write-downs of assets from continuing operations. Firms argue that ignoring these expenses gives a clearer picture of the underlying profitability of the firm. Comparisons with earlier periods probably would make more sense if those costs were excluded.

Even GAAP allow firms considerable discretion to manage earnings. For example, in the late 1990s, Kellogg took restructuring charges, which are supposed to be one-time events, nine quarters in a row. Were these really one-time events, or were they more appropriately treated as ordinary expenses? Given the available leeway in managing earnings, the justified P/E multiple becomes difficult to gauge.

A confounding factor in the use of P/E ratios is related to the business cycle. We were careful in deriving the DDM to define earnings as being net of *economic* depreciation, that is, the maximum flow of income that the firm could pay out without depleting its productive capacity. Reported earnings, as we note above, are computed in accordance with generally accepted accounting principles and need not correspond to economic earnings. Beyond this, however, notions of a normal or justified P/E ratio, as in equations 16.5 or 16.6, assume implicitly that earnings rise at a constant rate, or, put another way, on a smooth trend line. In contrast, reported earnings can fluctuate dramatically around a trend line over the course of the business cycle.

Figure 16.4

P/E ratios and inflation.

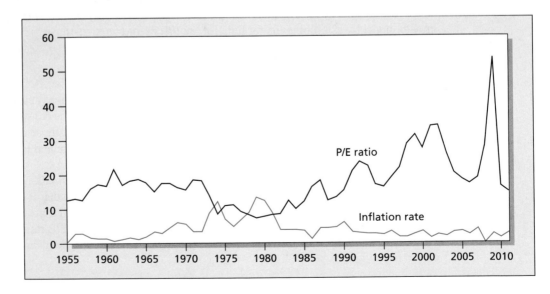

Figure 16.5

Normalized earnings per share for CNQ and Magna.

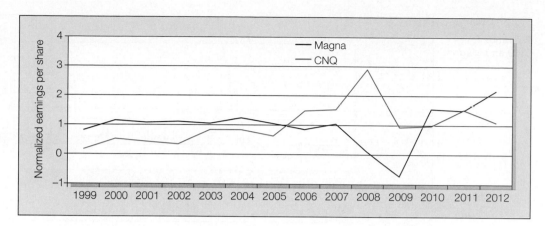

Another way to make this point is to note that the "normal" P/E ratio predicted by equation 16.6 is the ratio of today's price to the trend value of future earnings, E_1. The P/E ratio reported in the financial pages of the newspaper, by contrast, is the ratio of price to the most recent *past* accounting earnings. Current accounting earnings can differ considerably from future economic earnings. Because ownership of stock conveys the right to future as well as current earnings, the ratio of price to most recent earnings can vary substantially over the business cycle, as accounting earnings and the trend value of economic earnings diverge by greater and lesser amounts.

As an example, Figure 16.5 graphs the normalized earnings per share of Canadian Natural Resources (CNQ) and Magna International; normalization is the result of dividing the EPS before extraordinary items by the average EPS over the 14-year period. This enables us to see that the CNQ EPS varies considerably more than that of Magna (ignoring 2008 and 2009 results), with CNQ's steadily rising over the period before 2008; earnings since 2009 may be showing weakness, due to the natural gas glut resulting from increases U.S. supply. In fact, Magna's earnings had shown a barely rising trend, but have improved somewhat since 2009. Yet CNQ's have risen at an annual rate of 18 percent to almost 7 times their initial value. At the same time, CNQ's beta was approximately 1.89, in contrast to the lower 1.52 for Magna. (This is consistent with CNQ's higher systematic risk yielding a higher average gain in earnings.)

Figure 16.6 graphs the P/E ratios of the two firms. CNQ, with the more volatile earnings profile, also has a more volatile P/E profile, although Magna had no meaningful P/E during much of 2009 and 2010, as negative earnings demand a cessation to the P/E calculation. Note the spike in CNQ's P/E in 2006, based on the trailing EPS which fell in 2005. The market discounted the drop as temporary, with the price barely dropping through 2006. Magna's P/E only spiked in early 2009 on poor earnings results. (These P/E graphs respond to quarterly earnings.)

This example indicates why analysts must be careful in using P/E ratios. There is no way to say that the P/E ratio is overly high or low without referring to the company's long-run growth prospects, as well as to current earnings per share relative to the long-run trend line.

Since growth varies by industry, P/E ratios should also vary across industries, and in fact they do. Figure 16.7 shows P/E ratios in 2012 for a sample of industries. Notice that the industries with the highest multiples—such as business software or biotech—have attractive investment opportunities and relatively high growth rates, whereas the industries with the lowest ratios—for example, aerospace or computer manufacturers—are in more mature or less profitable industries with limited growth opportunities. The relationship between P/E and growth is not perfect, which is not surprising in light of the pitfalls discussed in this section, but as a general rule, the P/E multiple does appear to track growth opportunities.

Figure 16.6

P/E ratios for
CNQ and Magna.

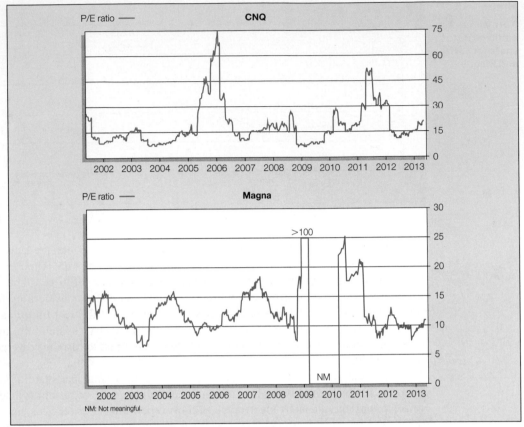

Figure 16.7

P/E ratios for
different
industries, 2012.

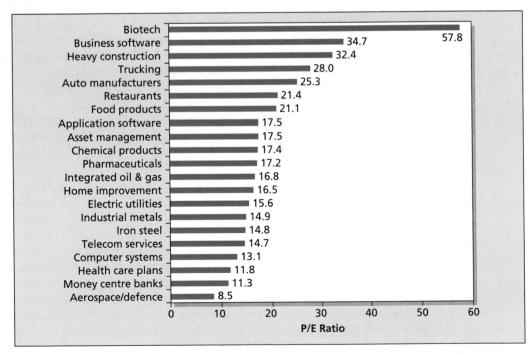

Source: Data from Yahoo Finance, September 12, 2012. Stock return is YTD from *Wall Street Journal*,
September 12, 2012.

Combining P/E Analysis and the DDM

Some analysts use P/E ratios in conjunction with earnings forecasts to estimate the price of a stock at an investor's horizon date. The Honda analysis in Figure 16.2 shows that Value Line forecasted a P/E ratio for 2016 of 14.0. EPS for 2016 were forecast at $4, implying a price in 2016 of $14 \times \$4.00 = \$56$. Given an estimate of $56 for the 2016 sales price, we would compute Honda's intrinsic value in 2016 as

$$V_{2012} = \frac{\$.78}{1.096} + \frac{\$.85}{(1.096)^2} + \frac{\$.92}{(1.096)^3} + \frac{\$1 + \$56}{(1.096)^5} = \$41.62$$

which turns out to be quite well above the $32.88 market price.

Other Comparative Valuation Ratios

The price-earnings ratio is an example of a comparative valuation ratio. Such ratios are used to assess the valuation of one firm versus another based on a fundamental indicator such as earnings. For example, an analyst might compare the P/E ratios of two firms in the same industry to test whether the market is valuing one firm "more aggressively" than the other. Other such comparative ratios are commonly used, which we will discuss in turn.

Price-to-Book Ratio

Price-to-Book Ratio   This is the ratio of price per share divided by book value per share. As we noted earlier in this chapter, some analysts view book value as a useful measure of value and therefore treat the ratio of price to book value as an indicator of how aggressively the market values the firm.

Price-to-Cash-Flow Ratio   Earnings as reported on the income statement can be affected by the company's choice of accounting practices, and thus are commonly viewed as subject to some imprecision and even manipulation. In contrast, cash flow—which tracks cash actually flowing into or out of the firm—is less affected by accounting decisions. As a result, some analysts prefer to use the ratio of price to cash flow per share rather than price to earnings per share. Some analysts use operating cash flow when calculating this ratio; others prefer "free cash flow," that is, operating cash flow net of new investment.

Price-to-Sales Ratio   Many start-up firms have no earnings. As a result, the price-earnings ratio for these firms is meaningless. The price-to-sales ratio (the ratio of stock price to the annual sales per share) has recently become a popular valuation benchmark for these firms. Of course, price-to-sales ratios can vary markedly across industries, since profit margins vary widely.

E-INVESTMENTS **Stock** **Screening** **Tools**	Stock screening tools allow one to sort through thousands of companies, according to predetermined criteria such as revenue and earnings growth, debt-equity maximums, profitability minimums, and so forth. Go to Yahoo's stock screening page at **screen.yahoo.com/stocks.html**. Select firms from any industry with P/E ratios below 20 and one-year growth estimates of more than 5 percent. Review the ranked list of companies provided from the screen and the variables listed. What are the top five companies, on the basis of this "screen"? Modify your list one variable at a time and observe the changes in the ranking. Next, select a stock category and an industry of interest to you. Using these screen variables, what companies are listed? (*Hint:* Do not make large changes in the range and/or the number of screening variables until you have a feel for the screening ranges, or you may find zero companies in your results!)

Figure 16.8

Market valuation statistics.

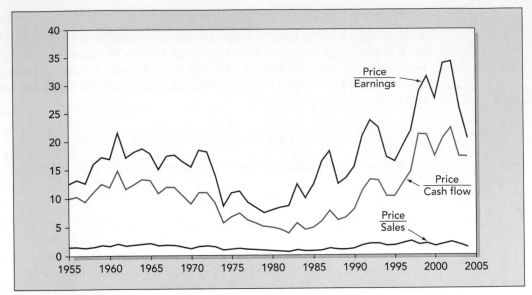

Figure 16.8 presents the behaviour of these valuation measures since 1955 for the broad market. (Again, up-to-date graphs would be non-meaningful.) While the levels of these ratios differ considerably, for the most part they track each other fairly closely, with upturns and downturns at the same times.

16.5 ▶ FREE CASH FLOW VALUATION

An alternative approach to the dividend discount model values the firm using free cash flow, that is, cash flow available to the firm or its equityholders net of capital expenditures. This approach is particularly useful for firms that pay no dividends, for which the dividend discount model would be difficult to implement. But free cash flow models may be applied to any firm and can provide useful insights about firm value beyond the DDM.

One approach is to discount the *free cash flow for the firm (FCFF)* at the weighted-average cost of capital to obtain the value of the firm, and subtract the then-existing value of debt to find the value of equity. Another is to focus from the start on the *free cash flow to equityholders (FCFE)*, discounting those directly at the cost of equity to obtain the market value of equity.

The free cash flow to the firm is the cash flow that accrues from the firm's operations, net of investments in capital and net working capital. It includes cash flows available to both debt- and equityholders.[6] It equals

$$\text{FCFF} = \text{EBIT}(1 - t_c) + \text{Depreciation} - \text{Capital expenditures} - \text{Increase in NWC} \quad (16.7)$$

where

$$\text{EBIT} = \text{earnings before interest and taxes}$$
$$t_c = \text{the corporate tax rate}$$
$$\text{NWC} = \text{net working capital}$$

---

[6]This is firm cash flow assuming all-equity financing. Any tax advantage to debt financing is recognized by using an after-tax cost of debt in the computation of weighted-average cost of capital. This issue is discussed in any introductory corporate finance text.

Alternatively, we can focus on cash flow available to equityholders. This will differ from free cash flow to the firm by after-tax interest expenditures, as well as by cash flow associated with net issuance or repurchase of debt (i.e., principal repayments minus proceeds from issuance of new debt).

$$\text{FCFE} = \text{FCFF} - \text{Interest expense} \times (1 - t_c) + \text{Increases in net debt} \quad (16.8)$$

A free cash flow to the firm valuation model discounts year-by-year cash flows plus some estimate of terminal value, P_T. In equation 16.9, we use the constant-growth model to estimate terminal value and discount at the weighted-average cost of capital (WACC).

$$\text{Firm value} = \sum_{t=1}^{T} \frac{\text{FCFF}_t}{(1 + \text{WACC})^t} + \frac{P_T}{(1 + \text{WACC})^T} \quad \text{where } P_T = \frac{\text{FCFF}_{T+1}}{\text{WACC} - g} \quad (16.9)$$

To find equity value, we subtract the existing market value of debt from the derived value of the firm.

Alternatively, we can discount *free cash flow to equity (FCFE)* at the cost of equity, k_E,

$$\text{Market value of equity} = \sum_{t=1}^{T} \frac{\text{FCFE}_t}{(1 + k_E)^t} + \frac{P_T}{(1 + k_E)^T} \quad \text{where } P_T = \frac{\text{FCFE}_{T+1}}{k_E - g} \quad (16.10)$$

As in the dividend discount model, free cash flow models use a terminal value to avoid adding the present values of an infinite sum of cash flows. That terminal value may simply be the present value of a constant-growth perpetuity (as in the formulas above) or it may be based on a multiple of EBIT, book value, earnings, or free cash flow. As a general rule, estimates of intrinsic value depend critically on terminal value.

Spreadsheet 16.2 presents a free cash flow valuation of Honda using the data supplied by Value Line in Figure 16.2. We start with the free cash flow to the firm approach given in equation 16.7. Panel A of the spreadsheet lays out values supplied by Value Line. Entries for middle years are interpolated from beginning and final values. Panel B calculates free cash flow. The sum of after-tax profits in row 11 (from Value Line) plus after-tax interest payments in row 12 (i.e., interest expense $\times$ [$1 - t_c$]) equals EBIT($1 - t_c$). In row 13 we subtract the change in net working capital, in row 14 we add back depreciation, and in row 15 we subtract capital expenditures. The result in row 17 is the free cash flow to the firm, FCFF, for each year between 2013 and 2016. (In the case of a bank, these adjustments are unnecessary; the application of this model is far more useful for corporations outside the financial industry.)

To find the present value of these cash flows, we will discount at WACC, which is calculated in panel C. WACC is the weighted average of the after-tax cost of debt and the cost of equity in each year. When computing WACC, we must account for the change in leverage forecast by Value Line. To compute the cost of equity, we will use the CAPM as in our earlier (dividend discount model) valuation exercise, but accounting for the fact that equity beta will decline each year as the firm reduces leverage.[7]

---

[7]Call β_L the firm's equity beta at the initial level of leverage as provided by Value Line. Equity betas reflect both business risk and financial risk. When a firm changes its capital structure (debt/equity mix), it changes financial risk, and therefore equity beta changes. How should we recognize the change in financial risk? As you may remember from an introductory corporate finance class, you must first un-leverage beta. This leaves us with business risk. We use the following formula to find unleveraged beta, β_U (where D/E is the firm's current debt-equity ratio):

$$\beta_U = \frac{\beta_L}{1 + (D/E)(1 - t_c)}$$

Then, we re-leverage beta in any particular year using the forecast capital structure for that year (which reintroduces the financial risk associated with that year's capital structure):

$$\beta_L = \beta_U[1 + (D/E)(1 - t_c)]$$

EXCEL SPREADSHEET 16.2 ⬀

Free cash valuation for Honda Motor Co.

	A	B	C	D	E	F	G	H	I	J	K	L	M
1			2012	2013	2014	2015	2016						
2	**A. Input data**												
3	P/E		14.35	14.25	14.17	14.08	14.00						
4	Cap spending/shr		2.65	2.70	2.82	2.93	3.05						
5	LT Debt		30000	28500	27333	26167	25000						
6	Shares		1800	1800	1798	1797	1795						
7	EPS		3.10	3.75	3.83	3.92	4.00						
8	Working Capital		36825	37750	41173	44597	48020						
9													
10	**B. Cash flow calculations**												
11	Profits (after tax)		5700.0	6850.0	6970.0	7090.0	7210.0						
12	Interest (after tax)		702.0	666.9	639.6	612.3	585.0			= (1-tax_rate) × r_debt × LT Debt			
13	Chg Working Cap			925.0	3423.3	3423.3	3423.3						
14	Depreciation		7000.0	7250.0	7166.67	7083	7000.0						
15	Cap Spending			4860.0	5064.9	5269.8	5474.8						
16								**Terminal value**					
17	FCFF			8981.9	6288.0	6092.5	5896.9	104098.2					
18	FCFE			6815.0	4481.8	4313.5	4145.3	83203.2		assumes fixed debt ratio after 2016			
19													
20	**C. Discount rate calculations**												
21	Current beta	0.95								from Value Line			
22	Unlevered beta	0.767								current beta/[1 + (1-tax)*debt/equity]			
23	terminal growth	0.02											
24	tax_rate	0.35								from Value Line			
25	r_debt	0.036								YTM in 2012 on A+ rated LT debt			
26	risk-free rate	0.02											
27	market risk prem	0.08											
28	MV equity		81795				100940			Row 3 × Row 11			
29	Debt/Value			0.27	0.25	0.23	0.22	0.20		linear trend from initial to final value			
30	Levered beta			0.950	0.934	0.919	0.904	0.891		unlevered beta × [1 + (1-tax)*debt/equity]			
31	k_equity			0.096	0.095	0.094	0.092	0.091	0.091	from CAPM and levered beta			
32	WACC			0.077	0.077	0.077	0.077	0.078	0.078	(1-t)*r_debt*D/V + k_equity*(1-D/V)			
33	PV factor for FCFF			1.000	0.929	0.862	0.800	0.742	0.742	Discount each year at WACC			
34	PV factor for FCFE			1.000	0.913	0.835	0.765	0.701	0.701	Discount each year at k_equity			
35													
36	**D. Present values**									Intrinsic val	Equity val	Intrin/share	
37	PV(FCFF)				8341	5421	4875	4378	77283	100298	70298	39.05	
38	PV(FCFE)				6225	3744	3299	2905	58307	74479	74479	41.38	

*2012 P/E ratio is from Yahoo Finance. Other inputs are from Value Line.

To find Honda's cost of debt, we note that long-term bonds were rated A+ in 2012 and that yields to maturity on this quality debt at the time were about 3.6 percent. Honda's debt-to-value ratio (assuming its debt is selling near par value) is computed in row 29. In 2012, the ratio was .27. Based on Value Line forecasts, it will fall to .20 by 2016. We interpolate the debt-to-value ratio for the intermediate years. WACC is computed in row 32. WACC increases slightly over time as the debt-to-value ratio declines between 2012 and 2016. The present value factor for cash flows accruing in each year is the previous year's factor divided by (1 + WACC) for that year. The present value of each cash flow (row 37) is the free cash flow times the cumulative discount factor.

The terminal value of the firm (cell H17) is computed from the constant-growth model as $FCFF_{2016} \times (1 + g)/(WACC_{2016} - g)$, where g (cell B23) is the assumed value for the steady growth rate. We assume in the spreadsheet that $g = .02$, which is comparable to the long-run growth rate of the broad economy.[8] Terminal value is also discounted back to 2012

---

[8]In the long run a firm can't grow forever at a rate higher than the aggregate economy. So by the time we assert that growth is in a stable stage, it seems reasonable that the growth rate should not be significantly greater than that of the overall economy (although it can be less if the firm is in a declining industry).

(cell H37), and the intrinsic value of the firm is thus found as the sum of discounted free cash flows between 2013 and 2016 plus the discounted terminal value. Finally, the value of debt in 2012 is subtracted from firm value to arrive at the intrinsic value of equity in 2012 (cell K37), and value per share is calculated in cell L37 as equity value divided by number of shares in 2012.

The free cash flow to equity approach yields a similar intrinsic value for the stock. FCFE (row 18) is obtained from FCFF by subtracting after-tax interest expense and net debt repurchases. The cash flows are then discounted at the equity rate. Like WACC, the cost of equity changes each period as leverage changes. The present value factor for equity cash flows is presented in row 34. Equity value is reported in cell H38, which is put on a per share basis in cell K38. The values found here are comparable to the value found for the three-stage growth model in Spreadsheet 16.1.

FCF Versus the DDM

In principle, the free cash flow approach is fully consistent with the dividend discount model and should provide the same estimate of intrinsic value if one can extrapolate to a period in which the firm begins to pay dividends growing at a constant rate. This was demonstrated in two famous papers by Modigliani and Miller.[9] However, in practice, you will find that values from these models may differ, sometimes substantially. This is due to the fact that in practice, analysts are always forced to make simplifying assumptions. For example, how long will it take the firm to enter a constant-growth stage? How should depreciation best be treated? What is the best estimate of ROE? Answers to questions like these can have a big impact on value, and it is not always easy to maintain consistent assumptions across the models.

We can value Honda using several approaches, with estimates of intrinsic value as follows:

Model	Intrinsic Value
Two-stage divided discount model	$38.81
DDM with earnings multiple terminal value	41.62
Three-stage DDM	40.29
Free cash flow to the firm	39.05
Free cash flow to equity	41.38
Market price (from Value Line)	32.88

What should we make of these differences? All the model estimates are somewhat higher than Honda's actual stock price, perhaps indicating that they use an unrealistically high value for the ultimate constant growth rate. For example, in the long run, it seems unlikely that Honda will be able to grow as rapidly as Value Line's forecast for 2016 growth, 7.5 percent. The two-stage dividend discount model is the most conservative of the estimates, largely because it assumes that Honda's dividend growth rate will fall to its terminal value after only three years. In contrast, the three-stage DDM allows growth to taper off over a longer period. Given the consistency with which all these estimates exceed market price, perhaps the stock is indeed underpriced compared to its intrinsic value.

On balance, however, this valuation exercise shows that finding bargains is not as easy as it seems. While these models are easy to apply, establishing proper inputs is more of a challenge. This should not be surprising. In even a moderately efficient market, finding profit opportunities will be more involved than analyzing Value Line data for a few hours. These models are extremely

---

[9]Franco Modigliani and M. Miller, "The Cost of Capital, Corporation Finance, and the Theory of Investment," *American Economic Review*, June 1958, and "Dividend Policy, Growth, and the Valuation of Shares," *Journal of Business*, October 1961.

useful to analysts however. They provide ballpark estimates of intrinsic value. More than that, they force rigorous thought about underlying assumptions and highlight the variables with the greatest impact on value and the greatest payoff to further analysis.

The Problem with DCF Models

Our estimates of Honda's intrinsic value are all based on discounted cash flow (DCF) models, in which we calculate the present value of forecasted cash flows and a terminal sales price at some future date. It is clear from the calculations for Honda that most of the action in these models is in the terminal value and that this value can be highly sensitive to even small changes in some input values (e.g., see Concept Check 4). Therefore, you must recognize that DCF valuation estimates are almost always going to be imprecise. Growth opportunities and future growth rates are especially hard to pin down.

For this reason, many value investors employ a hierarchy of valuation. They view the most reliable components of value as the items on the balance sheet that allow for the most precise estimates of market value. Real estate, plant, and equipment would fall in this category.

A somewhat less reliable component of value is the economic profit on assets already in place. For example, a company like Intel earns a far higher ROE on its investments in chip-making facilities than its cost of capital. The present value of these "economic profits," or economic value added,[10] is a major component of Intel's market value. This component of value is less certain than its balance sheet assets, however, because there is always a concern that new competitors will enter the market, force down prices and profit margins, and reduce the return on Intel's investments. Thus, one needs to carefully assess the barriers to entry that protect Intel's pricing and profit margins. We noted some of these barriers in the last chapter, where we discussed the role of industry analysis, market structure, and competitive position (see Section 15.6).

SUMMARY

1. One approach to estimating intrinsic value is to focus on the firm's book value, either as it appears on the balance sheet or as adjusted to reflect current replacement cost of assets or liquidation value. Another approach is to focus on the present value of expected future dividends, earnings, or free cash flow.

2. Dividend discount models give estimates of the intrinsic value of a stock. If price does not equal intrinsic value, the rate of return will differ from the equilibrium return based on the stock's risk. The actual return will depend on the rate at which the stock price is predicted to revert to its intrinsic value.

3. The constant-growth version of the DDM asserts that if dividends are expected to grow at a constant rate forever, the intrinsic value of the stock is determined by the formula

$$V_0 = \frac{D_1}{k - g}$$

This version of the DDM is simplistic in its assumption of a constant value of g. There are more-sophisticated multistage versions of the model for more-complex environments. When the constant-growth assumption is reasonably satisfied and the stock is selling for its intrinsic value, the formula can be inverted to infer the market capitalization rate for the stock:

$$k = \frac{D_1}{P_0} + g$$

4. The constant-growth dividend discount model is best suited for firms that are expected to exhibit stable growth rates over the foreseeable future. In reality, however, firms progress through life cycles. In early years, attractive investment opportunities are ample and the firm responds with high plowback ratios and rapid dividend growth. Eventually, however, growth rates level off to more sustainable values. Three-stage growth models are well suited to such a pattern. These

---

[10]We discuss economic value added in greater detail in Chapter 17.

models allow for an initial period of rapid growth, a final period of steady dividend growth, and a middle, or transition, period in which the dividend growth rate declines from its initial high rate to the lower sustainable rate.

5. Stock market analysts devote considerable attention to a company's price-earnings ratio. The P/E ratio is a useful measure of the market's assessment of the firm's growth opportunities. Firms with no growth opportunities should have a P/E ratio that is just the reciprocal of the capitalization rate, k. As growth opportunities become a progressively more important component of the total value of the firm, the P/E ratio will increase.

6. The expected growth rate of earnings is related both to the firm's expected profitability and to its dividend policy. The relationship can be expressed as

g = (ROE on new investment) ×
(1 − Dividend payout ratio)

7. You can relate any DDM to a simple capitalized earnings model by comparing the expected ROE on future investments to the market capitalization rate, k. If the two rates are equal, then the stock's intrinsic value reduces to expected earnings per share (EPS) divided by k.

8. Many analysts form their estimate of a stock's value by multiplying their forecast of next year's EPS by a P/E multiple. Some analysts mix the P/E approach with the dividend discount model. They use an earnings multiplier to forecast the terminal value of shares at a future date, and add the present value of that terminal value with the present value of all interim dividend payments.

9. The free cash flow approach is the one used most often in corporate finance. The analyst first estimates the value of the entire firm as the present value of expected future free cash flows to the entire firm and then subtracts the value of all claims other than equity. Alternatively, the free cash flows to equity can be discounted at a discount rate appropriate to the risk of the stock.

KEY EQUATIONS

(16.1) $V_0 = \dfrac{D_1}{1+k} + \dfrac{D_2}{(1+k)^2} + \dfrac{D_3}{(1+k)^3} + \cdots = \dfrac{D_1 + P_1}{1+k}$

(16.2) $V_0 = \dfrac{D_1}{k-g}$

(16.3) $E(r) = k = \dfrac{D_1}{P_0} + g$

(16.4) $P_0 = \dfrac{E_1}{k} + \text{PVGO}$

(16.5) $\dfrac{P_0}{E_1} = \dfrac{1}{k}\left(1 + \dfrac{\text{PVGO}}{E/k}\right)$

(16.6) $\dfrac{P_0}{E_1} = \dfrac{1-b}{k - \text{ROE} \times b}$

(16.7) $\text{FCFF} = \text{EBIT}(1 - t_c) + \text{Depreciation} - \text{Capital expenditures} - \text{Increase in NWC}$

(16.8) $\text{FCFE} = \text{FCFF} - \text{Interest expense} \times (1 - t_c) + \text{Increases in net debt}$

(16.9) $\text{Firm value} = \displaystyle\sum_{t=1}^{T} \dfrac{\text{FCFF}_t}{(1+\text{WACC})^t} + \dfrac{P_T}{(1+\text{WACC})^T}$ where $P_T = \dfrac{\text{FCFF}_{T+1}}{\text{WACC} - g}$

(16.10) $\text{Market value of equity} = \displaystyle\sum_{t=1}^{T} \dfrac{\text{FCFE}_t}{(1+k_E)^t} + \dfrac{P_T}{(1+k_E)^T}$ where $P_T = \dfrac{\text{FCFE}_{T+1}}{k_E - g}$

PROBLEMS

Mc Graw Hill Education **connect**™ **Practise and learn online with Connect.**

1. In what circumstances would you choose to use a dividend discount model rather than a free cash flow model to value a firm?

2. In what circumstances is it most important to use multistage dividend discount models rather than constant-growth models?

3. If a security is underpriced (i.e., intrinsic value > price), what is the relationship between its market capitalization rate and its expected rate of return?

4. Deployment Specialists pays a current (annual) dividend of $1 and is expected to grow at 20 percent for 2 years and at 4 percent thereafter. If the required return for Deployment Specialists is 8.5 percent, what is the intrinsic value of their stock?

5. Jand, Inc. currently pays a dividend of $1.22, which is expected to grow indefinitely at 5 percent. If the current value of Jand's shares based on the constant-growth dividend discount model is $32.03, what is the required rate of return?

6. A firm pays a current dividend of $1 which is expected to grow at a rate of 5 percent indefinitely. If current value of the firm's shares is $35, what is the required return applicable to the investment based on the constant-growth dividend discount model (DDM)?

7. Tri-coat Paints has a current market value of $41 per share with earnings of $3.64. What is the present value of its growth opportunities (PVGO) if the required return is 9 percent?

8. The market consensus is that Analog Electronic Corporation has an ROE of 9 percent, has a beta of 1.25, and plans to maintain indefinitely its traditional plowback ratio of 2/3. This year's earnings were $3 per share. The annual dividend was just paid. The consensus estimate of the coming year's market return is 14 percent, and T-bills currently offer a 6 percent return.

   a. Find the price at which Analog stock should sell.

   b. Calculate the P/E ratio.

   c. Calculate the present value of growth opportunities.

   d. Suppose your research convinces you Analog will announce momentarily that it will immediately reduce its plowback ratio to 1/3. Find the intrinsic value of the stock. The market is still unaware of this decision. Explain why V_0 no longer equals P_0 and why V_0 is greater or less than P_0.

9. a. Computer stocks currently provide an expected rate of return of 16 percent. MBI, a large computer company, will pay a year-end dividend of $2 per share. If the stock is selling at $50 per share, what must be the market's expectation of the growth rate of MBI dividends?

   b. If dividend growth forecasts for MBI are revised downward to 5 percent per year, what will happen to the price of MBI stock? What (qualitatively) will happen to the company's price-earnings ratio?

10. a. MF Corp. has an ROE of 16 percent and a plowback ratio of 50 percent. If the coming year's earnings are expected to be $2 per share, at what price will the stock sell? The market capitalization rate is 12 percent.

   b. What price do you expect MF shares to sell for in three years?

11. If the expected rate of return of the market portfolio is 15 percent and a stock with a beta of 1.0 pays a dividend yield of 4 percent, what must the market believe is the expected rate of price appreciation on that stock?

12. The FI Corporation's dividends per share are expected to grow indefinitely by 5 percent per year.

    a. If this year's year-end dividend is $8 and the market capitalization rate is 10 percent per year, what must the current stock price be according to the DDM?

    b. If the expected earnings per share are $12, what is the implied value of the ROE on future investment opportunities?

    c. How much is the market paying per share for growth opportunities (i.e., for an ROE on future investments that exceeds the market capitalization rate)?

13. The stock of Nogro Corporation is currently selling for $10 per share. Earnings per share in the coming year are expected to be $2. The company has a policy of paying out 50 percent of its earnings each year in dividends. The rest is retained and invested in projects that earn a 20 percent rate of return per year. This situation is expected to continue indefinitely.

    a. Assuming the current market price of the stock reflects its intrinsic value as computed using the constant-growth DDM, what rate of return do Nogro's investors require?

    b. By how much does its value exceed what it would be if all earnings were paid as dividends and nothing were reinvested?

    c. If Nogro were to cut its dividend payout ratio to 25 percent, what would happen to its stock price? What if Nogro eliminated the dividend?

14. Chiptech, Inc. is an established computer chip firm with several profitable existing products as well as some promising new products in development. The company earned $1 a share last year, and just paid out a dividend of $.50 per share. Investors believe the company plans to maintain its dividend payout ratio at 50 percent. ROE equals 20 percent. Everyone in the market expects this situation to persist indefinitely.

    a. What is the market price of Chiptech stock? The required return for the computer chip industry is 15 percent, and the company has just gone ex-dividend (i.e., the next dividend will be paid a year from now, at $t = 1$).

    b. Suppose you discover that Chiptech's competitor has developed a new chip that will eliminate Chiptech's current technological advantage in this market. This new product, which will be ready to come to the market in 2 years, will force Chiptech to reduce the prices of its chips to remain competitive. This will decrease ROE to 15 percent, and, because of falling demand for its product, Chiptech will decrease the plowback ratio to .40. The plowback ratio will be decreased at the end of the second year, at $t = 2$; the annual year-end dividend for the second year (paid at $t = 2$) will be 60 percent of that year's earnings. What is your estimate of Chiptech's intrinsic value per share? (*Hint:* Carefully prepare a table of Chiptech's earnings and dividends for each of the next three years. Pay close attention to the change in the payout ratio in $t = 2$.)

    c. No one else in the market perceives the threat to Chiptech's market. In fact, you are confident that no one else will become aware of the change in Chiptech's competitive status until the competitor firm publicly announces its discovery near the end of year 2. What will be the rate of return on Chiptech stock in the coming year (i.e., between $t = 0$ and $t = 1$)? In the second year (between $t = 1$ and $t = 2$)? The third year (between $t = 2$ and $t = 3$)? (*Hint:* Pay attention to when the *market* catches on to the new situation. A table of dividends and market prices over time might help.)

15. The risk-free rate of return is 8 percent, the expected rate of return on the market portfolio is 15 percent, and the stock of Xyrong Corporation has a beta coefficient of 1.2. Xyrong pays out 40 percent of its earnings in dividends, and the latest earnings announced were $10 per share. Dividends were just paid and are expected to be paid annually. You expect that Xyrong will earn an ROE of 20 percent per year on all reinvested earnings forever.

    a. What is the intrinsic value of a share of Xyrong stock?

    b. If the market price of a share is currently $100, and you expect the market price to be equal to the intrinsic value 1 year from now, what is your expected 1-year holding-period return on Xyrong stock?

16. Janet Ludlow's firm requires all its analysts to use a two-stage dividend discount model (DDM) and the capital asset pricing model (CAPM) to value stocks. Using the CAPM and DDM, Ludlow has valued QuickBrush Company at $63 per share. She now must value SmileWhite Corporation.

a. Calculate the required rate of return for SmileWhite by using the information in the following table:

	QuickBrush	SmileWhite
Beta	1.35	1.15
Market price	$45.00	$30.00
Intrinsic value	$63.00	?
Notes:		
Risk-free rate	4.50%	
Expected market return	14.50%	

b. Ludlow estimates the following EPS and dividend growth rates for SmileWhite:

First 3 years   12% per year
Years thereafter   9% per year

Estimate the intrinsic value of SmileWhite by using the table above, and the two-stage DDM. Dividends per share in the most recent year were $1.72.

c. Recommend QuickBrush or SmileWhite stock for purchase by comparing each company's intrinsic value with its current market price.

d. Describe one strength of the two-stage DDM in comparison with the constant-growth DDM. Describe one weakness inherent in all DDMs.

17. The Digital Electronic Quotation System (DEQS) Corporation pays no cash dividends currently and is not expected to for the next five years. Its latest EPS was $10, all of which was reinvested in the company. The firm's expected ROE for the next five years is 20 percent per year, and during this time it is expected to continue to reinvest all of its earnings. Starting six years from now the firm's ROE on new investments is expected to fall to 15 percent, and the company is expected to start paying out 40 percent of its earnings in cash dividends, which it will continue to do forever after. DEQS's market capitalization rate is 15 percent per year.

a. What is your estimate of DEQS's intrinsic value per share?

b. Assuming its current market price is equal to its intrinsic value, what do you expect to happen to its price over the next year? The year after?

c. What effect would it have on your estimate of DEQS's intrinsic value if you expected DEQS to pay out only 20 percent of earnings starting in year 6?

18. The Generic Genetic (GG) Corporation pays no cash dividends currently and is not expected to for the next four years. Its latest EPS was $5, all of which was reinvested in the company. The firm's expected ROE for the next four years is 20 percent per year, during which time it is expected to continue to reinvest all of its earnings. Starting five years from now, the firm's ROE on new investments is expected to fall to 15 percent per year. GG's market capitalization rate is 15 percent per year.

a. What is your estimate of GG's intrinsic value per share?

b. Assuming its current market price is equal to its intrinsic value, what do you expect to happen to its price over the next year?

19. The Duo Growth Company just paid a dividend of $1 per share. The dividend is expected to grow at a rate of 25 percent per year for the next three years and then to level off to

5 percent per year forever. You think the appropriate market capitalization rate is 20 percent per year.

a. What is your estimate of the intrinsic value of a share of the stock?

b. If the market price of a share is equal to this intrinsic value, what is the expected dividend yield?

c. What do you expect its price to be 1 year from now? Is the implied capital gain consistent with your estimate of the dividend yield and the market capitalization rate?

20. The MoMi Corporation's cash flow from operations before interest and taxes was $2 million in the year just ended, and it expects that this will grow by 5 percent per year forever. To make this happen, the firm will have to invest an amount equal to 20 percent of pretax cash flow each year. The tax rate is 35 percent. Depreciation was $200,000 in the year just ended and is expected to grow at the same rate as the operating cash flow. The appropriate market capitalization rate for the unleveraged cash flow is 12 percent per year, and the firm currently has debt of $4 million outstanding. Use the free cash flow approach to value the firm's equity.

The following problems are based on questions that have appeared in past CFA examinations.

21. Which of the following assumptions does the constant-growth dividend discount model require? Answer all that apply.

i. Dividends grow at a constant rate.

ii. The dividend growth rate continues indefinitely.

iii. The required rate of return is less than the dividend growth rate.

22. A common stock pays an annual dividend per share of $2.10. The risk-free rate is 7 percent, and the risk premium for this stock is 4 percent. If the annual dividend is expected to remain at $2.10, what is the value of the stock?

23. At Litchfield Chemical Corp. (LCC), a director of the company said that the use of dividend discount models by investors is "proof" that the higher the dividend, the higher the stock price.

a. Using a constant-growth dividend discount model as a basis of reference, evaluate the director's statement.

b. Explain how an increase in dividend payout would affect each of the following (holding all other factors constant):

i. Sustainable growth rate

ii. Growth in book value

24. Helen Morgan, CFA has been asked to use the DDM to determine the value of Sundanci, Inc. Morgan anticipates that Sundanci's earnings and dividends will grow at 32 percent for two years and 13 percent thereafter. Calculate the current value of a share of Sundanci stock by using a two-stage dividend discount model and the data from Tables 16A and 16B.

25. Abbey Naylor, CFA has been directed to determine the value of Sundanci's stock using the Free Cash Flow to Equity (FCFE) model. Naylor believes that Sundanci's FCFE will grow at 27 percent for two years and 13 percent thereafter. Capital expenditures, depreciation, and working capital are all expected to increase proportionately with FCFE

a. Calculate the amount of FCFE per share for the year 2013, using the data from Table 16A.

b. Calculate the current value of a share of Sundanci stock based on the two-stage FCFE model.

c. i. Describe one limitation of the two-stage DDM model that is addressed by using the two-stage FCFE model.

ii. Describe one limitation of the two-stage DDM model that is not addressed by using the two-stage FCFE model.

Income Statement	2012	2013
Revenue	$ 474	$ 598
Depreciation	20	23
Other operating costs	368	460
Income before taxes	86	115
Taxes	26	35
Net income	60	80
Dividends	18	24
Earnings per share	$.714	$.952
Dividend per share	$.214	$.286
Common shares outstanding (millions)	84.0	84.0

Balance Sheet	2012	2013
Current assets	$ 201	$ 326
Net property, plant, and equipment	474	489
Total assets	675	815
Current liabilities	57	141
Long-term debt	0	0
Total liabilities	57	141
Shareholders' equity	618	674
Total liabilities and equity	675	815
Capital expenditures	34	38

Required rate of return on equity	14%
Growth rate of industry	13%
Industry P/E ratio	26

26. Christie Johnson, CFA has been assigned to analyze Sundanci using the constant dividend growth price/earnings (P/E) ratio model. Johnson assumes that Sundanci's earnings and dividends will grow at a constant rate of 13 percent.

   a. Calculate the P/E ratio based on information in Tables 16A and 16B and on Johnson's assumptions for Sundanci.

   b. Identify, within the context of the constant dividend growth model, how each of the following factors would affect the P/E ratio.

   • Risk (beta) of Sundanci

   • Estimated growth rate of earnings and dividends

   • Market risk premium

27. Dynamic Communication is a U.S. industrial company with several electronics divisions. The company has just released its 2013 annual report. Tables 16C and 16D present a summary of Dynamic's financial statements for the years 2012 and 2013. Selected data from the financial statements for the years 2009 to 2011 are presented in Table 16E.

   a. A group of Dynamic shareholders has expressed concern about the zero growth rate of dividends in the past four years and has asked for information about the growth of the company. Calculate Dynamic's sustainable growth rates in 2010 and 2013. Your calculations should use beginning-of-year balance sheet data.

b. Determine how the change in Dynamic's sustainable growth rate (2013 compared to 2010) was affected by changes in its retention ratio and its financial leverage. *Note:* Your calculations should use beginning-of-year balance sheet data.

TABLE 16C

Dynamic Communication Balance Sheets

	US$ Millions	
	2013	**2012**
Cash and equivalents	$ 149	$ 83
Accounts receivable	295	265
Inventory	275	285
Total current assets	$ 719	$ 633
Gross fixed assets	9,350	8,900
Accumulated depreciation	(6,160)	(5,677)
Net fixed assets	$3,190	$3,223
Total assets	$3,909	$3,856
Accounts payable	$ 228	$ 220
Notes payable	0	0
Accrued taxes and expenses	0	0
Total current liabilities	228	$ 220
Long-term debt	$1,650	$1,800
Common stock	50	50
Additional paid-in capital	0	0
Retained earnings	1,981	1,786
Total shareholders' equity	$2,031	$1,836
Total liabilities and shareholder's equity	$3,909	$3,856

TABLE 16D

Dynamic Communication Statements of Income (US$ millions except for share data)

	2013	2012
Total revenues	$3,425	$3,300
Operating costs and expenses	2,379	2,319
Earnings before interest, taxes, depreciation, and amortization (EBITDA)	$1,046	$ 981
Depreciation and amortization	483	454
Operating income (EBIT)	$ 563	$ 527
Interest expense	104	107
Income before taxes	$ 459	$ 420
Taxes (40%)	184	168
Net income	$ 275	$ 252
Dividends	$ 80	$ 80
Change in retained earnings	$ 195	$ 172
Earnings per share	$ 2.75	$ 2.52
Dividends per share	$ .80	$ .80
Number of shares outstanding (millions)	100	100

	2011	2010	2009
Total revenues	$3,175	$3,075	$3,000
Operating income (EBIT)	495	448	433
Interest expense	104	101	99
Net income	$ 235	$ 208	$ 200
Dividends per share	$ .80	$ .80	$ .80
Total assets	$3,625	$3,414	$3,230
Long-term debt	$1,750	$1,700	$1,650
Total shareholders' equity	$1,664	$1,509	$1,380
Number of shares outstanding (millions)	100	100	100

28. Mike Brandreth, an analyst who specializes in the electronics industry, is preparing a research report on Dynamic Communication. A colleague suggests to Brandreth that he may be able to determine Dynamic's implied dividend growth rate from Dynamic's current common stock price, using the Gordon growth model. Brandreth believes that the appropriate required rate of return for Dynamic's equity is 8 percent.

    a. Assume that the firm's current stock price of $58.49 equals intrinsic value and dividend for the year is .8. What sustained rate of dividend growth as of December 2013 is implied by this value? Use the constant-growth dividend discount model (i.e., the Gordon growth model).

    b. The management of Dynamic has indicated to Brandreth and other analysts that the company's current dividend policy will be continued. Is the use of the Gordon growth model to value Dynamic's common stock appropriate or inappropriate? Justify your response using the assumptions of the Gordon growth model.

29. Peninsular Research is initiating coverage of a mature manufacturing industry. John Jones, CFA, head of the research department, gathered the following fundamental industry and market data to help in his analysis:

Forecast industry earnings retention rate	40%
Forecast industry return on equity	25%
Industry beta	1.2
Government bond yield	6%
Equity risk premium	5%

    a. Compute the price-earnings (P_0/E_1) ratio for the industry using these fundamental data.

    b. Jones wants to analyze how fundamental P/E ratios might differ among countries. He gathered the following economic and market data:

Fundamental Factors	Country A	Country B
Forecast growth in real GDP	5%	2%
Government bond yield	10%	6%
Equity risk premium	5%	4%

    Determine whether each of these fundamental factors would cause P/E ratios to be generally higher for country A or higher for country B.

30. Rio National Corp. is a U.S.-based company and the largest competitor in its industry. Tables 16F to 16I present financial statements and related information for the company. Table 16J presents relevant industry and market data.

TABLE 16F

Rio National Corp. Summary Year-End Balance Sheets (US$ millions)

	2013	2012
Cash	$ 13.00	$ 5.87
Accounts receivable	30.00	27.00
Inventory	209.06	189.06
Current assets	$252.06	$221.93
Gross fixed assets	474.47	409.47
Accumulated depreciation	(154.17)	(90.00)
Net fixed assets	320.30	319.47
Total assets	$572.36	$541.40
Accounts payable	$ 25.05	$ 26.05
Notes payable	0.00	0.00
Current portion of long-term debt	0.00	0.00
Current liabilities	$ 25.05	$ 26.05
Long-term debt	240.00	245.00
Total liabilities	$265.05	$271.05
Common stock	160.00	150.00
Retained earnings	147.31	120.35
Total shareholders' equity	$307.31	$270.35
Total liabilities and shareholders' equity	$572.36	$541.40

TABLE 16G

Rio National Corp. Summary Income Statement for the Year Ended December 31, 2013 (US$ millions)

Revenue	$300.80
Total operating expenses	(173.74)
Operating profit	127.06
Gain on sale	4.00
Earnings before interest, taxes, depreciation, and amortization (EBITDA)	131.06
Depreciation and amortization	(71.17)
Earnings before interest and taxes (EBIT)	59.89
Interest	(16.80)
Income tax expense	(12.93)
Net income	$ 30.16

TABLE 16H

Rio National Corp. Supplemental Notes for 2013

Note 1:   RIO National had $75 million in capital expenditures during the year.

Note 2:   A piece of equipment that was originally purchased for $10 million was sold for $7 million at year-end, when it had a net book value of $3 million. Equipment sales are unusual for Rio National.

Note 3:   The decrease in long-term debt represents an unscheduled principal repayment; there was no new borrowing during the year.

Note 4:   On January 1, 2013, the company received cash from issuing 400,000 shares of common equity at a price of $25 per share.

Note 5:   A new appraisal during the year increased the estimated market value of land held for investment by $2 million, which was not recognized in 2013 income.

Dividends paid (US$ millions)	$3.20
Weighted-average shares outstanding during 2002	16,000,000
Dividend per share	$.20
Earnings per share	$1.89
Beta	1.80

Note: The dividend payout ratio is expected to be constant.

Risk-free rate of return	4.00%
Expected rate of return on market index	9.00%
Median industry price-earnings (P/E) ratio	19.90
Expected industry earnings growth rate	12.00%

The portfolio manager of a large mutual fund comments to one of the fund's analysts, Katrina Shaar: "We have been considering the purchase of Rio National Corp. equity shares, so I would like you to analyze the value of the company. To begin, based on Rio National's past performance, you can assume that the company will grow at the same rate as the industry."

a. Calculate the value of a share of Rio National equity on December 31, 2013, using the Gordon growth model and the capital asset pricing model.

b. Calculate the sustainable growth rate of Rio National on December 31, 2013. Use 2013 beginning-of-year balance sheet values.

31. While valuing the equity of Rio National Corp. (from problem 30), Katrina Shaar is considering the use of either cash flow from operations (CFO) or free cash flow to equity (FCFE) in her valuation process.

a. State two adjustments that Shaar should make to cash flow from operations to obtain free cash flow to equity.

b. Shaar decides to calculate Rio National's FCFE for the year 2013, starting with net income. Determine for each of the five supplemental notes given in Table 16H whether an adjustment should be made to net income to calculate Rio National's free cash flow to equity for the year 2013, and the dollar amount of any adjustment.

c. Calculate Rio National's free cash flow to equity for the year 2013.

32. Shaar (from the previous problem) has revised slightly her estimated earnings growth rate for Rio National and, using normalized (underlying) EPS, which is adjusted for temporary impacts on earnings, now wants to compare the current value of Rio National's equity to that of the industry, on a growth-adjusted basis. Selected information about Rio National and the industry is given in Table 16K.

Compared to the industry, is Rio National's equity overvalued or undervalued on a P/E-to-growth (PEG) basis, using normalized (underlying) earnings per share? Assume that the risk of Rio National is similar to the risk of the industry.

33. Recalculate the intrinsic value of Honda in each of the following scenarios by using the three-stage growth model of Spreadsheet 16.1. Treat each scenario independently.

a. ROE in the constant-growth period will be 9 percent.

b. Honda's actual beta is 1.0.

c. The market risk premium is 8.5 percent.

TABLE 16K

Rio National Corp. Versus Industry

Rio National	
Estimated earnings growth rate	11.00%
Current share price	$25.00
Normalized (underlying) EPS for 2011	$1.71
Weighted-average shares outstanding during 2011	16,000,000
Industry	
Estimated earnings growth rate	12.00%
Median price-earnings (P/E) ratio	19.90

 34. Recalculate the intrinsic value of Honda shares using the free cash flow model of Spreadsheet 16.2. Treat each scenario independently.

    a. Honda's P/E ratio starting in 2016 will be 15.

    b. Honda's unlevered beta is .7.

    c. The market risk premium is 9 percent.

E-INVESTMENTS
Equity
Valuation

Go to the MoneyCentral Investor page at **moneycentral.msn.com/investor/home.asp**. Use the *Research Wizard* function to obtain fundamentals, price history, price target, catalysts, and comparison for Walmart (WMT). For comparison, use Target (TGT), BJ's Wholesale Club (BJ), and the Industry.

1. What has been the one-year sales and income growth for Walmart?

2. What has been the company's five-year profit margin? How does that compare with the other two firms' profit margins and the industry's profit margin?

3. What have been the percentage price changes for the last 3, 6, and 12 months? How do they compare with the other firms' price changes and the industry's price changes?

4. What are the estimated high and low prices for Walmart for the coming year based on its current P/E multiple?

5. Compare the price performance of Walmart with that of Target and BJ's. Which of the companies appears to be the most expensive in terms of current earnings? Which of the companies is the least expensive in terms of current earnings?

6. What are the firms' *Stock Scouter Ratings*? How are these ratings interpreted?

APPENDIX 16A: DERIVATION OF THE DIVIDEND DISCOUNT MODEL

Consider an investor who buys a share of Steady State Electronics stock, planning to hold it for one year. The intrinsic value of the share is the present value of the dividend to be received at the end of the first year, D_1, and the expected sales price, P_1. We will henceforth use the simplest notation P_1 instead of $E(P_1)$ to avoid clutter. Keep in mind, though, future prices and dividends are unknown, and we are dealing with expected values, not certain values. Discounting at the cost of equity, k,

$$V_0 = \frac{D_1 + P_1}{1 + k} \qquad (16A.1)$$

While dividends are fairly predictable given a company's history, you might ask how we can estimate P_1, the year-end price. According to equation 16A.1, V_1 (the year-end value) will be

$$V_1 = \frac{D_2 + P_2}{1 + k}$$

If we assume the stock will be selling for its intrinsic value next year, then $V_1 = P_1$, and we can substitute this value for P_1 into equation 16A.1 to find

$$V_0 = \frac{D_1}{1 + k} + \frac{D_2 + P_2}{(1 + k)^2}$$

This equation may be interpreted as the present value of dividends plus sales price for a two-year holding period. Of course, now we need to come up with a forecast of P_2. Continuing in the same way, we can replace P_2 by $(D_3 + P_3)/(1 + k)$, which relates P_0 to the value of dividends plus the expected sales price for a three-year holding period.

More generally, for a holding period of H years, we can write the stock value as the present value of dividends over the H years, plus the ultimate sale price, P_H:

$$V_0 = \frac{D_1}{1 + k} + \frac{D_2}{(1 + k)^2} + \cdots + \frac{D_H + P_H}{(1 + k)^H} \qquad (16A.2)$$

Note the similarity between this formula and the bond valuation formula developed in Chapter 12. Each relates price to the present value of a stream of payments (coupons in the case of bonds, dividends in the case of stocks) and a final payment (the face value of the bond, or the sales price of the stock). The key differences in the case of stocks are the uncertainty of dividends, the lack of a fixed maturity date, and the unknown sales price at the horizon date. Indeed, one can continue to substitute for price indefinitely to conclude

$$V_0 = \frac{D_1}{1 + k} + \frac{D_2}{(1 + k)^2} + \frac{D_3}{(1 + k)^3} + \cdots \qquad (16A.3)$$

Equation 16A.3 states that the stock price should equal the present value of all expected future dividends into perpetuity. As discussed in Section 16.3, this formula is called the *dividend discount model (DDM)* of stock prices.

It is tempting, but incorrect, to conclude from equation 16A.3 that the DDM focuses exclusively on dividends and ignores capital gains as a motive for investing in stock. Indeed, we assume explicitly in equation 16A.1 that capital gains (as reflected in the expected sales price, P_1) are part of the stock's value. At the same time, the price at which you can sell a stock in the future depends on dividend forecasts at that time.

The reason only dividends appear in equation 16A.3 is not that investors ignore capital gains. It is instead that those capital gains will be determined by dividend forecasts at the time the stock is sold. That is why in equation 16A.2 we can write the stock price as the present value of dividends plus sales price for *any* horizon date. P_H is the present value at time H of all dividends expected to be paid after the horizon date. That value is then discounted back to today, time 0. The DDM asserts that stock prices are determined ultimately by the cash flows accruing to shareholders, and those are dividends.[11]

---

[11]If investors never expected a dividend to be paid, then this model implies that the stock would have no value. To reconcile the fact that non-dividend-paying stocks do have a market value with this model, one must assume that investors expect it may someday pay out some cash, even if only a liquidating dividend.

The Constant-Growth DDM

Equation 16A.3 as it stands is still not very useful in valuing a stock, because it requires dividend forecasts for every year into the indefinite future. For a more structured valuation approach, we need to introduce some simplifying assumptions. A useful first pass at the problem is to assume that Steady State Electronics dividends are trending upward at a stable growth rate, which we will call g. Then if $g = .05$, and the most recently paid dividend was $D_0 = 3.81$, expected future dividends would be

$$D_1 = D_0(1 + g) = 3.81 \times 1.05 = 4.00$$
$$D_2 = D_0(1 + g)^2 = 3.81 \times (1.05)^2 = 4.20$$
$$D_3 = D_0(1 + g)^3 = 3.81 \times (1.05)^3 = 4.41$$

and so on.

Using these dividend forecasts in equation 16A.3, we solve for intrinsic value as

$$V_0 = \frac{D_0(1 + g)}{1 + k} + \frac{D_0(1 + g)^2}{(1 + k)^2} + \frac{D_0(1 + g)^3}{(1 + k)^3} + \cdots$$

This equation can be simplified to

$$V_0 = \frac{D_0(1 + g)}{k - g} = \frac{D_1}{k - g} \qquad (16A.4)$$

Note in equation 16A.4 that we divide D_1 (not D_0) by $k - g$ to calculate intrinsic value. If the market capitalization rate for Steady State is 12 percent, now we can use equation 16A.4 to show that the intrinsic value of a share of Steady State stock is

$$\frac{\$4}{.12 - .05} = \$57.14$$

Equation 16A.4 is called the *constant-growth DDM* or the *Gordon model*, after Myron J. Gordon, who popularized the model. It should remind you of the formula for the present value of a perpetuity. If dividends were expected not to grow, then the dividend stream would be a simple perpetuity, and the valuation formula would be $P_0 = D_1/k$. Equation 16A.4 is a generalization of the perpetuity formula to cover the case of a *growing* perpetuity. As g increases, the stock price also rises.[12]

---

[12]Here is a proof that the intrinsic value, V_0, of a stream of cash dividends growing at a constant rate, g, is equal to $\frac{D_1}{k - g}$. By definition,

$$V_0 = \frac{D_1}{1 + k} + \frac{D_1(1 + g)}{(1 + k)^2} + \frac{D_1(1 + g)^2}{(1 + k)^3} + \cdots$$

Multiplying through by $(1 + k)/(1 + g)$, we obtain

$$\frac{(1 + k)}{(1 + g)} V_0 = \frac{D_1}{(1 + g)} + \frac{D_1}{(1 + k)} + \frac{D_2(1 + g)}{(1 + k)^2} + \cdots$$

Subtracting the first equation from the second, we find that

$$\frac{(1 + k)}{(1 + g)} V_0 - V_0 = \frac{D_1}{(1 + g)}$$

which implies

$$\frac{(k - g) V_0}{(1 + g)} = \frac{D_1}{(1 + g)}$$

$$V_0 = \frac{D_1}{k - g}$$

The constant-growth DDM is valid only when g is less than k. If dividends were expected to grow forever at a rate faster than k, the value of the stock would be infinite. If an analyst derives an estimate of g that is greater than k, that growth rate must be unsustainable in the long run. The appropriate valuation model to use in this case is a multistage DDM such as that discussed in Section 16.3.

The constant-growth DDM is so widely used by stock market analysts that it is worth exploring some of its implications and limitations. It implies that a stock's value will be greater

1. The larger its expected dividend per share
2. The lower the market capitalization rate, k
3. The higher the expected growth rate of dividends

Another implication of the model is that the stock price is expected to grow at the same rate as dividends. To see this, suppose Steady State stock is selling at its intrinsic value of $57.14, so that $V_0 = P_0$. Then

$$P_0 = \frac{D_1}{k - g}$$

Note that price is proportional to dividends. Therefore, next year, when the dividends paid to Steady State shareholders are expected to be higher by $g = 5$ percent, price also should increase by 5 percent. To confirm this, note

$$D_2 = \$4(1.05) = \$4.20$$

$$P_1 = D_2/(k - g) = \$4.29/(.12 - .05) = \$60$$

which is 5 percent higher than the current price of $57.14. To generalize,

$$P_1 = \frac{D_2}{k - g} = \frac{D_1(1 + g)}{k - g} = \frac{D_1}{k - g}(1 + g)$$

$$P_0(1 + g)$$

Therefore, the DDM implies that in the case of constant growth of dividends, the rate of price appreciation in any year will equal that constant growth rate, g.

CHAPTER 17

Financial Statement Analysis

In the previous chapter, we explored equity valuation techniques. These techniques take as inputs the firm's dividends and earnings prospects. While the valuation analyst is interested in economic earnings streams, only financial accounting data are readily available. What can we learn from a company's accounting data that can help us estimate the intrinsic value of its common stock? In this chapter, we are not trying to develop the art of financial statement analysis, but rather to show how investors can use financial data as inputs into stock valuation analysis. We present much more complicated financial statements than are often seen in elementary corporate finance texts; this is to show the complexity and the potential variety of statements.

We start by reviewing the basic sources of such data—the income statement, the balance sheet, and the statement of cash flows. We note the difference between economic and accounting earnings. Although economic earnings are more important for issues of evaluation, they can at best be estimated, so in practice analysts always begin their evaluation of the firm using accounting data. We show how analysts use financial ratios to explore the sources of a firm's profitability and evaluate the "quality" of its earnings in a systematic fashion. We also examine the impact of debt policy on various financial ratios.

We conclude with a discussion of the challenges encountered when using financial statement analysis as a tool in uncovering mispriced securities. Some of these limitations are due to differences in firms' accounting procedures, while others arise from inflation-induced distortions in accounting numbers.

17.1   THE MAJOR FINANCIAL STATEMENTS

The Income Statement

The **income statement** is a summary of the profitability of the firm over a period of time, such as a year. It presents revenues generated during the operating period, the expenses incurred during that same period, and the company's net income, which is simply the difference between revenues and expenses.

It is useful to distinguish four broad classes of expenses: cost of goods sold (COGS), which is the direct cost attributable to producing the product sold by the firm; salaries, advertising, and other costs of operating the firm that are not directly attributable to production; interest expense on the firm's debt; and taxes on earnings owed to federal and local governments. Typically, this simple breakdown of expenses is not immediately recognizable in the income statements of larger firms.

Table 17.1 presents a 2012 income statement for George Weston Limited (dividend and retained earnings data are from their statement of equity). Weston chooses to isolate the inventory

AnnualReports. com
www. annualreports. com

TABLE 17.1

Income Statement for Weston, 2012

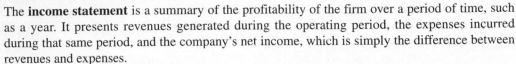

George Weston Limited Consolidated Statements of Earnings For the Years Ended December 31 ($ millions except where otherwise indicated)			
	2012	**2011**	**Percent of Revenue**
Sales (note 2)	$32,742	$32,376	100.0%
Operating Expenses			
Cost of inventories (note 11)	24,700	24,421	75.4%
Cost of selling general and administrative expenses (note 29)	6,650	6,346	20.3%
	31,350	$30,767	95.7%
Operating Income	1,392	1,609	4.25%
Net interest expense and other financing charges (note 5)	417	366	1.3%
Earnings Before Income Taxes	975	1,243	3.0%
Income taxes (note 6)	249	324	.8%
Net Earnings	726	919	2.2%
Attributable to:			
Shareholders of the company	486	635	1.5%
Non-controlling Interests	240	284	.7%
Net Earnings	$ 726	$ 919	2.2%
Net Earnings per Common Share—($) (note 7)	$ .52	$ 5.11	
Basic	$ 3.45	$ 4.58	
Diluted	$ 3.38	$ 4.55	
Dividends Declared			
Per common share ($)	$ 1.46	$ 1.44	
Retained earnings, beginning of year	4,496	4,311	
Retained earnings, end of year	4,736	4,496	

See accompanying notes to the consolidated financial statements.

cost, given that in the grocery business margins are fairly low, and this constitutes about 75 percent of their expenses. The major component of operating expense is cost of goods sold (COGS), but depreciation, goodwill impairment, and restructuring charges are typically additional expense. The remainder, called *operating income*, is equivalent to earnings before interest and taxes (EBIT). As a percentage, the operating margin is only 4.25 percent. Subtracting interest and income taxes and adjusting for minority interests leads to net earnings. Net income or earnings is the "bottom line" of the income statement.

Analysts also commonly prepare a *common-size income statement*, in which all items on the income statement are expressed as a fraction of total revenue. This makes it easier to compare firms of different sizes and yearly changes. We have added the right-hand column of Table 17.1, which is Weston's common-size income statement for 2012.

The Balance Sheet

While the income statement provides a measure of the profitability over a period of time, the **balance sheet** provides a snapshot of the financial condition of the firm at a particular point in time. The balance sheet is a list of the firm's assets and liabilities at that moment. The difference in assets and liabilities is the net worth of the firm, also called *shareholders' equity*. Like income statements, balance sheets are reasonably standardized in presentation. Table 17.2 is the balance sheet of Weston for year-end 2012.

The first section of the balance sheet gives a listing of the assets of the firm. Current assets are presented first. These are cash and other items such as accounts receivable or inventories that will be converted into cash within one year; Weston recognizes prepaid expenses separately from production inventories. The company lists long-term receivables together with investments it has made as well as goodwill and intangibles, in addition to the usual entry of the company's property, plant, and equipment. The sum of current and long-term assets, plus other adjustments, gives total assets, the last line of the assets side of the balance sheet.

The liability and shareholders' equity side is similarly arranged. First come short-term or current liabilities, such as accounts payable, accrued taxes, and debts due within one year. Following this is long-term debt and other liabilities due in more than a year, as well as other adjustments. The difference between total assets and total liabilities is shareholders' equity. This is the net worth or book value of the firm. Shareholders' equity may be divided between preferred and common shareholders. The latter section is usually divided into value of common shares, contributed surplus (additional paid-in capital), and retained earnings; the first two of these represent the proceeds realized from the sale of shares to the public, while retained earnings derive from the buildup of equity from profits plowed back into the firm.

To make it easier to compare firms of different sizes, analysts often present each item on the balance sheet as a percentage of total assets. This is called a *common-size balance sheet*; figures are presented this way in the second and fourth columns of Table 17.2, which we have added to the official statements.

The Statement of Changes in Financial Position

Market Wire
www.marketwire
.com

The **statement of changes in financial position** is also referred to as a *statement of cash flows* or *flow of funds statement*. It is a report of the cash flow generated by the firm's operations, investments, and financial activities. The income statement and balance sheet are based on accrual methods of accounting, which means revenues and expenses are recognized when incurred, even if no cash has yet been exchanged; this third statement, however, recognizes only the results of transactions in which cash changes hands. For example, if goods are sold now, with payment due in 60 days, the income statement will treat the revenue as generated when the sale occurs, and the balance sheet will be immediately augmented by accounts

TABLE 17.2 Balance Sheet for Weston, 2012

	2012	2012 as Percent of Total Assets	2011	2011 as Percent of Total Assets
George Weston Limited Consolidated Balance Sheets As at December 31 ($ millions)				
ASSETS				
Current Assets				
Cash and cash equivalents (note 8)	$ 1,589	7.29%	$ 1,372	6.43%
Short term investments (note 8)	2,138	9.81%	2,362	11.08%
Accounts receivable (note 9)	559	2.56%	559	2.62%
Credit card receivables (note 10)	2,305	10.57%	2,101	9.85%
Inventories (note 11)	2,132	9.78%	2,147	10.07%
Income taxes recoverable	37	0.17%	37	.17%
Prepaid expenses and other assets	83	0.38%	122	.57%
Assets held for sale (note 12)	30	0.14%	32	.15%
Total current assets	8,873	40.69%	8,732	40.95%
Fixed assets (note 13)	9,452	43.35%	9,172	43.01%
Investment properties (note 14)	100	0.46%	82	0.38%
Goodwill and intangible assets (note 15)	1,571	11.63%	1,555	0.38%
Deferred income taxes (note 6)	316	1.45%	295	7.29%
Security deposits (note 8)	348	1.60%	367	1.38%
Franchise loans receivable (note 29)	363	1.66%	331	1.72%
Other assets (note 16)	781	3.58%	789	3.70%
Total Assets	$21,804	100.00%	$21,323	100.00%
LIABILITIES				
Current Liabilities				
Bank indebtedness	—		$ 3	0.01%
Trade and other payables	$ 3,937	18.06%	3,940	18.48%
Provisions (note 17)	123	.56%	67	.31%
Short term debt (note 18)	1,319	6.05%	1,280	6.00%
Long term debt due within one year (note 19)	672	3.08%	87	.41%
Total Current Liabilities	6,051	27.75%	5,377	25.22%
Provisions (note 17)	94	.43%	94	.00%
Long term debt (note 19)	6,261	28.71%	6,757	31.69%
Deferred income taxes (note 6)	160	.73%	160	.75%
Other liabilities (note 20)	945	4.33%	1,033	4.84%
Capital securities (note 21)	223	1.02%	222	1.04%
Total Liabilities	13,734	62.99%	13,643	63.98%
EQUITY				
Share capital (note 22)	953	4.37%	950	4.46%
Contributed surplus (notes 23 & 26)	28	0.13%	24	.11%
Retained earnings	4,735	21.72%	4,496	21.09%
Accumulated other comprehensive loss	−24	−0.11%	−11	−.05%
Total Equity Attributable to Shareholders of the Company	5,692	26.11%	5,459	25.60%
Non-controlling Interests	2,378	10.91%	2,221	10.42%
Total Equity	8,070	37.01%	7,680	36.02%
Total Liabilities and Equity	$21,804	100.00%	$21,323	100.00%

Leases (note 28). Contingencies (note 31). Financial guarantees (note 32). Subsequent event (note 34).

Source: Reprinted by permission of George Weston Limited.

receivable less inventory; but the statement of changes in financial position will not recognize the transaction until the bill is paid and the cash is in hand.

Table 17.3 shows the 2012 consolidated statements of changes in financial position for Weston. The first item under cash from operating activities is net income. The next entries modify that figure by components of income that have been recognized, but for which cash has not yet been exchanged. An increase in accounts receivable, for example, means income has been claimed on the income statement, but cash has not yet been collected. Hence, decreases in accounts receivable increase the cash flows realized from operations in this period. Similarly, increases in accounts payable mean expenses have been incurred, but cash has not yet left the firm. Any payment delay increases the company's net cash flows in this period.

Another major difference between the income statement and the statement of changes in financial position involves depreciation, which is a major addition to income in the adjustment section of cash provided in Table 17.3. The income statement attempts to "smooth" large capital expenditures over time to reflect a measure of profitability not distorted by large infrequent expenditures. The depreciation expense on the income statement does this by recognizing capital expenditures over a period of many years rather than at the specific time of those expenditures.

TABLE 17.3

Consolidated Statements of Changes in Financial Position for Weston, 2012

George Weston Limited Consolidated Cash Flow Statements For the Years Ended December 31 ($ millions)		
	2012	**2011**
Operating Activities		
Net earnings	$ 726	$ 919
Income taxes (note 6)	249	324
Net interest expense and other financing charges (note 5)	417	366
Depreciation and amortization	840	762
Foreign currency translation loss (gain) (note 29)	24	−25
Income taxes paid	−261	−277
Interest received	65	76
Settlement of equity derivative contracts (note 29)		−22
Change in credit card receivables (note 10)	−204	−104
Change in non-cash working capital	43	−36
Fixed asset and other related impairments	19	7
Gain on disposal of assets (14) (18)	−14	−18
Other	−52	2
Cash Flows from Operating Activities	1,852	1,974
Investing Activities		
Fixed asset purchases (note 13)	−1,110	−1,027
Change in short term investments	181	929
Business acquisition—net of cash acquired		−12
Proceeds from fixed asset sales	64	57
Change in franchise investments and other receivables	−22	−18
Change in security deposits	14	74
Goodwill and intangible asset additions (note 15)	−43	−13
Other		−5
Cash Flows Used in Investing Activities	−916	−15

continued

George Weston Limited Consolidated Cash Flow Statements For the Years Ended December 31 ($ millions)		
	2012	**2011**
Financing Activities		
Change in bank indebtedness	−3	−8
Change in short term debt (note 18)	39	409
Long term debt (note 19)		
—Issued	111	635
—Retired	−115	−1,209
Share capital		
—Issued (notes 22 & 26)	2	1
—Retired (note 23)	−1	−61
Subsidiary share capital		
—Issued (notes 23 & 26)	22	21
—Retired (note 8)	−16	−39
Interest paid	−456	−489
Dividends		
—To common shareholders	−185	−1186
—To preferred shareholders	−44	−44
—To minority shareholders	−65	−79
Cash Flows Used in Financing Activities	−711	−2,049
Effect of Foreign Currency Exchange Rate Changes on Cash and Cash Equivalents	−8	9
Cash Flows (Used in) from Continuing Operations	−332	510
Change in Cash and Cash Equivalents	217	−81
Cash and Cash Equivalents, Beginning of Year	1,372	1,453
Cash and Cash Equivalents, End of Year	$1,589	$1,372

See accompanying notes to the consolidated financial statements.

Source: George Weston Limited, 2006 financial report. Reprinted by permission of George Weston Limited.

The statement of cash flows, however, recognizes the cash implication of a capital expenditure when it occurs. Therefore, it adds back the depreciation "expense" that was used to compute net income; instead, it acknowledges a capital expenditure when it is paid. It does so by reporting cash flows separately for operations, investing, and financing activities. This way, any large cash flows (such as those for big investments) can be recognized explicitly as nonrecurring, without affecting the measure of cash flow generated by operating activities.

The second section of the statement lists the cash flows resulting from investing activities. These entries are investments in the capital stock necessary for the firm to maintain or enhance its productive capacity, and other financial investments. For example, in 2012 Weston invested $1,110 million in fixed assets; while fixed-asset sales netted a less significant amount ($64 million) of cash.

Finally, the third section of the statement of cash flows is the accounting of cash flows from financing activities. Issuance of securities will contribute positive cash flows, while repurchasing or redeeming securities will consume cash. Note that Weston spent $115 million in repurchasing long-term debt while re-issuing an equivalent $111 million in 2012, in contrast to its 2011 retirement of twice as much debt as it issued. Notice that while dividends paid are included in the cash flows from the financing, interest payments on debt are included with operating activities, because, unlike dividends, interest payments are not discretionary. Nevertheless, Weston unusually reports interest payments in both the operating and financing segments of the cash flow statement. The final cash position increased by $217 million in 2012.

The statement of cash flows provides important evidence on the well-being of a firm. If a company cannot pay its dividends and maintain the productivity of its capital stock out of cash flow from operations, for example, and it must resort to borrowing to meet these demands, this is a serious warning that the firm cannot maintain dividend payout at its current level in the long run. The statement of cash flows will reveal this developing problem, when it shows that cash flow from operations is inadequate and that borrowing is being used to maintain dividend payments at unsustainable levels.

17.2 MEASURING FIRM PERFORMANCE

In Chapter 1, we noted that a natural goal of the firm is to maximize value, but that various agency problems, or conflicts of interest, may impede that goal. How can we measure how well the firm is actually performing? Financial analysts have come up with a vast list of financial ratios that measure many aspects of firm performance. To get a grasp on the problem we first need to consider what sorts of ratios may be related to the ultimate objective of added value.

Two broad activities are the responsibility of a firm's financial managers: investment decisions and financing decisions. Investment, or capital budgeting, decisions pertain to the firm's *use* of capital: the business activities in which it is engaged. Here, the questions we will wish to answer concern the profitability of those projects. How should profitability be measured? How does the acceptable level of profitability depend on risk and the opportunity cost of the funds used to pay for the firm's many projects? In contrast, financial decisions pertain to the firm's *sources* of capital. Is there a sufficient supply of financing to meet projected needs for growth? Does the financing plan rely too heavily on borrowed funds? Is there sufficient liquidity to deal with unexpected cash needs?

These questions suggest that we organize the ratios we choose to construct along the lines given in Figure 17.1. The figure shows that when evaluating the firm's investment activities, we will ask two questions: How efficiently does the firm deploy its assets, and how profitable are its sales? Aspects of both efficiency and profitability can be measured with a variety of ratios. Efficiency is typically assessed using several turnover ratios, while the profitability of sales is commonly measured with various profit margins. Similarly, when evaluating financing decisions, we look at both leverage and liquidity, and we will see that aspects of each of these two concepts also can be measured with an array of statistics.

Figure 17.1   Important financial questions and some ratios that help answer them.

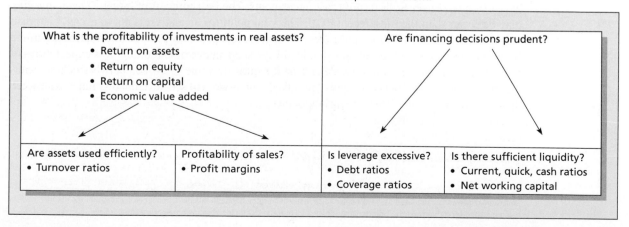

The next section shows how to calculate and interpret some of these key financial ratios and shows how many of them are related.

PROFITABILITY MEASURES AND THEIR ANALYSIS

Profitability measures focus on the firm's earnings. To facilitate comparisons across firms, total earnings are expressed on a per-dollar-invested basis. So return on capital, which measures profitability for all contributors of capital, is defined as earnings before interest and taxes divided by combined long-term capital. A very closely related measure, return on assets, focuses instead on the return—EBIT—to the total assets financed by that capital. Reflecting a different interest, return on equity, which measures profitability for contributors of equity capital, is defined as (after-tax) profits divided by the book value of equity.

To summarize, the three main profitability measures are:

- *Return on capital (ROC).* Return on capital expresses EBIT as a fraction of long-term capital, shareholder's equity plus long-term debt. It tells us the income earned per dollar of long-term capital invested in the firm.

$$ROC = EBIT/Long\text{-}term\ capital$$

- *Return on assets (ROA).* **Return on assets (ROA)** equals EBIT as a fraction of the firm's total assets.[1] The numerator of this ratio may be viewed as total operating income of the firm. Therefore, ROA tells us the income earned per dollar deployed in the firm.

$$ROA = EBIT/Total\ assets$$

- *Return on equity (ROE).* Whereas ROA and ROC measure profitability relative to funds raised by both debt and equity financing, **return on equity (ROE)** focuses only on the profitability of equity investments. It equals net income realized by shareholders per dollar they have invested in the firm.

$$ROE = Net\ income/Shareholders'\ equity$$

Past Versus Future ROE

We noted in Chapter 16 that ROE is one of the two basic factors in determining a firm's growth rate of earnings. There are two sides to using ROE. Sometimes it is reasonable to assume that future ROE will approximate its past value, but a high ROE in the past does not necessarily imply a firm's future ROE will be high. A declining ROE is evidence that the firm's new investments have offered a lower ROE than its past investments. The best forecast of future ROE in this case may be lower than the most recent ROE. The vital point for an analyst is not to accept historical values as indicators of future values. Data from the recent past may provide information regarding future performance, but the analyst should always keep an eye on the future. It is expectations of future dividends and earnings that determine the intrinsic value of the company's stock. Not surprisingly, returns on assets and equity are linked, but as we will see next, the relationship between them is affected by the firm's financial policies.

---

[1]ROA sometimes is computed using EBIT × (1 − Tax rate) in the numerator. Sometimes it is computed using after-tax operating income, that is,

$$Net\ income + Interest \times (1 - Tax\ rate)$$

Sometimes, it even is calculated using just net income in the numerator, although this definition ignores altogether the income the firm has generated for debt investors. Unfortunately, definitions of many key financial ratios are not fully standardized.

TABLE 17.4

Nodett's Profitability over the Business Cycle

Scenario	Sales ($ millions)	EBIT ($ millions)	ROA (% per year)	Net Profit ($ millions)	ROE ($ per year)
Bad year	80	5	5	3	3
Normal year	100	10	10	6	6
Good year	120	15	15	9	9

TABLE 17.5

Impact of Financial Leverage on ROE

		Nodett		Somdett	
Scenario	EBIT ($ millions)	Net Profits ($ millions)	ROE (%)	Net Profits* ($ millions)	ROE† (%)
Bad year	5	3	3	1.08	1.8
Normal year	10	6	6	4.08	6.8
Good year	15	9	9	7.08	11.8

*Somdett's after-tax profits are given by .6(EBIT − $3.2 million).
†Somdett's equity is only $60 million.

Financial Leverage and ROE

An analyst interpreting the past behaviour of a firm's ROE or forecasting its future value must pay careful attention to the firm's debt–equity mix and to the interest rate on its debt. An example will show why. Suppose Nodett is a firm that is all equity financed and has total assets of $100 million. Assume it pays corporate taxes at the rate of 40 percent of taxable earnings.

Table 17.4 shows the behaviour of sales, earnings before interest and taxes, and net profits under three scenarios representing phases of the business cycle. It also shows the behaviour of two of the most commonly used profitability measures: operating ROA, which equals EBIT/total assets, and ROE, which equals net profits/equity.

Somdett is a firm identical to Nodett, except that $40 million of its $100 million of assets are financed with debt bearing an interest rate of 8 percent. It pays annual interest expense of $3.2 million. Table 17.5 shows how Somdett's ROE differs from Nodett's.

Note that annual sales, EBIT, and therefore ROA for both firms are the same in each of the three scenarios, that is, business risk for the two companies is identical. It is their financial risk that differs. Although Nodett and Somdett have the same ROA in each scenario, Somdett's ROE exceeds that of Nodett in normal and good years and is lower in bad years.

We can summarize the exact relationship among ROE, ROA, and leverage in the following equation:[2]

$$\text{ROE} = (1 - \text{Tax rate})\left[\text{ROA} + (\text{ROA} - \text{Interest rate})\frac{\text{Debt}}{\text{Equity}} \right] \qquad (17.1)$$

---

[2]The derivation of equation 17.1 is as follows:

$$\text{ROE} = \frac{\text{Net profit}}{\text{Equity}}$$

$$= \frac{\text{EBIT} - \text{Interest} - \text{Taxes}}{\text{Equity}}$$

$$= (1 - \text{Tax rate}) \frac{(\text{ROA} \times \text{Assets} - \text{Interest rate} \times \text{Debt})}{\text{Equity}}$$

$$= (1 - \text{Tax rate})\left[\left(\text{ROA} \times \frac{(\text{Equity} + \text{Debt})}{\text{Equity}} - \text{Interest rate} \times \frac{\text{Debt}}{\text{Equity}} \right) \right]$$

$$= (1 - \text{Tax rate})\left[\text{ROA} + (\text{ROA} - \text{Interest rate})\frac{\text{Debt})}{\text{Equity}} \right]$$

The relationship has the following implications. If there is no debt or if the firm's ROA equals the interest rate on its debt, its ROE will simply equal $(1 - \text{Tax rate}) \times \text{ROA}$. If its ROA exceeds the interest rate, then its ROE will exceed $(1 - \text{Tax rate}) \times \text{ROA}$ by an amount that will be greater the higher the debt-to-equity ratio.

This result makes intuitive sense. If ROA exceeds the borrowing rate, the firm earns more on its money than it pays out to creditors. The surplus earnings are available to the firm's owners, the equityholders, which raises ROE. If, on the other hand, ROA is less than the interest rate, then ROE will decline by an amount that depends on the debt-to-equity ratio.

EXAMPLE 17.1   Leverage and ROE

To illustrate the application of equation 17.1, we can use the numerical example in Table 17.5. In a normal year, Nodett has an ROE of 6 percent, which is $.6(1 - \text{Tax rate}) \times$ its ROA of 10 percent. However, Somdett, which borrows at an interest rate of 8 percent and maintains a debt/equity ratio of $\frac{2}{3}$, has an ROE of 6.8 percent. The calculation using equation 17.1 is

$$\begin{aligned} \text{ROE} &= .6[10\% + (10\% - 8\%)\tfrac{2}{3}] \\ &= .6[10\% + \tfrac{4}{3}\%] \\ &= .6.8\% \end{aligned}$$

The important point to remember is that increased debt will make a positive contribution to a firm's ROE only if the firm's ROA exceeds the interest rate on the debt.

Note also that financial leverage increases the risk of the equityholder returns. Table 17.5 shows that ROE on Somdett is worse than that of Nodett in bad years. Conversely, in good years, Somdett outperforms Nodett because the excess of ROA over ROE provides additional funds for equityholders. The presence of debt makes Somdett more sensitive to the business cycle than Nodett. Even though the two companies have equal business risk (reflected in their identical EBITs in all three scenarios), Somdett's stockholders bear greater financial risk than Nodett's because all of the firm's business risk is absorbed by a smaller base of equity investors.

Even if financial leverage increases the expected ROE of Somdett relative to Nodett (as it seems to in Table 17.5), this does not imply the market value of Somdett's equity will be higher.[3] Financial leverage increases the risk of the firm's equity as surely as it raises the expected ROE, and the higher discount rate will offset the higher expected earnings.

Increased operating leverage has a similar effect in magnifying the results of increased sales into greater percentage increases in EBIT. Higher fixed costs work as do fixed financial charges; until sales reach a certain level, lower operating leverage will be superior in terms of EBIT. Given the principle of matching the financing of fixed assets with long-term capital, high-operating-leverage companies will probably have higher debt loads and interest charges. Thus total leverage, a product of financial and operating leverage, will be even higher, indicating a greater sensitivity to the sales cycle. Conceivably, lower operating leverage combined with higher financial leverage could make one firm equally sensitive to sales changes as another with the reverse leverage position; practically, it is unlikely to happen. Risk and cyclical response tend to be high or low by the nature of the particular industry, where optimal operating structures will suggest roughly equal degrees of operating leverage, financed with similar debt ratios.

---

[3]This is the essence of the debate on the Modigliani-Miller theorems regarding the effect of financial leverage on the value of the firm.

CC 1

CONCEPT CHECK

Mordett is a company with the same assets as Nodett and Somdett but a debt-to-equity ratio of 1.0 and an interest rate of 9 percent. What would its net profit and ROE be in a bad year, a normal year, and a good year?

Decomposition of ROE

To understand the factors affecting a firm's ROE, including its trend over time and its performance relative to competitors, analysts often "decompose" ROE into the product of a series of ratios. Each component ratio is in itself meaningful, and the process serves to focus the analyst's attention on the separate factors influencing performance.[4]

One useful decomposition of ROE is

$$\frac{\text{Net profit}}{\text{Equity}} = \underbrace{\frac{\text{Net profits}}{\text{Pretax profits}}}_{(1)} \times \underbrace{\frac{\text{Pretax profits}}{\text{EBIT}}}_{(2)} \times \underbrace{\frac{\text{EBIT}}{\text{Sales}}}_{(3)} \times \underbrace{\frac{\text{Sales}}{\text{Assets}}}_{(4)} \times \underbrace{\frac{\text{Assets}}{\text{Equity}}}_{(5)} \quad (17.2)$$

Table 17.6 shows all these ratios for Nodett and Somdett Corporations under the three different economic scenarios. Let us first focus on factors 3 and 4. Notice that their product, EBIT/Assets, gives us the firm's ROA.[5]

Factor 3 is known as the firm's operating **profit margin** or **return on sales (ROS)**. ROS shows operating profit per dollar of sales. In a normal year, ROS is .10, or 10 percent; in a bad year, it is .0625, or 6.25 percent; and in a good year, .125, or 12.5 percent.

Factor 4, the ratio of sales to assets, is known as **total asset turnover (total ATO)**. It indicates the efficiency of the firm's use of assets in the sense that it measures the annual sales generated by each dollar of assets. In a normal year, Nodett's ATO is 1.0 per year, meaning that sales of $1 per year were generated per dollar of assets. In a bad year, this ratio declines to .8 per year; in a good year, it rises to 1.2 per year.

TABLE 17.6

Ratio Decomposition Analysis for Nodett and Somdett

	ROE	(1) Net Profit/ Pretax Profit	(2) Pretax Profit/ EBIT	(3) EBIT/ Sales (ROS)	(4) Sales/ Assets (ATO)	(5) Assets/ Equity	(6) Compound Leverage Factor (2) × (5)
Bad Year							
Nodett	.030	.6	1.000	.0625	.800	1.000	1.000
Somdett	.018	.6	.360	.0625	.800	1.667	.600
Normal Year							
Nodett	.060	.6	1.000	.1000	1.000	1.000	1.000
Somdett	.068	.6	.680	.1000	1.000	1.667	1.134
Good Year							
Nodett	.090	.6	1.000	.1250	1.200	1.000	1.000
Somdett	.118	.6	.787	.1250	1.200	1.667	1.311

[4]This kind of decomposition of ROE is often called the *Du Pont system*.
[5]Balance sheet items may be calculated on the basis of either end-of-year values or average values; the latter are often preferred.

Comparing Nodett and Somdett, we see that factors 3 and 4 do not depend on a firm's financial leverage. The firms' ratios are equal to each other in all three scenarios. Similarly, factor 1, the ratio of net income after taxes to pretax profit, is the same for both firms. We call this the *tax-burden ratio*. Its value reflects both the government's tax code and the policies pursued by the firm in trying to minimize its tax burden. In our example it does not change over the business cycle, remaining a constant .6.

Although factors 1, 3, and 4 are not affected by a firm's capital structure, factors 2 and 5 are. Factor 2 is the ratio of pretax profits to EBIT. The firm's pretax profits will be greatest when there are no interest payments to be made to debtholders. In fact, another way to express this ratio is

$$\frac{\text{Pretax profits}}{\text{EBIT}} = \frac{\text{EBIT} - \text{Interest expense}}{\text{EBIT}}$$

We will call this factor the *interest-burden ratio (IB)*. It takes on its highest possible value, 1, for Nodett, which has no financial leverage. The higher the degree of financial leverage, the lower the IB ratio. Nodett's IB ratio does not vary over the business cycle. It is fixed at 1.0, reflecting the total absence of interest payments. For Somdett, however, because interest expense is fixed in a dollar amount while EBIT varies, the IB ratio varies from a low of .36 in a bad year to a high of .787 in a good year.

A closely related statistic to the interest burden ratio is the **interest coverage ratio**, or **times interest earned**. The ratio is defined as

$$\text{Interest coverage} = \text{EBIT/Interest expense}$$

A high coverage ratio indicates that the likelihood of bankruptcy is low because annual earnings are significantly greater than annual interest obligations. It is widely used by both lenders and borrowers in determining the firm's debt capacity and is a major determinant of the firm's bond rating.

Factor 5, the ratio of assets to equity, is a measure of the firm's degree of financial leverage. It is called the **leverage ratio** and is equal to 1 plus the debt-to-equity ratio.[6] In our numerical example in Table 17.6, Nodett has a leverage ratio of 1, while Somdett's is 1.667.

From our discussion in Section 17.2, we know that financial leverage helps boost ROE only if ROA is greater than the interest rate on the firm's debt. How is this fact reflected in the ratios of Table 17.6?

The answer is that to measure the full impact of leverage in this framework, the analyst must take the product of the IB and leverage ratios (i.e., factors 2 and 5, shown in Table 17.6 as column 6). For Nodett, factor 6, which we call the *compound leverage factor*, remains a constant 1.0 under all three scenarios. But for Somdett, we see that the compound leverage factor is greater than 1 in normal years (1.134) and in good years (1.311), indicating the positive contribution of financial leverage to ROE. It is less than 1 in bad years, reflecting the fact that when ROA falls below the interest rate, ROE falls with increased use of debt.

We can summarize all these relationships as follows:

$$\text{ROE} = \text{Tax burden} \times \text{Interest burden} \times \text{Margin} \times \text{Turnover} \times \text{Leverage}$$

Because

$$\text{ROA} = \text{Margin} \times \text{Turnover} \tag{17.3}$$

---

[6] $\dfrac{\text{Assets}}{\text{Equity}} = \dfrac{\text{Equity} + \text{Debt}}{\text{Equity}} = 1 + \dfrac{\text{Debt}}{\text{Equity}}$

and

$$\text{Compound leverage factor} = \text{Interest burden} \times \text{Leverage}$$

We can decompose ROE equivalently as follows:

$$\text{ROE} = \text{Tax burden} \times \text{ROA} \times \text{Compound leverage factor}$$

Equation 17.3 shows that ROA is the *product* of margin and turnover. High values of one of these ratios are often accompanied by low values of the other. For example, Walmart has low profit margins but high turnover, while Holt Renfrew has high margins but low turnover. High values for both margin and turnover is an enviable position, but this generally will not be possible: Retailers with high markups will sacrifice sales volume, and conversely those with low turnover need high margins just to remain viable. Therefore, comparing these ratios in isolation is usually meaningful only in evaluating firms following similar strategies in the same industry. Cross-industry comparison can be misleading.

Figure 17.2 shows evidence of the turnover–profit margin tradeoff. Industries with high turnover such as groceries or retail apparel tend to have low profit margins, while industries with high margins such as utilities tend to have low turnover. The two curved lines in the figure trace out turnover–margin combinations that result in an ROA of either 3 or 6 percent. You can see that most industries lie within this range, so ROA across industries demonstrates far less variation than either turnover or margin taken in isolation.

Figure 17.2   Median ROA, profit margin, and asset turnover for 23 industries, 1990–2004.

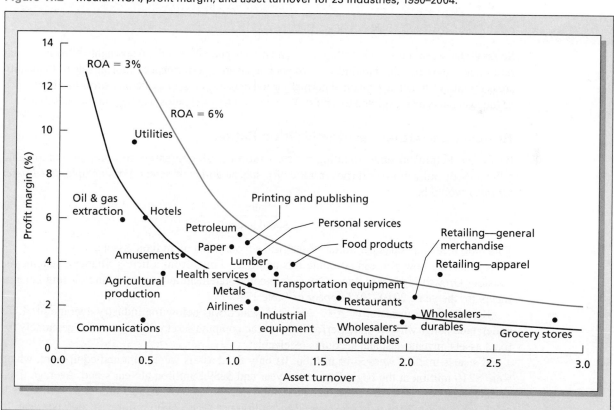

TABLE 17.7

Differences
Between ROS
and ATO Across
Industries

	ROS	×	ATO	=	ROA
Supermarket chain	2%		5.0		10%
Gas and electric utility	20%		.5		10%

EXAMPLE 17.2   Margin Versus Turnover

Consider two firms with the same ROA of 10 percent per year. The first is a supermarket chain, the second is a gas and electric utility.

As Table 17.7 shows, the supermarket chain has a "low" ROS of 2 percent and achieves a 10 percent ROA by "turning over" its assets five times per year. The capital-intensive utility, on the other hand, has a "low" ATO of only .5 times per year and achieves its 10 percent ROA by having an ROS of 20 percent. The point here is that a "low" ROS or ATO ratio need not indicate a troubled firm. Each ratio must be interpreted in light of industry norms.

CC 2

CONCEPT CHECK

Do a ratio decomposition analysis for Mordett of Concept Check 1, preparing a table similar to Table 17.6.

17.4   MORE RATIO ANALYSIS

So far we have examined profitability ratios and have begun to break them down into other important ratios that can be examined to find areas of poor or superior performance; these enable us to identify areas for improvement, to explain abnormally good or bad results, or to identify firms that have some advantage that can be expected to persist. We now turn to other ratios that help in this endeavour.

Turnover and Other Asset Utilization Ratios

It is often helpful in understanding a firm's ratio of sales to assets to compute comparable efficiency-of-utilization, or turnover, ratios for subcategories of assets. For example, *fixed-asset turnover* would be

$$\frac{\text{Sales}}{\text{Fixed assets}}$$

This ratio measures sales per dollar of the firm's money tied up in fixed assets.

To illustrate how you can compute this and other ratios from a firm's financial statements, consider Growth Industries, Inc. (GI). GI's income statement and opening and closing balance sheets for the years 2010–2013 appear in Table 17.8.

GI's total asset turnover in 2013 was .303, which was below the industry average of .4. To understand better why GI underperformed, we can compute asset utilization ratios separately for fixed assets, inventories, and accounts receivable.

GI's sales in 2013 were $144 million. Its only fixed assets were plant and equipment, which were $216 million at the beginning of the year and $259.2 million at year's end. Average fixed assets for the year were, therefore, $237.6 million ([$216 million + $259.2 million]/2). GI's fixed-asset turnover for 2013 therefore was $144 million per year/$237.6 million = .606 per year. In other words, for every dollar of fixed assets, there were $.606 in sales during the year 2013.

TABLE 17.8

Growth Industries Financial Statements, 2010–2013 ($ thousands)

	2010	2011	2012	2013
Income Statements				
Sales revenue		$100,000	$120,000	$144,000
Cost of goods sold (including depreciation)		55,000	66,000	79,200
Depreciation		15,000	18,000	21,600
Selling and administrative expenses		15,000	18,000	21,600
Operating income		30,000	36,000	43,200
Interest expense		10,500	19,095	34,391
Taxable income		19,500	16,905	8,809
Income tax (40% rate)		7,800	6,762	3,524
Net income		$ 11,700	$ 10,143	$ 5,285
Balance Sheets (end of year)				
Cash and marketable securities	$ 50,000	$ 60,000	$ 72,000	$ 86,400
Accounts receivable	25,000	30,000	36,000	43,200
Inventories	75,000	90,000	108,000	129,600
Net plant and equipment	150,000	180,000	216,000	259,200
Total assets	$300,000	$360,000	$432,000	$518,400
Accounts payable	$ 30,000	$ 36,000	$ 43,200	$ 51,840
Short-term debt	45,000	87,300	141,957	214,432
Long-term debt (8% bonds maturing in 2025)	75,000	75,000	75,000	75,000
Total liabilities	$150,000	$198,300	$260,157	$341,272
Shareholders' equity (1 million shares outstanding)	$150,000	$161,700	$171,843	$ 177,128
Other Data				
Market price per common share at year-end		$ 93.60	$ 61.00	$ 21.00

Comparable figures for the fixed-asset turnover ratio for 2011 and 2012 and the 2013 industry average are as follows:

2011	2012	2013	2013 Industry Average
.606	.606	.606	.700

GI's fixed-asset turnover has been stable over time and below the industry average.

Whenever a financial ratio includes one item from the income statement, which covers a period of time, and another from a balance sheet, which is a snapshot at a particular time, the practice is to take the average of the beginning and end-of-year balance sheet figures. Thus in computing the fixed-asset turnover ratio we divided sales (from the income statement) by average fixed assets (from the balance sheet).

Another widely followed turnover ratio is the inventory turnover ratio, which is the ratio of cost of goods sold per dollar of average inventory. The numerator is cost of goods sold instead of sales revenue because inventory is valued at cost. This ratio measures the speed with which inventory is turned over.

In 2011, GI's cost of goods sold (excluding depreciation) was $40 million, and its average inventory was $82.5 million ([$75 million + $90 million]/2). Its inventory turnover was .485 per year ($40 million/$82.5 million). In 2012 and 2013, inventory turnover remained the same, which was below the industry average of .5 per year.

Another measure of efficiency is the ratio of accounts receivable to sales. The accounts receivable ratio usually is computed as average accounts receivable/sales × 365. The result is a number called the **average collection period**, or **days' receivables**, which equals the total credit extended to customers per dollar of daily sales. It is the number of days' worth of sales tied up in accounts receivable. You can also think of it as the average lag between the date of sale and the date payment is received.

For GI in 2013 this number was 100.4 days:

$$\frac{(\$36 \text{ million} + \$43.2 \text{ million})/2}{\$144 \text{ million}} \times 365 = 100.4$$

The industry average was 60 days.

In summary, these ratios show us that GI's poor total asset turnover relative to the industry is in part caused by lower-than-average fixed-asset turnover and inventory turnover and higher-than-average days receivables. This suggests GI may be having problems with excess plant capacity along with poor inventory and receivables management procedures.

Liquidity Ratios

Leverage is one measure of the safety of a firm's debt. Debt ratios compare the firm's indebtedness broad measures of its assets, and coverage ratios compare various measures of earning power against the cash flow needed to satisfy debt obligations. Yet leverage is not the only determinant of financial prudence. You also want to know that a firm can lay its hands on cash either to pay its scheduled obligations or to meet unforeseen obligations. **Liquidity** is the ability to convert assets into cash at short notice. Liquidity is commonly measured using the current ratio, quick ratio, and cash ratio.

1. *Current ratio.* Current assets/Current liabilities. **Current ratio** measures the ability of the firm to pay off its current liabilities by liquidating its current assets (i.e., turning them into cash). It indicates the firm's ability to avoid insolvency in the short run. GI's current ratio in 2011, for example, was (60 + 30 + 90)/(36 + 87.3) = 1.46. In other years, it was as follows:

2011	2012	2013	2013 Industry Average
1.46	1.17	.97	2.0

This represents an unfavourable time trend and poor standing relative to the industry.

2. *Quick ratio.* (Cash + Marketable securities + Receivables)/Current liabilities. The **quick ratio** is also called the **acid test ratio**. It has the same denominator as the current ratio, but its numerator includes only cash, cash equivalents, and receivables. The quick ratio is a better measure of liquidity than the current ratio for firms whose inventory is not readily convertible into cash. GI's quick ratio shows the same disturbing trends as its current ratio:

2011	2012	2013	2013 Industry Average
.73	.58	.49	1.0

3. *Cash ratio.* A company's receivables are less liquid than its holdings of cash and marketable securities. Therefore, in addition to the quick ratio, analysts also compute a firm's **cash ratio**, defined as

$$\text{Cash ratio} = \frac{\text{Cash} + \text{Marketable securities}}{\text{Current liabilities}}$$

2011	2012	2013	2013 Industry Average
.487	.389	.324	.70

GI's liquidity ratios have fallen dramatically over this three-year period, and by 2013 its liquidity measures are far below industry averages. The decline in the liquidity ratios combined with the decline in coverage ratio (you can confirm that times interest earned has also fallen over this period) suggests that its credit rating has been declining as well, and, no doubt, GI is considered a relatively high credit risk in 2013.

Market Price Ratios: Growth Versus Value

Two important market price ratios are the market-to-book-value ratio and the price-to-earnings ratio.

The **market-to-book-value ratio (P/B)** equals the market price of a share of the firm's common stock divided by its *book value*, that is, shareholders' equity per share. Analysts sometimes consider the stock of a firm with a low market-to-book-value to be a "safer" investment, seeing the book value as a "floor" supporting the market price. In the previous chapter, we examined the balance sheet concept of valuation for firms. Analysts presumably view book value as the level below which market price will not fall because the firm always has the option to liquidate, or sell, its assets for their book values. However, this view is questionable. In fact, some firms do sell for less than book value. Two extreme cases were Citigroup and Bank of America, which sold for less than 50 percent of book value after the financial crisis, as investors questioned the permanence of their assets and the accuracy of their claims to liabilities. Nevertheless, low market-to-book-value ratio is seen by some as providing a "margin of safety," and some analysts will screen out or reject high-P/B firms in their stock selection process.

In fact, a better interpretation of the market-price-to-book ratio is as a measure of growth opportunities. Recall from the previous chapter that we may view the two components of firm value as assets in place and growth opportunities. As the next example illustrates, firms with greater growth opportunities will tend to exhibit higher multiples of market-price-to-book-value.

EXAMPLE 17.3   **Price-to-Book and Growth Options**

Consider two firms, both with book value per share of $10, both with a market capitalization rate of 15 percent, and both with plowback ratios of .60.

Bright Prospects has an ROE of 20 percent, well in excess of the market capitalization rate; this ROE implies that the firm is endowed with ample growth opportunities. With ROE = .20, Bright Prospects will earn $2 per share this year. With its plowback ratio of .60, it pays out a dividend of $D_1 = (1 - .6) \times \$2 = \$.80$, and has a growth rate of $g = b \times \text{ROE} = .60 \times .20 = .12$ and a stock price of $D_1/(k - g) = \$.80/(.15 - .12) = \$26.67$. Its price-to-book ratio is $26.67/10 = 2.667$.

continued

In contrast, Past Glory has an ROE of only 15 percent, just equal to the market capitalization rate. It therefore will earn $1.50 per share this year and will pay a dividend of $D_1 = .4 \times \$1.50 = \$.60$. Its growth rate is $g = b \times ROE = .60 \times .15 = .09$, and its stock price is $D_1/(k - g) = \$.60/(.15 - .09) = \$10$. Its price-to-book ratio is $\$10/\$10 = 1.0$. Not surprisingly, a firm that earns just the required rate of return on its investments will sell for book value, and no more.

We conclude that the market-price-to-book-value ratio is determined in large part by growth prospects.

Another measure used to place firms along a growth-versus-value spectrum is the **price-earnings (P/E) ratio**. In fact, we saw in the last chapter that the ratio of the present value of growth options to the value of assets in place largely determines the P/E multiple. While low-P/E stocks allow you to pay less per dollar of *current* earnings, the high-P/E stock may still be a better bargain if its earnings are expected to grow quickly enough.[7]

Many analysts nevertheless believe that low-P/E stocks are more attractive than high-P/E stocks. And in fact, low-P/E stocks have generally been positive-alpha investments using the CAPM as a benchmark. But an efficient market adherent would discount this track record, arguing that such a simple rule could not really generate abnormal returns, and that the CAPM may not be a good benchmark for returns in this case.

In any event, the important points to remember are that ownership of the stock conveys the right to future as well as current earnings, and therefore that a high P/E ratio might best be interpreted as a signal that the market views the firm as enjoying attractive growth opportunities.

Before leaving the P/B and P/E ratios, it is worth pointing out the relationship among these ratios and ROE:

$$ROE = \frac{\text{Earnings}}{\text{Book value}}$$

$$= \frac{\text{Market price}}{\text{Book value}} \div \frac{\text{Market price}}{\text{Earnings}}$$

$$= \text{P/B ratio} \div \text{P/E ratio}$$

By rearranging the terms, we find that a firm's **earnings yield**, the ratio of earnings to price, is equal to its ROE divided by the market-to-book-value ratio:

$$\frac{E}{P} = \frac{\text{ROE}}{\text{P/B}}$$

Thus a company with a high ROE can have a relatively low earnings yield because its P/B ratio is high. This indicates that a high ROE does not in and of itself imply the stock is a good buy: the price of the stock already may be bid up to reflect an attractive ROE. If so, the P/B ratio will be above 1.0, and the earnings yield to stockholders will be below the ROE, as the equation demonstrates. The relationship shows that a strategy of investing in the stock of high ROE firms may produce a lower holding-period return than investing in those with a low ROE.

---

[7]Remember, though, that P/E ratios reported in the financial pages are based on *past* earnings, while price is determined by the firm's prospects of *future* earnings. Therefore, reported P/E ratios may reflect variation in current earnings around a trend line.

Clayman[8] found that investing in the stocks of 29 "excellent" companies, with mean reported ROE of 19.05 percent during the period of 1976 to 1980, produced results much inferior to investing in 39 "unexcellent" companies, those with a mean ROE of 7.09 percent during the period. An investor putting equal dollar amounts in the stocks of unexcellent companies would have earned a portfolio rate of return over the 1981 to 1985 period that was 11.3 percent higher per year than the rate of return on a comparable portfolio of excellent company stocks.

CC 3

CONCEPT CHECK

What were GI's ROE, P/E, and P/B ratios in the year 2013? How do they compare to the industry average ratios, which were

$$ROE = 8.64\% \qquad P/E = 8 \qquad P/B = .69$$

How does GI's earnings yield in 2013 compare to the industry's average?

Table 17.9 presents a summary of the ratios that we have discussed.

TABLE 17.9

Summary of Key Financial Ratios

Leverage	
Interest burden	$\dfrac{\text{EBIT} - \text{Interest expense}}{\text{EBIT}}$
Interest coverage (times interest earned)	$\dfrac{\text{EBIT}}{\text{Interest expense}}$
Leverage	$\dfrac{\text{Assets}}{\text{Equity}} = 1 + \dfrac{\text{Debt}}{\text{Equity}}$
Compound leverage factor	Interest burden $\times$ Leverage
Asset utilization	
Total asset turnover	$\dfrac{\text{Sales}}{\text{Average total assets}}$
Fixed asset turnover	$\dfrac{\text{Sales}}{\text{Average fixed assets}}$
Inventory turnover	$\dfrac{\text{Cost of goods sold}}{\text{Average inventories}}$
Days' receivables	$\dfrac{\text{Average accounts receivable}}{\text{Annual sales}} \times 365$
Liquidity	
Current ratio	$\dfrac{\text{Current assets}}{\text{Current liabilities}}$
Quick ratio	$\dfrac{\text{Cash} + \text{Marketable securities} + \text{Receivables}}{\text{Current liabilities}}$
Cash ratio	$\dfrac{\text{Cash} + \text{Marketable securities}}{\text{Current liabilities}}$

continued

---

[8]Michelle Clayman, "In Search of Excellence: The Investor's Viewpoint," *Financial Analysts Journal*, May/June 1987.

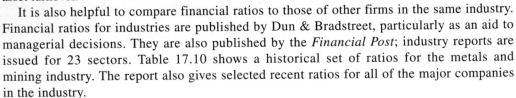

Profitability	
Return on assets	$\dfrac{\text{EBIT}}{\text{Average total assets}}$
Return on equity	$\dfrac{\text{Net income}}{\text{Average stockholders' equity}}$
Return on sales (Profit margin)	$\dfrac{\text{EBIT}}{\text{Sales}}$
Market price	
Market-to-book	$\dfrac{\text{Price per share}}{\text{Book value per share}}$
Price–earnings ratio	$\dfrac{\text{Price per share}}{\text{Earnings per share}}$
Earnings yield	$\dfrac{\text{Earnings per share}}{\text{Price per share}}$

Choosing a Benchmark

We have discussed how to calculate the principal financial ratios. To evaluate the performance of a given firm, however, you need a benchmark to which you can compare its ratios. One obvious benchmark is the set of ratios for the same company in earlier years. For example, Figure 17.3 shows Weston's asset turnover, profit margin, and return on assets for the past 20 years. You can see a clear correspondence between ROA and the margin over that period, with a decreasing asset turnover.

It is also helpful to compare financial ratios to those of other firms in the same industry. Financial ratios for industries are published by Dun & Bradstreet, particularly as an aid to managerial decisions. They are also published by the *Financial Post*; industry reports are issued for 23 sectors. Table 17.10 shows a historical set of ratios for the metals and mining industry. The report also gives selected recent ratios for all of the major companies in the industry.

Dun & Bradstreet
www.dnb.ca

Figure 17.3

Weston financial ratios.

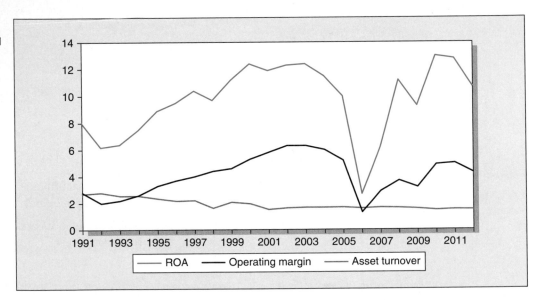

TABLE 17.10 Financial Ratios for Metals and Mining Industry, 2006–2012

Latest Quarterly Results (updated June 27, 2013)

	Quarter Ended	Latest Close	P/E Ratio	Divd Yield	Revenue $000s	Net Inc. $000s	Earns Per Sh	Assets $000s	Book Value
Teck Resources Limited	Q1: 03/13	22.24	14.8	4.00	2,330,000	329,000	0.55	34,617,000	30.572
First Quantum Minerals Ltd. (US$)*	Q1: 03/13	15.25	12.7	1.10	901,200	139,300	0.23	7,536,400	11.192
Sherritt International Corporation	Q1: 03/13	3.94	56.3	4.40	286,500	23,100	0.08	6,758,300	12.387
Pan American Silver Corp. (US$)*	Q1: 03/13	11.36	38.7	4.60	233,432	20,076	0.13	3,387,979	17.912
Silver Wheaton Corp. (US$)*	Q1: 03/13	19.12	11.3	2.60	205,761	133,421	0.38	3,189,337	8.768
Lundin Mining Corporation (US$)*	Q1: 03/13	4.00	19.1	n.a	185,137	50,055	0.09	3,990,451	5.951
HudBay Minerals Inc.	Q1: 03/13	6.78	n.m	2.90	119,881	1,907	0.01	3,487,824	10.226
Major Drilling Group International Inc.	Q4: 04/13	7.16	10.8	2.80	135,537	2,174	0.03	686,227	6.800
Noranda Income Fund	Q1: 03/13	5.06	n.m	9.90	154,079	22,162	n.a.	477,629	6.789
5N Plus Inc. (US$)*	Q1: 03/13	2.78	n.m	n.a	118,389	5,538	0.06	383,978	1.765

*Latest Close in Cdn$.

Industry Data Bank

Fiscal Year:	2012	2011	2010	2009	2008	2007	2006	7 Year Average
Screens								
Earnings—1 Yr Growth	(64.60)	16.81	123.26	69.33	(68.50)	(16.78)	112.96	24.64
Dividend Yield %	1.03	0.82	0.52	0.90	1.65	0.99	1.12	1.00
Avg Price/Earnings	27.03	18.38	23.29	25.91	25.14	18.47	16.86	22.15
Avg Price/Book Value	1.56	2.19	2.49	1.72	2.64	4.16	2.86	2.52
Avg Price/Sales	7.61	8.34	5.09	10.63	4.86	5.97	5.33	6.83
Avg Price/Cash Flow	13.14	16.92	14.07	17.40	17.36	12.20	17.21	15.47
Earnings Yield %	5.26	7.35	7.21	6.03	8.90	6.70	11.81	7.61
Estim Payback (yrs)	17.15	11.01	14.24	18.01	11.26	9.47	8.03	12.74
Safety								
Cash Flow/Total Debt %	59.73	103.77	162.84	97.78	117.41	49.12	157.82	106.92
Current Ratio	3.55	3.34	3.54	4.04	3.02	3.24	5.40	3.73
Acid Test (Quick Ratio)	2.73	2.55	2.81	3.04	2.24	2.53	4.63	2.93
Acct Rec/Acct Pay	1.05	1.07	1.30	1.08	0.94	1.14	1.37	1.13
Working Capital/Total Assets %	13.23	17.38	17.52	17.94	16.68	21.31	25.44	18.50
Long Term Debt/Common Equity	0.23	0.22	0.23	0.19	0.34	0.30	0.26	0.25
Total Debt/Common Equity	0.32	0.29	0.33	0.31	0.40	0.33	0.31	0.33
Cash Flow/Net Bef Disc	2.31	1.51	1.46	0.76	4.62	1.16	1.03	1.84
Interest Coverage	32.57	27.13	42.01	99.39	50.44	47.07	42.07	48.67
ROE/ROA	1.30	1.47	1.51	1.30	1.45	1.65	1.78	1.49
Earnings Quality								
EBIT Margin %	(25.86)	(12.96)	18.94	(68.72)	(6.44)	23.69	34.80	(5.22)
Asset Turnover	0.38	0.41	0.35	0.29	0.42	0.48	0.51	0.41
Interest Burden %	1.20	1.16	0.89	0.92	1.34	1.61	1.30	1.20
Retention %	76.70	76.98	81.06	57.04	53.52	85.86	80.27	73.06
After Tax Items/Assets %	(0.34)	(0.42)	(0.23)	(0.41)	(0.34)	(0.63)	(0.52)	(0.41)
Leverage	1.74	1.62	1.87	1.73	1.91	1.80	1.87	1.79

continued

Industry Data Bank								
Fiscal Year:	**2012**	**2011**	**2010**	**2009**	**2008**	**2007**	**2006**	**7 Year Average**
Apparent Tax Rate %	29.63	25.57	27.88	44.06	50.16	25.57	19.14	31.72
Sales—1 Yr Growth	(7.97)	33.38	53.68	(2.65)	10.19	53.91	116.12	36.67
Cash Flow Growth Y/Y%	36.31	48.37	104.46	(38.54)	51.82	11.57	151.35	52.19
Book Value/Share—1 Yr Growth	1.01	16.35	22.15	10.33	6.11	53.10	108.64	31.10
Dividends/Share—1 Yr Growth	37.03	38.01	211.90	(44.16)	5.08	22.74	90.83	51.63
Profitability and Efficiency %								
Operating Margin %	2.72	14.66	9.16	(57.75)	17.07	30.78	38.85	7.93
Pre-Tax Margin %	(31.85)	(17.74)	13.26	(77.17)	(11.52)	18.56	15.64	(12.97)
Net Profit Margin %	(35.67)	(24.51)	5.26	(83.74)	(15.22)	12.48	10.37	(18.72)
Return on Equity %	(5.61)	8.06	5.94	(2.56)	(5.21)	7.57	24.11	4.61
Return on Assets %	(0.36)	4.48	5.31	0.06	(2.02)	5.03	13.06	3.65
Return on Invested Capital %	4.95	12.36	10.55	10.58	5.45	8.55	23.36	10.83
Other Ratios								
Sales/Receivables	15.01	14.17	11.85	12.06	16.42	14.12	12.19	13.69
Sales/Inventory	6.57	7.76	8.18	7.11	7.79	9.30	11.17	8.27
Sales/Fixed Assets	1.11	1.25	1.00	0.76	1.07	1.41	1.60	1.17
Sales/Cash & Equiv.	23.18	17.88	13.99	9.92	12.83	30.33	12.23	17.19

Companies Included: Dominion Diamond Corporation; Dundee Precious Metals Inc.; Eastern Platinum Limited; First Quantum Minerals Ltd.; 5N Plus Inc.; HudBay Minerals Inc.; Imperial Metals Corporation; Labrador Iron Ore Royalty Corporation; Lundin Mining Corporation; MagIndustries Corp.; Major Drilling Group International Inc.; Mercator Minerals Ltd.; Noranda Income Fund; North American Palladium Ltd.; Pan American Silver Corp.; Sherritt International Corporation; Silver Standard Resources Inc.; Silver Wheaton Corp.; Silvercorp Metals Inc.; Taseko Mines Limited; Teck Resources Limited; Thompson Creek Metals Company Inc.; Turquoise Hill Resources Ltd.

17.5   ECONOMIC VALUE ADDED

While profitability measures such as ROA, ROC and ROE are commonly used to measure that performance, profitability is really not enough. A firm should be viewed as successful only if the return on its projects is better than the rate investors could expect to earn for themselves (on a risk-adjusted basis) in the capital market. Plowing back funds into the firm increases stock price *only* if the firm earns a higher rate of return on the reinvested funds than the opportunity cost of capital, that is, the market capitalization rate. To account for this opportunity cost, we might measure the success of the firm using the *difference* between the return on assets, ROA, and the opportunity cost of capital, k. **Economic value added** is the spread between ROA and k multiplied by the capital invested in the firm. It therefore measures the dollar value of the firm's return in excess of its opportunity cost. Another term for EVA (the term coined by proponents Stern Stewart) is **residual income**.[9]

EXAMPLE 17.4   Economic Value Added

In 2012, Intel had a weighted-average cost of capital of 7.8 percent (based on its cost of debt, its capital structure, its equity beta, and estimates derived from the CAPM for the cost of equity). Its return on assets was 13.9 percent, fully 6.1 percent greater than the opportunity cost of capital on its investments in plant, equipment, and know-how. In other words, each dollar invested by Intel earned about $.061 more than the return that investors could have anticipated by investing in equivalent-risk stocks. Intel earned this superior rate of return on a capital base of $56.34 billion. Its economic value added, that is, its return in excess of opportunity cost, was therefore $(.139 - .078) \times \$56.34 = \$3.44$ billion.

---

[9]Residual income can also be calculated as

$$RI = (ROE - k_e)(\text{beginning value of equity}) \quad \text{or} \quad RI = (ROIC - WACC)(\text{beginning value of capital})$$

TABLE 17.11

Economic Value
Added, 2012

	Ticker	EVA ($ billion)	Capital ($ billion)	ROA (%)	Cost of Capital (%)
Microsoft	MSFT	4.71	81.2	14.2	8.4
ExxonMobil	XOM	3.58	179.06	9.3	7.3
Intel	INTC	3.44	56.34	13.9	7.8
GlaxoSmithKline	GSK	2.13	38.1	11	5.4
Google	GOOG	1.37	75.95	10.5	8.7
Home Depot	HD	1.09	28.57	11.2	7.4
Hewlett-Packard	HPQ	−0.58	50.88	4.9	6
AT&T	T	−1.59	164.38	3.9	4.9

Source: Authors' calculations using data from http://finance.yahoo.com.

Table 17.11 shows EVA for a small sample of firms. The EVA leader in this sample was Microsoft. Notice that ExxonMobil's EVA was greater than Intel's, despite to a smaller margin between its ROA and the cost of capital. This is because ExxonMobil applied its margin to a much bigger capital base. At the other extreme, AT&T earned less than its opportunity cost of capital, which resulted in a negative EVA.

Notice that even the EVA "losers" in Table 17.11 reported positive accounting profits. For example, by conventional standards, AT&T was solidly profitable in 2012, with an ROA of 3.9 percent. But by virtue of its high business risk, its cost of capital was also higher, at 4.9 percent. By this standard, it did not cover its opportunity cost of capital, and returned a very negative EVA in 2012. EVA treats the opportunity cost of capital as a real cost that, like other costs, should be deducted from revenues to arrive at a more meaningful "bottom line." A firm that is earning profits but is not covering its opportunity cost might be able to redeploy its capital to better uses. Therefore, a growing number of firms now calculate EVA and tie managers' compensation to it.

17.6 AN ILLUSTRATION OF FINANCIAL STATEMENT ANALYSIS

In her 2013 annual report to the shareholders of Growth Industries, Inc., the president wrote: "2013 was another successful year for Growth Industries. As in 2012, sales, assets, and operating income all continued to grow at a rate of 20%."

Is she right?

We can evaluate her statement by conducting a full-scale ratio analysis of Growth Industries. Our purpose is to assess GI's performance in the recent past, to evaluate its future prospects, and to determine whether its market price reflects its intrinsic value.

Table 17.12 shows the key financial ratios we can compute from GI's financial statements. The president is certainly right about the growth rate in sales, assets, and operating income. Inspection of GI's key financial ratios, however, contradicts her first sentence: 2013 was not another successful year for GI—it appears to have been another miserable one.

ROE has been declining steadily from 7.51 percent in 2011 to 3.03 percent in 2013. A comparison of GI's 2013 ROE to the 2013 industry average of 8.64 percent makes the deteriorating time trend appear especially alarming. The low and falling market-to-book-value ratio and the falling price-earnings ratio indicate investors are less and less optimistic about the firm's future profitability.

The fact that ROA has not been declining, however, tells us that the source of the declining time trend in GI's ROE must be inappropriate use of financial leverage. And we see that as GI's leverage ratio climbed from 2.117 in 2011 to 2.723 in 2013, its interest-burden ratio (column 2) fell from .650 to .204—with the net result that the compound leverage factor fell from 1.376 to .556.

TABLE 17.12 Key Financial Ratios of Growth Industries, Inc.

Year	ROE (%)	(1) Net Profit/ Pretax Profit	(2) Pretax Profit/ EBIT	(3) EBIT/ Sales (%) (ROS)	(4) Sales/ Assets (ATO)	(5) Assets/ Equity	(6) Compound Leverage Factor (2) × (5)	(7) ROA (%) (3) × (4)	P/E	P/B
2011	7.51	.6	.650	30	.303	2.117	1.376	9.09	8	.58
2012	6.08	.6	.470	30	.303	2.375	1.116	9.09	6	.35
2013	3.03	.6	.204	30	.303	2.723	.556	9.09	4	.12
Industry average	8.64	.6	.800	30	.400	1.500	1.200	12.00	8	.69

The rapid increase in short-term debt from year to year and the concurrent increase in interest expense make it clear that to finance its 20 percent growth rate in sales, GI has incurred sizable amounts of short-term debt at high interest rates. The firm is paying rates of interest greater than the ROA it is earning on the investment financed with the new borrowing. As the firm has expanded, its situation has become ever more precarious.

In 2013, for example, the average interest rate on short-term debt was 20 percent versus an ROA of 9.09 percent. (You can calculate the interest rate on GI's short-term debt using the data in Table 17.8 as follows. The balance sheet shows us that the coupon rate on its long-term debt was 8 percent, and its par value was $75 million. Therefore the interest paid on the long-term debt was .08 × $75 million = $6 million. Total interest paid in 2013 was $34,391,000, so the interest paid on the short-term debt must have been $34,391,000 − $6,000,000 = $28,391,000. This is 20 percent of GI's short-term debt at the start of the year.)

GI's problems become clear when we examine its statement of cash flows in Table 17.13. The statement is derived from the income statement and balance sheet in Table 17.8. GI's cash

TABLE 17.13
Growth Industries Statement of Cash Flows ($ thousands)

	2011	2012	2013
Cash Flow from Operating Activities			
Net income	$ 11,700	$ 10,143	$ 5,285
+ Depreciation	15,000	18,000	21,600
+ Decrease (increase) in accounts receivable	(5,000)	(6,000)	(7,200)
+ Decrease (increase) in inventories	(15,000)	(18,000)	(21,600)
+ Increase in accounts payable	6,000	7,200	8,640
Cash provided by operations	$ 12,700	$ 11,343	$ 6,725
Cash Flow from Investing Activities			
Investment in plant and equipment*	$(45,000)	$(54,000)	$(64,800)
Cash Flow from Financing Activities			
Dividends paid†	$ 0	$ 0	$ 0
Short-term debt issued	42,300	54,657	72,475
Change in cash and marketable securities‡	$ 10,000	$ 12,000	$ 14,400

*Gross investment equals increase in net plant and equipment plus depreciation.
†We can conclude that no dividends are paid, because stockholders' equity increases each year by the full amount of net income, implying a plowback ratio of 1.0.
‡Equals cash flow from operations plus cash flow from investment activities plus cash flow from financing activities. Note that this equals the yearly change in cash and marketable securities on the balance sheet.

flow from operations is falling steadily, from $12,700,000 in 2011 to $6,725,000 in 2013. The firm's investment in plant and equipment, by contrast, has increased greatly. Net plant and equipment (i.e., net of depreciation) rose from $150,000,000 in 2010 to $259,200,000 in 2013. The firm's investment in plant and equipment, by contrast, has increased greatly. Net plant and equipment (i.e., net of depreciation) rose from $150,000,000 in 2012 to $259,200,000 in 2015. This near-doubling of the capital assets makes the decrease in cash flow from operations all the more troubling.

The source of the difficulty is GI's enormous amount of short-term borrowing. In a sense, the company is being run as a pyramid scheme. It borrows more and more each year to maintain its 20 percent growth rate in assets and income. However, the new assets are not generating enough cash flow to support the extra interest burden of the debt, as the falling cash flow from operations indicates. Eventually, when the firm loses its ability to borrow further, its growth will be at an end.

At this point GI stock might be an attractive investment. Its market price is only 12 percent of its book value, and with a P/E ratio of 4 its earnings yield is 25 percent per year. GI is a likely candidate for a takeover by another firm that might replace GI's management and build shareholder value through a radical change in policy.

CC 4   CONCEPT CHECK

You have the following information for IBX Corporation for the years 2013 and 2015 (all figures are in $ millions):

	2013	2015
Net income	$ 253.7	$ 239.0
Pretax income	411.9	375.6
EBIT	517.6	403.1
Average assets	4,857.9	3,459.7
Sales	6,679.3	4,537.0
Shareholders' equity	2,233.3	2,347.3

What is the trend in IBX's ROE, and how can you account for it in terms of tax burden, margin, turnover, and financial leverage?

17.7   COMPARABILITY PROBLEMS

Financial statement analysis gives us a good amount of ammunition for evaluating a company's performance and future prospects. But comparing financial results of different companies is not so simple. There is more than one acceptable way to represent various items of revenue and expense according to generally accepted accounting principles (GAAP). This means two firms may have exactly the same economic income yet very different accounting incomes.

Furthermore, interpreting a single firm's performance over time is complicated when inflation distorts the dollar measuring rod. Comparability problems are especially acute in this case because the impact of inflation on reported results often depends on the particular method the firm adopts to account for inventories and depreciation. The security analyst must adjust the earnings and the financial ratio figures to a uniform standard before attempting to compare financial results across firms and over time.

Comparability problems can arise out of the flexibility of GAAP guidelines in accounting for inventories and depreciation and in adjusting for the effects of inflation. Other important potential sources of noncomparability include the capitalization of leases and other expenses, the treatment of pension costs, and allowances for reserves.

Inventory Valuation

There are two commonly used ways to value inventories: **LIFO** (last-in, first-out), and **FIFO** (first-in, first-out). The difference is best explained using a numerical example. Suppose Generic Products Inc. (GPI) has a constant inventory of 1 million units of generic goods. The inventory turns over once per year, meaning that the ratio of cost of goods sold to inventory is 1.

The LIFO system calls for valuing the million units used up during the year at the current cost of production, so that the last goods produced are considered the first ones to be sold. They are valued at today's cost. The FIFO system assumes that the units used up or sold are the ones that were added to inventory first, and therefore that goods sold should be valued at original cost.

If the price of generic goods were constant, for example, at the level of $1, the book value of inventory and the cost of goods sold would be the same $1 million under both systems. But suppose the price of generic goods rises by 10 cents during the year as a result of general inflation. LIFO accounting would result in a cost of goods sold of $1.1 million, while the end-of-year balance sheet value of the one million units in inventory remains $1 million. The balance sheet value of inventories is measured as the cost of the goods still in inventory. Under LIFO, the last goods produced are assumed to be sold at the current cost of $1.10; the goods remaining are thus the previously produced goods, at a cost of only $1. You can see that although LIFO accounting accurately measures the cost of goods sold, it understates the current value of the remaining inventory in an inflationary environment.

In contrast, under FIFO accounting the cost of goods sold would be $1 million, and the end-of-year balance sheet value of the inventory would be $1.1 million. The result is that the LIFO firm has both a lower profit and a lower balance sheet of inventories than the FIFO firm.

LIFO is to be preferred to FIFO in computing economic earnings (i.e., real sustainable cash flow), because it uses up-to-date prices to evaluate the cost of goods sold. However, LIFO accounting induces balance sheet distortions when it values investment in inventories at original cost. This practice results in an upward bias in ROE, since the investment base on which return is earned is undervalued.

Canadian tax law requires that firms use FIFO accounting in determining their taxable income, but they are free to use LIFO in their internal or annual reporting. In the case of a discrepancy between accounting methods used, an adjustment must be made for the deferred tax credit or liability that is created with respect to the reported financial statements.

Depreciation

Another source of problems is the measurement of depreciation, which is a key factor in computing true earnings. The accounting and economic measures of depreciation can differ markedly. According to the *economic* definition, depreciation is the amount of a firm's operating cash flow that must be reinvested in the firm to sustain its real productive capacity at the current level.

The *accounting* measurement is quite different. Accounting depreciation or *amortization* is the amount of the original acquisition cost of an asset that is allocated to each accounting period over an arbitrarily specified life of the asset. This is the figure reported in financial statements.

Assume, for example, that a firm buys machines with a useful economic life of 20 years at $100,000 apiece. In its financial statement, however, the firm can depreciate the machines over 10 years using the straight-line method, for $10,000 per year in depreciation. Thus after 10 years a machine will be fully depreciated on the books, even though it remains a productive asset that will not need replacement for another 10 years.

In computing accounting earnings, this firm will overestimate depreciation in the first 10 years of the machine's economic life and underestimate it in the last 10 years. This will cause reported earnings to be understated compared with economic earnings in the first 10 years and overstated in the last 10 years.

Depreciation comparability problems include one more wrinkle. A firm can use different depreciation methods for tax purposes than for other reporting purposes. Canadian firms must use an accelerated depreciation method (declining balance for most depreciable assets) to calculate the capital cost allowance (CCA) for tax purposes; they are free, however, to use straight-line CCA in published financial statements. There are also differences across firms in their estimates of the depreciable life of plant, equipment, and other depreciable assets.

The major problem related to depreciation, however, is caused by inflation. Because conventional depreciation is based on historical costs rather than on the current replacement cost of assets, measured depreciation in periods of inflation is understated relative to replacement cost, and *real* economic income (sustainable cash flow) is correspondingly overstated.

The situation is similar to what happens in FIFO inventory accounting. Conventional depreciation and FIFO both result in an inflation-induced overstatement of real income, because both use original cost instead of current cost to calculate net income. For example, suppose Generic Products Inc. has a machine with a three-year useful life that originally cost $3 million. Annual straight-line depreciation is $1 million, regardless of what happens to the replacement cost of the machine. Suppose inflation in the first year turns out to be 10 percent. Then the true annual depreciation expense is $1.1 million in current terms, while conventionally measured depreciation remains fixed at $1 million per year. Accounting income therefore overstates *real* economic income by the inflation factor, $100,000.

Inflation and Interest Expense

Although inflation can cause distortions in the measurement of a firm's inventory and depreciation costs, it has perhaps an even greater effect on the calculation of *real* interest expense. Nominal interest rates include an inflation premium that compensates the lender for inflation-induced erosion in the *real* value of principal. From the perspective of both lender and borrower, part of what is conventionally measured as interest expense should be treated more properly as repayment of principal.

EXAMPLE 17.5   **Inflation and Real Income**

Suppose Generic Products has debt outstanding with a face value of $10 million, paying 10 percent per year. Interest expense, as conventionally measured, is therefore $1 million per year. However, suppose inflation during the year is 6 percent, so that the real interest rate is 4 percent. Then $600,000 of what appears as interest expense on the income statement is really an inflation premium, or compensation for the anticipated reduction in the real value of the $10 million principal; only $400,000 is *real* interest expense. The $600,000 reduction in the purchasing power of the outstanding principal may be thought of as repayment of principal, rather than as an interest expense. Real income of the firm is therefore understated by $600,000.

www.cica.ca

Mismeasurement of real interest means that inflation deflates the statement of real income. The effects of inflation on the reported values of inventories and depreciation that we have discussed work in the opposite direction. In both Canada and the United States, the responsible accounting bodies (in Canada, the Canadian Institute of Chartered Accountants, or CICA) have tried to impose a requirement for inflation-adjusted accounting reports as supplements to regular statements. Reportedly, however, security analysts by and large ignore the inflation-adjusted data, particularly since this adds another element of noncomparability. Consequently, the requirement has been dropped in both jurisdictions.

CC 5

CONCEPT CHECK

In a period of rapid inflation, companies ABC and XYZ have the same *reported* earnings. ABC uses LIFO inventory accounting, has relatively fewer depreciable assets, and has more debt than XYZ. XYZ uses FIFO inventory accounting. Which company has the higher *real* income, and why?

Fair Value Accounting

Many major assets and liabilities are not traded in financial markets and do not have easily observable values. For example, we cannot simply look up the values of employee stock options, health care benefits for retired employees, or buildings and other real estate. While the true financial status of a firm may depend critically on these values, which can swing widely over time, common practice has been to simply value them at historic cost. Proponents of **fair value accounting**, also known as **mark-to-market accounting**, argue that financial statements would give a truer picture of the firm if they better reflected the current market values of all assets and liabilities.

The U.S. Financial Accounting Standards Board's Statement No. 157 on fair value accounting places assets in one of three "buckets." Level 1 assets are traded in active markets and therefore should be valued at their market price. Level 2 assets are not actively traded, but their values still may be estimated using observable market data on similar assets. They can be "marked to a matrix" of comparable securities. Level 3 assets are hardest to value. Here it is difficult even to identify other assets that are similar enough to serve as benchmarks for their market values. One has to resort to pricing models to estimate their intrinsic values. Rather than mark to market, these values are often called "mark to model," although they are also disparagingly known as "mark-to-make-believe," as the estimates are so prone to manipulation by creative use of model inputs. Since 2012, firms have been required to disclose more about their methods and assumptions used in their valuation models and to describe the sensitivity of their valuation estimates to changes in their methodology.

Critics of fair value accounting argue that it relies too heavily on estimates. Such estimates potentially introduce considerable noise in firms' accounts and can induce great profit volatility as fluctuations in asset valuations are recognized. Even worse, subjective valuations may offer management a tempting tool to manipulate earnings or the apparent financial condition of the firm at opportune times. As just one example, Bergstresser, Desai, and Rauh[10] find that firms make more aggressive assumptions about returns on defined benefit pension plans (which lowers the computed present value of pension obligations) during periods in which executives are actively exercising their stock options.

---

[10]D. Bergstresser, M. Desai, and J. Rauh, "Earnings Manipulation, Pension Assumptions, and Managerial Investment Decisions," *Quarterly Journal of Economics* 121 (2006), pp. 157–95.

As banks and other institutions holding mortgage-backed securities revalued their portfolios throughout 2008, their net worth fell along with the value of those securities. The losses on these securities were painful enough, but their knock-on effects only increased the banks' woes. For example, banks are required to maintain adequate levels of capital relative to assets. If capital reserves decline, a bank may be forced to shrink until its remaining capital is once again adequate compared to its asset base. But such shrinkage may require the bank to cut back on its lending, which restricts its customers' access to credit. It may also require asset sales, and if many banks attempt to shrink their portfolios at once, waves of forced sales may put further pressure on prices, resulting in additional write-downs and reductions to capital in a self-feeding cycle. Critics of mark-to-market accounting therefore contend that it has exacerbated the problems of an already reeling economy.

Advocates, however, argue that the critics confuse the message with the messenger. Mark-to-market accounting makes transparent losses that have already been incurred, but it does not cause those losses. Critics retort that when markets are faltering, market prices may be unreliable. If trading activity has largely broken down, and assets can be sold only at fire-sale prices, then those prices may no longer be indicative of fundamental value. Markets cannot be efficient if they are not even functioning. In the turmoil surrounding the defaulted mortgages weighing down bank portfolios, one of the early proposals of then–Treasury secretary Henry Paulson was for the government to buy bad assets at "hold to maturity" prices based on estimates of intrinsic value in a normally functioning market. In that spirit, FASB approved new guidelines in 2009 allowing valuation based on an estimate of the price that would prevail in an orderly market rather than the one that could be received in a forced liquidation.

Waiving write-down requirements may best be viewed as thinly veiled regulatory forbearance. Regulators know that losses have been incurred and that capital has been impaired. But by allowing firms to carry assets on their books at model rather than market prices, the unpleasant implications of that fact for capital adequacy may be politely ignored for a time. Even so, if the goal is to avoid forced sales in a distressed market, transparency may nevertheless be the best policy. Better to acknowledge losses and explicitly modify capital regulations to help institutions recover their footing in a difficult economy than to deal with losses by ignoring them. After all, why bother preparing financial statements if they are allowed to obscure the true condition of the firm?

Before abandoning fair value accounting, it would be prudent to consider the alternative. Traditional historical-cost accounting, which would allow firms to carry assets on the books at their original purchase price, has even less to recommend it. It would leave investors without an accurate sense of the condition of shaky institutions, and by the same token lessen the pressure on those firms to get their houses in order. Dealing with losses must surely require acknowledging them.

A contentious debate over the application of fair value accounting to troubled financial institutions erupted in 2008 when even values of financial securities such as subprime mortgage pools and derivative contracts backed by these pools came into question as trading in these instruments dried up. Without well-functioning markets, estimating (much less observing) market values was, at best, a precarious exercise.

Many observers feel that mark-to-market accounting exacerbated the financial meltdown by forcing banks to excessively write down asset values; others felt that a failure to mark would have been tantamount to willfully ignoring reality and abdicating the responsibility to redress problems at nearly or already insolvent banks. The nearby box discusses the debate.

Quality of Earnings and Accounting Practices

Many firms will make accounting choices that present their financial statements in the best possible light. The different choices that firms can make give rise to the comparability problems we have discussed. As a result, earnings statements for different companies may be more or less rosy presentations of true economic earnings—sustainable cash flow that can be paid to shareholders without impairing the firm's productive capacity. Analysts commonly evaluate the **quality of earnings** reported by a firm. This concept refers to the realism and conservatism of the earnings number, in other words, the extent to which we might expect the reported level of earnings to be sustained.

Examples of the types of factors that influence quality of earnings are:

- *Allowance for bad debt.* Most firms sell goods using trade credit and must make an allowance for bad debt. An unrealistically low allowance reduces the quality of reported earnings.

- *Nonrecurring items.* Some items that affect earnings should not be expected to recur regularly. These include asset sales, effects of accounting changes, effects of exchange rate movements, or unusual investment income. For example, in 2003, which was a banner year for equity returns, some firms enjoyed large investment returns on securities held. These contributed to that year's earnings, but should not be expected to repeat regularly. They would be considered a "low-quality" component of 2003 earnings. Similarly, investment gains in corporate pension plans generated large but one-off contributions to reported earnings.

- *Earnings smoothing.* In 2003, Freddie Mac was the subject of an accounting scandal, when it emerged that it had improperly reclassified mortgages held in its portfolio in an attempt to *reduce* its current earnings. Similarly, in the 1990s, Why would it take such actions? Because later, if earnings turned down, Freddie could "release" earnings by reversing these transactions, and thereby create the appearance of steady earnings growth. Indeed, almost until its sudden collapse in 2008, Freddie Mac's nickname on Wall Street was "Steady Freddie." Similarly, in the four quarters ending in October 2012, the four largest U.S. banks released $18.2 billion in reserves, which accounted for nearly one-quarter of their pretax income.[11] Such "earnings" are clearly not sustainable over the long term and therefore must be considered of low quality.

- *Revenue recognition.* Under GAAP accounting, a firm is allowed to recognize a sale before it is paid. This is why firms have accounts receivable. But sometimes it can be hard to know when to recognize sales. For example, suppose a computer firm signs a contract to provide products and services over a five-year period. Should the revenue be booked immediately or spread out over five years? A more extreme version of this problem is called "channel stuffing," in which firms "sell" large quantities of goods to customers, but give them the right to later either refuse delivery or return the product. The revenue from the "sale" is booked now, but the likely returns are not recognized until they occur (in a future accounting period). Hewlett Packard argued in 2012 that it was led to overpay for its acquisition of Autonomy Corp. when Autonomy artificially enhanced its financial performance using channel stuffing. For example, Autonomy apparently sold software valued at over £4 billion to Tikit Group; it booked the entire deal as revenue but would not be paid until Tikit actually sold software to its clients.[12] Thus, several years' worth of only tentative future sales was recognized in 2010.

  If you see accounts receivable increasing far faster than sales, or becoming a larger percentage of total assets, beware of these practices. Given the wide latitude firms have to manipulate revenue, many analysts choose instead to concentrate on cash flow, which is far harder for a company to manipulate.

- *Off-balance-sheet assets and liabilities.* Suppose that one firm guarantees the outstanding debt of another firm, perhaps a firm in which it has an ownership stake. That obligation ought to be disclosed as a *contingent liability*, since it may require payments down the road. But these obligations may not be reported as part of the firm's outstanding debt. Similarly, leasing may be used to manage off-balance-sheet assets and liabilities. Airlines, for example, may show no aircraft on their balance sheets but have long-term leases that are virtually equivalent to debt-financed ownership. However, if the leases are treated as operating rather than capital leases, they may appear only as footnotes to the financial statements.

---

[11]Michael Rapoport, "Bank Profit Spigot to Draw Scrutiny," *Wall Street Journal*, October 1, 2012.
[12]Ben Worthen, Paul Sonne, and Justin Scheck, "Long Before H-P Deal, Autonomy's Red Flags," *Wall Street Journal*, November 26, 2012.

International Accounting Conventions

The examples cited above illustrate some of the problems that analysts can encounter when attempting to interpret financial data. Even greater problems arise in the interpretation of the financial statements of foreign firms. This is because these firms do not follow U.S. GAAP guidelines. Accounting practices in various countries differ to greater or lesser extents from U.S. standards. (As with currencies, the standard for comparison is U.S. practice.) Here are some of the major issues that you should be aware of when using the financial statements of foreign firms:

- *Reserving practices.* Many countries allow firms considerably more discretion in setting aside reserves for future contingencies than is typical in the United States. Because additions to reserves result in a charge against income, reported earnings are far more subject to managerial discretion than in the United States.

    Germany is a country that allows particularly wide discretion in reserve practice. When Daimler-Benz AG (producer of the Mercedes-Benz) decided to issue shares on the New York Stock Exchange in 1993, it had to revise its accounting statements in accordance with U.S. standards. The revisions transformed a small profit for the first half of 1993 using German accounting rules into a *loss* of a $592 million under more stringent U.S. rules.

- *Depreciation.* In the United States, firms typically maintain separate sets of accounts for tax and reporting purposes. For example, accelerated depreciation is typically used for tax purposes, whereas straight-line depreciation is used for reporting purposes. In contrast, most other countries do not allow dual sets of accounts, and most firms in foreign countries use accelerated depreciation to minimize taxes despite the fact that it results in lower reported earnings. This makes reported earnings of foreign firms lower than they would be if the firms were allowed to use the U.S. practice.

- *Intangibles.* Treatment of intangibles such as goodwill can vary widely. Are they amortized or expensed? If amortized, over what period? Such issues can have a large impact on reported profits.

Figure 17.4 summarizes some of the major differences in accounting rules in various countries. Note that Canadian and U.S. rules agree on these details. The effect of different accounting practices can be substantial. In a similar vein, a study by Speidell and Bavishi[13] recalculated the financial statements of firms in several countries using common accounting rules. The variation is considerable. While P/E multiples have changed considerably since this study was published, the results illustrate how different accounting rules can have a major impact on these ratios.

Some of the differences between U.S. and European accounting standards arise from different philosophies regarding regulating accounting practice. GAAP accounting in the U.S. is "rules-based," with detailed, explicit, and lengthy rules governing almost any circumstance that can be anticipated. In contrast, the **international financial reporting standards (IFRS)** used in the European Union are "principles-based," setting out general approaches for the preparation of financial statements. While EU rules are more flexible, firms must be prepared to demonstrate that their accounting choices are consistent with IFRS principles.

IFRS seem on their way to becoming global standards, even outside the European Union. By 2008, over 100 countries had adopted them, and they are making inroads even in the United States. In November 2007, the SEC began allowing foreign firms to issue securities in the U.S. if their financial statements are prepared using IFRS. In 2008, the SEC went even further when it proposed allowing large U.S. multinational firms to report earnings using IFRS rather than GAAP starting in 2010. A final integration of U.S. rules with IFRS has been long expected but

---

[13]Lawrence S. Speidell and Vinod Bavishi, "GAAP Arbitrage: Valuation Opportunities in International Accounting Standards," *Financial Analysts Journal,* November/December 1992, pp. 58–66.

Figure 17.4

Comparative accounting rules.

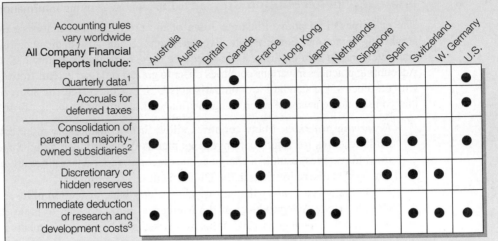

Accounting rules vary worldwide All Company Financial Reports Include:	Australia	Austria	Britain	Canada	France	Hong Kong	Japan	Netherlands	Singapore	Spain	Switzerland	W. Germany	U.S.
Quarterly data¹				●									●
Accruals for deferred taxes	●		●	●	●	●		●	●				●
Consolidation of parent and majority-owned subsidiaries²	●		●	●	●	●		●	●	●	●		●
Discretionary or hidden reserves		●			●					●	●	●	
Immediate deduction of research and development costs³	●		●	●	●		●	●			●	●	●

1   In Austria companies issue only annual data. Other countries besides the U.S. and Canada issue semiannual data. In the Netherlands, companies issue quarterly or semiannual data.
2   In Austria, Japan, Hong Kong, and West Germany, the minority of companies fully consolidate.
3   In Austria. Hong Kong, Singapore, and Spain, the accounting treatment for R&D costs—whether they are immediately deducted or capitalized and deducted over later years—isn't disclosed in financial reports.

Source: Center for International Financial Analysis and Research, Princeton, NJ; and Frederick D. S. Choi and Gerhard G. Mueller, *International Accounting*, 2nd ed. (Englewood Cliffs, NJ: Prentice Hall, 1992).

repeatedly delayed. However, even without formal adoption of IFRS, the widespread belief is that the United States will continue to change GAAP over time to more closely conform to IFRS rules. The goal is to make cross-border financial statements more consistent and comparable, improving the quality of information available to investors.

17.8   THE VALUE OF FUNDAMENTAL ANALYSIS

The Potential

The efficient market hypothesis (EMH) refutes the possibility of gleaning additional information of value from the published financial statements of a company. Yet, analysis must be valuable in order to justify the efforts of well-paid analysts in looking for mispriced assets; active management depends upon the identification of opportunities for investment. Financial theory has been slow to accept the possibility that financial statement analysis may have more than the smallest and shortest-lived effect in making extraordinary gains; instead it suggests that the practice of analysis adds to market information, which leads to efficient pricing. Accounting theorists have been more inclined to look for the value in their products and their analyses.

Michael Brennan[14] discusses two aspects of accounting information and its relation to stock prices in a review article. He presents the results of research on market reactions to the release of new information and on the use of accounting information in the determination of value and of stock prices. He suggests that the definition and presentation of accounting data must be carefully controlled when academic studies of the significance of accounting information are conducted.

[14] Michael J. Brennan, "A Perspective on Accounting and Stock Prices," *The Accounting Review* 66, no. 1 (January 1991), pp. 67–79.

Ou and Penman,[15] in two articles, demonstrate that accounting information presented in annual statements is not only retrospective but prospective in revealing future results. They claim that financial statements capture fundamentals that are not reflected in prices, contrary to the assertions of the semistrong form of efficiency; in fact, financial statements contain information that can predict future stock returns. Furthermore, they define an accounting measure from the released information that they assert is relevant to future earnings rather than the current earnings revealed in the income statement. The stock returns predicted by their measure are shown to be negatively correlated with the returns predicted by P/E ratios. Brockman, Mossman, and Olson[16] report also that use of accounting data and ratios to identify good and bad prospects can yield significant excess returns on long and short portfolios.

Value Investing: The Graham Technique

No presentation of fundamental security analysis would be complete without a discussion of the ideas of Benjamin Graham, the greatest of the investment gurus. Until the evolution of modern portfolio theory in the latter half of this century, Graham was the single most important thinker, writer, and teacher in the field of investment analysis. His influence on investment professionals remains very strong.

Graham's magnum opus is *Security Analysis*, written with Columbia Professor David Dodd in 1934. Its message is similar to the ideas presented in this chapter. Graham believed careful analysis of a firm's financial statements could turn up bargain stocks. Over the years, he developed many different rules for determining the most important financial ratios and the critical values for judging a stock to be undervalued. Through many editions, his book has been so influential and successful that widespread adoption of Graham's techniques has led to elimination of the very bargains they are designed to identify.

In a 1976 seminar Graham said:[17]

> I am no longer an advocate of elaborate techniques of security analysis in order to find superior value opportunities. This was a rewarding activity, say, forty years ago, when our textbook "Graham and Dodd" was first published; but the situation has changed a good deal since then. In the old days any well-trained security analyst could do a good professional job of selecting undervalued issues through detailed studies; but in the light of the enormous amount of research now being carried on, I doubt whether in most cases such extensive efforts will generate sufficiently superior selections to justify their cost. To that very limited extent I'm on the side of the "efficient market" school of thought now generally accepted by the professors.

Nonetheless, in that same seminar, Graham suggested a simplified approach to identifying bargain stocks:

> My first, more limited, technique confines itself to the purchase of common stocks at less than their working-capital value, or net current-asset value, giving no weight to the plant and other fixed assets, and deducting all liabilities in full from the current assets. We used this approach extensively in managing investment funds, and over a 30-odd-year period we must have earned an average of some 20 percent per year from this source. I consider it a foolproof method of systematic investment— once again, not on the basis of individual results but in terms of the expectable group income.

---

[15]Jane A. Ou and Stephen H. Penman, "Financial Statement Analysis and the Prediction of Stock Returns," *Journal of Accounting and Economics* 11 (1985), pp. 295–329; and "Accounting Measurement, Price-Earnings Ratio, and the Information Content of Security Prices," *Journal of Accounting Research* 27 (Spring 1989), pp. 111–144.

[16]Paul Brockman, Charles Mossman, and Dennis Olson, "What's the Value of Fundamental Analysis?" *Canadian Investment Review*, Fall 1997, pp. 10–15.

[17]As cited by John Train in *Money Masters* (New York: Harper & Row, 1987).

There are two convenient sources of information for those interested in trying out the Graham technique: both Standard & Poor's *Outlook* and *Value Line Investment Survey* carry lists of stocks selling below net working capital value.

SUMMARY

1. The primary focus of the security analyst should be the firm's real economic earnings rather than its reported earnings. Accounting earnings as reported in financial statements can be a biased estimate of real economic earnings, although empirical studies reveal that reported earnings convey considerable information concerning a firm's prospects.

2. A firm's ROE is a key determinant of the growth rate of its earnings. ROE is affected profoundly by the firm's degree of financial leverage. An increase in a firm's debt-to-equity ratio will raise its ROE and hence its growth rate only if the interest rate on the debt is less than the firm's return on assets.

3. It is often helpful to the analyst to decompose a firm's ROE ratio into the product of several accounting ratios and to analyze their separate behaviour over time and across companies within an industry. A useful breakdown is

$$\text{ROE} = \frac{\text{Net profits}}{\text{Pretax profits}} \times \frac{\text{Pretax profits}}{\text{EBIT}} \times \frac{\text{EBIT}}{\text{Sales}}$$
$$\times \frac{\text{Sales}}{\text{Assets}} \times \frac{\text{Assets}}{\text{Equity}}$$

4. Other accounting ratios that have a bearing on a firm's profitability and/or risk are fixed asset turnover, inventory turnover, days receivables, and current, quick, and interest coverage ratios.

5. Two ratios that make use of the market price of the firm's common stock in addition to its financial statements are the market-to-book-value ratio and the price-earnings ratio. Analysts sometimes take low values for these ratios as a margin of safety or a sign that the stock is a bargain.

6. A strategy of investing in stocks with high-reported ROE seems to produce a lower rate of return to the investor than investing in low-ROE stocks. This implies that high-reported-ROE stocks are overpriced compared with low-ROE stocks.

7. A major problem in the use of data obtained from a firm's financial statements is comparability. Firms have a great deal of latitude in how they choose to compute various items of revenue and expense. It is therefore necessary for the security analyst to adjust accounting earnings and financial ratios to a uniform standard before attempting to compare financial results across firms.

8. Comparability problems can be acute in a period of inflation. Inflation can create distortions in accounting for inventories, depreciation, and interest expense. Comparability is also an international issue.

9. Fair value or mark-to-market accounting requires that most assets be valued at current market value rather than historical cost. This policy has proved to be controversial because ascertaining true market

value in many instances is difficult, and critics contend that financial statements are therefore unduly volatile. Advocates argue that financial statements should reflect the best estimate of current asset values.

10. International financial reporting standards have become progressively accepted throughout the world, including the United States. They differ from traditional U.S. GAAP procedures in that they are "principles-based" rather than rules-based.

KEY EQUATIONS

(17.1) $$ROE = (1 - \text{Tax rate})\left[ROA + (ROA - \text{Interest rate})\frac{\text{Debt}}{\text{Equity}}\right]$$

(17.2) $$\frac{\text{Net profit}}{\text{Equity}} = \underset{(1)}{\frac{\text{Net profits}}{\text{Pretax profits}}} \times \underset{(2)}{\frac{\text{Pretax profits}}{\text{EBIT}}} \times \underset{(3)}{\frac{\text{EBIT}}{\text{Sales}}} \times \underset{(4)}{\frac{\text{Sales}}{\text{Assets}}} \times \underset{(5)}{\frac{\text{Assets}}{\text{Equity}}}$$

(17.3) $$ROA = \text{Margin} \times \text{Turnover}$$

PROBLEMS

Mc Graw Hill Education **connect**™ **Practise and learn online with Connect.**

1. What financial ratios would a credit rating agency such as Moody's or Standard & Poor's be most interested in? Which ratios would be of most interest to a stock market analyst deciding whether to buy a stock for a diversified portfolio?

2. If markets are truly efficient, does it matter whether firms engage in earnings management? On the other hand, if firms manage earnings, what does that say about management's view on efficient markets?

3. What is the major difference in approach of international financial reporting standards and U.S. GAAP accounting? What are the advantages and disadvantages of each?

4. The Crusty Pie Co., which specializes in apple turnovers, has a return on sales higher than the industry average, yet its ROA is the same as the industry average. How can you explain this?

5. The ABC Corporation has a profit margin on sales below the industry average, yet its ROA is above the industry average. What does this imply about its asset turnover?

6. Firm A and firm B have the same ROA, yet firm A's ROE is higher. How can you explain this?

7. Use the Du Pont system of financial analysis and the following data to find return on equity:
   - Leverage ratio (assets/equity)   2.2
   - Total asset turnover   2.0
   - Net profit margin   5.5%
   - Dividend payout ratio   31.8%

8. Recently, Galaxy Corporation lowered its allowance for doubtful accounts by reducing bad debt expense from 2 percent of sales to 1 percent of sales. Ignoring taxes, what are the immediate effects on
   a. Operating income?
   b. Operating cash flow?

Use the following case in answering problems 9–11.

Hatfield Industries is a large manufacturing conglomerate based in the United States with annual sales in excess of $300 million. Hatfield is currently under investigation by the Securities and Exchange Commission (SEC) for accounting irregularities and possible legal violations in the presentation of the company's financial statements. A due diligence team from the SEC has been sent to Hatfield's corporate headquarters in Philadelphia for a complete audit in order to further assess the situation.

Several unique circumstances at Hatfield are discovered by the SEC due diligence team during the course of the investigation:

- Management has been involved in ongoing negotiations with the local labor union, of which approximately 40 percent of its full-time labour force are members. Labour officials are seeking increased wages and pension benefits, which Hatfield's management states is not possible at this time due to decreased profitability and a tight cash flow situation. Labour officials have accused Hatfield's management of manipulating the company's financial statements to justify not granting any concessions during the course of negotiations.

- All new equipment obtained over the past several years has been established on Hatfield's books as operating leases, although past acquisitions of similar equipment were nearly always classified as capital leases. Financial statements of industry peers indicate that capital leases for this type of equipment are the norm. The SEC wants Hatfield's management to provide justification for this apparent deviation from "normal" accounting practices.

- Inventory on Hatfield's books has been steadily increasing for the past few years in comparison to sales growth. Management credits improved operating efficiencies in its production methods that have contributed to boosts in overall production. The SEC is seeking evidence that Hatfield somehow may have manipulated its inventory accounts.

The SEC due diligence team is not necessarily searching for evidence of fraud but of possible manipulation of accounting standards for the purpose of misleading shareholders and other interested parties. Initial review of Hatfield's financial statements indicates that at a minimum, certain practices have resulted in low-quality earnings.

9. Labour officials believe that the management of Hatfield is attempting to understate its net income to avoid making any concessions in the labour negotiations. Which of the following actions by management will *most likely* result in low-quality earnings?
   a. Lengthening the life of a depreciable asset in order to lower the depreciation expense
   b. Lowering the discount rate used in the valuation of the company's pension obligations
   c. The recognition of revenue at the time of delivery rather than when payment is received

10. Hatfield has begun recording all new equipment leases on its books as operating leases, a change from its consistent past use of capital leases, in which the present value of lease payments is classified as a debt obligation. What is the *most likely* motivation behind Hatfield's change in accounting methodology? Hatfield is attempting to
    a. Improve its leverage ratios and reduce its perceived leverage
    b. Reduce its cost of goods sold and increase its profitability
    c. Increase its operating margins relative to industry peers

11. The SEC due diligence team is searching for the reason behind Hatfield's inventory buildup relative to its sales growth. One way to identify a deliberate manipulation of financial results by Hatfield is to search for
    a. A decline in inventory turnover
    b. Receivables that are growing faster than sales
    c. A delay in the recognition of expenses

12. A firm has an ROE of 3 percent, a debt-to-equity ratio of .5, and a tax rate of 35 percent, and pays an interest rate of 6 percent on its debt. What is its operating ROA?

13. A firm has a tax burden ratio of .75, a leverage ratio of 1.25, an interest burden of .6, and a return on sales of 10 percent. The firm generates $2.40 in sales per dollar of assets. What is the firm's ROE?

14. Use the following cash flow data for Rocket Transport to find Rocket's

   a. Net cash provided by or used in investing activities

   b. Net cash provided by or used in financing activities

   c. Net increase or decrease in cash for the year

Cash dividend	$ 80,000
Purchase of bus	$ 33,000
Interest paid on debt	$ 25,000
Sales of old equipment	$ 72,000
Repurchase of stock	$ 55,000
Cash payments to suppliers	$ 95,000
Cash collections from customers	$300,000

15. Here are data on two firms.

	Equity ($ million)	Debt ($ million)	ROA (%)	Cost of capital (%)
Acme	100	50	17	9
Apex	450	150	15	10

   a. Which firm has the higher economic value added?

   b. Which has higher economic value added per dollar of invested capital?

The following problems are based on questions that have appeared in past CFA examinations.

16. The information in the table here comes from the financial statements of QuickBrush Company and SmileWhite Corporation. Determine which company has the higher quality of earnings by discussing each of the three notes.

	QuickBrush	SmileWhite
Goodwill	The company amortizes goodwill over 20 years.	The company amortizes goodwill over 5 years.
Property, plant, and equipment	The company uses a straight-line depreciation method over the economic lives of the assets, which range from 5 to 20 years for buildings.	The company uses an accelerated depreciation method over the economic lives of the assets, which range from 5 to 20 years for buildings.
Accounts receivable	The company uses a bad debt allowance of 2% of accounts receivable.	The company uses a bad debt allowance of 5% of accounts receivable.

17. Scott Kelly is reviewing MasterToy's financial statements in order to estimate its sustainable growth rate. Using the information presented in the table here for MasterToy,

   a. Identify and calculate the components of the Du Pont formula.

   b. Calculate the ROE for 2011 using the components of the Du Pont formula.

   c. Calculate the sustainable growth rate for 2011 from the firm's ROE and plowback ratios.

MasterToy, Inc. Actual 2010 and Estimated 2011 Financial Statements For Fiscal Year Ending December 31 ($ millions, except per-share data)			
	2010	2011 (est.)	Change (%)
Income Statement			
Revenue	$4,750	$5,140	8.2
Cost of goods sold	2,400	2,540	
Selling, general, and administrative	1,400	1,550	
Depreciation	180	210	
Goodwill amortization	10	10	
Operating income	$ 760	$ 830	9.2
Interest expense	20	25	
Income before taxes	$ 740	$ 805	
Income taxes	265	295	
Net income	$ 475	$ 510	
Earnings per share	$1.79	$1.96	9.5
Average shares outstanding (millions)	265	260	
Balance Sheet			
Cash	$ 400	$ 400	
Accounts receivable	680	700	
Inventories	570	600	
Net property, plant, and equipment	800	870	
Intangibles	500	530	
Total assets	$2,950	$3,100	
Current liabilities	550	600	
Long-term debt	300	300	
Total liabilities	$ 850	$ 900	
Stockholders' equity	2,100	2,200	
Total liabilities and equity	$2,950	$3,100	
Book value per share	$7.92	$8.46	
Annual dividend per share	$.55	$.60	

18. The cash flow data of Palomba Pizza Stores for the past financial year are as follows:

Cash payment of dividends	$ 35,000
Purchase of land	14,000
Cash payments for interest	10,000
Cash payments for salaries	45,000
Sale of equipment	38,000
Retirement of common stock	25,000
Purchase of equipment	30,000
Cash payments to suppliers	85,000
Cash collections from customers	250,000
Cash at beginning of year	50,000

a. Prepare a statement of cash flows for Palomba showing
- Net cash provided by operating activities
- Net cash provided by or used in investing activities
- Net cash provided by or used in financing activities

b. Discuss, from an analyst's viewpoint, the purpose of classifying cash flows into the three categories listed above.

19. This problem should be solved using the following data:

Cash payments for interest	$(12)
Retirement of common stock	(32)
Cash payments to merchandise suppliers	(85)
Purchase of land	(8)
Sale of equipment	30
Payments of dividends	(37)
Cash payment for salaries	(35)
Cash collection from customers	260
Purchase of equipment	(40)

a. What are cash flows from operating activities?

b. Using the data above, calculate cash flows from investing activities.

c. Using the data above, calculate cash flows from financing activities.

20. Janet Ludlow is a recently hired analyst. After describing the electric toothbrush industry, her first report focuses on two companies, QuickBrush Company and SmileWhite Corporation, and concludes: "QuickBrush is a more profitable company than SmileWhite, as indicated by the 40% sales growth and substantially higher margins it has produced over the last few years. Smile-White's sales and earnings are growing at a 10% rate and produce much lower margins. We do not think SmileWhite is capable of growing faster than its recent growth rate of 10% whereas Quick-Brush can sustain a 30% long-term growth rate."

a. Criticize Ludlow's analysis and conclusion that QuickBrush is more profitable, as defined by return on equity (ROE), than SmileWhite and that it has a higher sustainable growth rate. Use only the information provided in Tables 17A and 17B. Support your criticism by calculating and analyzing
- The five components that determine ROE
- The two ratios that determine sustainable growth: ROE and plowback

b. Explain how QuickBrush has produced an average annual earnings per share (EPS) growth rate of 40 percent over the last two years with an ROE that has been declining. Use only the information provided in Table 17A.

The following case should be used to solve problems 21–24.

21. Eastover Company (EO) is a large, diversified forest products company. Approximately 75 percent of its sales are from paper and forest products, with the remainder from financial services and real estate. The company owns 5.6 million acres of timberland, which is carried at very low historical cost on the balance sheet.

Peggy Mulroney, CFA is an analyst at the investment counselling firm of Centurion Investments. She is assigned the task of assessing the outlook for Eastover, which is being considered for purchase, and comparing it to another forest products company in Centurion's portfolios, Southampton Corporation (SHC). SHC is a major producer of lumber products in the United States. Building products, primarily lumber and plywood, account for 89 percent of SHC's sales,

TABLE 17A

QuickBrush Company Financial Statements: Yearly Data ($000 except per-share data)			
Income Statement	**December 2011**	**December 2012**	**December 2013**
Revenue	$3,480	$5,400	$ 7,760
Cost of goods sold	2,700	4,270	6,050
Selling, general, and administrative expense	500	690	1,000
Depreciation and amortization	30	40	50
Operating income (EBIT)	$ 250	$ 400	$ 660
Interest expense	0	0	0
Income before taxes	$ 250	$ 400	$ 660
Income taxes	60	110	215
Income after taxes	$ 190	$ 290	$ 445
Diluted EPS	$0.60	$0.84	$1.18
Average shares outstanding (000)	317	346	376

Financial Statistics	**December 2011**	**December 2012**	**December 2013**	**3-Year Average**
COGS as percent of sales	77.59%	79.07%	77.96%	78.21%
General and administrative expense as percent of sales	14.37	12.78	12.89	13.34
Operating margin	7.18	7.41	8.51	
Pretax income/EBIT	100.00	100.00	100.00	
Tax rate	24.00	27.50	32.58	

Balance Sheet	**December 2011**	**December 2012**	**December 2013**
Cash and cash equivalents	$ 460	$ 50	$ 480
Accounts receivable	540	720	950
Inventories	300	430	590
Net property, plant, and equipment	760	1,830	3,450
Total assets	$2,060	$3,030	$5,470
Current liabilities	$ 860	$ 1,110	$1,750
Total liabilities	$ 860	$ 1,110	$1,750
Stockholders' equity	1,200	1,920	3,720
Total liabilities and equity	$2,060	$3,030	$5,470
Market price per share	$21.00	$30.00	$45.00
Book value per share	$3.79	$5.55	$9.89
Annual dividend per share	$0.00	$0.00	$0.00

TABLE 17B

	SmileWhite Corporation Financial Statements: Yearly Data ($000 except per-share data)		
Income Statement	**December 2011**	**December 2012**	**December 2013**
Revenue	$104,000	$110,400	$119,200
Cost of goods sold	72,800	75,100	79,300
Selling, general, and administrative expense	20,300	22,800	23,900
Depreciation and amortization	4,200	5,600	8,300
Operating income	$ 6,700	$ 6,900	$ 7,700
Interest expense	600	350	350
Income before taxes	$ 6,100	$ 6,550	$ 7350
Income taxes	2,100	2,200	2500
Income after taxes	$ 4,000	$ 4,350	$ 4850
Diluted EPS	$2.16	$2.35	$2.62
Average shares outstanding (000)	1,850	1,850	1,850

Financial Statistics	**December 2011**	**December 2012**	**December 2013**	**3-Year Average**
COGS as percent of sales	70.00%	68.00%	66.53%	68.18%
General and administrative expense as percent of sales	19.52	20.65	20.05	20.07
Operating margin	6.44	6.25	6.46	
Pretax income/EBIT	91.04	94.93	95.45	
Tax rate	34.43	33.59	34.01	

Balance Sheet	**December 2011**	**December 2012**	**December 2013**
Cash and cash equivalents	$ 7900	$ 3,300	$ 1,700
Accounts receivable	7500	8,000	9,000
Inventories	6,300	6,300	5,900
Net property, plant, and equipment	12,000	14,500	17,000
Total assets	$33,700	$32,100	$33,600
Current liabilities	$ 6,200	$ 7,800	$ 6,600
Long-term debt	9,000	4,300	4,300
Total liabilities	$15,200	$12,100	$10,900
Stockholders' equity	18,500	20,000	22,700
Total liabilities and equity	$33,700	$32,100	$33,600
Market price per share	$23.00	$26.00	$30.00
Book value per share	$10.00	$10.81	$12.27
Annual dividend per share	$1.42	$1.53	$1.72

with pulp accounting for the remainder. SHC owns 1.4 million acres of timberland, which is also carried at historical cost on the balance sheet. In SHC's case, however, that cost is not as far below current market as Eastover's.

Mulroney began her examination of Eastover and Southampton by looking at the five components of return on equity (ROE) for each company. For her analysis, Mulroney elected to define equity as total shareholders' equity, including preferred stock. She also elected to use year-end data rather than averages for the balance sheet items.

a. Based on the data shown in Tables 17C and 17D, calculate each of the five ROE components for Eastover and Southampton in 2013. Using the five components, calculate ROE for both companies in 2013.

b. Referring to the components calculated in part (b), explain the difference in ROE for Eastover and Southampton in 2013.

c. Using 2013 data, calculate the sustainable growth rate for both Eastover and Southampton. Discuss the appropriateness of using these calculations as a basis for estimating future growth.

TABLE 17C   Eastover Company ($ millions, except shares outstanding)

	2009	2010	2011	2012	2013
Income Statement Summary					
Sales	$5,652	$6,990	$7,863	$8,281	$7,406
Earnings before interest and taxes (EBIT)	$ 568	$ 901	$1,037	$ 708	$ 795
Interest expense (net)	(147)	(188)	(186)	(194)	(195)
Income before taxes	$ 421	$ 713	$ 851	$ 514	$ 600
Income taxes	(144)	(266)	(286)	(173)	(206)
Tax rate	34%	37%	33%	34%	34%
Net income	$ 277	$ 447	$ 565	$ 341	$ 394
Preferred dividends	(28)	(17)	(17)	(17)	(0)
Net income to common	$ 249	$ 430	$ 548	$ 324	$ 394
Common shares outstanding (millions)	196	204	204	205	201
Balance Sheet Summary					
Current assets	$1,235	$1,491	$1,702	$1,585	$1,367
Timberland assets	649	625	621	612	615
Property, plant, and equipment	4,370	4,571	5,056	5,430	5,854
Other assets	360	555	473	472	429
Total assets	$6,614	$7,242	$7,852	$8,099	$8,265
Current liabilities	$1,226	$1,186	$1,206	$1,606	$1,816
Long-term debt	1,120	1,340	1,585	1,346	1,585
Deferred taxes	1,000	1,000	1,016	1,000	1,000
Equity—preferred	364	350	350	400	0
Equity—common	2,904	3,366	3,695	3,747	3,864
Total liabilities and equity	$6,614	$7,242	$7,852	$8,099	$8,265

TABLE 17D   Southampton Corporation ($ millions, except shares outstanding)

	2009	2010	2011	2012	2013
Income Statement Summary					
Sales	$1,306	$1,654	$1,799	$2,010	$1,793
Earnings before interest and taxes (EBIT)	$ 120	$ 230	$ 221	$ 304	$ 145
Interest expense (net)	(13)	(36)	(7)	(12)	(8)
Income before taxes	$ 107	$ 194	$ 214	$ 292	$ 137
Income taxes	(44)	(75)	(79)	(99)	(46)
Tax rate	41%	39%	37%	34%	34%
Net income	$ 63	$ 119	$ 135	$ 193	$ 91
Common shares outstanding (millions)	38	38	38	38	38
Balance Sheet Summary					
Current assets	$ 487	$ 504	$ 536	$ 654	$ 509
Timberland assets	512	513	508	513	518
Property, plant, and equipment	648	681	718	827	1,037
Other assets	141	151	34	38	40
Total assets	$1,788	$1,849	$1,796	$2,032	$2,104
Current liabilities	$ 185	$ 176	$ 162	$ 180	$ 195
Long-term debt	536	493	370	530	589
Deferred taxes	123	136	127	146	153
Equity	944	1,044	1,137	1,176	1,167
Total liabilities and equity	$1,788	$1,849	$1,796	$2,032	$2,104

22. *a.* Mulroney (see the previous problem) recalled from her CFA studies that the constant-growth discounted dividend model was one way to arrive at a valuation for a company's common stock. She collected current dividend and stock price data for Eastover and Southampton, shown in Table 17E. Using 11 percent as the required rate of return (i.e., discount rate) and a projected growth rate of 8 percent, compute a constant-growth DDM value for Eastover's stock and compare the computed value for Eastover to its stock price indicated in Table 17F.

b. Mulroney's supervisor commented that a two-stage DDM may be more appropriate for companies such as Eastover and Southampton. Mulroney believes that Eastover and Southampton could grow more rapidly over the next three years and then settle in at a lower but sustainable rate of growth beyond 2017. Her estimates are indicated in Table 17G. Using 11 percent as the required rate of return, compute the two-stage DDM value of Eastover's stock and compare that value to its stock price indicated in Table 17F.

c. Discuss advantages and disadvantages of using a constant-growth DDM. Briefly discuss how the two-stage DDM improves upon the constant-growth DDM.

23. In addition to the discounted-dividend-model approach, Mulroney (see previous problem) decided to look at the price-earnings ratio and price-book ratio, relative to the S&P 500, for both Eastover and Southampton. Mulroney elected to perform this analysis using 2010–2014 and current data.

a. Using the data in Tables 17E and 17F, compute both the current and the five-year (2010–2014) average relative price-earnings ratios and relative price-book ratios for Eastover and Southampton (i.e., ratios relative to those for the S&P 500). Discuss each company's current relative price-earnings ratio compared to its five-year average relative price-earnings ratio and each company's current relative price-book ratio as compared to its five-year average relative price-book ratio.

b. Briefly discuss one disadvantage for each of the relative price-earnings and relative price-book approaches to valuation.

TABLE 17E   Valuation of Eastover Company and Southampton Corporation Compared to S&P 500

	2006	2007	2008	2009	2010	2011	5-Year Average (2007–2011)
Eastover Company							
Earnings per share	$ 1.27	$ 2.12	$ 2.68	$ 1.56	$ 1.87	$ 0.90	
Dividends per share	0.87	0.90	1.15	1.20	1.20	1.20	
Book value per share	14.82	16.54	18.14	18.55	19.21	17.21	
Stock price:							
High	28	40	30	33	28	30	
Low	20	20	23	25	18	20	
Close	25	26	25	28	22	27	
Average P/E	18.9	14.2	9.9	18.6	12.3	27.8	
Average P/B	1.6	1.8	1.5	1.6	1.2	1.5	
Southampton Corporation							
Earnings per share	$ 1.66	$ 3.13	$ 3.55	$ 5.08	$ 2.46	$ 1.75	
Dividends per share	.77	.79	.89	.98	1.04	1.08	
Book value per share	24.84	27.47	29.92	30.95	31.54	32.21	
Stock price:							
High	34	40	38	43	45	46	
Low	21	22	26	28	20	26	
Close	31	27	28	39	27	44	
Average P/E	16.6	9.9	9.0	7.0	13.2	20.6	
Average P/B	1.1	1.1	1.1	1.2	1.0	1.1	
S&P 500							
Average P/E	15.8	16.0	11.1	13.9	15.6	19.2	15.2
Average P/B	1.8	2.1	1.9	2.2	2.1	2.3	2.1

TABLE 17F
Current
Information

	Current Share Price	Current Dividends per Share	2012 EPS Estimate	Current Book Value per Share
Eastover	$ 28	$ 1.20	$ 1.60	$ 17.32
Southampton	48	1.08	3.00	32.21
S&P 500	830	24.00	41.08	319.66

TABLE 17G
Projected Growth
Rates as of 2005

	Next Three Years (2012, 2013, 2014)	Growth Beyond 2014
Eastover	12%	8%
Southampton	13%	7%

24. Mulroney (see problems 21–23) previously calculated a valuation for Southampton for both the constant-growth and the two-stage DDM as shown below:

Constant-Growth Approach	Two-Stage Approach
$29	$35.50

Using only the information provided and your answers to problems 21–23, select the stock (EO or SHC) that Mulroney should recommend as the better value, and justify your selection.

25. In reviewing the financial statements of the Graceland Rock Company, you note that net income increased while cash flow from operations decreased from 2013 to 2014.

   a. Explain how net income could increase for Graceland Rock Company while cash flow from operations decreased. Give some illustrative examples.

   b. Explain why cash flow from operations may be a good indicator of a firm's "quality of earnings."

26. A firm has net sales of $3,000, cash expenses (including taxes) of $1,400, and depreciation of $500. If accounts receivable increase over the period by $400, what would be cash flow from operations?

27. A company's current ratio is 2.0. If the company uses cash to retire notes payable due within one year, would this transaction increase or decrease the current ratio and asset turnover ratio?

	Current Ratio	Asset Turnover Ratio
a.	Increase	Increase
b.	Increase	Decrease
c.	Decrease	Increase
d.	Decrease	Decrease

28. During a period of rising prices, the financial statements of a firm using FIFO reporting instead of LIFO reporting would show

   a. Higher total assets and higher net income

   b. Higher total assets and lower net income

   c. Lower total assets and higher net income

   d. Lower total assets and lower net income

29. In an inflationary period, the use of FIFO will make which one of the following more realistic than the use of LIFO?

   a. Balance sheet

   b. Income statement

   c. Cash flow statement

   d. None of the above

30. Jones Group has been generating stable after-tax ROE despite declining operating income. Explain how it might be able to maintain this stability.

31. The Du Pont formula defines the net return on shareholders' equity as a function of the following components:

   • Operating margin

   • Asset turnover

   • Interest burden

   • Financial leverage

   • Income tax rate

TABLE 17H

Income
Statements and
Balance Sheets
($ millions)

	2013	2014
Income Statement Data		
Revenues	$542	$979
Operating income	38	76
Depreciation and amortization	3	9
Interest expense	3	0
Pretax income	32	67
Income taxes	13	37
Net income after tax	19	30
Balance Sheet Data		
Fixed assets	$ 41	$ 70
Total assets	245	291
Working capital	123	157
Total debt	16	0
Total shareholders' equity	159	220

Using only the data in Table 17H,

a. Calculate each of the five components listed above for 2013 and 2014, and calculate the return on equity (ROE) for 2013 and 2014, using all of the five components.

b. Briefly discuss the impact of the changes in asset turnover and financial leverage on the change in ROE from 2013 to 2014.

**E-INVESTMENTS
Exercises**

This chapter introduced the idea of economic value added (EVA) as a means to measure firm performance. A related measure is market value added (MVA), which is the difference between the market value of a firm and its book value. You can find the firms with the best such measures at **www.evadimensions.com**. You will see there that EVA leaders do not necessarily have the highest return on capital. Why not? Are the EVA leaders also the MVA leaders? Why not?

18 CHAPTER

Options and Other Derivatives Markets: Introduction

Derivative securities, or more simply *derivatives*, play a large and increasingly important role in financial markets. These are securities whose prices are determined by, or "derive from," the prices of other securities. Options and futures contracts are both derivative securities. Their payoffs depend on the value of other securities. Swaps, which we will discuss in Chapter 20, also are derivatives. Because the value of derivatives depends on the value of other securities, they can be powerful tools for both hedging and speculation. We will investigate these applications in the next three chapters, starting in this chapter with options.

As is argued in the nearby box, option-like instruments have existed for a long time, but until recently they were considered relatively unimportant. Trading of standardized options contracts on a national exchange started in the United States in 1973 when the Chicago Board Options Exchange (CBOE) began listing call options. These contracts were almost immediately a great success, crowding out the previously existing over-the-counter options market.

Options contracts are traded now on several U.S. exchanges. They are written on common stock, stock indices, foreign exchange, agricultural commodities, precious metals, and interest rate futures. In addition, the over-the-counter market also has enjoyed a tremendous resurgence in recent years as trading in custom-tailored options has exploded. Popular and potent tools in modifying portfolio characteristics, options have become essential tools a portfolio manager must understand.

This chapter is an introduction to options markets. It explains how puts and calls work and examines their investment characteristics. Popular option strategies are considered next. Finally, the chapter provides a brief overview of securities with embedded options, such as callable or convertible bonds, as well as on some so-called exotic options.

Options have become ubiquitous financial instruments to manage risk across a host of different investment situations. Options are now so commonplace that they have become the focus of late-night infomercials promising lucrative profits through easy-to-learn trading strategies, for just three payments of $79.95 (plus postage and handling).

Usually regarded as a modern risk management tool developed by financial engineers in the early 1970s, options and their uses can be traced back to at least 600 BC. Aristotle is most often credited with recording the first use of call options in *Politics* written in 350 BC. To illustrate the art of accumulating wealth, Aristotle recounts the story of Thales of Miletus (620–546 BC). Tired of people pointing to his poverty as evidence of the uselessness of his academic pursuits (philosophy, astronomy and mathematics), Thales decided to apply his knowledge to the accumulation of material.

Using his astronomic skills, Thales foresaw a bumper crop of olives the coming year. With very little money, he placed deposits on all the olive presses in and around his region for their future use. Because no one was bidding against him, each deposit was small. When the bumper crop materialized, olive presses were in high demand all at once and Thales "let them out at any rate which he pleased, and made a quantity of money." With characteristic foresight, Aristotle underscored that the financial device used by Thales had "universal application."

Despite their use in early history, options remained on the financial sidelines for centuries. Well into the 1960s and early 1970s options were considered "specialized and relatively unimportant financial securities," this characterization made by Robert Merton in the opening paragraphs of his 1973 article, "The Theory of Rational Option Pricing."

With hindsight, the publication of Merton's article and the equally important "The Pricing of Options and Corporate Liabilities" by Fischer Black and Myron Scholes proved to be the tipping point for options. The elusive formula for valuing stock options had been found and it paved the way for the design, valuation and use of a host of new financial instruments that facilitated more efficient risk management in society. The 1973 co-discoveries earned the 1997 Nobel Prize in Economic Sciences.

Like Thales centuries before them, Merton and Scholes decided to use their academic expertise to make money and introduced the first option-based mutual fund in the United States. The strategy invested 10% of fund assets in a diversified portfolio of call options with the balance invested in short-term money market instruments. The open-ended mutual fund went live in February 1976. The fund performed in line with pre-launch simulations but was commercially unsuccessful. Readers will recognize the Merton-Scholes product as the precursor to the very profitable principal protection strategies that emerged over the subsequent two decades. They had a winning strategy, but the market was not ready for it.

Their second commercial venture, Long-Term Capital Management (LTCM), was co-founded in 1992 with a team of gifted financial engineers. It became wildly successful, earning billions for early investors by finding and leveraging mispriced securities. In early 1998, LTCM had US$130 billion under management and controlled a derivatives portfolio with a notional value of US$1.25 trillion. The credit crisis of August and September 1998 undermined LTCM's liquidity-sensitive strategies and, by the end of September, it had lost 90% of its value and had to be rescued to the tune of US$3.6 billion. Like Thales before them, Merton and Scholes returned to academia but unlike Thales they returned with their wealth very much reduced.

Source: John Ilkiw, *Canadian Investment Review* 19, no. 1 (Spring 2006), p. 9. Reprinted with permission.

18.1 THE OPTION CONTRACT

A **call option** gives its holder the right to purchase an asset for a specified price, called the **exercise** or **strike price**, on or before some specified expiration date. For example, a September call option on Research In Motion (RIM) stock with exercise price $14 entitles its owner to purchase RIM stock for a price of $14 at any time up to and including the expiration date in September. The holder of the call is not required to exercise the option. The holder will choose to exercise only if the market value of the asset to be purchased exceeds the exercise price. When the market price does exceed the exercise price, the optionholder may "call away" the asset for the exercise price. Otherwise, the option may be left unexercised. If it is not exercised before the expiration date of the contract, a call option simply expires and no longer has value. Therefore, if the stock price is greater than the exercise price on the expiration date, the value of the call option equals the difference between the stock price and the exercise price; but if the stock price is less than the exercise price at expiration, the call will be worthless. The *net profit* on the call is the value of the option minus the price originally paid to purchase it.

The purchase price of the option is called the *premium*. It represents the compensation the purchaser of the call must pay for the right to exercise the option only when exercise is desirable. Sellers of call options, who are said to *write* calls, receive premium income now as payment against the possibility they will be required at some later date to deliver the asset in return for an exercise price lower than the market value of the asset. If the option is left to expire worthless, however, then the writer of the call clears a profit equal to the premium income derived from the sale of the option.

But if the call is exercised, the profit to the option writer is the premium income minus the difference between the value of the stock that must be delivered and the exercise price that is paid for those shares. If that difference is larger than the initial premium, the writer will incur a loss.

EXAMPLE 18.1   Profits and Losses on a Call Option

Consider September 2013 maturity call options on RIM stock with an exercise price of $14 per share, which were selling on May 31, 2013 for $2.1. Exchange-traded stock options expire on the third Friday of the expiration month, which for this option was September 20, 2013. Until the expiration day, the purchaser of the calls was entitled to buy shares of RIM for $14. Because the stock price on May 31, 2013 was only $14.50, it clearly would not have made sense at that moment to exercise the option to buy at $14. Indeed, if RIM stock remained below $14 by the expiration date, the call would be left to expire worthless. If, on the other hand, RIM were selling above $14 at expiration, the call holder would find it optimal to exercise. For example, if RIM sold for $17 on September 20, the option would have been exercised since it would have given its holder the right to pay $14 for a stock worth $17. The value of the option on the expiration date would then be

$$\text{Value at expiration} = \text{Stock price} - \text{Exercise price} = \$17 - \$14 = \$3$$

Despite the $3 payoff at maturity, the call holder realizes a gain of only $0.9 on his investment, because the initial purchase price was $2.1:

$$\text{Profit} = \text{Final value} - \text{Original investment} = \$3 - \$2.1 = \$0.9$$

Even if the profit were negative, exercise of the call will be optimal at maturity if the stock price is above the exercise price, because the exercise proceeds will offset at least part of the investment in the option. The investor in the call will clear a profit if RIM is selling above $16.1 at the maturity date. At that stock price, the proceeds from exercise will just cover the original cost of the call.

A **put option** gives its holder the right to *sell* an asset for a specified exercise or strike price on or before some expiration date. A September 2013 put on RIM with exercise price $16 entitles its owner to sell RIM stock to the put writer at a price of $16 at any time before expiration in September even if the market price of RIM is less than $16. While profits on call options increase when the asset increases in value, profits on put options increase when the asset value falls. A put will be exercised only if the exercise price is greater than the price of the underlying asset, that is, only if its holder can deliver for the exercise price an asset with market value less than the exercise price. (One doesn't need to own the shares of RIM to exercise the RIM put option. Upon exercise, the investor's broker purchases the necessary shares of RIM at the market price and immediately delivers, or "puts" them, to an option writer for the exercise price. The owner of the put profits by the difference between the exercise price and market price.)

EXAMPLE 18.2   Profits and Losses on a Put Option

Consider the September 2013 maturity put option on RIM with an exercise price of $16 selling on May 31, 2013 for $2.88. It entitles its owner to sell a share of RIM for $16 at any time until September 20, the third Friday. If the holder of the put option bought a share of RIM and immediately exercised the right to sell at $15, net proceeds would be $16 − $14.50 = $1.50.

continued

Obviously, an investor who paid $2.88 for the put had no intention of exercising it immediately. If, on the other hand, RIM sold for $12 at expiration, the put would turn out to be a profitable investment. The value of the put on the expiration date would be

$$\text{Value at expiration} = \text{Exercise price} - \text{Stock price} = \$16 - \$12 = \$4$$

and the investor's profit would be $4 − $2.88 = $1.12. This is a holding-period return of 1.12/2.88 = .3889, or 38.89 percent—over less than four months! Obviously, put option sellers (who are on the other side of the transaction) did not consider this outcome very likely.

An option is described as **in the money** when its exercise would produce a positive cash flow. Therefore, a call option is in the money when the asset price is greater than the exercise price, and a put option is in the money when the asset price is less than the exercise price. Conversely, a call is **out of the money** when the asset price is less than the exercise price; no one would exercise the right to purchase for the strike price an asset worth less than that amount. A put option is out of the money when the exercise price is less than the asset price. Options are **at the money** when the exercise price and asset price are equal.

Options Trading

Some options trade on over-the-counter (OTC) markets. An OTC market offers the advantage that the terms of the option contract—the exercise price, maturity date, and number of shares committed—can be tailored to the needs of the traders. The costs of establishing an OTC option contract, however, are higher than for exchange-traded options. Today, most option trading takes place on organized exchanges but the OTC market in customized options is also thriving.

Options contracts traded on exchanges are standardized by allowable maturity dates and exercise prices for each listed option.[1] Each stock option contract provides for the right to buy or sell 100 shares of stock. (If stock splits occur after the contract is listed, adjustments are required. We discuss adjustments in option contract terms later in this section.)

Standardization of the terms of listed option contracts means that all market participants trade in a limited and uniform set of securities. This increases the depth of trading in any particular option, which lowers trading costs and results in a more competitive market. Exchanges therefore, offer three important benefits: ease of trading, which flows from a central marketplace where buyers and sellers or their representatives congregate; a liquid secondary market, where buyers and sellers of options can transact quickly and cheaply; and a guarantee by the exchange that both parties to the contract will fulfill their obligations.

Until recently, most options trading in the United States took place on the Chicago Board Options Exchange. However, by 2003 the International Securities Exchange, an electronic exchange based in New York, displaced the CBOE as the largest options market. Options trading in Europe is uniformly transacted in electronic exchanges.

In Canada, organized exchange trading of standardized option contracts began in 1975–1976 in Montreal and Toronto. The following year the two exchanges merged their options-clearing corporations, forming TransCanada Options Inc. (TCO). The Vancouver Stock Exchange joined TCO in 1984. Finally, in the year 1999 all derivatives trading in Canada (with the exception of agricultural futures) was transferred to the Montréal Exchange.

Figure 18.1 is a reproduction of a part of the listed stock option quotations for RIM from Montréal Exchange's Web site. At the top of the table, following the company name, it is indicated that the last recorded price on the Toronto Stock Exchange for RIM stock was $14.45 per share.

www.m-x.ca

---

[1]Although options trade in contracts of 100 units apiece, all quotes and examples are expressed on a per-unit basis.

FIGURE 18.1 Stock option quotations.

BB—Research In Motion Limited

Last Update: May 31, 2013 at 5.30 p.m.

Last Price: **14.450**   Net Change: **−0.420**   Bid Price: **14.450**   Ask Price: **14.500**   30-day historical volatility: **35.71%**

Calls					Puts				
Month/ Strike	Bid Price	Ask Price	Last Price	Open int.	Month/ Strike	Bid Price	Ask Price	Last Price	Open int.
Open interest: 68,200				Volume: 1,646	Open interest: 24,638				Volume: 493
13 JUN 11.000	3.400	3.550	3.550	509	13 JUN 11.000	0.010	0.050	0.050	113
13 JUN 12.000	2.490	2.560	2.560	1,962	13 JUN 12.000	0.050	0.070	0.070	695
13 JUN 13.000	1.610	1.680	1.680	1,201	13 JUN 13.000	0.160	0.200	0.200	457
13 JUN 14.000	0.910	0.970	0.970	2,127	13 JUN 14.000	0.440	0.490	0.490	849
13 JUN 15.000	0.440	0.500	0.500	2,415	13 JUN 15.000	0.980	1.020	1.020	11,176
13 JUN 16.000	0.180	0.210	0.210	3,301	13 JUN 16.000	1.700	1.770	1.770	335
13 JUN 17.000	0.080	0.130	0.130	2,004	13 JUN 17.000	2.590	2.670	2.670	105
13 JUL 12.000	2.800	2.870	2.870	36	13 JUL 12.000	0.370	0.420	0.420	84
13 JUL 13.000	2.110	2.190	2.190	16	13 JUL 13.000	0.670	0.720	0.720	170
13 JUL 14.000	1.480	1.590	1.590	63	13 JUL 14.000	1.110	1.150	1.150	80
13 JUL 15.000	1.090	1.140	1.140	370	13 JUL 15.000	1.640	1.700	1.700	60
13 JUL 16.000	0.760	0.800	0.800	413	13 JUL 16.000	2.260	2.370	2.370	65
13 JUL 17.000	0.520	0.560	0.560	230	13 JUL 17.000	3.050	3.150	3.150	20
13 SEP 11.000	3.850	3.950	3.950	248	13 SEP 11.000	0.470	0.520	0.520	379
13 SEP 12.000	3.150	3.300	3.300	406	13 SEP 12.000	0.740	0.800	0.800	394
13 SEP 13.000	2.540	2.630	2.630	349	13 SEP 13.000	1.130	1.180	1.180	193
13 SEP 14.000	2.020	2.100	2.100	358	13 SEP 14.000	1.600	1.660	1.660	312
13 SEP 15.000	1.600	1.690	1.690	683	13 SEP 15.000	2.170	2.260	2.260	404
13 SEP 16.000	1.250	1.320	1.320	932	13 SEP 16.000	2.800	2.880	2.880	45
13 SEP 17.000	0.980	1.040	1.040	1,041	13 SEP 17.000	3.500	3.650	3.650	96
13 DEC 11.000	4.250	4.350	4.350	10	13 DEC 11.000	0.860	0.910	0.910	247
13 DEC 12.000	3.600	3.700	3.700	50	13 DEC 12.000	1.200	1.300	1.300	602
13 DEC 13.000	3.050	3.150	3.150	20	13 DEC 13.000	1.640	1.760	1.760	108
13 DEC 14.000	2.590	2.760	2.760	40	13 DEC 14.000	2.160	2.240	2.240	221
13 DEC 15.000	2.190	2.280	2.280	52	13 DEC 15.000	2.740	2.840	2.840	57
13 DEC 16.000	1.850	1.950	1.950	271	13 DEC 16.000	3.350	3.500	3.500	90
13 DEC 17.000	1.560	1.670	1.670	78	13 DEC 17.000	4.100	4.200	4.200	95
14 JAN 11.000	4.300	4.450	4.450	358	14 JAN 11.000	0.930	1.040	1.040	107
14 JAN 12.000	3.600	3.700	3.700	6,383	14 JAN 12.000	1.270	1.340	1.340	284
14 JAN 13.000	3.100	3.200	3.200	7,046	14 JAN 13.000	1.710	1.800	1.800	100
14 JAN 14.000	2.700	2.810	2.810	260	14 JAN 14.000	2.260	2.350	2.350	508
14 JAN 15.000	2.320	2.420	2.420	4,204	14 JAN 15.000	2.870	2.960	2.960	84
14 JAN 16.000	1.970	2.080	2.080	1,028	14 JAN 16.000	3.500	3.650	3.650	166
14 JAN 17.000	1.680	1.770	1.770	432	14 JAN 17.000	4.200	4.350	4.350	100
15 JAN 11.000	5.550	6.000	6.000	68	15 JAN 11.000	1.990	2.210	2.210	20
15 JAN 12.000	5.100	5.450	5.450	95	15 JAN 12.000	2.470	2.760	2.760	10
15 JAN 13.000	4.650	4.950	4.950	55	15 JAN 13.000	3.000	3.300	3.300	53
15 JAN 14.000	4.200	4.550	4.550	23	15 JAN 14.000	3.550	3.850	3.850	6
15 JAN 15.000	3.800	4.200	4.200	86	15 JAN 15.000	4.150	4.450	4.450	40
15 JAN 16.000	3.450	3.850	3.850	23	15 JAN 16.000	4.750	5.100	5.100	0
15 JAN 17.000	3.150	3.550	3.550	233	15 JAN 17.000	5.400	5.800	5.800	0

Underlying equity quotations are a courtesy of the TSX and are delayed by at least 15 minutes.

Source: Bourse de Montréal (Canadian Derivatives Exchange) site, http://www.m-x.ca, May 31, 2013.

Options are traded on RIM at exercise prices varying in $1 or $2 increments. These values are also called *strike prices* and are given in the first column of numbers, next to the expiration month.

The exchanges offer options on stocks with exercise prices that bracket the stock price. Exercise prices generally are set at intervals of $1, $2, $2.5, $5, or $10, depending on the price of stock. If the stock price moves outside the range of exercise prices of the existing set of options, new options with appropriate exercise prices may be offered. Therefore, at any time both in-the-money and out-of-the-money options will be listed, as in the RIM example.

The following rows of numbers provide the bid, asked, and last trade prices as well as open interest (number of outstanding contracts) of call and put options on RIM shares that traded that day, with expiration dates of June, July, September, and December 2013 and January 2014 and 2015. Notice that the prices of RIM call options decrease as one moves down each column, toward progressively higher exercise prices. This makes sense, because the right to purchase a share at a given exercise price is worth less as that exercise price increases. At an exercise price of $14, the July RIM call had a closing price of $1.59, whereas the option to purchase for an exercise price of $16 sold for only $0.80. Conversely, put option prices increase with the exercise price: the July put option with $14 strike price sold for $1.15, while the put option with $16 strike sold at $2.37.

Many options may go an entire day without trading. Because trading is infrequent (especially in Canada), it is not unusual to find option prices that appear out of line with other prices. You might find, for example, two calls with different exercise prices that seem to sell for equal prices. This discrepancy arises because the last trades for these options may have occurred at different times during the day. At any moment the call with the lower exercise price must be worth more than an otherwise-identical call with a higher exercise price.

Expirations of most exchange-traded options tend to be fairly short, ranging up to only several months. For larger firms, however, longer-term options are traded with maturities ranging up to several years. These options are called LEAPS (for *long-term equity anticipation securities*). Figure 18.1 shows one such set of RIM options, maturing in January 2015.

CC 1

CONCEPT CHECK

a. What will be the proceeds and net profits to an investor who purchases the September-maturity RIM calls with exercise price $14 if the stock price at maturity is $12? What if the stock price at maturity is $18?

b. Now answer part (a) for an investor who purchases a September-maturity RIM put option with exercise price $14.

American and European Options

An **American option** allows its holder to exercise the right to purchase (call) or sell (put) the underlying asset on *or before* the expiration date. A **European option** allows for exercise of the option only on the expiration date. American options, because they allow more leeway than do their European counterparts, generally will be more valuable. Virtually all traded options in Canada and the United States are American. Foreign currency options and stock index options traded on the Chicago Board Options Exchange in the United States, and stock index options traded on the Canadian Derivatives Exchange in Canada, are notable exceptions to this rule, however.

www.cboe.com

Adjustments in Option Contract Terms

Because options convey the right to buy or sell shares at a stated price, stock splits would radically alter their value if the terms of the option contract were not adjusted to account for the stock split. For example, reconsider the call options in Figure 18.1.

If RIM were to announce a two-for-one split, its share price would fall from $14.45 to about $7.23. A call option with exercise price $14 would be just about worthless, with virtually no possibility that the stock would sell at more than $14 before the option expired.

To account for a stock split, the exercise price is reduced by the factor of the split, and the number of options held is increased by that factor. For example, the original RIM call option with exercise price of $14 would be altered after a two-for-one split to 2 new options, with each option carrying an exercise price of $7. A similar adjustment is made for stock dividends of more than 10 percent; the number of shares covered by each option is increased in proportion to the stock dividend, and the exercise price is reduced by that proportion.

In contrast to stock dividends, cash dividends do not affect the terms of an option contract. Because payment of a cash dividend reduces the selling price of the stock without inducing offsetting adjustments in the option contract, the value of the option is affected by dividend policy. Other things being equal, call option values are lower for high-dividend-payout policies, because such policies slow the rate of increase of stock prices; conversely, put values are higher for high dividend payouts. (Of course, the option values do not rise or fall on the dividend payment or ex-dividend dates. Dividend payments are anticipated, so the effect of the payment already is built into the original option price.)

CC 2

CONCEPT CHECK

Suppose that RIM stock price at the exercise date is $18, and the exercise price of the call is $14. What is the profit on one option contract? After a two-for-one split, the stock price is $9, the exercise price is $7, and the option holder now can purchase 200 shares. Show that the split leaves option profits unaffected.

The Option Clearing Corporation

The Option Clearing Corporation (OCC) is jointly owned by the U.S. exchanges on which stock options are traded. It is the clearinghouse for options trading in the U.S. In Canada, it is called Canadian Derivatives Clearing Corporation (CDCC), and is a subsidiary of the Canadian Derivatives Exchange, the English name of the Montréal Exchange (still called *Bourse de Montréal* in French).

Buyers and sellers of options who agree on a price will consummate the sale of the option. At this point the CDCC steps in, by placing itself between the two traders and becoming the effective buyer of the option from the writer and the effective writer of the option to the buyer. All individuals, therefore, deal only with the CDCC, which effectively guarantees contract performance.

When an option holder exercises an option, the CDCC arranges for a member firm with clients who have written that option to make good on the option obligation. The member firm, in turn, selects from its clients who have written that option to fulfill the contract. The selected client must deliver 100 shares of stock at a price equal to the exercise price for each call option contract written, or purchase 100 shares at the exercise price for each put option contract written.

Because the CDCC guarantees contract performances, it requires option writers to post margin amounts to guarantee that they can fulfill their contract obligations. The margin required is determined, in part, by the amount by which the option is in the money, because that value is an indicator of the potential obligation of the option writer upon exercise of the option. When the required margin exceeds the posted margin, the writer will receive a margin call. The holder of the option need not post margin, because the holder will exercise the option only if it is profitable to do so. After purchasing the option, no further money is at risk.

Margin requirements are determined, in part, by the other securities held in the investor's portfolio. For example, a call option writer owning the stock against which the option is written can satisfy the margin requirement simply by allowing a broker to hold that stock in the brokerage account. The stock is then guaranteed to be available for delivery should the call option be exercised. If the underlying security is not owned, however, the margin requirement is determined by both the value of the underlying security and the amount by which the option is in or out of the money. Out-of-the-money options require less margin from the writer, because expected payouts are lower.

Other Listed Options

Options on assets other than stocks also are widely traded, especially in the United States. These include options on market and industry indices; foreign currency; and even the future prices of agricultural products, gold, silver, fixed-income securities, and stock indices. We will discuss these in turn.

Index Options   An index option is a call or put based on a stock market index such as the S&P/TSX 60 or the S&P 500 Index. Index options are traded on several broad-based indices, as well as on several industry-specific indices, exchange-traded funds and even commodity price indices. We discussed many of these indices in Chapter 2.

The construction of the indices can vary across contracts or exchanges. For example, the S&P/TSX 60 index is a value-weighted average of 60 major Canadian stocks in the S&P/TSX Composite stock group. The weights are proportional to the market value of outstanding equity for each stock. The Dow Jones Industrial Index by contrast, is a price-weighted average of 30 U.S. stocks.

In contrast to stock options, index options do not require that the call writer actually "deliver the index" upon exercise, or that the put writer "purchase the index." Instead, a cash settlement procedure is used. The profits that would accrue upon exercise of the option are calculated, and the option writer simply pays that amount to the option holder. The profits are equal to the difference between the exercise price of the option and the value of the index. For example, if the S&P/TSX 60 index is at $760 when a call option on the index with exercise price $740 is exercised, the holder of the call receives a cash payment of $20 multiplied by the contract multiplier of 100, or $2,000 per contract. Options on the major indices—that is, the S&P 100 (often called the OEX after its ticker symbol), the S&P 500 (the SPX), the Nasdaq 100 (the NDX), and the Dow Jones Industrial (the DJX)—are the most actively traded contracts on the CBOE. Together, these contracts dominate CBOE volume.

Futures Options   Futures options give their holders the right to buy or sell a specified futures contract, using as a future price the exercise price of the option. Although the delivery process is slightly complicated, the terms of futures options contracts are designed, in effect, to allow the option to be written on the futures price itself. The option holder receives upon exercise a profit equal to the difference between the current futures price on the specified asset and the exercise price of the option. Thus, if the futures price is, for example, $37, and the call has an exercise price of $35, the holder who exercises the call option on the futures gets a payoff of $2.

Foreign Currency Options   A currency option offers the right to buy or sell a quantity of foreign currency for a specified amount of domestic currency.

Currency option contracts on U.S. exchanges call for purchase or sale of the currency in exchange for a specified number of U.S. dollars. Contracts are quoted in cents or fractions of a cent per unit of foreign currency. The size of each option contract is specified for each listing. Foreign currency options and other derivatives trade over the counter in Canada, with the total volume

TABLE 18.1

Foreign Exchange and Interest Rate Derivatives Trading in Canada, 1995–2010

Over-the-Counter (OTC) Derivatives Market Turnover in Canada Summary of Surveys (average daily turnover in billions of U.S. dollars)							
	Foreign Exchange Derivatives			Single-Currency Interest Rate Derivatives			
	Currency Swaps	Options	Total	Forward Rate Agreements	Interest Rate Swaps	Options	Total
1995	0.1	0.8	0.9	3.0	1.0	0.3	4.3
1998	0.3	0.8	1.1	2.4	2.9	1.1	6.4
2001	0.3	2.3	2.6	2.9	6.1	0.9	9.9
2004	0.6	4.8	5.4	3.4	7.3	1.4	12.1
2007	1.6	2.6	4.2	6.2	10.8	3.6	20.6
2010	1.2	2,2	3,5	6.5	34.6	0.6	41.7

Source: *Survey of Foreign Exchange and Derivatives Market Activity in Canada During April 2010*, Bank of Canada press release, August 31, 2010, available at http://www.bankofcanada.ca/wp-content/uploads/2010/09/pr010910.pdf.

increasing over the past 15 years. Table 18.1 documents the evolution of currency derivatives trading in Canada from 1995 to 2010.

There is an important difference between currency options and currency *futures* options. The former provide payoffs that depend on the difference between the exercise price and the exchange rate at maturity. The latter are foreign exchange futures options that provide payoffs that depend on the difference between the exercise price and the exchange rate *futures price* at maturity. Because exchange rates and exchange rate futures prices generally are not equal, the options and futures-options contracts will have different values, even with identical expiration dates and exercise prices. Trading volume in currency futures options dominates by far trading in currency options.

Interest Rate Options   Options on Canada bonds are traded on the Canadian Derivatives Exchange. There also are options on Canada Bond futures and bankers' acceptances futures.

Options are traded on U.S. Treasury notes and bonds, Treasury bills, and government bonds of other major economies such as the United Kingdom or Japan. Options on several interest rate futures, such as Treasury bonds, Treasury notes, municipal bonds, and LIBOR also trade on various U.S. exchanges.

18.2 ▸ VALUES OF OPTIONS AT EXPIRATION

Call Options

Recall that a call option gives the right to purchase a security at the exercise price. Suppose you hold a call option on FinCorp stock with an exercise price of $100 and FinCorp currently sells at $110. You can exercise your option to purchase the stock at $100 and simultaneously sell the shares at the market price of $110, clearing $10 per share. On the other hand, if the shares sell below $100, you can sit on the option and do nothing, realizing no further gain or loss. The value of the call option at expiration equals

$$\text{Payoff to call holder} = \begin{cases} S_T - X & \text{if } S_T > X, \\ 0 & \text{if } S_T \leq X \end{cases}$$

where S_T is the value of the stock at expiration and X is the exercise price. This formula emphasizes the option property, because the payoff cannot be negative. That is, the option is exercised

Figure 18.2

Payoff and profit to call option at expiration.

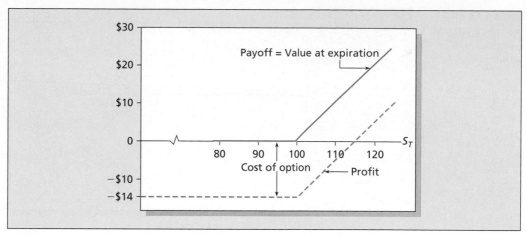

only if S_T exceeds X. If S_T is less than X, exercise does not occur and the option expires with zero value. The loss to the option holder in this case equals the price originally paid for the right to buy at the exercise price. More generally, the *profit* to the option holder is the option payoff at expiration minus the original purchase price.

The value at expiration of the call on FinCorp with exercise price $100 is given by the following schedule:

Stock price:	$90	$100	$110	$120	$130
Option value:	$ 0	$ 0	$ 10	$ 20	$ 30

For stock prices at or below $100, the option is worthless. Above $100, the option is worth the excess of the stock price over $100. The option's value increases by $1 for each dollar increase in the stock price. This relationship can be depicted graphically, as in the solid (top) line of Figure 18.2.

The solid line depicts the value of the call at maturity. The net *profit* to the holder of the call equals the gross payoff less the initial investment in the call. Suppose the call cost $14. Then the profit to the call holder would be as given in the broken (bottom) line of the figure. At option expiration, the investor has suffered a loss of $14 if the stock price is less than or equal to $100. Profits do not become positive unless the stock price at expiration exceeds $114. The breakeven point is $114, because at that point the payoff to the call, $S_T - X = \$114 - \$14 = \$14$, equals the cost paid to acquire the call. Hence, the call holder profits only if the stock price is higher.

Conversely, the writer of the call incurs losses if the stock price is high. In that scenario, the writer will receive a call and will be obligated to deliver a stock worth S_T for only X dollars:

$$\text{Payoff to call writer} = \begin{array}{ll} -(S_T - X) & \text{if } S_T \geq X \\ 0 & \text{if } S_T < X \end{array}$$

The call writer, who is exposed to losses if the stock increases in price, is willing to bear this risk in return for the option premium. Figure 18.3 depicts the payoff and profit diagrams for the call writer. Notice that these are just the mirror images of the corresponding diagrams for call holders. The breakeven point for the option writer also is $114. The (negative) payoff at that point just offsets the premium originally received when the option was written.

Figure 18.3
Payoff and profit
to call writers at
expiration.

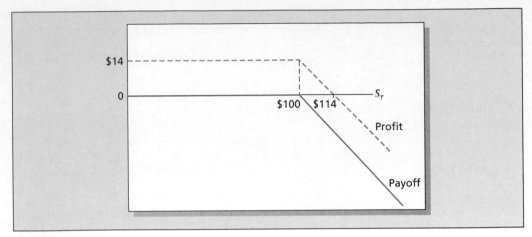

Put Options

A put option is the right to sell an asset at the exercise price. In this case, the holder will not exercise the option unless the asset sells for *less* than the exercise price. For example, if FinCorp shares were to fall to $90, a put option with exercise price $100 could be exercised to give a $10 profit to its holder. The holder would purchase a share for $90 and simultaneously deliver it to the put option writer for the exercise price of $100.

The value of a put option at expiration is

$$
\text{Payoff to put holder} = \begin{array}{ll} X - S_T & \text{if } S_T \leq X \\ 0 & \text{if } X_T > X \end{array}
$$

The solid (top) line in Figure 18.4 illustrates the payoff at maturity to the holder of a put option on FinCorp stock with an exercise price of $100. If the stock price at option maturity is above $100, the put has no value, because the right to sell the shares at $100 would not be exercised. Below a price of $100, the put value at expiration increases by $1 for each dollar that the stock price falls. The dashed (bottom) line in the figure is a graph of the put option owner's profit at expiration, net of the initial cost of the put.

Writing puts *naked* (i.e., writing a put without an offsetting position in the stock for hedging purposes) exposes the writer to losses if the market falls. Writing naked deep out-of-the-money

Figure 18.4
Payoff and profit
to put option at
expiration.

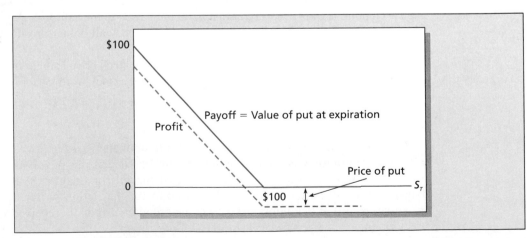

puts was once considered an attractive way to generate income, since it was believed that, as long as the market did not fall sharply before the option expiration, the option premium could be collected without the put holder ever exercising the option against the writer. Because only sharp drops in the market could result in losses to the writer of the put, the strategy was not viewed as overly risky. However, in the wake of the market crash of October 1987, such put writers suffered huge losses. Participants now perceive much greater risk to this strategy.

CC 3

CONCEPT CHECK

Consider these four option strategies: (i) buy a call; (ii) write a call; (iii) buy a put; (iv) write a put.
a. For each strategy, plot both the payoff and profit diagrams as a function of the final stock price.
b. Why might one characterize both buying calls and writing puts as "bullish" strategies? What is the difference between them?
c. Why might one characterize both buying puts and writing calls as "bearish" strategies? What is the difference between them?

Options Versus Stock Investments

Purchasing call options is a bullish strategy; that is, it provides profits when stock prices increase. Purchasing puts, in contrast, is a bearish strategy. Symmetrically, writing calls is bearish and writing puts is bullish. Because option values depend on the price of the underlying stock, purchase of options may be viewed as a substitute for direct purchase or sale of a stock. Why might an option strategy be preferable to direct stock transactions?

For example, why would you purchase a call option rather than buy shares of stock directly? Maybe you have some information that leads you to believe that the stock will increase in value from its current level, which in our examples we will take to be $100. You know your analysis could be incorrect, and that the shares also could fall in price. Suppose that a six-month maturity call option with exercise price $100 currently sells for $10, and that the interest rate for the period is 3 percent. Consider these three strategies for investing a sum of money, say $10,000. For simplicity, suppose that the firm will not pay any dividends until after the six-month period.

- *Strategy A*. Invest entirely in stock. Purchase 100 shares, each selling for $100.
- *Strategy B*. Invest entirely in at-the-money call options. Buy 1000 calls, each costing $10. (This would require 10 contracts, each for 100 shares.)
- *Strategy C*. Purchase 100 call options for $1,000. Invest the remaining $9,000 in six-month T-bills, to earn 3 percent interest. The bills will grow in value to 9,000 × 1.03 = $9,270.

Let us trace the possible values of these three portfolios when the options expire in six months as a function of the stock price at that time.

Stock Price	$95	$100	$105	$110	$115
Portfolio *A*: All stock	$9,500	$10,000	$10,500	$11,000	$11,500
Portfolio *B*: All calls	0	0	5,000	10,000	15,000
Portfolio *C*: Calls plus bills	9,270	9,270	9,770	10,270	11,270

Portfolio *A* will be worth 100 times the share price. Portfolio *B* is worthless unless shares sell for more than the exercise price of the call. Once that point is reached, the portfolio is worth 1,000 times the excess of the stock price over the exercise price. Finally, portfolio *C* is worth $9,270 from the investment in T-bills plus any profits from the 100 call options. Remember that each of these portfolios involves the same $10,000 initial investment. The rates of return on these three portfolios are as follows:

Share Price	$95	$100	$105	$110	$115
A (all stock)	−5.00%	0%	5.00%	10.00%	15.00%
B (all options)	−100.0%	−100.0%	−50%	0.0%	50.0%
C (options plus bills)	−7.3%	−7.3%	−2.3%	2.7%	7.7%

These rates of return are illustrated in Figure 18.5.

Comparing the returns to portfolios *B* and *C* to those of the simple investment in stock represented by portfolio *A*, we see that options offer two interesting features. First, an option offers leverage. Compare the returns of portfolio *B* and *A*. When the stock falls in price to $90, the value of portfolio *B* falls precipitously to zero, a rate of return of −100 percent. Conversely, if the stock price increases modestly, the all-option portfolio jumps in value disproportionately. For example, a 4.55 percent increase in the stock price from $110 to $115 would increase the rate of return on the call from 0 to 50 percent. In this sense, calls are a leveraged investment on the stock. Their values respond more than proportionately to changes in the stock value.

Figure 18.5 vividly illustrates this point. The slope of the all-option portfolio is far steeper than the all-stock portfolio, reflecting its greater proportional sensitivity to the value of the underlying security. The leverage factor is the reason that investors (illegally) exploiting inside information commonly choose options as their investment vehicle.

The potential insurance value of options is the second interesting feature, as portfolio *C* shows. The T-bill plus option portfolio cannot be worth less than $9,270 after six months, since the option can always be left to expire worthless. The worst possible rate of return on

Figure 18.5

Rates of return to three strategies.

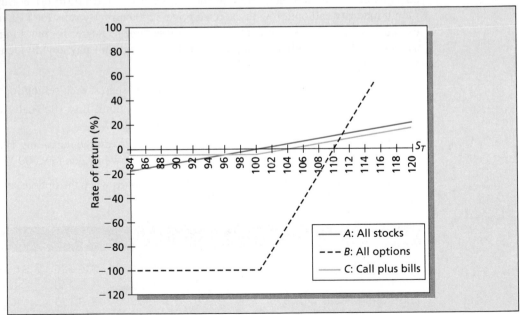

portfolio C is -7.3 percent, compared to a (theoretically) worst possible rate of return on the stock of -100 percent if the company were to go bankrupt. Of course, this insurance comes at a price: when the stock does well, portfolio C does not perform quite as well as portfolio A, the all-stock portfolio.

This simple example makes an important point. Although options can be used by speculators as effectively leveraged stock positions, as in portfolio B, they also can be used by investors who desire to tailor their risk exposures in creative ways, as in portfolio C. For example, the call-plus-bills strategy of portfolio C provides a rate-of-return profile quite unlike that of the stock alone. The absolute limitation on downside risk is a novel and attractive feature of this strategy. We next discuss several option strategies that provide other novel risk profiles that might be attractive to hedgers and other investors.

18.3   OPTION STRATEGIES

An unlimited variety of payoff patterns can be achieved by combining puts and calls with various exercise prices. The following subsections explain the motivation and structure of some of the more popular methods.

Protective Put

Imagine that you would like to invest in a stock, but you are unwilling to bear losses beyond some given level. Investing in the stock alone is quite risky, because in principle you might lose all the money you invest. Instead you might consider investing in stock together with a put option on the stock. Table 18.2 illustrates the total value of your portfolio at option expiration.

Whatever happens to the stock price, you are guaranteed a payoff equal to the put option's exercise price because the put gives you the right to sell shares for the exercise price even if the stock price is below that value.

EXAMPLE 18.3   Protective Put

Suppose the strike price is $X = \$100$ and the stock is selling at $97 at option expiration. Then the value of your total portfolio is $100. The stock is worth $97 and the value of the expiring put option is

$$X - S_T = \$100 - \$97 = \$3$$

Another way to look at it is that you are holding the stock and a put contract giving you the right to sell the stock for $100. The right to sell locks in a minimum portfolio value of $100. On the other hand, if the stock price is above $100, say $104, then the right to sell a share at $100 is worthless. You allow the put to expire unexercised, ending up with a share of stock worth $S_T = \$104$.

TABLE 18.2

Payoff to Protective Put Strategy

	$S_T \leq X$	$S_T > X$
Stock	S_T	S_T
Put	$X - S_T$	0
Total	X	S_T

Figure 18.6

Value of a
protective put
position at
expiration.

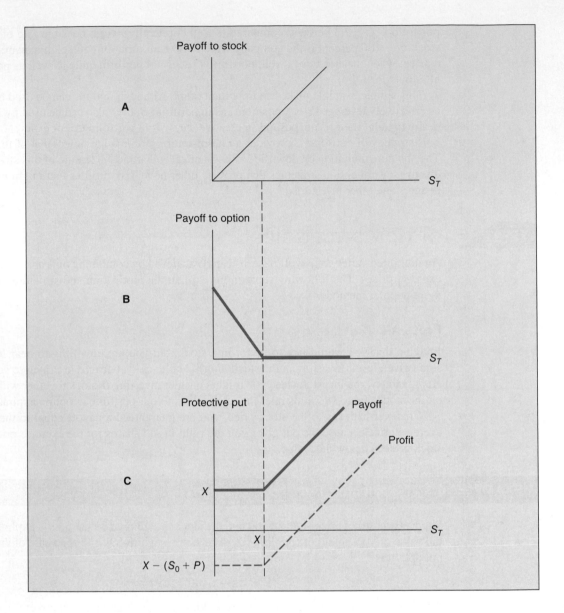

Figure 18.6 illustrates the payoff and profit to this **protective put** strategy. The solid line in the figure's panel C is the total payoff; the dashed line is displaced downward by the cost of establishing the position, $S_0 + P$. Notice that potential losses are indeed limited.

It is instructive to compare the profit to the protective put strategy with that of the stock investment. For simplicity, consider an at-the-money protective put, so that $X = S_0$. Figure 18.7 compares the profits for the two strategies. The profit on the stock is zero if the stock price remains unchanged, and $S_T = S_0$. It rises or falls by \$1 for every \$1 swing in the ultimate stock price. The profit on the stock plus put portfolio is negative and equal to the cost of the put if S_T is below S_0. The profit on the overall protective put position increases one for one with increases in the stock price, once S_T exceeds S_0.

Figure 18.7 makes it clear that the protective put offers some insurance against stock price declines in that it limits losses. Indeed, protective put strategies provide a form of *portfolio*

Figure 18.7

Protective put versus stock investment.

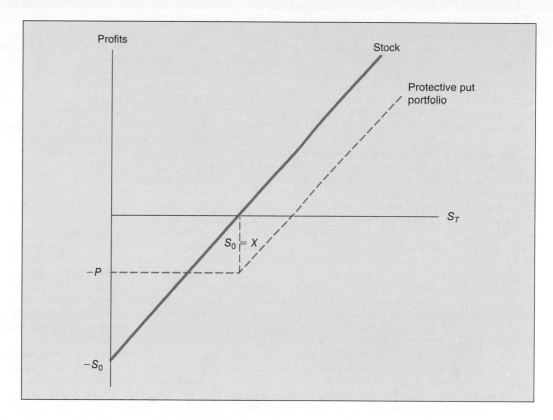

insurance. The cost of the protection is that, in the case of stock price increases, your profit is reduced by the cost of the put, which turned out to be unneeded.

This example also shows that despite the common perception that derivatives mean risk, derivative securities can be used effectively for *risk management.* In fact, such risk management is becoming accepted as part of the fiduciary responsibility of financial managers. Indeed, in one oft-cited U.S. court case, *Brane v. Roth*, a company's board of directors was successfully sued for failing to use derivatives to hedge the price risk of grain held in storage. Such hedging might have been accomplished using protective puts. Some observers believe that this case will soon lead to a broad legal obligation for firms to use derivatives and other techniques to manage risk.

The claim that derivatives are best viewed as risk management tools may seem surprising in light of the credit crisis of the last few years. The crisis was immediately precipitated when the highly risky positions that many financial institutions had established in credit derivatives blew up 2007–2008, resulting in large losses and government bailouts. Still, the same characteristics that make derivatives potent tools to increase risk also make them highly effective in managing risk, at least when used properly. Derivatives have aptly been compared to power tools: very useful in skilled hands, but also very dangerous when not handled with care. The nearby box makes the case for derivatives as central to risk management.

Covered Call

A **covered call** position is the purchase of a share of stock with a simultaneous sale of a call option on that stock. The position is "covered" because the obligation to deliver the stock can be satisfied using the stock held in the portfolio. Writing an option without an offsetting stock

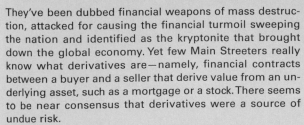

THE CASE FOR DERIVATIVES

They've been dubbed financial weapons of mass destruction, attacked for causing the financial turmoil sweeping the nation and identified as the kryptonite that brought down the global economy. Yet few Main Streeters really know what derivatives are—namely, financial contracts between a buyer and a seller that derive value from an underlying asset, such as a mortgage or a stock. There seems to be near consensus that derivatives were a source of undue risk.

And then there's Robert Shiller. The Yale economist believes just the opposite is true. A champion of financial innovation and an expert in management of risk, Shiller contends that derivatives, far from being a problem, are actually the solution. Derivatives, Shiller says, are merely a risk-management tool the same way insurance is. "You pay a premium and if an event happens, you get a payment." That tool can be used well or, as happened recently, used badly. Shiller warns that banishing the tool gets us nowhere.

For all the trillions in derivative trading, there were very few traders. Almost all the subprime mortgages that were bundled and turned into derivatives were sold by a handful of Wall Street institutions, working with a small number of large institutional buyers. It was a huge but illiquid and opaque market.

Meanwhile, the system was built on the myriad decisions of individual homeowners and lenders around the world. None of them, however, could hedge their bets the way large institutions can. Those buying a condo in Miami had no way to protect themselves if the market went down.

Derivatives, according to Shiller, could be used by homeowners—and, by extension, lenders—to insure themselves against falling prices. In Shiller's scenario, you would be able to go to your broker and buy a new type of financial instrument, perhaps a derivative that is inversely related to a regional home-price index. If the value of houses in your area declined, the financial instrument would increase in value, offsetting the loss. Lenders could do the same thing, which would help them hedge against foreclosures. The idea is to make the housing market more liquid. More buyers and sellers mean that markets stay liquid and functional even under pressure.

Some critics dismiss Shiller's basic premise that more derivatives would make the housing market more liquid and more stable. They point out that futures contracts haven't made equity markets or commodity markets immune from massive moves up and down. They add that a ballooning world of home-based derivatives wouldn't lead to homeowners' insurance: it would lead to a new playground for speculators.

In essence, Shiller is laying the intellectual groundwork for the next financial revolution. We are now suffering through the first major crisis of the Information Age economy. Shiller's answers may be counterintuitive, but no more so than those of doctors and scientists who centuries ago recognized that the cure for infectious diseases was not flight or quarantine, but purposely infecting more people through vaccinations. "We've had a major glitch in derivatives and securitization," says Shiller. "The *Titanic* sank almost a century ago, but we didn't stop sailing across the Atlantic."

Of course, people did think twice about getting on a ship, at least for a while. But if we listen only to our fears, we lose the very dynamism that has propelled us this far. That is the nub of Shiller's call for more derivatives and more innovation. Shiller's appeal is a tough sell at a time when derivatives have produced so much havoc. But he reminds us that the tools that got us here are not to blame; they can be used badly and they can be used well. And trying to stem the ineffable tide of human creativity is a fool's errand.

Source: Zachary Karabell, "The Case for Derivatives," *Newsweek*, February 2, 2009.

TABLE 18.3

Payoff to a Covered Call

	$S_T \leq X$	$S_T > X$
Payoff of stock	S_T	S_T
−Payoff of call	−0	$-(S_T - X)$
Total	S_T	X

position is called, by contrast, *naked option writing*. The payoff to a covered call, presented in Table 18.3, equals the stock value minus the payoff of the call. The call payoff is subtracted because the covered call position involves issuing a call to another investor who can choose to exercise it to profit at your expense.

The solid line in Figure 18.8, panel C illustrates the payoff pattern. We see that the total position is worth S_T when the stock price at time T is below X, and rises to a maximum of X

Figure 18.8
Value of a
covered call
position at
expiration.

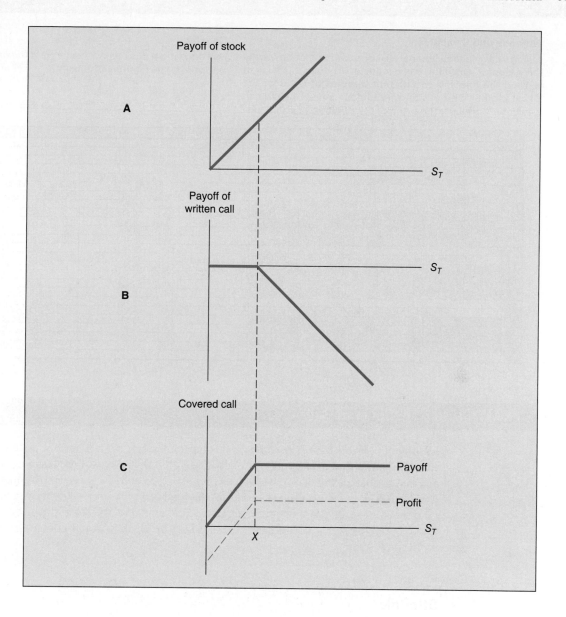

when S_T exceeds X. In essence, the sale of the call option means that the call writer has sold the claim to any stock value above X in return for the initial premium (the call price). Therefore, at expiration the position is worth, at most X. The dashed line of panel C is the net profit to the covered call.

Writing covered call options has been a popular investment strategy among institutional investors. Consider the managers of a fund invested largely in stocks. They might find it appealing to write calls on some or all of the stock in order to boost income by the premiums collected. Although they thereby forfeit potential capital gains should the stock price rise above the exercise price, if they view X as the price at which they plan to sell the stock anyway, then the call may be viewed as enforcing a kind of "sell discipline." The written call guarantees that the stock sale will take place as planned.

Spreads and Straddles

Using spreadsheets to analyze combinations of options is very helpful. Once the basic models are built, it is easy to extend the analysis to different bundles of options. The Excel model "Spreads and Straddles" shown below can be used to evaluate the profitability of different strategies.

Question

Use the data in this spreadsheet to plot the profit on a bullish spread (see Figure 18.10) with $X_1 = 120$ and $X_2 = 130$.

	A	B	C	D	E	F	G	H	I	J	K	L
1					Spreads and Straddles							
2												
3	Stock Prices											
4	Beginning Market Price	116.5										
5	Ending Market Price	130						X 110 Straddle			X 120 Straddle	
6							Ending	Profit		Ending	Profit	
7	Buying Options:						Stock Price	−15.40		Stock Price	−24.00	
8	Call Options Strike	Price	Payoff	Profit	Return %		50	24.60		50	36.00	
9	110	22.80	20.00	−2.80	−12.28%		60	14.60		60	26.00	
10	120	16.80	10.00	−6.80	−40.48%		70	4.60		70	16.00	
11	130	13.60	0.00	−13.60	−100.00%		80	−5.40		80	6.00	
12	140	10.30	0.00	−10.30	−100.00%		90	−15.40		90	−4.00	
13							100	−25.40		100	−14.00	
14	Put Options Strike	Price	Payoff	Profit	Return %		110	−35.40		110	−24.00	
15	110	12.60	0.00	−12.60	−100.00%		120	−25.40		120	−34.00	
16	120	17.20	0.00	−17.20	−100.00%		130	−15.40		130	−24.00	
17	130	23.60	0.00	−23.60	−100.00%		140	−5.40		140	−14.00	
18	140	30.50	10.00	−20.50	−67.21%		150	4.60		150	−4.00	
19							160	14.60		160	6.00	
20	Straddle	Price	Payoff	Profit	Return %		170	24.60		170	16.00	
21	110	35.40	20.00	−15.40	−43.50%		180	34.60		180	26.00	
22	120	34.00	10.00	−24.00	−70.59%		190	44.60		190	36.00	
23	130	37.20	0.00	−37.20	−100.00%		200	54.60		200	46.00	
24	140	40.80	10.00	−30.80	−75.49%		210	64.60		210	56.00	
25												

EXAMPLE 18.4 Covered Call

Assume a pension fund is holding 1,000 shares of stock, with a current price of $100 per share. Suppose that management intends to sell all 1,000 shares if the share price hits $110 and that a call expiring in 60 days with an exercise price of $110 is currently selling for $5. By writing 10 call contracts (100 shares each) the fund can pick up $5,000 in extra income. The fund would lose its share of profits from any movement of the stock price above $110 per share, but given that it would have sold its shares at $110, it would not have realized those profits anyway.

Straddle

A long **straddle** is established by buying both a call and a put on a stock, each with the same exercise price, X, and the same expiration date, T. Straddles are useful strategies for investors who believe that a stock will move a lot in price, but who are uncertain about the direction of the move. For example, suppose you believe that an important court case that will make or break a company is about to be settled, and the market is not yet aware of the situation. The stock will either double in value if the case is settled favourably, or it will drop by half if the settlement goes against the company. The straddle position will do well regardless of the outcome, because its value is highest when the stock price makes extreme upward or downward moves from X.

The worst-case scenario for a straddle is no movement in the stock price. If S_T equals X, both the call and the put expire worthless, and the investor's outlay for the purchase of the two positions is lost. Straddle positions, in other words, are bets on volatility. An investor who establishes a straddle must view the stock as more volatile than the market does. Conversely, investors who

TABLE 18.4

Payoff to a
Straddle

	$S_T \leq X$	$S_T > X$
Payoff of call	0	$S_T - X$
+Payoff of put	$+(X - S_T)$	$+0$
Total	$X - S_T$	$S_T - X$

write straddles—selling both a call and a put—must believe the stock is less volatile. They accept the option premiums now, hoping the stock price will not change much before option expiration.

The payoff to a straddle is presented in Table 18.4. The solid line in panel C of Figure 18.9 illustrates this payoff. Notice that the portfolio payoff is always positive, except at the one point

Figure 18.9

Payoff and profit
to a straddle at
expiration.

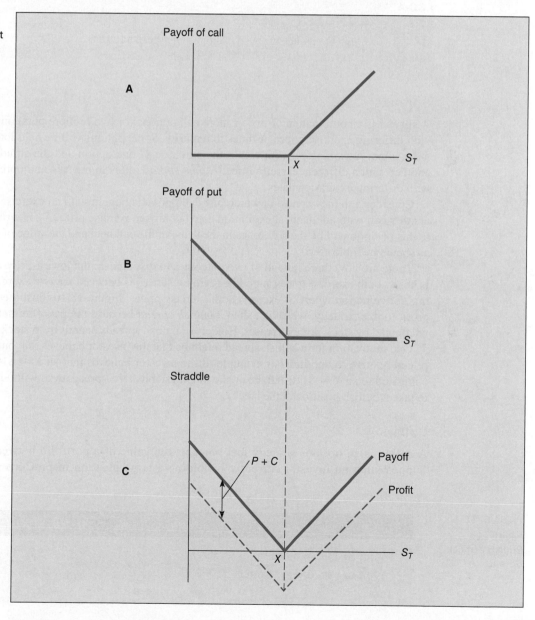

where the portfolio has zero value, $S_T = X$. You might wonder why all investors do not pursue such a no-lose strategy. Remember, however, that the straddle requires that both the put and call be purchased. The value of the portfolio at expiration, although never negative, still must exceed the initial cash outlay for the investor to clear a profit.

The broken line in Figure 18.9, panel C is the profit to the straddle. The profit line lies below the payoff line by the cost of purchasing the straddle, $P + C$. It is clear from the diagram that the straddle position generates a loss unless the stock price deviates substantially from X. The stock price must depart from X by the total amount expended to purchase the call and the put for the purchaser of the straddle to clear a profit.

Strips and *straps* are variations of straddles. A strip is two puts and one call on a security with the same exercise price and maturity date. A strap is two calls and one put.

CC 4

CONCEPT CHECK

Graph the profit and payoff diagrams for strips and straps.

Spreads

A **spread** is a combination of two or more call options (or two or more puts) on the same stock with differing exercise prices or times to maturity. Some options will be held long, while others are written. A *money spread* involves the purchase of one option and the simultaneous sale of another with a different exercise price. A *time spread* refers to the sale and purchase of options with differing expiration dates.

Consider a money spread in which one call option is bought with an exercise price X_1, while another call with an identical expiration date but higher exercise price, X_2, is written. The payoff to this position will be the difference in the value of the call held and the value of the call written, as shown in Table 18.5.

There are now three instead of two outcomes to distinguish: the lowest-price region where S_T is below both exercise prices, a middle region where S_T is between the two exercise prices, and a high-price region where S_T exceeds both exercise prices. Figure 18.10 illustrates the payoff and profit to this strategy, which is called a *bullish spread* because the payoff either increases or is unaffected by stock price increases. Holders of bullish spreads benefit from stock price increases.

One motivation for a bullish spread might be that the investor believes that one option is overpriced relative to another. For example, if the investor believes that an $X = \$100$ call is cheap compared to an $X = \$110$ call, he or she might establish the spread, even without a strong desire to take a bullish position in the stock.

Collars

A **collar** is an options strategy that brackets the value of a portfolio between two bounds. Suppose that an investor currently is holding a large position in FinCorp stock, which is

TABLE 18.5

Payoff to a Bullish Vertical Spread

	$S_T \leq X_1$	$X_1 < S_T \leq X_2$	$S_T > X_2$
Payoff of call, exercise price = X_1	0	$S_T - X_1$	$S_T - X_1$
$-$Payoff of call, exercise price = X_2	-0	-0	$-(S_T - X_2)$
Total	0	$S_T - X_1$	$X_2 - X_1$

Figure 18.10

Value of a bullish
spread position
at expiration.

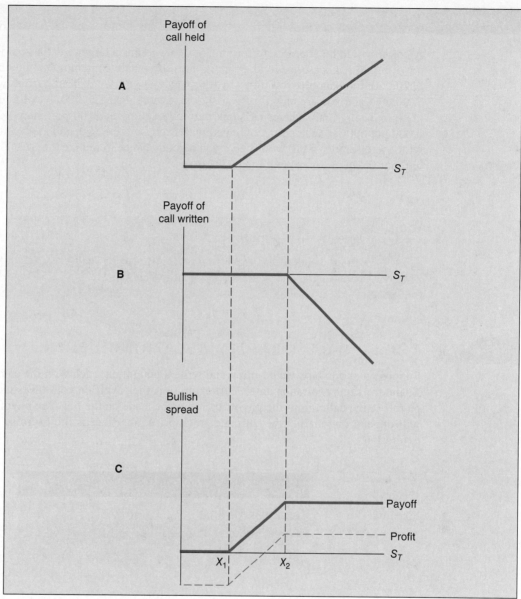

currently selling at $100 per share. A lower bound of $90 can be placed on the value of the portfolio by buying a protective put with exercise price $90. This protection, however, requires that the investor pay the put premium. To raise the money to pay for the put, the investor might write a call option, say with exercise price $110. The call might sell for roughly the same price as the put, meaning that the net outlay for the two options positions is approximately zero. Writing the call limits the portfolio's upside potential. Even if the stock price moves above $110, the investor will do no better than $110, because at a higher price the stock will be called away. Thus the investor obtains the downside protection represented by the exercise price of the put by selling her claim to any upside potential beyond the exercise price of the call.

EXAMPLE 18.5   Collars

A collar would be appropriate for an investor who has a target wealth goal in mind but is unwilling to risk losses beyond a certain level. If you are contemplating buying a house for $220,000, for example, you might set this figure as your goal. Your current wealth may be $200,000, and you are unwilling to risk losing more than $20,000. A collar established by (1) purchasing 2,000 shares of stock currently selling at $100 per share, (2) purchasing 2,000 put options (20 option contracts) with exercise price $90, and (3) writing 2,000 calls with exercise price $110 would give you a good chance to realize the $20,000 capital gain without risking a loss of more than $20,000.

CC 5

CONCEPT CHECK

Graph the payoff diagram for the collar just described with exercise price of the put equal to $90, and exercise price of the call equal to $110.

18.4   **THE PUT–CALL PARITY RELATIONSHIP**

Suppose that you buy a call option and write a put option, each with the same exercise price, X, and the same expiration date, T. At expiration, the payoff on your investment will equal the payoff to the call, minus the payoff that must be made on the put. The payoff for each option will depend on whether the ultimate stock price, S_T, exceeds the exercise price at contract expiration.

	$S_T \leq X$	$S_T > X$
Payoff of call held	0	$S_T - X$
Payoff of put written	$-(X - S_T)$	0
Total	$S_T - X$	$S_T - X$

Figure 18.11 illustrates this payoff pattern. Compare the payoff to that of a portfolio made up of the stock plus a borrowing position, where the money to be paid back will grow, with interest, to X dollars at the maturity of the loan. Such a position, in fact, is a *leveraged* equity position in which $X/(1 + r_f)^T$ dollars is borrowed today (so that X will be repaid at maturity) and S_0 dollars are invested in the stock. The total payoff of the leveraged equity position is $S_T - X$, the same as that of the option strategy. Thus the long call–short put position replicates the leveraged equity position. Again, we see that option trading allows us to construct artificial leverage.

Because the option portfolio has a payoff identical to that of the leveraged equity position, the costs of establishing the two positions must be equal. The net cost of establishing the option position is $C - P$; the call is purchased for C, while the written put generates premium income of P. Likewise, the leveraged equity position requires a net cash outlay of $S_0 - X/(1 + r_f)^T$, the cost of

Figure 18.11
The payoff pattern of a long call–short put position.

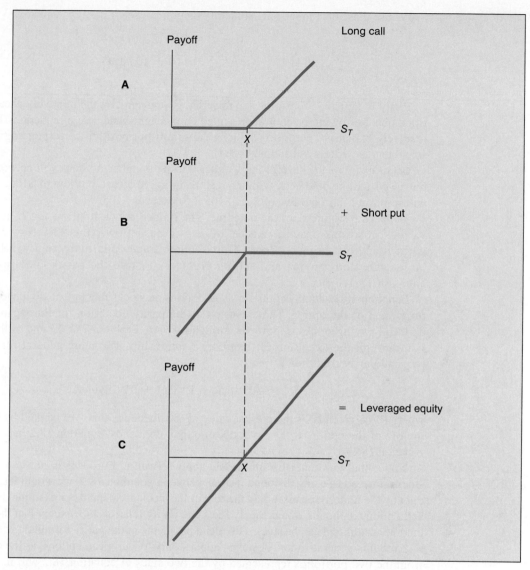

the stock less the proceeds from borrowing. Equating these costs, we conclude that

$$C - P = S_0 - X/(1 + r_f)^T \tag{18.1}$$

Equation 18.1 is called the **put–call parity theorem**, because it represents the proper relationship between put and call prices. If the parity relationship is ever violated, an arbitrage opportunity arises. For example, suppose that you confront these data for a certain stock:

Stock price	$110
Call price (1-year maturity, $X = \$105$)	$ 17
Put price (1-year maturity, $X = \$105$)	$ 5
Risk-free interest rate	5% per year

We use these data in the put–call parity theorem to see if parity is violated:

$$C - P \overset{?}{=} S_0 - X/(1 + r_f)^T$$
$$17 - 5 \overset{?}{=} 110 - 105/1.05$$
$$12 \overset{?}{=} 10$$

Parity is violated. To exploit the mispricing, you can buy the relatively cheap portfolio (the stock plus borrowing position represented on the right-hand side of equation 18.1) and sell the relatively expensive portfolio (the long call–short put position corresponding to the left-hand side—that is, write a call and buy a put).

Let us examine the payoff to this strategy. In six months, the stock will be worth S_T. The $100 borrowed will be paid back with interest, resulting in a cash outflow of $105. The written call will result in a cash outflow of $S_T - \$105$ if S_T exceeds $105.

Table 18.6 summarizes the outcome. The immediate cash inflow is $2. In six months, the various positions provide exactly offsetting cash flows: the $2 inflow is thus realized without any offsetting outflows. This is an arbitrage opportunity that will be pursued on a large scale until buying and selling pressures restore the parity condition expressed in equation 18.1.

Equation 18.1 actually applies only to options on stocks that pay no dividends before the maturity date of the option. The extension of the parity condition for European call options on dividend-paying stocks is, however, straightforward. Problem 7 at the end of this chapter leads you through the extension of the parity relationship. The more general formulation of the put–call parity condition is

$$P = C - S_0 + PV(X) + PV(\text{dividends}) \tag{18.2}$$

where PV(dividends) is the present value of the dividends that will be paid by the stock during the life of the option. If the stock does not pay dividends, equation 18.2 becomes identical to equation 18.1.

Notice that this generalization would apply as well to European options on assets other than stocks. Instead of using dividend income per se in equation 18.2, we would let any income paid only by the underlying asset play the role of the stock dividends. For example, European put and call options on bonds would satisfy the same parity relationship, except that the bond's coupon income would replace the stock's dividend payments in the parity formula.

Even this generalization, however, applies only to European options, as the cash flow stream from the two portfolios represented by the two sides of equation 18.2 will match only if each position is held until maturity. If a call and a put may be optimally exercised at different times before their common expiration date, then the equality of payoffs cannot be assured, or even expected, and the portfolio will have different values.

TABLE 18.6

Arbitrage Strategy

Position	Immediate Cash Flow	Cash Flow in 6 Months	
		$S_T \le 105$	$S_T > 105$
Buy stock	−110	S_T	S_T
Borrow $X/(1 + r_f)^T = \$100$	+100	−105	−105
Sell call	+ 17	0	$-(S_T - 105)$
Buy put	−5	$105 - S_T$	0
Total	2	0	0

EXAMPLE 18.6 Put–Call Parity

Let's see how well parity works with real data from Figure 18.1, using RIM options. The July call on RIM with exercise price $14 and time to expiration of 49 days till July 19, has an ask price of $1.59, while the put bid price was $1.11, RIM was selling for $14.50, and the annualized interest rate on this date for 49-day T-bills was 1.0 percent. According to parity, we should find that

$$\$1.59 - \$1.11 = \$14.50 - \frac{14}{(1.01)^{49/365}}$$

$$\$.48 \overset{?}{=} \$.52$$

In this case, parity is violated by 4 cents per share. Does this amount outweigh the brokerage fees involved in attempting to exploit the mispricing? Almost certainly not. Moreover, given the infrequent trading of options that we have noted, this discrepancy from parity could be due to "stale" prices, quotes at which you cannot actually trade.

18.5 OPTION-LIKE SECURITIES

Even if you never trade an option directly, you still need to appreciate the properties of options in formulating any investment plan. Why? Many other financial instruments and agreements have features that convey implicit or explicit options to one or more parties. To value and use these securities correctly, you must understand their option attributes.

Callable Bonds

You know from Chapter 12 that many corporate bonds are issued with call provisions entitling the issuer to buy bonds back from bondholders at some time in the future at a specified call price. This provision conveys a call option to the issuer, where the exercise price is equal to the price at which the bond can be repurchased. A callable bond arrangement is essentially a sale of a *straight bond* (a bond with no option features such as callability or convertibility) to the investor and the concurrent issuance of a call option by the investor to the bond-issuing firm.

There must be some compensation for offering this implicit call option to the firm. If the callable bond were issued with the same coupon rate as a straight bond, we would expect it to sell at a discount to the straight bond equal to the value of the call. To sell callable bonds at par, firms must issue them with coupon rates higher than the coupons on straight debt. The higher coupons are the investor's compensation for the call option retained by the issuer. Coupon rates usually are selected so that the newly issued bond will sell at par value.

Figure 18.12 illustrates the option-like property of a callable bond. The horizontal axis is the value of a straight bond with terms otherwise identical to the callable bond. The 45-degree dashed line represents the value of straight debt. The solid line is the value of the callable bond, and the dotted line is the value of the call option retained by the firm. A callable bond's potential for capital gains is limited by the firm's option to repurchase at the call price.

CC 6

CONCEPT CHECK

How is a callable bond similar to a covered call strategy on a straight bond?

Figure 18.12

Values of callable bonds compared with straight bonds.

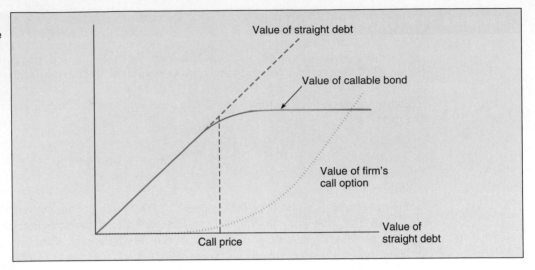

The option inherent in callable bonds is actually more complex than an ordinary call option, because usually it may be exercised only after some initial period of call protection. Also, the price at which the bond is callable may change over time. Unlike exchange-listed options, these features are defined in the initial bond offering and will depend on the needs of the issuing firm and its perception of the market's tastes.

CC 7

CONCEPT CHECK

Suppose that the period of call protection is extended. How will the coupon rate the company needs to offer on its bonds change to enable the issuer to sell the bonds at par value?

Convertible Securities

Convertible bonds and convertible preferred stock convey options to the holder of the security rather than to the issuing firm. The convertible security typically gives its holder the right to exchange each bond or share of preferred stock for a fixed number of shares of common stock, regardless of the market prices of the securities at the time.

CC 8

CONCEPT CHECK

Should a convertible bond issued at par value have a higher or lower coupon rate than a nonconvertible bond issued at par?

For example, a bond with a conversion ratio of 10 allows its holder to convert one bond of par value $1,000 into 10 shares of common stock. Alternatively, the conversion price in this case is $100: To receive 10 shares of stock, the investor sacrifices bonds with face value $1,000, or $100 of face value per share. If the present value of the bond's scheduled payments is less than 10 times the value of one share of stock, it may pay to convert; that is, the conversion option is in the money. A bond worth $950 with a conversion ratio of 10 could be converted profitably if the stock were selling above $95, since the value of the 10 shares received for each bond surrendered would exceed $950. Most convertible bonds are issued "deep out of the money"; that is, the issuer sets the conversion ratio so that conversion will not be profitable unless there is a substantial increase in stock prices and/or decrease in bond prices from the time of issue.

A bond's *conversion value* equals the value it would have if you converted it into stock immediately. Clearly, a bond must sell for at least its conversion value. If it did not, you could purchase the bond, convert it immediately, and clear a risk-free profit. This condition could never persist, because all investors would pursue such a strategy, which ultimately would bid up the price of the bond.

The straight bond value or "bond floor" is the value the bond would have if it were not convertible into stock. The bond must sell for more than its straight bond value because a convertible bond is in fact a straight bond plus a valuable call option. Therefore the convertible bond has two lower bounds on its market price: the conversion value and the straight bond value.

Figure 18.13, panel A illustrates the value of the straight debt as a function of the stock price of the issuing firm. For healthy firms the straight debt value is almost independent of the value of the stock because default risk is small. However, if the firm is close to bankruptcy (stock prices are low), default risk increases, and the straight bond value falls. Panel B shows the conversion value of the bond, and panel C compares the value of the convertible bond to these two lower bounds.

Figure 18.13

Value of a convertible bond as a function of stock price.
Panel A: Straight debt value, or bond floor.
Panel B: Conversion value of the bond.
Panel C: Total value of convertible bond.

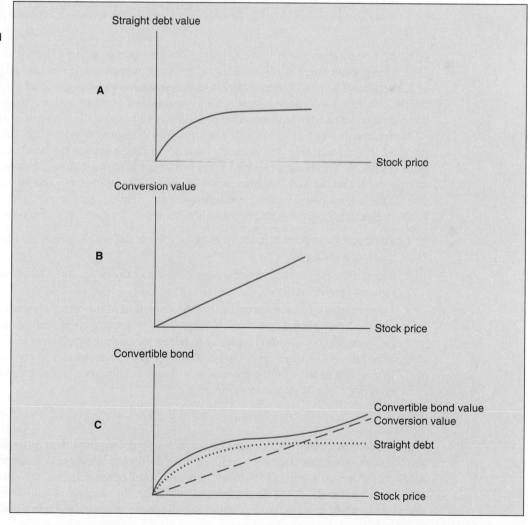

When stock prices are low, the straight bond value is the effective lower bound, and the conversion option is nearly irrelevant. The convertible will trade like straight debt. When stock prices are high, the bond's price is determined by its conversion value. With conversion all but guaranteed, the bond is essentially equity in disguise.

We can illustrate with two examples:

	Bond *A*	Bond *B*
Annual coupon	$80	$80
Maturity date	10 years	10 years
Quality rating	Baa	Baa
Conversion ratio	20	25
Stock price	$30	$50
Conversion value	$600	$1,250
Market yield on 10-year Baa-rated bonds	8.5%	8.5%
Value as straight debt	$967	$967
Actual bond price	$972	$1,255
Reported yield to maturity	8.42%	4.76%

Bond *A* has a conversion value of only $600. Its value as straight debt, in contrast, is $967. This is the present value of the coupon and principal payments at a market rate for straight debt of 8.5 percent. The bond's price is $972, so the premium over straight bond value is only $5, reflecting the low probability of conversion. Its reported yield to maturity based on scheduled coupon payments and the market price of $972 is 8.42 percent, close to that of straight debt.

The conversion option on bond *B* is in the money. Conversion value is $1,250, and the bond's price, $1,255, reflects its value as equity (plus $5 for the protection the bond offers against stock price declines). The bond's reported yield is 4.76 percent, far below the comparable yield on straight debt. The big yield sacrifice is attributable to the far greater value of the conversion option. In theory, we could value convertible bonds by treating them as straight debt plus call options. In practice, however, this approach is often impractical for several reasons:

1. The conversion price frequently increases over time, which means the exercise price for the option changes.

2. Stocks may pay several dividends over the life of the bond, further complicating the option valuation analysis.

3. Most convertibles also are callable at the discretion of the firm. In essence, the investor and the firm hold options on each other. If the firm exercises its call option to repurchase the bond, the bondholders typically have a month during which they still can convert. When firms use a call option, while knowing that bondholders will choose to convert, the firm is said to have *forced a conversion*. These conditions together mean that the actual maturity of the bond is indeterminate.

Warrants

Warrants are essentially call options issued by the firm. One important difference between calls and warrants is that exercise of a warrant requires the firm to issue a new share of stock—the total number of shares outstanding increases. Exercise of a call option requires only that the writer of the call deliver an already-issued share of stock to discharge the obligation. In that case, the number of shares outstanding remains fixed. Also unlike call options, warrants result in a cash flow to the firm when the exercise price is paid by the warrant holder. These differences mean that warrant values will differ somewhat from the values of call options with identical terms.

Like convertible debt, warrant terms may be tailored to meet the needs of the firm. Also like convertible debt, warrants generally are protected against stock splits and dividends in that the exercise price and the number of warrants held are adjusted to offset the effects of the split.

Warrants often are issued in conjunction with another security. Bonds, for example, may be packaged together with a warrant "sweetener," frequently a warrant that may be sold separately. This is called a *detachable warrant*.

The issue of warrants and convertible securities creates the potential for an increase in outstanding shares of stock if exercise occurs. Exercise obviously would affect financial statistics that are computed on a per-share basis, so annual reports must provide earnings-per-share (EPS) figures under the assumption that all convertible securities and warrants are exercised. These figures are called *fully diluted* earnings per share.[2]

The executive and employee stock options that became so popular in the past decade were actually warrants. Some of these grants were huge, with payoffs to top executives in excess of $100 million. Yet, until new reporting rules required such recognition, firms almost uniformly chose not to acknowledge these grants as expenses on their income statements until new reporting rules that took effect in 2006 required such recognition.

Collateralized Loans

Many loan arrangements require that the borrower put up collateral to guarantee that the loan will be paid back. In the event of default, the lender takes possession of the collateral. A *nonrecourse loan* gives the lender no recourse beyond the right to the collateral; that is, the lender may not sue the borrower for further payment if the collateral turns out not to be valuable enough to repay the loan.

This arrangement gives an implicit call option to the borrower. The borrower, for example, is obligated to pay back L dollars at the maturity of the loan. The collateral will be worth S_T dollars at maturity. (Its value today is S_0.) The borrower has the option to wait until loan maturity and repay the loan only if the collateral is worth more than the L dollars he or she borrowed. If the collateral is worth less than L, the borrower can default on the loan,[3] discharging the obligation by forfeiting the collateral, which is worth only S_T.

Another way of describing such a loan is to view the borrower as, in effect, turning over the collateral to the lender but retaining the right to reclaim it by paying off the loan. The transfer of the collateral with the right to claim it is equivalent to a payment of S_0 dollars, less a future recovery of a sum that resembles a call option with exercise price L. Basically, the borrower turns over collateral and keeps an option to "repurchase" it for L dollars at the maturity of the loan if L turns out to be less than S_T. This is, of course, a call option.

A third way to look at a collateralized loan is to assume the borrower will repay the L dollars with certainty but also retain the option to sell the collateral to the lender for L dollars, even if S_T is less than L. In this case, the sale of the collateral would generate the cash necessary to satisfy the loan. The ability to "sell" the collateral for a price of L dollars represents a put option, which guarantees that the borrower can raise enough money to satisfy the loan by turning over the collateral.

It is strange to think that we can describe the same loan as involving either a put option or a call option, since the payoffs to calls and puts are so different. Yet the equivalence of the

---

[2]We should note that the exercise of a convertible bond need not reduce EPS. Diluted EPS will be less than undiluted EPS only if interest saved (per share) on the converted bonds is less than the prior EPS.

[3]In reality, of course, defaulting on a loan is not so simple. There are losses of reputation involved as well as considerations of ethical behaviour. This is a description of a pure nonrecourse loan in which both parties agree from the outset that only the collateral backs the loan and that default is not to be taken as a sign of bad faith if the collateral is insufficient to repay the loan.

two approaches is nothing more than a reflection of the put–call parity relationship. In our call option description of the loan, the value of the borrower's liability is $S_0 - C$: the borrower turns over the asset, which is a transfer of S_0 dollars, but retains a call, which is worth C dollars. In the put-option description the borrower is obligated to pay L dollars but retains the put, which is worth P: the present value of this net obligation is $L/(1 + r_f)^T - P$. Because these alternative descriptions are equivalent ways of viewing the same loan, the value of the obligations must be equal:

$$S_0 - C = L/(1 + r_f)^T - P \tag{18.3}$$

Treating L as the exercise price of the option, equation 18.3 is simply the put–call parity relationship.

Figure 18.14, panel A illustrates the value of the payment to be received by the lender, which equals the minimum of S_T or L. Panel B shows that this amount can be expressed as S_T minus the payoff of the call implicitly written by the lender and held by the borrower. Panel C shows that it also can be viewed as a receipt of L dollars minus the proceeds of the put option.

Figure 18.14

Collateralized loan.

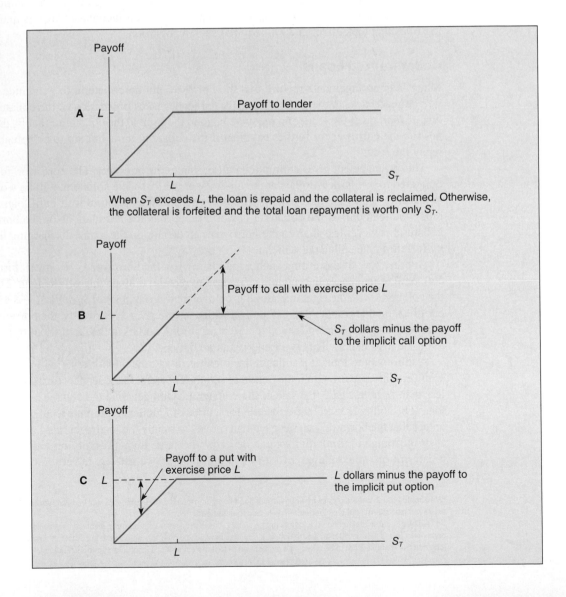

Levered Equity and Risky Debt

Investors holding stock in incorporated firms are protected by limited liability, which means that if the firm cannot pay its debts, the firm's creditors may attach only the firm's assets and may not sue the corporation's equityholders for further payment. In effect, any time the corporation borrows money, the maximum possible collateral for the loan is the total of the firm's assets. If the firm declares bankruptcy, we can interpret this as an admission that the assets of the firm are insufficient to satisfy the claims against it. The corporation may discharge its obligations by transferring ownership of the firm's assets to the creditors.

Just as with nonrecourse collateralized loans, the required payment to the creditors represents the exercise price of the implicit option, while the value of the firm is the underlying asset. The equityholders have a put option to transfer their ownership claims on the firm to the creditors in return for the face value of the firm's debt.

Alternatively, we may view the equityholders as retaining a call option. They have, in effect, already transferred their ownership claim on the firm to the creditors but have retained the right to reacquire the ownership claims on the firm by paying off the loan. Hence, the equityholders have the option to "buy back" the firm for a specified price—they have a call option.

The significance of this observation is that the values of corporate bonds can be estimated using option pricing techniques. The default premium required of risky debt, in principle, can be estimated using option valuation models. These will be considered in the next chapter.

18.6 FINANCIAL ENGINEERING

One of the attractions of options is the ability they provide to create investment positions with payoffs that depend in a variety of ways on the values of other securities. We have seen evidence of this capability in the various options strategies examined in Section 18.3. Options also can be used to custom-design new securities or portfolios with desired patterns of exposure to the price of an underlying security. In this sense, options (and futures contracts, to be discussed in Chapter 20) provide the ability to engage in *financial engineering*, the creation of portfolios with specified payoff patterns.

A simple example of a product engineered with options is the index-linked certificate of deposit. Unlike conventional CDs, which pay a fixed rate of interest, index-linked CDs pay depositors a specified fraction of the increase in the rate of return on a market index such as the S&P 500, while guaranteeing a minimum rate of return should the market fall. For example, the index-linked CD may offer 70 percent of any market increase, but protect its holder from any market decrease by guaranteeing at least no loss. The index-linked CD is clearly a type of call option. If the market rises, the depositor profits according to the *participation rate* or *multiplier*, in this case 70 percent; if the market falls, the investor is insured against loss. Just as clearly, the bank offering these CDs is in effect writing call options and can hedge its position by buying index calls in the options market. Figure 18.15 shows the nature of the issuer's obligation to its depositors.

How can the bank set the appropriate multiplier? To answer this, note various features of the option:

1. The price the depositor is paying for the options is the forgone interest on the conventional CD that could be purchased. Because interest is received at the end of the period, the present value of the interest payment on each dollar invested is $r_f/(1 + r_f)$. Therefore, the depositor trades a sure payment with present value per dollar invested of $r_f/(1 + r_f)$ for a return that depends on the market's performance. Conversely, the bank can fund its obligation using the interest that it would have paid on a conventional CD.

2. The option we have described is an at-the-money option, meaning that the exercise price equals the current value of the stock index. The option goes into the money as soon as the market index increases from its level at the inception of the contract.

Figure 18.15

Index-linked CD.

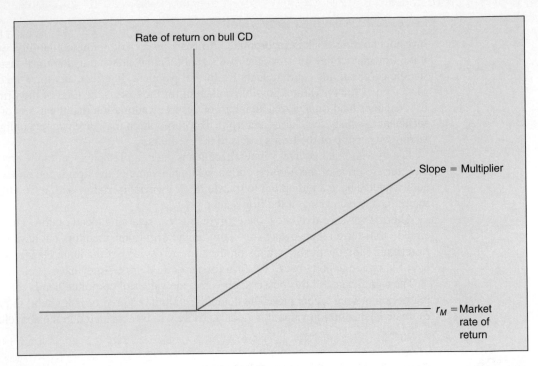

3. We can analyze the option on a per-dollar-invested basis. For example, the option costs the depositor $r_f/(1 + r_f)$ dollars per dollar placed in the index-linked CD. The market price of the option per dollar invested is C/S_0: the at-the-money option costs C dollars and is written on one unit of the market index, currently at S_0.

Now it is easy to determine the multiplier that the bank can offer on the CDs. It receives from its depositors a "payment" of $r_f/(1 + r_f)$ per dollar invested. It costs the bank C/S_0 to purchase the call option on a $1 investment in the market index. Therefore, if $r_f/(1 + r_f)$ is, for example, 70 percent of C/S_0, the bank can purchase at most .7 call option on the $1 investment and the multiplier will be .7. More generally, the break-even multiplier on an index linked CD is $r_f/(1 + r_f)$ divided by C/S_0.

EXAMPLE 18.7   Index-Linked CDs

Suppose that $r_f = 6\%$ per year (3% per six months) and that the index is currently at 1000. The six-month maturity at the money calls on the market index currently cost at $50. Then the option costs $50/$1,000 = $.05 per dollar of market value. The CD rate is 3 percent per six months, meaning that $r_f/(1 + r_f) = .03/1.03 = .0291$. Therefore, the multiplier would be $.0291/.05 = .5825$.

The index-linked CD has several variants. Investors can purchase similar CDs that guarantee a positive minimum return if they are willing to settle for a smaller multiplier. In this case, the option is "purchased" by the depositor for $(r_f - r_{min})/(1 + r_f)$ dollars per dollar invested, where r_{min} is the guaranteed minimum return. Because the purchase price is lower, fewer options can be purchased, which results in a lower multiplier. Another variant of the "bullish" CD we have described is the *bear CD*, which pays depositors a fraction of any *fall* in the market index. For example, a bear CD might offer a rate of return of .6 times any percentage decline in the S&P 500. The boxed article argues that most such instruments are not a good value.

NOTES FOR RISK-AVERSE OFFER SMALL PAYOFF

A fear of stocks afflicts a lot of Canadian investors these days. Even before the equity markets hit the skids last month, many people were shying away from exposure to stocks and equity funds in their investing. In driving terms, it's almost as if they've decided to stay off the highway because it's too scary.

You can see this in the news this week—conservative, income-oriented mutual funds remain more popular than straight equity funds, and also in the fast-growing popularity of a security called a principal protected note. With a principal protected note, you can get the benefit of returns from a grouping of mutual funds, hedge funds, stocks or stock indexes along with a guarantee from a major financial institution, usually a bank, that your capital will be returned to you on maturity. Arguably, they're the dream investment for the pathologically risk-averse.

However you describe principal protected notes, they're obviously a minor hit in the investing world. Consulting firm Investor Economics says there were 120 different issues in the market as of last June 30, more than double the 51 available at the end of 2001. Total assets as of June 30 were $3.4-billion, up from virtually zero in 1999.

Recent additions to the genre include NBC Blue Chip Notes, which are based on a portfolio of 20 blue-chip Canadian stocks and guaranteed by National Bank of Canada, and One Financial All-Star Portfolio Notes, which are based on the returns of five all-star mutual funds and guaranteed by the French bank BNP Paribas.

Some of the most popular principal protected notes have been issued by Canadian Imperial Bank of Commerce under the name FULPaY. These are based on returns of mutual funds baskets from such families as AGF, CI, Mackenzie and Franklin Templeton.

Would you classify yourself as a long-term investor with a prudently diversified portfolio? If the answer is yes, then cross off principal protected notes from your list of investment possibilities, with the possible exception of notes that offer exposure to hedge funds.

While the promise of capital protection and equity market returns is tempting, the costs and restrictions just aren't a good value.

There are four or so structures used by principal protected notes, but the general idea is the same in most cases. Part of the portfolio is invested in a bond to fund the capital guarantee, while the remainder is invested in various assets to generate gains. When the notes mature, you get your capital back, as well as any profits, which are treated as income for tax purposes in non-registered accounts.

Dundee Securities analyst James Gauthier recently issued a report on principal protected notes in which he outlined drawbacks like potentially high fees and a lack of liquidity. He said the secondary market for these notes is limited or non-existent, which is to say you may not be able to sell at your convenience prior to maturity. These notes are generally redeemable at set intervals, but there is no guarantee of capital until maturity.

Anyone who has experience with index-linked guaranteed investment certificates will know that one of their big limitations is that one's gains from the underlying index are limited through what's known as a "participation rate." The same concept often applies to principal protected notes, although the actual mechanics vary. Suffice it to say that the cost of your guarantee and the need for the notes sponsor to make money will give you significantly lower returns than if you invested in an asset directly.

Mr. Gauthier looked at a FULPaY issue based on three underlying mutual funds from a major fund family and found a cumulative two-year return of 24.5 per cent, which compared to 44 per cent for the funds themselves.

"We've reviewed dozens upon dozens of notes to date and one thing is clear to us: these tools are not the magic solution to anything," Mr. Gauthier concludes in his report. "Yes, they encourage peace of mind; however, our fear is that the cost of obtaining that peace of mind is lost on most investors and many advisers."

Let's go a little further than that and say the cost flat out isn't worth it unless you're traumatized by risk and can't bring yourself to invest the normal way.

Source: Rob Carrick, "Notes for Risk-Averse Offer Small Payoff," Report on Business, *The Globe and Mail*, May 22, 2004, p. B2. Reprinted by permission of The Globe and Mail.

CC 9

CONCEPT CHECK

Continue to assume that $r_f = 3$ percent per half-year, the at-the-money calls sell for $50, and the market index is at 1000. What would be the multiplier for 6-month bullish index-linked CDs offering a guaranteed minimum return of .5 percent over the term of the deposit?

18.7   EXOTIC OPTIONS

Options markets have been tremendously successful. Investors clearly value the portfolio strategies made possible by trading options; this is reflected in the heavy trading volume in these markets. Success breeds imitation, and in recent years we have witnessed considerable innovation in the range of option instruments available to investors. Part of this innovation has occurred in the market for customized options, which now trade in active over-the-counter markets. Many of these options have terms that would have been highly unusual even a few years ago; they are therefore called *exotic options*. In this section, we survey a few of the more interesting variants of these new instruments.

Asian Options

You already have been introduced to American and European options. *Asian options* are options with payoffs that depend on the *average* price of the underlying asset during at least some portion of the life of the option. For example, an Asian call option may have a payoff equal to the average stock price over the last three months minus the strike price if that value is positive, and zero otherwise. These options may be of interest, for example to firms that wish to hedge a profit stream that depends on the average price of a commodity over some period of time.

Barrier Options

Barrier options have payoffs that depend not only on some asset price at option expiration, but also on whether the underlying asset price has crossed through some "barrier." For example, a down-and-out option is one type of barrier option that automatically expires worthless if and when the stock price falls below some barrier price. Similarly, down-and-in options will not provide a payoff unless the stock price *does* fall below some barrier at least once during the life of the option. These options also are referred to as knock-out and knock-in options.

Lookback Options

Lookback options have payoffs that depend in part on the minimum or maximum price of the underlying asset during the life of the option. For example, a lookback call option might provide a payoff equal to the *maximum* stock price minus the exercise price. Such an option provides (for a fee, of course) a form of perfect market timing, providing the call holder with a payoff equal to the one that would accrue if the asset were purchased for X dollars and later sold at what turns out to be its high price.

Currency-Translated Options

Currency-translated options have either asset or exercise prices denominated in a foreign currency. A good example of such an option is the *quanto*, which allows an investor to fix in advance the exchange rate at which an investment in a foreign currency can be converted back into dollars. The right to translate a fixed amount of foreign currency into dollars at a given exchange rate is a simple foreign exchange option. Quantos are more interesting, however, because, the amount of currency that will be translated into dollars depends on the investment performance of the foreign security. Therefore, a quanto in effect provides a *random number* of options.

Digital Options

Digital options, also called *binary* or *"bet" options*, have fixed payoffs that depend on whether a condition is satisfied by the price of the underlying asset. For example, a digital call option might pay off a fixed amount of $100 if the stock price at maturity exceeds the exercise price.

SUMMARY

1. A call option is the right to buy an asset at an agreed-upon exercise price. A put option is the right to sell an asset at a given exercise price.

2. American options allow exercise on or before the expiration date. European options allow exercise only on the expiration date. Most traded options are American in nature.

3. Options are traded on stocks, stock indices, foreign currencies, fixed-income securities, and several futures contracts.

4. Options can be used either to increase an investor's exposure to an asset price or to provide insurance against volatility of asset prices. Popular option strategies include covered calls, protective puts, straddles, spreads, and collars.

5. The put–call parity theorem relates the prices of put and call options. If the relationship is violated, arbitrage

opportunities result. Specifically, the relationship that must be satisfied is that

$$P = C - S_0 + \text{PV}(X) + \text{PV}(\text{dividends})$$

where X is the exercise price of both the call and the put options; $\text{PV}(X)$ is the present value of a claim to X dollars to be paid at the expiration date of the options; and $\text{PV}(\text{dividends})$ is the present value of dividends to be paid before option expiration.

6. Many commonly traded securities embody option characteristics. Examples include callable bonds, convertible bonds and warrants. Other arrangements, such as collateralized loans and limited-liability borrowing can be analyzed as conveying implicit options to one or more parties.

7. Trading in so-called exotic options now takes place in an active over-the-counter market.

KEY EQUATIONS

(18.1) $C - P = S_0 - X/(1 + r_f)^T$

(18.2) $P = C - S_0 + \text{PV}(X) + \text{PV}(\text{dividends})$

(18.3) $S_0 - C = L/(1 + r_f)^T - P$

PROBLEMS

connect Practise and learn online with Connect.

1. Turn back to Figure 18.1, which lists prices of various RIM Ltd. options. Use the data in the figure to calculate the payoff and the profits for investments in each of the following September maturity options, assuming that the stock price on the maturity date is $14.
   a. Call option, $X = \$11$
   b. Put option, $X = \$11$
   c. Call option, $X = \$14$
   d. Put option, $X = \$14$
   e. Call option, $X = \$17$
   f. Put option, $X = \$17$

2. Suppose you think ABC stock is going to appreciate substantially in value in the next six months. Also suppose that the stock's current price, S_0, is $100, and the call option expiring in six months has an exercise price, X, of $100 and is selling at a price, C, of $10. With $10,000 to invest, you are considering three alternatives.

a. Invest all $10,000 in the stock, buying 100 shares.

b. Invest all $10,000 in 1,000 options (10 contracts).

c. Buy 100 options (one contract) for $1,000, and invest the remaining $9,000 in a money market fund paying 4 percent in interest over six months (8 percent per year).

What is your rate of return for each alternative for four stock prices six months from now? Summarize your results in the table and diagram that appear below.

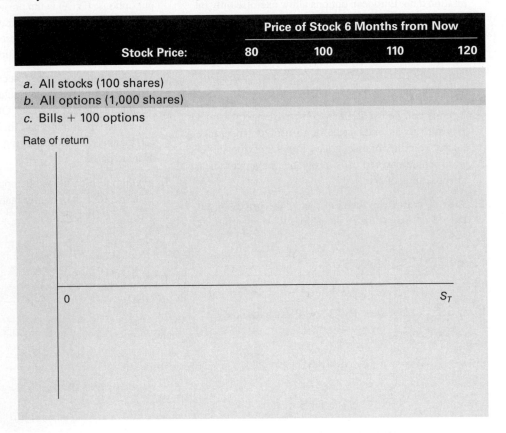

| | Price of Stock 6 Months from Now | | | |
Stock Price:	80	100	110	120
a. All stocks (100 shares)				
b. All options (1,000 shares)				
c. Bills + 100 options				

3. The common stock of the PUTT Corporation has been trading in a narrow price range for the past month, and you are convinced that it is going to break far out of that range in the next three months. You do not know whether it will go up or down, however. The current price of the stock is $100 per share, and the price of a three-month call option at an exercise price of $100 is $10. The stock will pay no dividends for the next three months.

a. If the risk-free interest rate is 10 percent per year, what must be the price of a three-month put option on PUTT stock at an exercise price of $100?

b. What would be a simple options strategy to exploit your conviction about the stock price's future movement? How far would it have to move in either direction for you to make a profit on your initial investment?

4. The common stock of the CALL Corporation has been trading in a narrow range around $50 per share for many months, and you are convinced that it is going to stay in that range for the next three months. The price of a three-month put option with an exercise price of $50 is $4. The stock will pay no dividends for the next three months.

a. If the risk-free interest rate is 10 percent per year, what must be the price of a three-month call option on CALL stock at an exercise price of $50 if it is at the money?

b. What would be a simple options strategy using a put and a call to explain your conviction about the stock price's future movement? What is the most money you can make on this position? How far can the stock price move in either direction before you lose money?

c. How can you create a position involving a put, a call, and risk-free lending that would have the same payoff structure as the stock at expiration? What is the net cost of establishing that position now?

5. You are a portfolio manager who uses options positions to customize the risk profile of your clients. In each case, what strategy is best given your client's objective?

a. • Performance to date: Up 16%.

   • Client objective: Earn at least 15%.

   • Your scenario: Good chance of large gains or large losses between now and end of year.

      i. Long straddle

      ii. Long bullish spread

      iii. Short straddle

b. • Performance to date: Up 16%.

   • Client objective: Earn at least 15%.

   • Your scenario: Good chance of large losses between now and end of year.

      i. Long put options

      ii. Short call options

      iii. Long call options

6. An investor purchases a stock for $38 and a put for $.50 with a strike price of $35. The investor sells a call for $.50 with a strike price of $40. What is the maximum profit and loss for this position? Draw the profit and loss diagram for this strategy as a function of the stock price at expiration.

7. In this problem, we derive the put–call parity relationship for European options on stocks that pay dividends before option expiration. For simplicity, assume that the stock makes one dividend payment of D per share at the expiration date of the option.

a. What is the value of a stock-plus-put position on the expiration date of the option?

b. Now consider a portfolio comprising a call option and a zero-coupon bond with the same maturity date as the option and with face value $(X + D)$. What is the value of this portfolio on the option expiration date? You should find that its value equals that of the stock-plus-put portfolio regardless of the stock price.

c. What is the cost of establishing the two portfolios in parts (*a*) and (*b*)? Equate the costs of these portfolio, and you will derive the put–call parity relationship, equation 18.2.

8. *a.* A butterfly spread is the purchase of one call at exercise price X_1, the sale of two calls at exercise price X_2, and the purchase of one call at exercise price X_3. X_1 is less than X_2, and X_2 is less than X_3 by equal amounts, and all calls have the same expiration date. Graph the payoff diagram to this strategy.

b. A vertical combination is the purchase of a call with exercise price X_2 and a put with exercise price X_1, with X_2 greater than X_1. Graph the payoff to this strategy.

9. A bearish spread is the purchase of a call with exercise price X_2 and the sale of a call with exercise price X_1, with X_2 greater than X_1. Graph the payoff to this strategy and compare it to Figure 18.10.

10. Joseph Jones, a manager at Computer Science, Inc. (CSI), received 10,000 shares of company stock as part of his compensation package. The stock currently sells at $40 a share. Joseph would like to defer selling the stock until the next tax year. In January, however, he will need to sell all his holdings to provide for a down payment on his new house. Joseph is worried about the price risk involved in keeping his shares. At current prices, he would receive $400,000 for the stock. If

the value of his stock holdings falls below $350,000, his ability to come up with the necessary down payment would be jeopardized. On the other hand, if the stock value rises to $450,000 he would be able to maintain a small cash reserve even after making the down payment. Joseph considers three investment strategies:

a. Strategy A is to write January call options on the CSI shares with strike price $45. These calls are currently selling for $3 each.

b. Strategy B is to buy January put options on CSI with strike price $35. These options also sell for $3 each.

c. Strategy C is to establish a zero-cost collar by writing the January calls and buying the January puts.

Evaluate each of these strategies with respect to Joseph's investment goals. What are the advantages and disadvantages of each? Which would you recommend?

11. Use the spreadsheet from the Excel Applications box on spreads and straddles to answer these questions.

a. Plot the payoff and profit diagrams to a straddle position with an exercise (strike) price of $130. Assume the options are priced as they are in the Excel Application.

b. Plot the payoff and profit diagrams to a bullish spread position with exercise (strike) prices of $120 and $130. Assume the options are priced as they are in the Excel Application.

12. You are attempting to formulate an investment strategy. On the one hand, you think there is great upward potential in the stock market and would like to participate in the upward move if it materializes. However, you are not able to afford substantial stock market losses and so cannot run the risk of a stock market collapse, which you also think is a possibility. Your investment advisor suggests a protective put position: buy both shares in a market index stock fund and put options on those shares with three-month maturity and exercise price of $780. The stock index is currently selling for $900. However, your uncle suggests you instead buy a three-month call option on the index fund with exercise price $840 and buy three-month T-bills with face value $840.

a. On the same graph, draw the *payoffs* to each of these strategies as a function of the stock fund value in three months. (*Hint:* Think of the options as being on one "share" of the stock index fund, with the current price of each share of the index equal to $900.)

b. Which portfolio must require a greater initial outlay to establish? (*Hint:* Does either portfolio provide a final payoff that is always at least as great as the payoff of the other portfolio?)

c. Suppose the market prices of the securities are as follows:

Stock fund	$900
T-bills (face value $840)	$810
Call (exercise price $840)	$120
Put (exercise price $780)	$ 6

Make a table of the profits realized for each portfolio for the following values of the stock price in three months: $S_T = \$700, \$840, \$900, \$960$.

Graph the profits to each portfolio as a function of S_T on a single graph.

d. Which strategy is riskier? Which should have a higher beta?

e. Explain why the data for the securities given in part (c) do *not* violate the put–call parity relationship.

13. The agricultural price support system guarantees farmers a minimum price for their output. Describe the program provisions as an option. What is the asset? The exercise price?

14. In what ways is owning a corporate bond similar to writing a put option? A call option?

15. An executive compensation scheme might provide a manager a bonus of $1,000 for every dollar by which the company's stock price exceeds some cutoff level. In what way is this arrangement equivalent to issuing the manager call options on the firm's stock?

16. Consider the following options portfolio. You write a December maturity call option on RIM with exercise price 13. You write a December RIM put option with exercise price 12.

    a. Graph the payoff of this portfolio at option expiration as a function of RIM's stock price at that time.

    b. What will be the profit/loss on this position if RIM is selling at 11 on the option maturity date? What if RIM is selling at 12.5? Use the listing from Figure 18.1 to answer this question.

    c. At what two stock prices will you just break even on your investment?

    d. What kind of "bet" is this investor making—that is, what must this investor believe about the RIM stock price in order to justify this position?

17. Consider the following portfolio. You write a put option with exercise price 90 and buy a put option on the same stock with the same maturity date with exercise price 95.

    a. Plot the value of the portfolio at the maturity date of the options.

    b. On the same graph, plot the profit of the portfolio. Which option must cost more?

18. A Ford put option with strike price 60 trading on the Acme options exchange sells for $2. To your amazement, Ford put with the same maturity selling on the Apex options exchange, but with strike price 62, also sells for $2. If you plan to hold the options positions to maturity, devise a zero-net-investment arbitrage strategy to exploit the pricing anomaly. Draw the profit diagram at maturity for your position.

19. You buy a share of stock, write a one-year call option with $X = \$10$, and buy a one-year put option with $X = \$10$. Your net outlay to establish the entire portfolio is $9.50. What is the risk-free interest rate? The stock pays no dividends.

20. FedEx is selling for $100 a share. A FedEx call option with one month until expiration and an exercise price of $105 sells for $2 while a put with the same strike and expiration sells for $6.94. What is the market price of a zero-coupon bond with face value $105 and 1 month maturity? What is the risk-free interest rate expressed as an effective annual yield?

21. Demonstrate that an at-the-money call option on a given stock must cost more than an at-the-money put option with the same maturity. (*Hint*: Use put–call parity.)

22. Using the RIM option prices in Figure 18.1, calculate the price of a riskless zero-coupon bond with face value $11 that matures in December on the same date as the listed options. Assume that the options are European and use the average of the bid and ask prices for the stock and the options.

23. You write a put option with $X = 100$ and buy a put with $X = 110$. The puts are on the same stock and have the same maturity date.

    a. Draw the payoff graph for this strategy.

    b. Draw the profit graph for this strategy.

    c. If the underlying stock has positive beta, does this portfolio have positive or negative beta?

24. Joe Finance has just purchased an indexed stock fund, currently selling at $400 per share. To protect against losses, Joe also purchased an at-the-money European put option on the fund for $20, with exercise price $400, and three-month time to expiration. Sally Calm, Joe's financial advisor, points out that Joe is spending a lot of money on the put. She notes that three-month puts with strike prices of $390 cost only $15 and suggests that Joe use the cheaper put.

    a. Analyze the strategies of Joe and Sally by drawing the *profit* diagrams for the stock-plus-put positions for various values of the stock fund in three months.

    b. When does Sally's strategy do better? When does it do worse?

    c. Which strategy entails greater systematic risk?

25. You write a call option with $X = 50$ and buy a call with $X = 60$. The options are on the same stock and have the same maturity date. One of the calls sells for $3; the other sells for $9.

   a. Draw the payoff graph for this strategy at the option maturity date.

   b. Draw the profit graph for this strategy.

   c. What is the breakeven point for this strategy? Is the investor bullish or bearish on the stock?

26. Devise a portfolio using only call options and shares of stock with the diagrammed value (payoff) at the option maturity date. If the stock price currently is 53, what kind of bet is the investor making?

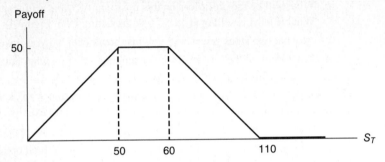

The following problems are based on questions that have appeared in past CFA examinations.

27. Donna Donie, CFA has a client who believes the common stock price of TRT Materials (currently $58 per share) could move substantially in either direction in reaction to an expected court decision involving the company. The client currently owns no TRT shares, but asks Donie for advice about implementing a "strangle" strategy to capitalize on the possible stock price movement. A *strangle* is a portfolio of a put and a call with different exercise prices but the same expiration date. Donie gathers the TRT option pricing data shown below.

Characteristic	Call Option	Put Option
Price	$5	$4
Strike price	$60	$55
Time to expiration	90 days from now	90 days from now

   a. Recommend whether Donie should choose a long strangle strategy or a short strangle strategy to achieve the client's objective.

   b. Calculate, at expiration for the appropriate strangle strategy in part (a), the

   i. Maximum possible loss per share

   ii. Maximum possible gain per share

   iii. Breakeven stock price(s)

28. Suresh Singh, CFA is analyzing a convertible bond. The characteristics of the bond and the underlying common stock are given in the following exhibit:

Convertible Bond Characteristics	
Par value	$1,000
Annual coupon rate (annual pay)	6.5%
Conversion ratio	22
Market price	105% of par value
Straight value	99% of par value
Underlying Stock Characteristics	
Current market price	$40 per share
Annual cash dividend	$1.20 per share

Compute the bond's

  i. Conversion value

  ii. Market conversion price

29. Rich Macdonald, CFA is evaluating his investment alternatives in Ytel Incorporated by analyzing a Ytel convertible bond and Ytel common equity. Characteristics of the two securities are given in the following exhibit:

Characteristics	Convertible Bond	Common Equity
Par value	$1,000	—
Coupon (annual payment)	4%	—
Current market price	$980	$35 per share
Straight bond value	$925	—
Conversion ratio	25	—
Conversion option	At any time	—
Dividend	—	$0
Expected market price in 1 year	$1,125	$45 per share

a. Calculate from the exhibit the

  i. Current market conversion price for the Ytel convertible bond

  ii. Expected one-year rate of return for the Ytel convertible bond

  iii. Expected one-year rate of return for the Ytel common equity

One year has passed and Ytel's common equity price has increased to $51 per share. Also, over the year, the interest rate on Ytel's nonconvertible bonds of the same maturity increased, while credit spreads remained unchanged.

b. Name the two components of the convertible bond's value. Indicate whether the value of each component should decrease, stay the same, or increase in response to the

  i. Increase in Ytel's common equity price

  ii. Increase in interest rates

30. a. Which one of the following comparative statements about common stock call options and warrants is correct?

		Call Option	Warrant
i.	Issued by the company	No	Yes
ii.	Sometimes attached to bonds	Yes	Yes
iii.	Maturity greater than one year	Yes	No
iv.	Convertible into the stock	Yes	No

b. Consider a bullish spread option strategy using a call option with a $25 exercise price priced at $4 and a call option with a $40 exercise price priced at $2.50. If the price of the stock increases to $50 at expiration and the option is exercised on the expiration date, the net profit per share at expiration (ignoring transaction costs) is

  i. $8.50

  ii. $13.50

  iii. $16.50

  iv. $23.50

c. A convertible bond sells at $1,000 par with a conversion ratio of 40 and an accompanying stock price of $20 per share. The conversion premium and (percentage) conversion premium, respectively, are

   i. $200 and 20%

  ii. $200 and 25%

 iii. $250 and 20%

 iv. $250 and 25%

d. A put on XYZ stock with a strike price of $40 is priced at $2 per share, while a call with a strike price of $40 is priced at $3.50. What is the maximum per-share loss to the writer of the uncovered put and the maximum per-share gain to the writer of the uncovered call?

	Maximum Loss to Put Writer	Maximum Gain to Call Writer
i.	$38	$ 3.50
ii.	$38	$36.50
iii.	$40	$ 3.50
iv.	$40	$40.00

e. You create a strap by buying two calls and one put on ABC stock, all with a strike price of $45. The calls cost $5 each, and the put costs $4. If you close your position when ABC is priced at $55, your per-share gain or loss is

   i. $4 loss

  ii. $6 gain

 iii. $10 gain

 iv. $20 gain

E-INVESTMENTS
Options and
Straddles

Go to **www.m-x.ca**, enter BCE in the quote section, and obtain an info quote for Bell Canada enterprises. Once you have the information quote, request the information on options. You will be able to access the prices and the market characteristics for all put and call options for Bell. Answer the following questions:

1. Examine the last prices for the call options. What is the relationship between the strike price and the last price? What is the pattern for the put options?
2. What are the prices for the put and call with the nearest expiration date?
3. What would be the cost of a straddle using the above options?
4. At expiration, what would be the breakeven stock prices for the above straddle?
5. What would be the percentage increase or decrease in the stock price required to break even?
6. What are the prices for the put and call with a later expiration date?
7. What would be the cost of a straddle using the later expiration date?
8. At expiration, what would be the breakeven stock prices for the above straddle?
9. What would be the percentage increase or decrease in the stock price required to break even?

Option Valuation

In the previous chapter, we examined option markets and strategies. We noted that many securities contain embedded options that affect both their values and their risk-return characteristics. In this chapter, we turn our attention to option valuation issues. To understand most option-valuation models requires considerable mathematical and statistical background. Still, many of the ideas and insights of these models can be demonstrated in simple examples, and we will concentrate on these.

We start with a discussion of the factors that ought to affect option prices. After this discussion, we present several bounds within which option prices must lie. Next, we turn to quantitative models. First, we examine an option valuation approach, called "two-state" or "binomial" option pricing, and its extensions. We continue with one particular valuation formula, the famous Black-Scholes model, one of the most significant breakthroughs in finance theory in the past four decades. We also look at some of the more important applications of option-pricing theory in portfolio management and control.

Option-pricing models allow us to "back out" market estimates of stock price volatility. Next we turn to some of the more important applications of option-pricing theory to risk management. We also look at some of the empirical evidence on option pricing and its implications concerning the limitations of the Black-Scholes model. Finally, we examine a generalization of the binomial model, the stochastic dominance option pricing model that converges at the limit to the Black-Scholes model but can also accommodate more complex models.

19.1 OPTION VALUATION: INTRODUCTION

Intrinsic and Time Values

Consider a call option that is out of the money at the moment, with the stock price below the exercise price. This does not mean the option is valueless. Even though immediate exercise today would be unprofitable, the call retains a positive value because there is always a chance the stock price will increase sufficiently by the expiration date to allow for profitable exercise. If not, the worst that can happen is that the option will expire with zero value.

The value $S_0 - X$ sometimes is called the **intrinsic value** of in-the-money call options, because it gives the payoff that could be obtained by immediate exercise. Intrinsic value is set equal to zero for out-of-the-money or at-the-money options. The difference between the actual call price and the intrinsic value commonly is called the *time value* of the option.

"Time value" is unfortunate terminology because it may confuse the option's time value with the time value of money. Time value in the options context refers simply to the difference between the option's price and the value the option would have if it were expiring immediately. It is the part of the option's value that may be attributed to the fact that it still has positive time to expiration.

Most of an option's time value typically is a type of "volatility value." As long as the option holder can choose not to exercise, the payoff cannot be worse than zero. Even if a call option is out of the money now, it still will sell for a positive price because it offers the potential for a profit if the stock price increases, while imposing no risk of additional loss should the stock price fall. The volatility value lies in the value of the right not to exercise the call if that action would be unprofitable. The option to exercise, as opposed to the obligation to exercise, provides insurance against poor stock price performance.

As the stock price increases substantially, it becomes more likely that the call option will be exercised by expiration. In this case, with exercise all but assured, the volatility value becomes minimal. As the stock price gets ever larger, the option value approaches the "adjusted" intrinsic value, the stock price minus the present value of the exercise price, $S_0 - PV(X)$.

Why should this be? If you are virtually certain the option will be exercised and the stock purchased for X dollars, it is as though you own the stock already. The stock certificate, with a value today of S_0, might as well be sitting in your safe-deposit box now, as it will be there in only a few months. You just haven't paid for it yet. The present value of your obligation is the present value of X, so the net value of the call option is $S_0 - PV(X)$.[1]

Figure 19.1 illustrates the call option valuation function. The value curve shows that when the stock price is very low, the option is nearly worthless because there is almost no chance that it will be exercised. When the stock price is very high, the option value approaches adjusted intrinsic value. In the midrange case, where the option is approximately at the money, the option curve diverges from the straight lines corresponding to adjusted intrinsic value. This is because although exercise today would have a negligible (or negative) payoff, the volatility value of the option is quite high in this region.

The call always increases in value with the stock price. The slope is greatest, however, when the option is deep in the money. In this case exercise is all but assured and the option increases in price one for one with the stock price.

---

[1]This discussion presumes the stock pays no dividends until after option expiration. If the stock does pay dividends before maturity, then there is a reason you would care about getting the stock now rather than at expiration—getting it now entitles you to the interim dividend payments. In this case, the adjusted intrinsic value of the option must subtract the value of the dividends the stock will pay out before the call is exercised. Adjusted intrinsic value would more generally be defined as $S_0 - PV(X) - PV(D)$, where D is the dividend to be paid before option expiration.

Figure 19.1

Call option value before expiration.

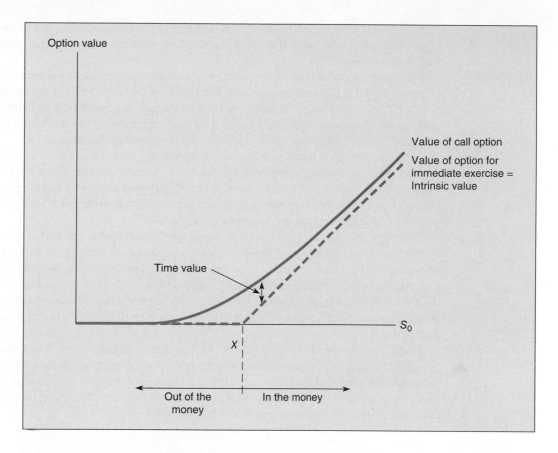

Determinants of Option Values

We can identify at least six factors that should affect the value of a call option: the stock price, the exercise price, the volatility of the stock price, the time to expiration, the interest rate, and the dividend rate of the stock. The call option should increase in value with the stock price and decrease in value with the exercise price because the payoff to a call, if exercised, equals $S_T - X$. The magnitude of the expected payoff increases with the difference $S_0 - X$.

Call option values also increase with the volatility of the underlying stock price. To see why, consider circumstances where possible stock prices at expiration may range from $10 to $50 compared with a situation where stock prices may range only from $20 to $40. In both cases the expected stock price will be $30. Suppose that the exercise price on a call option is also $30. What are the option payoffs?

High-Volatility Scenario				
Stock price	$10	$20	$30	$40	$50
Option payoff	0	0	0	$10	$20

Low-Volatility Scenario				
Stock price	$20	$25	$30	$35	$40
Option payoff	0	0	0	$ 5	$10

If each outcome is equally likely, with probability .2, the expected payoff to the option under high-volatility conditions will be $6, but under low-volatility conditions the expected payoff is half as much, only $3.

Despite the fact that the average stock price in each scenario is $30, the average option payoff is greater in the high-volatility scenario. The source of this extra value is the limited loss that an option holder can suffer, or the volatility value of the call. No matter how far below $30 the stock price drops, the option holder will get $0. Obviously, extremely poor stock price performance is no worse for the call option holder than is moderately poor performance.

In the case of good stock performance, however, the option will expire in the money, and it will be more profitable the higher the stock price. Thus, extremely good stock outcomes can improve the option payoff without limit, but extremely poor outcomes cannot worsen the payoff below zero. This asymmetry means that volatility in the underlying stock price increases the expected payoff to the option, thereby enhancing its value.[2]

Similarly, longer time to expiration increases the value of a call option. For more distant expiration dates, the range of likely stock prices expands, which has an effect similar to that of increased volatility. Moreover, as time to expiration increases, the present value of the exercise price falls, thereby benefiting the call option holder and increasing the option value. As a corollary to this issue, call option values are higher when interest rates rise (holding the stock price constant), because higher interest rates also reduce the present value of the exercise price.

Finally, the dividend payout policy of the firm affects option values. A high-dividend-payout policy puts a drag on the rate of growth of the stock price. For any expected total rate of return on the stock, a higher dividend yield must imply a lower expected rate of capital gain. This drag on stock price appreciation decreases the potential payoff from the call option, thereby lowering the call value. Table 19.1 summarizes these relationships.

CC 1

CONCEPT CHECK

Prepare a table like Table 19.1 for the determinants of put option values. How should American put values respond to increases in S, X, σ, T, r_f, and dividend payouts?

TABLE 19.1

Determinants of Call Option Values

Variable Increases	Value of a Call Option
Stock price, S	Increases
Exercise price, X	Decreases
Volatility, σ	Increases
Time to expiration, T	Increases
Interest rate, r_f	Increases
Cash dividend payouts	Decreases

[2]You should be careful interpreting the relationship between volatility and option value. Neither the focus of this analysis on total (as opposed to systematic) volatility nor the conclusion that options buyers seem to like volatility contradicts modern portfolio theory. In conventional discounted cash flow analysis, we find the discount rate appropriate for a *given* distribution of future cash flows. Greater risk implies a higher discount rate and lower present value. Here, however, the cash flow from the *option* depends on the volatility of the *stock*. The option value increases not because traders like risk but because the expected cash flow to the option holder increases along with the volatility of the underlying asset.

19.2   RESTRICTIONS ON OPTION VALUES

Several quantitative models of option pricing have been devised, and we will examine some of these in this chapter. All models, however, rely on simplifying assumptions. You might wonder which properties of option values are truly general and which depend on the particular simplifications. To start with, we will consider some of the more important general properties of option prices. Some of these properties have important implications for the effect of stock dividends on option values and the possible profitability of early exercise of an American option.

Restrictions on the Value of a Call Option

The most obvious restriction on the value of a call option is that its value must be zero or positive. Because the option need not be exercised, it cannot impose any liability on its holder; moreover, as long as there is any possibility that at some point it can be exercised profitably, the option will command a positive price. Its payoff must be zero at worst, and possibly positive, so it has some positive value.

We can place another lower bound on the value of a call option. Suppose that the stock will pay a dividend of D dollars just before the expiration date of the option, denoted by T (where today is time zero). Now compare two portfolios, one consisting of a call option on one share of stock and the other a leveraged equity position consisting of that share and borrowing of $(X + D)/(1 + r_f)^T$ dollars. The loan repayment is $X + D$ dollars, due on the expiration date of the option. For example, for a half-year maturity option with exercise price $70, dividends to be paid of $5, and effective annual interest of 10 percent, you would purchase one share of stock and borrow $75/(1.10)^{1/2} = \$71.51$. In six months, when the loan matures, the payment due is $75.

At that time, the payoff to the leveraged equity position would be:

	In General	Our Numbers
Stock value	$S_T + D$	$S_T + 5$
−Payback of loan	$-(X + D)$	$- 75$
Total	$S_T - X$	$S_T - 70$

where S_T denotes the stock price at the option expiration date. Notice that the payoff to the stock is the ex-dividend stock value plus dividends received. Whether the total payoff to the stock-plus-borrowing position is positive or negative depends on whether S_T exceeds X. The net cash outlay required to establish this leveraged equity position is $S_0 - \$71.51$, or, more generally, $S_0 - (X + D)/(1 + r_f)^T$, that is, the current price of the purchased stock, S_0, less the initial cash inflow from the borrowing position.

The payoff to the call option will be $S_T - X$ if the option expires in the money and zero otherwise. Thus, the option payoff is equal to the leveraged equity payoff when that payoff is positive and is greater when the leveraged equity position has a negative payoff. Because the option payoff always is greater than or equal to that of the leveraged equity position, the option price must exceed the cost of establishing that position.

In our case the value of the call must be greater than $S_0 - (X + D)/(1 + r_f)^T$, or, more generally,

$$C \geq S_0 - \text{PV}(X) - \text{PV}(D)$$

where $\text{PV}(X)$ denotes the present value of the exercise price and $\text{PV}(D)$ is the present value of the dividends the stock will pay at the option's expiration. More generally, we can interpret $\text{PV}(D)$ as the present value of any and all dividends to be paid prior to the option expiration date. Because we know already that the value of a call option must be non-negative, we may conclude that C is greater than the *maximum* of either 0 or $S_0 - \text{PV}(X) - \text{PV}(D)$.

Figure 19.2

Range of possible
call option
values.

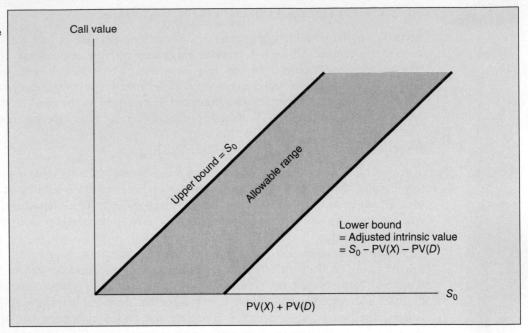

Figure 19.3

Call option value
as a function of
the stock price.

We also can put an upper bound on the possible value of the call: simply the stock price. No one would pay more than S_0 dollars for the right to purchase a stock currently worth S_0 dollars. Thus, $C \leq S_0$.

Figure 19.2 demonstrates graphically the range of prices that is ruled out by these upper and lower bounds for the value of a call option. Any option value outside the shaded area is not possible according to the restrictions we have derived. Before expiration, the call option value normally will be *within* the allowable range, touching neither the upper nor lower bound, as in Figure 19.3.

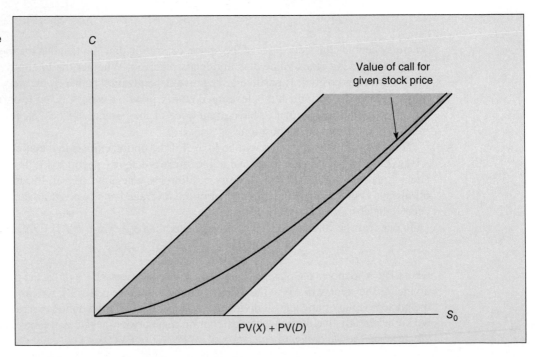

Early Exercise and Dividends

A call option holder who wants to close out that position has two choices: exercise the call or sell it. If the holder exercises at time t, the call will provide a profit of $S_t - X$, assuming, of course, that the option is in the money. We have just seen that the option can be sold for at least $S_t - \text{PV}(X) - \text{PV}(D)$. Therefore, for an option on a non-dividend-paying stock, C is greater than $S_t - \text{PV}(X)$. Because the present value of X is less than X itself, it follows that

$$C \ge S_t - \text{PV}(X) \ge S_t - X$$

The implication here is that the proceeds from a sale of the option (at price C) must exceed the proceeds from an exercise ($S_t - X$). It is economically more attractive to keep the call option "alive" rather than "killing" it through early exercise. In other words, calls on non-dividend-paying stocks are "worth more alive than dead."

If it never pays to exercise a call option before maturity, the right to exercise early actually must be valueless. We have to conclude that the values of otherwise-identical American and European call options on stocks paying no dividends are equal. This simplifies matters, because any valuation formula that applies to the European call for which only one exercise date need be considered, also must apply to an American call.

As most stocks do pay dividends, you may wonder whether this result is just a theoretical curiosity. It is not; reconsider our argument and you will see that all that we really require is that the stock pay no dividends *until the option expires*. This condition will be true for many real-world options.

Early Exercise of American Puts

For American *put options*, however, the optimality of early exercise is most definitely a possibility. To see why, consider a simple example. Suppose that you purchase a put option on a stock. Soon the firm goes bankrupt, and the stock price falls to zero. Of course you want to exercise now, because the stock price can fall no lower. Immediate exercise gives you immediate receipt of the exercise price, which can be invested to start generating income. Delay in exercise means a time-value-of-money cost. The right to early exercise of a put option before maturity must have value.

Now suppose instead that the firm is only nearly bankrupt, with the stock selling at just a few cents. Immediate exercise may still be optimal. After all, the stock price can fall by only a very small amount, meaning that the proceeds from future exercise cannot be more than a few cents greater than the proceeds from immediate exercise. Against this possibility of a tiny increase in proceeds must be weighed the time-value-of-money cost of deferring exercise. Clearly, there is some stock price below which early exercise is optimal.

This argument also proves that the American put must be worth more than its European counterpart. The American put allows you to exercise anytime before maturity. Because the right to exercise early may be useful in some circumstances, it will command a positive price in the capital market. The American put therefore will sell for a higher price than a European put with otherwise identical terms.

Figure 19.4, panel A illustrates the value of an American put option as a function of the current stock price, S_0. Once the stock price drops below a critical value, denoted S^* in the figure, exercise becomes optimal. From that point on, the option-pricing curve coincides with the straight line depicting the intrinsic value of the option. If and when the stock price reaches S^*, the put option is exercised and its payoff equals its intrinsic value.

In contrast, the value of the European put, which is graphed in panel B, is not asymptotic to the intrinsic value line. Because early exercise is prohibited, the maximum value of the European put is $\text{PV}(X)$, which occurs at the point $S_0 = 0$. Obviously, for a long enough horizon, $\text{PV}(X)$ can be made arbitrarily small.

Figure 19.4

Put option values as a function of the current stock price.

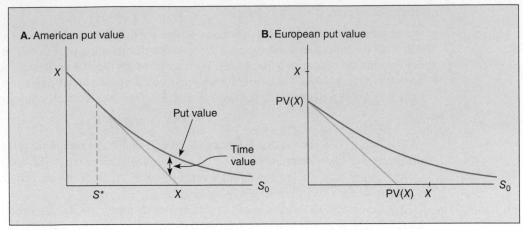

A. American put value

Put value

Time value

S_0

S^* X

B. European put value

X

PV(X)

PV(X) X

S_0

CC 2

CONCEPT CHECK

In the light of this discussion, explain why the put–call parity relationship is valid only for European options on non-dividend-paying stocks. If the stock pays no dividends, what *inequality* for American options would correspond to the parity theorem?

19.3

BINOMIAL OPTION PRICING

Two-State Option Pricing

A complete understanding of commonly used option-valuation formulas is difficult without a substantial mathematics background. Nevertheless, we can develop valuable insight into option valuation by considering a simple special case. Assume that a stock price can take only two possible values at option expiration: the stock will either increase to a given higher price or decrease to a given lower price. Although this may seem an extreme simplification, it allows us to come closer to understanding more complicated and realistic models. Moreover, we can extend this approach to describe far more reasonable specifications of stock price behaviour. In fact, several major financial firms employ variants of this simple model to value options and securities with option-like features.

Suppose that the stock currently sells at $S_0 = \$100$ and that by year-end the price will either increase by a factor of $u = 1.2$ to 120 or fall by a factor of $d = .9$ to 90 (u and d stand for "up" and "down," respectively). A call option on the stock might specify an exercise price of 110 and a time to expiration of one year. Suppose the interest rate is 10 percent. At year-end, the payoff to the holder of the call option either will be zero if the stock falls or 10 if the stock price goes to 120.

These possibilities are illustrated by the following value "trees":

100 ⟨ 120 / 90

Stock price

C ⟨ 10 / 0

Call option value

Compare the payoff of the call to that of a portfolio consisting of one share of the stock and borrowing of $81.82 at the interest rate of 10 percent. The payoff to this portfolio also depends on the stock price at year-end:

Value of stock	$90	$120
−Repayment of loan with interest	−90	−90
Total	$ 0	$ 30

We know the cash outlay to establish the portfolio is $18.18: $100 for the stock, less the $81.82 proceeds from borrowing. Therefore the portfolio's value tree is

The payoff of this portfolio is exactly three times that of the option for either value of the stock price. In other words, three call options will exactly replicate the payoff to the portfolio; it follows that three call options should have the same price as the cost of establishing the portfolio. Hence, the three calls should sell for the same price as this *replicating portfolio*. Therefore,

$$3C = \$100 - \$81.82 = \$18.18$$

or each call should sell at $C = \$6.06$. Thus, given the stock price, exercise price, interest rate, and volatility of the stock price (as represented by the spread between the up or down movements), we can derive the fair value for the call option.

This valuation approach relies heavily on the notion of replication. With only two possible end-of-year values of the stock, the returns to the leveraged stock portfolio replicate the returns to the call option and therefore command the same market price. This notion of replication is behind most option pricing formulas. For more complex price distributions for stocks, the replication technique is correspondingly more complex, but the principles remain the same.

One way to view the role of replication is to note that, using the numbers assumed for this example, a portfolio made up of one share of stock and three call options written is perfectly hedged. Its year-end value is independent of the ultimate stock price:

Stock value	$90	$120
−Obligations from two calls written	−0	−30
Net payoff	$90	$ 90

The investor has formed a risk-free portfolio, with a payout of $90. Its value must be the present value of $90, or $90/1.10 = $81.82. The value of the portfolio, which equals $100 from the stock held long, minus $3C$ from the two calls written, should equal $81.82. Hence, $100 − 3C = $81.82, or C = $6.06.

The ability to create a perfect hedge is the key to this argument. The hedge guarantees the end-of-year payout, which can be discounted using the risk-free interest rate. To find the value of the option in terms of the value of the stock, we do not need to know the option's or the stock's beta or expected rate of return. The perfect hedging, or replication, approach enables us to express the value of the option in terms of the current value of the stock without this information. With a hedged position the final stock price does not affect the investor's payoff, so the stock's risk-and-return parameters have no bearing.

The hedge ratio of this example is one share of stock to three calls, or one-third. This ratio has an easy interpretation in this context: it is the ratio of the range of the values of the option to those of the stock across the two possible outcomes. The option is worth either zero or $10, for a range of $10. The stock is worth either $90 or $120, for a range of $30. The ratio of ranges, 10/30, is one-third, which is the hedge ratio we have established.

The hedge ratio equals the ratio of ranges because the option and stock are perfectly correlated in this two-state example. Because they are perfectly correlated, a perfect hedge requires that they be held in a fraction determined only by relative volatility.

We can generalize the hedge ratio for the other two-state option problems as

$$H = \frac{C_u - C_d}{uS_0 - dS_0}$$

where C_u and C_d refer to the call option's value when the stock goes up or down, respectively, and uS_0 and dS_0 are the stock prices in the two states. The hedge ratio, H, is thus the ratio of the swings in the possible end-of-period values of the option and the stock. If the investor writes one option and holds H shares of stock, the value of the portfolio will be unaffected by the stock price. In this case, option pricing is easy: simply set the value of the hedged portfolio equal to the present value of the known payoff.

Using our example, the option pricing technique would proceed as follows:

1. Given the possible end-of-year stock prices, $uS_0 = 120$ and $dS_0 = 90$, and the exercise price of $110, calculate that $C_u = 10$ and $C_d = 0$. The stock price range is thus $30, while the option price range is $10.

2. Find that the hedge ratio is 10/30 = 1/3.

3. Find that a portfolio made up of 1/3 shares with one written option would have an end-of-year value of $30 with certainty.

4. Show that the present value of $30 with a one-year interest rate of 10 percent is $27.27.

5. Set the value of the hedged position to the present value of the certain payoff:

$$(1/3)S_0 - C_0 = 27.27$$
$$\$33.33 - C_0 = \$27.27$$

6. Solve for the call's value, $C_0 = \$6.06$.

What if the option were overpriced, perhaps selling for $6.50? Then you can make arbitrage profits. Here is how:

	Initial Cash Flow	Cash Flow in 1 Year for Each Possible Stock Price	
		$S = 90$	$S = 120$
1. Write three options	19.50	0	−30
2. Purchase one share	−100	90	120
3. Borrow $80.50 at 10% interest, and repay in 1 year	80.50	−88.55	−88.55
Total	0	1.45	1.45

Although the net initial investment is zero, the payoff in one year is positive and riskless. If the option were underpriced, one would simply reverse this arbitrage strategy: buy the option, and short-sell the stock to eliminate price risk. Note, by the way, that the present value of the profit to the arbitrage strategy above exactly equals three times the amount by which the option is overpriced. The present value of the risk-free profit of $1.45 at a 10 percent interest rate is $1.318. With three options written in this strategy, this translates to a profit of $.44 per option, exactly the amount by which the option was overpriced: $6.50 versus the "fair value" of $6.06.

Generalizing the Two-State Approach

Although the two-state stock price model seems simplistic, we can generalize it to incorporate more realistic assumptions. To start, suppose that we were to break up the year into two six-month segments, and then assert that over each half-year segment the stock price could take on two values. In this example, we will say it can increase 10 percent or decrease 5 percent (i.e., $u = 1.10$ and $d = .95$. A stock initially selling at 100 could follow these possible paths over the course of the year:

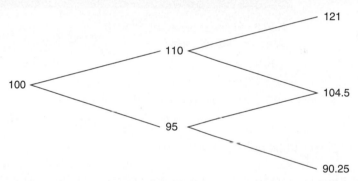

The midrange value of 104.5 can be attained by two paths: an increase of 10 percent followed by a decrease of 5 percent, or a decrease of 5 percent followed by a 10 percent increase.

There are now three possible end-of-year values for the stock and three for the option.

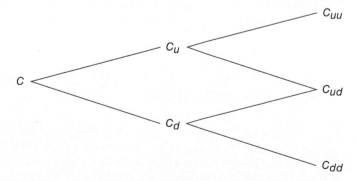

Using methods similar to those we followed above, we could value C_u from knowledge of C_{uu} and C_{ud} then value C_d from knowledge of C_{du} and C_{dd} and finally value C from knowledge of C_u and C_d. There is no reason to stop at six-month intervals. We could next break up the year into 4 three-month units, or 12 one-month units, or 365 one-day units, each of which would be posited to have a two-state process. Although the calculations become quite numerous and correspondingly tedious, they are easy to program into a computer, and such computer programs are used widely by participants in the options market.

EXAMPLE 19.1   Binomial Option Pricing

Suppose that the risk-free interest rate is 5 percent per six-month period and we wish to value a call option with exercise price $110 on the stock described in the two-period price tree just above. We start by finding the value of C_u. From this point, the call can rise to an expiration-date value of $C_{uu} = \$11$ (since at this point the stock price is $u \times u \times S_0 = \$121$) or fall to a final value of $C_{ud} = 0$ (since at this point, the stock price is $u \times d \times S_0 = \$104.50$, which is less than the $110 exercise price). Therefore the hedge ratio at this point is

$$H = \frac{C_{uu} - C_{ud}}{uuS_0 - udS_0} = \frac{\$11 - \$0}{\$121 - \$104.50} = \frac{2}{3}$$

Thus, the following portfolio will be worth $209 at option expiration regardless of the ultimate stock price:

	$udS_0 = \$104.50$	$uuS_0 = \$121$
Buy 2 shares at price $uS_0 = \$110$	$209	$242
Write 3 calls at price C_u	0	−33
Total	$209	$209

The portfolio must have a current market value equal to the present value of $209:

$$2 \times 110 - 3C_u = \$209/1.05 = \$199.047$$

Solve to find that $C_u = \$6.984$.

Next we find the value of C_d. It is easy to see that this value must be zero. If we reach this point (corresponding to a stock price of $95), the stock price at option maturity will be either $104.50 or $90.25; in either case, the option will expire out of the money. (More formally, we could note that with $C_{ud} = C_{dd} = 0$, the hedge ratio is zero, and a portfolio of *zero* shares will replicate the payoff of the call!)

Finally, we solve for C using the values of C_u and C_d. Concept Check 4 leads you through the calculations that show the option value to be $4.434.

CC 4

CONCEPT CHECK

Show that the initial value of the call option in Example 19.1 is $4.434.
a. Confirm that the spread in option values is $C_u - C_d = \$6.984$.
b. Confirm that the spread in stock values is $uS_0 - dS_0 = \$15$.
c. Confirm that the hedge ratio is .4656 shares purchased for each call written.
d. Demonstrate that the value in one period of a portfolio comprising .4656 shares and one call written is riskless.
e. Calculate the present value of this payoff.
f. Solve for the option value.

Making the Valuation Model Practical

As we break the year into progressively finer subintervals, the range of possible year-end stock prices expands. For example, when we increase the subperiods to three, the number of stock prices increases to four, as demonstrated in the following stock price tree and, in fact, will ultimately take on a lognormal distribution. This can be seen from an analysis of the event tree for the stock for a period with three subintervals:

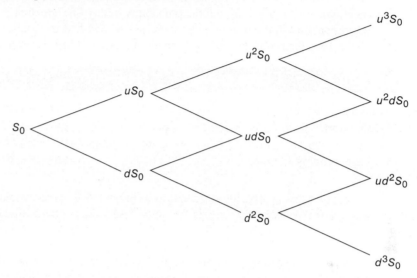

Thus, by allowing for an ever-greater number of subperiods, we can overcome one of the apparent limitations of the valuation model: that the number of possible end-of-period stock prices is small. Notice that extreme events such as u^3S_0 or d^3S_0 are relatively rare, since they require either three consecutive increases or decreases in the three subintervals. More moderate, or midrange, results such as u^2dS_0 can be arrived at by more than one path—any combination of two price increases and one decrease will result in stock price u^2dS_0. There are three of these paths, *uud, udu, duu*. In contrast, only one path, *uuu*, results in a stock price of u^3S_0. Thus, midrange values are more likely. As we make the model more realistic and break up the option maturity into more and more subperiods, the probability distribution for the final stock price begins to resemble the familiar bell-shaped curve with highly unlikely extreme outcomes and far more likely midrange outcomes. The probability of each outcome is given by the binomial distribution, and this multiperiod approach to option pricing is therefore called the **binomial model**.

But we still need to answer an important practical question. Before the binomial model can be used to value actual options, we need a way to choose reasonable values for u and d. The spread between up and down movements in the price of the stock reflects the volatility of its rate of return, so the choice for u and d should depend on that volatility. Call σ your estimate of the standard deviation of the stock's continuously compounded annualized rate of return, and Δt the length of each subperiod. To make the standard deviation of the stock in the binomial model match your estimate of σ, it turns out that you need to set $u = \exp(\sigma\sqrt{\Delta t})$ and $d = \exp(-\sigma\sqrt{\Delta t})$.[3] You can see that the proportional difference between u and d increases with both annualized volatility as well as the duration of the subperiod. This makes sense, as both higher σ and longer holding periods make future stock prices more uncertain. The following example illustrates how to use this calibration.

---

[3]Notice that $d = 1/u$. This is the most common but not the only way to calibrate the model to empirical volatility. For alternative methods, see Robert L. McDonald, *Derivatives Markets*, 2nd ed. (Boston: Pearson/Addison-Wesley, 2006), Ch.11, Section 11.3.

EXAMPLE 19.2   **Calibrating *u* and *d* to Stock Volatility**

Suppose you are using a 3-period model to value a one-year option on a stock with volatility (i.e., annualized standard deviation) of $\sigma = .30$. With a time to expiration of $T = 1$ year, and three subperiods, you would calculate $\Delta t = T/n = 1/3$, $u = \exp(\sigma\sqrt{\Delta t}) = \exp(.30\sqrt{1/3}) = 1.189$ and $d = \exp(-\sigma\sqrt{\Delta t}) = \exp(-.30\sqrt{1/3}) = .841$. Given the probability of an up movement, you could then work out the probability of any final stock price. For example, suppose the probability that the stock price increases is .554 and the probability that it decreases is .446.[4] Then the probability of stock prices at the end of the year would be as follows:

Event	Possible Paths	Probability		Final Stock Price
3 down movements	*ddd*	$.446^3$	$= .089$	$59.48 = 100 \times .841^3$
2 down and 1 up	*ddu, dud, udd*	$3 \times .446^2 \times .554 = .330$		$84.10 = 100 \times 1.189 \times .841^2$
1 down and 2 up	*uud, udu, duu*	$3 \times .446 \times .554^2 = .411$		$118.89 = 100 \times 1.189^2 \times .841$
3 up movements	*uuu*	$.554^3$	$= .170$	$168.09 = 100 \times 1.189^3$

We plot this probability distribution in Figure 19.5, panel A. Notice that the two middle end-of-period stock prices are, in fact, more likely than either extreme.

Now we can extend Example 19.2 by breaking up the option maturity into ever-shorter subintervals. As we do, the stock price distribution becomes increasingly plausible, as we demonstrate in Example 19.3.

EXAMPLE 19.3   **Increasing the Number of Subperiods**

In Example 19.2, we broke up the year into three subperiods. Let's now look at the cases of 6 and 20 subperiods.

Subperiods, *n*	$\Delta t = T/n$	$u = \exp(\sigma\sqrt{\Delta t})$	$d = \exp(-\sigma\sqrt{\Delta t})$
3	.333	$\exp(.173) = 1.189$	$\exp(-.173) = .841$
6	.167	$\exp(.123) = 1.130$	$\exp(-.095) = .885$
20	.015	$\exp(.067) = 1.069$	$\exp(-.067) = .935$

We plot the resulting probability distributions in panels B and C of Figure 19.5.[5]

Notice that the right tail of the distribution in panel C is noticeably longer than the left tail. In fact, as the number of intervals increases, the distribution progressively approaches the skewed lognormal (rather than the symmetric normal) distribution. Even if the stock price were to decline in *each* subinterval, it can never drop below zero. But there is no corresponding upper bound on its potential performance. This asymmetry gives rise to the skewness of the distribution.

[4]Using this probability, the continuously compounded expected rate of return on the stock is .10. In general, the formula relating the probability of an upward movement with the annual expected rate of return, *r*, is $p = \dfrac{\exp(r\Delta t) - d}{u - d}$.

[5]We adjust the probabilities of up versus down movements using the formula in footnote 4 to make the distributions in Figure 19.5 comparable. In each panel, *p* is chosen so that the stock's expected annualized, continuously compounded rate of return is 10 percent.

Figure 19.5 Probability distributions for final stock prices. Possible outcomes and associated probabilities. In each panel the stock's annualized continuously compounded expected rate of return is 10 percent and its standard deviation is 30 percent. **Panel A:** Three subintervals. In each subinterval the stock price can increase by 18.9 percent or decrease by 15.9 percent. **Panel B:** Six subintervals. In each subinterval the stock price can increase by 13.0 percent or fall by 11.5 percent. **Panel C:** Twenty subintervals. In each subinterval the stock can increase by 6.9 percent or fall by 6.5 percent.

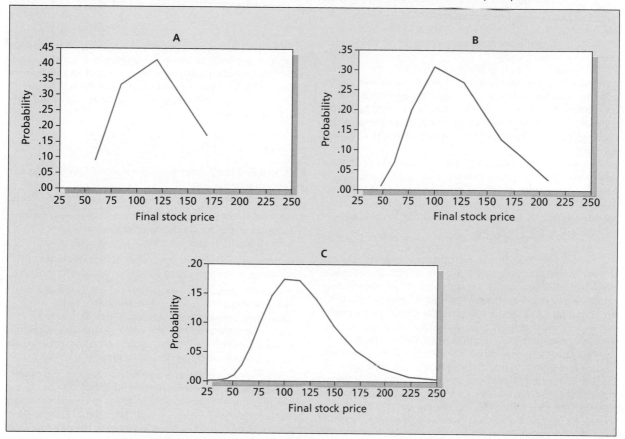

Eventually, as we divide the option maturity into an ever-greater number of subintervals each node of the event tree would correspond to an infinitesimally small time interval. The possible stock price movement within that time interval would be correspondingly small. As those many intervals pass, the end-of-period stock price would more and more closely resemble a lognormal distribution.[6] Thus the apparent oversimplification of the two-state model can be overcome by progressively subdividing any period into many subperiods.

At any node, one still could set up a portfolio that would be perfectly hedged over the next tiny time interval. Then, at the end of that interval, upon reaching the next node, a new hedge ratio could be computed and the portfolio composition could be revised to remain hedged over the coming small interval. By continuously revising the hedge position, the portfolio would remain hedged and would earn a riskless rate of return over each interval. This is called *dynamic*

---

[6]Actually, more complex considerations enter here. The limit of this process is lognormal only if we assume also that stock prices move continuously, by which we mean that over small time intervals only small price movements can occur. This rules out rare events such as sudden, extreme price moves in response to dramatic information (like a takeover attempt). For a treatment of this type of "jump process," see John C. Cox and Stephen A. Ross, "The Valuation of Options for Alternative Stochastic Processes," *Journal of Financial Economics* 3 (January–March 1976); or Robert C. Merton, "Option Pricing When Underlying Stock Returns Are Discontinuous," *Journal of Financial Economics* 3 (January–March 1976).

We pointed out earlier in the chapter that the binomial model valuation approach is arbitrage-based. We can value the option by replicating it with shares of stock plus borrowing. The ability to replicate the option means that its price relative to the stock and the interest rate must be based only on the technology of replication and *not* on risk preferences. It cannot depend on risk aversion or the capital asset pricing model or any other model of equilibrium risk-return relationships.

This insight—that the pricing model must be independent of risk aversion—leads to a very useful shortcut to valuing options. Imagine a *risk-neutral economy*, that is, an economy in which all investors are risk-neutral. This hypothetical economy must value options the same as our real one because risk aversion cannot affect the valuation formula.

In a risk-neutral economy, investors would not demand risk premiums and would therefore value all assets by discounting expected payoffs at the risk-free rate of interest. Therefore, a security such as a call option would be valued by discounting its expected cash flow at the risk-free rate:

$C = \dfrac{\text{"}E\text{"}(CF)}{1 + r_f}$. We put the expectation operator E in quotation marks to signify that this is not the true expectation, but the expectation that would prevail in the hypothetical risk-neutral economy. To be consistent, we must calculate this expected cash flow using the rate of return the stock *would* have in the risk-neutral economy as one of our inputs, *not* using its true rate of return. But if we successfully maintain consistency, the value derived for the hypothetical economy should match the one in our own.

How do we compute the expected cash flow from the option in the risk-neutral economy? Because there are no risk premia, the stock's expected rate of return must equal the risk-free rate. Call p the probability that the stock price increases. Then p must be chosen to equate the expected rate of increase of the stock price to the risk-free rate (we ignore dividends here):

$$\text{"}E\text{"}(S_1) = p(uS) + (1 - p)dS = (1 + r_f)S$$

This implies that $p = \dfrac{1 + r_f - d}{u - d}$. We call p a *risk-neutral probability* to distinguish it from the true, or "objective," probability. To illustrate, in our two-state example at the beginning of Section 19.3, we had $u = 1.2$, $d = .9$, and $r_f = .10$. Given these values, $p = \dfrac{1 + .10 - .9}{1.2 - 9} = \dfrac{2}{3}$.

Now let's see what happens if we use the discounted cash flow formula to value the option in the risk-neutral economy. We continue to use the two-state example from Section 19.3. We find the present value of the option payoff using the risk-neutral probability and discount at the risk-free interest rate:

$$C = \frac{\text{"}E\text{"}(CF)}{1 + r_f} = \frac{pC_u + (1 - p)C_d}{1 + r_f} = \frac{2/3 \times 10 + 1/3 \times 0}{1.10} = 6.06$$

This answer exactly matches the value we found using our no-arbitrage approach!

We repeat: This is not truly an expected discounted value.

- The *numerator* is not the true expected cash flow from the option because we use the risk-neutral probability, p, rather than the true probability.

- The *denominator* is not the proper discount rate for option cash flows because we do not account for the risk.

- In a sense, these two "errors" cancel out. But this is not just luck: We are *assured* to get the correct result because the no-arbitrage approach implies that risk preferences cannot affect the option value. Therefore, the value computed for the risk-neutral economy *must* equal the value that we obtain in our economy.

When we move to the more realistic multiperiod model, the calculations are more cumbersome, but the idea is the same. Footnote 4 shows how to relate p to any expected rate of return and volatility estimate. Simply set the expected rate of return on the stock equal to the risk-free rate, use the resulting probability to work out the expected payoff from the option, discount at the risk-free rate, and you will find the option value. These calculations are actually fairly easy to program in Excel.

---

hedging, the continued updating of the hedge ratio as time passes. As the dynamic hedge becomes ever finer, the resulting option-valuation procedure becomes more precise. The nearby box offers further refinements on the use of the binomial model.

CC 5

CONCEPT CHECK

In the table in Example 19.3, u and d both get closer to 1 (u is smaller and d is larger) as the time interval Δt shrinks. Why does this make sense? Does the fact that u and d are each closer to 1 mean that the total volatility of the stock over the remaining life of the option is lower?

19.4   BLACK-SCHOLES OPTION VALUATION

While the binomial model is extremely flexible, a computer is needed for it to be useful in actual trading. An option-pricing *formula* would be far easier to use than the tedious algorithm involved in the binomial model. It turns out that such a formula can be derived if one is willing to make just two more assumptions: that both the risk-free interest rate and stock price volatility are constant over the life of the option. In this case, as the time to expiration is divided into ever-more subperiods, the distribution of the stock price at expiration progressively approaches the lognormal distribution, as suggested by Figure 19.5. When the stock price distribution is actually lognormal, we can derive an exact option-pricing formula.

The Black-Scholes Formula

Financial economists searched for years for a workable option-pricing model before Black and Scholes[7] and Merton[8] derived a formula for the value of a call option. Scholes and Merton shared the 1997 Nobel Prize in economics for their accomplishment.[9] The **Black-Scholes pricing formula** for a call option, now widely used by options market participants, is

$$C_0 = S_0 N(d_1) - Xe^{-rT} N(d_2) \tag{19.1}$$

where

$$d_1 = \frac{\ln(S_0/X) + (r + \sigma^2/2)T}{\sigma\sqrt{T}}$$

$$d_2 = d_1 - \sigma\sqrt{T}$$

and where

C_0 = current call option value

S_0 = current stock price

$N(d)$ = probability that a random draw from a standard normal distribution will be less than d; this equals the area under the normal curve up to d, as in the shaded area of Figure 19.6; in Excel, this function is called NORMSDIST

X = exercise price

e = base of the natural log function, approximately 2.71828; in Excel, e^x can be evaluated using the function EXP(x)

r = risk-free interest rate (the annualized continuously compounded rate on a safe asset with the same maturity as the expiration date of the option, which is to be distinguished from r_f, the discrete period interest rate)

T = time to expiration of option, in years

ln = natural logarithm function; in Excel, ln(x) can be calculated as LN(x)

σ = standard deviation of the annualized continuously compounded rate of return of the stock

Notice a surprising feature of equation 19.1: the option value does *not* depend on the expected rate of return on the stock. In a sense, this information is already built into the formula with the inclusion of the stock price, which itself depends on the stock's risk and return characteristics. This version of the Black-Scholes formula is predicated on the assumption that the stock pays no dividends.

Although you may find the Black-Scholes formula intimidating, we can explain it first at a somewhat intuitive level. The trick is to view the $N(d)$ terms (loosely) as risk-adjusted probabilities

---

[7]Fischer Black and Myron Scholes, "The Pricing of Options and Corporate Liabilities," *Journal of Political Economy* 81 (May/June 1973).
[8]Robert C. Merton, "Theory of Rational Option Pricing," *Bell Journal of Economics and Management Science* 4 (Spring 1973).
[9]Fischer Black died in 1995.

Figure 19.6

A standard normal curve.

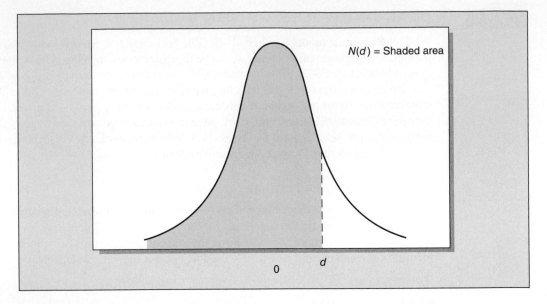

$N(d)$ = Shaded area

that the call option will expire in the money. First, look at equation 19.1 when both $N(d)$ terms are close to 1, indicating a very high probability that the option will be exercised. Then the call option value is equal to $S_0 - Xe^{-rT}$, which is what we called earlier the adjusted intrinsic value, $S_0 -$ PV(X). This makes sense: if exercise is certain, we have a claim on a stock with current value S_0 and an obligation with present value PV(X), or, with continuous compounding, Xe^{-rT}.

Now look at equation 19.1 when the $N(d)$ terms are close to zero, meaning that the option almost certainly will not be exercised. Then the equation confirms that the call is worth nothing. For middle-range values of $N(d)$ between 0 and 1, it tells us that the call value can be viewed as the present value of the call's potential payoff adjusting for the probability of in-the-money expiration.

How do the $N(d)$ terms serve as risk-adjusted probabilities? This question quickly leads us into advanced statistics. Notice, however, that d_1 and d_2 both increase as the stock price increases. Therefore, $N(d_1)$ and $N(d_2)$ also increase with higher stock prices. This is the property we would desire of our "probabilities." For higher stock prices relative to exercise prices, future exercise is more likely.

EXAMPLE 19.4   **Black-Scholes Valuation**

You can use the Black-Scholes formula fairly easily. Suppose that you want to value a call option under the following circumstances:

Stock price	$S_0 = 100$
Exercise price	$X = 95$
Interest rate	$r = .10$
Time to expiration	$T = .25$ (one-fourth year)
Standard deviation	$\sigma = .5$

First calculate

$$d_1 = \frac{\ln(100/95) + (.10 + .5^2/2) \times .25}{.5\sqrt{.25}} = .43$$

$$d_2 = .43 - .5\sqrt{.25} = .18$$

continued

Next find $N(d_1)$ and $N(d_2)$. The values of the normal distribution are tabulated and may be found in many statistics textbooks. The normal distribution function, $n(d)$, is provided in any spreadsheet program. In Microsoft Excel, for example, the function name is NORMSDIST. From the Excel program we find that

$$N(.43) = .6664$$
$$N(.18) = .5714$$

Thus, the value of the call option is

$$C = 100 \times .6664 - (95e^{-.10 \times .25}) \times .5714$$
$$= 66.64 - 52.94 = \$13.70$$

CC 6

CONCEPT CHECK

Calculate the call option value in Example 19.4 if the standard deviation on the stock were .6 instead of .5. Confirm that the option is worth more using this higher volatility.

What if the option price in our example were in fact $15? Is the option mispriced? Maybe, but before betting your fortune on that, you may want to reconsider the valuation analysis. First, like all models, the Black-Scholes formula is based on some simplifying abstractions that make the formula only approximately valid. Some of the important assumptions underlying the formula are the following:

1. The stock will pay no dividends until after the option expiration date.
2. Both the interest rate, r, and variance rate, σ^2, of the stock are constant (or in slightly more general versions of the formula, both are *known* functions of time—any changes are perfectly predictable).
3. Stock prices are continuous, meaning that sudden extreme jumps such as those in the aftermath of an announcement of a takeover attempt are ruled out.

Variants of the Black-Scholes formula have been developed to deal with some of these limitations.

Second, even within the context of the model, you must be sure of the accuracy of the parameters used in the formula. Four of these—S_0, X, T, and r—are straightforward. The stock price, exercise price, and time to maturity may be read directly from the option pages. The interest rate used is the money market rate for a maturity equal to that of the option. The last input, however, the standard deviation of the stock return, is not directly observable. It must be estimated from historical data, from scenario analysis, or from the prices of other options, as we will describe momentarily.

We saw in Chapter 4 that the historical variance of stock market returns can be calculated from n observations as follows:

$$\sigma^2 = \frac{n}{n-1} \sum_{t=1}^{n} \frac{(r_t - \bar{r})^2}{n}$$

where $\bar{r}$ is the average return over the sample period. The rate of return on day t is defined to be consistent with continuous compounding as $r_t = ln(S_t/S_{t-1})$. (We note again that the natural logarithm of a ratio is approximately the percentage difference between the numerator and denominator so that $ln(S_t/S_{t-1})$ is a measure of the rate of return of the stock from time $t - 1$ to time t.) Historical variance commonly is computed using daily returns over periods of several months. Because the standard deviation of stock returns must be estimated, however, it is always possible that discrepancies between an option price and its Black-Scholes value are simply artifacts of error in the estimation of the stock's volatility.

In fact, market participants often give the option valuation problem a different twist. Rather than calculating a Black-Scholes option value for a given stock standard deviation, they ask instead, "What standard deviation would be necessary for the option price that I can see to be consistent with the Black-Scholes formula?" This is called the **implied volatility** of the option, the volatility level for the stock that the option price implies. From the implied standard deviation, investors judge whether they think the actual stock standard deviation exceeds the implied volatility. If it does, the option is considered a good buy; if actual volatility seems greater than the implied volatility, its fair price would exceed the observed price.

CC 7

CONCEPT CHECK

Consider the option in the example selling for $15 with Black-Scholes value of $13.70. Is its implied volatility more or less than .5?

Another variation is to compare two options on the same stock with equal expiration dates but different exercise prices. The option with the higher implied volatility would be considered relatively expensive, because a higher standard deviation is required to justify its price. The analyst might consider buying the option with the lower implied volatility and writing the option with the higher implied volatility.

The Black-Scholes valuation formula, and the implied volatility, are easily calculated using an Excel spreadsheet such as Spreadsheet 19.1. The model inputs are provided in column B, and the outputs are given in column E. The formulas for d_1 and d_2 are provided in the spreadsheet, and the Excel formula NORMSDIST(d_1) is used to calculate $N(d_1)$. Cell E6 contains the Black-Scholes formula. (The formula in the spreadsheet actually includes an adjustment for dividends, as described in the next section.)

To compute an implied volatility, we can use the Goal Seek command from the Tools menu in Excel. Goal Seek asks us to change the value of one cell to make the value of another cell (called the target cell) equal to a specific value. For example, if we observe a call option selling for $7 with other inputs as given in the spreadsheet, we can use Goal Seek to change the value in cell B2 (the standard deviation of the stock) to set the option value in cell E6 equal to $7. The target cell, E6, is the call price, and the spreadsheet manipulates cell B2. When you click "OK," the spreadsheet finds that a standard deviation equal to .2783 is consistent with a call price of $7; this would be the option's implied volatility if it were selling at $7.

Figure 19.7 presents plots of the historical and implied standard deviation of the rate of return on the S&P 500 Index over the year ending in April 2007. The implied volatility is derived from prices of option contracts traded on the index. Notice that although both series have considerable

---

EXCEL SPREADSHEET 19.1 🔼

Calculating Black-Scholes option values.

	A	B	C	D	E	F	G	H	I	J
1	INPUTS			OUTPUTS			**FORMULA FOR OUTPUT IN COLUMN E**			
2	Standard deviation (annual)	0.2783		d1	0.0029		(LN(B5/B6)+(B4+.5*B2^2)*B3)/(B2*SQRT(B3))			
3	Maturity (in years)	0.5		d2	-0.1939		E2-B2*SQRT(B3)			
4	Risk-free rate (annual)	0.06		N(d1)	0.5012		NORMSDIST(E2)			
5	Stock price	100		N(d2)	0.4231		NORMSDIST(E3)			
6	Exercise price	105		B/S call value	7.0000		B5*E4-B6*EXP(-B4*B3)*E5			
7	Dividend yield (annual)	0		B/S put value	8.8968		B6*EXP(-B4*B3)*(1-E5)-B5*(1-E4)			

Figure 19.7

S&P 500 implied and historical volatility comparison.

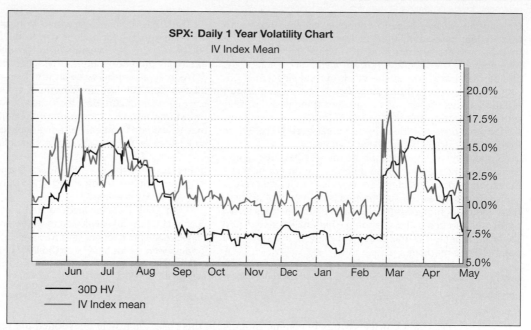

Source: Ivolatility.com site, http://www.ivolatility.com.

tendency to move together, there are considerable differences between the two estimates of volatility. In fact, these differences reflect a serious problem with the Black-Scholes model: its inability to reconcile empirical data drawn from two different markets, the options market and the market for the underlying asset.[10] More on this below.

The Chicago Board Options Exchange regularly computes the implied volatility of major stock indices. Figure 19.8 is a graph of the implied (30-day) volatility of the S&P 500 since 1990. During periods of turmoil, implied volatility can spike quickly. There are peaks in January 1991 (Gulf War); August 1998 (collapse of Long-Term Capital Management); September 11, 2001; 2002 (buildup to invasion of Iraq); and most dramatically during the credit crisis of 2008. Because implied volatility correlates with crisis, it is sometimes called an "investor fear gauge" and, as the nearby box makes clear, observers use it to infer the market's assessment of possible

Figure 19.8

Implied volatility of the S&P 500 (VIX Index).

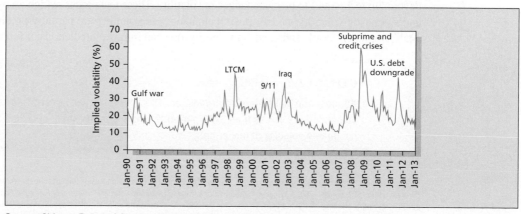

Source: Chicago Board of Options Exchange, http://www.cboe.com.

---

[10]For a recent review of this topic, see G. M. Constantinides, J. C. Jackwerth, and S. Perrakis, "Option Pricing: Real and Risk Neutral Distributions," in J. Birge and V. Linetsky, eds., *Handbooks in Operations Research and Management Science: Financial Engineering* (Amsterdam: Elsevier, 2007).

On the floor of the Chicago options exchange, those who trade in fear have seen little but calm. Measures of volatility in U.S. markets are pointing to relative calm, but some investors say the low readings are a sign of complacency. Unlike the rocky ride in the stock market since the U.S. presidential election, the Chicago Board Options Exchange's Volatility Index, or VIX, has registered tranquility. For four months, the so-called fear gauge of financial markets has traded below its two-decade historical average of 20, its longest such streak in more than five years.

Some investors worry that the low readings are a sign of complacency, and that the potential for further declines in response to unexpected bad news isn't reflected in stock prices. These investors say various barometers of skittishness could tick higher as the year-end deadline nears for an agreement on taxes and spending. That anxiety also would likely be reflected in increased volatility in the stock and commodities markets.

The VIX is an index calculated from the prices investors are willing to pay for options tied to the Standard & Poor's 500-stock index. As investors become nervous, they are willing to pay more for options, driving up the value of the VIX.

As market watchers search for clues about whether the relative calm can last, some of them are looking back to the early summer of 2011. Back then, the VIX was trading at levels close to today's, even though market pundits worried that lawmakers wouldn't agree to raise the debt ceiling. That scenario could have led the U.S. government to default on its debt.

Within a few weeks, as the debt-ceiling wrangling was going down to the wire, Standard & Poor's cut the U.S.'s long-term triple-A credit rating. The VIX nearly tripled to 48 in a span of two weeks.

"The whole situation leads me to believe that this lack of a cushion in the market will lead to wilder shocks" to markets if negative events happen, says Michael Palmer of Group One Trading who trades the VIX on the floor of the CBOE.

Source: Steven Russolillo and Kaitlyn Kiernan, "'Fear' Gauge Showing Little of It," *The Wall Street Journal*, November 26, 2012.

stock price swings in coming months. In this case, the article questioned the relatively low level of the VIX in light of tense political negotiations at the end of 2012 over the so-called fiscal cliff. The question was whether the price of the VIX contract indicated that investors were being too complacent about the potential for market disruption if those negotiations were to fail.

A futures contract on the 30-day implied volatility of the S&P 500 has traded on the CBOE Futures Exchange since 2004. The payoff of the contract depends on market implied volatility at the expiration of the contract. The ticker symbol of the contract is VIX.

Chicago Board
Options Exchange
www.cboe.com

Figure 19.8 also reveals an awkward empirical fact. While the Black-Scholes formula is derived assuming that stock volatility is constant, the time series of implied volatilities derived from that formula is in fact far from constant. This contradiction reminds us that the Black Scholes model (like all models) is a simplification that does not capture all aspects of real markets. In this particular context, extensions of the pricing model that allow stock volatility to evolve randomly over time would be desirable, and, in fact, many extensions of the model along these lines have been developed.[11]

The fact that volatility changes unpredictably means that it can be difficult to choose the proper volatility input to use in any option-pricing model. A considerable amount of recent research has been devoted to techniques to predict changes in volatility. These techniques, which go by the name ARCH and stochastic volatility models, posit that changes in volatility are partially predictable and that by analyzing recent levels and trends in volatility, one can improve predictions of future volatility.[12]

CC 8

CONCEPT CHECK ↗

Suppose the call option in Spreadsheet 19.1 is actually selling for $8. Is its implied volatility more or less than 27.83 percent? Use the spreadsheet and Goal Seek to find its implied volatility at this price.

[11]Influential articles on this topic are J. Hull and A. White, "The Pricing of Options on Assets with Stochastic Volatilities," *Journal of Finance*, June 1987, pp. 281–300; J. Wiggins, "Option Values Under Stochastic Volatility," *Journal of Financial Economics*, December 1987, pp. 351–72; and S. Heston, "A Closed-Form Solution for Options with Stochastic Volatility with Applications to Bonds and Currency Options," *Review of Financial Studies* 6 (1993), pp. 327–43. For a more recent review, see E. Ghysels, A. Harvey, and E. Renault, "Stochastic Volatility," in G. S. Maddala, ed., *Handbook of Statistics, Vol. 14: Statistical Methods in Finance* (Amsterdam: North Holland, 1996).
[12]For an introduction to these models, see C. Alexander, *Market Models* (Chichester, UK: Wiley, 2001).

Dividends and Call Option Valuation

We noted earlier that the Black-Scholes call option formula applies to stocks that do not pay dividends. When dividends are to be paid before the option expires, we need to adjust the formula. The payment of dividends raises the possibility of early exercise, and for most realistic dividend payout schemes the valuation formula becomes significantly more complex than the Black-Scholes equation.

We can apply some simple rules of thumb to approximate the option value, however. One popular approach, originally suggested by Black, calls for adjusting the stock price downward by the present value of any dividends that are to be paid before option expiration.[13] Therefore, we would simply replace S_0 with $S_0 -$ PV(dividends) in the Black-Scholes formula. Such an adjustment will take dividends into account by reflecting their eventual impact on the stock price. The option value then may be computed as before, assuming that the option will be held to expiration.

In one special case, the dividend adjustment takes a simple form. Suppose the underlying asset pays a continuous flow of income. This might be a reasonable assumption for options on a stock index, where different stocks in the index pay dividends on different days, so that dividend income arrives in a more or less continuous flow. If the dividend yield, denoted δ, is constant, one can show that the present value of that dividend flow accruing until the option maturity date is $S_0(1 - e^{-\delta T})$. (For intuition, notice that $e^{-\delta T}$ approximately equals $1 - \delta$, so the value of the dividend is approximately $\delta T S_0$.) In this case, $S_0 -$ PV(Div) $= S_0 e^{-\delta T}$, and we can derive a Black-Scholes call option formula on the dividend-paying asset simply by substituting $S_0 e^{-\delta T}$ for S_0 in the original formula. This approach is used in Spreadsheet 19.1.

These procedures would yield a very good approximation of option value for European call options that must be held until maturity, but they do not allow for the fact that the holder of an American call option might choose to exercise the option just before a dividend. The current value of a call option, assuming that it will be exercised just before the ex-dividend date, might be greater than the value of the option—assuming it will be held until maturity. Although holding the option until maturity allows greater effective time to expiration, which increases the option value, it also entails more dividend payments, lowering the expected stock price at maturity and thereby lowering the current option value.

For example, suppose that a stock selling at $20 will pay a $1 dividend in four months, whereas the call option on the stock does not expire for six months. The effective annual interest rate is 10 percent, so that the present value of the dividend is $\$1/(1.10)^{1/3} = \$.97$. Black suggests that we can compute the option value in one of two ways:

1. Apply the Black-Scholes formula assuming early exercise, thus using the actual stock price of $20 and a time to expiration of four months (the time until the dividend payment).

2. Apply the Black-Scholes formula assuming no early exercise, using the dividend-adjusted stock price of $20 - $.97 = $19.03 and a time to expiration of six months.

The greater of the two values is the estimate of the option value, recognizing that early exercise might be optimal. In other words, the so-called **pseudo-American call option value** is the maximum of the value derived by assuming that the option will be held until expiration and the value derived by assuming that the option will be exercised just before an ex-dividend date. Even this technique is not exact, however, for it assumes that the option holder makes an irrevocable decision now on when to exercise, when in fact the decision is not binding until exercise notice is given.[14]

---

[13]Fischer Black, "Fact and Fantasy in the Use of Options," *Financial Analysts Journal* 31 (July/August 1975).

[14]An exact formula for American call valuation on dividend-paying stocks has been developed in Richard Roll, "An Analytic Valuation Formula for Unprotected American Call Options on Stocks with Known Dividends," *Journal of Financial Economics* 5 (November 1977). The technique has been discussed and revised in Robert Geske, "A Note on an Analytical Formula for Unprotected American Call Options on Stocks with Known Dividends," *Journal of Financial Economics* 7 (December 1979); Robert E. Whaley, "On the Valuation of American Call Options on Stocks with Known Dividends," *Journal of Financial Economics* 9 (June 1981); and Giovanni Barone-Adesi and Robert E. Whaley, "Efficient Analytic Approximations of American Option Values," *Journal of Finance* 42, no. 2 (June 1987). These are difficult papers, however.

Put Option Valuation

We have concentrated so far on call option valuation. We can derive Black-Scholes European put option values from call option values using the put–call parity theorem. To value the put option, we simply calculate the value of the corresponding call option in equation 19.1 from the Black-Scholes formula, and solve for the put option value as

$$P = C + \text{PV}(X) - S_0 \tag{19.2}$$
$$= C + Xe^{-rT} - S_0$$

We must calculate the present value of the exercise price using continuous compounding to be consistent with the Black-Scholes formula.

Sometimes, it is easier to work with a put option valuation formula directly. If we substitute the Black-Scholes formula for a call in equation 19.2, we obtain the value of a European put option as

$$P = Xe^{-rT}[1 - N(d_2)] - S_0[1 - N(d_1)] \tag{19.3}$$

EXAMPLE 19.5   **Black-Scholes Put Valuation**

Using data from the Black-Scholes call option example ($C = \$13.70$; $X = \$95$; $S = \$100$; $r = .10$; and $T = .25$), we find that a European put option on that stock with identical exercise price and time to maturity is worth

$$P = \$13.70 + \$95e^{-.10 \times .25} - \$100 = \$6.35$$

As we noted traders can do, we might then compare this formula value to the actual put price as one step in formulating a trading strategy.

Equation 19.2 or 19.3 is valid for European puts on non-dividend-paying stocks. As we did for call options, if the underlying asset pays a dividend, we can find European put values by substituting $S_0 - \text{PV}(\text{dividends})$ for S_0. Cell E7 in Spreadsheet 19.1 allows for a continuous dividend flow with a dividend yield of d.

However, listed put options on stocks are American options that offer the opportunity of early exercise, and we have seen that the right to exercise puts early can turn out to be valuable. This means that an American option must be worth more than the corresponding European option. Therefore, equation 19.2 or 19.3 describes only the lower bound on the true value of the American put. However, in many applications the approximation is very accurate.[15]

19.5   ## USING THE BLACK-SCHOLES FORMULA

Hedge Ratios and the Black-Scholes Formula

In Chapter 18, Section 18.2, we considered two investments in FinCorp: 100 shares or 1,000 call options. We saw that the call option position was more sensitive to swings in the stock price than the all-stock position. To analyze the overall exposure to a stock price more precisely, however, it is necessary to quantify these relative sensitivities. We can summarize the overall exposure of

---

[15]For a more complete treatment of American put valuation, see R. Geske and H. E. Johnson, "The American Put Valued Analytically," *Journal of Finance* 39 (December 1984), pp. 1511–1524.

Figure 19.9

Call option value and hedge ratio.

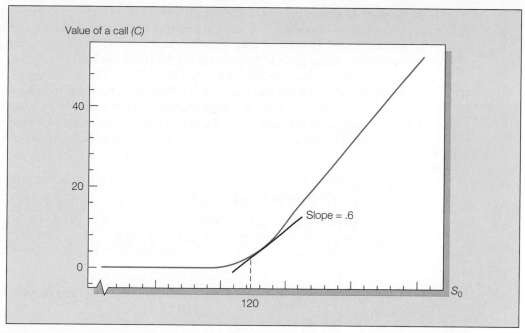

portfolios of options with various exercise prices and times to maturity using the **hedge ratio**, the change in option price for a $1 increase in the stock price. Therefore, a call option has a positive hedge ratio and a put option has a negative hedge ratio. The hedge ratio is commonly called the option's **delta**.

If you were to graph the option value as a function of the stock value as we have done for a call option in Figure 19.9, the hedge ratio is simply the slope of the value function evaluated at the current stock price. For example, suppose that the slope of the curve at $S_0 = \$120$ equals .60. As the stock increases in value by $1, the option increases by approximately $.60, as the figure shows.

For every call option written, .60 shares of stock would be needed to hedge the investor's portfolio. If one writes 10 options and holds six shares of stock, according to the hedge ratio of .6, a $1 increase in stock price will result in a gain of $6 on the stock holdings, whereas the loss on the 10 options written will be $10 \times \$0.60$, an equivalent $6. The stock price movement leaves total wealth unaltered, which is what a hedged position is required to do.

Black-Scholes hedge ratios are particularly easy to compute. It turns out that the hedge ratio for a call is $N(d_1)$, and the hedge ratio for a put is $N(d_1) - 1$. We defined $N(d_1)$ as part of the Black-Scholes formula (equation 19.1). Recall that $N(d)$ stands for the area under the standard normal curve up to d. Therefore, the call option hedge ratio must be positive and less than 1, whereas the put option hedge ratio is negative and of smaller absolute value than 1.

Figure 19.9 verifies that the slope of the call option valuation function is indeed less than 1, approaching 1 only as the stock price becomes much greater than the exercise price. This tells us that option values change less than one-for-one with changes in stock prices. Why should this be? Suppose that an option is so far in the money that you are absolutely certain it will be exercised. In that case, every dollar increase in the stock price would indeed increase the option value by $1. However, if there is a reasonable chance that the call option will expire out of the money even after a moderate stock price gain, a $1 increase in the stock price will not necessarily increase the ultimate payoff to the call; therefore, the call price will not respond by a full dollar.

The fact that hedge ratios are less than 1 does not conflict with our earlier observation that options offer leverage and are quite sensitive to stock price movements. Although *dollar* movements in option prices are slighter than dollar movements in the stock price, the *rate of return* volatility of options remains greater than stock return volatility because options sell at smaller prices. In our example, with the stock selling at $120 and a hedge ratio of .6, an option with exercise price $120 may sell for $5. If the stock price increases to $121, the call price would be expected to increase by only $.60, to $5.60. The percentage increase in the option value is $.60/$5 = 12 percent, however, whereas the stock price increase is only $1/$120 = .83 percent. The ratio of the percentage changes is 12 percent/.83 percent = 14.4. For every 1 percent increase in the stock price, the option price increases by 14.4 percent. This ratio, the percent change in option price per percent change in stock price, is called the **option elasticity**.

CC 9

CONCEPT CHECK

What is the elasticity of a put option currently selling for $4 with exercise price $120 and hedge ratio −.4, if the stock price is currently $122?

The hedge ratio is an essential tool in portfolio management and control.[16] An example will illustrate.

EXAMPLE 19.6   Hedge Ratios

Consider two portfolios, one holding 750 FinCorp calls and 200 shares of FinCorp, and the other holding 800 shares of FinCorp. Which portfolio has greater dollar exposure to FinCorp price movements? You can answer this question easily using the hedge ratio.

Each option changes in value by H dollars for each dollar change in stock price, where H stands for the hedge ratio. Thus, if H equals .6, the 750 options are equivalent to 450 (.6 × 750) shares in terms of the response of their market value to FinCorp stock price movements. The first portfolio has less dollar sensitivity to FinCorp, because the 450 share-equivalents of the options plus the 200 shares actually held are less than the 800 shares held in the second portfolio.

This is not to say, however, that the first portfolio is less sensitive to FinCorp in terms of its rate of return. As we noted in discussing option elasticities, the first portfolio may be of lower total value than the second, so despite its lower sensitivity in terms of total market value, it might have greater rate of return sensitivity. Because a call option has a lower market value than the stock, its price changes more than proportionally with stock price changes, even though its hedge ratio is less than 1.

Portfolio Insurance

In Chapter 18 we showed that protective put strategies offer a sort of insurance policy on an asset. The protective put has proved to be extremely popular with investors. Even if the asset price falls, the put conveys the right to sell the asset for the exercise price, which is a way to lock in a minimum portfolio value. With an at-the-money put ($X = S_0$), the maximum loss that can be realized is the cost of the put. The asset can be sold for X, which equals its original value, so even if the asset price falls, the investor's net loss over the period is just the cost of the put. If the asset

---

[16]See the comments by T. Higgins in "The Long and Short of Volatility," *Canadian Investment Review*, Spring 2004, p. R19.

Black-Scholes Option Valuation

The spreadsheet below can be used to determine option values using the Black-Scholes model. The inputs are the stock price, standard deviation, expiration of the option, exercise price, risk-free rate, and dividend yield. The call option is valued using equation 19.1 and the put is valued using equation 19.3. For both calls and puts, the dividend-adjusted Black-Scholes formula substitutes $Se^{-\delta T}$ for S, as outlined earlier under "Dividends and Call Option Valuation." The model also calculates the intrinsic and time value for both puts and calls.

Further, the model presents sensitivity analysis using the one-way data table. The first workbook presents the analysis of calls while the second workbook presents similar analysis for puts.

Questions

1. Find the value of the call and put options using the parameters given in this box but changing the standard deviation to .25. What happens to the value of each option?

2. What is implied volatility if the call option is selling for $9?

	A	B	C	D	E	F	G	H	I	J	K	L	M	N
1	Black-Scholes Option Pricing						LEGEND:							
2	Call Valuation & Call Time Premiums						Enter data							
3							Value calculated							
4							See comment							
5	Standard deviation (s)	0.27830												
6	Variance (annual, s^2)	0.07745			Call			Call			Call			Call
7	Time to expiration (years, T)	0.50		Standard	Option		Standard	Time		Stock	Option		Stock	Time
8	Risk-free rate (annual, r)	6.00%		Deviation	Value		Deviation	Value		Price	Value		Price	Value
9	Current stock price (S_0)	$100.00			7.000			7.000			7.000			7.000
10	Exercise price (X)	$105.00		0.15	3.388		0.150	3.388		$60	0.017		$60	0.017
11	Dividend yield (annual, d)	0.00%		0.18	4.089		0.175	4.089		$65	0.061		$65	0.061
12				0.20	4.792		0.200	4.792		$70	0.179		$70	0.179
13	d_1	0.0029095		0.23	5.497		0.225	5.497		$75	0.440		$75	0.440
14	d_2	−0.193878		0.25	6.202		0.250	6.202		$80	0.935		$80	0.935
15	$N(d_1)$	0.50116		0.28	6.907		0.275	6.907		$85	1.763		$85	1.763
16	$N(d_2)$	0.42314		0.30	7.612		0.300	7.612		$90	3.014		$90	3.014
17	Black-Scholes call value	$6.99992		0.33	8.317		0.325	8.317		$95	4.750		$95	4.750
18	Black-Scholes put value	$8.89670		0.35	9.022		0.350	9.022		$100	7.000		$100	7.000
19				0.38	9.726		0.375	9.726		$105	9.754		$105	9.754
20				0.40	10.429		0.400	10.429		$110	12.974		$110	7.974
21	Intrinsic value of call	$0.00000		0.43	11.132		0.425	11.132		$115	16.602		$115	6.602
22	Time value of call	6.99992		0.45	11.834		0.450	11.834		$120	20.572		$120	5.572
23				0.48	12.536		0.475	12.536		$125	24.817		$125	4.817
24	Intrinsic value of put	$5.00000		0.50	13.236		0.500	13.236		$130	29.275		$130	4.275
25	Time value of put	3.89670								$135.00	33.893		$135	3.893

value increases, however, upside potential is unlimited. Figure 19.10 graphs the profit or loss on a protective put position as a function of the change in the value of the underlying asset.

Although the protective put is a simple and convenient way to achieve **portfolio insurance**, that is, to limit the worst-case rate of return, there are practical difficulties in trying to insure a portfolio of stocks. First, unless the investor's portfolio corresponds to a standard market index for which puts are traded, a put option on the portfolio will not be available for purchase. In addition, if index puts are used to protect a non-indexed portfolio, tracking errors can result. For example, if the portfolio falls in value while the market index rises, the put will fail to provide the intended protection. Moreover, the maturities of traded options may not match the investor's horizon. Therefore rather than using option strategies, investors may use trading strategies that mimic the payoff to a protective put option.

Here is the general idea. Even if a put option on the desired portfolio with the desired expiration date does not exist, a theoretical option pricing model (such as the Black-Scholes model) can be used to determine how that option's price would respond to the portfolio's value if the option did in fact trade. For example, if stock prices were to fall, the put option would increase in value. The option model could quantify this relationship. The next exposure of the (hypothetical) protective put portfolio

Figure 19.10

Profit on a protective put strategy.

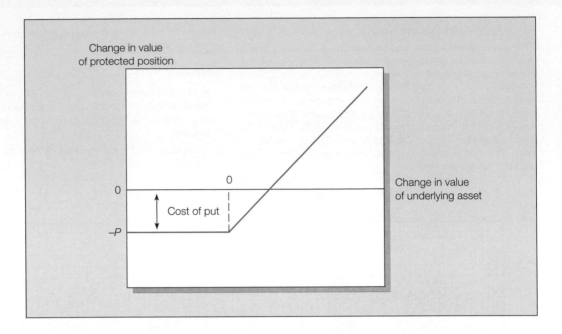

to swings in stock prices is the sum of the exposures of the two components of the portfolio, the stock and the put. The net exposure of the portfolio equals the equity exposure less the (offsetting) put option exposure. We can create "synthetic" protective put positions by holding a quantity of stocks with the same net exposure to market swings as the hypothetical protective put position.

We can create "synthetic" protective put positions by holding a quantity of stocks with the same net exposure to market swings as the hypothetical protective put position. The key to this strategy is the option's delta or hedge ratio, that is, the change in the price of the protective put option per change in the value of the underlying stock portfolio.

EXAMPLE 19.7   **Synthetic Protective Put Options**

Suppose that a portfolio is currently valued at $100 million. An at-the-money put option on the portfolio might have a hedge ratio or delta of −.6, meaning that the option's value swings $.60 for every dollar change in portfolio value, but in an opposite direction. Suppose the stock portfolio falls in value by 2 percent. The profit on a hypothetical protective put position (if the put existed) would be as follows (in millions of dollars):

Loss on stocks: 2% of $100	= $2.00
Gain on put: .6 × $2	= $1.20
Net loss	= $ .80

We create the synthetic option position by selling a proportion of shares equal to the put option's delta (i.e., selling 60 percent of the shares), and placing the proceeds in risk-free T-bills. The rationale is that the hypothetical put option would have offset 60 percent of any change in the stock portfolio's value, so one must reduce portfolio risk directly by selling off

continued

60 percent of the equity and putting the proceeds into a risk-free asset. Total return on a synthetic protective put position with $60 million in risk-free investments, such as T-bills, and $40 million in equity is:

Loss on stocks: 2% of $40	= $.80
Loss on bills	= 0
Net loss	= $.80

The synthetic and actual protective put positions have equal returns. We conclude that if you sell a proportion of shares equal to the put option's delta and place the proceeds in cash equivalents, your exposure to the stock market will equal that of the desired protective put position.

The difficulty with this procedure is that deltas constantly change. Figure 19.11 shows that, as the stock price falls, the magnitude of the appropriate hedge ratio increases. Therefore, market declines require extra hedging, that is, additional conversions of equity into cash. This constant updating of the hedge ratio is called **dynamic hedging** or **delta hedging**.

Dynamic hedging is one reason portfolio insurance has been said to contribute to market volatility. Market declines trigger additional sales of stock as portfolio insurers strive to increase their hedging. These additional sales are seen as reinforcing or exaggerating market downturns.

In practice, portfolio insurers often do not actually buy or sell stocks directly when they update their hedge positions. Instead, they minimize trading costs by buying or selling stock index futures as a substitute for sale of the stocks themselves. As you will see in the following chapter, stock prices and index futures prices usually are very tightly linked by cross-market arbitrageurs so that

Figure 19.11

Hedge ratios change as the stock price fluctuates.

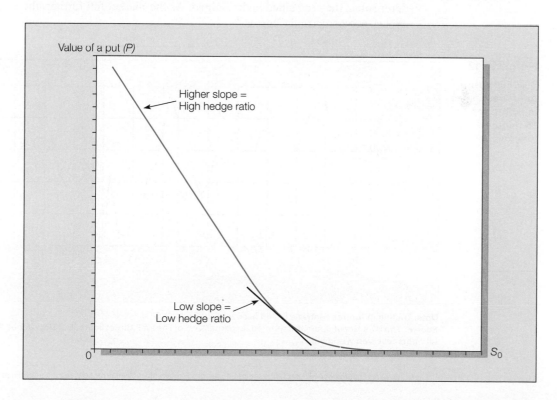

Value of a put (P)

Higher slope = High hedge ratio

Low slope = Low hedge ratio

S_0

futures transactions can be used as reliable proxies for stock transactions. Instead of selling equities based on the put option's delta, insurers will sell an equivalent number of futures contracts.[17]

Several U.S. portfolio insurers suffered great setbacks on October 19, 1987, when the market suffered an unprecedented one-day loss of about 20 percent. A description of what happened then should let you appreciate the complexities of applying a seemingly straightforward hedging concept:

1. Market volatility was much greater than ever encountered before. Put option deltas based on historical experience were too low, and insurers underhedged, held too much equity, and suffered excessive losses.

2. Prices moved so fast that insurers could not keep up with the necessary rebalancing. They were chasing deltas that kept getting away from them. In addition, the futures market saw a "gap" opening, where the opening price was nearly 10 percent below the previous day's close. The price dropped before insurers could update their hedge ratios.

3. Execution problems were severe. First, current market prices were unavailable, with the trade execution and price quotation system hours behind, which made computation of correct hedge ratios impossible. Moreover, trading in stocks and stock futures ceased altogether during some periods. The continuous rebalancing capability that is essential for a viable insurance program simply vanished during the precipitous market collapse.

4. Futures prices traded at steep discounts to their proper levels compared to reported stock prices, thereby making the sale of futures (as a proxy for equity sales) to increase hedging seem expensive. Although we will see in the next chapter that stock index futures prices normally exceed the value of the stock index, Figure 19.12 shows that on October 19, 1987, futures sold far below the stock index level. The so-called cash-to-futures spread was negative most of the day. When some insurers gambled that the futures price would recover to its usual premium over the stock index and chose to defer sales, they remained underhedged. As the market fell further, their portfolios experienced substantial losses.

Figure 19.12

S&P 500 cash-to-futures spread in points at 15-minute intervals.

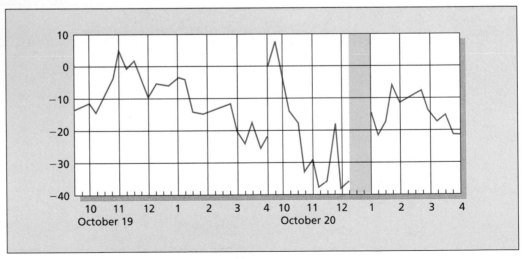

Note: Trading in futures contracts halted between 12:15 and 1:05.
Source: *The Wall Street Journal.* Reprinted by permission of The Wall Street Journal, © Dow Jones & Company Inc. All rights reserved worldwide.

---

[17]Notice, however, that the use of index futures reintroduces the problem of tracking error between the portfolio and the market index.

Although most observers believe that the portfolio insurance industry will never recover from the market crash, delta hedging is still alive and well on Wall Street. Dynamic hedges are widely used by large firms to hedge potential losses from options positions. For example, the nearby box notes that when Microsoft ended its employee stock option program and J. P. Morgan purchased many already-issued options of Microsoft employees, it was widely expected that Morgan would protect its options position by selling Microsoft stock in accordance with a delta-hedging strategy.

Option Pricing and the Crisis of 2008–2009

Merton[18] shows how option pricing models can provide insight into the financial crisis of 2008–2009. The key to understanding his argument is to remember that when banks lend to or buy the debt of firms with limited liability, they implicitly write a put option to the borrower (see Chapter 18, Section 18.5). If the borrower has sufficient assets to pay off the loan when it comes due, it will do so, and the lender will be fully repaid. But if the borrower has insufficient assets, it can declare bankruptcy and discharge its obligations by transferring ownership of the firm to its creditors. The borrower's ability to satisfy the loan by transferring ownership is equivalent to the right to "sell" itself to the creditor for the face value of the loan. This arrangement is therefore just like a put option on the firm with exercise price equal to the stipulated loan repayment.

Consider the payoff to the lender at loan maturity (time T) as a function of the value of the borrowing firm, V_T, when the loan, with face value L, comes due. If $V_T \geq L$, the lender is paid off in full. But if $V_T < L$, the lender gets the firm, which is worth less than the promised payment L.

We can write the payoff in a way that emphasizes the implicit put option:

$$\text{Payoff} = \begin{cases} L \\ V_T \end{cases} = L - \begin{cases} 0 & \text{if } V_T \geq L \\ L - V_T & \text{if } V_T < L \end{cases} \tag{19.4}$$

---

[18]This material is based on a lecture given by Robert Merton at MIT in March 2009. You can find the lecture online at http://mitworld.mit.edu/video/659.

Figure 19.13

Value of implicit put option on a loan guarantee as a percentage of the face value of debt. Debt maturity = 1 year; standard deviation of value of firm = 40%; risk-free rate = 6%.

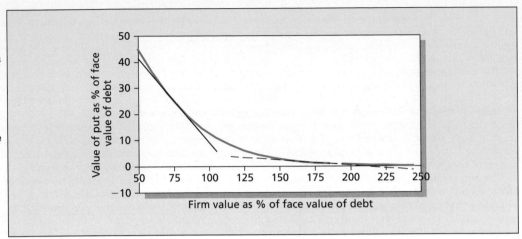

This equation shows that the payoff on the loan equals L (when the firm has sufficient assets to pay off the debt), *minus* the payoff of a put option on the value of the firm (V_T) with an exercise price of L. Therefore, we may view risky lending as a combination of safe lending, with a guaranteed payoff of L, combined with a short position in a put option on the borrower.

When firms sell credit default swaps (see Chapter 12, Section 12.5), the implicit put option is even clearer. Here, the CDS seller agrees to make up any losses due to the insolvency of a bond issuer. If the issuer goes bankrupt, leaving assets of only V_T for the creditors, the CDS seller is obligated to make up the difference, $L - V_T$. This is in essence a pure put option.

Now think about the exposure of these implicit put writers to changes in the financial health of the underlying firm. The value of a put option on V_T appears in Figure 19.13. When the firm is financially strong (i.e., V is far greater than L), the slope of the curve is nearly zero, implying that there is little exposure of the implicit put writer (either the bank or the CDS writer) to the value of the borrowing firm. For example, when firm value is 1.75 times the value of the debt, the dashed line drawn tangent to the put value curve has a slope of only $-.040$. But if there is a big shock to the economy, and firm value falls, not only does the value of the implicit put rise, but its slope is now steeper, implying that exposure to further shocks is now far greater. When firm value is only 75 percent of the value of the loan, the slope of the line tangent to the put value valuation curve is far steeper, $-.644$. You can see how as you get closer to the edge of the cliff, it gets easier and easier to slide right off.

We often hear people say that a shock to asset values of the magnitude of the financial crisis was a 10-sigma event, by which they mean that such an event was so extreme that it would be 10 standard deviations away from an expected outcome, making it virtually inconceivable. But this analysis shows that standard deviation may be a moving target, increasing dramatically as the firm weakens. As the economy falters and put options go further into the money, their sensitivity to further shocks increases, increasing the risk that even worse losses may be around the corner. The built-in instability of risk exposures makes a scenario like the crisis more plausible and should give us pause when we discount an extreme scenario as "almost impossible."

Option Pricing and Portfolio Theory

We've just seen that the option pricing model predicts that security risk characteristics can be unstable. For example, as the firm weakens, the risk of its debt can quickly accelerate. So too can equity risk change dramatically as the firm's financial condition deteriorates. We know from the last chapter (Section 17.5) that equity in a levered firm is like a call option on the value of the

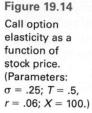

Figure 19.14

Call option elasticity as a function of stock price. (Parameters: $\sigma = .25$; $T = .5$, $r = .06$; $X = 100$.)

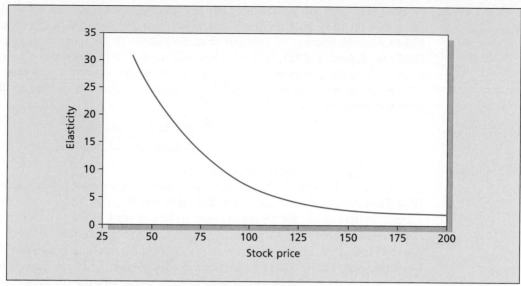

firm. If firm value exceeds the value of the firm's maturing debt, the firm can choose to pay off the debt, retaining the difference between firm value and the face value of its debt. If not, the firm can default on the loan, turning the firm over to its creditors, and the equity holders get nothing. In this sense, equity is a call option, and the firm's total value is the underlying asset.

In Section 19.5, we saw that the *elasticity* of an option measures the sensitivity of its rate of return to the rate of return on the underlying asset. For example, if a call option's elasticity is five, its rate of return will swing five times as widely as the rate of return on the underlying asset. This would imply that both the option's beta and its standard deviation are five times the beta and standard deviation of the underlying asset.

Therefore, when compiling the "input list" for creating an efficient portfolio, we may wish to think of equity as an implicit call option and compute its elasticity with respect to the total value of the firm. For example, if the covariance of the firm's *assets* with other securities is stable, then we can use elasticity to find the covariance of the firm's *equity* with those securities. This will allow us to calculate beta and standard deviation.

Unfortunately, elasticity can itself be a moving target. As the firm gets weaker, its elasticity will increase, potentially very quickly. Figure 19.14 uses the Black-Scholes model to plot call option elasticity as a function of the value of the underlying stock. Notice that as the option goes out of the money (the stock price falls below 100), elasticity increases rapidly and without limit. Similarly, as the firm gets closer to insolvency (the value of firm assets falls below the face value of debt), equity elasticity shoots up, and even small changes in financial condition can lead to major changes in risk. Elasticity is far more stable (and closer to 1) when the firm is healthy, that is, the implicit call option is deep in the money. Similarly, equity risk characteristics will be far more stable for healthy firms than for precarious ones.

Hedging Bets on Mispriced Options

Suppose you believe that the standard deviation of IBM stock returns will be 35 percent over the next few weeks, but IBM put options are selling at a price consistent with a volatility of 33 percent. Because the put's implied volatility is less than your forecast of the stock volatility, you believe the option is underpriced. Using your assessment of volatility in an option-pricing model like the Black-Scholes formula, you would estimate that the fair price for the puts exceeds the actual price.

Does this mean that you ought to buy put options? Perhaps it does, but by doing so, you risk great losses if IBM stock performs well, *even if* you are correct about the volatility. You would like to separate your bet on volatility from the "attached" bet inherent in purchasing a put that IBM's stock price will fall. In other words, you would like to speculate on the option mispricing by purchasing the put option, but hedge the resulting exposure to the performance of IBM stock.

The option *delta* can be interpreted as a hedge ratio that can be used for this purpose. The delta was defined as

$$\text{Delta} = \frac{\text{Change in value of option}}{\text{Change in value of stock}}$$

Therefore, delta is the slope of the option-pricing curve.

This ratio tells us precisely how many shares of stock we must hold to offset our exposure to IBM. For example, if the delta is $-.6$, then the put will fall by \$.60 in value for every one-point increase in IBM stock, and we need to hold .6 share of stock to hedge each put. If we purchase 10 option contracts, each for 100 shares, we would need to buy 600 shares of stock. If the stock price rises by \$1, each put option will decrease in value by \$.60, resulting in a loss of \$600. However, the loss on the puts will be offset by a gain on the stock holdings of \$1 per share $\times$ 600 shares.

To see how the profits on this strategy might develop, let's use the following example.

EXAMPLE 19.8   **Speculating on Mispriced Options**

Option maturity, T	60 days
Put price, P	\$4.495
Exercise price, X	\$90
Stock price, S	\$90
Risk-free rate, r	4%

We assume that the stock will not pay a dividend in the next 60 days. Given these data, the implied volatility on the option is 33 percent, as we posited. However, you believe the true volatility is 35 percent, implying that the fair put price is \$4.785. Therefore, if the market assessment of volatility is revised to the value you believe is correct, your profit will be \$.29 per put purchased.

Recall that the hedge ratio, or delta, of a put option equals $N(d_1) - 1$, where $N(\bullet)$ is the cumulative normal distribution function and

$$d_1 = \frac{\ln(S/X) + (r + \sigma^2/2)T}{\sigma\sqrt{T}}$$

Using your estimate of $\sigma = .35$, you find that the hedge ratio $N(d_1) - 1 - .453$.

Suppose, therefore, that you purchase 10 option contracts (1,000 puts) and purchase 453 shares of stock. Once the market "catches up" to your presumably better volatility estimate, the put options purchased will increase in value. If the market assessment of volatility changes as soon as you purchase the options, your profits should equal $1,000 \times \$.29 = \$290$. The option price will be affected as well by any change in the stock price, but this part of your exposure will be eliminated if the hedge ratio is chosen properly. Your profit should be based solely on the effect of the change in the implied volatility of the put, with the impact of the stock price hedged away.

Table 19.2 illustrates your profits as a function of the stock price assuming that the put price changes to reflect *your* estimate of volatility. Panel B shows that the put option alone can provide profits or losses depending on whether the stock price falls or rises. We see in panel C, however, that each *hedged* put option provides profits nearly equal to the original mispricing, regardless of the change in the stock price.

TABLE 19.2

Profit on Hedged Put Portfolio

A. Cost to Establish Hedged Position

1,000 put options @ $4.495/option	$ 4,495
453 shares @ $90/share	40,770
Total outlay	$45,265

B. Value of Put Option as a Function of the Stock Price at Implied Volatility of 35%

Stock Price:	89	90	91
Put price	$5.254	$4.785	$4.347
Profit (loss) on each put	.759	.290	(.148)

C. Value of and Profit on Hedged Put Portfolio

Stock Price:	89	90	91
Value of 1,000 put options	$ 5,254	$ 4,785	$ 4,347
Value of 453 shares	40,317	40,770	41,223
Total	$45,571	$45,555	$45,570
Profit (= Value − Cost from panel A)	306	290	305

CC 10

CONCEPT CHECK

Suppose you bet on volatility by purchasing calls instead of puts. How would you hedge your exposure to stock-price fluctuations? What is the hedge ratio?

Notice in Example 19.8 that the profit is not exactly independent of the stock price. This is because as the stock price changes, so do the deltas used to calculate the hedge ratio. The hedge ratio in principle would need to be continually adjusted as deltas evolve. The sensitivity of the delta to the stock price is called the **gamma** of the option. Option gammas are analogous to bond convexity. In both cases, the curvature of the value function means that hedge ratios or durations change with market conditions, making rebalancing a necessary part of hedging strategies.

A variant of this strategy in Example 19.8 involves cross-option speculation. Suppose you observe a 45-day maturity call option on IBM with strike price 95 selling at a price consistent with a volatility of $\sigma = 33$ percent while another 45-day call with strike price 90 has an implied volatility of only 27 percent. Because the underlying asset and maturity date are identical, you conclude that the call with the higher implied volatility is relatively overpriced. To exploit the mispricing, you might buy the cheap calls (with strike price 90 and implied volatility of 27 percent) and write the expensive calls (with strike price 95 and implied volatility 33 percent). If the risk-free rate is 4 percent and IBM is selling at $90 per share, the calls purchased will be priced at $3.6202 and the calls written will be priced at $2.3735.

Despite the fact that you are long one call and short another, your exposure to IBM stock-price uncertainty will not be hedged using this strategy. This is because calls with different strike prices have different sensitivities to the price of the underlying asset. The lower-strike-price call has a higher delta and therefore greater exposure to the price of IBM. If you take an equal number of positions in these two options, you will inadvertently establish a bullish position in IBM, as the calls you purchase have higher deltas than the calls you write. In fact, you may recall from Chapter 18 that this portfolio (long call with low exercise price and short call with high exercise price) is called a *bullish spread*.

To establish a hedged position, we can use the hedge ratio approach as follows. Consider the 95-strike-price options you write as the asset that hedges your exposure to the 90-strike-price options your purchase. Then the hedge ratio is

$$H = \frac{\text{Change in value of 90-strike-price call for \$1 change in IBM}}{\text{Change in value of 95-strike-price call for \$1 change in IBM}}$$

$$= \frac{\text{Delta of 90-strike-price call}}{\text{Delta of 95-strike-price call}} > 1$$

You need to write *more* than one call with the higher strike price to hedge the purchase of each call with the lower strike price. Because the prices of higher-strike-price calls are less sensitive to IBM prices, more of them are required to offset the exposure.

Suppose the true annual volatility of the stock is midway between the two implied volatilities, so $\sigma = 30$ percent. We know that the delta of a call option is $N(d_1)$. Therefore, the deltas of the two options and the hedge ratio are computed as follows:

Option with strike price 90:

$$d_1 = \frac{\ln(90/90) + (.04 + .30^2/2) \times 45/365}{.30\sqrt{45/365}} = .0995$$

$$N(d_1) = .5396$$

Option with strike price 95:

$$d_1 = \frac{\ln(90/95) + (.04 + .30^2/2) \times 45/365}{.30\sqrt{45/365}} = -.4138$$

$$N(d_1) = .3395$$

Hedge ratio:

$$\frac{.5396}{.3395} = 1.589$$

Therefore, for every 1,000 call options purchased with strike price 90, we need to write 1,589 call options with strike price 95. Following this strategy enables us to bet on the relative mispricing of the two options without taking a position on IBM. Panel A of Table 19.3 shows that the position will result in a cash inflow of $151.30. The premium income on the calls written exceeds the cost of the calls purchased.

When you establish a position in stocks and options that is hedged with respect to fluctuations in the price of the underlying asset, your portfolio is said to be **delta-neutral**, meaning that the portfolio has no tendency to either increase or decrease in value when the stock price fluctuates.

Let's check that our options position is in fact delta-neutral. Suppose that the implied volatilities of the two options come back into alignment just after you establish your position, so that both options are priced at implied volatilities of 30 percent. You expect to profit from the increase in the value of the call purchased as well as from the decrease in the value of the call written. The option prices at 30 percent volatility are given in panel B of Table 19.3 and the values of your position for various stock prices are presented in panel C. Although the profit or loss on each option is affected by the stock price, the value of the delta-neutral option portfolio is positive and essentially independent of the price of IBM. Moreover, we saw in panel A that the portfolio would have been established without ever requiring a cash outlay. You would have cash inflows both when you establish the portfolio *and* when you liquidate it after the implied volatilities converge to 30 percent.

This unusual profit opportunity arises because you have identified prices out of alignment. Such opportunities could not arise if prices were at equilibrium levels. By exploiting the pricing

TABLE 19.3
Profits on Delta-Neutral Options Portfolio

A. Cash Flow When Portfolio Is Established

Purchase 1,000 calls ($X = 90$) @ $3.6202
(option priced at implied volatility of 27%) $3,620.20 cash outflow
Write 1,589 calls ($X = 95$) @ $2.3735
(option priced at implied volatility of 27%)   3,771.50 cash inflow
   Total $ 151.30 net cash inflow

B. Option Prices at Implied Volatility of 30%

Stock Price:	89	90	91
90-strike-price calls	$3.478	$3.997	$4.557
95-strike-price calls	1.703	2.023	2.382

C. Value of Portfolio After Implied Volatilities Converge to 30%

Stock Price:	89	90	91
Value of 1,000 calls held	$3,478	$3,997	$4,557
−Value of 1,589 calls written	2,705	3,214	3,785
Total	$ 773	$ 783	$ 772

discrepancy using a delta-neutral strategy, you should earn profits regardless of the price movement in IBM stock.

Delta-neutral hedging strategies are also subject to practical problems, the most important of which is the difficulty in assessing the proper volatility for the coming period. If the volatility estimate is incorrect, so will be the deltas, and the overall position will not truly be hedged. Moreover, option or option-plus-stock positions generally will not be neutral with respect to changes in volatility. For example, a put option hedged by a stock might be delta-neutral, but it is not volatility neutral. Changes in the market assessments of volatility will affect the option price even if the stock price is unchanged.

These problems can be serious, because volatility estimates are never fully reliable. First, volatility cannot be observed directly, and must be estimated from past data which imparts measurement error to the forecast. Second, we've seen that both historical and implied volatilities fluctuate over time. Therefore, we are always shooting at a moving target. Although delta-neutral positions are hedged against changes in the price of the underlying asset, they still are subject to **volatility risk**, the risk incurred from unpredictable changes in volatility. The sensitivity of an option price to changes in volatility is called the option's **vega**. Thus, although delta-neutral option hedges might eliminate exposure to risk from fluctuations in the value of the underlying asset, they do not eliminate volatility risk.

19.6   STOCHASTIC DOMINANCE OPTION PRICING

Complete and Incomplete Markets

The binomial model described in Section 19.3 assumes that in every subinterval the stock price can take exactly two possible values, up or down by given amounts. We saw that in such a model it is possible to replicate the option with a portfolio containing exactly two assets, the stock and a riskless loan at the prevailing rate of interest. This correspondence of available assets and possible stock values in every subinterval is crucial to the use of the model for option pricing.

Consider again the example of Section 19.3, in which a stock that sells at $100 can by yearend either double to $200 or be cut in half to $50. Now, however, suppose that there is also a third possibility, that the stock keeps the original price of $100. If the interest rate is 8 percent, can we still use the replication method to value the option with exercise price of $125 and one year time to expiration?

The answer to this question is no. At year-end, the option payoff is either zero if the stock falls or stays the same or $75 if it rises. The portfolio that we examined in the previous section, with one share of the stock and borrowing of $46.30 at 8 percent, now yields the following contingent payoffs:

Value of stock	$50	$100	$200
Repayment of loan with interest	−50	−50	−50
Total	$ 0	$ 50	$150

The holder of this portfolio would get twice the option value when the stock goes up or down, *plus* $50 whenever the stock stays the same. Hence, the value of the portfolio can no longer be equal to twice that of the option, since it is clearly greater.

In fact, it can be shown that there is no portfolio involving only the stock and borrowed funds capable of replicating this option. Suppose that a replicating portfolio contains x shares and y of borrowed funds. Its future value must be equal to that of the option for all possible values of the stock. This means that

$$50x - 1.08y = 0, \ 100x - 1.08y = 0, \ 200x - 1.08y = 75$$

This system has no solution, since it has three equations and only two unknowns. This implies that there is no portfolio capable of replicating the option. The reason for this is that there are more possible future values of the stock than there are assets to form a replicating portfolio.

In the binomial model, there are only two future "states of the world" as far as the stock price is concerned. In our example, the stock can only go down to $50 (state 1), or up to $200 (state 2). Suppose also that we have two assets, also numbered 1 and 2, each one of them yielding a payoff equal to $1 if the corresponding state occurs, and 0 otherwise; their respective values are v_1 and v_2. These assets are known as *elementary* or *primitive* securities, and they are a very convenient analytical tool in valuing options or other derivative assets.

With these elementary assets we now can replicate every other asset in our binomial model. Thus, the stock is equivalent to a portfolio of 50 units of asset 1 and 200 units of asset 2, and any riskless investment corresponds to portfolios having equal numbers of units of assets 1 and 2. This helps us determine the two elementary assets' values, v_1 and v_2:

$$50v_1 + 200v_2 = 100$$
$$v_1 + v_2 = 1/1.08$$

Solving this system, we find $v_1 = .5679$, and $v_2 = .358$. With these prices it is now very easy to price the option with exercise price $125: it is simply equal to $75v_2 = 75 \times .358 = 26.85$, which is the value found in the previous section.

We now can see why the notion of replication can be applied to the binomial model but breaks down when there is a third "state of the world." In such a case we have three elementary assets, each one paying $1 when the corresponding state of the world occurs, and zero otherwise. Let us number them 1, 2, and 3, corresponding to the ascending order of future stock price, and denote their corresponding values by v_1, v_2, and v_3; then one share would be equivalent to a portfolio of 50 units of asset 1, 100 units of asset 2, and 200 units of asset 3.

However, we now have only *two* equations to determine the three unknown elementary asset values v_1, v_2, and v_3:

$$50v_1 + 100v_2 + 200v_3 = 100$$
$$v_1 + v_2 + v_3 = 1/1.08 \qquad (19.5)$$

Here, the observable stock price and rate of interest are insufficient to give us unique values of the three elementary assets. There are more states of the world (and, hence, elementary assets) than there are observable assets. This indeterminacy is the mirror image of the impossibility to find a portfolio replicating a given option.

A market that has as many independent observable assets as there are future states of the world is said to be *complete*. By contrast, **incomplete markets** are those that have fewer such assets than there are states of the world; real-world markets generally are assumed to be incomplete.[19] The binomial model is the only complete market model if our states of the world are classified by a stock's future payoffs and if we observe only the optioned stock and the riskless rate of interest.

Generalizing the Binomial Option Pricing Model

A unique set of elementary asset values consistent with the observed stock price and rate of interest does not exist in incomplete markets. Consequently, a unique option price cannot be derived by the replication method. For instance, there are infinitely many values of v_3, the elementary asset that pays $1 when the stock goes up and zero otherwise, that satisfy the two equations of equation 19.5 corresponding to the stock price and rate of interest. Each one of these v_3 values would yield a different value of the option with exercise price equal to $125, since the option's payoff is zero in all other states of the world.

This indeterminacy is rather disturbing, given that a stock price model with three (or more) states is otherwise very similar to the two-state model. In both types of models we can subdivide the year into progressively finer subintervals, approaching at the limit *the same* lognormal distribution. For such a distribution, the appropriate option value is given by the Black-Scholes formula. Do all admissible option values, derived from the values of v_3 satisfying the two equations in equation 19.5 similarly approach the Black-Scholes option price at the limit?

The answer is again no. While there are infinitely many option values consistent with the observed stock price and rate of interest, only a given subset of them, contained between an upper and a lower bound, converge at the limit to the Black-Scholes option value. The two bounds are known as *stochastic dominance bounds* on option prices. They constitute, therefore, the appropriate generalization of the binomial model when the number of possible future stock prices exceeds two.

The two bounds that define the appropriate option values depend not only on the size of the future stock prices, but also on their probabilities. Suppose, for instance, that in our previous example the stock price either could double or be cut in half, each with probability equal to .25, and could stay the same with probability equal to .5. The expected value of the stock price would be equal to

$$.25 \times 50 + .5 \times 100 + .25 \times 200 = 112.5$$

This corresponds to a return of 12.5 percent, which is higher than the rate on interest of 8 percent. For stock price distributions with expected returns higher than the rate of interest, it can be shown that upper and lower bounds on the admissible option values are equal to the expected

---

[19]See the remarks in W. Sharpe, *Investments*, 2nd ed. (Englewood Cliffs, NJ: Prentice Hall, 1988), pp. 99–101.

present values of the call payoff with the expectations taken over transformed[20] stock price distributions. In this example, the transformed probabilities for the upper bound are .304, .464, and .232 for stock prices of 50, 100, and 200, respectively; they give an upper bound equal to 75 × .232/1.08 = $16.11. The corresponding transformed probabilities for the lower bound are .263, .526, and .211, yielding a lower bound equal to 75 × .211/1.08 = $14.65.

Thus, option prices with an exercise price of $125 must lie between $15.86 and $16.11 in this three-state option pricing model. As we subdivide the time period into increasingly finer partitions, the distance between the two bounds tends to decrease. At the limit, both bounds become equal to the Black-Scholes option value.

In fact this bounding approach encompasses models of the underlying stock price distribution that are considerably more general than the binomial or the Black-Scholes model. Such models may include rare events such as sudden, extreme price moves in response to dramatic information like a takeover attempt.[21] More recently, the bounding approach has been extended to incorporate the existence of "frictions" or transaction costs in trading the underlying asset. Neither the binomial nor the Black-Scholes models are valid in the presence of such costs.[22]

19.7 EMPIRICAL EVIDENCE

The Black-Scholes option pricing model has been subjected to an enormous number of empirical tests. For the most part, the results of the studies have been positive in that the Black-Scholes model generates option values fairly close to the actual prices at which options trade. At the same time, some regular empirical failures of the model have been noted.

The biggest problem concerns volatility and was initially documented by Rubinstein.[23] If the model were accurate, the implied volatility of all options on a particular stock with the same expiration date would be equal—after all, the underlying asset and expiration date are the same for each option, so the volatility inferred from each also ought to be the same. But in fact, when one actually plots implied volatility as a function of exercise price, the typical results appear as in Figure 19.15, which treats S&P 500 index options as the underlying asset. Implied volatility steadily falls as the exercise price rises. Clearly, the Black-Scholes model is missing something. This something may be negative jumps in stock prices or the inability of the Black-Scholes model to incorporate transaction costs such as the bid–asked spread.[24]

Rubinstein points out that prior to the 1987 market crash, plots of implied volatility like the one in Figure 19.15 were relatively flat, consistent with the notion that the market was then less attuned to fears of a crash. However, post-crash plots have been consistently downward sloping, exhibiting a shape often called the *option smirk*. Option-pricing models that allow for more general stock price distributions, including crash risk and random changes in volatility, can generate

---

[20]Let p_1, p_2, and p_3 denote the three probabilities corresponding to the down, stay-the-same, and up states, respectively. Then for the upper bound the probabilities are transformed into $p_1 = Q + (1 - Q)p_1$, $p_2 = (1 - Q)p_2$, $p_3 = (1 - Q)p_3$, where Q is equal to $(112.5 - 108)/(112.5 - 50)$ in our example, the ratio of the difference between the expected future stock price and the rate of interest to the difference between the expected stock price and the lowest possible stock value. The transformation for the lower bound is slightly more complicated. See S. Perrakis, "Preference-Free Option Prices When the Stock Return Can Go Up, Go Down, or Stay the Same," *Advances in Futures and Options Research* 3 (1988), pp. 209–235.

[21]Stylianos Perrakis, "Options for Multinomial Stock Returns for Diffusion and Jump Processes," *Canadian Journal of Administrative Sciences* 10, no. 1 (1993), pp. 68–82.

[22]G. M. Constantinides and S. Perrakis, "Stochastic Dominance Bounds on Derivative Prices in a Multiperiod Economy with Proportional Transaction Costs," *Journal of Economic Dynamics and Control* 26 (2002), pp. 1323–1352.

[23]Mark Rubinstein, "Implied Binomial Trees," *Journal of Finance* 49 (July 1994), pp. 771–818.

[24]This latter issue is examined systematically in two empirical papers that show that index options may be subject to serious mispricing, to the point of creating opportunities for trading profits. See G. Constantinides, J. Jackwerth, and S. Perrakis, "Mispricing of S&P 500 Index Options," *Review of Financial Studies* 22, pp. 1247–1277; and G. Constantinides, M. Czerwonko, J. Jackwerth, and S. Perrakis, "Are Options on Index Futures Profitable for Risk Averse Investors? Empirical Evidence," *Journal of Finance* 66, 1407–1437.

Figure 19.15

Implied volatility of the S&P 500 index as a function of exercise price.

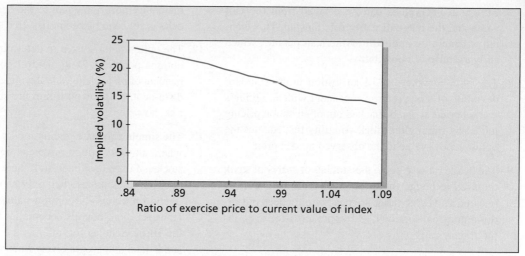

Source: Mark Rubinstein, "Implied Binomial Trees," *Journal of Finance*, July 1994, pp. 771–818.

downward-sloping implied volatility curves similar to the one observed in Figure 19.15. Nonetheless, the problem of reconciling these distributions extracted from the option market with those observed in the underlying asset market has so far not reached a satisfactory solution. Similarly, the option smirk observed in index options is not consistent with the equivalent plots derived from options on the stocks that constitute the index.[25] These issues continue to be lively research topics.

SUMMARY

1. Option values may be viewed as the sum of intrinsic value plus time or "volatility" value. The volatility value is the right to choose not to exercise if the stock price moves against the holder. Thus, option holders cannot lose more than the cost of the option regardless of stock price performance.

2. Call options are more valuable when the exercise price is lower, when the stock price is higher, when the interest rate is higher, when the time to maturity is greater, when the stock's volatility is greater, and when dividends are lower.

3. Call options must sell for at least the stock price less the present value of the exercise price and dividends to be paid before maturity. This implies that a call option on a non-dividend-paying stock may be sold for more than the proceeds from immediate exercise. Thus, European calls are worth as much as American calls on stocks that pay no dividends

because the right to exercise the American call early has no value.

4. Options may be priced relative to the underlying stock price using a simple two-period, two-state pricing model. As the number of periods increases, we may approximate more realistic stock price distributions. The Black-Scholes formula may be seen as a limiting case of the binomial option model as the holding period is divided into progressively smaller subperiods.

5. The Black-Scholes formula applies to options on stocks that pay no dividends. Dividend adjustments may be adequate to price European calls on dividend-paying stocks, but the proper treatment of American calls on dividend-paying stocks requires more complex formulas.

6. Put options may be exercised early whether the stock pays dividends or not. Therefore, American puts generally are worth more than European puts.

[25]See J. P. Driessen, J. Maenhout, and G. Vilkov, "The Price of Correlation Risk: Evidence from Equity Options," *Journal of Finance* 64 (2009), 1377–1406.

7. European put values can be derived from the call value and the put–call parity relationship. This technique cannot be applied to American puts for which early exercise is a possibility.

8. The implied volatility of an option is the standard deviation of stock returns consistent with an option's market price. It can be backed out of an option pricing model by finding the stock volatility that equates the option model value to the observed market price.

9. The hedge ratio refers to the number of shares of stock required to hedge the price risk involved in writing one option. Hedge ratios are near zero for deep out-of-the-money call options, and approach 1 for deep in-the-money calls.

10. Although hedge ratios are less than 1, call options have elasticities greater than 1. The rate of return on a call (as opposed to the dollar return) responds more than one-for-one with stock price movements.

11. Portfolio insurance can be obtained by purchasing a protective put option on an equity position. When the appropriate put is not traded, portfolio insurance entails a dynamic hedge strategy in which a fraction of

the equity portfolio equal to the desired put option's delta is sold and placed in risk-free securities.

12. The option delta is used to determine the hedge ratio options positions. Delta-neutral portfolios are independent of price changes in the underlying asset. Even delta-neutral option portfolios are subject to volatility risk, however.

13. The simple two-state pricing model is the only model where an exact option price can be derived from the stock and the rate of interest. If there are more than two possible stock prices, then only an upper and a lower bound on admissible option values can be defined. However, both bounds become, at the limit, equal to the Black-Scholes formula, as the holding period is subdivided into progressively finer subintervals.

14. Empirically, implied volatilities derived from the Black-Scholes model for a given option maturity exhibit systematic patterns with respect to the exercise price. These patterns differ between index and equity options, and may indicate index option mispricings sufficient to create trading profits. These empirical findings are inconsistent with the Black-Scholes assumptions.

KEY EQUATIONS

(19.1) $C_0 = S_0N(d_1) - Xe^{-rT}N(d_2)$

(19.2) $P = C + PV(X) - S_0$
$= C + Xe^{-rT} - S_0$

(19.3) $P = Xe^{-rT}[1 - N(d_2)] - S_0[1 - N(d_1)]$

(19.4) Payoff $= \begin{cases} L \\ V_T \end{cases} = L - \begin{cases} 0 & \text{if } V_T \geq L \\ L - V_T & \text{if } V_T < L \end{cases}$

(19.5) $v_1 + v_2 + v_3 = 1/1.08$

PROBLEMS

connect Practise and learn online with Connect.

1. We showed in the text that the value of a call option increases with the volatility of the stock. Is this also true of put option values? Use the put–call parity theorem as well as a numerical example to prove your answer.

2. In each of the following questions, you are asked to compare two options with parameters as given. The risk-free interest rate for *all* cases should be assumed to be 6 percent. Assume the stocks on which these options are written pay no dividends.

a.

Put	T	X	σ	Price of Option
A	.5	50	.20	$10
B	.5	50	.25	$10

Which put option must be written on the stock with the lower price?

   i. A

  ii. B

 iii. Not enough information

b.

Put	*T*	*X*	σ	Price of Option
A	.5	50	.2	$10
B	.5	50	.2	$12

Which call option must have the lower time to maturity?

   i. A

  ii. B

 iii. Not enough information

c.

Call	*S*	*X*	σ	Price of Option
A	50	50	.20	$12
B	55	50	.20	$10

Which call option is written on the stock with higher volatility?

   i. A

  ii. B

 iii. Not enough information

d.

Call	*T*	*X*	*S*	Price of Option
A	.5	50	55	$10
B	.5	50	55	$12

Which call option is written on the stock with higher volatility?

   i. A

  ii. B

 iii. Not enough information

e.

Call	*T*	*X*	*S*	Price of Option
A	.5	50	55	$10
B	.5	55	55	$ 7

Which call option is written on the stock with higher volatility?

   i. A

  ii. B

 iii. Not enough information

3. Reconsider the determination of the hedge ratio in the two-state model (in Section 19.3), where we showed that one-half share of stock would hedge one option. What is the hedge ratio at the following exercise prices: 120, 110, 100, 90? What do you conclude about the hedge ratio as the option becomes progressively more in the money?

4. Show that Black-Scholes call option hedge ratios also increase as the stock price increases. Consider a one-year option with exercise price $50 on a stock with annual standard deviation of 20 percent. The T-bill rate is 8 percent per year. Find $N(d_1)$ for stock prices $45, $50, and $55.

5. We will derive a two-state put option value in this problem. Data: $S_0 = 100$; $X = 110$; and $1 + r = 1.1$. The two possibilities for S_T are 130 and 80.

   a. Show that the range of S is 50 while that of P is 30 across the two states. What is the hedge ratio of the put?

   b. Form a portfolio of three shares of stock and five puts. What is the (non-random) payoff to this portfolio? What is the present value of the portfolio?

   c. Given that the stock currently is selling at $100, solve for the value of the put.

6. Calculate the value of the call option on the stock in problem 5 with an exercise price of $110. Verify that the put–call parity theorem is satisfied by your answers to problems 5 and 6. (Do not use continuous compounding to calculate the present value of X in this example because we are using a two-state model here, not a continuous-time Black-Scholes model.)

7. Use the Black-Scholes formula to find the value of a call option on the following stock:

Time to maturity	=	6 months
Standard deviation	=	50 percent per year
Exercise price	=	50
Stock price	=	50
Interest rate	=	3 percent

8. Recalculate the value of the option in problem 7, successively substituting one of the changes below while keeping the other parameters:

   a. Time to maturity = 3 months

   b. Standard deviation = 25 percent per year

   c. Exercise price = $55

   d. Stock price = $55

   e. Interest rate = 5 percent

   Consider each scenario independently. Confirm that the option value changes in accordance with the prediction of Table 19.1.

9. A call option with $X = \$50$ on a stock currently priced at $S = \$55$ is selling for $10. Using a volatility estimate of $\sigma = .30$, you find that $N(d_1) = .6$ and $N(d_2) = .5$. The risk-free interest rate is zero. Is the implied volatility based on the option price more or less than .30? Explain.

10. Would you expect a $1 increase in a call option's exercise price to lead to a decrease in the option's value of more or less than $1?

11. Is a put option on a high-beta stock worth more than one on a low-beta stock? The stocks have identical firm-specific risk.

12. All else being equal, is a call option on a stock with a lot of firm-specific risk worth more than one on a stock with little firm-specific risk? The betas of the two stocks are equal.

13. All else equal, will a call option with a high exercise price have a higher or lower hedge ratio than one with a low exercise price?

14. Should the rate of return of a call option on a long-term Treasury bond be more or less sensitive to changes in interest rates than the rate of return of the underlying bond?

15. If the stock price falls and the call price rises, then what has happened to the call option's implied volatility?

16. If the time to maturity falls and the put price rises, then what has happened to the put option's implied volatility?

17. According to the Black-Scholes formula, what will be the value of the hedge ratio of a call option as the stock price becomes infinitely large? Explain briefly.

18. According to the Black-Scholes formula, what will be the value of the hedge ratio of a put option for a very small exercise price?

19. What would be the Excel formula in Spreadsheet 19.1 for the Black-Scholes value of a straddle position?

20. The hedge ratio of an at-the-money call option on IBM is .4. The hedge ratio of an at-the-money put option is −.6. What is the hedge ratio of an at-the-money straddle position on IBM?

21. Consider a six-month expiration European call option with exercise price $105. The underlying stock sells for $100 a share and pays no dividends. The risk-free rate is 5 percent. What is the implied volatility of the option if the option currently sells for $8? Use Spreadsheet 19.1 to answer this question.

   a. Go to the Tools menu of the spreadsheet and select Goal Seek. The dialogue box will ask you for three pieces of information. In that dialogue box, you should *set cell E6 to value 8 by changing cell B2*. In other words, you ask the spreadsheet to find the value of standard deviation (which appears in cell B2) that forces the value of the option (in cell E6) equal to $8. Then click OK, and you should find that the call is now worth $8, and the entry for standard deviation has been changed to a level consistent with this value. This is the call's implied standard deviation at a price of $8.

   b. What happens to implied volatility if the option is selling at $9? Why has implied volatility increased?

   c. What happens to implied volatility if the option price is unchanged at $8, but option maturity is lower, say only four months? Why?

   d. What happens to implied volatility if the option price is unchanged at $8, but the exercise price is lower, say only $100? Why?

   e. What happens to implied volatility if the option price is unchanged at $8, but the stock price is lower, say only $98? Why?

22. A collar is established by buying a share of stock for $50, buying a 6-month put option with exercise price $45, and writing a six-month call option with exercise price $55. On the basis of the volatility of the stock, you calculate that for a strike price of $45 and maturity of 6 months, $N(d_1) = .60$, whereas for the exercise price of $55, $N(d_1) = .35$.

   a. What will be the gain or loss on the collar if the stock price increases by $1?

   b. What happens to the delta of the portfolio if the stock price becomes very large? Very small?

23. These three put options all are written on the same stock. One has a delta of −.9, one a delta of −.5, and one a delta of −.1. Assign deltas to the three puts by filling in this table.

Put	X	Delta
A	10	
B	20	
C	30	

24. You are *very* bullish (optimistic) on stock EFG, much more so than the rest of the market. In each question, choose the portfolio strategy that will give you the biggest dollar profit if your bullish forecast turns out to be correct. Explain your answer.

   a. *Choice A.* $10,000 invested in calls with $X = 50$
      Choice B. $10,000 invested in EFG stock

   b. *Choice A.* 10 call options contracts (for 100 shares each), with $X = 50$
      Choice B. 1,000 shares of EFG stock

25. Imagine you are a provider of portfolio insurance. You are establishing a four-year program. The portfolio you manage is currently worth $100 million, and you hope to provide a minimum return of 0 percent. The equity portfolio has a standard deviation of 25 percent per year, and T-bills pay 5 percent per year. Assume for simplicity that the portfolio pays no dividends (or that all dividends are reinvested).

    a. What fraction of the portfolio should be placed in bills? What fraction in equity?

    b. What should the manager do if the stock portfolio falls by 3 percent on the first day of trading?

26. You would like to be holding a protective put position on the stock of XYZ Co. to lock in a guaranteed minimum value of $100 at year-end. XYZ currently sells for $100. Over the next year, the stock price will increase by 10 percent or decrease by 10 percent. The T-bill rate is 5 percent. Unfortunately, no put options are traded on XYZ Co.

    a. Suppose the desired put option were traded. How much would it cost to purchase?

    b. What would have been the cost of the protective put portfolio?

    c. What portfolio position in stock and T-bills will ensure you a payoff equal to the payoff that would be provided by a protective put with $X = 100$? Show that the payoff to this portfolio and the cost of establishing the portfolio matches that of the desired protective put.

27. Suppose that the risk-free interest rate is zero. Would an American put option ever be exercised early? Explain.

28. Let $p(S,T,X)$ denote the value of a European put on a stock selling at S dollars, with time to maturity T, and with exercise price X, and let $P(S,T,X)$ be the value of an American put.

    a. Evaluate $p(0,T,X)$.

    b. Evaluate $P(0,T,X)$.

    c. Evaluate $p(S,T,0)$.

    d. Evaluate $P(S,T,0)$.

    e. What does your answer to (b) tell you about the possibility that American puts may be exercised early?

29. You are attempting to value a call option with an exercise price of $100 and one year to expiration. The underlying stock pays no dividends, its current price is $100, and you believe it has a 50 percent chance of increasing to $120 and a 50 percent chance of decreasing to $80. The risk-free rate of interest is 10 percent. Calculate the call option's value using the two-state stock price model.

30. Consider an increase in the volatility of the stock in the previous problem. Suppose that if the stock increases in price, it will increase to $130, and that if it falls, it will fall to $70. Show that the value of the call option is now higher than the value derived in the previous problem.

31. Calculate the value of a put option with exercise price $100 using the data in problem 29. Show that put–call parity is satisfied by your solution.

32. XYZ Corp. will pay a $2 per share dividend in two months. Its stock price currently is $60 per share. A call option on XYZ has an exercise price of $55 and three-month time to maturity. The risk-free interest rate is .5 percent per month, and the stock's volatility (standard deviation) = 7 percent per month. Find the pseudo-American option value. (*Hint:* Try defining one "period" as a month, rather than as a year.)

33. "The beta of a call option on General Motors is greater than the beta of a share of General Motors." True or false?

34. "The beta of a call option on the S&P 500 index with an exercise price of 1330 is greater than the beta of a call on the index with an exercise price of 1340." True or false?

35. What will happen to the hedge ratio of a convertible bond as the stock price becomes very large?

36. ABC Finances believes that market volatility will be 20 percent annually for the next three years. Three-year at-the-money call and put options on the market index sell at an implied volatility of 22 percent. What options portfolio can ABC establish to speculate on its volatility belief without taking a bullish or bearish position on the market? Using ABC's estimate of volatility, three-year at-the-money options have $N(d_1) = .6$.

37. Suppose that call options on ExxonMobil stock with time to maturity three months and strike price $90 are selling at an implied volatility of 30 percent. ExxonMobil stock currently is $90 per share, and the risk-free rate is 4 percent. If you believe the true volatility of the stock is 32 percent, how can you trade on your belief without taking on exposure to the performance of ExxonMobil? How many shares of stock will you hold for each option contract purchased or sold?

38. Using the data in problem 37, suppose that three-month put options with a strike price of $90 are selling at an implied volatility of 34 percent. Construct a delta-neutral portfolio comprising positions in calls and puts that will profit when the option prices come back into alignment.

39. Suppose that ABC Finance sells call options on $1.25 million worth of a stock portfolio with beta = 1.5. The option delta is .8. It wishes to hedge out its resultant exposure to a market advance by buying a market index portfolio.

   a. How many dollars' worth of the market index portfolio should it buy?

   b. What if ABC instead uses market index puts to hedge its exposure? Should it buy or sell puts? Each put option is on 100 units of the index, and the index at current prices represents $1,000 worth of stock.

40. You are holding call options on a stock. The stock's beta is .75, and you are concerned that the stock market is about to fall. The stock is currently selling for $5 and you hold 1 million options on the stock (i.e., you hold 10,000 contracts for 100 shares each). The option delta is .8. How much of the market index portfolio must you buy or sell to hedge your market exposure?

Use the following case in answering problems 41–46: Mark Washington, CFA, is an analyst with BIC. One year ago, BIC analysts predicted that the U.S. equity market would most likely experience a slight downturn and suggested delta-hedging the BIC portfolio. As predicted, the U.S. equity markets did indeed experience a downturn of approximately 4 percent over a 12-month period. However, portfolio performance for BIC was disappointing, lagging behind its peer group by nearly 10 percent. Washington has been told to review the options strategy to determine why the hedged portfolio did not perform as expected.

41. Which of the following *best* explains a delta-neutral portfolio? A delta-neutral portfolio is perfectly hedged against

   a. Small price changes in the underlying asset

   b. Small price decreases in the underlying asset

   c. All price changes in the underlying asset

42. After discussing the concept of a delta-neutral portfolio, Washington determines that he needs to further explain the concept of delta. Washington draws the value of an option as a function of the underlying stock price. Using this diagram, indicate how delta is interpreted. Delta is the

   a. Slope in the option price diagram

   b. Curvature of the option price graph

   c. Level in the option price diagram

43. Washington considers a put option that has a delta of $-.65$. If the price of the underlying asset decreases by $6, what is the best estimate of the change in option price?

44. BIC owns 51,750 shares of Smith & Oates. The shares are currently priced at $69. A call option on Smith & Oates with a strike price of $70 is selling at $3.50 and has a delta of .69. What is the number of call options necessary to create a delta-neutral hedge?

45. Return to the previous problem. Will the number of call options written for a delta-neutral hedge increase or decrease if the stock price falls?

46. Which of the following statements regarding the goal of a delta-neutral portfolio is *most* accurate? One example of a delta-neutral portfolio is to combine a

    a. Long position in a stock with a short position in call options so that the value of the portfolio does not change with changes in the value of the stock

    b. Long position in a stock with a short position in a call option so that the value of the portfolio changes with changes in the value of the stock

    c. Long position in a stock with a long position in call options so that the value of the portfolio does not change with changes in the value of the stock

47. Suppose you are attempting to value a one-year maturity option on a stock with volatility (i.e., annualized standard deviation) of $\sigma = .40$. What would be the appropriate values for u and d if your binomial model is set up using

    a. 1 period of one year?

    b. 4 subperiods, each 3 months?

    c. 12 subperiods, each 1 month?

48. You build a binomial model with one period and assert that over the course of a year, the stock price will either rise by a factor of 1.5 or fall by a factor of 2/3. What is your implicit assumption about the volatility of the stock's rate of return over the next year?

49. Use the put–call parity relationship to demonstrate that an at-the-money call option on a non-dividend-paying stock must cost more than an at-the-money put option. Show that the prices of the put and call will be equal if $S = X/(1 + r)^T$.

The following problems are based on questions that have appeared in past CFA examinations.

50. The board of directors of Abco Company is concerned about the downside risk of a $100 million equity portfolio in its pension plan. The board's consultant has proposed temporarily (for one month) hedging the portfolio with either futures or options. Referring to the following table, the consultant states:

    a. "The $100 million equity portfolio can be fully protected on the downside by selling (shorting) 2,000 futures contracts."

    b. "The cost of this protection is that the portfolio's expected rate of return will be zero percent."

Market, Portfolio, and Contract Data	
Equity index level	99.00
Equity futures price	100.00
Futures contract multiplier	500
Portfolio beta	1.20
Contract expiration (months)	3

Assess the accuracy of each of the consultant's two statements.

51. Michael Weber, CFA is analyzing several aspects of option valuation, including the determinants of the value of an option, the characteristics of various models used to value options, and the potential for divergence of calculated option values from observed market prices.

    a. What is the expected effect on the value of a call option on common stock if the volatility of the underlying stock price decreases? If the time to expiration of the option increases?

  b. Using the Black-Scholes option-pricing model, Weber calculates the price of a three-month call option and notices the option's calculated value is different from its market price. With respect to Weber's use of the Black-Scholes option-pricing model,

    i. Discuss why the calculated value of an out-of-the-money European option might differ from its market price.

    ii. Discuss why the calculated value of an American option might differ from its market price.

52. Joel Franklin is a portfolio manager responsible for derivatives. Franklin observes an American-style option and a European-style option with the same strike price, expiration, and underlying stock. Franklin believes that the European-style option will have a higher premium than the American-style option.

  a. Critique Franklin's belief that the European-style option will have a higher premium.

  Franklin is asked to value a 1-year European-style call option for Abaco Ltd. common stock, which last traded at $43. He has collected the information in the following table.

Closing stock price	$43.00
Call and put option exercise price	$45
1-year put option price	$4
1-year Treasury bill rate	5.50%
Time to expiration	One year

  b. Calculate, using put–call parity and the information provided in the table, the European-style call option value.

  c. State the effect, if any, of each of the following three variables on the value of a call option. (No calculations required.)

    i. An increase in short-term interest rate

    ii. An increase in stock price volatility

    iii. A decrease in time to option expiration

53. A stock index is currently trading at 50. Paul Tripp, CFA wants to value two-year index options using the binomial model. The stock will either increase in value by 20 percent or fall in value by 20 percent. The annual risk-free interest rate is 6 percent. No dividends are paid on any of the underlying securities in the index.

  a. Construct a two-period binomial tree for the value of the stock index.

  b. Calculate the value of a European call option on the index with an exercise price of 60.

  c. Calculate the value of a European put option on the index with an exercise price of 60.

  d. Confirm that your solutions for the values of the call and the put satisfy put–call parity.

54. Ken Webster manages a $100 million equity portfolio benchmarked to the S&P 500 index. Over the past two years, the S&P 500 Index has appreciated 60 percent. Webster believes the market is overvalued when measured by several traditional fundamental/economic indicators. He is concerned about maintaining the excellent gains the portfolio has experienced in the past two years but recognizes that the S&P 500 Index could still move above its current 668 level.

  Webster is considering the following *option collar* strategy:

  • Protection for the portfolio can be attained by purchasing an S&P 500 Index put with a strike price of 665 (just out of the money).

  • The put can be financed by selling two 675 calls (further out of the money) for every put purchased.

  • Because the combined delta of the two calls is less than 1 (i.e., $2 \times .36 = .72$), the options will not lose more than the underlying portfolio will gain if the market advances.

The information in the following table describes the two options used to create the collar.

Options to Create the Collar

Characteristics	675 Call	665 Put
Option price	$4.30	$8.05
Option implied volatility	11.00%	14.00%
Option's delta	.36	−0.44
Contracts needed for collar	602	301

Notes:
- Ignore transaction costs.
- S&P 500 historical 30-day volatility is 12.00 percent.
- Time to option expiration is 30 days.

a. *Describe* the potential returns of the combined portfolio (the underlying portfolio plus the option collar) if after 30 days the S&P 500 index has

   i. Risen approximately 5 percent to 701.00

   ii. Remained at 668 (no change)

   iii. Declined by approximately 5 percent to 635.00

   (No calculations are necessary.)

b. *Discuss* the effect on the hedge ratio (delta) of *each* option as the S&P 500 approaches the level for *each* of the potential outcomes listed in part (*a*).

c. *Evaluate* the pricing of *each* of the following in relation to the volatility data provided:

   i. The put

   ii. The call

E-INVESTMENTS
Option Price
Differences

Select a Canadian stock for which options are listed on the CBOE Web site (**www.cboe.com**), such as Bell Canada (BCE) or Canadian Pacific (CP). The price data for captions can be found on the *delayed quotes* menu option. Enter a ticker symbol for a stock of your choice and pull up its option price data.

Using daily price data from **http://finance.yahoo.com** calculate the annualized standard deviation of the daily percentage change in the stock price. Create a Black-Scholes option-pricing model in a spreadsheet, or use our Spreadsheet 19.1. Using the standard deviation and a risk-free rate found at **www.bloomberg.com/markets/rates/index.html**, calculate the value of the call options.

How do the calculated values compare to the market prices of the options? On the basis of the difference between the price you calculated using historical volatility and the actual price of the option, what do you conclude about expected trends in market volatility?

Futures, Forwards, and Swap Markets

Futures and forward contracts are similar to options in that they specify the purchase or sale of some underlying security at some future date. The key difference is that the holder of an option to buy is not compelled to buy and will not do so if it is to his or her disadvantage. A futures or forward contract, on the other hand, carries the obligation to go through with the agreed-upon transaction.

A forward contract is not an investment in the strict sense that funds are paid for an asset—it is only a commitment today to transact in the future. Forward arrangements are part of our study of investments, however, because they offer a powerful means to hedge other investments and generally modify portfolio characteristics.

Forward markets for future delivery of various commodities go back in time at least to ancient Greece. Organized *futures markets*, though, are a relatively modern development, dating only to the nineteenth century. Futures markets replace informal forward contracts with highly standardized, exchange-traded securities.

While futures markets have their roots in agricultural products and commodities, the markets today are dominated by trading in financial futures such as those on stock indices, interest-rate-dependent securities such as government bonds, and foreign exchange. The markets themselves have also changed, with trading today largely taking place in electronic markets.

This chapter describes the workings of futures markets and the mechanics of trading in these markets. We show how futures contracts are useful investment vehicles for both hedgers and speculators and how the futures price relates to the spot price of an asset. We also show how futures can be used in several risk management applications.

This chapter deals with both principles of futures markets in general and specific futures markets in some detail.

20.1 ▸ THE FUTURES CONTRACT

To see how futures and forwards work and how they might be useful, consider the portfolio diversification problem facing a farmer growing a single crop, say wheat. The entire planting season's revenue depends critically on the highly volatile crop price. The farmer can't easily diversify his position because virtually his entire wealth is tied up in the crop.

The miller who must purchase wheat for processing faces a risk management problem that is the mirror image of the farmer's. He is subject to profit uncertainty because of the unpredictable cost of the wheat.

Both parties can hedge their risk by entering into a **forward contract** requiring the farmer to deliver the wheat when harvested at a price agreed upon now, regardless of the market price at harvest time. No money need change hands at this time. A forward contract is simply a deferred-delivery sale of some asset with the sales price agreed on now. All that is required is that each party be willing to lock in the ultimate delivery price. The contract protects each party from future price fluctuations.

Futures markets formalize and standardize forward contracting. Buyers and sellers trade in a centralized futures exchange. The exchange standardizes the types of contracts that may be traded: it establishes contract size, the acceptable grade of commodity, contract delivery dates, and so forth. Although standardization eliminates much of the flexibility available in forward contracting, it has the offsetting advantage of liquidity because many traders will concentrate on the same small set of contracts. Futures contracts also differ from forward contracts in that they call for a daily settling up of any gains or losses on the contract. By contrast, no money changes hands in forward contracts until the delivery date.

The centralized market, standardization of contracts, and depth of trading in each contract allows futures positions to be liquidated easily through a broker rather than renegotiated with the other party to the contract. Because the exchange guarantees the performance of each party, costly credit checks on other traders are not necessary. Instead, each trader simply posts a good-faith deposit, called the *margin*, to guarantee contract performance.

The Basics of Futures Contracts

The **futures contract** calls for delivery of a commodity at a specified delivery or maturity date, for an agreed-upon price (called the **futures price**), to be paid at contract maturity. The contract specifies precise requirements for the commodity. For agricultural commodities, allowable grades (e.g., No. 2 hard winter wheat, or No. 1 soft red wheat) are set by the exchange. The place or means of delivery of the commodity is specified as well. For agricultural commodities, delivery is made by transfer of warehouse receipts issued by approved warehouses. For financial futures, delivery may be made by wire transfer; in the case of index futures, delivery may be accomplished by a cash settlement procedure such as those for index options. Although the futures contract technically calls for delivery of an asset, delivery in fact rarely occurs. Instead, traders much more commonly close out their positions before contract maturity, taking gains or losses in cash.

Because the futures exchange completely specifies the terms of the contract, the traders need bargain only over the futures prices. The trader taking the **long position** commits to purchasing the commodity on the delivery date, while the trader who takes the **short position** commits to delivering the commodity at contract maturity. The trader in the long position is said to "buy" a contract; the short-side trader "sells" a contract. The words *buy* and *sell* are figurative only, because a contract is not really bought or sold like a stock or bond, but is entered into by mutual agreement. At the time the contract is entered into, no money changes hands.

Figure 20.1   Prices for Canadian commodity futures.

		Electronic Daily Price Range			Settle		Current Day	Previous Day						
Commodity Name	Contract Month	Open	High	Low	Price	Change	Trades	Trades	EFPs/ EFRs	NOS/ Cabinet	Total Volume**	Deliveries	OI*	Change in OI*
Canola Futures														
RS	July 2013	628.20	628.90	618.60	619.90	−9.60	6,463	7,795	37	0	7,832	0	42,598	−3,712
RS	November 2013	564.50	564.50	554.50	556.40	−8.10	12,690	9,446	41	0	9,487	0	95,546	3,782
RS	January 2014	565.60	566.20	557.50	557.40	−8.70	501	750	0	0	750	0	5,903	463
RS	March 2014	558.80	558.80	558.40	553.90	−8.40	67	97	0	0	97	0	905	62
RS	May 2014				549.20	−6.70	30	10	0	0	10	0	254	0
RS	July 2014				547.30	−6.70	0	0	0	0	0	0	7	0
RS	November 2014				517.10	−6.70	0	0	0	0	0	0	0	0
RS	January 2015				517.10	−6.70	0	0	0	0	0	0	0	0
RS	March 2015				517.10	−6.70	0	0	0	0	0	0	0	0
RS	May 2015				517.10	−6.70	0	0	0	0	0	0	0	0
RS	July 2015				517.10	−6.70	0	0	0	0	0	0	0	0

Title row above table: **Daily Market Data / Canola Futures Settlement Prices / 06-Jun-2013**

*In addition to trades, EFPs, and deliveries, open interest in a given contract month may change due to position adjustments.

**Volume is aggregated and representative of each futures market strip including applicable TAS trading activity.

Source: ICE Report Center, https://www.theice.com/marketdata/reportcenter/reports.htm. Reprinted with permission.

Intercontinental Exchange Group www.theice.com

Figure 20.1 shows end-of-day prices for canola agricultural futures contracts trading on the Intercontinental Exchange (ICE) for June 6, 2013.[1] Each contract calls for delivery of 20 tonnes, and prices are quoted in Canadian dollars per tonne. The next several rows detail price data for contracts expiring on various dates. The January 2014 maturity canola contract, for example, opened during the date at a futures price of $565.60 per tonne. The highest futures price during the day was $566.20, the lowest was $557.50, and the settlement price (a representative trading price during the last few minutes of trading) was $557.40. The settlement price declined by $8.70 from the previous trading day. There were 501 trades during the day. Finally, open interest, or the number of outstanding contracts, was 5,903 at the beginning of the day, an increase of 463 from the previous day. No contracts were closed by physical delivery that date. A similar report exists for western barley, the other Canadian futures contract trading on ICE Futures Canada.

The trader holding the long position, who will purchase the good, profits from price increases. Suppose that in January 2014 the price of canola turns out to be $570 per tonne. The long-position trader who entered into the contract at the futures price of $557.40 on June 6, 2013 would pay the agreed-upon $337.40 per tonne to receive canola that, at contract maturity, is worth $570 per tonne in the market. Since each contract calls for delivery of 20 tonnes, ignoring brokerage fees, the profit to the long position is 20($570 − $557.40) = $252. Conversely, the short position must deliver 20 tonnes of canola, each with value $570, for the previously-agreed-upon futures price of only $557.40. The short position's loss equals the long position's gain.

---

[1]Until September 2007 Canadian agricultural commodity futures were traded in the Winnipeg Commodity Exchange (WCE). The WCE became a subsidiary of ICE and is now known as ICE Futures Canada.

Figure 20.2   Profits to buyers and sellers of futures and options contracts.

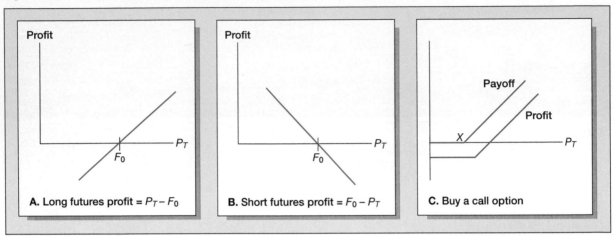

A. Long futures profit = $P_T - F_0$

B. Short futures profit = $F_0 - P_T$

C. Buy a call option

To summarize, at maturity:

$$\text{Profit to long} = \text{Spot price at maturity} - \text{Original futures price}$$
$$\text{Profit to short} = \text{Original futures prices} - \text{Spot price at maturity}$$

where the spot price is the actual market price of the commodity at the time of delivery.

The futures contract is therefore a zero-sum game, with losses and gains to all positions netting out to zero. Every long position is offset by a short position. The aggregate profits to futures trading, summing over all investors, also must be zero, as is the net exposure to changes in the commodity price. For this reason, the establishment of a futures market in a commodity should not have a major impact on the spot market for that commodity.

Figure 20.2, panel A is a plot of the profits realized by an investor who enters the long side of a futures contract as a function of the price of the asset on the maturity date. Notice that profit is zero when the ultimate spot price, P_T, equals the initial futures price, F_0. Profit per unit of the underlying asset rises or falls one-for-one with changes in the final spot price. Unlike the payoff of a call option, the payoff of the long futures position can be negative: this will be the case if the spot price falls below the original futures price. Unlike the holder of a call, who has an *option* to buy, the long futures position trader cannot simply walk away from the contract. Also unlike options, in the case of futures there is no need to distinguish gross payoffs from net profits. This is because the futures contract is not purchased; it is simply a contract that is agreed to by two parties. The futures price adjusts to make the present value of either side of the contract equal to zero.

The distinction between futures and options is highlighted by comparing panel A of Figure 20.2 to the payoff and profit diagrams for an investor in a call option with exercise price, X, chosen equal to the futures price F_0 (see panel C). The futures investor is exposed to considerable losses if the asset price falls. In contrast, the investor in the call cannot lose more than the cost of the option.

Panel B is a plot of the profits realized by an investor who enters the short side of a futures contract. It is the mirror image of the profit diagram for the long position.

CC 1

CONCEPT CHECK

a. Compare the profit diagram in Figure 20.2B to the payoff diagram for a long position in a put option. Assume the exercise price of the option equals the initial futures price.

b. Compare the profit diagram in Figure 20.2B to the payoff diagram for an investor who writes a call option.

Existing Contracts

Futures and forward contracts are traded on a wide variety of goods in four broad categories: agricultural commodities, metals and minerals (including energy commodities), foreign currencies, and financial futures (fixed-income securities and stock market indices). Innovation in financial futures has been rapid and is ongoing. In addition to indices one can now trade **single-stock futures** on individual stocks and narrowly based indices on OneChicago, a joint venture of the Chicago Board of Options Exchange (CBOE) and the Chicago Mercantile Exchange (CME). The exchange maintains futures markets in actively traded stocks with the most liquidity as well as in some popular ETFs such as those on the S&P 500 (ticker SPY), the Nasdaq-100 (QQQ), and the Dow Jones Industrial Average (DIA). However, trading volume in single-stock futures has to date been somewhat disappointing.

Table 20.1 offers a sample of the various contracts trading in the United States in 2013. Contracts now trade on items that would not have been considered possible only a few years ago. For example, there are now electricity as well as weather futures and options contracts. Weather derivatives (which trade on the Chicago Mercantile Exchange) have payoffs that depend on the number of degree-days by which the temperature in a region exceeds or falls short of 65 degrees Fahrenheit. The potential use of these derivatives in managing the risk surrounding electricity or oil and natural gas use should be evident.

TABLE 20.1   Sample of Futures Contracts

Currency	Agricultural	Metals and Energy	Interest Rate Futures	Equity Indices
British pound	Corn	Copper	Eurodollars	S&P 500 index
Canadian dollar	Oats	Aluminum	Euroyen	Dow Jones Industrials
Japanese yen	Soybeans	Gold	Euro-denominated bond	S&P Midcap 400
Euro	Soybeans meal	Platinum	Euroswiss	Nasdaq 100
Swiss franc	Soybean oil	Palladium	Sterling	NYSE index
Australian dollar	Wheat	Silver	British government bond	Russell 2000 index
Mexican peso	Barley	Crude oil	German government bond	Nikkei 225 (Japanese)
Brazilian real	Flaxseed	Heating oil	Italian government bond	FTSE index (British)
	Canola	Gas oil	Canadian government bond	CAC-40 (French)
	Rye	Natural gas	Treasury bonds	DAX-30 (German)
	Cattle	Gasoline	Treasury notes	All ordinary (Australian)
	Hogs	Propane	Treasury bills	S&P/TSX 60 (Canadian)
	Pork bellies	Commodity index	LIBOR	Dow Jones Euro STOXX 50
	Cocoa	Electricity	EURIBOR	Industry indices, e.g.:
	Coffee	Weather	Municipal bond index	• Banking
	Cotton		Federal funds rate	• Telecom
	Milk		Bankers' acceptance	• Utilities
	Orange juice		Interest rate swaps	• Health care
	Sugar			• Technology
	Lumber			
	Rice			

PREDICTION MARKETS

If you find S&P 500 or T-bond contracts a bit dry, perhaps you'd be interested in futures contacts with payoffs that depend on the winner of a presidential election, or the severity of the next influenza season, or the host city of the 2024 Olympics. You can now find "futures markets" in these events and many others.

For example, both Intrade (www.intrade.com) and Iowa Electronic Markets (www.biz.uiowa.edu/iem) maintain presidential futures markets.

In July 2011, you could have purchased a contract that would pay off $1 in November 2012 if the Republican candidate won the presidential race but nothing if he lost. The contract price (expressed as a percentage of face value) therefore may be viewed as the probability of a Republican victory, at least according to the consensus view of market participants at the time. If you believed in July that the probability of a Republican victory was 55 percent, you would have been prepared to pay up to $.55 for the contract. Alternatively, if you had wished to bet against the

Republicans, you could have *sold* the contract. Similarly, you could bet on (or against) a Democrat victory using the Democrat contract. (When there are only two relevant parties, betting on one is equivalent to betting against the other; but in other elections, such as primaries, in which there are several viable candidates, selling one contract is not the same as buying another's.)

The figure here shows the price of each contract from July 2011 through Election Day 2012. The price clearly tracks each candidate's perceived prospects. You can see Obama's price rise dramatically in the days shortly before the election as it became ever clearer that he would win the election.

Interpreting prediction market prices as probabilities actually requires a caveat. Because the contract payoff is risky, the price of the contract may reflect a risk premium. Therefore, to be precise, these probabilities are actually risk-neutral probabilities (see Chapter 19). In practice, however, it seems unlikely that the risk premium associated with these contracts is substantial.

Prediction markets for the 2012 presidential election. Contract on each party pays $1 if the party wins the election. Price is in cents.

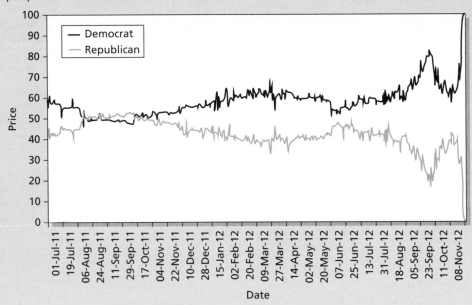

Source: Iowa Electronic Markets, downloaded January 25, 2013.

In Canada, futures contracts for several major agricultural commodities have been trading for a long time at the Winnipeg Commodity Exchange, which became part of the Intercontinental Exchange (ICE) in 2007. All other futures contracts, as well as all option contracts, have been trading since 1999 at the Montréal Exchange, which was renamed the Canadian Derivatives Exchange. The early 1980s saw the introduction of several precious metal, stock index, and interest rate futures, together with options on stock indices, foreign currencies, and bonds. By the end of the decade, most of these instruments had failed. By 2013, apart from the agricultural commodities on the ICE, the only active futures trading in Canada was in S&P/TSX Composite and

S&P/TSX 60 contracts, various S&P/TSX sectoral indices, bankers' acceptances, the overnight repo rate, overnight index swap futures, Canada bond futures, and options on the U.S. dollar, on Canada bond futures, and on bankers' acceptances. Low liquidity, thin trading, and the ready availability of comparable financial instruments in the United States are major reasons for the relative failure of financial innovations in Canadian futures markets.[2]

While Table 20.1 includes many contracts, the large and ever-growing array of markets makes this list necessarily incomplete. The nearby box discusses some comparatively fanciful futures markets, sometimes called *prediction markets*, in which payoffs may be tied to the winner of presidential elections, the box office receipts of a particular movie, or anything else in which participants are willing to take positions.

Outside the futures markets, a fairly developed network of banks and brokers has established a forward market in foreign exchange. This forward market is not a formal exchange in the sense that the exchange specifies the terms of the traded contract. Instead, participants in a forward contract may negotiate for delivery of any quantity of goods, as distinguished from futures markets where contract size is set by the exchange. In forward arrangements, banks and brokers simply negotiate contracts for clients (or themselves) as needed. This market is huge. In London alone, the largest currency market, around $US2 trillion of currency trades each day.

20.2   MECHANICS OF TRADING IN FUTURES MARKETS

The Clearinghouse and Open Interest

Until relatively recently, most futures trades in the United States and Canada occurred among floor traders in the "trading pit" for each contract. Today, however, trading is overwhelmingly conducted through electronic networks, particularly for financial futures.

The impetus for this shift originated in Europe, where electronic trading is the norm. Eurex, which is jointly owned by the Deutsche Börse and Swiss exchange, is currently the world's largest futures and options exchange. It operates a fully electronic trading and clearing platform and, in 2004, received clearance from regulators to list contracts in the U.S. In response, the Chicago Board of Trade adopted an electronic platform provided by Eurex's European rival Euronext. liffe,[3] and the CBOT's Treasury contracts are now traded electronically. The Chicago Mercantile Exchange maintains another electronic trading system called Globex. The CBOT and CME merged in 2007 into one combined company, named the CME Group, with all electronic trading moving from both exchanges onto Globex. In 2001 the Montréal Exchange introduced its electronic trading system, SAM. These electronic exchanges enable trading around the clock.

Once a trade is agreed to, the **clearinghouse** enters the picture. Rather than having the long and short traders hold contracts with each other, the clearinghouse becomes the seller of the contract for the long position and the buyer of the contract for the short position. The clearinghouse is obligated to deliver the commodity to the long position and to pay for delivery from the short; consequently, the clearinghouse's position nets to zero. This arrangement makes the clearinghouse the trading partner of each trader, both long and short. The clearinghouse, bound to perform on its side of each contract, is the only party that can be hurt by the failure of any trader to fulfill the obligations of the futures contract. This arrangement is necessary, because a futures contract calls for future performance, which cannot be guaranteed as easily as an immediate stock transaction.

---

[2]A more extensive treatment of the reasons for the failure of many new Canadian futures instruments can be found in E. Kirzner, "The Evolving Derivatives Story," *Canadian Investment Review* 11 (Winter 1998).

[3]Euronext.liffe is the international derivatives market of Euronext. It resulted from Euronext's purchase of LIFFE (the London International Financial Futures and Options Exchange) and a merger with the Lisbon exchange in 2002. Euronext was itself the result of a 2000 merger of the exchanges of Amsterdam, Brussels, and Paris.

Figure 20.3
Panel A: Trading without the clearinghouse.
Panel B: Trading with the clearinghouse.

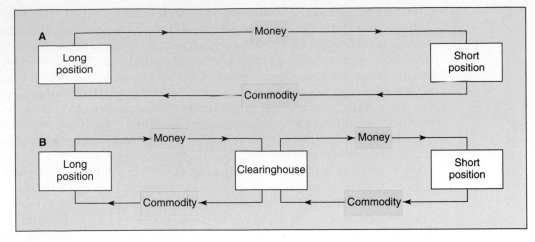

Figure 20.3, illustrates the role of the clearinghouse. Panel A shows what would happen in the absence of the clearinghouse. The trader in the long position would be obligated to pay the futures price to the short position trader; the trader in the short position would be obligated to deliver the commodity. Panel B shows how the clearinghouse becomes an intermediary, acting as the trading partner for each side of the contract. The clearinghouse's position is neutral, since it takes a long and a short position for each transaction.

The clearinghouse makes it possible for traders to liquidate positions easily. If you are currently long in a contract and want to undo your position, you simply instruct your broker to enter the short side of a contract to close out your position. This is called a **reversing trade**. The exchange nets out your long and short positions, reducing your net position to zero. Your zero net position with the clearinghouse eliminates the need to fulfill at maturity either the original long or the reversing short position.

The **open interest** on the contract is the number of contracts outstanding. (Long and short positions are not counted separately, meaning that open interest can be defined as the number of either long or short contracts outstanding.) The clearinghouse's position nets out to zero, of course, and so is not counted in the computation of open interest. When contracts begin trading, open interest is zero. As time passes, open interest increases as progressively more contracts are entered. Almost all traders, however, liquidate their positions before the contract maturity date. Instead of actually taking or making delivery of the commodity, virtually all traders enter reversing trades to cancel their original positions, thereby realizing the profits or losses on the contract. Actual deliveries and purchases of commodities are then made via regular channels of supply. The percentage of contracts that result in actual delivery is estimated to range from less than 1 percent to 3 percent, depending on the commodity and the activity in the contract. The image of a trader awakening one delivery date with a hog in the front yard is amusing, but unlikely. In the unusual case of actual deliveries of commodities, they occur via regular channels of supply, most often warehouse receipts.

You can see the typical pattern of open interest in Figure 20.1. In the canola contracts, for example, the November contract has the largest open interest. The more distant November 2014 to July 2015 maturity contracts have no open interest, because the contracts have only recently been available for trading.

Marking to Market and the Margin Account

The total profit or loss realized by the long trader who buys a contract at time zero, and closes or reverses it at time t, is just the change in the futures price over the period $F_t - F_0$. Symmetrically, the short trader earns $F_0 - F_t$.

The process by which profits or losses accrue to traders is called **marking to market**. At initial execution of a trade, each trader establishes a margin account. The margin is a security account consisting of cash and/or near-cash securities, such as Treasury bills, which ensure that the trader is able to satisfy the obligations of the futures contract. Because both parties to a futures contract are exposed to losses, both must post margin. This is in contrast to options, where only the option writer has an obligation and thus needs to post margin. If the initial margin for canola, for example, is 10 percent, then the trader who opens a position early on June 6, 2013 on the January 2014 contract must post $1,131.20 per contract of the margin account. This is 10 percent of the contract value of $565.60 per tonne times 20 tonnes per contract. Because the margin may be satisfied with interest-earning securities, posting the margin does not impose a significant opportunity cost of funds on the trader. The initial margin usually is set between 5 percent and 15 percent of the total value of the contract. Contracts written on assets with more volatile prices require higher margins.

On any day that futures markets trade, futures prices may rise or fall. Instead of waiting until the maturity date for traders to realize all gains and losses, the clearinghouse requires all positions to recognize profits as they accrue daily. If the futures price of canola at the ICE rises from $565.60 to $570.60 per tonne, the clearinghouse credits the margin account of the long position for 20 tonnes (which is the standard size of the canola-futures contract) multiplied by $5 per tonne, or $100 per contract. Conversely, for the short position the clearinghouse takes this amount from the margin account for each contract held. This daily settling is marking to market.

Therefore, the maturity date of the contract does not govern realization of profit or loss. Marking to market ensures that, as futures prices change, the proceeds accrue to the trader's margin account immediately.

CC 2

CONCEPT CHECK

What must be the net inflow or outlay from marking to market for the clearinghouse?

If a trader accrues sustained losses from daily marking to market, the margin account may fall below a critical value called the **maintenance margin**. If the value of the account falls below this value, the trader receives a margin call, requiring that the margin account be replenished or the position to be reduced to a size commensurate with the remaining funds. Margins and margin calls safeguard the position of the clearinghouse. Positions are closed out before the margin account is exhausted—the trader's losses are covered and the clearinghouse is not put at risk.

EXAMPLE 20.1 **Maintenance Margin**

Suppose the maintenance margin is 5 percent while the initial margin was 10 percent of the value of canola, or $1,131.20. Then a margin call will go out when the original margin account has fallen to just about half, or by $565.60. Each $1 decline in the canola price results in a $20 loss to the long position. Therefore, the futures price need only fall by $28.28 to trigger a margin call.

Marking to market is the major way in which futures and forward contracts differ, besides contract standardization. Futures follow a pay-(or receive-)as-you-go-method. Forward contracts are simply held until maturity, and no funds are transferred until that date, although the contracts may be traded.

On the contract delivery date the futures price will equal the spot price. Since a maturing contract calls for immediate delivery, the futures price on that day must equal the spot price—the cost of the commodity from the two competing sources is equalized in a competitive market.[4] You may obtain the delivery of the commodity either by purchasing it directly in the spot market or by entering the long side of a futures contract.

A commodity available from two sources (spot or futures market) must be priced identically, or else investors will rush to purchase it from the cheap source in order to sell it in the higher-priced market. Such arbitrage activity could not persist without prices adjusting to eliminate the arbitrage opportunity. Therefore, the futures price and spot price must converge at maturity. This is called the **convergence property**.

For an investor who establishes a long position in a contract now (time 0) and holds that position until maturity (time T), the sum of all daily settlements will equal $F_T - F_0$, where F_T stands for the futures price at contract maturity. Because of convergence, however, the futures price at maturity equals the spot price, P_T, so total futures profits also may be expressed as $P_T - F_0$. Thus we see that profits on a futures contract held to maturity perfectly track changes in the value of the underlying asset.

EXAMPLE 20.2   Marking to Market

Assume the current futures price for silver for delivery five days from today is US$30.10 per ounce. Suppose that over the next five days the futures price evolves as follows:

Day	Futures Price
0 (today)	$30.10
1	$30.20
2	$30.25
3	$30.18
4	$30.18
5 (delivery)	$30.21

The daily marking-to-market settlements for each contract held by the long position will be as follows:

Day	Profit (Loss) per Ounce	×	5,000 Ounces/Contract = Daily Proceeds
1	30.20 − 30.10 = .10		$500
2	30.25 − 30.20 = .05		250
3	30.18 − 30.25 = −.07		−350
4	30.18 − 30.18 = 0		0
5	30.21 − 30.18 = .03		150
			$550

continued

---

[4]Small differences between the spot and futures prices at maturity may persist because of transportation costs, but this is a minor factor.

The profit on day 1 is the increase in the futures price from the previous day, or ($30.20 − $30.10) per ounce. Because each silver contract on the Commodity Exchange (CMX) calls for purchase and delivery of 5,000 ounces, the total profit per contract is 5,000 multiplied by $.10, or $500. On day three, when the futures price falls, the long position's margin account will be debited by $350. By day five, the sum of all daily proceeds is $550. This is exactly equal to 5,000 times the difference between the final futures price of $30.21 and the original futures price of $30.10. Thus the sum of all the daily proceeds (per ounce of silver held long) equals $P_T − F_0$.

Cash Versus Actual Delivery

Most futures markets call for delivery of an actual commodity, such as a particular grade of wheat or a specified amount of foreign currency, if the contract is not reversed before maturity. For agricultural commodities where quality of the delivered good may vary, the exchange sets quality standards as part of the futures contract. In some cases, contracts may be settled with higher- or lower-grade commodities. In these cases, a premium or discount is applied to the delivered commodity to adjust for the quality difference.

Some futures contracts call for **cash delivery**. An example is a stock index futures contract where the underlying asset is an index such as the S&P/TSX 60 or the S&P 500 index. Delivery of every stock in the index clearly would be impractical. Hence the contract calls for "delivery" of a cash amount equal to the value that the index attains on the maturity date of the contract. The sum of all the daily settlements from marking to market results in the long position realizing total profits or losses of $S_T − F_0$, where S_T is the value of the stock index on the maturity date T, and F_0 is the original futures price. Cash settlement closely mimics actual delivery, except the cash value of the asset rather than the asset itself is delivered.

More concretely, the S&P/TSX 60 index contract calls for delivery of $200 multiplied by the value of the index. At maturity, the index might list at 800, a market-value-weighted index of the prices of all 60 stocks in the index. The cash settlement contract calls for delivery of $200 × 800, or $160,000, in return for 200 times the futures price. This yields exactly the same profit as would result from directly purchasing 200 units of the index for $160,000 and then delivering it for 200 times the original futures price.

Regulations

Futures markets in Canada are under the jurisdiction of the provincial securities commissions. Most futures trading is self-regulated, although some provinces have passed commodity futures acts.

In the United States, futures markets are regulated by the Commodities Futures Trading Commission (CFTC), a federal agency. The CFTC sets capital requirements for member firms of the futures exchanges, authorizes trading in new contracts, and oversees maintenance of daily trading records.

The futures exchange may set limits on the amount by which futures prices may change from one day to the next. In the S&P/TSX 60 the Montréal Exchange halts trading in conjunction with the triggering of "circuit breakers" set in coordination with the NYSE and the TSX. Suppose, for example, the price limit on the S&P/TSX 60 futures contract is set at $4,000, corresponding to a change of 20 ($4,000/$200) in the index. This means that if S&P/TSX 60 futures close today at 800, trades tomorrow in the S&P/TSX 60 index may vary only between 820 and 780. Likewise, if the price limit on silver contracts traded on the Chicago Board of Trade is $1, this means that if silver futures close today at $30.10 per ounce, trades in silver tomorrow may vary only between $29.10 and $31.10 per ounce. The exchanges may increase or reduce price limits in response to perceived increases or decreases in price volatility of the contract. Price limits often are eliminated as contracts approach maturity, usually in the last month of trading.

Price limits traditionally are viewed as a means to limit violent price fluctuations. This reasoning seems dubious. Suppose that an international monetary crisis overnight drives up the spot price of silver to $40. No one would sell silver futures at prices for future delivery as low as $30.10. Instead, the futures price would rise each day by the $1 limit, although the quoted price would represent only an unfilled bid order—no contracts would trade at the low quoted price. After several days of limit moves of $1 per day, the futures price would finally reach its equilibrium level, and trading would occur again. This process means no one could unload a position until the price reached its equilibrium level. This example shows that price limits offer no real protection against price fluctuation.

Taxation

Because of the marking-to-market procedure, investors do not have control over the tax year in which they realize gains or losses. Instead, price changes are realized gradually, with each daily settlement. Therefore, taxes are paid at year-end on accumulated profits or losses, regardless of whether the position has been closed out.

20.3   FUTURES MARKETS STRATEGIES

Hedging and Speculating

Hedging and speculating are two polar uses of futures markets. A speculator uses a futures contract to profit from movements in futures prices; a hedger, to protect against price movement. If speculators believe that prices will increase, they will take a long position for expected profits. Conversely, they will exploit expected price declines by taking a short position.

EXAMPLE 20.3   **Speculating with Bond Futures**

Let's consider the use of the 10-year Canada bond futures contract, the listing for which appears online at www.m-x.ca under the symbol CGB. Each Canada bond contract on the Montréal Exchange calls for delivery of $100,000 par value of bonds. Suppose you believed that interest rates would decrease and, therefore, bond prices would increase. You may then decide to purchase Canada bond futures. If the futures price for delivery in March is 116.730, then this means that the market price of the underlying bonds is 116.73 percent of par, or $116,730. Therefore, for every increase of one point in the Canada bond futures price (e.g., to 117.73), the long position gains $1,000, and the short loses that amount. Therefore, if you are bullish on bond prices, you might speculate by buying Canada bond futures contracts.

If the Canada bond futures price at contract maturity date increases by one point to 117.73, then you profit by $1,000 per contract. If the forecast is incorrect, and Canada bond futures prices decline, you lose $1,000 times the decrease in the futures price for each contract purchased. Speculators bet on the direction of futures price movements.

Why does a speculator buy a Canada bond futures contract? Why not buy Canada bonds directly? One reason lies in transaction costs, which are far smaller in futures markets.

Another important reason is the leverage futures trading provides. Recall that futures contracts require traders to post margin considerably less than the value of the asset underlying the contract. Therefore, they allow speculators to achieve much greater leverage than is available from direct trading in a commodity.

EXAMPLE 20.4   **Futures and Leverage**

Each Canada bond contract calls for delivery of $100,000 par value, worth $116,730 in our example. Suppose the initial margin required for this account is 10%, or $11,673. A one-point increase in the bond futures price yields a $1,000 per contract gain translates into a $1,000/$11,673 = 8.57 percent return on the money put up, despite the fact that the Canada bond futures price increases only 1/116.73 = .857%. The futures margin in this case yields tem times as large return as the increase in bond prices. The 10-to-1 ratio of percentage changes reflects the leverage inherent in the futures position, because the contract was established with an initial margin of one-tenth the value of the underlying asset.

Hedgers by contrast use futures markets to protect themselves against price movements. An investor holding a Canada bond portfolio, for example, might anticipate a period of interest rate volatility and want to protect the value of the portfolio against price fluctuations. In this case, the investor has no desire to bet on price movements in either direction. To achieve such protection, a hedger takes a short position in Canada bond futures, which obligates him to deliver Canada bonds at the contract maturity date for the current futures price. This locks in the sales price for the bonds and guarantees that the total value of the bond-plus-futures position at the maturity date is the futures price.[5]

EXAMPLE 20.5   **Hedging with Bond Futures**

Suppose as in Example 20.3 that the futures price for March delivery (rounding to the nearest dollar) is $117 per $100 par value, and that the only three possible Canada bond prices in March are $116, $117, and $118. If the investor currently holds 200 bonds, each with par value $1,000, he would take short positions in two contracts, each for $100,000 par value. Protecting the value of a portfolio with short futures positions is called *short hedging*. Taking the futures position requires no current investment. (The initial margin requirement is small relative to the size of the contract, and because it may be posted in interest-bearing securities, it does not represent a time-value or opportunity cost.)

The profits in March from each of the two short futures contracts will be 1,000 times any decrease in the futures price. At maturity, the convergence property ensures that the final futures price will equal the spot price of the Canada bonds. Hence the futures profit will be 2,000 times $(F_0 - P_T)$, where P_T is the price of the bonds on the delivery date and F_0 is the original futures price, $117.

Now consider the hedged portfolio consisting of the bonds and the short futures positions. The portfolio value as a function of the bond price in March can be computed as follows:

	Canada Bond Price in March		
	$116	**$117**	**$118**
Bond holdings (value = $2,000P_T$)	$232,000	$234,000	$236,000
Futures profits or losses	2,000	0	−2,000
Total	$234,000	$234,000	$234,000

continued

---

[5]To keep things simple, we will assume that the Canada bond futures contract calls for delivery of a bond with the same coupon and maturity as that in the investor's portfolio. In practice, a variety of bonds may be delivered to satisfy the contract, and a "conversion factor" is used to adjust for the relative values of the eligible delivery bonds. We will ignore this complication.

The total portfolio value is unaffected by the eventual bond price, which is what the hedger wants. The gains or losses on the bond holdings are exactly offset by those on the two contracts held short.

For example, if bond prices fall to $116, the losses on the bond portfolio are offset by the $2,000 gain on the futures contracts. That profit equals the difference between the futures price on the maturity date (which equals the spot price on that date of $116) and the originally contracted futures price of $117. For short contracts, a profit of $1 per $100 par value is realized from the fall in the spot price. Because two contracts call for delivery of $200,000 par value, this results in a $2,000 gain that offsets the decline in the value of the bonds held in portfolio. In contrast to a speculator, a hedger is indifferent to the ultimate price of the asset. The short hedger who has in essence arranged to sell the asset for an agreed-upon price need not be concerned about further developments in the market price.

To generalize this example, you can note that the bond will be worth P_T at maturity, whereas the profit on the futures contract is $F_0 - P_T$. The sum of the two positions is F_0 dollars, which is independent of the eventual bond price.

A *long hedge* is the analogue to a short hedge for a purchaser of an asset. Consider, for example, a pension fund manager who anticipates a cash inflow in two months that will be invested in fixed-income securities. The manager views Canada bonds as very attractively priced now and would like to lock in current prices and yields until the investment actually can be made two months hence. The manager can lock in the effective cost of the purchase by entering the long side of a contract, which commits her to purchasing at the current futures price.

CC 3

CONCEPT CHECK

Suppose, as in our example, that the futures price is 115 and that Canada bonds will be priced at $114, $115, or $116 in one month. Show that the cost in June of purchasing $200,000 par value of Canada bonds net of the profit/loss on two long Canada bond contracts will be $230,000 regardless of the eventual bond price.

Exact futures hedging may be impossible for some goods because the necessary futures contract is not traded. For example, a portfolio manager might want to hedge the value of a diversified, actively managed portfolio for a period of time. However, futures contracts are listed only on indexed portfolios. Nevertheless, because returns on the manager's diversified portfolio will have a high correlation with returns on broad-based indexed portfolios, an effective hedge may be established by selling index futures contracts. Hedging a position using futures on another asset is called *cross-hedging*.

Basis Risk and Hedging

The **basis** is the difference between the futures price and the spot price.[6] As we have noted, on the maturity date of a contract the basis must be zero: The convergence property implies that $F_T - P_T = 0$. Before maturity, however, the futures price for later delivery may differ substantially from the current spot price.

---

[6]Usage of the word *basis* is somewhat loose. It is sometimes used to refer to F-P and sometimes to P-F. We will consistently call the basis F-P.

In Example 20.5 we discussed the case of a short hedger who holds an asset and a short position to deliver that asset in the future. If the asset and futures contract are held until maturity, the hedger bears no risk, because the ultimate value of the portfolio on the delivery date is determined completely by the current futures price. Risk is eliminated because the futures price and spot price at contract maturity must be equal: gains and losses on the futures and the commodity position will exactly cancel. If the contract and asset are to be liquidated early, however, the hedger bears **basis risk**, because the futures price and spot price need not move in perfect lockstep at all times before the delivery date. In this case, gains and losses on the contract and the asset need not exactly offset each other.

CC 4

CONCEPT CHECK

What are the sources of risk to an investor who uses stock index futures to hedge an actively managed stock portfolio?

Some speculators try to profit from movements in the basis. Rather than betting on the direction of the futures or spot prices per se, they bet on the changes in the difference between the two. A long spot–short futures position will profit when the basis narrows.

EXAMPLE 20.6   **Speculating on the Basis**

Consider an investor holding 100 ounces of gold, who is short one gold futures contract. Suppose that gold sells today for $1,591 per ounce, while the futures price for next-year delivery is $1,596 an ounce The basis is therefore $5. Tomorrow, the spot price might increase to $1,505, while the futures price might increase to $1,599. The basis has narrowed to $4. The investor realizes a capital gain of $1,595 − $1,591 = $4 per ounce on her gold holdings and a loss of $1,599 − $1,596 = $3 per ounce from the increase in the futures price. The net gain is the decrease in basis, or $1 per ounce.

A related strategy is a calendar **spread** position where the investor takes a long position in a futures contract of one maturity and a short position in a contract on the same commodity, but with a different maturity. Profits accrue if the difference in futures prices between the two contracts changes in the hoped-for direction; that is, if the futures price on the contract held long increases by more (or decreases by less) than the futures price on the contract held short. Like basis strategies, spread positions aim to exploit movements in relative price structures rather than to profit from movements in the general level of prices.

20.4   **FUTURES PRICES**

The Spot–Futures Parity Theorem

We have seen that a futures contract can be used to hedge changes in the value of the underlying asset. If the hedge is perfect, meaning that the asset-plus-futures portfolio has no risk, then the hedged position must provide a rate of return equal to the rate on other risk-free investments. Otherwise, there will be arbitrage opportunities that investors will exploit until prices are brought back into line. This insight can be used to derive the theoretical relationship between a futures price and the price of its underlying asset.

Suppose for simplicity that the S&P/TSX 60 index currently is at 800 and an investor who holds $800 in a mutual fund indexed to the S&P/TSX 60 wishes to temporarily hedge her exposure to market risk. Assume that the indexed portfolio pays dividends totalling $10 over the course of the year and, for simplicity, that all dividends are paid at year-end. Finally, assume that the futures price for year-end delivery on the S&P/TSX 60 contract is 816.[7] Let's examine the end-of-year proceeds for various values of the stock index if the investor hedges her portfolio by entering the short side of the futures contract.

Value of stock portfolio	$760	$780	$800	$810	$820	$840
Payoff from short futures position (equals $F_0 - F_T = \$816 - S_T$)	56	36	16	6	−4	−24
Dividend income	10	10	10	10	10	10
Total	$826	$826	$826	$826	$826	$826

The payoff from the short futures position equals the difference between the original futures price, $816, and the year-end stock price. This is due to convergence: the futures price at contract maturity will equal the stock price at that time.

Notice that the overall position is perfectly hedged. Any increase in the value of the indexed stock portfolio is offset by an equal decrease in the payoff of the short futures position, resulting in a final value independent of the stock price. The $826 payoff is the sum of the current futures price, $F_0 = \$816$, and the $10 dividend. It is as though the investor arranged to sell the stock at year-end for the current futures price, thereby eliminating price risk and locking in total proceeds equal to the sales price plus dividends paid before the sale.

What rate of return is earned on this riskless position? The stock investment requires an initial outlay of $800, while the futures position is established without an initial cash outflow. Therefore, the $800 portfolio grows to a year-end value of $826, providing a rate of return of 3.25 percent. More generally, a total investment of S_0, the current stock price, grows to a final value of $F_0 + D$, where D is the dividend payout on the portfolio. The rate of return is therefore

$$\text{Rate of return on perfectly hedged stock portfolio} = \frac{(F_0 + D) - S_0}{S_0}$$

This return is essentially riskless. We observe F_0 at the beginning of the period when we enter the futures contract. While dividend payouts are not perfectly riskless, they are highly predictable over short periods, especially for diversified portfolios. Any uncertainty is *extremely* small compared to the uncertainty of stock prices.

Presumably, 3.25 percent must be the rate of return available on other riskless investments. If not, then investors would face two competing risk-free strategies with different rates of return, a situation that could not last. Therefore, we conclude that

$$\frac{(F_0 + D) - S_0}{S_0} = r_f$$

Rearranging, we find that the futures price must be

$$F_0 = S_0(1 + r_f) - D = S_0(1 + r_f - d) \tag{20.1}$$

---

[7]Actually, the futures contract calls for delivery of $200 times the value of the S&P/TSX 60 index, so that each contract would be settled for $200 times 816. We will simplify by assuming that you can buy a contract for one unit rather than 200 units of the index. In practice, one contract would hedge about $200 × 800 = $160,000 worth of stock. Of course, institutional investors would consider a stock portfolio of this size to be quite small.

where d is the dividend yield on the stock portfolio, defined as D/S_0. This result is called the **spot–futures parity theorem**. It gives the normal or theoretically correct relationship between spot and futures prices.

EXAMPLE 20.7 **Futures Market Arbitrage**

Suppose that parity were violated. For example, suppose the risk-free interest rate in the economy were only 2 percent, so that according to parity, the futures price should be $\$800(1 + .02) - \$10 = \$806$. The actual futures price, $F_0 = \$816$, is $\$10$ higher than its "appropriate" value. This implies that an investor can make arbitrage profits by shorting the relatively overpriced futures contract and buying the relatively underpriced stock portfolio using money borrowed at the 2 percent market interest rate. The proceeds from this strategy would be as follows:

Action	Initial Cash Flow	Cash Flow in One Year
Borrow $800, repay with interest in one year	+$800	$-800(1.02) = -\$816$
Buy stock for $800	−$800	$S_T + \$10$ dividend
Enter short futures position ($F_0 = \$816$)	0	$\$816 - S_T$
Total	0	$10

The net initial investment of the strategy is zero. But its cash flow in one year is positive and riskless. The payoff is $\$10$ regardless of the stock price. This payoff is precisely equal to the mispricing of the futures contract relative to its parity value.

When parity is violated, the strategy to exploit the mispricing produces an arbitrage profit—a riskless profit requiring no initial net investment. If such an opportunity existed, all market participants would rush to take advantage of it. The results? The stock price would be bid up, and/or the futures price offered would be bid down until equation 20.1 was satisfied. A similar analysis applies to the possibility that F_0 is less than $\$806$. In this case, you simply reverse the strategy above to earn riskless profits. We conclude, therefore, that in a well-functioning market in which arbitrage opportunities are competed away, $F_0 = S_0(1 + r_f) - D$.

The arbitrage strategy of Example 20.7 can be represented more generally as follows:

Action	Initial Cash Flow	Cash Flow in One Year
1. Borrow S_0 dollars	S_0	$-S_0(1 + r_f)$
2. Buy stock for S_0	$-S_0$	$S_T + D$
3. Enter short futures position	0	$F_0 - S_T$
Total	0	$F_0 - S_0(1 + r_f) + D$

The initial cash flow is zero by construction: the money necessary to purchase the stock in step 1 is borrowed in step 2, and the futures position in step 3, which is used to hedge the value of the stock position, does not require an initial outlay. Moreover, the total cash flow to the strategy at year-end is riskless, because it involves only terms that are already known when the contract is entered. If the final cash flow were not zero, all investors would try to cash in on the arbitrage opportunity. Ultimately prices would change until the year-end cash flow is reduced to zero, at which point F_0 would equal $S_0(1 + r_f) - D$.

CC 5

CONCEPT CHECK

What are the three steps of the arbitrage strategy in Example 20.7 if F_0 is equal to $802? Work out the cash flows of the strategy now and in one year in a table like the one above.

The parity relationship also is called the **cost-of-carry relationship** because it asserts that the futures price is determined by the relative costs of buying a stock with deferred delivery in the futures market versus buying it in the spot market with immediate delivery and "carrying" it in inventory. If you buy the stock now, you tie up your funds and incur a time-value-of-money cost of r_f per period. On the other hand, you receive dividend payments with a current yield of d. The net carrying-cost advantage of deferring delivery of the stock is therefore $r_f - d$ per period. This advantage must be offset by a differential between the futures price and the spot price. The price differential just offsets the cost-of-carry advantage when $F_0 = S_0(1 + r_f - d)$.

The parity relationship is easily generalized to multiperiod applications. We simply recognize that the difference between the futures and spot prices will be larger as the maturity of the contract is longer. This reflects the longer period to which we apply the net cost of carry. For contract maturity of T periods, the parity relationship is

$$F_0 = S_0(1 + r_f - d)^T \tag{20.2}$$

Notice that when the dividend yield is less than the risk-free rate, equation 20.2 implies that futures prices will exceed spot prices, and by greater amounts for longer times to contract maturity. But when $d > r_f$, as is generally the case today, the income yield on the stock exceeds the forgone (risk-free) interest that might be earned on the money invested; in this event, the futures price will be less than the current stock price, again by greater amounts for longer maturities. For instance, on July 18, 2013 the S&P/TSX 60 index closed at 726.59, while the settlement prices of the September 2013, December 2013, and March 2014 contracts were 723.60, 720.60, and 717.60 respectively. On the other hand, for futures on assets like gold, which pay no "dividend yield," we can set $d = 0$ and conclude that F *must* increase as time to maturity increases.

Although dividends of individual securities may fluctuate unpredictably, the annualized dividend yield of a broad-based index such as the S&P 500 is fairly stable, recently in the neighbourhood of a bit more than 2 percent per year. The yield is seasonal, however, with regular peaks and troughs, so the dividend yield for the relevant months must be the one used. Figure 20.4 illustrates the yield pattern for the S&P 500. Some months, such as January or April, have consistently low yields, while others, such as May, have consistently high ones.[8]

We have described parity in terms of stocks and stock index futures, but it should be clear that the logic applies as well to any financial futures contract. For gold futures, for example, we would simply set the dividend yield to zero. For bond contracts, we would let the coupon income on the bond play the role of dividend payments. In both cases, the parity relationship would be essentially the same as equation 20.2.

The arbitrage strategy described above should convince you that these parity relationships are more than just theoretical results. Any violations of the parity relationship give rise to arbitrage opportunities that can provide large profits to traders. We will see shortly that index arbitrage in the stock market is a tool to exploit violations of the parity relationship for stock index futures contracts.

---

[8]The very high dividend yield of November 2004 was due to Microsoft's special one-time dividend of $3 per share.

Figure 20.4

S&P 500 monthly dividend yield.

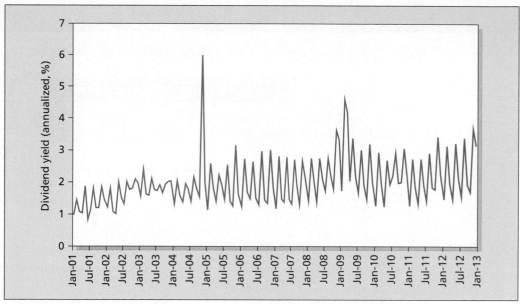

Spreads

Just as we can predict the relationship between spot and futures prices, there are similar methods to determine the proper relationships among futures prices for contracts of different maturity dates. These relationships are simple generalizations of the spot–futures parity relationship.

Call $F(T_1)$ the current futures price for delivery at date T_1, and $F(T_2)$ the futures price for delivery at T_2. Let d be the dividend yield of the stock between T_1 and T_2. We know from the parity equation 20.2 that[9]

$$F(T_1) = S_0(1 + r_f - d)^{T_1}$$
$$F(T_2) = S_0(1 + r_f - d)^{T_2}$$

As a result,

$$F(T_2)/F(T_1) = (1 + r_f - d)^{(T_2 - T_1)}$$

Therefore, the basic parity relationship for spreads is

$$F(T_2)/F(T_1) = (1 + r_f - d)^{(T_2 - T_1)} \tag{20.3}$$

Equation 20.3 should remind you of to the spot–futures parity relationship. The major difference is in the substitution of $F(T_1)$ for the current spot price. The intuition also is similar. Delaying delivery from T_1 to T_2 assures the long position that the stock will be purchased for $F(T_2)$ dollars at T_2 but does not require that money be tied up in the stock until T_2. The savings realized are the cost of carry between T_1 and T_2 of the money that would have been paid at T_1. Delaying delivery from T_1 until T_2 frees up $F(T_1)$ dollars, which earn risk-free interest at rate r_f. The delayed delivery of the stock also results in the lost dividend yield between T_1 and T_2. The net cost of carry saved by delaying the delivery is thus $r_f - d$. This gives the proportional increase in the futures price required to compensate market participants for the delayed delivery of the stock and postponement of the payment of the futures price. If the parity condition for spreads is violated, arbitrage opportunities will arise. (Problem 5 at the end of this chapter explores this phenomenon.)

---

[9]We also assume that r_f is the same for all maturities, which implies that the pure yield curve that we saw in Chapter 13 is "flat."

EXAMPLE 20.8   Spread Pricing

To see how to use equation 20.3, consider the following data for a hypothetical contract:

Contract Maturity	Date Futures Price
January 15	105
March 15	104.75

Suppose that the effective annual T-bill rate is 1 percent and that the dividend yield is 2 percent per year. The "correct" March futures price relative to the January price is, according to equation 20.3,

$$105(1 + .01 - .02)^{1/6} = 104.82$$

The actual March futures price is 104.75, meaning that the March futures contract is slightly underpriced compared to the January futures, and that, aside from transaction costs, an arbitrage opportunity seems to be present.

Equation 20.3 shows that futures prices should all move together. This is not surprising, because all are linked to the same spot price through the parity relationship. Figure 20.5 plots futures prices on gold for three maturity dates. It is apparent that the prices move in virtual lockstep and that the more distant delivery dates require higher futures prices, as equation 20.3 predicts.

Forward Versus Futures Pricing

Until now we have paid little attention to the differing time profile of returns of futures and forward contracts. Instead, we have taken the sum of daily marking-to-market proceeds to the long position as $P_T - F_0$ and assumed for convenience that the entire profit accrues on the delivery date. The parity theorems apply only to forward pricing because they assume that contract proceeds are realized only on delivery. In contrast, the actual timing of cash flows conceivably might affect the futures price.

Figure 20.5
Gold futures prices.

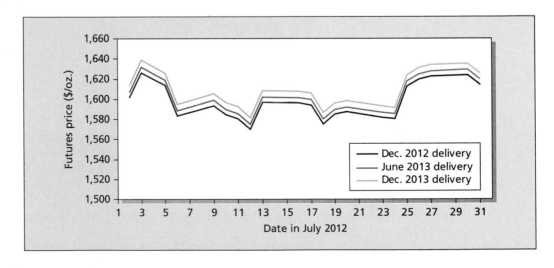

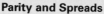
Parity and Spreads

The parity spreadsheet allows you to calculate futures prices corresponding to a spot price for different maturities, interest rates, and income yields. You can use the spreadsheet to see how prices of more distant contracts will fluctuate with spot prices and the cost of carry. You can learn more about this spreadsheet by using the version available on this book's Web site.

Questions

1. Experiment with different values for both income yield and interest rate. What happens to the size of the time spread (the difference in futures prices for the long versus short maturity contracts) if the interest rate increases by 2 percent?
2. What happens to the time spread if the income yield increases by 2 percent?
3. What happens to the spread if the income yield equals the interest rate?

Spot Futures Parity and Time Spreads					
Spot price	100				
Income yield (%)	2		Futures prices versus maturity		
Interest rate (%)	4.5				
Today's date	5/14/13		Spot price		100.00
Maturity date 1	11/17/13		Futures 1		101.26
Maturity date 2	1/2/14		Futures 2		101.58
Maturity date 3	6/7/14		Futures 3		102.66
Time to maturity 1	0.51				
Time to maturity 2	0.63				
Time to maturity 3	1.06				

Futures prices will deviate from parity values when marking to market gives a systematic advantage to either the long or short position. If marking to market tends to favour the long position, for example, the futures price should exceed the forward price, since the long position will be willing to pay a premium for the advantage of marking to market.

When will marking to market favour either the long or short trader? A trader will benefit if daily settlements are received (and can be invested) when the interest rate is high and are paid (and can be financed) when the interest rate is low. Because long positions will benefit if futures prices tend to rise when interest rates are high, they will be willing to accept a higher futures price. Therefore, a positive correlation between interest rates and changes in futures prices implies that the "fair" futures price will exceed the forward price. Conversely, a negative correlation means that marking to market favours the short position and implies that the equilibrium futures price should be below the forward price.

For most contracts, the covariance between futures prices and interest rates is so low that the difference between futures prices and forward prices will be negligible. However, contracts on long-term fixed-income securities are an important exception to this rule. In this case, because prices have a high correlation with interest rates, the covariance can be large enough to generate a meaningful spread between forward and future prices.

20.5 COMMODITY FUTURES PRICING

Commodity futures prices are governed by the same general considerations as stock futures. One difference, however, is that the cost of carrying commodities, especially those subject to spoilage, is greater than the cost of carrying financial assets. The underlying asset for some contracts, such as electricity futures, simply cannot be "carried" or held in portfolio. Finally, spot prices for some commodities demonstrate marked seasonal patterns that can affect futures pricing.

Pricing with Storage Costs

The cost of carrying commodities includes (in addition to interest costs) storage costs, insurance costs, and an allowance for spoilage of goods in storage. To price commodity futures, let us reconsider the earlier arbitrage strategy that calls for holding both the asset and a short position in the futures contract on the asset. In this case, we will denote the price of the commodity at time T as P_T, and assume for simplicity that all non-interest-carrying costs (C) are paid in one lump sum at time T, the contract maturity. Carrying costs appear in the final cash flow.

Action	Initial Cash Flow	Cash Flow at Time T
Buy asset; pay carrying costs at T	$-P_0$	$P_T - C$
Borrow P_0; repay with interest at time T	P_0	$-P_0(1 + r_f)$
Short futures position	0	$F_0 - P_T$
Total	0	$F_0 - P_0(1 + r_f) - C$

Because market prices should not allow for arbitrage opportunities, the terminal cash flow of this zero net investment, risk-free strategy should be zero.

If the cash flow were positive, this strategy would yield guaranteed profits for no investment. If the cash flow were negative, the reverse of this strategy also would yield profits. In practice, the reverse strategy would involve a short sale of the commodity. This is unusual but may be done as long as the short sale contract appropriately accounts for storage costs.[10] Thus we conclude that

$$F_0 = P_0(1 + r_f) + C$$

Finally, if we call $c = C/P_0$, and interpret c as the percentage "rate" of carrying costs, we may write

$$F_0 = P_0(1 + r_f + c) \tag{20.4}$$

which is a (one-year) parity relationship for futures involving storage costs. Compare equation 20.4 to the first parity relationship for stocks, equation 20.2, and you will see that they are very similar. In fact, if we think of carrying costs as a "negative dividend," the equations are identical. This treatment makes intuitive sense because, instead of receiving a dividend yield of d, the storer of the commodity must pay a storage cost of c. Obviously, this parity relationship is simply an extension of those we have seen already.

Although we have called c the carrying cost of the commodity, we may interpret it more generally as the *net* carrying cost, that is, the carrying cost net of the benefits derived from holding the commodity in inventory. For example, part of the "convenience yield" of goods held in inventory is the protection against stocking out, which may result in lost production or sales.

It is vital to note that we derive equation 20.4 assuming that the asset will be bought and stored; it therefore applies only to goods that currently *are* being stored. Two kinds of commodities cannot be expected to be stored. The first kind is commodities such as electricity or highly perishable goods, for which storage is technologically not feasible. The second includes goods that are not stored for economic reasons. For example, it would be foolish to buy wheat now, planning to store it for ultimate use in three years. Instead, it is clearly preferable to delay the purchase of the wheat until after the harvest of the third year. The wheat is then obtained without incurring the storage costs. Moreover, if the wheat harvest in the third year is comparable to this

---

[10]Robert A. Jarrow and George S. Oldfield, "Forward Contracts and Futures Contracts," *Journal of Financial Economics* 9 (1981).

year's, you could obtain it at roughly the same price as you would pay this year. By waiting to purchase, you avoid both interest and storage costs.

CC 6

CONCEPT CHECK

People are willing to buy and "store" shares of stock despite the fact that their purchase ties up capital. Most people, however, are not willing to buy and store soybeans. What is the difference in the properties of the expected evolution of stock prices versus soybean prices that accounts for this result?

Because storage across harvests is costly, equation 20.4 should not be expected to apply for holding periods that span harvest times, nor should it apply to perishable goods that are available only "in season." Whereas the futures price for gold, which is a stored commodity, increases steadily with the maturity of the contract, the futures price for wheat is seasonal; it typically falls across harvests between March and July as new supplies become available.

Figure 20.6 is a stylized version of this seasonal price pattern for an agricultural product. Clearly, this pattern differs sharply from financial assets, such as stocks or gold, for which there is no seasonal price movement. Financial assets are priced so that holding them produces a fair return. Agricultural prices, by contrast, are subject to steep periodic drops as each crop is harvested, which makes storage across harvests consequently unprofitable.

Futures pricing across seasons requires a different approach that is not based on storage across harvest periods. In place of general no-arbitrage restrictions we rely instead on risk premium theory and discounted cash flow (DCF) analysis.

Discounted Cash Flow Analysis for Commodity Futures

Given the current expectation of the spot price of the commodity at some future date and a measure of the risk characteristics of that price, we can measure the present value of a claim to

Figure 20.6

Typical commodity price pattern over the season. Prices adjusted for inflation.

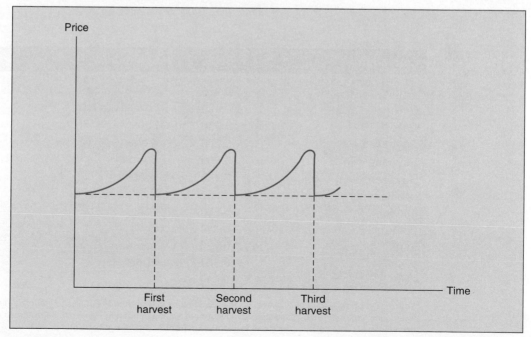

receive the commodity at that future date. We simply calculate the appropriate risk premium from a model such as the CAPM or APT and discount the expected spot price at the appropriate risk-adjusted interest rate.

EXAMPLE 20.9   Commodity Futures Pricing

Table 20.2, which presents betas on a variety of commodities, shows that the beta of orange juice, for example, was estimated to be .117 over the period. If the T-bill rate is currently 5 percent, and the historical market risk premium has been about 8 percent, the appropriate discount rate for orange juice would be given by the CAPM as

$$5\% + .117(8\%) = 5.94\%$$

If the expected spot price for orange juice six months from now is $1.45 per pound, the present value of a six-month deferred claim to a pound of orange juice is simply

$$\$1.45/(1.0594)^{1/2} = \$1.409$$

What would the proper futures price for orange juice be? The contract calls for the ultimate exchange of orange juice for the futures price. We have just shown that the present value of the juice is $1.409. This should equal the present value of the futures price that will be paid for the juice. A commitment to a payment of F_0 dollars in six months has a present value of $F_0/(1.05)^{1/2} = .976 \times F_0$. (Note that the discount rate is the risk-free rate of 5 percent, because the promised payment is fixed and therefore independent of market conditions.)

To equate the present values of the promised payment of F_0 and the promised receipt of orange juice, we would set

$$.976F_0 = \$1.409$$

or

$$F_0 = \$1.444$$

TABLE 20.2
Commodity
Betas

Commodity	Beta	Commodity	Beta
Wheat	−0.370	Orange juice	0.117
Corn	−0.429	Propane	−3.851
Oats	0.000	Coca	−0.291
Soybeans	−0.266	Silver	−0.272
Soybean oil	−0.650	Copper	0.005
Soybean meal	0.239	Cattle	0.365
Broilers	−1.692	Hogs	−0.148
Plywood	0.660	Pork bellies	−0.062
Potatoes	−0.610	Eggs	−0.293
Platinum	0.221	Lumber	−0.131
Wool	0.307	Sugar	−2.403
Cotton	−0.015		

Source: Zvi Bodie and Victor Rosansky, "Risk and Return in Commodity Futures," *Financial Analysts Journal* 36 (May/June 1980). © 1980, Association for Investment Management and Research. Reproduced and republished from Financial Analysts Federation with permission from AIMR. All rights reserved.

The general rule, then, to determine the appropriate futures price is to equate the present value of the future payment of F_0 and the present value of the commodity to be received. This implies

$$\frac{F_0}{(1 + r_f)^T} = \frac{E(P_T)}{(1 + k)^T}$$

or

$$F_0 = E(P_T)\left(\frac{1 + r_f}{1 + k}\right)^T \tag{20.5}$$

where k is the required rate of return on the commodity, which may be obtained from a model of asset market equilibrium such as the CAPM.

Note that equation 20.5 is perfectly consistent with the spot–futures parity relationship. For example, apply equation 20.5 to the futures price for a stock paying no dividends. Because the entire return on the stock is in the form of capital gains, the expected rate of capital gains must equal k, the required rate of return on the stock. Consequently, the expected price of the stock is its current price times $(1 + k)^T$, or $E(P^T) = P_0(1 + k)^T$. Substituting this expression into equation 20.5 results in $F_0 = P_0(1 + r_f)^T$, which is exactly the parity relationship.

CONCEPT CHECK

Suppose that the systematic risk of orange juice were to increase, holding the expected time T price of juice constant. If the expected spot price is unchanged, would the futures price change? In what direction? What is the intuition behind your answer?

Futures Prices Versus Expected Spot Prices

The above analysis sheds light upon one of the oldest controversies in the theory of futures pricing: the relationship between the futures price and the expected value of the spot price of the commodity at some *future* date. Three traditional theories have been put forth: the expectations hypothesis, normal backwardation, and contango. Today's consensus is that all of these traditional hypotheses are subsumed by the insights provided by modern portfolio theory. Figure 20.7 shows the expected path of futures prices under the three traditional hypotheses.

Expectations Hypothesis

The *expectations hypothesis* is the simplest theory of futures pricing. It states that the futures price equals the expected value of the future spot price: $F_0 = E(P_T)$. Under this theory, the expected profit to either position of a futures contract would equal zero: the short position's expected profit is $F_0 - E(P_T)$, while the long's is $E(P_T) - F_0$. With $F_0 = E(P_T)$, the expected profit to either side is zero. This hypothesis relies on a notion of risk neutrality. If all market participants are risk-neutral, they should agree on a futures price that provides an expected profit of zero to all parties.

The expectations hypothesis resembles market equilibrium in a world with no uncertainty; that is, if prices of goods at all future dates are currently known, then the futures price for delivery at any particular date would simply equal the currently known future spot price for that date. It is a tempting but incorrect leap to assert next that under uncertainty the futures price should equal the currently expected spot price. This view ignores the risk premiums that must be built into futures prices when ultimate spot prices are uncertain.

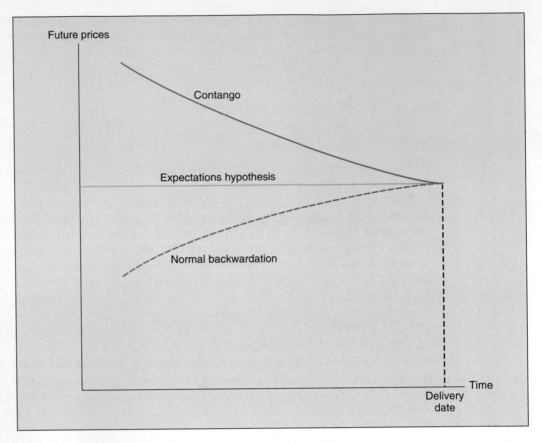

Normal Backwardation

This theory is associated with the famous British economists John Maynard Keynes and John Hicks. They argued that for most commodities there are natural hedgers who desire to shed risk. For example, wheat farmers will desire to shed the risk of uncertain wheat prices. These farmers will take short positions to deliver wheat at a guaranteed price; they will short hedge. To induce speculators to take the corresponding long positions, the farmers need to offer them an expectation of profit. Speculators will enter the long side of the contract only if the futures price is below the expected spot price of wheat, for an expected profit of $E(P_T) - F_0$. The speculator's expected profit is the farmer's expected loss, but farmers are willing to bear this expected loss to shed the risk of uncertain wheat prices. The theory of *normal backwardation* thus suggests that the futures price will be bid down to a level below the expected spot price and will rise over the life of the contract until the maturity date, at which point $F_T = P_T$.

Although this theory recognizes the important role of risk premiums in futures markets, it is based on total variability rather than on systematic risk. (This is not surprising, as Keynes wrote almost 40 years before the development of modern portfolio theory.) The modern view refines the measure of risk used to determine appropriate risk premiums.

Contango

The polar hypothesis to backwardation holds that the natural hedgers are the purchasers of a commodity, rather than the suppliers. In the case of wheat, for example, we would view grain processors as willing to pay a premium to lock in the price that they must pay for wheat. These processors hedge by taking a long position in the futures market; therefore, they are called long hedgers, whereas farmers are short hedgers. Because long hedgers will agree to pay high futures prices to shed risk, and because speculators must be paid a premium to enter into the short position, the *contango* theory holds that F_0 must exceed $E(P_T)$.

It is clear that any commodity will have both natural long hedgers and short hedgers. The compromise traditional view, called the *net hedging hypothesis*, is that F_0 will be less than $E(P_T)$ when short hedgers outnumber long hedgers, and vice versa. The strong side of the market will be the side (short or long) that has more natural hedgers. The strong side must pay a premium to induce speculators to enter into enough contracts to balance the "natural" supply of long and short hedgers.

Modern Portfolio Theory

The three traditional hypotheses all envision a mass of speculators willing to enter either side of the futures market if they are sufficiently compensated for the risk they incur. Modern portfolio theory fine-tunes this approach by refining the notion of risk used in the determination of risk premiums.

As we saw, futures price and expected spot price at a future date are related through equation 20.5. You can see immediately from that equation that F_0 will be less than the expectation of P_T whenever k is greater than r_f, which will be the case for any positive-beta asset. This means that the long side of the contract will make an expected profit (F_0 will be lower than $E(P_T)$) when the commodity exhibits positive systematic risk (k is greater than r_f).

Why should this be? A long futures position will provide a profit (or loss) of $P_T - F_0$. If the ultimate value of P_T entails positive systematic risk, so will the profit to the long position. Speculators with well-diversified portfolios will be willing to enter long futures positions only if they receive compensation for bearing that risk in the form of positive expected profits. Their expected profits will be positive only if $E(P_T)$ is greater than F_0. The short position's profit is the negative of the long's and will have negative systematic risk. Diversified investors in the short position will be willing to suffer that expected loss to lower portfolio risk and will be willing to enter the contract even when F_0 is less than $E(P_T)$. Therefore, if P_T has positive beta, F_0 must be less than the expectation of P_T. The analysis is reversed for negative-beta commodities.

CC 8

CONCEPT CHECK

What must be true of the risk of the spot price of an asset if the futures price is an unbiased estimate of the ultimate spot price?

20.6   STOCK INDEX FUTURES

The Contracts

In contrast to most futures contracts, which call for delivery of a specified commodity, stock index contracts are settled by a cash amount equal to the value of the stock index in question on the contract maturity date times a multiplier that scales the size of the contract. The total profit to the long position is $S_T - F_0$, where S_T is the value of the stock index on the maturity date. Cash settlement avoids the costs that would be incurred if the short trader had to purchase the stocks in the index and deliver them to the long position, and if the long position then had to sell the stock for cash. Instead, the long trader's profit is $S_T - F_0$ dollars, and the short trader's is $F_0 - S_T$ dollars. These profits duplicate those that would arise with actual delivery.

As noted earlier, several index futures contracts are currently trading in Canada, including the S&P/TSX Composite (SCF) and the S&P/TSX 60 (SXF), which trade in the Montréal Exchange (ME) with multipliers equal to $5 and $200, respectively. Several sectoral index futures, the Info Tech, Financial, Energy, and Gold Index futures, also trade in the ME. In the United States and overseas many more stock index futures contracts are currently traded. Table 20.3 lists the major ones, showing under contract size the multiplier used to calculate contract settlements. An S&P 500 contract, for example, with a futures price of 1,400 and a final index value of 1,405 would result in a profit for the long side of $250 × (1,405 − 1,400) = $1,250. The S&P 500 contract by far dominates the market in stock index futures.[11]

The broad-based U.S. stock market indices are all highly correlated. Table 20.4 is a correlation matrix for four well-known indices: the S&P 500, the Dow Jones Industrial Average, the Russell 2000 index of small-capitalization stocks, and the Nasdaq 100. The highest correlation, .979, is between the two large-cap indices, the S&P 500 and the DJIA. The Nasdaq 100, which is dominated by technology firms, and the Russell 2000 index of small-cap firms have smaller correlations with the large-cap indices and with each other, but even these are above .85.

Creating Synthetic Stock Positions: An Asset Allocation Tool

One reason why stock index futures are so popular is that they substitute for holdings in the underlying stocks themselves. Index futures let investors participate in broad market movements without actually buying or selling large numbers of stocks.

TABLE 20.3   Major Stock Index Futures

Contract	Underlying Market Index	Contract Size	Exchange
S&P 500	Standard & Poor's 500 index; a value-weighted arithmetic average of 500 stocks	$250 times the S&P 500 index	Chicago Mercantile Exchange
Dow Jones Industrial Average	Dow Jones Industrial Average; price-weighted average of 30 firms	$10 times the index	Chicago Board of Trade
Russell 2000	Index of 2,000 smaller firms	$100 times the index	Intercontinental Exchange (ICE)
Nasdaq 100	Value-weighted arithmetic average of 100 of the largest over-the-counter stocks	$100 times the index	Chicago Mercantile Exchange
Nikkei 225	Nikkei 225 stock average	$5 times the Nikkei Index	Chicago Mercantile Exchange
FT-SE 100	Financial Times–Share Exchange Index of 100 U.K. firms	£10 times the FT-SE Index	London International Financial Futures Exchange
DAX-30	Index of 30 German stocks	25 Euros times the index	Eurex
CAC-40	Index of 40 French stocks	10 Euros times the index	Euronext Paris
Hang Seng	Value-weighted index of largest firms in Hong Kong	50 Hong Kong dollars times the index	Hong Kong Exchange

---

[11]We should point out that while the multipliers on these contracts may make the resulting positions too large for many small investors, there are effectively equivalent futures contracts with smaller multipliers (typically one-fifth the value of the standard contract) called *E-minis*.

	DJIA	Nasdaq	S&P 500	Russell 2000
DJIA	1.000			
Nasdaq	.876	1.000		
S&P 500	.979	.928	1.000	
Russell 2000	.908	.898	.948	1.000

Because of this, we say futures represent "synthetic" holdings of the market portfolio. Instead of holding the market directly, the investor takes a long futures position in the index. The transaction costs involved in establishing and liquidating futures positions are much lower than taking actual spot positions. Investors who wish to frequently buy and sell market positions find it much less costly to play the futures market rather than the underlying spot market. "Market timers," who speculate on broad market moves rather than on individual securities, are large players in stock index futures for this reason.

One means to market time, for example, is to shift between Treasury bills and broad-based stock market holdings. Timers attempt to shift from bills into the market before market upturns and to shift back into bills to avoid market downturns, thereby profiting from broad market movements. Market timing of this sort, however, can result in huge trading costs. An attractive alternative is to invest in Treasury bills and hold varying amounts of market index futures contracts, which are far cheaper to trade.

The strategy works like this: When timers are bullish, they will establish many long futures positions that they can liquidate quickly and cheaply when expectations turn bearish. Rather than shifting back and forth between T-bills and stocks, they buy and hold T-bills, and adjust only the futures position.

You can construct a T-bill plus index futures position that duplicates the payoff to holding the stock index itself. Here is how:

1. Hold as many market index futures contracts long as you need to purchase your desired stock position. A desired holding of $1,000 multiplied by the S&P/TSX 60 index, for example, would require the purchase of five contracts because each contract calls for delivery of $200 multiplied by the index.

2. Invest enough money in T-bills to cover the payment of the futures price at the contract's maturity date. The necessary investment is simply the present value of the futures price.

EXAMPLE 20.10   Synthetic Positions Using Stock Index Futures

Suppose that an institutional investor wants to invest $80 million in the Canadian equity market for one month and, to minimize trading costs, chooses to buy the S&P/TSX 60 futures contract as a substitute for actual stock holdings. If the index is now at 800, the one-month delivery futures price is 808, and the T-bill rate is 1 percent per month, the investor would buy 500 contracts. (Each contract controls $200 \times 800 = \$160,000$ worth of stock, and $\$80$ million/$\$160,000 = 500$.) The institution thus has a long position of $100,000 \times$ the S&P/TSX 60 index (500 contracts $\times$ the contract multiplier of $200). To cover payment of the futures price, it must invest $100,000 \times$ the present value of the futures price in T-bills. This equals $100,000 \times (808/1.01) = \$80$ million market value of bills. Notice that the

continued

$80 million outlay in bills is precisely equal to the amount that would have been needed to buy the stock directly. The bills will increase in value in one month to $80.8 million.

This is an artificial, or synthetic, stock position. What is the value of this portfolio at the maturity date? Call S_T the value of the stock index on the maturity date T, and, as usual, let F_0 be the original futures price:

	In General (per unit of the index)	Our Numbers
1. Profits from contract	$(S_T - F_0)$	$100,000(S_T - 808)$
2. Value of T-bills	F_0	$80,800,000$
Total	S_T	$100,000S_T$

The total payoff on the contract maturity date is exactly proportional to the value of the stock index. In other words, adopting this portfolio strategy is equivalent to holding the stock index itself, aside from the issue of interim dividend distributions and tax treatment.

The bills-plus-futures strategy may be viewed as a 100 percent stock strategy. At the other extreme, investing in zero futures results in a 100 percent bills position. Moreover, a short futures position will result in a portfolio equivalent to that obtained by short selling the stock market index, because in both cases the investor gains from decreases in the stock price. Bills-plus-futures mixtures clearly allow for a flexible and low transaction-cost approach to market timing. The futures positions may be established or reversed quickly and cheaply. Also, since the short futures position allows the investor to earn interest on T-bills, it is superior to a conventional short sale of the stock, where the investor typically earns no interest on the proceeds of the short sale.

The nearby box illustrates that it is now commonplace for money managers to use futures contracts to create synthetic equity positions in stock markets. The article notes that futures positions can be particularly helpful in establishing synthetic positions in foreign equities, where trading costs tend to be greater and markets tend to be less liquid.

CC 9

CONCEPT CHECK

The market timing strategy of Example 20.10 can also be achieved by an investor who holds an indexed stock portfolio and "synthetically exits" the position using futures if and when he or she turns pessimistic concerning the market. Suppose the investor holds $80 million of stock. What futures position added to the stockholdings would create a synthetic T-bill exposure when he or she is bearish on the market? Confirm that the profits are effectively risk-free using a table like that in Example 20.10.

Index Arbitrage

Whenever the actual futures price falls outside the no-arbitrage band, there is an opportunity for profit. This is why the parity relationships are so important. Far from being theoretical academic constructs, they are in fact a guide to trading rules that can generate large profits. One of the most notable developments in trading activity has been the advent of **index arbitrage**, an investment strategy that exploits divergences between the actual futures price and its theoretically correct parity value.

As investors go increasingly global and market turbulence grows, stock-index futures are emerging as the favorite way for nimble money managers to deploy their funds. Indeed, in most major markets, trading in stock futures now exceeds the buying and selling of actual shares.

What's the big appeal? Speed, ease and cheapness. For most major markets, stock futures not only boast greater liquidity but also lower transaction costs than traditional trading methods.

"When I decide it's time to move into France, Germany or Britain, I don't necessarily want to wait around until I find exactly the right stocks," says Fabrizio Pierallini, manager of New York–based Vontobel Ltd.'s Euro Pacific Fund.

Mr. Pierallini says he later fine-tunes his market picks by gradually shifting out of futures into favorite stocks. To the extent Mr. Pierallini's stocks outperform the market, futures provide a means to preserve those gains, even while hedging against market declines.

For instance, by selling futures equal to the value of the underlying portfolio, a manager can almost completely insulate a portfolio from market moves. Say a manager succeeds in outperforming the market, but still loses 3% while the market as a whole falls 10%. Hedging with futures would capture that margin of out-performance, transforming the loss into a profit of roughly 7%.

Among futures-intensive strategies is "global tactical asset allocation," which involves trading whole markets worldwide as traditional managers might trade stocks. The growing popularity of such asset-allocation strategies has given futures a big boost in recent years.

To capitalize on global market swings, "futures do the job for us better than stocks, and they're cheaper," said Jarrod Wilcox, director of global investments at PanAgora Asset Management, a Boston-based asset allocator. Even when PanAgora does take positions in individual stocks, it often employs futures to modify its position, such as by hedging part of its exposure to that particular stock market.

When it comes to investing overseas, Mr. Wilcox noted, futures are often the only vehicle that makes sense from a cost standpoint. Abroad, transaction taxes and sky-high commissions can wipe out more than 1% of the money deployed on each trade. By contrast, a comparable trade in futures costs as little as 0.05%.

In principle, index arbitrage is simple. If the futures price is too high, short the futures contract and buy the stocks in the index. If it is too low, go long in futures and short the stocks. You can perfectly hedge your position and should earn arbitrage profits equal to the mispricing of the contract.

In practice, however, index arbitrage can be difficult to implement. The problem lies in buying "the stocks in the index." Selling or purchasing shares in all stocks in an index is impractical for two reasons. The first is transaction costs, which may outweigh any profits to be made from the arbitrage. Second, index arbitrage calls for the purchase or sale of shares of many different firms simultaneously, and any lags in the execution of such a strategy can destroy the effectiveness of a plan to exploit temporary price discrepancies. Note that others may also try to exploit deviations from parity, and if they trade first they may move prices before your trade is executed.

Arbitrageurs need to trade an entire portfolio of stocks quickly and simultaneously if they hope to exploit disparities between the futures price and its corresponding stock index. For this they need a coordinated trading program; hence the term **program trading**, which refers to coordinated purchases or sales of entire portfolios of stocks. Electronic trading enables traders to submit coordinated buy or sell programs to the stock market at once.

The success of these arbitrage positions and associated program trades depends on only two things: the relative levels of spot and futures prices and synchronized trading in the two markets. Because arbitrageurs exploit disparities in futures and spot prices, absolute price levels are unimportant.

20.7 FOREIGN EXCHANGE FUTURES

The Markets

Exchange rates between currencies vary continually and often quite substantially. This variability can be a source of concern for anyone involved in international business. A Canadian exporter who sells goods in England, for example, will be paid in British pounds, and the dollar value of those pounds depends on the exchange rate at the time payment is made. Until that date, the Canadian exporter is exposed to foreign exchange rate risk. This risk, however, is easily hedged through currency futures or forward markets. For example, if you know you will receive £100,000 in 90 days, you can sell those pounds forward today in the forward market and lock in an exchange rate equal to today's forward price.

The forward market in foreign exchange is fairly informal. It is simply a network of banks and brokers that allows customers to enter forward contracts to purchase or sell currency in the future at a currently agreed-upon rate of exchange. The bank market in currencies is among the largest in the world, and most large traders with sufficient creditworthiness execute their trades here rather than in futures markets. Unlike those in futures markets, these contracts are not standardized in a formal market setting. Instead, each is negotiated separately. Moreover, there is no marking to market as would occur in futures markets. Currency forward contracts call for execution only at the maturity date. Participants need to consider *counterparty risk*, the possibility that a trading partner may not be able to make good on its obligations under the contract if prices move against it. For this reason, traders who participate in forward markets must have solid creditworthiness.

Currency futures, however, trade in formal markets. As already noted, trading in such futures was introduced by the Montréal Exchange but did not meet with any success; by 1991, it had been eliminated. Elsewhere, however, currency futures markets were established by the Chicago Mercantile Exchange (International Monetary Market), or the London International Financial Futures Exchange. In these exchanges, contracts are standardized by size, and daily marking to market is observed. Moreover, there are standard clearing arrangements that allow traders to enter or reverse positions easily. Margin positions are used to ensure contract performance, which is in turn guaranteed by the exchange's clearinghouse, so the identity and creditworthiness of the counterparty to a trade are less of a concern.

Chicago
Mercantile
Exchange
www.cme.com

Figure 20.8 reproduces a listing of foreign exchange spot cross rates for major currencies, as well as the forward rates for the Canadian dollar in terms of $US. The listing gives the number of U.S. dollars required to purchase one Canadian dollar. Figure 20.9 reproduces similar Canadian dollar futures listings from the CME. The forward quotations in Figure 20.8 always apply to delivery in one month, three months, six months, or one year. Thus, tomorrow's forward listings will apply to a maturity date one day later than today's listing. In contrast, the futures contracts mature in March, June, September, and December, and these four maturity days are the only dates each year when futures contracts settle.

Interest Rate Parity

As is true of stocks and stock futures, there is a spot-futures exchange rate relationship that will prevail in well-functioning markets. Should this so-called **interest rate parity relationship** be violated, arbitrageurs will be able to make risk-free profits in foreign exchange markets with zero net investment. Their actions will force futures and spot exchange rates back into alignment. Another term for interest rate parity is the **covered interest arbitrage relationship**.

We can illustrate the interest rate parity theorem by using two currencies, the Canadian dollar and the British (U.K.) pound. Call E_0 the current exchange rate between the two currencies, that is, E_0 dollars are required to purchase one pound. F_0, the forward price, is the number of dollars that is agreed to today for purchase of one pound at time T. Call the risk-free interest rates in Canada and the United Kingdom r_{CAN} and r_{UK}, respectively.

The interest rate parity theorem then states that the proper relationship between E_0 and F_0 is

$$F_0 = E_0 \left(\frac{1 + r_{CAN}}{1 + r_{UK}} \right)^T \tag{20.6}$$

Figure 20.8   Foreign exchange listing, July 19, 2013.

Cross Rates								
	USD	EUR	GBP	JP1	CHF	CAD	AUD	MXN
USD		1.3141	1.5258	0.9968	1.0636	0.9650	0.9199	0.0797
EUR	0.7610		1.1611	0.7586	0.8094	0.7343	0.7000	0.0606
GBP	0.6554	0.8612		0.6533	0.6971	0.6324	0.6029	0.0522
JPY	100.32	131.83	153.07		106.70	96.805	92.284	7.9913
CHF	0.9402	1.2355	1.4346	0.9372		0.9073	0.8649	0.0749
CAD	1.0363	1.3618	1.5812	1.0330	1.1022		0.9533	0.0825
AUD	1.0871	1.4285	1.6587	1.0836	1.1562	1.0490		0.0866
MXN	12.554	16.497	19.155	12.514	13.352	12.114	11.548	

Recent as of Friday, July 19, 2013. Explanations: USD: U.S. Dollar; EUR: European Euro; GBP: British Pound; JPY: Japanese Yen; JP1: 100 Japanese Yen; CHF: Swiss Franc; CAD: Canadian Dollar; AUD: Australian Dollar; MXN: Mexican Peso. Read vertically to find how much each currency buys. The "USD" column shows how many EUR, GBP etc. you get for 1 USD. Read horizontally to find the price of foreign currencies. The "USD" row shows how many USD one has to pay for 1 EUR, 1 GBP etc.

Canadian Dollar Forward Rates

The table shows the forward rates, in U.S. Dollars per 1 Canadian Dollar on **Friday, July 19, 2013**. Also reported are the implied forward premium (+) or discount (−) in basis points (100ths of a US cent), and the implied foreign interest rate differential at an annualized rate FIRD$=100[(f/s)^{(1/d)}-1]$, where f and s are the forward and spot rate, and d is the forward time in years.

	Rate	Premium	FIRD
Spot	0.9650		
1 month	0.9643	−6	−0.77%
2 months	0.9638	−12	−0.75%
3 months	0.9631	−19	−0.77%
6 months	0.9611	−39	−0.81%
9 months	0.9591	−59	−0.81%
1 year	0.9570	−79	−0.82%
2 years	0.9471	−179	−0.93%
5 years	0.9279	−371	−0.78%

Source: Sauder School of Business, "Canadian Dollar Forward Rates," University of British Columbia, http://fx.sauder.ubc.ca/CAD/forward.html.

For example, if $r_{CAN} = .06$ and $r_{UK} = .05$ annually, while $E_0 = \$2.10$ per pound, then the proper futures price for a one-year contract would be

$$\$2.10\left(\frac{1.06}{1.05}\right) = \$2.12 \text{ per pound}$$

Consider the intuition behind equation 20.6. If r_{CAN} is greater than r_{UK}, money invested in Canada will grow at a faster rate than money invested in the United Kingdom. If this is so, why

Figure 20.9

Canadian dollar futures on the CME, July 19, 2013.

Month	Last	Chg	Open	High	Low	Volume	OpenInt
Sep '13	0.9631s	0.0014	0.9616	0.9616	0.9616	0	123630
Dec '13	0.9610s	0.0014	0.9610	0.9610	0.9610	0	5854
Mar '14	0.9589s	0.0014	0.9589	0.9589	0.9589	0	933
Jun '14	0.9568s	0.0014	0.9568	0.9568	0.9568	0	310
Sep '14	0.9548s	0.0014	0.9548	0.9548	0.9548	0	37
Dec '14	0.9525s	0.0014	0.9525	0.9525	0.9525	0	7

Source: Interactive Data, July 20, 2013, 23:18:29 GMT; all quotes Greenwich Mean Time, http://online.wsj.com/mdc/public/page/2_3028.html?category=Other&subcategory=Currency&contract=Canadian%2520Dollar%2520Comp.%2520-%2520cme&catandsubcat=Other%7CCurrency&contractset=Canadian%2520Dollar%2520Comp.%2520.

wouldn't all investors decide to invest their money in Canada? One important reason why not is that the dollar may be depreciating relative to the pound. Although dollar investments in Canada grow faster than pound investments in the United Kingdom, each dollar may be worth fewer pounds in the forward market than in the spot market. Such a forward premium can exactly offset the advantage of the higher Canadian interest rate.

To complete the argument, we ask how a depreciating dollar would show up in equation 20.6. If the dollar is depreciating, more dollars are required to purchase each pound, and the forward exchange rate F_0 (in dollars per pound) will exceed E_0, the current exchange rate. This is exactly what equation 20.6 tells us: when r_{CAN} exceeds r_{UK}, F_0 must exceed E_0. The forward discount of the dollar embodied in the ratio of F_0 to E_0 exactly compensates for the difference in interest rates available in the two countries. Of course, the argument also works in reverse: if r_{CAN} is less than r_{UK}, then F_0 is less than E_0.

EXAMPLE 20.11   **Covered Interest Arbitrage**

What if the interest rate parity relationship is violated? For example, suppose the futures price is $2.11 instead of $2.12. You could adopt the following strategy to reap arbitrage profits. In this example, let E_1 denote the exchange rate that will prevail in one year. E_1 is, of course, a random variable from the perspective of today's investors.

Action	Initial Cash Flow ($)	Cash Flow in One Year ($)
1. Borrow one U.K. pound in London. Convert to dollars.	2.10	$-E_1(1.05)$
2. Lend $2.10 in Canada.	−2.10	2.10(1.06)
3. Enter a contract to purchase 1.05 pounds at a (futures) price of $F_0 = \$2.11$.	0	$1.05(E_1 - 2.11)$
Total	0	$.0105

In step 1, you exchange the one pound borrowed in the United Kingdom for $2.10 at the current exchange rate. After one year you must repay the pound borrowed with interest. Since the

continued

loan is made in the United Kingdom at the U.K. interest rate, you would repay 1.05 pounds, which would be worth $E_1(1.05)$ dollars. The Canadian loan in step 2 is made at the Canadian interest rate of 6 percent. The futures position in step 3 results in receipt of 1.05 pounds, for which you would first pay F_0 dollars each, and then trade into dollars at rate E_1.

Note that the exchange rate risk here is exactly offset between the pound obligation in step 1 and the futures position in step 3. The profit from the strategy is therefore risk-free and requires no net investment.

To generalize this strategy:

Action	Initial Cash Flow ($)	Cash Flow in One Year ($)
1. Borrow one U.K. pound in London. Convert to $.	E_0	$-\$E_1(1 + r_{UK})$
2. Use proceeds of borrowing in London to lend in Canada.	$-\$E_0$	$\$E_0(1 + r_{CAN})$
3. Enter $(1 + r_{UK})$ futures positions to purchase one pound for F_0 dollars.	0	$(1 + r_{UK})(E_1 - F_0)$
Total	0	$E_0(1 + r_{CAN}) - F_0(1 + r_{UK})$

Let us again review the stages of the arbitrage operation. The first step requires borrowing one pound in the United Kingdom. With a current exchange rate of E_0, the one pound is converted into E_0 dollars, which is a cash inflow. In one year the British loan must be paid off with interest, requiring a payment in pounds of $(1 + r_{UK})$, or in dollars $E_1(1 + r_{UK})$. In the second step the proceeds of the British loan are invested in Canada. This involves an initial cash outflow of $\$E_0$, and a cash inflow of $\$E_0(1 + r_{CAN})$ in one year. Finally, the exchange risk involved in the British borrowing is hedged in step 3. Here, the $(1 + r_{UK})$ pounds necessary to satisfy the British loan are purchased ahead in the futures contract.

The net proceeds to the arbitrage portfolio are risk-free and given by $E_0(1 + r_{CAN}) - F_0(1 + r_{UK})$. If this value is positive, borrow in the United Kingdom, lend in Canada, and enter a long futures position to eliminate foreign exchange risk. If the value is negative, borrow in Canada, lend in the United Kingdom, and take a short position in pound futures. When prices preclude arbitrage opportunities, the expression must equal zero. This no arbitrage condition implies that

$$F_0 = \frac{1 + r_{CAN}}{1 + r_{UK}} E_0 \qquad (20.7)$$

which is the interest rate parity theorem for a one-year horizon.

CC 10

CONCEPT CHECK

What are the arbitrage strategy and associated profits in Example 20.11 if the initial futures price is $F_0 = \$2.14/\text{pound}$?

Ample empirical evidence bears out this theoretical relationship. For two other currencies, for example, on July 19, 2013, *The Globe and Mail* listed the two-year U.S. interest rate at .30 percent and the two-year Canadian rate at 1.09 percent. The U.S. dollar was then worth 1.0363 Canadian dollars. Substituting these values into equation 20.7 gives $F_0 = 1.0363 \times (1.0109/1.003)^2 = 1.053$. The actual forward price at that time for two-year delivery was from Figure 20.8 equal to $(.09471)^{-1} = \$1.056$ per U.S. dollar, so close to the parity value that transaction costs would prevent arbitrageurs from profiting from the discrepancy.

20.8

INTEREST RATE FUTURES

The Markets

The late 1970s and 1980s saw a dramatic increase in the volatility of interest rates, leading to investor desire to hedge returns on fixed-income securities against changes in interest rates. As one example, thrift institutions that had loaned money on home mortgages before 1975 suffered substantial capital losses on those loans when interest rates later increased. An interest rate futures contract could have protected banks against such large swings in yields. The significance of these losses has spurred trading in interest rate futures.

Montréal
Exchange
www.me.org

As with other futures contracts, several Canadian interest rate futures were introduced in the past by the TFE and Montréal Exchange.[12] Bankers' acceptances, two-, five-, ten-, and thirty-year Canada bonds, and overnight repo rate futures were the contracts trading in the Montréal Exchange in 2013.

Interest rate futures contracts call for delivery of a bond, bill, or note. Should interest rates rise, the market value of the security at delivery will be less than the original futures price, and the deliverer will profit. Hence, the short position in the interest rate futures contract gains when interest rates rise.

In the United States, the major interest rate contracts currently traded are on Treasury bills, Treasury notes, Treasury bonds, and a municipal bond index. These securities thus provide an opportunity to hedge against a wide spectrum of maturities from very short- (T-bills) to long-term (T-bonds). In addition, futures contracts trade on Eurodollar rates and interest rates in Germany, Japan, Switzerland, Italy, Canada, and the United Kingdom and are listed in the major U.S. financial publications.

Hedging Interest Rate Risk

Like equity managers, fixed-income managers may desire to separate security-specific decisions from bets on movements in the entire structure of interest rates. Consider, for example, these problems:

1. A fixed-income manager holds a bond portfolio on which capital gains have been earned. She foresees an increase in interest rates but is reluctant to sell her portfolio and replace it with a lower-duration mix of bonds because such rebalancing would result in large trading costs as well as realization of capital gains for tax purposes. Still, she would like to hedge her exposure to interest rate increases.

2. A corporation plans to issue bonds to the public. It believes that now is a good time to act, but it cannot issue the bonds for another three months because of the lags inherent in SEC registration. It would like to hedge the uncertainty surrounding the yield at which it eventually will be able to sell the bonds.

3. A pension fund will receive a large cash inflow next month that it plans to invest in long-term bonds. It is concerned that interest rates may fall by the time it can make the investment, and would like to lock in the yield currently available on long-term issues.

---

[12]The two have now been merged into the Canadian Derivatives Exchange, located in Montreal.

In each of these cases, the investment manager wishes to hedge interest rate uncertainty. This hedging takes place by using two properties of fixed-income securities that we saw in Chapter 14. The first one is that the sensitivity of these securities to changes in the rate of interest is approximately proportional to the size of their *modified duration*. The second one is that the duration of a portfolio of fixed-income securities is equal to the "portfolio" of durations, the weighted average of the durations of the securities in the portfolio. Hedging interest rate risk, therefore, is the process of changing the duration of our fixed-income portfolio, by taking an appropriate position (long or short) in interest rate futures contracts. This combination of the futures contract position and the original portfolio would have duration equal to the weighted average of the durations of the position and the portfolio.

The hedge ratio, the appropriate number of long or short contracts, depends on the ratios of the sizes and the modified durations of the portfolio and the instrument underlying the futures contract. The exact procedure will be illustrated in detail when we discuss hedging in Chapter 22 by an example of a bond portfolio manager, as in case 1 above. Hedging interest rate risk can either set the duration equal to zero or reduce it to a desired value. An example where this last case arises is in a financial corporation in which the duration of the assets is lower than that of its liabilities. By taking appropriate positions in interest rate futures it is possible to reduce the duration of the liabilities to match that of the assets and reduce the balance sheet exposure to interest rate risk.

20.9 SWAPS

Swaps are multiperiod extensions of forward contracts. For example, rather than agreeing to exchange British pounds for Canadian dollars at an agreed-upon forward price at one single date, a **foreign exchange swap** would call for an exchange of currencies on several future dates. The parties might exchange $2 million for £1 million in each of the next 5 years. Similarly, **interest rate swaps** call for the exchange of a series of cash flows proportional to a given interest rate for a corresponding series of cash flows proportional to a floating interest rate.[13] One party might exchange a variable cash flow equal to $1 million times a short-term interest rate for $1 million times a fixed interest rate of 5 percent for each of the next 7 years.

The swap market is a huge component of the derivatives market, with well over $500 trillion in swap agreements outstanding. We will illustrate how these contracts work by using a simple interest rate swap as an example.

EXAMPLE 20.12   **Interest Rate Swap**

Consider the manager of a large portfolio that currently includes $100 million par value of long-term bonds paying an average coupon rate of 7 percent. The manager believes that interest rates are about to rise. As a result, he would like to sell the bonds and replace them with either short-term or floating-rate issues. However, it would be exceedingly expensive in terms of transaction costs to replace the portfolio every time the forecast for interest rates is updated. A cheaper and more flexible approach is for the managers to "swap" the $7 million a year in interest income the portfolio currently generates for an amount of money tied to the short-term interest rate. That way, if rates do rise, so will the portfolio's interest income.

continued

---

[13]Interest rate swaps have nothing to do with the Homer-Liebowitz bond swap taxonomy described in Chapter 14.

A swap dealer might advertise its willingness to exchange, or "swap," a cash flow based on the six-month LIBOR rate for one based on a fixed rate of 7 percent. (The LIBOR, or London Interbank Offered Rate, is the interest rate at which banks borrow from each other in the Euro-dollar market. It is the most commonly used short-term interest rate in the swap market.) The portfolio manager would then enter into a swap agreement with the dealer to *pay* 7 percent on **notional principal** of $100 million and *receive* payment of the LIBOR rate on that amount of notional principal.[14] In other words, the manager swaps a payment of $.07 \times \$100$ million for a payment of LIBOR $\times \$100$ million. The manager's *net* cash flow from the swap agreement is therefore (LIBOR $- .07) \times \$100$ million. Note that the swap arrangement does not mean that a loan has been made. The participants have agreed only to exchange a fixed cash flow for a variable one.

	LIBOR Rate		
	6.5%	**7.0%**	**7.5%**
Interest income from bond portfolio (= 7% of $100 million bond portfolio)	$7,000,000	$7,000,000	$7,000,000
Cash flow from swap [= (LIBOR − 7%) × Notional principal of $100 million]	(500,000)	0	500,000
Total (= LIBOR × $100 million)	$6,500,000	$7,000,000	$7,500,000

Notice that the total income on the overall position—bonds plus swap agreement—equals the LIBOR rate in each scenario times $100 million. The manager has, in effect, converted a fixed-rate bond portfolio into a synthetic floating-rate portfolio.

Swaps and Balance Sheet Restructuring

Example 20.12 illustrates why swaps have tremendous appeal to fixed-income managers. These contracts provide a means to quickly, cheaply, and anonymously restructure the balance sheet. Suppose a corporation that has issued fixed-rate debt believes that interest rates are likely to fall; it might prefer to have issued floating-rate debt. In principle, it could issue floating-rate debt and use the proceeds to buy back the outstanding fixed-rate debt. In practice, however, this would be enormously expensive in terms of transaction costs. Instead, the firm can convert the outstanding fixed-rate debt into synthetic floating-rate debt by entering a swap to receive a fixed interest rate (offsetting its fixed-rate coupon obligation) and paying a floating rate.

Conversely, a bank that pays current market interest rates to its depositors, and thus is exposed to increases in rates, might wish to convert some of its financing to a fixed-rate basis. It would enter a swap to receive a floating rate and pay a fixed rate on some amount of notional principle. This swap position, added to its floating-rate deposit liability, would result in a net liability of a fixed stream of cash. The bank might then be able to invest in long-term fixed-rate loans without encountering interest rate risk.

For another example, consider a fixed-income portfolio manager. Swaps enable the manager to switch back and forth between a fixed- or floating-rate profile quickly and cheaply as the

---

[14]The participants to the swap do not loan each other money. They agree only to exchange a fixed cash flow for a variable cash flow that depends on the short-term interest rate. This is why the principal is described as *notional*. The notional principal is simply a way to describe the size of the swap agreement. In this example, a 7 percent fixed rate is exchanged for the LIBOR rate; the difference between LIBOR and 7 percent is multiplied by notional principal to determine the net cash flow.

forecast for the interest rate changes. A manager who holds a fixed-rate portfolio can transform it into a synthetic floating-rate portfolio by entering a pay fixed–receive floating swap and can later transform it back by entering the opposite side of a similar swap.

Foreign exchange swaps also enable the firm to quickly and cheaply restructure its balance sheet. Suppose, for example, that a firm issues $10 million in debt at an 8 percent coupon rate, but actually prefers that its interest obligations be denominated in British pounds. For example, the issuing firm might be a British corporation that perceives advantageous financing opportunities in the United States but prefers pound-denominated liabilities. Then the firm, whose debt currently obliges it to make dollar-denominated payments of $800,000, can agree to swap a given number of pounds each year for $800,000. By so doing, it effectively covers its dollar obligation and replaces it with a new pound-denominated obligation.

CC 11

CONCEPT CHECK

Show how a firm that has issued a floating-rate bond with a coupon equal to the LIBOR rate can use swaps to convert that bond into synthetic fixed-rate debt. Assume the terms of the swap allow an exchange of LIBOR for a fixed rate of 8 percent.

The Swap Dealer

What about the swap dealer? Why is the dealer, which is typically a financial intermediary such as a bank, willing to take on the opposite side of the swaps desired by these participants in these hypothetical swaps?

Consider a dealer who takes on one side of a swap, let's say paying LIBOR and receiving a fixed rate. The dealer will search for another trader in the swap market who wishes to receive a fixed rate and pay LIBOR. For example, company A may have issued a 7 percent coupon fixed-rate bond that it wishes to convert into synthetic floating-rate debt, while company B may have issued a floating-rate bond tied to LIBOR that it wishes to convert into synthetic fixed-rate debt. The dealer will enter a swap with company A in which it pays a fixed rate and receives LIBOR, and will enter another swap with company B in which it pays LIBOR and receives a fixed rate. When the two swaps are combined, the dealer's position is effectively neutral on interest rates, paying LIBOR on one swap and receiving it on another. Similarly, the dealer pays a fixed rate on one swap and receives it on another. The dealer becomes little more than an intermediary, funnelling payments from one party to the other.[15] The dealer finds this activity profitable because it will charge a bid–asked spread on the transaction.

This rearrangement is illustrated in Figure 20.10. Company A has issued 7 percent fixed-rate debt (the leftmost arrow in the figure) but enters a swap to pay the dealer LIBOR and receive a 6.95 percent fixed rate. Therefore, the company's net payment is 7% + (LIBOR − 6.95%) = LIBOR + .05%. It has thus transformed its fixed-rate debt into synthetic floating-rate debt. Conversely, company B has issued floating-rate debt paying LIBOR (the rightmost arrow), but enters a swap to pay a 7.05 percent fixed rate in return for LIBOR. Therefore, its net payment is LIBOR + (7.05% − LIBOR) = 7.05%. It has thus transformed its floating-rate debt into synthetic fixed-rate debt. The bid–asked spread, the source of the dealer's profit, in the example illustrated in Figure 20.10 is .10 percent of notional principal each year.

---

[15]Actually, things are a bit more complicated. The dealer is more than just an intermediary because it bears the credit risk that one or the other of the parties to the swap might default on the obligation. Referring to Figure 20.10, if company A defaults on its obligation, for example, the swap dealer still must maintain its commitment to company B. In this sense, the dealer does more than simply pass through cash flows to the other swap participants.

Figure 20.10 Interest rate swap. Company B pays a fixed rate of 7.05 percent to the swap dealer in return for LIBOR. Company A receives 6.95 percent from the dealer in return for LIBOR. The swap dealer realizes a cash flow each period equal to .10 percent of notional principal.

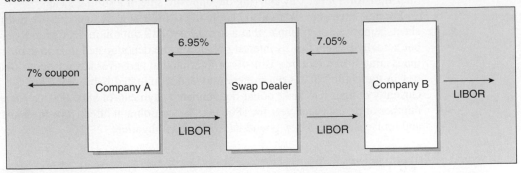

CC 12

CONCEPT CHECK

A pension fund holds a portfolio of money market securities that the manager believes are paying excellent yields compared to other comparable-risk short-term securities. However, the manager believes that interest rates are about to fall. What type of swap will allow the fund to continue to hold its portfolio of short-term securities while at the same time benefiting from a decline in rates?

Other Interest Rate Contracts

Swaps are multiperiod forward contracts that trade over the counter. There are also exchange-listed contracts that trade on interest rates. The biggest of these in terms of trading activity is the Eurodollar contract, the listing for which we reproduce in Figure 20.11. The profit on this contract is proportional to the difference between the LIBOR rate at contract maturity and the contract rate entered into at contract inception. There are analogous rates on interbank loans in other currencies. For example, one close cousin of LIBOR is EURIBOR, which is the rate at which euro-denominated interbank loans within the Eurozone are offered by one prime bank to another.

The listing conventions for this contract are a bit peculiar. Consider, for example, the first contract listed, which matures in February 2013. The settlement price is presented as $F_0 = 99.7075$, or approximately 99.71. However, this value is not really a price. In effect, participants in the contract negotiate over the contract interest rate, and the so-called futures price is actually set equal to $100 - $ contract rate. Since the futures price is listed as 99.71, the contract rate

Figure 20.11

Interest rate futures.

			Contract				Open
	Open	High	Hi Lo	Low	Settle	Chg	Interest
Eurodollar (CME) $1,000,000; pts of 100%							
Feb	99.7100	99.7100	▲	99.7075	**99.7075**	...	78,171
March	99.7000	99.7100		99.6800	**99.7050**	.0050	918,700
June	99.6850	99.6950		99.6650	**99.6850**	...	789,137
Dec	99.6250	99.6450		99.6050	**99.6250**	...	736,966

Source: *The Wall Street Journal*, February 9, 2013. Reprinted by permission of The Wall Street Journal, © 2013 Dow Jones & Company, Inc. All rights reserved worldwide.

is $100 - 99.71 = .29$ percent. Similarly, the final futures price on contract maturity date will be marked to $F_T = 100 - \text{LIBOR}_T$. Thus, profits to the buyer of the contract will be proportional to

$$F_T - F_0 = (100 - \text{LIBOR}_T) - (100 - \text{Contract rate}) = \text{Contract rate} - \text{LIBOR}_T$$

Thus, the contract design allows participants to trade directly on the LIBOR rate. The contract multiplier is $1 million, but the LIBOR rate on which the contract is written is a three-month (quarterly) rate; for each basis point that the (annualized) LIBOR increases, the quarterly interest rate increases by only $\frac{1}{4}$ of a basis point, and the profit to the buyer decreases by

$$.0001 \times \frac{1}{4} \times \$1,000,000 = \$25$$

Examine the payoff on the contract, and you will see that, in effect, the Eurodollar contract allows traders to "swap" a fixed interest rate (the contract rate) for a floating rate (LIBOR). Thus, this is in effect a one-period interest rate swap. Notice in Figure 20.11 that the total open interest on this contract is enormous—almost three million contracts for maturities extending to one year. Moreover, while not presented in *The Wall Street Journal*, significant trading in Eurodollars takes place for contract maturities extending out to ten years. Contracts with such long-term maturities are quite unusual. They reflect the fact that the Eurodollar contract is used by dealers in long-term interest rate swaps as a hedging tool.

Swap Pricing

How can the fair swap rate be determined? For example, do we know that an exchange of LIBOR is a fair trade for a fixed rate of 6 percent? Or what is the fair swap rate between dollars and pounds for the foreign exchange swap we considered? To answer these questions we can exploit the analogy between a swap agreement and a forward or futures contract.

Consider a swap agreement to exchange dollars for pounds for one period only. Next year, for example, one might exchange $1 million for £.5 million. This is no more than a simple forward contract in foreign exchange. The dollar-paying party is contracting to buy British pounds in one year for a number of dollars agreed upon today. The forward exchange rate for one year delivery is $F_1 = \$2/\text{pound}$. We know from the interest rate parity relationship that this forward price should be related to the spot exchange rate, E_0, by the formula $F_1 = E_0(1 + r_{\text{CAN}})/(1 + r_{\text{UK}})$. Because a one-period swap is in fact a forward contract, the fair swap rate also is given by the parity relationship.

Now consider an agreement to trade foreign exchange for two periods. This agreement could be structured as a portfolio of two separate forward contracts. If so, the forward price for the exchange of currencies in one year would be $F_1 = E_0(1 + r_{\text{CAN}})/(1 + r_{\text{UK}})$, while the forward price for the exchange in the second year would be $F_2 = E_0[(1 + r_{\text{CAN}})/(1 + r_{\text{UK}})]^2$. As an example, suppose that $E_0 = \$2.038/\text{pound}$, $r_{\text{CAN}} = 5$ percent, and $r_{\text{UK}} = 7$ percent. Then, using the parity relationship, we would have prices for forward delivery of $F_1 = \$2.038/\pounds \times (1.05/1.07) = \$2.00/\pounds$ and $F_2 = \$2.038/\pounds \times (1.05/1.07)^2 = \$1.9625/\pounds$. Figure 20.12, panel A illustrates this sequence of cash exchanges assuming that the swap calls for delivery of one pound in each year. While the dollars to be paid in each of the two years are known today, they vary from year to year.

In contrast, a swap agreement to exchange currency for two years would call for a fixed exchange rate to be used for the duration of the swap. This means that the same number of dollars would be paid per pound in each year, as illustrated in panel B. Because the forward prices for delivery in each of the next two years are $2/£ and $1.9625/£, the fixed exchange rate that makes the two-period swap a fair deal must be between these two values. Therefore, the dollar payer underpays for the pound in the first year (compared to the forward exchange rate) and overpays in the second year. Thus, the swap can be viewed as a portfolio of forward transactions, but instead of each transaction being priced independently, one forward price is applied to all of the transactions.

Figure 20.12
Forward
contracts
versus swaps.
Panel A:
Two forward
contracts,
each priced
independently.
Panel B:
Two-year swap
agreement.

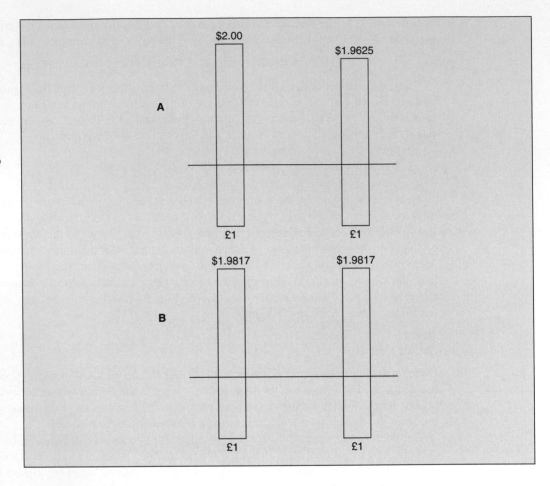

Given this insight, it is easy to determine the fair swap price. If we were to purchase one pound per year for two years using two independent forward rate agreements, we would pay F_1 dollars in one year and F_2 dollars in two years. If, instead, we enter a swap, we pay a constant rate of F^* dollars per pound. Because both strategies must be equally costly, we conclude that

$$\frac{F_1}{1 + y_1} + \frac{F_2}{(1 + y_2)^2} = \frac{F^*}{1 + y_1} + \frac{F^*}{(1 + y_2)^2}$$

where y_1 and y_2 are the appropriate yields from the yield curve for discounting dollar cash flows of one and two years' maturity, respectively. In our example, where we have assumed a flat Canadian yield curve at 5 percent, we would solve

$$\frac{2.00}{1.05} + \frac{1.9625}{1.05^2} = \frac{F^*}{1.05} + \frac{F^*}{1.05^2}$$

which implies that $F^* = 1.9817$. The same principle would apply to a foreign exchange swap of any other maturity. In essence, we need to find the level annuity, F^*, with the same present value as the sequence of annual cash flows that would be incurred in a sequence of forward rate agreements.

Interest rate swaps can be subjected to precisely the same analysis. Here, the forward contract is on an interest rate. For example, if you swap LIBOR for a 7 percent fixed rate with notional principal of $100, then you have entered a forward contract for delivery of $100 times r_{LIBOR} for a fixed "forward" price of $7. If the swap agreement is for many periods, the fair spread will be determined by the entire sequence of interest rate forward prices over the life of the swap.

Credit Risk in the Swap Market

The rapid growth of the swap market has given rise to increasing concern about credit risk in these markets. Actually, although credit risk in the swap market is certainly not trivial, it is not nearly as large as the magnitude of the notional principal in these markets would suggest. To see why, consider a simple interest rate swap of LIBOR for a fixed rate. At the time the transaction is initiated, it has zero net present value to both parties for the same reason that a futures contract has zero value at inception: both are simply contracts to exchange cash in the future at terms established today that make both parties willing to enter into the deal. Even if one party were to back out of the deal at this moment, it would not cost the counterparty anything, because another trader could be found to take its place.

Once interest or exchange rates change, however, the situation is not as simple. Suppose, for example, that interest rates increase shortly after an interest-rate swap agreement has begun. The floating-rate payer therefore suffers a loss, while the fixed-rate payer enjoys a gain. If the floating-rate payer reneges on its commitment at this point, the fixed-rate payer suffers a loss. However, that loss is not as large as the notional principal of the swap, for the default of the floating-rate payer relieves the fixed-rate payer from its obligation as well. The loss is only the *difference* between the values of the fixed-rate and floating-rate obligations, not the *total* value of the payments that the floating-rate payer was obligated to make.

EXAMPLE 20.13   **Credit Risk in Swaps**

Consider a swap written on $1 million of notional principal that calls for exchange of LIBOR for a fixed rate of 8 percent for five years. Suppose, for simplicity, that the yield curve is currently flat at 8 percent. With LIBOR thus equal to 8 percent, no cash flows will be exchanged unless interest rates change. But now suppose that the yield curve immediately shifts up to 9 percent. The floating-rate payer now is obligated to pay a cash flow of $(.09 - .08) \times \$1$ million $= \$10,000$ each year to the fixed-rate payer (as long as rates remain at 9 percent). If the floating-rate payer defaults on the swap, the fixed-rate payer loses the prospect of that five-year annuity. The present value of that annuity is $\$10,000 \times$ Annuity factor$(9\%, 5$ years$) = \$38,897$. This loss may not be trivial, but it is less than 4 percent of notional principal. We conclude that the credit risk of the swap is far less than notional principal.

Credit Default Swaps

Despite the similarity in names, a **credit default swap (CDS)** is not the same type of instrument as interest rate or currency swaps. Payment on a CDS is tied to the financial status of one or more reference firms; the CDS therefore allows two counterparties to take positions on the credit risk of those firms. When a particular "credit event" is triggered, say default on an outstanding bond or failure to pay interest, the seller of protection is expected to cover the loss in the market value of the bond. For example, the swap seller may be obligated to pay par value to take delivery of the defaulted bond (in which case the swap is said to entail *physical settlement*) or may instead pay the swap buyer the difference between the par value and market value of the bond (termed *cash settlement*). The swap purchaser pays a periodic fee to the seller for this protection against credit events.

Unlike interest rate swaps, credit default swaps do not entail periodic netting of one reference rate against another. They are in fact more like insurance policies written on particular credit events. Bondholders may buy these swaps to transfer their credit risk exposure to the swap seller, effectively enhancing the credit quality of their portfolios. Unlike with insurance policies, however, the swapholder need not hold the bonds underlying the CDS contract; therefore, credit default swaps can be used purely to speculate on changes in the credit standing of the reference firms.

SUMMARY

1. Forward contracts call for future delivery of an asset at a currently agreed-upon price. The long trader purchases the good, and the short trader delivers it. If the price of the asset at the maturity of the contract exceeds the forward price, the long side benefits by virtue of acquiring the good at the contract price.

2. A futures contract is similar to a forward contract, differing most importantly in the aspects of standardization and marking to market, which is the process by which gains and losses on futures contract positions are settled daily. In contrast, forward contracts call for no cash transfers until contract maturity.

3. Futures contracts are traded on organized exchanges that standardize the size of the contract, the grade of the deliverable asset, the delivery date, and the delivery location. Traders negotiate only over the contract price. This standardization increases liquidity and means buyers and sellers can easily find many traders for a desired purchase or sale.

4. The clearinghouse steps in between each pair of traders, acting as the short position for each long, and as the long position for each short. In this way, traders need not be concerned about the performance of the trader on the opposite side of the contract. In turn, traders post margins to guarantee their own performance.

5. The long position's gain or loss between time 0 and t is $F_t - F_0$. Because $F_T = P_T$, the long's profit if the contract is held until maturity is $P_T - F_0$, where P_T is the spot price at time T and F_0 is the original futures price. The gain or loss to the short position is $F_0 - P_T$.

6. Futures contracts may be used for hedging or speculating. Speculators use the contracts to take a stand on the ultimate price of an asset. Short hedgers take short positions in contracts to offset any gains or losses on the value of an asset already held in inventory. Long hedgers take long positions to offset gains or losses in the purchase price of a good.

7. The spot–futures parity relationship states that the equilibrium futures price on an asset providing no services or payments (such as dividends) is $F_0 = P_0(1 + r_f)^T$. If the futures price deviates from this value, then market participants can earn arbitrage profits.

8. If the asset provides services or payments with yield d, the parity relationship becomes $F_0 = P_0(1 + r_f - d)^T$. This model also is called the cost-of-carry model,

because it states that the futures price must exceed the spot price by the net cost of carrying the asset until maturity date T.

9. Commodity futures pricing is complicated by costs for storage of the underlying commodity. When the asset is willingly stored by investors, then the storage costs enter the futures pricing equation as follows:

$$F_0 = P_0(1 + r_f + c)^T$$

The non-interest-carrying costs, c, play the role of a "negative dividend" in this context.

10. When commodities are not stored for investment purposes, the correct futures price must be determined using general risk–return principles. In this event

$$F_0 = E(P_T)\left(\frac{1 + r_f}{1 + k}\right)^T$$

The equilibrium (risk–return) and the no-arbitrage predictions of the proper futures price are consistent with one another.

11. The equilibrium futures price will be less than the currently expected time T spot price if the spot price exhibits systematic risk, in which case $k > r_f$. This provides an expected profit for the long position that bears the risk and imposes an expected loss on the short position that is willing to accept that expected loss as a means to shed risk.

12. Futures contracts calling for cash settlement are traded on the S&P/TSX 60 in Canada and in various U.S. stock market indices. The contracts may be mixed with Treasury bills to construct artificial equity positions, which makes them potentially valuable tools for market timers. Market index contracts also are used by arbitrageurs who attempt to profit from violations of the parity relationship.

13. Foreign exchange futures trade in the United States. on several foreign currencies, as well as on a European currency index. The interest rate parity relationship for foreign exchange futures is

$$F_0 = E_0\left(\frac{1 + r_{US}}{1 + r_{foreign}}\right)^T$$

Deviations of the futures price from this value imply arbitrage opportunity. Empirical evidence, however, suggests that generally the parity relationship is satisfied.

14. Interest rate futures allow for hedging against interest rate fluctuations in several different markets. Several such contracts are currently actively traded in Canada.

15. Swaps, which call for the exchange of a series of cash flows, may be viewed as portfolios of forward contracts. Each transaction may be viewed as a separate forward agreement. However, instead of pricing each exchange independently, the swap sets one "forward price" that applies to all of the transactions. Therefore, the swap price will be an average of the futures prices that would prevail if each exchange were priced separately.

KEY EQUATIONS

(20.1) $F_0 = S_0(1 + r_f) - D = S_0(1 + r_f - d)$

(20.2) $F_0 = S_0(1 + r_f - d)^T$

(20.3) $F(T_2)/F(T_1) = (1 + r_f - d)^{(T_2 - T_1)}$

(20.4) $F_0 = P_0(1 + r_f + c)$

(20.5) $F_0 = E(P_T)\left(\dfrac{1 + r_f}{1 + k}\right)^T$

(20.6) $F_0 = E_0\left(\dfrac{1 + r_{CAN}}{1 + r_{UK}}\right)^T$

(20.7) $F_0 = \dfrac{1 + r_{CAN}}{1 + r_{UK}} E_0$

PROBLEMS

McGraw Hill Education **connect**™ **Practise and learn online with Connect.**

1. Why is there no futures market in cement?

2. Why might an investor choose to purchase futures contracts rather than the underlying asset?

3. What is the difference in cash flow between short selling an asset and entering a short futures position?

4. In each of the following cases discuss how you, as a portfolio manager, would use financial futures to protect the portfolio.

   a. You own a large position in a relatively illiquid bond that you want to sell.

   b. You have a large gain on one of your long Treasuries and want to sell it, but you would like to defer the gain until the next accounting period, which begins in four weeks.

   c. You will receive a large contribution next month that you hope to invest in long-term corporate bonds on a yield basis as favourable as is now available.

5. Consider this arbitrage strategy to derive the parity relationship for spreads: (1) enter a long futures position with maturity date T_1 and futures price $F(T_1)$; (2) enter a short position with maturity T_2 and futures price $F(T_2)$; and (3) at T_1, when the first contract expires, buy the asset and borrow $F(T_1)$ dollars at rate r_f and pay back the loan with interest at time T_2.

   a. What are the total cash flows to this strategy at times 0, T_1, and T_2?

   b. Why must profits at time T_2 be zero if no arbitrage opportunities are present?

   c. What must be the relationship between $F(T_1)$ and $F(T_2)$ for the profits at T_2 to be equal to zero? This relationship is the parity relationship for spreads.

6. Consider a stock that pays no dividends on which a futures contract, a call option, and a put option trade. The maturity date for all three contracts is T, the exercise price of the put and the call are both X, and the futures price is F. Show that if $X = F$, then the call price equals the put price. Use parity conditions to guide your demonstration.

7. Suppose that an investor in a 50 percent tax bracket purchases three soybean futures contracts at a price of $5.40 a bushel and closes them out at a price of $5.80. What are the after-tax profits to the position?

8. These questions address stock futures contracts:

   a. A hypothetical futures contract on a non-dividend-paying stock with current price $150 has a maturity of one year. If the T-bill rate is 6 percent, what is the futures price?

   b. What should be the futures price if the maturity of the contract is three years?

   c. What if the interest rate is 8 percent and the maturity of the contract is three years?

9. You suddenly receive information that indicates to you that the stock market is about to rise substantially. The market is unaware of this information. What should you do?

10. Suppose the value of the S&P/TSX 60 stock index is currently 800. If the one-year T-bill rate is 5 percent and the expected dividend yield on the S&P/TSX 60 is 2 percent, what should the one-year maturity futures price be?

11. It is now January. The current interest rate is 5 percent annually. The June futures price for gold is $546.30, while the December futures price is $560. Is there an arbitrage opportunity here? If so, how would you exploit it?

12. The Montréal Exchange has just introduced a new futures contract on Brandex stock, a company that currently pays no dividends. Each contract calls for delivery of 1,000 shares of stock in one year. The T-bill rate is 6 percent per year.

   a. If Brandex stock now sells at $120 per share, what should be the futures price?

   b. If Brandex stock immediately decreases by 3 percent, what will be the change in the futures price and the change in the investor's margin account?

   c. If the margin on the contract is $12,000, what is the percentage return on the investor's position?

13. The multiplier for a futures contract on the stock market index is 250. The maturity of the contract is one year, the current level of the index is 1300, and the risk-free interest rate is .5 percent per month. The dividend yield on the index is .2 percent per month. Suppose that after one month, the level of the stock index is 1320.

   a. Find the cash flow from the marking-to-market proceeds on the contract. Assume that the parity condition always holds exactly.

   b. Find the holding-period return if the initial margin on the contract is $13,000.

14. You are a corporate treasurer who will purchase $1 million of bonds for the sinking fund in three months. You believe rates will soon fall, and you would like to repurchase the company's sinking fund bonds (which currently are selling below par) in advance of requirements. Unfortunately, you must obtain approval from the board of directors for such a purchase, and this can take up to two months. What action can you take in the futures market to hedge any adverse movements in bond yields and prices until you can actually buy the bonds? Will you be long or short? Why? A qualitative answer is fine.

15. The spot–futures parity relationship can be used to find a "term structure of futures prices," that is, futures prices for various maturity dates.

   a. Suppose that today is January 1, 2013. Assume the interest rate is 3 percent per year and a stock index currently at 1,500 pays a dividend yield of 1.5 percent. Find the futures price for contract maturity dates of February 14, 2013, May 21, 2013, and November 18, 2013.

   b. What happens to the term structure of futures prices if the dividend yield is higher than the risk-free rate? For example, what if the dividend yield is 4 percent?

16. a. How should the parity condition (equation 20.2) for stocks be modified for futures contracts on Treasury bonds? What should play the role of the dividend yield in that equation?

b. In an environment with an upward-sloping yield curve, should T-bond futures prices on more-distant contracts be higher or lower than those on near-term contracts?

17. Consider the futures contract written on the S&P 500 index and maturing in six months. The interest rate is 3 percent per six-month period, and the future value of dividends expected to be paid over the next six months is $15. The current index level is 1425. Assume that you can short sell the S&P 500 index.

   a. Suppose the expected rate of return on the market is 6 percent per six-month period. What is the expected level of the index in six months?

   b. What is the theoretical no-arbitrage price for a six-month futures contract on the S&P 500 stock index?

   c. Suppose the futures price is 1,422. Is there an arbitrage opportunity here? If so, how would you exploit it?

18. Suppose that the value of the S&P 500 stock index is 1350.

   a. If each futures contract costs $25 to trade with a discount broker, how much is the transaction cost per dollar of stock controlled by the futures contract?

   b. If the average price of a share on the NYSE is about $40, how much is the transaction cost per "typical share" controlled by one futures contract?

   c. For small investors, the typical transaction cost per share in stocks directly is about 10 cents per share. How many times the transactions costs in futures markets is this?

19. The one-year futures price on a stock-index portfolio is 812, the level of the stock index currently is 800, the one-year risk-free interest rate is 3 percent, and the year-end dividend that will be paid on a $800 investment in the market index portfolio is $10.

   a. By how much is the contract mispriced?

   b. Formulate a zero-net-investment arbitrage portfolio and show that you can lock in riskless profits equal to the futures mispricing.

   c. Now assume (as is true for small investors) that if you short-sell the stocks in the market index, the proceeds of the short sale are kept with the broker, and you do not receive any interest income on the funds. Is there still an arbitrage opportunity (assuming you don't already own the shares in the index)? Explain.

   d. Given the short-sale rules, what is the no-arbitrage band for the stock-futures price relationship? That is, given a stock index level of 800, how high and how low can the futures price be without giving rise to arbitrage opportunities?

20. Consider these futures market data for the June delivery S&P 500 contract, exactly six months hence. The S&P 500 index is at 1,350, and the June maturity contract is at $F_0 = 1,351$.

   a. If the current interest rate is 2.2 percent semiannually, and the average dividend rate of the stocks in the index is 1.2 percent semiannually, what fraction of the proceeds of stock short sales would need to be available for you to earn arbitrage profits?

   b. Suppose that you, in fact, have access to 90 percent of the proceeds from a short sale. What is the lower bound on the futures price that rules out arbitrage opportunities? By how much does the actual futures price fall below the no-arbitrage bound? Formulate the appropriate arbitrage strategy and calculate the profits to that strategy.

21. What is the difference between the futures price and the value of the futures contract?

22. If the spot price of gold is $1500 per troy ounce, the risk-free interest rate is 4 percent, and storage and insurance costs are zero, what should the forward price of gold be for delivery in one year? Use an arbitrage argument to prove your answer, and include a numerical example showing how you could make risk-free arbitrage profits if the forward price exceeded its upper-bound value.

23. If the wheat harvest today is poor, would you expect this fact to have any effect on today's futures prices for wheat to be delivered (post-harvest) two years from today? Under what circumstances will there be no effect?

24. Suppose that the price of corn is risky, with a beta of .5. The monthly storage cost is $.03, and the current spot price is $5.50, with an expected spot price in three months of $5.88. If the expected rate of return on the market is .9 percent per month, with a risk-free rate of .5 percent per month, would you store corn for three months?

25. Use the information in the table below in solving this problem.

- *Situation A.* A fixed-income manager holding a $20 million market value position of U.S. Treasury $11\frac{3}{4}$ percent bonds maturing November 15, 2024, expects the economic growth rate and the inflation rate to be above market expectations in the near future. Institutional rigidities prevent any existing bonds in the portfolio from being sold in the cash market.

- *Situation B.* The treasurer of XYZ Corporation has recently become convinced that interest rates will decline in the near future. He believes it is an opportune time to purchase his company's sinking fund bonds in advance of requirements since these bonds are trading at a discount from par value. He is preparing to purchase in the open market $20 million par value XYZ Corporation $12\frac{1}{2}$ percent bonds maturing June 1, 2015. A $20 million par value position of these bonds is currently offered in the open market at 93. Unfortunately, the treasurer must obtain approval from the board of directors for such a purchase, and this approval process can take up to two months. The board of directors' approval in this instance is only a formality.

Issue	Price	Yield to Maturity	Modified Duration*
U.S. Treasury bond $11\frac{3}{4}$% maturing November 15, 2024	100	11.75%	7.6 years
U.S. Treasury long bond futures contract (contract expiration in 6 months)	63.33	11.85%	8.0 years
XYZ Corporation bond $121\frac{1}{4}$% maturing June 1, 2015 (sinking fund debenture, rated AAA)	93	13.50%	7.2 years
Volatility of AAA corporate bond yields relative to U.S. Treasury bond yields = 1.25 to 1.0 (1.25 times).			
Assume no commission and no margin requirements on U.S. Treasury long bond futures contracts. Assume no taxes.			
One U.S. Treasury bond futures contract is a claim on $100,000 par value long-term U.S. Treasury bonds.			

*Modified duration = Duration/$(1 + y)$.

For each of these situations, demonstrate how interest rate risk can be hedged using the Treasury bond futures contract. Show all calculations, including the number of futures contracts used.

26. You manage a $13.5 million portfolio, currently all invested in equities, and believe that you have extraordinary market-timing skills. You believe that the market is on the verge of a big but short-lived downturn; you would move your portfolio temporarily into T-bills, but you do not want to incur the transaction costs of liquidating and reestablishing your equity position. Instead, you decide to temporarily hedge your equity holdings with S&P 500 index futures contracts.

    a. Should you be long or short the contracts? Why?

    b. If your equity holdings are invested in a market index fund, into how many contracts should you enter? The S&P 500 index is now at 1,350 and the contract multiplier is $250.

    c. How does your answer to (b) change if the beta of your portfolio is .6?

27. Suppose that the spot price of the Euro is currently US$1.50. The one-year futures price is US$1.55. Is the interest rate higher in the United States or the Eurozone?

28. *a.* The spot price of the British pound is currently $1.60. If the risk-free interest rate on one-year government bonds is 4 percent in the United States and 8 percent in the United Kingdom, what must be the forward price of the pound for delivery one year from now?

    b. How could an investor make risk-free arbitrage profits if the forward price were higher than the price you gave in answer to (*a*)? Give a numerical example.

29. Consider the following information:

$$r_{US} = 4\% \qquad r_{UK} = 7\%$$
$$E_0 = 1.60 \text{ dollars per pound}$$
$$F_0 = 1.58 \text{ (1-year delivery)}$$

    where the interest rates are annual yields on U.S. or U.K. bills. Given this information,

    a. Where would you lend?

    b. Where would you borrow?

    c. How could you arbitrage?

30. The U.S. yield curve is flat at 5 percent and the euro yield curve is flat at 4 percent. The current exchange rate is $1.20 per euro. What will be the swap rate on an agreement to exchange currency over a three-year period? The swap will call for the exchange of one million euros for a given number of dollars in each year.

31. Desert Trading Company has issued $100 million worth of long-term bonds at a fixed rate of 7 percent. The firm then enters into an interest rate swap where it pays LIBOR and receives a fixed 6 percent on notional principal of $100 million. What is the firm's overall cost of funds?

32. Firm ABC enters a five-year swap with firm XYZ to pay LIBOR in return for a fixed 8 percent rate on notional principal of $10 million. Two years from now, the market rate on three-year swaps is LIBOR for 7 percent; at this time, firm XYZ goes bankrupt and defaults on its swap obligation.

    a. Why is firm ABC harmed by the default?

    b. What is the market value of the loss incurred by ABC as a result of the default?

    c. Suppose instead that ABC had gone bankrupt. How do you think the swap would be treated in the reorganization of the firm?

33. At the present time, one can enter five-year swaps that exchange LIBOR for 8 percent. An *off-market swap* would then be defined as a swap of LIBOR for a fixed rate other than 8 percent. For example, a firm with 10 percent coupon debt outstanding might like to convert to synthetic floating-rate debt by entering a swap in which it pays LIBOR and receives a fixed rate of 10 percent. What up-front payment will be required to induce a counterparty to take the other side of this swap? Assume notional principal is $10 million.

The following problems are based on questions that have appeared in past CFA examinations.

34. Michelle Industries issued a Swiss franc–denominated five-year discount note for SFr200 million. The proceeds were converted to U.S. dollars to purchase capital equipment in the United States. The company wants to hedge this currency exposure and is considering the following alternatives:

    • At-the-money Swiss franc call options

    • Swiss franc forwards

    • Swiss franc futures

    a. Contrast the essential characteristics of each of these three derivative instruments.

    b. Evaluate the suitability of each in relation to Michelle's hedging objective, including both advantages and disadvantages.

35. Identify the fundamental distinction between a futures contract and an option contract, and briefly explain the difference in the manner that futures and options modify portfolio risk.

36. Maria VanHusen, CFA suggests that using forward contracts on fixed-income securities can be used to protect the value of the Star Hospital Pension Plan's bond portfolio against the possibility of rising interest rates. VanHusen prepares the following example to illustrate how such protection would work:

- A 10-year bond with a face value of $1,000 is issued today at par value. The bond pays an annual coupon.
- An investor intends to buy this bond today and sell it in six months.
- The six-month risk-free interest rate today is 5.00 percent (annualized).
- A six-month forward contract on this bond is available, with a forward price of $1,024.70.
- In six months, the price of the bond, including accrued interest, is forecast to fall to $978.40 as a result of a rise in interest rates.

  a. State whether the investor should buy or sell the forward contract to protect the value of the bond against rising interest rates during the holding period.

  b. Calculate the value of the forward contract for the investor at the maturity of the forward contract if VanHusen's bond-price forecast turns out to be accurate.

  c. Calculate the change in value of the combined portfolio (the underlying bond and the appropriate forward contract position) six months after contract initiation.

37. Sandra Kapple asks Maria VanHusen about using futures contracts to protect the value of the Star Hospital Pension Plan's bond portfolio if interest rates rise. VanHusen states:

  a. "Selling a bond futures contract will generate positive cash flow in a rising interest rate environment prior to the maturity of the futures contract."

  b. "The cost of carry causes bond futures contracts to trade for a higher price than the spot price of the underlying bond prior to the maturity of the futures contract."

Comment on the accuracy of each of VanHusen's statements.

38. Joan Tam, CFA believes she has identified an arbitrage opportunity for a commodity as indicated by the information given here:

Spot price for commodity	$120
Futures price for commodity expiring in 1 year	$125
Interest rate for 1 year	8%

  a. Describe the transactions necessary to take advantage of this specific arbitrage opportunity.

  b. Calculate the arbitrage profit.

39. Janice Delsing, a U.S.-based portfolio manager, manages an $800 million portfolio ($600 million in stocks and $200 million in bonds). In reaction to anticipated short-term market events, Delsing wishes to adjust the allocation to 50 percent stock and 50 percent bonds through the use of futures. Her position will be held only until "the time is right to restore the original asset allocation." Delsing determines a financial futures-based asset allocation strategy is appropriate. The stock futures index multiplier is $250 and the denomination of the bond futures contract is $100,000. Other information relevant to a futures-based strategy is as follows:

Bond portfolio modified duration	5 years
Bond portfolio yield to maturity	7%
Basis point value (BPV) of bond futures	$97.85
Stock index futures price	1,378
Stock portfolio beta	1.0

   a. Describe the financial futures–based strategy needed and explain how the strategy allows Delsing to implement her allocation adjustment. No calculations are necessary.

   b. Compute the number of each of the following needed to implement Delsing's asset allocation strategy:

       i. Bond futures contracts

       ii. Stock index futures contracts

40. *a.* Pamela Itsuji, a currency trader for a Japanese bank, is evaluating the price of a six-month Japanese yen/U.S. dollar currency futures contract. She gathers the following currency and interest rate data:

Japanese yen/U.S. dollar spot currency exchange rate	¥124.30/$1
6-month Japanese interest rate	.10%
6-month U.S. interest rate	3.80%

   Calculate the theoretical price for a six-month Japanese yen/U.S. dollar currency futures contract, using the data above.

   b. Itsuji is also reviewing the price of a three-month Japanese yen/U.S. dollar currency futures contract, using the currency and interest rate data shown below. Because the three-month Japanese interest rate has just increased to .50 percent, Itsuji recognizes that an arbitrage opportunity exists and decides to borrow US$1 million to purchase Japanese yen. Calculate the yen arbitrage profit from Itsuji's strategy, using the following data:

Japanese yen/U.S. dollar spot currency exchange rate	¥124.30/$1
New 3-month Japanese interest rate	.50%
3-month U.S. interest rate	3.50%
3-month currency futures contract value	¥123.2605/$1

41. Donna Doni, CFA wants to explore potential inefficiencies in the futures market. The TOBEC stock index has a spot value of 185.00. TOBEC futures contracts are settled in cash and underlying contract values are determined by multiplying $100 times the index value. The current annual risk-free interest rate is 6.0 percent. For the other necessary data use the information in the table of problem 25.

   a. Calculate the theoretical price of the futures contract expiring six months from now, using the cost-of-carry model. The index pays no dividends.
   The total (round-trip) transaction cost for trading a futures contract is $15.

   b. Calculate the lower bound for the price of the futures contract expiring six months from now.

42. Suppose your client says, "I am invested in Japanese stocks but want to eliminate my exposure to this market for a period of time. Can I accomplish this without the cost and inconvenience of selling out and buying back in again if my expectations change?"

   a. Briefly describe a strategy to hedge both the local market risk and the currency risk of investing in Japanese stocks.

   b. Briefly explain why the hedge strategy you described in part (*a*) might not be fully effective.

43. René Michaels, CFA plans to invest $1 million in U.S. government cash equivalents for the next 90 days. Michaels's client has authorized her to use non–U.S. government cash equivalents, but only if the currency risk is hedged to U.S. dollars by using forward currency contracts.

   a. Calculate the U.S. dollar value of the hedged investment at the end of 90 days for each of the two cash equivalents in the table below. Show all calculations.

   b. Briefly explain the theory that best accounts for your results.

c. Based on this theory, estimate the implied interest rate for a 90-day U.S. government cash equivalent.

Interest Rates
90-Day Cash Equivalents

Japanese government	7.6%
Swiss government	8.6%

Exchange Rates
Currency Units per U.S. Dollar

	Spot	90-Day Forward
Japanese yen	133.05	133.47
Swiss franc	1.5260	1.5348

44. You ran a regression of the yield of KC Company's 10-year bond on the 10-year U.S. Treasury benchmark's yield using month-end data for the past year. You found the following result:

$$\text{Yield}_{KC} = .54 + 1.22 \times \text{Yield}_{\text{Treasury}}$$

where Yield_{KC} is the yield on the KC bond and $\text{Yield}_{\text{Treasury}}$ is the yield on the U.S. Treasury bond. The modified duration on the 10-year U.S. Treasury is 7.0 years, and modified duration on the KC bond is 6.93 years.

a. Calculate the percentage change in the price of the 10-year U.S. Treasury, assuming a 50-basis-point change in the yield on the 10-year U.S. Treasury.

b. Calculate the percentage change in the price of the KC bond, using the regression equation above, assuming a 50-basis-point change in the yield on the 10-year U.S. Treasury.

E-INVESTMENTS **Contract** **Specifications** **for Financial** **Futures and** **Options**	Go to the Chicago Mercantile Exchange site (**www.cme.com**). From the *Products & Trading* tab select the link to *Equity Index* and then to U.S. indices and to the *E-mini NASDAQ-100* contract. Now find the tab for *Contract Specs*. 1. What is the contract size for the futures contract? 2. What is the settlement procedure for the futures contract? 3. For what months are the futures contracts available? 4. Click *View price limits details* and then *Equity limits*. What is the current value of the 5 percent price limit for this contract? 5. Click on *View calendar*. What is the settlement date of the shortest-maturity outstanding contract? The longest-maturity contract?

E-INVESTMENTS **Foreign** **Currency** **Futures**	Go to the Chicago Mercantile Exchange site (**www.cme.com**) and go to the tab for *CME Products*, then *Foreign Exchange* (FX). Click *Canadian Dollar* contracts and answer the following questions about the futures contract (see *Contract Specifications*): 1. What is the size (units of $C) of each contract? 2. What is the tick size (minimum price increment) for the contract? 3. In what time period during the day is the contract traded? 4. If the delivery option is exercised, when and where does delivery take place?

PART 7

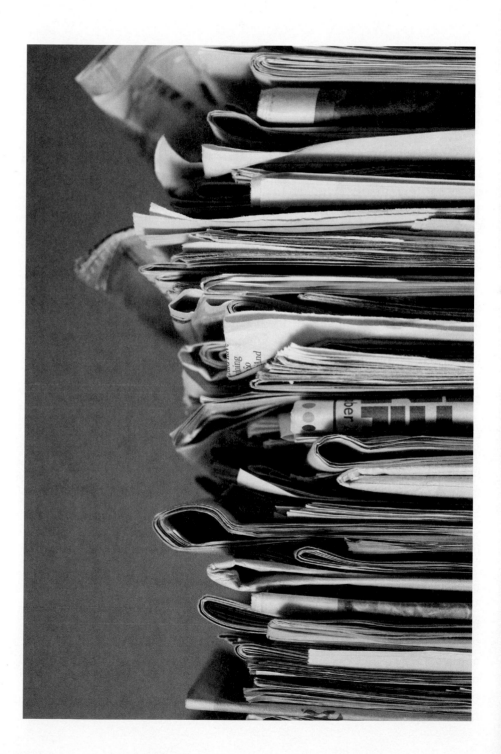

CHAPTER

21

Active Management and Performance Measurement

In the first Parts of this book, we presented the concept of asset pricing under a portfolio theory approach that led to the notion of efficient markets. This demonstrated why assets should be efficiently priced and why the market portfolio represents the appropriate equity investment choice. The theory implies that a passive strategy of holding the market portfolio of equities, in conjunction with investments in bonds and cash, is optimal. Chapter 9 on market efficiency summarized this conclusion. Subsequently, we investigated techniques for evaluating stocks, bonds and derivatives; the result of this valuation process should be the prices that these assets would command in the efficient market. Were the results of these analyses to produce values that differed from observed market prices, we would have to reject either our analysis or the notion of rigid market efficiency; in the latter case, this would give rise to active rather than passive management.

Despite the efficient market hypothesis, there are reasons to believe that active management can have effective results, but these need to be verified after the fact. It is possible to evaluate the performance of a portfolio manager, but it is not a simple matter; what the manager is trying to do as an investment strategy, and how this relates to individual investors, will cause different measures of performance to apply. Although the subject may seem technical, a close and accurate appraisal of performance is needed to cut through the arbitrary or nonspecific claims of success made by many professional managers.

We begin with a discussion of what one might expect from active management but illustrate how active management causes problems in evaluation. We then review the conventional approaches to risk adjustment for performance evaluation. We show the problems inherent in these approaches, even though they involve the use of specific theoretical measures, when they are applied in a complex world. We also present some newer alternatives to performance appraisal. Next we deal specifically with the issue of market timing, in which asset allocations between the three components are modified in response to macroeconomic factors. Following this, we present a discussion regarding the evaluation of actual performance. We conclude with a means of identifying the sources of performance results attributable to specific strategies. The appendix to this chapter presents an advanced analysis for assessing timing ability as an option.

21.1 THE OBJECTIVE OF ACTIVE MANAGEMENT

How can a theory of active portfolio management be reconciled with the notion that markets are in equilibrium? Market efficiency prevails when many investors are willing to depart from maximum diversification, or a passive strategy, by adding mispriced securities to their portfolios in the hope of realizing abnormal returns. The competition for such returns ensures that prices will be near their "true" values. Most managers will not beat the passive strategy on a risk-adjusted basis. However, in the competition for rewards to investing, exceptional managers might beat the average forecasts built into market prices.

There is both economic logic and some empirical evidence to indicate that exceptional portfolio managers can beat the average forecast. Let us discuss economic logic first. We must assume that, if no analyst can beat the passive strategy, investors will be smart enough to divert their funds from strategies entailing expensive analysis to less expensive passive strategies. With less capital under active management and less research being produced, prices will no longer reflect sophisticated forecasts. The potential profit resulting from research will then increase and active managers using this research will again have superior performance.[1]

As for empirical evidence, consider the following: (1) some portfolio managers have produced streaks of abnormal returns that are hard to label as lucky outcomes; (2) the "noise" in realized rates is enough to prevent us from rejecting outright the hypothesis that some money managers have beaten the passive strategy by a statistically small, yet economically significant, margin; and (3) some anomalies in realized returns have been sufficiently persistent to suggest that portfolio managers who identified them in a timely fashion could have beaten the passive strategy over prolonged periods.

These conclusions persuade us that there is a role for a theory of active portfolio management. Active management has an inevitable lure even if investors agree that security markets are nearly efficient.

Suppose that capital markets are perfectly efficient, an easily accessible market index portfolio is available, and this portfolio is, for all practical purposes, the efficient risky portfolio. Clearly, in this case security selection would be a futile endeavour. You would be better off with a passive strategy of allocating funds to a money market fund (the safe asset) and the market index portfolio. Under these simplifying assumptions the optimal investment strategy seems to require no effort or know-how.

Such a conclusion, however, is too hasty. Recall that the proper allocation of investment funds to the risk-free and risky portfolios requires some analysis because y, the fraction to be invested in the risky market portfolio, M, is given by

$$y = \frac{E(r_M) - r_f}{A\sigma_M^2} \tag{21.1}$$

where $E(r_M) - r_f$ is the risk premium on M, σ_M^2 its variance, and A the investor's coefficient of risk aversion. Any rational allocation therefore requires an estimate of σ_M and $E(r_M)$. Even a passive investor needs to do some forecasting, in other words.

---

[1] This point is worked out fully in Sanford J. Grossman and Joseph E. Stiglitz, "On the Impossibility of Informationally Efficient Markets," *American Economic Review* 70 (June 1980).

Forecasting $E(r_M)$ and σ_M is further complicated by the existence of security classes that are affected by different environmental factors. Long-term bond returns, for example, are driven largely by changes in the term structure of interest rates, whereas equity returns depend on changes in the broader economic environment, including macroeconomic factors beyond interest rates. Once our investor determines relevant forecasts for separate sorts of investments, she might as well use an optimization program to determine the proper mix for the portfolio. It is easy to see how the investor may be lured away from a purely passive strategy, and we have not even considered temptations such as international stock and bond portfolios or sector portfolios.

In fact, even the definition of a "purely passive strategy" is problematic, because simple strategies involving only the market-index portfolio and risk-free assets now seem to call for market analysis. For our purposes we define purely passive strategies as those that use only index funds *and* weight those funds by fixed proportions that do not vary in response to perceived market conditions. For example, a portfolio strategy that always places 60 percent in a stock market index fund, 30 percent in a bond index fund, and 10 percent in a money market fund is a purely passive strategy.

More important, the lure into active management may be extremely strong because the potential profit from active strategies is enormous. At the same time, competition among the multitude of active managers creates the force driving market prices to near-efficiency levels. Although enormous profits may be increasingly difficult to earn, decent profits to the better analysts should be the rule rather than the exception. For prices to remain efficient to some degree, some analysts must be able to eke out a reasonable profit. Absence of profits would decimate the active investment management industry, eventually allowing prices to stray from informationally efficient levels. The theory of managing active portfolios is the concern of this chapter.

Evidence of market efficiency is strong, but not conclusive, that markets are perfectly efficient, 100 percent of the time. If markets are not entirely efficient, investing in the market portfolio and in index funds will be suboptimal. The activities of thousands of investment professionals can then be justified not merely on the basis of protecting investors from their own mistakes and building portfolios that serve the interest of those investors; instead they will be able to identify departures in the pricing of assets from their inherent values and turn these into profits for investors. This may be through modification of asset allocations over time or by the over- and underweighting of assets in a diversified portfolio. This potential, if realized, certainly justifies the salaries of the analysts paid to determine the appropriate values of equities and bonds, and portfolio managers who determine their weights in active portfolios.

One study has indicated that most portfolio managers have sufficient predictive ability to beat an index fund; yet this ability does not translate into the performance of their portfolios. This predictive ability, if measured directly, rather than by fund performance, was shown to exist and when the predictions were used efficiently in portfolio design, the ability was sufficient to outperform index funds. The efficient design involves the use of good portfolio design methodology to combine stocks with nonzero alphas with an index fund in such a way as to increase expected return without undue increase in risk and yield a more efficient mean-variance combination with a higher Sharpe ratio. (The technique, known as the Treynor-Black approach, is presented in the next chapter.) This is a strong finding, and it encourages us to make the efforts required to conduct fundamental analysis, while explaining partially the failure of fund managers to succeed in beating the market. It also justifies the search by investors for good portfolio managers.

What does an investor expect from a professional portfolio manager, and how does this expectation affect the operation of the manager? If the client were risk-neutral, that is, indifferent to risk, the answer would be straightforward. The investor would expect the portfolio manager to construct a portfolio with the highest possible expected rate of return. The portfolio manager follows this dictum and is judged by the realized average rate of return.

When the client is risk-averse, the answer is more difficult. Without a normative theory of portfolio management, the manager would have to consult each client before making any portfolio decision in order to ascertain that reward (average return) is commensurate with risk. Massive and constant input would be needed from the client-investors, and the economic value of professional management would be questionable.

Fortunately, the theory of mean-variance efficient portfolio management allows us to separate the "product decision," which is how to construct a mean-variance efficient risky portfolio, and the "consumption decision," or the investor's allocation of funds between the efficient risky portfolio and the safe asset. We have seen that construction of the optimal risky portfolio is purely a technical problem, resulting in a single optimal risky portfolio appropriate for all investors. Investors will differ only in how they apportion investment to that risky portfolio and the safe asset.

Another feature of the mean-variance theory that affects portfolio management decisions is the criterion for choosing the optimal risky portfolio. In Chapter 8 we established that the optimal risky portfolio for any investor is the one that maximizes the reward-to-variability ratio, or the expected excess rate of return (over the risk-free rate) divided by the standard deviation. A manager who uses this Markowitz methodology to construct the optimal risky portfolio will satisfy all clients regardless of risk aversion. Clients, for their part, can evaluate managers using statistical methods to draw inferences from realized rates of return about prospective, or ex ante, reward-to-variability ratios.

William Sharpe's assessment of mutual fund performance[2] is the seminal work in the area of portfolio performance evaluation. The Sharpe ratio, the reward-to-variability ratio or excess return over standard deviation, $(\bar{r}_P - \bar{r}_f)/\sigma_P$, is now a common criterion for tracking performance of professionally managed portfolios. We introduced it in Chapter 4, and take it as a suitable basis for comparison.

Briefly, mean-variance portfolio theory implies that the objective of professional portfolio managers is to maximize the (ex ante) Sharpe ratio, which entails maximizing the slope of the capital allocation line (CAL). A "good" manager is one whose CAL is steeper than the CAL representing the passive strategy of holding a market index portfolio. Clients can observe rates of return and compute the realized Sharpe ratio (the ex post CAL) to evaluate the relative performance of their manager.

Ideally, clients would like to invest their funds with the most able manager, one who consistently obtains the highest Sharpe ratio and presumably has real forecasting ability. This is true for all clients, regardless of their degree of risk aversion. At the same time, each client must decide what fraction of investment funds to allocate to this manager, putting the remainder in a safe fund. If the manager's Sharpe ratio is constant over time (and can be estimated by clients), the investor can compute the optimal fraction to be invested with the manager from equation 6.12, based on the portfolio long-term average return and variance. The remainder will be invested in a money market fund.

The manager's ex ante Sharpe ratio from updated forecasts will be constantly varying. Clients may wish to increase their allocation to the risky portfolio when the forecasts are optimistic, and vice versa. However, it would be impractical to constantly communicate updated forecasts to clients and for them to constantly revise their allocation between the risky portfolios and risk-free asset.

Allowing managers to shift funds between their optimal risky portfolio and a safe asset according to their forecasts alleviates the problem. Indeed, many stock funds allow the managers reasonable flexibility to do just that. Managers can be assessed on their decisions of timing, when to invest in risky or safe portfolios, and selectivity (i.e., which risky assets to choose).

---

[2]William F. Sharpe, "Mutual Fund Performance," *Journal of Business, Supplement on Security Prices* 39 (January 1966).

Performance Measurement Under Active Management

We know that the high variance of stock returns requires a very long observation period to determine performance levels with any statistical significance, even if portfolio returns are distributed with constant mean and variance. Imagine how this problem is compounded when portfolio return distributions are constantly changing.

It is acceptable to assume that the return distributions of passive strategies have constant mean and variance when the measurement interval is not too long. However, under an active strategy return distributions change by design, as the portfolio manager updates the portfolio in accordance with the dictates of financial analysis. In such a case, estimating various statistics from a sample period assuming a constant mean and variance may lead to substantial errors. Let us look at an example.

EXAMPLE 21.1   **Changing Portfolio Risk**

Suppose that the Sharpe ratio of the passive strategy is .4. Over an initial period of 52 weeks, the portfolio manager executes a low-risk strategy with an annualized mean excess return of 1 percent and standard deviation of 2 percent. This makes for a Sharpe ratio of .5, which beats the passive strategy. Over the next 52-week period this manager finds that a *high*-risk strategy is optimal, with an annual mean excess return of 9 percent and standard deviation of 18 percent. Here again, the Sharpe ratio is .5. Over the two-year period our manager maintains a better-than-passive Sharpe ratio.

Figure 21.1 shows a pattern of (annualized) quarterly returns that are consistent with our description of the manager's strategy over two years. In the first four quarters the excess returns are −1 percent, 3 percent, −1 percent, and 3 percent, making for an average of 1 percent and standard deviation of 2 percent. In the next four quarters the returns are: −9 percent, 27 percent,

Figure 21.1
Portfolio returns.

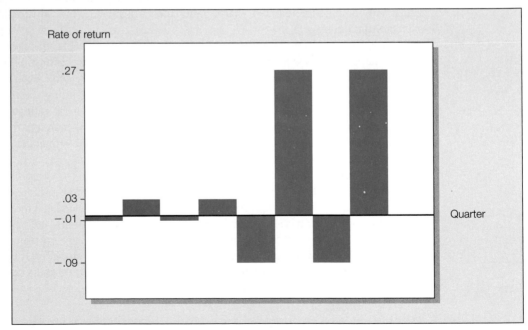

−9 percent, and 27 percent, making for an average of 9 percent and a standard deviation of 18 percent. Since the Sharpe ratio is average excess return divided by standard deviation, both years yield a ratio of .5. However, if we take the eight-quarter sequence as a single measurement period and measure the portfolio's mean and standard deviation over that full period, we will obtain an average excess return of 5 percent and standard deviation of 13.42 percent, making for a Sharpe ratio of only .37. Since a higher Sharpe ratio is considered better, the active strategy is apparently inferior to the passive strategy!

What happened? The shift in the mean from the first four quarters to the next was not recognized as a shift in strategy. Instead, the difference in mean returns in the two years added to the *appearance* of volatility in portfolio returns. The active strategy with shifting means appears riskier than it really is and biases the estimate of the Sharpe ratio downward. We conclude that for actively managed portfolios it is crucial to keep track of portfolio composition and changes in portfolio mean and risk.

21.2   MEASURING RETURNS AND CALCULATING AVERAGES

In order to evaluate the performance of a portfolio manager, we will need both a measurement of the returns of the portfolio and a way of comparing those returns to one or more benchmarks considering the risk involved. The first problem is not quite as trivial as it might seem, as it also implies the question of whether the past performance is indicative of future performance. The second process depends greatly on the context in which the comparison is made.

Average Rates of Return

We defined the holding-period return (HPR) in Section 4.4 of Chapter 4 and explained the differences between arithmetic and geometric averages in Section 4.5. Suppose we evaluate the performance of a portfolio over a period of 5 years from 20 quarterly rates of return. The arithmetic average would be the best estimate of the expected rate of return of the portfolio for the next quarter. The geometric average, which can differ substantially from the arithmetic, is the constant quarterly return over the 20 quarters that would yield the same total or cumulative return.

The geometric average, r_G, for the 20-quarter investment period is computed from the quarterly rates of return[3] as

$$1 + r_G = [(1 + r_1)(1 + r_2) \cdots (1 + r_{20})]^{1/20}$$

Each return has an equal weight in the geometric average. For this reason, the geometric average is referred to as a **time-weighted average**.

To set the stage for discussing the more subtle issues that follow, let us start with a trivial example. Consider a stock paying a dividend of $2 annually that currently sells for $50. You purchase the stock today and collect the $2 dividend, and then you sell the stock for $53 at year-end. Your rate of return is

$$\frac{\text{Total proceeds}}{\text{Initial investment}} = \frac{\text{Income} + \text{Capital gain}}{50} = \frac{2 + 3}{50} = .10, \text{ or } 10\%$$

---

[3] This formula gives the geometric average as a quarterly rate of return, consistent with the quarterly rates used to compute it. In general, when the observation period is of length h years (1/4 in this example), the *annualized* compounded rate is defined by

$1 + r_{GA} = (1 + r_{Gh})^{1/h}$. In general, the annualized geometric average of T observations, each of length h, is $1 + r_{GA} = \left(\prod_{t=1}^{T} (1 + r_t) \right)^{1/hT}$

where Π is the product operator. In our example with $T = 20$ quarterly observations, each of length $h = \frac{1}{4}$ year, $1/hT = 1/5$, so to find the annualized geometric average, we would take the fifth root of the cumulative return over the five-year investment period.

Another way to derive the rate of return that is useful in the more difficult multiperiod case is to set up the investment as a discounted cash flow problem. Call r the rate of return that equates the present value of all cash flows from the investment with the initial outlay. In our example the stock is purchased for $50 and generates cash flows at year-end of $2 (dividend) plus $53 (sale of stock). Therefore, we solve $50 = (2 + 53)/(1 + r)$ to find again that $r = 10$ percent.

Time-Weighted Returns Versus Dollar-Weighted Returns

When we consider investments over a period during which cash was added to or withdrawn from the portfolio, measuring the rate of return becomes more difficult. To continue our example, suppose that you were to purchase a second share of the same stock at the end of the first year, and hold both shares until the end of year 2, at which point you sell each share for $54.

Total cash outlays are:

Time	Outlay
0	$50 to purchase first share
1	$53 to purchase second share a year later
	Proceeds
1	$2 dividend from initially purchased share
2	$4 dividend from the 2 shares held in the second year, plus $108 received from selling both shares at $54 each

Using the discounted cash flow (DCF) approach, we can solve for the average return over the two years by equating the present values of the cash inflows and outflows:

$$50 + \frac{53}{1 + r} = \frac{2}{1 + r} + \frac{112}{(1 + r)^2}$$

resulting in $r = 7.117$ percent.

This value is called the *internal rate of return*, or **dollar-weighted rate of return** on the investment. It is "dollar-weighted" because the stock's performance in the second year, when two shares of stock are held, has a greater influence on the average overall return than the first-year return, when only one share is held.

Notice that the time-weighted (geometric average) return in this example is 7.83 percent:

$$r_1 = \frac{53 + 2 - 50}{50} = .10 = 10\% \qquad r_2 = \frac{54 + 2 - 53}{53} = .0566 = 5.66\%$$

$$r_G = (1.10 \times 1.0566)^{1/2} - 1 = .0781 = 7.81\%$$

The dollar-weighted average was less than the time-weighted average in this example because the return in the second year, when more money was invested, was lower.

Dollar-Weighted Return and Investment Performance

Every household faces several daunting saving goals, for example, the education of children and retirement. Many of these goals allow for tax-sheltered savings, for example RRSPs or TFSAs for retirement and RESPs for college expenses. These accounts are, by their nature, separated from other household assets. Household have considerable latitude in choices of investment venues and will want to check results from time to time. How should they do this? The answer here is quite simple. First, the household must maintain a spreadsheet of time-dated cash inflows and outflows. It is a simple task to record the current value of the investment account. In this setting, the dollar-weighted average over any investment period will yield the effective rate of return earned for the period.[4]

21.3   RISK-ADJUSTED PERFORMANCE MEASURES

Risk Adjustment Techniques

Calculating average portfolio returns does not mean the task is done—returns must be adjusted for risk before they can be compared meaningfully. The simplest and most popular way to adjust returns for portfolio risk is to compare rates of return with those of other investment funds with similar risk characteristics. For example, high-yield bond portfolios are grouped into one "universe," growth stock, equity funds are grouped into another universe, and so on. Then the (usually time-weighted) average returns of each fund within the universe are ordered, and each portfolio manager receives a percentile ranking depending on relative performance within the **comparison universe**. For example, the manager with the ninth-best performance in a universe of 100 funds would be the 90th percentile manager: his performance was better than 90 percent of all competing funds over the evaluation period.[5]

These relative rankings usually are displayed in a chart such as that in Figure 21.2. The chart summarizes performance rankings over five periods: one quarter, one year, three years, five years, and ten years. The top and bottom lines of each box are drawn at the rate of return of the 95th and 5th percentile managers. The three dotted lines correspond to the rates of return of the 75th, 50th (median), and 25th percentile managers. The diamond is drawn at the average return of a particular fund and the rectangle is drawn at the return of a benchmark index such as the S&P/TSX Composite. The placement of the diamond within the box is an easy-to-read representation of the performance of the fund relative to the comparison universe.

This comparison of performance with other managers of similar investment style is a useful first step in evaluating performance. However, such rankings can be misleading. Within a particular universe, some managers may concentrate on particular subgroups, so that portfolio characteristics are not truly comparable. For example, within the equity universe, one manager may concentrate on high-beta or aggressive growth stocks. Similarly, within fixed-income universes, durations can vary across managers. These considerations suggest that a more precise means of risk adjustment is desirable.

Methods of risk-adjusted performance evaluation using mean-variance criteria came on stage simultaneously with the capital asset pricing model. Jack Treynor,[6] William Sharpe,[7] and Michael Jensen[8] recognized immediately the implications of the CAPM for rating the performance of managers.

---

[4]Excel's function XIRR allows you to input sums at any date. The function provides the IRR between any two dates given a starting value, cash flows at various dates in between (with additions given as negative numbers, and withdrawals as positive values), and a final value on the closing date.

[5]In previous chapters (particularly in Chapter 9 on the efficient market hypothesis), we have examined whether actively managed portfolios can outperform a passive index. For this purpose we looked at the distribution of alpha values for samples of mutual funds. We noted that any conclusion from such samples was subject to error due to survivorship bias if funds that failed during the sample period were excluded from the sample. In this chapter, we are interested in how to assess the performance of individual funds (or other portfolios) of interest. When a particular portfolio is chosen today for inspection of its returns going forward, survivorship bias is not an issue. However, comparison groups must be free of survivorship bias. A sample comprising only surviving funds will bias the return of the benchmark group upward and the *relative* performance of any particular fund downward.

[6]Jack L. Treynor, "How to Rate Management Investment Funds," *Harvard Business Review* 43 (January/February 1966).

[7]William F. Sharpe, "Mutual Fund Performance," *Journal of Business* 39 (January 1966).

[8]Michael C. Jensen, "The Performance of Mutual Funds in the Period 1945–1964," *Journal of Finance*, May 1968; and "Risk, the Pricing of Capital Assets, and the Evaluation of Investment Portfolios," *Journal of Business*, April 1969.

Figure 21.2
Universe
comparison.

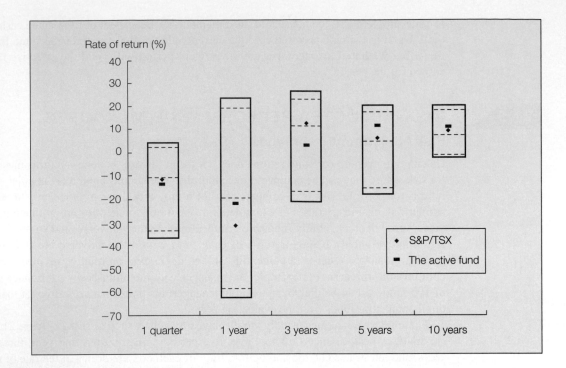

Within a short time, academicians were in command of a battery of performance measures, and a bounty of scholarly investigation of mutual fund performance was pouring from ivory towers. Shortly thereafter, agents emerged who were willing to supply rating services to portfolio managers and their clients.

Yet, while widely used, risk-adjusted performance measures each have their own limitations. Moreover, their reliability requires quite a long history of consistent management with a steady level of performance and a representative sample of investment environments, bull as well as bear markets.

We will start, however, by cataloguing some possible risk-adjusted performance measures for a portfolio P, and examining the circumstances in which each measure might be most relevant.

1. Sharpe's ratio: $(\bar{r}_P - \bar{r}_f)/\sigma_P$

   Sharpe's ratio divides average portfolio excess return over the sample period by the standard *deviation* of returns over that period. It measures the reward-to-variability ratio.[9]

2. Treynor's measure: $(\bar{r}_P - \bar{r}_f)/\beta_P$

   Like the Sharpe ratio, **Treynor's measure** gives excess return per unit of risk, but uses systematic risk instead of total risk.

3. Jensen's alpha: $\alpha_P = \bar{r}_P - [\bar{r}_f + \beta_P(\bar{r}_M - \bar{r}_f)]$

   Alpha is the average return on the portfolio over and above that predicted by the CAPM, given the portfolio's beta and the average market return.[10]

---

[9]We place bars over r_f as well as r_P to denote the fact that since the risk-free rate may not be constant over the measurement period, we are taking a sample average, just as we do for r_P.

[10]In many cases performance evaluation assumes a multifactor market. For example, when the Fama-French 3-factor model is used, Jensen's alpha will be $\alpha_P = \bar{r}_P - \bar{r}_f - \beta_{PM}(\bar{r}_M - \bar{r}_f) - s_P\bar{r}_{SMB} - h_P\bar{r}_{HML}$ where s_P is the loading on the SMB portfolio and h_P is the loading on the HML portfolio. A multifactor version of the Treynor measure also exists. See footnote 15.

4. Information ratio: $\alpha_P/\sigma(e_P)$

    The **information ratio** divides the alpha of the portfolio by the nonsystematic risk of the portfolio. It measures abnormal return per unit of risk that in principle could be diversified away by holding a market index portfolio.

5. Morningstar risk-adjusted return: $\text{MRAR}(\gamma) = \left[\dfrac{1}{T} \sum_{t=1}^{T} \left(\dfrac{1 + r_t}{1 + r_{ft}} \right)^{-\gamma} \right]^{\frac{12}{\gamma}} - 1$

    The Morningstar rating is a sort of harmonic average of excess returns, where $t = 1, \ldots, T$ are monthly observations,[11] and γ measures risk aversion. Higher γ means greater punishment for risk. For mutual funds, Morningstar uses $\gamma = 2$, which is considered a reasonable coefficient for an average retail client.[12] MRAR can be interpreted as the risk-free equivalent excess return of the portfolio for an investor with risk aversion measured by γ.

Each measure has some appeal. But each does not necessarily provide consistent assessments of performance, since the risk measures used to adjust returns differ substantially.

CC 1

CONCEPT CHECK

Consider the following data for a particular sample period:

	Portfolio *P*	Market *M*
Average return	.35	.28
Beta	1.20	1.00
Standard deviation	.42	.30
Nonsystematic risk, $\sigma(e)$	.18	.00

Calculate the following performance measures for portfolio *P* and the market: Sharpe, Jensen (alpha), Treynor, and information ratio. The T-bill rate during the period was .06. By which measures did portfolio *P* outperform the market?

The M^2 Measure of Performance

While the Sharpe ratio can be used to rank portfolio performance, its numerical value is not easy to interpret. Comparing the ratios for portfolios M and P in Concept Check 1, you should have found that $S_P = .69$ and $S_M = .73$. This suggests that portfolio P underperformed the market index. But is a difference of .04 in the Sharpe ratio economically meaningful? We are used to comparing rates of return, but these ratios are difficult to interpret.

A variant of Sharpe's ratio was proposed by Graham and Harvey, and later popularized by Leah Modigliani of Morgan Stanley and her grandfather Franco Modigliani, past winner of the

---

[11]The fraction $(1 + r_t)/(1 + r_{ft})$ is well approximated by 1 plus the excess return, R_t.

[12]The MRAR measure is the *certainty-equivalent geometric average excess return* derived from a more sophisticated utility function than the mean-variance function we used in Chapter 5. The utility function is called *constant relative risk aversion (CRRA)*. When investors have CRRA, their capital allocation (the fraction of the portfolio placed in risk-free versus risky assets) does not change with wealth. The coefficient of risk aversion is: $A = 1 + \gamma$. When $\gamma = 0$ (equivalently, $A = 1$), the utility function is just the geometric average of gross excess returns:

$$\text{MRAR}(0) = \left[\prod_{t=1}^{T} (1 + R_t) \right]^{\frac{12}{T}} - 1$$

Nobel Prize for economics.[13] Their approach has been dubbed the M^2 measure (for "Modigliani-squared"). Like the Sharpe ratio, the M^2 measure focuses on total volatility as a measure of risk, but its risk adjustment leads to an easy-to-interpret differential return relative to the benchmark index.

To compute the M^2 measure, we imagine that a managed portfolio, P, is mixed with a position in T-bills so that the complete, or "adjusted," portfolio matches the volatility of a market index such as the S&P/TSX Composite. If the managed portfolio has 1.5 times the standard deviation of the index, the adjusted portfolio would be two-thirds invested in the managed portfolio and one-third in bills. The adjusted portfolio, which we call P^*, would then have the same standard deviation as the index. (If the managed portfolio had *lower* standard deviation than the index, it would be leveraged by borrowing money and investing the proceeds in the portfolio.) Because the market index and portfolio P^* have the same standard deviation, we may compare their performance simply by comparing returns. This is the M^2 measure for portfolio P:

$$M_P^2 = r_{P*} - r_M \tag{21.2}$$

EXAMPLE 21.2 M^2 **Measure**

Using the data of Concept Check 1, P has a standard deviation of 42 percent versus a market standard deviation of 30 percent. Therefore, the adjusted portfolio P^* would be formed by mixing bills and portfolio P with weights $30/42 = .714$ in P and $1 - .714 = .286$ in bills. The expected return on this portfolio would be $(.286 \times 6\%) + (.714 \times 35\%) = 26.7$ percent, which is 1.3 percent less than the market return. Thus portfolio P has an M^2 measure of -1.3 percent.

A graphical representation of the M_P^2 appears in Figure 21.3. We move down the capital allocation line corresponding to portfolio P (by mixing P with T-bills) until we reduce the standard deviation of the adjusted portfolio to match that of the market index. The M_P^2 measure is then the vertical distance (i.e., the difference in expected returns) between portfolios P^* and M. You can see from Figure 21.3 that P will have an M_P^2 below that of the market when its capital allocation line is less steep than the capital market line, that is, when its Sharpe ratio is less than that of the market index.[14]

The Sharpe Ratio as the Criterion for Overall Portfolios

Suppose that Jane d'Arque constructs a portfolio and holds it for a considerable period of time. She makes no changes in portfolio composition during the period. In addition, suppose that the daily rates of return on all securities have constant means, variances, and covariances. These assumptions are unrealistic, and the need for them illustrates the shortcoming of conventional applications of performance measurement.

---

[13]John R. Graham and Campbell R. Harvey, "Market Timing Ability and Volatility Implied in Investment Advisors' Asset Allocation Recommendations," National Bureau of Economic Research Working Paper 4890, October 1994. The part of this paper dealing with volatility-adjusted returns was ultimately published as "Grading the Performance of Market Timing Newsletters," *Financial Analysts Journal* 53 (November/December 1997), pp. 54–66. Franco Modigliani and Leah Modigliani, "Risk-Adjusted Performance," *Journal of Portfolio Management*, Winter 1997, pp. 45–54.

[14]M^2 is positive when the portfolio's Sharpe ratio exceeds the market's. Letting R denote excess returns and S denote Sharpe measures, the geometry of Figure 21.3 implies that $R_{P^*} = S_P\sigma_M$, and therefore that $M^2 = r_{P^*} - r_M = R_{P^*} - R_M = S_P\sigma_M - S_M\sigma_M = (S_P - S_M)\sigma_M$.

Figure 21.3
M^2 of portfolio P.

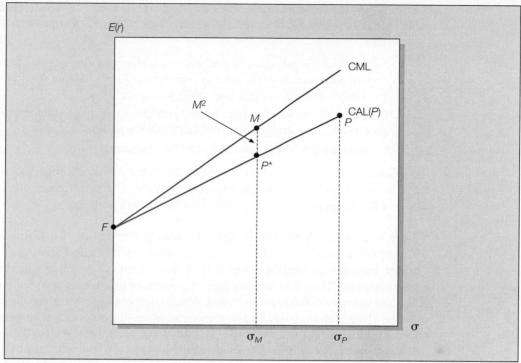

Now we want to evaluate the performance of Jane's portfolio. Has she made a good choice of securities? This is really a three-pronged question. First, good choice compared with what alternatives? Second, in choosing between two distinct alternatives, what are the appropriate criteria to use to evaluate performance? Finally, having identified the alternatives and the performance criteria, is there a rule that will separate basic ability from the random luck of the draw?

Earlier chapters of this text help to determine portfolio choice criteria. If investor preferences can be summarized by a mean-variance utility function such as that introduced in Chapter 4, we can arrive at a relatively simple criterion. The particular utility function that we have used in this text is

$$U = E(r_P) - \tfrac{1}{2}A\sigma_P^2$$

where A is the coefficient of risk aversion. With mean-variance preferences, Jane will want to maximize the Sharpe ratio $[E(r_P) - r_f]/P$ of her *complete* portfolio of assets. Recall that this is the criterion that led to the selection of the tangency portfolio in Chapter 5. Jane's problem reduces to that of whether her overall portfolio is the one with the highest possible Sharpe ratio.

Appropriate Performance Measures in Two Scenarios

To evaluate Jane's portfolio choice, we first ask whether this portfolio is her exclusive investment vehicle. If the answer is no, we need to know her "complementary" portfolio—the portfolio to which she is adding the one in question. The appropriate measure of portfolio performance depends critically on whether the portfolio is the entire investment fund or only a portion of the investor's overall wealth.

Jane's Portfolio Is Her Entire Risky Investment Fund   In this simplest case, we need to ascertain only whether Jane's portfolio has the highest possible Sharpe ratio. We can proceed in three steps:

1. Assume that her past security performance is representative of expected future performance, meaning that security returns over Jane's holding period exhibit averages and sample covariances that Jane might have anticipated.
2. Determine the benchmark (alternative) portfolio that Jane would have held if she had chosen a passive strategy (e.g., the S&P/TSX Composite).
3. Compare Jane's Sharpe ratio to that of the alternative.

In essence, when Jane's portfolio represents her entire investment fund, the benchmark alternative is the market index or another specific portfolio. The performance criterion is the Sharpe ratio of the actual portfolio versus that of the benchmark portfolio.

Jane's Choice Portfolio Is One of Many Portfolios Combined into a Large Investment Fund   This case might describe the situation where Jane, as a corporate financial officer, manages the corporate pension fund. She parcels out the entire fund to a number of portfolio managers. Then she evaluates the performance of individual managers to reallocate parts of the fund to improve future performance. What is the correct performance measure?

The Sharpe ratio is based on average excess return (the reward) against total SD (total portfolio risk). It measures the slope of the CAL. However, when Jane employs a number of managers, non-systematic risk will be largely diversified away, so systematic risk becomes the relevant measure of risk. The appropriate performance metric is now Treynor's, which takes the ratio of average excess return to beta (because systematic SD = $\beta \times$ market SD).

Consider portfolios P and Q in Table 21.1, and graph in Figure 21.4. We plot P and Q in the mean return–beta (rather than the mean–standard deviation) plane, because we assume that P and Q are two of many subportfolios in the fund, and thus that nonsystematic risk will be largely diversified away. The security market line (SML) shows the value of α_P and α_Q as the distance of P and Q above the SML.

If we invest w_Q in Q and $w_F = 1 - w_Q$ in T-bills, the resulting portfolio, Q^*, will have alpha and beta values proportional to Q's alpha and beta and to w_Q:

$$\alpha_{Q^*} = w_Q \alpha_Q$$
$$\beta_{Q^*} = w_Q \beta_Q$$

Thus, all portfolios Q^* generated from mixes of Q and T-bills plot on a straight line from the origin through Q. We call it *the T-line for the Treynor measure*, which is the slope of this line.

Figure 21.4 shows the T-line for portfolio P as well. P has a steeper T-line; despite its lower alpha, P is a better portfolio in this case after all. For any *given* beta, a mixture of P with T-bills will give a better alpha than a mixture of Q with T-bills.

TABLE 21.1

Portfolio Performance

	Portfolio P	Portfolio Q	Market
Beta	.90	1.60	1.0
Excess return $(\bar{r} - \bar{r}_f)$	.11	.19	.10
Alpha*	.02	.03	0

*Alpha = Excess return − (Beta × Market excess return)
    = $(\bar{r} - \bar{r}_f) - \beta(\bar{r}_M - \bar{r}_f)$
    = $\bar{r} - [\bar{r}_f + \beta(\bar{r}_M - \bar{r}_f)]$

Figure 21.4

Treynor measure.

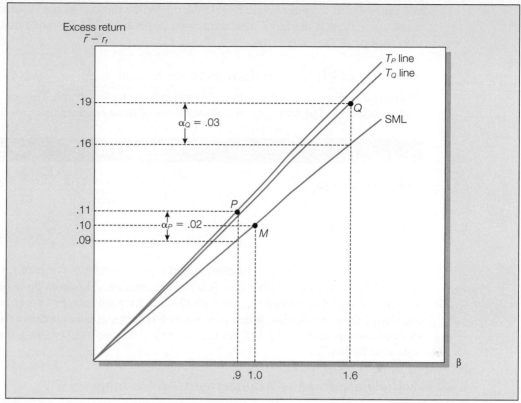

EXAMPLE 21.3   Equalizing Beta

Suppose that we choose to mix Q with T-bills to create a portfolio Q^* with a beta equal to that of P. We find the necessary proportion by solving for w_Q:

$$w_Q\beta_Q = 1.6w_Q = \beta_P = .9$$
$$w_Q = \tfrac{9}{16}$$

Portfolio Q^* therefore has an alpha of

$$\alpha_{Q^*} = \tfrac{9}{16} \times 3 = 1.69\%$$

which, in fact, is less than that of P.

In other words, the slope of the T-line is the appropriate performance criterion for the third case. The slope of the T-line for P, denoted T_P, is given by

$$T_P = \frac{\bar{r}_P - \bar{r}_f}{\beta_P}$$

Like M^2, Treynor's measure is a percentage. If you subtract the market excess return from Treynor's measure, you will obtain the difference between the return on the T_P line in Figure 21.4

and the SML, at the point where $\beta = 1$. We might dub this difference T^2, analogous to M^2. Be aware, though, that M^2 and T^2 are as different as Sharpe's and Treynor's measures. They may well rank portfolios differently.

The Role of Alpha in Performance Measures

With some algebra we can derive the relationship between the Sharpe, Treynor, and alpha performance measures. The following table shows some of these relationships.

	Treynor (T_P)	Sharpe* (S_P)
Relation to alpha	$\dfrac{E(r_P) - r_f}{\beta_P} = \dfrac{\alpha_P}{\beta_P} + T_M$	$\dfrac{E(r_P) - r_f}{\sigma_P} = \dfrac{\alpha_P}{\sigma_P} + \rho S_M$
Deviation from market performance	$T_P^2 = T_P - T_M = \dfrac{\alpha_P}{\beta_P}$	$S_P - S_M = \dfrac{\alpha_P}{\sigma_P} - (1 - \rho)S_M$

All of these measures are consistent in that superior performance requires a positive alpha. Hence, alpha is the most widely used performance measure. However, positive alpha alone cannot guarantee a better Sharpe ratio for a portfolio. Taking advantage of mispricing means departing from full diversification, which entails a cost in terms of nonsystematic risk. A mutual fund can achieve a positive alpha, yet, at the same time, increase its SD enough that its Sharpe ratio will actually fall.[15]

Actual Performance Measurement: An Example

Now that we have examined possible criteria for performance evaluation, we need to deal with a statistical issue: How can we derive an appropriate performance measure for ex ante decisions using ex post data? Before we plunge into a discussion of this problem, let us look at the rate of return on Jane's portfolio over the last 12 months. Table 21.2 shows the excess return recorded each month for Jane's portfolio P, one of her alternative portfolios, Q, and the benchmark market index portfolio M. The last rows in Table 21.2 give sample averages and standard deviations. From these, and regressions of P and Q on M, we obtain the necessary performance statistics.

The performance statistics in Table 21.3 show that portfolio Q is more aggressive than P, in the sense that its beta is significantly higher (1.40 versus .70). At the same time, P is better diversified, as seen by its residual standard deviation (2.02 percent versus 9.81 percent). Both portfolios outperformed the benchmark market index portfolio, as is evident from their larger Sharpe ratios (and thus positive M^2), positive alphas, and better Morningstar RARs.

Which portfolio is more attractive on the basis of reported performance? If P or Q represents the entire investment fund, Q would be preferable on the basis of its higher Sharpe ratio (.49 versus .43) and better M^2 (2.66 percent versus 2.16 percent). For the second scenario,

---

[15]With a multifactor model, alpha must be adjusted for the additional factors. When you have K factors, $k = 1, \ldots, K$ (the first of which, $k = 1$, is the market index M), a portfolio P's average realized excess return is given by: $\bar{R}_P = \alpha_P + \sum_{k=1}^{K} \beta_{Pk}\bar{R}_k$, where $\bar{R}_k$ is the average return on the zero-investment factor portfolio, or the average excess rate when the direct factor growth rate is used. Hence, the adjusted Jensen's alpha measure is now $\alpha_P^K = \alpha_P - \sum_{k=2}^{K} \beta_{Pk}\bar{R}_k$. The generalized Treynor measure that accounts for all K factors is given by $GT_P = \alpha_P^K \dfrac{\sum_k \beta_{kM}\bar{R}_k}{\sum_k \beta_{Pk}\bar{R}_k}$, where β_{kM} is the beta of factor k on the index M, and β_{Pk} is the beta of P on factor k. (This measure was developed Georges Hubner [HEC School of Management, yet unpublished]). Notice that with just one factor, the alpha reduces to the original Jensen's alpha and GT to the single-index Treynor measure.

TABLE 21.2

Excess Returns for Portfolios P and Q and the Benchmark M over 12 Months

Month	Jane's Portfolio P	Alternative Q	Benchmark M
1	3.58	2.81	2.20
2	−4.91	−1.15	−8.41
3	6.51	2.53	3.27
4	11.13	37.09	14.41
5	8.78	12.88	7.71
6	9.38	39.08	14.36
7	−3.66	−8.84	−6.15
8	5.56	.83	2.74
9	−7.72	.85	−15.27
10	7.76	12.09	6.49
11	−4.01	−5.68	−3.13
12	.78	−1.77	1.41
Year's average	2.77	7.56	1.64
Standard deviation	6.45	15.55	8.84

TABLE 21.3

Performance Statistics

	Portfolio P	Portfolio Q	Portfolio M
Sharpe ratio	0.43	0.49	0.19
M^2	2.16	2.66	0.00
Morningstar RAR	0.30	0.80	0.07
SCL Regression Statistics			
Alpha	1.63	5.26	0.00
Beta	0.70	1.40	1.00
Treynor	3.97	5.38	1.64
T^2	2.34	3.74	0.00
$\sigma(e)$	2.02	9.81	0.00
Information ratio	0.81	0.54	0.00
R-squared	0.91	0.64	1.00

where P and Q are competing for a role as one of a number of subportfolios, Q also dominates, because its Treynor measure is higher (5.38 versus 3.97). However, as an active portfolio to be mixed with the index portfolio, P is to be preferred, because its information ratio (IR = $\alpha/\sigma(e)$) is larger (.81 versus .54). Thus, the example illustrates that the right way to evaluate a portfolio depends in large part on how the portfolio fits into the investor's overall wealth.

Performance Manipulation and the Morningstar Risk-Adjusted Rating

Performance evaluation so far has been based on this assumption: Rates of return in each period are independent and drawn from the same distribution; in statistical jargon, returns are independent and identically distributed. This assumption can crumble in an insidious way when managers, whose compensation depends on performance, try to game the system. They may employ strategies designed to improve *measured* performance even if they harm investors. Managers' compensation may then lose its anchor to beneficial performance.

Performance Measurement

The following performance measurement spreadsheet computes all the performance measures discussed in this section. You can see how relative ranking differs according to the criterion selected.

This analysis is based on 12 months of data only, a period too short to lend statistical significance to the conclusions. Even longer observation intervals may not be enough to make the decision clear-cut, which represents a further problem.

Questions

1. Examine the performance measures of the funds included in the spreadsheet. Rank performance and determine whether the rankings are consistent using each measure. What explains these results?
2. Which fund would you choose if you were considering investing the entire risky portion of your portfolio? What if you were considering adding a small position in one of these funds to a portfolio currently invested in the market index?

	A	B	C	D	E	F	G	H	I	J	K
1	Performance Measurement								LEGEND		
2									Entered data		
3									Value calculated		
4									See comment		
5											
6					Non-						
7		Average	Standard	Beta	systematic	Sharpe's	Treynor's	Jensen's	M2	T2	Appraisal
8	Fund	Return	Deviation	Coefficient	Risk	Measure	Measure	Measure	Measure	Measure	Ratio
9	Alpha	28.00%	27.00%	1.7000	5.00%	0.8148	0.1294	-0.0180	-0.0015	-0.0106	-0.3600
10	Omega	31.00%	26.00%	1.6200	6.00%	0.9615	0.1543	0.0232	0.0235	0.0143	0.3867
11	Omicron	22.00%	21.00%	0.8500	2.00%	0.7619	0.1882	0.0410	-0.0105	0.0482	2.0500
12	Millennium	40.00%	33.00%	2.5000	27.00%	1.0303	0.1360	-0.0100	0.0352	-0.0040	-0.0370
13	Big Value	15.00%	13.00%	0.9000	3.00%	0.6923	0.1000	-0.0360	-0.0223	-0.0400	-1.2000
14	Momentum Watcher	29.00%	24.00%	1.4000	16.00%	0.9583	0.1643	0.0340	0.0229	0.0243	0.2125
15	Big Potential	15.00%	11.00%	0.5500	1.50%	0.8182	0.1636	0.0130	-0.0009	0.0236	0.8667
16	S&P Index Return	20.00%	17.00%	1.0000	0.00%	0.8235	0.1400	0.0000	0.0000	0.0000	0.0000
17	T-Bill Return	6.00%		0.0000							
18											
19	Ranking By Sharpe's Measure				Non-						
20		Average	Standard	Beta	systematic	Sharpe's	Treynor's	Jensen's	M2	T2	Appraisal
21	Fund	Return	Deviation	Coefficient	Risk	Measure	Measure	Measure	Measure	Measure	Ratio
	Millennium	~.00%	33.00%		27.00%	1.03~~		-0.0100	~~	~.0040	-0.0370

Managers can affect performance measures over a given evaluation period because they observe how returns unfold over the course of the period and can adjust portfolios accordingly. Once they do so, rates of return in the later part of the evaluation period come to depend on rates in the beginning of the period. Ingersoll, Spiegel, Goetzmann, and Welch[16] show how all but one of the performance measures covered in this chapter can be manipulated. The sole exception is the Morningstar RAR, which is in fact a manipulation-proof performance measure (MPPM). While the details of their model are challenging, the logic is straightforward, as we now illustrate using the Sharpe ratio.

As we saw when analyzing capital allocation (Chapter 5), investment in the risk-free asset (lending or borrowing) will not affect the Sharpe ratio of the portfolio. Put differently, the Sharpe ratio is invariant to the fraction y in the risky portfolio (leverage occurs when $y > 1$). The reason is that excess returns are proportional to y and therefore so are both the risk premium and SD, leaving the Sharpe ratio unchanged. But what if y is changed during a period? If the decision to change leverage in midstream is made before any performance is observed, again, the Sharpe ratio will not be affected because rates in the two portions of the period will still be uncorrelated.

But imagine a manager already partway into an evaluation period. While realized excess returns (average return, SD, and Sharpe ratio) are now known for the first part of the evaluation period, the distribution of the remaining future rates is still the same as before. The overall Sharpe ratio will be some (complicated) average of the known Sharpe ratio in the first leg and the yet unknown ratio in the second leg of the evaluation period. Increasing leverage during the second leg will increase the weight of that performance in the average because leverage will amplify

[16]Jonathan Ingersoll, Matthew Spiegel, William Goetzmann, and Ivo Welch, "Portfolio Performance Manipulation and Manipulation Proof Performance Measures," *Review of Financial Studies* 20 (2007).

returns, both good and bad. Therefore, managers will wish to increase leverage in the first part of the period if early returns are poor.[17] Conversely, good first-part performance calls for deleveraging to increase the weight on the initial period. With an extremely good first leg, a manager will shift almost the entire portfolio to the risk-free asset. This strategy induces a (negative) correlation between returns in the first and second legs of the evaluation period.

Investors lose, on average, from this strategy. Even if the fund's expected Sharpe ratio is same throughout the period, the average switch is to higher leverage and is less preferable to the typical investor. More fundamentally, arbitrary variation in leverage (and therefore risk) is utility-reducing. It benefits managers only because it allows them to adjust the weighting scheme of the two subperiods over the full evaluation/compensation period after observing their initial performance.[18] Hence investors would like to prohibit or at least eliminate the incentive to pursue this strategy.

Unfortunately, only one performance measure is impossible to manipulate. A manipulation-proof performance measure (MPPM) must fulfill four requirements:

1. The measure should produce a single-value score to rank a portfolio.
2. The score should not depend on the dollar value of the portfolio.
3. An uninformed investor should not expect to improve the expected score by deviating from the benchmark portfolio.
4. The measure should be consistent with standard financial market equilibrium conditions.

Ingersoll et al. prove that the Morningstar RAR fulfills these requirements. Interestingly, when it developed the MRAR, Morningstar was not aiming to create an MPPM, but simply attempting to accommodate investors with CRRA.

Panel A of Figure 21.5 shows a scatter plot of Sharpe ratios against MRAR of 100 portfolios based on statistical simulation. Thirty-six excess returns were randomly generated for each portfolio, all with an annual expected return of 7 percent and SDs varying from 10 to 30 percent. Thus, the true Sharpe ratios of these simulated "mutual funds" are in the range of .7 to .23, with a mean of .39. Because of sampling variation, the actual 100 Sharpe ratios in the simulation differ quite a bit from these population parameters—from −1.02 to 2.46 and average .32. The 100 MRARs range from −28 to 37 percent and average .7 percent. The correlation between the measures was .94, suggesting that Sharpe ratios track MRAR quite well. Indeed the scatter is quite tight along a line with a slope of .19.

Panel B of Figure 21.5 (drawn on the same scale as panel A) illustrates the effect of manipulation when one leverage change is allowed after initial performance is observed, specifically in the middle of the 36-month evaluation period.[19] The effect of manipulation is evident from the extreme-value portfolios. For high-positive initial MRARs, the switch toward the risk-free rate preserves the first-half high Sharpe ratios that would otherwise be diluted or possibly even reversed in the second half. For the high-negative initial MRARs, when leverage ratios are increased, we see two effects. First, MRARs look worse because of cases in which the high leverage backfired and worsened the MRARs compared to panel A (points move to the left). In contrast, Sharpe ratios look better than in panel A (they move upward). Some Sharpe ratios move from negative to positive values, while others do not look worse (because the increased SD in the second period reduced the absolute value of the negative Sharpe ratios).

The statistics in the box of panel B quantify the improvement of measured Sharpe ratios; in contrast, MRARs clearly deteriorated from a slight positive value to a certainty equivalent

---

[17]Managers who are precluded from increasing leverage will instead shift to high-beta stocks. If this is a widespread phenomenon, it could help explain why high-beta stocks appear, on average, to be overpriced relative to low-beta ones.

[18]One way to reduce the potency of manipulation is to evaluate performance more frequently. This will reduce the statistical precision of the measure, however.

[19]To keep the exercise realistic, leverage ratios were capped at 2 (a debt-to-equity ratio of 1.0).

Figure 21.5
MRAR scores and Sharpe ratios with and without manipulation.

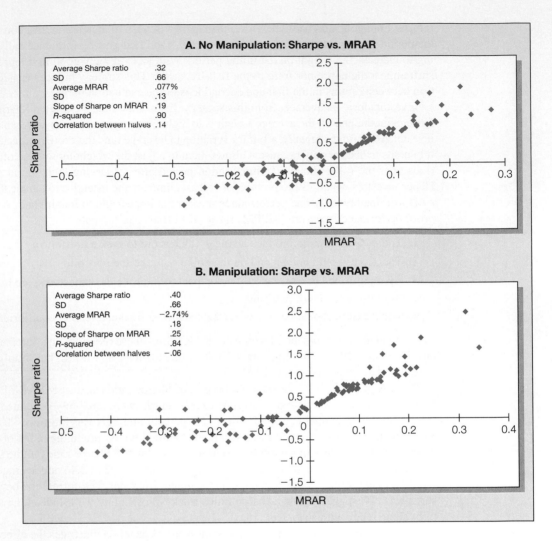

A. No Manipulation: Sharpe vs. MRAR

Average Sharpe ratio	.32
SD	.66
Average MRAR	.077%
SD	.13
Slope of Sharpe on MRAR	.19
R-squared	.90
Correlation between halves	.14

B. Manipulation: Sharpe vs. MRAR

Average Sharpe ratio	.40
SD	.66
Average MRAR	−2.74%
SD	.18
Slope of Sharpe on MRAR	.25
R-squared	.84
Corelation between halves	−.06

of −2.74 percent per year! As predicted, the correlation between average returns in the first and second legs of the period changes from positive to negative. All this happened because of an average increase in leverage from 1.0 to 1.39.[20]

Morningstar introduced the MRAR in 2002. It is particularly relevant to hedge funds, where managers have great latitude and incentive to manipulate. See Chapter 23 for further discussion. Given its immunity to manipulation, we would expect the MRAR measure to become a standard performance statistic sometime in the future, one required especially of managers who have the most discretion over investment policy.

Realized Returns Versus Expected Returns

When evaluating a portfolio, the evaluator knows neither the portfolio manager's original expectations nor whether those expectations made sense. One can only observe performance after the fact and hope that random results are not taken for, or do not hide, true underlying ability. But risky asset returns are "noisy," which complicates the inference problem. To avoid making

---

[20]Out of 100 funds, the leverage ratio was decreased in 38 portfolios, was increased to less than 2 in 14 portfolios, and was increased to 2 (and would have been increased even more absent the cap) in 48 portfolios.

mistakes, we have to determine the "significance level" of a performance measure to know whether it reliably indicates ability.

Consider Joe Dark, a portfolio manager. Suppose that his portfolio has an alpha of 20 basis points per month, which makes for a hefty 2.4 percent per year before compounding. Let us assume that the return distribution of Joe's portfolio has constant mean, beta, and alpha—a big assumption, but one in line with the usual treatment of performance measurement. Suppose that for the measurement period Joe's portfolio beta is 1.2 and the monthly standard deviation of the residual (nonsystematic risk) is .02 (2 percent). With a market index standard deviation of 6.5 percent per month (22.5 percent per year), Joe's portfolio systematic variance is

$$\beta^2 \sigma_M^2 = 1.2^2 \times 6.5^2 = 60.84$$

and hence the correlation coefficient between his portfolio and the market index is

$$\rho = \left[\frac{\beta^2 \sigma_M^2}{\beta^2 \sigma_M^2 + \sigma^2(e)} \right]^{1/2} = \left[\frac{60.84}{60.84 + 4} \right]^{1/2} = .97$$

which shows that his portfolio is quite well diversified.

To estimate Joe's portfolio alpha from the security characteristic line (SCL), we regress the portfolio excess returns on the market index. Suppose that we are in luck and the regression estimates yield the true parameters. That means that our SCL estimates for the N months are

$$\hat{\alpha} = .2\%, \qquad \hat{\beta} = 1.2, \qquad \hat{\sigma}(e) = 2\%$$

The evaluator who runs such a regression, however, does not know the true values, and hence must compute the t-statistic of the alpha estimate to determine whether to reject the hypothesis that Joe's alpha is zero, that is, that he has no superior ability.

The standard error of the alpha estimate in the SCL regression is approximately

$$\sigma(\hat{\alpha}) = \frac{\hat{\sigma}(e)}{\sqrt{N}}$$

where N is the number of observations and $\hat{\sigma}(e)$ is the sample estimate of nonsystematic risk. The t-statistic for the alpha estimate is then

$$t(\hat{\alpha}) = \frac{\hat{\alpha}}{\hat{\sigma}(\alpha)} = \frac{\hat{\alpha}\sqrt{N}}{\hat{\sigma}(e)} \qquad (21.3)$$

Suppose that we require a significance level of 5 percent. This requires a $t(\hat{\alpha})$ value of 1.96 if N is large. With $\hat{\alpha} = .2$ and $\hat{\sigma}(e) = 2$, we solve equation 21.3 for N and find that

$$1.96 = \frac{.2\sqrt{N}}{2}$$

$$N = 384 \text{ months}$$

or 32 years!

What have we shown? Here is an analyst who has very substantial ability. The example is biased in his favour in the sense that we have assumed away statistical problems. Nothing changes in the parameters over a long period of time. Furthermore, the sample period "behaves" perfectly. Regression estimates are all perfect. Still, it will take Joe's entire working career to get to the point where statistics will confirm his true ability. We have to conclude that the problem of statistical inference makes performance evaluation extremely difficult in practice.

Now add to the imprecision of performance estimates the fact that the average tenure of a fund manager is only about 4.5 years. By the time you are lucky enough to find a fund whose historic superior performance you are confident of, its manager is likely to be about to move, or has already moved elsewhere. The nearby box explores this topic further.

The whole idea of investing in a mutual fund is to leave the stock and bond picking to the professionals. But frequently, events don't turn out quite as expected—the manager resigns, gets transferred or dies. A big part of the investor's decision to buy a managed fund is based on the manager's record, so changes like these can come as an unsettling surprise.

There are no rules about what happens in the wake of a manager's departure. It turns out, however, that there is strong evidence to suggest that the managers' real contribution to fund performance is highly overrated. For example, research company Morningstar compared funds that experienced management changes between 1990 and 1995 with those that kept the same managers. In the five years ending in June 2000, the top-performing funds of the previous five years tended to keep beating their peers—despite losing any fund managers. Those funds that performed badly in the first half of the 1990s continued to do badly, regardless of management changes. While mutual fund management companies will undoubtedly continue to create star managers and tout their past records, investors should stay focused on fund performance.

Funds are promoted on their managers' track records, which normally span a three-to-five-year period. But performance data that goes back only a few years is hardly a valid measure of talent. To be statistically sound, evidence of a manager's track record needs to span, at a minimum, 10 years or more.

The mutual fund industry may look like a merry-go-round of managers, but that shouldn't worry most investors. Many mutual funds are designed to go through little or no change when a manager leaves. That is because, according to a strategy designed to reduce volatility and succession worries, mutual funds are managed by teams of stock pickers, who each run a portion of the assets, rather than by a solo manager with co-captains. Meanwhile, even so-called star managers are nearly always surrounded by researchers and analysts, who can play as much of a role in performance as the manager who gets the headlines.

Don't forget that if a manager does leave, the investment is still there. The holdings in the fund haven't changed. It is not the same as a chief executive leaving a company whose share price subsequently falls. The best thing to do is to monitor the fund more closely to be on top of any changes that hurt its fundamental investment qualities.

In addition, don't underestimate the breadth and depth of a fund company's "managerial bench." The larger, established investment companies generally have a large pool of talent to draw on. They are also well aware that investors are prone to depart from a fund when a managerial change occurs.

Lastly, for investors who worry about management changes, there is a solution: index funds. These mutual funds buy stocks and bonds that track a benchmark index like the S&P 500 rather than relying on star managers to actively pick securities. In this case, it doesn't really matter if the manager leaves. At the same time, index investors don't have to pay tax bills that come from switching out of funds when managers leave. Most importantly, index fund investors are not charged the steep fees that are needed to pay star management salaries.

Source: Shauna Carther, "Should You Follow Your Fund Manager?" *Investopedia.com*, March 3, 2010. Provided by Forbes.

CC 2

CONCEPT CHECK

Suppose an analyst has a measured alpha of .2 percent with a standard error of 2 percent, as in our example. What is the probability that the positive alpha is due to luck of the draw and that true ability is zero?

21.4 STYLE ANALYSIS

Style analysis was introduced by Nobel laureate William Sharpe.[21] The popularity of the concept was aided by a well-known study[22] concluding that 91.5 percent of the variation in returns of 82 mutual funds could be explained by the funds' asset allocation to bills, bonds, and stocks. Later studies that considered asset allocation across a broader range of asset classes found that as much as 97 percent of fund returns can be explained by asset allocation alone.

Sharpe's idea was to regress fund returns on indices representing a range of asset classes. The regression coefficient on each index would then measure the fund's implicit allocation to that

[21]William F. Sharpe, "Asset Allocation: Management Style and Performance Evaluation," *Journal of Portfolio Management*, Winter 1992, pp. 7–19.

[22]Gary Brinson, Brian Singer, and Gilbert Beebower, "Determinants of Portfolio Performance," *Financial Analysts Journal*, May/June 1991.

TABLE 21.4

Style Analysis for Fidelity's Magellan Fund

Style Portfolio	Regression Coefficient
T-bill	0
Small cap	0
Medium cap	35
Large cap	60
High P/E (growth)	5
Medium P/E	0
Low P/E (value)	0
Total	100
R-squared	97.5

Source: Authors' calculations. Return data for Magellan from http://finance.yahoo.com/funds and return data for style portfolios from Web page of Professor Kenneth French, http://mba.tuck.dartmouth.edu/pages/faculty/ken.french/data_library.html.

"style." Because funds are barred from short positions, the regression coefficients are constrained to be either zero or positive and to sum to 100 percent, so as to represent a complete asset allocation. The R-squared of the regression would then measure the percentage of return variability attributable to style or asset allocation, while the remainder of return variability would be attributable either to security selection or to market timing by periodic changes in the asset-class weights.

To illustrate Sharpe's approach, we use monthly returns on Fidelity Magellan's Fund over the five-year period from October 1986 to September 1991, with results shown in Table 21.4. While seven asset classes are included in this analysis (of which six are represented by stock indices and one is the T-bill alternative), the regression coefficients are positive for only three, namely large-capitalization stocks, medium-cap stocks, and high-P/E (growth) stocks. These portfolios alone explain 97.5 percent of the variance of Magellan's returns. In other words, a tracking portfolio made up of the three style portfolios, with weights as given in Table 21.4, would explain the vast majority of Magellan's variation in monthly performance. We conclude that the fund returns are well represented by three style portfolios.

The proportion of return variability *not* explained by asset allocation can be attributed to security selection within asset classes, as well as timing that shows up as periodic changes in allocation. For Magellan, residual variability was $100 - 97.5 = 2.5$ percent. This sort of result is commonly used to play down the importance of security selection and timing in fund performance, but such a conclusion misses the important role of the intercept in this regression. (The R-squared of the regression can be 100 percent, and yet the intercept can be nonzero due to a superior risk-adjusted abnormal return.) For Magellan, the intercept was 32 basis points per month, resulting in a cumulative abnormal return over the five-year period of 19.19 percent.

The superior performance of Magellan is displayed in Figure 21.6, which plots the cumulative impact of the intercept plus monthly residuals relative to the tracking portfolio composed of the style portfolios. Except for the period surrounding the crash of October 1987, Magellan's return consistently increased relative to the benchmark portfolio.

Style analysis provides an alternative to performance evaluation based on the security market line (SML) of the CAPM. The SML uses only one comparison portfolio, the broad market index, whereas style analysis more freely constructs a tracking portfolio from many more specialized indices. To compare the two approaches, the security characteristic line (SCL) of Magellan was estimated by regressing its excess return on the excess return of a market index composed of all

Figure 21.6

Fidelity Magellan
Fund cumulative
returns
difference: Fund
versus style
benchmark and
fund versus SML
benchmark.

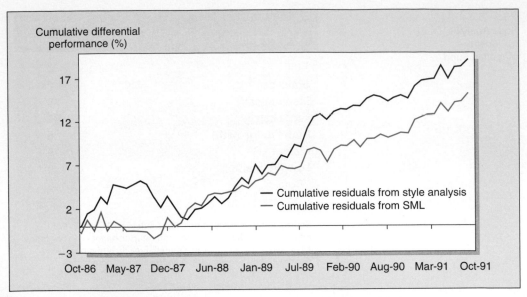

Source: Authors' calculations.

NYSE, Amex, and Nasdaq stocks. The beta estimate of Magellan was 1.11 and the R-squared of the regression was .99. The alpha value (intercept) of this regression was "only" 25 basis points per month, reflected in a cumulative abnormal return of 15.19 percent for the period.

How can we explain the higher R-squared of the regression with only one factor (the market index) relative to the style regression, which deploys six stock indices? The answer is that style analysis imposes extra constraints on the regression coefficients: it forces them to be positive and to sum to 1.0. This "neat" representation may not be consistent with actual portfolio weights that are constantly changing over time. So which representation better gauges Magellan's performance over the period? There is no clear-cut answer. The SML benchmark is a better representation of performance relative to the theoretically prescribed passive portfolio, that is, the broadest market index available. On the other hand, style analysis reveals the strategy that most closely tracks the fund's activity and measures performance relative to this strategy. If the strategy revealed by the style analysis method is consistent with the one stated in the fund prospectus (a rare event), then the performance relative to this strategy is the correct measure of the fund's success.

Figure 21.7 shows the frequency distribution of average residuals across 636 mutual funds from Sharpe's style analysis. The distribution has the familiar bell shape with a slightly negative mean of $-.074$ percent per month. As in Sharpe's study, these risk-adjusted returns plot as a bell-shaped curve with slightly negative mean.

Style Analysis and Multifactor Benchmarks

Style analysis raises an interesting question for performance evaluation. Suppose a growth-index portfolio exhibited superior performance relative to a mutual fund benchmark such as the S&P 500 over some measurement period. Including this growth index in a style analysis would eliminate this superior performance from the portfolio's estimated alpha value. Is this proper? Quite plausibly, the fund's analysts predicted that an active portfolio of growth stocks was underpriced and tilted the portfolio to take advantage of it. Clearly, the contribution of this decision to an alpha value relative to the benchmark is a legitimate part of the overall alpha value of the fund, and should not be eliminated by style analysis. This brings up a related question.

Figure 21.7

Average tracking error for 636 mutual funds, 1985–1989.

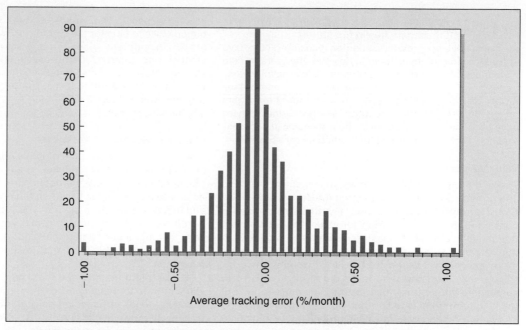

Average tracking error (%/month)

Source: William F. Sharpe, "Asset Allocation: Management Style and Performance Evaluation," *Journal of Portfolio Management,* Winter 1992, pp. 7–19. Copyrighted material is reprinted with permission from Institutional Investor, 225 Park Avenue South, New York, NY 10003. Email: info@iijournals.com.

In Chapter 9 it was pointed out that the conventional performance benchmark today is a four-factor model, which employs the three Fama-French factors (the return on the market index, and returns to portfolios based on size and book-to-market ratio) augmented by a momentum factor (a portfolio constructed based on prior-year stock return). Alphas estimated from these four factor portfolios control for a wide range of style choices that may affect average returns. But using alpha values from a multifactor model presupposes that a passive strategy would include the aforementioned factor portfolios. When is this reasonable?

Use of any benchmark other than the fund's single-index benchmark is legitimate only if we assume that the factor portfolios in question are part of the fund's alternative passive strategy. This assumption may be unrealistic in many cases where a single-index benchmark is used for performance evaluation even if research shows a multifactor model better explains asset returns. In Section 21.7 on performance attribution we show how portfolio managers attempt to uncover which decisions contributed to superior performance. This performance attribution procedure starts with benchmark allocations to various indices and attributes performance to asset allocation on the basis of deviation of actual from benchmark allocations. The performance benchmark may be and often is specified in advance without regard to any particular style portfolio.

Style Analysis in Excel

Style analysis has become very popular in the investment management industry and has spawned quite a few variations on Sharpe's methodology. Many portfolio managers utilize Web sites that help investors identify their style and stock selection performance. The alpha/beta controversy is addressed in the boxed article here.

You can do style analysis with Excel's Solver. The strategy is to regress a fund's rate of return on those of a number of style portfolios (as in Table 21.4). The style portfolios are passive (index) funds that represent a style alternative to asset allocation. Suppose you choose

Investment styles have been evolving over time. Will alpha set investment managers free in the future?

From value to growth, Canadian pension funds have looked to different investment styles over the years to help them meet their returns and manage risk. In examining style trends among Canadian plan sponsors, one need not look further than some of the fastest-growing money managers on our Top 40 list for their thoughts. Which investment styles have been the most prevalent in the last couple of decades? And how is alpha expanding the traditional style boxes?

Value Versus Growth

Two of the key styles in investment management are value and growth. Bill Chinery, managing director with Barclays Global Investors Canada in Toronto, says that, today, Canadian pension funds are still looking for value. "My view is that there's still a big value bias in pension plans in general. It makes sense to buy things cheap to sell when they get more expensive." When it comes to growth, however, there's been less long-term focus among funds. "Growth comes into vogue from time to time," he points out. "But the long-term trend is to see that value is preeminent."

For Rob Vanderhooft, however, growth is all about creating returns over the long term. Vanderhooft, who is chief executive officer and chief investment officer with growth-oriented Greystone Managed Investments Inc. in Regina, notes, "growth and value are not mutually exclusive."

Instead, he says, it's all about how you define it. "Growth tends to involve strong quarter-over-quarter earnings and other factors that correlate well with earnings growth and, more importantly, with stock price performance." And, he says, it is possible to add growth without taking more risks in the area of valuation.

While value and growth continue to be resilient styles in pension investment, the landscape is beginning to change. According to David Cameron, chief investment officer of Boston-based Mellon Institutional Asset Management's affiliate The Boston Company, the advent of alpha onto the investment scene has challenged the traditional notions of style, such as large-cap, small-cap, mid-cap, value, core and growth.

Those "style boxes," says Cameron, can be very limiting for managers working to tightly wrap performance around a specific benchmark—and the result is getting a bit too close to beta for the comfort of investors. "The buyers of investment management services are getting smarter and smarter," Cameron explains. "If managers stick too closely to the style boxes, then they're too close to the market and the indexes. That's beta—it's cheap to produce and it doesn't take much skill. No one wants to pay big fees for beta."

Managers Set Free

Cameron says that portable alpha is unshackling managers from the style boxing issue. Mixing and matching alpha and beta exposure, he notes, "frees up managers to be true to a style that is based on their core competencies and to move away from the box. You can create alpha and port it on top of any beta portfolio you want." Cameron says that alpha is a "genie that's not going back into the bottle" and that this is changing the investment style landscape.

Looking into the future, it looks as if investment styles will continue to evolve and change in order to meet the changing needs of Canadian pension funds. Chinery sees the current move toward liability driven investing as having an influence on styles in the future.

At the same time, he sees more and more pension funds moving into fixed income. "There will be a lot of focus on this in the next five to 10 years due to accounting changes and the fact that many plans have converted to defined contribution," says Chinery. Indeed, according to him, British drugstore chain, Boots PLC's move into a 100% fixed income portfolio in 2000 just might be something that will become a lot more prevalent in Canada.

Porting alternative strategies onto other strategies such as fixed income is likely what more and more pension funds will be doing in the years to come. Chinery says they might also "get forced into value" as the equities pendulum continues to shift away from the strong returns of the 1980s and '90s along with the equity risk premium.

Whatever happens, it looks as if investment styles are set to get a boost from the alpha–beta split that is happening within many pension funds in Canada and around the world. The investment style landscape is set to get even more interesting in the years ahead.

Source: © 2006 Rogers Publishing Ltd. This article first appeared in the September 2006 edition of *Benefits Canada* magazine. Caroline Cakebread is the editor of *Canadian Investment Review*. Caroline.cakebread@rogers.com.

three style portfolios, labelled 1–3. Then the coefficients in your style regression are alpha (the intercept that measures abnormal performance) and three slope coefficients, one for each style index. The slope coefficients reveal how sensitively the performance of the fund follows the return of each passive style portfolio. The residuals from this regression, $e(t)$, represent "noise," that is, fund performance at each date, t, that is independent of any of the style portfolios. We cannot use a standard regression package in this analysis, however, because we wish to constrain each coefficient to be nonnegative and sum to 1.0, representing a portfolio of styles.

To do style analysis using Solver, start with arbitrary coefficients (e.g., you can set $\alpha = 0$ and set each $\beta = 1/3$). Use these to compute the time series of residuals from the style regression according to

$$e(t) = R(t) - [\alpha - \beta_1 R_1(t) - \beta_2 R_2(t) - \beta_3 R_3(t)] \tag{21.4}$$

where

$R(t)$ = excess return on the measured fund for date t

$R_i(t)$ = excess return on the ith style portfolio ($i = 1,2,3$)

$\quad \alpha$ = abnormal performance of the fund over the sample period

$\quad \beta_i$ = beta of the fund on the ith style portfolio

Equation 21.4 yields the time series of residuals from your "regression equation" with those arbitrary coefficients. Now square each residual and sum the squares. At this point, you call on the Solver to minimize the sum of squares by changing the value of the four coefficients. You will use the "by changing variables" command. You also add four constraints to the optimization: three that force the betas to be nonnegative and one that forces them to sum to 1.0.

Solver's output will give you the three style coefficients, as well as the estimate of the fund's unique, abnormal performance as measured by the intercept. The sum of squares also allows you to calculate the R-squared of the regression and p-values as explained in Chapter 8.

Other Performance Measures

Style is not the only alternative to the traditional mean-variance measures of performance, which increasingly are coming under attack. The assumption that these first two moments of the return distributions are the only factors in investors' risk aversion is often challenged. Furthermore, the normality or lognormality of returns is also questioned. Earlier work has considered third and fourth moments (i.e., skewness and kurtosis) in appraising portfolios. Reactions to anomalous findings, according to the CAPM, in returns lead to alternative explanations for valuation. For example, the Fama and French studies have pointed to the inability of the CAPM to determine returns. Consequently, researchers have looked for other measures that might reveal superior management.

In a short article, Wilfred Vos examines measures that also capture skewness and proposes his own rating system, the Vos Value Ratio (VVR), which is broken down into three different modules: a performance module (VVR P), a risk module (VVR R), and a best balance module (VVR B), combining the previous two.[23] He states:

> Post Modern Portfolio Theory, which is gaining acceptance with institutional investors world-wide, replaces standard deviation with downside risk, which differentiates between upside and downside variability. In so doing, it treats as risky only those returns that have fallen below some target or benchmark return. . . . Intuitively, short-fall probability is perhaps most closely related to what risk is for the mutual fund investor. This is the idea that the probability of making a gain in any standardized time period is what is most relevant.

[23]See Wilfred Vos, "Measuring Mutual Fund Performance," *Canadian Investment Review*, Winter 1998, and also articles referenced by him: Brian M. Rom and Kathleen W. Ferguson, "New Breed of Tools Available to Assess Risk," *Pensions & Investments*, November 13, 1995; and Lawrence Kryzanowski and Simon Lalancette, "Conditioning for Better Performance Evaluations," *Canadian Investment Review*, Fall 1997.

21.5 ► MARKET TIMING

In the example in the first section, we considered the problem posed by a portfolio manager who changed her portfolio strategy between high risk and low risk over time. This was an example of predicting periods of higher or lower return and adjusting portfolio composition in response to these changing expectations. We refer to the practice of adjusting portfolios to suit such forecasts as *market timing*.

The Potential Value of Market Timing

Suppose we define perfect **market timing** as the ability to tell (with certainty) at the beginning of each year whether the S&P 500 portfolio will outperform the strategy of rolling over one-month T-bills throughout the year. Accordingly, at the beginning of each year, the market timer shifts all funds into either cash equivalents (T-bills) or equities (the U.S. stock portfolio), which-ever is predicted to do better. Beginning with $1 on January 1, 1927, how would the perfect timer end the 86-year experiment on December 31, 2012 in comparison with investors who kept their funds in either equity or T-bills for the entire period?

Table 21.5, columns 1–3, presents summary statistics for each of the three strategies, com-puted from the historical annual returns of bills and equities. From the returns on stocks and bills, we calculate wealth indices of the all-bills and all-equity investments and show terminal values for these investors at the end of 2012. The return for the perfect timer in each year is the *maxi-mum* of the return on stocks and the return on bills.

The first row in Table 21.5 tells all. The terminal value of investing $1 in bills over the 86 years (1926–2012) is about $20, while the terminal value of the same initial investment in equities is about $2,652. We saw a similar pattern for a 25-year investment in Chapter 4; the much larger terminal values (and difference between them) when extending the horizon from 25 to 86 years is just another manifestation of the power of compounding. We argued in Chapter 4 that as impressive as the difference in terminal values is, it is best interpreted as no more than fair compensation for the risk borne by equity investors. Notice that the standard deviation of the all-equity investor was a hefty 20.39 percent. This is also why the geometric average of large stocks for the period is "only" 9.60 percent, as against the arithmetic average of 11.63 percent. (The difference between the two averages increases with volatility.)

Now observe that the terminal value of the perfect timer is about $353,000, a 133-fold increase over the already large terminal value of the all-equity strategy! In fact, this result is even better than it looks, since the return to the market timer is truly risk-free. This is the classic case in

TABLE 21.5

Performance of Bills, Equities, and (Annual) Timers, Perfect and Imperfect

Strategy	Bills	Equities	Perfect Timer	Imperfect Timer*
Terminal value	20	2,652	352,796	8,859
Arithmetic average	3.59	11.63	16.75	11.98
Standard deviation	3.12	20.39	13.49	14.36
Geometric average	3.54	9.60	16.01	11.09
LPSD (relative to bills)	0	21.18	0	17.15
Minimum†	−.04	−44.00	−.02	−27.09
Maximum	14.72	57.42	57.42	57.42
Skew	.99	−.42	.72	.71
Kurtosis	.98	.02	−.13	1.50

*The imperfect timer has $P_1 = .7$ and $P_2 = .7$. $P_1 + P_2 - 1 = .4$.
†A negative rate on "bills" of −.06 percent was observed in 1940. The Treasury security used in the data series for this year actually was not a T-bill, but a T-bond with a short remaining maturity.

which a large standard deviation (13.49 percent) has nothing to do with risk. Since the timer never delivers a return below the risk-free rate, the standard deviation is a measure of *good* surprises only. The positive skew of the distribution (compared with the small negative skew of equities) is a manifestation of the fact that the extreme values are all positive. Another indication of this stellar performance is the minimum and maximum returns—the minimum return equals the minimum return on bills (in 1940) and the maximum return is that of equities (in 1933)—so that all negative returns on equities (as low as −44 percent in 1931) were avoided by the timer. Finally, the best indication of the performance of the timer is a lower partial standard deviation, LPSD.[24] The LPSD of the all-equity portfolio is only slightly greater than the conventional standard deviation, but it is necessarily zero for the perfect timer.

If we interpret the terminal value of the all-equity portfolio in excess of the value for the T-bill portfolio entirely as a risk-premium commensurate with investment risk, we must conclude that the risk-adjusted equivalent value of the all-equity terminal value is the same as that of the T-bill portfolio, $20.[25] In contrast, the perfect timer's portfolio has no risk, and so receives no discount for risk. Hence, it is fair to say that the forecasting ability of the perfect timer converts an $20 final value to a value of $352,796 free of risk.

The Value of Imperfect Forecasting

A weather forecaster in Tucson, Arizona who *always* predicts no rain, may be right 90 percent of the time; but a high success rate for a "stopped-clock" strategy clearly is not evidence of forecasting ability. Similarly, the appropriate measure of market forecasting ability is not the overall proportion of correct forecasts. If the market is up two days out of three and a forecaster always predicts market advance, the two-thirds success rate is not a measure of forecasting ability. We need to examine the proportion of bull markets ($r_M > r_f$) correctly forecast *and* the proportion of bear markets ($r_M < r_f$) correctly forecast.

If we call P_1 the proportion of the correct forecasts of bull markets and P_2 the proportion for bear markets, then $P = P_1 + P_2 - 1$ is the correct measure of timing ability. For example, a forecaster who always guesses correctly will have $P_1 = P_2 = 1$, and will show ability of $P = 1$ (100 percent). An analyst who always bets on a bear market will mispredict all bull markets ($P_1 = 0$), will correctly "predict" all bear markets ($P_2 = 1$), and will end up with timing ability of $P = P_1 + P_2 - 1 = 0$.

CC 3

> **CONCEPT CHECK**
>
> What is the market timing score of someone who flips a fair coin to predict the market?

When timing is imperfect, Merton shows that if we measure overall accuracy by the statistic $P = P_1 + P_2 - 1$, the market value of the services of an imperfect timer is simply

$$P \times C = (P_1 + P_2 - 1)[2N(\sigma_M \sqrt{T}) - 1] \qquad (21.5)$$

The last column in Table 21.5 provides an assessment of the imperfect market timer. To simulate the performance of an imperfect timer, we drew random numbers to capture the possibility that the timer will sometimes issue an incorrect forecast (we assumed here both P_1 and $P_2 = .7$)

---

[24]The conventional LPSD is based on the average squared deviation below the mean. Since the threshold performance in this application is the risk-free rate, we modify the LPSD for this discussion by taking squared deviations from that rate.

[25]It may seem hard to attribute such a big difference in final outcome solely to risk aversion. But think of it this way: the final value of the equity position is about 125 times that of the bills' position ($2,300 versus $18.35). Over 80 years, this implies a reasonable annualized risk premium of 6.2 percent: $125^{1/80} = 1.062$.

and compiled results for the 86 years of history.[26] The statistics of this exercise resulted in a terminal value for the timer of "only" $8,859, compared with the perfect timer's $352,796, but still considerably superior to the $2,652 for the all-equity investments.

A further variation on the valuation of market timing is a case in which the timer does not shift fully from one asset to the other. In particular, if the timer knows her forecasts are imperfect, one would not expect her to shift fully between markets. She presumably would moderate her positions. Suppose that she shifts a fraction ω of the portfolio between T-bills and equities. In that case, equation 21.5 can be generalized as follows:

$$MV(\text{Imperfect timer}) = \omega \times P \times C = \omega(P_1 + P_2 - 1)[2N(\sigma_M\sqrt{T}) - 1]$$

If the shift is $\omega = .50$ (50 percent of the portfolio), the timer's value will be one-half of the value we would obtain for full shifting, for which $\omega = 1.0$.

Identifying Timing Ability

In its pure form, market timing involves shifting funds between a market index portfolio and a safe asset, such as T-bills or a money market fund, depending on whether the market as a whole is expected to outperform the safe asset. In practice, of course, most managers do not shift fully between T-bills and the market. How might we measure partial shifts into the market when it is expected to perform well?

To simplify, suppose that the investor holds only the market index portfolio and T-bills. If the weight on the market were constant, for example, .6, then the portfolio beta also would be constant, and the SCL would plot as a straight line with slope .6, as in Figure 21.8, panel A. If, however, the investor could correctly time the market, and shift funds into it in periods when the market does well, the SCL would plot as in panel B. A timer who can predict bull and bear

Figure 21.8

Characteristic lines. **Panel A:** No market timing, beta is constant. **Panel B:** Market timing, beta increases with expected market excess return. **Panel C:** Market timing with only two values of beta.

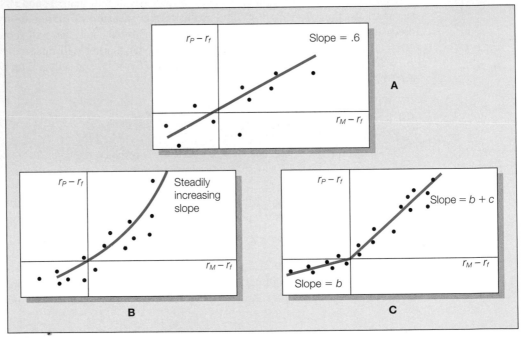

---

[26]In each year, we started with the correct forecast, but then used a random number generator to occasionally change the timer's forecast to an incorrect prediction. We set the probability that the timer's forecast would be correct equal to .70 for both up and down markets.

markets will shift more into the market when the market is about to go up. The portfolio beta and the slope of the characteristic line will be higher when r_M is higher, resulting in the curved line that appears in panel B.

Treynor and Mazuy[27] proposed that such a line can be estimated by adding a squared term to the usual linear index model:

$$r_P - r_f = a + b(r_M - r_f) + c(r_M - r_f)^2 + e_P$$

where r_P is the portfolio return, and a, b, and c are estimated by regression analysis. If c turns out to be positive, we have evidence of timing ability, because this last term will make the characteristic line steeper as $r_M - r_f$ is larger. Treynor and Mazuy estimated this equation for a number of mutual funds but found little evidence of timing ability.

A similar and simpler methodology was proposed by Henriksson and Merton.[28] These authors suggested that the beta of the portfolio can take only two values: a large value if the market is expected to do well and a small value otherwise. Under this scheme, the portfolio characteristic line appears as panel C. Such a line appears in regression form as

$$r_P - r_f = a + b(r_M - r_f) + c(r_M - r_f)D + e_P$$

where D is a dummy variable that equals 1 for $r_M > r_f$ and zero otherwise. Hence the beta of the portfolio is b in bear markets and $b + c$ in bull markets. Again, a positive value of c implies market timing ability.

Henriksson[29] estimated this equation for 116 mutual funds over the period 1968–1980. He found that the average value of c for the funds was *negative*, and equal to $-.07$. In sum, the results showed little evidence of market timing ability. Perhaps this should be expected; given the tremendous values to be reaped by a successful market timer, it would be surprising in nearly efficient markets to uncover clear-cut evidence of such skills.[30]

To illustrate a test for market timing, return to Table 24.2. Regressing the excess returns of portfolios P and Q on the excess returns of M and the square of these returns,

$$r_P - r_f = a_P + b_P(r_M - r_f) + c_P(r_M - r_f)^2 + e_P$$
$$r_Q - r_f = a_Q + b_Q(r_M - r_f) + c_Q(r_M - r_f)^2 + e_Q$$

we derive the following statistics:

	Portfolio	
Estimate	P	Q
Alpha (*a*)	1.77 (1.63)	−2.29 (5.28)
Beta (*b*)	.70 (0.69)	1.10 (1.40)
Timing (*c*)	.00	.10
R-squared	.91 (0.91)	.98 (.64)

The numbers in parentheses are the regression estimates from the single variable regression reported in Table 24.3. The results reveal that portfolio P shows no timing. It is not clear whether this is a result of Jane's making no attempt at timing or that the effort to time the market was in vain and served only to increase portfolio variance unnecessarily.

---

[27]Jack L. Treynor and Kay Mazuy, "Can Mutual Funds Outguess the Market?" *Harvard Business Review* 43 (July/August 1966).
[28]Roy D. Henriksson and R. C. Merton, "On Market Timing and Investment Performance. II: Statistical Procedures for Evaluating Forecasting Skills," *Journal of Business* 54 (October 1981).
[29]Roy D. Henriksson, "Market Timing and Mutual Fund Performance: An Empirical Investigation," *Journal of Business* 57 (January 1984).
[30]Also see John Rumsey, "Can We Detect Market Timing Ability Using an Option Model?" *Canadian Journal of Administrative Sciences* 17, no. 3 (September 2000), pp. 269–279; the author finds the answer is negative, even if timing is successful.

The results for portfolio Q, however, reveal that timing has, in all likelihood, successfully been attempted. The timing coefficient, c, is estimated at .10. The evidence thus suggests successful timing (positive c) offset by unsuccessful stock selection (negative a). Note that the alpha estimate, a, is now -2.29 percent as opposed to the 5.28 percent estimate derived from the regression equation that did not allow for the possibility of timing activity.

This example illustrates the inadequacy of conventional performance evaluation techniques that assume constant mean returns and constant risk. The market timer constantly shifts beta and mean return, moving into and out of the market. Whereas the expanded regression captures this phenomenon, the simple SCL does not. The relative desirability of portfolios P and Q remains unclear in the sense that the value of the timing success and selectivity failure of Q compared with P has yet to be evaluated. The important point for performance evaluation, however, is that expanded regressions can capture many of the effects of portfolio composition change that would confound the more conventional mean-variance measures.

21.6   PERFORMANCE EVALUATION

Performance evaluation has two very basic problems:

1. Many observations are needed for significant results even when portfolio mean and variance are constant.
2. Shifting parameters when portfolios are actively managed make accurate performance evaluation all the more elusive.

Although these objective difficulties cannot be overcome completely, it is clear that to obtain reasonably reliable performance measures we need to do the following:

1. Maximize the number of observations by taking more frequent return readings
2. Specify the exact makeup of the portfolio to obtain better estimates of the risk parameters at each observation period

Suppose an evaluator knows the exact portfolio composition at the opening of each day. Because the daily return on each security is available, the total daily return on the portfolio can be calculated. Furthermore, the exact portfolio composition allows the evaluator to estimate the risk characteristics (variance, beta, residual variance) for each day. Thus, daily risk-adjusted rates of return can be obtained. Although a performance measure for one day is statistically unreliable, the number of days with such rich data accumulates quickly. Performance evaluation that accounts for frequent revision in portfolio composition is superior by far to evaluation that assumes constant risk characteristics over the entire measurement period.

What sort of evaluation takes place in practice? Performance reports for portfolio managers traditionally have been based on quarterly data over 5–10 years. Currently, managers of mutual funds are required to disclose the exact composition of their portfolios only quarterly. Trading activity that immediately precedes the reporting date is known as "window dressing." Window dressing involves changes in portfolio composition to make it look as if the manager chose successful stocks. If Bombardier performed well over the quarter, for example, a portfolio manager will make sure that his or her portfolio includes a lot of Bombardier on the reporting date, whether or not it did during the quarter and whether or not Bombardier is expected to perform as well over the next quarter. Of course, portfolio managers deny such activity, and we know of no published evidence to substantiate the allegation. However, if window dressing is quantitatively significant, even the reported quarterly composition data can be misleading. Mutual funds publish portfolio values on a daily basis, which means the rate of return for each day is publicly available, but portfolio composition is not.

Moreover, mutual fund managers have had considerable leeway in the presentation of both past investment performance and fees charged for management services. The resultant noncomparability of net-of-expense performance numbers has made meaningful comparison of funds difficult. This may be changing, however; the OSC has moved toward greater disclosure in the reporting of fees. Awareness of the fees may help to evaluate performance based on the actual invested capital.

Portfolio managers reveal their portfolio composition only when they have to, which so far is quarterly. This is not nearly sufficient for adequate evaluation. However, current computer and communication technology makes it easy to use daily composition data for evaluation purposes. If the technology required for meaningful evaluation is in place, implementation of more accurate performance measurement techniques could improve welfare by enabling the public to identify the truly talented investment managers. In the United States, the Association of Investment Management and Research has published an extensive set of performance presentation standards encouraging the presentation of regular reporting periods and intervals, comparative indices, and expense effects.

The additional information may help. But this still leaves performance evaluation with the problem known as **survivorship bias**, which refers to the measurement of results from a population whose membership varies over time; put more simply, badly performing funds disappear, and their poor results are not counted in determining average performance. Thus the reported returns used for comparison are upwardly biased, making outperformance more difficult. A number of articles have examined the question of performance persistence by mutual fund managers, with Brown and Goetzmann[31] reporting on the effect of survival bias in such studies. A 1995 study of this phenomenon for Canadian funds is summarized by Curwood et al.[32]

21.7 PERFORMANCE ATTRIBUTION PROCEDURES

Traditionally, portfolio managers have distinguished themselves as either market timers or stock pickers. In this way, some have claimed an aptitude for timing the broad market swings by macroeconomic analysis; others, doubting the feasibility of this, have relied on **selectivity**—identifying equities that would perform well in particular economic climates. More recently, we have seen the emergence of managers who despair of either ability and operate index funds. Earlier in the chapter, we described a number of measures used to assess the success of managers' efforts.

Rather than focus on risk-adjusted returns, practitioners often want simply to ascertain which decisions resulted in superior or inferior performance. Superior investment performance depends on an ability to be in the "right" securities at the right time. Such timing and selection ability may be considered broadly, for instance, being in equities as opposed to fixed-income securities when the stock market is performing well. Or it may be defined at a more detailed level, such as choosing the relatively better-performing stocks within a particular industry.

Recent characterizations of performance ability have extended the simpler timing–selectivity dichotomy by adding a policy variable representing asset allocation. Market-timers do not actually switch from T-bills to index funds; rather, they have a standard or base allocation of portfolio weights to T-bills, government bonds, corporate bonds, domestic equities, foreign equities, and perhaps other assets. From this base allocation they shift weights as they see the various assets responding more favourably to changing market conditions.

Attribution studies start from the broadest asset allocation choices and progressively focus on ever-finer details of portfolio choice. The difference between a managed portfolio's performance

[31]S. J. Brown and W. N. Goetzmann, "Performance Persistence," *The Journal of Finance* 50 (June 1995), pp. 679–698.
[32]B. Curwood, S. Hadjiyannakis, P. Halpern, and K. Taylor, "How Survivorship Bias Skews Results of Comparative Measurement Universes," *Canadian Investment Review* 8 (Winter 1995/1996), pp. 9–12.

and that of a benchmark portfolio then may be expressed as the sum of the contributions to performance of a series of decisions made at the various levels of the portfolio construction process. For example, one common attribution system breaks performance down into three components: (1) broad-asset market allocation choices across equity, fixed-income, and money markets, (2) industry (sector) choice within each market, and (3) security choice within each sector.

The attribution method explains the difference in returns between a managed portfolio, P, and a selected benchmark portfolio, B, called the **bogey**. Suppose that the universe of assets for P and B includes n asset classes such as equities, bonds, and bills. For each asset class, a benchmark index portfolio is determined. For example, the S&P/TSX 60 may be chosen as benchmark for equities. The bogey portfolio is set to have fixed weights in each asset class, and its rate of return is given by

$$r_B = \sum_{i=1}^{n} w_{Bi} r_{Bi}$$

where w_{Bi} is the weight of the bogey in asset class i, and r_{Bi} is the return on the benchmark portfolio of that class over the evaluation period. The portfolio managers choose weights in each class, w_{Pi}, based on their capital market expectations, and they choose a portfolio of the securities within each class on the basis of their security analysis, which earns r_{Pi} over the evaluation period. Thus the return of the managed portfolio will be

$$r_P = \sum_{i=1}^{n} w_{Pi} r_{Pi}$$

The difference between the two rates of return, therefore, is

$$r_P - r_B = \sum_{i=1}^{n} w_{Pi} r_{Pi} - \sum_{i=1}^{n} w_{Bi} r_{Bi} = \sum_{i=1}^{n} (w_{Pi} r_{Pi} - w_{Bi} r_{Bi}) \tag{21.6}$$

Each term in the summation of equation 21.6 can be rewritten in a way that shows how asset allocation decisions versus security selection decisions for each asset class contributed to overall performance. We decompose each term of the summation into a sum of two terms as follows. Note that the two terms we have labelled contributions from asset allocation and security selection in the following decomposition do in fact sum to the total contribution of each asset class to overall performance.

Contribution from asset allocation	$(w_{Pi} - w_{Bi}) r_{Bi}$
+ Contribution from security selection	$w_{Pi}(r_{Pi} - r_{Bi})$
= Total contribution from asset class i	$w_{Pi} r_{Pi} - w_{Bi} r_{Bi}$

The first term of the sum measures the impact of asset allocation because it shows how deviations of the actual weight from the benchmark weight for that asset class multiplied by the index return for the asset class added to or subtracted from total performance. The second term of the sum measures the impact of security selection because it shows how the manager's excess return *within* the asset class compared to the benchmark return for that class multiplied by the portfolio weight for that class added to or subtracted from total performance. Figure 21.9 presents a graphical interpretation of the attribution of overall performance into security selection versus asset allocation.

To illustrate this method, consider the attribution results for a hypothetical portfolio. The portfolio invests in stocks, bonds, and money market securities. An attribution analysis appears in Tables 21.6 to 21.9. The portfolio return over the month is 5.34 percent.

The first step is to establish a benchmark level of performance against which performance ought to be compared. This benchmark, again, is called the bogey. The bogey portfolio represents

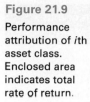

Figure 21.9

Performance attribution of *i*th asset class. Enclosed area indicates total rate of return.

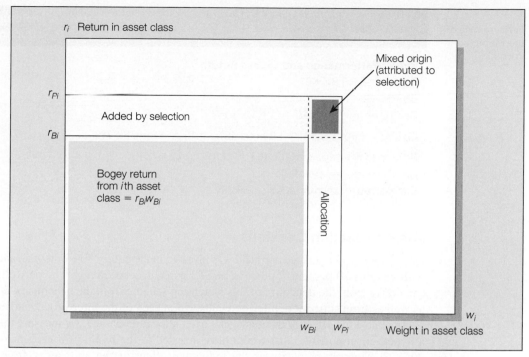

what the portfolio manager would have earned by a passive strategy. "Passive" has two attributes. First, it means that the allocation of funds across broad asset classes is set in accord with a notion of "usual," or neutral, allocation across sectors. This would be considered a passive asset-market allocation. Second, it means that *within* each asset class, the portfolio manager holds an indexed portfolio such as the S&P 500 index for the equity sector. In such a manner, the passive strategy used as a performance benchmark rules out asset allocation as well as security selection decisions. Any departure from the benchmark's return by the manager's return must be due to either asset allocation (departure from the neutral allocation across markets) or security selection (departure from the passive index within asset classes), or both.

While we have already discussed in earlier chapters the justification for indexing within sectors, it is worth briefly explaining the determination of the neutral allocation of funds across the broad asset classes. Weights that are designated as "neutral" will depend on the risk tolerance of the investor and must be determined in consultation with the client. For example, risk-tolerant clients may place a large fraction of their portfolio in the equity market, perhaps directing the fund manager to set neutral weights of 75 percent equity, 15 percent bonds, and 10 percent cash equivalents. Any deviation from these weights must be justified by a belief that one or another market will either over- or underperform its usual risk–return profile. In contrast, more risk-averse clients may set neutral weights of 45/35/20 for the three markets. Therefore, their portfolios in normal circumstances will be exposed to less risk than that of the risk-tolerant client. Only intentional bets on market performance will result in departures from this profile.

In Table 21.6, the neutral weights are 60 percent equity, 30 percent fixed-income, and 10 percent cash (money market securities). The bogey portfolio, composed of investments in each index with the 60/30/10 weights, returned 3.97 percent. The managed portfolio's measure of performance is positive and equal to its actual return less the return of the bogey: $5.34 - 3.97 = 1.37$ percent. The next step is to allocate the 1.37 percent excess return to the separate decisions that contributed to it.

TABLE 21.6

Performance of the Managed Portfolio

Component	Benchmark Weight	Return of Index During Month (%)
Bogey Performance and Excess Return		
Equity (S&P/TSX 60)	.60	5.81
Bonds (Scotia Capital)	.30	1.45
Cash (money market)	.10	.48
Bogey = (.60 × 5.81) + (.30 × 1.45) + (.10 × .48) = 3.97%		
Return of managed portfolio		5.34%
Return of bogey portfolio		3.97%
Excess return of managed portfolio		1.37%

Asset Allocation Decisions

Our hypothetical managed portfolio was invested in the equity, fixed-income, and money markets with weights 70 percent, 7 percent, and 23 percent, respectively. The portfolio's performance can derive from the departure of this weighting scheme from the benchmark 60/30/10 weights, as well as from superior or inferior results *within* each of the three broad markets.

To isolate the effect of the manager's asset allocation choice, we measure the performance of a hypothetical portfolio that would have invested in the *indices* for each market with weights 70/7/23. This return measures the individual effect of the shift away from the benchmark 60/30/10 weights, without allowing for any effects attributable to active management of the securities selected within each market. Superior performance relative to the bogey is achieved by overweighting investments in markets that turn out to perform relatively well and by underweighting poorly performing markets. The contribution of asset allocation to superior performance equals the sum over all markets of the excess weight (or *active weight* in the industry) in each market multiplied by the return of the market index.

Panel A of Table 21.7 demonstrates that asset allocation contributed almost 31 basis points to the portfolio's overall excess return of 137 basis points. The major factor contributing to superior performance in this month was the heavy weighting of the equity market in a month when the equity market had an excellent return of 5.81 percent.

Sector and Security Allocation Decisions

If .31 percent of the excess performance can be attributed to advantageous asset allocation across markets, the remaining 1.06 percent must be attributable to sector and security selection within each market. Panel B of Table 21.7 details the contribution of the managed portfolio's sector and security selection to total performance.

Panel B shows that the equity component of the managed portfolio had a return of 7.28 percent versus a return of 5.81 percent for the S&P/TSX 60. The fixed-income return was 1.89 percent versus 1.45 percent for the Scotia Capital index. The superior performance in equity and fixed-income markets weighted by the portfolio proportions invested in each market sums to the 1.06 percent contribution to performance attributable to sector and security selection.

Table 21.8 documents the sources of the equity component performance by each sector within the market. The first three columns detail the allocation of funds to the sectors in the equity market compared with their (hypothetical) representation in the S&P/TSX 60. Column 4 shows the rate of return of each sector, and column 5 documents the performance of each sector relative to the return of the S&P/TSX 60. The contribution of each sector's allocation presented in column 6 equals the product of the difference in the sector weight and the sector's relative performance.

Scotiabank
www.gbm.
scotiabank.com

TABLE 21.7   Performance Attribution

Market	(1) Actual Weight in Market	(2) Benchmark Weight in Market	(3) Excess Weight	(4) Market Return (%)	(5) = (3) × (4) Contribution to Performance (%)
A. Contribution of Asset Allocation to Performance					
Equity	.70	.60	.10	5.81	.5810
Fixed income	.07	.30	−.23	1.45	−.3335
Cash	.23	.10	.13	.48	−.0624
Contribution of asset allocation					.3099

Market	(1) Portfolio Performance (%)	(2) Index Performance (%)	(3) Excess Performance (%)	(4) Portfolio Weight	(5) = (3) × (4) Contribution (%)
B. Contribution of Selection to Total Performance					
Equity	7.28	5.81	1.47	.70	1.03
Fixed income	1.89	1.45	.44	.07	.03
Contribution of selection within markets					1.06

TABLE 21.8   Sector Selection Within the Equity Market

Sector	(1) Beginning-of-Month Weights (%) Portfolio	(2) Beginning-of-Month Weights (%) S&P/TSX 60	(3) Difference in Weights	(4) Sector Return	(5) Sector Over-/Under-performance*	(6) = (3) × (5) Sector Allocation Contribution
Interest-sensitive	29.72	31.99	−2.27	6.4	.9	−2.04
Consumer	9.54	17.46	−7.92	5.4	−.1	.79
Resource	10.31	21.52	−11.21	3.7	−1.8	20.18
Energy	24.29	9.31	14.98	8.4	2.9	43.44
Industrial products	19.03	9.83	9.2	8.3	2.8	25.76
Transportation	2.32	3.70	−1.38	−.2	−5.7	7.87
Management companies	4.79	6.19	−1.4	2.1	−3.4	4.76
Total						100.76 basis points

*S&P/TSX 60 performance, excluding dividends, was 5.5 percent. Returns compared net of dividends.

Note that good performance (a positive contribution) derives from overweighting well-performing sectors, such as energy, or underweighting poorly performing sectors, such as transportation. The excess return of the equity component of the portfolio attributable to sector allocation alone is 1.01 percent. Since the equity component of the portfolio outperformed the S&P/TSX 60 by 1.47 percent (Table 21.7, panel B, column 3), we conclude that the effect of security selection within sectors must have contributed an additional 1.47 − 1.01 = .46 percent to the performance of the equity component of the portfolio.

A similar sector analysis can be applied to the fixed-income portion of the portfolio, but we do not show those results here.

Performance Attribution

The performance attribution spreadsheet develops the attribution analysis that is presented in this section. Additional data can be used in the analysis of performance for other sets of portfolios. The model can be used to analyze performance of mutual funds and other managed portfolios.

Questions

1. What would happen to the contribution of asset allocation to overall performance if the actual weights had been 75/12/13 instead of 70/7/23? Explain your result.
2. What would happen to the contribution of security selection to overall performance if the actual return on the equity portfolio had been 6.81 percent instead of 5.81 percent and the return on the bond portfolio had been 0.45 percent instead of 1.45 percent? Explain your result.

	A	B	C	D	E	F
1	**Performance Attribution**					
2						
3						
4	**Bogey**					
5	**Portfolio**		**Benchmark**	**Return on**	**Portfolio**	
6	**Component**	**Index**	**Weight**	**Index**	**Return**	
7	Equity	S&P/TSX 60	0.60	5.8100%	3.4860%	
8	Bonds	Scotia Capital	0.30	1.4500%	0.4350%	
9	Cash	Money Market	0.10	0.4800%	0.0480%	
10				Return on Bogey	3.9690%	
11						
12		**Managed**				
13		**Portfolio**	**Portfolio**	**Actual**	**Portfolio**	
14		**Component**	**Weight**	**Return**	**Return**	
15		Equity	0.70	5.8100%	5.0960%	
16		Bonds	0.07	1.4500%	0.1323%	
17		Cash	0.23	0.4800%	0.1104%	
18				Return on Managed	5.3387%	
19				Excess Return	1.3697%	

Summing up Component Contributions

In this particular month, all facets of the portfolio selection process were successful. Table 21.9 details the contribution of each aspect of performance. Asset allocation across the major security markets contributes 31 basis points. Sector and security allocation within those markets contributes 106 basis points, for total excess portfolio performance of 137 basis points. The sector and security allocation of 106 basis points can be partitioned further. Sector allocation within the equity market results in excess performance of 100.76 basis points, and security selection within sectors contributes 46 basis points. (The total equity excess performance of 147 basis points is multiplied by the 70 percent weight in equity to obtain contribution to portfolio performance.) Similar partitioning could be done for the fixed-income sector.

CC 4

CONCEPT CHECK

a. Suppose the benchmark weights had been set at 70 percent equity, 25 percent fixed-income, and 5 percent cash equivalents. What then are the contributions of the manager's asset allocation choices?

b. Suppose the S&P/TSX 60 return is 5 percent. Compute the new value of the manager's security selection choices.

TABLE 21.9

Portfolio Attribution: Summary

	Contribution (basis points)
1. Asset allocation	31.0
2. Selection	
a. Equity excess return	
i. Sector allocation 101	
ii. Security allocation 46	
147 × .70 (portfolio weight) = 102.9	
b. Fixed-income excess return 44 × .07 (portfolio weight) =	3.1
Total excess return of portfolio	<u>137.0</u> basis points

SUMMARY

1. A truly passive portfolio strategy entails holding the market index portfolio and a money market fund. Determining the optimal allocation to the market portfolio requires an estimate of its expected return and variance, which in turn suggests delegating some analysis to professionals.

2. Active portfolio managers attempt to construct a risky portfolio that maximizes the reward-to-variability (Sharpe) ratio.

3. The shifting mean and variance of actively managed portfolios make it even harder to assess performance. A typical example is the attempt of portfolio managers to time the market, resulting in ever-changing portfolio betas.

4. The appropriate performance measure depends on the role of the portfolio to be evaluated. Appropriate performance measures are as follows:

   a. *Sharpe.* When the portfolio represents the entire investment fund.

   b. *Information ratio.* When the portfolio represents the active portfolio to be optimally mixed with the passive portfolio.

   c. *Treynor* or *Jensen.* When the portfolio represents one subportfolio of many.

   d. *Morningstar.* When the portfolio has the characteristics of a mutual fund and an alternative to the mean-variance utility function is desired.

5. Many observations are required to eliminate the effect of the "luck of the draw" from the evaluation process, because portfolio returns commonly are very "noisy."

6. The value of perfect market timing ability is considerable. The rate of return to a perfect market timer will be uncertain. However, its risk characteristics are not measurable by standard measures of portfolio risk, because perfect timing dominates a passive strategy, providing "good surprises" only.

7. With imperfect timing, the value of a timer who attempts to forecast whether stocks will outperform bills is given by the conditional probabilities of the true outcome given the forecasts: $P_1 + P_2 - 1$. Thus, if the value of perfect timing is given by the option value, C, then imperfect timing has the value $(P_1 + P_2 - 1)C$.

8. The Morningstar rating method compares each fund to a peer group represented by a style portfolio within four asset classes. Risk-adjusted ratings (RAR) are based on fund returns relative to the peer group and used to award each fund one to five stars based on the rank of its RAR.

9. Style analysis uses a multiple regression model where the factors are category (style) portfolios such as bills, bonds, and stocks. A regression of fund returns on the style portfolio returns generates residuals that represent the value added of stock selection in each period. These residuals can be used to gauge fund performance relative to similar-style funds.

10. A simple way to measure timing and selection success simultaneously is to estimate an expanded SCL, with a quadratic term added to the usual index model.

11. Common attribution procedures partition performance improvements to asset allocation, sector selection, and security selection. Performance is assessed by calculating departures of portfolio composition from a benchmark or neutral portfolio.

KEY EQUATIONS

(21.1) $y = \dfrac{E(r_M) - r_f}{A\sigma_M^2}$

(21.2) $M_P^2 = r_{P*} - r_M$

(21.3) $t(\hat{\alpha}) = \dfrac{\hat{\alpha}}{\hat{\sigma}(\alpha)} = \dfrac{\hat{\alpha}\sqrt{N}}{\hat{\sigma}(e)}$

(21.4) $e(t) = R(t) - [\alpha - \beta_1 R_1(t) - \beta_2 R_2(t) - \beta_3 R_3(t)]$

(21.5) $P \times C = (P_1 + P_2 - 1)[2N(\sigma_M\sqrt{T}) - 1]$

(21.6) $r_P - r_B = \sum\limits_{i=1}^{n} w_{Pi} r_{Pi} - \sum\limits_{i=1}^{n} w_{Bi} r_{Bi} = \sum\limits_{i=1}^{n} (w_{Pi} r_{Pi} - w_{Bi} r_{Bi})$

PROBLEMS

connect   Practise and learn online with Connect.

1. A household (HH) saving-account spreadsheet shows the following entries:

Date	Additions	Withdrawals	Value
1/1/10			148,000
1/3/10	2,500		
3/20/10	4,000		
7/5/10	1,500		
12/2/10	13,460		
3/10/11		23,000	
4/7/11	3,000		
5/3/11			198,000

Calculate the dollar-weighted average return on the HH saving account between the first and final dates.

2. Is it possible that a positive alpha will be associated with inferior performance? Explain.

3. We know that the geometric average (time-weighted return) on a risky investment is always lower than the corresponding arithmetic average. Can the IRR (the dollar-weighted return) similarly be ranked relative to these other two averages?

4. We have seen that market timing has tremendous potential value. Would it therefore be wise to shift resources to timing at the expense of security selection?

5. Consider the rate of return of stocks ABC and XYZ.

Year	r_{ABC}	r_{XYZ}
1	.20	.30
2	.12	.12
3	.14	.18
4	.03	.00
5	.01	−.10

a. Calculate the arithmetic average return on these stocks over the sample period.

b. Which stock has greater dispersion around the mean?

c. Calculate the geometric average returns of each stock. What do you conclude?

 d. If you were equally likely to earn a return of 20 percent, 12 percent, 14 percent, 3 percent, or 1 percent in each of the five annual returns for stock ABC, what would be your expected rate of return? What if the five outcomes were those of stock XYZ?

6. XYZ stock price and dividend history are as follows:

Year	Beginning-of-Year Price	Dividend Paid at Year-End
2010	$100	$4
2011	$120	$4
2012	$ 90	$4
2013	$100	$4

An investor buys three shares of XYZ at the beginning of 2010, buys another two shares at the beginning of 2011, sells one share at the beginning of 2012, and sells all four remaining shares at the beginning of 2013.

 a. What are the arithmetic and geometric average time-weighted rates of return for the investor?

 b. What is the dollar-weighted rate of return? (*Hint:* Carefully prepare a chart of cash flows for the *four* dates corresponding to the turn of the year for January 1, 2010 to December 31, 2013. If your calculator cannot calculate internal rate of return, you will have to use trial and error.)

7. A manager buys three shares of stock today, and then sells one of those shares each year for the next three years. His actions and the price history of the stock are summarized below. The stock pays no dividends.

Time	Price	Action
0	$ 90	Buy 3 shares
1	100	Sell 1 share
2	100	Sell 1 share
3	100	Sell 1 share

 a. Calculate the time-weighted geometric average return on this portfolio.

 b. Calculate the time-weighted arithmetic average return on this portfolio.

 c. Calculate the dollar-weighted average return on this portfolio.

8. Based on current dividend yields and expected capital gains, the expected rates of return on portfolios A and B are .12 and .16, respectively. The beta of A is .7, while that of B is 1.4. The T-bill rate is currently .05, while the expected rate of return of the S&P/TSX index is .13. The standard deviation of portfolio A is .12 annually, that of B is .31, and that of the S&P/TSX index is .18.

 a. If you currently hold a market-index portfolio, would you choose to add either of these portfolios to your holdings? Explain.

 b. If instead you could invest *only* in T-bills and *one* of these portfolios, which would you choose?

9. Consider the two (excess return) index-model regression results for stocks A and B. The risk-free rate over the period was 6 percent, and the market's average return was 14 percent. Performance was measured using an index model regression on excess returns.

	Stock *A*	Stock *B*
Index model regression estimates	$1\% + 1.2(r_M - r_f)$	$2\% + .8(r_M - r_f)$
R-squared	.576	.436
Residual standard deviation, $\sigma(e)$	10.3%	19.1%
Standard deviation of excess returns	21.6%	24.9%

  a. Calculate the following statistics for each stock:
    i. Alpha
    ii. Appraisal/information ratio
    iii. Sharpe ratio
    iv. Treynor measure
  b. Which stock is the best choice under the following circumstances?
    i. This is the only risky asset to be held by the investor.
    ii. This stock will be mixed with the rest of the investor's portfolio, currently composed solely of holdings in the market index fund.
    iii. This is one of many stocks that the investor is analyzing to form an actively managed stock portfolio.

10. Evaluate the timing and selection abilities of four managers whose performances are plotted in the following four scatter diagrams:

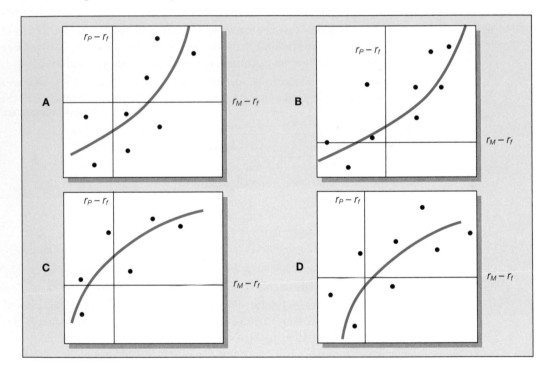

11. James Chan is reviewing the performance of the global equity managers of the Jarvis University endowment fund. Williamson Capital is currently the endowment fund's only large-capitalization global equity manager. Performance data for Williamson Capital are shown in Table 21A.

    Chan also presents the endowment fund's investment committee with performance information for Joyner Asset Management, which is another large-capitalization global equity manager. Performance data for Joyner Asset Management are shown in Table 21B. Performance data for the relevant risk-free asset and market index are shown in Table 21C.

  a. Calculate the Sharpe ratio and Treynor measure for both Williamson Capital and Joyner Asset Management.
  b. The Investment Committee notices that using the Sharpe ratio versus the Treynor measure produces different performance rankings of Williamson and Joyner. Explain why these criteria may result in different rankings.

TABLE 21A

Williamson
Capital
Performance
Data, 2000–2011

Average annual rate of return	22.1%
Beta	1.2
Standard deviation of returns	16.8%

TABLE 21B

Joyner Asset
Management
Performance
Data 2000–2011

Average annual rate of return	24.2%
Beta	.8
Standard deviation of returns	20.2%

TABLE 21C

Relevant Risk-
Free Asset and
Market Index
Performance
Data, 2000–2011

Risk-Free Asset	
Average annual rate of return	5.0%
Market Index	
Average annual rate of return	18.9%
Standard deviation of returns	13.8%

12. Conventional wisdom says that one should measure a manager's investment performance over an entire market cycle. What arguments support this contention? What arguments contradict it?

13. Does the use of universes of managers with similar investment styles to evaluate relative investment performance overcome the statistical problems associated with instability of beta or total variability?

14. During a particular year, the T-bill rate was 6 percent, the market return was 14 percent, and a portfolio manager with beta of .5 realized a return of 10 percent.

    a. Evaluate the manager based on the portfolio alpha.

    b. Reconsider your answer to part (a) in view of the Black-Jensen-Scholes finding that the security market line is too flat. Now how do you assess the manager's performance?

15. Consider the following information regarding the performance of a money manager in a recent month. The table represents the actual return of each sector of the manager's portfolio in column 1, the fraction of the portfolio allocated to each sector in column 2, the benchmark or neutral sector allocations in column 3, and the returns of sector indices in column 4.

	Actual Return (%)	Actual Weight	Benchmark Weight	Index Return (%)
Equity	2	.70	.60	2.5 (S&P 60)
Bonds	1	.20	.30	1.2 (Scotia Capital)
Cash	.5	.10	.10	.5

    a. What was the manager's return in the month? What was her overperformance or underperformance?

    b. What was the contribution of security selection to relative performance?

    c. What was the contribution of asset allocation to relative performance? Confirm that the sum of selection and allocation contributions equals her total "excess" return relative to the bogey.

16. A pension fund portfolio begins with $500,000 and earns 15 percent the first year and 10 percent the second year. At the beginning of the second year, the sponsor contributes another $500,000. What were the time-weighted and dollar-weighted rates of return?

17. Bill Smith is evaluating the performance of four large-cap equity portfolios: Funds A, B, C, and D. As part of his analysis, Smith computed the Sharpe ratio and the Treynor measure for all four funds. Based on his finding, the ranks assigned to the four funds are as follows:

Fund	Treynor Measure Rank	Sharpe Ratio Rank
A	1	4
B	2	3
C	3	2
D	4	1

The difference in rankings for funds A and D is most likely due to which of the following explanations:

a. A lack of diversification in fund A as compared to fund D

b. Different benchmarks used to evaluate each fund's performance

c. A difference in risk premiums

Use the following information to answer problems 18–21: Primo Management Co. is looking at how best to evaluate the performance of its managers. Primo has been hearing more and more about benchmark portfolios and is interested in trying this approach. Consequently, the company hired Sally Jones, CFA, as a consultant to educate the managers on the best methods for constructing a benchmark portfolio, how best to choose a benchmark, whether the style of the fund under management matters, and what they should do with their global funds in terms of benchmarking.

For the sake of discussion, Jones put together some comparative two-year performance numbers that relate to Primo's current domestic funds under management and a potential benchmark.

Style Category	Weight		Return (%)	
	Primo	**Benchmark**	**Primo**	**Benchmark**
Large-cap growth	60	.50	17	16
Mid-cap growth	.15	.40	24	26
Small-cap growth	.25	.10	20	18

As part of her analysis, Jones also takes a look at one of Primo's global funds. In this particular portfolio, Primo is invested 75 percent in Dutch stocks and 25 percent in British stocks. The benchmark invested 50 percent in each—Dutch and British stocks. On average, the British stocks outperformed the Dutch stocks. The euro appreciated 6 percent versus the U.S. dollar over the holding period while the pound depreciated 2 percent versus the dollar. In terms of the local return, Primo outperformed the benchmark with the Dutch investments, but underperformed the index with respect to the British stocks.

18. What is the within-sector selection effect for each individual sector?

19. Calculate the amount by which the Primo portfolio out- (or under-)performed the market over the period, as well as the contribution to performance of the pure sector allocation and security selection decisions.

20. If Primo decides to use return-based style analysis, will the R^2 of the regression equation of a passively managed fund be higher or lower than that of an actively managed fund?

21. Which of the following statements about Primo's global fund is most correct? Primo appears to have a positive currency allocation effect as well as

a. A negative market allocation effect and a positive security allocation effect

b. A negative market allocation effect and a negative security allocation effect

c. A positive market allocation effect and a negative security allocation effect

22. Kelli Blakely is a portfolio manager for the Miranda Fund (Miranda), a core large-cap equity fund. The market proxy and benchmark for performance measurement purposes is the S&P 500. Although the Miranda portfolio generally mirrors the asset class and sector weightings of the S&P, Blakely is allowed a significant amount of leeway in managing the fund. Her portfolio holds only stocks found in the S&P 500 and cash. Blakely was able to produce exceptional returns last year (as outlined in the table below) through her market timing and security selection skills. At the outset of the year, she became extremely concerned that the combination of a weak economy and geopolitical uncertainties would negatively impact the market. Taking a bold step, she changed her market allocation. For the entire year her asset class exposures averaged 50 percent in stocks and 50 percent in cash. The S&P's allocation between stocks and cash during period was a constant 97 percent and 3 percent, respectively. The risk-free rate of return was 2 percent.

| | One-Year Trailing Returns | |
	Miranda Fund	S&P 500
Return	10.2%	−22.5%
Standard deviation	37%	44%
Beta	1.10	1.00

  a. What are the Sharpe ratios for the Miranda Fund and the S&P 500?

  b. What are the M^2 measures for Miranda and the S&P 500?

  c. What is the Treynor measure for the Miranda Fund and the S&P 500?

  d. What is the Jensen measure for the Miranda Fund?

23. Go to Kenneth French's data library site, http://mba.tuck.dartmouth.edu/pages/faculty/ken.french/data_library.html. Select any two industry portfolios and download 36 months of data. Download other data from the site as needed to perform the following tasks.

  a. Compare the portfolio's performance to that of the market index on the basis of the various performance measures discussed in the chapter. Plot the monthly values of alpha plus residual return.

  b. Now use the Fama-French three-factor model as the return benchmark. Compute plots of alpha plus residual return using the FF model. How does performance change using this benchmark instead of the market index?

The following problems are based on questions that have appeared in past CFA examinations.

24. In measuring the comparative performance of different fund managers, the preferred method of calculating rate of return is

  a. Internal   b. Time-weighted

  c. Dollar-weighted   d. Income

25. Which *one* of the following is a valid benchmark against which a portfolio's performance can be measured over a given time period?

  a. The portfolio's dollar-weighted rate of return

  b. The portfolio's time-weighted rate of return

  c. The portfolio manager's "normal" portfolio

  d. The average beta of the portfolio

26. Assume you invested in an asset for two years. The first year you earned a 15 percent return, and the second year you earned a *negative* 10 percent return. What was your annual geometric return?

27. Assume you purchased a rental property for $50,000 and sold it one year later for $55,000 (there was no mortgage on the property). At the time of the sale, you paid $2,000 in commissions and

$600 in taxes. If you received $6,000 in rental income (all of it received at the end of the year), what annual rate of return did you earn?

 a. 15.3 percent   *b.* 15.9 percent

 c. 16.8 percent   *d.* 17.1 percent

28. A portfolio of stocks generates a −9 percent return in 2012, a 23 percent return in 2013, and a 17 percent return in 2014. What is the annualized return (geometric mean) for the entire period?

29. A two-year investment of $2,000 results in a return of $150 at the end of the first year and a return of $150 at the end of the second year, in addition to the return of the original investment. What is the internal rate of return on the investment?

30. In measuring the performance of a portfolio, the time-weighted rate of return is superior to the dollar-weighted rate of return because

 a. When the rate of return varies, the time-weighted return is higher

 b. The dollar-weighted return assumes all portfolio deposits are made on day 1

 c. The dollar-weighted return can only be estimated

 d. The time-weighted return is unaffected by the timing of portfolio contributions and withdrawals

31. The annual rate of return for JSI's common stock has been:

	2005	2006	2007	2008
Return	14%	19%	−10%	14%

 a. What is the arithmetic mean of the rate of return for JSI's common stock over the four years?

 b. What is the geometric mean of the rate of return for JSI's common stock over the four years?

32. The difference between an arithmetic average and a geometric average of returns

 a. Increases as variability of the returns increases

 b. Increases as the variability of the returns decreases

 c. Is always negative

 d. Depends on the specific returns being averaged, but is not necessarily sensitive to their variability

Use the following data in solving problems 33 and 34.

The administrator of a large pension fund wants to evaluate the performance of three portfolio managers. Each portfolio manager invests only in U.S. common stocks. Assume that during the most recent five-year period, the average annual total rate of return including dividends on the S&P 500 was 14 percent, and the average nominal rate of return on government Treasury bills was 8 percent. The following table shows risk and return measures for each portfolio:

Portfolio	Average Annual Rate of Return (%)	Standard Deviation (%)	Beta
P	17	20	1.1
Q	24	18	2.1
R	11	10	0.5
S&P 500	14	12	1.0

33. What is the Treynor performance measure for portfolio P?

34. What is the Sharpe performance measure for portfolio Q?

35. An analyst wants to evaluate portfolio X, consisting entirely of U.S. common stocks, using both the Treynor and Sharpe measures of portfolio performance. The following table provides the

average annual rate of return for portfolio *X*, the market portfolio (as measured by the S&P 500), and U.S. Treasury bills during the past eight years:

	Average Annual Rate of Return (%)	Standard Deviation (%)	Beta
Portfolio *X*	10	18	.60
S&P 500	12	13	1.00
T-bills	6	NA	NA

a. Calculate the Treynor and Sharpe measures for both portfolio *X* and the S&P 500. Briefly explain whether portfolio *X* underperformed, equalled, or outperformed the S&P 500 on a risk-adjusted basis using both the Treynor measure and the Sharpe ratio.

b. In view of the performance of portfolio *X* relative to the S&P 500 calculated in part (*a*), briefly explain the reason for the conflicting results when using the Treynor measure versus the Sharpe ratio.

36. During the annual review of Acme's pension plan, several trustees questioned their investment consultant about various aspects of performance measurement and risk assessment.

a. Comment on the appropriateness of using each of the following benchmarks for performance evaluation:
   • Market index
   • Benchmark normal portfolio
   • Median of the manager universe

b. Distinguish among the following performance measures:
   • The Sharpe ratio
   • The Treynor measure
   • Jensen's alpha

   i. Describe how each of the three performance measures is calculated.

   ii. State whether each measure assumes that the relevant risk is systematic, unsystematic, or total. Explain how each measure relates excess return and the relevant risk.

37. Trustees of the Pallor Corp. pension plan ask consultant Donald Millip to comment on the following statements. What should his response be?

   i. Median manager benchmarks are statistically unbiased measures of performance over long periods of time.

   ii. Median manager benchmarks are unambiguous and are therefore easily replicated by managers wishing to adopt a passive/indexed approach.

   iii. Median manager benchmarks are not appropriate in all circumstances because the median manager universe encompasses many investment styles.

38. The chairperson provides you with the following data, covering one year, concerning the portfolios of two of the fund's equity managers (firm A and firm B). Although the portfolios consist primarily of common stocks, cash reserves are included in the calculation of both portfolio betas and performance. By way of perspective, selected data for the financial markets are included in the following table:

	Total Return (%)	Beta
Firm A	24.0	1.0
Firm B	30.0	1.5
S&P/TSX Composite	21.0	
ScotiaMcLeod Total Bond Index	31.0	
91-day Treasury bills	12.0	

　　a. Calculate and compare the risk-adjusted performance of the two firms relative to each other and to the S&P/TSX Composite.

　　b. Explain *two* reasons the conclusions drawn from this calculation may be misleading.

39. Carl Karl, a portfolio manager for the Alpine Trust Company, has been responsible since 2010 for the City of Alpine's Employee Retirement Plan, a municipal pension fund. Alpine is a growing community, and city services and employee payrolls have expanded in each of the past ten years. Contributions to the plan in fiscal 2015 exceeded benefit payments by a three-to-one ratio.

　　The plan's Board of Trustees directed Karl five years ago to invest for total return over the long term. However, as trustees of this highly visible public fund, they cautioned him that volatile or erratic results could cause them embarrassment. They also noted a state statute that mandates that not more than 25 percent of the plan's assets (at cost) be invested in common stocks.

　　At the annual meeting of the trustees in November 2015, Karl presented the following portfolio and performance report to the board:

Alpine Employee Retirement Plan

Asset Mix as of 9/30/2015	At Cost (millions)		At Market (millions)	
Fixed-Income Assets				
Short-term securities	$ 4.5	11.0%	$ 4.5	11.4%
Long-term bonds and mortgages	26.5	64.7	23.5	59.5
Common stocks	10.0	24.3	11.5	29.1
	$41.0	100.0%	$39.5	100.0%

Investment Performance

	Annual Rates of Return for Period Ending 9/30/2015	
	5 Years	**1 Year**
Total Alpine Fund:		
Time-weighted	8.2%	5.2%
Dollar-weighted (internal)	7.7%	4.8%
Assumed actuarial return	6.0%	6.0%
U.S. Treasury bills	7.5%	11.3%
Large sample of pension funds (average 60% equities, 40% fixed income)	10.1%	14.3%
Common stocks—Alpine Fund	13.3%	14.3%
Average portfolio beta coefficient	0.90	0.89
Standard & Poor's 500 stock index	13.8%	21.1%
Fixed-income securities—Alpine Fund	6.7%	1.0%
Salomon Brothers' bond index	4.0%	−11.4%

Karl was proud of his performance, and thus he was chagrined when a trustee made the following critical observations:

　　a. "Our one-year results were terrible, and it's what you've done for us lately that counts most."

　　b. "Our total fund performance was clearly inferior compared to the large sample of other pension funds for the last five years. What else could this reflect except poor management judgment?"

c. "Our common stock performance was especially poor for the five-year period."

d. "Why bother to compare your returns to the return from Treasury bills and the actuarial assumption rate? What your competition could have earned for us or how we would have fared if invested in a passive index [which doesn't charge a fee] are the only relevant measures of performance."

e. "Who cares about time-weighted return? If it can't pay pensions, what good is it?"

Appraise the merits of each of these statements and give counterarguments that Mr. Karl can use.

40. The Retired Fund is an open-ended mutual fund composed of $500 million in U.S. bonds and U.S. Treasury bills. This fund has had a portfolio duration (including T-bills) of between three and nine years. Retired has shown first-quartile performance over the past five years, as measured by an independent fixed-income measurement service. However, the directors of the fund would like to measure the market timing skill of the fund's sole bond investment manager. An external consulting firm has suggested the following three methods:

 i. Method I examines the value of the bond portfolio at the beginning of every year and then calculates the return that would have been achieved had that same portfolio been held throughout the year. This return would then be compared with the return actually obtained by the fund.

 ii. Method II calculates the average weighting of the portfolio in bonds and T-bills for each year. Instead of using the actual bond portfolio, the return on a long-bond market index and T-bill index would be used. For example, if the portfolio on average was 65 percent in bonds and 35 percent in T-bills, the annual return on a portfolio invested 65 percent in a long-bond index and 35 percent in T-bills would be calculated. This return is compared with the annual return that would have been generated using the indices and the manager's actual bond/T-bill weighting for each quarter of the year.

 iii. Method III examines the net bond purchase activity (market value of purchases less sales) for each quarter of the year. If net purchases were positive (negative) in any quarter, the performance of the bonds would be evaluated until the net purchase activity became negative (positive). Positive (negative) net purchases would be viewed as a bullish (bearish) view taken by the manager. The correctness of this view would be measured.

Critique *each* method with regard to market timing measurement problems.

41. A plan sponsor with a portfolio manager who invests in small-capitalization, high-growth stocks should have the plan sponsor's performance measured against which *one* of the following?

a. S&P 500 index

b. Wilshire 5000 index

c. Dow Jones Industrial Average

d. S&P 400 index

42. Strict market timers attempt to maintain a _____ portfolio beta and a _____ portfolio alpha.

a. constant; shifting

b. shifting; zero

c. shifting; shifting

d. zero; zero

43. Which of the following methods measures the reward-to-variability tradeoff by dividing the average portfolio excess return over the standard deviation of return?

a. Sharpe ratio

b. Treynor's measure

c. Jensen's alpha

d. Information ratio

APPENDIX 21A: VALUING MARKET TIMING AS A CALL OPTION

The key to valuing market timing ability is to recognize that perfect foresight is equivalent to holding a call option on the equity portfolio. The perfect timer invests 100 percent in either the safe asset or the equity portfolio, whichever will provide the higher return. The rate of return is *at least* the risk-free rate. This is shown in Figure 21A.1.

To see the value of information as an option, suppose that the market index currently is at S_0 and that a call option on the index has an exercise price of $X = S_0(1 + r_f)$. If the market outperforms bills over the coming period, S_T will exceed X, whereas it will be less than X otherwise. Now look at the payoff to a portfolio consisting of this option and S_0 dollars invested in bills:

	$S_T < X$	$S_T \geq X$
Bills	$S_0(1 + r_f)$	$S_0(1 + r_f)$
Option	0	$S_T - X$
Total	$S_0(1 + r_f)$	S_T

Figure 21A.1

Rate of return of a perfect market timer as a function of the rate of return on the market index.

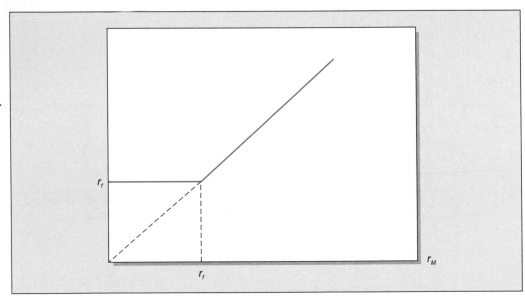

Figure 21A.2   Scatter diagram of timer performance.

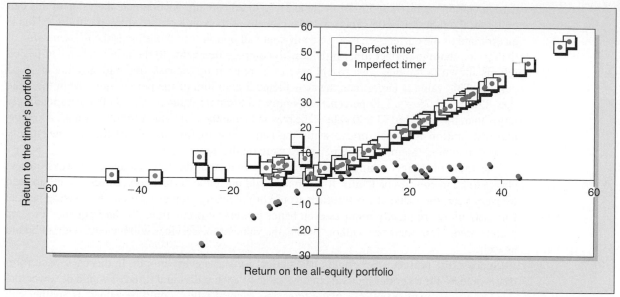

The portfolio pays the risk-free return when the market is bearish (i.e., the market return is less than the risk-free rate), and it pays the market return when the market is bullish and beats bills. Such a portfolio is a perfect market timer.[33]

Figure 21A.2 illustrates the actual pattern of returns to the perfect timer relative to the all-equity investor using historical data. The squares in the scatter diagram show the return to the perfect timer paired with the return in that period on the all-equity portfolio. When the market does well (i.e., when $r_M > r_f$), the return of the perfect timer matches the market's and falls on the 45-degree line. When the market does poorly, the timer earns the T-bill rate. If the risk-free rate were constant, the plot would precisely match that of the payoff to a call option as in Figure 21A.1, flat when $r_M < r_f$ and with a slope of 1.0 when $r_M > r_f$. The only reason the actual pattern deviates from the simple call-option graph is that the risk-free rate is not constant.

Because the ability to predict the better-performing investment is equivalent to holding a call option on the market, in any given period, when the risk-free rate is known, we can use option-pricing models to assign a dollar value to the potential contribution of perfect timing ability. This contribution would constitute the fair fee that a perfect timer could charge investors for his or her services. Placing a value on perfect timing also enables us to assign value to less-than-perfect timers.

The exercise price of the perfect-timer call option on $1 of the equity portfolio is the final value of the T-bill investment. Using continuous compounding, this is $1 \times e^{rT}$. When you use this exercise price in the Black-Scholes formula for the value of the call option, the formula simplifies considerably to[34]

$$\text{MV(Perfect timer)} = C = 2N(\sigma_M \sqrt{T}) - 1 \qquad (21A.1)$$

---

[33]The analogy between market timing and call options, and the valuation formulas that follow from it, were developed in Robert C. Merton, "On Market Timing and Investment Performance: An Equilibrium Theory of Value for Market Forecasts," *Journal of Business*, July 1981.

[34]If you substitute $S_0 = 1 for the current value of the equity portfolio and $X = $1 \times e^{rT}$ in equation 19.1 of Chapter 19, you will obtain equation 21A.1.

We have so far assumed annual forecasts, that is, $T = 1$ year. Using the estimate for the standard deviation of the S&P 500 from Table 21.5, 20.26 percent, we compute the value of this call option in the table as 16.05 cents, or 16.05 percent of the value of the equity portfolio.[35] This is an estimate of the current price of the equivalent call option, and therefore is the *present value* of the service that the perfect timer provides. To compare this value to the historical end-of-period returns shown in the table, we would have to increase it by the risk-free rate, arriving at 16.65 percent. This value is larger than the actual annual premium of the perfect timer from the table (i.e., $17.04 - 3.75 = 13.29$ percent) and implies a terminal value of $225,000, correspondingly larger than the actual $173,000 value. The reason is that the call value formula assumes a lognormal distribution for stock prices while the actual distribution in this period was negatively skewed, meaning that more extreme values were on the negative side.

The value of perfect timing depends on the frequency of the forecast and the always-correct choice to be in equities or T-bills. If the timer could make the correct choice every month instead of every year, the value of the forecasts would dramatically increase. Of course, making perfect forecasts more frequently requires even better powers of prediction. As the frequency of such perfect predictions increases without bound, the value of the services will increase without bound as well.

Suppose the perfect timer could make perfect forecasts every month. In this case, each forecast would be for a shorter interval, and the value of each individual forecast would be lower, but there would be twelve times as many forecasts, each of which could be valued as another call option. The net result is a big increase in total value. With monthly predictions, the value of the call will be $2N(.2026 \times \sqrt{1/12}) - 1 = .0466$. Using a monthly T-bill rate of 3.75%/12, the present value of a 1-year string of such monthly calls, each worth $.0466, is $.5486. Thus, the value of the monthly perfect timer is 54.86 cents on the dollar, compared to 16.05 cents for an annual timer. For an investment period of 80 years, the forecast future value of a $1 investment would be a staggering $(1 + .5486 \times 1.0375)^{80} = \$4.5$ million.

---

[35]Notice that this is a call option with a maturity of one year, and hence it is equivalent to shortfall insurance for one year. (Recall that shortfall insurance is insurance against underperforming some benchmark, in this case T-bills, and pays off any underperformance over some specified investment horizon.) We can obtain the value of implicit shortfall insurance provided by perfect timing over a 25-year period by multiplying the annual standard deviation by $\sqrt{25}$ to obtain cumulative volatility for the 25-year horizon. The resulting insurance value is 58 cents per dollar invested. The sensitivity of the insurance premium to volatility is self-evident.

Portfolio Management Techniques

In the previous chapter, we explored active portfolio management and how the success of those who reject a passive approach can be assessed. Active management takes the form of either the selection of assets that are expected to outperform the market index or the allocation of funds between equities, bonds and cash so as to place capital where it will earn the highest return over shorter periods. In this chapter, we discuss just how active management is executed, that is, what specific techniques can be used to invest in accordance with the results of selectivity or timing analysis.

We shall begin with a discussion of how investment policy is framed. Next we explain the passive strategy of indexing, or how purchasing the market portfolio is achieved. Then we discuss how active or passive positions can be hedged by the use of derivatives. An active manager can establish a position in a sector or an individual asset and then hedge away the systematic risk involved in the active choice. That choice can also be affected by interest rate changes, so this effect can also be hedged. We then continue with the issue of asset allocation, which turns passive strategies with respect to selectivity into active timing.

In the following sections, we demonstrate how selectivity can be optimally conducted, while respecting the notions of portfolio optimization; this is effected by purchasing an index portfolio, but also adding specific equity positions that respond to security analysis decisions. This process, known as the Treynor-Black model, is extended by the Black-Litterman model presented in two more sections. We conclude with a discussion of the value of active management based on the incorporation of active portfolios.

A FRAMEWORK FOR INVESTMENT POLICY

Investors can be differentiated as individuals and institutions. A frequent lament is that individuals appear to be abandoning the markets to the institutions. As small investors, individuals are thought to provide liquidity to the market, which institutional portfolios are too large to do. Nevertheless, individuals provide the funds to the institutions to invest; although individuals have no immediate control over pension funds, mutual funds must respond by buying and selling as their investors add or withdraw cash. This process should still channel funds to the best investment opportunities.

Institutions must attempt to interpret and serve the requirements of households in making their investment decisions. Generally, the household sector equates to individuals, but occasionally there will be **personal trusts**.[1] The institutions that respond to household needs by investing in stock and bond markets include mutual funds, pension funds, endowment funds, and life insurance companies. Casualty insurance companies, like banks and trust companies, tend to have more conservative investments, with shorter maturities, due to the nature of their cash payouts. Each of the institutions must tailor its policies to the needs of its clients and the regulations or circumstances guiding it. We shall examine how these respond accordingly, with particular attention to mutual funds and pension funds.

A formal process for making investment decisions has been established by the CFA Institute, formerly the Association for Investment Management and Research (AIMR), established by the merger of the Financial Analysts Federation (FAF) with the Institute of Chartered Financial Analysts (ICFA). The idea is to subdivide the major steps (objectives, constraints, and policies) into concrete considerations of the various aspects, making the process more tractable. The standard format appears in Table 22.1, and we shall discuss the three parts of the process in turn.

CFA Institute
www.cfainstitute
.org

Institutions and Their Objectives

Portfolio objectives centre on the risk-return tradeoff between the expected return the investors want (*return requirements* in the first column of Table 22.1) and how much risk they are willing to assume (*risk tolerance*). Investment managers must know the level of risk that can be tolerated in the pursuit of a better rate of return. Table 22.2 lists factors governing return requirements and risk attitudes for each of the seven major investor categories discussed.

For mutual funds, the objectives are spelled out precisely in the prospectus. Individuals and trustees can be guided by those statements, even if the objectives are not guaranteed to be met. A detailed discussion follows in the next section.

Pension funds are usually categorized as defined-contribution plans or defined-benefit plans. The former are, in effect, tax-deferred retirement savings accounts established by the firm in trust for its employees; the employees bear all the risk and receive all the return from the plans' assets. In the second form, the assets serve as collateral for the liabilities that the firm sponsoring the

TABLE 22.1

Determination of Portfolio Policies

Objectives	Constraints	Policies
Return requirements	Liquidity	Asset allocation
Risk tolerance	Horizon	Diversification
	Regulations	Risk positioning
	Taxes	Tax positioning
	Unique needs	Income generation

[1]These are established when an individual confers legal title to another person or institution (the trustee) to manage that property for one or more beneficiaries. The beneficiaries are of two types, essentially, those entitled to a life income and those entitled to the remaining principal upon death of the former. By definition of the objective of the trust, the options of the trustee are limited; the requirements have been made much clearer for the trustee than for individuals.

TABLE 22.2   Matrix of Objectives

Type of Investor	Return Requirement	Risk Tolerance
Individual and personal trusts	Life cycle (education, children, retirement)	Life cycle (younger: more risk-tolerant)
Mutual funds	Variable	Variable
Pension funds	Assumed actuarial rate	Depends on proximity of payouts
Endowment funds	Determined by current income needs and need for asset growth to maintain real value	Generally conservative
Life insurance companies	Should exceed new money rate by sufficient margin to meet expenses and profit objectives; also actuarial rates important	Conservative
Nonlife insurance companies	No minimum	Conservative
Banks	Interest spread	Variable

plan owes to the plan beneficiaries. The difference between the two is crucial to how the objective is defined and how the plan will be directed, as we will see in Appendix 22B.

Endowment funds are organizations chartered to use their money for specific nonprofit purposes. They are financed by gifts from one or more sponsors and are typically managed by educational, cultural, and charitable organizations or by independent foundations established solely to carry out the fund's specific purposes. Generally, the investment objectives of an endowment fund are to produce a steady flow of income subject to only a moderate degree of risk. Trustees of an endowment fund, however, can specify other objectives as dictated by the circumstances of the particular endowment fund.

Life insurance companies generally try to invest so as to hedge their liabilities, which are defined by the policies they write. Thus, there are as many objectives as there are distinct types of policies. Until a decade or so ago there were only two types of life insurance policies available for individuals: whole-life and term. A whole-life insurance policy combines a death benefit with a kind of savings plan that provides for a gradual buildup of cash value that the policyholder can withdraw at a later point in life, usually at age 65. Term insurance, on the other hand, provides death benefits only, with no buildup of cash value.

The interest rate embedded in the schedule of cash value accumulation promised under a whole-life policy is a fixed rate; life insurance companies try to hedge this liability by investing in long-term bonds. Often, the insured individual has the right to borrow at a prespecified fixed interest rate against the cash value of the policy.

During the inflationary years of the 1970s and early 1980s, when many older whole-life policies carried contractual borrowing rates as low as 4 percent or 5 percent per year, policyholders borrowed heavily against the cash value to invest in money market mutual funds paying double-digit yields. Other actual and potential policyholders abandoned whole-life policies and took out term insurance, investing the difference in the premiums on their own.

In response to the public's change in tastes, the insurance industry came up with some new policy types, of which two are of particular interest to investors: variable life and universal life.[2] Under a variable life policy, the insured's premium buys a fixed death benefit plus a cash value that can be invested in a variety of mutual funds from which the policyholder can choose. With a universal life policy, policyholders can increase or reduce the premium or death benefit

---

[2]A third type was *adjustable life*, which enabled the policyholder to vary benefits and premiums according to his or her changing needs.

according to their changing needs. Furthermore, the interest rate on the cash value component changes with market interest rates. These two plans effectively unbundle the charges for insurance and savings. The great advantage of variable and universal life insurance policies is that earnings on the cash value are not taxed until the money is withdrawn.[3]

The life insurance industry also provides services or products in the pension area, these being the sale of annuities and pension fund management service. Prior to the introduction of the registered retirement savings plan (RRSP) for individual retirement planning, the monopolistic sale by insurance companies of annuities was a major source of income. The insurance industry must now compete with other financial intermediaries for the sale of RRSPs. The RRSP must, however, be collapsed into an annuity or a registered retirement income fund (RRIF); since RRIFs are less popular than annuities, which may only be offered by insurance companies, the industry has benefited from the wide adoption of RRSPs.

Since the cash flow characteristics of life insurance and pensions are quite similar, insurance companies have developed expertise in fund management that is transferable to the pension industry. One example of this is the insured defined-benefit pension. A firm sponsoring a pension plan enters into a contractual agreement by which an insurance company assumes all liability for the benefits accrued under the plan. This guarantee is given in return for an annual premium based on the benefit formula and the number and characteristics of the employees covered by the plan.

Constraints

Even with identical attitudes toward risk, different households and institutions might choose different investment portfolios because of their differing circumstances. These circumstances include tax status, requirements for liquidity or a flow of income from the portfolio, or various regulatory restrictions; naturally, they impose constraints on investor choice. Together, objectives and constraints determine investment policy.

As an example of a personal circumstance, if a family has children about to enter college, there will be a high demand for liquidity since cash will be needed to pay tuition bills. Other times, however, constraints are imposed externally. For example, banks and trusts are subject to legal limitations on the types of assets they may hold in their portfolios. Finally, some constraints are self-imposed, such as "social investing" by which investors will not hold shares of firms involved in ethically objectionable activities. Some criteria that have been used to judge firms as ineligible for a portfolio are involvement in countries with human rights abuses, production of tobacco or alcohol, and participation in polluting activities. The constraints can be classified broadly as liquidity needs, investment horizon, regulations, and tax considerations.

Liquidity is the ease (speed) with which an asset can be sold and still fetch a fair price. It is a relationship between the time dimension (how long will it take to dispose) and the price dimension (what discount from fair market price) of an investment asset.

When an actual concrete measure of liquidity is necessary, one thinks of the discount when an immediate sale is unavoidable.[4] Cash and money market instruments, such as Treasury bills and commercial paper, where the bid–asked spread is a fraction of 1 percent, are the most liquid assets, and real estate is among the least liquid. Office buildings and manufacturing structures can easily be assessed a 50 percent liquidity discount.

Both individual and institutional investors must consider how likely they are to dispose of assets at short notice. From this likelihood, they establish the minimum level of liquid assets they want in the investment portfolio.

---

[3]Investment contracts with insurance features also may be protected against seizure in bankruptcy.

[4]In most cases, it is impossible to know the liquidity of an asset with certainty, before it is put up for sale. In dealer markets (described in Chapter 3), however, the liquidity of the traded assets can be observed from the bid–asked spread that is quoted by the dealers, that is, the difference between the "bid" quote (the lower price the dealer will pay the owner) and the "asked" quote (the higher price a buyer would have to pay the dealer).

The **investment horizon** is the planned liquidation date of all or part of the investment; for example, it might be the time to fund college education or the retirement date for a wage earner. For a university endowment, an investment horizon could relate to the time needed to fund a major campus construction project. Horizon needs to be considered when investors choose between assets of various maturities, such as bonds, which pay off at specified future dates. For example, the maturity date of a bond might make it a more attractive investment if it coincides with a date on which cash is needed. This idea is analogous to the matching principle from corporate finance: Strive to match financing maturity to the economic life of the financed asset.

Only professional and institutional investors are constrained by *regulations*. First and foremost is the **prudent person law**. That is, professional investors who manage other people's money have a fiduciary responsibility to restrict investment to assets that would have been approved by a prudent investor. The law is purposely nonspecific. Every professional investor must stand ready to defend an investment policy in a court of law, and interpretation may differ according to the standards of the times.

Also, specific regulations apply to various institutional investors. For instance, provincial legislation governs mutual fund holdings, imposing a maximum on the percentage of ownership in a single corporation; this regulation keeps professional investors from getting involved in the actual management of corporations.

Tax consequences are central to investment decisions. The performance of any investment strategy should be measured by how much it yields in real, after-tax investment returns. For household and institutional investors who face significant tax rates, tax sheltering and deferral of tax obligations may be pivotal in their investment strategy.

Unique Needs

Virtually every investor faces special circumstances. Imagine husband-and-wife aeronautical engineers holding high-paying jobs in the same aerospace corporation. The entire human capital of that household is tied to a single player in a rather cyclical industry. This couple would need to hedge the risk (find investment assets that yield more when the risk materializes, thus partly insuring against the risk) of a deterioration in the economic well-being of the aerospace industry.

Human capital is usually an individual's biggest "asset," and the unique risk profile that results from employment must play a major role in determining a suitable investment portfolio.

An example of a unique need for an institutional investor is a university whose trustees let the administration use only cash income from the endowment fund. This constraint would translate into a preference for high-dividend-paying assets.

Table 22.3 presents a summary of the importance of each of the general constraints to each of the seven types of investors.

TABLE 22.3   Matrix of Constraints

Type of Investor	Liquidity	Horizon	Regulatory	Taxes
Individuals and personal trusts	Variable	Life cycle	None	Variable
Mutual funds	Low	Short	Little	None
Pension funds	Young, low; mature, high	Long	Some (federal)	None
Endowment funds	Little	Long	Little	None
Life insurance companies	Low	Long	Complex	Yes
Nonlife insurance companies	High	Short	Little	Yes
Banks	Low	Short	Changing	Yes

22.2   INDEXING

Portfolio theory is substantiated by a considerable body of evidence that points to (1) the relatively accurate pricing of financial assets by the CAPM, (2) the lack of success of portfolio managers in beating the market, whether by timing or selectivity, and (3) the general refutation of apparent anomalies and violations of weak and semistrong forms of market efficiency. In consequence, investors have been advised to diversify and to buy-and-hold. Since perfect diversification is virtually impossible because of transactions costs, investors can either buy a relatively small portfolio that will still eliminate almost all diversifiable risk if chosen optimally, or they can purchase mutual funds (which unfortunately are likely to charge 1 to 2 percent per annum for the benefits of diversification, management and accounting services). As will be noted in Chapter 23, the average mutual fund will probably underperform the market approximately by the size of its management fee percentage.

Index Strategies

Investors appear to be faced with the dismal prospect of doing worse than the well-known dartboard strategy by relying on mutual funds; in fact, they have a better option. A reasonable solution is to buy a low-cost mutual fund which does not charge for its management skills. Such funds may be relatively passive funds, which simply reduce their fees and probably have low portfolio turnover; this saves the investor transactions fees in their portfolios (even with low commissions to funds, the bid–asked spread will still impose a noticeable cost), and reduces the capital gains tax burden. Alternatively, the funds may be **index funds**, whose stated policy is to hold only those equities which compose one of the popular market indices, such as the S&P/TSX Composite or S&P 500. Some turnover still occurs, when the index is adjusted to replace one asset by another; at this point the index fund must sell and buy accordingly. Nevertheless, the major expense of maintaining a research team is eliminated as well as most of the transactions costs. Examples of such funds include the BMO Equity Index and its older and much larger U.S. equivalent, the Vanguard 500 Portfolio, which tracks the S&P 500 index. Added to these benefits is the evidence in the middle nineties that the market indices and index funds outperformed the vast majority of managed funds, giving them increasing publicity for unsophisticated investors.

A lower-cost alternative has emerged more recently. Investors in Canada can duplicate the S&P/TSX 60 index by purchasing iUnits, for instance; these securities are traded on the TSX as ordinary shares, but replicate the index in the same way as an index fund. This is achieved at almost no cost to the investor. The management expenses, for maintaining the portfolio and occasionally adjusting it in line with the index, are covered by retaining the dividends received on the stocks until the end of the quarter, at which time the aggregated dividends are paid to the investor's account; the interest earned on the funds is sufficient to cover the expense, with any excess also paid out. The U.S. equivalent goes by the name of "Spiders," from the name S&P Depositary Receipts, based on the S&P 500 index, but there are also "Diamonds" for the Dow-Jones Industrials, and "Cubes" for the Nasdaq 100.

In both Canada and the United States, one can also invest in various sector indices, such as high-tech or energy sector indices based on the major representatives of those fields. These can be invested in as ETFs relatively inexpensively. As an alternative, one can buy mutual funds that are restricted to sectors, such as Fidelity's "Select" funds in the U.S.; this turns out to be an expensive alternative, with higher fees than the average funds. At this point, we are departing from the notion of replicating the market portfolio and turning to playing bets on sector performance; this represents a compromise position based on sector selectivity rather than individual stock selectivity, and can be explained (as we shall see) as a timing or asset allocation play.

For the equity component of a portfolio then, the efficient and low-cost method to holding the market portfolio has come to be known as **indexing**; it is achieved by purchasing some kind of index security whose performance will track almost perfectly that of the market portfolio. In the United

Since 1997, the FPX indices have stood the test of time as portfolio benchmarks. There are three model portfolio benchmarks: the FPX Income Index, the FPX Balanced Index and the FPX Growth Index.

If you follow these portfolio benchmarks, you know that on April 1 we rebalance the indices back to near their target weights. The goal is to bring it back into line from deviations caused by fluctuations in market values. We say "near" to the target weights because the reallocation is not precise. We do not, for example, purchase fractional shares, bonds or units.

Why is an annual rebalancing necessary? There are really two answers to that question, one simple and one complicated.

The simple reason is that over time, the cash, fixed-income, and equity asset classes move at different speeds, and sometimes even in different directions. At the end of the year, then, one asset class may have a disproportionately large representation in the portfolio, while another has too little. Rebalancing the indices back to their original percentage weightings is akin to lining up the horses at the starting gate before the next race begins.

The more complex reason, for rebalancing the FPX indices in particular, comes from the reason they were created in the first place. They were designed as investable, diversified, passive, and realistic portfolios with an assumed portfolio size of $100,000, which was, at the time they were created, representative of the average investment portfolio held by *Financial Post* readers.

More importantly, they were designed as a benchmark against which an investor could measure the performance of their investment advisor, their portfolio manager, or even themselves. The portfolios must be reset, then, to provide a consistent benchmark for measuring the performance of alternative approaches.

This year, the rebalancing of the three portfolios will mean increasing the amount of fixed-income securities held in each, and decreasing the equity component. Think about that: We are going to sell from the asset class that has done well, and buy the asset class that has done relatively poorly. In other words, we're going to sell high and buy low.

What active portfolio managers call "dynamic asset allocation" and some investors call "the contrarian method" is, in this passive-portfolio case, nothing more than a simple rebalancing. It is not meant as a recommendation; however, if you feel it is also a very wise move at this point in the market (and you may be right), the FPX indices can serve as your benchmark a year from now to see if you were right. Just remember, this rebalancing is a reaction to the past year's market, not a suggestion for next year's.

Within each FPX Index, we hold "on-the-run" (or bellwether and therefore liquid) 3-, 10-, and 30-year Government of Canada bonds. The new three-year bond that will be part of this rebalancing will be the Government of Canada 5.5 percent, June 1, 2010; the 10-year will be the Government of Canada 4 percent June 1, 2017; and the 30-year will be the Government of Canada 5 percent June 1, 2037.

For investors looking to replicate these benchmarks—and why not, they have been first- or second-quartile performers in almost all measuring periods—consider using bond ETFs that trade on the Toronto Stock Exchange. There are a number of such animals, the most liquid being Barclays Broad Bond iShares (XBB/TSX), which is designed to track a well-known institutional bond benchmark, the Scotia Capital Bond Universe.

Bond ETFs have some interesting advantages over holding the actual bonds. First, actual bonds tend to mature over time. An investor who holds a five-year bond this year will end up with a four-year bond next year. Unless, of course, they go through the process of selling at the end of each year and reinvesting one year further out. This is not necessary with the iShares, since they do this automatically within the fund.

Second, the iShares may do it cheaper: Their MERs are capped at .30 percent. Try doing a bond switch for that kind of spread. Third, the ETF buys bonds in bulk ($88 million to $91 million a pop), leading to better wholesale pricing and, theoretically, better yields.

Another nice feature of these ETFs is their transparency. They can be bought and sold every day on the Toronto Stock Exchange, just like a stock. They were underwritten by a group of major Canadian investment dealers, and two of those dealers serve as market makers to maintain liquidity. And best of all in terms of transparency, their prices are quoted every day in your newspaper.

So is the ETF approach always better than buying the bonds? Not necessarily. From a portfolio perspective, the purpose of adding a fixed-income component, or any part of the asset mix, for that matter, is to improve the risk/reward ratio of the overall portfolio. Academics call this measure the *coefficient of variation*, as calculated by the standard deviation of the portfolio divided by its expected return.

The negative correlation of different asset classes is a factor in moving the portfolio nearer to the efficient frontier, and ultimately to an optimal position. The inclusion of bond ETFs in a portfolio will assist in accomplishing this better than, say, a five-year laddered portfolio.

Critical to this whole portfolio-building business is the conviction that risk is defined as the uncertainty of future returns. Risk is not the absence of safety.

Having said that, if safety is the goal of a particular individual investor, a laddered bond portfolio in most cases will do the job better than a bond ETF. It just won't be as efficient.

States there are also a number of alternative indices aimed at different slices of the whole market: the Russell 2000 and S&P 400, for the somewhat lower-capitalization equities, or the Wilshire 5000, for almost the entire set of listed securities. These are intended as benchmarks for portfolio performance comparison purposes, but derivatives can also be based upon them and used for hedging purposes. The purchase of the index security fulfills the aim of acquiring a well-diversified proxy for the market portfolio. It allows an investor to follow the dictates of modern portfolio theory and has the added benefit of avoiding the realization of any capital gains through portfolio rebalancing.

In addition to the passive strategy of indexing, the index security and sector indices can be used as part of an active management scheme. A basic strategy for risk reduction involves shorting an index security (either a future or index option) against a portfolio; this can be done for timing (after a sustained up-move) or for reducing the systematic risk of an active portfolio imperfectly correlated with the index. Similarly, a portfolio of securities drawn from a particular sector can be hedged by shorting the sector index securities. (This process is explained in Section 22.3.)[5]

As noted in the bond portfolio management chapter, bond indexing can be achieved through a cellular portfolio, but this is not really a practical investment. Instead the more traditional opportunities are personal construction of laddered or barbell portfolios, or the purchase of a professionally managed bond mutual fund; in the latter case, it is generally accepted that the lowest-cost (management fees) fund is likely to be the best. (Others recommend the direct purchase of a medium-term bond, on issue, from the Bank of Canada, which is rolled over at maturity; this is claimed to have realized returns at least as good as those of mutual funds, whose portfolio durations are generally of similar length as the initial bond maturity.)

Finally for cash, a money market fund, invested either in government securities alone or in prime corporate issues as well, provides the best yields for the ultimate liquidity that a "cash" component is expected to have. See the boxed article here for comments on indexing and asset allocation.

22.3 HEDGING

We have seen two methods of reacting to information based on analysis of either macroeconomic scenarios or individual security returns, recognizing powers of either timing or selectivity. In both cases, underlying portfolios are based on index replication. Under these strategies, investors remain exposed to market risk and its effect on their total portfolios, tempered as they may be by the adjustments made through active management. By using derivatives, this market risk can be further reduced; stock index futures can be sold short against the value of the equity portfolio, while interest rate futures can be shorted against the value of the bond portfolio. In this section we describe the actual construction of the hedges based on the size and beta or duration of the two portfolios. As well, investors can buy hedge funds to exercise these strategies and others for them.

Hedging Systematic Risk

We saw in Chapter 20 that pure market timers might use a combination of money market securities and stock index futures contracts to adjust market exposure in response to changing forecasts about stock market performance. When the outlook is bullish, more contracts would be added to the fixed position in cash equivalents.

This form of timing is a bit restrictive, however, in that it allows for equity positions in only the stock index. How might a manager of a more actively constructed portfolio hedge market exposure? Suppose, for example, that you manage a $30 million portfolio with a beta of .8. You are bullish on the market over the long term, but you are afraid that over the next two months, the market is vulnerable to a sharp downturn. If trading were costless, you could sell your portfolio, place the proceeds in T-bills for two months, and then reestablish your position after you perceive that the risk of the downturn has passed. In practice, however, this strategy would result in unacceptable trading costs,

---

[5]See Lorne Switzer and Rana Zoghaib, "Index Participation Units, Market Tracking Risk, and Equity Market Demand," *Canadian Journal of Administrative Sciences* 16, no. 3 (September 1999), pp. 243–255.

not to mention tax problems resulting from the realization of capital gains or losses on the portfolio. An alternative approach would be to use stock index futures to hedge your market exposure.

EXAMPLE 22.1   Hedging Market Risk

Suppose that the S&P/TSX 60 index currently is at 800. A decrease in the index to 790 would represent a drop of 1.25 percent. Given the beta of your portfolio, you would expect a loss of .8 × 1.25% = 1 percent, or in dollar terms, .01 × $30 million = $300,000. Therefore, the sensitivity of your portfolio value to market movements is $300,000 per 10-point movement in the S&P 60 index.

To hedge this risk, you could sell stock index futures. When your portfolio falls in value along with declines in the broad market, the futures contract will provide an offsetting profit.

The sensitivity of a futures contract to market movements is easy to determine. With its contract multiplier of $200, the profit on the S&P/TSX 60 futures contract varies by $2,000 for every 10-point swing in the index. Therefore, to hedge your market exposure for two months, you could calculate the **hedge ratio** as follows:

$$H = \frac{\text{Change in portfolio value}}{\text{Profit on one futures contract}} = \frac{\$300,000}{\$2,000} = 150 \text{ contracts (short)}$$

You would enter the short side of the contracts, because you want profits from the contract to offset the exposure of your portfolio to the market. Because your portfolio does poorly when the market falls, you need a position that will do well when the market falls.

We also could approach the hedging problem using the regression procedure illustrated above. The predicted value of the portfolio is graphed in Figure 22.1 as a function of the value of the S&P/TSX 60 index. With a beta of .8, the slope of the relationship is 60,000: a 1.25 percent increase in the index, from 800 to 810 results in a capital gain of 1 percent of $30 million, or $300,000. Therefore, your portfolio will increase in value by $30,000 for each increase of one point in the index. As a result, you should enter a short position on 30,000 units of the S&P/TSX 60 index to fully offset your exposure to marketwide movements. Because the contract multiplier is $200 times the index, you need to sell 30,000/200 = 150 contracts.

Notice that when the slope of the regression line relating your unprotected position to the value of an asset is positive, your hedge strategy calls for a *short* position in that asset. The hedge ratio is the negative of the regression slope. This is because the hedge position should offset your initial exposure. If you do poorly when the asset value falls, you need a hedge vehicle that will do well when the asset value falls. This calls for a short position in the asset.

Active managers sometimes believe that a particular asset is underpriced, but that the market as a whole is about to fall. Even if the asset is a good buy relative to other stocks in the market, it still might perform poorly in a broad market downturn. To solve this problem, the manager would like to separate the bet on the firm from the bet on the market: the bet on the company must be offset with a hedge against the market exposure that normally would accompany a purchase of the stock.

In other words, the manager seeks a **market-neutral bet** on the stock, by which we mean that a position on the stock is taken to capture its alpha (its abnormal risk-adjusted expected return), but that market exposure is fully hedged, resulting in a position beta of zero.

By allowing investors to hedge market performance, the futures contract allows the portfolio manager to make stock picks without concern for the market exposure of the stocks chosen. After the stocks are chosen, the resulting market risk of the portfolio can be modulated to any degree using the stock futures contracts. Here again, the stock's beta is the key to the hedging strategy.

Figure 22.1

Predicted value of the portfolio as a function of the market index.

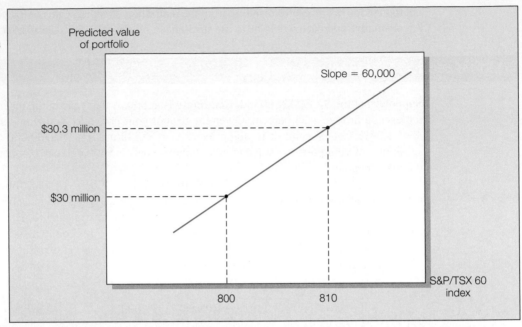

Predicted value of portfolio

Slope = 60,000

$30.3 million

$30 million

800   810

S&P/TSX 60 index

EXAMPLE 22.2   **Market-Neutral Active Stock Selection**

Suppose the beta of the stock is $^2/_3$, and the manager purchases $480,000 worth of the stock. For every 3 percent drop in the broad market, the stock would be expected to respond with a drop of $^2/_3 \times 3\% = 2$ percent, or $9,600. The S&P/TSX 60 contract will fall by 24 points from a current value of 800 if the market drops 3 percent. With the contract multiplier of $200, this would entail a profit to a short futures position of $24 \times \$200 = \$4,800$ per contract. Therefore, the market risk of the stock can be offset by shorting two S&P/TSX 60 contracts. More formally, we could calculate the hedge ratio as

$$H = \frac{\text{Expected change in stock value per 3\% market drop}}{\text{Profit on one short contract per 3\% market drop}}$$

$$= \frac{\$9,600 \text{ swing in unprotected position}}{\$4,800 \text{ profit per contract}}$$

$$= 2 \text{ contracts}$$

Now that market risk is hedged, the only source of variability in the performance of the stock-plus-futures portfolio will be the firm-specific performance of the stock.

Hedging Interest Rate Risk

Like equity managers, fixed-income managers also desire to hedge market risk, in this case resulting from movements in the entire structure of interest rates. Consider, for example, these problems:

1. A fixed-income manager holds a bond portfolio on which considerable capital gains have been earned. She foresees an increase in interest rates but is reluctant to sell her portfolio and replace it with a lower-duration mix of bonds because such rebalancing would result in large trading costs as well as realization of capital gains for tax purposes. Still, she would like to hedge her exposure to interest rate increases.

2. A corporation plans to issue bonds to the public. It believes that now is a good time to act, but it cannot issue the bonds for another three months because of the lags inherent in registration. It would like to hedge the uncertainty surrounding the yield at which it eventually will be able to sell the bonds.

3. A pension fund will receive a large cash inflow next month that it plans to invest in long-term bonds. It is concerned that interest rates may fall by the time it can make the investment and would like to lock in the yield currently available on long-term issues.

In each of these cases, the investment manager wishes to hedge interest rate uncertainty. To illustrate the procedures that might be followed, we will focus on the first example, and suppose that the portfolio manager has a $10 million bond portfolio with a modified duration of nine years.[6] If, as feared, market interest rates increase and the bond portfolio's yield also rises, say by 10 basis points (.1 percent), the fund will suffer a capital loss. Recall from Chapter 14 that the capital loss in percentage terms will be the product of modified duration, D^*, and the change in the portfolio yield. Therefore, the loss will be

$$D^* \times \Delta y = 9 \times .1\% = .9\%$$

or $90,000. This establishes that the sensitivity of the value of the unprotected portfolio to changes in market yields is $9,000 per 1 basis point change in the yield. Market practitioners call this ratio the **price value of a basis point**, or PVBP. The PVBP represents the sensitivity of the dollar value of the portfolio to changes in interest rates. Here, we've shown that

$$\text{PVBP} = \frac{\text{Change in portfolio value}}{\text{Predicted change in yield}} = \frac{\$90,000}{10 \text{ basis points}} = \$9,000 \text{ per basis point}$$

One way to hedge this risk is to take an offsetting position in an interest rate futures contract, for example the Canada bond contract. The bond nominally calls for delivery of $100,000 par value bonds with 9 percent coupons and 10-year maturity. In practice, the contract delivery terms are fairly complicated because many bonds with different coupon rates and maturities may be substituted to settle the contract. However, we will assume that the bond to be delivered already is known and has a modified duration of 10 years. Finally, suppose that the futures price currently is $90 per $100 par value. Because the contract requires delivery of $100,000 par value of bonds, the contract multiplier is $1,000.

Given these data, we can calculate the PVBP for the futures contract. If the yield on the delivery bond increases by 10 basis points, the bond value will fall by $D^* \times .1\% = 10 \times .1\% = 1$ percent. The futures price also will decline 1% from 90 to 89.10.[7] Because the contract multiplier is $1,000, the gain on each short contract will be $1,000 \times .90 = $900. Therefore, the PVBP for one futures contract is $900/10-basis-point change, or $90 for a change in yield of 1 basis point.

Now we can easily calculate the hedge ratio as follows:

$$H = \frac{\text{PVBP of portfolio}}{\text{PVBP of hedge vehicle}} = \frac{\$9,000}{\$90 \text{ per contract}} = 100 \text{ contracts}$$

Therefore, 100 Canada bond futures contracts will offset the portfolio's exposure to interest rate fluctuations.

---

[6]Recall that modified duration, D^*, is related to duration, D, by the formula $D^* = D/(1 + y)$, where y is the bond's yield to maturity. If the bond pays coupons semiannually, then y should be measured as a semiannual yield. For simplicity, we will assume annual coupon payments, and treat y as the effective annual yield to maturity.

[7]This assumes the futures price will be exactly proportional to the bond price, which ought to be nearly true.

Notice that this is another example of a market-neutral strategy. In Example 22.2, which illustrated an equity-hedging strategy, stock-index futures were used to drive a portfolio beta to zero. In this application, we used a bond contract to drive the interest rate exposure of a bond position to zero. The hedged fixed-income position has a duration (or a PVBP) of zero. The source of risk differs, but the hedging strategy is essentially the same.

Although the hedge ratio is easy to compute, the hedging problem in practice is more difficult. We assumed in our example that the yields on the bond contract and the bond portfolio would move perfectly in unison. Although interest rates on various fixed-income instruments do tend to vary in tandem, there is considerable slippage across sectors of the fixed-income market. For example, Figure 22.2 shows that the spread between long-term corporate and Canada bond yields has fluctuated considerably over time. Our hedging strategy would be fully effective only if the yield spread across the two sectors of the fixed-income market were constant (or at least perfectly predictable) so that yield changes in both sectors were equal.

This problem highlights the fact that most hedging activity is in fact **cross-hedging**, meaning that the hedge vehicle is a different asset than the one to be hedged. To the extent that there is slippage between prices or yields of the two assets, the hedge will not be perfect. Cross-hedges can eliminate a large fraction of the total risk of the unprotected portfolio, but you should be aware that they typically are far from risk-free positions.

Figure 22.2   Yield spread between AA corporate and long-term government bonds.

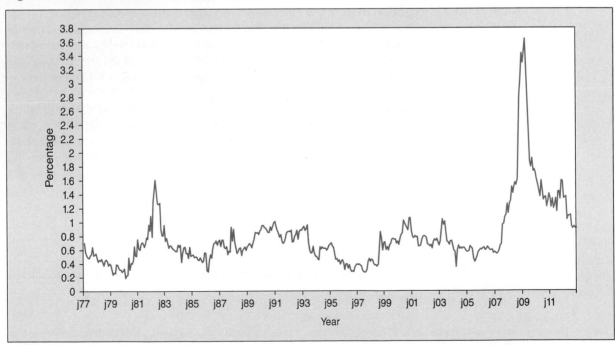

Source: Scotia Capital, *Debt Market Indices,* various years.

22.4 ASSET ALLOCATION

Market timing in its simplest form would entail buying an index fund of equities when the investor predicted that the market would be yielding higher than a money market fund and selling it when the prediction reversed, as in the previous chapter. With fixed income securities added to the portfolio, the prediction would have to include whether bonds, stocks or cash would have the highest return and the resultant action would require switching to whichever asset was chosen. In fact, since perfect predictions are not expected, one is more likely to talk about the risk-adjusted returns predicted for each asset. Professional advisors determine the probabilities of each of the three assets outperforming the others, and then recommend portfolio proportions for the three assets which respond to the strength of the probabilities. The recommended proportions are then referred to as asset allocations.

A passive asset allocation approach would specify the three proportions and keep them unmodified under a long-term, buy-and-hold strategy. Such a strategy is, once again, supported by the empirical evidence describing the average results of those who try to time the market. The only question in that prescription is answered by our earliest conclusion in portfolio theory—that of the location along the capital allocation line representing the proportion of wealth placed in the risky portfolio. We would amplify that simple two-asset allocation as presented in Chapter 6, where risky capital was first allocated between what was described as a (less risky) bond portfolio and a (more risky) stock portfolio, and then the capital allocation question was resolved.

We should note at this point that the prescription of Chapter 6 is not followed strictly in the markets. Essentially, the markets are segmented into bond and equity (and others), and optimal portfolios are constructed separately. The proportions in each of the two asset classes plus cash are determined as a distinct decision. The first result of determining an allocation of capital between cash, bonds, and equities is taken as a neutral or baseline allocation. The resultant weights designated as neutral will depend on the risk tolerance of the individual investor, and must be determined by a manager in consultation with the client. For example, risk-tolerant clients may put a large fraction of their capital in the equity market, perhaps directing the portfolio manager to set neutral weights of 75 percent equity, 15 percent bonds, and 10 percent cash equivalents. In contrast, more risk-averse clients may set neutral weights of 45/35/20 percent for the three markets; thus their portfolios in normal circumstances will be exposed to less risk than that of the risk-tolerant client. Any deviation from these weights, by either type of client, must be justified by a belief that one or the other market will either under- or overperform its usual risk–return profile. This would be an intentional departure from the neutral position based on macro analysis.

The previous risk tolerance approach to baseline portfolios applies to individual clients and their financial advisors. Brokerage houses tend to identify a broader portfolio for their general clients. This approach is defined by the establishment of a baseline portfolio position for at least two types of investors; thus there may exist model portfolios described as the "balanced portfolio" and the "growth portfolio." Each of these might hold the same bond and stock portfolios, but in different proportions. (There are opportunities for expansion at this point; the equity portfolio could be redefined for different representative investors having objectives of "preservation of capital" or "aggressive growth," but these objectives could also be satisfied simply by moving along the capital allocation line.)

The two portfolios above were described as baseline positions. Under an active asset allocation approach, proportions are adjusted from the **baseline allocation** in response to the predictions about asset performance. These predictions are initially based on a macroeconomic analysis indicating such results as (1) increasing activity leading to higher interest rates that would lower bond prices but perhaps increase corporate profits and equity prices or (2) higher inflation leading to both higher interest rates with falling bond prices and squeezed profits with higher discount factors causing equity declines also. The resultant asset allocation decisions in these two cases would be switching funds out of bonds and into stocks, and reducing positions in both bonds and stocks and increasing the cash proportion.

Brokerage houses regularly report on the asset allocation proportions in their two-or-more-model portfolios, giving their current allocations and reminding their clients of the neutral positions. They also tend to indicate the maximum and minimum levels for each asset proportion to indicate the strength of their convictions about market prospects. Thus, a balanced portfolio might have a neutral weighting of stocks, bonds, and cash (60 percent, 30 percent, 10 percent) with a stated range of 30–70 percent, 20–40 percent, 5–25 percent; with a recommendation of 68 percent, 25 percent, 7 percent, the broker would be indicating a very bullish perspective on equities; while a 50 percent, 35 percent, 15 percent posture would suggest a somewhat cautious outlook.

Asset allocation is also described more specifically as "swing fund management" and "tactical asset allocation," with the first term referring to a more general and subjective version based on economic conditions. Assessment of interest rates for short- and long-term debt instruments and predicted returns on the market index quickly leads to an increase or decrease in each of the current proportions to provide the next allocation. Subjectively, if the differences between predicted short and long rates and equity returns shrink, then capital will be moved toward bonds and cash, while if the differences are expanding the allocation will shift toward equities. This loose and intuitive approach is given the more impressive "tactical" label when more formal computational techniques are employed. Extensive analysis of time series and their changes, using sophisticated statistical techniques and even the latest technologies such as neural networks and chaos theory, requires extensive sessions on higher powered computers to produce (perhaps) more reliable estimates of the optimal proportions. One should note, however, that research in this area by some foremost financial researchers concludes that the essential ingredients in the analysis are still the predicted returns on short- and long-term debt securities and on the market index, with much attention paid to their relative levels both to each other and to their historical values, as well as current economic conditions.

The economic analysis can be extended further, using the fundamental approach previously described in Chapter 15. This would reveal that certain sectors of the market are expected to perform better at different stages of the economic cycle in general, which is linked to the assessment of where the cycle currently is to identify superior prospects; alternatively, specific sectors can be expected to outperform due to particular economic conditions that are occurring. Such predictions would lead to overweighting of these sectors, either through their representative companies or through a sector fund or index, with a corresponding underweighting of all other sectors or of some predicted to underperform. This adjustment of the equity portfolio would constitute a finer level of asset allocation; we addressed the assessment of the success of such decisions specifically by the technique of performance attribution presented in Section 20.7.

| **E-INVESTMENTS**
Asset
Allocation
Plans | Use the interactive asset allocator offered by the Iowa Public Employees Retirement System at **www.ipers .org/members/calculators/calculators_5.html**. See what happens to the recommended allocations for each of the seven asset classes as the inputs change. |

Under the CFA approach, the process of asset allocation consists of the following steps:

1. *Specify asset classes to be included in the portfolio.* The major classes usually considered are the following:
   a. Money market instruments (usually called *cash*)
   b. Fixed-income securities (usually called *bonds*)
   c. Stocks
   d. Real estate
   e. Precious metals
   f. Other

   Institutional investors will rarely invest in more than the first four categories, whereas individual investors may include precious metals and other more exotic types of investments in their portfolios.

2. *Specify capital market expectations.* This step consists of using both historical data and economic *analysis* to determine your expectations of future rates of return over the relevant holding period on the assets to be considered for inclusion in the portfolio.

3. *Derive the efficient portfolio frontier.* This step consists of finding portfolios that achieve the *maximum* expected return for any given degree of risk.

4. *Find the optimal asset mix.* This step consists of selecting the efficient portfolio that best meets your risk *and* return objectives while satisfying the constraints you face.

22.5   SECURITY SELECTION: THE TREYNOR-BLACK MODEL

Alpha and Security Analysis

Security analysis is the other form of active portfolio management besides timing the overall market. Suppose that you are an analyst studying individual securities. It is quite likely that you will turn up several securities that appear to be mispriced. They offer positive anticipated alphas to the investor. But how do you exploit your analysis? Concentrating a portfolio on these securities entails a cost, namely, the firm-specific risk that you could shed by more fully diversifying. As an active manager you must strike a balance between aggressive exploitation of perceived security mispricing and diversification motives that dictate that a few stocks should not dominate the portfolio.

Treynor and Black[8] developed an optimizing model for portfolio managers who use security analysis. It represents a portfolio management theory that assumes security markets are *nearly* efficient in the context of the single-index model. The essence of the model is this:

1. Security analysts in an active investment management organization can analyze in depth only a relatively small number of stocks out of the entire universe of securities. The securities not analyzed are assumed to be fairly priced.

2. For the purpose of efficient diversification, the market index portfolio is the baseline portfolio, which the model treats as the passive portfolio.

3. The macro forecasting unit of the investment management firm provides forecasts of the expected rate of return and variance of the passive (market index) portfolio.

4. The objective of security analysis is to form an active portfolio of a necessarily limited number of securities. Perceived nonzero alphas of the analyzed securities are what guide the composition of this active portfolio.

---

[8]Jack L. Treynor and Fischer Black, "How to Use Security Analysis to Improve Portfolio Selection," *Journal of Business*, January 1973.

5. Analysts follow several steps to make up the active portfolio and evaluate its expected performance:

   a. Estimate the beta of each analyzed security and its residual risk. From the beta and the macro forecast, $E(r_M) - r_f$, determine the *required* rate of return of the security.

   b. Given the degree of mispricing of each security, determine its expected return and expected *abnormal* return (alpha).

   c. Calculate the cost of less than full diversification. The nonsystematic risk of the mispriced stock, the variance of the stock's residual, offsets the benefit (alpha) of specializing in an underpriced security.

   d. Use the estimates for the values of alpha, beta, and residual risk to determine the optimal weight of each security in the active portfolio.

   e. Estimate the alpha, beta, and residual risk for the active portfolio according to the weights of the securities in the portfolio.

6. The macroeconomic forecasts for the passive index portfolio and the composite forecasts for the active portfolio are used to determine the optimal risky portfolio, which will be a combination of the passive and active portfolios.

Security analysis of the sort Treynor and Black propose has enormous value, deriving from mispriced securities with nonzero alphas.

In the context of portfolio construction, alpha is more than just one of the components of expected return. It is the key variable that tells us whether a security is a good or a bad buy. Consider an individual stock for which we have a beta estimate from statistical considerations and an alpha value from security analysis. We easily can find many other securities with identical betas and therefore identical systematic components of their risk premiums. Therefore, what really makes a security attractive or unattractive to a portfolio manager is its alpha value. In fact, we've suggested that a security with a positive alpha is providing a premium over and above the premium it derives from its tendency to track the market index. This security is a bargain and therefore should be overweighted in the overall portfolio compared to the passive alternative of using the market-index portfolio as the risky vehicle. Conversely, a negative-alpha security is overpriced and, other things equal, its portfolio weight should be reduced. In more extreme cases, the desired portfolio weight might even be negative, that is, a short position (if permitted) would be desirable.

The Index Portfolio as an Investment Asset

The process of charting the efficient frontier using the single-index model can be pursued much like the procedure using the Markowitz model to find the optimal risky portfolio. Here, however, we can benefit from the simplification the index model offers for deriving the input list. Moreover, portfolio optimization highlights another advantage of the single-index model, namely, a simple and intuitively revealing representation of the optimal risky portfolio. Before we get into the mechanics of optimization in this setting, however, we start by considering the role of the index portfolio in the optimal portfolio.

Suppose the prospectus of an investment company limits the universe of investable assets to only stocks included in the S&P 500[9] portfolio. In this case, the S&P 500 index captures the impact of the economy on the large stocks the firm may include in its portfolio. Suppose that the resources of the company allow coverage of only a relatively small subset of this so-called

---

[9]We use the S&P 500 because of the stocks in the example that follows.

investable universe. If these analyzed firms are the only ones allowed in the portfolio, the portfolio manager may well be worried about limited diversification.

A simple way to avoid inadequate diversification is to include the S&P 500 portfolio as one of the assets of the portfolio. If we treat the S&P 500 portfolio as the market index, it will have a beta of 1.0 (its sensitivity to itself), no firm-specific risk, and an alpha of zero—there is no non-market component in its expected return. Also, the covariance of any security, i, with the index is $\beta_i \sigma^2_M$. To distinguish the S&P 500 from the n securities covered by the firm, we will designate it the $(n + 1)$th asset. We can think of the S&P 500 as a *passive portfolio* that the manager would select in the absence of security analysis. It gives broad market exposure without the need for expensive security analysis. However, if the manager is willing to engage in such research, she may devise an *active portfolio* that can be mixed with the index to provide an even better risk-return tradeoff.

Input List   If the portfolio manager plans to compile a portfolio from a list of n actively researched firms plus a passive market index portfolio, the input list will include the following estimates:

1. Risk premium on the S&P 500 portfolio
2. Standard deviation of the S&P 500 portfolio
3. n sets of estimates of (a) beta coefficients, (b) stock residual variances, and (c) alpha values (The alpha values, together with the risk premium of the S&P 500 and the beta of each security, determine the expected return on each security.)

The Optimal Risky Portfolio in the Single-Index Model

The single-index model allows us to solve for the optimal risky portfolio directly and to gain insight into the nature of the solution. First we confirm that we easily can set up the optimization process to chart the efficient frontier in this framework along the lines of the Markowitz model. Recall the formulation of the single-index model:

$$E(R_i) = \alpha_i + \beta_i E(R_M) \tag{22.1}$$

$$\text{Cov}(r_i, r_j) = \beta_i \beta_j \sigma^2_M \tag{22.2}$$

With the estimates of the beta and alpha coefficients, plus the risk premium of the index portfolio, we can generate the $n + 1$ expected returns using equation 22.1. With the estimates of the beta coefficients and residual variances, together with the variance of the index portfolio, we can construct the covariance matrix using equation 22.2. Given a column of risk premiums and the covariance matrix; we can conduct the optimization program described in Chapter 7.

We can take the description of how diversification works in the single-index framework of Section 8.2 a step further. We showed earlier that the alpha, beta, and residual variance of an equally weighted portfolio are the simple averages of those parameters across component securities. This result is not limited to equally weighted portfolios. It applies to any portfolio, where we need only replace "simple average" with "weighted average," using the portfolio weights. Specifically,

$$\alpha_P = \sum_{i=1}^{n1} w_i \alpha_i \qquad ; \quad \text{for the index } \alpha_{n+1} = \alpha_M = 0$$

$$\beta_P = \sum_{i=1}^{n1} w_i \beta_i \qquad ; \quad \text{for the index } \beta_{n+1} = \beta_M = 1 \tag{22.3}$$

$$\sigma^2(e_P) = \sum_{i=1}^{n1} w_i^2 \sigma^2(e_i); \quad \text{for the index } \sigma^2(e_{n+1}) = \sigma^2(e_M) = 0$$

The objective is to maximize the Sharpe ratio of the portfolio by using portfolio weights, $w_1, \ldots,$ w_{n+1}. With this set of weights, the expected return, standard deviation, and Sharpe ratio of the portfolio are

$$E(R_P) = \alpha_P + E(R_M)\beta_P = \sum_{i=1}^{n1} w_i\alpha_i + E(R_M)\sum_{i=1}^{n1} w_i\beta_i$$

$$\sigma_P = [\beta_P^2\sigma_M^2 + \sigma^2(e_P)^{1/2}] = \left[\sigma_M^2\left(\sum_{i=1}^{n+1} w_i\beta_i\right)^2 + \sum_{i=1}^{n+1} w_i^2\sigma^2(e_i)\right]^{1/2} \qquad (22.4)$$

$$S_P = \frac{E(R_P)}{\sigma_P}$$

At this point, as in the Markowitz procedure, we could use Excel's optimization program to maximize the Sharpe ratio subject to the adding-up constraint that the portfolio weights sum to 1.0. However, this is not necessary because when returns follow the index model, the optimal portfolio can be derived explicitly, and the solution for the optimal portfolio provides insight into the efficient use of security analysis in portfolio construction. It is instructive to outline the logical thread of the solution. We will not show every algebraic step, but will instead present the major results and interpretations of the procedure.

Before delving into the results, let us first explain the basic tradeoff the model reveals. If we were interested only in diversification, we would just hold the market index. Security analysis gives us the chance to uncover securities with a nonzero alpha and to take a differential position in those securities. The cost of that differential position is a departure from efficient diversification, in other words, the assumption of unnecessary firm-specific risk. The model shows us that the optimal risky portfolio trades off the search for alpha against the departure from efficient diversification.

The optimal risky portfolio turns out to be a combination of two component portfolios: (1) an *active portfolio*, denoted A, comprising the n analyzed securities (which we call the *active* portfolio because it follows from active security analysis) and (2) the market-index portfolio, the $(n + 1)$th asset we include to aid in diversification, which we call the *passive portfolio* and denote M.

Assume first that the active portfolio has a beta of 1.0. In that case, the optimal weight in the active portfolio would be proportional to the ratio $\propto_A/\sigma^2(e_A)$. This ratio balances the contribution of the active portfolio (its alpha) against its contribution to the portfolio variance (via residual variance). The analogous ratio for the index portfolio is $E(R_M)/\sigma_M^2$, and hence the initial position in the active portfolio (i.e., if its beta were 1) is

$$w_A^0 = \left[\frac{\dfrac{\alpha_A}{\sigma^2(e_A)}}{\dfrac{E(R_M)}{\alpha_M^2}}\right] \qquad (22.5)$$

Next, we amend this position to account for the actual beta of the active portfolio. For any level of σ_A^2, the correlation between the active and passive portfolios is greater when the beta of the active portfolio is higher. This implies less diversification benefit from the passive portfolio and a lower position in it. Correspondingly, the position in the active portfolio increases. The precise modification for the position in the active portfolio is as follows:[10]

$$w_A^* = \frac{w_A^0}{1 + (1 - \beta_A)w_A^0} \qquad (22.6)$$

---

[10]The definition of correlation implies that $\rho(R_A, R_M) = \text{Cov}(R_A, R_M)/\sigma_A\sigma_M = \beta_A\sigma_A/\sigma_M$. Therefore, given the ratio of SD, a higher beta implies higher correlation and smaller benefit from diversification than when $\beta = 1$ in equation 22.5. This requires the modification in equation 22.6.

The Information Ratio

Equations 22.5 and 22.6 yield the optimal position in the active portfolio once we know its alpha, beta, and residual variance. With w_A^* in the active portfolio and $1 - w_A^*$ invested in the index portfolio, we can compute the expected return, standard deviation, and Sharpe ratio of the optimal risky portfolio. The Sharpe ratio of an optimally constructed risky portfolio will exceed that of the index portfolio (the passive strategy). The exact relationship is

$$S_P^2 = S_M^2 + \left[\frac{\alpha_A}{\sigma(e_A)} \right]^2 \tag{22.7}$$

Equation 22.7 shows us that the contribution of the active portfolio (when held in its optimal weight, w_A^*) to the Sharpe ratio of the overall risky portfolio is determined by the ratio of its alpha to its residual standard deviation. This is the *information ratio,* which measures the extra return we can obtain from security analysis compared to the firm-specific risk we incur when we over-or underweight securities relative to the passive market index. Equation 22.7 therefore implies that to maximize the overall Sharpe ratio, we must maximize the information ratio of the active portfolio.

It turns out that the information ratio of the active portfolio will be maximized if we invest in each security in proportion to its ratio of $\alpha_i / \sigma^2(e_i)$. Scaling this ratio so that the total position in the active portfolio adds up to w_A^*, the weight in each security is

$$w_A^0 = \frac{\dfrac{\alpha_i}{\sigma^2(e_i)}}{\displaystyle\sum_{i=1}^{n} \dfrac{\alpha_i}{\sigma^2(e_i)}} \tag{22.8}$$

With this set of weights, the contribution of each security to the information ratio of the active portfolio is the square of its *own* information ratio, that is,

$$\left[\frac{\alpha_A}{\sigma(e_A)} \right]^2 = \sum_{i=1}^{n} \left[\frac{\alpha_i}{\sigma(e_i)} \right]^2 \tag{22.9}$$

The model thus reveals the central role of the information ratio in efficiently taking advantage of security analysis. The positive contribution of a security to the portfolio is made by its addition to the nonmarket risk premium (its alpha). Its negative impact is to increase the portfolio variance through its firm-specific risk (residual variance).

In contrast to alpha, the market (systematic) component of the risk premium, $\beta_i E(R_M)$, is offset by the security's nondiversifiable (market) risk, $\beta_i^2 \sigma_M^2$, and both are driven by the same beta. This tradeoff is not unique to any security, as any security with the same beta makes the same balanced contribution to both risk and return. Put differently, the beta of a security is neither vice nor virtue. It is a property that simultaneously affects the risk *and* risk premium of a security. Hence we are concerned only with the aggregate beta of the active portfolio, rather than the beta of each individual security.

We see from equation 22.8 that if a security's alpha is negative, the security will assume a short position in the optimal risky portfolio. If short positions are prohibited, a negative-alpha security would simply be taken out of the optimization program and assigned a portfolio weight of zero. As the number of securities with nonzero alpha values (or the number with positive alphas if short positions are prohibited) increases, the active portfolio will itself be better diversified and its weight in the overall risky portfolio will increase at the expense of the passive index portfolio.

Finally, we note that the index portfolio is an efficient portfolio only if all alpha values are zero. This makes intuitive sense. Unless security analysis reveals that a security has a nonzero alpha, including it in the active portfolio would make the portfolio less attractive. In addition to the security's systematic risk, which is compensated for by the market risk premium (through beta), the security would add its firm-specific risk to portfolio variance. With a zero alpha, however, the latter is not compensated by an addition to the nonmarket risk premium. Hence, if all securities have zero alphas, the optimal weight in the active portfolio will be zero, and the weight in the index portfolio will be 1.0. However, when security analysis uncovers securities with nonmarket risk premiums (nonzero alphas), the index portfolio is no longer efficient.

Summary of Optimization Procedure

Once security analysis is complete, the optimal risky portfolio is formed from the index-model estimates of security and market index parameters using these steps:

1. Compute the initial position of each security in the active portfolio as $w_i^0 = \alpha_i / \sigma^2(e_i)$.

2. Scale those initial positions to force portfolio weights to sum to 1 by dividing by their sum, that is, $w_i = \dfrac{w_i^0}{\displaystyle\sum_{i=1}^{n} w_i^0}$.

3. Compute the alpha of the active portfolio: $\alpha_A = \displaystyle\sum_{i=1}^{n} w_i \alpha_i$.

4. Compute the residual variance of the active portfolio: $\sigma^2(e_A) = \displaystyle\sum_{i=1}^{n} w_i^2 \sigma^2(e_i)$.

5. Compute the initial position in the active portfolio: $w_i^0 = \left[\dfrac{\alpha_A / \sigma^2(e_A)}{E(R_M)/\sigma_M^2}\right]$.

6. Compute the beta of the active portfolio: $\beta_A = \displaystyle\sum_{i=1}^{n} w_i \beta_i$.

7. Adjust the initial position in the active portfolio: $w_A^* = \dfrac{w_A^0}{1 + (1 - \beta_A)w_A^0}$.

8. *Note:* The optimal risky portfolio now has weights: $w_M^* = 1 - w_A^*$; $w_i^* = w_A^* w_i$.

9. Calculate the risk premium of the optimal risky portfolio from the risk premium of the index portfolio and the alpha of the active portfolio: $E(R_P) = (w_M^* + w_A^* \beta_A)E(R_M) + w_A^* \alpha_A$. Notice that the beta of the risky portfolio is $w_M^* + w_A^* \beta_A$ because the beta of the index portfolio is 1.0.

10. Compute the variance of the optimal risky portfolio from the variance of the index portfolio and the residual variance of the active portfolio: $\sigma_P^2 = (w_M^* + w_A^* \beta_A)^2 \sigma_M^2 + [w_M^* \sigma(e_A)]^2$.

An Example

We can illustrate the implementation of the index model by constructing an optimal portfolio from the S&P 500 index and the six stocks in Spreadsheet 22.1.

This example entails only six analyzed stocks, but by virtue of selecting three *pairs* of firms from the same industry with relatively high residual correlations, we put the index model to a severe test. This is because the model ignores the correlation between residuals when producing estimates for the covariance matrix. Therefore, comparison of results from the index model with the full-blown covariance (Markowitz) model should be instructive.

Risk Premium Forecasts   Panel 4 of Spreadsheet 22.1 contains estimates of alpha and the risk premium for each stock. These alphas would be the most important production of the investment company in a real-life procedure. Statistics plays a small role here; in this arena, macro/security analysis is king. In this example, we simply use illustrative values to demonstrate the portfolio construction process and possible results. You may wonder why we have chosen such

EXCEL SPREADSHEET 22.1 ↗

Implementing the index model.

	A	B	C	D	E	F	G	H	I	J
1	Panel 1: Risk Parameters of the Investable Universe (annualized)									
2										
3		SD of excess return	Beta	SD of Systematic component	SD of Residual	Correlation with the S&P 500				
4	S&P 500	0.1358	1.00	0.1358	0	1				
5	HP	0.3817	2.03	0.2762	0.2656	0.72				
6	DELL	0.2901	1.23	0.1672	0.2392	0.58				
7	WMT	0.1935	0.62	0.0841	0.1757	0.43				
8	TARGET	0.2611	1.27	0.1720	0.1981	0.66				
9	BP	0.1822	0.47	0.0634	0.1722	0.35				
10	SHELL	0.1988	0.67	0.0914	0.1780	0.46				
11										
12	Panel 2: Correlation of Residuals									
13										
14		HP	DELL	WMT	TARGET	BP				
15	HP	1								
16	DELL	0.08	1							
17	WMT	−0.34	0.17	1						
18	TARGET	−0.10	0.12	0.50	1					
19	BP	−0.20	−0.28	−0.19	−0.13	1				
20	SHELL	−0.06	−0.19	−0.24	−0.22	0.70				
21										
22	Panel 3: The Index Model Covariance Matrix									
23										
24			S&P 500	HP	DELL	WMT	TARGET	BP	SHELL	
25		Beta	1.00	2.03	1.23	0.62	1.27	0.47	0.67	
26	S&P 500	1.00	0.0184	0.0375	0.0227	0.0114	0.0234	0.0086	0.0124	
27	HP	2.03	0.0375	0.1457	0.0462	0.0232	0.0475	0.0175	0.0253	
28	DELL	1.23	0.0227	0.0462	0.0842	0.0141	0.0288	0.0106	0.0153	
29	WMT	0.62	0.0114	0.0232	0.0141	0.0374	0.0145	0.0053	0.0077	
30	TARGET	1.27	0.0234	0.0475	0.0288	0.0145	0.0682	0.0109	0.0157	
31	BP	0.47	0.0086	0.0175	0.0106	0.0053	0.0109	0.0332	0.0058	
32	SHELL	0.67	0.0124	0.0253	0.0153	0.0077	0.0157	0.0058	0.0395	
33										
34	Cells on the diagonal (shadowed) equal to variance									
35			formula in cell C26	$= B4^{\wedge}2$						
36	Off-diagonal cells equal to covariance									
37			formula in cell C27	$= C\$25^{*}\$B27^{*}\$B\$4^{\wedge}2$						
38			multiplies beta from row and column by index variance							
39										
40	Panel 4: Macro Forecast and Forecasts of Alpha Values									
41										
42										
43		S&P 500	HP	DELL	WMT	TARGET	BP	SHELL		
44	Alpha	0	0.0150	−0.0100	−0.0050	0.0075	0.012	0.0025		
45	Risk premium	0.0600	0.0750	0.1121	0.0689	0.0447	0.0880	0.0305		
46										
47	Panel 5: Computation of the Optimal Risky Portfolio									
48										
49		S&P 500	Active Pf A	HP	DELL	WMT	TARGET	BP	SHELL	Overall Pf
50	$\sigma^2(e)$			0.0705	0.0572	0.0309	0.0392	0.0297	0.0317	
51	$\alpha/\sigma^2(e)$		0.5505	0.2126	−0.1748	−0.1619	0.1911	0.4045	0.0789	
52	$w^0(i)$		1.0000	0.3863	−0.3176	−0.2941	0.3472	0.7349	0.1433	
53	$[w^0(i)]^2$			0.1492	0.1009	0.0865	0.1205	0.5400	0.0205	
54	α_A		0.0222							
55	$\sigma^2(e_A)$		0.0404							
56	w_A^0		0.1691							
57	w^*(Risky portf)	0.8282	0.1718							
58	Beta	1	1.0922	0.0663	−0.0546	−0.0505	0.0596	0.1262	0.0246	1.0158
59	Risk premium	0.06	0.0878	0.0750	0.1121	0.0689	0.0447	0.0880	0.0305	0.0648
60	SD	0.1358	0.2497							0.1422
61	Sharpe Ratio	0.44	0.35							0.46

small, forecast alpha values. The reason is that even when security analysis uncovers a large apparent mispricing, that is, large alpha values, these forecasts must be substantially trimmed to account for the fact that such forecasts are subject to large estimation error. We discuss the important procedure of adjusting actual forecasts in the following section.

The Optimal Risky Portfolio   Panel 5 of Spreadsheet 22.1 displays calculations for the optimal risky portfolio. They follow the summary procedure (you should try to replicate these calculations in your own spreadsheet). In this example we allow short sales. Notice that the weight of each security in the active portfolio (see row 52) has the same sign as the alpha value. Allowing short sales, the positions in the active portfolio are quite large (e.g., the position in BP is .7349); this is an aggressive portfolio. As a result, the alpha of the active portfolio (2.22 percent) is larger than that of any of the individual alpha forecasts. However, this aggressive stance also results in a large residual variance (.0404, which corresponds to a residual standard deviation of 20 percent). Therefore, the position in the active portfolio is scaled down (see equation 22.5) and ends up quite modest (.1718; cell C57), reinforcing the notion that diversification considerations are paramount in the optimal risky portfolio.

The optimal risky portfolio has a risk premium of 6.48 percent, standard deviation of 14.22 percent, and a Sharpe ratio of .46 (cells J58–J61). By comparison, the Sharpe ratio of the index portfolio is .06/.1358 = .44 (cell B61), which is quite close to that of the optimal risky portfolio. The small improvement is a result of the modest alpha forecasts that we used. In Chapter 9 on market efficiency, we demonstrate that such results are common in the mutual fund industry. Of course, a few portfolio managers can and do produce portfolios with better performance.

The interesting question here is the extent to which the index model produces results that are inferior to that of the-full-covariance (Markowitz) model. Figure 22.3 shows the efficient frontiers from the two models with the example data. We find that the difference is in fact small. Table 22.4 compares the compositions and expected performance of the global minimum variance (*G*) and the optimal risky portfolios derived from the two models. The standard deviations of efficient portfolios produced from the Markowitz model and the index model are calculated from the covariance matrixes used in each model. As discussed earlier, we cannot be sure that the covariance estimates from the full covariance model are more accurate than those from the more restrictive single-index model. However, by assuming the full covariance model to be more accurate, we get an idea of how far off the two models can be.

Figure 22.3
Efficient frontiers with the index model and full-covariance matrix.

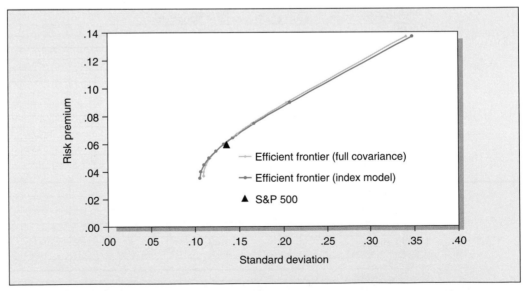

TABLE 22.4

Comparison of Portfolios from Single-Index and Full-Covariance Models

	Global Minimum-Variance Portfolio		Optimal Portfolio	
	Full-Covariance Model	Index Model	Full-Covariance Model	Index Model
Mean	.0371	.0354	.0677	.0649
SD	.1089	.1052	.1471	.1423
Sharpe ratio	.3409	.3370	.4605	.4558
Portfolio Weights				
S&P 500	.88	.83	.75	.83
HP	−.11	−.17	.10	.07
Dell	−.01	−.05	−.04	−.06
WMT	.23	.14	−.03	−.05
Target	−.18	−.08	.10	.06
BP	.22	.20	.25	.13
Shell	−.02	.12	−.12	.03

Figure 22.3 shows that for conservative portfolios (closer to the minimum-variance portfolio G), the index model underestimates the volatility and hence overestimates performance. The reverse happens with portfolios that are riskier than the index, which also include the region near the optimal portfolio. Despite these differences, what stands out from this comparison is that the outputs of the two models are in fact extremely similar, with the index model perhaps calling for a more conservative position. This is where we would like to be with a model relying on approximations.

22.6 THE BLACK-LITTERMAN MODEL

Fischer Black, famous not only for the Black-Scholes option-pricing formula but also for the Treynor-Black model, teamed up with Robert Litterman to produce a truly elegant model that allows portfolio managers to quantify complex forecasts (which they call *views*) and apply them to portfolio construction.[11] We begin the discussion of the BL model with an illustration of a simple problem of asset allocation. Although we devote the next section to a comparison of the two models, some comments on commonalities of the models will help us better understand the BL model.

A Black-Litterman Asset Allocation Decision

Consider a portfolio manager labouring over **asset allocation** to bills, bonds, and stocks for the next month. The risky portfolio will be constructed from bonds and stocks so as to maximize the Sharpe ratio. So far this is no more than the problem described in Section 6.3 of Chapter 6. There, we were concerned with optimizing the portfolio given a set of data inputs. In real life, however, optimization using a given data set is the least of the manager's problems. The real issue that dogs any portfolio manager is how to come by that input data. Black and Litterman propose an approach that uses past data, equilibrium considerations, and the private views of the portfolio manager about the near future.

Data enter the BL model from two sources: history and forecasts, called *views*, about the future. The historical sample is used to estimate the covariance matrix of the asset classes involved in the asset allocation decision. That estimated covariance matrix, combined with a model of equilibrium returns (e.g., the CAPM) is used to produce baseline forecasts that would be the basis of a passive strategy. In the next step, views are introduced and quantified. The views

[11]Fischer Black and Robert Litterman, "Global Portfolio Optimization," *Financial Analysts Journal*, September/October 1992. Originally published by Goldman Sachs Company, © 1991.

represent a departure from the baseline forecast and result in a revised set of expected returns. With the new set of inputs (just as with alpha forecasts in the Treynor-Black model), an optimal risky portfolio is designed to replace the (no-longer-efficient) passive portfolio.

A Five-Step Process

Step 1: Creation of the Covariance Matrix from Historical Data   This straightforward task is the first in the chain that makes up the BL model. Suppose step 1 results in the following covariance matrix, estimated from recent historical excess returns:

	Bonds (B)	Stocks (S)
Standard deviation	.08	.17
Correlation (bonds/stocks)	.3	
Covariance:		
Bonds	.0064	.00408
Stocks	.00408	.0289

Notice that step 1 is common to both the BL and the Treynor-Black (TB) model. This activity appears in the organizational chart in Figure 22A.4 in Appendix A to this chapter.

Step 2: Determination of a Baseline Forecast   Since past data are of such limited use in inferring expected returns for the next month, BL propose an alternative approach. They start with a baseline forecast derived from the assumption that the market is in equilibrium where current prices of stocks and bonds reflect all available information and, as a result, the theoretical market portfolio with weights equal to market-value proportions is efficient. Suppose that current market values of outstanding bonds and stocks imply that the weight of bonds in the baseline portfolio is $w_B = .25$, and the weight of stocks is $w_S = .75$. When we apply these portfolio weights to the covariance matrix from step 1, the variance of the baseline portfolio emerges as

$$\text{Var}(R_M) = w_B^2\text{Var}(R_B) + w_S^2\text{Var}(R_S) + 2w_Bw_S\text{Cov}(R_B, R_S)$$
$$= .25^2 \times .0064 + .75^2 \times .0289 + 2 \times .25 \times .75 \times .00408 = .018186$$

The CAPM equation (equation 7.2 in Chapter 7) gives the relationship between the market portfolio risk (variance) and its risk premium (expected excess return) as

$$E(R_M) = \overline{A} \times \text{Var}(R_M) \tag{22.10}$$

where $\overline{A}$ is the average coefficient of risk aversion. Assuming $\overline{A} = 3$ yields the equilibrium risk premium of the baseline portfolio as

$$E(R_M) = 3 \times .018186 = .0546 = 5.46\%$$

The equilibrium risk premiums on bonds and stocks can be inferred from their betas on the baseline portfolio:

$$ER_B = \frac{\text{Cov}(R_B, R_M)}{\text{Var}(R_M)}E(R_M)$$

$$\text{Cov}(R_B, R_M) = \text{Cov}(R_B, w_BR_B + w_SR_S) = .25 \times .0064 + .75 \times .00408 = .00466$$

$$E(R_B) = \frac{.00466}{.018186} \times 5.46\% = 1.40\% \text{ (bond beta } = .26)$$

$$E(R_S) = \frac{.75 \times .0289 + .25 \times .00408}{.018186} \times 5.46\% = 6.81\% \text{ (stock beta } = 1.25)$$

Thus, step 2 ends up with baseline forecasts of a risk premium for bonds of 1.40 percent and for stocks of 6.81 percent.

The final element in step 2 is to determine the covariance matrix of the baseline forecasts. This is a statement about the *precision* of these forecasts, which is different from the covariance matrix of realized excess returns on the bond and stock portfolios. We are looking for the precision of the *estimate* of expected return, as opposed the volatility of the actual returns. A conventional rule of thumb in this application is to use a standard deviation that is 10 percent of the standard deviation of returns (or equivalently, a variance that is 1 percent of the return variance). Imagine that the covariance matrix of actual returns was estimated from the returns of the last 100 months. The variance of the average return (which is the forecast of the expected return) would then be 1 percent of the variance of the actual return. Hence in this case it would be correct to use .01 times the covariance matrix of returns for the expected return. Thus step 2 ends with a forecast and covariance matrix shown as follows.

	Bonds (B)	Stocks (S)
Expected return (%)	.0140	.0681
Covariance matrix of baseline forecasts:		
Bonds	.000064	.0000408
Stocks	.0000408	.000289

Now that we have backed out market expectations, it is time to integrate the manager's private views into our analysis.

Step 3: Integration of the Manager's Private Views   The BL model allows the manager to introduce any number of views about the baseline forecasts into the optimization process. Appended to the views is the manager's degree of confidence in each. Views in the BL model are expressed as values of various linear combinations of excess returns, and the confidence in them as a covariance matrix of errors in these values.

EXAMPLE 22.3   **Views in the Black-Litterman Model**

Suppose the manager takes a contrarian view concerning the baseline forecasts; that is, he believes that in the next month bonds will outperform stocks by .5 percent. The following equation expresses this:

$$1 \times R_B + (-1) \times R_S = .5\%$$

More generally, any view that is a linear combination of the relevant excess returns can be presented as an array (in Excel, an array would be a column of numbers) that multiplies another array (column) of excess returns. In this case, the array of weights is $P = (1, -1)$ and the array of excess returns is (R_B, R_S). The value of this linear combination, denoted Q, that reflects the manager's view, in this case .5 percent, must be taken into account in optimizing the portfolio.[12]

---

[12]A simpler view that, say, bonds will return 3 percent is also legitimate. In that case $P = (1, 0)$ and the view is really like an alpha forecast in the Treynor-Black model. If all views were like this simple one, there would be no difference between the TB and BL models.

A view must come with a degree of confidence, that is, a standard deviation to measure the precision of Q. The manager's view is really $Q + \varepsilon$, where ε represents zero-mean error in the view with a standard deviation that reflects the manager's less than perfect confidence. Noticing that the standard deviation of the difference between the expected rates on stocks and bonds is 1.65 percent (calculated below), suppose that the manager assigns a value of $\sigma(\varepsilon) = 1.73$ percent.[13] To summarize, if we denote the array of returns by $R = (R_B, R_S)$, then the manager's view, P, applied to these returns is[14]

$$PR' = Q + \varepsilon$$
$$P = (1, -1)$$
$$R = (R_B, R_S)$$
$$Q = .5\% = .005$$
$$\sigma^2(\varepsilon) = .0173^2 = .0003$$

Step 4: Revised (Posterior) Expectations The baseline forecasts of expected returns derived from market values and their covariance matrix make up the prior distribution of the rates of return on bonds and stocks. The manager's view, together with its confidence measure, provides the probability distribution arising from the "experiment," that is, the additional information that must be optimally integrated with the prior distribution. The result is the posterior: a new set of expected returns, conditioned on the manager's views.

To acquire intuition about the solution, consider what the baseline expected returns imply about the view. The expectations derived from market data were that the expected return on bonds is 1.40 percent and on stocks 6.81 percent. Therefore, the baseline view is that $E(R_B) - E(R_S) = 5.41$ percent. In contrast, the manager thinks this difference is $Q = R_B - R_S = .5$ percent. Using the BL linear-equation notation for market expectations:

$$Q^E = PR_E^T$$
$$P = (1, -1)$$
$$R = [E(R_B), E(R_S)] = (1.40\%, 6.81\%)$$
$$Q^E = 1.40 - 6.81 = -5.41\%$$

Thus, the baseline "view" is -5.41 percent (i.e., stocks will outperform bonds), which is vastly different from the manager's view. The difference, D, and its variance are

$$D = Q - Q^E = .005 - (-.0541) = .0591$$
$$\sigma^2(D) = \sigma^2(\varepsilon) + \sigma^2(Q^E) = .0003 + \sigma^2(Q^E)$$
$$\sigma^2(Q^E) = \mathrm{Var}[E(R_B) - E(R_S)] = \sigma^2_{E(R_B)} + \sigma^2_{E(R_S)} - 2\mathrm{Cov}[E(R_B), E(R_S)]$$
$$= .000064 + .000289 - 2 \times .0000408 = .0002714$$
$$\sigma^2(D) = .0003 + .0002714 = .0005714$$

Given the large difference between the manager's and the baseline views, we expect a significant change in the conditional expected returns from those of the baseline and, as result, a very different optimal portfolio.

---

[13]Absent specific information shedding light on the SD of the view, for example the track record of the source of the view, the SD calculated from the covariance matrix of the baseline forecasts is commonly used. In that case, the SD would be that of Q^E in the equation above: $\sigma(Q^E) = \sqrt{.0002714} = .0165$ (1.65 percent).

[14]Notice that the view is expressed as a line vector with as many elements as there are risky assets (here, two) applied to the line vector of returns. The manager's view (Q) is obtained from the vector, P, marking the assets included in the view, times their actual returns. We denote the return line vector, R, with a superscript "T" (for transpose—turning a row vector into a column), and therefore compute the "sumproduct" of the two vectors.

The expected returns conditional on the view are a function of four elements: the baseline expectations, $E(R)$; the difference, D, between the manager's view and the baseline view (see equation above); the contribution of the asset return to the variance of D; and the total variance of D. The result is

$$E(R|\text{View}) = R + D\left(\frac{\text{Contribution of asset to } \sigma_D^2}{\sigma_D^2}\right)$$

$$E(R_B|P) = E(R_B) + \frac{D\{\sigma_{E(R_B)}^2 - \text{Cov}[E(R_B), E(R_S)]\}}{\sigma_D^2}$$

$$= .0140 + \frac{.0591(.000064 - .0000408)}{.0005714} = .0140 + .0024 = .0164$$

$$E(R_S|P) = E(R_S) + \frac{D\{\text{Cov}[E(R_B), E(R_S)]\sigma_{E(R_S)}^2\}}{\sigma_D^2}$$

$$= .0681 + \frac{.0591(.0000408 - .000289)}{.0005714} = .0681 - .0257 = .0424$$

We see that the manager increases expected returns on bonds by .24 percent to 1.64 percent, and reduces expected return on stocks by 2.57 percent to 4.24 percent. The difference between the expected returns on stocks and bonds is reduced from 5.41 percent to 2.60 percent. While this is a very large change, we also realize that the manager's private view that $Q = .5$ percent has been greatly tempered by the prior distribution to a value roughly halfway between the private view and the baseline view. In general, the degree of compromise between the views will depend on the precision assigned to them.

The example we have described contains only two assets and one view. It can easily be generalized to any number of assets with any number of views about future returns. The views can be more complex than a simple difference between a pair of returns. Views can assign a value to *any* linear combination of the assets in the universe, and the confidence level (the covariance matrix of the set of ε values of the views) can allow for dependence across views. This flexibility gives the model great potential by quantifying a rich set of information that is unique to a portfolio manager. Appendix 22B to this chapter presents the general BL model.

Step 5: Portfolio Optimization
At this point, the portfolio optimization follows the Markowitz procedure of Chapter 6, with an input list that replaces baseline expectations with the conditional expectations arising from the manager's view.

Spreadsheet 22.2 presents the calculations of the BL model. Table 1 of the spreadsheet shows the calculation of the benchmark forecasts and Table 2 incorporates a view to arrive at the revised (conditional) expectations. Figure 22.4 shows portfolio performance measured by M-squared for various levels of confidence in the view when the view is correct and incorrect. The weight in bonds declines as the confidence in the view falls (the SD of the view increases). With no confidence in the view (SD very large), the weight in bonds falls to .3, determined by the baseline forecast. At this point, the portfolio is passive; its M-squared is zero.

Notice that the M-squared profile is asymmetric. With great confidence in the view and the resultant large position in bonds, the gain in M-squared when the view is correct is smaller than the loss in M-squared when the view is incorrect. With less confidence and therefore a smaller position in bonds, the "game" becomes more symmetric between a correct and incorrect view. Since determination of the SD of a view is quite abstract, the graph tells us that to err on the side of skepticism may well be the prudent choice.

EXCEL SPREADSHEET 22.2 ↗

Sensitivity of the Black-Litterman portfolio to confidence in views.

	A	B	C	D	E	F	G	H	I
1									
2									
3									
4	Table 1: Bordered Covariance Matrix Based on Historical Excess Returns								
5	and Market-Value Weights and Calculation of Baseline Forecasts								
6									
7			Bonds	Stocks					
8		Weights	0.25	0.75					
9	Bonds	0.25	0.006400	0.004080					
10	Stocks	0.75	0.004080	0.028900					
11		sumproduct	0.001165	0.017021					
12	Market portfolio variance V(M) = sum(c11:d11) =					0.018186			
13	Coefficient of risk aversion of representative investor =					3			
14	Baseline market portfolio risk premium = A V(M) =					0.0546			
15	Covariance with R_M		0.00466	0.022695					
16	Baseline risk premiums		0.01	0.07					
17									
18	Proportion of covariance attributed to expected returns:					0.01			
19	Covariance matrix of expected returns								
20			Bonds	Stocks					
21		Bonds	0.000064	0.0000408					
22		Stocks	0.0000408	0.000289					
23									
24	Table 2: Views, Confidence and Revised (Posterior) Expectations								
25									
26	View: Difference between returns on bonds and stocks, Q =					0.0050			
27	View embedded in baseline forecasts Q^E =					−0.0541			
28	Variance of Q^E = Var(R_B − R_S)					0.000271			
29	Var[E(R_B)] − Cov[E(R_B),E(R_S)] =					0.000023			
30	Cov[E(R_B),E(R_S)] − Var[E(R_B)] =					−0.000248			
31	Difference between view and baseline data, D =					0.0591			
32	Confidence measured by standard deviation of view Q								
33	Possible SD	0	0.0100	0.0173	0.0300	0.0600			
34	Variance	0	0.0015	0.0003	0.0009	0.0036	Baseline		
35	E(R_B|P)	0.0190	0.0148	0.0164	0.0152	0.0143	0.0140		
36	E(R_S|P)	0.0140	0.0598	0.0424	0.0556	0.0643	0.0681		

Figure 22.4

Sensitivity of Black-Litterman portfolio performance to confidence level.

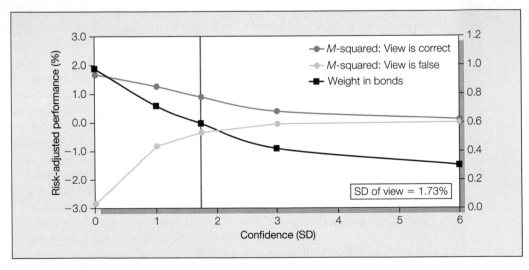

22.7

THE TWO MODELS: COMPLEMENTS, NOT SUBSTITUTES

Treynor, Black, and Litterman have earned a place among the important innovators of the investments industry. Wide implementation of their models might contribute much to the industry. The comparative analysis of their models presented here is not aimed at elevating one at the expense of the other—in any case, we find them complementary—but rather to clarify the relative merits of each.

First and foremost, once you reach the optimization stage, the models are identical. Put differently, if users of either model arrive at identical input lists, they will choose identical portfolios and realize identical performance measures. In Section 22.8, we show that these levels of performance should be far superior to passive strategies, as well as to active strategies that do not take advantage of the quantitative techniques of these models. The models differ primarily in the way they arrive at the input list, and analysis of these differences shows that the models are true complements and are best used in tandem.

Enhancement or Replacement of TB by BL

The Treynor-Black (TB) model is really oriented to individual security analysis. This can be seen from the way the active portfolio is constructed. The alpha values assigned to securities must be determined relative to the passive portfolio. This portfolio is the one that would be held if all alpha values turned out to be zero. Now suppose an investment company prospectus mandates a portfolio invested 70 percent in a U.S. universe of large stocks, say the S&P 500, and 30 percent in a well-defined universe of large European stocks. In that case, the macro analysis of the organization would have to be split, and the TB model would have to be run as two separate divisions. In each division, security analysts would compile values of alpha relative to their own passive portfolio. The product of this organization would thus include four portfolios, two passive and two active. But this scheme might prove to be unworkable, as the parameters relevant to portfolio construction (such as alpha, beta, or residual return) make sense only when computed relative to a common market index, not different benchmarks for different securities. Thus, the U.S. and European portfolios would first be *separately* optimized, and the final portfolio would be constructed as an asset allocation problem.

The resulting portfolio could be improved using the BL approach. First, views about the relative performance of the U.S. and European markets can be expected to add information to the independent macro forecasts for the two economies. For reasons of specialization, the U.S. and European macro analysts must focus on their respective economies; there is no way for them to incorporate a variable that explicitly represents a view about the relative performance of the two economies. Obviously, when more country or regional portfolios are added to the company's universe, the need for decentralization becomes more compelling, and the potential of applying the BL model to the TB product greater. Moreover, the foreign-stock portfolios will result in various positions in local currencies. This is a clear area of international finance, and the only way to import forecasts from this analysis is with the BL technique.[15]

So Why Not Replace TB with BL? This question is raised by the need to use the BL technique if the overall portfolio is to include forecasts from comparative economic and international finance analyses. It is indeed possible to use the BL model for the entire process of constructing the efficient portfolio. The reason is that the alpha compiled for the TB model can be replaced with BL views. To take a simple example, suppose only one security makes up the active portfolio. With the TB model, we have macro forecasts, $E(R_M)$ and σ_M, as well as alpha, beta, and

---

[15]The BL model can also be used to introduce views about relative performance of various U.S. and foreign corporations.

residual variance for the active portfolio. This input list also can be represented in the following form, along the lines of the BL framework:

$$R = [E(R_M), E(R_A) = \beta_A E(R_M)]$$
$$P = [0, 1 + \alpha_A/(\beta_A E(R_M))]$$
$$PR' = Q + \varepsilon = \alpha_A + \varepsilon$$
$$Q_E = 0$$
$$D = \alpha_A$$
$$\sigma^2(\varepsilon) = \text{Var(Forecasting error) in equation 22A.6}$$
$$\sigma^2(D) = \sigma_2(\varepsilon) + \sigma_2(e)$$

In this light, the BL model can be viewed as a generalization of the TB model. The BL model allows you to adjust expected return from views about alpha values as in the TB model, but it also allows you to express views about *relative* performance that cannot be incorporated in the TB model.

However, this conclusion might produce a false impression that is consequential to investment management. To understand the point, we first discuss the degree of confidence, which is essential to fully represent a view in the BL model. Spreadsheet 22.2 and Figure 22.4 illustrate that the optimal portfolio weights and performance are highly sensitive to the degree of confidence in the BL views. Thus, the validity of the model rests in large part on the way the confidence about views is arrived at.

When a BL view is structured to replace a direct alpha estimate in a TB framework, we must use the variance of the forecasting error of alpha. This is how "confidence" is quantified in the BL model. Whereas in the TB framework one can measure forecast accuracy by computing the correlation between analysts' alpha forecasts and subsequent realizations, such a procedure is not as easily applied to BL views about relative performance. Managers' views may be expressed about different quantities in different time periods, and, therefore, we will not have long forecast histories on a particular variable with which to assess accuracy. To our knowledge, no promotion of any kind of how to quantify "confidence" appears in academic or industry publications about the BL model.

This raises the issue of adjusting forecasts in the TB model. We have never seen evidence that analysts' track records are systematically compiled and used to adjust alpha forecasts, although we cannot assert that such effort is nowhere expended. However, indirect evidence confirms the impression that alphas are usually not adjusted, specifically, the common "complaint" that the TB model is not applied in the field because it results in "wild" portfolio weights. Yet it is known that those wild portfolio weights are a consequence of failing to adjust alpha values to reflect forecast precision. Any realistic *R*-squared that can be obtained even by excellent forecasters will result in moderate portfolio weights. Even when "wild" weights do occasionally materialize, they can be "tamed" by a straightforward restriction on benchmark risk.

It is therefore useful to keep the two models separate and distinct; the TB model for the management of security analysis with proper adjustment of forecasts and the BL model for asset allocation where views about relative performance are useful *despite* the fact that the degree of confidence must in practice be inaccurately estimated.

22.8 THE VALUE OF ACTIVE MANAGEMENT

We showed in Chapter 21 that the value of successful market timing is enormous. Even a forecaster with far-from-perfect predictive power would contribute significant value. Nevertheless, active portfolio management based on security analysis has even far greater potential. Even if each individual security analyst has only modest forecasting power, the power of a *portfolio* of analysts is potentially unbounded.

The value of market timing was derived from the value of an equivalent number of call options that mimic the return to the timer's portfolio. Thus, we were able to derive an unambiguous market value to timing ability; that is, we could price the implicit call in the timer's services. We cannot get quite that far with valuation of active portfolio management, but we can do the next best thing: calculate what a representative investor would pay for such services.

The Contribution of the Information Ratio

Kane, Marcus, and Trippi[16] derive an annuitized value of portfolio performance measured as a percent of funds under management. The percentage fee, f, that investors would be willing to pay for active services can be related to the difference between the square of the portfolio Sharpe ratio and that of the passive portfolio as

$$f = (S_P^2 - S_M^2)/2A \tag{22.11}$$

where A is the coefficient of the investor's risk aversion.

The source of the power of the active portfolio is the additive value of the squared information ratios (information ratio $= \frac{\alpha_i}{\sigma(e_i)}$ and precision of individual analysts. Recall the expression for the square of the Sharpe ratio of the optimized risky portfolio:

$$S_P^2 = S_M^2 + \sum_{i=1}^{n} \left[\frac{\alpha}{\sigma(e_i)} \right]^2$$

Therefore,

$$f = \frac{1}{2A} \sum_{i=1}^{n} \left[\frac{\alpha_i}{\sigma(e_i)} \right]^2 \tag{22.12}$$

Thus, the fee that can be charged, f, depends on three factors: (1) the coefficient of risk aversion, (2) the distribution of the squared information ratio in the universe of securities, and (3) the precision of the security analysts. Notice that this fee is in excess of what an index fund would charge. If an index fund charges about 30 basis points, the active manager could charge incremental fees above that level by the percentage given in the equation above.

Kane, Marcus, and Trippi investigated the distribution of the squared IR for all S&P 500 stocks over two five-year periods and estimated that this (annualized) expectation, $E(IR_2)$, is in the range of .845 to 1.122. With a coefficient of risk aversion of 3, a portfolio manager who covers 100 stocks with security analysts whose R-squared of forecasts with realized alpha is only .001 would still be able to charge an annual fee that is 4.88 percent higher than that of an index fund. This fee is based on the lower end of the range of the expected squared information ratio.

One limitation of this study is that it assumes that the portfolio manager knows the quality of the forecasts, however low they may be. As we have seen, portfolio weights are sensitive to forecast quality, and when that quality is estimated with error, performance will be further reduced.

The Performance of Alternative Forecasts

A study of actual forecasts by Kane, Kim, and White (see footnote 21 in Appendix 22A to this chapter) found the distribution of over 11,000 alpha forecasts for over 600 stocks over 37 months presented in Figure 22A.3. The average forecast precision from this database of forecasts provided an R-squared of .00108 using ordinary least squares (OLS) regressions and .00151 when allowing separate coefficients for positive and negative forecasts. These are only marginally better than the precision used to interpret the Kane, Marcus, and Trippi study of the distribution of realized information value. Kane, Kim, and White use these R-squareds to adjust the forecasts in their database and form optimal portfolios from 105 stocks selected randomly from the 646 covered by the investment company.

Kane, Kim, and White assume that forecast quality is the same each month for all alpha forecasts for the 105 stocks, but act as though they do not know that quality. Thus, the adjustment

---

[16]Alex Kane, Alan Marcus, and Robert R. Trippi, "The Valuation of Security Analysis," *Journal of Portfolio Management* 25 (Spring 1999).

TABLE 22.5

M-Squared for
the Portfolio,
Actual Forecasts

Forecast Adjustment	Diagonal Model	Covariance Model
Line*	2.67	3.01
Kinked†	4.25	6.31

*Same coefficients for positive and negative forecasts.
†Different coefficients for positive and negative forecasts.

TABLE 22.6

M-Squared of
Simulated
Portfolios

Stocks in Portfolio	Forecast Record (months)		
	36	48	60
100	.96	3.12	6.36
300	.60	5.88	12.72
500	3.00	5.88	15.12

process is performed each month by using past forecasts. This introduces another source of estimation error that compounds the difficulty of low forecast quality. To dull the impact of this real-life difficulty, the estimation of forecast quality adopts improved econometric technique. They find that least absolute deviation (LAD) regressions perform uniformly better than OLS regressions. The optimization model used both the diagonal index model (as in TB) as well as the full-covariance model (the Markowitz algorithm).

The annualized *M*-squared measures of performance are shown in Table 22.5. The *M*-squared values, which range from 2.67 to 6.31 percent, are quite impressive. The results in the table also show that using the residual covariance matrix can significantly improve performance when many stocks are covered, contrary to the small difference when only six stocks are covered, as in Spreadsheet 22.1.

To investigate the role of the forecasting record in performance with low-quality forecasts, Kane, Kim, and White simulate a market with the S&P 500 index portfolio as benchmark and 500 stocks with the same characteristics as the S&P 500 universe.[17] Various sizes of active portfolios are constructed by selecting stocks randomly from this universe with available forecasting records of only 36 to 60 months. To avoid estimation techniques that may not be available to portfolio managers, all estimates in this study are obtained from OLS regressions.

The portfolio manager in the simulation must deploy a full-blown "organizational structure" to capture performance under realistic conditions. At any point, the manager uses only past returns and past forecast records to produce forward-looking estimates which include (1) the benchmark risk premium and standard deviation, (2) beta coefficients for the stocks in the active portfolio, and (3) the forecasting quality of each security analyst. At this point, the manager receives a set of alpha forecasts from the security analysts and proceeds to construct the optimal portfolio. The portfolio is optimized on the basis of macro forecasts for the benchmark portfolio, and alpha forecasts adjusted for quality using the past record of performance for each analyst. Finally, the next month returns are simulated and the performance of the portfolio is recorded.

Table 22.6 summarizes the results for portfolios when, unbeknownst to the portfolio manager, security-analyst forecasts are generated with an *R*-squared of .001. *M*-squared clearly increases when performance records are longer. The results also show that, in general, performance improves with the size of the portfolio.

---

[17]Alex Kane, Tae-Hwan Kim, and Halbert White, "Forecast Precision and Portfolio Performance," UCSD working paper, University of California–San Diego, April 2006.

The results of all three studies show that even the smallest forecast ability can result in greatly improved performance. Moreover, with better estimation techniques, performance can be further enhanced. We believe that one reason the proposed procedures are not widely used in the industry is that security analysts believe that low individual correlations imply low aggregate forecasting value and thus wish to avoid the estimation of their abilities. We hope that results of studies of the type discussed here will lure investment companies to adopt these techniques and move the industry to new levels of performance.

SUMMARY

1. Indexing represents the adoption of a passive strategy with respect to the asset class; it is achieved by purchase of a proxy to the market such as an index mutual fund or an exchange-traded index security.

2. Hedging requires investors to purchase assets that will offset the sensitivity of their portfolios to particular sources of risk. A hedged position requires that the hedging vehicle provide profits that vary inversely with the value of the position to be protected.

3. The hedge ratio is the number of hedging vehicles such as futures contracts required to offset the risk of the unprotected position. The hedge ratio for systematic market risk is proportional to the size and beta of the underlying stock portfolio. The hedge ratio for fixed-income portfolios is proportional to the price value of a basis point, which in turn is proportional to modified duration and the size of the portfolio.

4. Asset allocation refers to the proportions of capital invested in the three asset classes of stocks, bonds, and cash.

5. Passive asset allocation corresponds to a stable investment in the baseline allocation that suits an investor's risk preferences; in contrast, active asset allocation occurs when adjustments to the baseline position are adopted in response to macroeconomic forecasts.

6. The Treynor-Black security selection model envisions that a macroeconomic forecast for market performance is available and that security analysts estimate abnormal expected rates of return, α, for various securities. Alpha is the expected rate of return on a security beyond that explained by its beta and the security market line. In the Treynor-Black model, the weight of each analyzed security is proportional to the ratio of its alpha to its nonsystematic risk, $\sigma^2(e)$.

7. Once the active portfolio is constructed, its alpha value, nonsystematic risk, and beta can be determined from the properties of the component securities. The optimal risky portfolio, P, is then constructed by holding a position in the active portfolio according to the ratio of α_P to $\sigma^2(e_P)$, divided by the analogous ratio for the market index portfolio. Finally, this position is adjusted by the beta of the active portfolio.

8. When the overall risky portfolio is constructed using the optimal proportions of the active portfolio and passive portfolio, its performance, as measured by the square of Sharpe's measure, is improved (over that of the passive, market index portfolio) by the amount $[\alpha_A/\sigma(e_A)]^2$.

9. The contribution of each security to the overall improvement in the performance of the active portfolio is determined by its degree of mispricing and nonsystematic risk. The contribution of each security to portfolio performance equals $[\alpha_i/\sigma(e_i)]^2$, so that for the optimal risky portfolio,

$$S_P^2 = \left[\frac{E(r_M) - r_f}{\sigma_M}\right]^2 + \sum_{i=1}^{n}\left[\frac{\alpha_i}{\sigma(e_i)}\right]^2$$

10. The Black-Litterman model allows the private views of the portfolio manager to be incorporated with market data in the optimization procedure.

11. The Treynor-Black and Black-Litterman models are complementary tools. Both should be used: the TB model is more geared toward security analysis, while the BL model more naturally fits asset allocation problems.

12. Even low-quality forecasts are valuable. Imperceptible R-squareds of only .001 in regressions of realizations on analysts' forecasts can be used to substantially improve portfolio performance.

KEY EQUATIONS

(22.1)　$E(R_i) = \alpha_i + \beta_i E(R_M)$

(22.2)　$\text{Cov}(r_i, r_j) = \beta_i \beta_j \sigma_M^2$

(22.3)　$\alpha_P = \sum_{i1}^{n1} w_i \alpha_i$　　　；　for the index $\alpha_{n+1} = \alpha_M = 0$

$\beta_P = \sum_{i=1}^{n1} w_i \beta_i$　　　；　for the index $\beta_{n+1} = \beta_M = 1$

$\sigma^2(e_P) = \sum_{i=1}^{n1} w_i^2 \sigma^2(e_i);$　for the index $\sigma^2(e_{n+1}) = \sigma^2(e_M) = 0$

(22.4)　$E(R_P) = \alpha_P + E(R_M)\beta_P = \sum_{i=1}^{n1} w_i \alpha_i + E(R_M) \sum_{i=1}^{n1} w_i \beta_i$

$\sigma_P = [\beta_P^2 \sigma_M^2 + \sigma^2(e_P)^{1/2}] = \left[\sigma_M^2 \left(\sum_{i=1}^{n+1} w_i \beta_i \right)^2 + \sum_{i=1}^{n+1} w_i^2 \sigma^2(e_i) \right]^{1/2}$

$S_P = \dfrac{E(R_P)}{\sigma_P}$

(22.5)　$w_A^0 = \left[\dfrac{\dfrac{\alpha_A}{\sigma^2(e_A)}}{\dfrac{E(R_M)}{\alpha_M^2}} \right]$

(22.6)　$w_A^* = \dfrac{w_A^0}{1 + (1 - \beta_A)w_A^0}$

(22.7)　$S_P^2 = S_M^2 + \left[\dfrac{\alpha_A}{\sigma(e_A)} \right]^2$

(22.8)　$w_A^0 = \dfrac{\dfrac{\alpha_i}{\sigma^2(e_i)}}{\sum_{i=1}^{n} \dfrac{\alpha_i}{\sigma^2(e_i)}}$

(22.9)　$\left[\dfrac{\alpha_A}{\sigma(e_A)} \right]^2 = \sum_{i=1}^{n} \left[\dfrac{\alpha_i}{\sigma(e_i)} \right]^2$

(22.10)　$E(R_M) = \bar{A} \times \text{Var}(R_M)$

(22.11)　$f = (S_P^2 - S_M^2)/2A$

(22.12)　$f = \dfrac{1}{2A} \sum_{i=1}^{n} \left[\dfrac{\alpha_i}{\sigma(e_i)} \right]^2$

PROBLEMS

Mc Graw Hill Education **connect**™ **Practise and learn online with Connect.**

1. What is the least-risky asset for each of the following investors?

   a. A person investing for her three-year-old child's college tuition.

   b. A defined-benefit pension fund with benefit obligations that have an average duration of 10 years. The benefits are not inflation-protected.

   c. A defined-benefit pension fund with benefit obligations that have an average duration of 10 years. The benefits are inflation-protected.

2. Your client says, "With the unrealized gains in my portfolio, I have almost saved enough money for my daughter to go to college in eight years, but educational costs keep going up." On the basis of this statement alone, which of the following looks least important to your client's investment policy?

   a. Time horizon

   b. Purchasing power risk

   c. Liquidity

   d. Taxes

3. Your neighbour has heard that you have successfully completed a course in investments and comes for your advice. She and her husband are both 50 years old. They have just finished making their last payments on their condominium and for their children's college education, and are planning for retirement. What advice on investing their retirement savings would you give them? If they are very risk-averse, what would you advise in that case?

4. What are the implications of placing your entire equity portfolio in iUnits, or some management company's index mutual fund?

5. How would the application of the BL model to a stock and bond portfolio (as the example in the text) affect security analysis? What does this suggest about the hierarchy of use of the BL and TB models?

6. A manager is holding a $1 million stock portfolio with a beta of 1.25. She would like to hedge the risk of the portfolio using the S&P/TSX 60 stock index futures contract. How many dollars' worth of the index should she sell in the futures market to minimize the volatility of her position?

7. A manager is holding a $1 million bond portfolio with a modified duration of eight years. She would like to hedge the risk of the portfolio by short-selling Canada bonds. The modified duration of Canadas is 10 years. How many dollars' worth of Canadas should she sell to minimize the variance of her position?

8. Yields on short-term bonds tend to be more volatile than yields on long-term bonds. Suppose that you have estimated that the yield on 20-year bonds changes by 10 basis points for every 15-basis-point move in the yield on 5-year bonds. You hold a $1 million portfolio of 5-year-maturity bonds with modified duration 4 years and desire to hedge your interest rate exposure with Canada bond futures, which currently have modified duration nine years and sell at $F_0 = \$95$. How many futures contracts should you sell?

9. You hold an $8 million stock portfolio with a beta of 1.0. You believe that the risk-adjusted abnormal return on the portfolio (the alpha) over the next three months is 2 percent. The S&P/TSX 60 index currently is at 800 and the risk-free rate is 1 percent per quarter.

   a. What will be the futures price on the three-month maturity S&P/TSX 60 futures contract?

   b. How many S&P/TSX 60 futures contracts are needed to hedge the stock portfolio?

   c. What will be the profit on that futures position in three months as a function of the value of the S&P/TSX 60 index on the maturity date?

   d. If the alpha of the portfolio is 2 percent, show that the expected rate of return (in decimal form) on the portfolio as a function of the market return is $r_p = .03 + 1.0 \times (r_M - .01)$.

   e. Let S_T be the value of the index in three months. Then $S_T/S_0 = S_T/800 = 1 + r_M$. (We are ignoring dividends here to keep things simple.) Substitute this expression in the equation for the portfolio return, r_p, and calculate the expected value of the hedged (stock-plus-futures) portfolio in three months as a function of the value of the index.

   f. Show that the hedged portfolio provides an expected rate of return of 3 percent over the next three months.

   g. What is the beta of the hedged portfolio? What is the alpha of the hedged portfolio?

10. Suppose that the relationship between the rate of return on IBM stock, the market index, and a computer industry index can be described by the following regression equation: $r_{IBM} = .5r_M + .75r_{industry}$. If a futures contract on the computer industry is traded, how would you hedge the exposure to the systematic and industry factors affecting the performance of IBM stock? How many dollars' worth of the market and industry index contracts would you buy or sell for each dollar held in IBM?

11. BMO Nesbitt believes that market volatility will be 20 percent annually for the next three years. Three-year at-the-money call and put options on the market index sell at an implied volatility of 22 percent. What options portfolio can BMO Nesbitt establish to speculate on its volatility belief without taking a bullish or bearish position on the market? Using BMO Nesbitt's estimate of volatility, three-year at-the-money options have $N(d_1) = .6$.

12. Suppose that Scotia Capital sells call options on $1.25 million worth of a stock portfolio with beta $= 1.5$. The option delta is .8. It wishes to hedge out its resultant exposure to a market advance by buying market index futures contracts. If the current value of the market index is 1,000 and the contract multiplier is $250, how many contracts should it buy?

13. A portfolio manager summarizes the input from the macro and micro forecasters in the following tables:

Micro Forecasts

Asset	Expected Return (%)	Beta	Residual Standard Deviation
Stock A	20	1.3	58
Stock B	18	1.8	71
Stock C	17	.7	60
Stock D	12	1.0	55

Macro Forecasts

Macro	Expected Return (%)	Standard Deviation
T-bills	8	0
Passive equity portfolio	16	23

   a. Calculate expected excess returns, alpha values, and residual variances for these stocks.

   b. Construct the optimal risky portfolio.

   c. What is Sharpe's measure for the optimal portfolio, and how much of it is contributed by the active portfolio?

   d. What should be the exact makeup of the complete portfolio for an investor with a coefficient of risk aversion of 2.8?

14. Recalculate problem 13 for a portfolio manager who is not allowed to short-sell securities.

    a. What is the cost of the restriction in terms of Sharpe's measure?

    b. What is the utility loss to the investor ($A = 2.8$) given his new complete portfolio?

15. Suppose that on the basis of an analyst's past record, you estimate that the relationship between forecast and actual alpha is

    $$\text{Actual abnormal return} = .3 \times \text{Forecast of alpha}$$

    Use the alphas from problem 13. How much is expected performance affected by recognizing the imprecision of alpha forecasts?

  16. Make up new alpha forecasts and replace those in Spreadsheet 22.1. Find the optimal portfolio and its expected performance.

 17. Make up a view and replace the one in Spreadsheet 22.2. Recalculate the optimal asset allocation and portfolio expected performance.

CFA®
PROBLEMS

The following problems are based on questions that have appeared in past CFA examinations.

18. You have $100,000 to invest in equities, and have decided to use iUnits (S&P/TSX 60s) as your index portfolio; use a newspaper listing or the Internet to determine how many units you could buy with your capital.

19. On June 1, 2009, Byron Henry was examining a new fixed-income account that his firm, Hawaiian Advisors, had accepted. Included in the new portfolio was a $10 million par value position in Procter & Gamble (PG) $8\frac{5}{8}$ percent bonds due April 1, 2036.

    Henry was concerned about this position for three reasons: (1) there was an unrealized loss on the PG bonds due to a widening in the yield spread between U.S. Treasuries and high-grade corporate bonds; (2) he felt that the PG bonds represented too large a portion of the $100 million portfolio; and (3) he feared that interest rates would move higher over the short term.

    Hawaiian Advisors has the capability to do short sales and to use financial futures as well as options on futures. With this in mind, Henry collected some information on the PG bonds and on some alternative vehicles, shown in Tables 22.7 and 22.8.

    Henry recalled that the formula for calculating a hedge ratio is

    $$\text{Hedge ratio} = \text{Yield beta} \times \frac{\text{PVBP}(y)}{\text{PVBP}(x)}$$

TABLE 22.7 Bonds

Name	Coupon	Maturity	Price	Yield	Duration (years)	Price Value of a Basis Point
Procter & Gamble	$8\frac{5}{8}$%	4/1/2036	86.36	10.10%	10.08	.08286
U.S. Treasury bond	$9\frac{1}{8}$%	5/15/2033	99.125	9.21%	9.25	.08766

TABLE 22.8 Futures (contract size = $100,000)

Contract	Expiration	Settlement Price	Yield	Price Value of a Basis Point	Conversion Factor
U.S. Treasury bond future	Dec. 2009	86.3125	9.51%	.0902	1.1257

where

PVBP(*y*) = price change for a one-basis-point change (PVBP) in the target vehicle (the PG bond)

PVBP(*x*) = price change for a one-basis-point change (PVBP) in the hedge vehicle (the U.S. Treasury bond or the U.S. Treasury bond future)

Henry did a regression using *Y* (the dependent variable) as the yield of the PG bonds, and *X* (the independent variable) as the yield of the U.S. Treasury bonds. The result was the following equation:

$$Y = 1.75 + .89X \ (R\text{-squared} = .81)$$

Henry did a second regression using *Y* (the dependent variable) as the yield of the PG bonds, and *X* (the independent variable) as the yield on the futures contract. The result was the following equation:

$$Y = 5.25 + .47X \ (R\text{-squared} = .49)$$

For tax reasons, Henry does not want to sell the PG bonds now but would like to protect the portfolio from any further price decline. Formulate two hedging strategies, using only the investment vehicles cited in Tables 22.7 and 22.8, that would protect against any further decline in the price of the PG bonds. Calculate the relevant hedge ratio for each strategy. Comment on the appropriateness of each of these strategies for this portfolio.

E-INVESTMENTS
Asset Allocation and Financial Planning

Visit the *Asset Allocation Wizard* site, which provides suggestions about portfolio asset proportions based on your time frame and attitude toward risk: **http://cgi.money.cnn.com/tools/assetallocwizard/assetallocwizard.html**. After you run the calculator with your preferences, change your inputs slightly to see what effect that would have on the results.

E-INVESTMENTS
Tracking Error

Visit **www.jpmorganfunds.com**. Enter "tracking error" in the *Keyword Search* box, and you will be directed to a discussion about the measurement of tracking error. What factors are mentioned as possible causes of high tracking error? What is the relationship between high tracking error and a manager's generation of high positive alphas? How can the tracking error measurement and the Sharpe ratio be used to assess a manager's performance?

APPENDIX 22A: REFINEMENTS TO TREYNOR-BLACK

Forecasts of Alpha Values and Extreme Portfolio Weights

The overriding impression from Spreadsheet 22.1 is apparently meagre performance improvement: panel 5 of the spreadsheet shows an improvement of .0136 in the Sharpe ratio. If we calculate *M*-squared for the overall portfolio, it is only 19 basis points, while that of the active portfolio is actually negative (−.0123). Correspondingly, the Sharpe ratio of the active portfolio is inferior to that of the passive portfolio (due to its large standard deviation). But the active

TABLE 22A.1   Stock Prices and Analysts' Target Prices, June 1, 2006

Stock	HP	Dell	WMT	Target	BP	Shell
Current price	32.15	25.39	48.14	49.01	70.8	68.7
Target price	36.88	29.84	57.44	62.8	83.52	71.15
Implied alpha	.1471	.1753	.1932	.2814	.1797	.0357

portfolio is mixed with the passive portfolio, so total volatility is not its appropriate measure of risk. When combined with the passive portfolio, it does offer some improvement in performance, albeit quite modest. This is the best that can be had given the alpha values uncovered by the security analysts (see panel 4). Notice that the position in the active portfolio amounts to 17 percent, financed in part by a combined short position in Dell and Walmart of about 10 percent. Since the figures in Spreadsheet 22.1 are annualized, this performance is equivalent to a 1-year HPR.

The alpha values we used in Spreadsheet 22.1 are actually small by the standard of typical analysts' forecasts. On June 1, we downloaded the current prices of the six stocks in the example, as well as analysts' 1-year target prices for each firm. These data and the implied annual alpha values are shown in Table 22A.1. Notice that all alphas are positive, indicating an optimistic view for this group of stocks. Figure 22A.1 shows the graphs of the stock prices, as well as the S&P 500 index (ticker = GSPC), for the previous year. The graph shows that the optimistic views in Table 22A.1 are not a result of extrapolating rates from the past.

Table 22A.2 shows the optimal portfolio using the analysts' forecasts rather than the original alpha values in panel 4 of Spreadsheet 22.1. The difference in performance is striking. The Sharpe ratio of the new optimal portfolio has increased from .44 to 2.32, amounting to a huge risk-adjusted return advantage. This shows up in an *M*-squared of 25.53 percent! However, these results also expose the presumed major problem with the Treynor-Black model. The optimal portfolio calls for extreme long/short positions that are simply infeasible for a real-world

Figure 22A.1   Rates of return on the S&P 500 (GSPC) and the six stocks.

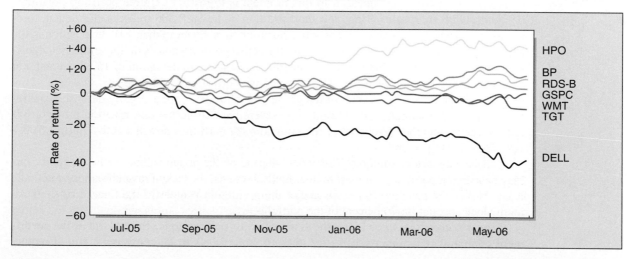

TABLE 22A.2 Optimal Risky Portfolio with Analysts' New Forecasts

	S&P 500	Active Portfolio A		HP	Dell	WMT	Target	BP	Shell
			$\sigma^2(e)$	.0705	.0572	.0309	.0392	.0297	.0317
		25.7562	$\alpha/\sigma^2(e)$	2.0855	3.0641	6.2544	7.1701	6.0566	1.1255
		1.0000	$w_0(i)$	.0810	.1190	.2428	.2784	.2352	.0437
			$[w_0(i)]^2$	.0066	.0142	.0590	.0775	.0553	.0019
α_A		.2018							
$\sigma^2(e_A)$		.0078							
w_0		7.9116							
w^*	−4.7937	5.7937		.4691163	.6892459	1.4069035	1.6128803	1.3624061	.2531855
		Overall Portfolio							
Beta	1	.9538	.7323	.4691	.6892	1.4069	1.6129	1.3624	.2532
Risk premium	.06	.2590	1.2132	.0750	.1121	.0689	.0447	.0880	.0305
SD	.1358	.1568	.5224	.3817	.2901	.1935	.2611	.1822	.1988
Sharpe ratio	.44	1.65	2.3223						
M-squared	0	.1642	.2553						
Benchmark risk			.5146						

portfolio manager. For example, the model calls for a position of 5.79 (579 percent) in the active portfolio, largely financed by a short position of −4.79 in the S&P 500 index. Moreover, the standard deviation of this optimal portfolio is 52.24 percent, a level of risk that only extremely aggressive hedge funds would be willing to bear. It is important to notice that this risk is largely nonsystematic since the beta of the active portfolio, at .95, is less than 1.0, and the beta of the overall risky portfolio is even lower, only .73, because of the short position in the passive portfolio.

A somewhat common approach to this problem is to restrict extreme portfolio positions, beginning with short sales. When the short position in the S&P 500 index is eliminated, forcing us to constrain the position in the active portfolio to be no more than 1.0, the position in the passive portfolio (the S&P 500) is zero, and the active portfolio makes up the entire risky position. Table 22A.3 shows that the active portfolio has a standard deviation of 15.68 percent, not overwhelmingly greater than the SD of the passive portfolio (13.58 percent). The beta of the overall risky portfolio is now that of the active portfolio (.95), still a slightly defensive portfolio in terms of systematic risk. Despite this severe restriction, the optimization procedure is still powerful, and the M-squared of the optimal risky portfolio (now the active portfolio) is a very large 16.42 percent.

Is this a satisfactory solution? This would depend on the organization. For hedge funds, this may be a dream portfolio. For most mutual funds, however, the lack of diversification would rule it out. Notice the positions in the six stocks; the position in Walmart, Target, and British Petroleum alone account for 76 percent of the portfolio.

Here we have to acknowledge the limitations of our example. Surely, when the investment company covers more securities, the problem of lack of diversification would largely

TABLE 22A.3   Optimal Risky Portfolio with Constraint on Active Portfolio ($w_A \leq 1$)

	S&P 500	Active Portfolio A		HP	Dell	WMT	Target	BP	Shell
			$\sigma^2(e)$	.0705	.0572	.0309	.0392	.0297	.0317
		25.7562	$\alpha/\sigma^2(e)$	2.0855	3.0641	6.2544	7.1701	6.0566	1.1255
		1.0000	$w_0(i)$	.0810	.1190	.2428	.2784	.2352	.0437
			$[w_0(i)]^2$	.0066	.0142	.0590	.0775	.0553	.0019
α_A		.2018							
$\sigma^2(e_A)$		.0078							
w_0		7.9116							
w^*	.0000	1.0000		.0810	.1190	.2428	.2784	.2352	.0437
		Overall Portfolio							
Beta	1	.9538	.9538	.0810	.1190	.2428	.2784	.2352	.0437
Risk premium	.06	.2590	.2590	.0750	.1121	.0689	.0447	.0880	.0305
SD	.1358	.1568	.1568	.3817	.2901	.1935	.2611	.1822	.1988
Sharpe ratio	.44	1.65	1.6515						
M-squared	0	.1642	.1642						
Benchmark risk			.0887						

vanish. But it turns out that the problem with extreme long/short positions typically persists even when we consider a larger number of firms, and this can gut the practical value of the optimization model. Consider this conclusion from an important article by Black and Litterman:[18]

> … the mean-variance optimization used in standard asset allocation models is extremely sensitive to expected return assumptions the investor must provide…. The optimal portfolio, given its sensitivity to the expected returns, often appears to bear little or no relation to the views the investor wishes to express. In practice, therefore, despite obvious conceptual attractions of a quantitative approach, few global investment managers regularly allow quantitative models to play a major role in their asset allocation decisions.

This statement is more complex than it reads at first blush. Note the general conclusion that "few global investment managers regularly allow quantitative models to play a major role in their asset allocation decisions." In fact, this statement also applies to many portfolio managers who avoid the mean-variance optimization process altogether for other reasons.

Restriction of Benchmark Risk

Black and Litterman point out a related important practical issue. Many investment managers are judged against the performance of a benchmark, and a benchmark index is provided in the mutual fund prospectus. Implied in our analysis so far is that the passive portfolio, the S&P 500, is that benchmark. Such commitment raises the importance of what is called tracking error. Tracking

---

[18]Fischer Black and Robert Litterman, "Global Portfolio Optimization," *Financial Analysts Journal*, September/October 1992. Originally published by Goldman Sachs Company, © 1991.

Figure 22A.2   Reduced efficiency when benchmark risk is lowered.

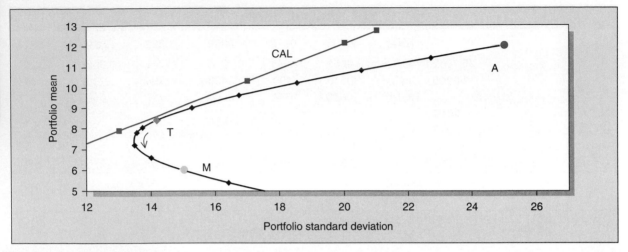

error is defined as the difference between the returns on the overall risky portfolio versus the benchmark return, that is, $T_E = R_P - R_M$. The portfolio manager must be mindful of benchmark risk, that is, the standard deviation of the tracking error.

The tracking error of the optimized risky portfolio can be expressed in terms of the beta of the portfolio and thus reveals the benchmark risk:

$$\text{Tracking error} = T_E = R_P - R_M$$
$$R_P = w_A^* \alpha_A + [1 - w_A^* A(1 - \beta_A)]R_M + w_A^* e_A$$
$$T_E = w_A^* \alpha_A - w_A^*(1 - \beta_A)R_M + w_A^* e_A \tag{22A.1}$$
$$\text{Var}(T_E) = [w_A^*(1 - \beta_A)]^2 \text{Var}(R_M) + \text{Var}(w_A^* e_A)$$
$$= [w_A^*(1 - \beta_A)]^2 \sigma_M^2 + [w_A^* \sigma(e_A)]^2$$
$$\text{Benchmark risk} = \sigma(T_E)$$
$$= w_A^* \sqrt{(1 - \beta_A)^2 \sigma_M^2 + [\sigma(e_A)]^2}$$

Equation 22A.1 shows us how to calculate the volatility of tracking error (i.e., benchmark risk) and how to set the position in the active portfolio, w_A^*, to restrict tracking risk to any desired level. For a unit investment in the active portfolio, that is, for $w_A^* = 1$, benchmark risk is

$$\sigma(T_E; w_A^* = 1) = \sqrt{(1 - \beta_A)^2 \sigma_M^2 + [\sigma(e_A)]^2} \tag{22A.2}$$

For a desired benchmark risk of $\sigma_0(T_E)$ we would restrict the weight of the active portfolio to

$$w_A(T_E) = \frac{\sigma_0(T_E)}{\sigma(T_E; w_A^* = 1)} \tag{22A.3}$$

Obviously, introducing a constraint on tracking risk entails a cost. We must shift weight from the active to the passive portfolio. Figure 22A.2 illustrates the cost. The portfolio optimization would lead us to portfolio T, the tangency of the capital allocation line (CAL), which is the ray from the risk-free rate to the efficient frontier formed from A and M. Reducing risk by shifting weight from T to M takes us down the efficient frontier, instead of along the CAL, to a lower risk position, reducing the Sharpe ratio and M-squared of the constrained portfolio.

Notice that the standard deviation of tracking error using the "meagre" alpha forecasts in Spreadsheet 22.1 is only 3.45 percent because the weight in the active portfolio is only 17 percent. Using the larger alphas based on analysts' forecasts with no restriction on portfolio weights, the

TABLE 22A.4 Optimal Risky Portfolio with Analysts' New Forecasts (benchmark risk constrained to 3.85%)

	S&P 500	Active Portfolio A		HP	Dell	WMT	Target	BP	Shell
			$\sigma^2(e)$	.0705	.0572	.0309	.0392	.0297	.0317
		25.7562	$\alpha/\sigma^2(e)$	2.0855	3.0641	6.2544	7.1701	6.0566	1.1255
		1.0000	$w_0(i)$	.0810	.1190	.2428	.2784	.2352	.0437
			$[w_0(i)]^2$	.0066	.0142	.0590	.0775	.0553	.0019
α_A		.2018							
$\sigma^2(e_A)$		.0078							
w_0		7.9116							
w^*	.5661	.4339		.0351	.0516	.1054	.1208	.1020	.0190
		Overall Portfolio							
Beta	1	.9538	.9800	.0351	.0516	.1054	.1208	.1020	.0190
Risk premium	.06	.2590	.1464	.0750	.1121	.0689	.0447	.0880	.0305
Standard deviation	.1358	.1568	.1385	.3817	.2901	.1935	.2611	.1822	.1988
Sharpe ratio	.44	1.65	1.6515						
M-squared	0	.1642	.0835						
Benchmark risk			.0385						

standard deviation of tracking error is 51.46 percent (see Table 22A.2), more than any real-life manager who is evaluated against a benchmark would be willing to bear. However, with the constraint on the active portfolio in equation 22A.2, the benchmark risk falls to 8.87 percent (Table 22A.3).

Finally, suppose a manager wishes to restrict benchmark risk to the same level as it was using the original forecasts, that is, to 3.45 percent. Equations 22A.2 and 22A.3 instruct us how to set the weight in the active portfolio. Applying these equations to the data in Spreadsheet 22.1, we obtain the results in Table 22A.4. This portfolio is moderate, yet superior in performance: (1) its standard deviation is slightly lower than that of the passive portfolio, 13.85 percent; (2) its beta is .98; (3) the standard deviation of tracking error is extremely low, 3.45 percent; (4) given that we have only six securities, the largest position of 12 percent (in Target) is quite low and would be lower still if more securities were covered; yet (5) the Sharpe ratio is a whopping 1.06, and the *M*-squared is a very impressive 8.35 percent. Thus, by controlling benchmark risk we can avoid the flaws of the unconstrained portfolio and still maintain superior performance.

Imperfect Forecast and Adjustments to Alpha

Suppose the risky portfolio of your retirement portfolio is currently in an index fund, and you are pondering whether you should take some extra risk and allocate some funds to Weston's stock, the high-performing discounter. You know that, absent research analysis, you should assume the alpha of any stock is zero. Hence, the mean of your prior distribution of Weston's alpha is zero. Downloading return data for Weston and the index reveals a residual standard deviation of 19.8 percent. Given this volatility, the prior mean of zero, and an assumption of normality, you now have the entire prior distribution of Weston's alpha.

One can make a decision using a prior distribution, or refine that distribution by expending effort to obtain additional data. In jargon, this effort is called *the experiment*. The experiment as a stand-alone venture would yield a probability distribution of possible outcomes.

The optimal statistical procedure is to combine one's prior distribution for alpha with the information derived from the experiment to form a posterior distribution that reflects both. This posterior distribution is then used for decision making.

A "tight" prior, that is, a distribution with a small standard deviation, implies a high degree of confidence in the likely range of possible alpha values even before looking at the data. In this case, the experiment may not be sufficiently convincing to affect your beliefs, meaning that the posterior will be little changed from the prior.[19] In the context of the present discussion, an active forecast of alpha and its precision provides the experiment that may induce you to update your prior beliefs about its value. The role of the portfolio manager is to form a posterior distribution of alpha that serves portfolio construction.

Adjusting Forecasts for the Precision of Alpha

Imagine you have just downloaded from Yahoo Finance the analysts' forecasts we used in the previous section, implying that Weston's alpha is 28.1 percent. Should you conclude that the optimal position in Weston, before adjusting for beta, is $.281/.198^2 = 7.17$ (717 percent)? Naturally, before committing to such an extreme position, any reasonable manager would first ask: "How accurate is this forecast?" and "How should I adjust my position to take account of forecast imprecision?"

Treynor and Black[20] asked this question and supplied an answer. The logic of the answer is quite straightforward; you must quantify the uncertainty about this forecast, just as you would the risk of the underlying asset or portfolio. A Web surfer may not have a way to assess the precision of a downloaded forecast, but the employer of the analyst who issued the forecast does. How? By examining the forecasting record of previous forecasts issued by the same forecaster.

Suppose that a security analyst provides the portfolio manager with forecasts of alpha at regular intervals, say the beginning of each month. The investor portfolio is updated using the forecast and held until the update of next month's forecast. At the end of each month, T, the realized abnormal return of Weston's stock is the sum of alpha plus a residual:

$$u(T) = R_{TGT}(T) - \beta R_M(T) = \alpha(T) + e(T) \tag{22A.4}$$

where beta is estimated from Weston's security characteristic line (SCL) using data for periods prior to T,

$$SCL: R_{TGT}(t) = \alpha + \beta R_M(t) + e(t), t < T \tag{22A.5}$$

The one-month, forward-looking forecast $\alpha^f(T)$ issued by the analyst at the beginning of month T is aimed at the abnormal return, $u(T)$, in equation 22A.4. In order to decide on how to use the forecast for month T, the portfolio manager uses the analyst's forecasting record. The analyst's record is the paired time series of all past forecasts, $\alpha^f(T)$, and realizations, $u(T)$. To assess forecast accuracy, that is, the relationship between forecast and realized alphas, the manager uses this record to estimate the regression:

$$u(t) = a_0 + a_1 \alpha^f(t) + \varepsilon(t) \tag{22A.6}$$

Our goal is to adjust alpha forecasts to properly account for their imprecision. We will form an adjusted alpha forecast $\alpha(T)$ for the coming month by using the original forecasts $\alpha^f(T)$ by applying the estimates from the regression equation 22A.6, that is,

$$\alpha(T) = a_0 + \alpha_1 \alpha^f(T) \tag{22A.7}$$

---

[19]When applied to debates about social issues, you might define a fanatic as one who enters the debate with a prior that is so tight that no argument will influence his posterior, making the debate altogether a waste of time.

[20]Jack Treynor and Fischer Black, "How to Use Security Analysis to Improve Portfolio Selection," *Journal of Business*, January 1973.

The properties of the regression estimates assure us that the adjusted forecast is the "best linear unbiased estimator" of the abnormal return on Weston in the coming month, T. "Best" in this context means it has the lowest possible variance among unbiased forecasts that are linear functions of the original forecast. Regression analysis implies that the value we should use for a_1 in equation 22A.7 is the R-squared of the regression equation 22A.6. Because R-squared is less than 1, this implies that we "shrink" the forecast toward zero. The lower the precision of the original forecast (the lower its R-squared), the more we shrink the adjusted alpha back toward zero. The coefficient a_0 adjusts the forecast upward if the forecaster has been consistently pessimistic, and downward for consistent optimism.

Distribution of Alpha Values

Equation 22A.7 implies that the quality of security analysts' forecasts, as measured by the R-squared in regressions of realized abnormal returns on their forecasts, is a critical issue for construction of optimal portfolios and resultant performance. Unfortunately, these numbers are usually impossible to come by.

Kane, Kim, and White[21] obtained a unique database of analysts' forecasts from an investment company specializing in large stocks with the S&P 500 as a benchmark portfolio. Their database includes a set of 37 monthly pairs of forecasts of alpha and beta values for between 646 and 771 stocks over the period December 1992 to December 1995—23,902 forecasts in all. The investment company policy was to truncate alpha forecasts at $+14$ percent and -12 percent per month.[22] The histogram of these forecasts is shown in Figure 22A.3. Returns of large stocks over these years were about average, as shown in the following table, including one average year (1993), one bad year (1994), and one good year (1995):

	1993	1994	1995	1926–1999 Average	SD (%)
Rate of return, %	9.87	1.29	37.71	12.50	20.39

The histogram shows that the distribution of alpha forecasts was positively skewed, with a larger number of pessimistic forecasts. The adjusted R-squared in a regression of these forecasts with actual alphas was .001134, implying a tiny correlation coefficient of .0337. As it turned out, the optimistic forecasts were of superior quality to the pessimistic ones. When the regression allowed separate coefficients for positive and negative forecasts, the R-squared increased to .001536, and the correlation coefficient to .0392.

These results contain "good" and "bad" news. The "good" news is that after adjusting even the wildest forecast, say an alpha of 12 percent for the next month, the value to be used by a forecaster when R-squared is .001 would be .012 percent, just 1.2 basis points per month. On an annual basis, this would amount to .14 percent, which is on the order of the alpha forecasts of the example in Spreadsheet 22.1. With forecasts of this small magnitude, the problem of extreme portfolio weights would never arise. The bad news arises from the same data: the performance of the active portfolio will be no better than in our example—implying an M-squared of only 19 basis points.

An investment company that delivers such limited performance will not be able to cover its cost. However, this performance is based on an active portfolio that includes only six stocks. As we showed in Section 22.8, even small information ratios of individual stocks can add up

---

[21]Alex Kane, Tae-Hwan Kim, and Halbert White, "Active Portfolio Management: The Power of the Treynor-Black Model," in *Progress in Financial Market Research*, ed. C. Kyrtsou (New York: Nova, 2004).

[22]These constraints on forecasts make sense, as on an annual basis they imply a stock would rise by more than 380 percent or fall below 22 percent of its beginning-of-year value.

Figure 22A.3

Histogram of alpha forecast.

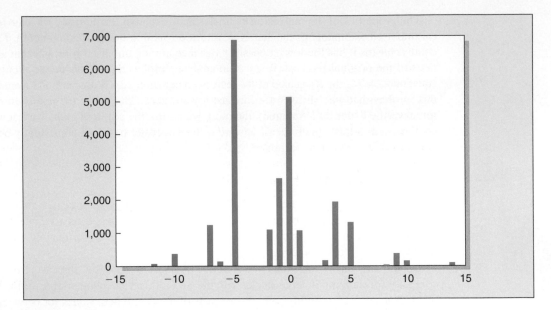

(see equation 22.7). Thus, when many forecasts of even low precision are used to form a large active portfolio, large profits can be made.

So far we have assumed that forecast errors of various stocks are independent, an assumption that may not be valid. When forecasts are correlated across stocks, precision is measured by a covariance matrix of forecasting errors, which can be estimated from past forecasts. While the necessary adjustment to the forecasts in this case is algebraically messy, it is just a technical detail. As we might guess, correlations among forecast errors will call for us to further shrink the adjusted forecasts toward zero.

Organizational Structure and Performance

The mathematical property of the optimal risky portfolio reveals a central feature of investment companies, namely, economies of scale. From the Sharpe measure of the optimized portfolio, it is evident that performance as measured by the Sharpe ratio and M-squared grows monotonically with the squared information ratio of the active portfolio (see equation 22.7 for a review), which in turn is the sum of the squared information ratios of the covered securities (see equation 22.9). Hence, a larger force of security analysts is sure to improve performance, at least before adjustment for cost. Moreover, a larger universe will also improve the diversification of the active portfolio and mitigate the need to hold positions in the neutral passive portfolio, perhaps even allowing a profitable short position in it. Additionally, a larger universe allows for an increase in the size of the fund without the need to trade larger blocks of single securities. Finally, as we showed in some detail in Section 22.8, increasing the universe of securities creates another diversification effect, that of forecasting errors by analysts.

The increases in the universe of the active portfolio in pursuit of better performance naturally come at a cost, as security analysts of quality do not come cheap. However, the other units of the organization can handle increased activity with little increase in cost. All this suggests economies of scale for larger investment companies provided the organizational structure is efficient.

Optimizing the risky portfolio entails a number of tasks of different nature in terms of expertise and need for independence. As a result, the organizational chart of the portfolio management outfit requires a degree of decentralization and proper controls. Figure 22A.4 shows an organizational chart designed to achieve these goals. The figure is largely self-explanatory and the structure is consistent with the theoretical considerations worked out in previous chapters. It can go a long way in forging sound underpinnings to the daily work of portfolio management. A few comments are in order, though.

The control units responsible for forecasting records and determining forecast adjustments will directly affect the advancement and bonuses of security analysts and estimation experts. This implies that these units must be independent and insulated from organizational pressures.

An important issue is the conflict between independence of security analysts' opinions and the need for cooperation and coordination in the use of resources and contacts with corporate and government personnel. The relative size of the security analysis unit will further complicate the solution to this conflict. In contrast, the macro forecast unit might become *too* insulated from the security analysis unit. An effort to create an interface and channels of communications between these units is warranted.

Finally, econometric techniques that are invaluable to the organization have seen a quantum leap in sophistication in recent years, and this process seems still to be accelerating. It is critical to keep the units that deal with estimation updated and on top of the latest developments.

Figure 22A.4 Organizational chart for portfolio management.

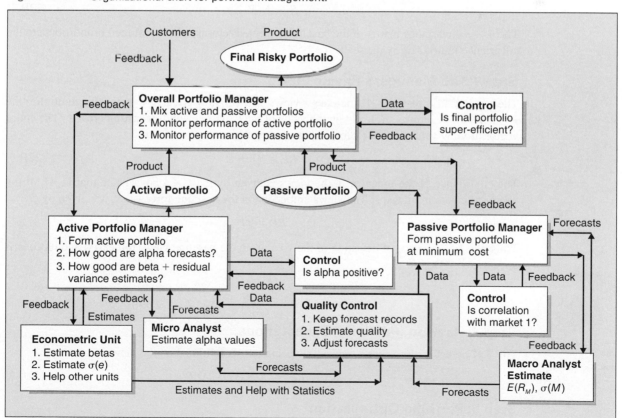

Source: Adapted from Robert C. Merton, *Finance Theory* (Boston: Harvard Business School), Ch. 12.

APPENDIX 22B: THE GENERAL BLACK-LITTERMAN MODEL

The BL model is easiest to write using matrix notation. We describe the model according to the steps in Section 22.6.

Steps 1 and 2: The Covariance Matrix and Baseline Forecasts

A sample of past excess returns of the universe of n assets is used to estimate the $n \times n$ covariance matrix, denoted by Σ. It is assumed that the excess returns are normally distributed.

Market values of the universe assets are obtained and used to compute the $1 \times n$ vector of weights, w_M, in the baseline equilibrium portfolio. The variance of the baseline portfolio is calculated from

$$\sigma_M^2 = w_M \Sigma w_M' \tag{22B.1}$$

A coefficient of risk aversion for the representative investor in the economy, $\bar{A}$, is applied to the CAPM equation to obtain the baseline macro forecast for the market portfolio risk premium,

$$E(R_M) = \bar{A}\sigma_M^2 \tag{22B.2}$$

The $1 \times n$ vector of baseline forecasts for the universe securities risk premiums, R, is computed from the macro forecast, and the covariance matrix by R is computed from the macro forecast and the covariance matrix by

$$R' = E(R_M)\Sigma w_M' \tag{22B.3}$$

The data so far describe the prior (baseline) distribution of the rates of return of the asset universe by

$$\tilde{R} \sim N(R, \Sigma) \tag{22B.4}$$

The $n \times n$ covariance matrix of the baseline expected returns, $\tau\Sigma$, is assumed proportional to the covariance matrix, Σ, by the scalar τ.

Step 3: The Manager's Private Views

The $k \times n$ matrix of views, P, includes k views. The ith view is a $1 \times k$ vector that multiplies the $1 \times n$ vector of returns, $\tilde{R}$, to obtain the value of the view, Q_i, with forecasting error ε_i. The entire vector of view values and their forecasting errors is given by

$$RP = Q + \varepsilon \tag{22B.5}$$

The confidence of the manager in the views is given by the $k \times k$ covariance matrix, Ω, of the vector of errors in views, ε. The views embedded in the baseline forecast, R, are given by Q^E:

$$RP = Q^E$$

Thus, the $1 \times k$ vector of deviation of the view from the baseline view (forecasts) and its covariance matrix SD is

$$D = Q^E - Q \tag{22B.6}$$
$$S_D = \tau P \Sigma P' + \Omega$$

Step 4: Revised (Posterior) Expectations

The $1 \times n$ vector of posterior (revised) expectations conditional on the views is given by

$$R^* = R|P = R + \tau D S_D^{-1} \Sigma P' \tag{22B.7}$$

Step 5: Portfolio Optimization

The vector of revised expectations is used in conjunction with the covariance matrix of excess returns to produce the optimal portfolio weights with the Markowitz algorithm.

Managed Funds

Chapter 3 introduced you to the mechanics of trading securities and the structure of the markets in which securities trade. Increasingly, however, individual investors are choosing not to trade securities directly for their own accounts, as this requires personal attention that many investors feel they have neither time nor expertise to give; rather, they entrust investment decisions to institutional management.

The most important institution to manage individual assets is the mutual fund industry, and this chapter focuses on this branch of professional investment management. We begin by presenting a classification of the variety of investment companies available to investors, before describing the particular form known as mutual funds, which we categorize according to their policies and styles; we also discuss how these policies affect the taxation of their results in investors' hands. We continue with a look at the increasingly important sector of hedge funds, used by wealthier individuals and other institutions. Following this, we examine the expenses associated with management and how costs and fees affect the returns for both mutual and hedge funds. This leads to the topic of just how good the performance of professional managers is in directing mutual funds. In conclusion, we indicate where information, primarily an accurate assessment of performance, can be obtained.

In Appendix 23A, we present a summary of the tax system, as it affects investing; this detail is essential for determining what investment promises to provide the highest risk-adjusted, after-tax returns. Appendix 23B is a general overview of the pension fund industry with a focus on the defined-benefit and defined-contribution dichotomy.

23.1   INVESTMENT COMPANIES

Investment companies are financial intermediaries that collect funds from individual investors and invest those funds in a potentially wide range of securities or other assets. Pooling of assets is the key idea behind investment companies. Each investor has a claim to the portfolio established by the investment company in proportion to the amount invested. These companies thus provide a mechanism for small investors to team up to obtain the benefits of large-scale investing.

Investment companies perform several important functions for their investors:

1. *Record keeping and administration.* Investment companies issue periodic status reports, keeping track of capital gains distributions, dividends, investments, and redemptions, and they may reinvest dividend and interest income for shareholders.

2. *Diversification and divisibility.* By pooling their money, investment companies enable investors to hold fractional shares of many different securities. They can act as large investors even if any individual shareholder cannot.

3. *Professional management.* Many, but not all, investment companies have full-time staffs of security analysts and portfolio managers who attempt to achieve superior investment results for their investors. High individual search costs are reduced when institutional research is conducted.

4. *Lower transaction costs.* Because they trade large blocks of securities, investment companies can achieve substantial savings on brokerage fees and commissions.

While all investment companies pool assets of individual investors, they also need to divide claims to those assets among those investors. Investors buy shares in investment companies, and ownership is proportional to the number of shares purchased. The value of each share is called the **net asset value**, or **NAV**. Net asset value equals assets minus liabilities expressed on a per-share basis:

$$\text{Net asset value} = \frac{\text{Market value of assets minus liabilities}}{\text{Shares outstanding}}$$

Consider a mutual fund that manages a portfolio of securities worth $120 million. Suppose the fund owes $4 million to its investment advisors and owes another $1 million for rent, wages due, and miscellaneous expenses. The fund has 5 million shareholders. Then

$$\text{Net asset value} = \frac{\$120 \text{ million} - \$5 \text{ million}}{5 \text{ million}} = \$23 \text{ per share}$$

> **CC 1**
>
> ### CONCEPT CHECK
>
> Consider these data from the October 27, 2013 balance sheet of Evergrow Fund. What was the net asset value of the portfolio?
>
> | | |
> |---|---|
> | Assets | $90,686.10 million |
> | Liabilities | $866.15 million |
> | Shares | 3,135.68 million |

Funds under the administration of investment companies are usually referred to as **managed funds**, so named because securities in their investment portfolios are continually being managed by purchase and sale.

AGF Management
Limited
www.agf.com

There are two types of managed companies: closed-end and open-end. In both cases, the fund's board of directors, which is elected by shareholders, hires a management company to manage the portfolio for an annual fee that typically ranges from .2 percent to 1.5 percent of assets. In many cases the management company is the firm that organized the fund. For example, AGF Management Limited sponsors many AGF mutual funds and is responsible for managing the portfolios. It assesses a management fee on each AGF fund. In other cases, a mutual fund will hire an outside portfolio manager. AGF has hired Nomura Asset Management as the investment advisor for both its Japan and its China funds. Most management companies have contracts to manage several funds.

Open-end funds stand ready to redeem or issue shares at their net asset value (although both purchases and redemptions may involve sales charges). When investors in open-end funds wish to cash out their shares, they sell them back to the fund at NAV. In contrast, **closed-end funds** do not redeem or issue shares. Investors in closed-end funds who wish to cash out must sell their shares to other investors. Shares of closed-end funds are traded on organized exchanges and can be purchased through brokers just like other common stock; their prices therefore can differ from NAV. Listings of closed-end fund information usually give three key figures: the fund's most recent net asset value, the closing share price, and the percentage difference between the two, which is (Price − NAV)/NAV. Typically, more funds sell at discounts to NAV (indicated by negative differences) than premiums.

The common divergence of price from net asset value, often by wide margins, is a puzzle. To see why, consider a closed-end fund selling at a discount from net asset value. If the fund were to sell all the assets in the portfolio, it would realize proceeds equal to net asset value. The difference between the market price of the fund and the fund's NAV would represent the per-share increase in the wealth of the fund's investors. Moreover, several studies[1] have shown that on average, fund premiums or discounts tend to dissipate over time, so funds selling at a discount get a boost to their rate of return as the discount shrinks. Pontiff[2] estimates that a fund selling at a 20 percent discount would have an expected 12-month return more than 6 percent greater than funds selling at net asset value.

Strangely, while many closed-end funds sell at a discount from net asset value, the prices of these funds when originally issued are typically above NAV. This is a further puzzle, as it is hard to explain why investors would purchase these newly issued funds at a premium to NAV when the shares tend to fall to a discount shortly after issue.

In contrast to closed-end funds, the price of open-end funds cannot fall below NAV, because these funds stand ready to redeem shares at NAV. The offering price will exceed NAV, however, if the fund carries a **load**. A load is, in effect, a sales charge, which is paid to the seller. Load funds are sold by securities brokers and directly by mutual fund groups. Unlike closed-end funds, open-end mutual funds do not trade on organized exchanges. Instead, investors simply buy shares from and liquidate through the investment company at net asset value. Thus the number of outstanding shares of these funds changes daily.

Other Investment Organizations

There are intermediaries not formally organized or regulated as investment companies that nevertheless serve functions similar to investment companies. Five of the more important are commingled funds, real estate investment trusts, segregated funds, private equity, and hedge funds.

Commingled funds are partnerships of investors that pool their funds. The management firm that organizes the partnership, for example, a bank or insurance company, manages the funds for a fee.

[1]See, for example, Rex Thompson, "The Information Content of Discounts and Premiums on Closed-End Fund Shares," *Journal of Financial Economics* 6 (1978), pp. 151–86.
[2]Jeffrey Pontiff, "Costly Arbitrage: Evidence from Closed-End Funds," *Quarterly Journal of Economics* 111 (November 1996), pp. 1135–51.

Typical partners in a commingled fund might be trust or retirement accounts which have portfolios that are much larger than those of most individual investors but are still too small to warrant managing on a separate basis.

Commingled funds are similar in form to open-end mutual funds. Instead of shares, though, the fund offers units, which are bought and sold at net asset value. A bank or insurance company may offer an array of different commingled funds from which trust or retirement accounts can choose. Examples are a money market fund, a bond fund, and a common stock fund. In certain cases, these funds may be formed as *unit investment trusts* as a means of avoiding realization of gains when assets are sold and the proceeds reinvested. The holding in the trust is not deemed to be realized, so that tax or other regulatory consequences can be avoided, but the composition of the portfolio can be adjusted to meet market conditions. (The concept of "unit investment trust" has another interpretation in the United States.)

A **real estate investment trust (REIT)** is similar to a closed-end fund, with the purpose of investing in real estate or loans secured by real estate. Thus they take the form of either an equity or a mortgage trust. REITs generally are established by banks, insurance companies, or mortgage companies, which then serve as investment managers to earn a fee. An alternative is the **real estate limited partnership (RELP)**, which will have a somewhat different tax structure and be less liquid. Both forms use extensive leverage to purchase property or issue mortgages, typically with a debt ratio of 70 percent.

Segregated funds are essentially mutual funds with an attached guarantee for a minimum value. They are typically sold by insurance companies, with estate planning aspects, tying the performance of a mutual fund to the payoff but allowing 75 or 100 percent of the initial investment (or a reset value at a later date) to be a guaranteed payout at maturity or upon death of the investor. The "reset" feature makes for difficult valuation of the product; high fees paid for funds management and the insurance guarantee make these funds far less attractive than they appear to be.

Private Equity and Hedge Funds

In recent years, the phenomenon of exclusive investment pools reserved for wealthy investors with many millions to invest has received much press. Reports of high returns for those with sufficient capital to enjoy special treatment have piqued the interest of financial commentators and academics. In theory, efficient markets should not permit excess returns on large capital bases; nearly efficient markets would allow occasional high returns on temporary opportunities for small investments. The existence of hedge funds ought to guarantee that equilibrium relationships are quickly reestablished in the financial markets. Yet these large capital pools have apparently been successful in two specific areas, leveraged buyouts and hedge funds, with decidedly high returns.

Private Equity   Private equity is actively pursuing these opportunities, as it provides capital directly to firms in need of funds without making disclosure. This capital can be injected directly into successful firms, provided to management or other teams as tranches of funds involved in leveraged buyouts (LBOs), or contributed to hedge funds. LBOs have been around since the 1980s, when they were the most sensational financial news items. Reports of the returns from working out the repayments of highly leveraged, bought-out firms leave the impression that they yield excess returns. Yet many LBOs resulted in failure, Canadian real estate mogul Robert Campeau's foray into retailing being a notable example. LBOs are high-risk endeavours that require expertise and effort, and hence earn higher rewards. The current surge in LBO activity is directed at increasingly large targets, leading to consolidation in many industries. Private equity is actively involved here, and regulators express concern over the cooperation, rather than competition, in the bidding for targets.

Last Friday, May 22, Ontario Teachers' Pension Plan (OTPP) quietly sold much of its stake in Canadian Bell (BCE Inc.) thus ending the tumultuous relationship between the institutional investor and Canada's largest telecom company. For BCE, there had been 18 months of buyout-related distractions, including regulatory hearings, near-constant pressure from cash-strapped banks, a bondholder lawsuit that went all the way to the country's highest court, all of which took a toll on the company's competitive position. . . .

At the credit boom's peak in June 2007, OTPP and three private equity firms, including Providence Equity Partners and Madison Dearborn Partners[,] agreed to buy BCE, including all outstanding debt, and accounting for currency fluctuations. In January 2008, OTPP proposed a $52 billion takeover of Bell Canada. The buyout was to be the largest leveraged buyout in Canadian history and possibly of the world.

OTPP was to be the bond holder of $33 billion of debt after the cheering stopped. . . .

By Spring 2008, the proposed buyout was starting to have problems. From January to June, the deal had been in front of the Supreme Court of Canada who finally gave them the go ahead. . . .

During Spring 2008, OTPP and their partners were still negotiating with banks for financing after the banks tried to tighten their financing terms. Citigroup, Deutsche Bank, Royal Bank of Scotland and Toronto-Dominion Bank were the four banks that had committed to financing the debt portion of the largest leveraged buyout deal. In a jointly issued statement they then said they still backed the proposed sale. Later in Fall of 2008, these were the same banks that received "bailout money" from their countries' government.

Citigroup's November bailout money, the U.S. Treasury's Troubled Asset Relief Program (TARP) funds, seemed to give a surge of confidence that the $52 billion takeover of Bell Canada would close on schedule in December 2008. Of the $33 billion of debt being used to finance the buyout,

Citigroup was responsible for about $11 billion (USD). By then the subprime mortgage crisis and credit crisis was in full swing, which had all but frozen the secondary market for leveraged debt. Last fall, the four banks that agreed to finance the deal were then thought to have planned to keep the debt on their balance sheets. . . .

[Then] along came the auditing firm KPMG with a very unfavourable opinion about the transaction's so-called solvency test. The deal's debt and market conditions were working against it. . . .

George Cope, the chief executive of Bell Canada's parent, said that no one on the phone company's deal team, including an army of high-priced lawyers, had ever raised a flag about the transaction's so-called solvency test prior to November 26. That was the day BCE revealed that accounting firm KPMG had delivered an unfavourable opinion that effectively killed the deal. BCE had actually hired a second auditor, PricewaterhouseCoopers, in an attempt to gain an endorsement for the deal and influence KPMG's final opinion on the matter. That brings into question some of the official statements by BCE's CEO.

Then there is BCE's demand that the buyout group, led by OTPP, pay the phone company the deal's $1.187 billion "reverse breakup fee" because of a termination notice that was delivered to BCE "prematurely." OTPP on the other side doesn't believe any break fees are owed because the deal failed on KPMG's solvency opinion. The independent auditor's solvency test opinion was a condition to which both sides had originally agreed. . . .

At the end of 2008, BCE was the single largest holding in Teachers' $80.16 billion portfolio. The pension plan had a 50.8-million-share stake in BCE worth $1.19 billion, but in its last regulatory filing as of March 31, 2009, the stake had shrunk to 39.8 million shares. When the deal was first signed in June 2007, BCE was selling at $39.20 per share. Friday, May 21 OTPP BCE shares sold for $21.09 each, approximate return was $839,382,000.

Source: Thomas Gordon, at *Bright Side of News*, May 30, 2009, http://www.brightsideofnews.com/news/2009/5/30/bell-canada-ends-era2c-ontario-teachers-pension-plan-sell-stake.aspx, accessed November 15, 2010.

The case of BCE (Bell Canada) and the Ontario Teachers' pension fund illustrates many of the issues involved in the takeover of public companies by private equity funds. (See the nearby box.) BCE had experienced several years of poor results blamed on management strategy. Academics argue that the threat of takeover by other corporations or more recent private equity pools leads to more efficient use of real resources. For their part, managers, who often participate either as principals or as agents in the takeovers, appreciate the absence of myopic public oversight. The principal–agent conflict is also reduced by the direct relationship between the few owners and their managers.

Hedge Funds   *Hedge funds* (see Section 23.3) have mushroomed in quantity and importance. Hedge Fund Research (HFR) provides estimates of 610 funds controlling $39 billion of assets in 1990; by 2000 these numbers had increased to 3,873 funds and $490 billion; despite the folding of many unsuccessful funds, assets under management exceeded $2 trillion by 2013. Like mutual funds, hedge funds are vehicles that allow private investors to pool assets to be invested by a fund manager. Unlike mutual funds, however, hedge funds are commonly structured as private partnerships and are subject to only minimal regulation. Typically they are open only to wealthy or institutional investors. Many require investors to agree to initial **lock-up periods**—that is, periods as long as several years in which investments cannot be withdrawn. Lock-ups allow hedge funds to invest in illiquid assets without worrying about meeting demands for redemption of funds. Moreover, because hedge funds are only lightly regulated, their managers can pursue investment strategies involving, for example, heavy use of derivatives, short sales, and leverage; such strategies are not usually open to mutual fund managers. Hedge funds by design are empowered to invest in a wide range of investments, with various funds focusing on derivatives, distressed funds, currency speculation, convertible bonds, emerging markets, merger arbitrage, and so on. Other funds may jump from one asset class to another as perceived investment opportunities shift.

In Canada, varying estimates put the hedge fund market at about $30 billion of assets in 2012, double its size in 2009. The asset-weighted Scotiabank Canadian Hedge Fund Index reported a drop of almost 5 percent in 2012, while the TSX was rising 4 percent. Median performance for hedge funds since 2000 has been poor relative to the general market performance, although this should be seen as reasonable given that they are hedges to the market, which has enjoyed exceptionally good returns. With their smaller size, Canadian funds offer hope for better returns than the giant American and British funds; smaller pools of capital can be moved more easily without affecting prices so much. Some larger sponsors are Sprott, Man Group, Dynamic and Horizons.

23.2 MUTUAL FUNDS

Mutual funds are by far the most popular form of investment vehicle open to individuals. The value of the funds under management by mutual funds grew immensely during the decade of the 1990s as investors recognized the unprecedented growth in equity values during that period. We shall see, however, that the general increase in market valuation has indicated to investors that the option of index funds has become an extremely attractive form of mutual fund that competes with the traditional forms. In what follows, the term *mutual fund* refers to open-ended investment companies.

By January 2013, there were 145 members in the Investment Funds Institute of Canada managing 2,256 mutual funds with assets of $850 billion. Of these, money market funds held approximately 3.5 percent of the total assets; this is a very low percentage, probably reflecting the low yield available for short-term funds. Figure 23.1 demonstrates the substantial growth that has occurred in the Canadian market; Table 23.1 gives a breakdown of the types and sizes of mutual funds in December 2012.

Investment Policies

Every mutual fund has a specified investment policy, which is described in the fund's prospectus. For example, money market mutual funds hold the short-term, low-risk instruments of the money market (see Chapter 2 for a review of these securities), while bond funds hold fixed-income securities. Some funds, such as fixed-income funds, have even more narrowly defined mandates: for example, some will hold primarily government-issue bonds, and others primarily mortgage-backed securities.

Management companies manage a family, or "complex," of mutual funds. They organize an entire collection of funds and then collect a management fee for operating them. By managing a collection of funds under one umbrella, these companies make it easy for investors to allocate assets across market sectors and to switch assets across funds while still benefiting from centralized record keeping.

Some of the more important fund types, classified by investment policy, are discussed next.

Figure 23.1

Growth of mutual fund assets in Canada, January 1995–2012 ($ billions; number of funds above bars).

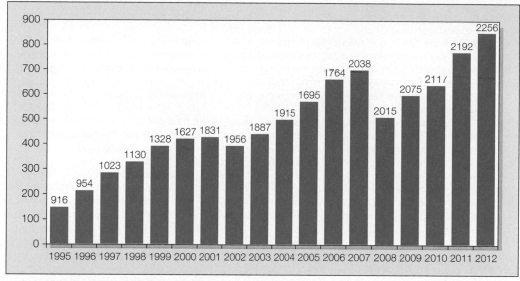

Source: Investment Funds Institute of Canada.

Money Market Funds   These funds invest in money market securities, including government and corporate issues. They usually offer cheque-writing features, and net asset value of a share is fixed, so that there are no tax implications such as capital gains or losses associated with redemption of shares. The credit crisis brought a new experience to the money market industry, as noted in the boxed article.

Fixed-Income Funds   As the name suggests, these funds specialize in the fixed-income sector. Within that sector, however, there is considerable room for specialization. For example, various funds will concentrate on corporate bonds, Canada bonds, or mortgage-backed securities.

TABLE 23.1

Types and Assets of Mutual Funds, December 31, 2012

Fund Type	Total Assets ($000)	% Share of Market
Equity Funds	267,230,198	31.40%
Domestic equity	153,373,588	18.00%
Global and international equity	68,225,728	8.00%
U.S. equity	28,722,602	3.40%
Sector equity	16,908,280	2.00%
Balanced Funds	388,911,212	45.80%
Domestic balanced	195,139,543	23.00%
Global balanced	193,771,669	22.80%
Bond Funds	131,504,263	15.50%
Domestic fixed income	103,456,128	12.20%
Global and high-yield fixed income	28,048,135	3.30%
Specialty Funds	32,368,422	3.80%
Long-Term Funds Total	820,014,095	96.50%
Money Market Funds	29,724,321	3.50%
Short-Term Funds Total	29,724,321	3.50%
All Funds	849,738,417	100.00%

Source: The Investment Funds Institute of Canada.

Money market funds are mutual funds that invest in the short-term debt instruments that make up the money market. In 2008, these funds had investments totalling about $3.4 trillion. They are required to hold only short-maturity debt of the highest quality: the average maturity of their holdings must be maintained at less than three months. Their biggest investments tend to be in commercial paper, but they also hold sizable fractions of their portfolios in certificates of deposit, repurchase agreements, and Treasury securities. Because of this very conservative investment profile, money market funds typically present extremely low price risk. Investors for their part usually acquire cheque-writing privileges with their funds and often use them as a close substitute for a bank account. This is feasible because the funds almost always maintain share value at $1 and pass along all investment earnings to their investors as interest.

Until 2008, only one fund had "broken the buck," that is, suffered losses large enough to force value per share below $1. But when Lehman Brothers filed for bankruptcy protection on September 15, 2008, several funds that had invested heavily in its commercial paper suffered large losses. The next day, Reserve Primary Fund, the oldest money market fund, broke the buck when its value per share fell to only $.97.

The realization that money market funds were at risk in the credit crisis led to a wave of investor redemptions similar to a run on a bank. Only three days after the Lehman bankruptcy, Putman's Prime Money Market Fund announced that it was liquidating due to heavy redemptions. Fearing further outflows, the U.S. Treasury announced that it would make federal insurance available to money market funds willing to pay an insurance fee. This program would thus be similar to FDIC bank insurance. With the federal insurance in place, the outflows were quelled.

However, the turmoil in Wall Street's money market funds had already spilled over into "Main Street." Fearing further investor redemptions, money market funds had become afraid to commit funds even over short periods, and their demand for commercial paper had effectively dried up. Firms that had been able to borrow at 2 percent interest in previous weeks now had to pay up to 8 percent, and the commercial paper market was on the verge of freezing up altogether. Firms throughout the economy had come to depend on those markets as a major source of short-term finance to fund expenditures ranging from salaries to inventories. Further breakdown in the money markets would have had an immediate crippling effect on the broad economy. Within days, the federal government put forth its first plan to spend $700 billion to stabilize the credit markets.

Many funds will also specialize by the maturity of the securities, ranging from short-term to intermediate to long-term, or by the credit risk of the issuer, ranging from very safe to high-yield or "junk" bonds.

Balanced and Income Funds   Some funds are designed to be candidates for an individual's entire investment portfolio. Therefore, they hold both equities and fixed-income securities in relatively stable proportions. According to Wiesenberger, such funds are classified as income or balanced funds. *Income funds* strive to maintain safety of principal consistent with "as liberal a current income from investments as possible," while *balanced funds* "minimize investment risks so far as this is possible without unduly sacrificing possibilities for long-term growth and current income." *Dividend funds* hold preferred shares and high-quality common shares that pay consistent dividends.

Asset Allocation Funds   These funds are similar to balanced funds in that they hold both stocks and bonds. However, asset allocation funds may dramatically vary the proportions allocated to each market in accord with the portfolio manager's forecast of the relative performance of each sector. Hence these funds are engaged in market timing and are not designed to be low-risk investment vehicles.

Equity Funds   Equity funds invest primarily in stock, although they may, at the portfolio manager's discretion, also hold fixed-income or other types of securities. Funds will commonly hold at least some money market securities to provide liquidity necessary to meet potential redemption of shares.

It is traditional to classify stock funds according to their emphasis on capital appreciation versus current income. Thus, *income funds* tend to hold shares of firms with high dividend yields, which provide high current income. *Growth funds* are willing to forgo current income, focusing instead on prospects for capital gains. While the classification of these funds is couched in terms of income versus capital gains, in practice the more relevant distinction concerns the level of risk these funds assume. Growth stocks and therefore growth funds are typically riskier and respond far more dramatically to changes in economic conditions than do income funds.

Index Funds   An index fund tries to match the performance of a broad market index. The fund buys shares in securities included in a particular index in proportion to the security's representation in that index. For example, CIBC's Canadian Index Fund is a mutual fund that replicates the composition of the S&P/TSX Composite Index. Because the TSX is a value-weighted index, the fund buys shares in each company in proportion to the market value of that company's outstanding equity. Investment in an index fund is a low-cost way for small investors to pursue a passive investment strategy—that is, to invest without engaging in security analysis. In 2012, about 15 percent of equity funds were index funds. Of course, index funds can be tied to nonequity indices as well.

Specialized Sector Funds   Some funds concentrate on a particular industry. For example, in the United States, Fidelity markets dozens of "select funds," each of which invests in a specific industry such as biotechnology, utilities, precious metals, or telecommunications. Other funds specialize in securities of particular countries. Emerging-market, regional (e.g., Latin American), or global funds have become increasingly popular as the importance of global diversification is realized.

How Funds Are Sold

Mutual funds are generally marketed to the public either directly by the fund underwriter or indirectly through brokers or their parent banks on behalf of the underwriter. Direct-marketed funds are sold through the mail, various offices of the fund, over the phone, and, increasingly, over the Internet. Investors contact the fund directly to purchase shares.

About half of fund sales today are distributed through a sales force. Brokers or financial advisors receive a commission for selling shares to investors. (Ultimately, the commission is paid by the investor.)

Investors who rely on their broker's advice to select their mutual funds should be aware that brokers may have a conflict of interest with regard to fund selection. This can arise from a practice called *revenue sharing*, in which fund companies pay the brokerage firm for preferential treatment when making investment recommendations. The payment sometimes comes in the form of direct payments, computed either as a one-time payment based on sales of the mutual fund or as an ongoing payment or trailer fee based on fund assets held by the brokerage's clients.

The larger of the members of the Investment Funds Institute of Canada are likely to have approximately a hundred different types of funds under management. These different funds will include equity, income, money market, index, international, and other more narrowly focused funds of the types mentioned above; these may be managed internally or delegated to outside specialized professional managers. Table 23.2 lists the 10 largest families and the assets under management as of December 2012. The total assets of $687 billion of these 10 fund managers constitute about 81 percent of the total assets ($850 billion) managed by the member firms. (We should note here, however, that about 18 percent of managed firms are not included in the IFIC statistics.)

Taxation of Mutual Fund Proceeds

Under the Canadian tax system, the returns on investment made by mutual funds is taxable in the hands of the investors and not to the management company or the fund, provided that the proceeds are paid out annually to the investors (hence being taxable for them). Every year, the

TABLE 23.2

Ten Largest Canadian Mutual Fund Families, December 2012*

Rank	Fund Family	Total Net Assets ($ thousands)
1	RBC Global Asset Management	124,700,665
2	IGM Financial Inc	103,598,487
	Investors Group Inc.	60,594,467
	Mackenzie Financial Corporation	40,345,334
	Counsel Portfolio Services Inc.	2,658,686
3	TD Asset Management	69,515,182
4	Scotia Global Asset Management	67,682,271
5	CIBC Asset Management	58,690,112
6	Fidelity Investments Canada ULC	55,331,478
7	BMO Financial Group	43,138,290
8	Manulife Mutual Funds	20,697,532
9	Franklin Templeton	20,113,188
10	AGF Investments Inc.	19,571,691

*Only includes IFIC members.
Source: The Investment Funds Institute of Canada.

mutual fund will issue a statement to the investor as to the amount of taxable capital gains and dividend or interest income that has been recognized. This practice can be viewed favourably as ensuring that there is no liability being built up for taxes, contingent upon disposal of the shares in the mutual fund; on the other hand, it is necessary to keep track of the accumulated annual declarations when the shares are finally sold. Typically, the recognized proceeds are not distributed but are reinvested in additional shares, even though the taxes must be paid annually. Consequently, the holding in the fund grows in keeping with its performance; however, the difference in value, as of disposition, from its original value does not reflect the recognizable gain that must be declared.

The pass-through of investment income has one important disadvantage for individual investors. If you manage your own portfolio, you decide when to realize capital gains and losses on any security; therefore, you can time those realizations to efficiently manage your tax liabilities. When you invest through a mutual fund, however, the timing of the sale of securities from the portfolio is out of your control, which reduces your ability to engage in tax management. Of course, if the mutual fund is held in a tax-deferred retirement account such as an RRSP account, these tax management issues are irrelevant.

A fund with a high portfolio turnover rate can be particularly "tax-inefficient." **Turnover** is the ratio of the trading activity of a portfolio to the assets of the portfolio. It measures the fraction of the portfolio that is "replaced" each year. For example, a $100 million portfolio with $50 million in sales of some securities with purchases of other securities would have a turnover rate of 50 percent. High turnover means that capital gains or losses are being realized constantly, and therefore that the investor cannot time the realizations to manage his or her overall tax obligation.

A recent concept available in Canada, the **corporate class** of funds, has an appealing structure for tax purposes. Consider an investor with a portfolio of two mutual funds, one a growth equity fund and the other a dividend income fund with an initial allocation of 60–40 in growth and dividend. Assume that after a year of good returns particularly in the growth fund, the investor decides to rebalance holdings to 40–60 in growth and dividend. Sale of a portion of the growth fund would attract capital gains tax. Imagine that some successful timing of switching between the funds occurs with tax liabilities each time. One thing is for sure: each sale would reduce the wealth of the investor, and if financed by sales of the portfolio would also reduce the invested capital in the portfolio.

Under the corporate class scheme, the investor places funds in the broad class of funds available, encompassing a wide range of investment possibilities, rather than in the individual funds. Choosing to perform occasional switches in sector emphasis triggers no capital gains (or losses), as the investor is still fully invested in the broad corporate class—effectively in a single umbrella fund. Only when funds are actually withdrawn from the portfolio are capital gains and losses assessed. Even this can be managed by designating withdrawals as return of capital, having no immediate tax consequence, but reducing the cost base.

CC 2

CONCEPT CHECK

An investor's portfolio currently is worth $1 million. During the year, the investor sells 1,000 shares of Weston at a price of $80 per share and 4,000 shares of Teck at a price of $20 per share. The proceeds are used to buy 2,000 shares of CIBC at $80 per share.
a. What was the portfolio turnover rate?
b. If the shares in Weston were originally purchased for $70 each and those in Teck were purchased for $17.50, and the investor's tax rate on capital gains income is 20 percent, how much extra will the investor owe on this year's taxes as a result of these transactions?

23.3   HEDGE FUNDS: STRATEGIES AND ALPHA

Like mutual funds, the basic idea behind **hedge funds** is investment pooling. Investors buy shares in these funds, which then invest the pooled assets on their behalf. The net asset value of each share represents the value of the investor's stake in the portfolio. In this regard, hedge funds operate much like mutual funds. However, there are important differences between the two.

Transparency   American mutual funds are subject to the U.S. *Securities Act* of 1933 and *Investment Company Act* of 1940 (designed to protect unsophisticated investors), which require transparency and predictability of strategy. Canadian mutual funds are similarly regulated. They periodically must provide the public with information on portfolio composition. In contrast, hedge funds are usually set up as limited liability partnerships, and provide minimal information about portfolio composition and strategy to their investors only.

Investors   Hedge funds traditionally have no more than 100 "sophisticated" investors, in practice usually defined by minimum net worth and income requirements. They generally do not advertise to the general public, and minimum investments are usually between $250,000 and $1 million, although there has been a recent trend to open them to smaller investors.

Investment Strategies   Mutual funds lay out their general investment approach (e.g., large, value stock orientation versus small-cap growth orientation) in their prospectus. They face pressure to avoid *style drift* (departures from their stated investment orientation), especially given the importance of retirement funds to the industry, and the demand of such plans for predictable strategies. Most mutual funds promise to limit their use of short-selling and leverage, and their use of derivatives is highly restricted. (In recent years, some so-called "130/30" funds have opened, primarily for institutional clients, with prospectuses that explicitly allow for more active short-selling and derivatives positions, but even these have less flexibility than hedge funds. (See the box here.) In contrast, hedge funds may effectively partake in any investment strategy and may act opportunistically as conditions evolve. For this reason, it would be a mistake to view hedge funds as anything remotely like a uniform asset class. Hedge funds by design are empowered to invest in a

Hedge funds and their elaborate strategies—particularly their ability to short-sell assets perceived as overpriced—have long been open only to wealthy or institutional clients. The U.S. *Investment Companies Act* of 1940 makes it more difficult for mutual funds to short-sell, requiring that they set aside in a separate account liquid securities that can be used to close out short positions. Nevertheless, short-selling has become more common among some funds.

More recently, smaller investors have been able to invest in 130/30 funds that mimic some of the features of hedge funds. These are funds that may sell short up to 30 percent of the value of their portfolios, using the proceeds of the sale to increase their positions in invested assets. So for every $100 in net assets, the fund could sell short $30, investing the proceeds to increase its long positions to $130. This gives rise to the "130/30" moniker. These funds have been among the fastest-growing segments of the institutional money management sector. Variations range from 110/10 funds to 150/50 funds.

These funds are promoted as maintaining full exposure to the market (e.g., the net exposure of a 130/30 fund is 130 percent long minus the 30 percent short position, or 100 percent) while still providing the fund manager the opportunity to enhance alpha by selling overpriced securities. In contrast, conventional long-only mutual funds can produce alpha only by identifying and purchasing underpriced securities.

wide range of investments, with various funds focusing on derivatives, distressed firms, currency speculation, convertible bonds, emerging markets, merger arbitrage, and so on. Other funds may jump from one asset class to another as perceived investment opportunities shift.

Liquidity Hedge funds often impose lock-up periods, that is, periods as long as several years in which investments cannot be withdrawn. Many also employ redemption notices that require investors to provide notice weeks or months in advance of their desire to redeem funds. These restrictions limit the liquidity of investors but in turn enable the funds to invest in illiquid assets where returns may be higher, without worrying about meeting unanticipated demands for redemptions.

Compensation Structure Hedge funds also differ from mutual funds in their fee structure. Whereas mutual funds assess management fees equal to a fixed percentage of assets, for example, between .5 and 1.5 percent annually for typical equity funds, hedge funds charge a management fee, usually between 1 and 2 percent of assets, *plus* a substantial *incentive fee* equal to a fraction of any investment profits beyond some benchmark. The incentive fee is often 20 percent. The threshold return to earn the incentive fee is often a money market rate such as LIBOR. Indeed, some observers characterize hedge funds, only half-jokingly, as "a compensation scheme masquerading as an asset class."

Hedge Fund Strategies

Table 23.3 lists most of the common investment themes found in the hedge fund industry. The list comprises a wide diversity of styles and suggests how hard it can be to speak generically about hedge funds as a group. We can, however, divide hedge fund strategies into two general categories: directional and nondirectional.

Directional and Nondirectional Strategies **Directional strategies** are easy to understand. They are simply bets that one sector or another will outperform other sectors of the market.

In contrast, **nondirectional strategies** are usually designed to exploit temporary misalignments in security valuations. For example, if the yield on corporate bonds seems abnormally high compared to that on Treasury bonds, the hedge fund would buy corporates and short-sell Treasury securities. Notice that the fund is *not* betting on broad movements in the entire bond market: it buys one type of bond and sells another. By taking a long corporate–short Treasury position, the fund hedges its interest rate exposure, while making a bet on the *relative* valuation across the two sectors. The idea is that when yield spreads converge back to their "normal" relationship, the fund will profit from the realignment regardless of the general trend in the level of interest rates.

TABLE 23.3   Hedge Fund Styles

Convertible arbitrage	Hedged investing in convertible securities, typically long convertible bonds and short stock.
Dedicated short bias	Net short position, usually in equities, as opposed to pure short exposure.
Emerging markets	Goal is to exploit market inefficiencies in emerging markets. Typically long-only, because short-selling is not feasible in many of these markets.
Equity-market-neutral	Commonly uses long/short hedges. Typically controls for industry, sector, size, and other exposures, and establishes market-neutral positions designed to exploit some market inefficiency. Commonly involves leverage.
Event-driven	Attempts to profit from situations such as mergers, acquisitions, restructuring, bankruptcy, or reorganization.
Fixed-income arbitrage	Attempts to profit from price anomalies in related interest-rate securities. Includes interest rate swap arbitrage, U.S. versus non-U.S. government bond arbitrage, yield-curve arbitrage, and mortgage-backed arbitrage.
Global macro	Involves long and short positions in capital or derivative markets across the world. Portfolio positions reflect views on broad market conditions and major economic trends.
Long/short equity hedge	Equity-oriented positions on either side of the market (i.e., long or short), depending on outlook. *Not* meant to be market-neutral. May establish a concentrated focus regionally (e.g., U.S. or Europe) or on a specific sector (e.g., tech or health care stocks). Derivatives may be used to hedge positions.
Managed futures	Uses financial, currency, or commodity futures. May make use of technical trading rules or a less structured judgmental approach.
Multistrategy	Opportunistic choice of strategy depending on outlook.
Fund of funds	Fund allocates its cash to several other hedge funds to be managed.

Note: CS/TASS (Credit Suisse/Tremont Advisors Shareholder Services) maintains one of the most comprehensive databases on hedge fund performance. It categorizes hedge funds into these 11 different investment styles.

In this respect, it strives to be **market-neutral**, or hedged with respect to the direction of interest rates, which gives rise to the term "hedge fund."

Nondirectional strategies are sometimes further divided into convergence or relative value positions. The difference between convergence and relative value is a time horizon at which one can say with confidence that any mispricing ought to be resolved. An example of a convergence strategy would entail mispricing of a futures contract that must be corrected by the time the contract matures. In contrast, the corporate versus Treasury spread we just discussed would be a relative value strategy, because there is no obvious horizon during which the yield spread would "correct" from unusual levels.

EXAMPLE 23.1   Market-Neutral Positions

We can illustrate a market-neutral position with a strategy used extensively by several hedge funds, which have observed that newly issued 30-year on-the-run Treasury bonds regularly sell at higher prices (lower yields) than 29½-year bonds with almost identical duration. The yield spread presumably is a premium due to the greater liquidity of the on-the-run bonds. Hedge funds, which have relatively low liquidity needs, therefore buy the 29½-year bond and sell the

continued

30-year bond. This is a hedged, or market-neutral, position that will generate a profit whenever the yields on the two bonds converge, as typically happens when the 30-year bonds age, are no longer the most liquid on-the-run bond, and are no longer priced at a premium.

Notice that this strategy should generate profits regardless of the general direction of interest rates. The long-short position will return a profit as long as the 30-year bonds underperform the 29½-year bonds, as they should when the liquidity premium dissipates. Because the pricing discrepancies between these two securities almost necessarily *must* disappear at a given date, this strategy is an example of convergence arbitrage. While the convergence date in this application is not quite as definite as the maturity of a futures contract, one can be sure that the currently on-the-run T-bonds will lose that status by the time the Treasury next issues 30-year bonds.

Long–short positions such as in Example 23.1 are characteristic of hedged strategies. They are designed to *isolate* a bet on some mispricing without taking on market exposure. Profits are made regardless of broad market movements once prices "converge" or return to their "proper" levels. Hence, use of short positions and derivatives is part and parcel of the industry.

A more complex long–short strategy is *convertible bond arbitrage*, one of the more prominent sectors of the hedge-fund universe. Noting that a convertible bond may be viewed as a straight bond plus a call option on the underlying stock, the market-neutral strategy in this case involves a position in the bond offset by an opposite position in the stock. For example, if the convertible is viewed as underpriced, the fund will buy it, and offset its resultant exposure to declines in the stock price by shorting the stock.

Although these market-neutral positions are hedged, they are *not* risk-free arbitrage strategies. Rather they should be viewed as **pure plays**, that is, bets on *particular* (perceived) mispricing between two sectors or securities, with extraneous sources of risk such as general market exposure hedged away. Moreover, because the funds often operate with considerable leverage, returns can be quite volatile.

> **CC 3**
>
> **CONCEPT CHECK**
>
> Classify each of the following strategies as directional or nondirectional.
> a. The fund buys shares in the India Investment Fund, a closed-end fund selling at a discount to net asset value, and sells the MSCI India Index Swap.
> b. The fund buys shares in Petrie Stores and sells Toys 'Я' Us, a major component of Petrie's balance sheet.
> c. The fund buys shares in Generic Pharmaceuticals betting that it will be acquired at a premium by Pfizer.

Statistical Arbitrage

Statistical arbitrage is a version of a market-neutral strategy, but one that merits its own discussion. It differs from pure arbitrage in that it does not exploit risk-free positions based on unambiguous mispricing (such as index arbitrage). Instead, it uses quantitative and often automated trading systems that seek out many temporary misalignments in prices among securities. By taking relatively small positions in many of these opportunities, the law of averages would make the probability of profiting from the collection of ostensibly positive-value bets very high, ideally almost a "statistical certainty." Of course, this strategy presumes that the fund's modelling techniques can actually identify reliable, if small, market inefficiencies. The law of averages will work for the fund only if the expected return is positive!

Statistical arbitrage often involves trading in hundreds of securities a day with holding periods that can be measured in minutes or less. Such rapid and heavy trading requires extensive use of quantitative tools such as automated trading and mathematical algorithms to identify profit opportunities and efficient diversification across positions. These strategies try to profit from the smallest of perceived mispricing opportunities, and require the fastest trading technology and the lowest possible trading costs. They would not be possible without the electronic communication networks discussed in Chapter 3.

A particular form of statistical arbitrage is **pairs trading**, in which stocks are paired up on the basis of an analysis of either fundamental similarities or market exposures (betas). The general approach is to pair up similar companies whose returns are highly correlated but wherein one company seems to be priced more aggressively than the other.[3] Market-neutral positions can be formed by buying the relatively cheap firm and selling the expensive one. Many such pairs make up the hedge fund's overall portfolio. Each pair may have an uncertain outcome, but with many such matched pairs, the presumption is that the large number of long–short bets will provide a very high probability of a positive abnormal return. More general versions of pairs trading allow for positions in clusters of stocks that may be relatively mispriced.

Statistical arbitrage is commonly associated with **data mining**, which refers to sorting through huge amounts of historical data to uncover systematic patterns in returns that can be exploited by traders. The risk of data mining, and statistical arbitrage in general, is that historical relationships may break down when fundamental economic conditions change or, indeed, that the apparent patterns in the data may be due to pure chance. Enough analysis applied to enough data is sure to produce apparent patterns that do not reflect real relationships that can be counted on to persist.

Portable Alpha

An important implication of the market-neutral pure play is the notion of **portable alpha**. Suppose you wish to speculate on a stock you think is underpriced, but you believe that the market is about to fall. Even if you are right about the stock being *relatively* underpriced, you still might lose money investing in it if it falls along with the broad market. You would like to separate the stock-specific bet from the implicit asset allocation bet on market performance that arises because the stock's beta is positive. The solution is to buy the stock and eliminate the resultant market exposure by selling enough index futures to drive beta to zero. This long stock–short futures strategy gives you a pure play or, equivalently, a *market-neutral* position on the stock.

More generally, you might wish to separate asset allocation from security selection. The idea is to invest wherever you can "find alpha." You would then hedge the systematic risk of that investment to isolate its alpha from the asset market where it was found. Finally, you establish exposure to desired market sectors by using passive products such as indexed mutual funds, ETFs, or index securities. In other words, you have created portable alpha that can be mixed with an exposure to whatever sector of the market you choose. This procedure is also called **alpha transfer**, because you transfer alpha from the sector where you find it to the asset class in which you finally establish exposure. Finding alpha requires skill. By contrast, beta, or market exposure, is a "commodity" that can be supplied cheaply through index products, and offers little value added.

An Example of a Pure Play   Suppose you manage a $1.4 million portfolio. You believe that the alpha of the portfolio is positive, $\alpha > 0$, but also that the market is about to fall, that is, that $r_M < 0$. You would therefore try to establish a pure play on the perceived mispricing.

---

[3]Rules for deciding relative "aggressiveness" of pricing may vary. In one approach, a computer scans for stocks whose prices historically have tracked very closely but have recently diverged. If the differential in cumulative return typically dissipates, the fund will buy the recently underperforming stock and sell the outperforming one. In other variants, pricing aggressiveness may be determined by evaluating the stocks based on some measure of price to intrinsic value.

The return on portfolio over the next month may be described by equation 23.1, which states that the portfolio return will equal its "fair" CAPM return (the first two terms on the right-hand side), plus firm-specific risk reflected in the "residual," e, plus an alpha that reflects perceived mispricing:

$$r_{\text{portfolio}} = r_f + \beta(r_M - r_f) + e + \alpha \tag{23.1}$$

To be concrete, suppose that $\beta = 1.20$, $\alpha = .02$, $r_f = .01$, the current value of the S&P 500 index is $S_0 = 1,344$, and, for simplicity, that the portfolio pays no dividends. You want to capture the positive alpha of 2 percent per month, but you don't want the positive beta that the stock entails because you are worried about a market decline. So you choose to hedge your exposure by selling S&P 500 futures contracts.

Because the S&P contracts have a multiplier of $250, and the portfolio has a beta of 1.20, your stock position can be hedged for 1 month by *selling* five futures contracts:[4]

$$\text{Hedge ratio} = \frac{\$1,400,000}{1,334 \times \$250} = 5 \text{ contracts}$$

The dollar value of your portfolio after 1 month will be

$$
\begin{aligned}
\$1,400,000 \times (1 + r_{\text{portfolio}}) &= \$1,400,000[1 + .01 + 1.20(r_M - .01) + .02 + e] \\
&= \$1,425,200 + \$1,680,000 \times r_M + \$1,400,000 \times e
\end{aligned}
$$

The dollar proceeds from your futures position will be:

$5 \times \$250 \times (F_0 - F_1)$	Mark to market on 5 contracts sold
$= \$1,250 \times [S_0(1.01 - S_1)]$	Substitute for futures prices from parity relationship
$= \$1,250 \times S_0[1.01 - (1 + r_M)]$	Because $S_1 = S_0(1 + r_M)$ when no dividends are paid
$= \$1,250 \times [S_0(.01 - r_M)]$	Simplify
$= \$16,800 - \$1,680,000 \times r_M$	Because $S_0 = 1,344$

The total value of the stock plus futures position at month's end will be the sum of the portfolio value plus the futures proceeds, which equals

$$\text{Hedged proceeds} = \$1,442,000 + \$1,400,000 \times e \tag{23.2}$$

Notice that the dollar exposure to the market from your futures position precisely offsets your exposure from the stock portfolio. In other words, you have reduced beta to zero. Your investment is $1.4 million, so your total monthly rate of return is 3 percent plus the remaining nonsystematic risk (the second term of equation 23.2). The fair or equilibrium expected rate of return on such a zero-beta position is the risk-free rate, 1 percent, so you have preserved your alpha of 2 percent, while eliminating the market exposure of the stock portfolio.

This is an idealized example of a pure play. In particular, it simplifies by assuming a known and fixed portfolio beta, but it illustrates that the goal is to speculate on the stock while hedging out the undesired market exposure. Once this is accomplished, you can establish any desired exposure to other sources of systematic risk by buying indices or entering index futures contracts in those markets. Thus, you have made alpha portable.

Figure 23.2 gives a graphical analysis of this pure play. Panel A shows the *excess* returns to betting on a positive-alpha stock portfolio "naked," that is, unhedged. Your *expected* return is better than an equilibrium return given your risk, but because of your market exposure you still

---

[4]We simplify here by assuming that the maturity of the futures contract precisely equals the hedging horizon, in this case one month. If the contract maturity were longer, one would have to slightly reduce the hedge ratio in a process called "tailing the hedge."

Figure 23.2

A pure play.
Panel A:
Unhedged
position.
Panel B:
Hedged position.

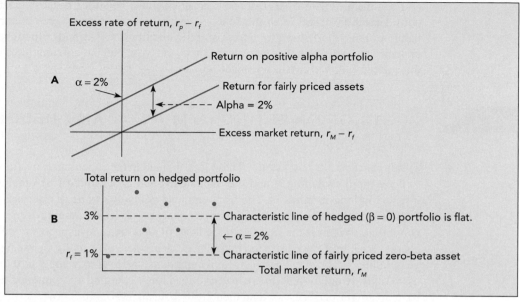

can lose if the market declines. Panel B shows the characteristic line for the position with systematic risk hedged out. There is no market exposure.

A warning: Even market-neutral positions are still bets, and they can go wrong. This is not true arbitrage because your profits still depend on whether your analysis (your perceived alpha) is correct. Moreover, you can be done in by simple bad luck, that is, your analysis may be correct but a bad realization of idiosyncratic risk (negative values of e in equation 23.1 or 23.2) can still result in losses.

CC 4

CONCEPT CHECK

What would be the dollar value and rate of return on the market-neutral position if the value of the residual turns out to be −4 percent? If the market return in that month is 5 percent, where would the plot of the strategy return lie in each panel of Figure 23.2?

EXAMPLE 23.2   LTCM: A Market-Neutral Play Gone Wrong

An apparently market-neutral bet misfired in 1998. While the 30- versus 29½-year maturity T-bond strategy (see Example 23.1) worked well over several years, it blew up when Russia defaulted on its debt, triggering massive investment demand for the safest, most liquid assets that drove up the price of the 30-year Treasury relative to its 29½-year counterpart. The big losses that ensued illustrate that even the safest bet—one based on convergence arbitrage— carries risks. Although the T-bond spread had to converge eventually, and in fact it did several weeks later, Long Term Capital Management and other hedge funds suffered large losses on their positions when the spread widened temporarily. The ultimate convergence came too late for LTCM, which was also facing massive losses on its other positions and had to be bailed out.

Even market-neutral bets can result in considerable volatility, because most hedge funds use considerable leverage. Most incidents of relative mispricing are fairly minor, and the hedged nature of long-short strategies makes overall volatility low. The hedge funds respond by scaling up their bets. This amplifies gains when their bets work out, but also amplifies losses. In the end, the volatility of the funds is not small.

23.4 COSTS OF INVESTING IN MUTUAL AND HEDGE FUNDS

Fee Structure

Front- and Back-End Load These fees are paid to cover commissions for selling agents and to deter rapid switching in and out of funds, which is detrimental to keeping the assets fully invested in long-term assets. The front-end load typically can be as high as 8 percent, so that a $1,000 investment only leaves $920 invested in a portfolio; discount brokers will often cut their commission to lower the load fee to the investor, and larger investments rapidly lead to a lower charge. Back-end loads leave the initial investment intact but usually charge 6 percent in the first year, falling by a percent per year, for redemptions; the load may apply to the initial or the final asset value. In addition, there are many no-load funds charging no front-end fee, which appear to have no poorer performance than their costly cousins.

Operating Expenses These expenses refer to the costs incurred by the mutual fund in operating the portfolio, including administrative expenses and advisory fees paid to the investment manager. These expenses usually are expressed as a percent of total assets under management and may range from .2 to 2.5 percent. Shareholders do not receive an explicit bill for these operating expenses; however, the expenses are periodically deducted from the assets of the fund. Shareholders pay these expenses through the reduced value of the portfolio. The average expense ratio of actively managed funds is considerably higher than that of indexed funds, one estimate being .93 percent versus .14 percent (weighted by assets under management).

Other Charges These refer to charges against the asset value for expenses due to distribution costs such as advertising, promotional literature including prospectuses and annual reports, and commissions paid to brokers (which may be alternative or additional to load fees and which include the trailer fees). (These are specifically referred to in the United States as "12b-1 charges.")

The combination of operating expenses and other charges is expressed as a ratio of total assets and is then referred to as the **management expense ratio**. Other expenses such as switching fees between funds in the family may be charged. The *Mutual Fund Sourcebook* published by Southam Information Products Ltd. provides data on fees for Canadian funds.

Fees and Mutual Fund Returns

The rate of return on an investment in a mutual fund is measured as the increase or decrease in net asset value plus income distributions such as dividends or distributions of capital gains expressed as a fraction of net asset value at the beginning of the investment period. If we denote the net asset value at the start and end of the period as NAV_0 and NAV_1, respectively, then

$$\text{Rate of return} = \frac{NAV_1 - NAV_0 + \text{Income and capital gain distributions}}{NAV_0}$$

For example, if a fund has an initial NAV of $20 at the start of the month, makes income distributions of $.15 and capital gain distributions of $.05, and ends the month with NAV of $20.10, the monthly rate of return is computed as

$$\text{Rate of return} = \frac{\$20.10 - \$20 + \$.15 + \$.05}{\$20} = .15 \text{ or } 1.5\%$$

Notice that this measure of the rate of return ignores any commissions such as front-end loads paid to purchase the fund.

On the other hand, the rate of return is affected by the fund's expenses and other fees. This is because such charges are periodically deducted from the portfolio, which reduces net asset value. Thus the investor's rate of return equals the gross return on the underlying portfolio minus the total expense ratio.

EXAMPLE 23.3   Fees and Net Returns

To see how expenses can affect rate of return, consider a fund with $100 million in assets at the start of the year and with 10 million shares outstanding. The fund invests in a portfolio of stocks that provides no income but increases in value by 10 percent. The expense ratio, including other charges, is 1 percent. What is the rate of return for an investor in the fund?

The initial NAV equals $100 million/10 million shares = $10 per share. In the absence of expenses, fund assets would grow to $110 million and NAV would grow to $11 per share, for a 10 percent rate of return. However, the expense ratio of the fund is 1 percent. Therefore, $1 million will be deducted from the fund to pay these fees, leaving the portfolio worth only $109 million, and NAV equal to $10.90. The rate of return on the fund is only 9 percent, which equals the gross return on the underlying portfolio minus the total expense ratio.

Fees can have a big effect on performance. Table 23.4 considers an investor who starts with $10,000 and can choose between three funds that all earn an annual 12 percent return on investment before fees but have different fee structures. The table shows the cumulative amount in each fund after several investment horizons. Fund A has total operating expenses of .5 percent, no load, and no other charges. This might represent an index fund. Fund B has no load but has 1 percent in management expenses and .5 percent in other charges. This level of charges is fairly typical of

TABLE 23.4

Impact of Costs on Investment Performance

	Cumulative Proceeds (all dividends reinvested)		
	Fund *A*	Fund *B*	Fund *C*
Initial investment*	$10,000	$10,000	$ 9,200
5 years	17,234	16,474	15,503
10 years	29,699	27,141	26,123
15 years	51,183	44,713	44,018
20 years	88,206	73,662	74,173

*After front-end load, if any.

Notes:
1. Fund *A* is no-load with .5 percent expense ratio.
2. Fund *B* is no-load with 1.5 percent expense ratio.
3. Fund *C* has an 8 percent load on purchase and reinvested dividends, with a 1 percent expense ratio.
4. Gross return on all funds is 12 percent per year before expenses. Net returns are 1.12(1 − *x*%).

actively managed equity funds. Finally, fund *C* has 1 percent in management expenses, no other charges, but assesses an 8 percent front-end load on purchases. Note the substantial return advantage of low-cost fund *A*. Moreover, that differential is greater for longer investment horizons.

Although expenses can have a big impact on net investment performance, it is sometimes difficult for the investor in a mutual fund to measure true expenses accurately. This is because of the common practice of paying for some expenses in **soft dollars**. A portfolio manager earns soft-dollar credits with a stockbroker by directing the fund's trades to that broker. On the basis of those credits, the broker will pay for some of the mutual fund's expenses, such as databases, computer hardware, or stock quotation systems. The soft-dollar arrangement means that the stockbroker effectively returns part of the trading commission to the fund. Purchases made with soft dollars are not included in the fund's expenses, so funds with extensive soft-dollar arrangements may report artificially low expense ratios to the public. The fund may, however, have paid the broker needlessly high commissions to obtain the soft-dollar "rebate." The impact of the higher trading commission shows up in net investment performance rather than in the reported expense ratio. Soft-dollar arrangements make it difficult for investors to compare fund expenses, and periodically these arrangements come under attack. Canadian regulations limit the soft-dollar arrangements that may be made.

CC 5

CONCEPT CHECK

The Equity Fund sells Class A shares with a front-end load of 4 percent and Class B shares with other charges of .5 percent annually as well as back-end load fees that start at 5 percent and fall by 1 percent for each full year the investor holds the portfolio (until the fifth year). Assume the rate of return on the fund portfolio net of operating expenses is 10 percent annually. What will be the value of a $10,000 investment in Class A and Class B shares if the shares are sold after (a) one year, (b) four years, (c) ten years? Which fee structure provides higher net proceeds at the end of each investment horizon?

Fee Structure in Hedge Funds

The typical hedge fund fee structure is a management fee of 1 percent to 2 percent of assets plus an **incentive fee** equal to 20 percent of investment profits beyond a stipulated benchmark performance annually. Incentive fees are effectively call options on the portfolio with a strike price equal to (Current portfolio value $\times$ 1 + Benchmark return). The manager gets the fee if the portfolio value rises sufficiently but loses nothing if it falls. This constitutes a call option for the fund managers that effectively can more than double a stated management fee of 2 percent. The major complication to this description of the typical compensation structure is the **high-water mark**. If a fund experiences losses, it may not be able to charge an incentive fee unless and until it recovers to its previous higher value. With large losses, this may be difficult. High-water marks therefore give managers an incentive to shut down funds that have performed poorly, and are likely to be the cause of the high attrition rate for funds that we see below.

One of the fastest-growing sectors in the hedge fund universe has been in **funds of funds**—hedge funds that invest in several other such funds. Optionality can have a big impact on expected fees in these funds. This is because the fund of funds pays an incentive fee to each underlying fund that outperforms its benchmark, even if the aggregate performance of the fund of funds is poor. In this case, diversification can hurt you.

The idea behind funds of funds is to spread risk across several different funds. Investors need to be aware, however, that funds of funds operate with considerable leverage on top of the leverage of the primary funds in which they invest, which can make returns highly volatile. Moreover, if the various hedge funds in which these funds invest have similar investment styles, the diversification benefits may be illusory—but the extra layer of steep management fees paid to the manager of the fund of funds certainly is not; the diversification benefit is more than offset by the payment of incentive fees to the individual hedge fund that achieve their thresholds. Part of the Bernie Madoff scandal involved hedge funds of funds that contributed to his Ponzi scheme, which says something about the benefits of diversification.

23.5 INVESTMENT PERFORMANCE OF MANAGED FUNDS

We noted earlier that one of the benefits of managed funds for the individual investor is the ability to delegate management of the portfolio to investment professionals. The investor retains control over the broad features of the overall portfolio through the asset allocation decision: each individual chooses the percentages of the portfolio to invest in bond funds versus equity funds versus money market funds, and so forth, but can leave the specific security selection decisions within each investment class to the managers of each fund. Shareholders hope that these portfolio managers can achieve better investment performance than they could obtain on their own.

Mutual Fund Performance

What is the investment record of the mutual fund industry? This seemingly straightforward question is deceptively difficult to answer because we need a standard against which to evaluate performance. For example, we clearly would not want to compare the investment performance of an equity fund to the rate of return available in the money market. The vast differences in the risk of these two markets dictate that year-by-year as well as average performance will differ considerably. We would expect to find that equity funds outperform money market funds (on average) as compensation to investors for the extra risk incurred in equity markets. How then can we determine whether mutual fund portfolio managers are performing up to par *given* the level of risk they incur? In other words, what is the proper benchmark against which investment performance ought to be evaluated?

Measuring portfolio risk properly and using such measures to choose an appropriate benchmark is far from straightforward. We devote all of Parts Two and Three of this text to issues surrounding the proper measurement of portfolio risk and the tradeoff between risk and return. In this chapter, therefore, we will content ourselves with a first look at the question of fund performance by using only very simple performance benchmarks and ignoring the more subtle issues of risk differences across funds.

Here[5] we use as a benchmark for the performance of equity fund managers the rate of return on the Wilshire 5000 Index. Recall from Chapter 2 that this is a value-weighted index of about 7,000 stocks that trade on the NYSE, Nasdaq, and Amex stock markets. It is the most inclusive index of the performance of U.S. equities. The performance of the Wilshire 5000 is a useful benchmark with which to evaluate professional managers because it corresponds to a simple passive investment strategy: buy all the shares in the index in proportion to their outstanding market value. Moreover, this is a feasible strategy for even small investors, because the Vanguard Group offers an index fund (its Total Stock Market Portfolio) designed to replicate the performance of the Wilshire 5000 Index. The expense ratio of the fund is extremely small by the standards of other equity funds, only .25 percent per year. Using the Wilshire 5000 Index as a benchmark, we may pose the problem of evaluating the performance of mutual fund portfolio managers this way: How does the typical performance of actively managed equity mutual funds compare to the performance of a passively managed portfolio that simply replicates the composition of a broad index of the stock market?

NYSE Euronext
https://nyse.nyx
.com

---

[5]We use U.S. data here due to the extensive study conducted.

Figure 23.3

Rates of return on actively managed equity funds versus Wilshire 5000 index, 1971–2011.

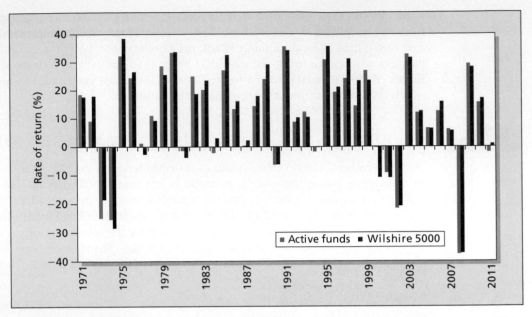

Casual comparisons of the performance of the Wilshire 5000 index versus that of professionally managed mutual fund portfolios show disappointing results for active managers. Figure 23.3 shows that the average return on diversified equity funds was below the return on the Wilshire index in 25 of the 41 years from 1971 to 2011. The average annual return on the index was 11.75 percent, exceeding that of the average mutual fund by 1 percent.[6]

This result may seem surprising to you. After all, it would not seem unreasonable to expect that professional money managers should be able to outperform a very simple rule such as "hold an indexed portfolio." As it turns out, however, there may be good reasons to expect such a result. We explored them in detail in Chapter 9, where we discussed the efficient market hypothesis.

Persistence in Performance

Of course, one might argue that there are good managers and bad managers, and that the good managers can, in fact, consistently outperform the index. To test this notion, we examine whether managers with good performance in one year are likely to repeat that performance in a following year. In other words, is superior performance in any particular year due to luck, and therefore random, or due to skill, and therefore consistent from year to year?

To answer this question, we can examine the performance of a large sample of equity mutual fund portfolios, divide the funds into two groups based on total investment return, and ask: "Do funds with investment returns in the top half of the sample in one period continue to perform well in a subsequent period?"

Table 23.5 presents such an analysis from a study by Malkiel.[7] The table shows the fraction of "winners" (i.e., top-half performers) in each year that turn out to be winners or losers in the following year. If performance were purely random from one period to the next, there would be

---

[6]Of course, actual funds incur trading costs while indices do not, so a fair comparison between the returns on actively managed funds versus those on a passive index should first reduce the return on the Wilshire 5000 by an estimate of such costs. Vanguard's Total Stock Market Index portfolio, which tracks the Wilshire 5000 fund, charges an expense ratio of less than .10 percent, and, because it engages in little trading, it incurs low trading costs. Therefore, it would be reasonable to reduce the returns on the index by about .15 percent. This reduction would not erase the difference in average performance.

[7]Burton G. Malkiel, "Returns from Investing in Equity Funds 1971–1991," *Journal of Finance* 50 (June 1995), pp. 549–72.

TABLE 23.5

Consistency of
Investment
Results

Initial-Period Performance	Successive-Period Performance (%)	
	Top Half	Bottom Half
A. Malkiel Study, 1970s		
Top half	65.1	34.9
Bottom half	35.5	64.5
B. Malkiel Study, 1980s		
Top half	51.7	48.3
Bottom half	47.5	52.5

Source: Burton G. Malkiel, "Returns from Investing in Equity Mutual Funds 1971–1991," *Journal of Finance* 50 (June 1995), pp. 549–572. Reprinted by permission of the publisher, Blackwell Publishing, Inc.

entries of 50 percent in each cell of the table, as top- or bottom-half performers would be equally likely to perform in either the top or bottom half of the sample in the following period. On the other hand, if performance were due entirely to skill, with no randomness, we would expect to see entries of 100 percent on the diagonals and entries of 0 percent on the off-diagonals: top-half performers would all remain in the top half while bottom-half performers similarly would all remain in the bottom half. In fact, the table shows that 65.1 percent of initial top-half performers fall in the top half of the sample in the following period, while 64.5 percent of initial bottom-half performers fall in the bottom half in the following period. This evidence is consistent with the notion that at least part of a fund's performance is a function of skill as opposed to luck, so that relative performance tends to persist from one period to the next.[8]

On the other hand, this relationship does not seem stable across different sample periods. While initial-year performance predicts subsequent-year performance in the 1970s (panel A), the pattern of persistence in performance virtually disappears in the 1980s (panel B). To summarize, the evidence that performance is consistent from one period to the next is suggestive, but it is inconclusive.

There have been a number of studies of Canadian fund performance, which have focused on various effects such as size, inflation, performance in up and down markets, and signs of managerial expertise. Fund performance for the period 1967–1984 was analyzed by Bishara,[9] who concluded that Canadian funds could not outperform the market. He subdivided his fund universe into balanced, income, and growth funds and considered their returns over boom and recession periods. His findings concluded that while growth funds managed to match the index return, the balanced and income funds were inferior to the index over the whole period and during one boom. A study by Calvet and Lefoll[10] used 17 mutual funds and considered the effect of inflation. Only one of the funds was able to outperform the market by one measure of performance and none did by other traditional measures; inflation offered no explanation for the results.

Other studies suggest that there is little performance persistence among professional managers, and if anything, bad performance is more likely to persist than good performance. This makes some sense: it is easy to identify fund characteristics that will predictably lead to consistently poor investment performance, notably high expense ratios, and high turnover ratios with

---

[8]Another possibility is that performance consistency is due to variation in fee structure across funds. We dealt with this possibility in Chapter 9.

[9]H. Bishara, "Evaluation of the Performance of Canadian Mutual Funds (1967–1984)," *Proceedings of the Administrative Sciences Association of Canada* 1, part 1 (1987), p. 18.

[10]A. L. Calvet and J. Lefoll, "The CAPM Under Inflation and the Performance of Canadian Mutual Funds," *Journal of Business Administration* 12, no. 1 (Fall 1980).

associated trading costs. It is far harder to identify the secrets of successful stock picking. (If it were easy, we would all be rich!) Thus the consistency we do observe in fund performance may be due in large part to the poor performers. On the other hand, the phenomenon of *survivorship bias*—the worst performers go out of business—implies that statistics based on surviving funds are upwardly biased. This suggests that the real value of past performance data is to avoid truly poor funds, even if identifying the future top performers is still a daunting task.

CC 6

CONCEPT CHECK

Suppose you observe the investment performance of 200 portfolio managers and rank them by investment returns during the year. Of the managers in the top half of the sample, 40 percent are truly skilled, but the other 60 percent fell in the top half purely because of good luck. What fraction of these top-half managers would you expect to be top-half performers next year?

Hedge Fund Performance

Because hedge funds can follow a variety of investment strategies, including both market-neutral, or nondirectional, and directional types, the returns are highly dependent on a number of different factors. As a result, a performance analyst would want to measure the fund's exposure to the various asset classes or factors. For a market-neutral fund, there would be no sensitivity, but a directional fund will exhibit significant betas or loadings on whichever factors the fund is betting on. Consequently, the style analysis introduced in Chapter 21 is particularly appropriate for hedge funds. An effective hedge fund assessment is provided by a simple style analysis with the following four systematic factors:

- *Interest rates.* The return on long-term U.S. Treasury bonds
- *Equity markets.* The return on the S&P 500
- *Credit conditions.* The difference in the return on Baa-rated bonds over Treasury bonds
- *Foreign exchange.* The percentage change in the value of the U.S. dollar against a basket of foreign currencies

Analyzing 13 hedge funds indices for their exposure to these factors, reveals that most funds are in fact directional with very clear exposures to one or more of the four factors. Moreover, the estimated factor betas seem reasonable in terms of the funds' stated style. For example:

- The equity market-neutral funds have uniformly low sector betas, as one would expect of a market-neutral posture.
- Dedicated short bias funds exhibit substantial negative betas on the S&P index.
- Distressed firm funds have significant exposure to credit conditions (more positive credit spreads in this table indicate better economic conditions) as well as to the S&P 500. This exposure arises because restructuring activities often depend on access to borrowing, and successful restructuring depends on the state of the economy.
- Global macro funds show negative exposure to a stronger U.S. dollar, which would make the dollar value of foreign investments less valuable.

We conclude that, by and large, most hedge funds are making very explicit directional bets on a wide array of economic factors.

Table 23.6 shows basic performance data for a collection of hedge fund indices computed from the standard index model with the S&P 500 used as the market benchmark. The model is

TABLE 23.6   Index Model Regressions for Hedge Fund Indices

	Beta	Serial Correlation	Alpha	Sharpe Ratio
Hedge fund composite index	.355	.321	.2	.123
Event-driven: Distressed	.324	.57	.206	.12
Event-driven: Merger arbitrage	.153	.254	.273	.287
Event-driven: All	.368	.466	.216	.128
Market-neutral	.09	.133	.007	.007
Short bias	−.668	.147	−.169	−.076
Emerging markets	.618	.357	.415	.133
Long/short hedge	.506	.306	.097	.061
Fund of funds	.261	.361	−.016	.012
Relative value	.245	.576	.3	.204
Fixed income: Asset-backed	.088	.57	.468	.468
Fixed income: Convertible arbitrage	.435	.597	.163	.072
Fixed income: Corporate	.322	.585	.113	.075
Multistrategy	.241	.565	.136	.1
S&P 500	1	.218	0	.031
Average across hedge funds	.238	.415	.171	.123

Note: Estimation period: January 2005–November 2011.

Source: Authors' calculations using data downloaded from Hedge Fund Research Inc., http://www.hedgefundresearch.com, March 2012.

estimated using monthly excess returns over the period January 2005 through November 2011. We report for each index the beta relative to the S&P 500, the serial correlation of returns, the alpha, and the Sharpe ratio. Betas tend to be considerably less than one; not surprisingly, the beta of the short bias index is large and negative. The market-neutral index has a beta near zero.

By and large, hedge fund performance is impressive. Most of the alpha estimates are positive, and the average alpha is substantial, .17 percent per month. Similarly, most Sharpe ratios exceed that of the S&P 500, and the average Sharpe ratio across hedge fund groups, .123, is four times that of the S&P 500. What might be the source of such seemingly impressive performance?

One possibility, of course, is the obvious one: these results may reflect a high degree of skill among hedge fund managers. Another possibility is that funds maintain some exposure to omitted risk factors that convey a positive risk premium, but given the extensive list of included factors, this seems unlikely. However, there are several other factors that make hedge fund performance difficult to evaluate, and these are worth considering.

Liquidity and Hedge Fund Performance   One explanation for apparently attractive hedge fund performance is liquidity. Recall from Chapter 7 that one of the more important extensions of the CAPM is a version that allows for the possibility of a return premium for investors willing to hold less liquid assets. Hedge funds tend to hold more illiquid assets than other institutional investors such as mutual funds. They can do so because of restrictions such as the lock-up provisions that commit investors to keep their investment in the fund for some period of time. Therefore, it is important to control for liquidity when evaluating performance. If it is ignored, what may be no more than compensation for illiquidity may appear to be true alpha, that is, risk-adjusted abnormal returns.

Aragon[11] demonstrates that hedge funds with lock-up restrictions do tend to hold less liquid portfolios. Moreover, once he controlled for lock-ups or other share restrictions (such as

[11]George O. Aragon, "Share Restrictions and Asset Pricing: Evidence from the Hedge Fund Industry," *Journal of Financial Economics* 83 (2007), pp. 33–58.

redemption notice periods), the apparently positive average alpha of those funds turned insignificant. Aragon's work suggests that the typical "alpha" exhibited by hedge funds may be better interpreted as an equilibrium liquidity premium rather than a sign of stock-picking ability, in other words a "fair" reward for providing liquidity to other investors.

One symptom of illiquid assets is serial correlation in returns. Positive serial correlation means that positive returns are more likely to be followed by positive than by negative returns. Such a pattern is often taken as an indicator of less liquid markets for the following reason. When prices are not available because an asset is not actively traded, the hedge fund must estimate its value to calculate net asset value and rates of return. But such procedures are at best imperfect and, as demonstrated by Getmansky, Lo, and Makarov,[12] tend to result in serial correlation in prices as firms either smooth out their value estimates or only gradually mark prices to true market values. Positive serial correlation is therefore often interpreted as evidence of liquidity problems; in nearly efficient markets with frictionless trading, we would expect serial correlation or other predictable patterns in prices to be minimal. Most mutual funds show almost no evidence of such correlation in their returns and, as Table 23.6 documents, the serial correlation of the S&P 500 in most periods is just about zero.[13]

In a study on a sample of hedge funds, Hasanhodzic and Lo[14] find that hedge fund returns in fact exhibit significant serial correlation. This suggestion of smoothed prices has two important implications. First, it lends further support to the hypothesis that hedge funds are holding less liquid assets and that their apparent alphas may in fact be liquidity premiums. Second, it implies that their performance measures are upward-biased, because any smoothing in the estimates of portfolio value will reduce total volatility (increasing the Sharpe ratio) as well as covariances and therefore betas with systematic factors (increasing risk-adjusted alphas).

In fact, Figure 23.4 shows that both the alphas and the Sharpe ratios of the hedge fund indices in Table 23.6 increase with the serial correlation of returns. These results are consistent with the fund-specific results of Hasanhodzic and Lo and suggest that price smoothing may account for some part of the apparently superior average hedge fund performance.

Whereas Aragon focuses on the average *level* of liquidity, Sadka addresses the liquidity *risk* of hedge funds.[15] He shows that exposure to unexpected declines in market liquidity is an important determinant of average hedge fund returns, and that the spread in average returns across the funds with the highest and the lowest liquidity exposure may be as much as 6 percent annually. Hedge fund performance may therefore reflect significant compensation for liquidity risk.

Returns can be even more difficult to interpret if a hedge fund takes advantage of illiquid markets to manipulate returns by purposely misvaluing illiquid assets. In this regard, it is worth noting that, on average, reported hedge fund returns in December are substantially greater than their average returns in other months.[16] The pattern is stronger for lower-liquidity funds and funds that are near or beyond the threshold return at which performance incentive fees kick in. It appears that some funds use their discretion in valuing assets to move returns to December when that will enhance their annual incentive fees. It also appears that some hedge funds attempt to

[12]Mila Getmansky, Andrew W. Lo, and Igor Makarov, "An Econometric Model of Serial Correlation and Illiquidity in Hedge Fund Returns," *Journal of Financial Economics* 74 (2004), pp. 529–609.

[13]The 2005–2011 period, in which the serial correlation of monthly excess returns for the S&P 500 was .218 (see Table 23.6), is a striking exception to this general rule. This aberration arises from the period of the financial crash, when the return on the S&P 500 was strongly negative in sequential months (September–November 2008, and then again in January and February of 2009). These sequences of large, consecutive negative returns resulted in positive serial correlation over the sample period, a highly unusual outcome for the index. Note, however, that even in this period the average serial correlation of the hedge fund indices is nearly twice that of the S&P 500.

[14]Jasmina Hasanhodzic and Andrew P. Lo, "Can Hedge Fund Returns Be Replicated? The Linear Case," *Journal of Investment Management* 5 (2007), pp. 5–45.

[15]Ronnie Sadka, "Liquidity Risk and the Cross-Section of Hedge-Fund Returns," *Journal of Financial Economics* 98 (October 2010), pp. 54–71.

[16]Vikas Agarwal, Naveen D. Daniel, and Narayan Y. Naik, "Why Is Santa So Kind to Hedge Funds? The December Return Puzzle!" March 29, 2007, http://ssrn.com/abstract=891169.

Figure 23.4

Hedge funds with higher serial correlation in returns, an indicator of illiquid portfolio holdings, exhibit higher alphas **(panel A)** and higher Sharpe ratios **(panel B)**.

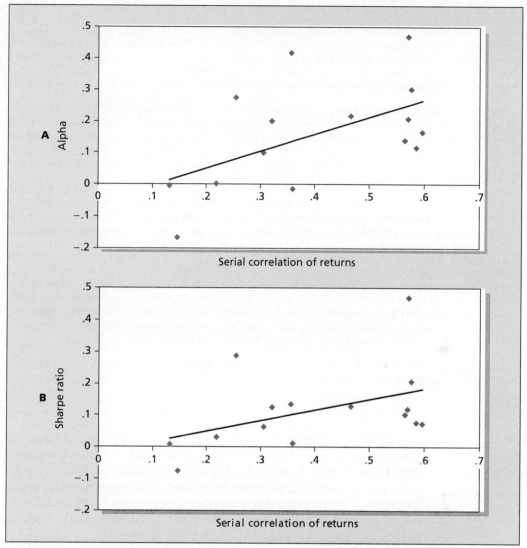

Source: Plotted from data in Table 23.6.

manipulate their measured performance by buying additional shares in stocks they already own in an effort to push up their prices.[17] The buying takes place just before market close at the end of the month when hedge fund performance is reported. Moreover, the effort is concentrated in less liquid stocks where the price impact would be expected to be greater. If, as these papers suggest, funds take advantage of illiquid markets to manage returns, then accurate performance measurement becomes almost impossible. The box here discusses problems in obtaining reliable price quotes for infrequently traded hedge fund assets.

Hedge Fund Performance and Survivorship Bias   We already know that survivorship bias (when only successful funds are included in a database) can affect the measured performance of a sample of mutual funds. The same problems, as well as related ones, apply to hedge funds.

[17]Itzhak Ben-David, Francesco Franzoni, Augustin Landier, and Rabih Moussawi, "Do Hedge Funds Manipulate Stock Prices?" *Journal of Finance* 68 (2013), pp. 2383–2434.

Since the invention of the ticker tape 140 years ago, America has been able to boast of having the world's most transparent financial markets. These days, after a decade of frantic growth in mortgage-backed securities and other complex investments traded off exchanges, that clarity is gone. Large parts of American financial markets have become a hall of mirrors.

Today, "way less than half" of all securities trade on exchanges with readily available price information, according to Goldman Sachs Group Inc. analyst Daniel Harris. As a result, money managers can no longer gauge with certainty the value of some assets in mutual funds, hedge funds and other investment vehicles—a process known as marking to market.

For years, one of the bedrocks of U.S. financial markets had been that clear prices were available to all. When prices went up or down, investors knew it right away, and they could usually figure out why. The credit crunch that struck earlier this year highlighted a danger lurking in markets for newfangled securities: When buyers pull back and nothing trades, investors can be in for unpleasant surprises.

During this summer's credit crunch, more than 80% of investors in bonds tied to the mortgage market said they had trouble obtaining price quotes from their bond dealers, according to a survey of 251 institutional investors by Greenwich Associates, a Connecticut consulting firm.

Moreover, some Wall Streeters have a motive to inflate marks: Their bonuses often are tied to the value of their holdings. "Everyone has an incentive in the short run to put the best face" on valuations, says Peter J. Solomon, a former Lehman vice chairman who now heads an investment bank.

The SEC is examining how accurately mutual funds and other investors "value their hard-to-value" securities, according to Douglas Scheidt, an associate director in the SEC's division of investment management. Investment funds are supposed to adjust their price marks if they sell assets at a different price level, says Mr. Scheidt. But when turmoil hit the market for subprime-mortgage securities, some funds were either "obtaining quotes that didn't seem to reflect what was going on in the market, or the dealer they had been using stopped providing quotes, yet the funds continued using stale quotes for several weeks," he says.

Since the recent market turmoil, some traders seem to be trying to set prices simply by offering them for sale, according to some investors who say they've talked to traders. The position is then marked at the "offer" price, these investors say. That's akin to a home-owner valuing a house based on how much he wants for it—not how much a buyer is willing to pay.

Source: Susan Pulliam, Randall Smith, and Michael Siconolfi, *The Wall Street Journal*, October 12, 2007, p. A1. © 2007 Dow Jones & Company, Inc. All rights reserved worldwide.

Backfill bias arises because hedge funds report returns to database publishers only if they choose to. Funds started with seed capital will open to the public and therefore enter standard databases only if their past performance is deemed sufficiently successful to attract clients. Therefore, the prior performance of funds that are eventually included in the sample may not be representative of typical performance. **Survivorship bias** arises when unsuccessful funds that cease operation stop reporting returns and leave a database, leaving behind only the successful funds. Malkiel and Saha[18] find that attrition rates for hedge funds are far higher than for mutual funds—in fact, commonly more than double the attrition rate of mutual funds—making this an important issue to address. Malkiel and Saha estimate survivorship bias at 4.4 percent, but most other studies find somewhat smaller values.[19]

Hedge Fund Performance and Changing Factor Loadings

In Chapter 21, we pointed out that an important assumption underlying conventional performance evaluation is that the portfolio manager maintains a reasonably stable risk profile over time. But hedge funds are designed to be opportunistic and have considerable flexibility to change that profile. This too can make performance evaluation tricky. If risk is not constant, then estimated alphas will be biased if we use a standard, linear index model. And if the risk profile changes in systematic manner with the expected return on the market, performance evaluation is even more difficult.

To see why, look at Figure 23.5, which illustrates the characteristic line of a perfect market timer (see Chapter 21, Section 21.5) who engages in no security selection but moves funds from

---

[18]Burton G. Malkiel and Atanu Saha, "Hedge Funds: Risk and Return," *Financial Analysts Journal* 61 (2005), pp. 80–88.

[19]For example, G. Amin and H. Kat, "Stocks, Bonds and Hedge Funds: Not a Free Lunch!" *Journal of Portfolio Management* 29 (Summer 2003), pp. 113–20, find a bias of about 2 percent, and William Fung and David Hsieh, "Performance Characteristics of Hedge Funds and CTA Funds: Natural Versus Spurious Biases," *Journal of Financial and Quantitative Analysis* 35 (2000), pp. 291–307, find a bias of about 3.6 percent.

Figure 23.5 Characteristic line of a perfect market timer. The true characteristic line is kinked, with a shape like that of a call option. Fitting a straight line to the relationship will result in misestimated slope and intercept.

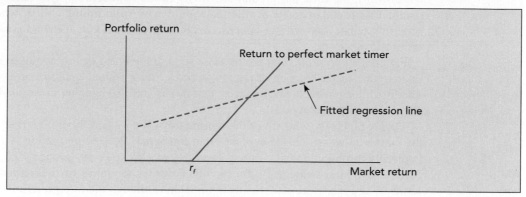

T-bills into the market portfolio only when the market will outperform bills. The characteristic line is nonlinear, with a slope of 0 when the market's excess return is negative, and a slope of 1 when it is positive. But a naïve attempt to estimate a regression equation from this pattern would result in a fitted line with a slope between 0 and 1, and a positive alpha. Neither statistic accurately describes the fund.

As we noted in Chapter 21, and as is evident from Figure 23.5, an ability to conduct perfect market timing is much like obtaining a call option on the underlying portfolio without having to pay for it. Similar nonlinearities would arise if the fund actually buys or writes options. Figure 23.6, panel A, illustrates the case of a fund that holds a stock portfolio and writes put

Figure 23.6

Characteristic lines of stock portfolio with written options. **Panel A:** Buy stock, write put. Here, the fund writes fewer puts than the number of shares it holds. **Panel B:** Buy stock, write calls. Here, the fund writes fewer calls than the number of shares it holds.

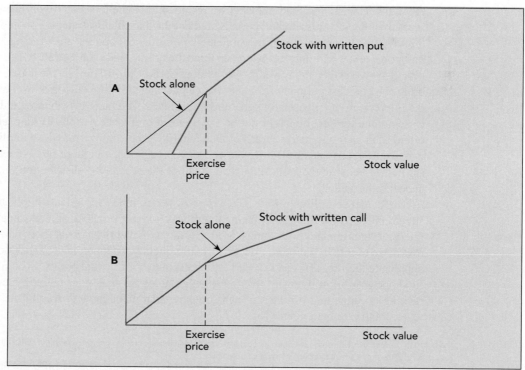

options on it, and panel B illustrates the case of a fund that holds a stock portfolio and writes call options. In both cases, the characteristic line is steeper when portfolio returns are poor—in other words, the fund has greater sensitivity to the market when it is falling than when it is rising. This is the opposite profile that would arise from timing ability, which is much like acquiring rather than writing options, and therefore would give the fund greater sensitivity to market advances.[20]

Figure 23.7 presents evidence on these sorts of nonlinearities. A nonlinear regression line is fitted to the scatter diagram of returns on hedge funds plotted against returns on the S&P 500. The fitted lines in each panel suggest that these funds have higher down-market betas (higher slopes) than up-market betas.

This is precisely what investors presumably do *not* want: higher market sensitivity when the market is weak. This is evidence that funds may be *writing* options, either explicitly or implicitly through dynamic trading strategies (see Chapter 19, Section 19.5, for a discussion of such dynamic strategies). On the other hand, the alphas of these funds are uniformly positive, and many are statistically significant (although the interpretation of these alphas is subject to the caveats discussed in this section, such as liquidity, survivorship bias, and price accuracy).

Just as hedge fund betas may be unstable, so may be other aspects of their risk profile, for example, total volatility of returns. Because they have great discretion to use leverage and to trade in derivatives, these funds have tremendous capacity to alter their risk exposures. Recall from Chapter 22 that when portfolio managers can change risk within any measurement period, they can also manipulate standard measures of risk-adjusted return. Thus, one would like them to compute and report manipulation-proof performance measures such as Morningstar's risk-adjusted return.

Tail Events and Hedge Fund Performance

Imagine a hedge fund whose entire investment strategy is to hold an S&P 500 index fund and write deep-out-of-the-money put options on the index. Clearly the fund manager brings no skill to the job. But if you knew only his or her investment results over limited periods, and not the underlying strategy, you might be fooled into thinking that he or she is extremely talented. For if the put options are written sufficiently out-of-the-money, they will only rarely end up imposing a loss, and such a strategy can appear over long periods—even over many years—to be consistently profitable. In most periods, the strategy brings in a modest premium from the written puts and therefore outperforms the S&P 500, giving the impression of consistently superior performance. The huge loss that might be incurred in an extreme market decline might not be experienced even over periods as long as years. Every so often, such as in the market crash of October 1987, the strategy may lose multiples of its entire gain over the last decade. But if you are lucky enough to avoid these rare but extreme *tail events* (so named because they fall in the far-left tail of the probability distribution), the strategy might appear to be gilded.

The evidence in Figure 23.7 indicating that hedge funds are at least implicitly option writers should make us nervous about taking their measured performance at face value. The problem in interpreting strategies with exposure to extreme tail events (such as short options positions) is that these events by definition occur very infrequently, so it can take *decades* of results to fully appreciate their true risk and reward attributes. In two influential books,[21] Nassim Taleb, a hedge fund operator himself, argues that many hedge funds are analogous to our hypothetical manager, racking up fame and fortune through strategies that make money *most* of the time, but expose investors to rare but extreme losses.

---

[20]But the fund that writes options would at least receive fair compensation for the unattractive shape of its characteristic line in the form of the premium received when it writes the options.

[21]Nassim N. Taleb, *Fooled by Randomness: The Hidden Role of Chance in Life and in the Markets* (New York: TEXERE [Thomson], 2004); Nassim N. Taleb, *The Black Swan: The Impact of the Highly Improbable* (New York: Random House, 2007).

Figure 23.7 Monthly return on hedge fund indices versus return on the S&P 500, 1993–2009. **Panel A:** Hedge fund index. **Panel B:** Market-neutral funds. **Panel C:** Short-bias funds.

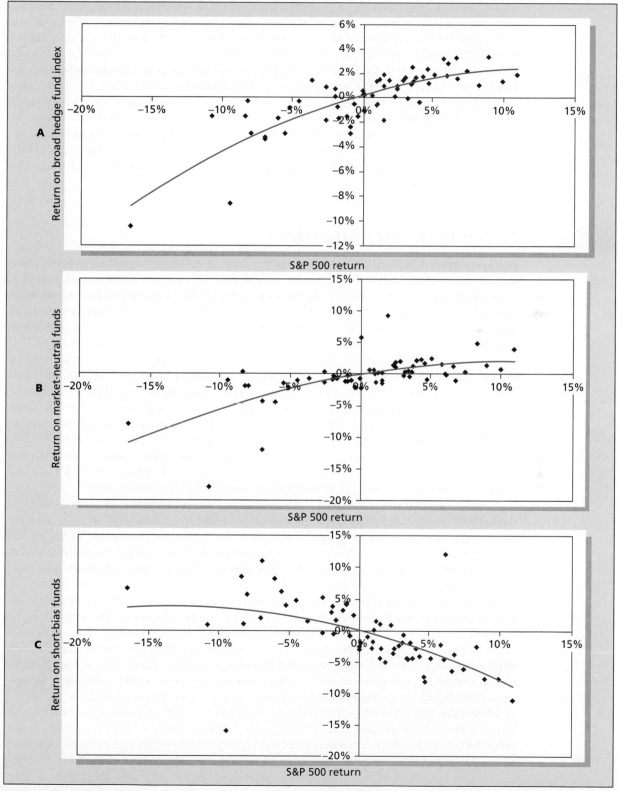

Source: Data downloaded from Credit Suisse Hedge Index, http://www.hedgeindex.com, and Yahoo Finance, http://finance.yahoo.com.

Taleb uses the metaphor of the black swan to discuss the importance of highly improbable, but highly impactful, events. Until the discovery of Australia, Europeans believed that all swans were white: they had never encountered swans that were not white. In their experience, the black swan was outside the realm of reasonable possibility, in statistical jargon, an extreme outlier relative to their sample of observations. Taleb argues that the world is filled with black swans, deeply important developments that simply could not have been predicted from the range of accumulated experience to date. While we can't predict which black swans to expect, we nevertheless know that one may be making an appearance at any moment. The October 1987 crash, when the market fell by more than 20 percent in one day, might be viewed as a black swan—an event that had never taken place before, one that most market observers would have dismissed as impossible and certainly not worth modelling, but with high impact. These sorts of events seemingly come out of the blue, and they caution us to show great humility when we use past experience to evaluate the future risk of our actions. With this in mind, consider again the example of Long Term Capital Management.

23.6 EXCHANGE-TRADED FUNDS

Exchange-traded funds (ETFs) are products that allow investors to trade index portfolios just as they do shares of individual stocks. The first ETF was the TIP (Toronto Index Participation unit), which represented a share of the TSE 35 index value; this predated the first U.S. ETF known as the "spider," a nickname for SPDR or S&P Depository Receipt, which was a unit investment trust holding a portfolio based on the S&P 500 index. TIPs were expanded by the creation of TIPs on the TSE 100, which is a closer approximation of a broad index such as the S&P 500.

These ETFs give investors the diversification advantage of a large mutual fund but allow trading throughout the day, like ordinary shares, rather than at the closing value like mutual funds. The U.S. market added to spiders by devising the "cubes" (from the symbol QQQ for the Nasdaq 100 index unit), the "diamonds" (from DIA for the Dow-Jones Industrials), and WEBS (World Equity Benchmark Shares); these permitted investments in either the technology-heavy Nasdaq, the conservative Dow, or foreign stock market indices. Cubes and spiders are consistently the most heavily traded securities on U.S. exchanges, with average daily volume of 40 million and over 100 million, respectively; by 2012, over $1 trillion was invested in more than 1100 U.S. ETFs. For Canadian investors, these are excellent vehicles for U.S. diversification.

With the creation of the new S&P/TSX 60 Index, TIPs were replaced by iUnits, called the i60s. iUnits are index securities issued by BlackRock based on the S&P/TSX 60 Index and subindices. The i60, trading under the symbol XIU, is the basic index security for the TSX. Canadian ETFs include a variety of products with a capped index, portfolios of IT, financial, energy, and gold companies, fixed-income funds on 5- and 10-year Canadas, and a Canadian-listed S&P 500 fund. These have been designed to reflect the primary interests of Canadian investors.

Technically, ETFs are securities that participate in an open-ended fund. In the case of i60s, the fund is established by BlackRock and holds a portfolio of the 60 stocks in the index. They are listed like common shares and pay dividends, as well as being marginable. These units allow small investors to hold a portfolio of senior Canadian firms diversified across the economy, similarly to owning a mutual fund but escaping the management fee. Acceptance is high, with the i60 being the largest Canadian mutual fund for Canadian securities, and the second most actively traded security on the exchange in 2012.

Many other ETFs now exist. BMO has numerous ETFs, including Canadian sector ETFs capturing banks, oil and gas, utilities, industrials, and REITs, as well as fixed-income ETFs, U.S. broad and sector indices, international and other equities, commodities, and more. Foreign index shares can be bought as part of the S&P international index portfolio as iShares based on either

TABLE 23.7

ETF Sponsors and Products

A. ETF Sponsors

Sponsor	Product Name
BlackRock	i-Shares
Merrill Lynch	HOLDRs (Holding Company Depository Receipts: "Holders")
State Street/Merrill Lynch	Select Sector SPDRs (S&P Depository Receipts: "Spiders")
Vanguard	VIPERs (Vanguard Index Participation Equity Receipts: "Vipers")

B. Sample of ETF Products

Name	Ticker	Index Tracked
Canadian Indices		
iShares Composite	XIC	S&P/TSX Composite
iShares 60 Index	XIU	S&P/TSX 60
iShares Energy	XEG	S&P/TSX Capped Energy Index
iShares Financial	XFN	S&P/TSX Capped Financial Index
iShares Gold	XGD	S&P/TSX Global Gold Index
iShares Bond	XBB	Scotia Capital Universe Bond Index
iShares Real Return Bond	XRB	Scotia Capital Real Return Bond Index
iShares MSCI EAFE	XIN	MSCI EAFE 100% Hedged Index
Broad U.S. Indices		
Spiders	SPY	S&P 500
Diamonds	DIA	Dow Jones Industrials
Cubes	QQQ	Nasdaq 100
iShares Russell 2000	IWM	Russell 2000
VIPERS	VTI	Wilshire 5000
International Indices		
WEBS United Kingdom	EWU	MCSI U.K. Index
WEBS France	EWQ	MCSI France Index
WEBS Japan	EWJ	MCSI Japan Index

S&P global funds or Morgan Stanley country indices (MSCI). Sectors of the U.S. market can be bought again as iShares linked to almost all the recognized U.S. indices, as SPDR Selects on industry groups, as Merrill Lynch HOLDRs (Holding Company Depository Receipts), and as S&P Global industry sector indices. (See Table 23.7 for a list of some issuers and products.) In addition, chartered banks may trade their index funds as ETFs.

ETFs offer several advantages over conventional mutual funds. First, as we just noted, a mutual fund's net asset value is quoted—and therefore, investors can buy or sell their shares in the fund—only once a day. In contrast, ETFs trade continuously. Moreover, like other shares, but unlike mutual funds, ETFs can be sold short or purchased on margin.

ETFs also offer a potential tax advantage over mutual funds. When large numbers of mutual fund investors redeem their shares, the fund must sell securities to meet the redemptions. This can trigger large capital gains taxes, which are passed through to and must be paid by the remaining shareholders. In contrast, when small investors wish to redeem their position in an ETF, they simply sell their shares to other traders, with no need for the fund to sell any of the underlying portfolio. Again, a redemption does not trigger a stock sale by the fund sponsor.

Figure 23.8

ETF asset value
growth.

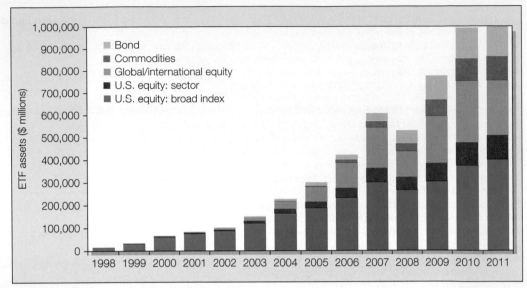

Source: *2012 Investment Company Fact Book: A Review of Trends and Activity in the U.S. Investment Company Industry* (Washington, DC: Investment Company Institute, 2012).

Large investors can exchange their ETF shares for shares in the underlying portfolio, avoiding a tax liability. This potential ensures that the price of an ETF cannot depart significantly from the net asset value of that portfolio. A significant discrepancy would give rise to an arbitrage opportunity for large traders, eliminating the disparity.

ETFs are also cheaper than mutual funds. Investors who buy ETFs do so through brokers rather than buying directly from the fund. Therefore, the fund saves the cost of marketing itself directly to small investors. This reduction in expenses translates into lower management fees. For example, Barclays charges annual expenses of just over 9 basis points (i.e., .09 percent) of net asset value per year on its S&P 500 ETF, whereas Vanguard charges 18 basis points on its S&P 500 index mutual fund.

More recently, a variety of new ETF products have been devised. Among these are leveraged ETFs, with daily returns that are a targeted *multiple* of the returns on an index, and inverse ETFs, which move in the opposite direction to an index. In addition, there is now a small number of actively managed ETF funds that, like actively managed mutual funds, attempt to outperform market indices. But these account for only about 3 percent of assets under management in the ETF industry. Figure 23.8 shows both the growth in asset value of ETFs and the expansion of more exotic categories of ETFs.

Other even more exotic variations are so-called synthetic ETFs such as exchange-traded notes (ETNs) or exchange-traded vehicles (ETVs). These are nominally debt securities, but with payoffs linked to the performance of an index. Often that index measures the performance of an illiquid and thinly traded asset class, so the ETF gives the investor the opportunity to add that asset class to his or her portfolio. However, rather than invest in those assets directly, the ETF achieves this exposure by entering a "total return swap" with an investment bank in which the bank agrees to pay the ETF the return on the index in exchange for a relatively fixed fee. These have become controversial, as the ETF is then exposed to risk that in a period of financial stress the investment bank will be unable to fulfill its obligation, leaving investors without the returns they were promised.

There are some disadvantages to ETFs, however. Because they trade as securities, there is the possibility that their prices can depart by small amounts from net asset value. Although a large amount would be arbitraged, even small discrepancies can easily swamp the cost advantage of

Exchange-traded funds are at the centre of one of the biggest transformations in the indexing world, a no-frills fund category launched by U.S. firm Vanguard Group in 1976. As ETFs have spread to every corner of the stock market, both in North America and abroad, financial advisors small and large have been turning to these products for their flexibility, tax efficiency, low cost and, in some cases, market beating returns. A decade ago, 19 ETFs held just US$6.7-billion. Now there are 387, according to State Street, that hold US$422-billion. That's still a small sliver of the US$10-trillion sitting in mutual funds, but the impact has been swift and dramatic.

With the ETF universe growing at warp speed, the question arises whether it would be possible to create an all-ETF portfolio—and whether that would be a wise strategy. ETFs do offer some attractive advantages over other investments. For one, investors don't have to worry about finding the best pharmaceutical or retail stock, for example. They can just buy the industry ETF. In addition, since ETFs constantly change hands investors can jump in and out of the market quickly, a huge selling point for active traders. In most cases, they can also be shorted. And for the most part they charge cheap fees and have better tax efficiency than mutual funds since their low turnover doesn't typically lead to big capital-gains hits. A new generation of ETFs is even allowing small-time investors to get access to some sophisticated strategies that in the past were reserved for a select few.

In the wrong hands, though, those benefits can cause problems. After all, the original idea behind index funds was to give investors access to the entire market through a product that shunned sales and marketing charges while eliminating turnover. Being able to trade index funds throughout the day—in addition to shorting them, too—is anathema to John Bogle, Vanguard's founder. "If long-term investing was the paradigm for the classic index fund," he said in the *Wall Street Journal* last week, "trading ETFs can only be described as short-term speculation."

He has a point. Most of the newer products are untested and designed with institutional or hedge-fund clients in mind. Today, many ETFs track benchmarks that did not exist just two years ago. Finally, there's also a profit motive at play: ETFs generate about US$1-billion in management fees. That does not include the trading commissions that fall into the pockets of brokerages and wire houses.

That said, there are two essential products to any standard ETF portfolio: one that tracks the market cap–weighted S&P 500 index, and another that does the same internationally. These funds would represent the core of a portfolio, garnering 50% or of assets. They will provide broad exposure to the stock market while charging some of the lowest fees.

The most popular option for U.S. exposure is State Street's SPDR, which holds US$63-billion, or 15% of the industry's assets. It has returned an average annual 10.7% since then, the same returns as the broad market minus fees. Other alternatives include the Vanguard Total Stock Market (VTI) ETF, along with a series of funds designed around the Russell 3000. These funds invest in a wider universe of stocks—more than double the number of the S&P 500—that are smaller than the average S&P 500 member.

Those core holdings could be rounded out with new fixed-income ETFs that were just released by iShares. These offerings track well-established Lehman bond indexes that cover corporate and government paper, along with U.S. treasuries in various durations. These funds charge between 0.15% and 0.20%. Some additional risk could be added by selecting some ETFs that specialize in certain stocks, like growth firms or value plays.

Most fund families have ETFs that track energy, technology, consumer staples, utilities, financial services and health care, among other industries. Making the right bet on a part of the market can pay off big.

Source: Rob Wherry, *National Post*, February 16, 2007, p. FP.13. Copyright National Post 2007. Don Mills, ON.

ETFs over mutual funds. Second, while mutual funds can be bought at no expense from no-load funds, ETFs must be purchased from brokers for a fee; discount commissions make this relatively minor. (See the boxed article.)

A very popular category is commodity ETFs which grew from $1 billion in 2004 to $109 billion by 2011; ETFs have been the main vehicle for speculation in precious metals. Critics have noted that the explosion of narrowly defined indices or focuses tracked by ETFs has resulted in many cases of poorly designed funds which are insufficiently hedged against rare events and composed of relatively illiquid assets. In the so-called flash crash of May 6, 2010, when the Dow Jones Industrial Average fell by 583 points in *seven minutes*, leaving it down nearly 1,000 points for the day. Remarkably, the index recovered more than 600 points in the next 10 minutes. In the wake of this incredible volatility, the stock exchanges canceled many trades that had gone off at what were viewed as distorted prices. Around one-fifth of all ETFs changed hands on that day at prices less than one-half of their closing price, and ETFs accounted for about two-thirds of all cancelled trades. At least two problems were exposed in this episode. First, when markets are not working properly, it can be hard to measure the net asset value of the ETF portfolio, especially for ETFs that track less liquid assets. And, reinforcing this problem, some ETFs may be supported by only a very small number of dealers. If they drop out of the market during a period of turmoil, prices may swing wildly.

Another problem is that index tracking ETFs, particularly for foreign markets, are designed to replicate an index by statistical analysis and hold a far smaller number of assets than the actual index; in fact, all too many such ETFs depart noticeably from the realized index return over quarterly periods. This is tracking error, and these price discrepancies can easily swamp the cost advantage that ETFs otherwise offer.

23.7 INFORMATION ON MUTUAL FUNDS

Besides the tax effects on mutual fund returns, which apply to all funds, there are two major issues particular to the choice of specified funds, namely the fees that are charged by the management companies and the success that they have in managing the funds. Both of these crucial pieces of information can be obtained *in one form or another.* That qualifying phrase is there to indicate that what funds may advertise about their fees and performance will tend to cast them in a favourable light that may omit some of the relevant factors; for example, the advertised return is likely to be for the best-performing funds without mention of the benchmark index or the risk involved. What is needed is an independent appraisal service that presents information in a consistent and complete manner.

Globefunds.com
www.globefunds
.com
Morningstar
Research Inc.
www.morningstar
.ca

Analyses of fund performance should include information relevant to the type of fund in question. As a means of providing meaningful comparisons, funds must be grouped by type, including: balanced, dividend (income), Canadian equity, U.S. equity, international equity, and money market, bond, mortgage, and real estate funds. There must also be a measure of volatility and a list of returns for periods ranging from three months to 10 years, where these are net of management fees and include reinvestment of dividends. The compound annual rate of return over different periods should also appear. Other details such as sales commissions or "loads" and contact numbers would also be typical. Online sources include Globefunds.com, http://finance.yahoo. com/funds, and Morningstar.ca.

A far more informative appraisal is provided by firms whose primary purpose is to track performance of managers for funds that are their clients. Individual components of performance are measured to examine the success or failure of the manager in beating the index or the average of similar-objective funds. Four major services specialize in providing these analyses in Canada: SEI Financial Services, Comstat Capital Sciences, and Intersec Research Corp. Between them they track performance for over 2,000 investment portfolios.

Software providing similar information is also available to individuals to aid in the assessment of funds. For instance, Morningstar Canada provides statistical information about mutual funds on line through software called *PALTrak.* The data provided include performance, management expense ratios and load structures, characterization as to purpose, asset allocation, NAV, dividend payouts, and other relevant material. Similar material on U.S. mutual funds is available in Morningstar Inc.'s principal software. Figure 23.9 shows a sample of PALTrak analysis.

The PALTrak analysis comprises information of a tabular and graphical nature, the latter including a comparative historical summary of the fund's returns, a breakdown of asset composition, and, in this example, a breakdown of the source of income. Tabular results include the major holdings and historical performance data such as returns and the net asset value. "General Information" summarizes the fees and MER, with a capsule description of the return and risk of the fund. Other fundamental analysis classifies ratios such as P/E and price to book in order to characterize the risk of the fund.

Morningstar Canada's parent, Morningstar Inc., issues reports on U.S. mutual funds that provide a more extensive range of useful information in descriptive, tabular, and graphical form.

Figure 23.9   PALTrak analysis.

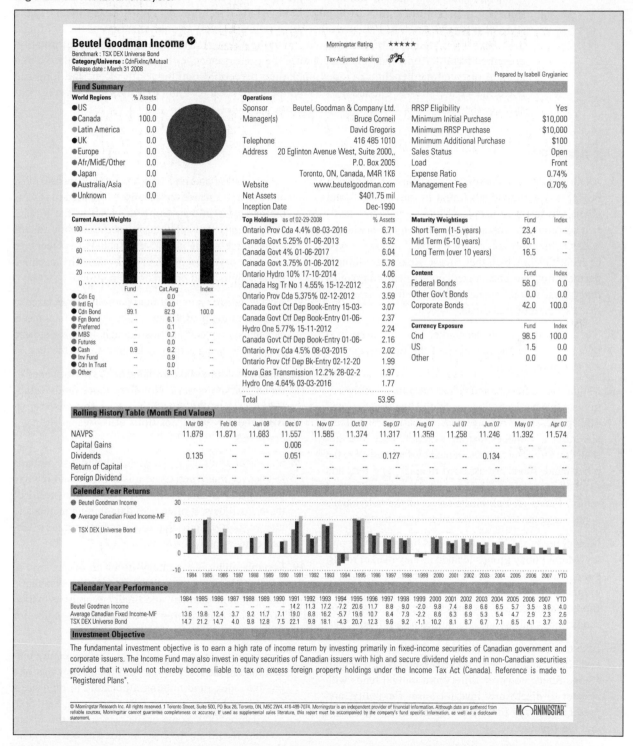

A list and analysis of the top holdings of the fund is given, as well as the weighting of the portfolio across economic sectors. A number of key statistics are presented that help to identify the style of the fund, such as P/E and other price ratios, as well as capitalization of the holdings; these reveal the style with respect to size and to the value/growth dichotomy. Other information presented in tables and charts helps appraise the performance, either absolutely or relative to a general or category benchmark index, including percentile ranking; both recent and long-run performance are shown. The analysis also presents data on fees and expenses, and several measures of the fund's risk and return characteristics.

SUMMARY

1. As an alternative to investing in securities through a broker, many individuals invest in mutual funds and other investment companies. Mutual funds are classified according to whether they are open-end or closed-end, whether they are load or no-load, and by the type of securities in which they invest. Real estate limited partnerships are specialized investment companies that invest in real estate; mortgage funds invest in loans secured by real estate.

2. Net asset value equals the market value of assets held by a fund minus the liabilities of the fund divided by the shares outstanding.

3. Mutual funds free the individual from many of the administrative burdens of owning individual securities and offer professional management of the portfolio. They also offer advantages that are available only to large-scale investors, such as discounted trading costs. On the other hand, funds are assessed management fees and incur other expenses, which reduce the investor's rate of return. Funds also eliminate some of the individual's control over the timing of capital gains realizations.

4. Mutual funds are often categorized by investment policy. Major policy groups include money market funds; equity funds, which are further grouped according to emphasis on income versus growth; fixed-income funds; balanced and income funds; asset allocation funds; index funds; and specialized sector funds.

5. Like mutual funds, hedge funds pool the assets of several clients and managed pooled assets on their behalf. Hedge funds, however, differ from mutual funds with respect to disclosure, investor base, flexibility, and predictability of investment orientation, regulation, and fee structure.

6. Costs of investing in mutual funds include front-end loads, which are sales charges; back-end loads, which are redemption fees or, more properly, contingent-deferred sales charges; fund operating expenses; and other charges, which are recurring fees used to pay for the expenses of marketing the fund to the public. Hedge funds typically charge investors both a management fee and an incentive fee equal to a percentage of profits beyond some threshold value. The incentive fee is akin to a call option on the portfolio.

7. Income earned on mutual fund portfolios is not taxed at the level of the fund. Instead, as long as the fund meets certain requirements for pass-through status, the income is treated as being earned by the investors in the fund.

8. Directional funds take a stance on the performance of broad market sectors. Nondirectional funds establish market-neutral positions on relative mispricing. Even these hedged positions still present idiosyncratic risk.

9. Statistical arbitrage is the use of quantitative systems to uncover many perceived misalignments in relative pricing and ensure profits by averaging over all of these small bets. It often uses data-mining methods to uncover past patterns that form the basis for the established investment positions.

10. Portable alpha is a strategy in which one invests in positive alpha positions, then hedges the systematic risk of that investment, and finally establishes market exposure where desired by using passive indices or futures contracts.

11. The average rate of return of the average equity mutual fund in the last 25 years has been below that of a passive index fund holding a portfolio to replicate a broad-based index like the TSX Composite, S&P 500, or Wilshire 5000. Some of the reasons for this disappointing record are the costs incurred by actively managed funds, such as the expense of conducting the research to guide stock-picking activities, and trading costs due to higher portfolio turnover. The record on

the consistency of fund performance is mixed. In some sample periods, the better-performing funds continue to perform well in the following periods; in other sample periods they do not.

12. Performance evaluation of hedge funds is complicated by survivorship bias, by the potential instability of risk attributes, by the existence of liquidity premiums, and by unreliable market valuations of infrequently traded assets. Performance evaluation is particularly difficult when the fund engages in option positions. Tail events make it hard to assess the true performance of positions involving options without extremely long histories of returns.

13. Exchange-traded funds (ETFs) are index securities trading on the exchanges that provide low-cost alternatives to mutual funds.

KEY EQUATIONS

(23.1) $r_{\text{portfolio}} = r_f + \beta(r_M - r_f) + e + \alpha$

PROBLEMS

Connect Practise and learn online with Connect.

1. Would you expect a typical open-end fixed-income mutual fund to have higher or lower operating expenses than a fixed-income unit investment trust? Why?

2. An open-end fund has a net asset value of $10.70 per share. It is sold with a front-end load of 6 percent. What is the offering price?

3. If the offering price of an open-end fund is $12.30 per share and the fund is sold with a front-end load of 5 percent, what is its net asset value?

4. The composition of the Fingroup Fund portfolio is as follows:

Stock	Shares	Price ($)
A	200,000	35
B	300,000	40
C	400,000	20
D	600,000	25

The fund has not borrowed any funds, but its accrued management fee with the portfolio manager currently totals $30,000. There are 4 million shares outstanding. What is the net asset value of the fund?

5. Reconsider the Fingroup Fund in the previous problem. If during the year the portfolio manager sells all of the holdings of stock D and replaced it with 200,000 shares of stock E at $50 per share and 200,000 shares of stock F at $25 per share, what is the portfolio turnover rate?

6. The Closed Fund is a closed-end investment company with a portfolio currently worth $200 million. It has liabilities of $3 million and 5 million shares outstanding.

   a. What is the NAV of the fund?

   b. If the fund sells for $36 per share, what is the percentage premium or discount that will appear in the listings in the financial pages?

7. Corporate Fund started the year with a net asset value of $12.50. By year-end, its NAV equalled $12.10. The fund paid year-end distributions of income and capital gains of $1.50. What was the rate of return to an investor in the fund?

8. A closed-end fund starts the year with a net asset value of $12. By year-end, NAV equals $12.10. At the beginning of the year, the fund was selling at a 2 percent premium to NAV. By the end of the year, the fund is selling at a 7 percent discount to NAV. The fund paid year-end distributions of income and capital gains of $1.50.

   a. What is the rate of return to an investor in the fund during the year?

   b. What would have been the rate of return to an investor who held the same securities as the fund manager during the year?

9. What are some comparative advantages of investing in each of the following?

   a. Closed-end mutual funds

   b. Open-end mutual funds

   c. Individual stocks and bonds that you choose for yourself

10. Open-end equity mutual funds find it necessary to keep a significant percentage of total investments, typically around 5 percent of the portfolio, in very liquid money market assets. Closed-end funds do not have to maintain such a position in "cash-equivalent" securities. What difference between open-end and closed-end funds might account for their differing policies?

11. Balanced funds and asset allocation funds invest in both the stock and the bond market. What is the difference between these types of funds?

12. a. Impressive Fund had excellent investment performance last year, with portfolio returns that placed it in the top 10 percent of all funds with the same investment policy. Do you expect it to be a top performer next year? Why or why not?

   b. Suppose instead that the fund was among the poorest performers in its comparison group. Would you be more or less likely to believe its relative performance will persist into the following year? Why?

13. Consider a mutual fund with $200 million in assets at the start of the year and with 10 million shares outstanding. The fund invests in a portfolio of stocks that provides dividend income at the end of the year of $2 million. The stocks included in the fund's portfolio increase in price by 8 percent, but no securities are sold, and there are no capital gains distributions. The fund charges other fees of 1 percent, which are deducted from portfolio assets at year-end. What is net asset value at the start and end of the year? What is the rate of return for an investor in the fund?

14. The New Fund had average daily assets of $2.2 billion in 2010. The fund sold $400 million worth of stock and purchased $500 million during the year. What was its turnover ratio?

15. If New Funds' expense ratio (see problem 14) was 1.1 percent and the management fee was .7 percent, what were the total fees paid to the fund's investment managers during the year? What were other administrative expenses?

16. You purchased 1,000 shares of the New Fund at a price of $20 per share at the beginning of the year. You paid a front-end load of 4 percent. The securities in which the fund invests increase in value by 12 percent during the year. The fund's expense ratio if 1.2 percent. What is your rate of return on the fund if you sell your shares at the end of the year?

17. The Investments Fund sells Class A shares with a front-end load of 6 percent and Class B shares with other charges of .5 percent annually as well as backend load fees that start at 5 percent and fall by 1 percent for each full year the investor holds the portfolio (until the fifth year). Assume the portfolio rate of return net of operating expenses is 10 percent annually. If you plan to sell the fund after four years, are Class A or Class B shares the better choice for you? What if you plan to sell after 15 years?

18. Suppose you observe the investment performance of 350 portfolio managers for five years, and rank them by investment returns during each year. After five years, you find that 11 of the funds have investment returns that place the fund in the top half of the sample in each and every year of your sample. Such consistency of performance indicates to you that these must be the funds whose managers are in fact skilled, and you invest your money in these funds. Is your conclusion warranted?

19. You are considering an investment in a mutual fund with a 4 percent load and expense ratio of .5 percent. You can invest instead in a bank GIC paying 6 percent interest.

    a. If you plan to invest for two years, what annual rate of return must the fund portfolio earn for you to be better off in the fund than in the GIC? Assume annual compounding of returns.

    b. How does your answer change if you plan to invest for six years? Why does your answer change?

    c. Now suppose that instead of a front-end load the fund assesses another charge of .75 percent per year. What annual rate of return must the fund portfolio earn for you to be better off in the fund than in the GIC? Does your answer in this case depend on your time horizon?

20. Suppose that every time a fund manager trades stock, transaction costs such as commissions and bid–asked spreads amount to .4 percent of the value of the trade. If the portfolio turnover rate is 50 percent, by how much is the total return of the portfolio reduced by trading costs?

21. A front-end load mutual fund has a net asset value of $25 per share. It has a sales charge of 7 percent. Calculate the offering price and round your answer to two decimal places.

22. If an investor's investment objectives were protection of capital, cash flows and the possibility of capital gains, the investor would probably choose a

    a. Money market fund

    b. Dividend and income fund

    c. Growth fund

    d. Balanced fund

23. Loaded-Up Fund charges another fee of 1.0 percent and maintains an expense ratio of .75 percent. Economy Fund charges a front-end load of 2 percent but has no other fees and an expense ratio of .25 percent. Assume the rate of return on both funds' portfolios (before any fees) is 6 percent per year. Assuming $1,000 investment, how much will an investment in each fund grow to after

    a. 1 year

    b. 3 years

    c. 10 years

24. City Street Fund has a portfolio of $450 million and liabilities of $10 million.

    a. If 44 million shares are outstanding, what is net asset value?

    b. If a large investor redeems 1 million shares, what happens to the portfolio value, to shares outstanding, and to NAV?

25. Why can closed-end funds sell at prices that differ from net asset value while open-end funds do not?

26. What are the advantages and disadvantages of exchange-traded funds versus mutual funds?

27. Would a market-neutral hedge fund be a good candidate for an investor's entire retirement portfolio? If not, would there be a role for the hedge fund in the overall portfolio of such an investor?

28. How might the incentive fee of a hedge fund affect the manager's proclivity to take on high-risk assets in the portfolio?

29. Why is it harder to assess the performance of a hedge fund portfolio manager than that of a typical mutual fund manager?

30. Which of the following is *most* accurate in describing the problems of survivorship bias and backfill bias in the performance evaluation of hedge funds?

    a. Survivorship bias and backfill bias both result in upwardly biased hedge fund index returns.

    b. Survivorship bias and backfill bias both result in downwardly biased hedge fund index returns.

    c. Survivorship bias results in upwardly biased hedge fund index returns, but backfill bias results in downwardly biased hedge fund index returns.

31. Which of the following would be the *most* appropriate benchmark to use for hedge fund evaluation?

a. A multifactor model

b. The S&P 500

c. The risk-free rate

32. With respect to hedge fund investing, the net return to an investor in a fund of funds would be lower than that earned from an individual hedge fund because of

a. Both the extra layer of fees and the higher liquidity offered

b. No reason; fund of funds earn returns that are equal to those of individual hedge funds

c. The extra layer of fees only

33. Which of the following hedge fund types is *most likely* to have a return that is closest to risk-free?

a. A market-neutral hedge fund

b. An event-driven hedge fund

c. A long/short hedge fund

34. Is statistical arbitrage true arbitrage? Explain.

35. A hedge fund with $1 billion of assets charges a management fee of 2 percent and an incentive fee of 20 percent of returns over a money market rate, which currently is 5 percent. Calculate total fees, both in dollars and as a percent of assets under management, for portfolio returns of

a. −5 percent

b. 0

c. 5 percent

d. 10 percent

36. The following is part of the computer output from a regression of monthly returns on Waterworks stock against the S&P 500 index. A hedge fund manager believes that Waterworks is underpriced, with an alpha of 2 percent over the coming month.

Beta	R-squared	Standard Deviation of Residuals
.75	.65	.06 (i.e., 6% monthly)

a. If he holds a $2 million portfolio of Waterworks stock, and wishes to hedge market exposure for the next month using one-month maturity S&P 500 futures contracts, how many contracts should he enter? Should he buy or sell contracts? The S&P 500 currently is at 1,000 and the contract multiplier is $250.

b. What is the standard deviation of the monthly return of the hedged portfolio?

c. Assuming that monthly returns are approximately normally distributed, what is the probability that this market-neutral strategy will lose money over the next month? Assume the risk-free rate is .5 percent per month.

37. Refer to problem 36.

a. Suppose you hold an equally weighted portfolio of 100 stocks with the same alpha, beta, and residual standard deviation as Waterworks. Assume the residual returns (the *e* terms in equations 23.1 and 23.2) on each of these stocks are independent of each other. What is the residual standard deviation of the portfolio?

b. Recalculate the probability of a loss on a market-neutral strategy involving equally weighted, market-hedged positions in the 100 stocks over the next month.

38. Refer again to problem 36. Now suppose that the manager misestimates the beta of Waterworks stock, believing it to be .50 instead of .75. The standard deviation of the monthly market rate of return is 5 percent.

   a. What is the standard deviation of the (now improperly) hedged portfolio?

   b. What is the probability of incurring a loss over the next month if the monthly market return has an expected value of 1 percent and a standard deviation of 5 percent? Compare your answer to the probability you found in problem 36.

   c. What would be the probability of a loss using the data in problem 29 if the manager similarly misestimated beta as .50 instead of .75? Compare your answer to the probability you found in problem 37.

   d. Why does the misestimation of beta matter so much more for the 100-stock portfolio than it does for the one-stock portfolio?

39. A hedge fund with net asset value of $62 per share currently has a high-water mark of $66. Is the value of its incentive fee more or less than it would be if the high-water mark were $67?

40. Reconsider the hedge fund in the previous problem. Suppose it is January 1, the standard deviation of the fund's annual returns is 50 percent, and the risk-free rate is 4 percent. The fund has an incentive fee of 20 percent, but its current high-water mark is $66, and net asset value is $62.

   a. What is the value of the annual incentive fee according to the Black-Scholes formula?

   b. What would the annual incentive fee be worth if the fund had no high-water mark and it earned its incentive fee on its total return?

   c. What would the annual incentive fee be worth if the fund had no high-water mark and it earned its incentive fee on its return in excess of the risk-free rate? (Treat the risk-free rate as a continuously compounded value to maintain consistency with the Black-Scholes formula.)

   d. Recalculate the incentive fee value for part (*b*) now assuming that an increase in fund leverage increases volatility to 60 percent.

41. Go to the Connect site for this book, Chapter 23, and find there a spreadsheet containing monthly values of the S&P 500 index. Suppose that in each month you had written an out-of-the-money put option on one unit of the index with an exercise price 5 percent lower than the current value of the index.

   a. What would have been the average value of your gross monthly payouts on the puts over the 10-year period October 1977–September 1987? The standard deviation?

   b. Now extend your sample by one month to include October 1987, and recalculate the average payout and standard deviation of the put-writing strategy. What do you conclude about tail risk in naked put writing?

42. Suppose a hedge fund follows the following strategy. Each month it holds $100 million of an S&P 500 index fund and writes out-of-the-money put options on $100 million of the index with exercise price 5 percent lower than the current value of the index. Suppose the premium it receives for writing each put is $.25 million, which is roughly in line with the actual value of the puts.

   a. Calculate the Sharpe ratio the fund would have realized in the period October 1982–September 1987. Compare its Sharpe ratio to that of the S&P 500. Use the data from problem 41, available at the Connect site for this book, and assume the monthly risk-free interest rate over this period was .7 percent.

   b. Now calculate the Sharpe ratio the fund would have realized if we extend the sample period by one month to include October 1987. What do you conclude about performance evaluation and tail risk for funds pursuing option-like strategies?

43. Here are data on three hedge funds. Each fund charges its investors an incentive fee of 20 percent of total returns. Suppose initially that a fund of funds (FF) manager buys equal amounts of each of these funds, and also charges its investors a 20 percent incentive fee. For simplicity, assume also that management fees other than incentive fees are zero for all funds.

	Hedge Fund 1	Hedge Fund 2	Hedge Fund 3
Start-of-year value (millions)	$100	$100	$100
Gross portfolio rate of return	20%	10%	30%

a. Compute the rate of return after incentive fees to an investor in the fund of funds.

b. Suppose that instead of buying shares in each of the three hedge funds, a stand-alone (SA) hedge fund purchases the same *portfolio* as the three underlying funds. The total value and composition of the SA fund is therefore identical to the one that would result from aggregating the three hedge funds. Consider an investor in the SA fund. After paying 20 percent incentive fees, what would be the value of the investor's portfolio at the end of the year?

c. Confirm that the investor's rate of return in SA is higher than in FF by an amount equal to the extra layer of fees charged by the fund of funds.

d. Now suppose that the return on the portfolio held by hedge fund 3 were -30 percent rather than $+30$ percent. Recalculate your answers to parts (*a*) and (*b*). Will either FF or SA charge an incentive fee in this scenario? Why then does the investor in FF still do worse than the investor in SA?

**E-INVESTMENTS
Choosing a
Mutual Fund**

Here are the Web sites for three of the largest mutual fund companies:

- Fidelity Investments   **www.fidelity.ca**
- Invesco Trimark Investments   **www.invescotrimark.com**
- Investors Group   **www.investorsgroup.ca**

Pick three or four funds from one of these sites. What are the investment objectives of each fund? Find the expense ratio of each fund. Which fund has had the best recent performance? What are the major holdings of each fund? Compare your answers with information at **www.morningstar.ca**.

**E-INVESTMENTS
Hedge Fund
Styles and
Results**

Log on to **www.hedgeindex.com**, a site run by Credit Suisse/Tremont, which maintains the TASS Hedge Funds Data Base of the performance of more than 2,000 hedge funds, and produces indices of investment performance for several hedge fund classes. Click the *Downloads* tab (free registration is required for access to this part of the site). From the downloads page, you can access historical rates of return on each of the hedge fund subclasses (e.g., market-neutral, event-driven, dedicated short bias, and so on). Download five years of monthly returns for each subclass and download returns on the S&P 500 for the same period from **http://finance.yahoo. com**. Calculate the beta of the equity-market-neutral and dedicated short-bias funds. Do the results seem reasonable in terms of the orientation of these funds? Next, look at the year-by-year performance of each hedge fund class. How does the variability of performance results in different years compare to that of the S&P 500?

APPENDIX 23A: TAXATION AND TAX SHELTERING

The Canadian Tax System

Investment choice by individuals is a process of placing funds temporarily under the control of others in the hope of obtaining a future cash flow greater than the amount invested. Governments consider the increase in funds, or the return on investment, to be taxable, like earned income. For the investor, the return available after tax is what is relevant. Frequently, the tax payable may reflect the risk involved in the investment; hence, the government may encourage risky invest- ments by exempting part, or even all, of their returns from income tax. In order to stimulate in- vestment in certain areas or of certain types, the government may legislate particularly favourable tax treatment. Thus, tax policy is often (many would say always) a reflection of social policy.

In Canada, the three major characteristics of income tax that are relevant to investment are the treatment of interest, dividends, and capital gains. The receipt of interest is predictable and rela- tively certain (barring default by the borrower), leading the government to tax it as ordinary in- come. Since equity is more risky than debt for investors, but safer for corporations, equity investment is encouraged by offering a lower effective tax rate. Dividends being more assured than capital gains, we would expect a higher tax rate on dividends than on capital gains. Thus, the system rewards long-term equity investment for growth more than equity investment for dividend income, and in turn, dividend income more than interest income.

Although the system has changed extensively since the introduction of the capital gains tax in 1972, we now have a system that favours dividends through a complicated adjustment procedure and capital gains by exclusion of some of the gain from taxable income. Dividends are currently "grossed up" by increasing the actual amount by 25 percent and including this in taxable income; then a tax credit of 19 percent (federal) of the grossed-up amount is granted against taxes due. Dividends are actually now classified as "eligible" if issued by large public corporations and "other than eligible" as when issued by small private corporations. Actual capital gains are re- duced by 50 percent and then included in taxable income.

Capital losses are deductible against capital gains, and can be carried back and forward if in- sufficient gains exist in a year. One is hindered from taking losses as they occur by the **superfi- cial loss rule**, which governs the sale of an asset at a loss within 30 days of purchase. Thus if a stock has been bought for $30 and is currently trading at $20, one can only recognize the loss of $10 provided that the stock is not re-bought within 30 days of the sale or even 30 days before (in anticipation of the sale); this prevents investors from taking the loss but maintaining a long-term position on the assumption that the stock price will rebound. If the stock were sold for $20 and re-bought a week later for $18, the cost base would be adjusted to $28 ($30 − $20 + $18) for determination of the effective gain or loss; that gain or loss is ultimately recognized when the stock is sold (and not re-bought during the 60-day window).

Table 23A.1 illustrates the calculation of taxes and the after-tax return for an income of $1,000 from the three types of investment income: interest, dividends, and capital gains. This table uses

TABLE 23A.1 Calculation of Tax Payable on Forms of Investment Income (excluding surtaxes)

Source	Interest ($)	Dividend ($)	Capital Gain ($)
Income	1,000	1,000	1,000
Dividend gross-up (25%)		250	
Capital gain exclusion			−500
Taxable income	1,000	1,250	500
Federal tax (29%)	−290	−362.5	−145
Dividend tax credit (19%)		187.75	
Basic federal tax	−290	−174.75	−145
Ontario tax (17.41%)	−174.1	−217.625	−87.05
Dividend tax credit (6.4%)		80	
Ontario tax	−174.1	−137.625	−87.05
Total tax	−464.1	−312.375	−232.05
After-tax income	536	688	768
Retention ratio	53.59%	68.76%	76.80%

TABLE 23A.2

After-Tax
Retention of
Income from
Interest,
Dividends, and
Capital Gains,
2013

	Ontario	Quebec	British Columbia
Combined federal and provincial tax rate	46.41%	49.97%	43.70%
Retention rate on:			
Interest	53.59	50.03	56.30
Eligible dividends	70.46	68.76	74.22
Capital gains	76.80	75.01	78.15

Source: Deloitte & Touche.

Ontario's 2013 rates before surtaxes for an investor with "high" income still below the $500,000 level (taxed even more highly). As we see in Table 23A.2, comparing the after-tax retention rates (excluding surtaxes) in Ontario, Quebec, and British Columbia, capital gains are currently taxed less than dividends, although the difference is small. The fact that capital gains can be accrued over a period of time, but are taxable only upon realization, causes their treatment to be even more favourable in reality. This makes ETFs even better investments relative to mutual funds; the latter must distribute annual capital gains on portfolio changes to unitholders, but ETFs have only minimal portfolio adjustments. Purchase of ETFs defers virtually all capital gains until the final sale.

Timing is an important detail in the effect of taxation. Generally, income is taxed in the year that it is received, although corporations may account for income on an accrual basis. Bond interest is then taxed when received, which is determined as the payment date by the issuer; similarly, dividends are taxed as of the payment date (not to be confused with the declaration or record dates). Capital gains are based on the years of purchase and sale; because of transfer delays, the date for tax purposes—the **settlement date**—is formally three business days after the actual trade date (this makes the days prior to Christmas an active period of trading, as annual gains and losses are established).

One exception to the actual receipt of cash occurs for so-called **zero-coupon bonds**, or **zeroes**, and similarly for compound interest savings bonds. Although no actual interest is paid, interest is imputed from the increase in value over the life of the zero-coupon bond; similarly, the savings bonds' interest is not received until redemption. In both cases, the income tax is paid annually on the imputed interest, making these negative cash flow instruments. Note that the government is precluding the possibility of an investor claiming the increase in value of the zero, from its initial discounted value to its redemption value, as a capital gain to be taxed at the preferential rate.

Besides timing, location of the source of income is important. As international investments become more common, income from foreign sources is likely to become part of taxable income. It is fortunate that agreements between taxing authorities permit the recognition of foreign income tax as a credit against Canadian taxes, although only to the extent that that tax would have been charged under Canadian law. Note that it is the source of the income that causes a country to tax it first, that is, U.S.-source income will be taxed there. Capital gains on foreign assets, however, are taxable in Canada and generally are not taxable under the foreign tax regime.

The significance of the after-tax returns on different forms of investment is that the prices of financial assets are determined by the returns, on an after-tax basis, that are required by investors in recompense for the risks posed by the assets. Investment choices in response to tax policies must be made from the available set of instruments that are competitively priced to appeal to the investing public. As previously mentioned, occasionally governments may judge that the investment appeal of certain assets does not attract sufficient capital; in such cases, additional incentives may be offered to increase their appeal.

Tax Deferral and Shelters

There are five important tax-sheltering options that can radically affect the optimal asset allocation for individual investors. The first is the tax-deferral option, which arises from the fact that you do not have to pay tax on a capital gain until you choose to realize the gain. The second, third, and fourth options are similar; they are called tax-deferred retirement plans, such as the registered retirement savings plan (RRSP), tax-free savings accounts (TFSAs), and tax-deferred annuities, which are offered by life insurance companies. The fourth option is the class of investments known as tax shelters. We will discuss each of these options in more detail below.

A fundamental feature of the *Income Tax Act* is that tax on the capital gain of an asset is payable only when the asset is sold,[22] this is the **tax-deferral option**. The investor, therefore, can control the timing of the tax payment. From a tax perspective, this option makes stocks in general preferable to fixed-income securities.

To see this, compare BCE stock with a BCE bond. Suppose both offer an expected total return of 15 percent this year. The stock has a dividend yield of 5 percent and an expected appreciation in price of 10 percent, whereas the bond has an interest rate of 15 percent. The bond investor must pay tax on the bond's interest in the year it is earned, whereas the BCE shareholder pays tax only on the dividend and defers paying tax on the capital gain until the stock is sold.

Suppose the investor is investing $1,000 for five years and is in a 40 percent tax bracket. An investment in the bond will earn an after-tax return of 9.0 percent per year ($.60 \times 15$ percent). The yield after taxes at the end of five years is

$$\$1,000 \times 1.09^5 = \$1,538.62$$

For the stock, dividend yield after taxes will be 3.4775 percent per year ($[1.0 - 1.45(.40 - .19)] \times 5\%$).[23] Because no taxes are paid on the capital gain until year 5, the return before paying the capital gains tax is

$$\$1,000 \times (1 + .034775 + .10)^5 = \$1,000(1.134775)^5$$
$$= \$1,881.69$$

In year 5, the capital gain is

$$\$1,000(1.10^5 - 1) = \$1,610.51 - \$1,000 = \$610.51$$

Taxes due are $122.10, leaving $1,759.59 of the year 5 return, which is $220.97 more than the bond investment yields. Deferral of the capital gains tax allows the investment to compound at a faster rate until the tax is actually paid.

Note that the more of one's total return that is in the form of price appreciation, the greater the value of the tax-deferral option.

Recent years have seen the establishment of **tax-deferred retirement plans** in which investors can choose how to allocate assets. Such plans include self-directed RRSPs and employer-sponsored "tax-qualified" defined-contribution plans. A feature they all have in common is that contributions and earnings are subject to neither federal nor provincial income tax until the individual withdraws them as benefits.

---

[22]The only exception to this rule occurs in futures investing, where National Revenue treats a gain as taxable in the year it occurs, regardless of whether the investor closes the position. Note also that on pure discount bonds, imputed interest is taxable, even though no interest payment is received until sale or maturity (making these very popular in RRSPs). Additionally, note that there are capital gains exemptions for principal residences and small businesses.

[23]We have used .19 as the dividend tax credit rate.

Typically, an individual may have some investment in the form of such qualified retirement accounts and some in the form of ordinary taxable accounts. The basic investment principle that applies is to keep whatever bonds you want to hold in the retirement account while placing equities in the ordinary account. You maximize the tax advantage of the retirement account by holding in it the security that is the least tax-advantaged.

To see this point, consider the following example. Suppose Eloise has $200,000 of wealth, $100,000 of it in a tax-qualified retirement account. She has decided to invest half of her wealth in bonds and half in stocks, so she allocates half of her retirement account and half of her nonretirement funds to each. By doing this, Eloise is not maximizing her after-tax returns. She could reduce her tax bill with no change in before-tax returns simply by shifting her bonds into the retirement account and holding all her stocks outside the retirement account.

Deferred annuities are accounts offered by life insurance companies that combine the option of withdrawing one's funds in the form of a life annuity with some tax sheltering. Variable annuity contracts offer the additional advantage of mutual fund investing. One major difference between a RRSP and a variable annuity contract is that, whereas the amount one can contribute to a RRSP is tax-deductible and extremely limited as to maximum amount, the amount one can contribute to a deferred annuity is unlimited, but not tax-deductible. The TFSA is a hybrid with a $5,000 limit but no tax-deductibility.

The defining characteristic of a life annuity is that its payments continue as long as the recipient is alive, although virtually all deferred annuity contracts have several withdrawal options, including a lump sum of cash paid out at any time. You need not worry about running out of money before you die. Like CPP, therefore, life annuities offer longevity insurance and would seem to be an ideal asset for someone in the retirement years. Indeed, theory suggests that where there are no bequest motives, it would be optimal for people to invest heavily in actuarially fair life annuities.[24]

There are two types of life annuities, **fixed annuities** and **variable annuities**. A fixed annuity pays a fixed nominal sum of money per period (usually each month), whereas a variable annuity pays a periodic amount linked to the investment performance of some underlying portfolio.

In pricing annuities, insurance companies use **mortality tables** that show the probabilities that individuals of various ages will die within a year. These tables enable the insurer to compute with reasonable accuracy how many of a large number of people in a given age group will die in each future year. If it sells life annuities to a large group, the insurance company can estimate fairly accurately the amount of money it will have to pay in each future year to meet its obligations.

Variable annuities are structured so that the investment risk of the underlying asset portfolio is passed through to the recipient, much as shareholders bear the risk of a mutual fund. There are two stages in a variable annuity contract: an accumulation phase and a payout phase. During the *accumulation* phase, the investor contributes money periodically to one or more open-end mutual funds and accumulates shares. The second, or *payout*, stage usually starts at retirement, when the investor typically has several options, including the following:

1. Taking the market value of the shares in a lump-sum payment
2. Receiving a fixed annuity until death
3. Receiving a variable amount of money each period that is computed according to a certain procedure

---

[24]For an elaboration of this point, see Laurence J. Kotlikoff and Avia Spivak, "The Family as an Incomplete Annuities Market," *Journal of Political Economy* 89 (April 1981).

ILLUSTRATION OF A VARIABLE ANNUITY

Starting accumulation = $100,000

R_t = Rate of return on underlying portfolio in year t

Assumed investment return (AIR) = 4 percent per year

B_t = Benefit received at end of year t

$$= B_{t-1}\frac{1 + R_t}{1 + \text{AIR}}$$

B_0 = $36,035, hypothetical constant payment, which has a present value of $100,000, using a discount rate of 4 percent per year

A_t = Remaining balance after B_t is withdrawn

t	R_t	B_t	Remaining Balance = $A_t = A_{t-1} \times (1 + R_t) - B_t$
0			$100,000
1	6%	$36,728	69,272
2	2	36,022	34,635
3	4	36,022	0

This procedure is best explained by the following example. Assume that, at retirement, John Shortlife has $100,000 accumulated in a variable annuity contract. The initial annuity payment is determined by setting an *assumed investment return* (AIR), 4 percent per year in this example, and an assumption about mortality probabilities. In Shortlife's case, we assume he will live for only three years after retirement and will receive three annual payments starting one year from now.

The benefit payment in each year, B_t, is given by the recursive formula

$$B_t = B_{t-1}[(1 + R_t)/(1 + \text{AIR})] \tag{23A.1}$$

where R_t is the actual holding period return on the underlying portfolio in year t. In other words, each year the amount Shortlife receives equals the previous year's benefit multiplied by a factor that reflects the actual investment return compared with the assumed investment return. In our example, if the actual return equals 4 percent, the factor will be one, and this year's benefit will equal last year's. If R_t is greater than 4 percent, the benefit will increase, and if R_t is less than 4 percent, the benefit will decrease.

CC 23A.1

CONCEPT CHECK

Suppose Eloise earns a 10 percent per year rate of interest on bonds and 15 percent per year on stocks, all in the form of price appreciation. In five years she will withdraw all her funds and spend them. By how much will she increase her final accumulation if she shifts all bonds into the retirement account and holds all stocks outside the retirement account? She is in a 28 percent tax bracket.

The starting benefit is found by computing a hypothetical constant payment with a present value of $100,000 using the 4 percent AIR to discount future values and multiplying it by the first year's performance factor. In our example, the hypothetical constant payment is $36,035.

The "Illustration of a Variable Annuity" box summarizes the computation and shows what the payment will be in each of three years if R_t is 6 percent, then 2 percent, and finally 4 percent. The last column shows the balance in the fund after each payment.

This method guarantees that the initial $100,000 will be sufficient to pay all benefits due, regardless of what actual holding period returns turn out to be. In this way, the variable annuity contract passes all portfolio risk through to the annuitant.

By selecting an appropriate mix of underlying assets, such as stocks, bonds, and cash, an investor can create a stream of variable annuity payments with a wide variety of risk–return combinations. Naturally, the investor wants to select a combination that offers the highest expected level of payments for any specified level of risk.[25]

Variable life insurance is another tax-deferred investment vehicle offered by the life insurance industry. A variable life insurance policy combines life insurance with the tax-deferred annuities described earlier.

To invest in this product, you pay either a single premium or a series of premiums. In each case there is a stated death benefit, and the policyholder can allocate the money invested to several portfolios, which generally include a money market fund, a bond fund, and at least one common stock fund. The allocation can be changed at any time.

CC 23A.2

CONCEPT CHECK

Assume Victor is now 75 years old and is expected to live until age 80. He has $100,000 in a variable annuity account. If the assumed investment return is 4 percent per year, what is the initial annuity payment? Suppose the annuity's asset base is the TSX Composite equity portfolio and its holding period return for the next five years is each of the following: 4 percent, 10 percent, −8 percent, 25 percent, and 0. How much would Victor receive each year? Verify that the insurance company would wind up using exactly $100,000 to fund Victor's benefits.

A variable life policy has a cash surrender value equal to the investment base minus any surrender charges. Typically, there is a surrender charge (about 5 percent of the purchase payments) if you surrender the policy during the first several years, but not thereafter. At policy surrender, income taxes become due on all investment gains.

Variable life insurance policies offer a death benefit that is the greater of the stated face value or the market value of the investment base. In other words, the death benefit may rise with favourable investment performance, but it will not go below the guaranteed face value. Furthermore, the surviving beneficiary is not subject to income tax on the death benefit.

The policyholder can choose from a number of income options to convert the policy into a stream of income, either on surrender of the contract or as a partial withdrawal. In all cases, income taxes are payable on the part of any distribution representing investment gains.

The insured can gain access to the investment without having to pay income tax by borrowing against the cash surrender value. Policy loans of up to 90 percent of the cash value are available at any time at a contractually specified interest rate.

Tax shelters are investment opportunities under which most, if not all, of the investment can be deducted from ordinary income over a few years' horizon. These generally are structured as *limited partnerships* (LPs) for the investors, with a general partner who is usually related to the sponsor of the shelter. The advantage of this arrangement is that there is only minimal risk of any further assessment of liability against the limited partners, while a share of LP expenses are deductible against income; if the structure involved a limited liability corporation, these expenses would *not* be deductible. Tax regulations allow the writeoff of these expenses over three years, typically, with administrative expenses of setting up and selling the LP requiring five years to write off.

---

[25]For an elaboration on possible combinations, see Zvi Bodie, "An Innovation for Stable Real Retirement Income," *Journal of Portfolio Management*, Fall 1980; and Zvi Bodie and James E. Pesando, "Retirement Annuity Design in an Inflationary Climate," Ch. 11 in Zvi Bodie and J. B. Shoven (eds.), *Financial Aspects of the United States Pension Systems* (Chicago: University of Chicago Press, 1983).

The consequences of entering into an LP include the generation of a cash flow of income from the business for the life of the LP, often 10 years or even much longer, against which the amortized expenses can be deducted for income tax purposes. If a partner wishes to sell his share, however, the adjusted cost basis is likely to be zero for the purpose of determining the taxable capital gain. Such a sale is further impeded by illiquidity in the (OTC) resale market, with large bid–asked spreads.

Shelters are created to raise capital to finance investment in various areas, including commercial real estate (such as multiple-unit residential buildings, or MURBs), filmmaking, and railroad boxcars. Two more popular forms have been the flow-through share program of the 1980s and mutual fund LPs, in favour until the mid-1990s.

Flow-through shares were issued to allow mining and energy companies to pass through their exploration and resource depletion expenses to shareholders who would be able to use the deduction against income; the companies themselves usually did not have enough taxable income to make use of the expenses. Companies were able to raise significant amounts of capital to finance resource exploration and development in this way. The federal government originally encouraged this arrangement to increase activity and employment in the mining and energy sectors. As capital was squandered on marginal prospects, and tax revenues suffered from helping in the financing, the government greatly reduced the attractiveness of the shares by reducing the writeoff allowances; this virtually killed the program.

Mutual fund LPs raised capital to pay for the commissions paid to salespersons for back-end load funds. Since no front-end fee was collected, the fund managers did not have the cash to pay the commissions. In return for financing the commissions, partners were entitled to receive all the resulting back-end load fees, as well as a percentage of the regular management fees paid by mutual fund shareholders. This income was received for 10 or more years through the LP. The load income and management fee income tend to offset each other as fund performance varies. Ultimately, the after-tax cash flow is correlated with the performance of the underlying mutual fund; having much lower risk, it dominates direct investment in the fund.[26] Resale of the LPs was costly, with many investors trying to sell after the three-year writeoff period; attempts were made to improve liquidity by consolidating the partnerships into TSX-traded securities. The government again killed these shelters by disallowing writeoffs.

Many tax shelters, such as MURB investments, have turned out to have very poor results. Although taxes were saved originally, little of the after-tax investment was returned. Although early flow-through share partnerships were extremely profitable, the later ones resulted in investment in low-quality mining companies and yielded little payoff. The saving of taxes must be a secondary consideration to the overall profitability of the investment when choosing a shelter. Given the complexity of the tax consequences, the advice of a tax accountant, rather than that of the selling broker, is strongly recommended to prospective investors. That advice ought to include some appraisal of the investment prospects, as well as tax planning.

PROBLEMS

1. Your neighbour has heard that you have just successfully completed a course in investments and has come to seek your advice. She and her husband are both 50 years old. They have just finished making their last payments for their condominium and their children's college education and are planning for retirement. Until now, neither of them has been able to set aside any savings for retirement, and so have not participated in their employers' voluntary tax-sheltered savings plan, nor have they opened RRSPs. Both of them work, and their combined after-tax income last year

---

[26]See Peter J. Ryan, "Gimme More Than Shelter," *Canadian Investment Review*, Fall 1995, pp. 22–27.

was $50,000. They are both in the 42 percent marginal tax bracket. They plan to retire at age 65 and would like to maintain the same standard of living in retirement as they enjoy now.

a. Devise a simple plan for them on the assumption of a combined CPP income of $10,000 per year. How much should they start saving? (Assume they will live to age 80, can shelter as much retirement savings as they want from tax, and will earn a zero real rate of return.)

b. Redo part (a) with the following changes:

   i.   The real interest rate is assumed to be 3 -percent per year.

   ii. Your neighbours are 40 years old instead of 50.

   iii. The tax bracket after retirement drops to 15 percent.

c. What advice on investing their retirement savings would you give them? If they are very risk-averse, what would you advise?

The following problem is based on a question that appeared in past CFA examinations.

2. Investors in high marginal tax brackets probably would be least interested in a

   a. Portfolio of diversified stocks

   b. Tax-deferred retirement fund

   c. Commodity pool

   d. High-income bond fund

APPENDIX 23B: PENSION FUNDS

By far the most important institution in the retirement income system is the employer-sponsored pension plan. These plans vary in form and complexity, but they all have certain common elements in every country. In general, investment strategy depends on the type of plan.

Pension plans are defined by the terms specifying the "who," "when," and "how much," for both the plan benefits and the plan contributions used to pay for those benefits. The *pension fund* of the plan is the cumulation of assets created from contributions and the investment earnings on those contributions, less any payments of benefits from the fund. In the United States, contributions to the fund by either employer or employee are tax-deductible, and investment income of the fund is not taxed. Distributions from the fund, whether to the employer or the employee, are taxed as ordinary income. There are two "pure" types of pension plans: *defined-contribution* and *defined-benefit.*

Defined-Contribution Plans

In a defined-contribution plan, a formula specifies contributions but not benefit payments. Contribution rules usually are specified as a predetermined fraction of salary (e.g., the employer contributes 15 percent of the employee's annual wages to the plan), although that fraction need not be constant over the course of an employee's career. The pension fund consists of a set of individual investment accounts, one for each employee. Pension benefits are not specified, other than that at retirement the employee may apply that total accumulated value of contributions and earnings on those contributions to purchase an annuity. The employee often has some choice over both the level of contributions and the way the account is invested.

In principle, contributions could be invested in any security, although in practice most plans limit investment choices to bond, stock, and money market funds. The employee bears all the investment risk; the retirement account is, by definition, fully funded by the contributions, and the employer has no legal obligation beyond making its periodic contributions.

For defined-contribution plans, investment policy is essentially the same as for a tax-qualified individual retirement account. Indeed, the main providers of investment products for these plans are the same institutions such as mutual funds and insurance companies that serve the general investment needs of individuals. Therefore, in a defined-contribution plan much of the task of setting and achieving the income-replacement goal falls on the employee.

CC 23B.1

CONCEPT CHECK

An employee is 45 years old. Her salary is $40,000 per year, and she has $100,000 accumulated in her self-directed defined-contribution pension plan. Every year she contributes 5 percent of her salary to the plan, and her employer matches it with another 5 percent. She plans to retire at age 65. The plan offers a choice of two funds: a guaranteed return fund that pays a risk-free real interest rate of 3 percent per year and a stock index fund that has an expected real rate of return of 6 percent per year and a standard deviation of 20 percent. Her current asset mix in the plan is $50,000 in the guaranteed fund and $50,000 in the stock index fund. She plans to reinvest all investment earnings in each fund in that same fund and to allocate her annual contribution equally between the two funds. If her salary grows at the same rate as the cost of living, how much can she expect to have at retirement? How much can she be *sure* of having?

Defined-Benefit Plans

In a defined-benefit plan, a formula specifies benefits, but not the manner, including contributions, in which these benefits are funded. The benefit formula typically takes into account years of service for the employer and level of wages or salary (e.g., the employer pays the employee for life, beginning at age 65, a yearly amount equal to 1 percent of his final annual wage for each year of service). The employer (called the "plan sponsor") or an insurance company hired by the sponsor guarantees the benefits and thus absorbs the investment risk. The obligation of the plan sponsor to pay the promised benefits is like a long-term debt liability of the employer.

As measured both by number of plan participants and the value of total pension liabilities, the defined-benefit form dominates in most countries around the world. This is so in the United States, although the trend since the mid-1970s is for sponsors to choose the defined-contribution form when starting new plans. But the two plan types are not mutually exclusive. Many sponsors adopt defined-benefit plans as their primary plan, in which participation is mandatory, and supplement them with voluntary defined-contribution plans.

With defined-benefit plans, there is an important distinction between the pension *plan* and the pension *fund*. The plan is the contractual arrangement setting out the rights and obligations of all parties; the fund is a separate pool of assets set aside to provide collateral for the promised benefits. In defined-contribution plans, by definition, the value of the benefits equals that of the assets, so the plan is always fully funded. But in defined-benefit plans, there is a continuum of possibilities. There may be no separate fund, in which case the plan is said to be unfunded. When there is a separate fund with assets worth less than the present value of the promised benefits, the plan is underfunded. And if the plan's assets have a market value that exceeds the present value of the plan's liabilities, it is said to be overfunded.

Alternative Perspectives on Defined-Benefit Pension Obligations

As previously described, in a defined-benefit plan, the pension benefit is determined by a formula that takes into account the employee's history of service and wages or salary. The plan sponsor provides this benefit regardless of the investment performance of the pension fund assets. The annuity promised to the employee is therefore the employer's liability. What is the nature of this liability?

There is a widespread belief that pension benefits in final-pay formula plans are protected against inflation at least up to the date of retirement. But this is a misperception. Unlike social benefits, whose starting value is indexed to a general index of wages, pension benefits even in final-pay private-sector plans are "indexed" only to the extent that (1) the employee continues to work for the same employer, (2) the employee's own wage or salary keeps pace with the general price index, and (3) the employer continues to maintain the same plan. In Canada, most private pension plans are indexed to inflation in whole or in part. However, in the United States, very few private corporations offer pension benefits that are automatically indexed for inflation; thus workers who change jobs wind up with lower pension benefits at retirement than otherwise identical workers who stay with the same employer, even if the employers have defined-benefit plans with the same final-pay benefit formula. This is referred to as the *portability problem.*

Corporate pension liabilities are measured for balance sheet purposes by the accumulated benefit obligation (ABO)—that is, the present value of pension benefits owed to employees under the plan's benefit formula absent any salary projections and discounted at a nominal rate of interest. The ABO is thus a key element in a pension fund's investment strategy. It affects a corporation's reported balance sheet liabilities; it also reflects economic reality. An additional measure of a defined-benefit plan's liability is the projected benefit obligation (PBO). The PBO is a measure of the sponsor's pension liability that includes projected increases in salary up to the expected age of retirement.

Pension Investment Strategies

The special tax status of pension funds creates the same incentive for both defined-contribution and defined-benefit plans to tilt their asset mix toward assets with the largest spread between pretax and after-tax rates of return. In a defined-contribution plan, because the participant bears all the investment risk, the optimal asset mix also depends on the risk tolerance of the participant.

In defined-benefit plans, optimal investment policy may be different because the sponsor absorbs the investment risk. If the sponsor has to share some of the upside potential of the pension assets with plan participants, there is an incentive to eliminate all investment risk by investing in securities that match the promised benefits. If, for example, the plan sponsor has to pay $100 per year for the next five years, it can provide this stream of benefit payments by buying a set of five zero-coupon bonds each with a face value of $100 and maturing sequentially. By so doing, the sponsor eliminates the risk of a shortfall. This is an example of **immunization** of the pension liability.

If a corporate pension fund has an ABO that exceeds the market value of its assets, accounting standards require that the corporation recognize the unfunded liability on its balance sheet. If, however, the pension assets exceed the ABO, the corporation cannot include the surplus on its balance sheet. This asymmetric accounting treatment expresses a deeply held view about defined-benefit pension funds. Representatives of organized labour, some politicians, and even a few pension professionals believe that the sponsoring corporation, as guarantor of the accumulated pension benefits, is liable for pension asset shortfalls but does not have a clear right to the entire surplus in case of pension overfunding.

If the pension fund is overfunded, a 100 percent fixed-income portfolio is no longer required to minimize the cost of the corporate pension guarantee. Management can invest surplus pension assets in equities, provided it reduces the proportion so invested when the market value of pension assets comes close to the value of the ABO. Such an investment strategy, first introduced in Chapter 14, is known as *contingent immunization.*

Investing in Equities   If the only goal guiding corporate pension policy were shareholder wealth maximization, it is hard to understand why a financially sound pension sponsor would invest in equities at all. A policy of 100 percent bond investment would minimize the cost of guaranteeing the defined benefits.

In addition to the reasons given for a fully funded pension plan to invest only in fixed-income securities, there is a tax reason for doing so too. The tax advantage of a pension fund stems from the ability of the sponsor to earn the pretax interest rate on pension investments. To maximize the value of this tax shelter, it is necessary to invest entirely in assets offering the highest pretax interest rate. Because capital gains on stocks can be deferred and dividends are taxed at a lower rate than interest on bonds, corporate pension funds should invest entirely in taxable bonds and other fixed-income investments. Yet we know that in general pension funds invest from 40 to 60 percent of their portfolios in equity securities. Even a casual perusal of the practitioner literature suggests that they do so for a variety of reasons—some right and some wrong. There are three possible correct reasons.

CC 23B.2

CONCEPT CHECK

An employee is 40 years old and has been working for the firm for 15 years. If normal retirement age is 65, the interest rate is 8 percent, and the employee's life expectancy is 80, what is the present value of the accrued pension benefit per dollar?

The first is that corporate management views the pension plan as a trust for the employees and manages fund assets as if it were a defined-contribution plan. It believes that a successful policy of investment in equities might allow it to pay extra benefits to employees and is therefore worth taking the risk.

The second possible correct reason is that management believes that through superior market timing and security selection it is possible to create value in excess of management fees and expenses. Many executives in nonfinancial corporations are used to creating value in excess of cost in their businesses. They assume that it can also be done in the area of portfolio management. Of course, if that is true, then one must ask why they do not do it on their corporate account rather than in the pension fund. That way they could have their tax-shelter "cake" and eat it too. It is important to realize, however, that to accomplish this feat, the plan must beat the market, not merely match it.

Note that a very weak form of the efficient market hypothesis would imply that management cannot create shareholder value simply by shifting the pension portfolio out of bonds and into stocks. Even when the entire pension surplus belongs to the shareholders, investing in stocks just moves the shareholders along the capital market line (the market tradeoff between risk and return for passive investors) and does not create value. When the net cost of providing plan beneficiaries with shortfall risk insurance is taken into account, increasing the pension fund equity exposure reduces shareholder value unless the equity investment can put the firm above the capital market line. This implies that it makes sense for a pension fund to invest in equities only *if* it intends to pursue an active strategy of beating the market either through superior timing or security selection. A completely passive strategy will add no value to shareholders.

For an underfunded plan of a corporation in financial distress there is another possible reason for investing in stocks and other risky assets—federal pension insurance. Firms in financial distress have an incentive to invest pension fund money in the riskiest assets, just as troubled thrift institutions insured by the Federal Savings and Loan Insurance Corporation (FSLIC) in the 1980s had similar motivation with respect to their loan portfolios.

Wrong Reasons to Invest in Equities The wrong reasons for a pension fund to invest in equities stem from interrelated fallacies. The first is the notion that stocks are not risky in the long run. This fallacy was discussed at length in Chapter 4. Another, related fallacy is the notion that stocks are a hedge against inflation. The reasoning behind this fallacy is that stocks are an ownership claim over real physical capital. Real profits are either unaffected or enhanced when there is unanticipated inflation, so owners of real capital should not be hurt by it.

Let us assume that this proposition is true, and that the real rate of return on stocks is uncorrelated or slightly positively correlated with inflation. If stocks are to be a good hedge against inflation risk in the conventional sense, however, the nominal return on stocks has to be *highly* positively correlated with inflation. However, empirical studies show that stock returns have been negatively correlated with inflation in the past with a low *R*-squared. Thus, even in the best of circumstances, stocks can offer only a limited hedge against inflation risk.

In Canada, this argument is particularly pertinent due to an institutional difference. Unlike in the United States, defined-benefit plans are usually partly or entirely inflation-indexed. This can be accommodated by the use of real-return bonds, but the supply of Canadian real-return bonds is insufficient for the volume of pension funds. In order, therefore, to provide an inflation hedge, pension managers seek equity protection. If in fact equities do not provide strong positive correlation with inflation, their inclusion is not as justified as supposed by the managers.

Pension Fund Appraisal

Institutions operating pension funds for their employees can assess the performance both of their funds and of the professional managers they hire for portions of the funds. Several organizations, the largest being SEI, will evaluate performance by comparing the realized returns to benchmarks based on selected categories such as long-term bonds, small-cap equities, or market indices. The overall performance over various time periods can be compared to results of other institutions in general or of a similar type, such as universities or hospitals.

If an institution has been using a number of managers for different purposes, or if it is considering a change to other potential managers, it can obtain information about the results they have obtained. Combining the realized returns with the variability of results over different periods will permit the identification of managers who will satisfy the objectives of the pension fund.

SUMMARY

1. The Canadian tax system is designed to make investment in equity more favourable than investment in debt, by offering a dividend tax credit and excluding some of the capital gains from taxation. Capital gains and dividends are taxed at approximately the same effective rate.

2. There are four ways to shelter investment income from federal income taxes. The first is by investing in assets whose returns take the form of appreciation in value, such as common stocks or real estate. As long as capital gains taxes are not paid until the asset is sold, the tax can be deferred indefinitely. The second way of tax sheltering is through investing in tax-deferred retirement plans, such as RRSPs. The general

investment rule is to hold the least tax-advantaged assets in the plan and the most tax-advantaged assets outside of it. The third way of sheltering is to invest in the tax-advantaged products offered by the life insurance industry—tax-deferred annuities and variable and universal life insurance. They combine the flexibility of mutual fund investing with the tax advantages of tax deferral. Finally, there are investments in tax shelters, which finance investment in mutual funds, real estate, or other assets. Poor prospects with tax benefits make bad investments.

3. Pension plans are either defined-contribution or defined-benefit plans. Defined-contribution plans are, in effect, retirement funds held in trust for the employee

by the employer. The employees in such plans bear all the risk of the plan's assets and often have some choice in the allocation of those assets. Defined-benefit plans give the employees a claim to a money-fixed annuity at retirement. The annuity level is determined by a formula that takes into account years of service and the employee's wage or salary history.

4. If the only goal guiding corporate pension policy were shareholder wealth maximization, it is hard to understand why a financially sound pension sponsor would invest in equities at all. A policy of 100 percent bond investment would both maximize the tax advantage of funding the pension plan and minimize the cost of guaranteeing the defined benefits.

PROBLEMS

1. John Oliver, formerly a senior partner of a large management consulting firm, has been elected president of Mid-South Trucking Company. He has contacted you, a portfolio manager for a large investment advisory firm, to discuss the company's defined-benefit pension plans. Upon assuming his duties, Oliver learned that Mid-South's pension plan was 100 percent in bonds, with a maximum maturity of 10 years. He believes that "a pension plan should be managed so as to maximize return within well-defined risk parameters," and "anyone can buy bonds and sit on them." Mr. Oliver has suggested that he meet with you, as an objective advisor, and the plan's actuary to discuss possible changes in plan asset mix. To aid you in preparing for the meeting, Mr. Oliver has provided the current portfolio (Table 23B.1). He also has provided the following information about the company and its pension plans.

Company

Mid-South is the eighth-largest domestic trucking company, with annual revenues of $500 million. Revenues have grown about 8 percent per year over the past five years, with one down year. The company employs about 7,000 people, as against 6,500 five years ago. The annual payroll is about $300 million. The average age of the workforce is 43 years. Company profits last year were $20 million, compared with $12 million five years ago.

Pension Plan

Mid-South's pension plan is a defined-benefit plan that was established in 1975. The company annually contributes 7 percent of payroll to fund the plan. During the past five years, portfolio income has been used to meet payments for retirees, while company contributions have been available for investment. Although the plan is adequately funded on a current basis, unfunded past service liabilities are equal to 40 percent of plan assets. The liability is to be funded over the next 35 years. Plan assets are valued annually on a rolling four-year average for actuarial purposes.

Whereas FASB No. 87 requires an annual reassessment of the assumed rate of return, for purposes of this analysis, Mid-South's management, in consultation with the actuary, has decided to use an assumed annual rate of 7 percent. This compares with actual plan results that have averaged 10 percent per year over the past 20 years. Wages and salaries are assumed to increase 5 percent per year, which is identical with past company experience.

TABLE 23B.1
Current Portfolio

	Cost	Market Value	Current Yield	Yield to Maturity
Short-term reserves	$ 10,000,000	$ 10,000,000	5.8%	5.8%
Notes, 90 days to 1 year	25,000,000	25,500,000	6.5	6.4
Notes, 1 to 5 years	110,000,000	115,000,000	8.0	7.8
Bonds, 5 to 10 years	115,000,000	127,500,000	8.8	8.5
Total	$260,000,000	$278,000,000	8.1%	7.9%

Before the meeting, you review your firm's investment projections, dated March 31, 1997. Your firm believes that continued prosperity is the most likely outlook for the next three to five years but has allowed for two alternatives, a return to high inflation or a move into deflation/depression. The details of the projections are shown in Table 23B.2.

a. Using this information, create an investment policy statement for the Mid-South Trucking Company's pension plan. On the basis of your policy statement and the expectations shown, recommend an appropriate asset allocation strategy for Mid-South's pension plan limited to the same asset classes shown. Justify your changes, if any, from the current portfolio. Your allocation must add up to 100 percent.

b. At the meeting, the actuary suggests that Mid-South consider terminating the defined-benefit plan, purchasing annuities for retirees and vested employees with the proceeds, and establishing a defined-contribution plan. The company would continue to contribute 7 percent of payroll to the defined-contribution plan.

Compare the key features of a defined-benefit plan and a defined-contribution plan. Assuming Mid-South were to adopt and retain responsibility for a defined-contribution plan, briefly explain any revisions to your asset allocation strategy developed in part (a) above. Again, your allocation must sum to 100 percent and be limited to the same asset classes shown.

CFA® PROBLEMS

The following problem is based on a question that appeared in past CFA examinations.

2. You are Mr. R. J. Certain, a retired CFA, who formerly was the chief investment officer of a major investment management organization. Although you have over 30 years of experience in the investment business, you have kept up with the literature and developed a reputation for your knowledge and ability to blend modern portfolio theory and traditional portfolio methods.

The chairperson of the board of Morgan Industries has asked you to serve as a consultant to him and the other members of the board of trustees of the company's pension fund. Since you are interested in developing a consulting practice and in keeping actively involved in the investment management business, you welcome the opportunity to develop a portfolio management decision-making process for Morgan Industries that you could apply to all types of investment portfolios.

Morgan Industries is a company in transition. Its long-established business, dating back to the early years of the century, is the production of steel. Since the 1960s, however, Morgan gradually has built a highly profitable stake in the domestic production of oil and gas.

TABLE 23B.2

Investment Projections

Scenarios	Expected Annual Total Return (%)
Continued Prosperity (60% probability)	
Short-term reserves (Treasury bills)	6.0
Stocks (S&P 500 index)	12.0
Bonds (S&P high-grade bond index)	8.0
High-Inflation Scenario (25% probability)	
Short-term reserves (Treasury bills)	10.0
Stocks (S&P 500 index)	15.0
Bonds (S&P high-grade bond index)	3.0
Deflation/Depression Scenario (15% probability)	
Short-term reserves (Treasury bills)	2.0
Stocks (S&P 500 index)	−6.0
Bonds (S&P high-grade bond index)	12.0

Most of the company's 1982 sales of $4 billion were still derived from steel operations. Because Morgan occupies a relatively stable niche in a specialized segment of the steel industry, its losses on steel during the 1982 recession were moderate compared to industry experience. At the same time, profit margins for Morgan's oil and gas business remained satisfactory despite all the problems in the world oil market. This segment of the company's operations accounted for the entire 1982 net profit of $150 million. Even when steel operations recover, oil and gas operations are expected to contribute, on average, over half of Morgan's annual profits.

Judging from the combination of the two segments of the company's operations, the overall cyclicality of company earnings appears to be approximately the same as that of the S&P 500. Several well-regarded security analysts, citing the outlook for recovery in steel operations, as well as further gains in oil and gas production, project earnings progress for Morgan over the next five years at about the same rate as for the S&P 500. Debt makes up about 35 percent of the long-term capital structure, and the beta (market risk) for the company's common stock is also about the same as for the S&P 500.

Morgan's defined-benefit pension plan covers 25,000 active employees, vested and unvested, and 15,000 retired employees, with the latter projected to exceed 20,000 in five years. The burden of pension liabilities is large because the steel industry has long been labour-intensive and the company's current labour force in this area of operations is not as large as it was some years ago. Oil and gas operations, although growing at a significant rate, account for only 10 percent of the active plan participants and for even less of the retired beneficiaries.

Pension assets amounted to $1 billion of market value at the end of 1982. For the purpose of planning investment policy, the present value of the unfunded pension liability is calculated at $500 million. Although the company's outstanding debt is $600 million, it is clear that the unfunded pension liability adds significantly to the leverage in the capital structure.

Pension expenses charged to company income—and reflected in company contributions to the pension trust—were $80 million in 1982. The level of expenses, which are projected to rise with payroll, reflects current assumptions concerning inflation, the rate of return on pension assets, wage and salary increases, and benefits changes. If these assumptions were to prove completely correct, the current method of funding would amortize the unfunded pension liability over 20 years. Since assumptions are subject to change in the light of new information, they must be reviewed periodically. Revision by one percentage point in the assumed rate of investment return, for example, would require a current change in the level of pension expenses by $15 million before taxes, or about $7 million after taxes. The current actuarially assumed rate of return is 8.5 percent.

Pension investment policy, through its influence on pension expenses, unfunded pension liability, and the company's earnings progress, is a critical issue for Morgan's management. The chairperson is strongly committed to the corporate goal of achieving a total investment return for shareholders superior to that of other large industrial companies. He recognizes that a more aggressive pension investment policy—if successful—would facilitate attainment of the corporate goal through a significant reduction in pension expenses and unfunded pension liability. He also worries, however, that a significant drop in the market value of the company's pension fund—now $1 billion—could result in a major setback in the company's growth strategy. Current pension investment policy is based on an asset mix of approximately 50 percent common stocks and 50 percent fixed-income securities.

The chairperson is concerned about the overall investment management and direction of the pension fund and is very interested in your informed and objective evaluation.

What recommendations would you make and why?

International Investing

Although it is common in Canada to consider the S&P/TSX 60 as the market index portfolio, such practice is rather limited in scope. Equities actually make up 10 percent of total Canadian wealth and a far smaller percentage of world wealth. In one sense, international investing may be viewed as no more than a straightforward generalization of our earlier treatment of portfolio selection with a larger menu of assets from which to construct a portfolio. One faces similar issues of diversification, security analysis, security selection, and asset allocation. On the other hand, international investments pose some problems not encountered in domestic markets. Among these are the presence of exchange rate risk, restrictions on capital flows across national boundaries, an added dimension of political risk and country-specific regulations, and different accounting practices in different countries.

In this chapter we review the major topics covered in the rest of the book, emphasizing their international aspects. We start with the central concept of portfolio theory—diversification. We will see the importance of world markets and the benefits of global diversification for risk–return tradeoffs; we also introduce the possibilities for making international investments. We then examine the associated factors of political risk and the effect of currency fluctuations on returns. We next turn to passive and active investment styles in the international context. We will consider some of the special problems involved in the interpretation of passive index portfolios, and we will show how active asset allocation can be generalized to incorporate country and currency choices in addition to traditional domestic asset class choices. Finally, we demonstrate performance attribution for international investments.

24.1 ▶

INTERNATIONAL INVESTMENTS

The World Equity Portfolio

Canadian investors have shown themselves to be far less prone than their American neighbours to limit their investment horizons to the national boundaries. The presence and influence of foreign investors and markets serve to focus Canadian attention on alternatives to domestic investment; while the proximity of the United States makes it the dominant figure in our international perspective, European and Far Eastern nations already and increasingly are receiving substantial attention from investors. The internationalization of trade, beyond the traditional markets for major corporations such as Bombardier, Teck, and the banks, implies that Canadians can and must diversify their portfolio holdings into foreign assets in order to hedge foreign currency and economic fluctuations.

The portfolio holdings of an investor in any country should serve to protect his or her future consumption opportunities, given the prices faced domestically; but these prices are affected by foreign economic conditions and pricing relative to the proportion that foreign trade represents in the domestic economy. Thus in the United States, where domestic production and consumption represent the vast majority of economic activity, foreign economic events have had less and later effect on domestic conditions; in contrast, Canadian conditions react swiftly and directly to external events, particularly those in the United States. Canadians, therefore, have far more need to link themselves to foreign financial markets in order to hedge their portfolios and their consumption opportunities from adverse international events.

Canadians, by nature, may be more inclined to underestimate the size of their securities markets rather than the opposite. The Canadian market values in 2011 represented only 4.1 percent; that left about US$37 trillion of foreign equities for investment opportunities. As we noted in Chapter 1, Canadians can easily invest in U.S. securities; but these represented only some 36 percent of the equity markets. The United States itself accounts for only about a third of world stock market capitalization. Furthermore, we shall see that for Canadian portfolios, U.S. securities offer little in the way of diversification, which is the key opportunity to be exploited in considering foreign securities.

International Diversification

You can easily invest today in capital markets of nearly 100 countries and obtain up-to-date data about your investments in each of them. By 2011, 52 countries had stock markets with aggregate market capitalization above $1 billion. The data and discussion in this chapter are based on these countries.

The investments industry commonly distinguishes between "developed" and "emerging" markets. **Developed countries** (wealthier countries with modern financial systems, arbitrarily defined as having per capita income [in 2005] exceeding $10,000.) made up 68 percent of world gross domestic product in 2010, and 85 percent of the world market capitalization. Clearly, investors can attain better risk–return tradeoffs if they extend their search for attractive securities to both developed and emerging markets. Developed countries have broad stock indices that are generally less risky than those of emerging markets, but both offer opportunities for improved diversification. A typical emerging economy still is undergoing industrialization, is growing faster than developed economies, and its capital markets usually entail greater risk. (We use the FTSE[1] criteria, which emphasize capital market conditions, to classify markets as emerging or developed.)

---

[1]FTSE Index Co. (the sponsor of the British FTSE [Financial Times Share Exchange] stock market index) uses 14 specific criteria to divide countries into "developed" and "emerging" lists. Our list of developed countries includes all 25 countries that appear on FTSE's list.

The economic events of the past decade and of the end of the 1990s might incline investors to believe that international markets are highly correlated. The financial collapse caused an immediate and predictable global decline in equity markets. Previously also, the "Asian flu" that began with Thailand's currency and stock market collapse swept around Asia and then to Europe and the Americas. One country's financial troubles indicated the potential for the same, and led to the realization of those fears in a number of similar and supposedly healthier nations. Fears of a global financial crisis and the drastic retrenchment in Asian economies caused the stocks of multinational banks and firms to fall. As stability returned and fears subsided, a new crisis arose in Russia and Brazil; again the news struck multinationals and banks in various countries proportionately to their exposure. What was evident was that all the markets and economies were interlinked. What then was the point of trying to diversify risk by spreading investments across these different financial markets?

While the evidence of correlation was strong, the level of that correlation is demonstrably lower than one might suspect. The discussion of diversification in Chapter 6 indicates that any assets that are less than perfectly correlated will improve the reward-to-volatility ratio. The addition of foreign securities to a portfolio will, therefore, always serve to extend diversification. In considering their contribution, we usually distinguish between developed countries and emerging markets.

Developed Countries   To appreciate the myopia of an exclusive investment focus on U.S. stocks and bonds, consider the data in Table 24.1. The first two columns of Table 24.1 show market capitalization over the years 2000 and 2011 for developed markets. The first line shows capitalization for all world exchanges, showing total capitalization of corporate equity in 2011 as $38.2 trillion, of which combined Canadian and U.S. stock exchanges made up $15.5 trillion or 40.5 percent. The year-to-year changes in the figures in these columns demonstrate the volatility of these markets.

The next three columns show country equity capitalization as a percentage of the world's in 2000 and 2011, and the growth in capitalization over those 12 years. The two crises of the first dozen years of the twenty-first century, the bursting of the tech bubble in 2000–2001, and the financial crisis of 2008–2009 hit the developed countries hardest. Average growth of developed-country equity markets over these years was an anaemic 1.7 percent, as against a world average of 2.79 percent boosted by 16.3 percent for emerging markets. Clearly, a portfolio of Canadian and U.S. stocks alone is missing much of the available growth potential.

The last three columns of the table show GDP, per capita GDP, and equity capitalization as a percentage of GDP in 2010. Although per capita GDP in developed countries is not as variable across countries as total GDP, which is determined in part by total population, market capitalization as a percentage of GDP is quite variable. This suggests widespread differences in economic structure even across developed countries. We return to this issue in the next section.

Emerging Markets   For a passive strategy one could argue that a portfolio of equities of just the six countries with the largest capitalization would make up 64 percent (in 2011) of the world portfolio and may be sufficiently diversified. This argument will not hold for active portfolios that seek to tilt investments toward promising assets. Active portfolios will naturally include many stocks or even indices of emerging markets.

Table 24.2 makes the point. Surely, active portfolio managers must prudently scour stocks in markets such as China, Brazil, or Russia. The table shows data from the 20 largest emerging markets, the most notable of which is China with annual growth of over 35.2 percent over the ten-year period. But managers also would not want to have missed other markets such as Indonesia, Malaysia, and Thailand with annual growth of over 20 percent over the same years.

TABLE 24.1 Market Capitalization of Stock Exchanges in Developed Countries

| | Market Capitalization | | | | Annual Growth (%) | GDP | GDP per Capita | Market Capitalization as % of GDP |
| | Billions of U.S. Dollars | | Percent of World | | | | | |
	2000	2011	2000	2011	2000–2011	2010	2010	2010
World	**27,473**	**38,200**	**100%**	**100%**	**2.8**	**63,124**	**9,228**	**68**
U.S.	12,900	13,917	47.0	36.4	0.6	14,587	47,199	98
Japan	3,140	3,289	11.4	8.6	0.4	5,459	42,831	69
U.K.	2,566	2,794	9.3	7.3	0.7	2,249	36,144	133
Canada	615	1,581	2.2	4.1	8.2	1,577	46,236	114
France	1,278	1,455	4.7	3.8	1.1	2,560	39,460	70
Hong Kong	564	1,369	2.1	3.6	7.7	225	31,758	701
Germany	1,061	1,177	3.9	3.1	0.9	3,281	40,152	43
Switzerland	783	1,062	2.9	2.8	2.6	528	67,464	224
Australia	349	1,039	1.3	2.7	9.5	925	42,131	132
Korea	123	763	0.4	2.0	16.4	1,015	20,757	86
Spain	331	546	1.2	1.4	4.2	1,407	30,542	44
Italy	716	460	2.6	1.2	-3.6	2,051	33,917	28
Sweden	274	440	1.0	1.2	4.0	459	48,936	118
Netherlands	680	376	2.5	1.0	-4.8	779	46,915	60
Mexico	112	372	0.4	1.0	10.5	1,035	9,123	39
Norway	52	238	0.2	0.6	13.5	413	84,538	61
Chile	44	229	0.2	0.6	14.7	213	12,431	136
Belgium	159	216	0.6	0.6	2.6	469	43,144	54
Denmark	99	176	0.4	0.5	4.9	310	55,891	67
Turkey	50	164	0.2	0.4	10.4	734	10,094	34
Finland	280	139	1.0	0.4	-5.7	239	44,512	86
Israel	46	119	0.2	0.3	8.3	217	28,504	80
Poland	27	112	0.1	0.3	12.5	469	12,293	34
Austria	28	85	0.1	0.2	9.8	379	45,209	33
Ireland	82	65	0.3	0.2	-1.9	211	47,170	30
Portugal	64	59	0.2	0.2	-0.6	229	21,505	35
Czech Rep.	12	39	0.0	0.1	10.4	192	18,245	23
New Zealand	20	35	0.1	0.1	5.0	136	31,067	35
Luxemburg	28	34	0.1	0.1	1.7	53	105,438	79
Greece	72	29	0.3	0.1	-7.1	301	26,600	21
Hungary	12	19	0.0	0.0	4.1	129	12,852	22
Slovenia	2	6	0.0	0.0	11.2	47	22,851	18

Source: *Market capitalization:* Datastream, http://online.thomsonreuters.com/datastream; *GDP and GDP per capita:* The World Bank, http://data.worldbank.org.

TABLE 24.2 Market Capitalization of Stock Exchanges in Emerging Countries

| | Market Capitalization | | | | | | | Market Capitalization as % of GDP |
| | Billions of U.S. Dollars | | Percent of World | | Annual Growth (%) | GDP | GDP per Capita | |
	2000	2011	2000	2011	2000–2011	2010	2010	2010
Brazil	180	1,056	0.7	2.8	15.9	2,088	10,710	66
India	107	868	0.4	2.3	19.0	1,727	1,475	69
Russia	19	694	0.1	1.8	34.9	1,480	10,440	58
China	13	499	0.0	1.3	35.2	5,927	4,428	11
Taiwan	177	455	0.6	1.2	8.2	430	18,300	134
Singapore	136	428	0.5	1.1	10.1	209	41,122	241
South Africa	104	405	0.4	1.1	12.0	364	7,275	134
Malaysia	83	330	0.3	0.9	12.1	238	8,373	135
Indonesia	21	301	0.1	0.8	24.8	707	2,946	41
Thailand	23	219	0.1	0.6	20.7	319	4,608	70
Colombia	4	191	0.0	0.5	37.3	288	6,225	70
Philippines	20	141	0.1	0.4	17.6	200	2,140	67
Peru	5	77	0.0	0.2	25.9	157	5,401	64
Argentina	24	36	0.1	0.1	3.6	369	9,124	15
Pakistan	5	26	0.0	0.1	15.2	177	1,019	17
Sri Lanka	1	14	0.0	0.0	27.5	50	2,375	31
Romania	0	14	0.0	0.0	36.9	162	7,538	9
Venezuela	6	6	0.0	0.0	−0.2	392	13,590	3
Cyprus	9	3	0.0	0.0	−9.7	23	28,779	28
Bulgaria	0	2	0.0	0.0	29.6	48	6,325	4

Source: Market capitalization: Datastream, http://online.thomsonreuters.com/datastream; GDP and GDP per capita: The World Bank, http://data.worldbank.org.

These 20 emerging markets constituted 24 percent of the world GDP and, together with the 32 developed markets in Table 24.1, make up 92 percent of the world GDP. Per capita GDP in these countries was quite variable, ranging from $1,019 (Pakistan) to $41,122 (Singapore, debatably emerging). Market capitalization as a percentage of GDP ranges from 3 or 4 percent to 241 percent (Singapore), while in the so-called BRIC countries (Brazil, Russia, India, and China) it is still below 70 percent and only 11 percent in China; this suggests that these markets are expected to show significant growth over the coming years, even without spectacular growth in GDP.

E-INVESTMENTS **International** **Fundamental** **Analysis**	Research a country and/or an industry or company in a specific country at Wright Investor's Service (**www.wisi.com**). Pull down the menu bar under *Wright Research Center*, make your selection, and then review the companies. This is an excellent site for researching international companies and industries.

The growth of capitalization in emerging markets over 2002–2007 was very large and much more volatile than growth in developed countries, suggesting that both risk and rewards in this segment of the globe may be substantial.

Market Capitalization and GDP

The contemporary view of economic development (rigorously stated in de Soto)[2] holds that a major requirement for economic advancement is a developed code of business laws, institutions, and regulation that allows citizens to legally own, capitalize, and trade capital assets. As a corollary, we expect that development of equity markets will serve as catalysts for enrichment of the population, that is, that countries with larger relative capitalization of equities will tend to be richer. For rich countries, with already-large equity markets, this relationship will be weaker.

Figure 24.1 depicts the relationship[3] between per capita GDP and market capitalization (where both variables have been transformed to log 10 scale). Figure 24.1, panel A shows a scatter diagram and regression line for 2000; the situation in 2011 is shown in panel B. While developed markets are mostly above the line and emerging markets mostly below, the latter dramatically moved up in relative market capitalization over these years. This move was sufficient to greatly moderate the slope of the line. One can also easily see the upward shift of the whole world on the vertical axis that measures per capita GDP.

The regression slope coefficient measures the average percent change in per capita income when market capitalization increases by 1 percent. In 2000, this value was .64, but it fell to .35 in 2011. The scatter around the regression line has also visibly grown, as reflected in an R-squared of .52 in 2000 but only .10 in 2011.

Home-Country Bias

Home-country bias refers to the common tendency of investors to underweight foreign equities in their portfolio of risky assets. If investors allocated their stock investments across countries in proportion to outstanding equity, Canadian investors in 2011 would have placed only

---

[2]Hernando de Soto, *The Mystery of Capital* (New York: Basic Books, 2000).
[3]This simple single-variable regression is put forward not as a causal model but simply as a way to describe the relation between per capita GDP and the size of markets.

Figure 24.1

Per capita GDP and market capitalization as percentage of GDP. **Panel A:** Log scale, 2000 data. **Panel B:** Log scale, 2010 data.

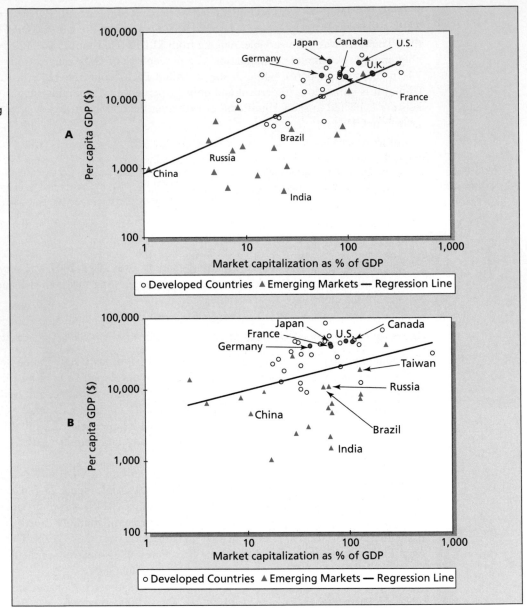

4.1 percent of their equity in Canadian firms (see Table 24.1) with the remaining 95.9 percent held in foreign markets. In fact, most investors show a pronounced bias toward holding stock in their home countries. On the other hand, U.S. investors' holdings of foreign stocks and long-term bonds, and foreigners' holdings of U.S stocks and long-term bonds, have tripled in 2001 and 2011, and this trend toward internationalization of portfolios has spread around the world, reducing the bias.

Techniques for Investing Internationally

Investors have a number of alternatives for achieving international exposure in their portfolios, the most direct being difficult for individuals. Large, or institutional, investors can invest directly in shares of companies trading on foreign exchanges, except in certain developing markets where foreign investment is restricted. Small investors still have satisfactory opportunities that include the purchase of

1. Foreign shares on U.S. markets
2. International closed-end mutual funds
3. International open-end mutual funds
4. International ETFs

General Electric
www.ge.com

Before describing these options, we should recall that among the stocks available for investment, there are both domestic and foreign companies, which are commonly known as *multinational firms*. Almost all large banks and major oil companies would qualify for this label, but there are also numerous nonfinancial enterprises, such as Philip Morris, Nestlé, GE, and Unilever. Such firms can be characterized as conducting many, if not all, of their primary activities, including obtaining raw materials, production, sales, and financing, in a large number of countries. Typically, these firms derive a majority of their profits from foreign sales. Hence, we can conclude that their financial results will depend on the economic conditions all around the world, and thus are themselves internationally diversified. Analysis of multinationals requires a more widely based approach than does analysis of purely domestic firms.[4]

NYSE Euronext
www.nyse.com

These firms may be bought on Canadian or U.S. exchanges in most cases, with the largest Canadian multinationals trading on both. In addition to the U.S. multinationals, one can, of course, purchase other U.S. firms for specific U.S. exposure. There are also a number of the largest European, Japanese, and Mexican companies that trade on the NYSE in the form of **American Depository Receipts (ADRs)**. ADRs are issued by U.S. financial institutions, or by the firms themselves, and represent claims to a number of shares in the foreign firm, issued abroad but held on deposit in the United States. A U.S. financial institution like a bank will purchase shares of a foreign firm in that firm's country, then issue claims to those shares in the United States. Each ADR is then a claim on a given number of the shares of stock held by the bank. Some stocks sell in the U.S. both directly and as ADRs.

There is also a wide array of mutual funds with an international focus. **Single-country funds** are mutual funds that invest in the shares of only one country. These tend to be closed-end funds; there are also regional funds, many of which are closed. Many of the large mutual fund families have a variety of open-end funds with an international focus. A new trend is to focus on global sector diversification; rather than a domestic fund for pharmaceuticals or high tech, or a fund for regional or single-country large-cap firms, portfolios are designed by internationally diversifying holdings in pharmaceuticals or high-tech companies.

Just as returns on actively managed domestic funds are dominated by index securities, so in general are the open- and closed-end international funds. Morgan Stanley's iShares and WEBS (World Equity Benchmark Shares) are a set of passive investments based on foreign market indices that can be bought on U.S. exchanges like stocks.

Tokyo Stock
Exchange
www.tse.or.jp

U.S. investors also can trade derivative securities based on prices in foreign security markets. For example, they can trade options and futures on the Nikkei stock index of 225 stocks traded on the Tokyo stock exchange, or on FTSE (Financial Times Share Exchange) indices of U.K. and European stocks. All of the above strategies are accessible to Canadians.

Although closed-end funds typically trade at a discount to asset value, foreign funds tend to trade at a premium, as they offer a service, diversification, that investors cannot provide

---

[4]A study on the effectiveness of diversification through multinationals reveals, however, that the price of this diversification may be lower risk-adjusted performance; see S. Foerster, R. Reinders, and M. Thorfinnson, "Are Investors Rewarded for the Foreign Exposure of Canadian Corporations?" *Canadian Investment Review* 5, no. 1 (Spring 1992).

themselves in foreign markets.[5] In this case, it would seem better to invest in open-end funds, which sell at asset value. As an interesting note on the investment policies of closed- and open-end funds, Franklin Templeton and Morgan Stanley offer both types of funds managed by the same advisors. On one occasion, it was observed that, for both these firms, the performance of the closed-end versions exceeded the open-end fund results by almost exactly the amount of the premium, suggesting excellent market efficiency in pricing. How could this happen? Closed-end funds are able to be fully invested if desired, since the investors' funds have been collected and need not be refunded. The open-end funds, on the other hand, must always maintain a cash reserve for investors who wish to cash in, so their returns must be lower due to the short-term rates; given the higher volatility of foreign markets, and the investor reactions, cash reserves for international funds are quite high.

24.2   RISK ISSUES IN INTERNATIONAL INVESTING

International investing poses unique challenges and a variety of new risks for Canadian investors. In principle, security analysis at the macroeconomic, industry, and firm-specific level is similar in all countries. Such analysis aims to provide estimates of expected returns and risk of individual assets and portfolios. However, to achieve the same quality of information about assets in a foreign country is by nature more difficult and hence more expensive. Assessment of foreign assets is impeded when information is less timely and more difficult to come by, as well as being reported according to standards and regulations that may differ from North American practice. Moreover, the risk of coming by false or misleading information is greater. Essentially, the investment environment in most foreign countries is less transparent than in North American markets.

Political Risk

One particular concern is referred to as **political risk**. The term is used to describe the possibility of the expropriation of assets, changes in tax policy, the institution of restrictions on the exchange of foreign currency for domestic currency and the repatriation of profits, or other changes in the business climate of a country. An extreme example of this happened to a Canadian company engaged in diamond mining in Angola in 1998. The mine operators found themselves under attack by guerrillas wanting to either take over the property or extract a "royalty" to permit the operation to continue. Protection money or slightly less obvious taxes imposed by forms of corruption are common in less developed countries. Multinationals and foreign companies may be forced to deliver a percentage of their returns to local influences, and must weigh these and additional uncertainty against the potential profits.

In the past, when international investing was novel, the added risk was referred to as political risk and its assessment was an art. As cross-border investment has increased and more resources have been utilized, the quality of related analysis has improved. A leading organization in the field (which is quite competitive) is the PRS Group, (Political Risk Services), which publishes two methodologies, *Political Risk Services* (PRS, the one presented here, and *International Country Risk Guide* (ICRG).[6]

---

[5]On the other hand, the premium on foreign funds appears to be related to investment restrictions in the particular countries involved. See C. Bonser-Neal, G. Brauer, R. Neal, and S. Wheatley, "International Investment Restrictions and Closed-End Country Fund Prices," *Journal of Finance* 45 (June 1990).
[6]You can find more information on the PRS Group Web site, www.prsgroup.com.

TABLE 24.3   Composite Risk Ratings for January 2011 Versus February 2010

Rank in January 2011	Country	Composite Risk Rating January 2011	Composite Risk Rating February 2012	January 2011 Versus February 2010	Rank in February 2010
	Very low risk				
1	Norway	**90.5**	90.00	0.50	1
11	Germany	**83.5**	83.50	0.00	5
13	Canada	**82.8**	82.75	0.00	6
16	Qatar	**82.0**	81.25	0.75	11
19	Japan	**81.0**	80.00	1.00	17
	Low risk				
31	United Kingdom	**77.3**	73.75	3.50	39
32	United States	**77.0**	77.25	−0.25	26
39	China, People's Rep.	**75.0**	76.25	−1.25	30
44	Brazil	**74.5**	72.75	1.75	46
68	Spain	**70.0**	71.00	−1.00	58
	Moderate risk				
78	Indonesia	**68.5**	67.25	1.25	81
86	India	**67.3**	70.50	−3.25	62
104	Egypt	**64.5**	66.50	−2.00	84
111	Turkey	**63.3**	63.50	−0.25	100
	High risk				
124	Venezuela	**59.5**	53.75	5.75	133
127	Iraq	**58.5**	59.25	−0.75	119
129	Pakistan	**57.3**	57.00	0.25	125
	Very high risk				
138	Haiti	**48.5**	49.75	−1.25	137
140	Somalia	**41.5**	36.75	4.75	140

Source: *International Country Risk Guide*, January 2011, Table 1, The PRS Group, Inc. Used with permission.

PRS's country risk analysis results in a country composite risk rating on a scale of 0 (most risky) to 100 (least risky). Countries are then ranked by the composite risk measure and divided into five categories: very low risk (100–80), low risk (79.9–70), moderate risk (69.9–60), high risk (59.9–50), and very high risk (less than 50). To illustrate, Table 24.3 shows the placement of selected countries in the January 2011 issue of the ICRG. It is not surprising to find Norway at the top of the very-low-risk list, and small emerging markets at the bottom, with Somalia (ranked 140) closing the list. Canada is clearly very-low-risk. What may be surprising is the fairly mediocre ranking of the United States (rank 32), comparable to Libya (20) and Bahrain (29), all three appearing in the low-risk category.

The composite risk rating is a weighted average of three measures: political risk, financial risk, and economic risk. Political risk is measured on a scale of 100–0, while financial and economic risk are measured on a scale of 50–0. The three measures are added and divided by two to obtain the composite rating. The variables used by PRS to determine the composite risk rating from the three measures are shown in Table 24.4.

TABLE 24.4

The Three Ratings Making Up ICRG's Composite Risk Rating

Political Risk Variables	Financial Risk Variables	Economic Risk Variables
• Government stability • Socioeconomic conditions • Investment profile • Internal conflicts • External conflicts • Corruption • Military in politics • Religious tensions • Law and order • Ethnic tensions • Democratic accountability • Bureaucracy quality	• Foreign debt (% of GDP) • Foreign debt service (% of GDP) • Current account (% of exports) • Net liquidity in months of imports • Exchange rate stability	• GDP per capita • Real annual GDP growth • Annual inflation rate • Budget balance (% of GDP) • Current account balance (% GDP)

Table 24.5 shows the three risk measures for seven of the countries in Table 24.3, in order of the January 2011 ranking of the composite risk ratings. The table shows that by political risk, the United States ranked third, but in the financial risk measure, the U.S. ranked *sixth* among these countries. The surprisingly poor performance of the U.S. in this dimension is probably due to its exceedingly large government and balance-of-trade deficits, which have put considerable pressure on its exchange rate. Exchange rate stability, foreign trade imbalance, and foreign indebtedness all enter into ICRG's computation of financial risk. The financial crisis that began in August of 2008 was a striking vindication of PRS's judgment of assigning relatively low financial scores to the U.S. and other major markets.

Country risk is captured in greater depth by scenario analysis for the composite measure and each of its components. Table 24.6 (panels A and B) shows one- and five-year worst-case and best-case scenarios for the composite ratings and for the political risk measure. Risk stability is based on the difference in the rating between the best- and the worst-case scenario and is quite large in most instances. The worst-case scenario can move a country to

TABLE 24.5   Current Risk Ratings and Composite Risk Forecasts

Country	Composite Ratings		Current Ratings		
	Year Ago February 2010	Current January 2011	Political Risk January 2011	Financial Risk January 2011	Economic Risk January 2011
Norway	90.00	**90.50**	88.5	46.5	46.0
Canada	82.75	**82.75**	86.5	40.0	39.0
Japan	80.00	**81.00**	78.5	44.0	39.5
United States	77.25	**77.00**	81.5	37.0	35.5
China, People's Rep.	76.25	**75.00**	62.5	48.0	39.5
India	70.50	**67.25**	58.5	43.5	32.5
Turkey	63.50	**63.25**	57.0	34.5	35.0

Source: *International Country Risk Guide*, January 2011, Table 2B, The PRS Group, Inc. Used with permission.

TABLE 24.6   Composite and Political Risk Forecasts

A. Composite risk forecasts

Country	Current Rating January 2011	One Year Ahead			Five Years Ahead		
		Worst Case	Best Case	Risk Stability	Worst Case	Best Case	Risk Stability
Norway	90.5	88.3	93.3	5.0	83.3	92.8	9.5
Canada	82.8	78.3	84.3	6.0	75.3	86.5	11.3
Japan	81.0	77.0	84.3	7.3	72.5	87.5	15.0
United States	77.0	73.3	80.3	7.0	69.5	83.0	13.5
China, People's Rep.	75.0	70.8	79.0	8.3	61.3	82.0	20.8
India	67.3	64.0	72.3	8.3	57.5	77.0	19.5
Turkey	63.3	57.8	67.5	9.8	53.8	71.5	17.8

B. Political risk forecasts

Country	Current Rating January 2011	One Year Ahead			Five Years Ahead		
		Worst Case	Best Case	Risk Stability	Worst Case	Best Case	Risk Stability
Norway	88.5	88.0	92.0	4.0	86.0	89.5	3.5
Canada	86.5	83.0	88.5	5.5	81.5	89.5	8.0
Japan	78.5	75.5	84.0	8.5	72.0	88.0	16.0
United States	81.5	77.5	85.5	8.0	76.0	87.0	11.0
China, People's Rep.	62.5	58.5	68.5	10.0	55.0	73.0	18.0
India	58.5	55.0	64.0	9.0	53.5	71.0	17.5
Turkey	57.0	52.5	63.5	11.0	51.5	69.0	17.5

Source: *Panel A: International Country Risk Guide*, January 2011, Table 2C. *Panel B: International Country Risk Guide*, January 2011, Table 3C. The PRS Group, Inc. Used with permission.

a higher-risk category. For example, Table 24.6, panel B shows that in the worst-case five-year scenario, China and Turkey were particularly vulnerable to deterioration in the political environment.

Finally, Table 24.7 shows ratings of political risk by each of its 12 components. Corruption (variable F) in Japan is rated worse than in the United States, but better than in China and India. In democratic accountability (variable K), China ranked worst and the United States, Canada, and India best, while China ranked best in government stability (variable A).

Each monthly issue of the *International Country Risk Guide* of the PRS Group includes great detail and holds some 250 pages. Other organizations compete in supplying such evaluations. The result is that today's investor can become well equipped to properly assess the risk involved in international investing.

Exchange Rate Risk

Beyond these risks, international investing entails **exchange rate risk**. The dollar return from a foreign investment depends not only on the returns in the foreign currency, but also on the exchange rate between the dollar and that currency, as we see from the following example.

TABLE 24.7 Political Risk Points by Component, January 2011

This table lists the total points for each of the following political risk components out of the maximum points indicated. The final columns in the table show the overall political risk rating (the sum of the points awarded to each component) and the change from 2010.

A	Government stability	12	G	Military in politics	6
B	Socioeconomic conditions	12	H	Religious tensions	6
C	Investment profile	12	I	Law and order	6
D	Internal conflict	12	J	Ethnic tensions	6
E	External conflict	12	K	Democratic accountability	6
F	Corruption	6	L	Bureaucracy quality	4

Country	A	B	C	D	E	F	G	H	I	J	K	L	Risk Rating January 2011	Change from December 2010
Canada	8.5	9.0	11.5	11.0	11.0	5.0	6.0	6.0	5.5	3.5	5.5	4.0	86.5	0.5
China, People's Rep.	9.0	8.0	6.5	9.0	9.0	2.0	3.0	5.0	4.0	3.5	1.5	2.0	62.5	0.0
India	6.0	4.5	8.5	6.0	9.5	2.0	4.0	2.5	4.0	2.5	6.0	3.0	58.5	−1.5
Japan	5.0	8.5	11.5	10.0	9.0	4.5	5.0	5.5	5.0	5.5	5.0	4.0	78.5	−0.5
Norway	7.5	10.5	11.5	11.0	11.0	5.0	6.0	5.5	6.0	4.5	6.0	4.0	88.5	0.0
Turkey	8.5	5.5	7.5	7.5	7.5	2.5	2.0	4.0	3.5	2.0	4.5	2.0	57.0	0.0
United States	8.0	8.5	12.0	10.0	9.5	4.0	4.0	5.5	5.0	5.0	6.0	4.0	81.5	0.5

Source: *International Country Risk Guide,* January 2011, Table 3B, The PRS Group, Inc. Used with permission.

EXAMPLE 24.1 **Exchange Rate Risk**

Consider an investment in England in risk-free British government bills paying 10 percent annual interest in British pounds. Although these U.K. bills would be the risk-free asset to a British investor, this is not the case for a Canadian investor. Suppose, for example, the current exchange rate is $2 per pound, and the Canadian investor starts with $20,000. That amount can be exchanged for £10,000 and invested at a riskless 10 percent rate in the United Kingdom to provide £11,000 in one year.

What happens if the dollar-pound exchange rate varies over the year? Say that during the year, the pound depreciates relative to the dollar, so that by year-end only $1.80 is required to purchase £1. The £11,000 can be exchanged at the year-end exchange rate for only $19,800 (£11,000 × $1.80/£), resulting in a loss of $200 relative to the initial $20,000 investment. Despite the positive 10 percent pound-denominated return, the dollar-denominated return is −1 percent.

We can generalize from these results. The $20,000 is exchanged for $20,000/$E_0$ pounds, where E_0 denotes the original exchange rate ($2/£). The U.K. investment grows to $(20,000/E_0)$ $[1 + r_f(\text{UK})]$ British pounds, where $r_f(\text{UK})$ is the risk-free rate in the United Kingdom. The pound proceeds ultimately are converted back to dollars at the subsequent exchange rate E_1, for total dollar proceeds of $20,000(E_1/E_0)[1 + r_f(\text{UK})]$. The dollar-denominated return on the investment in British bills, therefore, is

$$1 + r(\text{C}) = [1 + r_f(\text{UK})]E_1/E_0 \qquad (24.1)$$

We see in equation 24.1 that the dollar-denominated return for a Canadian investor equals the pound-denominated return times the exchange rate "return." For a Canadian investor, the investment in the British bill is a combination of a safe investment in the United Kingdom and a risky investment in the performance of the pound relative to the dollar. Here, the pound fared poorly, falling from a value of $2 to only $1.80. The loss on the pound more than offsets the earnings on the British bill.

Figure 24.2 illustrates this point. It presents returns on stock market indices in some of the larger foreign stock markets during 2012. The lower boxes depict returns in local currencies, whereas the upper boxes depict returns in U.S. dollars, adjusting for exchange rate movements. It is clear that exchange rate fluctuations over this period had large effects on dollar-denominated returns. For example, Norway's 13.3 percent gain in krone became a 22.5 percent gain in U.S. dollars after currency appreciation, while Japan's 22.9 percent gain in yen shrank to an 8.5 percent gain in U.S. dollars after currency depreciation.

CC 1

CONCEPT CHECK

Using the data in Example 24.1, calculate the rate of return in dollars to a Canadian investor holding the British bill if the year-end exchange rate is

a. $E_1 = \$2/£$ b. $E_1 = \$2.20/£$

Pure exchange rate risk is the risk borne by investments in foreign safe assets. The investor in U.K. bills of Example 24.1 bears only the risk of the U.K./Canadian exchange rate. We can

Figure 24.2   Stock market returns for 2012.

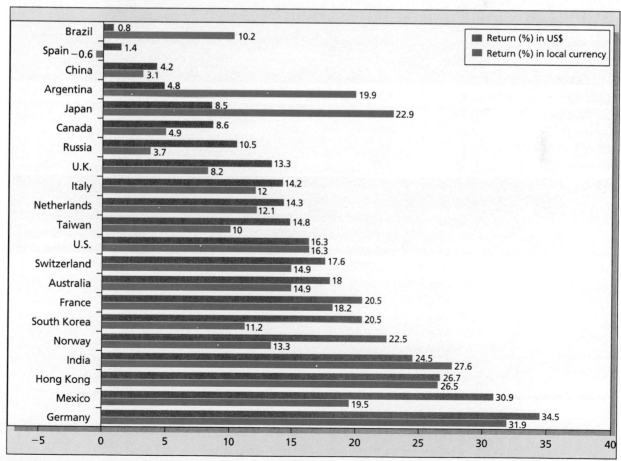

assess the magnitude of exchange rate risk by examination of historical rates of change in various exchange rates and their correlations.

Table 24.8, panel A shows historical exchange rate risk measured by the standard deviation of monthly percent changes in the exchange rates of major currencies against the U.S. dollar over the period 2001–2011.[7] The data show that currency risk is quite high. The annualized standard deviation of the percent changes in the exchange rate ranged from 9.13 percent (Japanese yen) to 13.87 percent (Australian dollar). The standard deviation of monthly returns on U.S. large stocks for the same period was 16 percent (low by historical standards). Hence, currency exchange risk was roughly 70 percent of that of the volatility of stocks. Clearly, an active investor who believes that a foreign stock is underpriced, but has no information about any mispricing of the Japanese yen, would be advised to hedge the currency risk exposure when tilting the portfolio toward the stock. Exchange rate risk of the major currencies has been relatively high this century. For example, a study by Solnik[8] for the period 1971–1998 finds lower standard deviations, ranging from 4.8 percent (Canadian dollar) to 12.0 percent (Japanese yen).

In the context of international portfolios, exchange rate risk may be mostly diversifiable. This is evident from the low correlation coefficients in Table 24.8, panel B. (There are notable exceptions

TABLE 24.8   Rates of Change in Major Currencies Against the U.S. Dollar, 2002–2011 (annualized monthly rate)

A. Standard deviation (annualized %)

Euro (€)	U.K. (£)	Switzerland (SF)	Japan (¥)	Australia (A$)	Canada (C$)
11.04	9.32	11.94	9.13	13.87	10.04

B. Correlation matrix

	Euro (€)	U.K. (£)	Switzerland (SF)	Japan (¥)	Australia (A$)	Canada (C$)
U.K. (£)	0.63	1				
Switzerland (SF)	0.83	0.51	1			
Japan (¥)	0.27	0.08	0.42	1		
Australia (A$)	0.75	0.6	0.61	0.05	1	
Canada (C$)	0.51	0.49	0.37	−0.02	0.72	1

C. Average annual returns from rolling over one-month LIBOR rates (%)

Country	Currency	Return in Local Currency	Expected Gain from Currency	Actual Gain from Currency	Actual Return in U.S. Dollars	Surprise Component of Return	SD of Annual Return
U.S.	$	2.18			2.18		
Euro	€	2.38	−0.20	4.38	6.77	4.58	11.04
U.K.	£	3.51	−1.32	1.09	4.60	2.41	9.32
SF	SF	0.90	1.28	6.46	7.36	5.17	11.94
Japan	¥	0.24	1.94	5.75	5.99	3.81	9.13
Australia	A$	5.25	−3.07	7.94	13.19	11.01	13.87
Canada	C$	2.50	−0.31	5.01	7.51	5.32	10.04

Source: *Exchange rates:* Datastream, http://online.thomsonreuters.com/datastream; *LIBOR rates:* http://www.economagic.com.

[7] Note that currencies and returns are in U.S. dollars; the discussion proceeding from Table 24.8 is from the perspective of a U.S. dollar portfolio.

[8] B. Solnick, *International Investing*, 4th ed. (Reading, MA: Addison-Wesley, 1999).

in the table, though, and this observation will be reinforced when we compare the risk of hedged and unhedged country portfolios in a later section.) Thus, passive investors with well-diversified international portfolios need not be concerned with hedging their exposure to foreign currencies.

The effect of exchange rate fluctuations also shows up in Table 24.8, panel C, which presents the returns on money market investments in different countries. While these investments are virtually risk-free in local currency, they are risky in dollar terms because of exchange rate risk. International investment flows by currency speculators should roughly equalize the expected dollar returns in various currencies, adjusted for risk. Moreover, exchange rate risk is largely diversifiable, as panel B shows, and hence we would expect similar dollar returns from cash investments in major currencies.

We can illustrate exchange rate risk using a yen-denominated investment during this period. The low yen-denominated LIBOR rate, .24 percent, compared to the U.S.-dollar LIBOR rate, 2.18 percent, suggests that investors expected the yen to appreciate against the dollar by around 1.94 percent, the interest rate differential across the two countries. But those expectations were not realized; in fact, the yen actually appreciated against the dollar at an annual rate of 5.75 percent, leading to an annual dollar-denominated return on a yen investment of 5.99 percent (the .24 percent yen interest rate together with the realized exchange rate appreciation of 5.75 percent). However, such deviations between prior expectations and actual returns of this magnitude are not shocking. The "surprise" return in a yen LIBOR investment (converted into dollars) was the difference between the actual return in dollars, 5.99 percent, and the dollar-denominated LIBOR rate of 2.18 percent, amounting to 3.81 percent. This surprise is actually considerably less than the yen standard deviation of 9.13 percent. In fact, none of the six surprises exceeded the standard deviation, which is actually the surprising event here. (See the boxed article for a non-hedging discussion.)

The investor in our example could have hedged the exchange rate risk using a forward or futures contract in foreign exchange. Recall that a forward or futures contract on foreign exchange calls for delivery or acceptance of one currency for another at a stipulated exchange rate. Here, to hedge her exposure to the British pound, the Canadian investor would agree to deliver pounds for dollars at a fixed exchange rate, thereby eliminating the future risk involved with conversion of the pound investment back into dollars.

EXAMPLE 24.2   **Hedging Exchange Rate Risk**

If the forward exchange rate in Example 24.1 had been $F_0 = \$1.93/\pounds$ when the investment was made, the Canadian investor could have assured a riskless dollar-denominated return by arranging to deliver the £11,000 at the forward exchange rate of $1.93/£. In this case, the riskless Canadian return would have been 6.15 percent:

$$[1 + r_f(\text{UK})]F_0/E_0 = (1.10)1.93/2 = 1.0615$$

Here are the steps to take to lock in the dollar-denominated returns. The futures contract entered in the second step exactly offsets the exchange rate risk incurred in step 1.

Initial Transaction	End-of-Year Proceeds in Dollars
Exchange $20,000 for £10,000 and invest at 10% in the United Kingdom	$\pounds 11,000 \times E_1$
Enter a contract to deliver £11,000 for dollars at the (forward) exchange rate $1.93/£	$\pounds 11,000(1.93 - E_1)$
Total	$\pounds 11,000 \times \$1.93/\pounds = \$21,32$

It may just be a case of buying the euro or the yen before a vacation in Europe or Japan, and then reconverting the remainder after returning home and awaiting an opportune moment. Unfortunately, this is unlikely to be profitable, especially if you are buying and selling through your local bank. The spread alone would eliminate any chance for profit, even if the currency had gained against the dollar during your vacation. But professionals also frequently get it wrong.

Currency traders can often profit from the presence of "non-profit-maximizing" individuals. These could be vacationers or businesses whose main interest is in selling goods and repatriating the revenues in dollars, with little attention to the currency fluctuations. This is the most reliable source of gain for professional traders, because on the whole it must be a zero-sum game.

Investors can choose to diversify their portfolios by investing in foreign assets such as equities and bonds. This enables them to benefit when a particular country's economy is flourishing, as is the case for many emerging markets. One source of expanding profits for foreign firms might be a cheap currency that aids exports. Investing in such firms might be profitable in the foreign currency, but it might be much less in domestic dollars if the currency depreciates to help export sales.

At the same time, a strong economy might well lead to an appreciating currency, as capital flows into the country to invest in expanding industries. One good example has been Australia, which has benefited from resource sales to China. While most of the world suffered from the financial crisis, Australia's exports were barely affected by a slight slowdown in Chinese demand. The Australian dollar, which some years ago approached $.50 to the U.S. dollar and always traded for less than the Canadian dollar, had by the end of 2010 marched past parity with the U.S. dollar and exceeded the Canadian dollar.

Currency traders seek to predict the direction of currency fluctuations. This requires a better model for market behaviour than reliance on purchasing-power parity. The latter means simply that similar baskets of goods should be priced the same in all currencies. Unfortunately, this is oversimplified, as most citizens of different countries demand and consume different products and have vastly different costs of living. Also, the timing of adjustment to parity is unpredictable.

More complex models include recognition of other factors such as the "carry trade." This term refers to the practice of borrowing money in currencies that have low interest rates and using the funds to buy currencies of countries with high interest rates or assets with high growth prospects denominated in those currencies. For many years (especially in the 1990s), investors took advantage of Japan's economic woes and low-yielding currency to borrow yen and convert these funds into U.S. dollars. That had the added benefit of acting to lower the yen further and raise the dollar. These days, the U.S. dollar is being borrowed instead.

Another factor is simple momentum. Traders can see that one currency is hot and another cold. Following that momentum results in herd behaviour of purchasing the hot one and selling the cold one, which reinforces the heat and the cold. Vigilant observers will be able to tell when the momentum is disappearing and cancel or reverse their investments.

These two factors, among other less obvious ones, are anomalous in that the purchasing-power parity theorem must prevail in the long-run, and they run counter to the economic logic. Yet they are realistic in recognizing what is occurring rather than stubbornly insisting on the necessity for cold economic logic to prevail at all times. It appears that many professionals are betting on the reality rather than the theory. Models used today attempt to combine the conflicting forces.

You may recall that this is the same type of hedging strategy at the heart of the spot-futures parity relationship discussed in Chapter 20. In both instances, forward or futures markets are used to eliminate the risk of holding another asset. The Canadian investor can lock in a riskless dollar-denominated return either by investing in the United Kingdom and hedging exchange rate risk or by investing in riskless Canadian assets. Because the returns on two riskless strategies must provide equal returns, we conclude

$$[1 + r_f(\text{UK})]\frac{F_0}{E_0} = 1 + r_f(\text{C}),$$

which can be rearranged to

$$F_0/E_0 = [1 + r_f(\text{C})]/[1 + r_f(\text{UK})] \qquad (24.2)$$

This relationship is called **interest rate parity** or the **covered interest arbitrage relationship**, which we first encountered in Chapter 20.

Unfortunately, such perfect exchange rate hedging is usually not so easy. In our example, we knew exactly how many pounds to sell in the forward or futures market, because the pound-denominated proceeds in the United Kingdom were riskless. If the U.K. investment had not been in bills, but instead had been in risky U.K. equity, we would know neither the ultimate value in pounds of our U.K. investment nor how many pounds to sell forward. That is, the hedging opportunity offered by foreign exchange forward contracts would be imperfect.

To summarize, the generalization of equation 24.1 is

$$1 + r(C) = [1 + r(\text{foreign})]E_1/E_0 \tag{24.3}$$

where $r(\text{foreign})$ is the possibly risky return earned in the currency of the foreign investment. You can set up a perfect hedge only in the special case that $r(\text{foreign})$ is itself a known number. In that case, you know you must sell in the forward or futures market an amount of foreign currency equal to $[1 + r(\text{foreign})]$ for each unit of that currency you purchase today.

CC 2

CONCEPT CHECK

How many pounds would need to be sold forward to hedge exchange rate risk in the above example if

a. $r(\text{UK}) = 20$ percent?

b. $r(\text{UK}) = 30$ percent?

Using Futures to Manage Exchange Rate Risk

We have just seen an illustration of using the futures exchange rate to lock in the return on the investment in U.K. bills. Using futures is a more precise operation, as we saw in Chapter 20, and there are some details to clarify for foreign exchange hedging. International currencies are quoted in cross rates against each other, particularly for major currencies; futures, however, are traded on the International Monetary Market (IMM, a division of the Chicago Mercantile Exchange) on the basis of individual currencies against the U.S. dollar. Suppose that a Canadian institution has made an investment in the United Kingdom and wishes to hedge the returns against dollar-pound exchange fluctuations. Instead of using forwards between the Canadian dollar and British pound, the firm could use futures of the Canadian dollar against the U.S. dollar, and again of the U.S. dollar against the pound. Then again, it might be content to hedge the U.S./U.K. risk and retain the Canada/U.S. risk due to other investments.

Let us examine the use of futures to control the U.S./U.K. risk, so that the following references to dollars are in U.S. currency. The institution has a portfolio of two million pounds that will lose $200,000 for every $.10 depreciation in the pound against the dollar. To hedge this, it arranges to deliver pounds for dollars at an exchange rate determined today. Thus, in delivering pounds, it is on the short side of the pound futures contract, which will benefit from a pound depreciation.

For example, suppose that the futures price is currently $1.50 per pound for delivery in three months. If the firm enters a futures contract with a futures price of $1.50 per pound, and the exchange rate in three months is $1.40 per pound, then the profit on the transaction is $.10 per pound. The futures price converges at the maturity date to the spot exchange rate of $1.40 and the profit to the short position is therefore $F_0 - F_T = \$1.50 - \$1.40 = \$.10$ per pound.

How many pounds should be sold in the futures market to most fully offset the exposure to exchange rate fluctuations? We need to find the number of pounds we should commit to delivering in order to provide a $200,000 profit for every $.10 that the pound depreciates. Therefore, we need a futures position to deliver 2,000,000 pounds. As we have just seen, the profit per pound on the futures contract equals the difference in the current futures price and the ultimate exchange rate; therefore, the foreign exchange profits resulting from a \$.10 depreciation[9] will equal \$.10 $\times$ 2,000,000 = \$200,000.

The proper hedge position in pound futures is independent of the actual depreciation in the pound as long as the relationship between profits and exchange rates is approximately linear. For example, if the pound depreciates by only half as much, \$.05, the investment would lose only \$100,000. The futures position would also return half the profits: \$.05 $\times$ 2,000,000 = \$100,000, again just offsetting the exposure. If the pound *appreciates*, the hedge position still (unfortunately in this case) offsets the exposure. If the pound appreciates by \$.05, the firm might gain \$100,000 from the enhanced value of the pound; however, it will lose that amount on its obligation to deliver the pounds for the original futures price.

The hedge ratio is the number of futures positions necessary to hedge the risk of the unprotected portfolio. In general, we can think of the hedge ratio as the number of hedging vehicles (e.g., futures contracts) one would establish to offset the risk of a particular unprotected position. The hedge ratio, H, in this case is

$$H = \frac{\text{Change in value of unprotected position for a given change in exchange rate}}{\text{Profit derived from one futures position for the same change in exchange rate}}$$

$$= \frac{\$200,000 \text{ per } \$.10 \text{ change in } \$/\pounds \text{ exchange rate}}{\$.10 \text{ profit } \textit{per pound} \text{ delivered per } \$.10 \text{ change in } \$/\pounds \text{ exchange rate}}$$

$$= 2,000,000 \text{ pounds to be delivered}$$

Because each pound-futures contract on the IMM calls for delivery of 62,500 pounds, you would need to short 2,000,000/62,500 per contract = 32 contracts.

One interpretation of the hedge ratio is as a ratio of sensitivities to the underlying source of uncertainty. The sensitivity of operating profits is \$200,000 per swing of \$.10 in the exchange rate. The sensitivity of futures profits is \$.10 per pound to be delivered per swing of \$.10 in the exchange rate. Therefore, the hedge ratio is 200,000/.10 = 2,000,000 pounds.

We could just as easily have defined the hedge ratio in terms of futures contracts rather than in terms of pounds. Because each contract calls for delivery of 62,500 pounds, the profit on each contract per swing of \$.10 in the exchange rate is \$6,250. Therefore, the hedge ratio defined in units of futures contracts is \$200,000/\$6,250 = 32 contracts, as derived above.

Although one might well wish to hedge the exchange rate risk, another opinion maintains that domestic consumption is dependent upon the prices of foreign goods and thus, currency fluctuations in one's portfolio actually help to hedge this risk to consumption. As such, once a foreign component has been determined for a portfolio, it may be best to leave it unhedged. A study by Auger and Parisien[10] for 1973–1987 data including Canadian assets, U.S. equities (S&P 500), and international equities (Morgan Stanley's EAFE index, described in Section 24.5) analyzes the effect of foreign currency hedging on internationally diversified portfolios for Canadian investors. While the unhedged EAFE portfolio had a slightly higher rate of return of 17.7 percent for volatility of 27.2 percent, the hedged equivalent return of 16.0 percent was obtained for a volatility of only 19.3 percent. Table 24.9, reproduced from their study, shows the returns and volatilities for various portfolios and periods; the results show the local currency returns and the Canadian dollar equivalents, with and without hedging. Note that the TSE 300 (now known as the S&P/TSX Composite) is clearly dominated by the hedged EAFE portfolio.

---

[9]Actually, the profit on the contract depends on the changes in the futures price, not the spot exchange rate. For simplicity, we call the decline in the futures price the depreciation in the pound.

[10]Robert Auger and Denis Parisien, "The Risks and Rewards of Global Investing," *Canadian Investment Review* 2, no. 1 (Spring 1989).

TABLE 24.9 Domestic and Foreign Investments: Annualized Returns and Return Standard Deviations for 1973–1987

Period	TSE 300	Unhedged EAFE	Local EAFE	Hedged EAFE	Unhedged S&P 500	Local S&P 500	Hedged S&P 500	Canadian Paper	Canadian Bonds
1973–1987									
Return	11.0	17.7	12.0	16.0	11.8	9.8	10.7	10.8	9.7
Standard deviation	22.2	27.2	17.3	19.3	17.8	18.0	18.5	1.2	14.5
1973–1977									
Return	1.6	4.6	−.2	.2	1.7	−.2	.8	8.6	7.2
Standard deviation	12.4	21.6	18.0	19.5	18.8	18.2	19.2	1.7	8.5
1978–1982									
Return	18.3	14.5	13.8	20.8	16.8	14.0	14.5	14.0	8.1
Standard deviation	26.1	18.6	7.9	7.6	12.4	12.8	12.3	4.1	13.9
1983–1987									
Return	13.8	36.2	23.7	29.0	17.5	16.4	17.7	9.9	13.9
Standard deviation	20.4	27.1	11.6	12.4	14.4	15.5	16.0	1.5	14.9

Source: Robert Auger and Denis Parisien, "The Risks and Rewards of Global Investing," *Canadian Investment Review* 2, no. 1 (Spring 1989). Reprinted by permission.

24.3 RISK, RETURN, AND BENEFITS FROM INTERNATIONAL DIVERSIFICATION

Integration of Markets

Integration Versus Segmentation Investigation of the benefits of international investment leads immediately to the question of whether assets listed in different capital markets offer the same risk-return characteristics. Interlisting of stocks on various world exchanges makes them accessible to investors in those markets and places them in direct competition as financial assets with the domestic securities of those markets. One might suspect that the inevitable result of this would be that all assets in all markets would display the same risk-return characteristics, at least relative to some world index or common factors. Were this the case, we would describe the markets as being fully integrated. In contrast to this, if assets in different markets retained different risk-return characteristics or were priced according to different and country-specific factors, we would describe these markets as segmented.

The existence of market segmentation is ascribed to both indirect and legal barriers to investment by all potential investors in all potential assets. Indirect barriers are defined as those previously mentioned problems besetting the foreign investor, such as lack of access to financial information or ability to trade efficiently in the securities. Legal barriers include restrictions on foreign ownership or of foreign investment by individuals or institutions, such as the limitation placed on Canadian pension funds. Interlisting of securities tends to alleviate the indirect barriers but usually cannot solve legal barriers.

Studies indicate that various important financial ratios vary widely across the different markets. This might be taken as evidence of clear segmentation of the many markets, possibly excepting the Canadian and U.S. markets with their similar ratios, given the relevance of these ratios to market valuation. Yet these statistics must be recognized as dependent upon the market conditions under which they were compiled; prices are high relative to earnings during recessions. Furthermore, the different markets are not homogeneous in terms of the firms that comprise the indices; the Canadian market is disproportionately high in natural resource companies. Financial ratios vary appropriately across different industries, and the different comparisons of specific national markets leads to a variety of aggregates of ratios.

Consideration of financial ratios is a dated approach to valuation, however, and cannot provide reliable evidence as to market segmentation. Modern financial theory prescribes the comparison of ex post risk–return measures and the sensitivity to market factors as evidence. Recent interest in the subject of market integration and segmentation has led to a number of theoretical and empirical studies to test which of the two descriptions is accurate. Generally, these tests involve attempts to price international assets by appeal to multifactor models, as described in the previous section; both multifactor CAPM and APT models have been used. Modelling the effects of barriers causing segmentation is difficult, however, given the problem of defining and quantifying imperfections in the markets. Hence, the risk premiums for the various factors cannot be reliably established. Alternatively, theory suggests that the integration of a smaller market with larger markets will result in a lowering of expected returns in the smaller market, due to increased liquidity and demand, but more importantly, due to a lowering of the risk premium. Interlisting of securities should produce a lowering of risk premiums for these securities at least; thus the event of interlisting can be studied to test for an observed reduction as of the occurrence of the event.[11]

Canadian and U.S. Integration   Canadian markets offer a unique opportunity to researchers to study the question of segmentation versus integration since they are close to U.S. markets both institutionally and geographically; the economies are closely linked, corporations are governed by essentially similar rules and practices, and both debt and equity instruments of both countries are sold to and traded by investors of both countries, with interlisting of many stocks. Yet the different tax treatment of dividends in the two countries implies that ex-dividend-day returns should differ for stocks in the two markets; interlisted stocks were shown by Booth and Johnston[12] to behave differently from domestically traded stocks. Comparison of interlisted and domestic stocks can provide statistically significant results to demonstrate segmentation. Furthermore, a case for integration between the two markets can be made more strongly than for integration of a third market with either of the two. Statistical methods can be used to test for the different characteristics of integration as would be expected under the closely linked versus distant markets.

Most empirical studies of Canadian and U.S. returns differ in their conclusions as to whether the two markets are truly integrated. Hatch and White[13] examined the comparative returns of U.S. and Canadian stock markets, and noted that U.S. stocks had a higher return than did Canadian but had a slightly lower risk; they rationalized this as resulting from a lower beta for Canadian stocks, relative to a world index. Brennan and Schwartz[14] rejected integration of the two markets over the period 1968–1980 based on a combined index, but their analysis does not correct for the substantial double-counting of interlisted stocks. Extending the period to 1982, Jorion and Schwartz[15] found the same result by using a two-factor CAPM

---

[11]Gordon J. Alexander, Cheol S. Eun, and S. Janakiramanan, "Asset Pricing and Dual Listing on Foreign Capital Markets: A Note," *Journal of Finance* 42 (March 1987).

[12]L. D. Booth and D. J. Johnston, "The Ex-Dividend Day Behavior of Canadian Stock Prices: Tax Changes and Clientele Effects," *Journal of Finance* 39 (June 1984).

[13]J. E. Hatch and R. W. White, "A Canadian Perspective on Canadian and United States Capital Market Returns: 1950–1983," *Financial Analysts Journal* 42 (May/June 1986).

[14]M. J. Brennan and E. Schwartz, "Asset Pricing in a Small Economy: A Test of the Omitted Assets Model," in K. Spremann, ed., *Survey of Developments in Modern Finance* (New York: Springer-Verlag, 1986).

[15]P. Jorion and E. Schwartz, "Integration vs. Segmentation in the Canadian Stock Market," *Journal of Finance* 41 (July 1986).

approach; the model was designed to eliminate the commonality between the domestic and international components. They found that the international index did not account for all the returns in Canadian stocks, leaving a priceable national component; hence, they concluded there was evidence of segmentation. A study by Mittoo[16] finds evidence that both time and interlisting are significant in explaining the segmentation issue. Using both CAPM and APT approaches, it is revealed that data prior to 1982 support segmentation, while integration is indicated afterward; furthermore, interlisted stocks after 1982 show integration, but domestically listed stocks suggest segregation. The data were restricted to TSE 35 companies to avoid thin-trading problems and natural resource factor loading, and to a time period where regulatory impediments to integration were absent. Alexander, Eun, and Janakiramanan[17] tested the reduction in expected required returns following interlisting for the period 1969–1982. They investigated both Canadian and non–North American stocks that were listed on the NYSE, AMEX, or Nasdaq, and found a significant distinction between the Canadian and non-Canadian groups; as hypothesized, the Canadian stocks experienced a much smaller return reduction than did the others. In fact, the Canadian results were found to be insignificant, leading them to the conclusion that the foreign markets are definitely segmented from the U.S., but that the Canadian market may not have been.

Nasdaq Stock
Market
www.nasdaq.com

In conclusion, we can say that there are institutional and sectoral explanations for an apparent segmentation of Canadian and U.S. markets; at the same time, similarities and accessibility of the two markets suggest little if any differential pricing is likely and that virtual integration is possible.

Risk and Return: Summary Statistics

Illustrations for most of our discussions in the remaining part of this chapter derive from a database of country market-index returns. We use 10 years of monthly returns over 2002–2011 for 48 non-U.S. country market indices as well as the U.S. S&P 500. This decade stretches from the beginning of the recovery from the bursting of the tech bubble in 2001, through the low–interest rate boom period that followed and the ensuing financial crisis of 2008, and, finally, to the beginning of the slow recovery from that crisis.

Analysis of risky assets typically focuses on *excess* returns over the risk-free rate. This alone adds a perplexing aspect to international investing, since the appropriate risk-free rate varies around the globe. Rates of return on identical indices (and on individual assets) will generate different excess returns when safe bonds are denominated in different currencies. Although our perspective is U.S.-based, our methodology would serve investors in any country, yet the numbers may differ when applied to risk-free rates denominated in other currencies.

The tumultuous period we analyze resulted in unexpected low average excess returns, primarily in developed markets, while most emerging markets continued unabated growth. This fact alone conveys an important lesson. It provides an extreme example of the general observation that realized returns are very noisy reflections of investor expectations and cannot provide accurate forecasts of future returns. Past returns do, however, provide an indication of risk, at least for the near future. While the near-efficient market hypothesis applies to expected returns (to wit, future returns cannot be forecast from past returns), it does *not* apply to forecasting risk. Thus our exercise will allow us to demonstrate the distinction between what you can and cannot learn from historical returns that evidently departed from prior expectations.

---

[16]Usha R. Mittoo, "Additional Evidence on Integration in the Canadian Stock Market," *Journal of Finance* 47 (December 1992).

[17]Gordon J. Alexander, Cheol S. Eun, and S. Janakiramanan, "International Listings and Stock Returns: Some Empirical Evidence," *Journal of Financial and Quantitative Analysis* 23 (1988). This is a typical example of the event study methodology, described in Chapter 9.

TABLE 24.10   Market Value and Performance of Country Portfolio Combinations Compared with Regional-Index Portfolios

Country-Index Portfolios	Market Value ($ billion)			Performance 2002–2011 ($-denom. returns)		
	2001	2006	2011	Average	SD	Sharpe Ratio
U.S.	11,850	15,520	13,917	0.21	4.63	0.0444
Developed excluding U.S.	10,756	22,065	18,487	0.48	5.48	0.0869
Emerging	1,230	5,319	5,765	1.35	6.86	0.1971
Developed + EM	11,987	27,384	24,251	0.61	5.63	0.1077
U.S. + Developed	22,606	37,585	32,403	0.34	4.99	0.0680
U.S. + EM	13,080	20,839	19,681	0.36	4.94	0.0736
World	23,836	42,904	38,168	0.50	5.32	0.0948
Regional-Index Portfolios						
MSCI EAFE (Europe + Australia + Far East) = Developed				0.42	5.41	0.0771
MSCI emerging markets				1.21	7.00	0.1734
MSCI World excluding U.S.				0.46	5.41	0.0841
World				0.31	4.90	0.0637

Source: Datastream.

While active-strategy managers engage in individual-market asset allocation and security selection, we will restrict our international diversification to country market-index portfolios, keeping us on the side of an enhanced passive strategy. Nevertheless, our analysis illustrates the essential features of extended active management as well.

We begin with an investigation of the characteristics of individual markets and then proceed to analyze the benefits of diversification, using portfolios constructed from these individual markets. The market capitalization of individual-country indices can be found in Tables 24.1 and 24.2, and the aggregated results for the portfolios are shown in Table 24.10. This table also displays the performance of two types of portfolios: portfolios aggregated from country indices and regional-index portfolios. The performances of individual-country-index portfolios are shown in Table 24.11.

For the aggregated country-index portfolios, we examine a strategy that constructs value-weighted portfolios of developed and emerging markets based on market capitalizations at the beginning of 2002. These portfolios are rebalanced after five years, in 2007, based on capitalizations at the end of 2006, and held for another five years. (Dividends are reinvested throughout the 10-year experiment.) Such a strategy is feasible to a large degree, since many (although, admittedly, not all) country-index portfolios are investable as index funds or ETFs. Because not all country indices are investable, this hypothetical strategy perhaps generates a bit more efficient diversification than is actually possible. On the other hand, if actually held, these value-weighted portfolios would automatically be rebalanced to value weights continually. In contrast, we rebalance only once after five years, which slightly attenuates diversification benefits. On balance, then, we expect these hypothesized portfolios to perform about as well as a feasible country-based, passive international strategy.

These portfolios are contrasted with completely feasible international diversification by investing in regional-index funds, which are also shown in Table 24.10. This comparison is based on standard performance statistics, namely, average and standard deviation of excess returns (denominated in U.S. dollars), as well as beta and alpha estimated against a U.S.-only portfolio.

TABLE 24.11   Performance of Individual-Country-Index Portfolios, Monthly Excess Returns in U.S. Dollars over 2002–2011

Individual-Country-Index Portfolios	Average	SD	Sharpe Ratio	Regression Against U.S.				
				Corr. w/U.S.	Beta	Alpha	Residual SD	Info Ratio
Developed								
U.S.	0.21	4.63	0.0444	1	1	0	0	0
Australia	1.17	6.75	0.1728	0.82	1.20	0.92	3.84	0.24
Austria	0.78	8.87	0.0876	0.74	1.42	0.49	6.00	0.08
Belgium	0.32	7.47	0.0434	0.79	1.28	0.06	4.56	0.01
Canada	0.99	6.33	0.1557	0.80	1.10	0.76	3.77	0.20
Denmark	0.97	6.48	0.1496	0.78	1.10	0.74	4.04	0.18
Finland	0.09	8.93	0.0101	0.77	1.49	−0.22	5.72	−0.04
France	0.37	6.76	0.0548	0.88	1.29	0.11	3.19	0.03
Germany	0.58	7.80	0.0743	0.89	1.49	0.27	3.64	0.08
Greece	−0.51	10.10	−0.0506	0.66	1.43	−0.81	7.65	−0.11
Hong Kong	0.74	6.33	0.1175	0.69	0.94	0.55	4.61	0.12
Ireland	−0.37	7.69	−0.0477	0.79	1.31	−0.64	4.73	−0.13
Israel	0.56	6.19	0.0904	0.64	0.86	0.38	4.76	0.08
Italy	0.21	7.18	0.0291	0.82	1.27	−0.05	4.11	−0.01
Japan	0.23	4.95	0.0463	0.56	0.60	0.11	4.11	0.03
Netherlands	0.41	6.95	0.0589	0.88	1.32	0.14	3.32	0.04
New Zealand	0.97	6.22	0.1554	0.67	0.90	0.78	4.64	0.17
Norway	1.35	8.98	0.1507	0.78	1.51	1.04	5.68	0.18
Portugal	0.35	6.74	0.0524	0.73	1.06	0.13	4.63	0.03
Singapore	0.99	6.71	0.1475	0.75	1.09	0.77	4.43	0.17
Spain	0.76	7.53	0.1009	0.79	1.29	0.49	4.62	0.11
Sweden	0.94	8.01	0.1177	0.86	1.49	0.64	4.11	0.16
Switzerland	0.60	5.04	0.1194	0.79	0.86	0.42	3.10	0.14
U.K.	0.38	5.29	0.0725	0.87	1.00	0.18	2.60	0.07
Emerging								
Argentina	1.32	11.05	0.1191	0.44	0.44	1.05	1.10	0.96
Brazil	2.10	10.86	0.1931	0.71	0.71	1.66	1.76	0.94
Chile	1.46	6.69	0.2179	0.63	0.63	0.91	1.27	0.72
China	1.37	8.13	0.1683	0.62	0.62	1.10	1.14	0.96
Colombia	2.95	8.76	0.3367	0.53	0.53	1.00	2.74	0.36
Czech Republic	2.06	7.93	0.2593	0.62	0.62	1.06	1.84	0.58
Egypt	2.17	10.29	0.2111	0.40	0.40	0.89	1.99	0.45
Hungary	1.25	10.78	0.1155	0.70	0.70	1.64	0.91	1.80
India	1.53	9.13	0.1676	0.62	0.62	1.21	1.28	0.95
Indonesia	2.77	10.01	0.2766	0.54	0.54	1.17	2.53	0.46
Jordan	0.59	6.32	0.0932	0.28	0.28	0.38	0.51	0.75
Malaysia	1.07	5.27	0.2033	0.59	0.59	0.67	0.93	0.71
Mexico	1.28	7.09	0.1809	0.83	0.83	1.27	1.02	1.24
Morocco	1.18	6.01	0.1970	0.31	0.31	0.41	1.10	0.37

continued

Individual-Country-Index Portfolios	Average	SD	Sharpe Ratio	Regression Against U.S.				
				Corr. w/U.S.	Beta	Alpha	Residual SD	Info Ratio
Pakistan	1.87	10.09	0.1849	0.14	0.14	0.31	1.80	0.17
Peru	2.53	9.54	0.2655	0.52	0.52	1.08	2.31	0.47
Philippines	1.27	7.37	0.1725	0.48	0.48	0.77	1.11	0.69
Poland	1.19	10.24	0.1162	0.75	0.75	1.65	0.85	1.94
Russia	1.50	10.30	0.1457	0.61	0.61	1.35	1.22	1.10
South Africa	1.61	7.93	0.2031	0.68	0.68	1.16	1.37	0.84
Korea	1.34	8.76	0.1526	0.75	0.75	1.41	1.05	1.35
Sri Lanka	1.82	10.92	0.1663	0.19	0.19	0.45	1.72	0.26
Taiwan	0.52	7.44	0.0697	0.70	0.70	1.12	0.29	3.86
Thailand	1.92	8.34	0.2298	0.57	0.57	1.03	1.70	0.61
Turkey	1.66	13.14	0.1267	0.59	0.59	1.67	1.32	1.27

Source: Datastream.

We will assess these performance statistics after we first take a broad-brush look at the return behaviour of developed versus emerging market indices.

Are Investments in Emerging Markets Riskier?

In Figure 24.3, countries in both developed and emerging markets are ordered separately from low to high standard deviation. The standard deviations of investments in emerging markets are charted with those in developed countries. The graphs clearly show that, considered as total portfolios, emerging markets are generally riskier than developed countries, since risk is measured by total volatility of returns. Still, you can find emerging markets that appear safer than some developed

Figure 24.3 Monthly standard deviation of excess (dollar-denominated) returns in developed and emerging markets, 2002–2011.*

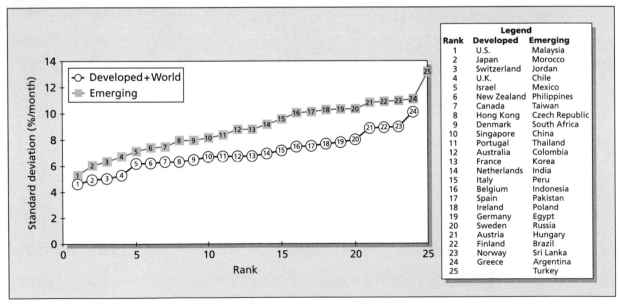

*Developed and emerging markets are ranked by SD of returns (low to high).

Figure 24.4 Beta against the U.S. market of developed and emerging markets, 2002–2011.*

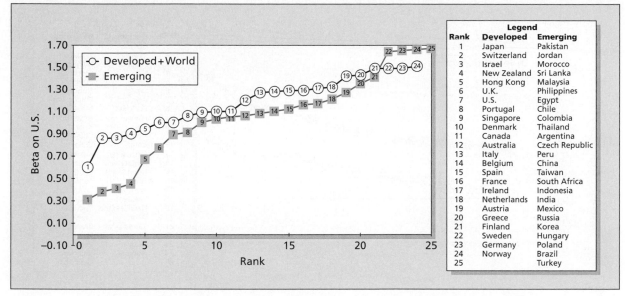

	Legend	
Rank	**Developed**	**Emerging**
1	Japan	Pakistan
2	Switzerland	Jordan
3	Israel	Morocco
4	New Zealand	Sri Lanka
5	Hong Kong	Malaysia
6	U.K.	Philippines
7	U.S.	Egypt
8	Portugal	Chile
9	Singapore	Colombia
10	Denmark	Thailand
11	Canada	Argentina
12	Australia	Czech Republic
13	Italy	Peru
14	Belgium	China
15	Spain	Taiwan
16	France	South Africa
17	Ireland	Indonesia
18	Netherlands	India
19	Austria	Mexico
20	Greece	Russia
21	Finland	Korea
22	Sweden	Hungary
23	Germany	Poland
24	Norway	Brazil
25		Turkey

*Markets are sorted by beta, from low to high.

countries. However, if one considers adding an investment in a country index to an indexed U.S. portfolio, the more relevant risk measure is the country's beta against the United States.[18]

Figure 24.4 ranks and charts the betas of country returns (in U.S. dollars) against the U.S. index. It shows that betas of six developed and eight emerging markets were estimated to be below 1. Notice, however, that this is only about one-third of all 48 foreign markets. Thus we can foresee the conclusion: A well-diversified international portfolio may well be riskier than the U.S. alone, which has consistently exhibited the lowest standard deviation of all countries. This is not to say, however, that an international portfolio with higher variance would be inferior. In fact, when a risk-free asset is available, minimum-variance portfolios are never efficient (they are dominated by the maximum Sharpe ratio, or tangency, portfolio on the efficient frontier). But, then, the international portfolio must show a sufficiently larger average return to provide a larger Sharpe ratio.

Comparison between developed and emerging markets' betas in Figure 24.4 shows that, in contrast to the picture painted by standard deviation, emerging markets are not meaningfully riskier to U.S. investors than developed markets. This is the most important lesson from this exercise.

Are Average Returns in Emerging Markets Greater?

Figure 24.5 repeats the previous exercises for average excess returns. The graphs show that over the period 2002–2011 emerging markets generally provided higher average returns than developed countries. The fact that only 2 (developed) of the 49 markets averaged a lower rate than the risk-free alternative is quite unusual given the volatility of these markets. However, this result is partially due to the weak U.S. dollar over these years. When returns are hedged, that is, returns are measured in local currencies, returns in eight countries, all developed, average below U.S. T-bills over the 10-year period. Beyond that, we see that countries with relatively low betas (e.g., Pakistan) earned higher returns than countries with relatively high betas, even the highest-beta country, Turkey. Further, average returns in emerging markets were generally higher than those in developed

---

[18]A sufficient condition to reduce the standard deviation of a portfolio by adding an asset is that the beta of the asset on the portfolio be less than 1.

Figure 24.5　Average dollar-denominated excess returns of developing and emerging markets, 2002–2011.*

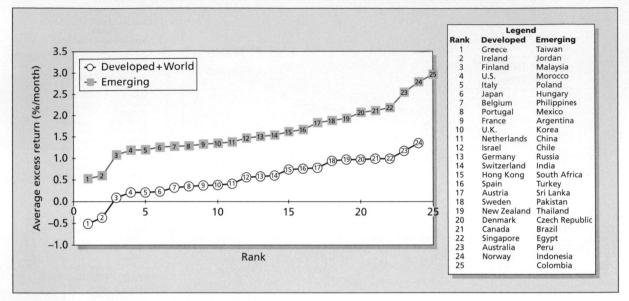

*Markets are sorted by average return, from low to high.

countries despite the fact that emerging market betas were not higher, implying that emerging markets provided better diversification opportunities than developed markets in this period.

We shouldn't be too surprised by these results. Remember again that the SD of an average estimated over 120 months (without serial correlation, which is very low) is given by SD(10-year average) = SD(1-month average)/$\sqrt{120}$. Thus, the SD of the 10-year average monthly return for Pakistan would be about .92 percent, and that of Turkey about 1.20 percent. An outcome of one SD in opposite directions for these two portfolios would span a distance of about 2.12 percent, while the difference in average returns is only .21 percent. The conclusion is one we've noted before: We cannot read too much into realized averages even over periods as long as 10 years.

Instinct calls for estimating alpha or information ratios for individual markets, to see whether they are distributed around zero. Recall from our discussion of performance evaluation in Chapter 21 that, without positive alpha, we cannot conclude that an asset has shown superior performance on any measure. The information ratio measures the potential increase in the Sharpe ratio if the country index were to be added in an optimal proportion to the U.S index.

Figure 24.6 verifies that information ratios in emerging markets were, on the whole, clearly better than those in developed markets. This is a result of inferior performance of the eight markets most affected by the financial crisis, all developed countries, and four stellar emerging market performers. The performance of the other 36 markets cannot be distinguished in terms of emerging versus developed. Here again, given the high volatilities, finding four outperformers and eight underperformers in a group of 48 countries is not surprising or significant.

One striking result is the inferior performance of the United States. We see this in Table 24.10. Although the U.S. has the lowest standard deviation among all countries, it still ranks near the bottom in terms of the Sharpe ratio. This may be explained by the financial crisis and/or by the steady decline in the international economic position of the United States, as reflected by the steady decline in the value of the dollar.[19]

---

[19]The decline of the U.S. dollar has so far been sporadically interrupted by international crises. A regular feature of those crises has been a flight to the safety of dollar instruments.

Figure 24.6   Information ratios of developed and emerging markets against U.S.-dollar-denominated returns, 2002–2011.*

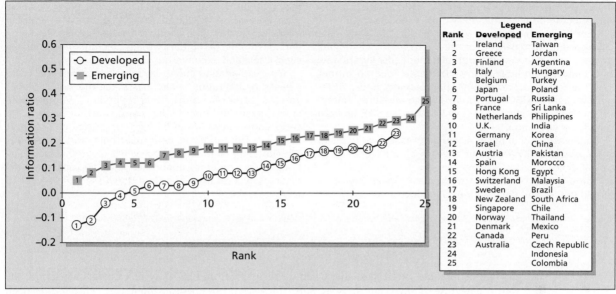

*Markets are sorted by information ratio, from low to high.

Spurious Benefits from Diversification

The baseline technique for constructing efficient portfolios is the efficient frontier. A useful efficient frontier is constructed from *expected* returns and an estimate of the covariance matrix of returns. This frontier combined with cash assets generates the capital allocation line, the set of efficient complete portfolios, as elaborated in Chapter 6. The benefit from this efficient diversification is reflected in the curvature of the efficient frontier. Other things equal, the lower the covariance across stocks, the greater the curvature of the efficient frontier and the greater the risk reduction for any desired *expected* return. So far, so good. But suppose we replace *expected* returns with *realized* average returns from a sample period to construct an efficient frontier. What is the possible use of this graph?

The ex post efficient frontier (derived from realized returns) describes the portfolio of only one investor—the clairvoyant who actually expected the precise averages of realized returns on all assets and estimated a covariance matrix that materialized, precisely, in the actual realizations of the sample period returns on all assets. Obviously, we are talking about a slim to empty set of investors. For all other, less-than-clairvoyant investors, such a frontier may have value only for purposes of performance evaluation.

In the world of volatile stocks, some stocks are bound to realize large, *unexpected* average returns. This will be reflected in ex post efficient frontiers of enormous "potential." They will, however, suggest exaggerated diversification benefits. Such (elusive) potential was enumerated in Chapter 21 on performance evaluation. It has no meaning as a tool to discuss the potential for future investments for real-life investors.

Realistic Benefits from Diversification

In developed markets, correlations between their returns and those of the United States have been significantly increasing over the past few decades (Canada is a notable exception, but see the boxed article). Hence, the benefits of diversification can be expected to emanate from countries with relatively lower correlations. Table 24.11 shows that such low correlations are found mostly in the emerging markets. On the other hand, the standard

It's one of the golden rules of investing: Reduce risk by diversifying your money into a variety of holdings—stock funds, bonds, commodities—that don't move in lockstep with one another. And it's a rule that's getting tougher to obey.

According to recent research, an array of investments whose prices used to rise and fall independently are now increasingly correlated. For an example, look no further than the roller coaster in emerging-markets stocks of recent weeks. The MSCI EAFE index, which measures emerging markets, now shows .96 correlation to the S&P, up from just .32 six years ago.

For investors, that poses a troubling issue: how to maintain a portfolio diversified enough so all the pieces don't tank at once.

The current correlation trend doesn't mean investors should go out and ditch their existing investments. It's just

that they may not be "getting the same diversification" they thought if the investment decisions were made some time ago, says Mr. Ezrati, chief economist at money-management firm Lord Abbett & Co. He adds that over long periods of time, going back decades, sometimes varied asset classes tend to converge.

One explanation for today's higher correlation is increased globalization, which has made the economies of various countries more interdependent. International stocks, even with their higher correlations of present, deserve some allocation in a long-term investor's holdings, says Jeff Tjornehoj, an analyst at data firm Lipper Inc. Mr. Tjornehoj is among those who believe these correlations are a temporary phenomenon, and expects that the diversity will return some time down the line—a year or few years.

deviations in Table 24.10 show that when we diversify from U.S.-only investments whether to the entire world or to emerging markets only, the risk of the portfolio increases. This results from higher standard deviations of foreign markets that are not offset by the relatively low correlations of emerging markets.

Nevertheless, the objective of diversification is not merely risk reduction. Rather, it is to increase the Sharpe ratio. Here we see that, in any configuration, the Sharpe ratio of internationally diversified portfolios is significantly higher than that of the U.S. alone. Thus the data clearly indicate that despite increasing correlations, even a passive strategy of holding a world ETF is still superior to the U.S.-only portfolio. Figure 24.7 shows diversification benefits based on 1995 correlations and

Figure 24.7

International diversification: Portfolio standard deviation as a percent of the average standard deviation of a one-stock portfolio.

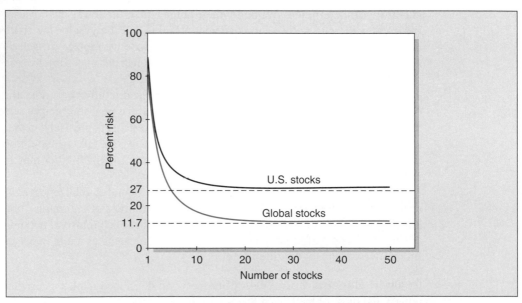

Source: B. Solnik, "Why Not Diversify Internationally Rather Than Domestically?" Copyright 1976, CFA Institute. Reproduced and republished from *Financial Analysts Journal* with permission from the CFA Institute. All rights reserved.

Figure 24.8

Ex post efficient frontier of country portfolios, 2001–2005.

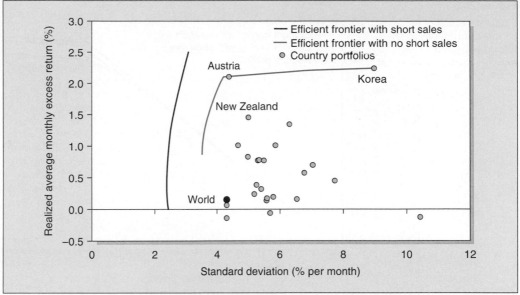

diversification into randomly selected stocks from around the world compared with a one-stock portfolio. This representation no longer serves the purpose of analyzing the true benefits from international diversification, which accrue from improved risk-adjusted performance.

While recent realized returns can be highly misleading estimates of expected future returns, they are more useful for measuring prospective risk. There are two compelling reasons for this. First, market efficiency (or even near-efficiency) implies that stock prices will be difficult to predict with any accuracy, but no such implication applies to risk measures. Second, it is a statistical fact that errors in estimates of standard deviation and correlation from realized data are of a lower order of magnitude than estimates of expected returns. For these reasons, using risk estimates from realized returns does not exaggerate as much the potential benefits from diversification.

Figure 24.8 shows the efficient frontier using realized average monthly returns on the stock indices of the 25 developed countries, with and without short sales. Even when the (ex post) efficient frontier is constrained to preclude short sales, it greatly exaggerates the benefits from diversification. Unfortunately, such misleading efficient frontiers are presented in many articles and texts on the benefits of diversification.

A more realistic description of diversification is achievable only when we input reasonable equilibrium expected returns. Absent superior information, such expected returns are best based on appropriate risk measures of the assets. The capital asset pricing model (CAPM) suggests using the beta of the stock against the world portfolio. To generate expected excess returns (over the risk-free rate) for all assets, we specify the expected excess return on the world portfolio. We obtain the expected excess return on each asset by multiplying the beta of the asset by the world portfolio expected excess return. This procedure presupposes that the world portfolio will lie on the efficient frontier, at the point of tangency with the world capital market line. The curvature of the efficient frontier will not be affected by the estimate of the world portfolio excess return. A higher estimate will simply shift the curve upward.

We perform this procedure with risk measures estimated from actual returns and further impose the likely applicable constraint on short sales. We use the betas to compute the expected return on individual markets, assuming the expected excess return on the world

Figure 24.9

Efficient frontier of country portfolios (world expected excess return = .6% per month).

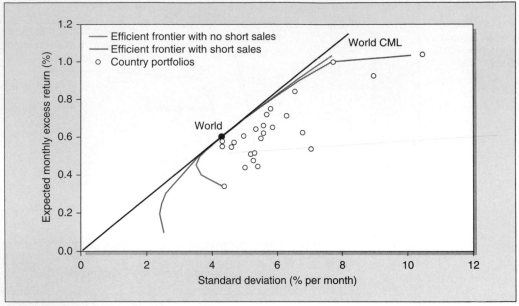

portfolio is .6 percent per month. This excess return is in line with the average return over the previous 50 years. Varying this estimate would not qualitatively affect the results shown in Figure 24.9 (which is drawn on the same scale as Figure 24.8). The figure shows a realistic assessment that reveals modest but significant benefits from international diversification using only developed markets. Incorporating emerging markets would slightly increase these benefits.

Benefits in Bear Markets   Some studies[20] suggest that correlation in country portfolio returns increases during periods of turbulence in capital markets. If so, benefits from diversification would be lost exactly when they are needed the most. For example, a study by Roll[21] of the crash of October 1987 shows that all 23 country indices studied declined over the crash period of October 12–26. This correlation is reflected in the movements of regional indices depicted in Figure 24.10. Roll found that the beta of a country index on the world index (estimated prior to the crash) was the best predictor of that index's response to the October crash of the U.S. stock market. This suggests a common factor underlying the movement of stocks around the world. This model predicts that a macroeconomic shock would affect all countries and that diversification can only mitigate country-specific events.

The 2008 crash of stock markets around the world allows us to test Roll's prediction. The data in Figure 24.11 include average monthly rates of return for both the ten-year period 1999–2008 and the crisis period corresponding to the last four months of 2008, in addition to the beta on the U.S. market and monthly standard deviation for several portfolios. The graph shows that both the country-index standard deviation and beta against the United States explain the difference

[20]F. Longin and B. Solnik, "Is the Correlation in International Equity Returns Constant: 1960–1990?" *Journal of International Money and Finance* 14 (1995), pp. 3–26; and Eric Jacquier and Alan Marcus, "Asset Allocation Models and Market Volatility," *Financial Analysts Journal* 57 (March/April 2001), pp. 16–30.
[21]Richard Roll, "The International Crash of October 1987," *Financial Analysts Journal*, September/October 1988.

Figure 24.10

Regional indices around the crash, October 14–October 26, 1987.

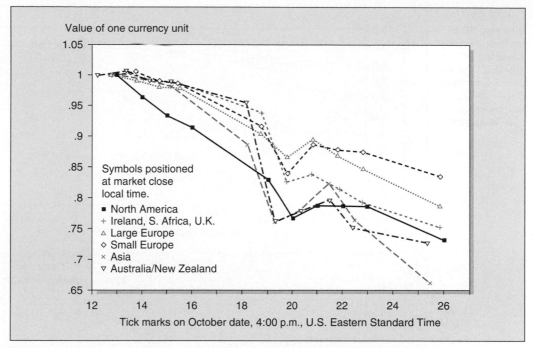

between crisis period returns and overall period averages. Market behaviour during the 1987 crisis, that is, larger correlations in extreme bad times, repeated itself in the crisis of 2008, vindicating Roll's prediction.

The Home Bias

Scholars have indirectly questioned passive as well as active investors for the apparent home bias (i.e., preference for domestic securities) demonstrated in their portfolio choices. A certain degree of home bias may be justified on theoretical grounds. Investor consumption consists in large part of goods and services produced in the home country, and prices of these goods and services may be correlated with home-country stock prices. To illustrate, consider an investor who lives in Silicon Valley. Prices of homes and other big-ticket items will be correlated with the success of local corporations. These prices therefore can be partially hedged by investing in the equity of local firms.[22] Moreover, "keeping up with the Joneses" of Silicon Valley also calls for tilting your portfolio toward local investment opportunities to keep your wealth aligned with that of your neighbours.

How exactly does one measure home bias? At first blush the question seems simple. Home bias is the excess weight of your country relative to its weight in the otherwise efficient portfolio. The problem is that we must identify that efficient portfolio. If a world CAPM is in force, then a portfolio weighted by market capitalization would be the efficient portfolio for all

---

[22]For a formal analysis of this idea, see Peter M. De Marzo, Ron Kaniel, and Ilan Kremer, "Diversification as a Public Good: Community Effects in Portfolio Choice," *Journal of Finance* 59 (August 2004).

Figure 24.11

Beta and SD of portfolios against deviation of monthly return over September–December 2008 from average over 1999–2008.

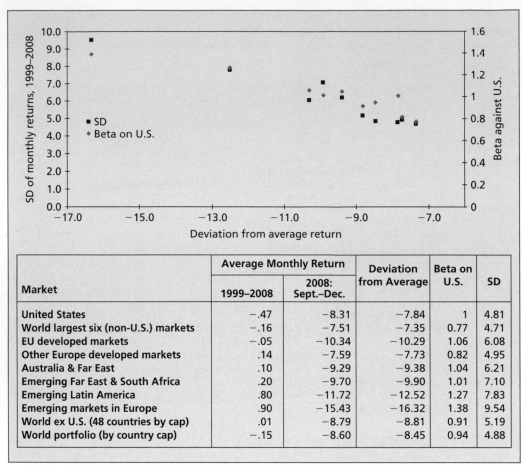

Market	Average Monthly Return		Deviation from Average	Beta on U.S.	SD
	1999–2008	2008: Sept.–Dec.			
United States	−.47	−8.31	−7.84	1	4.81
World largest six (non-U.S.) markets	−.16	−7.51	−7.35	0.77	4.71
EU developed markets	−.05	−10.34	−10.29	1.06	6.08
Other Europe developed markets	.14	−7.59	−7.73	0.82	4.95
Australia & Far East	.10	−9.29	−9.38	1.04	6.21
Emerging Far East & South Africa	.20	−9.70	−9.90	1.01	7.10
Emerging Latin America	.80	−11.72	−12.52	1.27	7.83
Emerging markets in Europe	.90	−15.43	−16.32	1.38	9.54
World ex U.S. (48 countries by cap)	.01	−8.79	−8.81	0.91	5.19
World portfolio (by country cap)	−.15	−8.60	−8.45	0.94	4.88

Source: Authors' calculations.

investors. There is, however, no evidence that the world portfolio is efficient. Neither is there support for a model in which the expected return–beta equation is based on a beta against the U.S. market. At minimum, however, we would expect international diversification to reduce portfolio variance.

24.4   ASSESSING THE POTENTIAL OF INTERNATIONAL INVESTING

We focus first on investors who wish to hold largely passive portfolios. Their objective is to maximize diversification with limited expense and effort. Passive investment is simple: rely on market efficiency to guarantee that a broad stock portfolio will yield the best possible Sharpe ratio. Estimate the mean and standard deviation of the optimal risky portfolio, and select a capital allocation to achieve the highest expected return at a level of risk you are willing to bear. But now, a passive investor must also decide whether to add an international component to the more convenient home-country index portfolio.

Suppose the passive investor could rely on efficient markets as well as a world CAPM. Then the world capitalization–weighted portfolio would be optimal. Abiding by this theoretically simple solution is also practical. An index fund like MSCI's (Morgan Stanley Capital International's) ACWI (All Country World Index) would do the trick. Over the period 2000–2009, the performance of this portfolio and that of a U.S.-only portfolio can be summarized (using monthly return statistics from Table 24.10) as follows:

Portfolio	ACWI	U.S. Only
Average return (%)	−.01	−.20
Standard deviation (%)	5.34	5.14

These results are instructive. First, the negative average returns on these broad portfolios (which must be lower than prior expectations, as investors would not have invested in them expecting a negative return) remind us again of the all-important fact that historical averages are unreliable. We also see that U.S. stocks make for a relatively low-risk portfolio. While the U.S. portfolio may lie inside the world efficient frontier, and thus may offer a lower Sharpe ratio than the world portfolio, it nevertheless may be of less risk than the better-diversified world portfolio.

Things are more complicated when we recognize that the data do not support the validity of the world CAPM, and hence we cannot be certain that the world portfolio is the most efficient risky portfolio. We do observe that higher country standard deviations tend to be rewarded with higher average returns. A passive investor may therefore wish to examine simple rules of thumb for including a small number of countries (via international index funds of various combinations) in an attempt to dull the effect of high individual-country standard deviations and yet improve the Sharpe ratio of the overall portfolio. In all three of these rules, we assume the perspective of a U.S. investor, using dollar-denominated returns. We include countries on the basis of market capitalization for two reasons: (1) the resultant portfolio will be at least reasonably close to the theoretically efficient portfolio, and (2) the weights of any foreign country will not be too large. We estimate the risk of progressively more diversified portfolios relative to the number of foreign countries included, and the total portfolio weight of the international component.

The three rules of thumb are to include country indices in order of:

1. *Market capitalization (from high to low).* This rule is motivated by a world CAPM consideration in which the optimal portfolio is capitalization weighted.

2. *Beta against the U.S. (from low to high).* This rule concentrates on diversifying the risk associated with investments in higher-risk countries.

3. *Country index standard deviation (from high to low).* This rule is motivated by the observation that higher country standard deviations (SDs) are correlated with higher average returns. It relies on diversification to mitigate individual-country risk.

These alternatives illustrate the potential risks and rewards of international diversification.

Results of this exercise appear in Table 24.12 and Figure 24.12. First turn to Figure 24.12, panel A, which vividly shows how portfolio SD progresses as we diversify the U.S. portfolio using the three rules. Clearly, adding countries in order of beta (or covariance with the U.S. market), from low to high, quickly reduces portfolio risk despite the fact that the standard deviations of all 12 included countries are higher than those of the United States. However, once we have adequate diversification, adding these higher-volatility indices eventually begins to increase portfolio standard deviation. Adding countries in order of standard deviation (but this time from high to low to improve expected returns, which are correlated with volatility) incurs the greatest increase in portfolio SD, as we would expect.

Figure 24.12, panel B shows that average returns increase along with the standard deviation of returns. Average returns also increase with beta, at least for low-beta countries, suggesting that at

TABLE 24.12   Standard Deviation of International Portfolios by Degree of Diversification

Portfolio Composition	Weight in World Portfolio	Weight of U.S. in Portfolio	Std. Dev.	Average Return
A. Inclusion based on capitalization				
1 U.S. only	0.33	1	5.17	−0.20
2 Portfolio 1 plus Japan*	0.42	0.79	4.95	−0.24
3 Portfolio 2 plus U.K.*	0.49	0.67	4.97	−0.20
4 Portfolio 3 plus France*	0.54	0.61	5.02	−0.16
5 Portfolio 4 plus Canada*	0.58	0.57	5.07	−0.10
6 Portfolio 5 plus Hong Kong*	0.62	0.54	5.06	−0.07
7 Portfolio 6 plus Germany*	0.65	0.51	5.11	−0.06
8 Portfolio 7 plus Brazil*	0.68	0.49	5.19	0.03
9 Portfolio 8 plus Australia*	0.71	0.46	5.19	0.07
10 Portfolio 9 plus Switzerland*	0.74	0.45	5.18	0.08
11 Portfolio 10 plus China*	0.76	0.44	5.19	0.10
12 Portfolio 11 plus Taiwan*	0.77	0.43	5.19	0.10
13 Portfolio 12 plus Netherlands*	0.78	0.42	5.20	0.10
B. Inclusion based on beta				
1 U.S. only	0.33	1	5.17	−0.20
2 Portfolio 1 plus Pakistan*	0.33	1.00	5.16	−0.20
3 Portfolio 2 plus Malaysia*	0.34	0.98	5.12	−0.18
4 Portfolio 3 plus Japan*	0.43	0.78	4.85	−0.22
5 Portfolio 4 plus Philippines*	0.43	0.77	4.84	−0.22
6 Portfolio 5 plus Portugal*	0.43	0.77	4.84	−0.22
7 Portfolio 6 plus Chile*	0.44	0.76	4.83	−0.20
8 Portfolio 7 plus Israel*	0.44	0.75	4.83	−0.19
9 Portfolio 8 plus Hong Kong*	0.48	0.70	4.83	−0.15
10 Portfolio 9 plus Switzerland*	0.50	0.66	4.81	−0.12
11 Portfolio 10 plus Colombia*	0.51	0.65	4.82	−0.10
12 Portfolio 11 plus U.K.*	0.58	0.57	4.84	−0.09
13 Portfolio 12 plus New Zealand*	0.58	0.57	4.84	−0.09
C. Inclusion based on standard deviation				
1 U.S. only	0.33	1	5.17	−0.20
2 Portfolio 1 plus Turkey*	0.34	0.98	5.25	−0.18
3 Portfolio 2 plus Argentina*	0.34	0.98	5.25	−0.17
4 Portfolio 3 plus Russia*	0.36	0.93	5.39	−0.08
5 Portfolio 4 plus Indonesia*	0.36	0.92	5.41	−0.05
6 Portfolio 5 plus Pakistan*	0.36	0.92	5.40	−0.05
7 Portfolio 6 plus Brazil*	0.39	0.84	5.66	0.10
8 Portfolio 7 plus Finland*	0.40	0.83	5.69	0.10
9 Portfolio 8 plus Poland*	0.40	0.83	5.70	0.11
10 Portfolio 9 plus Hungary*	0.40	0.83	5.70	0.11
11 Portfolio 10 plus Korea*	0.42	0.79	5.80	0.15
12 Portfolio 11 plus India*	0.44	0.74	5.87	0.22
13 Portfolio 12 plus Thailand*	0.45	0.74	5.87	0.23

continued

D. All countries with various weighting schemes

Equally weighted	0.99	0.33	6.14	0.76
By capitalization	0.99	0.33	5.60	0.27
World portfolio actual return**	1.00	0.33	5.34	−0.01
Minimum variance portfolio—no short sales	0.99	0.33	4.14	0.02
Minimum variance portfolio—no restrictions	0.99	0.33	2.21	0.32

*Portfolio weighted by capitalization of included countries.
**All countries (including five omitted here) capitalization-weighted.

Figure 24.12

Risks and rewards of international portfolios, 2000–2009.
Panel A: Standard deviations for international portfolios.
Panel B: Average return of international portfolios.

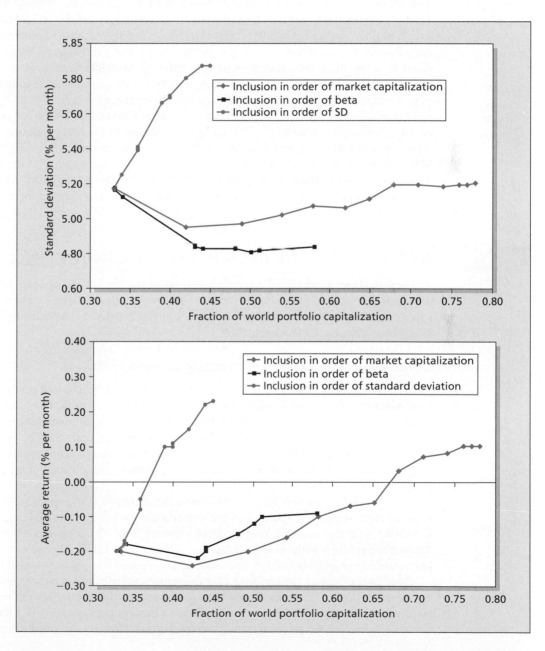

a qualitative level, world-systematic risk affects asset pricing, consistent with an international CAPM. Broadly speaking, these results are consistent with logic of the previous chapters. First, diversification pays, and risk is rewarded. Second, even with strong home-country bias, covariance risk still plays a role internationally. We also see that when confined to domestic markets, risk aversion across the world is not too different: higher country standard deviations match up with higher average returns.

In panel D of Table 24.12, we examine risk and reward from fuller international diversification. Observe first that an equally weighted portfolio of all countries is the riskiest in the group. At the same time, because this portfolio assigns much larger weights to the smaller, high-volatility–high-return countries, it also provides a higher average return. At the other extreme, consider the minimum-variance portfolios, with and without short-sale constraints. Without the short-sale restriction, the minimum-variance portfolio attains the amazingly low SD of 2.21 percent, less than half that of the lowest-SD country (the U.S.). However, this portfolio is probably not practical, including 22 short positions, the largest being 215 percent (in Sweden). When short sales are disallowed, the SD is far higher, 4.14 percent, offering much less improvement over the capitalization-weighted portfolio. Moreover, these portfolio weights also would be impractical, with the largest weight in Malaysia (29 percent), and only 7 percent in the U.S.

One puzzling and instructive feature of the results in Table 24.12 is the lower average return on the actual world portfolio (ACWI) compared with the 44-country portfolios. The difference arises because MSCI country-index portfolios are not capitalization-weighted portfolios. MSCI uses industry-weighted portfolios, which places greater weights on the larger stocks in each country. Since small stocks performed better over 2000–2009, the ACWI portfolio had a lower average return. This pattern is not guaranteed, or necessarily even likely, to apply to future returns.

24.5   ASSESSMENT OF INTERNATIONAL INVESTING

The benefits from international diversification may be modest for passive investors, but for active managers international investing offers greater opportunities. International investing calls for specialization in additional fields of analysis: currency, country and worldwide industry, as well as a greater universe for stock selection.

Constructing a Benchmark Portfolio of Foreign Assets

Active international investing, as well as passive, requires a benchmark portfolio (the bogey). One widely used index of non-U.S. stocks is the **Europe, Australia, Far East (EAFE) index** computed by Morgan Stanley Capital International (MSCI). Additional indices of world equity performance are published by MSCI, Salomon Brothers, Credit Suisse, First Boston, and Goldman Sachs. Portfolios designed to mirror or even replicate the country, currency, and company representation of these indices would be the obvious generalization of the purely domestic passive equity strategy.

An issue that sometimes arises in the international context is the appropriateness of market-capitalization weighting schemes in the construction of international indices. Capitalization weighting is far and away the most common approach. However, some argue that it might not be the best weighting scheme in an international context. This is in part because different countries have differing proportions of their corporate sector organized as publicly traded firms.

Table 24.13 shows 1998 and 2011 data for market capitalization weights versus the GDP for countries in the EAFE index. These data reveal substantial disparities between the relative sizes of market capitalization versus GDP. Since market capitalization is a stock figure (the value of equity at one point in time), while GDP is a flow figure (production of goods and

TABLE 24.13

Weighting Schemes for EAFE Countries

Country	2011		1998	
	% of EAFE Market Capitalization	% of EAFE GDP	% of EAFE Market Capitalization	% of EAFE GDP
Japan	21.1%	23.7%	26.8%	29.1%
United Kingdom	17.9	9.8	22.4	10.5
France	9.3	11.1	7.2	10.7
Germany	7.5	14.2	8.9	15.8
Switzerland	6.8	2.3	6.0	1.9
Italy	2.9	8.9	3.9	8.8
Netherlands	2.4	3.4	5.9	2.9
Hong Kong	8.8	1.0	4.0	1.2
Australia	6.7	4.0	2.9	2.7
Spain	3.5	6.1	2.7	4.3
Sweden	2.8	2.0	2.4	1.8
Finland	0.9	1.0	0.7	1.0
Belgium	1.4	2.0	1.4	1.8
Singapore	2.7	0.9	1.1	0.6
Denmark	1.1	1.3	0.9	1.3
Norway	1.5	1.8	0.6	1.1
Ireland	0.4	0.9	0.5	0.6
Greece	0.2	1.3	0.3	0.9
Portugal	0.4	1.0	0.6	0.8
Austria	0.5	1.6	0.4	1.6
New Zealand	0.2	0.6	0.4	0.4

Source: Datastream, http://online.thomsonreuters.com/datastream.

services during the entire year), we expect capitalization to be more volatile and the relative shares to be variable over time. Some discrepancies are persistent, however. For example, Hong Kong's share of capitalization in 2011 is about eight times its share of GDP, while Germany's share of capitalization is much less than its share of GDP. These disparities indicate that a greater proportion of economic activity is conducted by publicly traded firms in the Hong Kong than in Germany.

Some argue that it would be more appropriate to weight international indices by GDP rather than market capitalization. The justification for this view is that an internationally diversified portfolio should purchase shares in proportion to the broad asset base of each country, and GDP might be a better measure of the importance of a country in the international economy than the value of its outstanding stocks. Others have even suggested weights proportional to the import share of various countries. The argument is that investors who wish to hedge the price of imported goods might choose to hold securities in foreign firms in proportion to the goods imported from those countries.

Performance Attribution   Active portfolio management in an international context may be viewed similarly as an extension of active domestic management. In principle, one would form an efficient frontier from the full menu of world securities and determine the optimal risky portfolio. We saw in Chapter 5 that even in the domestic context, the need for specialization in various asset classes usually calls for a two-step procedure in which asset allocation is

International Portfolios

This Excel model provides an efficient frontier analysis similar to that in Chapter 6. In Chapter 6 the frontier was based on individual securities, whereas this model examines the returns on international exchange-traded funds and enables us to analyze the benefits of international diversification.

Questions

1. Find three points on the efficient frontier corresponding to three different expected returns. What are the portfolio standard deviations corresponding to each expected return?

2. Now assume that the correlation between the S&P 500 and the other country indices is cut in half. Find the new standard deviations corresponding to each of the three expected returns. Are they higher or lower? Why?

	A	B	C	D	E	F	G	H	I	J
58		Bordered Covariance Matrix for Target Return Portfolio								
59		EWD	EWH	EWI	EWJ	EWL	EWP	EWW	SP 500	
60	Weights	0.00	0.00	0.08	0.38	0.02	0.00	0.00	0.52	
61	0.0000	0.00	0.00	0.00	0.00	0.00	0.00	0.00	0.00	
62	0.0000	0.00	0.00	0.00	0.00	0.00	0.00	0.00	0.00	
63	0.0826	0.00	0.00	4.63	3.21	0.55	0.00	0.00	7.69	
64	0.3805	0.00	0.00	3.21	98.41	1.82	0.00	0.00	53.79	
65	0.0171	0.00	0.00	0.55	1.82	0.14	0.00	0.00	2.09	
66	0.0000	0.00	0.00	0.00	0.00	0.00	0.00	0.00	0.00	
67	0.0000	0.00	0.00	0.00	0.00	0.00	0.00	0.00	0.00	
68	0.5198	0.00	0.00	7.69	53.79	2.09	0.00	0.00	79.90	
69	1.0000	0.00	0.00	16.07	157.23	4.59	0.00	0.00	143.47	
70										
71	Port Via	321.36								
72	Port S.D.	17.93								
73	Port Mean	12.00								
74										
75										
76					Weights					
77	Mean	St. Dev	EWD	EWH	EWI	EWJ	EWL	EWP	EWW	SP 500
78	6	21.89	0.02	0.00	0.00	0.71	0.00	0.02	0.00	0.26
79	9	19.66	0.02	0.00	0.02	0.53	0.02	0.00	0.00	0.41
80	12	17.93	0.00	0.00	0.08	0.38	0.02	0.00	0.00	0.52
81	15	16.81	0.00	0.00	0.14	0.22	0.02	0.00	0.00	0.62
82	18	16.46	0.00	0.00	0.19	0.07	0.02	0.00	0.00	0.73
83	21	17.37	0.00	0.00	0.40	0.00	0.00	0.00	0.00	0.60
84	24	21.19	0.00	0.00	0.72	0.00	0.00	0.00	0.00	0.28
85	27	26.05	0.00	0.00	1.00	0.00	0.00	0.00	0.00	0.00
86										
87										

fixed initially, and then security selection within each asset class is determined. The complexities of the international market argue even more strongly for the primacy of asset allocation, and this is the perspective often taken in the evaluation of active portfolio management. Performance attribution of international managers focuses on these potential sources of abnormal returns: currency selection, country selection, stock selection within countries, and cash-bond selection within countries.

We can measure the contribution of each of these factors following a manner similar to the performance attribution techniques introduced in Chapter 21.

1. **Currency selection** measures the contribution to total portfolio performance attributable to exchange rate fluctuations relative to the investor's benchmark currency, which we will take to be the U.S. dollar. We might use a benchmark like the EAFE index to compare a portfolio's currency selection for a particular period to a passive benchmark. EAFE currency selection would be computed as the weighted average of the currency appreciation of the currencies represented in the EAFE portfolio using as weights the fraction of the EAFE portfolio invested in each currency.

TABLE 24.14

Example of Performance Attribution: International

	EAFE Weight	Return on Equity Index	Currency Appreciation $E_1/E_0 - 1$	Manager's Weight	Manager's Return
Europe	.30	10%	10%	.35	8%
Australia	.10	5	−10	.10	7
Far East	.60	15	30	.55	18

Currency Selection

EAFE: $(.30 \times 10\%) + (.10 \times -10\%) + (.60 \times 30\%) = 20\%$ appreciation

Manager: $(.35 \times 10\%) + (.10 \times -10\%) + (.55 \times 30\%) = 19\%$ appreciation

Loss of 1% relative to EAFE

Country Selection

EAFE: $(.30 \times 10\%) + (.10 \times 5\%) + (.60 \times 15\%) = 12.5\%$

Manager: $(.35 \times 10\%) + (.10 \times 5\%) + (.55 \times 15\%) = 12.25\%$

Loss of .25% relative to EAFE

Stock Selection

$(8\% - 10\%).35 + (7\% - 5\%).10 + (18\% - 15\%).55 = 1.15\%$

Contribution of 1.15% relative to EAFE

Sum of attributions (equal to overall performance):

Currency (−1%) + country (−.25%) + selection (1.15%) = −.10%

2. **Country selection** measures the contribution to performance attributable to investing in the better-performing stock markets of the world. It can be measured as the weighted average of the equity *index* returns of each country using as weights the share of the manager's portfolio in each country. We use index returns to abstract from the effect of security selection within countries. To measure a manager's contribution relative to a passive strategy, we might compare country selection to the weighted average across countries of equity index returns using as weights the share of the EAFE portfolio in each country.

3. **Stock selection** ability may, as in Chapter 21, be measured as the weighted average of equity returns *in excess of the equity index* in each country. Here, we would use local currency returns and use as weights the investments in each country.

4. **Cash/bond selection** may be measured as the excess return derived from weighting bonds and bills differently from some benchmark weights.

Table 24.14 gives an example of how to measure the contribution of the decisions an international portfolio manager might make.

CC 3

CONCEPT CHECK

Using the data in Table 24.14, compute the manager's country and currency selection if portfolio weights had been 40 percent in Europe, 20 percent in Australia, and 40 percent in the Far East.

SUMMARY

1. Canadian assets make up only a small fraction of the world wealth portfolio. International capital markets offer important opportunities for portfolio diversification with enhanced risk-return characteristics.

2. Investors can diversify internationally by buying multinational firms on Canadian or U.S. markets or by buying closed- or open-ended mutual funds that invest in specific countries, regions, or internationally in general.

3. International investing entails country-specific risk from political and other factors; assessments of that risk are available.

4. Exchange rate risk imparts an extra source of uncertainty to investments denominated in foreign currencies. Much of that risk can be hedged in foreign exchange futures or

forward markets, but unless the foreign currency rate of return is known, a perfect hedge is not feasible.

5. Financial markets in different countries may be integrated or segmented, depending on whether factors that influence security prices are universal or specific to the countries.

6. The benefits and risks of international diversification require careful examination to eliminate fictitious claims; changes to the efficient frontier and correlation between markets over time are particularly important.

7. Several world market indices can form a basis for passive international investing. Active international management can be partitioned into currency selection, country selection, stock selection, and cash/bond selection.

KEY EQUATIONS

(24.1) $\quad 1 + r(C) = [1 + r_f(UK)]E_1/E_0$

(24.2) $\quad F_0/E_0 = [1 + r_f(C)]/[1 + r_f(UK)]$

(24.3) $\quad 1 + r(C) = [1 + r(\text{foreign})]E_1/E_0$

PROBLEMS

 Practise and learn online with Connect.

1. Much of this subject is based on the perspective of a U.S. investor, but we have illustrated many issues from a Canadian perspective. Suppose you are advising an investor living in a small country (choose one to be concrete). How might the lessons of this chapter need to be modified for such an investor?

2. In Figure 25.2, we provide stock market returns in both local and dollar-denominated terms. Which of these is more relevant? What does this have to do with whether the foreign exchange risk of an investment has been hedged?

3. Suppose a Canadian investor wishes to invest in a British firm currently selling for £40 per share. The investor has $10,000 to invest, and the current exchange rate is $2/£.

   a. How many shares can the investor purchase?

   b. Fill in the table below for rates of return after one year in each of the nine scenarios (three possible prices per share in pounds times three possible exchange rates).

Price per Share (£)	Pound-Denominated Return (%)	Dollar-Denominated Return for Year-End Exchange Rate		
		$1.80/£	$2/£	$2.20/£
£35	—	—	—	—
£40	—	—	—	—
£45	—	—	—	—

   c. When is the dollar-denominated return equal to the pound-denominated return?

4. If each of the nine outcomes in problem 3 is equally likely, find the standard deviation of both the pound-and dollar-denominated rates of return.

5. Now suppose that the investor in problem 3 also sells forward £5,000 at a forward exchange rate of $2.10/£.

   a. Recalculate the dollar-denominated returns of each scenario.

   b. What happens to the standard deviation of the dollar-denominated return? Compare it both to its old value and the standard deviation of the pound-denominated return.

6. Calculate the contribution to total performance from currency, country, and stock selection for the manager in the example below. (E_1/E_0 is foreign currency units per dollar.)

	EAFE Weight	Return on Equity Index	$E_1/E_0 - 1$	Manager's Weight	Manager's Return
Europe	.30	20%	−10%	.35	18%
Australia	.10	15	0	.15	20
Far East	.60	25	+10	.50	20

7. If the current exchange rate is $1.75/£, the one-year forward exchange rate is $1.85/£, and the interest rate on British government bills is 8 percent per year, what risk-free dollar-denominated return can be locked in by investing in the British bills?

8. If you were to invest $10,000 in the British bills of problem 7, how would you lock in the dollar-denominated return?

9. Suppose two all-equity-financed firms, ABC and XYZ, both have $100 million of equity outstanding. Each firm now issues $10 million of new stock and uses the proceeds to purchase the other's shares.

   a. What happens to the sum of the value of outstanding equity of the two firms?

   b. What happens to the value of the equity in these firms held by the noncorporate sector of the economy?

   c. Prepare the balance sheet for these two firms before and after the stock issues.

   d. If both of these firms were in an index, what would happen to their weights in the index?

10. A global equity manager is assigned to select stocks from a universe of large stocks throughout the world. The manager will be evaluated by comparing her returns to the return on the MSCI World Market Portfolio, but she is free to hold stocks from various countries in whatever proportions she finds desirable. Results for a given month are contained in the table below.

Country	Weight in MSCI Index	Manager's Weight	Manager's Return in Country	Return of Index Stock for That Country
United Kingdom	.15	.30	20%	12%
Japan	.30	.10	15	15
United states	.45	.40	10	14
Germany	.10	.20	5	12

   a. Calculate the total value added of all the manager's decisions this period.

   b. Calculate the value added (or subtracted) by her *country* allocation decisions.

   c. Calculate the value added from her stock selection ability within countries. Confirm that the sum of the contributions to value added from her country allocation plus security selection decisions equals total over- or underperformance.

The following problems are based on questions that have appeared in past CFA examinations.

11. You are a Canadian investor who purchased British securities for £2,000 one year ago when the British pound cost C$1.50. What is your total return (based on Canadian dollars) if the value of the securities is now £2,400 and the pound is worth C$1.75? No dividends or interest was paid during this period.

12. The correlation coefficient between the returns on a broad index of U.S. stocks and the returns on indices of the stocks of other industrialized countries is mostly _____, and the correlation coefficient between the returns on various diversified portfolios of U.S. stocks is mostly _____.

    a. less than .8; greater than .8
    b. greater than .8; less than .8
    c. less than 0; greater than 0
    d. greater than 0; less than 0

13. An investor in the common stock of companies in a foreign country may wish to hedge against the _____ of the investor's home currency and can do so by _____ the foreign currency in the forward market.

    a. depreciation; selling
    b. appreciation; purchasing
    c. appreciation; selling
    d. depreciation; purchasing

14. John Irish, CFA is an independent investment advisor who is assisting Alfred Darwin, the head of the Investment Committee of General Technology Corporation, to establish a new pension fund. Darwin asks Irish about international equities and whether the Investment Committee should consider them as an additional asset for the pension fund.

    a. Explain the rationale for including international equities in General's equity portfolio. Identify and describe three relevant considerations in formulating your answer.

    b. List three possible arguments against international equity investment and briefly discuss the significance of each.

    c. To illustrate several aspects of the performance of international securities over time, Irish shows Darwin the following graph of investment results experienced by a U.S. pension fund in

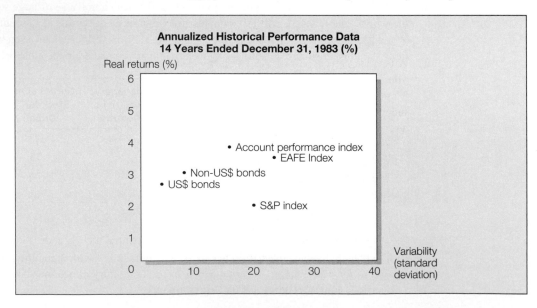

the recent past. Compare the performance of the U.S. dollar and non–U.S. dollar equity and fixed-income asset categories, and explain the significance of the result of the Account Performance Index relative to the results of the four individual asset class indices.

15. You are a U.S. investor considering purchase of one of the following securities. Assume that the currency risk of the German government bond will be hedged, and the six-month discount on Canadian dollar forward contracts is −.75 percent versus the U.S. dollar.

Bond	Maturity	Coupon	Price
U.S. government	6 months	6.50%	100.00
Canadian government	6 months	7.50%	100.00

Calculate the expected price change required in the Canadian government bond that would result in the two bonds having equal total returns in U.S. dollars over a six-month horizon. Assume that the yield on the U.S. bond is expected to remain unchanged.

16. A global manager plans to invest $1 million in U.S. government cash equivalents for the next 90 days. However, she is also authorized to use non–U.S. government cash equivalents, as long as the currency risk is hedged to U.S. dollars using forward currency contracts.

    a. What rate of return will the manager earn if she invests in money market instruments in either Canada or Japan and hedges the dollar value of her investment? Use the data in the following table.

Interest Rates (APR) 90–Day Cash Equivalents	
Japanese government	2.52%
Canadian government	6.74%

Exchange Rates Dollars per Unit of Foreign Currency		
	Spot	90-Day Forward
Japanese yen	.0119	.0120
Canadian dollar	.7284	.7269

    b. What must be the approximate value of the 90-day interest rate available on U.S. government securities?

17. After much research on the developing economy and capital markets of the country of Otunia, your firm, GAC, has decided to include an investment in the Otunia stock market in its Emerging Markets Commingled Fund. However, GAC has not yet decided whether to invest actively or by indexing. Your opinion on the active-versus-indexing decision has been solicited. The following is a summary of the research findings:

Otunia's economy is fairly well diversified across agricultural and natural resources, manufacturing (both consumer and durable goods), and a growing finance sector. Transaction costs in securities markets are relatively large in Otunia because of high commissions and government "stamp taxes" on securities trades. Accounting standards and disclosure regulations are quite detailed, resulting in wide public availability of reliable information about companies' financial performance.

Capital flows into and out of Otunia, and foreign ownership of Otunia securities, is strictly regulated by an agency of the national government. The settlement procedures under these ownership rules often cause long delays in settling trades made by nonresidents. Senior finance officials in the government are working to deregulate capital flows and foreign ownership, but GAC's political consultant believes that isolationist sentiment may prevent much real progress in the short run.

a. Briefly discuss aspects of the Otunia environment that favour investing actively, and aspects that favour indexing.

b. Recommend whether GAC should invest in Otunia actively or by indexing. Justify your recommendation based on the factors identified in part (*a*).

18. You and a prospective client are considering the measurement of investment performance, particularly with respect to international portfolios for the past five years. The data you discussed are presented in the following table:

International Manager or Index	Total Return	Country and Security Return	Currency Return
Manager A	−6.0%	2.0%	−8.0%
Manager B	−2.0	−1.0	−1.0
International index	−5.0	.2	−5.2

a. Assume that the data for manager A and manager B accurately reflect their investment skills and that both managers actively manage currency exposure. Briefly describe one strength and one weakness for each manager.

b. Recommend and justify a strategy that would enable your fund to take advantage of the strengths of each of the two managers while minimizing their weaknesses.

19. The Windsor Foundation, a U.S.-based, not-for-profit charitable organization, has a diversified investment portfolio of $100 million. Windsor's board of directors is considering an initial investment in emerging market equities. Robert Houston, treasurer of the foundation, has made the following four comments:

a. "For an investor holding only developed market equities, the existence of stable emerging market currencies is one of several preconditions necessary for that investor to realize strong emerging market performance."

b. "Local currency depreciation against the dollar has been a frequent occurrence for U.S. investors in emerging markets. U.S. investors have consistently seen large percentages of their returns erased by currency depreciation. This is true even for long-term investors."

c. "Historically, the addition of emerging market stocks to a U.S. equity portfolio such as the S&P 500 index has reduced volatility; volatility has also been reduced when emerging market stocks are combined with an international portfolio such as the MSCI EAFE index."

d. "Although correlations among emerging markets can change over the short term, such correlations show evidence of stability over the long term. Thus, an emerging markets portfolio that lies on the efficient frontier in one period tends to remain close to the frontier in subsequent periods."

Discuss *each* of these four comments, stating whether it is correct or incorrect.

abnormal return. Return on a stock beyond what would be predicted by market movements alone. See also *cumulative abnormal return (CAR)*.

accounting earnings. Earnings of a firm as reported on its *income statement*.

acid test ratio. *See quick ratio*.

active management. Attempts to achieve portfolio returns more than commensurate with risk, either by forecasting broad market trends or by identifying particular mispriced sectors of a market or securities in a market.

active portfolio. In the context of the Treynor-Black *model*, the portfolio formed by mixing analyzed stocks of perceived non-zero *alpha* values. This portfolio is ultimately mixed with the passive market index portfolio.

agency problem. The conflict of interest between stockholders, bondholders, and managers, and the resultant suboptimal decisions.

agency theory. The study of conflicts of interest between stockholders, bondholders, and managers of a firm.

alpha transfer. See *portable alpha*.

alpha. The abnormal rate of return on a security in excess of what would be predicted by an equilibrium *model* such as the *capital asset pricing model (CAPM) or arbitrage pricing theory (APT)*.

American Depository Receipts (ADR). The instrument traded on the NYSE which represents an equity interest in a (foreign) company; ADRs are equivalent to a number of shares in the company, as traded in that company's home market, and are entitled to proportional payments of dividends.

American option. An option that can be exercised before and up to its expiration date. See also *European option*.

announcement date. Date on which particular news concerning a given company is announced to the public. Used in *event studies*, which researchers use to evaluate the economic impact of events of interest.

annual percentage rates (APRs). Rates on short-term investments that are often annualized using simple rather than compound interest.

anomalies. Patterns of returns that seem to contradict the *efficient market hypothesis*.

arbitrage. A zero-risk, zero-net investment strategy that still generates profits.

arbitrage pricing theory (APT). An asset pricing theory that is derived from a *factor model*, using diversification and *arbitrage* arguments. The theory describes the relationship between *expected returns* on securities, given that there are no opportunities to create wealth through risk-free arbitrage investments.

ask price. The price at which a dealer will sell a security.

asset allocation. The choice made by investors between broad asset classes, in particular cash, stocks, and bonds, as well as other assets such as commodities.

at the money. Said of an option whose *exercise price* equals its asset value. See also *in the money* and *out of the money*.

auction market. A market where all traders in an asset meet at one place to buy or sell. The TSX is an example.

average collection period. The ratio of accounts receivable to sales, or the total amount of credit extended per dollar of daily sales (Average AR/ Sales × 365).

backfill bias. Bias in the average returns of a sample of funds induced by including past returns on funds that entered the sample only if they were successful.

balance sheet. A financial statement of the assets, liabilities, and net worth of the firm as of a particular date.

bank discount yield. An annualized *interest rate* assuming simple interest and a 360-day year, and using the *face value* of the security rather than purchase price to compute return per dollar invested.

bankers' acceptance. A money market instrument consisting of an order to a bank by a customer to pay a fixed amount at a future debt; the bank has "accepted" this order.

baseline allocation. Neutral allocation of funds to *equities*, fixed income, and cash used as a portfolio starting point from which modifications are made in response to predictions of asset performance.

baseline forecast. Forecast of security returns based on the assumption that the market is in equilibrium with current prices of assets reflecting all available information, and the efficiency of the theoretical market portfolio.

basis risk. Risk attributable to uncertain movements in the *spread* between a *futures price* and a spot price.

basis. The difference between the *futures price* and the spot price.

bear CD. Pays the holder a fraction of any fall in a given market index. See also *bull CD*.

bearer deposit notes (BDNs). Negotiable bank time deposits (in Canada).

bearish. Pessimistic; used to describe investor attitudes. Also used in the term *bear market*. See also *bullish*.

behavioural finance. A set of theoretical hypotheses that attribute departures from market efficiency to systematic patterns of investor behaviour that seemingly contradict rationality.

benchmark error. Use of an inappropriate *proxy* for the true *market portfolio*.

beta. The measure of the systematic risk of a security. The tendency of a security's returns to respond to swings in the broad market.

bid price. The price at which a dealer is willing to purchase a security.

bid–asked spread. The difference between a dealer's *bid price* and *asked price*.

binomial model. An option valuation *model* predicated on the assumption that stock prices can move to only two values over any short time period.

Black-Scholes pricing formula. An equation to value a *call option* that uses the stock price, the *exercise price*, the riskfree *interest rate*, the time to maturity, and the *standard deviation* of the stock return.

block house. Brokerage firms that help to find potential buyers or sellers of large block trades.

block sale. A sale of more than 10,000 shares of stock.

block transactions. Large transactions in which at least 10,000 shares of stock are bought or sold. Brokers or *block houses* often search directly for other large traders rather than bringing the trade to the *stock exchange*.

board lots. Standard volumes of traded securities, generally equal to 100 shares per lot. Can be larger (smaller) for low-priced (high-priced) securities.

bogey. The return an investment manager is compared to for performance evaluation.

bond. A security issued by a borrower that obligates the issuer to make specified payments to the holder over a specified period. A *coupon bond* obligates the issuer to make interest payments called coupon payments over the life of the bond, then to repay the *principal* at maturity.

bond equivalent yield. Bond yield calculated on an *annual percentage rate* method. Differs from *effective annual yield*.

bond indenture. See *indenture*.

bond index portfolio. A portfolio of bonds stratified to include representatives of available grades, coupons, and maturities in weights proportional to the actual bond universe.

bond reconstitution. Buying individual *zero-coupon bonds* in the strip market, then reassembling the cash flows into a *coupon bond* and selling the whole bond for more than the cost of pieces.

bond stripping. Selling bond cash flows (either coupon or *principal* payments) as stand-alone *zero-coupon bonds*.

book value. An accounting measure describing the net worth of common equity according to a firm's *balance sheet*.

book-to-market effects. The ratio of the *book value* of the firm's equity to the market value of the equity, used as a predictor of the return on the firm's securities.

breadth. A technical indicator measuring the extent to which movement in a market index is reflected in the price movements of all stocks.

brokered market. A market where an intermediary (a broker) offers search services to buyers and sellers.

bull CD. Pays its holder a specified percentage of the increase in return on a specified market index while guaranteeing a minimum rate of return. See also *bear CD*.

bullish. Optimistic; used to describe investor attitudes. Also used in the term *bull market*. See also *bearish*.

bundling. The creation of securities either by combining primitive and derivative securities into one hybrid or by separating returns on an asset into classes.

business cycle. The sequence of expansion and contraction of activity in the economy, observable after the fact.

call option. The right to buy an asset at a specified *exercise price* on or before a specified expiration date.

callable. The feature of *bonds* or preferred shares allowing the issuer to repurchase the security at a fixed price in some specified period.

callable bonds. *Bonds* that the issuer may repurchase at a given price in some specified period.

capital allocation line (CAL). A graph showing all feasible risk–return combinations of a *risky* and risk-free asset.

capital asset pricing model (CAPM). A *model* of financial market equilibrium that allows the computation of the riskadjusted equilibrium rates of return for various *financial assets*.

capital gains. The amount by which the sale price of a security exceeds the purchase price.

capital market line (CML). The *capital allocation line* provided by one-month *Treasury bills* and a broad index of *common stocks*.

capital markets. The markets for longer-term, relatively riskier securities.

cash/bond selection. *Asset allocation* in which the choice is between short-term cash equivalents and longer-term bonds.

cash delivery. The provision of some *futures contracts* that requires no delivery of the underlying assets (as in agricultural futures) but settlement according to the cash value of the asset.

cash flow matching. A form of *immunization*, matching cash flows from a bond with an obligation.

cash ratio. Measure of *liquidity* of a firm; ratio of cash and marketable securities to current liabilities.

cash settlement. The provision of certain options (*index options*) or *futures contracts* that requires, not delivery of the underlying asset, but settlement by the cash value of the asset.

CDOs. See *collateralized debt obligations*.

CDS. See *credit default swap*.

certainty equivalent rate. A rate that risk-free investments would need to offer with certainty to be considered equally attractive to a particular risky portfolio.

certainty equivalent. The certain return providing the same utility as a risky portfolio.

certificate of deposit (CD). A bank time deposit.

clearinghouse. Established by *exchanges* to facilitate transfer of securities resulting from trades. For options and *futures contracts*, the clearinghouse may interpose itself as a middleman between two traders.

closed-end funds. Funds whose shares are traded through brokers at market prices; the fund will not redeem shares at their *net asset value (NAV)*. The market price of the fund can differ from the net asset value.

collar. An option strategy that brackets the value of the underlying asset between two bounds.

collateral. A specific asset pledged against possible default on a bond. *Mortgage* bonds are backed by claims on property. *Collateral trust bonds* are backed by claims on other securities. *Equipment obligation bonds* are backed by claims on equipment.

collateralized debt obligations (CDOs). A pool of loans sliced into several *tranches* with different levels of risk.

collateralized mortgage obligations (CMOs). Mortgage *pass-through securities* that partition cash flows from underlying mortgages into successive maturity groups, called *tranches*, that receive *principal* payments according to different maturities.

commercial paper. Short-term unsecured paper (or note) issues by large corporations.

commingled funds. Investment pools of funds for accounts that are too small for individual attention and are managed as a group.

common stocks. *Equities*, or equity securities, issued as ownership shares in a publicly held corporation. Shareholders have voting rights and may receive dividends based on their proportionate ownership.

comparison universe. The collection of money managers of similar investment style used for assessing relative performance of a portfolio manager.

complete portfolio. A portfolio that includes both risky and risk-free investments.

conditional tail expectation (CTE). Expectation of a random variable conditional on it falling below some threshold value. Often used as measure of "downside risk."

confidence index. The ratio of the average yield on ten toprated *corporate bonds* divided by the average yield on ten intermediate-grade corporate bonds; a technical indicator that is *bullish* when the index approaches 100 percent, implying low-risk premiums.

conservatism. A decision-making bias by which investors are too slow in updating their beliefs in response to new evidence.

constant-growth DDM. A form of the *dividend discount model (DDM)* that assumes dividends will grow at a constant rate.

consumption timing. The decision of individuals who use funds for investment or consumption in different periods of their lives, generally entailing investing in *financial assets* at the beginning and later selling those assets for the consumption needs.

contango theory. Holds that the *futures price* must exceed the expected future spot price.

contingent claims. Claims whose value is directly dependent on or is contingent on the value of some underlying assets.

contingent immunization. A mixed passive-active strategy that immunizes a portfolio if necessary to guarantee a minimum acceptable return but otherwise allows *active management*.

convergence arbitrage. A *hedging* strategy based on the misalignment of two or more prices based on the expectation that pricing discrepancies between the securities will disappear over time.

convergence property. The convergence of *futures prices* and spot prices at the maturity of the *futures contract*.

convertible bonds. Bonds with an option allowing the bondholder to exchange the bond for a number of shares. The *market conversion price* is the current value of the shares for which the bond may be exchanged. The *conversion premium* is the excess of the bond's value over the conversion price.

convexity. The property of curvature in the graph which expresses the rate of change in bond value in response to changes in the *interest rate*; higher *coupon bonds* have greater convexity than lower or *zero-coupon bonds* of the same duration.

corporate bonds. Long-term debt issued by private corporations typically paying semiannual coupons and returning the *face value* of the bond at maturity.

corporate class. A specific fund within a mutual fund corporation (as opposed to a trust), containing a group of focus funds, such as small-cap stocks, Canadian *equities*, international equities, etc. An investor can typically move from one corporate class fund to another without incurring an immediate tax penalty. Instead, taxes are deferred until the investment is withdrawn from the corporation.

correlation coefficient. A statistic that scales the **covariance** to a value between minus one (perfect negative correlation) and plus one (perfect positive correlation).

cost-of-carry relationship. See *spot–futures parity theorem*.

counterparty risk. The risk that a trading partner might fail to satisfy his or her obligations under a security contract.

country selection. A type of active international management that measures the contribution to performance attributable to investing in the better-performing stock markets of the world.

coupon bond. Obligates the issuer to make interest payments called *coupon* payments over the life of the bond, then to repay the *principal* at maturity.

coupon rate. A bond's interest payments per dollar of *par value*.

covariance. A measure of the degree to which returns on two risky assets move in tandem. A *positive* covariance means that asset returns move together. A *negative* covariance means they vary inversely.

covered call. A combination of selling a call on a stock together with buying the stock.

covered interest arbitrage relationship. See *interest rate parity relationship*.

credit default swap (CDS). A derivative contract in which one party sells insurance concerning the credit risk of another firm.

credit enhancement. Purchase of the financial guarantee of a large insurance company to raise funds.

cross-hedging. Hedging a position in one asset using futures on another commodity.

cumulative abnormal return (CAR). The total *abnormal return* for the period surrounding an announcement or the release of information.

currency selection. *Asset allocation* in which the investor chooses among investments denominated in different currencies.

current ratio. A ratio representing the ability of the firm to pay off its current liabilities by liquidating current assets (current assets/current liabilities).

dark pools. Trading venues or trading systems in which participants can buy or sell large blocks of securities without showing their activities. Buyers and sellers in dark pools are hidden from the public. If dark-pool trades are reported, they may be lumped with other trades to obscure information about particular participants. While they preserve anonymity, they also affect market *liquidity*.

data mining. Sorting through large amounts of historical data to uncover systematic patterns that can be exploited.

days' receivables. See *average collection period*.

dealer markets. Markets where traders specializing in particular commodities buy and sell assets for their own accounts. The *over-the-counter (OTC) market* is an example.

debenture. A bond not backed by specific *collateral*. Also known as *unsecured bond*.

debt securities. Also known as *fixed-income securities*. They are issued by borrowers who will pay interest at a rate determined by the perceived repayment ability of the borrower and the time to maturity of the obligation. May be short-term (less than one year to maturity), medium-term (three-to-ten-year maturity), or long-term (over ten years to maturity). Debt securities include government bonds, corporate bonds, *CDs*, municipal bonds, *preferred stock*, *collateralized* securities (such as *CDOs*, *CMOs*, GNMAs (Government National Mortgage Association pass-through certificates), and *zero-coupon* securities.

dedication strategy. Refers to multiperiod *cash flow matching*.

default premium. A differential in promised yield that compensates the investor for the risk inherent in purchasing a corporate bond that entails some risk of default.

deferred annuities. Tax-advantaged life insurance product. Deferred annuities offer deferral of taxes with the option of withdrawing one's funds in the form of a life annuity.

degree of operating leverage (DOL). Percentage change in profits corresponding to a 1 percent change in sales.

delta. See *hedge ratio (for an option)*.

delta hedging. Offsetting positions in an option and its underlying security to reduce the risk of the resulting portfolio from changes in the security's price. For example, a long call position may be delta hedged by shorting the underlying stock. The change in premium (price of option) for each basis-point change in price of the underlying security is the *delta* and the relationship between the two movements is the delta *hedge ratio*.

delta-neutral. A position in options and the underlying stock that is insensitive to changes in the price of the stock.

demand shock. An event affecting the aggregate demand for goods and services, thereby influencing the state of the economy.

derivative assets, or contingent claims. Securities providing payoffs that depend on or are contingent on the values of other assets such as commodity prices, bond and stock prices, or market index values. Examples are futures and options.

desk traders. Representatives of securities firms who are limited to executing trades on behalf of clients of the firms; they may not trade for their firm's accounts.

developed countries. Wealthier countries with modern financial systems, arbitrarily defined as having per capita income (in 2005) exceeding $10,000.

direct search market. A market in which buyers and sellers seek each other directly and transact directly.

directional strategies. Speculation that one sector or another will outperform other sectors of the market.

discount bonds. *Bonds* selling below par value.

discretionary account. An account of a customer who gives a broker the authority to make buy-and-sell decisions on the customer's behalf.

diversifiable risk. Risk attributable to *firm-specific risk*, or non-market risk. *Nondiversifiable risk* refers to *systematic* or *market risk*.

diversification. Spreading a portfolio over many investments to avoid excessive exposure to any one source of risk.

dividend discount model (DDM). A formula to estimate the intrinsic value of shares by calculating the present value of all expected future dividends.

dividend payout ratio. Percentage of earnings paid out as dividends.

dividend yield. The percent rate of return provided by a stock's *dividend* payments.

dividends. Payments made from earnings to holders of *common* or *preferred* shares.

dollar-cost averaging. A strategy for investing by which the same sum of money is invested at regular time intervals; as an alternative to buying the same number of shares, this results in lower average cost for the portfolio.

dollar-weighted rate of return. An average giving the internal rate of return on an investment.

Dow theory. A long-standing approach to forecasting stock market direction by identification of long-term trends; the Dow Jones Industrial and Transportation Averages were used by Charles Dow to identify and confirm underlying trends.

duration. A measure of the average life of a bond, defined as the weighted average of the times until each payment is made, with weights proportional to the present value of the payment.

dynamic hedging. Constant updating of hedge positions as market conditions change.

earnings management. The practice of using flexibility in accounting rules to manipulate the reported profitability of a firm.

earnings yield. The ratio of earnings to price (E/P).

economic earnings. The real flow of cash that a firm could pay out forever in the absence of any change in the firm's productive capacity.

economic value added (EVA). The dollar value of a firm's return in excess of its opportunity cost measured by the *spread* between *return on assets (ROA)* and the opportunity cost of capital, times the capital invested in the firm.

effective annual rate (EAR). The percentage increase in funds invested over a one-year horizon.

effective annual yield. Annualized *interest rate* on a security computed using compound interest techniques.

effective duration. The proportional change in a bond price per unit change in market interest rates for bonds with embedded options.

efficient diversification. The organizing principle of *modern portfolio theory*, which maintains that any *risk-averse* investor will search for the highest *expected return* for any level of portfolio risk.

efficient frontier. Graph representing a set of portfolios that maximize *expected return* at each level of portfolio risk.

efficient market hypothesis (EMH). The prices of securities fully reflect available information. Investors buying securities in an efficient market should expect to obtain an equilibrium rate of return. *Weak-form* EMH asserts that stock prices already reflect all information contained in the history of past prices. The *semistrong-form* hypothesis asserts that stock prices already reflect all publicly available information. The *strong-form* hypothesis asserts that stock prices reflect all relevant information including insider information.

electronic communication networks (ECNs). Direct links between traders that avoid the formal *exchanges* and dealer markets.

equities. See *common stock*.

ES. See *expected shortfall*.

Eurodollars. Dollar-denominated deposits at foreign banks or foreign branches of American banks.

European option. A European option can be exercised only on the expiration date. See also *American option*.

Europe, Australia, Far East (EAFE) index. A widely used index of non-Western-Hemisphere stocks computed by Morgan Stanley.

event study. Research methodology designed to measure the impact of an event of interest on stock returns.

event tree. A diagram showing possible outcomes branching off over a period of time.

excess return. The difference between the actual rate of return on a risky asset and the *risk-free rate*.

exchange. A national or regional auction market providing a facility for members to trade securities. A *seat* is a *membership on an exchange*.

exchange rate. Price of a unit of one country's currency in terms of another country's currency.

exchange rate risk. The uncertainty in asset returns due to movements in the *exchange rates* between the dollar and foreign currencies.

exchange-traded funds (ETFs). Investment securities designed to represent an index or sub-index that are exchangetraded; an alternative to open or *closed-end mutual funds*.

exercise or strike price. Price set for calling (buying) an asset or putting (selling) an asset.

expectations hypothesis. Theory that *forward interest rates* are unbiased estimates of expected future interest rates.

expected return. The probability-weighted average of the possible outcomes.

expected return–beta (or mean–beta) relationship. Implication of the *capital asset pricing model* (*CAPM*) that security *risk premiums* (expected *excess returns*) will be proportional to *beta*.

expected shortfall (ES). A measure of the market risk or credit risk of a portfolio. The "expected shortfall at the *p%* level" is the expected return on the portfolio conditional on being in the worst *p%* of the return distribution.

extendible bond. A *bond* giving the holder the option to redeem the bond later than the stated maturity date. See also *retractable bond*.

face value. See *par value*.

factor model. A way of decomposing the factors that influence a security's rate of return into common and firm-specific influences.

factor portfolio. A *well-diversified portfolio* constructed to have a *beta* of 1.0 on one factor and a beta of zero on any other factor.

fair game. A prospect that has a zero-risk premium.

fair value accounting. An amount at which an asset could be exchanged between knowledgeable and willing parties in an arm's-length transaction, as defined by the International Accounting Standards Board (IASB).

FIFO. The first-in, first-out accounting method of inventory valuation. See also *LIFO*.

financial assets. Claims to the income generated by real assets or claims on income from the government. See also *real assets*.

financial engineering. Innovative security design and repackaging of investments.

financial intermediaries. Institutions such as a banks, mutual funds, *investment companies*, or insurance companies that serve to connect the household and business sectors so households can invest and businesses can finance production.

financial investment. The investment of capital in financial instruments and assets, rather than in real, physical goods (real investment).

firm-specific risk. Risk peculiar to an individual firm that is independent of *market risk*.

first-pass regression. A time series regression to estimate the *betas* of securities or portfolios.

fiscal policy. The use of taxes and government spending to affect aggregate demand as well as other objectives of macroeconomic policy.

fixed annuities. Annuity contracts in which the insurance company pays a fixed dollar amount of money per period.

fixed-income security. A security such as a bond that pays a specified cash flow over a specific period.

flight to quality. Describes the tendency of investors to require larger default premiums on investments under uncertain economic conditions.

float. Used to indicate the sale of new securities by firms to the public; the term also refers to the amount of stock available for public trading.

floating-rate bonds. Bonds whose *interest rate* is reset periodically according to a specified market rate.

foreign exchange swap. The exchange of cash flows denominated in one currency for cash flows denominated in another currency, in order to manage the foreign exchange risk.

forward interest rate. Rate of interest for a future period that would equate the total return of a long-term bond with that of a strategy of rolling over shorter-term bonds. The forward rate is inferred from the term structure.

framed. Said of choices when they are described in a certain way. For example, a risky prospect framed in terms of the risk surrounding possible gains is viewed differently than if framed in terms of the risk surrounding losses.

funds of funds. *Hedge funds* that invest in several other funds.

fundamental analysis. Research to predict stock value that focuses on such determinants as earnings and dividends prospects, expectations for future *interest rates*, and risk evaluation of the firm.

fundamental risk. The risk that no *arbitrage* opportunity will exist for an asset that is mispriced, since the mispricing can increase before price eventually converges to intrinsic value.

futures contract. Obliges traders to purchase or sell an asset at an agreed-upon price on a specified future date. The *long position* is held by the trader who commits to purchase. The *short position* is held by the trader who commits to sell. Futures differ from forward contracts in their standardization, exchange trading, *margin* requirements, and daily settling (marking to market).

futures option. The right to enter a specified *futures contract* at a *futures price* equal to the stipulated *exercise price*.

futures price. The price at which a futures trader commits to make or take delivery of the underlying asset.

gamma. The sensitivity of the *hedge ratio* of an option to the stock price.

globalization. Tendency toward a worldwide investment environment, and the *integration* of national capital markets.

growth company. A company for which the growth rate is greater than the market average due to superior opportunities for reinvestment.

guaranteed investment certificate (GIC). A fixed-term deposit with a trust company that pays interest and *principal* upon maturity and is non-transferable. See also *certificate of deposit*.

hedge funds. Private investment pools, open to institutions or wealthy investors, that are largely exempt from regulation and can pursue more speculative policies than mutual funds.

hedge ratio. For a bond, the number of contracts held to offset a bond portfolio's risk. For an option, the number of stocks required to hedge against the price risk of holding one option; also called the option's *delta*.

hedging. Investing in an asset to reduce the overall risk of a portfolio.

high-water mark. The previous value of a portfolio that must be re-attained before a *hedge fund* can charge *incentive fees*.

holding-period return (HPR). The rate of return over a given period.

homogenous expectations. The assumption that all investors use the same *expected returns* and *covariance* matrix of security returns as inputs in *security analysis*.

horizon analysis. The forecasting of the realized compound yield over various holding periods or *investment horizons*.

IFRS. See *international financial reporting standards*.

illiquidity. The ease and speed with which an asset can be sold at a fair market value in a timely fashion.

illiquidity premium. Increase in the *expected return* of illiquid assets to compensate for their higher transaction costs.

immunization. A strategy that matches durations of assets and liabilities so as to make net worth unaffected by *interest rate* movements.

implied volatility. The *standard deviation* of stock returns that is consistent with an option's market value according to the Black-Scholes *model*.

in the money. Said of an option whose exercise would be profitable. See *also at the money* and *out of the money*.

incentive fee. A fee charged by a *hedge fund* equal to a share of any investment returns beyond a stipulated benchmark performance.

income statement. A financial statement summarizing the profitability of the firm over a period of time, such as a year;

income trusts. Pooled investments held in trust that generate high current income through distribution of income from assets held by a firm, often including non-taxable distributions of capital.

incomplete markets. Financial markets in which the number of available independent securities is less than the number of distinct future states of the world.

indenture. The document defining the contract between the bond issuer and the bondholder.

index arbitrage. An investment strategy that exploits divergences between actual *futures prices* and their theoretically correct parity values to make a profit.

index funds. Mutual funds holding shares in proportion to their representation in a market index such as the S&P/TSX composite.

indexing. Holding a portfolio composed of the *market portfolio* in the case of *equities* (or a cellular bond portfolio).

index model. A *model* of stock returns using a market index such as the S&P/TSX composite to represent common or *systematic risk* factors.

index option. A *call option* or *put option* based on a stock market index.

indifference curve. A curve connecting all portfolios with the same utility according to their means and *standard deviations*.

industry life cycle. The set of stages in the evolution of an industry from innovative development to maturity and decline, which define the expectable returns for member firms.

information ratio. The signal-to-noise ratio of an analyst's forecasts. The ratio of *alpha* to residual *standard deviation*.

informational role. The role played by *financial assets* that enables the efficient allocation of capital to *real assets* by establishing prices that convey information about the value of those assets.

initial public offering. Stock issued to the public for the first time by a formerly privately owned company.

input list. The set of estimates of expected rates of return and *covariances* for the securities that will constitute portfolios forming the efficient frontier.

inside information. Non-public knowledge about a corporation possessed by corporate officers, major owners, or other individuals with privileged access to information about a firm.

insider transactions. Transactions by officers, directors, and major stockholders in their firm's securities; these transactions must be reported publicly at regular intervals.

insurance principle. The law of averages. The average outcome for many independent trials of an experiment will approach the expected value of the experiment.

interest coverage ratio, or times interest earned. A financial leverage measure (EBIT divided by interest expense).

interest rate. The number of dollars earned per dollar invested per period.

interest rate parity relationship. An equation—which should hold in well-functioning financial markets—yielding the futures *exchange rate* as a function of the *spot rate* and the *interest rates* prevailing in the two countries. Also known as *covered interest arbitrage*.

interest rate swaps. A method of managing interest rate risk in which parties trade the cash flows corresponding to different securities without actually exchanging securities directly.

intermarket spread swap. Switching from one segment of the bond market to another (from Treasuries to corporates, for example).

international financial reporting standards (IFRS). A set of international accounting standards issued by the International Accounting Standards Board stating how particular types of transactions and other events should be reported in financial statements. IFRS rely more on principles and less on rules compared to U.S. standards.

intrinsic value. Of a share of stock: The present value of a firm's expected future cash flows discounted by the required rate of return less the market value of debt, then divided by the number of shares outstanding. Of an option: Stock price minus *exercise price*, or the profit that could be attained by immediate exercise of an in-the-money option.

intrinsic value (of a firm). The present value of a firm's expected future net cash flows discounted by the required rate of return.

investment bankers. Firms specializing in the sale of new securities to the public, typically by *underwriting* the issue. Also known in Canada as *investment dealers*.

investment companies. Firms managing funds for investors. An investment company may manage several mutual funds.

investment dealers. A person or firm in the business of buying and selling securities for their own account, through a broker or otherwise. A dealer is defined by the fact that it acts as *principal* in trading for its own account, as opposed to a broker, which acts as an agent in executing orders on behalf of its clients. *Public offerings* of both stocks and *bonds* in Canada are typically marketed via an *underwriting* by investment dealers (also known as *investment bankers*)

investment horizon. Period of time for purposes of investment decisions.

investment-grade bond. Bond rated BBB and above or Baa and above. Lower-rated bonds are classified as *speculative-grade* or *junk bonds*.

junk bond. See *speculative-grade bond*.

kurtosis. The measure of the degree of "fat-tailed" distribution.

latency. The time it takes a trading system to detect an *arbitrage* opportunity and to successfully exploit that opportunity. Low latency refers to the rapid execution of a transaction.

Law of One Price. The rule stipulating that securities or portfolios with equal returns under all circumstances must sell at equal prices to preclude *arbitrage* opportunities. revenues and expenses are listed and their difference is calculated as net income.

leading economic indicators. A collection of economic series shown to precede changes in overall economic activity; these include retail sales, financial, manufacturing, house sales measures, and the U.S. index.

leverage ratio. Measure of debt to total capitalization of a firm.

LIBOR. See *London Interbank Offered Rate*.

LIFO. The last-in, first-out accounting method of valuing inventories. See also *FIFO*.

limited liability. The fact that shareholders have no personal liability to the creditors of the corporation in the event of failure.

liquidation value. Net amount that could be realized by selling the assets of a firm after paying the debt.

liquidity. The ease or speed with which an asset can be converted to cash without significant discount to its value.

liquidity preference theory. Theory that the forward rate exceeds expected future *interest rates*.

liquidity premium. Forward rate minus expected future *short interest* rate.

load. The fee charged as a commission for purchasing a mutual fund.

load fund. A mutual fund with a sales commission, or load.

lock-up periods. Periods in which investors cannot redeem funds invested in a *hedge fund*.

London Interbank Offered Rate (LIBOR). Rate that most creditworthy banks charge one another for large loans of Eurodollars in the London market.

long position. Protecting the future cost of a purchase by taking a long futures position to protect against changes in the price of the asset.

lower partial standard deviation (LPSD). The *standard deviation* computed solely from values below the expected return; a measure of "downside risk."

maintenance margin. A term used in the United States for the established value below which a trader's *margin* ratio cannot fall, in order to avoid a margin call.

managed funds. A generic term for funds under the administration of investment companies.

management expense ratio. The combination of operating expenses and other charges expressed as a ratio of total assets in a mutual fund.

margin. Describes securities purchased with money borrowed from a broker. Current maximum margin is 50 percent.

market. An organized forum for the exchange of assets. Also used to describe the general aggregate of securities.

market capitalization rate. The market-consensus estimate of the appropriate discount rate for a firm's cash flows.

market making. The act of receiving orders to buy and sell securities and dealing in those securities, thereby establishing market *liquidity* and a price for the securities.

market order. A buy or sell order to be executed immediately at current market prices.

market portfolio. The portfolio for which each security is held in proportion to its market value.

market price of risk. A measure of the extra return, or *risk premium*, that investors demand to bear risk. The reward-to-risk ratio of the *market portfolio*.

market risk. Risk attributable to common macro-economic factors. See also *firm-specific risk*.

market timing. *Asset allocation* in which the investment in the market is increased if one forecasts that the market will outperform *Treasury bills*.

market-neutral. A strategy designed to exploit relative mispricing within a market, but which is hedged to avoid taking a stance on the direction of the broad market.

market-neutral bet. A position taken on an investment to capture its *alpha* with market exposure fully hedged, resulting in a position *beta* of zero.

market-to-book-value ratio (P/B). Market price of a share divided by *book value* per share.

market-value-weighted index. An index of a group of securities computed by calculating a weighted average of the returns of each security in the index, with weights proportional to outstanding market value.

mark-to-market accounting. Refers to accounting for the *fair value* of an asset or liability using the current market price, or for similar assets and liabilities, as opposed to some other measure (such as the historical price).

marking to market. The daily settlement of obligations on futures positions. **MBS See *mortgage-backed security*.**

mean return. See *expected return*.

mean-variance (M-V) criterion. The selection of portfolios on the basis of the means and *variances* of their returns. The choice of the higher *expected return* portfolio for a given level of variance or the lower variance portfolio for a given expected return.

membership or seat on an exchange. A limited number of *exchange* positions that enable the holder to trade for the holder's own accounts and charge clients for the execution of trades for their accounts.

mental accounting. The mental segregation of assets by individuals into independent accounts rather than viewing them as part of a unified portfolio.

minimum-variance frontier. Graph of the lowest possible portfolio *variance* that is attainable for a given portfolio *expected return*.

minimum-variance portfolio. The portfolio of risk assets with lowest *variance*.

models. Abstract representations of real-world financial situations.

modern portfolio theory (MPT). Principles underlying analysis and evaluation of rational portfolio choices on the basis of *risk–return tradeoffs* and *efficient diversification*.

modified duration. Macaulay's duration divided by (1 + *Yield to maturity*). Measures interest rate sensitivity of the *bond*.

momentum effect. The phenomenon by which good or bad recent performance of particular stocks persists over time (as contrasted with reversals).

monetary policy. The manipulation of the money supply to influence economic activity and the level of *interest rates*.

money market. Includes short-term, highly liquid, and relatively low-risk debt instruments.

mortality tables. Tables of probabilities that individuals of various ages will die within a year.

mortgage-backed security (MBS). Ownership claim in a pool of mortgages or an obligation that is secured by such a pool. Also called a *pass-through security*, because payments are passed along from the mortgage originator to the purchaser of the mortgage-backed security.

moving average. A rolling average of stock prices, based on a short, intermediate, or long period, serving as a reference point for the current price; displayed on a chart.

multifactor. A characteristic of *models* of stock returns that decompose the factors that affect the returns into more than one common influence, as well as a firm-specific influence.

mutual fund theorem. A result associated with the *capital asset pricing model (CAPM)*, asserting that investors will choose to invest their entire risky portfolio in a market-index mutual fund.

M-V criterion. See *mean-variance criterion*.

NAICS codes. North American Industry Classification System (NAICS) codes that use numerical values to identify industries.

naked option writing. Writing an option without an offsetting stock position.

Nasdaq Stock Market. The automated quotation system for the OTC market, showing current bid–asked prices for thousands of stocks.

neglected-firm effect. That investments in stock of lesswell-known firms have generated *abnormal returns*.

net asset value (NAV). The value per share or unit of an investment in a pool of investments, determined as assets minus liabilities divided by the number of shares outstanding.

nominal interest rate. The *interest rate* in terms of nominal (not adjusted for purchasing power) dollars.

nondirectional strategies. Positions designed to exploit temporary misalignments in relative pricing. Typically involve a long position in one security hedged with a short position in a related security.

nondiversifiable risk. See *systematic risk*.

nonsystematic risk. Non-market or *firm-specific risk* factors that can be eliminated by diversification. Also called *unique risk* or *diversifiable risk*. *Systematic risk* refers to risk factors common to the entire economy.

normal backwardation theory. Holds that the *futures price* will be bid down to a level below the expected spot price.

normal distribution. A statistical distribution that has these properties: (1) it is symmetric and completely described by two parameters, its mean and standard deviation; (2) a weighted average of variables that are normally distributed will also be normally distributed. Can be applied to stock returns.

notional principal. *Principal* amount used to calculate swap payments.

odd-lot theory. Assessment of market tops and bottoms by observation of the net buying and selling of odd-lots (shares sold in less than round or *board lots*); used as a contrarian measure so that odd-lot buying suggests a top.

on-the-run yield curve. A *yield curve* that plots yield as a function of maturity for recently issued coupon bonds selling at or near par value.

open interest. The number of *futures contracts* outstanding.

open-end funds. Funds that issue or redeem their own shares at *net asset value (NAV)*.

optimal risky portfolio. An investor's best combination of risky assets to be mixed with safe assets to form the *complete portfolio*.

option elasticity. The percentage increase in an option's value given a 1 percent change in the value of the underlying security.

original issue discount bond. A bond issued with a low *coupon rate* that sells at a discount from *par value*.

OTC. See *over-the-counter markets*.

out of the money. Said of an option whose exercise would not be profitable. See also *in the money* and *at the money*.

over-the-counter (OTC) markets. Informal networks of brokers and dealers who negotiate sales of securities.

pairs trading. Trading in which stocks are paired up on the basis of underlying similarities, and long-short positions are established to exploit any relative mispricing between them.

par value. The *face value* of the bond.

passive investment strategy. See *passive management*.

passive management. Buying a *well-diversified portfolio* to represent a broad-based market index without attempting to search out mispriced securities.

passive portfolio. A market index portfolio.

passive strategy. See *passive management*.

pass-throughs. Pools of loans (such as mortgages) sold in a package, and entitling the owner to receive all *principal* and interest payments made by the borrowers.

pass-through securities. Pools of loans (such as home mortgage loans) sold in one package. Owners of pass-throughs receive all *principal* and interest payments made by the borrowers.

P/B. See *market-to-book-value ratio*.

P/E effect. That portfolios of low P/E stocks have exhibited higher average risk-adjusted returns than high P/E stocks.

P/E ratio. See *price-earnings ratio*.

personal trusts. An interest in an asset held by a trustee for the benefit of another person.

plowback ratio. The proportion of the firm's earnings reinvested in the business (and not paid out as dividends). The plowback ratio equals 1 minus the *dividend payout ratio*.

political risk. Possibility of the expropriation of assets, changes in tax policy, restrictions on the exchange of foreign currency for domestic currency, or other changes in the business climate of a country.

portable alpha. A strategy in which one invests in positive *alpha* positions, then hedges the systematic risk of that investment, and finally establishes market exposure where one wants it by using passive indices. Also known as *alpha transfer*.

portfolio insurance. The practice of using options or *dynamic hedging* strategies to provide protection against investment losses while maintaining upside potential.

portfolio management. Process of combining securities in a portfolio tailored to the investor's preferences and needs, monitoring that portfolio, and evaluating its performance.

portfolio opportunity set. The possible *expected return–standard deviation* pairs of all portfolios that can be constructed from a given set of assets.

preferred stock. Non-voting shares in a corporation, paying a fixed or variable stream of dividends.

premium. The purchase price of an option.

premium bonds. *Bonds* selling above *par value*.

present value of growth opportunities (PVGO). A value determined by the NPV of investment opportunities.

price-earnings (P/E) ratio. The ratio of a stock's price to its earnings per share. Also referred to as the *P/E multiple*.

price value of a basis point. The change in the value of a fixed-income asset resulting from a one-basis-point change in the asset's *yield to maturity*.

price-earnings multiple. See *price-earnings ratio*.

price-weighted average. Computed by adding the prices of 30 companies and dividing by the divisor.

primary market. A market in which issues of securities are offered to the public.

principal. The outstanding balance on a loan.

private placement. *Bonds* sold directly to a limited number of institutional investors. See also *public offering*.

profit margin. Profit percentage defined as EBIT divided by total sales.

program trading. Coordinated buy orders and sell orders of entire portfolios, usually with the aid of computers, and often to achieve index *arbitrage* objectives.

prospect theory. A modification of the analytic description of rational *risk-averse* investors found in standard financial theory, by which the utility function is defined in terms of losses relative to current wealth, that is, changes in wealth rather than levels of wealth.

prospectus. A final and approved *registration statement* including the price at which a security issue is offered.

protective put. Purchase of stock combined with a *put option* that guarantees minimum proceeds equal to the put's *exercise price*.

proxy. An instrument empowering an agent to vote in the name of a shareholder.

prudent person law. A regulation on investment managers whereby they have a fiduciary responsibility to restrict investment to assets that would have been approved by a prudent investor.

pseudo-American call option value. The maximum of the value derived by assuming that the option will be held until expiration and the value derived by assuming that the option will be exercised just before an ex-dividend date.

public offering. *Bonds* sold in the *primary market* to the general public. See also *private placement*.

pure plays. Positions on perceived sources of mispricing in which all other influences on prices are hedged.

pure yield curve. A curve that shows the *spot rates*, the yields on *zero-coupon bonds*, as functions of the maturities of those bonds.

pure yield pickup swap. Moving to higher-yield bonds.

put/call ratio. The ratio of outstanding *put options* to outstanding *call options*, used as an indicator of market sentiment.

put–call parity theorem. An equation representing the proper relationship between put and call prices. Violation of parity allows *arbitrage* opportunities.

put option. The right to sell an asset at a specified *exercise price* on or before a specified expiration date.

quality of earnings. The extent to which one can expect the reported level of a firm's earnings to be continued.

quick ratio. A measure of *liquidity* similar to the *current ratio* except for exclusion of inventories (cash plus receivables divided by current liabilities).

random walk. The notion that stock price changes are random and unpredictable.

rate anticipation swap. A switch made in response to forecasts of *interest rates*.

real assets. Land, buildings, and equipment used to produce goods and services. See also *financial assets*.

real estate investment trust (REIT). A form of investment vehicle similar to a *closed-end* mutual fund that issues shares for investments in real estate or loans secured by real estate.

real estate limited partnership (RELP). A pool of funds that uses leverage to purchase real estate, and hence must be structured as a partnership rather than a mutual fund.

real interest rate. The excess of the *interest rate* over the inflation rate. The growth rate of purchasing power derived from an investment.

real investment. The investment of capital in physical goods, such as equipment or plant, resulting in expansion of the productive base of the economy.

realized compound return. Yield assuming that coupon payments are invested at the going market interest rate at the time of their receipt and rolled over until the bond matures.

rebalancing. Realigning the proportion of assets in a portfolio as needed.

registered traders. Traders who make a market in the shares of one or more firms and who maintain a "fair and orderly market" by dealing personally in the stock; known as *specialists* in the United States.

registration statement. A document required to be filed with the SEC to describe the issue of a new security.

regression equation. An equation that describes the average relationship between a dependent variable and a set of explanatory variables.

regret avoidance. A decision-making bias by which losses due to decisions engender more regret if the decision was more unconventional.

reinvestment rate risk. A source of offsetting risk that may be operative when interest rates change on a bond. When prices fall it reduces the value of the bond portfolio; however, reinvested coupon income may compound more rapidly at those higher rates.

REIT. See *real estate investment trust*.

relative strength. The ratio of an individual stock price to a price index for the relevant industry; a technical indicator of the out- or underperformance of a company relative to the industry or market.

RELP. See *real estate limited partnership*.

replacement cost. Cost to replace a firm's assets. "Reproduction" cost.

repos (RPs). See *repurchase agreements*.

representativeness. Basing decisions on overly small samples in on the mistaken premise that a small sample is just as representative of the population as a large one.

repurchase agreements. Short-term, often overnight, sales of government securities with an agreement to repurchase the securities at a slightly higher price. A *reverse repo* is a purchase with an agreement to resell at a specified price on a future date.

residual. Part of stock returns not explained by the explanatory variable (the market-index return). Measures the impact of firm-specific events during a particular period.

residual claim. The remainder of firm assets due shareholders, given that they occupy the last position to receive value in the event of failure or bankruptcy.

residual income. See *economic value added (EVA)*.

resistance level. A price level above which it is supposedly difficult for a stock or stock index to rise.

restricted shares. A special type of shares that have no voting rights, or only limited voting rights, but otherwise participate fully in the financial benefits of share ownership.

retractable bond. A bond that gives the right to the holder to redeem early at *par value*, instead of holding it till maturity date.

return on assets (ROA). A profitability ratio; earnings before interest and taxes divided by total assets.

return on equity (ROE). An accounting ratio of net profits divided by equity.

return on sales (ROS). Profit percentage defined as EBIT divided by total sales.

reversal effect. The tendency of poorly performing stocks and well-performing stocks in one period to experience reversals in following periods.

reversing trade. Entering the opposite side of a currently held futures position to close out the position.

reward-to-variability ratio. The excess *expected return* of a portfolio over the riskless rate of interest, divided by the *standard deviation* of the portfolio return.

reward-to-volatility ratio. Ratio of *excess return* to portfolio *standard deviation*.

risk arbitrage. *Speculation* on perceived mispriced securities, usually in connection with merger and acquisition targets.

risk-averse, risk-neutral, risk lover. A *risk-averse* investor will consider risky portfolios only if they provide compensation for risk via a *risk premium*. A *risk-neutral* investor finds the level of risk irrelevant and considers only the *expected return* of risk prospects. A *risk lover* is willing to accept lower *expected returns* on prospects with higher amounts of risk.

risk aversion. The preference of investors for assets with certain returns over assets with risky returns whose expectation is equal to the certain return.

risk premium. An *expected return* in excess of that on riskfree securities. The premium provides compensation for the risk of an investment.

risk-free rate. The *interest rate* that can be earned with certainty.

risk lover. An investor willing to engage in fair games and gambles; he or she adjusts the expected return upward to take into account the "fun" of confronting the prospect's risk.

risk-neutral. See *risk-averse*.

risk–return tradeoff. If an investor is willing to take on risk, there is the reward of higher *expected returns*.

ROA. See *return on assets*.

ROE. See *return on equity*.

ROS. See *return on sales*.

RPs. See *repurchase agreements*.

scatter diagram. A plot of the observed values of the dependent variable versus those of the independent variable of a regression equation.

SCL. See *security characteristic line*.

secondary market. Already-existing securities are bought and sold on the exchanges or in the OTC market.

second-pass regression. A cross-sectional regression of portfolio returns on *betas*. The estimated slope is the measurement of the reward for bearing *systematic risk* during the period.

sector rotation. *Rebalancing* of a portfolio to emphasize economic sectors expected to outperform the market index.

securitization. Pooling loans for various purposes into standardized securities backed by those loans, which can then be traded like any other security.

security analysis. Determining the correct value of a security in the marketplace.

security characteristic line (SCL). A plot of the expected *excess return* on a security over the *risk-free rate* as a function of the excess return on the market.

security market line (SML). Graphical representation of the *expected return–beta relationship* of the *capital asset pricing model (CAPM)*.

security selection. The choice made by investors of which particular securities to hold within an asset class.

segregated funds. Mutual funds (usually issued by insurance companies) with an attached guarantee for a minimum payment.

selectivity. The ability to select individual stocks that will perform well in particular economic climates.

semistrong-form. A form of the *efficient market hypothesis*.

separation of ownership and management. The division in a corporation between the owners or stockholders of a firm and their agents who are the managers hired to direct the firm.

separation property. The property that portfolio choice can be separated into two independent tasks: (1) determination of the optimal risky portfolio, which is a purely technical problem and (2) the personal choice of the best mix of the risky portfolio and the risk-free asset.

serial bond issue. An issue of bonds with staggered maturity dates that spreads out the *principal* repayment burden over time.

settlement date. The date at which capital gains are recognized for tax purposes; usually five business days after the actual trade date.

Sharpe's ratio. *Reward-to-volatility ratio*; ratio of portfolio *excess return* to *standard deviation*.

short hedge. See *short position*.

short interest. The total number of shares of stock held short in the market; considered *bullish* in that short holdings must be covered by purchases (latent demand), but *bearish* in that sophisticated traders (who are more likely to short) predict better.

short position. Protecting the value of an asset held by taking a short position in a *futures contract*. Also called *short hedge*.

short rate. A one-period *interest rate*.

short sale. The sale of shares not owned by the investor but borrowed through a broker and later repurchased to replace the loan. Profit comes from initial sale at a higher price than the repurchase price.

simple prospect. An investment opportunity in which a certain initial wealth is placed at risk and only two outcomes are possible.

single-country funds. Mutual funds that invest solely in the securities of a single country.

single-factor model. The *model* of security returns that acknowledges only one common factor. See *factor model*.

single-index model. A *model* of stock returns that decomposes influences on returns into a systematic factor, as measured by the return on a broad market index, and firm-specific factors.

single-stock futures. Futures contracts on a single stock rather than an index.

sinking fund. A procedure that allows for the repayment of *principal* at maturity by calling for the bond issuer to repurchase some proportion of the outstanding bonds either in the open market or at a special call price associated with the sinking fund provision.

skew. A measure of asymmetry of a distribution that uses the ratio of the average cubed deviations from the main, called the *third moment*, to the cubed *standard deviation*.

skip-day settlement. A convention for calculating yield that assumes a *Treasury bill* sale is not settled until two days after quotation of the *Treasury bill* price.

small-firm effect. That investments in stocks of small firms appear to have earned *abnormal returns*.

SML. See *security market line*.

soft dollars. The value of research services that brokerage houses supply to investment managers "free of charge" in exchange for the investment manager's business.

specialist. See *registered trader*.

speculation. Undertaking a risky investment with the objective of earning a positive profit compared with investment in a risk-free alternative (a *risk premium*).

speculative-grade bonds. Bonds rated Ba or lower by Moody's, or BB or lower by Standard & Poor's, or an unrated bond.

spot–futures parity theorem. Describes the theoretically correct relationship between spot and *futures prices*. Violation of the parity relationship gives rise to *arbitrage* opportunities. Also known as *cost-of-carry relationship*.

spot rate. The current *interest rate* appropriate for discounting a cash flow of some given maturity.

spread. Futures: Taking a *long position* in a *futures contract* of one maturity and a *short position* in a contract of different maturity, both on the same commodity. Options: A combination of two or more *call options* or *put options* on the same stock with differing *exercise prices* or times to expiration. A *vertical* or *money spread* refers to a spread with different exercise price; a *horizontal* or *time spread* refers to differing expiration date.

standard deviation. Square root of the *variance*.

statement of changes in financial position. A listing of the sources and uses of funds through operations, financing, and investments; over the specific time period, the net addition to the cash position is determined.

statistical arbitrage. Use of quantitative systems to uncover many perceived misalignments in relative pricing and ensure profit by averaging over all these small bets.

stock exchanges. *Secondary markets* where already issued securities are bought and sold by members.

stock selection. An active *portfolio management* technique that focuses on advantageous selection of particular stocks rather than on broad *asset allocation* choices.

stock split. Issue by a corporation of a given number of shares in exchange for the current number of shares held by stockholders. Splits may go in either direction, either increasing or decreasing the number of shares outstanding. A *reverse split* decreases the number outstanding.

stop-loss orders. Conditional sell orders to be executed if the price of the stock falls below a stipulated level.

straddle. A combination of buying both a call and a put, each with the same *exercise price* and expiration date. The purpose is to profit from expected volatility in either direction.

strap, strip. Variants of a straddle. A *strip* is two puts and one call on a stock; a *strap* is two calls and one put, both with the same *exercise price* and expiration date.

street name. Describes securities held by a broker on behalf of a client but registered in the name of the firm.

strike price. See *exercise price.*

strip. See *strap.*

stripped of coupons. Describes the practice of some investment banks that sell "synthetic" *zero-coupon bonds* by marketing the rights to a single payment backed by a coupon-paying *Treasury bond.*

strong-form EMH. See *efficient market hypothesis.*

subordinated debentures. Unsecured bonds that have been made inferior as claims to higher-ranked borrowings of a firm.

subordination clauses. Provisions in a *bond indenture* that restrict the issuer's future borrowing by subordinating the new leaders' claims on the firm to those of the existing bondholders. Claims of *subordinated* or *junior* debtholders are not paid until the prior debt is paid.

substitution swap. Exchange of one bond for a bond with similar attributes but more attractively priced.

superficial loss rule. A tax regulation that prohibits the recognition of capital losses if a security is purchased within 30 days of its sale.

supply shock. An event affecting the aggregate supply of goods and services, thereby influencing the state of the economy.

support level. A price level below which it is supposedly difficult for a stock or stock index to fall.

survivorship bias. An upward bias to measured returns of a group of mutual funds that stems from the fact that failed funds are automatically excluded from the group.

swap. An agreement between two parties to exchange a set of liabilities with different payments over multiple periods.

systematic risk. Risk factors common to the whole economy, for example *nondiversifiable risk*; see *market risk.*

tax-deferral option. The feature of the U.S. Internal Revenue Code that the capital gains tax on an asset is payable only when the gain is realized by selling the asset.

tax-deferred retirement plans. Employer-sponsored and other plans that allow contributions and earnings to be made and accumulate tax free until they are paid out as benefits.

tax shelters. Investment opportunities whereby most, if not all, of the investment can be deducted from ordinary income for tax purposes over a year's horizon.

tax swap. Swapping two similar bonds to receive a tax benefit.

technical analysis. Research to identify mispriced securities that focuses on recurrent and predictable stock price patterns and on *proxies* for buy or sell pressure in the market.

term structure of interest rates. The pattern of *interest rates* appropriate for discounting cash flows of various maturities.

thin trading. Persistently infrequent trading, including long intervals without any recorded transactions, for a given security.

time value (of an option). The part of the value of an option that is due to its positive time to expiration. Not to be confused with present value or the time value of money.

times interest earned. See *interest coverage ratio.*

time-weighted average. An average of the period-by-period *holding-period returns* of an investment.

Tobin's q. Ratio of market value of the firm to *replacement cost.*

total asset turnover (total ATO). The annual sales generated by each dollar of assets.

total ATO. See *total asset turnover.*

total excess return of portfolio. The return on a portfolio in excess of the risk-free rate or in excess of a given benchmark.

tracking portfolio. A portfolio constructed to have returns with the highest possible correlation with a systematic risk factor.

tranche. See *collateralized mortgage obligation.*

Treasury bills (T-bills). Short-term, highly liquid government securities issued at a discount from the *face value* and returning the face amount at maturity.

Treasury bond or note. Debt obligations of the U.S. federal government that make semiannual coupon payments and are sold at or near *par value* in denominations of $1,000 or more.

Treynor's measure. Ratio of *excess return* to *beta.*

trin statistic. The ratio of the number of advancing to declining stocks divided by the ratio of volume in advancing versus declining stocks; a technical indicator of market strength that is *bullish* when the value is less than one.

turnover. The ratio of trading activity in a portfolio to the assets of the portfolio.

unbundling. See *bundling.*

underwriting. Underwriters (*investment bankers*) purchase securities from the issuing company and resell them. Usually a syndicate of investment bankers is organized behind a lead firm.

underwriting syndicate. A group of other investment dealers that a lead firm forms in order to share the responsibility for a stock issue.

unique risk. See *diversifiable risk.*

unsecured bond. See *debenture.*

utility. The measure of the welfare or satisfaction of an investor.

utility value. The welfare a given investor assigns to an investment with a certain return and risk.

value at risk (VaR). A risk measure that highlights the potential loss from extreme negative returns; another name for the quantile of a distribution.

VaR. See *value at risk.*

variable annuities. Annuity contracts in which the insurance company pays a periodic amount linked to the investment performance of an underlying portfolio.

variable-rate mortgage. A conventional mortgage loan with interest payment varying in response to market rates.

variance. A measure of the dispersion of a random variable. Equals the expected value of the squared deviation from the mean.

vega. The amount by which an option price changes in reaction to a 1 percent change in the volatility of the underlying asset.

views. In the Black-Litterman *model*, analysts' opinions on the likely performance of a stock or sector, as compared to the market consensus opinion.

volatility risk. The risk of a portfolio containing options that arises from unpredictable changes in the volatility of the underlying asset.

warrants. An option issued by the firm to purchase shares of the firm's stock.

weak-form. One form of the efficient market hypothesis. See *efficient market hypothesis.*

well-diversified portfolio. A portfolio spread out over many securities in such a way that the weight in any one security is close to zero.

workout period. Realignment period of a temporary misaligned yield relationship.

writing a call. Selling a *call option.*

yield curve. A graph of *yield to maturity* as a function of time to maturity.

yield to maturity. The *interest rate* that discounts the cash flows of a security to equal the price of the security.

YTM. See *yield to maturity.*

zero-beta portfolio. The *minimum-variance portfolio* uncorrelated with a chosen efficient portfolio.

zero-coupon bonds (zeroes). A bond paying no coupons that sells at a discount and provides payment of the *principal* only at maturity.

Commonly Used Notation

b	Retention or plowback ratio
C	Call option value
CF	Cash flow
D	Duration
E	Exchange rate
$E(x)$	Expected value of random variable x
F	Futures price
e	2.718, the base for the natural logarithm, used for continuous compounding
e_{it}	The firm-specific return, also called the residual return, of security i in period t
f	Forward rate of interest
g	Growth rate of dividends
H	Hedge ratio for an option, sometimes called the option's delta
i	Inflation rate
k	Market capitalization rate, the required rate of return on a firm's stock
$\ln$	Natural logarithm function
M	The market portfolio
$N(d)$	Cumulative normal function, the probability that a standard normal random variable will have value less than d
p	Probability
P	Put value
PV	Present value
P/E	Price-to-earnings multiple
r	Rate of return on a security; for fixed-income securities, r may denote the rate of interest for a particular period

r_f	The risk-free rate of interest
r_M	The rate of return on the market portfolio
ROE	Return on equity, incremental economic earnings per dollar reinvested in the firm
S_p	Sharpe ratio, also called the *reward-to-volatility ratio*; the excess expected return divided by the standard deviation
t	Time
T_p	Treynor's measure for a portfolio, excess expected return divided by beta
V	Intrinsic value of a firm, the present value of future dividends per share
X	Exercise price of an option
y	Yield to maturity
α	Rate of return beyond the value that would be forecast from the market's return and the systematic risk of the security
β	Systematic or market risk of a security
ρ_{ij}	Correlation coefficient between returns on securities i and j
σ	Standard deviation
σ^2	Variance
$Cov(r_i, r_j)$	Covariance between returns on securities i and j

Useful Formulas

Measures of Risk

Variance of returns: $\sigma^2 = \sum_s p(s)[r(s) - E(r)]^2$

Standard deviation: $\sigma = \sqrt{\sigma^2}$

Covariance between returns: $\text{Cov}(r_i, r_j) = \sum_s p(s)[r_i(s) - E(r_i)][r_j(s) - E(r_j)]$

Beta of security i: $\beta_i = \dfrac{\text{Cov}(r_i, r_M)}{\text{Var}(r_M)}$

Portfolio Theory

Expected rate of return on a portfolio with weights w_i in each security: $E(r_p) = \sum_{i=1}^{n} w_i E(r_i)$

Variance of portfolio rate of return: $\sigma_p^2 = \sum_{j=1}^{n} \sum_{i=1}^{n} w_j w_i \, \text{Cov}(r_i, r_j)$

Market Equilibrium

The security market line: $E(r_i) = r_f + \beta_i[E(r_M) - r_f]$

Multifactor security market line (in excess returns): $E(R_i) = \beta_{iM} E(R_M) + \sum_{k=1}^{K} E(R_k)$

Fixed-Income Analysis

Present value of \$1:

Discrete period compounding: $PV = 1/(1 + r)^T$

Continuous compounding: $PV = e^{-rT}$

Forward rate of interest for period T: $f_T = \dfrac{(1 + y_T)^T}{(1 + y_{T-1})^{T-1}} - 1$

Real interest rate: $r_r = \dfrac{1 + r_n}{1 + i} - 1$

where r_n is the nominal interest rate and i is the inflation rate

Duration of a security: $D = \sum_{t=1}^{T} t \times \dfrac{CF_t}{(1 + y)^t} \bigg/ \text{Price}$

Modified duration: $D^* = D/(1 + y)$